THE OXFORD ENCYCLOPEDIA OF
MESOAMERICAN CULTURES

THE OXFORD ENCYCLOPEDIA

OF

MESOAMERICAN CULTURES

THE CIVILIZATIONS OF MEXICO AND CENTRAL AMERICA

DAVÍD CARRASCO

Editor in Chief

VOLUME 1

UNIVERSITY PRESS

2001

OXFORD
UNIVERSITY PRESS

Oxford   New York
Athens Auckland Bangkok Bogotá Buenos Aires Calcutta
Cape Town Chennai Dar es Salaam Delhi Florence Hong Kong Istanbul
Karachi Kuala Lumpur Madrid Melbourne Mexico City Mumbai
Nairobi Paris São Paulo Shanghai Singapore Taipei Tokyo Toronto Warsaw
and associated companies in
Berlin Ibadan

Copyright © 2001 by Oxford University Press, Inc.

Published by Oxford University Press, Inc.
198 Madison Avenue, New York, New York 10016
www.oup.com

Oxford is a registered trademark of Oxford University Press

Library of Congress Cataloging-in-Publication Data
The Oxford encyclopedia of Mesoamerican cultures:
the civilizations of Mexico and Central America
/ Davíd Carrasco, editor in chief.
p. cm.
Includes bibliographical references and index.
ISBN 0-19-510815-9 (set)—ISBN 0-19-514255-1 (vol. 1)—
ISBN 0-19-514256-X (vol. 2)—ISBN 0-19-514257-8 (vol. 3)
1. Indians of Mexico—Antiquities—Encyclopedias.
2. Indians of Central America—Antiquities—Encyclopedias.
3. Mexico—Antiquities—Encyclopedias.
4. Central America—Antiquities—Encyclopedias.
I. Carrasco, Davíd.
F1218.6 .O95   2000
972′.01—dc21   00-032624

EDITORIAL AND PRODUCTION STAFF

Commissioning Editor: Christopher Collins
Development Editor: Scott Sessions
Managing Editor: Mark Mones
Project Editor: Mark Gallagher
Production Editor: Cynthia Garver
Copyeditors: Martha Goldstein, Jane McGary, Laura Daly
Proofreaders: Susan Gilad, Joy Matkowski
Cartographer: Bill Nelson
Indexer: Catherine Goddard
Manufacturing Controller: Genieve Shaw
Book Designer: Joan Greenfield
Publisher: Karen Casey

1 3 5 7 9 8 6 4 2

Printed in the United States of America
on acid-free paper

Contents

THE OXFORD ENCYCLOPEDIA OF

MESOAMERICAN CULTURES

Editorial Board

Preface

WHY *THE OXFORD ENCYCLOPEDIA OF MESOAMERICAN CULTURES*? At the most general level, because Mesoamerica, designated by scholars as a geographical and cultural area involving the southern two thirds of mainland Mexico, as well as Guatemala, Belize, El Salvador, and parts of Honduras, Nicaragua, and Costa Rica, is the site of two major cultural transformations in Western Hemisphere history. First, Mesoamerica was one of the seven areas of primary urban generation—the complex evolution from the social world of the village to urbanized cultures. Only the civilizations of Mesopotamia, Egypt, the Indus Valley, China, Peru, and Nigeria share the significance of this historical evolution. It was within the cultural world of socially stratified, sometimes monumentally constructed ceremonial centers and cities that significant aspects of indigenous cultures were generated, expressed, and periodically transformed—including social organization, public architecture, religion, economic exchange, and hierarchical political order. Although these cultures survive largely through their cultural remains, they continually provoke our awareness in today's developing world of global communications. For example, as governments in Mexico and Central America work to modernize and industrialize their economies through building projects and renewals, such as subways, they periodically uncover the remains of settlements, pottery, pyramids, palaces, and other impressive evidence of pre-Hispanic and Colonial-era indigenous cultures.

Second, Mesoamerica was also one of the places where the encounter between Europe and the Americas fundamentally changed the course of human history. It was in Mesoamerica where, in the words of Elizabeth Wilder Weismann, "Two (or more) different kinds of life absorbed each other and produced things new and different from anything else in the world." While it was in the Caribbean islands that the initial sites were established for sixteenth-century transatlantic contacts and exchanges, European culture first took firm root in Mesoamerica, where it was significantly changed by the indigenous peoples and *mestizos*. As scholars have shown, the complex social process known as "colonialism" first emerged in Mesoamerica as natives, European settlers, and slaves from sub-Saharan Africa formed distinctive and complex social, religious, and political relationships. There, they developed new ways of being and of constructing culture. These colonial patterns are also periodically brought back to our contemporary consciousness, as demonstrated in the attention given to the recent Zapatista insurrection in Chiapas, Mexico.

More specific reasons for a major reference work that organizes and interprets new knowledge concerning Mesoamerican cultures include the impressive number of archaeological, linguistic, and other scholarly and popular developments since the 1960s. First, there have been major archaeological excavations throughout Mesoamerica that are changing our understanding of the diversity of paths, including the indigenous urban tradition, which Mesoamerican societies followed prior to European intervention. New archaeological discoveries at the Olmec sites in the Gulf Coast region, at Maya sites in Southern Mexico and Central America, at the Mixtec and Zapotec areas of Oaxaca and Guerrero, and at the Central Mexican sites of Teotihuacan, Tula, Tenochtitlan, Xochicalco, and Cholula, as well as a host of others, have revealed the following: widespread evidence of internal complexity; local and regional diversity; and surprising interchanges between social communities and ethnic groups—developments scarcely believed possible even as late as the 1980s. Important new excavations have revitalized the long debate on the emergence, nature, and legacy of Teotihuacan; the rise, florescence, and collapse of the Classic Maya and the Oaxacan kingdoms; the extent of Toltec cultural influence upon the Maya of Yucatán; and Central Mesoamerican connections with the indigenous cultures of the American Southwest.

A second source of new knowledge is the substantial advance in Maya, Nahuatl, and other linguistic studies, highlighted by the breathtaking advances in the decipherment of the Maya hieroglyphic writing system. The partial breaking of the Maya code has allowed researchers to plumb greater depths in understanding Maya peoples in their own region, as well as in their interactions with a number of other cities and cultures in parts of Mesoamerica distant from the Maya realm. Collaborative scholarship and academic meetings that addressed the social and symbolic patterns of Maya cultures emanating from this linguistic breakthrough have resulted in comparative studies concerning gods, rites, lineages, symbols, as well as religious, cultural, and economic exchange. Fresh gleanings from other primary sources have also emerged from the publication of high-quality facsimiles of the *Codices Mexicanos* series and from state-of-the-art commentaries on pre-Hispanic and early Colonial-period pictorial manuscripts, including the *Codex Borbonicus, Codex Vindobonensis, Codex Mendoza, Codex Borgia, Codex Telleriano-Remensis, Primeros Memoriales*, and others.

A third reason for a major reference work on Mesoamerica stems from the significant advances in the study of colonial and modern Mesoamerica, including new translations of Colonial-era manuscripts, as well as intensive studies of ecclesiastical and legal documents that enable us to understand substantially more about New Spain. Among these are new translations and analyses of such conquest narratives as Fernando Cortés's *Cartas de relacion* and Diego Duran's *History of the Indies*, and the indigenous Colonial-period manuscripts in native languages like the *Popul Vuh* and the *Codex Chimalpopoca* and a significant number of "mundane" indigenous documents, such as wills, retrieved from a variety of archives. As our discussion of the *Handbook of Middle American Indians* below will show, studies of New Spain and the national period of Mesoamerican cultures have been reactivated, in part, by the useful inventories and descriptions of documentary evidence (some unpublished) that were written by Indians, *mestizos*, and Euro-Americans. Also, new approaches to the evidence for the rise of modern Mesoamerica have illuminated the story of nationalisms and the impact of the rise of capitalism on all the peoples of Mesoamerica.

As our encyclopedia shows, Mesoamerica is not to be understood only in pre-Hispanic terms. The coming of various cultural groups of Europeans and their encounters with very diverse native communities—and the introduction of peoples from Africa with a variety of religious and ethnic orientations—were in addition to a conquest and destruction of indigenous society, religion, and culture also a formation of a New World for Europeans, for the natives, and for the various groups of *mestizos* and mulattoes. While there have been other important overviews of Mesoamerican cultures, no other reference work treats the long history of Mesoamerica (as a pre-Hispanic, colonial, and modern world) so fully. Our work draws directly on the recent methods and insights of archaeology, anthropology, linguistics, history, ethnohistory, art history, history of religions, astronomy, and literature and literary interpretation to understand the complexity of Mesoamerican societies. This includes the complex ways that indigenous Mesoamerican societies—with their history, symbols, architectural and social styles—interacted with both European and African cultural elements, and continue to this day, contributing to the vitality and struggles of Mesoamerican peoples.

The editors have been faced, in some cases, with the thorny problem of finding the appropriate "names" for indigenous peoples. Scholarship has not always been thoughtful, kind, or accurate in using the names that identify a group or a people—such as the "Aztec," for example—and the result is that some peoples have not been called what they call themselves. Aztec was a name made popular by William Prescott's famous writings on Mexico and not a term used by the Mexicas or Chichimecas or Tenochcas to designate themselves. Yet its widespread use makes it impossible to just ignore the term, so we have kept it as a headword although the essay on *Aztec* clarifies the problem. In a number of cases, such as the "Olmec" or the people of Teotihuacan, we do not know what these people called themselves and have resorted to using names designated by scholarly consensus. Still, our intention has been to demonstrate respect for the names, languages, and traditions of Mesoamerican peoples. We have included, whenever possible, indigenous names alongside the "official" names that have worked their way into general parlance and scholarly literature in order to identify the subjects of the essays.

It is important to note that in many cases, today's indigenous peoples call themselves by names associated with their lineage, language, village, community, region, or ethnic group. Other peoples whose names have been changed by journalists, scholars, or governments, to give just a few examples, include the Benizaa (Zapotecs), Ñudzahui (Mixtecs), Purépecha (Tarascans), and Rarámuri (Tarahumara), as well as several Maya peoples. It is our belief that as more indigenous, African, and *mestizo* peoples make known their histories, traditions, and worldviews, our shared nomenclature will increasingly reflect knowledge of both their ancient and modern names and the profound meanings behind those names.

Foundations. In various important ways, this encyclopedia builds on the remarkable and still very useful work of the monumental *Handbook of Middle American Indians* published in sixteen volumes from 1964 to 1976 under the general editorship of Robert Wauchope and with the assistance of a number of leading Mesoamerican scholars. It covered many topics in Mesoamerican studies in focused, descriptive articles that also developed empirical generalizations about regularities and variations in Mesoamerican geography, archaeology, physical anthropology, linguistics, social anthropology, ethnology, and ethnohistorical documents. Overall, it was written from an anthropological perspective, and its editors felt in the early 1980s a need, based in part on new data and methodological developments in the field, to publish a number of supplemental volumes on archaeology, linguistics, indigenous literatures, ethnohistory, and epigraphy, which have been edited by Victoria Bricker. Relevant to appreciating our encyclopedia's extensive historical vision was the state of the art of Colonial- and national-period Mesoamerican studies when the *Handbook of Middle American Indians* decided to publish as volumes 13–15 of the *HMAI*, between 1972 and 1975, the "Guide to Ethnohistorical Sources." In his introductory essay, Howard Cline, the general editor, described the decision of the editorial board of the *Handbook of Middle American Indians* to *not* write "substantive articles on Indian groups of Middle America in the Colonial period" because of a general lack of knowledge about the sources and the lack of trained interpreters who could utilize them to interpret social realities of this period of Mesoamerican ethnohistory. Instead, the decision was made to inventory the substantial body of written materials created by Indians and *mestizos* or in the native style and those produced by Europeans or in the European tradition. This project was completed with impressive results in 1975, and in the last quarter century scholars have been reading and interpreting the mass of Mesoamerican ethnohistorical documentation, including pre-Hispanic and Colonial-era religious/ritual and historical pictorials, colonial *Relaciones Geográficas*, *lienzos*, and maps, as well as legal and ecclesiastical records. *The Oxford Encyclopedia of Mesoamerican Cultures* benefits from the multidisciplinary interpretation of specialists who have read back from, through, and beyond these largely Colonial-period works. It is important to note, however, that they have aided our understandings of not only colonial Mesoamerica but also the pre-Hispanic and the contemporary indigenous world. A new wave of scholarship in colonial and contemporary Mesoamerican studies has been able to interpret various ways that Indian communities today are engaging globalization pressures by both incorporating new cultural and trade patterns and reasserting their indigenous identities.

Since the publication of the *Handbook*, a new generation of monographs and collections of essays have been published on politics and states, religion and symbolism, social history and economic institutions, and missionaries and lay societies in colonial Mexico, Guatemala, El Salvador, Belize, Honduras, and other parts of Mesoamerica. In addition, scholars have undertaken productive new research on the impacts of the slave trade and Africans on Mesoamerican cultural formation in the Colonial period. While these kinds of specific and general studies have been burgeoning, the field of Mesoamerican studies has been enriched by the development and application of new disciplinary orientations, such as archaeoastronomy, gender studies, ethnobotany, comparative philosophy, semiotics, poetics, and performance studies. Never before in the history of Mesoamerican or New World studies have new orientations in scholarship met such rich resources and growth of evidence, which have led to new questions of method and theory as well as a new mapping of future research projects. A concomitant development that enriches the social context of Mesoamerican studies has been the publication of various extensive, well-researched catalogs in conjunction with major museum exhibitions in Mexico, the United States, and Europe that featured various Mesoamerican cultures and New World encounters. Also, scholars and lay people have been galvanized into several long-term forums of informational and interpretive exchange at such places as Dumbarton Oaks, the Palenque Round Tables, the Maya Workshops at the University of Texas, the Peabody Museum of Archaeology and Ethnology at Harvard University, Tulane University, the University of California at Los Angeles (UCLA), the Moses Mesoamerican Archive at the University of Colorado, and Princeton University. *The Oxford Encyclopedia of Mesoamerican Cultures* is the new resource through which this scholarship and collaboration is presented and passes into the public domain; through it, the scholar or the curious can return to review or question the state of the discipline.

Orientations. At the beginning of our work, the editorial team made several general decisions that guided the nature of the writing. First, we wrestled with the definitions and historical and geographical boundaries of Mesoamerica to be used. We were mindful of previous influential definitions and descriptions of Mesoamerica by Paul Kirchhoff, Jaime Litvak King, and Gordon Willey. Kirchhoff's work emphasized Mesoamerica as a culture area with considerable pre-Hispanic time depth that underwent intense interactions among cultures. The *Handbook of Middle American Indians* and almost all students of Mesoamerica developed this approach, working to refine and give sharper definition to the geographical, linguistic, and temporal boundaries of the region. Eventually, scholars realized that Mesoamerica could best be understood with more attention to the intercommunication networks that linked local, regional, and imperial settlements. Since the 1970s, our research has benefited from a more diversified vision of Mesoamerica as an evolving series of local and regional cultures, with many ethic groups who, after the decline of Teotihuacan, moved toward multiethnic political organizations, often in oscillating contact and conflict with one another. For example, it was once thought that the Maya and the "Mexicans" of the Central Highlands, as well as other cultural groups, were, for the most part, discrete units in cultural orientation, cosmology, social order, and history. Recent research shows the variety of ways that these and a number of other Mesoamerican communities shared a common ideological tradition and material culture—enriched through continuous, sustained exchanges of matter, information, and ideas throughout several millennia. As a number of articles relating to pre-Hispanic Mesoamerica make clear, many communities from the Formative (Preclassic) period onward participated in a latticework of social and symbolic interaction that connected people of many different language groups and ecological settings.

The editorial board decided to use both a focused and a flexible definition of Mesoamerica, which was respectful of the traditional geographic and historical maps but was also open to new scholarship that addressed the permeable and moveable boundaries of Mesoamerica throughout its history. Recent historical research has shown how various Mesoamerican frontiers moved and were permeable to exchanges with extra-Mesoamerican cultures. While the majority of the essays about the pre-Hispanic period focus on the ceremonial centers, sites, and settlements, articles on cultures existing at the frontiers were also included, so while not in an integral sense Mesoamerican, they nevertheless exhibit important exchanges with and effects on Mesoamerican peoples. To guide the reader's sense of sociogeographical organization in Mesoamerica, we expanded the six ethnohistorical regions that guided, in part, the *Handbook of Middle American Indians*; we have employed a division of eleven regions. These are Central Mexico, Oaxaca, Maya Highlands, Northern Maya Lowlands, Southern Maya Lowlands, Gulf Coast, North Central Mexico, Northwestern Mexico, Northeastern Mexico, Western Mexico, and Southern Mesoamerica.

On the matter of temporal patterns of Mesoamerican cultures, we decided to emphasize the long history of Mesoamerica, which has sequences spanning thousands of years and includes not only the heterogeneity of pre-Hispanic cultures but also the complex combinations developed in the Colonial and, to a lesser extent, in the Post-Colonial and contemporary periods. As members of the committee communicated with each other and evaluated the evolving literature on historical reconstruction, it became clear that chronology poses a hazardous if fascinating problem. In order to control the complexities of historical reconstruction we asked authors not only to describe but also to interpret the problems of historical sequence and regional boundaries. As guides we chose such chronological overviews as Early Development and the Archaic period (before 2000 BCE), the Formative (Preclassic) period (2000 BCE–250 CE), the Classic period (250–900 CE), the Postclassic period (900–1521), the Colonial period (1521–1821), and the Post-Colonial period (1821–present). To extend the scope of the presentation, we also decided to include a modest number of articles about the contemporary influences and uses of Mesoamerican ideas and social patterns among Latinos in the United States today.

Part of the purpose of *The Oxford Encyclopedia of Mesoamerican Cultures* is to contribute to a vigorous public discourse in colleges, libraries, and museums via well-written essays. To ensure balanced coverage, thought was given by the editorial team comprised of a vigorous group of area editors and a distinguished editorial board. To ensure broad coverage of the developments in archaeology, I invited William Fash and Linda Manzanilla to collaborate on designing and assigning articles on the full range of archaeological sites, issues, and methods, based on their long field experience at a variety of Mesoamerican sites. I was especially mindful of the need to provide an overall balance between the Central Mexican cultures and the Maya, Gulf Coast, Oaxacan, and other important and dynamic culture areas. Elizabeth Boone's expertise in reading and interpreting a wide range of pre-Hispanic and Colonial manuscripts and traditions of writing and representation enabled a wide coverage of primary and secondary sources associated with the art and writing of Mesoamerica. Anthony Aveni was particularly qualified to organize articles on Mesoamerican cosmovision, ethnoscience, and numerous sites where archaeology and architecture expressed ideological concepts. Eduardo Matos Moctezuma, H. B. Nicholson, and Doris Heyden served as senior advisers enabling us to include important articles on the archaeological and ethnohistorical record and a number of major figures and stylistic trends, as well as discussions of the symbolic landscape. Our commitment to representing the Colonial and national periods of Mesoamerica in less extensive but strategic ways depended on the contributions and guidance of William B. Taylor and John Chance. Taylor's and Chance's extensive research and writing in Mexican Colonial history helped us ensure ample coverage of multiple perspectives on the various institutions and phases of change in economic, social, and religious dimensions of Colonial and Post-Colonial life in the sixteenth through twentieth centuries. As a number of articles show, our authors focused on the varieties and differences among colonial institutions, rates and styles of change in Indian communities, the clashes of royal and political elites with poorer communities, and the need for multiple perspectives in organizing new knowledge about Mesoamerica. We were fortunate to draw on the advice and critical understandings of an enthusiastic group of editorial advisers who engaged Mexican, Guatemalan, and other Latin American scholars in the project.

The editorial board, with the integrative efforts of our development editor, Scott Sessions, worked to devise a synoptic outline that would reflect both traditional approaches and new trends in the study of Mesoamerican cultures. This included articles grouped under the geography and history of Mesoamerica; Mesoamerican studies with special attention to the approaches, methods, and institutions that have contributed to our evolving knowledge; written and oral sources; economy and subsistence with special attention to trade and exchange; social and political organization and especially the problem of social differentiation; cultural interaction and processes of social change that highlight the dynamics of Mesoamerican history and culture; cosmovision and ritual performance; creative expression and material forms, which included attention to the styles, movements, and forms of art and architecture; and substantial attention to the range of sites, cities, and civic-ceremonial centers that organized Mesoamerica. In addition, we were interested in the biographical record of the major contributors to the history of Mesoamerica—those individuals who have both animated and illuminated its study.

In the end, we feel that our common effort has presented a picture of consensus and innovation in Mesoamerican studies while raising new issues and problems. More than three hundred historians, anthropologists, archaeologists, historians of religion, art historians, epigraphers, gender theorists, sociologists, filmmakers, and others have written the 617 entries for the encyclopedia. Our collective result creates new debates about the issues of sociopolitical organization and settlement, social change and syncretism, sacred and public architecture, ethnography and native testimonies, interregional contact and exchange, European domination and native resistance, chronology and synoptic histories, the state of archaeology and hermeneutics, and the various ways of representing native and *mestizo* cultures. It was also our intention, wherever appropriate, to have articles cover an issue, problem, or theme across the boundaries of change between the pre-Hispanic and the Colonial and contemporary periods. In some cases, a single article explores patterns and changes throughout these periods; in other cases, a composite group of articles serves the purpose.

Origin of the Work. *The Oxford Encyclopedia of Mesoamerican Cultures* descends from many origins, including a modest beginning in 1979 at the Raphael and Fletcher Lee Moses Mesoamerican Archive and Research Project, first located at the University of Colorado in Boulder and then at Princeton University. This research, teaching, and publishing project began when Eduardo Matos Moctezuma, Davíd Carrasco, and William B. Taylor collaborated to organize the first international conference on the stunning discoveries at the 1978–1979 excavation of the Templo Mayor of Tenochtitlan in Mexico City. Entitled "Center and Periphery: The Great Temple and the Aztec Empire," the conference focused on the exemplary role of the Templo Mayor in the organization and expansion of Aztec urbanism and brought together diverse intellectual interests and disciplinary approaches, including archaeology, history of religion, art history, colonial history, sociology, linguistics, and urban geography. The impressive public interest and the rich intellectual content of the papers convinced Carrasco and Matos that a longer range, collaborative group should be established to share scholarship, identify key issues, and attack a series of conceptual problems in ongoing seminars. For eighteen years, these seminars were held in Boulder, Mexico City, Teotihuacan, Colgate University, and Princeton as a means of developing new models for understanding not only the Mexica traditions of Central Mexico but also, increasingly, the Maya, Oaxacan, and Teotihuacan cultural and religious traditions of the wider Mesoamerican region.

Another important aspect of the long-term project was the overt strategy to nurture a working group of scholars as they interacted for almost two decades by focusing on sets of research problems of common interest within the field of Mesoamerican studies. In time, we began to see Mesoamerican studies as focused not only on such "centered masses" as temples, cities, palaces, and other forms of architecture but also on "sensitive grids," that is, the numerous interrelationships between centers and peripheries, diverse city-states and villages, economies and ritual, kingships, warriors, and commoners. This resulted in conferences on Tlatelolco and especially Teotihuacan, as well as the problems of understanding the nature, spread, and influence of the Classic cultures in Mesoamerica. Through the good offices of Luther Wilson, Director of the University Press of Colorado, a series of books were published that recorded this collaboration and its exciting results. In recounting this history, two other points must be kept in mind. The first is that the growing group of scholars yearned for a constantly larger understanding of Mesoamerican patterns, so we increased our efforts to talk with, learn from, and include Mayanists and researchers working in Oaxaca and other cultural areas, as well as those studying colonial New Spain. The second point was a conviction that our work could assist in a more public understanding of Mesoamerican history, cultures, and scholarship. Our conviction resulted in two major public exhibitions: the first was held in Mexico City at the Museo del Templo Mayor, entitled "Ofrendas de Tlatelolco" and viewed by more than a million people in 1990; the second, "Aztec: The World of Moctezuma," was held at the Denver Museum of Natural History in 1992–1993 and was attended by almost a million.

During the years just before the planning of this encyclopedia, our working group was enhanced by collaboration with William and Barbara Fash, David Stuart, Karl Taube, and Geoffrey McCafferty, whose work in a variety of cultures within and beyond Central Mexico provided the solid base on which to develop the general plan. At Oxford University Press, Claude Conyers and Christopher Collins encouraged and enabled us to form the Editorial Board that devised and carried out the extensive plans for this reference, research, and teaching resource. Along the way, the project was greatly enhanced by the organizational and conceptual abilities of editors Mark Mones, Mark Gallagher, and Kathy Moreau. It was clear to our editorial group that the entire Oxford staff was interested and imaginatively involved in the success of this encyclopedia. We are particularly grateful for the wise guidance and firm support of Karen Casey, Senior Vice President and Publisher of Scholarly and Professional Reference, who in all difficult moments helped us find reasonable and meaningful solutions.

In many parts of the Americas, people are becoming increasingly aware of the ways in which their daily life participates in the heritage of Mesoamerica. Most immediately, the United States shares a 3,000-kilometer (2,000-mile) long border with Mexico, along which and through which occur complex exchanges of culture, goods, people, and ideas. An increasing number of emigrants from Mexico and Central America speak Indian languages, not Spanish, as their first language. Some of these refugees contribute to international forums concerning indigenous rights in Latin America and the United States. There is increasing interest in the oppression of contemporary Indian cultures in Mesoamerica, as well as in understanding and stimulating cultural connections with Mesoamerican refugee communities in the United States. Mesoamerican legacies—including the long domestication of maize, beans, squash, chili peppers, tomatoes, and cacao (source of chocolate), and the use of tortillas and such architectural forms as ranch houses, patios, and plazas—become more of a presence in the United States every year. Mesoamerican artistic productions of pottery, jewelry, weaving, and other folk arts, sometimes rooted in myth and legend, have stimulated a new discourse on aesthetics in the Americas. There has also been some appropriation of such Mesoamerican spiritual traditions as *curanderismo* and *Dia de los Muertos* observances within U.S. society. Although hardly ever acknowledged, the cowboy culture so celebrated in the United States is Mexican in origin. Further, Mexican Spanish is becoming a widespread public and literary language that shows no sign of waning in influence. There are Mesoamerican *salsas*—in our foods and in our multicultural music. Mesoamerica is, in every way, a living world of complex and dynamic cultures. *The Oxford Encyclopedia of Mesoamerican Cultures* is the most recent attempt to describe, interpret, and raise issues of meaning and significance about all these patterns and developments.

DAVÍD CARRASCO

A Note on Mesoamerican Orthographies

Because of the linguistic diversity of Native Mesoamerica, it is inevitable that there should also be diversity in Roman orthographies, and that is reflected in this publication. The practice of the Colonial period, in the works of missionaries and chroniclers, was to adapt the orthographic practices of Spanish; thus a Nahuatl word that might be written phonemically as /tenočtitlan/ was spelled Tenochtitlan. As it happened, Spanish spelling was relatively adaptable to Nahuatl phonology; and the resulting system, with some variants, is still widely used by scholars. In other cases, as with Otomí, the "fit" was much poorer, and Colonial-period documents are harder to interpret.

In the twentieth century, linguists introduced systematic phonemic orthographies for many languages. These are valuable for scholarly use, but they often involve the use of phonetic symbols, which make them awkward typographically and difficult for practical use. For example, the Tarascan name for their own language, sometimes written in Spanish as Porépecha, can be written phonemically as /pʰorépeča/.

Still, there has been an increasing trend to compromise between scholarly and practical criteria, substituting ordinary Roman letters for some of the phonetic symbols—to write, for example, *Phorhépecha*. In Guatemala, a compromise orthography of this type, recommended by the official Academia de las Lenguas Mayas de Guatemala, and adaptable to all languages of the Mayan family, has now been widely adopted.

WILLIAM BRIGHT

THE OXFORD ENCYCLOPEDIA OF

MESOAMERICAN CULTURES

A

ACATEC. *See* Q'anjob'al.

ACCULTURATION. Anthropologists have traditionally conceptualized cultural change as originating within or outside sociocultural systems, a rough dichotomy that classes internal change as either evolutionary or revolutionary, depending on the rapidity with which it takes place. External change has received the most attention and has been studied in terms of two main concepts: diffusion and acculturation. Acculturation involves the institutional presence of large numbers of persons in the process of change, while diffusion does not.

Redfield, Linton, and Herskovits formulated the following landmark definition in 1936: "Acculturation comprehends those phenomena which result when groups of individuals having different cultures come into continuous first-hand contact, with subsequent changes in the original cultural patterns of either or both groups." Moreover, they distinguished acculturation from culture change, asserting that the former is only one aspect of the latter; from assimilation, which is usually one of the results of acculturation; and from diffusion, which constitutes just one aspect of acculturation but is always present when it occurs, and sometimes present when it does not. Subsequently, anthropologists began to define and use the concept of acculturation in different ways, often employing it in the widest sense as synonymous with the process of culture change.

Despite some disagreement among anthropologists engaged with these issues since the 1950s, the concept of acculturation has a rather high "common denominator," which may be summarized as follows. A culture different from either of its source traditions arises when two cultures come into direct contact in their full institutional array, and with the presence of the entire attendant societies or a large number of their personnel, in contexts that may include voluntary interaction, forced acceptance, selective adoption, and/or social, religious, political, and economic pressures. The novelty of the new culture results from the inequality of borrowing and transmission, which are internalized and reinterpreted according to a process of action and reaction that affects the final cultural product. In such a situation, the structure of the new sociocultural system is the result of the mutual changes that are produced in the two original systems.

Although acculturation has several forms, it occurs under two main conditions: in the presence of social, economic, political, and/or religious dominance of one cultural tradition over another, or in the absence of any kind of dominance. Anthropologists, historians, and sociologists have studied acculturation with dominance almost exclusively, primarily in the context of colonialism, as a result of the expansion of western European peoples throughout the world during the past five centuries. This was the type of acculturation that structured the multiethnic configuration of Mexico and Guatemala from pre-Hispanic times through the Spanish conquest to the middle of the nineteenth century.

Most of the considerable body of work on the transformation of Indian cultures in Mesoamerica and elsewhere in the New World has addressed specific periods and has concentrated on specific social and cultural domains. Ethnohistorians have been most successful in handling acculturation in more historical depth, as well as in taking a more systematic approach empirically and analytically. Topically, ethnohistorians have studied a large array of ethnographic and ethnologic domains—religion, social organization, economics, political organization, demography, and ethnicity. Most ethnohistorical work has been concerned with the long-range historical perspective from the pre-Hispanic situation to the middle of the nineteenth century. The short-range historical perspective—three to five generations from the ethnographic present, as it can be reconstructed from living informants and local written sources—has been the domain of anthropologists anchored to specific field situations. It is probably in Mesoamerica that the ethnohistorical study of acculturation has been most successful. Studies there have shown that the basic sectors of Indians, *mestizos*, and *criollos*, as well as the different levels of the rural–urban continuum, were structured toward the end of the seventeenth century. Between 1700 and about 1850, the multiethnic sectors were subject to a series of cultural cycles and epicycles that brought new elements of Western culture which, in interaction with the established Indian–

1

Spanish synthesis, gave the cultural mosaic of rural Mexico and Guatemala its contemporary form.

The results of acculturation in Mesoamerica, as in many other colonized parts of the world, have been asymmetrical, produced by various kinds of dominance of one cultural tradition over another. Mesoamerican Indians, for example, were forced to convert to Catholicism, and this form of dominance conditioned many aspects of the changes that took place. However, many of the complexes that came into being included elements that resulted from selective adoption and voluntary interaction—an indication that acculturation was not a rigid process. Even such central acculturative-syncretic institutions as the cult of the saints and the *mayordomía* system, as they exist today, indicate that there was a significant amount of choice and enough flexibility to mitigate the rigidity of dominance and outright imposition. This is even more evident in the domains of material culture (dress, diet), economics, and social and political organization, where the ultimate synthesis of structural and ideological elements is significantly more symmetrical.

In short, acculturation, with an emphasis on the antagonistic confrontation of entire institutions and different ideologies, is the most adequate concept for understanding how multiethnic societies come into being. This is attested by the fact that in most of Mexico and Guatemala, the multiethnic structure has not changed fundamentally for a century and a half, despite the many upheavals that these countries have undergone. The modern and contemporary context of change is no longer characterized by the antagonistic confrontation of different cultural traditions or extensive institutional complexes mutually influencing each other, but rather by the adoption of new elements by one of the multiethnic sectors. What is lacking now is the mutual cultural interchange that is the hallmark of the acculturative process. Thus, change in Mesoamerica during the last 150 years is best understood in terms of the concepts of cultural diffusion—more specifically, modernization—and secularization. Furthermore, it seems that one of the inevitable results of sociocultural change in the modern and contemporary context is the erosion of ethnocultural differences and the eventual disappearance of the multiethnic society as such.

[*See also* Transculturation.]

BIBLIOGRAPHY

Aguirre Beltrán, Gonzalo. *La población negra de México.* Mexico City, 1946. The best account of the settlement and evolution of the Black population in Mexico and its tribal African origins.

Aguirre Beltrán, Gonzalo. *El proceso de acculturación y el cambio sociocultural en México.* Mexico City, 1970. Excellent discussion of acculturation in Mexico and the differential changes it has produced in various regions.

Alberro, Solange. *Inquisition et société au Mexique, 1571–1700.* Mexico City, 1988. Brilliant study of the Inquisition in Mexico and its role in the formation of the Colonial mentality.

Barnett, Homer G. "Applied Anthropology in 1860." *Applied Anthropology* 1.2 (1941), 19–24. Insightful account of guided acculturative syncretism among the Tsimshian Indians of British Columbia in the late 1950s.

Beals, Ralph L. "The History of Acculturation in Mexico." In *Homenaje al Dr. Alfonso Caso.* Mexico City, 1951. Useful for understanding the relationship of syncretism to acculturation in Mesoamerica.

Carrasco, Davíd. *Daily Life of the Aztecs: People of the Sun and Earth.* Greenwood, Conn., 1998. Excellent account of cosmology, geography, and society among the pre-Hispanic peoples of Central Mexico; contains many illuminating analyses of ritual and ceremonialism.

Carrasco, Pedro. *Tarascan Folk Religion: An Analysis of Economic, Social, and Religious Integration.* Tulane University Middle American Research Institute, 17. New Orleans, 1952. Excellent statement on characteristics of syncretism and acculturation and their relationship to the wider aspects of social structure.

Chance, John K. *Race and Class in Colonial Oaxaca.* Stanford, 1978. Insightful study of the formation of a regional multiethnic society.

Gamio, Manuel. *La población del Valle de Teotihuacán.* Mexico City, 1922. The earliest work on acculturation in a Mesoamerican region.

Gibson, Charles. *The Aztecs under Spanish Rule: The History of the Indians of the Valley of Mexico 1519–1810.* Stanford, 1964. The best reconstruction of a Mesoamerican regional society as the result of contact throughout the Colonial period.

Gruzinski, Serge. *La colonisation de l'imaginaire: Sociétés indigène et occidentalisation dans le Mexique Espagnol XVIᵉ–XVIIᵉ siècle.* Paris, 1988. Important for understanding the formation of the Colonial mentality in New Spain; full of insights and concrete analyses of the interaction of Indian and Spanish society.

Kirchhoff, Paul. "Los pueblos de la historia Tolteca-Chichimeca: Sus migraciones y parentesco." *Revista mexicana de estudios antropológicos* 4. 1–2 (1943). An indispensable source for the study of the acculturative history of Central Mexico during the three centuries before the Spanish conquest.

Kubler, George. "The Quechua in the Colonial World." In *Handbook of South American Indians*, edited by Julian Steward. Washington, D.C., 1946. One of the best studies of Indian Colonial acculturation; a model for organizing the long-range transformation of a group's culture and society.

La Farge, Oliver. "Maya Ethnology: The Sequence of Cultures." In *The Maya and Their Neighbors.* New York, 1940. Important article on the periodization that all long-range cases of acculturation must include, and a model that has often been used to organize the description of this process.

López Austin, Alfredo. *Hombre-Dios: Religión y política en el mundo Náhuatl.* Mexico City, 1973. Probably the best study on pre-Hispanic Mesoamerican religion; excellent background for understanding the acculturative-syncretic development of Indian-Spanish Catholicism.

Nutini, Hugo G. *Todos Santos in Rural Tlaxcala: A Syncretic, Expressive, and Symbolic Analysis of the Cult of the Dead.* Princeton, 1988. Contains many descriptions of the acculturative process that accompanied the syncretic development of Indian-Spanish Catholicism in Mesoamerica.

Nutini, Hugo G., and Betty Bell. *Ritual Kinship: The Structure and Historical Development of the Compadrazgo System in Rural Tlaxcala.* Princeton, 1980. Exhaustive account of the acculturative development of *compadrazgo* from the sixteenth century to the present.

Nutini, Hugo G., and Barry L. Issac. *Los pueblos de habla Nahuatl de la región de Tlaxcala y Puebla*. Mexico City, 1974. Includes analysis of acculturation and diffusion as two different forms of change, the latter in terms of modernization and secularization.

Redfield, R., R. Linton, and M. Herskovits. "Memorandum on the Study of Acculturation." *American Anthropologist* 38 (1936), 149–152. Contains the earliest definition of acculturation.

Reyes, Luis. *Cuauhtinchan del siglo XII al XVI: Formación social y desarrollo histórico de un señorío prehispánico*. Wiesbaden, 1977. Good study of acculturative development of Nahuatl-speaking peoples of Central Mexico during the four centuries before the Spanish Conquest.

Wolf, Eric R. *Sons of the Shaking Earth*. Chicago, 1962. Arguably the best acculturative and syncretic account of Mesoamerican peoples from pre-Hispanic times to the twentieth century.

HUGO G. NUTINI

ACOLHUA. *See* Triple Alliance.

ACOSTA, JOSEPH DE (1540–1600), Spanish Jesuit and historian. Born in Medina del Campo, he studied at the College of Alcalá. From 1562 to 1565, he resided in Rome. In 1572, he went to America destined for Peru, where he carried out missionary work in Lima, Cuzco, Arequipa, and other locations. He was principal of the College of Lima. In 1576, he wrote the missionary treatise *De procuranda indorum salute*; in 1581, the treatise *De natura novi orbis* (both in Latin). In these writings, he expressed his interest in the nature of the New World and his ideas about the universe. In 1586, he was sent north to New Spain and lived one year in Mexico City. There he met Juan de Tovar, a fellow Jesuit who provided him with information about the ancient Mexicans. In 1586, Acosta received a royal license from Madrid for publishing the treatises he wrote in Peru; these texts are the basis for his 1590 *Historia natural y moral de las Indias* (in Spanish), part of which was published in Latin in Seville, Spain. In 1590, he published other treatises, which are Latin versions of his sermons preached in the Americas. During those years, he traveled to Rome and Spain, attending to some political issues for his order. In 1597, he became dean of the College of Salamanca, and retained that position until his death in 1600.

Acosta's most important contribution was the 1590 publication of the *Historia* in Seville. In this seven-volume work, he presents sixteenth-century European ideas about the existence and nature of the New World. The last two volumes treat the histories of the pre-Hispanic Inca and Mexica. His source for the Inca was the information provided by Polo de Ondegardo, governor of Peru. For information on the Mexica, Acosta followed Juan de Tovar's *Relación del origen de los indios que habitan esta Nueva España según sus historias*, a possible summary of Fray Diego Durán's *Historia de las Indias de Nueva España e islas de Tierra Firme*—in turn derived in part from an anonymous Nahuatl history of Mexico-Tenochtitlan, known as the *Crónica X*.

Acosta held, like most philosophers of his time, that the physical world was composed of the basic elements—earth, water, air, and fire—along with their combinations or substances—the mineral, vegetable, and animal. As a second part of the *Historia*, he included the moral or humanistic aspects of the inhabitants of the New World. Following Aristotle, Acosta believed that there existed both animate and inanimate things. Minerals are inanimate; flora are beings with nutritious souls; animals have both nutritious and sensitive souls; humans pertain to the latter kind of beings, but they also have a rational and immortal soul, capable of salvation. This is why Acosta assumed as obvious his plan of exposition, from natural history to moral (human) history.

Acosta conceived the universe as a finite sphere, with a center and eleven other spheres, which contained the different elements, planets, and stars—all composed of masses of matter, that is, the four elements. The planet Earth was considered dominated by land and water, with five zones: two polar, two temperate, and the middle zone that was equatorial, "torrid," or "burned." Only the temperate zones were considered suitable for human habitation, although this was contradicted by the Spanish experience in the sixteenth century. Acosta's books explain the presence of people in the Americas as part of the human and the Christian experience. Acosta's views were the result of his concluding that the New World is an integral part of the universe, composed of the same materials and sharing the same natures as other living beings. In sum, according to Acosta, the indigenous peoples of the Americas were humans with nutritious, sensitive, and rational souls—to be saved by Christian doctrine.

BIBLIOGRAPHY

O'Gorman, Edmundo. *The Invention of America*. Westport, Conn., 1972. Discusses the concept of America as a sixteenth-century invention, starting from the work of Acosta and exploring the ideas of other contemporary authors.

O'Gorman, Edmundo. "Prologo." In *Historia natural y moral de las Indias*, by Joseph de Acosta, pp. xi–cl. Mexico City, 1979. Presents an erudite discussion of the structure and significance of the work of Acosta and some debates about his writings that occurred in the eighteenth and nineteenth centuries.

BLAS ROMAN CASTELLON HUERTA

AGRICULTURE. In the Americas, the domestication of plants and some animals and the development of agriculture and irrigation were the result of prolonged local processes. These processes were originated by the peoples of two areas: Middle Americans (Mexico and Central America) and Andeans. Each took its own path, and there was only sporadic contact (evidenced by some plants and metal implements). Agriculture and irrigation in Mesoamerica cannot be characterized as simple, uniform, or primitive—providing the bases for the support of the ancient civilizations, large urban populations, and complex states.

The processes that led to these achievements were ecological, biological, agricultural, and organizational. Ecologically, a type of resource management was developed that bridged microenvironmental differences—both vertical (mountainous areas) and horizontal (plains)—to take advantage of the great diversities of soil, climate, vegetation, and humidity. Biologically, a wide range of plant species (second-largest after China) was domesticated by a process of selection and horticulture, resulting in genetic manipulation. Agriculturally, labor-intensive methods and techniques were practiced in the production cycle, as well as in the construction and maintenance of irrigation and terracing. Organizationally, labor groups larger than the family were created to manage the seasonal requirements of farming and water use (burning, weeding, harvesting, irrigation, construction and maintenance of works, clearing drains), as well as any external needs (tribute, exchange, marketing). These led to forms of cooperation and social reciprocity of variable scale and complexity.

The domestication of about seventy plant species occurred throughout a long period, beginning some 10,000 years BP (before present), according to the most recent dating of *Cucurbita* species remains from Oaxaca (Smith 1997). The domestication of maize and some other plants was a geographically diverse process that occurred simultaneously in various regions (MacNeish 1964). The subcenters were Tamaulipas, where squash and beans were first cultivated, followed much later by maize; Puebla, where avocados and chilies were first grown, then maize; Oaxaca, with the oldest cultivated squashes; and the Basin of Mexico, with maize followed by squashes. This evidence comes from the few sites with the longest archaeological sequences, and they may not be representative of the whole. Also, there are no examples from the tropical lowlands, where preservation conditions are not good for such remains.

The long period in which domestication and the first agricultural and hydraulic practices were originated is called the era of proto-agriculture or incipient cultivation. The diffusion of species from their places of origin to all of Mesoamerica—especially maize, beans, squashes, and chilies—occurred around 2000 BCE. From 1500 to 1000 BCE, small settlements of sedentary agriculturalists were formed, which produced baskets, ceramics, and stone objects by the first specialists. During this period, called the Formative (Preclassic), agricultural activity was transformed into an essential aspect of existence (Wolf 1966), when the basic patterns of Mesoamerican civilization were originated and tested: technology, architecture, artisanal specialization, social differentiation, and religious specialization.

According to Mangelsdorf, MacNeish, and Willey (1964), "the agricultural complex of Mesoamerica . . . was the richest group of edible plants in the Western Hemisphere." This group comprised eighty-eight species, seventy-one originated in the Mexican–Central American area and seventeen introduced from elsewhere, with a few genera having a number of species: *Phaseolus*, *Curcubita*, *Agave*, *Anona*, *Opuntia*, *Theobroma*, and *Dahlia*. By the sixteenth century, the plants of basic consumption (maize, beans, squashes, chilies, amaranths, and chias) were grown throughout the agricultural region, while other more specialized plants were cultivated only in certain areas (cotton, cacao, fruits, aromatics, and medicinal plants). The cases of squashes and maize illustrate the processes of domestication.

- *Curcubita* spp.: Twenty-three of the twenty-six wild and cultivated species of the genus—among which are squashes, *chilacayote*, and gourds—are native to Mexico and constitute the oldest domesticated New World plants. In Tehuacán, the remains of *C. pepo* (summer squash or pumpkin), *C. mixta* (walnut squash), and *C. moschata* (cushaw squash) date from 6,000 to 9,000 BP, while *Lagenaria siceraria* (bottle gourd) dates from 9,000 BP in Tamaulipas and Oaxaca. At first, only the seeds—rich in oils—were exploited, since the pulp of the squashes was very bitter, thin, and tough; once domesticated, nearly all parts could be consumed.

- *Zea mays*: The origin of this cereal is not fully known. The increase in the size of its ear is the most visible morphological change produced by domestication—from 5 centimeters (2 inches) in prehistoric Tehuacán to more than 30 centimeters (12 inches) in some modern varieties. Today, there are forty-eight distinct varieties—additional evidence of the effects of human action. Its domestication possibly occurred about 5000 BCE in the highlands of central and southern Mexico; by 2000 BCE, it was grown throughout the agricultural region; by 1519, it was cultivated at elevations ranging from sea level to 3,000 meters (9,300 feet).

The agriculture of Mesoamerica became varied, complex, and productive. The agricultural techniques were diverse. It is useful to review the systems of agricultural management according to the following criteria: agricultural intensity (frequency of land use over time), water sources (rain, humidity, irrigation, capillary action), management during the production cycle (techniques, methods, and implements), and long-term structures (modification of the topography with terraces, *bancales*, drains, and irrigation works). Mesoamerican agricultural systems may be organized into four groups: extensive seasonal systems, medium-intensive seasonal systems, intensive systems, and special systems (gardens and groves).

Extensive seasonal systems. The forest and shrub vegetation of the area to be cultivated was cut, felled, and burned; the soil was not tilled but depended on rainwater and, in rare instances, terracing. The energy and implements used were axes, fire, and the planting stick (*uitzoctli* in Nahuatl) for clearing, hoeing, depositing seeds or plants, and weeding. In the sixteenth century, such systems existed on hillsides and piedmonts of the Sierra Madre Oriental, Occidental, and del Sur, and to a lesser degree in the Neo-Volcanic Axis, as well as on the coastal plain of the Gulf of Mexico (ranging from the Huasteca to the Yucatán Peninsula). A parcel of land was cultivated with maize, some species of bean or squash, or else chia, amaranth, sweet potato, yucca, or jicama; useful trees and shrubs were left in the ground to surround the parcel, as well as scattered about. There were long fallow periods after the harvest.

Medium-intensive seasonal systems. Shrubs and grasses on the land were cut and burned; the soil was not conditioned, except for sowing in small holes or weeding with a work implement. This system had no irrigation works, but sometimes terraces were used to retain rainwater and prevent soil runoff. Axes were used for cutting and weeding and the *coa de hoja* (*uictli de hoja*, the Nahuatl word used generically here). There were one or two cultivation cycles each year—the first depending on the summer rains, the second (*tonamil*) on the winter rains (the *nortes* on the slopes of the Gulf Coast). These systems have often been confused with those of the forests because both involve slash-and-burn, or swidden, agriculture, but it is important to differentiate, for medium-intensive seasonal systems use several forms of management. Those of less intensity were practiced in noncontiguous areas, on the hillsides and ridges of the three great mountain ranges, in regions such as the Huasteca, the Sierra de Puebla, and the Chinantla (Oaxaca), and on the coastal plains of the Gulf of Mexico (the Chontalpa).

Intensive systems. These systems were used in various places throughout the agricultural region, in highlands and lowlands, some associated with irrigation, others with summer rains. With them, a short fallow period (one to two years) was used. Generally, their distribution coincided with the highlands of central, southern, and southeastern Mexico and Central America. On the hillsides, terraces and *metepantles* (wide terraces with maguey plants

on the edges) were constructed, to trap water and prevent erosion. Valleys and land near mountain bases were often irrigated, while soil reclamation (raised fields and *chinampas*) was used in wetlands. The soils were conditioned for sowing, with small compartments (*cajetes* or *pocetas*) formed, or mounds (*montones*), or raised beds (*camellones*) with furrows. The basic practices were oriented to increasing yield, with forms of manual cultivation—plant by plant—employed in making seedbeds, applying fertilizer (vegetal, lime, bat guano, ant colonies), sowing, weeding, hilling, and with such daily practices as the association, rotation, and arrangement of crops. Implements included the *uictli de hoja* (the most popular), *uictli axoquen* (a small stick with a zoomorphic magus), and *uictli grande* (a large stick).

Special systems. The permanent cultivation of special lands included garden plots near homes (*solar, milpa de casa, calmil*) as well as the groves of fruit trees, cacao, avodacos, cochineal cactus, ornamentals, and most probably maguey. These were stable parcels, for everyday use, with high yields. They were generally situated close to living spaces, for security and for fertilization with domestic waste material. Their composition was mixed, so they produced at staggered but continuous intervals.

Annual Planting. The yearly cycle began with the selection and preparation of the land for sowing. In the intensive and medium-intensive systems, the work minimally included examining, selecting, measuring, and marking out the parcel; opening the underbrush; cutting, felling, spreading, and chopping the underbrush, shrubs, or grass, accordingly; cleaning the firebreaks; and burning. A common practice was to combine a *milpa* slashed during the annual cycle with an older one of two or more years' use, which reduced the work and spread out the risks of loss. Burning converted the vegetal carpet into a layer of ash and embers, whose nutrients were utilized immediately by the crop plants. When summer sowing was followed by a second planting during the dry season, to take advantage of winter rains or residual moisture, the vegetation was cut but not burned, to avoid moisture loss. In contrast, preparation of the land for intensive agriculture included some amount of working the soil—digging, breaking up, loosening, and conditioning—to receive the seeds. Kernels of maize (often with seeds for beans, squash, or *chilacayote* or tubers for sweet potato, yucca, or jicama), were placed by hand into small holes dug at the time of sowing in the *pocetas, cajetes, camellones,* or *montones* of previously loosened earth. Planting by hand was common to all Mesoamerican cultivation systems. The seeds or plant parts were placed one by one into the earth; each plant and each *mata* (group of plants) received attention. The careful selection of the seeds and plant parts was also important. In the intensive systems, such as *chinampas*, the preparation of seedbeds (*almácigas*) was a common practice. The soil was helped by weeding—done by killing the weed in a simultaneous operation of grubbing and hilling or loosening and removing the soil around the *matas* to uproot and smother the harmful weed. Bringing the soil up against a plant resulted in additional light, air, and support. Weeding might also consist of cutting or uprooting weeds by hand. Maize harvesting techniques—by removing the ear of kernels with or without the bracts—were similar in all the systems. Storage and conservation of the previous maize seed (mainly by drying), as well as harvesting and caring for the rest of the plants, were involved processes.

Lowland Maya agriculture. For many years it was considered absolute truth that swidden agriculture was practiced universally by Maya *campesinos*. According to modern versions, slash-and-burn agriculture was complemented with groves of perennial plants (arboriculture), and intensive agriculture was practiced in areas close to the great urban and ceremonial centers, where production was controlled by the elite. Today's more accepted interpretation does not conceive of only one model for the entire Maya Lowlands throughout its history; rather, it provides a diversified model that combines swidden with long and short fallow periods, crop rotation, the association of crops, fertilization, mulching, diversified cultivation of annuals (including tubers and trees), domestic gardens, terracing, and drained and raised fields, among others.

Irrigation. The importance of irrigated lands in Mesoamerican agriculture since ancient times has been amply demonstrated. During the Postclassic period, some were widely dispersed and of medium and small scale, although others were concentrated, and complex, large-scale examples, such as those in the Basin of Mexico. The coincidence of irrigation with the geographical limits of Mesoamerica in the sixteenth century—and the correlation with areas of high demographic, urban, political, and economic density—is clear. In direct relation to climatic factors, irrigation had its greatest significance in the high plains of western, central, and southern Mesoamerica. Most of the irrigation works were of a permanent nature—dams, canals, and aqueducts—but there were also the ephemeral ditches, runoff channels, and diversion dams. Doolittle (1990) has reviewed the technology, chronology, and irrigation areas of twenty-eight pre-Hispanic canal systems, concluding that: "there were very few things pertaining to the technology of irrigation canals that were not developed in Mexico prior to the arrival of Spaniards in the sixteenth century." Yet he found no "board-type sluice gates, arched aqueducts, [or such] assortment of masonry devices as flow control boxes, drop structures, chutes, pipes, and inverted siphons."

Dating irrigation works and terraces is a complex problem, but not impossible with some new methods; nevertheless, the only sure way is based on remains sealed within their structures. Such is the case in the Olmec system of Teopantecuanitlán in Guerrero, which consists of a canal of large stone blocks and the retaining wall of a dam that possibly led to a reservoir (1200–1000 BCE). The oldest Mesoamerican canal irrigation system known, however, is at Santa Clara Coatitla, in the Basin of Mexico, which was dated to about 1000 BCE.

Contemporary Agriculture in Historical Perspective. Mesoamerican agriculture underwent profound transformations after the Spanish conquest. The drastic demographic decline caused by Old World contagious diseases shaped history and the agrarian landscape. Two other phenomena important for ecological and social effects were the introduced livestock and the incorporation of new plants and other animals (including pests). The biological contact between the Old and New World produced a genuine ecological revolution, as well as changes in various modes of production. Yet indigenous societies and their cultures not only persisted but also played an active role in this revolution. Native populations soon appropriated new biological and technical elements, with the related knowledge, and incorporated them into their everyday practices, which were thus enriched and diversified. As indigenous economies and societies were transformed, so too were forms of agricultural and water management. The persistence, until today, of many agricultural-management practices—old and new—results from basic changes and experiments.

In the extensive and seasonal systems with long fallow periods, slashing and weeding continue to be done manually, but now with steel axes and machetes; planting is conducted with the old wooden planting stick, but now with a metal point; and the same *picador*, now made of iron, is used for harvesting. Commercial herbicides are often employed in the exhausting task of weeding. Today, the extensive systems have become less common, owing to the growing scarcity of forested lands needed to form a good layer of vegetal ash. Such systems are exposed to strong pressures that have shortened fallow periods and led to reductions in yields. *Milpas* can still be found, but maize monoculture predominates where herbicides destroy adjacent plants. In areas with winter rains, a second cycle of beans or maize is still planted. In medium-intensive systems, the management forms and the tools for swidden remain similar to those described, but iron *coas*, *palos*, and *azadones* (broad hoes) are used in sowing and weeding, or the plow and draft animal are used in combination with these manual tools. Today, land pressure increasingly promotes herbicides and chemical fertilizers for successful farming.

In the wake of the Conquest, intensively managed parcels and garden plots were modified the most. They were located in valleys or plains and on moderately sloped hillsides, and they depended on such structures as irrigation works, leveling, and terracing. Therefore, they first aroused the greed of the Spaniards, who obtained them either by royal dispensation or plunder. The agricultural practices on lands that indigenous communities retained were perhaps the most transformed—after the plow, tools, animal fertilizers, and new technical elements of irrigation were incorporated.

More general changes affected all of rural indigenous society. In many areas, especially those that suffered the greatest population losses, raising livestock—mainly horses, cattle, and sheep—became the principal activity, practiced on the savannas and agricultural lands abandoned with the disappearance of the *campesinos*. In the domestic sphere, European bees, domesticated fowl (especially chickens), pigs, goats, burros, and mules, as well as the livestock, were adopted as draft animals, for agriculture, or as sources of new products (meat, fertilizer, fats, honey, hides, milk, eggs, feathers, bones, etc.). Raising horses and cattle, combined with carts and other implements, produced a revolution in labor, transportation, and agriculture, lightening some of the work of *campesinos* and carriers, but also creating new tasks to provide their food (maize, forage) and care (apiaries, corrals, pens, chicken coops).

Growing Old World plants unleashed effects that ranged from complementation, to displacement and substitution (cotton for sugar cane). Diverse results included complex agricultural calendars, with new crop rotations and associated labor, expansion of the altitudinal and longitudinal frontiers and the autumn-winter cycle, and an increase in production from new species resistant to lower temperatures (cereals, legumes, fruits, and vegetables). All occurred alongside the increase in the cultivation of many native plants (maize, maguey, beans, cotton, chilies, squash, cacao, prickly-pear and cochineal cactus, and indigo). Produce went to *campesinos*, to the new inhabitants, and to export, with its associated labor. Today, the blend of old and new agricultural practices is continued on general and specialized crops, for local use and worldwide markets.

[*See also* Amaranth; Cacao; Chinampa Agriculture; Maize, *article on* Origin, Domestication, and Development.]

BIBLIOGRAPHY

Armillas, Pedro. "Notas sobre sistemas de cultivo en Mesoamérica: Cultivos de riego y humedad en la cuenca del río Balsas." *Anales del INAH* 3 (1949), 85–113. Pioneering study, based on historical sources and field observation, analyzing the agriculture practiced in the Balsas river basin.

Crosby, Alfred W., Jr. *The Columbian Exchange: Biological and Cultural Consequences of 1492.* Westport, Conn., 1973. Good account of the ecological and social effects of the interaction between the ecosystems of the New and Old Worlds that resulted from the contact and exchange of persons, plants, animals, and germs.

Doolittle, William E. *Canal Irrigation in Prehistoric Mexico: The Sequence of Technological Change.* Austin, Tex., 1990. Systematizes, with exceptional rigor, the extant information on prehistoric canal irrigation, to better understand its role in pre-Hispanic Mexican agriculture.

Flannery, Kent V., ed. *Guilá Naquitz: Archaic Foraging and Early Agriculture in Oaxaca, Mexico.* Orlando, Fla., 1986. Brings together the results of an interdisciplinary study on the origins of agriculture in the highlands of Southern Mexico, from the pre-agricultural era to the appearance of the first evidence of cultivated plants at the Guilá Naquitz cave in Oaxaca.

MacLung de Tapía, Emily, and Judith Zurita Noguera. "Las primeras sociedades sedentarias." In *Historia antigua de México*, edited by Linda Manzanilla and Leonardo López Luján, vol. 1, pp. 209–246. Mexico City, 1994. Synthesis of sedentarization and the factors associated with it in Mesoamerica.

MacNeish, Richard S. "The Food Gathering and Incipient Agriculture Stage of Prehistoric Middle America." In *Handbook of Middle American Indians*, edited by Robert Wauchope, vol. 1, edited by Robert C. West, pp. 413–426. Austin, Tex., 1964. Useful synthesis of the evidence extant at that time.

Mangelsdorf, Paul C., Richard S. MacNeish, and Gordon R. Willey. "Origins of Agriculture in Middle America." In *Handbook of Middle American Indians*, edited by Robert Wauchope, vol. 1, edited by Robert C. West, pp. 427–445. Austin, Tex., 1964. Authoritative review of the principal proposals on the origin of agriculture, the archaeological evidence, and the repertory of plants in Middle America.

Melville, Elinor G. K. *A Plague of Sheep: Environmental Consequences of the Conquest of Mexico.* Cambridge, 1994. Study of the biological conquest of the New World, based on the case of sixteenth-century Central Mexico; analyzes environmental changes associated with the introduction of grazing animals and compares them with processes that occurred in Australia.

Niederberger, Christine. "Las sociedades mesoamericanas: Las civilizaciones antiguas y su nacimiento." In *Historia general de América Latina: Las sociedades originarias*, edited by Teresa Rojas Rabiela and John V. Murra, vol. 1, pp. 117–150. Madrid, 1999. Revealing examination that separates the different processes of "Neolithicization"—the permanent occupation and use of cultivated plants—from the birth of Mesoamerican civilization (the Olmec cultural system).

Ochoa, Lorenzo. "Formaciones regionales de Mesoamérica: Tierras mayas." In *Historia general de América Latina: Las sociedades originarias*, edited by Teresa Rojas Rabiela and John V. Murra, vol. 1, Madríd, 1999. Panorama of Maya development that discusses, among others, the problems of economic bases, agriculture, and irrigation.

Palerm, Ángel. "Agricultural Systems and Food Patterns." In *Handbook of Middle American Indians*, edited by Robert Wauchope, vol. 6, edited by Manning Nash, pp. 26–52. Austin, Tex., 1967. One of the most authoritative and consulted works on the indigenous agriculture of contemporary Middle America.

Palerm, Ángel. "Distribuición geográfica de los regadíos prehispánicos en el área central de Mesoamérica (1954)." In *Agricultura y civilización en Mesoamérica*, edited by Ángel Palerm and Eric Wolf, pp. 30–54. Mexico City, 1972. Systematic review of the historical evidence on irrigated land in Mesoamerica.

Rojas Rabiela, Teresa. *Las siembras de ayer: La agricultura indígena del siglo XVI.* Mexico City, 1988. Detailed reconstruction of pre-

Hispanic agriculture and irrigation of the sixteenth century, based on archaeological and historical sources, with new propositions concerning their practices, instruments, and general function.

Rojas Rabiela, Teresa. "La tecnología agrícola." In *Historia antigua de México*, edited by Linda Manzanilla and Leonardo López Luján, vol 4. Mexico City, 2000. Up-to-date presentation of pre-Hispanic agriculture and irrigation, from their origins to the sixteenth century.

Smith, Bruce D. "Initial Domestication of *Curcubita pepo* in the Americas 10,000 Years Ago." *Science* 276 (1997), 932–934. Latest results derived from the analysis of *C. pepo* remains from the Guilá Naquitz cave (Oaxaca), the oldest domesticated plant in America (c.8000 BCE).

Wilken, Gene C. *Good Farmers: Traditional Agricultural Resource Management in Mexico and Central America*. Berkeley, Calif., 1987. From a detailed catalog of traditional agricultural practices of Mexico and Central America, some principles are formulated concerning the management of resources, with comparative ends; suggests that challenges are common to traditional as well as modern agriculturalists—that both require comparable management responses.

Wolf, Eric R. *Peasants*. Englewood Cliffs, N.J., 1966. Fundamental theoretical work.

TERESA ROJAS RABIELA
Translated from Spanish by Scott Sessions

AGUACATEC. *See* Mamean.

AGUIRRE BELTRÁN, GONZALO (1908–1996), Mexican anthropologist. Aguirre Beltrán was born into a prominent physician's family in Tlacotalpan, Veracruz. He completed his medical studies at age twenty-three at the Universidad Nacional Autónoma de México (UNAM) in Mexico City, then returned to Veracruz to practice medicine for ten years in the small town of Huatusco, where his interest in local history led to writing his first monograph, *El señorío de Cuauhtocho: Luchas agrarias en México durante el virreinato* (1940). This pioneering study of peasant movements proved to be the first step along an incredibly productive lifelong journey as an anthropologist committed to advancing anthropological theory, as an administrator concerned with the cultures of Mexico's indigenous peoples, and as a social critic confident in the power of civilized debate in an emerging democratic society.

In 1942, a decisive event took place in Aguirre Beltrán's life when he met the well-known Mexican anthropologist Manuel Gamio, then head of the demographic department of the Secretariat of Government and head of the Archivo General de la Nación in Mexico City. [*See the biography of Gamio.*] As a result of their meeting, Aguirre Beltrán took up the study of a previously ignored group, the blacks of Mexico, particularly those living along the *costa chica* ("little coast") in the Mexican state of Guerrero. Based on archival and field research, he collected materials that resulted in three significant works: *La*

población negra de México, 1519–1810: Estudio etnohistórico (1946), *Cuijla: Esbozo etnográfico de un pueblo* (1957), and *Medicina y magia: El proceso de aculturación en la estructura colonial* (1963).

Upon the recommendation of the French ethnologist Alfred Métraux, Aguirre Beltrán had gone to the United States for the 1945–1946 academic year to study at Northwestern University with two anthropologists—Melville J. Herskovits and A. Irving Hallowell—internationally known for their work on acculturation among African-American and Native American populations. Returning to Mexico, Aguirre Beltrán then put aside his medical practice to become a full-time anthropologist. He served as the director of Indigenous Affairs in the Secretariat of Public Education from 1946 to 1949 before becoming a researcher in the Tarascan region of Michoacán for the Instituto Nacional Indigenista (INI) from 1949 to 1950. He moved to Chiapas as coordinator of INI's Tzeltal-Tzotzil area (1951–1952), before returning to Mexico City as INI's subdirector (1952–1956). In 1956, Aguirre Beltrán was called back to his native state to be rector of the Universidad Veracruzana, where he served with distinction until 1961, when he entered the political arena as a federal deputy for the triennium of 1961 to 1964. He then left politics and returned to anthropological administration when he accepted the directorship of the Instituto Indigenista Interamericano (based in Mexico City), where he greatly expanded its role in indigenous affairs from 1966 to 1970.

From 1970 to 1976, Aguirre Beltrán served with distinction as subsecretary of the Department of Popular Culture and Continuing Education in the Secretariat of Education; there he initiated three major publication series that resulted in hundreds of anthropological studies being made available to the Mexican public at economical prices. At the same time, he did double duty as INI's director, in which capacity he helped Angel Palerm and Guillermo Bonfil Batalla establish a center for advanced studies in social anthropology within the Instituto Nacional de Antropología e Historia (INAH). In 1977, Aguirre Beltrán retired from these important administrative positions and was appointed to the Instituto de Investigaciones Antropológicas at UNAM. Subsequently, he moved back to Jalapa, Veracruz, where he was involved in creating a center for social anthropology for the Gulf region (1982) and a graduate program in social anthropology at Jalapa (1988).

His many contributions to the discipline of anthropology and the indigenous peoples of Mexico brought Aguirre Beltrán numerous awards and honors, including the 1973 Malinowski Award of the Society for Applied Anthropology, the 1975 Sourasky Prize, the 1978 Manuel Gamio Award, the 1979 National Social Science Prize, and the 1991 Belisario Domínguez Medal. In September 1995, just four months before he died, Aguirre Beltrán was the focus of a National Celebration in Jalapa.

His career involved major contributions in many areas of anthropology, including ethnohistory, political anthropology, regional studies, medical anthropology, and educational policy. Many of his publications blended these interests. Thus, *Formas de gobierno indígena* (1953) offered a wide-ranging assessment of three populations—Tarahumara, Tzeltal-Tzotzil, and Tarascan—whose political forms had been changed since pre-Conquest times. *El proceso de aculturación* (1957) and *Regiones de refugio: El desarrollo de la comunidad y el proceso dominical en mestizoamérica* (1967) represented ground-breaking efforts to understand the problems of indigenous communities in the face of external exploitation. The depth of his regional approach to Mexican cultures was manifested not only in theoretical works but also in ethnographic studies, such as *Problemas de la población indígena de la cuenca del Tepalcatepec* (1953) and *Zongólica: Encuentro de dioses y santos patrones* (1986). Aguirre Beltrán's distinctive approach to medical anthropology, blending theory and practice with the expertise of a scholar trained in both medicine and anthropology, is illustrated by his well-known volumes *Programas de salud en la situación intercultural* (1955) and *Antropología médica* (1986). His important work in educational policy is seen in *Teoría y práctica de la educación indígena* (1973) and in *Lenguas vernáculas: Su uso y desuso en la enseñanza, la experiencia de México* (1983).

Beyond his scholarly contributions, Aguirre Beltrán was an active participant in discussions on the development of contemporary Mexican society. Many of his essays on social issues are gathered in *Obra polémica* (1976), while his commentaries on the historical dialogue between anthropology and Indianist policies are assembled in *Crítica antropológica: Contribuciones al estudio del pensamiento social en México* (1990).

The grand scope of Aguirre Beltrán's accomplishments as anthropological theorist, program administrator, and social critic are manifest in the republication of his major works in a sixteen-volume set by the prestigious Fondo de Cultura Económica (1989–1995). In addition, two appreciations of his life and works have appeared, the first published by the Instituto Indigenista Interamericano in 1973, under the title *Homenaje a Gonzalo Aguirre Beltrán*, and the second by the Universidad Veracruzana in 1996 as *Gonzalo Aguirre Beltrán: Homenaje nacional—memorias*. In this last-named volume, the well-known Mexican anthropologist Arturo Warman describes Aguirre Beltrán as "a master of tolerance, civilized dialogue, patience, and even good humor—all essential elements of a democratic spirit" (p. 25).

Gonzalo Aguirre Beltrán was a spirited activist, devoted throughout his long career to understanding the diversity of Mexican history while challenging the relations of culture and power in contemporary Mexico. Although only one of his major monographs has been translated into English (*Regions of Refuge*, issued by the Society for Applied Anthropology in 1979), his work remains required reading for those concerned with ethnic and indigenous issues, acculturation of populations in local and regional contexts, and educational and medical theories and practices in Mesoamerica.

BIBLIOGRAPHY

Aguirre Beltrán, Gonzalo. *La población negra de México, 1519–1810: Estudio etnohistórico*. Mexico City, 1946. Based on archival and field research; first significant academic treatment of the African-*mestizo* population in Mexico.

Aguirre Beltrán, Gonzalo. *Formas de gobierno indígena*. Mexico City, 1953. Ethnohistorical assessment of political behavior and governmental structures among the Tarahumaras, Tzotzil-Tzeltal, and Tarascan populations of rural Mexico.

Aguirre Beltrán, Gonzalo. *El proceso de aculturación*. Mexico City, 1957. Examination of sociocultural transformations in Mexico within the framework of acculturation theories.

Aguirre Beltrán, Gonzalo. *Medicina y magia: El proceso de aculturación en la estructura colonial*. Mexico City, 1963. Application of the author's theory of acculturation to the domain of medicine in Mexico, with special attention to the interaction of pre-Hispanic and European medical theories and practices.

Aguirre Beltrán, Gonzalo. *Regiones de refugio: El desarrollo de la comunidad y el proceso dominical en mestizoamérica*. Mexico City, 1967. [Translated as: *Regions of Refuge*. Washington, D.C., 1979]. Important work about relations between the economically developed "metropolis" and the less-developed rural "periphery"; explains how diverse Indian populations have been dominated by *mestizo, ladino*, and national powers.

Aguirre Beltrán, Gonzalo. *Obra antropológica* (16 volumes). Mexico City, 1989–1995. Comprehensive republication of the author's major monographs and essays; offers an excellent opportunity to assess the continuing value of Aguirre Beltrán's theoretical and applied perspectives.

Instituto Indigenista Interamericano. *Homenaje a Gonzalo Aguirre Beltrán*. Mexico City, 1973–74. The first two volumes contain twenty-three contributions by distinguished scholars from throughout Mexico and the rest of the Americas; the third volume offers a comprehensive bibliography of Aguirre Beltrán's articles, books, and other works from 1939 to 1973.

Peña, Guillermo de la. "Gonzalo Aguirre Beltrán." *La antropología en México, panorama histórico*, coordinadores Lina Odena Güemes and Carlos García Mora, pp. 63–95. Mexico City, 1988. Excellent summary and critical appreciation of Aguirre Beltrán's career as a leader in the field of Mexican *indigenismo*.

ROBERT V. KEMPER

ALCALDES. *See* Corregidores and Alcaldes Mayores.

ALL SAINTS' DAY. *See* Day of the Dead and Todos Santos.

ALTARS. The term "altar" is applied to a variety of objects from Mesoamerica. Generally, altars were large stone sculptures, more horizontal than vertical, often carved with iconography, that served as focal points in ritual activity. Altars were sometimes associated with stelae. Although some scholars argue that thrones and pedestals are sculptural categories with distinct functions, it seems that these objects, plus platform altars and zoomorphs, shared a loose web of ideological correspondences. Thrones and low pedestals served as seats of power for humans and as foci for ritual offerings. Murals at Chichén Itzá illustrated human sacrifice occurring on circular pedestals, as well as on the bodies of serpents, which suggests that pedestals and zoomorphs may have functioned as tables for sacrifice. Some toad effigies, the supernatural head incense burners, and some circular pedestals served as receptacles for burning incense or other offerings. Imagery on many forms of altars expressed the understanding that supernatural origins, time, and ritual sacrifice were the foundations of rulership.

Thrones. Many authors use "throne" and "altar" interchangeably when describing a single monument.

The Gulf Coast Olmec produced basalt "tabletop altars" that functioned as thrones. One of the largest, La Venta Altar 4, measures 390 by 190 centimeters (12 by 6 feet)

Temple stone found at Motecuhzoma's palace. (Height: 48 inches.) *Courtesy of Museo Nacional de Antropología, México, D.F. Photograph by Salvador Guil'liem Arroyo.*

and is 160 centimeters (5 feet) high. A typical theme of these monuments is a high-relief image of a ruler emerging from a cavelike niche, either holding an apparently lifeless infant or grasping a rope leading to bas-relief figures on the sides of the monument. These likely illustrated a myth of chthonic origins for early rulers. That these functioned as thrones was demonstrated by David Grove (1973), who pointed out that a painted throne supporting a winged human at Oxtotitlan, Guerrero, is similar to La Venta Altar 4.

The Gulf Coast Olmec also fashioned monolithic three-dimensional figures seated or kneeling on blocky thrones. On some of these, such as San Lorenzo Monument 15, carved pairs of ropes crisscross them, as if to tie them for transport. Similarly, many Maya reliefs illustrate figures seated on circular pedestals, so these may have functioned as thrones. The Olmec, Maya, and Aztec often placed sculptures of humans and supernaturals on pedestals.

At many Maya sites, a ruler was inaugurated on the throne of his predecessor. Some such thrones took the form of a large slab supported by four legs. As on Piedras Negras Throne 1, the legs, backrests, and sides of the slab could be elaborated sculpturally and with hieroglyphs. Benches built into interiors of vaulted rooms also served as thrones for humans or sculptures and were carved.

In the Epiclassic and Postclassic periods, thrones became simpler benches, with reliefs along the bases (Palacio Quemado, Tula, and Templo Mayor, Tenochtitlan) or with three-dimensional atlantean figures as legs (Temple of the Warriors, Chichén Itzá).

Pedestals. At Gulf Coast Olmec sites, as well as cities throughout Mesoamerica, there were plain circular and rectangular low pedestals. The Maya exercised great variety in embellishing pedestals.

In the Formative period, circular pedestals were carved in relief on top, with a contortionist doing a backbend, his feet on his head. This was a posture of disciplined effort (Carolyn Tate, "Art in Olmec Culture," in Michael Coe et al., *The Olmec World: Ritual and Rulership,* Princeton, 1995).

Similar to the Olmec "bound" thrones with attached seated figures are Maya pedestals with reliefs of ropes. There are several at Tikal. At Copán, the Altar of Stela I has knotted bands on its sides. According to David Stuart (1996), its hieroglyphic text states that the stone was ritually fastened or bound.

Related to the Olmec niche-thrones, some Early Classic Maya pedestals have a quatrefoil shape that forms an enclosure, signifying the mouth of a cave or earth supernatural. It indicates that what is within the enclosure existed in a distinct space and/or time from what surrounded it. Supernaturals within quatrefoils are shown offering bowls on the sides of Tikal Altar 4. Some quatrefoils on the top of a pedestal enclose a seated figure. Karen Bassie-Sweet (*From the Mouth of the Dark Cave*, Norman, 1991) links the quatrefoil with the 260-day cycle.

Several Maya circular pedestals incorporate imagery relating to time, specifically to the days on which a new temporal cycle began. These "Giant Ahaw" altars feature, as a large central image on the upper surface, the day sign Ahaw (from the 260-day cycle) on which the 365-day *haab* always began. These probably related to the notion of "binding" time. Stuart (1996) thinks that the term *tun* refers to stones that embody periods of time rather than periods of 360 days.

Besides time and seated figures, prisoners are "bound" on pedestals, such as Tikal Altar 10. On its upper surface, a prisoner is superimposed over a quatrefoil. On its sides, bound prisoners alternate with matting and rope. Because many Maya stelae show bound sacrificial victims at the feet of rulers, it has been supposed that rulers stood on such "bound prisoner" altars. Epiclassic-period *chacmools*, partially reclining figures that hold sacrificial basins over their navels, replaced pedestals at Chichén Itzá and Tula.

Remarkable among square pedestals is Copán Altar Q (763 CE), a large rectangular pedestal/throne raised on four small legs and carved on its four sides with reliefs of King Yax Pac and his fifteen ancestors. Hieroglyphs enrich the upper surface. Below it, in a masonry crypt, are cached fifteen jaguars, one for each ancestor.

Low circular pedestals with relief imagery also appeared in Maya ballcourts, thus marking it as an interface with chthonic, or underworld, imagery and tying the game to notions of time and rulership.

The Aztec Stone of Tizoc, on the sides of which Tizoc documented the accumulated conquered peoples and territories of his dynasty, was a larger example of the ancient circular pedestal. Like Maya "time" pedestals, it has a sun disk on its upper surface and a concave basin for offerings at its center. The Calendar Stone, with its evocations of five temporal eras and sacrificial fire, also relates to the themes of Mesoamerican altars. The Coyolxauhqui relief is a circular pedestal showing a sacrificial victim and, simultaneously, the end of the era prior to the arrival of the Mexica.

Zoomorphs and Supernatural Heads. La Venta Altar 1 is a zoomorphic or supernatural head altar. On the rectangular block, giant paw-wings on each side flank a monster head on the front. At Kaminaljuyú were found six toad altars, some with concave "basins" in which to burn incense. Similar to these are colossal incense burners in the form of supernatural heads from Kaminaljuyú, and one from Altar de Sacrificios.

Among the Late Classic Maya, the well-known zoomorphic boulder sculptures from Copán and Quiriguá revived the zoomorphic altar form. These multiple-headed creatures, often inscribed with texts relating to the current ruler and his burden of time, reached 255 by 160 by 101 centimeters (8 by 5 by 3 feet) at Copán (Monument 25) and even larger at Quiriguá, where they replaced stelae about 790 CE. Associated with zoomorphs at Quiriguá are irregular, flat boulder altars (Monuments 23 and 24), on which supernaturals, stepping from the otherworld, dance the world into being. The larger measures 360 centimeters (12 feet) in diameter and is 50 centimeters (1.6 feet) high.

Temple/Platforms. Throughout central Mexico, altars took the form of platforms supporting temple constructions. Cuicuilco, a Formative-period circular platform, had a double altar of stone and mud at its summit. Similar constructions existed in western Mexico. At Teotihuacan, altars in the form of small *talud-tablero* platforms were constructed in residential patios. These often contained burials. Also in the form of a temple is the Aztec Throne of Motecuhzoma. The backrest illustrates Motecuhzoma and his lineage patron, Huitzilopochtli, carrying water and fire signs, referring to war. They flank the present era or sun. Offering bowls and dates appear on the front of the temple/throne.

[*See also* Art and Architecture, *articles on* Pre-Hispanic Period *and* Colonial Period.]

BIBLIOGRAPHY

WORKS ADDRESSING THE FUNCTIONS OF ALTARS

Grove, David C. "Olmec Altars and Myths." *Archaeology* 26.2 (1973), 129–135.

Stuart, David. "Kings of Stone: A Consideration of Stelae in Ancient Maya Ritual and Representation." *Res: Anthropology and Aesthetics* 29.30 (1996), 148–170.

WORKS DOCUMENTING ALTARS AT SPECIFIC SITES, RELATED SITES, OR TIME PERIODS

Baudez, Claude-François. *Maya Sculpture of Copán: The Iconography.* Norman, Okla., 1994.

Clancy, Flora S. *Sculpture in the Ancient Maya Plaza: The Early Classic Period.* Albuquerque, N.M., 1999.

Fuente, Beatriz de la. *Los Hombres de Piedra: Escultura Olmeca.* 2d ed. Mexico City, 1984.

Jones, Christopher, and Linton Satterthwaite. *The Monuments and Inscriptions of Tikal: The Carved Monuments.* Tikal Reports 33, pt. A. Philadelphia, 1982.

Norman, V. Garth. *Izapa Sculpture: Parts I and II.* Papers of the New World Archaeological Foundation 30. Provo, Utah, 1973, 1976.

Parsons, Lee Allen. *The Origins of Maya Art: Monumental Stone Sculpture of Kaminaljuyu, Guatemala, and the Southern Pacific Coast.* Studies in Pre-Columbian Art and Archaeology, 28. Washington, D.C., 1986.

Pasztory, Esther. *Aztec Art.* New York, 1983.

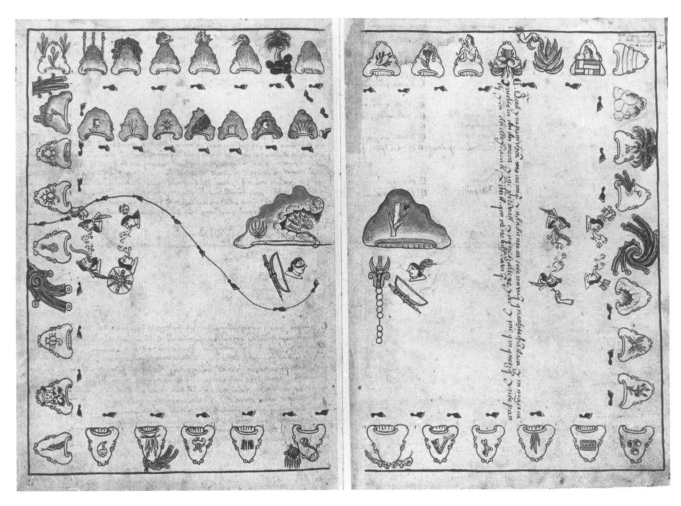

The founding of Cuauhtinchan and the *altepetl*'s boundaries. From the *Historia Tolteca-Chichimeca* (folio 35v–36r) c.1545–1565. Colored pigments on paper. *Photo courtesy of Bibliothèque Nationale, Paris.*

Sharer, Robert S. *Quirigua: A Classic Maya Center and Its Sculpture.* Durham, N.C., 1990.
Townsend, Richard F. *The Aztecs.* London and New York, 1992.

CAROLYN E. TATE

ALTEPETL. *Altepetl* (plural, *altepeme*) in the Nahuatl language is a "metaphorical doublet." Literally translated, it means "hill-water." Its equivalent in Mixtec is *ñuu*; the corresponding term in the language of the Yucatecan Maya is *batabil*. The significance of *altepetl* among the Nahuas of the Late Postclassic and Early Colonial periods has received the most attention from scholars because there are extensive Nahua sources available.

Altepetl is usually taken to denote an indigenous city, village, or town, with geographical limits and a well-defined political governmental organization. The institution of the *altepetl* survived the Spanish conquest in several regions of Mesoamerica and played an important role in the organization of native populations.

According to Alfredo López Austin (1996), *altepetl*, in the cosmovision of the pre-Hispanic Nahuas, was related to a series of principles concerned with important agricultural cycles. Its glyph depicts a bell-shaped hill that contains in its interior a pool of water with the forces of germination distributed through the rain. Of considerable importance was the belief that a patron god (or goddess, in many instances) inhabited the interior of the *altepetl*. This was the titular deity of a specific ethnic population, a group of immigrants, a city, a town, or even a neighborhood or ward. The patron god, or divine ancestor, was both the creator and the protector of some large or small group of individuals. He guided his people on a pilgrimage and bestowed a promised land on them. In addition, he provided them with water, rendered the land fertile, and gave the people both the knowledge and the tools necessary for their occupations. The patron god protected his people from disease and the evil attacks of neighboring deities; he punished his people for moral transgressions or for abandoning traditions. A pyramid with a temple at the top was built in his honor, or he was worshiped on a hill that he had chosen as his residence.

These important religious ideas embodied by the term *altepetl* were the basis of landownership and social cohesion; however, not all pre-Hispanic or Colonial settlements enjoyed the status of *altepetl*, and a full understanding of the concept is elusive. Nevertheless, James Lockhart (1993) has defined the elements basic to an *altepetl*: (a) a delineated territory, large or small; (b) an autonomous government; (c) "a predetermined set of named constituent parts"; and (d) a dynastic rulership. Other common elements are a pyramid and a market. Considering these features, the *altepetl* can be defined as a "city-state," closely resembling those that flourished in the ancient Near East and Classical Greece. The territory of the *altepetl* was politically divided into two important levels: the *cabecera* ("head town") and its *sujetos* ("subject communities"). Both were organized into wards, or *barrios*, called *calpulli* or *tlaxilacalli*; although these might vary in size and political power, they were the cellular system of the *altepetl*.

Leadership of the *altepetl* seems to have borne a relationship, though not a clear one, with the status of *tlatocayotl*, a term translated as "kingship" (*señorío*). In some *altepeme*, a *tlatoani* ("king") was recognized as the highest political leader. However, the concepts of *altepetl* and *tlatocayotl* are not considered synonymous, because they seem to belong to different concepts of government. These, however, may have been complementary at certain periods.

The *altepetl* survived the first disruptive impact of the Spanish conquest. Its components contributed to the establishment of municipal governments and the *encomienda* system in Early Colonial times. Lockhart comments, "Everything the Spanish organized outside their own settlements in the sixteenth century . . . was built solidly upon individual, already existing *altepetl*." The Colonial *altepetl* assimilated various features of the Spanish *cabildo*, or town council, which rendered it more democratic. By the second half of the seventeenth century, however, the existing *altepeme* entered into an irreversible process of impoverishment, atomization, and simplification, losing most of their original characteristics. Today, two aspects of the *altépetl* remain: the continuing use of ancient place names, and a few ancestral territorial boundaries.

BIBLIOGRAPHY

Carrasco, Pedro. *La estructura político-territorial del imperio tenochca: La triple alianza de Tenochtitlan, Tetzcoco y Tlacopan*. Mexico City, 1996. See Introduction and chapter titled "La estructura tripartita y las categorías territoriales." Among other important issues, Carrasco explains the differences between *altepetl* and *hueialtepetl*.

García Martínez, Bernardo. "El *altépetl* o pueblo de indios. Expresión básica del cuerpo político mesoamericano." *Arqueología mexicana* 6.32 (1998), 58–65. Brief but well-documented article gives an overview of current knowledge about *altepetl*.

Lockhart, James. *The Nahuas after the Conquest: A Social and Cultural History of the Indians of Central Mexico, Sixteenth through Eighteenth Centuries*. Stanford, 1993. Chapter 2 deals with the definition and problems of pre-Hispanic and Colonial *altepetl*; a basic source on the subject.

López Austin, Alfredo. "Los mexicas y su cosmos." *Dioses del México antiguo*. Mexico City, 1996. Concise and useful article on pre-Hispanic Nahuatl worldviews; published as one of the introductory texts for an exhibition catalog.

XAVIER NOGUEZ

AMARANTH. Also known as *alegría*, *huauhtli* (in Nahuatl), *quiwicha*, and *quinua de castilla*, among other names, amaranth is a plant of the genus *Amaranthus*, belonging to the family Amaranthaceae, which consists of some sixty genera and approximately eight hundred species. Amaranth is cultivated primarily for the production of grain, verdure, and, in some cases, forage, as an ornamental, and for dye. The species used in the production of grain are *A. cruentas*, *A. caudatus*, *A. edulis*, and *A. hypochondriacus*, all of which are of American origin. The species used for verdure are *A. tricolor*, *A. dubius*, and some forms of *A. cruentus* and *A. hybridus*. The first is of Asian origin.

In pre-Hispanic times, amaranth was cultivated by the Aztec and their tributary communities in a quantity very similar to maize. Amaranth also had religious and ceremonial uses. Amaranth grains were used to make figures of Aztec deities, such as Huitzilopochtli and the rain gods, and were consumed at the end of religious ceremonies. A survey conducted in 1890 by the Mexican government demonstrated the total disappearance of its cultivation, which, it suggested, could be related to the prohibition of the practice on the part of the Spaniards, who, it is believed, considered it a symbol of paganism. However, there is no evidence of this Spanish prohibition. Today, 1000 to 2000 hectares (2,470 to 4,940 acres) are cultivated in the productive zones of Mexico, which is one of the centers of the origin and diversity of the genus. The most important system of cultivation is monoculture, although there are also cases of mixed and associated cultivation.

One of the attributes of this plant is its capacity for prospering in conditions of high temperatures and low humidity, which makes it a good alternative in desert agriculture. Another aspect is its high nutritional value because of its 17 percent content of protein 13, above all the high biological value of the protein, which is superior to all of the cereals, legumes, and cow's milk, because the balanced proportion of amino acids is very close to that of the ideal protein. In particular, amaranth contains twice as much of the essential amino acid lysine than the common grains maize, wheat, and rice. Because of this, amaranth can be used to complement processed foods with the aforementioned cereals. In the time of the Aztec, amaranth was consumed in the form of tamales, pinole, masa, and atoles. After the Spanish conquest, its principal use was in the form of sweet *alegría*, which consisted of the popped grain and honey. The seeds pop when heated on a clay *comal de barro*, or griddle. Popping makes the seeds taste better while raising their protein value. Today, sweet *alegría* continues to be the principal use of amaranth in Mexico, although its use is diversifying in the forms of cereals, atoles, creams, crackers, bread, tortillas, pastries, marzipans, granolas, flours, pinoles, tamales, sweets, and protein concentrates.

[*See also* Agriculture; Cuisine; Nutrition.]

BIBLIOGRAPHY

Bale, Judith R., and Charles S. Kauffman, eds. "Special Issue on Grain Amaranth: New Potential for an Old Crop." *Food Reviews International* 8.1 (1992), 8755–9129.

Cole, John N. *Amaranth from the Past for the Future*. Emmaus, Pa., 1979.

Joshi, B. D., and Rana, R. S. *Grain Amaranths: The Future Food Crop*. Shimla, India, 1991.

Paredes, O., A. P. Barba de la Rosa, D. Hernández, and A. Carabez. *Amaranto: Características alimentarias y aprovechamiento agroindustrial*. Washington, D.C., 1990.

Williams, John T., and D. Brenner. "Grain Amaranth (*Amaranthus* Species)." In *Cereals and Pseudocereals*, edited by John T. Williams, pp. 129–186. London, 1995.

CRISTINA MAPES
and EDUARDO ESPITIA
Translated from Spanish by Scott Sessions

AMATL. *See* Papermaking.

AMUZGO. The Amuzgo people live in the lower parts of the Sierra Madre del Sur in the states of Guerrero and Oaxaca, between 16° and 17° north latitude and 98° and 99° west longitude, at altitudes between 500 and 600 meters, in a semi-humid climate. Xochistlahuaca, Tlacoachistlahuaca, and Ometepec in Guerrero and San Pedro Amuzgo and Santa María Ipalapa in Oaxaca are their main towns. The Amuzgo language belongs to the Otomanguean linguistic group and comprises at least two dialects, one in Guerrero and one in Oaxaca. The current population surpasses 32,000 (27,000 in Guerrero; 5,000 in Oaxaca), of whom about 40 percent are monolingual in Amuzgo.

The settlements are nucleated. The traditional house, or *redondo*, is built of interwoven twigs covered with mud, with a conical palm roof, showing African cultural influence. Quadrangular mud houses, however, are more frequent. The economy is based on slash-and-burn agriculture and animal husbandry. The kinship system features undifferentiated (cognatic) descent, with a patrilineal bias centered on the domestic group. The kinship terminology is of the Eskimo type, with a classificatory subsystem by age. The traditional marriage ritual consists of a petition for the bride, the *quedamento* (social commitment), a religious wedding, and advice to the couple.

Social life is based on ritual kinship (*compadrazgo*), the *cargo* system, and the religious fiesta cycle. The *cargo* system (civil-religious hierarchy) consists of a ladder of ranked offices; incumbents must perform various communal, political, and religious duties. Individuals gain prestige as they move up to higher posts, the highest being *principal* in the elders' council. Roman Catholicism is the dominant religion, although Protestant groups exist. Singers and shamans organize healing and some festivities according to the indigenous ritual calendar. Other festivities are associated with the Catholic calendar: Carnival, Holy Week, All Saints' and All Souls' days, and the patron saint's day. Dances are an essential part of these celebrations, especially "Macho Mule," "Turtle," "Tiger," "The Conquest," "The Twelve Peers of France," and "The Little Bulls," which are accompanied by flute and drum or band music. Rain rituals are performed in the fields, using stone figures and offerings of animal blood.

Women spin cotton yarn and weave using back-strap looms and make garments, mainly *huipiles* (women's tunics). Older women still wear the *pasahuanque*, a tightly wrapped skirt extending from waist to ankles, called *enagua* in Guerrero. Symbolic figures woven into *huipiles* include butterflies (which represent insects, spiders, and worms), and also flowers with branches and leaves. Men's garments consist of a *cotón* (shirt) and white *calzón* (pants).

Amuzgos share the Mesoamerican belief in *nahualismo* (the power of certain people—mainly healers and shamans—to turn into animals). Illness and other misfortunes may be attributed to *nahuales*. The most frequent disorders so diagnosed are "anger," affecting one who listens to a dispute; "fright," with various motives and circumstances; and "whim," diagnosed by movements or by spots on the face and hands of the patient which resemble the animal that caused it. Healing and diagnostic techniques include *pulsar*: the pulse is conceived to be minute animals in the bloodstream; a slow rhythm is associated with cold, and fast with heat. To cure a person of "fright," a healer chooses a "good" weekday and inscribes a cross in the ground with five small pits; the afflicted person drinks water containing a pinch of earth from the pits.

BIBLIOGRAPHY

Cruz Hernández, Modesta. *N'on nan kobijind'ue n'an tzjon noan: Los usos de la madera entre los Amuzgos.* Mexico City, 1993. Classification of woods used for objects and tools.

Franco Pellotier, Victor M. "Terminología de parentesco, usos y actitudes verbales entre los amuzgos de Oaxaca." In *Cultura y Comunicación: Edmund Leach, In Memoriam,* edited by Jesús Jáuregui et al., pp. 75–103. Mexico City, 1996. General view of parenthood systems and verbal attitudes in the matrimonial ritual.

Ravicz, Robert, and A. Kimball Romney. "The Amuzgo." In *Handbook of Middle American Indians,* edited by Evon Vogt, vol. 7, pp. 417–433. Austin, Tex., 1969. One of the most complete outlines of the Amuzgos.

Smith Stark, Thomas. "Estado actual de los estudios de las lenguas mixtecanas y zapotecanas." In *Panorama de los estudios de las lenguas indígenas de México,* edited by Doris Bartholomew et al., vol. 2. Quito, 1995. General overview of linguistic studies and educational materials written in Amuzgo.

Tapia García, Fermín. *Las plantas curativas y su conocimiento entre los amuzgos: Arboles grandes y arbustos.* Mexico City, 1985. Botanical ethnoclassification of tree and shrub types, with information about their medicinal uses.

VÍCTOR FRANCO PELLOTIER

ANÁHUAC. The word *anáhuac* derives from Nahuatl *atl* ("water") and *nahuac* ("near"); it therefore translates literally as "near the water," or empirically as "coast." The term is usually applied to the Pacific and Gulf coastal regions but has also been used in reference to island cities, to the Valley of Mexico generally, and, even more broadly, to the Mexican nation.

Conceptually, the ancient Central Mexicans viewed the earth as a disk or an enormous alligator floating on and surrounded by water, symbolized as a ring of turquoises. Geographically, the areas called *anáhuac* comprised the coasts of the Pacific and Gulf Lowlands. The chroniclers of sixteenth-century Central Mexico most commonly applied the term *anáhuac* to coastal areas in the southern reaches of the Aztec Empire. For example, the Franciscan friar and ethnographer Bernardino de Sahagún (*Florentine Codex,* book 9) describes merchant expeditions to Anáhuac Xicalanco (on the Gulf coast, south of present-day Veracruz) and Anáhuac Ayotlan (on the Pacific coast, near present-day Tehuantepec). These lands were rich in luxury goods coveted by the Mexica, and such important trading enclaves as Xicalanco (Gulf coast), Tehuantepec, and Xoconochco (Pacific coast) emerged as quasi-neutral ports of trade. In pre-Hispanic times, Anáhuac Xicalanco

was probably home to the Nonoalca, with Tehuantepec home to the "Anauaca Tzapoteca" (Seler 1993, 11, 109).

The term *anáhuac* is related to and sometimes confused with another commonly used word, *cemanáhuac,* translated as "the world," by Alonso de Molina (*Vocabulario en lengua castellana y mexicana y mexicana y castellana*) and as "place surrounded by water" (Broda 1987). Aztlán, the Mexica place of origin, was an island site and qualified as *cemanáhuac,* as did the Mexica's island capital city of Tenochtitlan (Matos Moctezuma 1987). In fact, Tenochtitlan was viewed by the Mexica as the center of their known world. The similarity between the words *anáhuac* and *cemanáhuac* has undoubtedly given rise to the use of *anáhuac* in a very generalized sense to refer to the highland Valley of Mexico, and even to Mexico itself (Florescano 1994).

BIBLIOGRAPHY

Broda, Johanna. "The Provenience of the Offerings: Tribute and Cosmovision." In *The Aztec Templo Mayor,* edited by Elizabeth Hill Boone, pp. 211–256. Washington, D.C., 1987. Discusses geographic symbolism, including the meaning of *cemanáhuac.*

Florescano, Enrique. *Memory, Myth, and Time in Mexico.* Austin, Tex., 1994. Includes brief discussion of the extension of the term *anáhuac* to the Mexican nation.

Matos Moctezuma, Eduardo. "Symbolism of the Templo Mayor." In *The Aztec Templo Mayor,* edited by Elizabeth Hill Boone, pp. 185–209. Washington, D.C., 1987. Insightful analysis of the Great Temple of Tenochtitlan, with a discussion of the conceptual notion of *cemanáhuac.*

Seler, Eduard. *Collected Works in Mesoamerican Linguistics and Archaeology.* Vol. 4. Culver City, Calif., 1993. In various articles, Seler elucidates the concept and meaning of *anáhuac.*

FRANCES F. BERDAN

ANALES DE CUAUHTITLÁN. *See* Chimalpopoca, Codex.

ANCESTOR WORSHIP. The term "ancestor worship" or "ancestor veneration" denotes rites for deceased ancestors that are performed regularly, often by kinsmen, after the funeral and mourning period. Its presence in Mesoamerica is difficult to verify for periods and regions documented only by archaeological data. Among the Olmec, the first civilization that left monuments with diversified iconography, ancestor veneration may be suggested by elaborate tombs, by the possible depiction of ancestors on stelae (La Venta, Stela 2 and Stela 3) that show rulers surrounded by numerous "flying" figures, and especially by the importance of ancestors among the Maya, whose culture was in many respects a continuation of the Olmec.

Celestial ancestors depicted above Maya rulers on stelae appear from the Protoclassic or the Early Classic period onward at Abaj Takalik, Tikal, Copán, Ixlú, and Yaxchilán. On Altar Q at Copán (763 CE), the first and the last rulers of the city face each other, and the first one may be handing his scepter to the new ruler on the day of his accession. The ancestors seem to have been protectors of the rulers and guarantors of their legitimacy; from them, the rulers received the power that they were to transmit to their heirs. They were the representatives on earth of the gods, from whom their ancestors descended or by whom they were created. When rulers died, they became divine—probably as sky-bearers, as indicated by the ceremonial celestial bar they wore, and as was the case among the later and better-documented Aztec.

The nature of the rites is also a matter of speculation. There are depictions of bloodletting associated with ancestors who appear in the mouth of a serpent on lintels at Yaxchilán. Rulers are figured on stelae standing behind altars on which human and other sacrifices are offered. Stelae often were erected before pyramids where rulers were buried with rich offerings and sacrificed humans and animals; these were primarily monuments to the deceased rulers, who are also represented on huge crests or in sanctuaries. Among nobles and commoners, the dead were often buried and worshiped in shrines constructed within household clusters. In Postclassic times (900–1200 CE), according to the sixteenth-century bishop of Yucatán, Diego de Landa, a major source on the Maya, nobles were cremated and their ashes placed in urns, above which their families constructed temples, or in wooden or pottery effigies that were placed among the statues of the gods and worshiped, especially on festival days, when food was offered them. People sometimes kept parts of skulls ornamented with modeled features of the deceased.

In other regions, ancestor worship is probable but difficult to verify before the Postclassic. A good case can be made for its presence among the Zapotec, especially if the celebrated effigy urns and the personages depicted on the tomb murals are indeed ancestors, as has recently been suggested; they buried their dead in elaborate tombs situated in pyramids or under palaces. After the Monte Albán III phase (200–700 CE), genealogical reliefs bear witness to the importance of the deceased forebears of rulers. In Gulf Coast cultures, burials were frequently in pyramids.

Our best information on the Mesoamerican cult of the dead comes from sixteenth-century sources relating to the Aztec. We know that many Aztec gods were regarded as their ancestors, and that Aztec rulers were burned and their ashes buried in pyramids. Since the cult addressed to them lasted no longer than four years, however, it is problematic whether it should be classed as ancestor worship.

During the eighty days following a ruler's death, slaves were sacrificed to accompany him in the afterworld. For four years, offerings of food and drink were made during specific festivals by the families of the deceased on their tombs; after this period, they were supposed to have reached their permanent abode in the afterworld.

Six of the eighteen 20-day "months" featured rituals associated with the dead. Four belong to the "nocturnal" part of the year, corresponding to the rainy season, and two to the end of the dry season, that of the "day." In the month of Tepeilhuitl, a festival of the mountain and rain gods, the Tlalocs, images of amaranth-seed dough were made of those who had died by drowning, lightning, or supposedly "aquatic" illnesses—that is, those who had been chosen by the Tlalocs; the images were ritually bathed, offered food and incense, and finally eaten. Quecholli, the month dedicated to the warriors, witnessed offerings to those fallen in battle. Sixty days later, in the month of Tititl, offerings were made again to the heroic dead, especially to women who had died in childbirth and who were regarded as heroic warriors. During the next festival, Izcalli, tamales were given to the fire and laid as offerings on tombs.

The main commemoration of the deceased took place nine months later, during both the Small and the Great Festival of the Dead. During the Small Festival, flowers, food, and drink were placed on tombs. The following month was dedicated to the fire god. People went onto the roofs of their houses and called for their dead, saying they awaited them. Since it was the end of the "day," the deceased warriors were expected to descend from heaven and make the earth fertile, acting together with the setting sun and other heavenly bodies. A branchless tree, symbolizing the link with the otherworld, was erected; then a dead effigy bundle, called "fruit," was placed on top of it. Youths climbed the tree and made the "fruit" fall like seed on the earth. A well-known variant of this ritual is the *volador*, a dance performance still widely practiced. There is reason to believe that these festivals were very ancient, with their roots in the Classic period.

Today, despite Roman Catholic influence, the ancient beliefs and rituals persist in more or less altered form. The deceased are still buried with some of their belongings or with grave goods for the journey. Usually there is only one festival of the deceased, before or around the Christian Day of the Dead, 2 November, when cemeteries are visited and flowers offered. In some places, a minor festival two weeks earlier honors those who died a violent death or who drowned. During that period the deceased are believed to come back among the living—they are welcomed by vigils, by offerings of food and drink on domestic altars or tombs, and by the making of images of corpses or skeletons. It is thought that the dead must be honored when they return because they are kin, and in order to avoid their malevolence, but this propitiation may not properly constitute "ancestor worship." Perhaps this problematic concept is another example of the ambiguity of pre-Hispanic vis-à-vis modern Indian relationships with elders and ancients, who are much respected—although Mesoamerican myth often stresses the victory of poor, young newcomers over their old, rich, decadent elders.

[*See also* Day of the Dead and Todos Santos.]

BIBLIOGRAPHY

Baudez, Claude-François. "El espacio mítico del rey maya en el periodo Clásico." *Trace* 28 (Dec. 1995), 29–52.

Baudez, Claude-François. *Maya Sculpture of Copán: The Iconography.* Norman, Okla., 1994. Both works by Baudez offer very valuable new interpretation of Maya divine kingship.

Graulich, Michel. "Miccailhuitl: The Aztec Festivals of the Deceased." *Numen* 36 (1989), 43–71.

Graulich, Michel. *Rituales aztecas: Las fiestas de las veintenas.* Mexico City, in press. A detailed analysis of the eighteen "monthly" festivals of the solar year.

Ichon, Alain. *La religión de los totonacas de la Sierra.* Mexico City, 1973. Excellent descriptions of present-day funeral rites and the festival of the dead among the Sierra Totonac.

Marcus, Joyce. *Mesoamerican Writing Systems: Propaganda, Myth and History in Four Ancient Civilizations.* Princeton, 1992. Contains many insightful interpretations of data on royal ancestors among the Zapotec, Mixtec, Aztec, and Maya.

Schele, Linda, and David Freidel. *A Forest of Kings: The Untold Story of the Ancient Maya.* New York, 1990. Important for possible Maya rituals associated with the royal ancestors, although some statements should be considered with caution.

MICHEL GRAULICH

ANNALS. In Mesoamerica, annals and annalistic histories were created primarily, if not exclusively, in Central Mexico. Today no pre-Hispanic annals are known. Yet evidence suggests that Nahuatl-speakers kept such histories prior to the Spanish conquest and the introduction of the Roman alphabet. Even so, annals seem to have become important only in the Late Postclassic period (c.1350–1520 CE). Because annals originated in, and circulated through, the region of Mesoamerica dominated by the Mexica (Aztec Empire) they may be a genre of history-keeping associated with Mexica claims to political power. After the Spanish defeat of the Mexica in 1521, annals-writing persisted; in fact, throughout the Colonial period it embodied a significant mode for documenting indigenous historical knowledge.

Mesoamerican annals share many of the literary and conceptual forms that appear in annals from other regions of the world. Perhaps the most important aspect is time; measured year by year, it structures annalistic histories. Nahuatl words that refer to annals-writing include *xiuhpohualli* ("year count," "year relation"), *xiuhtlacuilolli* ("year writing"), and *xiuhamatl* ("year paper"), all of which reference yearly units of time. Moreover, although the opening year and initial event may vary from annals to annals, all known Mesoamerican examples respect the constancy and logic of annual chronology. Depending on the annalist, then, years may be identified through the Christian calendar (e.g., 1591, 1592), an indigenous calendar (e.g., 1 Flint Knife, 2 Reed), or both. Regardless of the calendrical system used, each set of annals registers events according to the year of their occurrence. Annals writers adhere to this yearly framework so consistently that they even record those years in which "nothing happened." Among the events most commonly mentioned in Mesoamerican annals: changes in political leadership; droughts, famines, and epidemics; comets and eclipses; the founding of new markets or communities; and the deaths of notable people. In some years, annalists might register multiple events; in others, nothing may have been worthy of note. Consequently, annals are histories in which full years and empty years together constitute the whole.

Two implicit narratives organize the histories set forth in Mesoamerican (and other) annals. First, annalistic histories tell a story of regularity. Within any set of annals, some years may be more momentous than others. Yet because annals organize human experiences in yearly units, and because this form of time-keeping is both sequential and predictable, annals present worldly events in discrete, well-ordered chapters, with each one year long. Second, and in contrast to this ordering effect, annals imply that history is a series of chance occurrences. An eclipse, a famine, and the death of a political leader may all occur in a single year and thus appear together in an annalistic account; yet no causal link—except the coincidence of timing—may bind them together. Annals are, then, a mix of both prescriptive and incidental history. The commitment to temporal regularity endows them with a prescriptive quality; as long as the years are counted and recorded, there is the opportunity to organize new events into the usual meaningful pattern. At the same time, chance occurrences and daily experiences lend each set of annals its texture and specificity; these events, annals suggest, may occur unexpectedly but can, and therefore ought to, be noted.

The tension between order and happenstance is fundamental to the annals genre. Whether Mesoamerican annalists ever explored or discussed these concepts is not known at present. Only a few texts have survived from the post-Conquest period that hint at the way annalists went about their task. The indigenous and *mestizo* annalists who worked in the sixteenth century through the eighteenth were educated men, literate in Nahuatl and/or Spanish. Don Hernando de Alvarado Tezozomoc, who wrote annals in Nahuatl and chronicles in Spanish, is somewhat exceptional, since annalists tended to write in only one language. Mesoamerican annalists would have become familiar, however, with other modes of documentary writing, including notarial and church documents. Even so, when annals writers composed their histories, they consulted other record-forms only rarely, preferring to find source material and guides for writing in the work of other annalists and their own experiences. This preference suggests that annals represented a specific modality of history-keeping in Mesoamerica; and, given this, indigenous and *mestizo* annalists were probably cognizant of several other features of the genre. For example, by their nature, annals are accretive records that typically register history event by event, in piecemeal fashion, which results in a processual pattern of observation. In addition, no predetermined moment or pre-established method existed for ending a set of annals. If some annals draw to a formal close, others break off midway, which implies that an author died or secured no one to carry on the work. Annals are also partisan accounts. Someone—and in post-Conquest Mexico, usually the annals' author—determines which events will be registered, which overlooked. Annals thus exhibit the biases of those who penned them. Related to this, most annals are concerned with a restricted geographical region. Events of consequence tend to be those that transpire within a single community (usually the home or region of the author) and its environs. For example, the *Codex Aubin*, which dates to the late sixteenth and early seventeenth century, centers attention on San Juan Tenochtitlan, an *altepetl* in Mexico City. Some annals from the Mexican state of Puebla include events that occurred in Mexico City or even in Spain, such as the arrival of a new viceroy or the death of a king. Typically, however, the purview of post-Conquest annals is more narrow than expansive.

While we do not know specifically why most Mesoamerican annalists took up their pens, annals tend to be driven by personal, rather than community, ambitions; most annalists wrote anonymously. Scholars believe that pre-Hispanic models played a significant role in shaping post-Conquest historical practices, especially in the Early Colonial period. Yet the absence of such pre-Hispanic annals makes it impossible to know how the post-Conquest annals mirror their pre-Conquest counterparts. Through careful analysis of Early Colonial annals, however, connections with pre-Hispanic modes of record-keeping—in terms of concept and content—can be suggested. For example, such annals as the *Codex Aubin, Codex Telleriano-Remensis, Codex Mexicanus, Tira de Tepechpan,* and *Historia Tolteca-Chichimeca,* all of which date before 1585, combine pictorial and alphabetic forms of record-keeping. Yet all betray keen memory of pre-Hispanic conventions for keeping oral and glyphic records. In the *Tira de*

Tepechpan, the pre-Hispanic-style year glyphs provide the visual and temporal framework. Key events are registered through both pre-Conquest-style images and glyphic signs for named individuals and places. Then, too, alphabetic writing in the *Tira* functions largely to gloss or explain these pictures, much as oral recitations might have filled out the historical account in pre-Conquest times. In addition to these attributes, sixteenth-century annals frequently reference pre-Conquest events. This is certainly true of the annalistic portions of the *Codex Telleriano-Remensis* and the *Historia Tolteca-Chichimeca*, both of which cover events from the late twelfth century through the mid-sixteenth; although later annals tighten much pre-Hispanic history, emphasizing instead the period closest to the writer's own life, these two works—and others of this period—lavish attention on pre-Conquest times.

In many sixteenth-century Mesoamerican annals, events associated with the Spanish conquest and colonization are integrated into the same literary framework that registers pre-Hispanic events. In fact, the changes wrought by Europeans were often acknowledged as mere disruptions in the pre-Conquest historical fabric. For example, many sixteenth-century annals note, but do not emphasize, the Conquest. Moreover, different Mesoamerican annals stress distinct aspects of the Conquest. Some focus on military events, others diplomatic ceremony, still others the advent of Christianity or the tragedy of epidemic disease. Indigenous annals of sixteenth-century New Spain are thus notable for two crucial absences: the lack of moral or political consensus about the Spanish conquest and its import; and the failure of European introductions to remake indigenous history-keeping in any radical way. Instead, each community, and even more specifically, each annalist, integrated events associated with the Conquest and colonization into the larger tales—wherein pre-Hispanic kings rose, fell, and conquered enemies as their people survived droughts and earthquakes and marveled at comets. Beyond this, the presentation of post-Conquest topics in sixteenth-century annals often parallels those recorded for ancient times. Lists of elected officials and *cabildo* leaders frequently resemble accounts of pre-Conquest dynastic succession, while legal battles and community conflicts find parallels in pre-Hispanic wars and conquests. Ancestral migrations, ritual events, and community foundations—all of which surface in the pre-Conquest sections of sixteenth-century annals—become less common after 1550, when the founding of new markets, towns, and churches occurs. Mesoamerican annalists did not find post-Conquest equivalents for every pre-Hispanic event; rather they capitalized on concerns and occurrences that seemed (or could be made to seem) analogous. Ultimately, then, the rupture of the Conquest was presented—if not perceived—as a far less catastrophic event than modern historians are wont to recognize.

Another key feature of Mesoamerican annals are speeches by, and conversations between, historical actors. These take form as matter-of-fact, highly dramatic, or ironic scenes—depending on the annalist and the events. Overall, such verbal exchanges and orations lend immediacy to annals and, because of their varied tones and textures, imbue these histories with distinct personalities. Most post-Conquest annals also have two discernible parts: an early section that recounts key events from prior generations (if not centuries), and a section that articulates events the annalist experienced or was apprised of personally. In the sixteenth century, the first section, especially if focused on pre-Hispanic times, is often the more copious, frequently recording ritual actions, ancestral migrations, and dynastic successions. In the seventeenth and eighteenth centuries, such ancient events tend to receive summary notice. Although exceptions can be found, in later documents the incidents that transpired during the writer's own lifetime (or in the very recent past) accrue fuller, and often more animated, exposition.

Throughout the colonial period, the interest of annalists in pre-Hispanic traditions and concerns clearly wanes. In seventeenth-century annals, as in other Nahua documents of the time, pictorial images and glyphs appear only infrequently. The writings of the most accomplished Nahua annalist, Domingo de San Antón Muñón Chimalpahin Quauhtlehuanitzin (known as Chimalpahin), date from the late sixteenth century through the early seventeenth, and they are fully alphabetic. So, too, are the writings of nearly all annalists working after 1620, when in addition, their presentations of Spanish institutions, vocabulary, and individuals burgeon. By the late seventeenth century, events of the distant past tend to be those of a hundred years earlier—events of the Colonial period—and not the pre-Hispanic. Even when later annalists do register pre-Hispanic occurrences, their reports tend to lack the coherence of earlier documents. Thus, as is the case with other forms of expression, the annals produced early in the Colonial period retained the most replete grasp of pre-Hispanic events and sources. As one might surmise, with the passage of time, people who had direct experiences of pre-Conquest life died; pre-Conquest memories faded as they were passed from generation to generation; and pre-Conquest documents became increasingly scarce. Annals written later in the Colonial period therefore offer far more abbreviated descriptions of the pre-Hispanic world.

Even though annals produced after the sixteenth century only reference pre-Hispanic times, they still provide vital information about indigenous lives and experiences.

The later annals record events crucial to community identity—intense storms and agricultural failures, notorious murders, consecrations of new buildings, elections of officials, and spectacular parades. They also register many personal details and opinions, thus providing insight into the daily lives of post-Conquest Nahuas. For example, the annals of Juan Buenaventura de Zapata, written in Tlaxcala in the second half of the seventeenth century, recall not only public ceremonies and local political rivalries but also the night that thieves broke into his house in May of 1675.

Several Mesoamerican annals, including anonymous works from the towns of Quecholac, Tepeaca, Puebla, and Tlaxcala, as well as those by such well-known authors as Tezozomoc, cover broad swaths of time—from pre-Conquest centuries to the Colonial-era present. These suggest that annalists were privy to a variety of documentary sources; scholars also presume that, at least on occasion, Mesoamerican annalists interviewed elders and community leaders to fill gaps in their own knowledge and sources. Most annals writers, however, remain mute about their historical sources. Chimalpahin is the most explicit on this point; he claims to have relied on pre-Hispanic pictorial works, textual documents written soon after the Conquest, and interviews with elders who were alive both before and after the imposition of European rule. Although other annalists rarely give such detailed information about their working methods, many—especially in the sixteenth and early seventeenth centuries—must have relied on similar sources. The annalist of the *Historia Tolteca-Chichimeca* does not name his sources, yet he betrays their existence in multiple ways. For example, he records in detail the conversations of ancestral heroes who lived three to four centuries before his lifetime; other entries about pre-Hispanic times were punctuated with the abbreviation for *et cetera*; and errors in the account have been crossed out and then corrected. Painted images in the *Historia* have also been traced to older pictorial documents. All such features indicate that it registers not merely a single individual's memories of bygone times, but that the most ancient sections derive from the selective copying, editing, and recompiling of disparate sources.

How regularly annalists culled information from pictorial, alphabetic, or oral sources is not known. Regardless of the way each annalist worked, most seem to have depended on their own memories and experiences more than on extensive research in archives. Although annals writers would have known about, if not themselves written, other kinds of civic records, rarely has information from notarial or other documents been incorporated into annalistic histories. Post-Conquest annals nevertheless demonstrate that the redaction of earlier sources—presumably other annals or pictorial images—was essential; thus as each annalist took up the pen, he winnowed events from the distant and intermediate past, deciding which were most relevant to his narrative and thus worthy of record and remembrance. Each set of Mesoamerican annals, then, represents both a construction and a reconstrual of history, rather than a full compendium of all surviving historical knowledge to that time.

Since the 1960s, by means of the increased translation of Nahuatl annals, analyses of the formal and physical features of documents, and comparisons among annalistic histories, much has been learned about indigenous history-writing. Still poorly understood are the conditions that annals writers encountered as they worked; local and personal motivations for preserving and curating annals; and the meanings that individuals and communities lent such histories. For example, little is known about how they obtained inks and papers, or the price of such materials. Moreover, the daily circumstances and specific motivations that prompted them to write annals are still not fully understood. Analyses of inks and handwriting indicate that in some communities, a single person might bear full responsibility for creating a set of annals; in other cases, there was a collaborative enterprise. The lettering in certain documents betrays a single hand writing over many years; in others, the penmanship of two of three hands are in a single document, implying some collaboration; some documents reveal that one writer started his annals and then, after a period of years, passed the document on to another. How such arrangements were made—or why collaborations were sometimes preferred—are still to be answered.

The significance attached to the annals—as books, objects, and documents—by their communities, lineages, or individuals is also a topic that warrants further research. Although annals and other manuscripts were held by Nahua families and communities throughout the Colonial period, for only a few is it known how specific documents were collected, bequeathed, or preserved. Usually, this process becomes traceable when writers are well known, when documents leave their communities, or when annals pass into the hands of scholarly collectors. For example, manuscripts written and owned by Fernando de Alva Ixtlilxochitl, a *mestizo* descendent of Texcoco's pre-Hispanic rulers (whose works date from c.1600–1645), became part of the collection owned by Carlos Sigüenza y Góngora, the renowned seventeenth-century Mexican scholar; they later went to the library of the Jesuit college of San Pedro y San Pablo. Also documented is the transfer of sixteenth-century annals and painted histories from the town of Cuauhtinchan first to the Italian collector Lorenzo Boturini in the eighteenth century, then to the

French collector Joseph Aubin in the nineteenth century, and finally to the Bibliothèque Nationale in Paris. Apart from these and a few other cases, however, the circumstances that led writers, families, or communities to preserve, forfeit, or sell their documents remain poorly understood. That we know so little about how annals were cared for or passed from one historian to the next should not be surprising, since evidence that could illuminate the ways in which people handled documents and their practices for preserving books is scarce. In fact, the daily curation of objects is a topic that, in general, has not yet been thoroughly explored in Mesoamerican history. At present, scholars understand the events that the indigenous annals record far better than they grasp the meanings that people invested in the annals, as documents and objects.

Within the scholarship on Mesoamerican annals, since the early 1900s, a suite of themes has dominated research: the historical veracity of each set of annals; the relationships among the writings of specific annalists; indigenous concepts of temporality and history; and most recently, the language and vocabulary used to register times past. Before 1980, a primary concern was the accuracy of indigenous and *mestizo* annals. Many scholars tried to analyze the post-Conquest annals, in an effort to distinguish mythic history from verifiable events. Since the late 1980s, myth versus history debates have become more reasoned, with the greater understanding about the constructed and contingent nature of history (both in Euro-American and other traditions). Moreover, since many of the basic relationships among annalistic histories have been well established, other issues have moved to the fore, and scholars have become increasingly interested in charting how within Central Mexico the social and cultural practices differed from community to community, family to family, and document to document. The result is that analyses of language and paleography are playing a more significant role. Then, too, there are the questions about how indigenous historical consciousness took form—and then changed—within the Colonial period. The research on concepts and vocabularies (especially for annals written in Nahuatl) continues, as do explorations of the textual structure, syntax, and style of specific annals; and the formal features and visual appearance of annals (pictorial components, handwriting, and deployment of paper and ink) are also receiving attention.

As objects and as texts, Mesoamerican annals exemplify indigenous engagements with and remembrance of the past. Consequently, for modern and colonial readers, they offer extraordinary insights into Mesoamerica—both before, and after, the arrival of Europeans.

BIBLIOGRAPHY

Anderson, Arthur J. O., and Susan Schroeder. *Codex Chimalpahin: Society and Politics in Mexico Tenochtitlan, Tlatelolco, Texcoco, Culhuacan and Other Nahua Altepetl in Central Mexico.* 2 vols. Norman, Okla., 1997. English translation of Nahuatl histories written in the seventeenth century by Chimalpahin; includes a useful introduction to his work and milieu.

Boone, Elizabeth Hill. *Stories in Red and Black: Pictorial Histories of the Aztecs and Mixtecs.* Austin, Tex., 2000. Analysis of pre-Hispanic and post-Conquest historical manuscripts that are largely pictorial; addresses the forms, contents, and visual principles of annals, genealogies, and cartographic-histories. Extensive discussion of the value and importance Mesoamericans placed on history-keeping.

Gibson, Charles. "A Survey of Middle American Prose Manuscripts in the Native Historical Tradition." In *Handbook of Middle American Indians,* edited by Howard F. Cline, vol. 15, *Guide to Ethnohistorical Sources,* part 4, pp. 311–321. Austin, Tex., 1975. Discusses the types of prose documents that were focused on historical themes and written by native authors after the Spanish conquest; considers annals, titles, and the transition from oral and pictorial record-keeping to alphabetic writing.

Gibson, Charles, and John B. Glass. "A Census of Middle American Prose Manuscripts in the Native Historical Tradition." In *Handbook of Middle American Indians,* edited by Howard F. Cline, vol. 15, *Guide to Ethnohistorical Sources,* part 4, pp. 322–400. Austin, Tex., 1975. Summarizes the contents, collection history, and publication of alphabetic documents that feature indigenous histories; emphasizes writings of the sixteenth and seventeenth centuries by indigenous people, although later works, especially from the Maya area, receive attention.

Lockhart, James. *The Nahuas after the Conquest: A Social and Cultural History of the Indians of Central Mexico, Sixteenth through Eighteenth Centuries.* Stanford, Calif., 1992. Foundational work on post-Conquest Nahua social organization, cultural life, language, and forms of expression; analysis rests on extensive work with texts in Nahuatl, including wills, annals, songs, and land documents. Also provides extended discussion of the transition from oral and pictorial record-keeping to alphabetic writing.

DANA LEIBSOHN

ANTHROPOLOGY. [*This entry comprises two articles. The first article is an overview of the history and development of sociocultural anthropology in light of its contributions to Mesoamerican studies; the second article is an overview of the history and development of archaeology in light of its contributions to Mesoamerican studies. For related discussions, see* Archaeoastronomy; Epigraphy; Gender Studies; Linguistics; *and* Mesoamerican Studies.]

Sociocultural Anthropology

The sociocultural anthropology of Mesoamerica has developed in relation to intellectual interests in the broader discipline, to the government policies of Mexico and Guatemala, and to the changing conditions of life of the peoples of Mesoamerica. These influences are reflected in the kinds of field work carried out by ethnographers, the kinds of theoretical statements that drive research in the area, and the institutional missions of the organizations that support the sociocultural anthropology of the region.

Nineteenth Century and Early Twentieth Century. The earliest modern ethnological reports on Mesoamerica were anthropologically informed travelers' accounts. Sir Edward Tylor's *Anahuac; or Mexico and the Mexicans, Ancient and Modern* (1861) is probably the best-known example, with John Lloyd Stephens's *Incidents of Travel in the Yucatan* (1841) in the same genre. The full-blown anthropological expedition eventually developed from this, as presented in Frans Blom and Oliver La Farge's two-volume *Tribes and Temples* (1926–1927); it recounts the Tulane University expedition through Southern Mesoamerica in 1925. Although expeditionary anthropology lasted a bit longer in the Mesoamerican region than elsewhere, its limitations—researchers seldom stayed in a place long enough to make anything other than superficial observations—led to its eclipse by long-term research in a single setting, even at the time of Blom and La Farge's study.

German-speaking scholars developed a rich ethnograhic literature alongside the nineteenth-century travelers' accounts and the early-twentieth-century expeditionary reports. Unlike Stephens or Blom and LaFarge, many had been long-term colonists, with links to the coffee trade. Their association with Mesoamericans on remote plantations often resulted in a command of indigenous languages. Some also had training in the natural sciences, committing them to precise observation and description. Thus the ethnographers Karl Sapper, Otto Stoll, and Leonhard Schultze Jena based their reports on thorough empirical research; the literary embellishments and romantic reconstructions that are seen in other early accounts of indigenous people are absent. Other ethnographers, such as Konrad Preuss, who were influenced by philological and linguistic concerns, systematically recorded texts in indigenous languages for the first time since the Colonial period.

Throughout the nineteenth century and well into the twentieth, the ethnographic understanding of contemporary Mesoamerican societies was subordinate to the use of ethnography in reconstructing the past, particularly the pre-Hispanic past. Living indigenous peoples were seen as the bearers of a particular historical tradition, which anthropologists would uncover with their special tools. Philologists like Eduard Seler studied indigenous languages to help decipher ancient scripts. Alfred Tozzer hunted for survivals of Maya religious rituals in his 1907 *Comparative Study of the Mayas and the Lancandons.* Indigenous groups that used the 260-day calendar came under ethnographic scrutiny for an understanding of the pre-Conquest versions. This historicist orientation was reinforced by the German-trained Franz Boas, whose pioneering students from Columbia University worked in Mexico and Guatemala (including Elise Clews Parsons and Paul Radin in Oaxaca; Ruth Bunzel in Guatemala). Boas also participated in the training of many Mexican anthropologists, and he carried out some archaeological work in Mexico as part of his general interest in human and cultural variation. In this era, ethnography sometimes became a subproject of an archaeological expedition. Alfred Tozzer (see above) is usually identified as an archaeologist; the Maya archaeologist Sir Eric Thompson published an important study of the Maya of Belize in 1930, *Ethnology of the Mayans of Southern and Central British Honduras*; and the French archaeologist Alain Ichon wrote a very rich ethnographic description of the religious life of a Mesoamerican people: *La religión de los totonacos de la Sierra*. Archaeologists continue to carry out studies of material culture with an ethnoarchaeological focus, even when such interest has lapsed among contemporary sociocultural anthropologists.

Several anthropological institutions played key roles in the development of the field during the early twentieth century. One of the most important was the Museo Nacional de Antropología in Mexico City. While primarily concerned with Mexico's archaeological remains, early researchers supported ethnographic work among indigenous populations and produced a widely disseminated periodical, *Anales del Museo Nacional*, which was begun in 1886. The influential International School of Archeology and American Ethnography, which was founded within the Museo Nacional in 1911, brought together anthropologists from Germany, France, Mexico, and the United States to undertake research and the training of students; participants included Franz Boas, Alfred Tozzer, Eduard Seler, J. Alden Mason, and Isabel Ramírez Castañeda.

Synchronic Ethnography, Model Building, and Applied Anthropology. Beginning in the late 1920s, a number of alternatives began to emerge to the dominant historicist orientation in sociocultural anthropology. One of the most influential figures of this period, Manuel Gamio, established a distinctive Mexican anthropology. Gamio had studied with Boas at Columbia University in New York, and his research was supervised by Seler. Much of Gamio's doctoral dissertation, published in 1922 as *La Población del Valle de Teotihuacan*, is dedicated to the archaeology and history of the Central Highlands of Mexico. In addition, its careful documentation of the then standard of living of the people in the Teotihuacan Valley, its sponsorship by the new post-revolution Mexican government, and its policy implications prefigure the large

multidisciplinary, regional, holistic, and development-oriented projects that came to be favored by Mexican anthropology. Gamio worked to ensure that anthropology played an important role in governmental policy formulation, and he served in a number of government posts, beginning with the Secretariat of Agriculture. At the end of his career, Gamio distinguished himself as the director of the Instituto Indigenista Americano, which advocated indigenous peoples' interests throughout the Americas. Moisés Sáenz, also trained by Boas (as well as by John Dewey) at Columbia University, was another important pioneer; during the 1920s and 1930s, he helped develop a national school system in Mexico for the indigenous areas as a high official within the Secretaría de Educación Pública.

A second alternative to the historicism of the late nineteenth and early twentieth century emerged in the work of Robert Redfield, a North American anthropologist trained at the University of Chicago, where anthropology and sociology were combined in a single academic department. Redfield and his students, particularly Sol Tax, identified the community (or *municipio*) as the basic social unit for the study of Mesoamerica, then developed theoretical statements that placed the community within a comparative typology of human groups. Redfield carried out the first of what became known as the "community study" during field research in Morelos in 1926 and 1927, which he published as *Tepotzlán, a Mexican Village* (1930). Afterward, at the behest of Sylvanus Morley and supported by the Carnegie Foundation, Redfield moved into the Mayan-speaking region of Mexico and Guatemala. There, he carried out important ethnographic investigations in the Yucatán Peninsula from 1930 to 1935 with the Mexican anthropologist Alfonso Villa Rojas. Redfield developed the Folk-Urban continuum as a structural model for understanding settlement types and social variation in the region, which was published in 1941 as *The Folk Culture of Yucatan*. He also collaborated with Tax on projects in the Guatemala Highlands.

Redfield's work moved Mesoamerican ethnology to the forefront of the developing area of peasant studies, and it attracted the attention of metropolitan (or urban) anthropologists. As an international discipline, anthropology was then moving away from an exclusive focus on the so-called primitive groups, where research was aimed at uncovering elementary social forms, to a post–World War II concern with more complex social entities and the study of socioeconomic change. The term *peasant* was defined as a household-based, small-scale agriculturalist, who produced both for subsistence and for the market; that made peasants quite unlike tribal people, since peasants were components of the broader society whose urban sector drained off rural surpluses. This anthropological reorientation profoundly influenced the way researchers came to frame the problems faced by the rural sectors of Mexico and Guatemala, as well as the programs that national governments and international agencies developed for improving standards of living and facilitating the integration of the various peasant societies into national life.

In Mexico, anthropology developed a pronounced radical current that was nurtured by government administrations; these often linked Mexican nationalism to anti-imperialism and utilized the practical experience of anthropologists who had been involved in programs of social and economic transformation, such as the post-Revolution agrarian reforms. Also important was the intellectual input of the Spanish and the German-speaking refugees from fascism who began to come to Mexico in the 1930s. Consequently, from the late 1930s through the early 1960s, a series of programmatic statements and methodologically innovative studies on Mexico's indigenous societies had a profound impact on anthropology as a whole as well as on Mesoamerican ethnology. In Mexico, these statements placed causal emphasis on the material conditions of life, gave priority to structure over culture, and viewed peasant social formations as a product of their changing interactions with broader social and economic systems. Researchers such as Angel Palerm began focusing on the development of agriculture and irrigation; ethnographers such as Bronislaw Malinowski and Julio de la Fuente undertook detailed studies of regional social and economic systems; theorists such as Gonzalo Aguirre Beltrán, Fernando Cámara, and Eric Wolf placed the structural features of the peasant community in the context of Colonial and post-Colonial period sociopolitical and socioeconomic relations; John Gillen and Melvin Tumin studied issues of status hierarchy in complex culture; and Oscar Lewis restudied Redfield's village of Tepoztlán, calling attention to the unequal distribution of resources and the political conflict in the region.

After World War II, a number of important institutions supported ethnographic research in Mesoamerica. Each was infused with a strong focus on applied anthropology, so almost all the leading researchers premised field work on the need for economic development and social integration. In Guatemala, the Instituto Indigenista was founded in 1944 to accomplish these goals; it had little impact since its leadership was chosen for political rather than intellectual reasons, and it was chronically underfunded. In Washington, D.C., the Institute for Social Anthropology was created within the Smithsonian Institution, to foster cooperation between U.S. scholars and those in other countries. One of its most significant programs was with Mexico's Escuela Nacional de Antropología of the Instituto Nacional de Antropología e Historia

(a later manifestation of the Museo Nacional de Antropología), which brought together Ralph Beals, George Foster, Isabel Kelly, Pedro Carrasco, and Angel Palerm in the Tarascan and Totonac regional projects. Perhaps the institution that had the broadest and longest lasting impact was the Instituto Nacional Indigenista of Mexico (INI), created in 1948 and first headed by Alfonso Caso. Informed by the theoretical developments of the postwar period and the *indigenismo* goals of modernizing peasant communities through education, health care, and economic development, the INI established numerous coordinating centers in indigenous areas—the first was in San Cristóbal de las Casas, directed by Gonzalo Aguirre Beltrán. From this position Aguirre Beltrán, who eventually became head of the INI and Mexico's minister of education, put into operation his concept of the "region of refuge," which embodied both an analysis of the indigenous situation and a program of directed change. For Aguirre Beltrán, peasant societies were viewed as parts of regional systems of exploitation and unequal exchange; regional systems were controlled by a "dominical city," such as San Cristóbal, whose nonindigenous populations subordinated their own region by controlling its connections to national political institutions and to national and international markets. Through programs of education, economic development, and health care, INI Coordinating Centers were designed to break the dominical city's stranglehold on indigenous areas and allow the people to acquire the skills and resources needed to bypass nonindigenous mediators. Although the INI never received the resources necessary to shift the balance of power in these regions, INI's directors sponsored the work of many Mexican and non-Mexican anthropologists; it has also served as an important publication outlet for ethnographic and ethnological works.

Last Decades of the Twentieth Century. As interests in development and national integration came to dominate ethnographic work in Mesoamerica, other approaches were not excluded. Anthropologists John Gillen and Robert Paul, for example, focused on personality formation and viewed curing practices in social-psychological terms; Hugo Nutini and his collaborators did important work on kinship and social organization. Even these perspectives were sometimes integrated with an applied interest. Only in the late 1960s did ethnographic work in Mesoamerica begin to reflect a variety of other theoretical interests; this was due in part to the waning of anthropology's dominant acculturation and functionalist approaches, which made room for new perspectives to develop. In part it was due to the many anthropologists working in Mesoamerica and the increased funding that had become available for anthropological research.

One far-reaching development of this time was the sustained critique, launched in 1970 by an influential group of Mexican anthropologists, of national and international policy toward indigenous peoples. Although the goals were (1) to provide the social and cultural tools they needed to protect themselves from exploitation, (2) to lift themselves out of poverty, and (3) to participate fully in the life of the nation, in practice these amounted to a kind of ethnocide—as when schoolteachers forbade the use of indigenous language and dress, and discouraged participation in religious and other local institutions. The anthropologists began to argue for the preservation of indigenous and other local traditions, and they wanted to increase the input of indigenous groups into decisions that affected their lives. One institution to emerge as a result of this shift in perspectives is the Centro de Investigaciones y Estudios Superiores en Antropología Social (CIESAS). Under the directorship of Guillermo Bonfil Batalla, it was begun with the assumption that the culture of indigenous people is an important resource, not only for indigenous people but also for the nation as a whole. As a consequence, CIESAS supports the work of indigenous scholars; it has instituted programs that promote the use of indigenous languages; and it has attacked attitudes that devalue indigenous cultures. In Guatemala, organizations with similar goals are the Proyecto Lingüístico Francisco Marroquín (PLFM) and the Academia de Lenguas Mayas de Guatemala (ALMG). The PLFM—begun in the early 1970s by Peace Corps volunteers, by academics, and by Mayan speakers—has emphasized indigenous language training, general perspectives, and cultural resources that are central to the awakening of indigenous pride among Guatemalans. The ALMG is a government-sponsored organization that is developing national language policy so that all the official languages of Guatemala will be supported.

By the 1980s, Mexico had shed its overt assimilationist policy. Criticism had caused it to refocus on development programs from the dependency-theory perspective; then, beginning in the 1980s, there was an ongoing scrutiny of internal programs of rural development, including dam projects, whose social costs were initially borne by indigenous groups flooded out and displaced by the dam while other sectors reaped the benefits. Similar developments have occurred in Guatemala in the 1990s, with the end of counterinsurgency and the return to civilian rule.

In the 1960s, there was a rising standard for ethnographic reporting in Mesoamerica. Although this occurred in almost all areas of ethnographic inquiry, it was most fully manifested in studies of indigenous cosmologies and religious practices. Those concerned with these topics—influenced by such theoretical trends as structuralism, cognitive anthropology, symbolic anthropology, and hermeneutics—tended to be the ones who learned indigenous languages and carried out prolonged fieldwork. Evon Vogt's 1976 *Tortillas for the Gods* is a noteworthy example. The focus on indigenous languages soon led many of these anthropologists into analyses of indigenous texts from the Colonial and Pre-Colonial periods; this merged with the deeper current within Mesoamerican ethnology, which remained interested in using ethnographic tools to recover the past of Mesoamerican peoples. The works of Alfredo López Austin, Victoria Bricker, Miguel León-Portilla, and Dennis Tedlock are perhaps the most prominent expressions of a view that treats the indigenous peoples of Mesoamerica as bearers of various distinct civilizations. Although crudely dismissed by some as "essentializing," this research was premised on a deep respect for indigenous traditions and has transformed our understanding of the practice of religion in native Mesoamerica; the approach continues to draw researchers to the field.

A great deal of ethnographic work in Mesoamerica, particularly in the decades after the 1970s, was organized by the concept of ethnicity, which proved to be particularly appropriate in rural areas—where politics, unequal access to resources, economic insecurities, and a constant struggle for power accentuate the significance of such identity markers as dress, language, and residence. It has been argued that *indios* and *ladino* cultural premises and behavioral practices are so oppositional and inverse but meaningfully interrelated that they should be considered components of an integrated, rather than a pluralistic, colonial culture. As this suggests, ethnicity in Mesoamerica functions in most of these schemes as symbolic of something else; this led to interesting discussions not only of the relationships between *ladinos*, *mestizos*, and *indios* but also of the relationship between class and identity. In the 1990s, the focus of study shifted to processes of resistance and accommodation, local formulations of social action, and the intensification of ethnic discourse in group mobilization and the struggle for power. In the process, indigenous people are now represented not as passive subjects—as in the acculturation literature—but as strategic actors whose own agendas help shape the processes of change.

Mesoamerican peoples have changed in important ways since the 1950s. Like other rural populations throughout Latin America, they participated in the massive rural-to-urban migration of the postwar period. Although Gamio's *Mexican Immigration to the United States* was published in 1930, Oscar Lewis and his students realized that the phenomenon they were witnessing required anthropologists to carry out something other than the community study to produce a new kind of ethnographic monograph. Lewis directed a team of researchers in Mexico City and in Tepoztlán, where they worked among migrants and urban dwellers. His book, *Five Families*, is a harsh portrait, a pastiche, of the typical day in the homes of each of five families—distinguished from one another by a number of socioeconomic factors. Then, Lourdes Arzipe, Douglas Butterworth, Robert Van Kemper, and others documented the constant movement back and forth between city and country, demonstrating that communities did not so much lose people to migration as acquire an urban component. Researchers have continued to follow Mesoamericans who have migrated in increasing numbers to the United States and Canada; new conceptual categories have emerged to describe this process, while ethnographers struggle with the problem of how to meet the high standards for ethnographic reporting as they work among far-flung villages and diversely organized populations.

Rural-to-urban and transnational migration, the expansion of educational opportunities, and the possibilities of steady employment in such government programs as bilingual education have meant that an indigenous identity is no longer synonymous in Mesoamerica with being a peasant—part of a rural farming household. The variety of life careers now open to indigenous peoples has led to ethnographies that are similarly diverse. Alongside typical community studies, one also finds published studies of indigenous teachers, activists, refugees, internationally recognized artists and artisans, poets, and novelists. Since this is, in many ways, uncharted terrain, ethnographers have experimented with "postmodernist" writing strategies, often emphasizing the dialogic and collaborative nature of fieldwork, writing themselves into the narrative to make the relative positions of researcher and subject more visible. Although this move has sometimes alienated traditional readerships, other postmodernist concerns—multisited ethnography among geographically dispersed populations and close attention to the interaction of localizing and transnational processes—have become standard fare in Mesoamerican ethnology for many decades (although not always phrased in the language of postmodernism). Directly confronting the situation of today's Mesoamericans, many sociocultural anthropologists have shifted their focus away from the structural analysis of rural institutions and cross-cultural generalization, to produce a kind of "thick" political reportage, with attention to the conduct of the counterinsurgency program of the Guatemalan military or the Zapatista rebellion in Chiapas. Such anthropologists have documented state terror; the predicament of "being caught between two armies"; and the devastation these events brought to the lives of ordinary Mesoamericans.

Indigenous people, now trained as professional anthropologists and linguists, have also begun to produce substantial ethnographic work. In some areas, such as Oa-

xaca, they published close to half the ethnographies that have appeared since 1980. Some, on their own or in collaboration, have also created a genre of ethnographic reporting not previously seen in Mesoamerica—the testimonial narrative—such as Victor Montejo's *Testimony: Death of a Guatemalan Village* (1987) or the controversial *I, Rigoberta Menchú* (1984) by Elizabeth Burgos.

BIBLIOGRAPHY

Bonfil Batalla, Guillermo, et al. *De eso que llaman la antropología mexicana*. Mexico City, 1970. Pioneering critique of assimilationist programs in Mexico.

Chambers, Erve J., and Philip D. Young. "Mesoamerican Community Studies: The Past Decade." *Annual Review of Anthropology* 8 (1979), 45–69. Review of theoretical and methodological issues in Mesoamerican ethnology in the decade of the 1970s.

García Mora, Carlos, ed. *La antropología en México: Panorama histórico*. 15 vols. Mexico City, 1988. Comprehensive examination of the history and development of anthropology in Mexico.

Handbook of Middle American Indians, vol. 6, *Social Anthropology*. Austin, 1967. Encyclopedic treatment of the characteristic institutions of rural Mexico and Guatemala.

Handbook of Middle American Indians: Ethnology Supplement. Austin, 2000. Contains chapters on major ethnographic regions in Mesoamerica, as well as topical syntheses of work on social organization, religious practices, and politicized ethnic movements.

Hewitt de Alcántara, Cynthia. *Anthropological Perspectives on Rural Mexico*. London, 1984. Intellectual history of anthropology in Mexico, with particular emphasis on materialist and development perspectives.

Kendall, Carl, John Hawkins, and Laurel Bossen. *Heritage of Conquest: Thirty Years Later*. Albuquerque, 1983. Synthesis of the major theoretical and ethnological topics in Mesoamerican anthropology one generation after the effort by Sol Tax (1952) and his colleagues.

Tax, Sol, ed. *Heritage of Conquest*. Glencoe, Ill., 1952. For Mesoamerica, the first comprehensive attempt of ethnological synthesis, with chapters contributed by leading researchers in the field.

Warren, Kay. *Indigenous Movements and Their Critics*. Princeton, 1998. Account of the emergence of work of indigenous intellectuals in Guatemala; also much information on the development of anthropology in Guatemala for some thirty years.

JOHN MONAGHAN
and JOHN P. HAWKINS

Archaeology

Profound interest in the Mesoamerican past and the contributions of its great cultures is a phenomenon of considerable antiquity. Numerous pre-Hispanic graves documented from many different regions and epochs contain portable art objects that were centuries older than the individual with whom they were buried. The Aztec chronicler Bernardino de Sahagún recorded that there were specialists who devoted themselves to unearthing antiquities in the Valley of Mexico in the early sixteenth century. Evidence from the excavations of the Templo Mayor of Mexico-Tenochtitlan suggests that the Culhua Mexica commissioned such specialists to excavate at the ruins of Teotihuacan, at Tula, and very likely at sites in many other regions of Mesoamerica, to reveal temple architecture and to obtain portable works of ancient art to offer to the gods in their Great Temple. In like vein, the early Western explorers Alexander von Humboldt and John Lloyd Stephens rekindled interest in the ancient civilizations by seeking and extolling the magnificent, the monumental, and the aesthetically exquisite, legitimating their own work by glorifying the Mesoamerican cultures of yore.

As the discipline of archaeology came of age, however, the fascination with precious objects yielded to concerns with broader historical and anthropological questions. Derived from the Greek, the term *archaeology* literally means "the study of ancient history." The first century of archaeology in the Americas was, indeed, devoted to reconstructing the culture histories of all the cultures whose remains it uncovered. As the twentieth century proceeded, however, Mesoamerican archaeologists sought to look beyond the great man, and great woman, to the varied roles of the commoners, the slaves, the merchants and warriors, the landed nobility, and the many social factions that created and maintained complex societies throughout the area. The role of the physical environment and the diversity of adaptations that people made to it have proved fundamental to understanding the origins of sedentary life and the later development of all of the major cities, states, and civilizations that rose to greatness and eventually fell, prior to the arrival of Europeans. The strong participation of historians, social anthropologists, linguists, and physical anthropologists in the interpretation of the archaeological cultures of Mesoamerica, and in crafting the theoretical constructs of the discipline, has resulted in a particularly rich and rewarding field of anthropological inquiry.

Archaeology has enabled us to appreciate the tremendous time depth of the Mesoamerican cultural tradition, and through chronometric dating techniques has clarified the temporal order and relationships of its most long-lived and influential cultures. The intricacies of the economic and social organization of its villages, towns, and cities have been reconstructed through a variety of means, including settlement-pattern surveys, ecological and subsistence studies, household archaeology, craft specialization studies, chemical compositional analyses of raw material sources, and evidence for their redistribution networks. The reconstruction of dynastic and political histories through hieroglyphic studies has given names to faces, and meaning to dates, in the dynastic and genealogical records that continue to be unearthed by archaeologists. Concurrently, studies of pictorial symbolism, astronomical texts, and building/site alignments have increased our understanding of cosmovision and the perceived place of the rulers and their subjects in the

larger universe of being. Archaeology has also come to grips with its responsibilities in educating the public about the past and in conserving the priceless cultural patrimony of Mesoamerican cultures for future generations.

The first post-Mexica archaeology in Mesoamerica came centuries after the Spanish conquest, when the monumental Sun Stone and Coatlicue sculptures were found in the Zocalo of Mexico City in 1790. At a time when Mexico was gearing up for independence from Spain, these awe-inspiring monuments came to symbolize the pride of the nation, a role that the Sun Stone still bears today. The early nineteenth century was to witness a number of discoveries of remarkable antiquities and the beginnings of careful descriptions and visual records of the sites and monuments of Mesoamerica. In the 1890s, several archaeological expeditions were undertaken in the Basin of Mexico, Xochicalco, Morelos, the Valley of Oaxaca, the peninsula of Yucatán, and as far south as Copán in Honduras. These were primarily focused upon clearing and recording—and in some cases digging and restoring—monumental architecture and sculpture. Much of this work was sponsored by the Mexican government or, in the case of much of the research in the Maya area, by the Peabody Museum of Archaeology and Ethnology of Harvard University. In Mexico, the work of Leopoldo Batres at Xochicalco, at Monte Albán, and particularly at Teotihuacan was focused on reconstructing the monumental architecture, again as a means of signalling the greatness of the pre-Hispanic past in Mexico. Peñafiel and Del Paso y Troncoso also conducted archaeological excavations at this time in Mexico.

Reconstructing Culture History. It was not until the "stratigraphic revolution" initiated by the Mexican anthropologist Manuel Gamio in 1911 that archaeological research entered a new stage, referred to by Gordon Willey and Jeremy Sabloff in their *History of American Archaeology* (1993) as the "Classificatory Historical Period" in American archaeology. Gamio's research was undertaken as one of the first investigations of the newly founded Escuela Internacional de Arqueología y Etnología, which came to life in 1911 and was to have profound influence on the future of archaeology in Mexico. Its directors read like a "who's who" of anthropology at the time, all of them distinguished ethnologists with deep interest in the Pre-Columbian cultures of the Americas: Eduard Seler, Franz Boas, Alfred Tozzer, and Gamio himself. This interplay of social anthropology and archaeology was to characterize Mexican archaeology from that time forward, much to the betterment of the profession. Gamio dug a very deep test pit in the vicinity of Azcapotzalco, a site of great importance in the rise of the Aztec Triple Alliance. In the excavations and subsequent analysis of the artifacts, he documented that materials from the great Teotihuacan civilization were found beneath, and were therefore (following geological principles) earlier than, those of the Aztec. The Teotihuacan levels were in turn underlain (and therefore, preceded) by those of the Aztec. The Teotihuacan levels were in turn underlain (and therefore, preceded) by those of the so-called Tipo de los Cerros (later known as "Archaic," now called Formative or Preclassic) cultures of the Valley of Mexico.

This research provided the stratigraphic and relative position in time of the epochs that are now known as the Formative (or Preclassic), Classic, and Postclassic periods in Mesoamerican prehistory and enabled all future investigators to place their ceramics in time relative to those of the Valley of Mexico. The North American scholars Herbert Joseph Spinden, Alfred Kroeber, and George Vaillant were to contribute important treatises on the "Archaic" cultures of Mesoamerica and on the evolution of figurine styles, based on their presence and stratigraphic placement in sites throughout Mexico and upper Central America. Ceramics and figurines, through their abundance and their changes in style with the passage of time, became the fundamental tools of reconstructing the history of this large and complex culture area. The larger aim of the intellectual tradition that Gamio started was to produce culture-historical syntheses of regions and areas, based on statigraphic, seriational, and classificatory methods. In the view of one of Mexico's most prominent anthropological archaeologists (and public figures), Ignacio Bernal, the era from 1910–1950 was that of "Potsherds Victorious."

However, the rich historical record provided by the Postclassic codices, and the insights provided by ethnohistory and ethnography, enabled Mesoamericanists to have a much broader and richer understanding of human agency, foreign affairs, and dynastic traditions than could be provided by archaeology alone. The work of such scholars as Alfonso Caso and Ignacio Bernal on the Aztec, Zapotec, and Mixtec set the standard for the conjoined archaeological and historiographic studies of pre-Hispanic Mesoamerican cultures. For Teotihuacan, Gamio's classic monograph *La poblacion del Valle de Teotihuacan* (1922) served as a model of conceptualization, research, and reporting, discussing archaeology, demography, ethnography, and geography from the Archaic period to the present, as well as concerning itself with conservation and the cataloguing of archaeological zones. In the Maya area, culture-historical research was greatly aided by the presence of hieroglyphic dates recorded in the Long Count linear time-reckoning system, which were being deciphered just as quickly as researchers like Alfred Percival Maudslay, Teobert Maler, the members of the Peabody Museum expeditions in Copán, and Sylvanus

Griswold Morley could record and publish them. The calendric and astronomical portions of the Classic Maya inscriptions had largely been worked out by Ernst Forstemann, J. T. Goodman, William Gates, and Charles Bowditch, enabling them to correlate the Maya dates to those of the Christian calendar and thus providing the first absolute chronology in Mesoamerican archaeology.

Although in his early writings Morley left open the possibility that the Classic Maya inscriptions recorded historical data, place-names, and other secular matters, with time he was to become a great champion of the idea that the Maya texts were used exclusively to record calendric and astronomical data. This perspective was reinforced by the tendency, in early Maya studies, for Morley and other archaeologists to focus on the monumental centers (or "site-cores," as they are now known), in their quest to find new inscriptions. This zeal for the monumental meant that the hundreds of thousands of house-mounds that surrounded the large public architecture and represented the dwellings of the supporting population went virtually unnoticed. The view became entrenched that the major Maya sites were "vacant ceremonial centers," inhabited by a small group of calendar-priests who oversaw periodic public ceremonies which drew in the peasant agriculturalists, who were thought to have resided in simple hamlets and villages in the countryside. Greatly to his credit, Morley was also instrumental in securing the participation of the Carnegie Institution of Washington, D.C., in archaeology, a period (1920–1956) that many archaeologists still think of as a golden age in Maya studies. Happily, this overlapped with what has likewise been referred to as a golden age of social anthropology in Mexico (1940–1964), enhancing the dialogue between Mesoamericanist ethnologists and archaeologists that continues to shape professionals in both realms.

Under the direction of Alfred V. Kidder, the Carnegie's Division of Historical Studies engaged in a multidisciplinary research agenda that spanned the whole spectrum of humanist and scientific investigation of the Maya. On the humanist side, the Carnegie program actively engaged ethnographic studies by Robert Redfield and Alfonso Villa Rojas; ethnohistoric research by Ralph Roys and Robert Chamberlin; numerous large-scale excavation projects at such sites as Chichén Itzá, Copán, Kaminaljuyú, Mayapán, and Uaxactún; important regional site surveys in the Petén and on the east coast of the Yucatán Peninsula; epigraphic surveys (Morley's monumental *Inscriptions of Peten*); and a settlement survey in Uaxactún. Morley proved prescient not only in promoting a multidisciplinary approach to Maya archaeology, but in hiring the Russian-American architect Tatiana Proskouriakoff to do architectural renderings of the ancient Maya sites. She went on to produce innovative studies of Classic

Maya sculpture and, eventually, to lay bare the essentially historical nature of Classic Maya inscriptions. The Carnegie Institution also made a strong contribution to the field of conservation, with the architectural restoration programs that it carried out at the ruins of Chichén Itzá in Yucatán and at Copán in Honduras.

Mexico already had an invaluable precedent for this kind of work in the model research and restoration project that was conducted by Ignacio Marquina at the ruins of Tenayuca in the Valley of Mexico. Marquina was able to expose and meticulously restore for the public several construction stages of the twin-pyramid of Tenayuca, and he tied the ceramics of each stage into an overall pottery sequence for the Aztec period. His work there was conducted under the auspices of Mexico's Departamento de Monumentos Prehispanicos (founded in 1925). Likewise, Alfonso Caso began a long-term project of investigation and restoration at Monte Albán in 1930, where he was to direct eighteen field seasons. In 1938, he was appointed the first director of Mexico's newly founded Instituto Nacional de Antropología e Historia. The architectural restoration projects at Tenayuca and at Chichén Itzá (which has seen a series of large-scale Mexican government projects after the Carnegie expedition) helped fulfill the important mission of conservation of archaeological sites, particularly the monumental architectural ones, that was so fundamental for fomenting the cultural, ethnic, and national identity of post-Revolutionary Mexico. In the case of Copán, the Carnegie project dug and restored major portions of the Acropolis temples there and the ballcourt, in a collaborative arrangement, wherein the government of Honduras supplied the labor and materials and the Carnegie Institution provided technical staff, expertise, equipment, and final scholarly publication.

On the "hard science" or natural history side, there were Carnegie-sponsored investigations of the soils, geology, vegetation, and modern land-use patterns in the Maya Lowlands, as well as path-breaking studies of the technological aspects of pottery-making. The vegetation, soils, land-use patterns studies, and ethnographic research in the Yucatán Peninsula led scholars to believe that Lowland Maya communities could never have held dense, urban populations. This conclusion lent credence to the idea that sites like Tikal, Palenque, and Copán were "vacant ceremonial centers," periodically accrued to by peasants scattered in villages and hamlets in the countryside. Carnegie Institution archaeologist and epigrapher J. Eric S. Thompson was to become the most outstanding proponent of this model, arguing from his observations of the sites themselves, their hieroglyphic inscriptions, and his considerable ethnographic and ethnohistoric expertise. He also provided a model for the multidisciplinary approach of Maya archaeology with his classic

monograph on his excavations at San José, Belize; there he combined relevant information from all fields of inquiry to the reconstruction of the life and times of this site in the culture history of the Maya Lowlands. There was a concern for reconstructing the role and development of this "minor ceremonial center" vis-à-vis the larger Maya capitals nearby and, as such, getting a better command of Maya civilization as a whole.

Winds of Change: 1940–1960. Thompson's monograph on San José reflected what Willey and Sabloff (1993) signal as "the concern with context and function" that swept American archaeology during the latter part of the Classificatory-Historical period, from 1940–1960. In their view, three new approaches were most important in expanding our understanding of ancient societies, in Mesoamerica and the rest of the American continent. The first was that artifacts are to be understood as the material relics of social and cultural behavior, yielding insights into the individuals and the societies that made them the cultural constructs that inspired their manufacture. The second was the concern with the way human societies distributed themselves across the landscape and the inferences that could be drawn from those choices, an approach that came to be known as settlement-patterns analysis. This approach was suggested to Gordon Willey by the ethnologist Julian Steward, who viewed it as a way of studying the relationships between culture and natural environment. The third, and a critically important new focus of archaeological research in the Americas, was the study of cultural ecology.

These new frontiers in archaeological inquiry were greatly enhanced by scientific applications from related disciplines, including radiocarbon dating, archaeomagnetism (also used for dating), obsidian hydration dating, aerial photography (and other noninvasive detection techniques), spectroscopy, geology, zoology, botany, and mathematics (particularly statistics). Bolstered in its methodology and broadened in the questions that it asked, the archaeological goals of reconstructing culture history thus became more deeply immersed in larger anthropological concerns of the nature and processes of cultural evolution.

The period from 1940 to 1960 started with a series of revelations in Mesoamerican archaeology. First came a dose of wisdom from the Harvard ethnologist Clyde Kluckhohn, who critiqued the field of Maya studies in 1940 for its lack of theory-building and its tendency to wallow in detail without any explicit theoretical or conceptual formulations. The following year, the distinguished Mexican ethnohistorian Wigberto Jiménez Moreno created quite a stir when, at the first Mesa Redonda de la Sociedad Mexicana de Antropología, he marshalled evidence from several chronicles in identifying the mythical city of Tollan with the ruins of Tula, Hidalgo. The excavations begun at Tula the previous year by the archaeologist Jorge R. Acosta came to play a critical role in the discussions, which ended in consensus that Jiménez Moreno was right. At the following Mesa Redonda in 1942, another important issue in Mesoamerican archaeology was also approached from the perspective of different data sets. The Olmec civilization of the Gulf Coast of Mexico had not been placed securely in time since its rediscovery by Blom and LaFarge in the 1920s. Based on Mathew Stirling's (1940) publications of a very early Long Count date on Stela C from Tres Zapotes, Jiménez Moreno's ethnohistoric research, and Alfonso Caso and Miguel Covarrubias's studies of the Olmec art style, it was concluded that the Olmec was the first civilization of Mexico. It was Caso, at this meeting, who coined the term "cultura madre" for the Olmec, considering it the font of all the subsequent great civilizations in the region. (Although the Mayanists, particularly Morley and Thompson, disagreed strongly with this conclusion at the time, subsequent radiocarbon dates from La Venta proved Stirling, Caso, Covarrubias, and Jiménez Moreno right: the Gulf Coast Olmec predated the Classic Maya tradition by a millennium.)

The next seminal contribution of this era was the publication, in 1943, of Paul Kirchhoff's definition of the cultural area of Mesoamerica. Based on linguistic, archaeological, ethnohistoric, and ethnographic data, Kirchhoff's fundamental contribution was to link the peoples and cultures of the region together culturally, in the minds of all subsequent researchers. Prior to that time, Maya archaeology was virtually a separate discipline from the archaeology of the rest of Mexico, but Kirchhoff's fundamental essay changed that, much for the better. The emphasis on languages was important, and soon to be followed by significant and influential historical linguistic studies by Morris Swadesh and, in later years, by Terrence Kaufman and Lyle Campbell. Kirchhoff also did a series of innovative environmental studies in Mesoamerica and neighboring culture areas that he defined ("Aridomerica," basically the north of Mexico, and "Oasisamerica," the area most archaeologists refer to as the American Southwest plus northernmost Mexico). In these, he sought to tie the environments to social structures and systems of subsistence strategies among pre-Hispanic populations. Kirchhoff was also a phenomenal teacher, giving classes on a wide array of topics, including Marxism, to a whole generation of scholars who would prove critical in the development of the archaeology of Mesoamerica. The 1940s in general was a time of great intellectual foment in Mexico, with a number of scholars espousing the writings of Marxist and materialist scholars.

Pedro Armillas was among the first to bring a heavily materialist theoretical orientation to bear in the study of Mesoamerican archaeology. A Spaniard who had emigrated to Mexico, Armillas had clearly been influenced by the theories of social evolution of the Australian archaeologist V. Gordon Childe. He was particularly interested in Childe's formulation of the "urban revolution" and sought to apply it to the rise of Teotihuacan. He established a series of cultural periods (tied to societal development) in 1949 that continues to be used today. He was the first anthropological archaeologist in Mexico to espouse an environmental approach for explaining social change. Thus, he was quick to take up the "irrigation hypothesis" for explaining the rise of the state that was adumbrated in Karl Wittfogel's 1957 book on *Oriental Despotism*. Armillas was to have a profound effect on the thinking and fieldwork of a number of anthropologists both in Mexico and the United States, among the latter most notably William T. Sanders. As part of a field "practicum" at the Escuela Nacional de Antropología (founded in 1937, as a training arm of Mexico's INAH, the Instituto Nacional de Antropología e Historia), Armillas did the first settlement-pattern survey in Mexico at the site of Xochicalco in Morelos (written up by Sanders in 1956). Angel Palerm and Eric Wolf (a student of Julian Steward) also concentrated their efforts on investigating the correlations between differing environments in Mesoamerica, agricultural techniques, and the development of civilization. In 1959 the National Autonomous University of Mexico (UNAM) founded the Centro de Estudios Mayas, and the Instituto de Investigaciones Antropológicas, to provide research facilities and teaching in these fields. The latter has provided training in archaeology to hundreds of students, many of whom have gone on to distinguished careers in the field.

The Archaeological and Epigraphic Revolutions of the 1960s and 1970s. In the 1960s a revolution of sorts took place in American archaeology. At the time, its practitioners called it the "New Archaeology," but with the passage of time it has acquired the name processual archaeology. The concern was no longer simply with what happened, where, and when, but why it happened in the first place. Archaeologists agreed that their most important mission was to study variability in the archaeological record, in order to understand cultural process. The mission was to employ scientific method to explain the past, not merely to describe it and place it in proper chronological relation to developments in other sites and regions. The cultural evolutionary frameworks that had been championed in the works of Armillas, Palerm, and Wolf were taken up and refined by a whole generation of scholars, for whom an evolutionary perspective provided the most satisfactory means of explaining how and why cultures changed through time and space. Human-land interaction and technological innovation (particularly but not exclusively in food domestication and craft specialization) were seen as the key variables in cultural evolution, a perspective well suited to the material remains that are best preserved in the archaeological record.

Beginning in 1960, Pedro Armillas's theories and approach were given substantive strength by the extensive surveys carried out in the Basin of Mexico by Sanders and his colleagues and students at the Pennsylvania State University, as well as the exemplary Teotihuacan Mapping Project of Rene Millon. In a tour de force of scientific method, Millon and his team mapped the entire urban center of Teotihuacan, with the aid of aerial photography and extensive on-ground measurements and checking of the aerial data. In both Sanders's Basin of Mexico project (Sanders et al. 1979) and Millon's Teotihuacan Mapping Project (Millon 1973), surface collections of artifacts enabled archaeologists to date the features visible on the modern landscape and obtain an idea of the presence of earlier occupations at the same locus. In this way, settlement-pattern studies could analyze issues of human ecology, site function, and sociopolitical organization through both time and space. The surface collections also enabled Millon and his team to identify specialized production activities for many of the site's apartment compounds and to isolate larger social units, which they called *barrios*. It was even possible to identify *barrios* occupied by immigrants from Oaxaca, and another termed the "Merchants' Barrio," which excavations eventually determined was occupied by migrants from the Gulf Coast. While Millon's mapping project represented the very best in both methodology and the results of the single-site approach, Sanders insisted that a larger, regional approach was the only way that any site could be placed in its true context, both ecological and culture-historical. Indeed, Sanders's finding that virtually all of the population of the Basin emigrated to Teotihuacan during the first century CE supported his thesis that only regional, 100 percent survey, could provide archaeologists with the answers to the broad questions of social theory that came to be the focus of the discipline.

The most influential North American practitioners of the ecological approach in Mesoamerica were Sanders, Richard ("Scotty") MacNeish of the Peabody Andover Institute, and Kent V. Flannery of the University of Michigan. Sanders and Barbara Price (1968) contended that, following Wittfogel, environmental limitations and potentials led inexorably to the development of irrigation agriculture, and explained the rise of urbanism, state-level organization, and civilization at Teotihuacan in the Basin of Mexico. MacNeish's Tehuacan Valley Archaeobotanical Project sought to document subsistence strategies—from the earliest migrants to the region, through the earliest times of plant collecting and incipient domestication, to the irrigation agriculture documented for the later eras—through a multidisciplinary approach and research team. Flannery's Valley of Oaxaca Human Ecology Project sought to document human adaptation, from initial arrivals to European contact, through survey and excavations of sites from caves and rock shelters to the great center of Monte Albán.

Flannery championed a systems-theory approach to understanding culture change, concerning himself with how changes in one aspect of the overall system of human adaptation to the environment affected other aspects or subsystems. He sought to isolate the factors in such "feedback loops" that either restored the system to equilibrium or resulted in further change to it. In incorporating ethnohistoric and ethnographic data in his analyses, Flannery took an expansive view of ecology, proclaiming that "anything that transmits information is within the realm of ecology." In holistic treatments of the interaction between people and their environment (broadly defined), Flannery and Joyce Marcus sought to document how people's perceptions of change and stasis in both the natural and supernatural world helped to shape their responses in Formative-period Oaxaca, in a long-term symbiotic relationship that had many checks and balances built into it. Flannery's emphasis on the ecosystem and systems analysis derived, in part, from his participation in MacNeish's Tehuacan Valley Project.

Another important contribution to the development of the "New" or processual archaeology in Mesoamerica was to come from beyond its borders, in the form of a theory of cultural evolution based on the cultures of Amazonia (in South America). The ethnologist Robert Carneiro had developed the theory of circumscription to explain how human cultures evolved in response to overpopulation and crowded conditions. The extremely limited potential for food production offered by the thin soils and tropical-forest resources of the Amazon Basin results in a pattern of "circumscription." In his view, such geographic barriers as mountains, the sea, or some other physical environmental constraints—including the presence of unyielding neighbors—create a vehicle for social evolution: with unrestricted population growth, people soon outgrow the carrying capacity of their well-defined ("circumscribed") domain. Thereafter, they must either fission off segments of the community (to seek and develop new lands elsewhere) or develop a more complex form of social organization, based on ranking. While based on Amazonian data, Carneiro and other anthropologists—most particularly archaeologists—quickly saw that his theory helped explain the development not only of "ranked" societies, but of stratified ones, leading to the development of urbanism and a state apparatus to maintain the status quo. Circumscription theory helped to explain why urbanism developed in the Basin of Mexico, with its clearly defined geographic boundaries. It also helped explain the development of urban centers in the Maya Lowlands, where it was argued that good soils (Sanders 1978) and hostile neighbors (Webster 1973) quickly set the boundaries beyond which Maya communities could not expand.

Research in the Maya Lowlands was led by Gordon Willey of Harvard University, who directed students and colleagues in a series of field projects spanning nearly three decades in the Belize River Valley, at Altar de Sacrificios and at Seibal in Guatemala, in the Copán Valley in Honduras, and at Chichén Itzá in Yucatán. Willey provided a model of forced research, timely and thorough reporting, and answers to the pressing questions of the day regarding the origins, development, and demise of the Classic Maya tradition. Harvard archaeology students also benefited enormously from the teaching of Evon Vogt, whose Harvard Chiapas Project also ran for thirty years and trained dozens of able ethnographers. The University of Pennsylvania was responsible for the highly influential, long-term and large-scale multidisciplinary project at Tikal, which provided research opportunities for a number of distinguished scholars. Similarly, in the Yucatán Peninsula, the Middle American Research Institute—under the direction of E. Wyllys Andrews IV, Robert Wauchope, and since 1978, E. Wyllys Andrews V—has trained many professionals and created a wealth of new knowledge and insights regarding the archaeology and ethnology of the Northern Maya Lowlands. The universities of Campeche and of Yucatán fulfilled this role admirably in Mexico, and continue to be the font of significant ongoing research projects in Maya archaeology, as is Mexico's University of the Americas, in Puebla, for Highland archaeology.

The dramatic shifts in theory, methodology, and research questions that began in the 1960s in Mesoamerican archaeology were tremendously enhanced by a revolution in an allied field, that of epigraphy. The discovery by Heinrich Berlin that each Maya kingdom recorded its own name (in what he referred to as its "emblem glyph"), and the concurrent but independent revelation by Tatiana Proskouriakoff that a pattern of dates on monuments in Piedras Negras showed conclusively that the Classic Maya stelae recorded historical events in the lives of named rulers, proved to be a watershed event in Maya studies. With the ensuing success of epigraphers in both the "historical approach" and the "phonetic approach" (championed first by the Russian philologist Yurii Knorosov and later, in the United States, by David Kelley and the linguist Floyd Lounsbury), archaeologists were for the first time privy to all manner of historical information

regarding the lives and times of the rulers of Classic Maya sites. Joyce Marcus's pathbreaking study of the distribution and hierarchical pattern of citation of emblem glyphs was the first step in mapping out areawide power relations between Maya centers and led to her later development of the powerful "dynamic model" of Lowland Maya political organization.

With time, it has been possible to learn so much of the dynastic and political histories of Maya realms that one of the foremost archaeologists in the field can now boldly state that "this historical information now structures most aspects of Classic period archaeology." The inscriptions are particularly revealing about the genealogical links, royal visits, political skirmishes, captures, sacrifices, long-term wars, and shifting alliances forged between the ruling families during the Late Classic period.

Recent Directions in Mesoamerican Archaeology. The role of warfare in social change has become a central concern of anthropological archaeology throughout the world, and Mesoamerica has helped to lead the charge. The publication of the murals of Bonampak by the Carnegie Institution in 1955, with their scenes of a pitched battle and the ensuing human sacrifice on a temple, provided the first concrete evidence against the view then current that Classic Maya society was ruled over by peace-loving priests who reviled warfare and human sacrifice. Simultaneously, the settlement pattern research then being conducted by Gordon Willey in the Belize River Valley, and subsequently carried out by the University of Pennsylvania's long-term project at Tikal in Guatemala, showed that the old idea of "vacant ceremonial centers" among the Maya was completely incorrect. The temple complexes were the civic as well as ceremonial centers for vast populations—calculated at some 70,000 people for central Tikal alone. While not as tightly packed as Teotihuacan, or Mexico-Tenochtitlan, nonetheless the largest Lowland Maya centers were clearly home to densely nucleated urban societies, with marked social ranking if not stratification. The evidence for defensive site placement at such locales as Aguateca, of a defensive ditch at Becan, and of earthworks (thought to have a defensive function) at Tikal, caused archaeologists like David Webster and Arthur Demarest to posit that warfare had a central role in the development, maintenance, and, in many cases, the collapse of many Maya cities.

Webster argued convincingly that circumscription led not just to more complex and inclusive forms of social organization, but to increasingly frequent and devastating hostilities between rival centers. He emphasized the role of warfare in the rise of Maya civilization, while Arthur Demarest has placed more emphasis on charting its role in the collapse of the Late Classic states. The research that he and his colleagues and students (from

Vanderbilt University and the Universidad de San Carlos in Guatemala) have conducted in the Petexbatun region of western Guatemala has shown conclusively that warfare became endemic there in the eighth and ninth centuries CE, with rapidly shifting alliances and devastating results for sites such as Dos Pilas, Seibal, Aguateca, and Punta de Chimino.

Hieroglyphic evidence has served to support the views expressed by Demarest and other proponents of the importance of Maya warfare, particularly for the Late Classic period. With the phenomenal advances in the decipherment of the Maya writing system, scholars know not only the dates of battles but also the names and origins of both the winners and losers. Tatiana Proskouriakoff was the pioneer in this arena during the early 1960s when she discovered, in the inscriptions of Yaxchilán, the glyphs (modestly referred by her as "event glyphs"; now known to be verbs) for capture, and titles for the number of captives taken. Since that time a number of epigraphers have detailed not only the individual battles between rulers and centers but also the shifting alliances between major and minor centers during the course of the Classic period in the Maya Lowlands. These textual references are wholly in keeping with what we know of such historical processes in Highland Mexico, both in Oaxaca and the Basin of Mexico, during the Postclassic period.

Some archaeologists have objected that they do not find direct archaeological evidence at their sites to support the specific findings of their epigrapher colleagues, in keeping with their (properly anthropological) skepticism about the reliability of official histories, carved in stone in what all agree are propagandistic monuments. Yet recent decipherments of records of battles in the texts of both the winning and the losing kingdom (e.g., at Quirigua and Copán, and at Palenque and Calakmul) show that records of such encounters cannot be dismissed as baseless propaganda, whether they be found in the Maya area, the Valley of Oaxaca, or the Valley of Mexico. The documentation through surveys and excavations of defensible locations, fortifications, and strategies, particularly in Postclassic Mesoamerica, is but one of many ways in which archaeology has and will continue to contribute to our understanding of warfare—a problem that besets all civilizations in world history.

The large-scale, multidisciplinary projects that have characterized Mesoamerican studies for nearly a century continue to thrive, but now with an even more stunning array of analytical tools and specializations. The example of the regional approach carried out in the Basin of Mexico project has inspired important work in the Tula region by Guadalupe Mastache, Robert Cobean, Richard Diehl, and Dan Healan; in the Valley of Oaxaca by Richard Blanton, Gary Feinman, and Steven Kowaleski; in the sustaining area of San Lorenzo by Ann Cyphers Guillen; in the Petexbatun region of Guatemala by Arthur Demarest and his colleagues; and in the Copán Valley by Sanders and Webster. It has its maximal example in the *Archaeological Atlas of Yucatan*, coordinated by Edward Kurjack and Sylvia Garza T. When combined with intense research into the dynastic center and extensive household archaeology, as at Chalcatzingo in Morelos directed by David Grove, the Petexbatun project, and the Copán project, these endeavors have provided a remarkably complete picture of life in ancient Mesoamerica, through several millennia and across immense distances.

In the give-and-take that has characterized the relationship between field archaeology and historical studies through the years, archaeology has complemented, as well as tested, historical records of dynastic history through the pursuit, documentation, and complete publication of the architectural and artifactual remains that lay buried beneath the final phase buildings of the larger, more long-lived sites. This approach was first employed by the Carnegie Institution projects at Uaxactún and Kaminaljuyú and was also to become one of the great contributions of the Tikal projects run by the University of Pennsylvania in the late 1950s to early 1970s and by the Government of Guatemala since then. More recently, tunneling and other strategies have proven extraordinarily informative in reconstructing the architectural and dynastic history of Copán, in the Honduran government–sponsored projects there. The documentation of the buildings, texts, portraits, and even the final resting places of Early Classic kings by these and other projects has put the lie to skeptical pronouncements by field archaeologists that Late Classic textual references to long lines of rulers were merely delusions of grandeur, that no such "putative kings" existed. The contextual information provided by ecological studies, settlement-pattern studies, and household archaeology, particularly if conducted in a way that the population history and social evolution of the populace can be gleaned, enables archaeologists to begin to grasp the economic and social context in which the monuments of Mesoamerican states, and the decisions of its rulers, were carried out.

The magnificent research at the Templo Mayor of the Culhua Mexica, directed by Eduardo Matos Moctezuma, has admirably revealed the form, content, and timing of the many rebuildings of that awe-inspiring edifice and the social context to which they responded. This research has ably drawn upon the extensive documentation available through the sixteenth-century chronicles of Aztec society to understand why each set of dedicatory offerings took the form that it did; this kind of historiography follows ably in the tradition of the work of Bernal and Caso in the Valley of Oaxaca, now deepened and broadened by the findings and interpretations there by Flannery and Marcus for the Zapotec, and more recently by John Pohl and Bruce Byland among the Mixtec. Likewise, many generations of Mayanists have made fruitful use of Landa's *Relacion*, the *Books of Chilam Balam*, the *Anals of the Cakchiquels*, the *Popol Vuh*, and other Colonial-period accounts in attempting to understand pre-Hispanic Maya history and religion.

Another significant development in this regard is the focus on ideology in reconstructing culture change in Mesoamerica. An early leader in this regard was Doris Heyden, whose interpretation of the cave beneath the Pyramid of the Sun was to have a profound effect on archaeological interpretations of the rise of the city, state, and civilization at Teotihuacan. Clara Millon and Rene Millon were to contribute strongly to this new focus, through their interpretations of the ideology behind the mural paintings and the nature of the household religion at the city. Flannery and Marcus's work on Formative Oaxaca and the Zapotec cosmos is a model of sophisticated analysis of the role of ideology in shaping human adaptations and culture change. The illuminating hieroglyphic decipherments of Classic Maya monument names by David Stuart and of place names, supernatural domains, and spiritual "co-essences" by Stuart and Stephen Houston have opened new vistas in our gazes upon a distant world. The decipherments in the Maya area have gone along with fresh interpretations of the pictorial symbolism that the texts often accompany. This has given new meaning to the aesthetics of Mesoamerican art, much of it related to the person of the ruler and the important ritual acts and the acts of war that he conducted in order to provide bounty for his people.

Studies of astronomical alignments of buildings and entire sites by anthropologists and astronomers like Anthony Aveni of Colgate, and dozens of decipherments of astronomical data in the inscriptions of the Maya by Floyd Lounsbury, Linda Schele, and other epigraphers, have given us a greatly enhanced understanding of the Maya's perception of their own role, and place, in the universe. Schele and David Freidel produced a trilogy of books that have been highly influential in examining the role of religious ideology in the conceptualization and practice of divine kingship among the Maya. Arthur Demarest has been instrumental in showing how social theory can explain the preponderance of ideology and political symbolism in the governing of Classic Maya kingdoms, through his analogies with theater-states (or "galactic polities") in Southeast Asia. The Moses Mesoamerican Archive of Princeton University and its Director, Davíd

Carrasco, have proven invaluable in promoting dialogue and consensus between scholars of many disciplinary backgrounds and nationalities in the quest to elucidate the religious foundations of civilized life in Mesoamerica, through time and space.

Like the discipline of archaeology as a whole, Mesoamerican archaeology has benefited enormously from the application of a more scientific methodology and the dozens of new analytical procedures and materials analyses developed in the hard sciences. Ceramics are no longer studied only for their chronological value or for gauging the degree of contact with neighboring societies; now ceramicists study the function of vessels through their form, thermal qualities, and residues, as a first step toward analyzing activities areas and economic organization more broadly. Chemical characterization studies of ceramic components allow archaeologists to determine the sources of the clays and pigments used in pottery manufacture, and these lend greater strength to their identifications and interpretations of workshop areas, redistribution networks, and the location and nature of markets. Likewise, obsidian analysis has profited enormously from sophisticated new laboratory techniques that enable secure source identifications and new revelations about the ways in which the finished (and recycled) tools were utilized, through use-wear analysis, and information about their relative ages through obsidian-hydration studies. Procurement, manufacturing techniques, workshop activities, and redistribution systems for obsidian, chert, and ground-stone tools have also increased in sophistication and significance as a result of new technology and archaeological theory. The study of long-distance commodity exchange by Anthony Andrews, Michael Smith, and Flannery and his colleagues Richard Bishop and Dorie Reents-Budet has provided new and important revelations about Mesoamerican macroeconomics. Studies of the Aztec tribute and market systems by Smith and Frances Berdan have been complemented by market studies in Oaxaca by Richard Blanton, Gary Feinman, and their colleagues. For the Maya area, the question of seafaring trade has been illuminated by the research of Anthony Andrews, Tomas Gallareta, Rafael Cobos, Jeremy Sabloff, and David Freidel.

The application of geographic information systems to Mesoamerican archaeology is now fully under way and will continue to be an extremely powerful tool in regional studies of cultural geography and human ecology. The use of laser technology in computer-assisted mapping of sites, features, and even the carved faces of stone monuments has enormously increased the precision and accuracy of archaeological and conservation recording. Like all other members of our global village, archaeologists are now avid devotees of Web sites, e-mail, and CD-ROMs, and these media will undoubtedly have a profound effect in increasing "readability" of data, communication between colleagues, and dissemination of results to both the professional and lay communities.

The final theoretical shift to affect American archaeology is what is referred to as the "post-processual" movement. Led by the British archaeologist Ian Hodder and a number of North American colleagues, these scholars believe that processual archaeology was too deeply ecological, evolutionist, and materialist. Hodder in particular believes that this approach is too narrow and restrictive, and that the most important kinds of inferences are those which fully take into account the social context of the actors. Archaeological remains constitute, in his view, "texts" to be read, in which scholars can deal with issues of gender, power, ideology, text, structure, and history. As we have seen, in Mesoamerican studies the significant documentation of the history of individual actors, the monuments they either added onto or created sui generis, the larger ideological and political networks in which they operated, and the social context to which they responded, have long been a part of the scholarly tradition of Mesoamerican archaeology and ethnohistory.

For most of the ancient cultures of Mesoamerica, the textual record is, however, inevitably focused exclusively on the elite segments of society. Given the concerns of processual archaeology to place the cultural evolution of civilizations in both an ecological and a social context, and of post-processual studies to incorporate historical and gender analysis, no amount of documentation and analysis of Mesoamerican (male) elites will provide the full measure of understanding of how and why societies developed, prospered, and disbanded in the particular ways that they did. For this, the ecological data, settlement patterns (and underlying systems of settlement and resource utilization), and household archaeology hold the key. Household archaeology in Mesoamerica can be said to have begun with the Carnegie Institution of Washington's final project in the Maya area at Mayapán in the 1950s. Since then it has been ably carried out all over Mesoamerica, yielding invaluable data on household economics, religion, social organization, and individual life histories. Given the concerns with "people's history" current in the social sciences today, this approach will likely be among the most powerful tools in the Mesoamerican field archaeologist's arsenal in the coming years. Efforts such as those of archaeologist Linda Manzanilla Naim of the Universidad Nacional Autónoma de México at the Teotihuacan apartment compounds of Oztoyahualco, Teopancaxco, and now (with Leonardo López Luján of INAH) at the Xalla compound, have revealed the economic, social, and religious organization of the different social strata of the city, with a level of precision and detail that represents a new model for the profession.

From its inception, Mesoamerican archaeology has been a major vehicle for education, conservation of cultural patrimony, and ethnic and national identity. Happily, conservation has now permeated all aspects of field research on most large-scale excavation projects, from initial conceptualization of research problem and design, to excavation and recording methods, to transport, conservation, and storage (or display) of objects, to long-term regional site management planning. From the time of the earliest monumental restoration projects in Highland Mexico and the Maya area, archaeologists have concerned themselves not only with identifying and protecting the most exalted monuments of antiquity but also of projecting their meanings—both ancient and newly created—to the world at large. Increasingly, archaeologists are confronted with balancing the needs of the government bodies and funding agencies that support their field research with those of the indigenous peoples whose ancestors created not only the towering temple-pyramids but the humble house-mounds that still have so much to tell us about people's history in ancient Mesoamerica. As the intellectuals in the pan-Maya movement and other indigenous groups continue their efforts not only to reinterpret but to create knowledge about their own past, Mesoamerican archaeology will take new and productive directions in the future.

[*Many of the people mentioned in this entry are the subjects of independent biographical entries.*]

BIBLIOGRAPHY

Bernal, Ignacio. *A History of Mexican Archaeology*. London and New York, 1980.

Carrasco, Davíd, ed. *To Change Place: Aztec Ceremonial Landscapes*. Boulder, Colo., 1999.

Coe, Michael D. *Breaking the Maya Code*. London and New York, 1992.

Flannery, Kent V., and Joyce Marcus, eds. *The Cloud People: Divergent Evolution of the Zapotec and Mixtec Civilizations*. New York City, 1983.

Gamio, Manuel. *La población del Valle de Teotihuacan*. Mexico City, 1922.

Kirchhoff, Paul. "Mesoamérica: sus limites geográficos, composición étnica, y caracteres culturales." *Acta Americana* 1 (1943), 92–107.

Mastache, Alba Guadalupe, and Robert H. Cobean. "La arqueología." In *La antropología en Mexico: Panorama Histórico*, edited by Carlos García Mora and María de la Luz del Valle, vol. 5, pp. 39–82. Mexico City, 1987.

Millon, Rene. *Urbanization at Teotihuacan, Mexico. Vol. 1: The Teotihuacan Map*. Austin, Tex., 1973.

Sanders, William T., Jeffrey Parsons, and Robert Santley. *The Basin of Mexico: Ecological Processes in the Evolution of Civilization*. New York, 1979.

Sanders, William T., and Barbara Price. *Mesoamerica: The Evolution of Civilization*. New York, 1968.

Sharer, Robert J. *The Ancient Maya*. Stanford, 1994.

Willey, Gordon R., and Jeremy Sabloff. *A History of American Archaeology*, 3d ed. New York, 1993.

WILLIAM L. FASH

APICULTURE. *See* Bees and Honey.

ARCHAEOASTRONOMY. Archaeoastronomy is the interdisciplinary study of ancient astronomical systems based on both the written and the unwritten record. It has become a meeting ground for at least three established inquiries into ancient astronomy: (1) astroarchaeology, though now a somewhat outdated term, a field methodology for retrieving astronomical information from the study of alignments associated with ancient architecture and the landscape; (2) history of astronomy, a traditional discipline that usually deals only with written texts, and is concerned with the means of acquisition and content of precise astronomical knowledge by ancient cultures, usually those of the Old World; and (3) ethnoastronomy, a branch of cultural anthropology that draws evidence from ethnographic studies of contemporary cultures, mostly non-Western. Since the early 1990s the term "cultural astronomy" has come to embrace all three of these endeavors.

Archaeoastronomy owes its origin in part to the development of astroarchaeology around the turn of the twentieth century, in particular to the influential British astronomer Sir J. Norman Lockyer. He suggested that walls, doorways, and axes of Egyptian temples and pyramids were arranged deliberately to align with the rising and setting positions of the sun (especially on the solstices, when the sun reaches its northernmost and southernmost standstill positions on the horizon), as well as other celestial bodies. But Lockyer's speculations about Egyptian religion and society emanating from his orientation studies led to condemnation of his work by archaeologists.

After a half century of dormancy, another astronomer, Gerald Hawkins, reawakened the interpretive conflict between the culture- and science-based disciplines by publishing a series of papers and a popular book advocating that Stonehenge was intended to function as a device for computing eclipses of the moon, these events having been foretold by the ancient sighting of solar and lunar horizon standstills through openings in the standing stones. Although Hawkins's conclusions were dramatically at odds with contemporary views on pan-European cultural diffusion, as well as the presumed intellectual level of prehistoric people in the British Isles about 3000 BCE, his efforts opened up the question of the level of sophistication of mensuration, mathematics, and astronomy in an-

cient societies in general. His studies also called attention to the work of the Scottish engineer Alexander Thom, who had systematically studied and surveyed more than 200 megalithic structures in the British Isles, exploring in greater detail many of the same questions entertained by Hawkins. By the early 1970s, the Thom paradigm—investigating the possibility that astronomy might have been a motivating factor in the placement and orientation of ancient architecture—crossed the Atlantic and took root in the Americas.

Mesoamerican archaeoastronomical studies have proven to be quite productive for a number of reasons. First, relevant evidence often can be derived from pre- and post-contact written records and historical documents, as well as numerous well-preserved archaeological materials from a relatively more recent past. Second, the living remains of indigenous cultures that might offer meaningful data persist from the southwestern United States through Central and South America. A number of conference volumes cited in the bibliography may be consulted for details.

Combined with evidence from allied disciplines, field studies have revealed that significant astronomical information is incorporated in a variety of Mesoamerican architectural works. In the space allotted, a few examples will be cited that demonstrate the methodology of archaeoastronomy and its contributions to Mesoamerican cultural studies.

As Teotihuacan was one of the great ideological centers of Mesoamerica in Early Classic times, it is no surprise to discover that calendric and astronomical knowledge was propagated throughout Mesoamerica from this sacred place. One means of doing so employed the use of orientation/day counting devices called pecked crosses. These consist of cuplike depressions pecked into the rock or stucco matrix with a percussive device. More than eighty petroglyphs of similar structure (usually double circles centered on a cross) have been found carved in the floors of buildings and on prominent rock outcrops at the edges of cliffs in the vicinity. Although they tend to cluster around Teotihuacan, where they probably originated, a few of the pecked crosses also have been found in the Maya region (e.g., at the ruins of Uaxactún and Seibal). The twenty holes that comprise each axis are a persistent design element (20 is the base of the Mesoamerican counting system). Other numbers of calendrical significance also make up segments of the design. Often the axes of the markers and visual lines passing over some distance from one marker to another can be matched favorably with astronomical building orientations, thus suggesting that the symbol may have functioned as an architectural benchmark.

About the beginning of the Christian era, when Teotihuacan was built, the Pleiades star group aligned precisely with the orientation of the Teotihuacan grid, which is oddly skewed 15.5 degrees clockwise from the cardinal directions. This orientation is also marked by a pair of pecked crosses 3 kilometers (1.9 miles) apart. Interestingly, the Pleiades star group underwent heliacal rise on the day the sun passed the zenith, or overhead position, at Teotihuacan. Moreover, the Pleiades also transited the zenith of highland Mexican skies, and the ethnohistoric record suggests they were employed in Aztec times to mark the beginning of a fifty-two-year sacred calendar round. Taken together, the evidence suggests that at Teotihuacan a star-sun timing mechanism was integrated into the urbanistic plan of the city as a way of both standardizing time and following possibly yet undisclosed religious dictates.

Given the developed nature of the Teotihuacan state, we might well anticipate that its rulers would seek a methodology for organizing the calendar and disseminating it to all points of influence. Part of a complex set of alignments, a summer solstice orientation is marked by pecked crosses at the ruins of Alta Vista (Chalchihuites) in northwest Mexico. Lying within 20 kilometers (12.4 miles) of the Tropic of Cancer, this site dates from the Tlamimilolpa-Xolalpan phase of the Teotihuacan. Solar alignments might be anticipated at the tropic, for this is the place where the sun turns around, reaching the zenith at noon precisely on the summer solstice. The Alta Vista markers closely resemble those at Teotihuacan 650 kilometers (400 miles) away and at Uaxactún, 1700 kilometers (1,050 miles) distant. The evidence suggests a rather specific and detailed common mode of transmission of knowledge of Mesoamerican space and time over a wide area of Mesoamerica. This has led to discussions of the possible political implications of the use of the pecked cross symbol in the Maya area.

Mesoamerican archaeoastronomers have paid considerable attention to the worship of Venus and to possible methods used by ancient astronomers to track its motion. [See Astronomy.] Native manuscripts attest to the care the Maya had given to following the wanderings of this bright planet, from which astrologers drew omens regarding affairs of state. For example, Venus is evident in the alignments and iconography of the House of the Governor at Uxmal. The principal doorway of this structure, likely a royal palace, is markedly skewed from the principal site axis to align with Venus rising at its southerly standstill reached every eight years. The line of view also intersects the largest structure at Cehtzuc, another site 6 kilometers (3.7 miles) away. The Venus orientation scheme is supported by the occurrence on the frieze of the building of more than three hundred carvings of the Venus hieroglyphic symbol, the same one that appears in the Venus Table in the *Dresden Codex*. Also, the number 8 in Maya dot-bar notation is carved on a pair of large rain-god masks that form part of the north and south cornerstones of the building. (Eight days is also the tabulated interval of disappearance of the planet prior to heliacal rise or first appearance before dawn.) Finally, a zodiacal band flanking an effigy of the ruler over the Venus-aligned doorway may refer to the timing of sky rituals that were conducted by the ruler in the large open space fronting the temple. The motivation for worship of the Venus deity Quetzalcoatl-Kukulcan may have included the religious need for the ruler to publicly demonstrate his relationship to the ancestor gods who lived in the sky, as well as a practical connection between setting timings of the planet with the maize-rain cycle.

Specialized architectural assemblages also were employed by the ancient Mesoamericans to standardize time by marking the sun at horizon, especially its solstices and equinoxes. At Uaxactún (c.400 CE), an observer standing on an east-facing radial pyramid viewed the sunrise over a series of three smaller buildings constructed on a common base to the east of it. When the sun reached summer and winter standstills, it would be positioned over the northern and southernmost of these buildings, respectively, while at the equinox it would be perched over the central one. Today, over forty variants of this architectural-solar calendar have been uncovered at sites in the Petén rain forest of Guatemala. At one time or another in their evolution, many may have incorporated variations of the solar orientation calendar to suit local agricultural needs. Still others may have included seminal dates in dynastic history.

The sun also was sighted directly when it crossed the zenith, by the passage of its light through vertical tubes built into the architecture; examples occur in Structure P at Monte Albán and in modified caves at the ruins of Xochicalco and Teotihuacan. There is no solid evidence that any of the cultures of Mesoamerica either divided the time of day or night or marked the solar course by following the shadow cast by a gnomon, practices that are found in early European astronomy. In Aztec Tenochtitlan, the most famous example occurs in the Templo Mayor, which, according to both the alignment studies and the historical record, was oriented to permit the sun at the equinox (just before the start of the rainy season) to rise between the twin temples as its summit. Here was a way of permanently affixing in stone the connection between Huitzilopochtli, the god of sun/war, and Tlaloc, the god of rain and fertility, whose dedicatory temples were erected atop the main platform.

Light and shadow phenomena have been proposed to explain a possible architectural hierophany involving the sun at Chichén Itzá in a Maya Toltec structure dating to about 1000 CE. An undulating shadow in the shape of a diamondback rattlesnake falls on the west side of the north balustrade of the Castillo or Temple of Kukulcan late in the afternoon around the equinoxes. Whether the phenomenon is a modern invention or may have been employed in ancient public rituals concerned with signaling the impending rainy season remains problematic. A testimony to the enduring power of the cosmos, today's version of the event has come to take on great public importance. Customarily, upwards of 40,000 pilgrims arrive on 21 March from all over the world to witness the spectacle. Recognizing that this date also coincides with the birthday of the liberator-president Benito Juárez, the Mexican government has turned it into a national holiday, thus creating a new version of what might be an old myth. In a time that seems to have given rise to a wide variety of new religions, today outsiders come to reinforce their own particular religious beliefs in the transcendent. At other sites (e.g., Dzibilchaltún, Chalchihuites, and Teotihuacan), eager hierophants turn out in numbers at the spring equinox despite the fact that hierophanies have not necessarily been proposed for these places at this specific time.

The few examples cited here show the interdisciplinary character of archaeoastronomical studies by demonstrating what kinds of knowledge it offers the allied disciplines and how it contributes to the understanding of Mesoamerican culture in general. More than mere precision-alignment hunting, contemporary archaeoastronomy has developed into an anthropology of astronomy that seeks to examine those endeavors by which people attempt to make their observations of the heavens understandable in terms that are meaningful in each particular society.

Despite these advances, the field of archaeoastronomy continues to struggle to free itself from association with those who would make outrageous claims about the astronomical endeavors of ancient cultures and to shed the image of an enterprise bent on merely collecting data with an ethnocentric view toward demonstrating to what extent "traditional" societies are precursors to modern science. Compared to other areas of the world, in Mesoamerican studies the integration among the disciplines that border on archaeoastronomy is relatively advanced. Joint work by scholars from relevant academic fields, the sharing of information among them, and the appearance of an increasing number of publications on archaeoastronomy in the established disciplinary journals demonstrate that archaeoastronomy has begun to grow roots in the culture-related disciplines by paying more attention to questions posed by the anthropologist, the religionist, the epigrapher, and others, for example, How do people perceive the sky? How do they interpret what they see?

and How do they integrate it into their worldview? Thus, archaeoastronomical studies are ever more shaped and motivated by issues of cultural needs and perceptions.

BIBLIOGRAPHY

Aveni, Anthony. *Skywatchers of Ancient Mexico.* Austin, 1980. (Revised edition 2001.) General text on Mesoamerican archaeoastronomy.
Aveni, Anthony. "Archaeoastronomy." *Advances in Archaeological Method and Theory* 4 (1981), 1–77. Details the methodology for field research.
Aveni, Anthony. "The Thom Paradigm in the Americas: The Case of the Cross-Circle Designs." In *Records in Stone, Papers in Memory of Alexandar Thom*, edited by Clive L. N. Ruggles, pp. 442–472. Cambridge, 1988. Survey of applications of archaeoastronomical methods in the Americas.
Aveni, Anthony. *World Archaeoastronomy.* Cambridge, 1989. Edited conference volume on archaeoastronomy.
Aveni, Anthony, and Horst Hartung. "Maya City Planning and the Calendar." *Transactions of the American Philosophical Society* 76 (No. 7) (1986). Monograph detailing alignment and calendar studies at the Maya sites.
Aveni, Anthony, Horst Hartung, and Beth Buckingham. "The Pecked Cross Symbol in Ancient Mesoamerica." *Science* 202 (1978), 267–279. Initial study of the pecked cross calendrical alignment device.
Aveni, Anthony, Horst Hartung, and J. Charles Kelley. "Alta Vista (Chalchihuites) Astronomical Implications of a Mesoamerican Ceremonial Outpost at the Tropic of Cancer." *American Antiquity* 47 (1982), 316–353. Study of extension of the Teotihuacan calendars and alignments to the remote northern reaches of Mesoamerica.
Coggins, Clemency. "Some Political Implications of a Four-Part Figure." *American Antiquity* 45 (1980), 727–739. Discussion of social questions arising from archaeoastronomical studies.
Galindo Trejo, Jesus. *Arqueoastronomía en la América Antigua.* Mexico City, 1994. Survey text detailing alignment studies in Mexico.
Ruggles, Clive L. N., and Nicholas Saunders, eds. *Astronomies and Cultures.* Niwot, Colo., 1993. Edited conference volume on archaeoastronomy, beginning with excellent survey/directive article on the kinds of questions archaeoastronomers should deal with.

ANTHONY F. AVENI

ARCHAEOLOGY. *See* Anthropology, *article on* Archaeology.

ARCHITECTURE. *See* Art and Architecture.

ARCHIVES AND LIBRARIES. Scholars interested in studying Mesoamerica can avail themselves of three general types of repositories wherein primary materials are held. They are depository archives, public libraries and archives, and private research libraries and collections. It is impossible in the limits of this article to outline all of the repositories, but at least a general description of the types of repositories and the types of documentation each holds will serve as an introduction to the topic.

Among depository archives, there are two subgroups:

local and regional archives, and national and international archives. They are all considered depository archives in that, by law or custom, all public documents were deposited in them, and consequently, they have the effect of being official repositories. The local and regional archives are still the largest group of untouched repositories for historians and other scholars of Mesoamerica. These institutions have suffered the vicissitudes of time, are normally not well preserved, and frequently have no professional archivist. Since the late 1960s scholars throughout Latin America have discovered the importance of notarial records. Similarly, scholars have begun to make valuable contributions using local parish records in population reconstruction and demographic investigations. These are but two examples of the types of research that depend heavily on local archives. But more than this, many local archives, municipal, parochial, and departments of state hold important records for ethnohistory, including codices and other important works from the earliest days of the Colonial period. Repositories of this type that have been used include Tlaxcala's Archivo General del Estado.

Scholars interested in Mesoamerica might well begin their search in local archives and libraries, because these are still the least well studied repositories. Some regional archives, such as those of Tlaxcala and of Yucatán, both in Mexico, have achieved renown through the work of scholars. Others, such as the papers of the *alcaldía mayor* of Tulancingo or of the *corregimiento* of Zacatecas, have been dispersed. The Tulancingo papers are held by the University of California, Los Angeles, the University of Texas (San Antonio) Library, and in private hands in California. Some of the Zacatecas papers are in the collection of the University of Michigan. But these are exceptional cases, and one must conclude that most local documentation, if it has survived to the present day, resides in the locale where it was produced. Nevertheless, it is frequently difficult to gain entry to local repositories.

Two important types of local repositories are church and notarial archives. Cathedrals and parishes hold extensive documentation for demographic and social research. Clearly, registers of births, marriages, and burials are important tools. Papers related to pious endowments, investments, and church property can also be useful to the scholar. Cathedral archives also hold papers relating to internal church administration and frequently have the minutes of the cathedral chapter (*cabildo eclesiástico*), a rich source for social and cultural history. The Church of Jesus Christ of Latter-day Saints (Mormon) has been engaged in a massive microfilming project over the last several decades, collecting vital statistics from local parishes throughout Mesoamerica. Scholars would do well to check the holdings of the Mormon church, which are available at any local Family History Center, also operated by the church. Similarly, much of this information is being made available on the World Wide Web (http://www.familysearch.org/Browse/BrowseLibrary.asp).

In Hispanic America, the notary was an important figure. Many documents had to be passed before a notary to attain legal standing. Moreover, the notary was required to maintain copies of all documents that he drafted. Consequently, notarial archives are rich sources of information about business ventures, property ownership, and landholding, among other topics. The holdings of notarial archives can be quite rich. For example, the Mexico City notarial archive contains records dating from the years immediately following the Spanish conquest, and the collection is fairly strong by the end of the sixteenth century. In Mérida, however, the *protocolos* ("notarized records") begin in 1689.

The second subgroup of depository archives is the national and international archives. These are the repositories to which scholars have traditionally had recourse in their investigations concerning Mesoamerica. By far the most important are the Archivo General de Centroamérica (AGCA), the Archivo General de la Nación (AGN), and the Archivo General de Indias (AGI). The AGCA is located in downtown Guatemala City on 4 Avenida between Calles 7 and 8. It is open Monday through Friday, although scholars should inquire about the exact hours of operation. The holdings include records from the Colonial period through the nineteenth century. Not only does the archive hold the papers of the territorial *audiencia*, it also holds most of the colonial papers of the municipal *cabildo*. The archive is divided into two large sections dealing with the Colonial and Post-Colonial periods, respectively. There is a catalog containing what is estimated to be in excess of 4.2 million cards, although it is widely recognized to be incomplete.

The AGN is currently located in the Palacio de Lecumberrí of downtown Mexico City. Over the past twenty-five years, this is the third locale for the repository, and discussions are under way concerning yet another move. The AGN holds a wealth of documents concerning Mexican history. Among other collections, the colonial section is probably best known. It holds the papers of the *audiencia* of Mexico, the viceroy, the Inquisition, and confiscated ecclesiastical records. The archive consists of some 170 *ramos* and a total of somewhere in excess of 68,500 bundles. The *ramos* of Tierras, Indios, Bienes Nacionales, and Inquisición are extremely important. Most of the available catalogs of *ramos* are on CD-ROM. Beyond the colonial section, the archive also houses the papers of several presidents, treasury records from the Colonial period to the nineteenth century, the papers of many governmental departments, documentation of the 1910 Revolution, and many other collections of great value.

The AGI is perhaps the most famous of all archives, especially for scholars researching the Colonial period. Its holdings consist of all Spanish government papers dealing with the New World from the time of first contact to the late eighteenth century. It is housed in the old Seville stock exchange, built in the sixteenth century by Phillip II's court architect, Juan de Herrera. The archive is open Monday through Friday. The holdings are organized according to the structure of colonial government. The largest single section is Gobernación, which is in turn divided according to political territories. For scholars of Mesoamerica, the most important subsections are Mexico, Guatemala, and Guadalajara. The archive was indexed in the eighteenth century, and the holdings are being digitized at present. Eventually, scholars will consult the manuscript only via digital image on computer screens. There are still important documents to be discovered in Seville.

The nations of Mesoamerica have many other depository archives that can be of potential assistance to the scholar. In Mexico, for example, the Archivo de Salubridad, of the Departamento de Salubridad Pública, holds papers of colonial and nineteenth-century hospitals that are especially valuable to demographers and economic historians. Similarly, the Archivo de Reforma Agraria holds many important papers dealing with landholding in Mexico.

The British Library and the U.S. Library of Congress are similar to these archives. Although they function largely like depository archives for their respective nations, they have acquired materials from other countries, as have other institutional libraries and archives in the United States and Europe. Among the institutional libraries and archives, one must consider the collections at the large research libraries of many universities in the United States and institutional libraries and archives in Mesoamerica. Public libraries in Europe and the Americas tend to make up in quality what they lack in quantity of documentation. These repositories tend to hold precious items acquired at some point in the past because of their collection value. The remaining examples of native codices tend to be held in public and private libraries. Several hold large collections of original documents from Mesoamerica; among these are the Latin American Library of Tulane University, Princeton University, the Bancroft Library of the University of California, the Peabody Museum of Archaeology and Ethnology and Library of Harvard University, the John Carter Brown Library at Brown University, The Benson Latin American Collection of the

University of Texas at Austin, the Pompa y Pompa Library of the Museo Nacional de Antropología e Historia of Mexico, and the Biblioteca Nacional, also of Mexico. In Europe, several public libraries and archives hold important Mesoamerican records, such as the Bibliothèque Nationale of Paris, the Biblioteca del Palacio Real in Madrid, the Biblioteca Nacional of Spain, the Biblioteca del Real Monasterio de El Escorial in Spain, and the Nationalbibliothek of Vienna.

Private collections, libraries, and archives hold some of the greatest allure for scholars. They range in quantity and quality from the private holdings of families in Latin America and Spain to the large private collections in those countries and the United States. Several famous examples in the United States are the Newberry Library of Chicago, the Huntington Library of Los Angeles, and the Gilcrease Library of Tulsa, Oklahoma. Although these libraries are all open to the public, they are private in nature and resulted largely from the collecting activities of a single person. They are similar in this manner to the Bancroft, which is now a public institution, part of the University of California. In Europe, some private collections hold important records for the study of Mesoamerica. Noble families such as the Dukes of Alba, the Dukes of the Infantado, and the Dukes of Medina Sidonia, because of their role in Spanish government during the age of exploration, acquired materials on the discovery, conquest, and settlement of Mesoamerica.

These public and private libraries hold many of the best known manuscripts, dating from before and immediately following the Conquest. Yet, because the original manuscripts have been dispersed from their original repositories and nations, discovering them, and then consulting them, can be extremely difficult. For example, the Library of Congress of the United States holds not only papers from the Mexican Inquisition but also native manuscripts such as the *Huejotzingo Codex*, part of the testimony relating to the so-called Cortés Conspiracy, early works written by Europeans in native languages, such as the *Arte de la lengua mexicana* by Fray Andrés de Olmos, and miscellaneous letters and government reports. The Library of Congress is not alone in holding papers of the Mexican Inquisition. Portions are also held by the Huntington Library in San Marino, the Gilcrease Library in Tulsa, and the Bancroft Library, as well as the largest portion still in the AGN in Mexico. The Latin American Library of Tulane also holds a wide range of materials, including some pictorial manuscripts, such as the "Ordenanza del Señor Motezuma," the *Codex Tulane*, manuscripts by Olmos and others in native languages, and a very rich collection of documents from both religious and governmental sources in the Colonial period. The works of Fray Bernardino de Sahagún have scattered to the Newberry Library in Chicago, the Biblioteca Medicea-Laurenziana in Florence, the Palacio Real and the Academia Real de la Historia in Madrid, the Vatican Library, and the Biblioteca Nacional in Mexico, to name but a few sites. For Maya materials, the Bibliothèque Nationale de Paris is an important repository. In its collections, one can find the *Codex Paris*, an eleven-leaf Maya screenfold manuscript. The *Books of Chilam Balam* are held in the Garrett Collection of Princeton University (Chumayel and Kaua) and the Museo Nacional de Antropología of Mexico (Ixil). In terms of published works, especially works published in Mesoamerica in the sixteenth and seventeenth centuries, several repositories stand out. First among these would be the John Carter Brown Library, which has sought to develop a nearly complete collection of early printed works from Latin America, either original works or microfilm copies. The Library of Congress has strong holdings, as does the Bancroft Library, the Sutro Library in San Francisco, and the American Antiquarian Society of Worcester, Massachusetts.

There are many types of documents that one can consult in the study of Mesoamerica. The two major types consist of pictorial manuscripts and manuscripts written in European characters. Pictorial manuscripts come in at least two different types: those composed before the Conquest, and those composed during European domination. Among the manuscripts from the Colonial period, there are two major types, one in which natives were responsible for the total production, the other in which part of the record was produced by Spaniards, with natives providing additional content. An important subgroup of colonial manuscripts are the so-called Techialoyan manuscripts. They are colonial documents for some central Mexico communities written in Nahuatl with native illustrations on native paper, usually created for the purpose of justifying native land claims. [*See* Primordial Titles.] Pictorial manuscripts as a whole can be further categorized by content. The general types include ritual-calendrical, historical-genealogical, cartographic, economic, and ethnographic. Many manuscripts include content from more than one type. The *Handbook of Middle American Indians* provides the best guide to pictorial manuscripts and their whereabouts. It is likely that more pictorial manuscripts will be uncovered as scholars continue to work in smaller, local archives and private collections, and as communities that hold pictorial manuscripts share them with scholars.

The manuscripts in European characters can also be divided into two large groups: those composed in native languages and those composed in Spanish. Although scholars have known of the large quantity of manuscripts written in native languages, it is only in the past quarter century that such manuscripts have been utilized extensively by scholars. Pioneering work by James Lockhart and others has pointed out the usefulness of these native language texts. Within Mesoamerica, many native languages were committed to European writing. Nevertheless, a few account for the vast majority of all manuscripts available. Nahuatl is by far the most common language in the written records. Others, in Mixtec and the various Maya languages, are also common. Yet others, such as Otomí, Purépecha, and Zapotec, are far less common. Manuscripts in European characters, largely in Spanish, have traditionally been the most important resources to our understanding the history of Mesoamerica. It is the collection and preservation of these materials that most archives and libraries have fostered. Guides to these materials, if guides exist, are normally the most extensive and well developed. Because these represent the internal papers of the Spanish colonial government and later modern states, they represent the most abundant single type of documentation available. Nevertheless, government records are not the only documents one can consult. As noted, notarial and ecclesiastical records are also very important. Increasingly, records of industries, sugar mills, and weaving mills have been used by scholars. Yet private archives with private papers can still be found and will greatly broaden our understanding of life in the region.

Because the Spanish imported printing presses to Mexico shortly after the Conquest, there is also an extensive corpus of printed material that can be of assistance to the scholar. The earliest works and the longest printed record come from Mexico City, although early presses were also established in Guatemala and Puebla. The vast majority of works were printed in Spanish, although there is strong evidence that the first work published in Mexico, and thus in the New World, was composed in Nahuatl. Moreover, as in the case of manuscripts, many books were published in native languages during the Colonial period. These tended to be doctrinal works and catechisms composed for the evangelization of the natives. But a significant number of grammatical works were published, along with dictionaries and other aids to language study. There were even works published for popular reading. The tales of saints and martyrs appear among the lists of books published in native languages. The languages committed to print include Nahuatl, Purépecha, Otomí, Timucua, and Maya, to name a few. Nearly every type of book common in Europe at the time was published in Spanish in Mesoamerica. As with works in native languages, these titles tend to reflect the needs of evangelization, with doctrinal and devotional works being the most common. Among the doctrinal books, one finds catechisms and *doctrinas*, confessional guides, and collections of sermons. By the end of the sixteenth century, there even emerged books for recreational reading but with religious topics, such as biographies of saints and collections of devotional songs.

Scholars should be aware that libraries and archives have suffered greatly over the years. In Mesoamerica, many ecclesiastical archives have been destroyed as a result of civil war in the nineteenth and twentieth centuries. Important repositories such as the AGI have suffered loss from fire. Civil wars and insurrections have also destroyed many governmental repositories. Unscrupulous persons in every age have attempted, and often succeeded, in taking for their personal possession the documents that represent the patrimony of the nation. In short, conducting research frequently resembles detective work more than anything else. Nevertheless, the archives and libraries, and the materials they contain, will continue to be the mainstay of research in Mesoamerica.

BIBLIOGRAPHY

Gómez Candeo, Lino. *Los archivos de la historia de América.* 2 vols. Mexico City, 1961.

Greenleaf, Richard E., and Michael C. Meyer. *Research in Mexican History.* Lincoln, Nebr., 1973.

Millares Carlo, Agustín. *Repertorio bibliográfico de los archivos mexicanos y de los europeos y norteamericanos de interés para la historia de México.* Mexico City, 1959.

Rodríguez Ochoa, Patricia, et al. *Guía general de los archivos estatales y municipales de México.* Mexico City, 1988.

Wauchope, Robert, and Howard Cline. *Handbook of Middle American Indians.* Austin, Tex., 1975.

JOHN F. SCHWALLER

Pedro Armillas (1914–1984). *Photograph courtesy of Mrs. Pedro Armillas.*

ARMILLAS, PEDRO (1914–1984), archaeologist and social anthropologist.

Armillas was born in San Sebastián, Spain. From 1932 to 1936, he studied the sciences, philosophy, letters, and art in Barcelona. His studies were interrupted by the Spanish Civil War, in which he fought on the Republican side and attained the rank of captain of artillery (1938–1939). He was wounded on the eastern front in March 1938 and later held prisoner in France. He went to Mexico in June 1939; he first worked there as a surveyor in Chiapas.

Between 1940 and 1946, Armillas studied in the recently inaugurated Escuela Nacional de Antropología (National School of Anthropology), where he became a professor. He conducted archaeological work for the Instituto Nacional de Antropología e Historia (National Institute of Anthropology and History) between 1942 and 1952. His accomplishments in the Viking Group at Teotihuacan and in Oztuma, Guerrero, deserve particular mention. He also worked for the New World Archaeological Foundation (1952–1953). Support for his research came from the Guggenheim Foundation, the Wenner-

Gren Foundation for Anthropological Research, the National Science Foundation, the American Philosophical Society, and the Research Foundation of the State University of New York. The greatest academic influence on Armillas was that of Paul Kirchhoff, who introduced him to historical materialism and cultural evolutionism, stressing the fundamental relationships between economics and society. Other significant influences were V. Gordon Childe and O. G. S. Crawford.

After some disagreements with the important archaeologist Alfonso Caso, Armillas established himself in the United States, where he taught at Bowdoin College (1955–1956), the University of Michigan at Ann Arbor (1959–1960), Southern Illinois University (1960–1966), the University of Chicago (1965–1968), the State University of New York at Stony Brook (1968), and the University of Illinois at Chicago (1972–1984). He died in Chicago, of heart disease. Particularly outstanding among his numerous publications are his works on Teotihuacan and on Mesoamerican cultivation systems. Some of his students became prominent researchers, including William T. Sanders and Eric Wolf; Armillas's influence is discernible in their cultural materialist perspective of the pre-Hispanic world.

BIBLIOGRAPHY

Armillas, Pedro. "Teotihuacán, Tula y los toltecas: Las culturas posarcaicas y pre-aztecas del centro de México: Excavaciones y estudios, 1922–1950." *Runa* (Buenos Aires) 3 (1950), 37–70.

Armillas, Pedro. "Tecnología, formaciones socio-económicas y religión en Mesoamérica." In *The Civilizations of Ancient America: Selected Papers from the 29th International Congress of Americanists, New York, 1949*, edited by Sol Tax, pp. 19–30. Chicago, 1951.

Armillas, Pedro. "Mesoamerican Fortifications." *Antiquity* 25.96 (June 1951), 77–86.

Armillas, Pedro. "Cronología y periodificación de la historia de América precolombina." *Cahiers d'historie mondiale* 3.2 (1956), 463–503.

Armillas, Pedro. *Program of the History of American Indians.* 2 vols. Washington, D.C., 1958–1960.

Armillas, Pedro. "Gardens on Swamps." *Science* 174.4010 (1971), 653–661.

Rojas, José Luis de. *La aventura intelectual de Pedro Armillas: Visión antropológica de la historia de América.* Zamora, Michoacán, 1987.

Rojas, Rabiela, Teresa, ed. *Pedro Armillas: Vida y obra.* 2 vols. Mexico City, 1991.

Eduardo Matos Moctezuma
Translated from Spanish by Scott Sessions

ART AND ARCHITECTURE. [*This entry comprises three articles:*

Pre-Hispanic Period
Colonial Period
Nineteenth and Twentieth Centuries

The first article presents a general conceptual overview and survey of the development of pre-Hispanic Mesoamerican art and architecture; the second article discusses the development of colonial art and architecture; the third article presents a survey of the development of nineteenth- and twentieth-century Mesoamerican art and architecture. For related discussions, see Altars; Baroque; Castas Paintings; Churches and Cathedrals; Crosses and Crucifixes; Masks; Murals; Painting; Pictorial Manuscripts; Plazas; Relics; *and* Retablos.]

Pre-Hispanic Period

Among the visual arts, sculpture is the one that evokes the sense of the touch. Architecture alludes as well to the vital temporality of humankind.

Sculpture. The interaction between the volume of the visible material and the surrounding space is the essence of sculpture. Certain common attributes give unity to Mesoamerican sculpture, while differences express regional and local characteristics.

Between 1300 BCE and 1521 CE—the moment of European contact—large and small sculptures in different for-

mats and materials reflect an extraordinary diversity of form and subject matter. Three-dimensional sculpture, or statuary, predominated in the early part of the Formative (Preclassic) period, in ceramic figurines found throughout Mesoamerica and in the stone monuments of the Olmec region. A vigorous disposition toward the predominance of mass is also patent in the Early Postclassic era and in the Toltec era, and it is pervasive in Mexica (Aztec) times. Although there are no absolutes and notable exceptions exist, Classic-period artists exhibited a planimetric disposition, adapted to the development of relief with various gradations.

There are two basic methods of producing sculpture: modeling and carving. In Mesoamerica, one or the other is dominant, and the image always is firmly rooted on the ground. In an Olmec colossal head, in the water goddesses of Teotihuacan, or in the Mexica images of Coatlicue, space encompasses and limits the volume and establishes it in a rigid mode. These and other examples also communicate monumentality.

There is, however, variation in sculptural styles. The most frequent is the closed volume characterized by an order of internal rhythm, apparent in visual axes joined at the center, as in the great Coatlicue. This principle of interior order within a general geometrical scheme is also observed in Olmec heads and other sculptures which achieve perfect harmony. There are other modes in which volume interacts with space; for example, apertures may pierce the mass in a regular way, such as the articulated legs of Mexica standing figures or the free arms of Huastec statuary. There is also a dynamic mode in which part of the mass erupts into space, creating a plastic and visual sense of movement; examples are the "Wrestler" of Uxpanapa, the irregular veins that perforate the "Guacamaya Head," the Xochicalco ballgame marker, or some *hachas* from central Veracruz. Massive forms often dominate, as in the statuary of Tula and of the Mexica; however, there are many notable exceptions, especially those executed in terracotta, as at El Zapotal during the Late Classic. Staticism is dominant in the Atlantes of Early Postclassic Tula, but there are other modes of expressing a visual dynamic: observe the "Danzantes" of Late Preclassic Monte Albán and the contemporaneous Dainzú "Ballplayers." Sometimes real movement is achieved, as in the jointed figures of Teotihuacan and the smiling figures of Veracruz, which are believed to have been amusing objects. The images of animals mounted on wheels, present from early times on the Gulf Coast, represent not only moving sculpture but also undeniable knowledge of the wheel. Another element to note is the "law of frontality," which gives great attention to the frontal portion, as in Olmec Monument 52 at San Lorenzo or in Huastec fertility deities.

Mask found in Offering 82 at the Great Temple of Tenochtitlan. *Courtesy of Museo del Templo Mayor, México, D.F.*

Plurality of expressions. It has been reiterated without foundation that pre-Hispanic volumetric figures lacked expression. However, it is easy to detect a great range: the minimal scheme of the icon, as in Mezcala lapidary; convention, accepted by the patron and repeated, as in Teotihuacan masks; clearly human expressions full of sensuality (e.g., the Cihuateteo of El Zapotal), tenderness, and passion (Jaina figurines of the Classic Maya); and portraits, such as the stucco heads of Palenque, the clay heads from central Veracruz, and the Olmec colossal heads. The smiles and laughter of the so-called smiling figures of Veracruz and the pain and sorrow in figures from West Mexico or the dismembered Mexica goddesses never cease to astonish us. This desire to reproduce natural behavior is particularly visible in the terracottas of West Mexico.

Relief. This technique is governed by its own rules. It does not partake of the three-dimensional reality of sculpture because it always emerges from a flat background. In relief, the form is never isolated in space; it creates a visual world located between illusory pictorial space and the real space of sculpture. Relief has always been intimately linked with the architecture of rubble masonry. By the Late Formative, in Monte Albán and Dainzú in Oaxaca, buildings were being covered with reliefs of stone and earth. From the Formative and Protoclassic on, in the central Maya area at Uaxactún and Tikal as well as to the north at Dzibichaltún, structures were enriched with reliefs executed in stucco. In the Maya region, the taste for adorning buildings culminated with the detachment of elements once fixed to the wall, which were now disposed almost like aerial figures on the roof comb. In the Central Highlands, buildings were covered with reliefs considerably detached from their background or smoothly modeled with modest projection, as in the Ciudadela at Teotihuacan or in the *coatepantli* (serpent walls) at Tula, Tenayuca, and Tenochtitlan. Walls covered predominantly with mosaics of geometric patterns in relief occur in central Veracruz and the Mixtec zone, and in the fantastic geometricized images at Puuc Maya sites.

Reliefs have been classified according to their degree of projection from the background plane. Some are embedded in the base, creating a bas-relief like the panel at the Temple of Inscriptions in Palenque. Others seem to emerge tenuously from a surface, as in Izapa stelae, or are superimposed on a plane of greater projection, like Altar Q at Copán. There are still others that we would call "high relief," such as the stelae and altars of Copán and Quiriguá. Relief favors descriptive narration and scenic development, and it was used widely in the stelae and lintels of Yaxchilán and Piedras Negras in the central Maya region and in the so-called sun stones or historical stones, which relate the deeds of Mexica rulers, such as the Tizoc Stone and the Archbishop's Stone. Although Mesoamerican sculptors did not employ perspective with a vanishing point, exceptional examples exist in which a close approximation to visual realism is achieved based on projection and recession, such as Lintel 2 and Stela 12 of Piedras Negras. An extraordinary manner of working in relief appears on the backs of thrones from Piedras Negras; on one, now at the Museo Amparo in the city of

Puebla, the figures in relief are detached as if cut out from a nonexistent background.

Materials. The majority of sculptural monuments that have survived are executed in stone of many types. Volcanic tufa was employed in the Central Highlands for the Atlantes of Tula and the Mexica jaguar *cuauhxicalli.* Limestone was used for reliefs on stelae, altars, tablets, and panels in the Maya area and sandstone for the carvings of Huastec and Veracruz. Grayish-green serpentine was worked by the Olmecs into the "Señor de las Limas" and smaller objects such as plaques, *hachuelas* (small axes), pendants, and figurines. Jade is the material of Olmec and Maya figurines and masks, and obsidian of Maya eccentrics, Teotihuacan masks, and Mexica human and animal figurines.

Fired clay is the material for anthropomorphic and zoomorphic figures in West Mexico, funerary urns in Oaxaca, and small figurines found throughout Mesoamerica. Terracotta cylinders with images of solar deities and celestial birds were profusely offered in the Temple of the Foliated Cross at Palenque. Wood was another medium for carving, though only a few examples remain, including the *chicozapote* lintels at Tikal, an Olmec figure in the Metropolitan Museum in New York, small Olmec effigies from El Manatí, and Mexica musical instruments. Stucco was an easily modeled material with which the façades, friezes, and roof combs of Maya buildings were covered. Bone—both animal and human—was utilized, especially in small bas-relief scenes of Zapotec and Maya cosmogony. Shells were engraved with ritual scenes and symbols of the elite.

Subject matter. Most of the subject matter depicted in sculptures and reliefs refers to religion—ritual acts (Stela 11 at Kaminaljuyú and ballgame accouterments from central Veracruz), images of deities, deity impersonators and their attributes (the terracotta Eagle Warriors at the Templo Mayor)—or to the authority symbols of the ruling classes. Among the latter are warfare (the battles of Tizoc), dominion and subjugation (Lintel 8 at Yaxchilán), acts legitimating accession to power (the Palace Tablet at Palenque), acts of alliance (an architectural relief at Xochicalco), and attempts to preserve images of officials and political rulers (portraits from central Veracruz and those of Shield Jaguar in Yaxchilán). Individuals and supernaturals are identified by name glyphs and by figurative and ascribed conventions superimposed on the head, held in the hands, or distinguished in the clothing (e.g., on a Zapotec earthenware urn or a large mask uncovered in the Ciudadela at Teotihuacan). Many sculptures and reliefs refer to myths: the Calendar Stone records the four previous cosmic eras in a manner removed from verifiable reality; the Olmec Twins of El Azuzul allude to the Maya creation myth in the *Popol Vuh*, in which the brothers Hunahpu and Ixbalanque are the protagonists. Themes of daily life were preferentially depicted in clay—from the "maquettes" of Nayarit neighborhoods, where dogs and children play among busy adults on the porticoes of the houses or the patios of the settlements, to the refined millers and weavers of the Maya necropolis in Jaina.

Finally, one must mention the different aesthetic preferences in pre-Hispanic sculpture. On the one hand, there is a reductionist schematism tending toward abstraction, as is apparent in the Olmec mosaic at La Venta. On the other hand, there is a fixation on visual reality, as in the stucco portraits on Palenque buildings. Between these extremes lies an enormous range of variation. A characteristic that appears in early times and continues throughout pre-Hispanic history is occult imagery, found in Olmec mosaic floors as well as in the Tlaltecuhtli depicted on the bottoms of numerous Mexica sculptures. Thus, many pre-Hispanic sculptural images possess a significance that transcends the visible.

Architecture and Urbanism. Architecture is one of the plastic arts that deal directly with human beings, because it concerns habitable spaces. Architecture and urbanism constitute an indissoluble whole resulting from the conjunction of open and closed areas and their functions. The following discussion identifies some general principles and then addresses certain important sites.

Urbanization in the highlands and lowlands of Mesoamerica. The two most important types of patterns are the dispersed and the concentrated. The first is based on large unoccupied spaces distinguished by buildings separated with ample clearance. The second suggests a greater proximity of construction—at times in direct contact—in which the unoccupied areas are smaller, such as small squares or domestic patios and passageways. Both types may coexist within a single city, as in Teotihuacan.

Likewise, there exist two specific urban patterns. One characterizes the highlands, as in Central Mexico, and the other the lowlands, particularly the coastal zones of Veracruz and the mountainous spurs of Chiapas. Both are intimately tied to topography: buildings are organized according to the terrain. The architecture does not imitate the surrounding natural relief—it modifies it, takes it as a pretext, and alters it to invent new types of surroundings, artificial mountains and valleys which exist in the social and religious imagination.

The first pattern is based on two central, perpendicular axes. Buildings are distributed according to a reticular plan in which symmetry emanating from straight lines and right angles predominates. To this fundamental characteristic in the plan must be added volumes emphasizing geometrical patterns with an ascending tendency, especially notable in public and religious constructions.

In the second pattern, there is greater freedom; the design does not follow the rectilinear canon, and the urban pattern is asymmetric and of varied proportions. Harmony is maintained between the dimensions of buildings and plazas, as well as between their different levels of elevation. Geometric volumes are softened, and the resulting assemblage is more dynamic.

Architectural types. The architectural plurality of Mesoamerica can be summarized in the following building types.

- Pyramids and platforms: superimposed truncated foundations whose apex serves as a base for temples or residential complexes. The number of constituent sections varies. Their exterior appearance is massive and solid. The most utilized plan is the rectangle, as in the Pyramids of the Sun and Moon at Teotihuacan; occasionally the plan is circular, as in Cuicuilco, or combines elements of both, like the *yácatas* of West Mexico.
- Plazas: open spaces of rectangular plan, delimited wholly or partially by platforms. They may contain altars or stelae, as at Tikal, Guatemala.
- Residential complexes: formed by the juxtaposition of rooms, porticoes (supported by pillars or columns), galleries, passageways, and patios (with or without altars), like the Palace at Palenque; containing one to six floors accessed by stairways, as in Cobá, Yucatán. The plans are usually rectangular but may vary considerably.
- Ballcourts: usually consisting of two parallel foundations that delimit the area of the game. When there are four foundations, they fill in the plan in the form of the letter "H," as at Monte Albán and Copán.

The buildings' functions include ritual and ceremonial and governmental, as well as housing for the nobility and for the common people. In some cities, the central zone comprises large religious and civil structures that are surrounded concentrically by the dwellings of rulers, the upper nobility, and finally the lower classes, as in Tenochtitlan. In other cities, the religious buildings are integrated with residences of nobility and common people, along with areas dedicated to agriculture; this results in peculiar, repetitive conglomerates accessed by causeways and roads, as in the Maya area. The harmony of the constructions is achieved through the interplay of openings and solid walls: the volumes of pyramids and platforms, and the enormity of space that contains them. Volumes define parts of spatial infinity; only in porticoed plazas, such as those at Tula and Chichén Itzá, is the space contained.

La Venta. The elements just mentioned appear at La Venta. By the Early Formative, the design of this Olmec city was defined through the linkage of platforms and large areas resembling plazas, all oriented along a north–south axis.

Complex A consists of an enormous plaza and various pyramids. To the north of the complex and circumscribing it is the largest construction of the group; the east and west sides are marked by various stone columns and low platforms, two of them of great length. Complex C lies to the south of Complex A. Mound C-1 is a pyramid of tamped earth, rising above a quadrangular base; it has a single section, more than 30 meters in height, whose appearance is now that of a truncated cone. Complex residential constructions have been found in which monolithic columns and aqueducts evidence an advanced stage of urbanism. The distribution of the buildings suggests symbolism related to Olmec cosmovision and astronomical knowledge.

Central valleys of Oaxaca. Monte Albán is a mountain city that controlled its surrounding valleys. Its central part, at the top, is clearly demarcated by numerous buildings arranged around a principal plaza, while other structures divide it lengthwise and eccentrically. Within this plaza, Mound J, called the Observatory, stands out with a pentagonal plan deviating southward from the principal axis of symmetry; this suggests the importance of astronomical orientation. On nearly all of the foundations, residential complexes are arranged around sunken patios accessed by corridors. Below them, vaulted tombs abound. The impact of Zapotec architecture is achieved by means of the "scapular panel": above a sloping wall rises another vertical wall, in the form of an inverted "U," with right angles and on two planes, so that the exterior seems to frame the interior.

Teotihuacan. The great Classic period metropolis of the Central Highlands is distinguished by its monumentality, its marked inclination toward horizontality, and its geometrization of volumes, which combine to produce overwhelming, superhuman scale. Its fundamental urban feature is its reticular design emanating from two perpendicular central axes, the most prominent being the Street or Avenue of the Dead. The two prominent pyramidal bases are the Pyramids of the Sun and the Moon, whose simple but extraordinary profiles mark visual pivots of the urban design. The platforms and foundations are defined by the *talud-tablero*—the city's distinctive architectural feature—consisting of a sloping panel which supports a vertical wall framed with a cornice. Dispersed among these great edifices are numerous complexes where the angular geometry of the forms is outstanding.

Mexico-Tenochtitlan. Many centuries after Teotihuacan was abandoned, the Mexica capital brought back the reticular design. Mexico-Tenochtitlan was also based on two perpendicular axes, with the sacred precinct of the city situated at the center. There, large pyramidal bases stood out, but with an innovation: the double stairway corresponding to the two shrines on top of the pyramids.

The stairway was surrounded by a *coatepantli,* or "serpent wall." The palatial precincts had porticoes and hypostyle (columned) galleries, with benches decorated with polychrome reliefs and elements inherited from Toltec architecture.

Streets and canals, along with *chinampas* (drained fields), defined the urban grid pattern. The lake was invaded by artificial terrain—wooden frames filled with earth and rubble—on which the houses of the common people were built. Sufficient space was left between them for foot traffic, complemented by bridges made of planks and canals for navigation by canoe.

Maya plurality. The varied topography of the Maya area led to an extraordinary richness of urban designs. Outstanding are certain architectural constants, such as the use of stone vaults and pediments on the roofs ("roof combs"), the distribution of large religious buildings and the residences of elites around plazas scattered with sculptures, and the organization of structures according to the natural topography. Among the most distinguished examples are Tikal, Palenque, and Chichén Itzá.

Tikal, in the Petén of Guatemala, is one of the most important and monumental urban centers. It is distinguished by an ascending impulse defined by the great vertical volume of the temples, whose massiveness contrasts strongly with the plazas and the relative horizontality of the residential complexes, or "acropolises." The main pyramid, Temple IV, measures 70 meters in height; the much lower Temple I exhibits graduated sections that consist of wide moldings, grooves between them, and recessed corners. A steep stairway without balustrades leads to the top, where a temple with thick walls and extremely small interior space supports a massive ornamented roof comb. Acropolises, temples, and plazas are joined by causeways. In Tikal there was great attention paid to the exterior aspect of buildings and their supernatural symbolism.

In contrast to the gigantism of Tikal, Palenque favors the human scale. This city, which brings together architecture and fine sculptural relief in an extraordinary manner, is distributed over a succession of artificial terraces that modify the mountainous topography. The Palace, the Group of the Crosses, and the Temple-Tomb of Inscriptions stand out. A large base with a trapezoidal plan serves as the foundation of the Palace, which consists of several buildings with large parallel galleries with wide bays and high vaults, as well as four asymmetrical patios. In one of them is the most unusual building in all Mesoamerica, the Tower.

In the Cross Group, the specificities of Palenque are most prominent. The vaulted temples are divided into various interior spaces. One of the temples has a portico with three entrances and a central room with a small sanctuary containing sculpted panels. Wide bays and narrow walls achieve ample and luminous interior spaces. The roofs are made lighter with perforations in the intradoses (inner curves) of the vaults. The exterior is finished with a light, fretted roof comb that once supported stucco figures.

The Temple of the Inscriptions is the earliest known building which, in addition to its stepped pyramidal base, contains an interior funerary space, wherein the ruler Pacal II was buried. Many other building-tombs have been found in the Maya area.

On the plains of Yucatán, Chichén Itzá stands out. It shares two artistic styles: one is Late Classic Maya (seventh–tenth centuries CE), and the other shows distinct traces of highland Mexico (Early Postclassic, tenth–thirteenth centuries CE). Although it is outside the Puuc region, Chichén Itzá's Late Classic buildings are linked to this regional style. Elaborately decorated sections alternate with plain surfaces on the building façades. Friezes and portals are covered with mosaics of polished stone presenting elements such as latticework, groups of small columns, images of thatched huts, and masks of large-nosed deities. Although the most notable example typifying the Puuc style is the Governor's Palace at Uxmal, in Chichén Itzá it is represented by buildings such as the Temple of the Three Lintels, the Nunnery (Las Monjas) and its Annex (Anexo), the Church (Iglesia) and Akab Dzib, and the Red House.

Other constructions exhibit strong influences from Central Mexico, including hypostyle galleries and precincts, columns and pillars simulating flying serpents with bodies raised to the sky, and sculpted benches. Examples are the Temple of the Warriors, the radially symmetric El Castillo pyramid, and the Great Ballcourt.

Western region. Although little of the architecture of this area has survived, we know of it through ceramic representations from Nayarit. These are maquettes— dioramas which depict buildings and activities of daily, nonritual life. The exterior walls and roofs are painted with geometric designs, such as undulant zigzag lines, triangles, and rhombi. Five varieties of extraordinary symmetry are depicted in the maquettes. The simplest is a platform on which a solitary room with two walls supports the roof. The second type includes two or three steps in front of the platform; the third has a smaller area placed in front; the fourth, two floors with steps; and the fifth, also with two floors, has various chambers and stairways. They reveal a spatial and temporal consciousness that multiplies and penetrates, moves, encloses, and opens up the mass. Recently, structures have been excavated that confirm the information provided from the maquettes.

Central Veracruz. One of the most outstanding and influential sites is El Tajín. Constructed on a series of hills, the city is governed by its surroundings: plazas are circumscribed by buildings dedicated to religion and habitation. Two sectors are distinguished: Tajín proper, and Tajín Chico, which occupies the highest part of the terrain. Typical architectural traits are manifested in panels with niches, flying cornices, frets, and volutes; thus, the buildings acquire a rhythmic chiaroscuro when plain surfaces are combined with niches and cornices. Straight lines and geometric profiles permeate the volumetry of the city, in which the Pyramid of the Niches and the Building of the Columns stand out, together with the ballcourts without *cabezales* (wider sections usually found at both ends of the court).

In terms of its construction technique, the Building of the Columns in Tajín Chico is revolutionary for Mesoamerica. It consists of two levels accessed by steep stairways, with porticoes and areas that employ columns made up of tambours (short cylindrical sections), which allow the creation of large interior spaces. These spaces are covered with a false tile of variable thickness, made of lime mortar consolidated with vegetation and ceramic fragments.

[*See also* Altars; Aztec; Cacaxtla; Calakmul; Cantona; Caracol; Casas Grandes; Cempoala; Chacmool; Chalcatzingo; Chalchihuites–Alta Vista; Chenes; Chichén Itzá; Cholula; Cobá; Copán; Cotzumalhuapa; Cuicuilco; El Tajín; Feathers and Featherwork; Huastec; Huexotzinco; Iximche; Izapa; Jaina; Kaminaljuyú; La Quemada; Lapidary; Lintels; Malinalco; Masks; Maya; Mayapán; Mérida-Ti'ho; Mezcala; Mining and Metalwork; Mitla; Mixtec, *article on* Pre-Hispanic and Colonial Periods; Mixteca-Puebla Style; Monte Albán; Murals; Nochixtlán Valley; Olmec; Painting; Palaces; Pictorial Manuscripts; Piedras Negras; Plazas; Putun; Puuc; Pyramids; Quiriguá; Remojadas; Río Bec; Río Viejo; San José Mogote; San Lorenzo–Tenochtitlan; Sculpture; Seibal; Skull Racks; Stucco; Sweatbaths; Tehuantepec, Isthmus of; Temple Complexes; Templo Mayor; Tenochtitlan; Teotihuacan; Tikal; Tilantongo; Tlapacoya; Tlatelolco; Toltec; Tombs; Totonac and Tepehua; Tula; Tulum; Tzintzuntzan; Uaxactún; Utlatlán; Uxmal; Veracruz Style; Weaving; Xochicalco; Xochitecatl; Zapotec, *articles on* Pre-Hispanic and Colonial Periods.]

BIBLIOGRAPHY

Amador Sellerier, Alberto. "Rasgos fundamentales de la arquitectura prehispánica." In *Historia del arte mexicano*, vol. 1, pp. 16–31. Mexico City, 1982.
Foncerrada de Molina, Marta. *La escultura arquitectónica de Uxmal.* Mexico City, 1965.
Fuente, Beatriz de la. *Escultura monumental olmeca.* Mexico City, 1973.
Fuente, Beatriz de la. "Escultura en el Occidente: Períodos preclásicos a clásico." In *Historia del arte mexicano*, vol. 2, pp. 202–218. Mexico City, 1982.
Fuente, Beatriz de la. *Arte prehispánico funerario: El Occidente de México.* 2nd ed. Mexico City, 1994.
Fuente, Beatriz de la, and Nelly Gutiérrez Solana. *Escultura huasteca en piedra.* Mexico City, 1980.
Fuente, Beatriz de la, et al. *Escultura en piedra de Tula.* Mexico City, 1988.
Fuente, Beatriz de la, et al. "El arte: Centinelas de la eternidad." In *Los mayas del período clásico*, pp. 141–225. Mexico City, 1997.
Gendrop, Paul. *Quince ciudades mayas.* Mexico City, 1977.
Gendrop, Paul. *Los estilos Río Bec, Chenés y Puuc en la arquitectura maya.* Mexico City, 1983.
Gendrop, Paul, and Doris Heyden. *Arquitectura mesoamericana.* Madrid, 1975.
Hardoy, Jorge E. *Ciudades precolombinas.* Buenos Aires, 1964.
Kubler, George. *The Art and Architecture of Ancient America.* Baltimore, 1962.
Marquina, Ignacio. *Arquitectura prehispánica.* 2 vols. Mexico City, 1951.
Pollock, Harry E. D. "The Architectural Survey." In *Year Book* 35 (1935): 122–125.
Pollock, Harry E. D. "Architecture of the Maya Lowlands." In *Handbook of Middle American Indians*, edited by Robert A. Wauchope, vol. 2, part 1, pp. 378–440. Austin, Tex., 1965.
Ruz Lhuillier, Alberto. *El Templo de las Inscripciones en Palenque.* Mexico City, 1973.
Stierlin, Henri. *Living Architecture: Mayan.* New York, 1946; reprinted, London, 1964.

BEATRIZ DE LA FUENTE
Translated from Spanish by Scott Sessions

Colonial Period

The term "colonial" designates the visual arts produced from 1521 to 1821 during the three centuries when Spain ruled the Viceroyalty of New Spain. Defined by these temporal parameters, colonial or viceregal art broadly encompasses a rich corpus of painting, sculpture, architecture, and the decorative arts. However convenient a label, "colonial" does not qualify the range and originality of artistic syntheses that occurred during this time frame nor should it convey pejorative implications of being derivative or inferior to European sources. Just as historians now depart from binary stereotypes of colonizer-colonized, so too the artistic relationship cannot be characterized as one of recipient-donor, that of a copyist's dependency on the models exported by the mother country. Although undeniably responsive to European styles and iconography, the arts of New Spain are singularly inventive and bear a complex relationship to those of Spain.

At the time of the Spanish conquest, Spain itself had accrued a layered artistic heritage that included Classical, Islamic, Gothic, and fifteenth-century Flemish characteristics; Italian Renaissance, Mannerist, and Baroque styles were subsequently absorbed to varying degrees, producing a mix that was distinct from its sources and uniquely Iberian. Thus, a blend of styles and motifs from Spain and other European countries was transmitted overseas in successive waves by way of itinerant artists and portable works of art. How these influences were variously received, selectively adopted, and creatively transformed by competing constituencies to meet the needs of a pluralistic society in the Spanish Americas are some of the more intriguing questions currently being addressed. Responses were tempered by a variety of factors, including, initially, the ethnicity and training of the artists as well as the availability of new materials. Even European architects working in New Spain were stimulated by the potential of contrasting *tezontle*, a dark red volcanic stone, with *chiluca*, a light, finely grained limestone more suitable for detailed carving. In different political and ritual contexts, how works of art functioned, including those almost identical to their Spanish prototypes, altered considerably their intended meaning(s). The veristic tradition of sculpting holy figures in polychromed wood, for example, became wildly popular in New Spain, where the physical agony of the bleeding and dead Jesus was graphically portrayed. Often commissioned by native brotherhoods (*cofradías*) and activated in ritual processions, these sculptures aroused an empathetic response among native American penitents, including an increase in ritual self-flagellation, perhaps a distant echo of the religious importance accorded blood sacrifice in their past. Certain subjects, when transposed to the New World, assumed greater importance, as did Saint Joseph and a host of archangels, particularly Saint Michael.

Images were one of the most effective means of communication and self-expression in New Spain, crossing barriers of language, geography, and cultural difference. Public billboard-sized murals, as well as widely circulating prints, were intended to disseminate the official messages of the Roman Catholic church and the Spanish Crown. However, in their reformulation by local artists, images became a potent means for advancing alternative agendas and promoting multiple, contested readings. The Assumption of the Virgin Mary, so frequently carved on church façades, was not only a carrier of esoteric Catholic dogma, but, when appropriated into the local pantheon of saints, also became a prominent signifier of communal pride and identity.

History, Styles, and Periods. Serious scholarship in colonial art began in the 1920s with Manuel Toussaint; thus, the contours of this field are still being mapped and the cataloguing of monuments is ongoing. With growing academic stature, colonial art historians increasingly relied on archival data, combining biography with social history to contextualize art production. Currently, although iconographic studies predominate, considerations of patronage, audience, gender, and ritual theory are being incorporated into analytical strategies.

Classifying artworks remains problematic, as there is no uniform system, and style designations tend to be idiosyncratic and elastic. Challenging a consistent nomenclature and chronology are the variety of artistic sources,

The serpent ("Evil") and the sparrow ("Good"). Detail in paradise garden murals in the lower cloister (east wall) of the Augustinian monastery in Malinalco, Mexico. *Photograph courtesy of Jeanette Favrot Peterson.*

their novel recombinations, and the time lag in style transmission, both transoceanic and provincial. As a consequence, stylistic responses developed their own rhythm in New Spain, at times partial and intermittent, as with the appearance of classical elements, at other times enduring longer than their European counterparts, such as Mannerist tendencies that continued into the eighteenth century in painting and strapwork ornament. In addition, the lasting, vivifying imprint of indigenous creativity blurs the boundaries between "fine" and "folk" art and disrupts the neat categorization of many regional monuments.

It may be useful to chart major style developments across media by century, recognizing that these are not discrete but porous units, with many of the important social, political, and artistic impulses developing in the final decades of one century and bearing fruit in the following century. Style names are modified as "Mexican" to emphasize that they must be evaluated independent of Europe's qualitative yardstick:

Sixteenth century	Mexican Renaissance
Seventeenth century	Mexican Early Baroque
Eighteenth century to 1781	Mexican Late Baroque
1781 to nineteenth century	Neoclassicism

Sixteenth Century. Soon after the Conquest, the arts, including city planning, were harnassed to advance the enormous task of hispanizing the new territories. Spanish communities were founded on standardized grid designs similar to the quadripartite division and centralized plans of many pre-Conquest cities. Because to civilize was to Christianize under the Hapsburg credo of the universal monarchy, a powerful colonizing effort was spearheaded among the indigenous population by the mendicant orders (Franciscans, Dominicans, and Augustinians). The friars exploited native expertise in stone masonry to erect some three hundred monastic complexes, which included a single-nave church, a cloister, an expansive forecourt or atrium (*atrio*), and orchards. This model of self-sufficiency was repeated in the string of missions that expanded over the next two centuries into the northern frontiers of New Spain (today the southwestern United States).

As centers for an ambitious educational program, monastic schools included curricula in the manual arts; native artisans expertly replicated, but also improvised on and modified, Euro-Christian illustrations from graphics and pattern books. Eclectic syntheses in style and iconography were common. A Gothic stone traceried window and wooden inlay ceiling of *mudéjar* (Moorish-Christian) origins might exist side by side within the same church, although Renaissance motifs and ideals provided the primary inspiration. Façades featured fluted columns and pediments of restrained geometry, or, more frequently,

classical portals were enlivened with intricate patterns, a predilection for surface ornamentation that persisted throughout the Colonial period. New liturgical needs prompted the development of innovative features, including the open chapel (*capilla abierta*), a portico or alcove from which Mass could be given to overflow crowds. Hybrid forms also arose from translating Christian subjects in indigenous techniques, such as the *Cristos de caña*, lightweight sculptures fabricated from cornstalk paste (*pasta de caña*). Although the melding of technologies, forms, and/or symbol systems is sometimes referred to as *tequitqui*, collaborative projects with significant bicultural input permeated much of the artistic production in the sixteenth century.

Moreover, although the earliest guild ordinances (1556) restricted the activities of non-Spaniards, in reality Indian artists competed successfully at every level. Some have only recently been recognized, such as Juan Gerson, a mural painter at Tecamachalco (Puebla) in 1562. Others attained notoriety in their day, as did Pedro Patiño Ixtolinque (1774–1834), a sculptor and director of the Academy of Arts in Mexico City. Talent and ambition overrode discrimination, as witnessed by the significant contributions of the mulatto Juan Correa (1645/50–1716) or the prestigious mestizo painter from Oaxaca Miguel Cabrera (1695–1768). It is ultimately unsatisfactory to attempt to identify "styles" based on race and place of birth, just as it is too facile and misleading to homogenize artistic contributions under the racially derived term *mestizaje* ("mixture").

By the final decades of the sixteenth century, the decimation of the Indian population through disease and abuse, as well as the influx of foreign artists and engravings, provoked a shift to more current European styles. In New Spain, the more disturbing, antinaturalistic elements of Mannerism were moderated to conform to Counter-Reformation mandates, that art should edify and move the viewer through orthodox themes; quiet, legible compositions that focused on biblical narratives became the rule. Two of the artists, the immigrant Baltasar Echave Orio (active 1580–1620) and Luis Juárez (active 1610–1637), were immensely influential. The Echave and Juárez families, in tandem, produced artistic dynasties that bred or apprenticed generations of successful painters, many of whom ultimately defined a national style.

Seventeenth Century. At no time was the tension between freedom of expression and the essential conservatism of the viceregal patron more fully felt than in the seventeenth century. Evolving over 150 years, Baroque manifestations in painting focused on didactic ends and thus remained relatively cautious pictorially. In architecture and *retablo*, or altar screen, ornamentation, however, the Mexican Baroque became exuberantly experimental.

Commissions for religious works continued to dominate art production, with patronage shifting to the ascendant ecclesiastical hierarchy. The stability and wealth of a mature colony were manifest in the completion of six of the seven major cathedrals, from Oaxaca to Guadalajara. Impressive exteriors displayed monumental orders consolidated around the cathedral portals; interiors also required artistic programs of commensurate scale and vigor. Tiered *retablos* were composite works requiring teams of artists. They became accurate indices of style change, showcasing and sometimes initiating salient architectural features, such as the Solomonic column, whose dynamic spiral also energized church façades. From lavish *retablos* to choir stalls, sculpture became a dominant art form, as in the work of Salvador de Ocampo (active 1696–1722).

In the decoration of the cathedral sacristy in Mexico City (1685–1691), all of the arts were coordinated to express a sophisticated theological program with dazzling theatricality. The Mexican Cristóbal de Villalpando (1644/45–1714) contributed several giant canvases, among them one celebrating the Church Militant and Triumphant. In theme and execution, Villalpando's compositions, with their vivid coloration, heroic figures, and sweeping energy, fully embodied the Baroque. He also adopted the mystical use of dramatic lighting (*tenebrism*) that had earlier been introduced through the work of Francisco de Zurbarán. Workshops, such as those of Villalpando, or his contemporary, Juan Correa, met the demands of the burgeoning class of American-born *criollos*. Among new subjects tailored to reflect the *criollos'* nationalistic ambitions were images of the dark-skinned American Virgin of Guadalupe and scenes of a romanticized pre-Hispanic past.

Eighteenth Century to 1781. The advent in 1700 of a new Bourbon dynasty in Spain introduced reforms that simultaneously imposed greater political controls and stimulated the economy. Prosperity from mining and trade was concentrated in private hands, creating an individualized patronage system (*patronazgo*) for the arts. Silver mine owner José de la Borda could sink one million pesos into the construction of a church for Taxco (Santa Prisca and San Sebastián) between 1751 and 1758 and boast: "God has given to Borda, and Borda gives to God." The main *retablo* in Santa Prisca is exemplary of the flamboyant Late Baroque, with its foliation, broken pediments, and *estípite*, a column-like inverted obelisk that earned eighteenth-century architecture the term "Estípite Baroque" (also Ultra or Churrigueresque Baroque). Like church façades, their counterparts in stone, altar screens were deeply undercut and fractured by their gilded, prismatic surfaces. This boldness in decoration did not extend to interiors, which adhered to traditional cruciform layouts. One outstanding exception was the oval plan for the Chapel of El Pocito (1779–1791) that covered the sacred well near the Virgin of Guadalupe's sanctuary. The architect, Francisco Antonio de Guerrero y Torres (1727–1792), was also responsible for several ornate town houses (*palacios*) that lined metropolitan streets and that, along with civic construction, hospitals, and country estates (*haciendas*), reflected the building boom of a flourishing economy. The enduring preference for coloristic ornament was satisfied through the combined use of white stucco, brick, and glazed tiles (*azulejos*).

The need to furnish these edifices and multiple parish churches stimulated decorative arts of a sophisticated elegance, including marquetry furniture, tooled leather, and ceramics. Silverworking, in which pre-Hispanic methods of casting precious metals had surpassed those of the Spanish in the sixteenth century, maintained its tradition of excellence. Trade with the Far East, initiated by the Manila Galleon to and from the Philippines, also brought oriental influences to bear on the decorative arts.

Virgin of the Immaculate Conception. Early-eighteenth-century polychrome wooden sculpture. Anonymous. (Height: 42.5 inches.) *Photograph courtesy of Jeanette Favrot Peterson.*

By the eighteenth century, Chinese blue-on-white porcelain was being liberally adopted by Puebla ceramicists, and oriental floral patterns were embellishing silk and cotton textiles.

To record the elevated status of the New World aristocracy, archbishops and landowners alike, painters such as José de Ibarra (1688–1756) and Miguel Cabrera created fashionable portraits, as well as new secular subjects, such as still lifes and genre series of castes (*castas*). The inventory of miscegenation in *casta* paintings was an Enlightenment exercise in classification and a Bourbon attempt to impose an idealized hierarchy on colonial society based on skin color. The demand for religious paintings remained unabated; however, haste sometimes sacrificed quality. Miguel Cabrera and his prodigious workshop completed a Jesuit commission for thirty-two canvases on the life of Saint Ignatius of Loyola in only thirteen months (1756–1757).

In contrast to painting's occasionally formulaic quality, freestanding sculpture attained a high point. Representations of angels and saints now pivoted, their garments taking on the same gravity-defying movements as the precarious position of the nonstructural *estípite* columns. These rococo traits were introduced through the Francophile tastes of the Bourbon court, corresponding to the lighter tones, delicacy, and sentimentality also found in painting. Particularly esteemed were the wooden polychrome sculptures exported from Guatemala, known for their *estofado*, a technique of emulating the floral patterns of brocade by engraving through layers of gold and silver leaf and colored pigments.

1781 to Nineteenth Century. The most definitive change occurred in 1781 with the opening of an arts academy in Mexico City, the Royal Academy of San Carlos. The multitalented Manuel Tolsá (1757–1816) encouraged a widespread adoption of the neoclassical canon that subsequently endured throughout the nineteenth century. In feverish programs to redecorate churches, altars deemed grotesquely (and sacrilegiously) overwrought were destroyed, replaced by the antiseptic standards of "modern" neoclassicism. Ironically, entry into the international arena was at the expense of forfeiting some of colonial art's most audacious and ingenious contributions.

[*See also* Altars; Baroque; Cabrera, Miguel; Castas Paintings; Churches and Cathedrals; Cristos de Caña; Crosses and Crucifixes; Masks; Monasteries and Convents; Murals; Painting; Pictorial Manuscripts; Plazas; Relics; Retablos; Sculpture; Tequitqui.]

BIBLIOGRAPHY

Baird, Joseph. *The Churches of Mexico: 1530–1810.* Berkeley and Los Angeles, 1962. Useful compendium of major monuments and style changes in viceregal architecture.

Bantel, Linda, and Marcus Burke. *Spain and New Spain: Mexican Colonial Arts in Their European Context.* Corpus Christi, Tex., 1979. Exhibition catalog from the Art Museum of South Texas, particularly strong in its coverage of painting and its Spanish antecedents; available only in libraries.

Kubler, George, and Martin Soria. *Art and Architecture in Spain and Portugal and Their American Dominions, 1500–1800.* Pelican History of Art. Harmondsworth, 1959. Still an excellent overview and reference, although the treatment of the arts in the Spanish colonies is somewhat Eurocentric.

Marco Dorta, Enrique. *Arte en America y Filipinas*, vol. 21, *Ars Hispaniae.* Madrid, 1973. Comprehensive, condensed review of all arts in the Spanish Americas, including the Philippines.

Mexico: Splendors of Thirty Centuries. Metropolitan Museum of Art. New York, 1990. "Viceregal Art" section in this catalog provides thoughtful essays on various facets of the colonial arts; superb illustrations and solid bibliography.

Mullen, Robert. *Architecture and Its Sculpture in Viceregal Mexico.* Austin, Tex., 1997. Concise inventory of major architectural monuments and building styles (except Yucatán).

Palmer, Gabrielle, and Donna Pierce. *Cambios: The Spirit of Transformation in Spanish Colonial Art.* Santa Barbara, Calif., 1992. Exhibition catalog from the Santa Barbara Museum of Art that covers selected examples from viceroyalties of New Spain and Peru; organized thematically.

Sebastián López, Santiago, José de Mesa Figueroa, and Teresa Gisbert de Mesa. *Arte Iberoamericano desde la Colonización a la Independencia*, vols. 28 and 29, *Summa Artis.* Madrid, 1989. Broad coverage of arts in Spanish Americas, with strength in its iconographic analyses and sources.

Toussaint, Manuel. *Colonial Art in Mexico.* Translated by Elizabeth Weismann. Austin, Tex., 1967. Classic work on the colonial arts, including decorative arts, by the pioneer Mexican art historian in this field.

Tovar de Teresa, Guillermo. *Pintura y Escultura en Nueva España (1557–1640).* Mexico City, 1992. Incisive study of painters and sculptors during the Renaissance/Mannerist period with excellent color images.

Weismann, Elizabeth W., and J. Hancock Sandoval. *Art and Time in Mexico: From the Conquest to the Revolution.* New York, 1985. Very accessible, almost poetic, commentary on the evolution of architecture and sculpture in viceregal Mexico.

JEANETTE FAVROT PETERSON

Nineteenth and Twentieth Centuries

Around the end of the eighteenth century, Mexican institutions and intellectuals found it useful to place ancient Mesoamerican culture at the center of an emerging national culture and identity. This intensified interest emerged within a complex web of Enlightenment practices, which included eighteenth-century Bourbon Spain's "reconquest" and investigation of its own colony of New Spain, as well as a desire to order the world scientifically in text and image. A valorization of the ancient Mexican past was also integral to the project of Mexico's pro-independence *criollos* (Mexican-born Spaniards), who sought justification for an independent nation in the authenticity of their own New World history rather than in Europe's. The representation of a unique, sophisticated, ancient high culture was also useful in the ongoing battle to counter the often denigrating and patronizing tales spun by Europeans about Mexico; the eradication of the stereotype of heathen cannibals that these narratives created was a goal shared across political lines. Despite the rancorous political antagonisms that were to characterize much of the nineteenth century, the ancient history and cultures often provided some common celebration.

Mexican society of the nineteenth century tended to promote ancient Aztec, which was Central Mexican, culture—not the Maya of southern Mesoamerica—as a kind of "golden age" or indigenous "classical past." In fact, Mexico City was standing on the physical remains of the Aztec capital, an ironic counterpoint of both burying the remnants of Colonial-era destruction and eventually providing a treasure trove of archaeological materials. For example, the discovery of the Aztec Calendar Stone in 1790, during the repaving of the Plaza Mayor, generated many literary works and images that touted the scientific and cultural achievements of the Aztec. Such objects, as well as heroic narratives based largely on sixteenth-century chronicles, helped to fortify the position of ancient Mexican culture within a venerable national history.

Major contributors to the pictorial and sculptural representation of ancient Mexico were the skilled painters and sculptors trained at the Academy of Fine Arts in Mexico City, founded in the late eighteenth century as the Academy of San Carlos. Throughout the nineteenth century, the academy's professors and students responded to the increasing interest in Mexico's ancient history with classicized and, later, more realistic representations of indigenous heroes and tales, which were stylistically consistent with the academic conventions of the time. Academic painters and sculptors contributed to the growing visual chronicle of national history with a variety of narratives that celebrated the indigenous "natural" patrimony, such as pulque and maize; certain political arrangements presented as parallels to modern democratic institutions, such as the "senate" of Tlaxcala; and key foundational figures, such as deity Quetzalcoatl or the Aztec rulers. Pictorial examples include José Obregón's "The Discovery of Pulque" (1869), Rodrigo Gutiérrez's "The Deliberation of the Senate of Tlaxcala" (1875), José Ibarrarán's "Quetzalcoatl Discovers Maize," versions of "The Foundation of Tenochtitlan" by Luis Coto and José Jara, and the "Torture of Cuauhtémoc" (1892) by Leandro Izaquirre. Scenes from the Spanish conquest of Mexico are organized around representations of pre-Hispanic ruins in Felix Parra's "Fray Bartolomé de las Casas" (1875) and his "Massacre of Cholula" (1877). These, as well as images made by non-Academic artists, were often displayed at public exhibitions at the Academy throughout most of the nineteenth century.

Academic sculptors shared subjects with painters. The Spanish-born director of sculpture at the academy, Manuel Vilar, cast plaster models intended for finished bronze sculptures—"Moctezuma" (1850), and "Tlahuicole" (1852), an early-sixteenth-century Tlaxcalan hero who became a figure of resistance for Mexico. Vilar's student Miguel Noreña exhibited a plaster cast of "Fray Bartolomé de las Casas Protecting the Indians" in 1865. Many of the themes represented in painting and sculpture could also be found in the lithographs that illustrated the growing corpus of books about ancient and modern Mexican history and culture, which were produced in the nineteenth century by both Mexicans and non-Mexicans. Vicente Riva Palacio's edited series, *México a través de los siglos* (1887–1889), for example, incorporates lithographs of both ancient artifacts and academic paintings.

Public sculptures of ancient Mesoamerican figures became significant in the decoration of plazas and boulevards, especially as Mexico City began to expand westward in the late nineteenth century. A small bust of the hero Cuauhtemoc—the last Aztec ruler, tortured and later hanged by the Spaniards—was erected in 1869 in the southeastern part of the city; its installation coincided with the restoration to political power of the Zapotec liberal politician Benito Juárez. A more critically successful, life-size bronze statue of Cuauhtemoc on an elaborate base eclipsed the earlier sculpture when it was installed in 1887 in a *glorieta* (intersection circle) in the prominent Paseo de la Reforma, the wide promenade modeled after the Champs Elyseés, the grand boulevard of Paris. The statue, sculpted by Miguel Noreña with bas-reliefs by Gabriel Guerra, was one of a series of bronzes placed along the center of the Paseo de la Reforma, effectively creating a condensed visual chronicle of Mexican history from the pre-Hispanic period through independence. Alejandro Casarín's late-nineteenth-century life-size pair of bronze statues, known as the "Indios Verdes," still stand as guardians to the northern entrance of this boulevard.

Another manifestation of the visual recuperation of ancient Mesoamerica was evident in the late-nineteenth-century debate about the development of a national architectural style. The debate revolved around the use of a neo-indigenous versus a European-based classical or even neo-Gothic architectural style for new public buildings. Much of Europe was then using the Beaux Arts style of elaborate classicism, as was the United States. This controversy arose within the context of self-conscious presence in various international arenas. Exemplary of the "neo-indigenist" style are the decorative bas-reliefs on the base of Noreña's statue of Cuauhtemoc, which are derived from a pre-Hispanic architectural "step-fret" motif, and several of the temporary triumphal arches erected in the Paseo de la Reforma in honor of President Porfirio Díaz's birthday in 1899 (the most notable of these was an arch based on the ruins of the Postclassic site of Mitla in Oaxaca, the state of Díaz's birth). The indigenist–classicist antagonism was most salient in the designs of pavilions for international expositions: one designed for the 1889 Paris World's Fair, for example, included Toltec-derived atlantid figures, as well as sculptor Jesús Contreras's relief panels of Cuauhtemoc and other pre-Hispanic historical and mythological figures.

Representations of pre-Hispanic themes continued to be a significant element in the twentieth century; such imagery proliferated across all media exponentially. This modern recuperation of the pre-Hispanic past became an integral part of post-Revolution ideology, which relied in part on a codified narrative of Mexican history beginning with the pre-Hispanic period. Its pictorial and public presence was negotiated in an intense realist style, often labeled "social realist" by artists, the best-known being Diego Rivera, José Clemente Orozco, and David Alfaro Siqueiros. Such artists received numerous commissions for mural cycles on the walls of public buildings from the 1920s through the 1950s. The heroic resistance of Cuautemoc and the wisdom of Quetzalcoatl were often enhanced in twentieth-century imagery (see, for example, Siqueiros's "Resurrection of Cuauhtémoc" (1950) in the Palacio de Bellas in Artes, in Mexico City or Orozco's "The Departure of Quetzalcoatl" (1932) from his *American Civilization* cycle in Baker Library at Dartmouth College in New Hampshire). Like many of his contemporaries, Rivera incorporated in his works pre-Hispanic figures that stood as mediators between Mexico's ancient past and its modern present—for example, in his 1953 "History of Medicine" in the Hospital de la Raza in Mexico City. There, the central motif of the Aztec deity Tlazolteotl, whom Rivera uses to symbolize health and cleanliness, divides the representation of modern medicine from that of ancient practices.

Architects, artists, and other intellectuals continued to negotiate the antagonism between a pre-Hispanic, indigenist style and an adaptation of Euro-American modernism or functionalism. For example, in the Museo Nacional de Antropología, designed and built in 1964 by Pedro Ramírez Vázquez, the sharp, planar wall surfaces are combined with sculpture, a large fountain, and window surfacing, to evoke both Aztec structures and the lakebed on which the ancient Aztec capital of Tenochtitlan was built. The interplay between modernist language and the evocation of ancient cultural history is also accomplished by the placement of modern buildings near pre-Hispanic ruins. A particularly striking example is the stadium located within the complex of structures at the the Ciudad Universitaria, site of UNAM (Universidad Nacional Autónoma de México), south of Mexico City's metropolitan area. The stadium was designed and built by August Pérez Palacios, Jorge Bravo, and Raúl Salinas from 1950 to 1952. The Ciudad Universitaria and stadium were built on an existing volcanic platform, near the late Formative (Preclassic) period (300 BCE–150 CE) site of Cuicuilco, which contains one of the earliest and largest monumental pyramidal structures in the New World. The stadium evoked this round, multilayered structure through the use of stepped terraces, volcanic-rock facing, and a *talud* profile. In addition, during the 1950s, the architect Luis Barragán made use of the natural volcanic rock outcrops covering the area, known as El Pedregal (the lava field), as building material for walls and as the substrate of a garden of native plants. His modernist steel and glass houses were built into this same natural environment, consciously used to conjure its ancient Mesoamerican foundation. The architect and painter Juan O'Gorman's own house, also built in the Pedregal, incorporates an eclectic array of motifs, including Toltec-based atlantid figures on its façade.

The interplay of ancient Mexican past and modern Mexican present, with its attendant contradictions and complexities, is perhaps best exemplified by the cityscape created since the late 1970s in Mexico City's Plaza Mayor. Next to the metropolitan cathedral and adjacent to the Palacio Nacional, which are situated over the ruins of the Aztec capital, stand the remains of the Aztec Templo Mayor. The structures and other artifacts systematically excavated during the 1980s and 1990s are material testimony to the importance of ancient Mesoamerica to modern Mexico. The continuing tension of this relationship is evident in the Mexican government's uneasy decision that destroyed a number of sixteenth-century buildings—at the time actively used for domestic and commercial purposes—to allow the excavations to proceed.

[*See also* Craft Production; Folk Art; Gamio, Manuel; Indigenismo and Pre-Hispanic Revivals; Kahlo, Frida; Masks; Mexican Mural Movement; Murals; Painting; Retablos; Rivera, Diego; Sculpture; Siqueiros, David Alfaro; Vasconcelos, José; Weaving.]

BIBLIOGRAPHY

Brown, Betty Ann. "The Past Idealized: Diego Rivera's Use of Pre-Columbian Imagery." In *Diego Rivera, A Retrospective*, pp. 138–155. New York and London, 1986. Deals with selective and idealized recuperation of pre-Hispanic images for contemporary murals in the context of revolutionary ideology.

Burian, Edward R. *Modernity and the Architecture of Mexico*. Austin, Tex., 1997. Essays and interviews about the trajectory of modern Mexican architecture.

Charlot, Jean. *Mexican Art and the Academy of San Carlos, 1785–1915*. Austin, Tex., 1964. First English study of the history of the Academy of San Carlos in Mexico City, viewed through the eyes of a foreign participant in the mural movement of the early twentieth century.

Rochfort, Desmond. *Mexican Muralists: Orozco, Rivera, Siqueiros.* San Francisco, 1993. Broad survey of works by the "big three," useful for basic chronology of mural production; numerous color plates.

Rodríguez Prampolini, Ida. "La figura del indio en la pintura del siglo XIX: Fondo ideológico." *Arte, sociedad, e ideología* 3 (Oct.– Nov. 1977), 56–66. Seminal article on the representation of the figure of the Indian in nineteenth-century Mexico; focuses on academic art.

Tenorio-Trillo, Mauricio. *Mexico at the World's Fairs: Crafting a Modern Nation.* Berkeley, 1996. Detailed study of activities connected with Mexico at international expositions; excellent for primary source references and illustrations of pavilions; covers key issues of the predicament of modernism and nationalism around the turn of the century.

Uribe, Eloisa, coord. *Y Todo . . . por una nación: Historia social de la producción plástica de la ciudad mexicana, 1761–1910.* Mexico City, 1987. Important survey of art production in Mexico City from the beginning of the Bourbon reforms to the Mexican Revolution; detailed accounts of monuments, patronage, institutional contexts; a key social history of nineteenth-century Mexican art; no illustrations.

Widdifield, Stacie G. *The Embodiment of the National in Late Nineteenth-Century Mexican Painting.* Tucson, Ariz., 1996. First English-language discussion of nationalism and nineteenth-century Mexican painting; discusses contemporary criticism and negotiation of meanings of categories of the "national," including *mestizaje*, assimilation, and gender; illustrated.

STACIE G. WIDDIFIELD

ART HISTORY. During the late eighteenth and early nineteenth centuries, European scholarly concerns about art and its history were being formalized into an academic discipline, which, interestingly, was turning its attention to ancient and alien arts. These efforts were linked to, and inspired by, philosophies of history put forward by Immanuel Kant (1724–1804) and Georg W. F. Hegel (1770–1831). Central to the development of historical attention to the arts of ancient Mesoamerica, however, was the philosophy of history put forward by the German philosopher Johann Gottfried von Herder (1744–1803), wherein he represented a relativist point of view that "the products of one society were conditioned by the purposes and ideas of that society, and that its purposes may not be ours." Thus, in 1841–1842, the German art historian Franz Theodor Kugler published *Handbuch der Kunstgeschichte* (Stuttgart) as the first attempt to write a history of world art, including the Americas. Kugler focused on monuments (*Denkmaler*), the arts of spatial form, as a universal framework by which to situate and explain the history of art.

During the late nineteenth and early twentieth centuries, art historians became less concerned with history per se, and more engaged with ideas of human behavior. Disciplinary linkages shifted from philosophy to the developing disciplines of psychology, anthropology/ethnology, and structural linguistics. Art objects came to be seen as social and cultural documents of human behavior, and so their aesthetic, formal qualities as indexes of historical place became of lesser interest. European art historians working and publishing at the turn of the twentieth century, such as Aby Warburg, were intent on developing rigorous, analytical methods. They were followed in this effort by Erwin Panofsky.

As Ignacio Bernal has pointed out, however, the perception that an art object is a cultural document for the time of its making can be traced back to the Classic period, and the understanding of ancient Mesoamerican art objects and architecture as documents revealing human intention and authentic meaning can be exemplified in the sixteenth century by Bishop Diego de Landa's description of the Castillo in the ancient site of Chichén Itzá; by Carlos de Sigüenza y Góngora's reported investigation of the Pyramid of the Sun at Teotihuacan, Mexico, in the seventeenth century; by Jose Antonio de Alzate Ramírez's eighteenth-century description of Xochicalco, Mexico; and by Guillermo DuPaix's study of Palenque, Chiapas, in the early nineteenth century.

The art object understood as a cultural document has been a central idea for both archaeological and art historical studies in Mesoamerica up to the middle of the twentieth century, at which point archaeology turned to other factors to define its discipline. Art historians, of course, continued to focus on objects.

Traditionally, art historical studies have taken two different approaches. One approach, by analyzing form and style, is concerned with the art object's cultural and historical dimensions, whereas the other considers more closely the art object's documentary functions by analyzing the images it displays. This last art historical method of analysis is now called iconography—the charting of icons or images. For ancient Mesoamerican art, iconography has been, and is, the most commonly used method of analysis. For both approaches—either iconography or the study of formal, stylistic features—comparison lies at the root of analysis.

It is a subjective task to identify any particular point in time when art history became an important discipline for scholars of ancient Mesoamerica. However, by the end of the nineteenth century, a requisite accumulation of factual material, along with a greater desire for scientific rigor, was well enough established for comparative analyses to be used effectively; analytical comparisons were possible of ancient forms, images, and architecture, aided by archaeological and ethnographic data, archival materials (codices [native books] and sixteenth-century chronicles), and knowledge of native languages.

Intensive comparative analysis was characteristic of the German botanist Eduard Seler (1849–1922). For many present-day scholars, Seler is still the foundation of their researches, not only as a rich and viable resource to consult but also for instruction in his methods of comparative analysis. In his article "Die Ruinen von Xochicalco" (reprinted in *Gesammelte Abhandlungen zur Amerikanischen Sprach- und Altertumskunde*, vol. 2, Graz, Austria, 1960:128–167), for example, Seler first describes the immediate geographical surroundings of Xochicalco, Mexico, then the general layout of the site itself. Following this introduction, he carefully describes the central monument, the Pyramid of the Feathered Serpent, starting with its plan, profile, and measurements and ending with the carved glyphs of the cellar wall. He then discusses sculptures found adjacent to the pyramid, widens his perspective out to comparative examples in the immediate surroundings of Xochicalco, then on to greater geographic distances for more and telling comparisons, all the while drawing on his extensive knowledge of the chronicles, the codices, the native language of Nahuatl, and the ethnographic present. His perspective is large when he starts, focused and detailed in his description and analyses, and large once again in his interpretative conclusions. Seler was aware that the archaeological knowledge of his time lacked precise chronological controls (see Willey and Sabloff 1980:85).

Seler's impact on the practice of art history in Mesoamerica is prodigious because most iconographical studies produced since his time, and at the time of this writing, are direct inheritors of his method of comparative analysis and his manner of representing his material, although he never called what he did iconography. In his article on Xochicalco, Seler illustrates the Pyramid of the Feathered Serpent with four photographs, but these photos do not illustrate the information he gathers and presents in his text; his line drawings do this. His drawings are usually done as outlines, and only on occasion does he render any suggestion of three dimensions when drawing from sculpture or relief-carved pieces. Figures 76 and 77 in the article on Xochicalco display so-called *chimalli* stones, natural boulders bearing singular, relief-carved dates and emblems. For these illustrations, Seler draws the boulders as three-dimensional objects, but the emblems and dates are two-dimensional line drawings that appear imposed on the stones. He has little use for relative scale, as comparable images from various objects tend to be drawn at the same scale. What is important to Seler, clearly, is the icon, not the medium in which it was rendered, nor its scale, nor its context, because most of his illustrations are images/icons taken out of their originating context. Basically, this is how iconography is practiced and represented today. An icon or set of icons is identified and compared to similar icons through illustrated ink line drawings. Although the geographic range of the icon is often an important factor, its more immediate context of medium or scale is seldom taken as pertinent to the decipherment of the icon's meaning (see, for example, *Maya Iconography*, Elizabeth Benson and Gillett Griffin, eds., Princeton, 1988).

In 1913, when Herbert Spinden (1879–1967) first published his Harvard doctoral dissertation, *A Study of Maya Art* (Cambridge), he had the chronological aid of the deciphered dates carved within the texts of ancient Maya monuments and was thus able to create an evolutionary, historical corpus. For monuments that lacked dates or whose dates were unreadable, Spinden used stylistic analysis, or, as Gordon Willey and Jeremy Sabloff (1980: 94) describe it, similary seriation, where the undated monuments were placed into a series of dated ones by reason of stylistic and formal similarities. Spinden's main criteria were human bodily proportions and depth of carved relief—criteria formed, unfortunately, by an imposed aesthetic valuation that assumes all figural styles will eventually coalesce into greatness by achieving natural human proportions and full sculpture in the round. His greatest success was with the stelae of Copán, Honduras; otherwise, without deciphered dates, his stylistic criteria were equivocal guides for establishing a historical sequence.

Spinden's heritage is less impressive than Seler's, with the major exception of Tatiana Proskouriakoff's *Study of Classic Maya Sculpture*, published in 1950. Using the graphic outline of images as an index of stylistic change through time and, like Spinden, keying these changes to the relative, but known, chronology for some ancient Maya sculptures, Proskouriakoff was able to produce a reliable stylistic seriation and history for Maya sculpture. Although she worked with more monuments and deciphered more dates than Spinden had, she also carefully divided her study into two parts. The first is a presentation of her seriation of graphic outlines for the human figure and the elements of its costuming. Here, she describes the evident temporal changes in graphic outline, making no judgments of value or of meaning. The second part, clearly separated from the first by a comprehensive, photographic corpus of monuments, is interpretative. It is a qualitative analysis of graphic outlines along with composition and carving techniques that suggested to Proskouriakoff meaningful historical groups labeled with aesthetic terms, such as the Ornate Phase and the Formative Phase.

Both Seler and Proskouriakoff relied on careful, close description to introduce their works, and both employed comparative analyses to come to their conclusions. However, Seler used comparative analyses to focus on the decipherment of meaning in imagery, not a history, whereas Proskouriakoff and Spinden focused on the style and forms of imagery in order to represent a history, not being so concerned with native meaning.

Eduard Seler did not believe he had enough information to undertake a broad synthesis of his work, and Spinden's and Proskouriakoff's more sweeping syntheses have had few followers. The closest productions in kind are grand exhibitions wherein the objects of the exhibition are represented historically while the catalog essays are thematic and topical. Two good examples are the exhibitions *Maya Treasures of an Ancient Civilization* and *Mexico: Forty Centuries of Splendor* (catalogs with the same titles published, respectively, Albuquerque and New York, 1985; New York, 1990).

Another strain of art historical concern related to ancient Mesoamerica has to do with aesthetic valuation of ancient artistry. This is a complex arena with many profound issues that cannot be fully tackled in this essay. Aesthetic valuations, explicitly or implicitly, can be found from the moment Europeans encountered and described, positively or negatively, ancient Mesoamerican art and architecture. During the late nineteenth century, however, a concern added to, or growing out of, aesthetic valuation is a project for eliciting from the work of art the essential, defining character of its own aesthetic energy, a psychological substance thought to be structurally embedded in the art object. Here the effort is to find and explain the indigenous aesthetic that informed the work of art, so to speak. Manuel Orozco y Berra (1816–1881) says of Aztec "deity" sculptures in his *História antigua y de la conquista de Mexico* (4 vols., Mexico, 1880), "[T]hey bear the stamp of an austere and harsh imagination." This type of interest is exemplified by W. H. Holmes (1916) and continues through the first half of the twentieth century. The Mexican art historian Salvador Toscano wrote *Arte precolombino de Mexico* (Mexico, 1944) within this idiom, followed by Paul Westheim's *Arte antiguo de Mexico* (Mexico, 1950), an effort at formal description framed by a psychology of art and aesthetics.

After the mid-twentieth century, aesthetic valuations are seldom evoked, and few scholars search for indigenous aesthetics through analysis of form and style. Since World War II, aesthetic valuation has been thought to impede rigorous historical or anthropological inquiry and is no longer a conscious project. Few present-day scholars consider psychological traits and aesthetic insights to be transcultural; that is, they cannot be transferred or truthfully understood from one culture or time to another.

In 1940, there appeared in *American Antiquity* (vol. 4, 360–362) a scathing review of Pal Keleman's book, *Battlefield of the Gods: Aspects of Mexican History, Art, and Exploration* (London, 1937), written by George Kubler, who believed Keleman's study lacked methodological rigor in its treatment of style and form. After Kubler published "The Cycle of Life and Death in Metropolitan Aztec Sculpture" (*Gazette des Beaux-Arts*, May 1943:257–268), Keleman responded (*American Antiquity*, vol. 11, 1946: 145–154) by accusing the young art historian of unfamiliarity with his material, his arbitrary selections, and of being a pompous tyro. This exchange illustrates early on the pitfalls of aesthetic valuation, and that applied methodologies were and are intensely scrutinized. Methods of analyses, not results, have become the hallmark of art historical rigor.

Kubler's article was an effort to find intrinsic meanings by combining iconographic analysis with formal and stylistic analyses. By doing this, he produced a historical sequence that was defined as much by its iconographic meanings as it was by changing aesthetics inherent in forms and styles. (It is likely that Keleman objected to this merging of the two, until now, distinct methodological, and philosophical, points of view.) Kubler's inclusive project resulted in two major works, both first published in 1962: *The Shape of Time* (New Haven) and *The Art and Architecture of Ancient America* (London).

Justino Fernandez's remarkable work, *Coatlicue. Estética del arte indígena antigua* (Mexico City, 1954), was researched and written in the inclusive manner, wherein all aspects of a work of art are investigated, in this case, the famous Aztec sculpture of Coatlicue, She-of-the-Serpent-Skirt.

In order to discuss the practices of art history and Mesoamerica since World War II, several issues and events need to be accounted for: the advent of "new archaeology" and its effect on the practice of art history and the advent of primary texts through the contributions of epigraphy.

During the 1950s, the discipline of archaeology substantially changed the focus of its questions from the recovery of material objects in efforts to establish a chronology and decipher function and meaning to questions of process—what ultimately drives change in human society. Thus, the problems and questions that structured archaeological projects centered on defining patterns of behavior: environmental conditions, settlement patterns, agricultural techniques and production, distribution of goods and the signifying patterns of their distribution, occupations, health, and so on. Julian Steward's *Theory of Culture Change* (Urbana, 1955) and the work of the anthropologist Lewis Binford were potent forces in shaping the philosophies and strategies of this new archaeology as they were and are practiced by archaeologists in Mesoamerica.

Concurrently, archaeologists were calling on other disciplines, such as zoology, sociology, osteology, ecology, economics, and agricultural science, to aid in answering their questions of processual interconnections. Although one could imagine that art history might have a role in this multidisciplinary project, the fact is that art historical concerns have to do primarily with the recovery of ancient meanings and ideologies. The new archaeologists considered meaning and ideology, both ancient and modern, to be epiphenomenal to the "actual" causes of social evolution and change, that is, demographics and environment.

The long-standing idea that ancient objects (monuments and architecture) embraced within themselves an authoritative source for ancient meaning was not only sidestepped but also rejected by many new archaeologists. The move from focusing on ancient material objects to ancient processes created, for the first time, a very real gap between the disciplines of archaeology and art history.

It is at this time that art historians working in Mesoamerica became affiliated first with the efforts of structural linguistics and then with epigraphy (the decipherment of hieroglyphs). In 1967, George Kubler published *The Iconography of the Art of Teotihuacan*, in which he suggested that the compound signs peculiar to the murals and painted ceramics of Teotihuacan, Mexico, held linguistic functions; that is, they operated like a grammar wherein images could be identified as nouns, adjectives, and verbs. He concluded that the art of Teotihuacan was essentially liturgical and therefore religious in content. Although it was an intriguing structural analysis, Kubler's effort to relate image patterns to grammatical structure did not yield the more intimate meanings for individual icons sought by today's scholars. Kubler discerned the meaningful, grammatical structure with which images are combined into compositions.

As Kubler was writing his article, epigraphers, students of ancient hieroglyphs, began to successfully open doors for the decipherment of ancient Maya texts. By the mid-1970s, the syllabic content of Maya glyphs was established, and tentative translations of glyphic texts were being offered. With primary texts there began a fruitful alignment between the methods of iconography and epigraphy, and a belief that this would achieve a greater precision for iconographic identification.

Clemency Coggins's Harvard dissertation, *Painting and Drawing Styles at Tikal: An Art Historical and Iconographic Reconstruction* (1975), is an early and successful example of working with image and text wherein she was able to match glyphic texts citing names of rulers, along with their dates and deeds, to actual burials and buildings of Tikal (Guatemala). Another important example comes from Peter Mathews and Linda Schele's work at Palenque, Chiapas (1974). The original names of ancient Maya rulers are now known, their genealogical relationships traced, and their ceremonial and ritual actions known through translation. Admittedly, what remains of the corpus of Maya hieroglyphic texts is not a prolific resource for the reconstruction of history. However, as almost all texts were carved or painted in conjunction with imagery, a reciprocal and positive relationship between text and image is the working assumption for the present. Interestingly enough, the type of iconography inspired by incorporating known, or hypothetically known, texts into the comparative analyses of imagery is very similar to that of Eduard Seler. Where Seler had used his knowledge of Nahuatl and sixteenth-century chronicles to arbitrate his close contextual analyses of images, the iconographer of ancient Maya images now uses original texts.

Although the very subjects and objects of the art historical discipline may be deemed by some archaeologists as epiphenomenal to any valid, systematic explanation of human evolution and change, the successful and productive marriage of epigraphy and iconography allowed for the reproduction of compelling histories. Epiphenomenal or not, these histories draw on the powerful aura of what is considered to be hard facts taken from ancient texts—names, dates, and events—and they have become so central in the field of ancient Maya studies that archaeologists and art historians have become partners. Art historians and epigraphers are members of archaeological research teams, and some archaeological projects are inspired by ancient texts or are designed to test the validity of the texts. The Copán (Honduras) Project (involving many institutions since it was initiated in the 1970s) is a prime example of this kind of collaboration, especially under the directorship of William Fash of Harvard University, as is the Caracol (Belize) Project, headed by Diane Chase and Arlen Chase, professors at the University of Florida in Gainesville.

At present, in other cultural, linguistic regions of ancient Mesoamerica, the partnership between art historian and archaeologist is less easily defined. Since the Spanish conquest, scholarly attention has always been focused on the Valley of Mexico, where the great urban centers of Teotihuacan and Tenochtitlan (now Mexico City) are located. Major archaeological projects at both sites have been more or less ongoing. The latest excavations have revealed the Templo Mayor of Tenochtitlan, just east of the cathedral in present-day Mexico City, and at Teotihuacan, excavations in the Ciudadela and the Pyramid of the Feathered Serpent have revealed an elaborate system of sacrificial burials of warriors apparently structured by calendrical cosmography. Both archaeological projects focus on major monuments and are in a sense more aligned to the older archaeological philosophies that did not exclude questions about history or ideology. However, after establishing chronology, one of the main questions for archaeology in central Mexico has been, and is, the formation and evolution of the state (as opposed to tribal organization), its structure, and its maintenance by the elite. The recent focus of art historians, therefore, has been to accept the archaeologists' theme and study the relationships between art and its more social functions within and for the state. (See *Art, Ideology, and the City of Teotihuacan*, edited by Janet Berlo, Washington, D.C., 1992; and *The Aztec Templo Mayor*, edited by Elizabeth Boone, Washington, D.C., 1987.)

The conjoining of iconographic and epigraphic studies with archaeological ones occurs with scholars working in the regions inhabited by the Zapotec and Mixtec peoples (modern Oaxaca) but here, too, there is a different focus to the research questions. The archaeologist Joyce Marcus (see *The Cloud People*, New York, 1983), working mainly with the ancient Zapotec remains, finds epigraphic and iconographic evidence for political and dynastic alliances or disputes rather than the records of elite ceremonialism attributed to the ancient Maya, or the cosmic justifications for rulership for the formation of statehood, as in the Valley of Mexico.

Iconography is a method of research developed within and by the discipline of art history, but in Mesoamerica the scholar utilizing this method may be trained as an archaeologist, an anthropologist, a historian, a photographer, or a bank manager (Seler was a botanist). However, if an art historian needing certain information decided to make a small excavation at, say, Monte Albán, he or she would probably be arrested. Although it seems curious that archaeologists and others are free to use the art historical method of iconography without any formal training in art history, it is also true that art history is a humanistic discipline and as such seems to be fair grounds for inquiry by anyone. Scientists regularly work in the humanities: physicists are philosophers; biologists are historians. Nonetheless, the analytical methods of art history—stylistic and formal analyses and/or iconographic, structural analyses—result in equivocal, subjective statements about the making of art (images) and its role within human history and human intention. This is so whether these methods are used by an art historian or an archaeologist. A work of art may be a cultural document, but the "languages" with which it is inscribed are profoundly and complexly intertwined.

[*See also* Conservation and Restoration.]

BIBLIOGRAPHY

Bernal, Ignacio. *A History of Mexican Archeology.* New York, 1980. Because of the close ties between art history and archaeology, this is a very useful, and erudite, overview.

Braun, Barbara. *Pre-Columbian Art and the Post-Columbian World: Ancient American Sources of Modern Art.* New York, 1993. Careful and insightful consideration of the intricate issues surrounding modern aesthetics and ancient art: pages 25 and following are most pertinent to this essay.

Coggins, Clemency. *Painting and Drawing Styles at Tikal: An Art Historical and Iconographic Reconstruction.* Ann Arbor, 1975. Although this study is exemplary for analyzing and matching text and image, it also is inclusive in its use of comparative, stylistic, and iconographic analyses.

Fernandez, Justino. *Coatlicue. Estética del arte indígena antigua.* Mexico City, 1954. Important essay, not only for the careful, inclusive analysis of the monument but also for its exhaustive review of aesthetic responses to ancient Mexican art.

Holmes, W. H. "Masterpieces of Aboriginal American Art: 4.—Sculpture in the Round." *Art and Archaeology* 3.2 (February 1916), 71–85. Early and exemplary effort to elicit native aesthetics. However, the author's own valuations are transparently imposed.

Honour, Hugh. *The New Golden Land: European Images of America from the Discoveries to the Present Time.* New York, 1975. Indispensable history of European responses to the Americas; especially interesting for the history of the development of the art historical and archaeological disciplines becoming attentive to the Americas.

Keen, Benjamin. *The Aztec Image in Western Thought.* New Brunswick, N.J., 1971 (paperback, 1990). Intellectual history that is an important companion to the history and development of art historical thought in regard to Mesoamerica.

Klein, Cecelia F. "The Relation of Mesoamerican Art History to Archaeology in the United States." In *Pre-Columbian Art History. Selected Readings*, edited by Alana Cordy-Collins, pp. 1–6. Palo Alto, Calif., 1982. Although this is a prescriptive article about the future goals for art historical studies, it does represent one of the few actual reviews of the role of art history in Mesoamerica, as it is practiced in the United States.

Kubler, George A. *The Shape of Time: Remarks on the History of Things.* New Haven, 1962. Theoretical tract that grew out of efforts to deal with the history of art in Mesoamerica. Important to art historians and artists in general.

Kubler, George A. *The Iconography of the Art of Teotihuacan.* Washington, D.C., 1967. Iconographic analysis influenced by structural linguistics.

Kubler, George A. *Esthetic Recognition of Ancient Amerindian Art.* New Haven, 1991. Although charting a particular history of aesthetics, this book, by focusing on individual scholars and writers through short biographical sketches, is a specially useful resource.

Kultermann, Udo. *The History of Art History.* Abaris Books, 1993. Concise but thorough discussions of art historians and their theoretical and practical accomplishments.

Mathews, Peter, and Linda Schele. "Lords of Palenque—The Glyphic Evidence." In *Primera Mesa Redonda de Palenque, Part 1*, edited by Merle Greene Robertson, pp. 63–76. Pebble Beach, Calif., 1974. Exemplary and early study of Maya glyphs revealing a dynastic king list.

Podro, Michael. *The Critical Historians of Art.* New Haven, 1982. Important overview focusing on art historians and their theories about ancient (Classic) and alien art (Egyptian, Near Eastern, and Asian).

Proskouriakoff, Tatiana. *A Study of Classic Maya Sculpture.* Washington, D.C., 1950. Exemplary formal and stylistic analysis.

Willey, Gordon R., and Jeremy A. Sabloff. *A History of American Archaeology.* New York, 1980. Very useful guide to philosophical developments in the discipline of archaeology, especially for the projects of "new archaeology."

FLORA S. CLANCY

ASTRONOMY. Western scientific astronomy attempts to define and categorize celestial phenomena according to materialistic, physical, and mathematical principles; indigenous Mesoamerican astronomy, by contrast, seems to have rested on a broader faith that the everyday human world was intimately related to the natural world, and that these worlds, mediated by human action, were intended to function in harmony. Ideally, the celestial and terrestrial worlds comprised a distinct whole, with all parts intricately linked together and each aspect influencing the others. The sky was the home of the gods, the divine ancestors of the rulers. Sky myths explained the unfolding of history, politics, social relations, and ideas about creation and life after death.

In this framework, the astronomer's goal was to follow the sky gods closely. This would help to maintain the alliance between the inherent power of the denizens of the cosmos and the physical well-being of the people and the state—that is, between divine knowledge and human action. We are inclined to label as "astrology" the practice of those who watched the Mesoamerican skies. These astronomers celebrated and expressed sky knowledge not only in written and pictorial texts but also in art, architecture, and sculpture. The calendars they developed, based on the appearance and motion of celestial objects, mimicked the other cycles they knew in everyday life.

Of all the native cultures of Mesoamerica, the Maya seem to have had the greatest interest in watching the skies. The Maya codices offer the closest link, at least in form, to ancient Babylonian and Greek tabulations of celestial motion with which historians and astronomers of the West are familiar. Tables of computed positions of Venus and Mars, along with an eclipse-warning table and season-reckoning tables, appear in the Maya *Dresden Codex*.

One is struck by the precision with which the occurrence of sky phenomena is predicted in these texts. For example, a correction page preceding the Venus table has been interpreted to render the ephemeris accurate to one day in five hundred years. Accompanying omens in hieroglyphic script warn of periods of danger to crops and to the welfare of the state. Decipherment of Stela 1 at La Mojarra, Veracruz, documents an interest in Venus and eclipses from the Epi-Olmec culture of the Gulf Coast (second century CE). In addition, the Paris Codex, which offers a pictorial zodiac containing a host of sky animals (e.g., tortoise, peccary, and scorpion), demonstrates that the Maya were concerned with following the movement of the planets relative to the stars. Research on astronomical events depicted in the Maya codices continues to be an active endeavor as the interpretive borderline between true astronomical ephemerides and simple day-counting almanacs becomes more diffuse.

The importance of astronomy is reinforced in Maya iconography. Zodiacs appear on friezes over doorways at Chichén Itzá and Uxmal. In each case, the effigy of a seated ruler is placed in a cosmic context beneath a zodiacal band; the scene gives the overall appearance of authorizing his divine origin. In the mural paintings of Bonampak, several zodiacal symbols decorated with Venus/star glyphs fill a band surmounting a scene showing the aftermath of a battle. Captors supplicate the ruler, who, adorned in elaborate costume, celebrates victory amid a scene of pageants. Dates carved on Bonampak stelae suggest that the battles were timed to the first and last appearances of Venus. Star war imagery, which includes Tlaloc-war effigies coupled with Venus glyphs, has been traced all the way back to Teotihuacan and seems to have played a prominent role at Copán, where a number of dates recording key points in the lives of several rulers appear to be associated with appearances of Venus as morning and evening star.

Astronomical alignments in Maya architecture suggest that horizon astronomy too was prominent in the Mesoamerican world. [*See* Archaeoastronomy.] Bolstering the evidence for Maya attentiveness to the position of Venus, Temple 22 at Copán contains a narrow window directed westward toward Venus, whose appearance signaled the arrival of the rainy season. The House of the Governor at Uxmal and the Caracol at Chichén Itzá, both oddly shaped or skewed structures, timed the arrival of Venus at its eight-year horizon extremes. Extraordinary attention was probably paid to Venus when the cyclic-minded Maya realized that a full cycle of appearances of that planet meshed with the seasonal year in the perfect ratio of 5 to 8; however, dates have also been found in the monumental inscriptions which many correlate with the observable periods of the other planets, such as Jupiter and Saturn.

Aztec pictorial manuscripts, particularly the linear year texts, peg dynastic history to natural events, many of them celestial. Among sky phenomena cited are eclipses, meteor showers, comets, the aurora borealis, sun pillars, and the zodiacal light. When the Aztec rewrote their history, they arranged historical and cosmic events which they perceived as like-in-kind at 52-year intervals. The sixteenth-century Franciscan missionary and ethnographer Bernadino de Sahagún tells us that the commencement of each period was marked by the overhead passage of the Pleiades star group. Astronomical considerations are also reflected in Central Mexican architecture. The Templo Mayor of Tenochtitlan was oriented to mark the sun at the equinox. Sahagún's detailed description of rituals to honor each of the months suggests that the movement of the Sun was watched closely. There is good evidence that, like the Maya, the Aztec tied the environment to their calendar by noting the arrival of the Sun at points of the horizon demarcating twenty-day intervals. This seems to have been an integral part of the mountain worship and sacred geography of the Valley of Mexico. While solar imagery dominates the cosmic iconographic record of the Aztecs, a host of images of decapitated lunar goddesses also links the symbolism of astronomy with politics and the seasonal cycle.

Like the Maya creation story in the *Popol Vuh*, the Aztec creation myth told to the chroniclers, and graphically symbolized on the Sun Stone and other sculptures, makes metaphoric use of the movement of celestial bodies. Thus, the multiple journeys of the Hero Twins into the underworld to set up the condition for the arrival of the Maya people on earth may be a deliberately veiled post-Conquest version of the movement of the Sun and Venus, as written in the *Dresden Codex*.

The Mesoamerican astronomical ethos lives on despite five centuries of conquest and colonialism. For example, astronomical terms and concepts of the Mixé of Oaxaca, the Chamula of Chiapas, and other groups appear to have been retained locally and even to have diffused to areas far removed from their original context. Native Maya still recognize the Three Stone Hearth (the region about the belt of Orion), which played a role in their creation story, and highland Guatemalan daykeepers still make prognostications according to the days of the *tzolkin*, or 260-day calendar, which formed the temporal centerpiece of the ancient codices.

[*See also* Comets; Eclipses; Meteors and Meteorites; Moon; Stars and Constellations; Sun; Venus.]

BIBLIOGRAPHY

Aveni, Anthony. *Skywatchers of Ancient Mexico.* Austin, Tex., 1980. (Revised edition, 2001). An overview of Mesoamerican astronomical practices.

Bricker, Victoria, and Harvey Bricker. "A Method for Cross-Dating Almanacs with Tables in the Dresden Codex." In *The Sky in Mayan Literature*, edited by Anthony Aveni, pp. 43–86. New York, 1992. Astronomy and seasonal cycles are explored.

Bricker, Victoria, and Harvey Bricker. "Astronomical References in the Throne Inscription of the Palace of the Governor at Uxmal." *Cambridge Archaeological Journal* 6 (1996), 191–229. Stellar related Venus timings at Uxmal.

Bricker, Harvey, and Victoria Bricker. "More on the Mars Table in the Dresden Codex." *Latin American Antiquity* 8 (1997), 384–397. References trace the exploration of astronomical information in the Mars table.

Broda, Johanna. "Astronomy, Cosmovisión and Ideology in Prehispanic Mesoamerica." In *Ethnoastronomy and Archaeoastronomy in the American Tropics*, edited by Anthony Aveni and Gary Urton, pp. 81–110. *Proceedings of the New York Academy of Sciences* 385 (1982). Overview of astronomy and its relation to mountain worship and social concepts.

Carlson, John. "Venus Regulated Warfare and Ritual Sacrifice in Mesoamerica." In *Astronomies and Cultures*, edited by Clive L. N. Ruggles and Nichoas Saunders, Niwot, Colo., 1993. Discusses star-war symbolism at Cacaxtla in highland Mexico.

Freidel, David, Linda Schele, and Joy Parker. *Maya Cosmos.* New York, 1993. See especially chapter 2, which explores continuity of astronomical practice into the present.

Justeson, John, and Terence Kaufmann. "A Decipherment of Epi-Olmec Hieroglyphic Writing." *Science* 259 (1993), 1003–1010. Early astronomic dates on Stela 1, La Mojarra.

Lipp, Frank. 1991 *The Mixe of Oaxaca.* Austin, Tex., 1991. Detailed compendium of contemporary highland astronomical practice.

Lounsbury, Floyd. "Astronomical Knowledge and Its Uses at Bonampak, Mexico." In *Archaeoastronomy in the New World*, edited by Anthony Aveni, pp. 143–168. Cambridge, 1982. On the relation of astronomical observations in the timing of ritual warfare.

Milbrath, Susan. "Decapitated Lunar Goddesses in Aztec Art, Myth, and Ritual." *Ancient Mesoamerica* 8 (1997), 185–206. A comprehensive discussion of symbolism relating to the moon.

Miller, Virginia. "Star Warriors at Chichén Itzá." In *Word and Image in Maya Culture: Explorations in Language, Writing and Representation*, edited by William Hanks and Donald Rice, pp. 287–305. Salt Lake City, 1989. Traces the timing of warfare to astronomical events.

Tedlock, Barbara. "The Road of Light: Theory and Practice of Mayan Skywatching." In *The Sky in Mayan Literature*, edited by Anthony Aveni, pp. 18–42, Oxford, 1992. An exploration of contemporary Maya astronomy and its ties to the past.

Vogt, Evon. "Cardinal Directions and Ceremonial Circuits in the Mayan and Southwestern Cosmology." *National Geographic Society Research Reports* 21 (1988), 487–496. Cross-cultural comparative study.

Vogt, Evon. "Zinacanteco Astronomy." *Mexicon* 19.6 (1988), 110–117. Caps a long tradition of ethnographic astronomical studies in Chiapas, Mexico.

ANTHONY F. AVENI

AUBIN, CODEX. A set of central Mexican annals, the *Codex Aubin* registers pre-Hispanic and colonial events through pictorial images and alphabetic writing in Nahuatl. [*See* Annals.] The indigenous cycle of years (Reed, Flint Knife, House, Rabbit) structures the account; however, the manuscript takes the form of a European-style book. The codex opens with the twelfth-century Mexica migration from Aztlan and ends with the arrival of a new viceroy and archbishop in Mexico City in 1607–1608. The writers and painters of the *Codex Aubin* probably came from San Juan Tenochtitlan (an *altepetl* in Mexico City), and they began their work sometime after 1560, using European paper, black ink, and colored pigments. Several hands can be discerned in the manuscript, indicating that the project was a collaborative enterprise executed over many years.

Like other Nahua annals, the *Codex Aubin* presents an anonymous but partisan record of the past. Throughout the codex, year-glyphs provide the armature for the account; true to the genre, the years in which nothing noteworthy transpired remain blank (here, the "empty" years dominate the earliest portions of the annals). The main narrative records a variety of events, many of which have parallels in other contemporary annals. Furthermore, the codex addresses themes significant to the Mexica Empire, as well as to the *altepetl* of San Juan Tenochtitlan. Among the more prominent events registered are the New Fire ceremony at Coatepec, the Mexica defeat at Chapultepec, the founding of Tenochtitlan, the installation and deaths of imperial *tlatoque*, enlargements of the Templo Mayor, comets and eclipses, the arrival of Spaniards, deaths from smallpox, local building projects, and changes in *altepetl* leadership.

The *Codex Aubin* is a small book (11 by 15 centimeters, 81 folios), but the main account has three sections, as well as an addendum that presents the succession of Mexica rulers and colonial officials. The three sections forming the body of the annals focus on the migration from Aztlan to Tenochtitlan, the imperial history of Tenochtitlan, and post-Conquest events. Each section opens with a prominent, full-page painting that parallels European codex images in function and placement; otherwise, each section exhibits a distinct arrangement of glyphs, texts, and images. Throughout the migration account, for example, year-glyphs appear in rectangular or L-shaped blocks. In contrast, the annals section that recounts imperial history situates the glyphs in vertical rows along the left side of each page, and after 1553, in the final portion of the codex, glyphs appear just one to a page. Correspondingly, the distribution and composition of images and written texts also vary by section. These different formats presumably derive from the annalists' sources as well as from diverse conceptions of history and personal choice. These distinctions further imply that among Nahuas of the sixteenth century, all memories of the past did not fill time the same way, nor did they warrant uniform modes of representation.

In structure, style, and conception, the *Codex Aubin* intermingles elements of pre-Hispanic and European origin. Annalistic histories seem to have pre-Conquest roots; evidence suggests that annals may have been a form of record-keeping closely bound to Mexica imperial ambitions. However, the book format of the *Codex Aubin*, the use of images like frontispieces, and a colophonic first page all point to considerable familiarity with European books. Consequently, the *Codex Aubin* should be understood as a colonial account that intertwines pre-Hispanic and European-style conventions to serve indigenous ends. To date, scholarship has emphasized two aspects of the *Codex Aubin*: the content of its pre-Hispanic account, and the relationships between pictorial and alphabetic exposition. The *Codex Aubin* represents an important example of indigenous record-keeping after the Conquest because it maintains strong interests in both pre-Hispanic and Colonial events. Moreover, it offers unique insights into Nahua responses to the changing status of pictorial imagery and alphabetic writing in the late sixteenth century.

The early viceregal history of the *Codex Aubin* is no longer known. Lorenzo Boturini Benaduci collected the document around the mid-eighteenth century, and like many of his other manuscripts, the annals passed into the hands of J. M. A. Aubin between 1830 and 1840. Aubin produced a lithographic reproduction of the manuscript in 1850 and renamed the document after himself. The *Codex Aubin* was also owned by J. Desportes before reaching its present home in the British Museum (Add. Ms. 31219). The manuscript was hand-copied and partially translated numerous times in the nineteenth and twentieth centuries; many of these copies are currently housed in collections in Europe and Mexico.

[*See also* Migrations; Pictorial Manuscripts.]

BIBLIOGRAPHY

Boone, Elizabeth Hill. *Stories in Red and Black: Pictorial Histories of the Aztecs and Mixtecs*. Austin, Tex., 2000. Discussion of structure and content of *Codex Aubin* and other Aztec annals, pp. 197–237.

Dibble, Charles, trans. and ed. *Historia de la Nación Mexicana: Reproducción de Códice de 1576 (Códice Aubin)*. Madrid, 1963. Color facsimile of the manuscript with translation of Nahuatl text into Spanish.

Glass, John B. "Codex Aubin." In "A Census of Native Middle American Pictorial Manuscripts," in *Handbook of Middle American Indians*, vol. 14, *Guide to Ethnohistorical Sources*, edited by Howard F. Cline, part 3, pp. 88–90. Austin, 1975. Summary of the physical attributes, contents, collection history, reproduction, and publication of the manuscript.

Lehmann, Walter, and Gerdt Kutscher, trans. and eds. *Geschichte der Azteken: Codex Aubin und verwandte Dokumente*. Berlin, 1981. Very good black-and-white facsimile of the codex and two related contemporary documents; includes translation of Nahuatl text into German, with brief commentary.

DANA LEIBSOHN

AUBIN TONALAMATL. The bark-paper screenfold known today as the *Aubin Tonalamatl* is a rare survival of a type of pre-Hispanic painted book called in Nahuatl *tonalamatl*, or "book of days." This divinatory handbook originally depicted pictorial symbols of the 260 days of the *tonalpohualli* ("count of days"). The screenfold's original twenty panels (or "pages") (24 by 27 centimeters) corresponded to the twenty 13-day periods (Spanish, *trecenas*) of the *tonalamatl*. Only eighteen *trecena* panels remain, the first two having been lost. Each densely organized panel, painted on only one side, displays figures whose influence on the fate of the *trecena* or of individual days in it was determined by a skilled diviner. Large deity images occupy a compartment in the upper left of each panel. An L-shaped series of 52 smaller compartments flanks it; each contains one of the thirteen day signs and mantic elements pertaining to them: nine "night lords," thirteen "day lords," and thirteen associated flying creatures.

The *Aubin Tonalamatl* has had a complicated history of ownership, the public record of which begins only in the eighteenth century. Identified as a "kalendario ydolatrico," it first surfaced in the 1743 inventory (no. 6–23) of the confiscated collection of ancient Mexican manuscripts gathered by the Italian aristocrat Lorenzo Boturini Benaduci, who was expelled from New Spain that same year. During the early nineteenth century, the screenfold (that is, panels 9–20) passed indirectly from the estate of the Mexican savant Antonio de León y Gama to two artist-travelers in Mexico: the German Karl Nebel, and then Jean-Frédéric Waldeck. In 1841 in Paris, Waldeck sold it to Joseph-Marius-Alexis Aubin, who added it to the extensive manuscript collection he had brought back from Mexico in 1840. It is not known where or when Aubin obtained the other panels (3–8); most likely, he brought them from Mexico. The rejoined screenfold was purchased by Eugène Goupil in Paris in 1889, along with the rest of the Aubin collection; in 1898, the screenfold was donated to the Bibliothèque Nationale of Paris by Goupil's widow. Taken from the Bibliothèque Nationale in 1982, the *Aubin Tonalamatl* is at present in the Biblioteca del Instituto Nacional de Antropología e Historia (INAH) in Mexico City.

Among surviving Central Mexican manuscripts, the *Aubin Tonalamatl*'s panels are comparable in pictorial complexity only to those of the *tonalamatl* that forms part of the early post-Conquest *Codex Borbonicus*. Although the two are similar iconographically, the *Aubin Tonalamatl* lacks the fine draftsmanship of the *Borbonicus* or other pre-Conquest screenfolds. It also contains copying errors. It is sometimes dated before the Conquest on the basis of its indigenous style, but it was more likely copied during the early years of the post-Conquest period. It apparently originated in the state of Tlaxcala, where Boturini collected it about 1740, and it is stylistically and iconographically related to the *Codex Huamantla* from the Otomí-speaking region of that state. With its wealth of pictorial information painted in native style and format, the *Aubin Tonalamatl* has contributed significantly to our understanding of Mesoamerican ritual and religion.

BIBLIOGRAPHY

Aguilera, Carmen. *El Tonalamatl de Aubin.* Tlaxcala, Codices y Manuscritos 1. Tlaxcala, 1981. Reprint of Seler's color lithograph and panel diagrams, with a general introductory essay on the screenfold's style and content, and interpretative tables based largely on Seler's work.

Seler, Eduard. *Das Tonalamatl der Aubinschen Sammlung: Eine altmexikanische Bilderhandschrift der Bibliothèque Nationale in Paris (Manuscrits mexicains nr. 18–19).* Berlin, 1900; English translation, Berlin and London, 1900–1901. Color lithograph of the screenfold, with a landmark though now somewhat outdated iconographic and ethnographic study.

ELOISE QUIÑONES KEBER

AUGUSTINIANS. The Order of the Hermits of St. Augustine of Hippo came to New Spain in 1533 and, beginning in 1535, was favored by the viceroy, Antonio de Mendoza. Its members were distributed in central Mesoamerica, including such distinct areas as the Sierra Alta and Huasteca of Hidalgo, the Sierra Madre Occidental of Guerrero, the Tierra Caliente of Michoacán, and the Chichimec frontier. Although they focused their attention on indigenous groups whose languages were difficult to learn (such as the Otomís or the Huastecs), or which had a small number of speakers (such as the Ocuiltecs, Tlapanecs, and Matlatzincas), they also worked among the Tarascans and Nahuas. Their labor was notable for the design and organization of communities, waterworks, and architecture; their urbanization and building interests left behind communities and monumental convents in their areas of influence that still stand today. The mural paintings that decorate the convents are of great interest; some, such as those of Ixmiquilpan, adapt and accept indigenous aesthetic and representational forms. Some Augustinian missionaries also permitted more participation by the Indians in spiritual and sacramental practices than did other orders.

The Augustinian presence in the indigenous realm is depicted in some codices painted during the sixteenth century. The Lienzo de Jucutácato, associated with the convent at Tiripitío, describes the evangelization of Tierra Caliente in Michoacán. The third section of the Codex Azoyú, from the region of Tlapa, Guerrero, recounts the work of Fray Gabriel Cortés and other Augustinian friars.

Like the Franciscans, the Augustinians were interested in the education of the native elite, as demonstrated by the presence of Antonio Huitzimengari, lord of Michoacán, at the Augustinian college in Tiripitío. This educational center was also distinguished for instruction in manual arts and music and trained many indigenous artists who worked throughout Michoacán. Another Augustinian activity was the foundation of hospitals, such as their collaboration with Vasco de Quiroga in his utopian experiments in the hospital community of Santa Fé.

The Augustinians often installed Christian elements in existing indigenous sanctuaries. At Chalma, for example,

Augustinian Monastery of Malinalco, Mexico. Sixteenth-century façade of church and cloister (c.1560–1580). *Photograph courtesy of Jeanette Favrot Peterson.*

the image of the crucified Christ took the place of an ancient cult dedicated to Oxtoteotl, lord of the caves, an advocation of the god Tezcatlipoca. This sanctuary was increased by a *mestizo* hermit and lay brother, Bartolomé de Torres. Other Augustinian images, such as the Christs of Ixmiquilpan and Totolapan, had an enormous impact among *mestizos* and *criollos* when they were transferred from indigenous towns to Mexico City.

The Augustinians also stand out as scholars of native languages. Fray Agustín de la Coruña wrote at least two Christian *doctrinas* (catechisms) in Nahuatl and a group of pious songs for the Indians of Chilapa. Fray Juan de Guevara and Fray Juan de la Cruz composed *doctrinas* in Huastec, and the latter compiled a grammar of that language. Fray Martín de Rada produced an *arte*, or grammar, of Otomí. In the seventeenth century, Fray Diego de Basalenque wrote a Christian *doctrina*, an *arte*, and a vocabulary in the Matlatzinca language and an *arte* in Tarascan.

The order played an important role in the defense of indigenous rights from a theological perspective. Fray Alonso de la Vera Cruz, master of theology and cofounder of the University of Mexico, formulated concepts on the injustice of wars of conquest; his attacks on the *encomienda* system and the excessive tribute levied on Indians were the same as those used by Fray Bartolomé de las Casas. He also wrote important texts attacking the bishops' collection of tithes from the Indians. His study of the administration of the sacrament of marriage is basic for theology concerning Native Americans.

Nevertheless, the Augustinians evinced little interest in the pre-Hispanic world. We have only a few *relaciones geográficas* from them reporting on the language and administration of their communities, in a series written in 1571 at the Crown's request. An exception is a *relación* of 1554 on the way the Indians of Meztitlán paid tribute before the Spaniards arrived, composed by a Dutch Augustinian, Nicolás de Witte or de San Pablo. This lack of interest in Indian traditions became more pronounced in most seventeenth-century Augustinian chronicles. The first of these, by Fray Juan de Grijalva, was printed in 1621 and is dedicated to discussing the Augustinians' work among the Indians. Fray Juan characterizes them as barbarous and their religion as inspired by the devil, not meriting the least attention. The Christians among them, in contrast, are considered good-natured but childish. The second published chronicle, by Fray Diego de Basalenque in Michoacán, also says little about the indigenous world. Nevertheless, this chronicler was a defender of the Indians against abuses that occurred during the process of *congregaciones* (resettlement in towns during the late sixteenth century); his pro-Indian voice, as well as his knowledge of native languages (exceptional among the Augustinians of the day), made him an exceptional thinker for his time. The Augustinians of the seventeenth and eighteenth centuries had more interest in the defense of their order's privileges vis-à-vis the secular clergy, who disputed their control of Indian parishes, than in the situation of their spiritual charges.

[*See also* Missionization, *overview article.*]

BIBLIOGRAPHY

Brinckmann, Lutz. *Die Augustinerrelationen Nueva España 1571–1573: Analyse eines zensus Manuskripts des 16 Jahrhunderts.* Hamburg, 1969. Quantitative demographic analysis of the *Relaciones geográficas* from communities administered by the Augustinians in the sixteenth century.

Ennis, Arthur J. *Fray Alonso de la Vera Cruz, O.S.A., 1507–1584: A*

Study of His Life and His Contribution to the Religious and Intellectual Affairs of Early Mexico. Louvain, 1957. The best study on the life and thought of Fray Alonso placed within the cultural and social context of his time.

Jaramillo, Roberto, comp. *Monumenta historica mexicana, seculum XVI.* Mexico City, 1993. First volume of a series containing unpublished or less-known documents concerning the Augustinians in Mexico, including, among others, the *relación* of Nicolás de Witte or de San Pablo about Metztitlán.

Rubial García, Antonio. *El convento augustino y la sociedad colonial, 1533–1630.* Mexico City, 1989. Study of the organization of the order's convents and parishes and changes it suffered while adapting to New Spain.

Vera Cruz, Alonso de la. *The Writings of Alonso de la Vera Cruz: The Original Texts with English Translation.* 5 vols. Edited by Ernest J. Burrus. Rome and St. Louis, Mo., 1968–1976. Collection and English translation of some of this Augustinian's theological and philosophical works.

ANTONIO RUBIAL GARCÍA
Translated from Spanish by Scott Sessions

AUTOSACRIFICE AND BLOODLETTING. On 8 January 1546, the *bachiller* Cristóbal de Lujo, *promotor fiscal* of the Inquisition, charged that a Mixtec noble named Don Juan, although ostensibly converted to Christianity, had recently "sacrificed blood taken from his ears and private parts with stone needles and blades, offering it to his idols in order to obtain knowledge about them, and to learn of the things of the past from the priests, and to ensure fortune and success in his undertakings" (Archivo General de la Nación, *Inquisición* 37, exp. II). The accused was deemed deserving of punishment for having reverted to pre-Conquest "pagan" ways, because the Roman Catholic church perceived as heretical this venerable pre-Hispanic practice, now called "autosacrifice" (the act of piercing one's own body with a sharp instrument for the purpose of making a blood offering). It thus disappeared by the end of the Colonial period.

Evidence of Mesoamerican autosacrifice appears in the archaeological record as early as the Late Middle Preclassic period. Stingray spines, often used for bloodletting, have been found at the Zapotec site of San José Mogote in Oaxaca, in burials dating from 850 to 500 BCE; a jade replica appeared in an elite Olmec tomb at La Venta in Tabasco, dating to about 400 BCE. For the ensuing centuries until the 1521 Spanish conquest of Mexico, we have archaeological, iconographic, and documentary evidence that bloodletting was being performed by most Mesoamerican peoples.

The instruments, like the parts of the body pierced for autosacrifice, varied from place to place through time. Stingray spines and obsidian or flint blades remained popular throughout, although animal and bird bones were also used. At the time of the Conquest, Aztec elites in Central Mexico often pierced their bodies with sharpened jag-

uar bones; commoners usually relied on maguey thorns. The elite Aztec inserted their used bloodletters into a plaited grass ball (*zacatapayolli*), which was publicly displayed for a time before the instruments were stored—in the case of the ruler, in a handsomely carved stone box. The bloodied thorns of the commoners, in contrast, were apparently discarded, while those used by priests were ritually burned in a special hearth at the ceremonial precinct of the city. Bloodletters have also been found in caches and in the offerings for building foundations.

The sixteenth-century Dominican friar Diego Durán in his *Book of the Gods and Rites* (Norman, Okla., 1971) says that the Aztec had "rules," determining the part of the body to be bled, and that these varied from town to town and from temple to temple. Aztec priests at the main temple had permanent notches in the outer edges of their ears as a result of their nightly bloodletting exercises; some of the blood they released was left smeared over their temples. Aztec priests are depicted in Colonial-era manuscripts piercing their tongues, thighs, and calves, and there are reports that others chose to bleed their penises, some going so far as to split it in two. The last practice was also documented by horrified Spanish observers living among the Maya in sixteenth-century Yucatán and Guatemala. The practice had a precedent in the Classic period: Maya imagery includes numerous depictions of elite males perforating their penises. In some of these scenes, the instrument used is elaborately decorated, as well as personified—perhaps signifying that it was regarded as a deity. In some scenes, the ruler scatters the blood he has gathered with his outstretched hand.

Although sixteenth-century sources indicate that bloodletting was usually expected of every man, woman, and child, only the Classic Maya depicted women performing the act. These women are invariably wives or mothers of a male ruler, who typically accompanies them in the image. The most famous example is Lintel 24 from Yaxchilan (Figure 1). In his sixteenth-century *Relación de las cosas de Yucatán*, the Franciscan bishop Diego de Landa reports that blood-spattered paper strips used in autosacrificial rites by the Conquest-period Yucatec Maya were eventually burned. The smoke from the burning bloodletters and bloodied papers was thought to transmit nourishment to the gods, since blood was perceived as an analogue of both fertilizing water and semen. Lintel 25 on the same Yaxchilan building shows large scrolls, representing smoke as it rises from a container filled with bloody papers.

The act of passing a cord through the tongue appears to have been restricted to royal women among the Classic Maya. In the Late Postclassic Maya *Codex Madrid*, male deities pass a cord through their bifurcated penises, and Landa relates a sixteenth-century Yucatec rite in which

FIGURE 1. Lady K'abal-Xoc performing auto-sacrifice by passing a cord with thorns through her tongue in honor of her husband Itzam-Balam I [Shield Jaguar I], who stands before her with a burning torch. Lintel 24, Yaxchilan, Mexico. Late Classic Maya. Limestone 130.1 × 86.3 × 10.1 cm. *Drawing by Ian Graham, courtesy of Peabody Museum of Archaeology and Ethnology, Harvard University.*

young men did the same. The practice is also documented for the Mixtec of western Oaxaca and Guerrero. The Aztec are said to have passed "straws" through their self-inflicted wounds, one for each transgression to be offset. The goal in all cases was probably the same: to increase the amount of blood that would flow. These efforts may have increased the risk of infection, though there is indirect evidence that the risk was reduced by application of a medicinal substance at the conclusion of the rite. Nonetheless, people occasionally died from such infections.

As Cristóbal de Lujo's complaint against Don Juan indicates, autosacrifice was seen as a form of payment to the gods for their assistance in ensuring the continuation of the cosmos, good health, life, and success in endeavors ranging from marriage to craftsmanship to food produc-

tion. It could be performed either as a petition for help or as an expression of gratitude for favors already received. *Maceua*, the root of the Aztec word for the act, *tlamaceua-liztli*, means "to deserve something," a clear reference to the fundamental concept of reciprocity between humans and their gods.

The Preclassic appearance of bloodletters in elite burials shows that Mesoamerican elites from early times adapted the ideology of autosacrifice to their own interests. At the time of the Conquest, the Aztec paramount rulers were performing autosacrifice at their election and again on installation in office, as a sign of their worthiness to assume political power. Together with their leading military officers, they also ritually shed their blood in thanksgiving for victory on the battlefield. Aztec youths, in training for the military, were required to shed their blood on a regular basis without expressing any sign of pain, since the ability to do so connoted their bravery and fitness to advance in the military hierarchy.

Tlaxcalan priests appear to have let their blood to induce visions in which they could communicate directly with the gods. Since their blood loss was typically accompanied by fasting, the release of certain chemicals in the body may have facilitated such experiences. Among the Classic Maya, the visions experienced by rulers or their wives were recorded in the form of stone carvings. In these images, the visions are represented as huge serpents, now referred to as "Vision Serpents" or "Blood Serpents." The function of Classic Maya royal bloodletting appears, however, to have differed somewhat from that elsewhere in Mesoamerica. To judge by the stone carvings, bloodletting by Maya royals called up their ancestors and so regenerated or gave birth to the gods. The Aztec, for their part, told how their god Quetzalcoatl created the present race of humankind by sprinkling blood from his penis on the bones of a previous people.

Both the Maya and the Aztec shed their own blood at the completion of a major temporal cycle. The Aztec did so during the time of the New Fire ceremony, for example, when the fifty-two-year calendrical "century" ended and there was fear that the universe might come to a cataclysmic end. Maya rulers let their blood during what we now call "period endings," which could mark the successful completion of a *katun* (twenty-year period), *baktun* (four-hundred-year period), or even longer time cycle. On those occasions, autosacrifice was intended to encourage the safe transition between the old cycle and the new, and thus the continuation of life.

[*See also* Sacrifice and Ritual Violence.]

BIBLIOGRAPHY

Furst, Peter. "Fertility, Vision Quest, and Autosacrifice: Some Thoughts on Ritual Blood-letting among the Maya." In *The Art, Iconography, and Dynastic History of Palenque, Part III*, edited by Merle Greene Robertson, pp. 181–193. Pebble Beach, Calif., 1976. Overview of evidence for a link between Classic Maya autosacrifice and visions.

Joralemon, David. "Ritual Blood-sacrifice among the Ancient Maya: Part I." In *Primera mesa redonda de Palenque, Part II*, edited by Merle Greene Robertson, pp. 59–75. Pebble Beach, Calif., 1974. A study of the penis-perforation rites of the Classic Maya, which identifies the art motif representing the perforator and argues that it was deified.

Klein, Cecelia F. "The Ideology of Autosacrifice at the Templo Mayor." In *The Aztec Templo Mayor*, edited by Elizabeth Hill Boone, pp. 293–370. Washington, D.C., 1987. A comprehensive examination of Aztec depictions of ceremonial bloodletting and the functions and meanings of the rite.

Nájera C., Martha Ilia. *El don de la sangre en el equilibrio cósmico: El sacrificio y el autosacrificio sangriento entre los antiguos mayas*. Mexico, 1987. Analysis of documentary and visual evidence of autosacrifice by the Classic Maya.

Nuttall, Zelia. "A Penitential Rite of the Ancient Mexicans." *Papers of the Peabody Museum of American Archaeology and Ethnology, Harvard University* 1.7 (1908), 439–465, plus plates. Pioneering work on bloodletting in pre-Hispanic Mexico, with emphasis on the Mixtec and Aztec.

Schele, Linda, and Mary Ellen Miller. *The Blood of Kings: Dynasty and Ritual in Maya Art*. Fort Worth, Tex., 1986; repr. New York, 1999. The first popularization of scholarly ideas about the ideology of bloodletting among Classic Maya dynasts.

Stuart, David. "Royal Auto-sacrifice among the Maya: A Study of Image and Meaning." *Res: Anthropology and Aesthetics* 7/8 (1984), 6–20. Identifies some of the key events and motifs related to Classic Maya autosacrifice, including the scattering ritual, the Blood Serpent, and birth.

Stuart, David. "Blood Symbolism in Maya Iconography." In *Maya Iconography*, edited by Elizabeth P. Benson and Gillett G. Griffin, pp. 175–221. Princeton, 1988. Expands on Stuart's 1984 study, with special attention to the Paddler Gods, the Celestial Monster, and the Quadripartite God.

CECELIA F. KLEIN

AZCATITLÁN, CODEX. The name of this important sixteenth-century Mexica pictorial manuscript was suggested by its first editor, Robert H. Barlow, who erroneously interpreted the anthill on page 2 as the glyph for "Aztlán." In the Bibliothèque Nationale of Paris, where it is housed, it is known as *Histoire mexicaine, [Manuscrit] Mexicain 59–64*. It belonged to the Milanese nobleman Lorenzo Boturini Benaduci (1702–1755), who mentions it in his *Idea de una nueva historia general de la América septentrional*. Later it was part of the collections of Joseph-Marius-Alexis Aubin and of Eugène Goupil in France. At the latter's death in 1898, it was donated to the Bibliothèque Nationale. Of the twenty-eight original leaves (21 by 28 centimeters), in European paper, three are lost (between pp. 8–9, 44–45, and 46–47). The writing of the glosses in Nahuatl suggests a date in the last third of the sixteenth century, but the glosses may not be contemporary with the drawings, since the glossarist did not always understand them correctly.

The codex has three sections: (1) the migration of the Mexica from Aztlán to Tenochitlan and Tlatelolco; (2) the rulers of Tenochtitlan from Acamapichtli to Motecuhzoma II, with their conquests and other important events of their reigns; and (3) the Spanish conquest and the beginning of the Colonial period. The unknown author or authors present information not only on the Mexica-Tenochca and Mexica-Tlatelolca, but occasionally also on Azcapotzalco, Tetzcoco, and even Chalco and Acolman, which may suggest that they used data from codices of different provenances, as was customary during the Colonial period. Barlow suggested that the dynastic section was the recollections of a single individual—perhaps an old warrior—because only a selection of conquests is registered. However, the timespan covered is much too long for a single individual, and the conquests figured in his-

The birth of Huitzilopochtli at Coatepec during the wanderings of the Aztec. *After the Codex. Drawing courtesy of Michel Graulich.*

torical documents are seldom exhaustive. He also suggests a provenance from the area Cuauhtitlan-Xaltocan-Tlatelolco and from the same workshop at the *Codex Cozcatzin*. The latter opinion is not substantiated. For the attribution to the Cuauhtitlan area, Barlow relies on rather uncertain interpretation of a scene he places in Cuauhtitlan (p. 22). To the contrary, everything in the codex points to an origin in Mexico-Tenochtitlan-Tlatelolco.

The drawings, by two different hands—one more schooled, and the other at times more daring—are sometimes unfinished, and the colors are scarce and light. European influence is obvious in the artists' (especially the schooled author of the first and last pages) endeavors to suggest volume and space by oblique views, shading, and overlapping; also Colonial are the varied postures, the animated groups with figures in frontal and back views, and the landscapes, especially two complex compositions figuring the wanderings through mountains and fishing in the lake of Mexico-Tenochtitlan. The drawings are so allusive that they may be incomprehensible to those unfamiliar with the mythical or historical events narrated (e.g., the victory of Huitzilopochtli at Coatepec, p. 6, or

Tlaloc welcoming the Mexica in the lake, p. 12): they served as memoranda for trained reciters.

The drawings referring to the migrations are more detailed, complete, and coherent than those in other codices. Their content is particularly close to Torquemada's version of the migration; less so to the codices *Aubin, Boturini,* and *Mexicanus,* to Chimalpahin's *Memorial breve,* the *Historia de los mexicanos por sus pinturas,* and the *Anales de Tlatelolco;* and still less to the *Anales de Cuauhtitlan,* the *Crónica Mexicáyotl,* and the *Crónica X.* Of particular interest are the information on Aztlán, divided into the same four quarters as Mexico; the events of Huey Colhuacan, Chicomóztoc, and Coatepec (this is the only pictorial source alluding to the myth of Huitzilopochtli's birth and victory there); the battles of Chapultepec, Xochimilco, and Colhuacan; the founding of Mexico; and the coronation of the first rulers of Tenochtitlan and Tlatelolco. Some important mythical fixtures and episodes are omitted: the conflict with Huitzilopochtli's witch sister Malinalxochitl; the shattered tree and the separation from the other migrating groups; the sacrifice of the Mimixcoa fallen from the sky; and the struggle against

Malinalxochitl's son Copil. These may have seemed too mythical for a "historical" account. The second part of the codex is interesting because of its peculiar series of conquests and the inclusion of other events such as plagues of grasshoppers, solemn rituals (e.g., the 1507 New Fire ceremony), and the construction of important buildings. The three incomplete scenes dedicated to the Spanish conquest center on the meeting between Motecuhzoma II and Cortés, an intriguing battle scene including Motecuhzoma's death, and episodes of the siege of Mexico. The Colonial part is the most difficult to elucidate because it refers to several unknown local events; it awaits in-depth study, as do the conquests of the dynastic part and several details of the migrations.

[*See also* Pictorial Manuscripts.]

BIBLIOGRAPHY

Codex Azcatitlan. Introduction by Michel Graulich; comments by Robert H. Barlow, revised by M. Graulich; translated into Spanish by Leonardo López Luján; translated into French and edited by D. Michelet. Paris, 1995.

MICHEL GRAULICH

AZTEC. The use of the term "Aztec" to denote the Mexica people is incorrect, as Robert Barlow pointed out in 1949. This erroneous designation stems from the early nineteenth-century work of the naturalist Alexander von Humboldt, who established a strong tradition of usage. The name derives from Aztlán, the Mexica's legendary place of origin. The reasons for their leaving Aztlán vary in the sources: their patron deity, Huitzilopochtli, commanded it; or they were oppressed there by the dominant people, the real "Aztecs." At the beginning of their migration, the Mexica assumed a new identity by order of their patron deity, leaving behind the name that connected them with the inhabitants of Aztlán.

The problem of the name "Aztec" involves not only historical impropriety but also ambiguity, since it has been used to designate ceramic types that have nothing to do with either the Mexica or the Aztec. At times, all the inhabitants of the Basin of Mexico in the Late Postclassic period have been called "Aztec," while at other times the term has included the culturally related inhabitants of the Puebla-Tlaxcala valleys. The term has been used to designate speakers of the Nahuatl language, or the language itself. It has been applied to the peoples who made up the Triple Alliance and has been extended to Mesoamericans who were not Mayan, or not from Oaxaca, and so on. In sum, this vague term, "Aztec," with its historical, ceramic, linguistic, cultural, ethnic, and political applications, invokes confusion when it is not precisely clear to whom it is referring.

Therefore, the term "Mexica" is used here to denote two groups: first, the peoples who are considered, historically, to have come from Aztlán and who founded the two settlements of Tenochtitlan and Tlatelolco (each known as Mexico); and second, those who inhabited these cities, regardless of whether they were descendants of the original founders.

Origin, Migration, and Rise of the Mexica in the Basin of Mexico. Accounts of the Mexica's origin—like those told by other Mesoamerican peoples—contain many supernatural sites, personages, and episodes. The reason for this joining of earthly and divine history stems from the search for legitimacy in the political context of the period, in which land tenure was justified above all through grants made by patron deities to their protected peoples.

Aztlán, the place of origin, appears in the documentary sources as a lacustrine or fluvial environment. [*See* Aztlán.] The Mexica asserted that they had left it under the advice of their patron deity, who guided them to a promised land. Sources say that the migration began at the beginning of the twelfth century and lasted for more than two hundred years, during which time the migrants traveled in groups called *calpultin* (singular, *calpulli*).

Around 1325, the Mexica managed to establish themselves on a few islands in the western part of Lake Tetzcoco. Although their limited land resources were made even scarcer by political conflicts in the surrounding communities, they sought to develop an economy based on lacustrine fishing, hunting, and gathering. On this site they founded the settlement of Tenochtitlan; thirteen years later, divided by land conflicts, some dissidents left to occupy a smaller island to the north, where they established Tlatelolco. The scarcity of available land forced the Mexica to begin reclaiming land from the lake, constructing arable parcels with their knowledge of *chinampa* agriculture; thus they built up fertile plots of marshland that extended into the lake. [*See* Chinampa Agriculture.]

Land Division and Distribution: The Calpulli. The Mexica territory was divided into four segments and a center occupied by the temple of Huitzilopochtli and other religious buildings. In each segment, land was parceled out and adjudicated by the various *calpultin*. These groups together formed the organizational foundation of the societies of the period. The documentary sources, however, disagree as to the number of the Mexica founding *calpultin*: between seven and twenty are mentioned.

Each *calpulli* consisted of a group of families who supposedly were united by a common deified ancestor, the *calpulteotl*. The ancestor had given his descendants a specialized profession, which augmented the cohesion of the group's members in production. The *calpulli* tended toward endogamy and endeavored to live in a coterminous territory. Thus, in the city, each *calpulli* occupied a ward or neighborhood. Considered the property of the group, the ward was divided up and distributed among the constituent families, each of which was given the right to exploit the land.

The *calpulli*, once integrated into the politico-administrative order of a city, was ruled by two types of government. The first type handled internal affairs and was run by the *teachcauh* ("elder brother"), assisted by a council. The *teachcauh* was a traditional governor named from among the members of the specific lineage of the *calpulli*. These internal affairs included the distribution of land, the establishment of temples and schools for particular rites, the defense of the group, the census, and the distribution of tributary obligations. The second type of government dealt with the affairs of the central government. The ruler in this case was the *tecuhtli*, a delegate named by the king. The *tecuhtli* was judge, military chief, tax collector, and mediator between the *calpulli* and the palace. In relation to the central government, the *calpulli* constituted a tributary unit, served as a military squadron under the command of the *tecuhtli*, and participated as a group in general religious obligations.

First Century of Lacustrine Life. One of the principal problems the Mexica faced was their lack of political recognition. In order to interact as peers with their neighbors, they had to be constituted into *tlatocayotl*, or kingdoms; to achieve this, they began to seek connections to the nearest dynasties. Finally the Mexica-Tenochca acquired Acamapichtli, a member of the royal family of Culhuacan, as their ruler; the Mexica-Tlatelolca placed on their throne Cuacuauhpitzahuac, one of the sons of the Tepanec king of Azcapotzalco. The two new kings governed in difficult circumstances in their impoverished, dependent kingdoms. The location of the islands they occupied placed the Mexica under the dominion of the Tepanecs of Azcapotzalco, to which they periodically delivered considerable tribute.

The precarious situation of the two nascent kingdoms improved with their participation as minor allies in the Azcapotzalco king's campaigns against his neighbors. The Mexica obtained tribute for their conquests and soon received a favorable informal agreement from their powerful allies. The political situation, however, took a turn that offered the opportunity for the Mexica to change sides and attack the Tepanecs as auxiliaries of their old enemies from Tetzcoco. Luck favored them: around 1430, Azcapotzalco was destroyed, and the Mexica became one of the dominant peoples in the Basin of Mexico.

Establishment of the *Excan Tlatoloyan*. With Azcapotzalco vanquished, the victors attempted to reestablish in the Basin the political order that had been broken by Tepanec ambitions. To achieve this, they reinstated a supra-state organization, which, according to tradition, had existed since the Toltec period: the *excan tlatoloyan* ("tribunal of three places"), also known as the "Triple Alliance." It consisted of three kings (*tlatoque*; singular, *tlatoani*) who functioned as representatives of the three principal ethnic groups of the region. Despite its name, the *excan tlatoloyan*'s attributes went beyond the mere exercise of jurisdiction. Its principal function was that of a military confederation. Neighboring peoples had to place themselves under its protection, for which the protected communities had to reciprocate with tribute. Communities that did not accept the *excan tlatoloyan*'s protection were considered hostile, and war was declared against them. Once defeated by the hegemonic powers, they were incorporated and forced to pay tribute to the victors. The alliance was more or less an instrument of hegemonic expansion in the hands of three powerful states and their allies, who organized the campaigns of conquest and established the rules for distributing the tribute seized from the vanquished.

The establishment of the *excan tlatoloyan* did not benefit the Mexica-Tlatelolca. In the division of responsibilities, the king of Tetzcoco retained his prewar standing, Mexico-Tenochtitlan took the place of Culhuacan, and Tlacopan—a Tepanec state that had participated little in the battle—inherited the position of Azcapotzalco. Mexico-Tlatelolco did not receive anything from the arrangement, which added to the enmity existing between the Tenochca and the Tlatelolca.

The three allied capitals immediately organized campaigns of conquest, first within and later beyond the Basin. Operations were divided among the members, and it was up to the Mexica-Tenochca to organize and direct the military campaigns. This gave them an advantage, since their orientation toward warfare favored their own interests of commercial expansion.

Mexico-Tenochtitlan's Internal Reorganization. Mexico-Tenochtitlan, once launched into the adventure of military expansion, had to change its internal organization. The first measures taken by its rulers Itzcoatl (r. 1427–1440) and Motecuhzoma Ilhuicamina (r. 1440–1469) were aimed at strengthening the central authority and implanting militarism. Itzcoatl, for example, affirmed the central authority by means such as confiscating and burning books accessible to commoners. He said it was not appropriate for everyone to be familiar with the codices, because there were some books that corrupted people with their lies and magic arts, causing many "to be taken as gods." His words reveal that the action was directed against the popular religious leaders whose sources of authority were in the sacred books. The new laws awarded goods, positions, and distinctions to the valiant in campaigns; they established a dress code that corresponded to military merit; they dignified public positions with exaggerated ceremonies; they instituted tribunals according to the rank of individuals; they organized public finances; they increased the number of priests and exempted them from taxes; and they intervened in the intellectual life of the *calpultin* by establishing the content of education, especially the lyrics of the songs taught in the schools.

Social Stratification. These reforms widened the gap between commoners (*macehualtin*; singular, *macehualli*) and nobles (*pipiltin*; singular, *pilli*). The principal difference between the two was in the paying of tribute. The majority of the population was made up of individuals free to arrange their own means of production as cultivators, artisans, merchants, or lenders of services. The *calpulli*'s lands were inalienable, and families made use of them. Nevertheless, the *macehualtin* had to contribute to sustaining the state with taxes they delivered in the form of goods and personal labor, participating in the construction and maintenance of public works.

The *pipiltin*, in contrast, were exempt from taxes, since their functions as administrators, judges, warriors of rank, or priests of the upper hierarchy were considered their contributions to public service. The nobility carried out most government activities, citing as qualifications lineal privileges, their education in rigorous schools called *calmecac*, and the rectitude they acquired in a family life with high moral values. Although distinguished *macehualtin* could achieve administrative, military, or scholarly positions of importance, this was the exception rather than the rule.

In addition to this distinction between *macehualtin* tributaries and *pipiltin* exempt functionaries, there were differences in their access to goods, their family structures, and the juridical regimes applicable to each class. For example, *pipiltin* rewarded for their military deeds could receive tribute generated in some of the conquered lands, called *pillalli*. They had the right to enter the royal palace and to use or consume certain prestige items, such as painted vases, cotton clothing, footwear, cacao, and jewels. Noblemen also practiced polygamy. The penal code was, however, much more rigid for the *pipiltin*, and they received severe penalties for acts not considered criminal or not warranting serious punishment if committed by *macehualtin*.

In the most inferior position were slaves (*tlatlacotin*), individuals obligated to deliver their labor to others as a consequence of a legal sentence, a debt, or a contract. They retained their basic rights of corporeal integrity, family, property, the recovery of their freedom, and even the exclusive execution of labors specified in their contract. They also maintained the right of not being transferred to another master without their consent. Nevertheless, the nonfulfillment of their obligations could reduce them to the unfortunate status of "collar slaves," which permitted their sale or conversion into sacrificial victims. Slavery, however, never constituted an important source of labor in pre-Hispanic Central Mexico.

Internal Political Organization. The basic political unit in the Basin of Mexico was the city (*altepetl*), and the most common type of government was the kingdom (*tlatocayotl*). The supreme command of the *tlatocayotl* fell to the *tlatoani* ("king"), a ruler elected for life from among the sons and grandsons of previous kings by a council of high nobles. The *cihuacoatl* served as his adjunct and also ruled for life; he acceded to the position by royal designation and was chosen from among the members of a specific lineage. The authority exercised by the *tlatoani* was very great, since he was considered the divinity's representative on earth. The concept of the Dual God made it necessary that the *tlatoani* share power with his coadjutor. Thus, the *tlatoani* incarnated celestial authority, while the *cihuacoatl* was the delegate of the terrestrial, feminine part of the cosmos.

Under the *tlatoani* and the *cihuacoatl* were councils who carried out various jurisdictional, administrative, military, and religious tasks. One of these councils, for example, consisted of the four governors of the four quadrants of Mexico-Tenochtitlan; another was made up of the grand electors charged with naming the successor of a deceased *tlatoani*.

The concept of cosmic duality was reproduced in many sectors of the government. There were two head priests, one dedicated to the sun deity and the other to the rain god; two supreme generals, whose names indicated their respective functions of commanding the armies and administering military resources; and two functionaries charged with the public finances, one to direct tax collection, the other to guard the proceeds.

Hegemonic Expansion. The restructuring of Itzcoatl and Motecuhzoma Ilhuicamina guided feverish military activity which was maintained until the time of the Spanish invasion. Motecuhzoma's successor, Axayacatl (r. 1469–1481), was one of the greatest conquerors. It fell to him to confront the sister city, Mexico-Tlatelolco, whose *tlatoani*, Moquihuix, died during the war; with the city's defeat, its autonomy was forever lost.

The armies of the *excan tlatoloyan* advanced in all directions. In the early years of the sixteenth century, after the reign of Ahuitzotl (r. 1486–1502), the Triple Alliance's dominions stretched from sea to sea, and a breach had been opened that allowed Mexica merchants free passage to the distant lands of Socunusco. Its forms of domination, however, were not firm. In most cases, the vanquished communities retained their own governments and their obligations were limited to the payment of tribute. The victors worried more about immediate economic profits than the consolidation of power, since they were confident in the military efficacy of their armies.

It was common for tribute to be stipulated at the moment of defeat. The vanquished were obligated to deliver products of the region, strictly appraised, to allow the armies of the *excan tlatoloyan* to pass freely through their territory, to remain within the trading radius of the victors, and to contribute men and material resources in the campaigns of expansion when required. Often some of the arable lands of the vanquished were encumbered so that the victorious kings could deliver their proceeds as awards to nobles who had distinguished themselves in combat. The amount of tribute assessed depended on the wealth of the vanquished, the resistance they had presented to the *excan tlatoloyan*, and prior relations; there was a rule that those who rebelled after being incorporated had to pay higher amounts.

Economic Rise of the Victors. The enormous conquered territory generated a constant flow of riches to the three capitals and their allies. Mexico-Tenochtitlan was the major beneficiary because its direction of warfare allowed it to lead campaigns into the best territories for supplying raw materials to its artisans and the best markets for its merchants. The *pochteca*, professional merchants belonging to specific *calpultin* and protected by the patron deity of merchants, possessed a complex organization because of the interrelationships among their *calpultin* of various cities. One of their most important centers of activity was Mexico-Tlatelolco. During Ahuitzotl's rule Tlatelolca merchants were amply favored by the state, and by way of compensation they served as spies, as ambassadors, and sporadically as combatants. Ahuitzotl had a stake in their profits, since he consigned goods to *pochteca* embarking on commercial expeditions.

Another favored group comprised the military professionals. Although all able-bodied males had to provide military service, those who proved valiant in war were selected to form units maintained at the expense of the central government. Undoubtedly, this was an onerous charge for the state.

Warrior Gods. The militarism characteristic of Late Postclassic communities reflected a religious emphasis on warfare. The Mexica were the prototype of the communities given to the sacred mission of maintaining cosmic equilibrium: they supported their bellicose actions religiously—attributing them to the obligation of sustaining the sun with the blood and hearts of their vanquished enemies. Although human sacrifice had ancient ritual forms in Mesoamerica, the hegemonic peoples of the Late Postclassic carried its practice to the extreme. Armies tried to capture great numbers of enemy captives in combat, to deliver them as victims (*mamaltin*) to the temples.

Among the myths that supported the exacerbation of bloody rites was that of the successive ages through which the creation of the world had passed. A god was charged with ruling the world, as the sun dominated each age, and on four previous occasions an age had ended in a great catastrophe. Humans had been born during the Fifth Sun, called "4 Movement" (*Nahui Ollin*), the definitive and ultimate age of the world's existence. Like the four earlier suns, "4 Movement" was also doomed to disappear. The Mexica assumed the mission of prolonging its existence, fortifying it with the delivery of victims.

Warrior Art. Mexica art was heir to important Mesoamerican traditions, mainly the Toltec and Tlaxcala-Puebla styles. Its originality stemmed both from the grandeur that political and economic ascendancy allowed and from its militaristic orientation. Militarism was manifested in three levels: a defensive urbanism adapted to the lacustrine sites of Mexico-Tenochtitlan and Mexico-Tlatelolco; an architecture appropriate to magnificent, multitudinous, and bloody rituals complemented with large-scale representations in music and dance; and an arts complex that was awe-inspiring, severe, vigorous, militarist, obsessed with death, and often monumental.

Mexico-Tlatelolco to the north and Mexico-Tenochtitlan to the south formed a single urban island locale connected to the mainland by straight causeways and aqueducts. Canals, streets on firm ground, or a combination of both served as its internal arteries. In the center of both cities were groups of religious buildings with adjacent government palaces. The great marketplace of Tlatelolco was one of the most renowned in Mesoamerica.

The largest architectural work was the Templo Mayor (Great Temple) of Mexico-Tenochtitlan, which, with the buildings comprising the ritual precinct, formed the heart of the city. [*See* Templo Mayor.] Its principal pyramid was divided in half and topped with two temples as a reflection of cosmic duality. The south side corresponded to the sun god, Huitzilopochtli, and the north side to the rain god, Tlaloc. Mexica sculpture stands out for its monumentality. Their image of the mother goddess, Coatlicue, is a terrifying depiction of the one who received all sustenance and to whom humans had to pay with their lives.

Splendor and Decline. Motecuhzoma Xocoyotzin (r. 1502–1520) was the *tlatoani* who ruled during the height of the Mexica florescence. His role was to consolidate a kingdom that had grown exceptionally quickly. The political and military power of the Mexica-Tenochca was such that in later times the other two member states of the *excan tlatoloyan* suffered greatly from their predominance.

At the peak of its glory, however, Mexico-Tenochtitlan suffered the invasion of Europeans. Many of the subject communities, weary of the abuses of Mexica domination, allied with the Spaniards and hastened the destruction of their old oppressors. In 1521, Mexico-Tenochtitlan and Mexico-Tlatelolco fell to the Spanish conquerors.

[*See also* Mexica; Nahuatl; Templo Mayor; Tenochtitlan; Tlatelolco; Triple Alliance.]

BIBLIOGRAPHY

Barlow, Robert. *The Extent of the Empire of the Culhua Mexica.* Berkeley, 1949. Classic study of the formation of Mexica hegemony and the territorial dominion of the Triple Alliance.

Berdan, Frances F. *The Aztecs of Central Mexico: An Imperial Society.* New York, 1982. Well-documented synthesis of Mexica history and culture, by a specialist.

Berdan, Frances F., Richard E. Blanton, Elizabeth Hill Boone, Mary G. Hodge, Michael E. Smith, and Emily Umberger. *Aztec Imperial Strategies.* Washington, D.C., 1996. One of the most complete collections of studies dedicated to the politics of the Triple Alliance and the extent of its dominions.

Boone, Elizabeth Hill, ed. *The Aztec Templo Mayor.* Washington, D.C., 1987. Collection of specialists' studies of religious, architectural, iconographic, and artistic aspects of the Mexica.

Boone, Elizabeth Hill. *The Aztec World.* Montreal, 1994. Well-illustrated synthesis of Mexica history and culture.

Carrasco, Davíd, and Eduardo Matos Moctezuma. *Moctezuma's Mexico: Visions of the Aztec World.* Niwot, Colo., 1992. Collection of specialists' studies on the cosmovision, urbanism, religion, and political history of the Mexica.

Carrasco, Pedro. "The Peoples of Central Mexico and Their Historical Traditions." In *Handbook of Middle American Indians,* edited by Robert A. Wauchope, vol. 11, pp. 459–473. Austin, Tex., 1971. Brief, authoritative view of the history of the Basin of Mexico during the period of the Mexica, based on many documentary sources.

Carrasco, Pedro. *Estructura político-territorial del Imperio Tenochca: La Triple Alianza de Tenochtitlan, Tetzcoco y Tlacopan.* Mexico City, 1996. One of the most complete studies of the political organization of the Triple Alliance; solid foundation in documentary sources.

Clendinnen, Inga. *Aztecs: An Interpretation.* Cambridge, 1991. General overview of Mexica culture and history.

Conrad, Geoffrey W., and Arthur A. Demarest. *Religion and Empire: The Dynamics of Aztec and Inca Expansionism.* Cambridge, 1984. Comparative interpretation of the religious and political processes leading to hegemonic expansion in the two most developed peoples of the ancient Americas.

Davies, Nigel. *The Aztecs: A History.* London, 1977. Excellent synthesis of Mexica political history.

Graulich, Michel. *Montezuma ou l'apologée et la chute de l'Empire Aztèque.* Paris, 1994. One of the best biographies of the Mexica king who had the misfortune of ruling Tenochtitlan at the time of the Spaniards' arrival.

Hassig, Ross. *Trade, Tribute, and Transportation: The Sixteenth-Century Political Economy of the Valley of Mexico.* Norman, Okla., 1985. Overview of the economic might of the Triple Alliance during its apogee.

Hassig, Ross. *Aztec Warfare, Imperial Expansion, and Political Control.* London, 1988. General overview of the hegemonic expansion of the Mexica and their allies in the Basin of Mexico.

Matos Moctezuma, Eduardo. *The Great Temple of the Aztecs: Treasures of Tenochtitlan.* New York, 1998. Discoveries at the Templo Mayor in Mexico-Tenochtitlan, by the director of the excavations.

Nicholson, H. B., and Eloise Quiñones Keber. *Art of Aztec Mexico: Treasures of Tenochtitlan.* Washington, D.C., 1983. One of the clearest interpretative studies of Mexica art; well illustrated.

Pasztory, Esther. *Aztec Art.* New York, 1983. General study of art of the people in the Basin of Mexico; excellent illustrations.

Sanders, William T., Jeffrey Parsons, and Robert Santley. *The Basin of Mexico: Ecological Process in the Evolution of Civilization.* New York, 1979. Excellent archaeological overview of the Basin of Mexico.

Smith, Michael. *The Aztecs.* Oxford and Cambridge, Mass., 1996. Very good synthesis of Mexica history, society, and customs.

Soustelle, Jacques. *Daily Life of the Aztecs on the Eve of the Spanish Conquest.* Stanford, 1961. Classic study of the life and customs of the Mexica and their contemporaries.

Townsend, Richard F. *The Aztecs.* London, 1992. Well-illustrated, general study of Mexica history, society, and customs.

Weaver, Muriel Porter. *The Aztecs, Maya, and Their Predecessors: Archaeology of Mesoamerica.* 3d ed. San Diego, 1993. General study of Mesoamerican archaeology, situating the Mexica as one of the heirs to a millenarian tradition.

ALFREDO LÓPEZ AUSTIN
Translated from Spanish by Scott Sessions

AZTLÁN. Aztlán stands in Nahuatl mythology as the original homeland from which the Mexica people migrated to the Valley of Mexico. The word *Aztlán* has been alternately translated as meaning "the place of whiteness" or "the place of the herons (or storks)." The narrative of the migration from Aztlán is recorded in many early colonial works such as the *Mapa Sigüenza*, the *Codex Boturini*, and the *Codex Mexicanus*, but the myth is most fully documented in the work of later chroniclers such as Fernando de Alvarado Tezozómoc and Bernal Díaz del Castillo, and especially in Diego Durán's *Historia de las Indias de Nueva España*.

The Mexica's ancestors dwelled in the Seven Caves, known as Chicomóztoc, located in Aztlán. Each cave corresponded to one of the seven groups that lived at Chicomóztoc: the Xochimilco, the Chalca, the Tepanec, the Colhua, the Tlalhuica, the Tlaxcala, and the group that was to become the Mexica. In time, all of these groups left Aztlán, although the last group, the future Mexica, stayed behind for 302 years after the others.

The southward migration of this last group began when their god Huitzilopochtli commanded their priests to move the people to a new home. The god prophesied events that would occur along their journey and promised that at the end they would find a land of plenty that would be recognized by a sign, namely, an eagle devouring a serpent while perched on a cactus. During their eighty-year trek, they faced many trials and obstacles, the most noteworthy of these being their ordeal at Coatepec. At this place, a number of the group decided that this must be their promised homeland and that they should travel no farther. This infuriated Huitzilopochtli, and his retribution was swift; the leaders of the offending faction were killed overnight by heart excision. This portion of the travel narrative is significant because it replays the myth of the birth of Huitzilopochtli—one of the offending leaders killed was a woman named Coyolxauhqui. This mythic trope is repeated again later at Tenochtitlan in the design of the Templo Mayor and the placement of the Coyolxauhqui stone.

After the events of Coatepec, the group adopts the name *Mexica*. Thus, the episode becomes a dividing line in the narrative of the pilgrimage from Aztlán. The section before Coatepec has a more ambiguous or mythic character, and the section following is more concrete and describes the founding of Tenochtitlan. The Mexica used the story of their migration from Aztlán to locate themselves historically and establish their legitimacy among the peoples of the Valley of Mexico.

Diego Durán (1994) tells us that the Mexica ruler Motecuhzoma Iluicamina (1440–1469) attempted to rediscover the location of Aztlán. He consulted with his court historian and sent magicians to find their ancestral homeland. They were able to travel to Aztlán by changing into animal form. Once they arrived, they met with the goddess Coatlique (Huitzilopochtli's mother) and discovered that Aztlán was a place where people never aged.

Durán further reports that Aztlán was believed to be north of Tenochtitlan, near La Florida, referring in Durán's time to what is now northeastern Mexico, southeastern Texas, and present-day Florida.

In recent years, the mythology of Aztlán has been reimagined and has become a powerful political symbol in the United States. The location and nature of Aztlán is a central concern of Chicano nationalism. The term was given its contemporary expression in the Plan Espiritual de Aztlán that was put forward at the Chicano National Liberation Youth Conference in 1969 in Denver. For Chicanos, Aztlán is a multivalent term, referring both to the lands ceded to the United States by Mexico in the Treaty of Guadalupe Hidalgo and to the spiritual and national unity of Chicanos wherever they may live.

BIBLIOGRAPHY

Anaya, Rudolfo A., and Francisco Lomeli, eds. *Aztlan: Essays on the Chicano Homeland*. Albuquerque, N.M., 1989.

Carrasco, Dávid, and Eduardo Matos Moctezuma. *Moctezuma's Mexico: Visions of the Aztec World*, Niwot, Colo., 1992.

Durán, Diego. *The History of the Indies of New Spain*. Translated by Doris Heyden. Norman, Okla., and London, 1994.

León-Portilla, Miguel. *The Aztec Image of Self and Society: An Introduction to Nahua Culture*. Edited by J. Jorge Klor de Alva. Salt Lake City, 1992.

ROBERTO LINT-SAGARENA

B

BACABS. In the sixteenth-century *Relación de las cosas de Yucatán*, Fray Diego de Landa mentions four beings called Bacabs who the Maya believed supported the sky at the four corners of the world. The Bacabs were also said to have caused the flood that destroyed the previous world. According to Diego López Cogolludo, the Bacabs were rain and wind deities as well as sky-bearers; colonial Yucatec texts also describe them as wind gods. In ancient Mesoamerica, quadripartite gods were commonly related to the four-sided maize field and, by extension, to forces of rain and agricultural fertility. In addition, the Maya sky-bearers were compared to four posts supporting the celestial roof of a great cosmic house. In both the maize field and house models of the cosmos, the Bacabs stand at the four corners, corresponding to the intercardinal points; however, it is clear that the Bacabs were also associated with the cardinal directions. Thus, Landa mentions that each Bacab was oriented to one of the four year-bearer days that name the series of fifty-two 365-day years, each year-bearer having its own color, cardinal direction, and significance for augury. Landa specifies the names of the four Bacabs and their world directions as follows: the Bacab of the south is Hobnil; of the east, Can Tizic Nal; of the north, Sac Cimi; and of the west, Hosan Ek.

According to Landa, the Bacabs played an important role in the Yucatec Uayeb ceremonies heralding the new year. The counterclockwise shift of directions each year, based on the succession of year-bearers, was played out in terms of the entire community, with offerings paid to the directions of the old as well as the new year. J. Eric S. Thompson (1934) compared the Yucatec Bacabs to the series of four sky-bearers in the *Borgia* and *Vaticanus B* codices of Central Mexico. In these two passages, a specific series of four gods holds up the night sky while standing on each of the four year-bearers. In Central Mexico, these sky-bearers were referred to as *tzitzimime*, star demons who threaten to destroy the world in times of darkness.

In Classic and Postclassic Maya art, there are abundant representations of the Bacabs, who often appear as grizzled old men wearing conch or turtle shells on their backs. In Maya studies, this figure is often referred to as

"God N," a designation coined by Paul Schellhas in his pioneering study of Maya gods that appear in the Post-classic codices. Ancient Maya texts reveal that the common Maya name for this being was Pauahtun, which Landa supplies as a variant name for Bacab. Although the term "Bacab" does appear as a political title in Late Classic Maya inscriptions, its meaning remains poorly known, and it cannot readily be related to the aged Pauahtun. Scenes in Classic Maya art, however, confirm that the quadripartite Pauahtun has the weighty office of supporting the sky. In addition, Late Classic subordinate lords bearing the title of "Sahal" commonly appear in the guise of Pauahtun, probably an allusion to their role in supporting the office of rulership. It is interesting, however, that despite his responsibility for supporting the cosmos, Pauahtun tends to appear as a rather decrepit old man with a penchant for excessive drink and attractive young women. Much like ritual clown characters of contemporary Mesoamerica and the American Southwest, Pauahtun seems to have been a favored figure for lampooning particular officeholders.

BIBLIOGRAPHY

Taube, Karl Andreas. *The Major Gods of Ancient Yucatan*. Dumbarton Oaks Studies in Pre-Columbian Art and Archaeology, 32. Washington, D.C., 1992. One chapter (pp. 92–99) concerns the history of study and the qualities of the god Pauahtun.

Thompson, J. Eric S. *Sky Bearers, Colors, and Directions in Maya and Mexican Religion*. Contributions to American Archaeology, Carnegie Institution of Washington, 436, no. 10, pp. 209–242. Washington, D.C., 1934. Concerns the concept of sky-bearers in Mesoamerica, along with their relation to world directions and calendrics.

Thompson, J. Eric S. The Bacabs: Their Portraits and Their Glyphs. In *Monographs and Papers in Maya Archaeology*, edited by William R. Bullard, Jr., pp. 469–485. Papers of the Peabody Museum of Archaeology and Ethnology, 48. Cambridge, Mass., 1970. Detailed discussion of the Bacabs; Thompson notes that Schellhas's "God N" of the pre-Hispanic codices should be considered the Bacab sky-bearer.

KARL A. TAUBE

BALLCOURTS. *See* Ballgame.

BALLGAME. The pre-Columbian peoples of Mesoamerica played several games that used a rubber ball. These games varied in regard to the size of the ball, the equipment used, the parts of the body that were deployed to project the ball, the type of location in which the game was played, and the context of the game.

Rubber was produced from the milky sap (latex) of various plants (especially the tree *Hevea brasilianus*) in the Gulf Coast region of Mexico by the Early Formative (Preclassic) period (1200–900 BCE). This substance had both ritual and medicinal uses throughout Mesoamerica: the latex sap was mixed with sap from the copal tree and burned as incense; pure rubber was burned in different forms for ceremonial purposes; effigy rubber balls were bounced in emulation of heavy rainfall for rain-petitioning rituals; or sap from the rubber tree might be ingested to relieve ailments.

Excavations at the site of El Manatí have yielded the earliest known rubber balls (solid rubber) in Mesoamerica, which date to 900 BCE. The Gulf Coast Olmec, the "rubber people" (a name later given them by the Aztec), probably noticed the rubber's resilient properties and developed the first Mesoamerican ballgames. [*See* Rubber.] One of the first to appear in the archaeological record is a handball game that used grapefruit-sized balls, such as those found at El Manatí, and protective helmets, such as those worn by the nobles represented in the Olmec colossal head statues. Early Olmec-style ceramic figurines depict athletes with handballs and caplike helmets. The handball game is found throughout time and space in Mesoamerica and may survive as the *juego de pelota mixteca* (Mixtec ballgame) played today in the Mexican state of Oaxaca and bordering states.

The hipball game was also invented by the Early Formative period, and probably by the Olmec peoples. This game was known as *ollama* (from *olli*, the word for "rubber," related to the term *ollin*, "motion") or *ullama* in Nahuatl, the language of the Aztec. The hipball game is still played in parts of northwestern Mexico with a smaller ball and in a field. Where the handball game could be played in an open, demarcated field, the hipball game apparently required a constructed court with a playing alley defined by two parallel mounds. Such courts appear during the Formative period in the Gulf Coast Olmec heartland and in the Soconusco region of southeastern Mesoamerica. This game used a larger ball, possibly 0.3 meter (1 foot) or so in diameter and weighing almost 3 kilos (more than 7 pounds) of solid rubber. Proportionately larger balls are represented in Maya Classic period art

Ballcourts, such as the North Ballcourt of Xochicalco seen here, are connected to the four directions of the Mesoamerican cosmos, the movement of astral bodies, and the confrontation of opposites. *Photograph courtesy of Norberto González Crespo.*

(300–900 CE); these balls might have been made with hollow centers (rubber over a gourd, perhaps). In the carved stone panels lining the Great Ballcourt at Chichén Itzá, large balls are shown with belching skulls at the center, so skulls of sacrificed, defeated ballplayers may have been used to form ball cores.

Stick-and-ball games are also known from Mesoamerica. The Classic period murals in the Tepantitla palace compound at the Central Mexican site of Teotihuacan illustrate one such game. Players are shown with sticks like those used in field hockey, batting around a small ball; this game was played in a field defined by two parallel mounds and standing stone (goal?) markers at either end of an alley.

Ballgame equipment varied with the nature of each game. Handball games usually required some form of helmet and protective clothing. At the Late Formative site of Dainzú in Oaxaca, stones carved with images of handball players show the use of helmets with facial grills, gauntlet-like gloves, padded clothing over the torso and legs, and knee pads. *Manoplas* (handstones) were used to project the ball in some handball games.

Variations on the hipball game employed different types of paraphernalia; however, common to all hipball games were padding around the waist and hips, and knee pads or some other protection for the lower limbs. Hip pads, known to archaeologists as "yokes," were often of stone; they ranged in size from thick belts encircling the hips to large protective devices covering most of the torso. During the course of the game, hipball players might slide along their upper thighs or drop onto one knee in order to check the ball; these athletes are often seen in pre-Columbian art wearing loin coverings and knee pads. Although an abundance of pre-Columbian ballgame equipment survives, these objects are principally carved in hard stone. Stone paraphernalia was most likely ceremonial or commemorative in nature. Lightweight materials such as fiber padding, leather, wicker, and wood were probably used for functional ballgame equipment. Apart from yokes and padding, *hachas, palmas*, and *manoplas* were also employed in some hipball games. *Hachas* and *palmas* are long, carved-stone projecting elements that may have been inserted into players' yokes to protect the chest, or they may have been used as ballgame-related architectural decoration around the ballcourt, like insignia or markers.

Most ballgames were played with two competing teams facing each other at either end of the playing field. Points were scored by hitting the ball toward markers along the alley or in the end zones, at or through rings along the alley walls. Use of the hands to strike the ball was not permitted, except in handball games; typically, the ball was hit with the thighs and upper arms. Bare hands or *manoplas* were employed only to set the ball into motion. Strength, athletic vigor, physical intensity, and a high degree of competition seem to have characterized Mesoamerican ballgames.

Constructed masonry courts are the best-known form of ballgame architecture. Ballcourts are essentially formed by two parallel mounds flanking a central alley. The Classic period ballcourt is defined by an I-shaped playing alley, with side benches and sloping side walls, and two end zones. Postclassic ballcourts have perpendicular side walls. Rooms were frequently built atop the parallel structures. Players may have used these rooms to prepare for the game, including steaming, bathing, and other ritual activities. Spectators were probably accommodated along platforms and structures outside each end zone. Some ritual ballgames were played on temple stairways and patios designed as symbolic ballcourts.

Mesoamerican ballgames were generally conducted within one of two broad contexts: sport and ritual. As pure sport, they were not unlike football, soccer, and baseball today. Scholars such as Linda Schele and Mary Ellen Miller (1987) have deduced from ethnohistoric and iconographic evidence that outstanding ballgame athletes were highly respected and even achieved starlike status. Communities competed with one another through their teams. Gambling was popular, and people bet desirable items such as fine cotton shirts on their favorite teams or players. Pre-Columbian ballgames are distinct from European-American ball sports, however, in their complexity of meaning and their connection to the cosmic events of creation and universal cycles.

Surviving Mesoamerican creation stories tell of primordial beings playing life-and-death ballgames in myth time. The sixteenth-century Quiché Maya community book, the *Popol Vuh*, and some Classic period hieroglyphic texts recount how the Hero Twins were summoned to the underworld to play a deadly ballgame with the deities there. The Twins survived several trials, defeated the underworld gods, and resurrected their father, the Maize God, in the ballcourt—named as the place of sacrifice. [*See* Hero Twins.] This tale explains how maize was brought into the world and provides a metaphor for the life cycle of birth, death, and regeneration that is dramatically experienced by agrarian societies in this geographic region, with its distinctive rainy and dry seasons. Certain ballgames were related to the coming of the rains and the subsequent fertility of the earth.

Mesoamerican ballgames were very early linked to political authority and the fundamental role of rulers as providers for their communities. Natural disasters such as drought and famine or political and military defeats might jeopardize the legitimacy of an individual's rule. Thus, some ballgames came to serve as public spectacles, full of courtly pomp and circumstance, for the ritual re-enactment of warfare and success on the battlefield. Captives were made to play staged, fixed "games" that were essentially mock combats with a predetermined outcome. The end result of these events was the sacrifice and, frequently, decapitation and dismemberment of defeated players. Severed heads taken as trophies in these ritualized ballgames were often displayed on nearby skull racks, known in Nahuatl as *tzompantli*.

The handball game known at Dainzú, Oaxaca, shows evidence of competitors using round stones rather than rubber balls in a symbolic game that was intended to draw blood. Heather Orr (1997) has shown that costume and other elements of this game were associated with the rain deity, and the echo of stone balls would have mimicked the sound of thunder. This game may have been analogous to the well-known *tigre* battles held today in some villages of the Mexican state of Guerrero. In these modern rituals, two players dressed in the jaguar costume of the local rain deity box with gloved fists or strike at their opponents with knotted ropes to produce blood. The flowing blood is said to be an offering to the rain deity, who also sheds his blood in the form of rain. These ritual events are held annually before the rainy season, to ensure the coming of the rains.

BIBLIOGRAPHY

Bernal, Ignacio, and Andy Seuffert. *The Ball Players of Dainzú*. Graz, 1979.

Borhegyi, Stephan F. de. "Ball-game Headstone and Ball-game Gloves." In *Essays in Precolumbian Art and Archaeology*, edited by Samuel Lothrop et al., pp. 126–151. Cambridge, Mass., 1961.

Borhegyi, Stephan F. de. *The Pre-Columbian Ballgames: A Pan-Meso-american Tradition*. Contributions in Anthropology and History, 1. Milwaukee, 1980.

Coe, Michael. "The Hero Twins: Myth and Image." In *Maya Vase Book I*, edited by Justin Kerr, pp. 161–184. New York, 1990.

Leyenaar, Ted, and Lee Parsons. *Ulama: The Ballgame of the Mayas and Aztecs, 2000 BC–AD 2000*. Leiden, 1988.

Miller, Mary Ellen, and Stephen D. Houston. Stairways and Ballcourt Glyphs: New Perspectives on the Classic Maya Ballgame. *RES* 14 (1987), 47–66.

Orr, Heather. "The Ball Players of Dainzú: Power Games in the Late Formative Valley of Oaxaca." Ph.D. diss., University of Texas at Austin, 1997.

Scarborough, Veron L., and David R. Wilcox, eds. *The Mesoamerican Ballgame*. Tucson, Ariz., 1991.

Stern, Theodore. *The Rubber-Ball Game of the Americas*. Monographs of the American Ethological Society, 17. New York, 1949.

Taladoire, Eric. "La pelota mixteca: Un juego contemporáneo, con origenes complejos." *XV Mesa Redonda* 1: 431–439. Mexico City, 1979.

Tedlock, Dennis, ed. and trans. *Popul Vuh: The Definitive Edition of the Mayan Book of the Dawn of Life and the Glories of Gods and Kings*. New York, 1985.

Thompson, J. Eric S. "Yokes or Ball Game Belts?" *American Antiquity* 6 (1941), 320–326.

HEATHER S. ORR

BAPTISM. Roman Catholic teaching on baptism, at the time of the arrival of Christianity in Mesoamerica, held that no one could obtain eternal salvation without this sacrament. In 1552, the doctrine was elevated to dogma by the Council of Trent. One of the most important activities of the first missionaries to Mexico, then, was the baptism of as many Indians as possible. There is only one known case of a dissenting opinion; according to the Spanish conqueror Nuño de Guzmán, the first bishop of Mexico, Fray Juan de Zumarraga, preached in a sermon in Tlatelolco, around 1529, that previous to the arrival of Christianity, many Indians had obtained salvation without baptism by observing natural law. This concept for converts had been discussed since the first centuries of the church, but the great baptismal activity of the friars demonstrates that it was not generally accepted.

The practices and ceremonies associated with baptism were well established in the church by the sixteenth century. The first missionaries to Mesoamerica made only minor changes in order to accommodate local conditions. A prerequisite was minimal instruction in Christian beliefs. Toribio de Benavente Motolinía, one of the early Franciscan missionaries, summarized this in four basic concepts: God, almighty and creator; the Virgin Mary; the soul's immortality; and the devil. Testimonies of this type of preparation are found in the so-called Testerian Catechisms, written in hieroglyphs in the 1530s. After baptism, a more detailed and systematic teaching of the Christian doctrine was imparted to children, adolescents, and adults. Catechisms printed in the 1540s are good examples of such ongoing Christian formation.

The baptismal ceremony in the early years of evangelization was quite short because of the great number of Indians who had to be baptized and the lack of materials for a solemn celebration, such as candles and chrism (consecrated oil). The essential rite of baptism consists of pouring water on the individual's head while reciting the formula "I baptize you in the name of the Father and the Son and the Holy Spirit," and the first Franciscans in the New World adopted the following method. They first baptized the children, using holy water for all of them but oil and candles for only two or three. Missionaries baptized the adults using the same procedure. The great number of Indians reported to be baptized by the friars was undoubtedly exaggerated. Pedro de Gante affirms in a letter written in 1529 that he and a companion baptized fourteen thousand persons in a single day. No document, however, confirms the practice reported by some missionaries of baptism by sprinkling water over the heads of a crowd.

The shortness of this ceremony was greatly debated after the arrival of other religious orders, the Dominicans in 1526 and the Augustinians in 1531. The Augustinians maintained that baptism had to be administered with great solemnity and only on the most important holidays of the year. In fact, these missionaries baptized only four times a year: on Christmas, Easter, Pentecost, and the feast day of St. Augustine. This debate was brought before Pope Paul III, who resolved in 1537 that the rapid administration of baptism was to be used only in emergencies. For ordinary cases, the missionaries had to use a solemn and complete ceremony. The Franciscans, much against their will, began to use the longer ceremony, but only for a short time. After a few months, asserting that the living conditions of the Indians were precarious, they declared an emergency and returned to the rapid formula of baptism.

Historians have long debated the missionaries' doubts about the Indians' capacity for receiving baptism. Conflicting interpretations had their origin in a "memorial" which the Dominican Bartolomé de Betanzos presented in 1532 to the Council of the Indies in Spain. This memorial was not about the Indians' capacity for receiving the sacraments but about their rights, which Betanzos ignored, to be humanely treated by the conquerors. The "memorial" was rejected in New Spain by both civil and ecclesiastical authorities. One of the strongest defenders of Indian rights on this occasion was the Dominican Bernardino de Minaya, who traveled to Spain to refute Betanzos's ideas. He also went to Rome carrying a letter from the first bishop of Tlaxcala, the Dominican Julian Garces, praising the Indians' abilities and their culture. With this document, Minaya obtained from Paul III the bull *Sublimis Deus* (2 June 1537), in which the pope solemnly defends Indians' rights to liberty and property—even if they are not baptized.

Some Mesoamerican cultures, such as the Nahuas, had rituals similar to Christian baptism. A Franciscan ethnographer, Fray Bernardino de Sahagún, uses the word "baptism" to describe an Indian ritual in the *Florentine Codex* (book 6, chap. 7). The Franciscan Motolinia considered this ancient rite to be a prophetical image of Christian baptism in his *History of the Indians of New Spain* (trat. 2 chap. 3). Such similarities might well explain the Indians' willing acceptance of the Christian ceremony. All the evidence now available shows us that by the mid-sixteenth century, the great majority of Mesoamerican Indians had been baptized; however, we should not forget the ambiguity surrounding the acceptance of this sacrament. Missionaries' frequent complaints of ancient religious practices persisting in Indian villages during the Colonial period indicate that Christian baptism had different meanings for missionaries and for Indians. For missionaries, it was a sign of conversion from paganism; for Indians, it was a way to be incorporated into the new society. These differences reflect what present-day ethnographers

call "public and private ritual." The first mediates supernatural and public life, whereas the second regulates the relationship between family and supernatural life. It is relatively easy to change public ritual, but private ones can persist.

[*See also* Augustinians; Dominicans; Franciscans.]

BIBLIOGRAPHY

Borobio, D. *Evangelización y sacramentos en la Nueva España (siglo XVI) según Jerónimo de Mendieta: Lecciones de ayer para hoy.* Murcia, 1992. Survey of the problems, discussions, and practices associated with the sacraments, according to the Franciscan chronicler Jerónimo de Mendieta.

Glass, John B. "A Census of Middle American Testerian Manuscripts." In *Handbook of Middle American Indians*, vol. 14, pp. 281–296. Austin, Tex., 1975. Illustrates the importance and teaching methods before baptism.

Ricard, Robert. *The Spiritual Conquest of Mexico.* Translated by Lesley Byrd Simpson. Berkeley, 1966. Includes a well-documented discussion of the practices of baptism during the early years of evangelization.

Sempat Assadourian, Carlos. "Hacia la *Sublimis Deus*: Las discordias entre los dominicos indianos y el enfrentamiento del franciscano padre Tastera con el padre Betanzos." *Historia Mexicana* 187 (1998), 465–536. Documented study on the origin, contents, and meaning of the bull *Sublimis Deus*.

Steck, Francis Borgia, ed. and trans. *Motolinia's History of the Indians of New Spain.* Washington, D.C., 1951. An account of the first experiences of the Franciscan missionaries in New Spain, written in the 1540s.

FRANCISCO MORALES

BAROQUE. The immediate appeal to the senses, emphatic unity, integration of various arts in a single work, dynamic movement, tension between idealism and naturalism, and all the other concepts that are used to describe the arts of Europe in the seventeenth and first half of the eighteenth centuries—the art that has been called Baroque—can also serve to characterize the art of New Spain of roughly the same epoch. However, like all the names given to artistic styles, Baroque is not an essence, but rather a history of judgments, applications, acceptances, and rejections, with a particular history in Mexico.

Although Baroque art had been despised or ignored by the Neoclassicists of the late eighteenth and nineteenth centuries, it began to attract positive attention in the 1880s. In Mexico, it became associated with the particular sensibility of the national culture, formed by the integration of pre-Columbian and Spanish traditions. The more usual term was "Churrigueresque," which referred to the more elaborate ornamental forms of the eighteenth century that would later be identified as a phase of the Baroque of New Spain. After the 1910 Mexican Revolution, specialized study came to more precise knowledge of key figures and works, and efforts were made to refine terminology. Eventually, "Churrigueresque" was largely dropped, and, as has happened with reference to the art of Europe, scholars now tend to speak in terms of specific dates and places, rather than with blanket terms like "Baroque."

In any case, Baroque in what had been Mesoamerica has to be seen within its own context of development to be properly understood. On 18 April, 1649, the cathedral of Puebla was dedicated. In the apse *retablo* or altar screen (the Retablo of the Kings), still preserved, albeit remodeled in the nineteenth century, as well as in the no longer extant baldachin, or canopy, over the freestanding main altar, twisted, or Solomonic, columns were used. The movement inherent in their form and the symbolism and prestige of the originals and of the versions by Giovanni Bernini in the Vatican ensured their presence in Baroque art throughout the Roman Catholic world. In New Spain, Solomonic is the first and founding stage of Baroque art, created in an urban context and with the patronage of the secular church.

Although Solomonic columns in many variations were to become basic elements in all subsequent *retablos* until about 1730, and in façades after about 1670, their presence alone is obviously not sufficient to characterize the architecture and architectural sculpture of that period in New Spain. The dome on a drum, also firmly established as a design element at the cathedral of Puebla, made possible the introduction of dramatic lighting focused on the main altar. Often decorated with tiles on the outside and with gesso, stone reliefs, or paintings on the inside, domes, along with the towers that enframed elaborate *retablo* façades, emphasized key points of the church buildings and marked the most important public urban spaces. Movement in plans is less frequent, and occurs about 1700 and later. An important aspect of Baroque in the late seventeenth century is its regionalization. Differences between one region and another became marked in materials, techniques, and formal qualities.

After about 1720 in *retablos* and 1740 in façade design, the use of the *estípite* in the Retablo of the Kings in Mexico City introduced a new vocabulary that contrasted strong geometric structural statements with relatively minute and naturalistic surface details. The freedom from canonical proportions in what is generally called Estípite Baroque permitted the eventual elimination of all explicit elements of architectural support in many later *retablo* designs. By around the middle of the eighteenth century, this was accompanied by a more vertical emphasis in building and larger windows that provided more diffuse lighting. In general, the continued use of European treatises by architects encouraged the persistence of a classical vocabulary in many buildings, despite the taste for rich ornament both outside and inside.

Painting in New Spain also became Baroque around the middle of the seventeenth century. Artists adopted the austere realism of Spanish painting, especially the contrasts and volumes of Francisco de Zurbarán, perhaps known in originals, and certainly known through prints, as were Jusepe de Ribera and Peter Paul Rubens. José Juárez is generally considered to have been the principal figure in Mexico City at this time. During the last quarter of the seventeenth and the first two decades of the eighteenth century, first Baltasar de Echave Rioja, then Cristóbal de Villalpando and Juan Correa, executed grand, monumental allegorical works largely inspired by Rubens in Mexico City and Puebla. The loose brushwork and brilliant color of Villalpando indicate that he had firsthand knowledge of European works, such as the paintings by the Madrid masters Francisco Rizi and Juan Carreño, which had been imported into New Spain. Villalpando also distinguished himself as an interpreter of iconography, creating original compositions from ideas in verbal instructions, written texts, and varied print sources. He must have been in contact with important literary and cultural contemporaries, such as Sor Juana Inés de la Cruz and Carlos de Sigüenza y Góngora, because he shared with them a delight in complex imagery and an interest in the pre-Columbian and early colonial past, as well as in subjects of popular, local devotion, such as the Virgin of Guadalupe and Saint Michael. The didactic narratives of earlier times had given way to conceptual conceits in both letters and visual imagery.

Painting in the eighteenth century adopted a generally calmer tone with respect to the grandiloquence of the earlier masters. In chronological order: Juan and Nicolás Rodríguez Juárez (grandsons of José Juárez), José de Ibarra, and Miguel Cabrera are the principal artists. Their compositions highlight quiet emotion and graceful figures. Toward the middle of the century, colors become more delicate and lighting more diffuse, while figures are given more ample spaces. There are intimations of Neoclassicism, especially among artists in Mexico City, who made several attempts at establishing an academy. Although compositions and ensembles in public buildings continued to be theatrical, there was a growing production of images for individual devotion, as well as an interest in portraiture, mythology, landscape, and still life for secular private spaces.

BIBLIOGRAPHY

Bargellini, Clara. *La arquitectura de la plata: iglesias monumentales del centro-norte de México, 1640–1750.* Madrid and Mexico City, 1991. Study of Baroque architecture based on regional and typological definitions.

Caudriello, Jaime, ed. *Juegos de ingenio y agudeza. La emblemática de la Nueva España.* Mexico City, 1994. Exhibition catalog; examines the emblematic tradition in New Spain.

Cuadriello, Jaime, ed. *Los pinceles de la historia. El origen del Reino de la Nueva España.* Mexico City, 1999. Exhibition catalog; works illustrating the treatment of the past in the art of New Spain of the seventeenth and eighteenth centuries.

Gutiérrez, Juana, et al. *Cristóbal de Villalpando.* Mexico City, 1997. Exhibition catalog; the most important painter of late-seventeenth-century New Spain.

Toussaint, Manual. *Arte colonial en México.* Mexico City, 1974. First ed. 1948. Translated by E. Weismann. Austin, Tex., 1967. Basic book by the founder of the studies of New Spanish art.

Vargaslugo, Elisa, et al. *Juan Correa: su vida y su obra.* Mexico City, 1985. This multivolume work is not yet complete, but it includes basic studies of an important painter and his milieu.

CLARA BARGELLINI

BARRIOS. Many Mesoamerican societies channel relations between the household and the community through an intermediate level of organization, the barrio. "Barrio" is one of several folk terms for this customary subdivision or social institution. Its basic characteristics are as follows. The subdivision is an alliance of households that cooperate in ceremonial, political, and other matters. The community—either a single settlement (*pueblo*) or a multisettlement township (*municipio*)—is composed of two or more subdivisions, which cooperate and compete with one another in the manner of a confederacy. Membership in the community requires membership in one of the subdivisions, and vice versa. Each subdivision has a distinctive name—for example, that of a Roman Catholic saint, a historical figure, or a geographic landmark. Depending on local custom, a person's subdivision affiliation is based on descent from a common ancestor or other kinship criteria, location of residence or property, birthplace, personal choice, or some combination of these criteria. As a consequence, the subdivision is not necessarily a territorial unit. Its members may be concentrated in a particular neighborhood or hamlet or scattered throughout the community.

In the most typical pattern (1) the subdivision has a home territory where the majority of the members reside; (2) children belong to the same subdivision as their father, by virtue of birthplace, residence, or descent; but (3) a woman upon marriage adopts her husband's subdivision affiliation if it differs from her own. This pattern reflects the widespread practice of residing with the husband's parents during the first years of a marriage and the preference for bequeathing land to sons rather than daughters. When the new couple builds a home of their own, it will probably be on land that the husband inherited, situated near his father's house.

A barrio in sixteenth-century Spain was always a territorial unit, either a neighborhood or ward within a town or a dependent settlement beyond the town boundaries. In contrast, pre-Columbian Mesoamericans used diverse strategies to segment their communities into subdivisions, including kinship, territorial criteria, ethnic iden-

tity, occupation, and patron–client relations with a noble house. Frequently, they based the number of subdivisions on a sacred principle (e.g., the four cardinal directions) or an origin myth (e.g., the "Seven Tribes of the Seven Caves"). Spanish colonial bureaucrats, faced with these unfamiliar forms of community organization, often classified the indigenous subdivisions as "barrios" for administrative purposes. Colonial policies led to the creation of new subdivisions as well. For example, in areas where the native population was especially dispersed, such as southern Mexico and Guatemala, the Spanish moved several whole communities and resettled them together in new towns, called *congregaciones*; each formerly independent group could retain its identity in the new town by becoming a separate subdivision.

Today, the word "barrio" has several colloquial meanings in Mexico and Guatemala, not all connected with Mesoamerican community organization. Some indigenous communities call their customary subdivisions "barrios," especially in central Mexico, but others do not. In highland Guatemala, the folk term is *parcialidad, cantón,* or *aldea*. In the Mexican state of Chiapas and some parts of highland Guatemala, the term is *paraje*. Additional terms are *calpulli* (Nahua of central Mexico), *calpul* or *culibal* (Tzotzil Maya of Chiapas), and *chinamit(l)* (Quiché Maya of Guatemala), and there are others.

Present-day communities vary in the degree of autonomy the subdivisions enjoy. Generally the subdivision has the authority to conscript labor for its own projects—with the consent of the members—and the obligation to provide labor for community projects. Each subdivision may have its own sanctuary, patron saint, titular deity, ceremonials, fiestas, lands to support civic and ritual expenditures, cash assessments on the membership, public works, officers or leaders, stewards in the community system of religious offices, and representatives in the local government. Rivalries between subdivisions are a common source of social friction. Serious disputes can lead a subdivision to break away and form an independent community. To counteract this tendency, some communities routinely include equal representation of all the subdivisions in any public enterprise. Another strategy, evident since pre-Columbian times, involves rotating community-level civil and religious obligations among the subdivisions in a fixed, ritual order. The rotation may follow the founding dates of the subdivisions, the dictates of an origin myth, or the cardinal directions; in the last case it is usually counterclockwise, based on the geographic location of the subdivisions' home territories. Changing the number of subdivisions requires adjusting the ritual order accordingly, as when a subdivision secedes from the confederacy, merges with another subdivision, or disappears altogether (i.e., all the members die without heirs), as well as when a new subdivision joins or an existing subdivision splits in two. The community can refuse to authorize these changes by refusing to amend the ritual order.

The structure of customary subdivision systems varies from simple to rather complex. In the simplest arrangement, the community consists of two opposing halves, an "upper" subdivision (*arriba*) and a "lower" subdivision (*abajo*). A road or other landmark serves as the dividing line. "Upper" and "lower" can refer to topography (uphill, downhill), water currents (upstream, downstream), or no attribute in particular. A more complex arrangement uses opposing halves to form an additional level of organization. The community has multiple subdivisions, but these are further grouped into two macro-divisions (e.g., barrios A, B, and C comprise *arriba*; barrios D and E comprise *abajo*). Another arrangement involves grouping some, but not all, of the subdivisions into macro-divisions (e.g., barrios A and B comprise *arriba*; barrios C and D comprise *abajo*; barrios E, F, and G are "neutral"). Yet another arrangement segments each subdivision into smaller micro-divisions (e.g., micro-divisions 1, 2, and 3 comprise barrio A; micro-divisions 4 and 5 comprise barrio B; and so on). Other variations exist.

The use of customary subdivisions is by no means universal in Mesoamerican community organization. This institution is closely associated with the two most populous groups in the region, the Highland Maya of southern Mexico and western Guatemala, and the Nahuas of central Mexico. It is also widespread among the post-Nahuas—that is, rural populations of Nahua ancestry who no longer consider themselves Indians. The practice is less prevalent among the Zapotecs in the state of Oaxaca (southern Mexico), and absent or socially unimportant among the Purépecha, formerly known as the Tarascans, in the state of Michoacán (western Mexico). The lowest incidence is among the Lowland Maya, a group whose territory extends across central Guatemala and Belize through the Mexican states of Quintana Roo, Yucatán, Campeche, Tabasco, and northern Chiapas.

BIBLIOGRAPHY

Chance, John K. "The Barrios of Colonial Tecali: Patronage, Kinship, and Territorial Relations in a Central Mexican Community." *Ethnology* 35 (1996), 107–139. Describes changes in the customary subdivision system of a Nahua town in the Mexican state of Puebla during the Late Colonial period, with special attention to the role of the indigenous nobility.

Flannery, Kent V. "Two Possible Village Subdivisions: The Courtyard Group and the Residential Ward." In *The Early Mesoamerican Village*, edited by Kent V. Flannery, pp. 25–72. New York, 1976. Analyzes Mesoamerican settlement patterns from 1500 to 500 BCE and concludes that larger villages may have been organized into residential wards.

Hill, Robert M. II, and John Monaghan. *Continuities in Highland Maya Social Organization.* Philadelphia, 1987. Innovative case study describes variations in the customary subdivision system of a Quiché Maya *municipio* (township) in the Guatemalan department of El Quiché from pre-Columbian times to the present.

Hunt, Eva M., and June Nash. "Local and Territorial Units." In *Handbook of Middle American Indians*, edited by Robert Wauchope, vol. 6, pp. 253–282. Austin, Tex., 1967. Widely quoted survey article confuses customary subdivisions as social institutions with territorial-political units, but the bibliography and ethnographic examples remain valuable.

Lockhart, James. *The Nahuas after the Conquest.* Stanford, 1992. Chapter 2 ("Altepetl") describes the multilevel system of customary subdivisions that characterized the Nahua ethnic state in Central Mexico shortly before the Spanish conquest.

Mulhare, Eileen M. "Barrio Matters: Toward an Ethnology of Mesoamerican Customary Social Units." *Ethnology* 35 (1996), 93–106. Comparative overview of customary subdivision systems in Mesoamerica, with extensive bibliography.

Thomas, Norman D. "The Mesoamerican Barrio: A Reciprocity Model for Community Organization." *Kroeber Anthropological Society Papers* 55–56 (1979), 45–58. Proposes an ideal type of customary subdivision, the civil-religious barrio, based on a survey of seventy-three indigenous and rural communities.

EILEEN M. MULHARE

BATAB. *See* Rulers and Dynasties.

BATS. The Mesoamerican area consists of a large quantity of diverse habitats containing more than 156 species of bats. These hematophagous, insectivorous, fructivorous, nocturnal creatures undoubtedly coexisted with humans, sharing caves and rock shelters, for more than thirty thousand years, since the time of the area's earliest evidence of settlement at El Cedral in the Mexican state of San Luis Potosí.

This coexistence invariably engendered a magico-religious cult among many Mesoamerican groups, including some that became closely identified with the flying mammal. For example, the ethnic designation "Tzotzil" and the place name "Zinacantán" respectively derive from the Mayan (*zotz*) and Nahuatl (*tzinacantli*) words for bat. In Mesoamerica, the animal has been related to deities such as Quetzalcoatl, Xochiquetzal, Mictlantecuhtli, and Xipe Totec, and symbolically associated with decapitation, blood, the jaguar, darkness, the underworld, fertility, night, and in some cultures, virginity, menstruation, and ejaculation.

Manifestations of this cult are evident in the Formative, Classic, and Postclassic periods and are preserved in native legends and myths from colonial times to the present. Representations of bats or bat deities are found in Zapotec stone and clay sculpture, including the extraordinary Formative jade mask from Monte Albán. They are most prevalent during the Classic period and appear on Maya architecture, vases, and plates, such as those from Uxmal and Copán. Although less numerous during the Postclassic, depictions of the Bat God (Tlacatzinacantli, in Nahuatl) are found in the *Borgia*, *Fejérváry-Mayer*, and *Vaticanus B* codices, and in stone and clay sculpture. Mythic references to bats occur in the *Codex Magliabechiano* (an early colonial manuscript from Central Mexico), the *Popol Vuh* (a sixteenth-century K'iche' [Quiché] Maya text), and contemporary oral accounts of several Mesoamerican peoples, including the Popoluca of southern Veracruz and the Tzotzil Maya of southern Chiapas.

Perhaps the most impressive representation, however, comes from San Mateo Tezoquipan, Miraflores, in the municipio of Chalco (Estado de México), in the southeast part of the Basin of Mexico, and dates from the Epiclassic. On 18 November 1990, archaeologists from the Instituto Nacional de Antropología e Historia uncovered approximately two hundred fragments belonging to a large clay anthropo-zoomorphic sculpture thought to be the Bat God. The exquisitely restored piece stands 2 meters (6.5 feet) high and consists of three mortise-and-tenoned sections corresponding to the head, torso, and lower extremities of the deity. The head has batlike features with an animal snout, upper and lower incisors exposed, a slightly split tongue, a nasal appendage between the eyes, two large circular ears, a stirrup-shaped handle on its forehead, a circle and three petals at the corners of its mouth, and circles and petals running ear-to-ear on its chin. From a collar modeled in a pattern characteristic of Xipe Totec hang three bells with clappers in the shape of human femurs. The torso and lower extremities are essentially human with a robust, naked chest, navel, arms (one complete, the other terminating above the elbow), and legs, though it has the paws of a feline with retractile claws. Around the waist is a belt with a *maxtlatl* loincloth hanging in front. Compositional analysis revealed that the sculpture was made of a coarse, dark paste irregularly fired at low temperature and painted with a black, ferrous-oxide pigment, possibly agglutinated with an organic vegetal material. This extraordinary piece is currently displayed at the Museo del Templo Mayor in Mexico City.

BIBLIOGRAPHY

Blaffer, Sarah C. *The Black-Man of Zinacantan: A Central American Legend*. Austin, Tex., 1972. Examines the ancient Mesoamerican "bat demon" in relation to the *h'ik'al* figure in contemporary Tzotzil Maya mythology.

Boone, Elizabeth H. *Codex Magliabechiano and the Lost Prototype of the Magliabechiano Group*. Berkeley, 1983. Folio 61 verso (p. 206). Presents a mythical episode concerning Quetzalcoatl, Xochiquetzal, and Mictlantecuhtli, which relates the bat to menstruation.

Foster, George M. *Sierra Popoluca Folklore and Belief*. Berkeley, 1945; reprinted 1971. Contains various stories collected in the early 1940s, including "The Origin of Maize" (pp. 191–196) wherein Homshuk (the young maize plant) enlists a bat to cut the throat of his grandfather who has come to kill him in his sleep.

Seler, Eduard. "The Bat God of the Maya Race." In *Mexican and Central American Antiquities, Calendar Systems, and History*. Washington, D.C., 1904. Discusses pictorial examples of the bat deity in Postclassic Mexican and Maya codices.

Tedlock, Dennis, ed. and trans. *Popol Vuh: The Mayan Book of the Dawn of Life*. New York, 1996. Contains the K'iche' account of Hunahpu and Xbalanque, who underwent several ordeals in the underworld, including a night in the "Bat House" where Hunahpu lost his head.

José Francisco Hinojosa Hinojosa
Translated from Spanish by Scott Sessions

BEANS. Bean seeds are one of three basic food elements in the Mesoamerican diet, along with maize and squash. Of the over fifty species of wild beans (*Phaseolus*) that grow throughout the American continents, only five have been cultivated and all in Mesoamerica: common bean (*P. vulgaris*), scarlet runner bean or cimatl (*P. coccineus*), polyanthus bean (*P. polyanthus*), lima bean (*P. lunatus*), and tepary bean (*P. acutifolius*).

Older archaeological materials from Peru and distinct genetic evidence suggest that the common and lima beans were also domesticated separately in South America. The amino acids of beans complement those of maize to provide a balanced protein diet. Beans have been cultivated as a single crop (especially the bush forms) or mixed in the multiple-crop *milpas* (cultivated fields, usually with many cultivated and encouraged plants that grow and are harvested based upon differential spatial and temporal patterns), where the vine forms climb the maize stalks. The common and scarlet runner beans grow in various ecological zones while the tepary tolerate the arid regions, and the lima are found in humid tropical zones. The polyanthus bean is not common and grows in semitropical areas. Each bean species has many forms that vary in the growth habit of the plant, the size, color, and pattern of the seed, as well as in culinary properties and flavors. In addition to the grain seed, the young leaves, flowers, green seeds, and young pods are cooked and eaten. Some wild species are used for medicinal purposes and to promote fermentation of alcoholic beverages.

Bean iconography in Mesoamerica is poor in comparison to that in South America. The murals at Teotihuacan (e.g., Tetitla, Zacuala) include seeds—some of which could be interpreted as those of beans. The beanlike seeds in a cavelike structure beneath the central figure (possibly Tlaloc) of Tlalocan of Tepantitla may be associated with the concept of fertility. The rareness of beans in Mesoamerican frescos, textiles, and ceramics is curious in light of the richness of other floristic elements.

The early colonial documents such as those written by Bernardino de Sahagún describe the diversity of beans. In particular, caution is given for cimatl (*P. coccineus*) with its medicinal and toxic properties. Beans were one of the grain tributes received by the Aztec Empire as recorded in the *Matrícula de Tributos*. Many indigenous names are applied to beans, the more generic ones being *etl* in Nahuatl and *ib* in Maya. While special colored beans are consumed for special ceremonies in some ethnic groups, the general preference for bean consumption is that of dark-colored beans in the south and the lighter-colored forms in the north.

BIBLIOGRAPHY
Kaplan, L., and T. F. Lynch. "Phaseolus (Fabaceae) in archaeology: AMS radiocarbon dates and their significance for pre-Columbian agriculture." *Economic Botany* 53 (1999), 261–273.
Manzanilla, Linda, and A. Delgado-Salinas. *"El frijol prehispanico." ICyT* 12.168 (1990), 52–56.

ROBERT A. BYE

BEES AND HONEY. Apiculture has a long history in Mesoamerica, dating back to the pre-Hispanic period when the first stingless bees (*Melipona beecheii*) were introduced to manmade hives. Stingless bees were raised primarily for their honey, which was traded extensively throughout Mesoamerica for use as a sweetener and as the basis of an alcoholic beverage for ceremonial consumption. In the Late Postclassic period in Central Mexico, honey was included in tribute payments, as illustrated in the *Codex Mendocino* (Nárez 1988). The chroniclers disagree about the importance of beeswax before the Conquest: Bernal Díaz del Castillo claimed that candlemaking techniques were introduced by the Spanish, but the pre-Hispanic Yucatec Maya calendar included a day named *kib*, meaning "candle, wax."

There are three sources for indigenous apiculture: native pictorial and hieroglyphic codices predating the Spanish conquest (in particular, the Maya *Madrid Codex*); ethnohistorical accounts written after the European invasion (summarized by Nárez); and present-day ethnographic descriptions of beekeeping practices in rural villages. In addition, material recovered from archaeological excavations contributes to the overall picture (see Terrones González 1994).

Despite the increasing importance of the European honeybee to the economy, stingless bees are still domesticated in parts of Mesoamerica, for example by the Popoluca of Veracruz, the Mixtec of Oaxaca, and communities of Yucatecan and Cholan Maya speakers in Mexico and Guatemala. The indigenous bee species plays a central role in ritual life that is not shared by its European counterpart.

Although cane sugar has largely replaced honey as a sweetener, honey is still commonly used in the preparation of ceremonial beverages, and it is also believed to have medicinal properties. In one Yucatec village, it has been reported to be given to women following childbirth. Elsewhere, it serves as an unguent on wounds and skin infections and as a remedy for sore throats and respiratory disorders. Honey is a proven antibacterial agent, so Mesoamerican uses are and were efficacious.

Throughout Mesoamerica, the beekeepers who raise stingless bees follow similar practices. Among the Yucatec Maya, hollow logs are fashioned into hives, which are grouped together within an open-walled palm-thatch structure. Honey is generally harvested two or three times

A bee ceremony conducted by a priest outside of a thatched structure built to house beehives. The ritual nature of the scene is suggested by the vessel containing food offerings that is pictured below the bee and by the glyphs for the four directions surrounding the picture. *Reproduced from Ferdinand Anders,* Codex Tro-Cortesianus (Codex Madrid), *Graz, 1967. Courtesy of Akademische Druck- u. Verlagsanstalt, Graz, Austria.*

in the spring and again in November or December. In some villages, beekeepers move their hives from place to place, to take advantage of the flowering cycles of certain plants. The *Madrid Codex* shows that the pre-Hispanic Maya housed their hives in thatched structures similar to those in use today.

Harvesting and other activities performed by contemporary Maya beekeepers are accompanied by rituals to both thank and appease the gods (*balams*) who protect the native bees. Bishop Diego de Landa, writing around 1566, described two beekeeping ceremonies that were governed by the yearly calendar. Examples of them may be illustrated in the *Madrid Codex*, as are scenes showing the extraction of honey from hives and the ritual of sweeping the hives to purify them.

BIBLIOGRAPHY

Foster, George M. "Indigenous Apiculture among the Popoluca of Veracruz." *American Anthropologist* 44 (1942), 538–542. Describes practices and rituals surrounding the native bee.

Nárez, Jesús. "Algunos datos sobre las abejas y la miel en la época prehispánica." *Revista mexicana de estudios antropológicos* 34 (1988), 123–140. Summarizes ethnohistorical sources relating to apiculture and the trade of honey, and discusses depictions of honey received as tribute in the *Codex Mendocino*.

Tec Poot, José, and Michel Bocara. "Abejas y hombres de la tierra maya." *Boletín de la Escuela de Ciencias Antropológicas de la Universidad de Yucatán* 7.42 (1980), 2–24. Discussion of indigenous beekeeping in Yucatán and the impact of the European bee on the economy; includes a detailed description of a ceremony in honor of the bee gods, with text in Yucatec Mayan and Spanish.

Terrones González, Enrique. "Apiarios prehispánicos." *Boletín de la Escuela de Ciencias Antropológicas de la Universidad de Yucatán* 20.117 (1994), 43–57. Summarizes evidence from archaeological excavations along the coast of Quintana Roo for the presence of structures identified as apiaries.

Vail, Gabrielle. "A Commentary on the Bee Almanacs in Codex Madrid." In *Códices y documentos sobre México, primer simposio*, edited by Constanza Vega Sosa, pp. 37–68. Mexico City, 1994. Provides a model for interpreting the calendrical interrelationship of the twenty-nine almanacs in the beekeeping section of the *Madrid Codex*.

Vásquez-Dávila, Marco Antonio, and María Beatríz Solís-Trejo. "Conocimiento, uso y manejo de la abeja nativa por los chontales de Tabasco." *Tierra y agua, la antropología en Tabasco* 2 (1991), 29–38. Describes the practices of beekeepers in the Chontal-speaking region of Tabasco, as well as the use of honey and wax in the native economy and religion.

Weaver, Nevin, and Elizabeth C. Weaver. "Beekeeping with the Stingless Bee *Melipona beecheii* by the Yucatecan Maya." *Bee World* 62 (1981), 7–19. Detailed description of beekeeping in the Maya village of Yaxcabá, including a ceremony in which the gods of the bees are invoked.

GABRIELLE VAIL

BEVERAGES. During their wanderings over arid Northwestern Mexico in search of a suitable place to settle, Mesoamericans quenched thirst with various extracts from juicy plants, the "thirst plants." These included extracts from maguey, a Mexican common name for the fleshy-leaved plants of the agave family—the prototype for today's agaves that are cultivated there for the beverages pulque and mezcal. Agave became an important plant in Mexican farming, second only to maize. Beverages of fermented agave sap, obtained from several varieties, were the most widespread. Pulque, however, was the most significant and was mostly produced in a large area of the Central Highlands. *Aguamiel* (maguey juice, but literally in Spanish "honey-water") is first obtained from the plant's core (a pool of sap collecting in the crater made by removing the plant's ovary and flower stalk). After a slight fermentation, it becomes *tlachique*, a product of young maguey plants; but when aged, it is called *octli*, ripe pulque, an alcoholic beverage. Maguey was regarded as a gift from the gods, associated with fertility and agricultural rites, and was integrated into the sacred worldview; as such, it had a prominent place in the complex Mesoamerican pantheon. Mayáhuel was the goddess "with four hundred heads," because she was changed into maguey, a plant with a juice that squirted four hundred (meaning "innumerable") forms of inebriation and dance. Maguey was also associated with aquatic deities and with water itself. In the *Codex Vaticanus B*, the innermost part of its *meyóllotl* (maguey core) is represented as an upside-down bowl full of water, with a fish. In the *Codex Borgia*, Mayáhuel is the goddess "of the four hundred teats" (the four hundred kinds of drunkenness?), breastfeeding a fish and showing the water sign on her dress.

The consumption of *octli*, as well as other activities, were ruled by the calendar; the drinking of the alcoholic beverage took place during certain religious festivities, to bring about a ritual inebriation. The rabbit (*tochtli*), an animal associated with the gods of pulque, was symbolic of inebriation and of crimes and misfortunes associated with that state. Those born on the days bearing the "2 Rabbit" calendar sign were thought to be inescapably doomed by the disastrous attraction of *octli*. Sixteenth-century informants to Bernardino de Sahagún reported that people became drunk during the Feast of the "Wine" Gods (Centzontotochtin, or "the four hundred rabbits"), and this was not viewed as a violation of the norm. According to the same sources, it was customary once every four years, during the feast of Izcalli ("growth"), to pierce the ears of newborn boys and girls. Their godfathers would let them drink pulque from some "tiny little cups"; it may be assumed that the container's size indicated restraint. War captives, courageous men sacrificed to honor the god Huitzilopochtli, drank *teoctli* ("fortified pulque"), to fill themselves with the strength of the gods before they died. Social and legal acceptance or rejection of drinking, therefore, resulted from the place and occasion, from the drinker's age and social status, and only to a lesser degree from the amount consumed or obvious signs of drunkenness. Those who failed to respect the norm faced punishment, ranging from reprimand to rejection by the community. In extreme cases, transgressors were hanged, beaten, or stoned to death. How often these harsh laws resulted in any given punishment is difficult to determine.

When not brewed for a ceremony, pulque was a syrup barely beginning to ferment, a young *tlachique*, with little alcohol content—viscous, sweet, and nourishing; it was likely to have been a regular drink for weddings and a popular beverage for everyday consumption and restrained use. Men and women drank it in different stages of life as a beverage-medicinal—women after childbirth and elders in acknowledgment of life's victory over death.

Mesoamericans were acquainted with additives that strengthened and accelerated the fermentation of their ritual beverages. These additives stimulated mystical or magical (psychoactive) enhancement of the beverage and ensured that the fermentation would proceed uniformly and free of impurities. Religious officers were not only entrusted with administering the beverage but also often in charge of its production. The Mexica (Aztec) added to *octli* the crushed bark of root of *ocpatli* or *cuapatle* (*Acacia angustissima*), which they called "the pulque's medicine." Once the ceremonial beverage had been strengthened, they called on the gods and they spilled some of the liquid as an offering; only then did they dare drink.

In the Yucatán Peninsula, Maya priests prepared a sacred honey-based alcoholic beverage, taken from wild bees. A characteristic element of Maya civilization, this fine, clear, aromatic drink was fermented and strengthened with the bark of the *balché* tree (*Lonchocarpus longistylus*), after which the drink was named. The ritual drinking of balché resulted in an inebriation with contortions and nonsensical mumblings, which enabled participants to go into a trance that facilitated their contact with the deity. It was also used in agricultural rites, in ceremonial sprinklings, and in force-feeding any birds that were to be sacrificed. The Maya ceremony, like the Mexica, ended in collective libation by participants. It was said that balché "cured," as did *octli* and *ocpatli* and other similar but less widespread local beverages; all shared a ritual-based controlled usage, and the plants that produced them were revered for their purifying significance.

Shortly after the fall of the Aztec capital to the Spanish, the Crown forbade the addition of roots to strengthen *octli*. Thus the beverage began to lose its ritual status—its rank as the wine of the gods—instead becoming a profane wine strengthened with other substances. *Octli* without *ocpatli* gradually changed into the popular drink now known as pulque. The encounter between two cultures with different ceremonial views, including clashing values concerning inebriating beverages, created a difficult situation. Mesoamericans did not tolerate individual drunkards, but they did permit inebriation under ceremonial circumstances. The Spaniards, like other Mediterranean peoples of Judeo-Christian tradition, penalized inebriation without regard to individuals or situations. In their view, once the senses were disturbed, men and women became less human, because they lost their resemblance to God, their creator.

The Spaniards gave unique cultural value to the wine extracted from grapes and used it in the Communion ceremony during Mass. To Mesoamericans, pulque was symbolic of permanence, providing a bridge to ancestral ideas; it also "illuminated" and provided contact with divinity. Wine, for them, represented the road toward a new, uncertain, and painful worldview and altered way of life. The unadulterated white pulque that was permitted to be sold during the Colonial period, as well as the other indigenous beverages that Spaniards branded as "forbidden," became the silent, lasting elements to be used as part of the local resistance to Westernization.

During the decades after the fall of the Aztec capital, the destruction of various codices (recorded both before and after the arrival of Cortés) disrupted the recorded memory of the religious and cultural contexts for the local fermented beverages. The loss was compounded by the decline in traditional controls against inebriation. Roman Catholicism faced serious difficulties in substituting new controls for the old. The introduction of catechisms and confession manuals imposed difficult standards on the newly baptized, who often resisted integrating their standards into an existing mental framework. Catholic priests gave the act of disorderly drinking a new meaning—that of sinning—and they imposed moral sanctions on sinners, many of which were not to take effect until the next world. They stressed that the effects of inebriation were reprehensible at all times, and they ignored the circumstances, which was contrary to traditional Mesoamerican practices.

Inebriation in Colonial times, defined as sinful in catechisms and manuals of confession, thus ranked as one of the most deeply entrenched and most destructive of social evils, particularly among the lower classes. Nevertheless, alcoholic beverages did not unavoidably lead to overindulgence; all indigenous drinkers were not drunkards; and there was no scourge of collective alcoholism. A jug of pulque was in every household in central New Spain, whether intended for consumption by the family, to entertain visiting friends, or to sell for a modest price. To drink, and to do so with restraint, was an everyday activity there as it was in other cultures.

The political conquest and subsequent economic and social limitations imposed by the Colonial-era government did not implement total destruction of indigenous lifeways. Provisional and continous adaptations took place, not only in rural communities but also among the new urban lower classes. In a large number of villages with no resident parish priest, people continued to drink in relative liberty, particularly in frequent community festivities that broke the monotonous rhythm of daily life. In the main population centers, occasions were more limited by the presence of the authorities and by the priest's inquisitive gaze within Indian barrios; paradoxically, in the barrios, the possibility of anonymity, impossible in remote communities, favored solitary inebriation and so contributed to some antisocial behavior.

At the end of the sixteenth century, Spaniards, *mestizos*, and mulattoes all began to engage in the increasingly profitable trade of pulque and other inebriating beverages, including wine from grapes, which enjoyed a unique status. Wine arrived from the Old World with the prerogatives of a Christian ritual beverage. Although frequently spoiled by the long journey from Spain, wine also took its place as a commercial product. Local authorities, supposedly entrusted with combating excessive indulgence, ironically became wine promoters, as the Crown encouraged the development of Spanish-style agriculture. Grape wine and the spirits derived from it (brandy) faced competition with local beverages, always available and less expensive. This partly accounts for the continued obstacles imposed by the authorities on the production and commerce in native alcoholic beverages. Despite such obstacles, many villages mainly engaged in farming (mostly in the highlands) depended on the pulque trade. From the seventeenth century onward, taxation of alcoholic beverages became a substantial source of financing for public works and other municipal projects. For this reason, white pulque (free from additives that increased inebriation effects) was the only authorized indigenous beverage.

The authorities pointed out the effects of excessive and disorderly drinking, not only in the context of private life but especially in public spaces, where bad examples might be emulated. Outlets for "permitted drinks" (pulque, grape wine, and other alcoholic beverages from Spain) were backed by official recognition and supervised by local authorities, a supervision not always adequate. All other alcoholic beverages were prohibited. The generic term "prohibited beverages" designated the alcoholic products for popular consumption—fermented or distilled, of doubtful origin, quality, and content—that were considered harmful and an inexhaustible source of conflicts.

Alcoholic beverages were obtained by two manufacturing processes: fermentation and distillation. Fermented beverages symbolized tradition. Most used *pulque curado*, a pulque that had been "fortified" with some variety of chili (hot pepper), fruit, corn syrup, or brown sugar—*guarapo* (from herbs with sugar cane or pineapple), *ojo de gallo* ("rooster's eye"), or *sangre de conejo* ("rabbit's blood"). Other fermented drinks were made from maize, like *quebrantahuesos* ("bone-breaker") and *tesgüino*. Some were even made from the peyote cactus (particularly prohibited) or based on fruits—apples, prickly pears, coconuts, and dates, among others. Distilled beverages were generically termed *aguardientes* ("fire water"). Previously unknown in the Americas, these had an aura of rebellious modernity, which contributed to their diffusion and success. To make them, stills were imported, along with sugar and sugar cane syrup from the West Indies. Stills could make beverages with a high alcohol content, including the two that attained the greatest popularity and were most harshly forbidden: mezcal and the type of *aguardiente* made from sugar cane syrup, known as *chinguirito*. In ancient times, the Zapotec and the Mayan Itzá brewed a fermented mezcal with the sap of local magueys, which differed from the species used in Central Mexico to make pulque. Stills made it possible to obtain mezcal as it is currently known, a product of fermentation followed by the distillation of sugars contained in the agave. The first mezcal to bear identification as a quality product was tequila. The difference among the various types of mezcal and tequila depends on the agave species used, improvements in the manufacturing process, and the place of origin (mainly in the Mexican state of Jalisco).

Another Mesoamerican beverage, a nonalcoholic drink, became the world-famous cocoa, or hot chocolate. As made today, from chocolate (*Theobroma cacao*) and milk sweetened with sugar, it is not the same as the pre-Hispanic beverage (nor is chocolate its original name). The drink that ancient Mesoamericans considered worthy of the gods, and one that Miguel León-Portilla (1997) presents with the alluring name of *atlaquetzalli* ("precious water"), was generally known as *cacaoatl* (cacao bean water). It was a cold drink that followed meals, prepared in water, and blended with spices and aromatic flowers that gave it a reddish hue and a touch of bitterness. The prized cacao beans were gathered from the large pods that grew on trees, which the Mexica also used as currency and obtained as tribute or by means of barter. The trees were grown mainly in the Maya lands of Soconusco, in Southeastern Mesoamerica. *Cacaoatl* was the excellent beverage reserved for nobles, poets, and sages. Priests avoided it, possibly as a sign of austerity and sacrifice. The *pochtecas* (Mexica merchants), who during their travels sometimes acted as "observer-spies," were regular consumers. Soldiers—the only group from lower-class background that drank it—were usually supplied for their campaigns with provisions that included not only toasted maize, chili, and beans but also portions of ground dried cacao formed into bars. Unlike other products of New World origin, cacao was never seriously questioned or outlawed by Europeans—perhaps because, along with its delicious flavor, it had the rare gift of not causing inebriation.

[*See also* Pulque.]

BIBLIOGRAPHY

Coe, Sophie D., and Michael D. Coe. *The True History of Chocolate*. London, 1996. Thorough study of the origins of cacao backed by little-known documents.

Corcuera de Mancera, Sonia. *El fraile el indio y el pulque. Evangelización y embriaguez en la Nueva España*. Mexico City, 1997. Problems of the evangelization of the Indians viewed through the first printed catechisms of New Spain.

Gonçalves de Lima, Oswaldo. *El maguey y el pulque en los códices mexicanos*. Mexico City, 1956. Pioneering study that highlights the important role of the maguey plant and pulque.

Informe de la Real Universidad sobre los inconvenientes de la bebida del pulque. Mexico City 1962. Written in the year of the "great pulque mutiny" in Mexico City. Housed in the National Library of Mexico.

León Pinelo, Antonio de. *Question moral. Si el chocolate quebranta el ayuno eclesiástico. Trátase de otras bebidas y confecciones que se usan en varias provincias*. Madrid, 1636. Excellent source; there is a facsimile edition (1994) published by the Centro de Estudios de Historia de México, Condumex (Center for the Study of Mexican History Condumex).

León-Portilla, Miguel. "Atlaquetzalli: Agua preciosa." In *Hazme cazón. Los historiadores y sus recetas de cocina*. Mexico City, 1997. Delicious interpretation of the uses of chocolate, by a highly qualified researcher of the Mesoamerican world.

Lozano Armendares, Teresa. *El chinguirito vindicado. El contrabando de aguardiente de caña y la política colonial*. Mexico City, 1995. Thorough study of colonial legislation on the so-called "forbidden drinks" and their economic consequences.

Motolinía, Toribio de Paredes. *Memoriales o libro de las cosas de la Nueva España y de los naturales que en ella viven*. Prepared by Edmundo O'Gorman. Mexico City, 1971. Eyewitness accounts of the world and life of Mesoamerica, by one of the first twelve Franciscan friars to arrive in New Spain (1524).

Sahagún, Bernardino de. *Códice Florentino*, edited by the Archivo General de la Nación. 3 vols. Mexico City, 1979. True encyclopedia of Nahua culture, including customs and beliefs related to beverages.

Taylor, William B. *Drinking, Homicide and Rebellion in Colonial Mexican Villages*. Stanford, Calif., 1979. Rigorous analysis of the effects of Spanish domination on peasant life during the Colonial period.

SONIA CORCUERA

BIRTH. In ancient Mesoamerica, human birth was not simply a biological event; it was related to some of the most basic and profound concepts of life, death, and cosmological order. The ritual acts and beliefs associated with parturition were directly concerned with such profound matters as the origins and nature of the soul, social roles and responsibilities, and the relationship of the individual to the gods and ancestors. Birth was also employed in metaphors to describe such acts as the conjuring of gods and ancestors through bloodletting and royal accession, as well as such abstract concepts as the origin and nature of the cosmos. The imagery surrounding human birth was an essential means by which the Mesoamerican peoples perceived themselves and their surrounding world.

The most detailed extant descriptions of birth ritual and symbolism pertain to the Aztec, particularly passages in book 6 of the *Florentine Codex*, which contain prayers and descriptions of pregnancy and rituals of birth, including the taking of sweatbaths and massages by the pregnant woman, the cutting and disposal of the umbilical cord, ritual bathing or baptism, and calendrical auguries concerning the future life of the child. According to Aztec belief, the infant is celestially conceived by drilling and blowing breath—basic acts of firemaking—and one passage of book 6 refers to the conception of a child as a shooting "spark." As Alfredo López Austin (1988, vol. 1, p. 209) notes, the gods blow the fiery *tonalli* life force to conceive the infant.

At birth, the severed umbilical cord was buried—that of a girl by the hearthstones in the "heart of the house," and that of a boy in a field of battle. The newborn was ritually bathed in honor of the water goddess, Chalchiuhtlicue, as a means of removing filth and contagion from previous acts committed by the parents. According to the early-seventeenth-century account of Hernando Ruíz de Alarcón, Chalchiuhtlicue was especially identified with childbirth because water was the first item touched by the newborn. In fact, in the codical "1 Reed" *trecena* scenes dedicated to Chalchiuhtlicue, infants are portrayed in a stream of water pouring from her loins, a motif clearly representing childbirth. After being kept near the constantly burning hearth for four days to protect its *tonalli*, the child was again ritually bathed at dawn and held aloft several times to the gods of the sky, and finally to the sun. The child then received its name and miniature forms of the accouterments of adulthood—warrior gear for boys and weaving implements for girls. An excellent depiction of this rite appears in the *Codex Mendoza*: an aged midwife holds an infant before a basin of water and miniature items of adulthood.

Aztec ideology portrayed childbirth as a courageous, warlike act in which the mother "captured" the infant for the state through painful blood battle. Women who died in childbirth were equated with heroic warriors slain in war. Just as the souls of male warriors carried the sun from the underworld to celestial zenith, the dead women accompanied it in its western descent into the underworld. Known as the *ciuapipiltin* or *mociuaquetzqui*, these celestial female spirits were greatly feared as fierce demonic beings, particularly on the days beginning the five western *trecenas*, when they were believed to dive headlong to earth to beguile and destroy unwary folk.

In Late Postclassic Central Mexican art, there are many portrayals of divine birth. In many cases, gods emerge not out of the loins but from the navel of the mother, which is often marked with the sign for jade. Quite frequently the face of the mother is turned sharply upward, as if she were facing the sky. A Late Postclassic polychrome vase attributed to Nayarit contains an elaborate scene of supernatural birth in the company of Tlaloc, Ehecatl, and other Central Mexican gods. The scene illustrates the birth ceremonies surrounding a pair of newborn twins. Among the depicted rites are the drilling of new fire, ceremonial bathing, and the use of the sweatbath (*temascal*)—all birth ceremonies also documented for the Aztec.

The importance of dynastic succession in ancient Mesoamerica made birth events a major component of elite historical texts. Still, the conventions for denoting birth varied considerably. The carved stone Late Classic Zapotec genealogical register, known as the Noriega Relief, indicates birth by portraying diminutive infants between adults. In the Postclassic Mixtec codices, birthdates—whether of historical individuals or of gods—are denoted by an umbilical cord connecting the individual to the year of birth. Although Classic Maya texts contain many references to the birth of particular historical figures, there are no explicit scenes of historical births in Classic Maya art; birth events are alluded to retroactively, usually when the individual is already an adult. The Classic Maya birth glyph is the upended head of the iguana, which in this context is to be read *siyah* ("is born").

Like the scenes and mythology of Late Postclassic Highland Mexico, Classic Maya inscriptions refer to the birth of gods as well as of historical individuals. The best-developed case occurs in the Cross Group at Palenque. The texts from the three temples contain detailed passages describing the divine birth of the Palenque Triad, and David Kelley has shown that each temple of the Cross Group corresponds to one of these three deities. Recent epigraphic research by Stephen Houston has established that the temples were referred to as *pib nah*, a Mayan term for "sweatbath." The role of the sweatbath in birth ceremonies continues to be widespread among contemporary native peoples of Mexico and Guatemala.

The most elaborate Classic scene of birth occurs on a four-sided vessel portraying birth within a cosmic house. Known as the Birth Vase, the vessel portrays a young goddess standing on a sacred mountain while holding onto a celestial rope formed of twisted serpents. Still today, in many regions of Mesoamerica, women give birth while holding onto a rope suspended from the roof beams of the house. In the terms of the Birth Vase, the birth rope also represents the sky umbilicus hanging from the center of the heavens. The celestial birth rope suggests that like the Aztec, the Classic Maya believed that at least part of the vitalizing force or forces—the soul—derived from the heavens. The Birth Vase portrays an old goddess embracing the young woman, with two others in the same scene. These aged deities are aspects of Chac Chel, the goddess of curing and midwives. The sixteenth-century account of Diego de Landa mentions that the Yucatec deity Ix Chel was "the goddess of making children." Although many have interpreted this to mean that she is a young, fertile woman, it actually refers to her role as a midwife; in many parts of Mesoamerica today, midwives are postmenopausal women.

BIBLIOGRAPHY
López Austin, Alfredo. *The Human Body and Ideology: Concepts of the Ancient Nahuas.* 2 vols. Translated by Thelma Ortiz de Montellano and Bernard Ortiz de Montellano. Salt Lake City, 1988. Detailed discussion of Aztec conceptions of birth and the origin and nature of animating principles of the human body; though focusing on sixteenth-century Nahuatl and Spanish sources, López Austin also includes ethnohistoric and ethnographic material from much of Mesoamerica.
Taube, Karl. "The Birth Vase: Natal Imagery in Ancient Maya Myth and Ritual." In *The Maya Vase Book*, vol. 4, edited by Barbara and Justin Kerr, pp. 652–685. New York, 1994. Analyzes the text and iconography of a Late Classic four-sided vase illustrating divine birth; discusses ancient Maya symbolism and deities of birth, Chac Chel; scenes are compared to birth rites and symbolism known for present-day Maya and other peoples of Mesoamerica.

KARL A. TAUBE

BLACK CARIB. *See* Garífuna.

BLOOD. *See* Human Body.

BLOODLETTING. *See* Autosacrifice and Bloodletting.

BODLEY, CODEX. The pre-Hispanic Mixtec pictorial manuscript known as *Codex Bodley 2858* is a screenfold book consisting of strips of deerskin glued together and folded into twenty-three pages measuring 26 by 29 centimeters. Twenty of these are painted on both sides, resulting in a pictorial text of forty numbered pages (twenty on the obverse of the codex, twenty on the reverse). Each page is subdivided into four or five horizontal "lines" by red guide lines in a *boustrophedon* (right-to-left, then left-to-right) reading pattern.

The codex is preserved in the Bodleian Library, Oxford. It was part of the collection made by Sir Thomas Bodley (1545–1613), after whom the library is named, and seems to have come into his possession during the years 1603–

1605, but it is not clear how. It has been speculated that it was among the books looted from the library of the bishop of Faro (Portugal) by Robert Devereux, earl of Essex, but there is no confirmation of this; it is also quite possible that the codex was bought by one of Bodley's agents, such as the London bookseller John Bill, who traveled widely through Europe and made a short visit to Spain.

The codex was probably made for Iya Qhcuaa 'Yaha Ndisi Nuu' (Lord 4 Deer "Sharp Eyed Eagle" or "Eagle of Tlaxiaco"), the last ruler of Tilantongo, who is mentioned in the document. He is also described by the *Relación geográfica* of Tilantongo as being the ruler of the place at the time of the Spanish conquest. He died shortly after and was not baptized. His father, Lord 10 Rain (Xico), is mentioned in archival documents, as is his brother, Lord 8 Death (Namahu), who became *cacique* of Yanhuitlan by marrying Lady 1 Flower (Cahuaco).

The contents of the codex are historical. The main structure of the story is relatively well understood, thanks to decipherment by Alfonso Caso, Nancy Troike, Emily Rabin, and several other scholars. The obverse side is essentially the genealogical history of Black Town, or Tilantongo (Ñuu Tnoo), a central *cacicazgo* or city-state in the Mixteca Alta (present-day Oaxaca, Mexico). It has a close parallel in the reverse of the *Codex Vindobonensis*.

The reverse side of *Codex Bodley* focuses on the closely related dynasties of "Temple of the Eye and the Crossed Beams or Legs," or Tlaxiaco (Ndisi Ñuu), and "Town of Flames," or Achitutla (Ñuu Ndecu), also in the Mixteca Alta. The last ruler here is also known from colonial sources: Iya Nacuañe "Dzavui Ndicandii" (Lord 8 Grass "Rain Sun") is described by Torquemada as the king of Tlaxiaco who opposed Motecuhzoma II. He was born in the year 7 Reed, which must be 1435 CE. Both lineages are said to descend from primordial personages who, in the sacred time of creation, were born from the tree or the river of Apoala. Both sides of the codex then refer to the three daughters of a couple who ruled in "Mountain that Opens-Insect," a sign that may represent Monte Albán. One of these princesses, Lady 5 Reed "Rain Quechquemitl," married the Mixtec Lord 9 Wind "Stone Skull"; together they became the founders of the Tilantongo dynasty. The other two married into the dynasty of "Town of the Xipe Bundle."

Detailed information is given on the early history of the Tilantongo dynasty. In the eleventh century, reigning power came into the hands of an important high priest, Lord 5 Alligator "Rain Sun," who, after having advanced through all priestly ranks, married twice. His eldest son of the second marriage, Lord 8 Deer "Jaguar Claw" (1063–1115 CE), became the most famous personage in Mixtec history. As a young man, Lord 8 Deer went to the Cave of Death (Huahi Cahi) with the princess of neighboring Jaltepec, Lady 6 Monkey, to invoke the help of the infernal guardian of that cave, the Cihuacoatl-like deity Lady 9 Grass. As a direct result, Lord 8 Deer became ruler of Tututepec on the Pacific coast. Later, when the untimely death of young Lord 2 Rain Ocoñaña brought the first dynasty of Tilantongo to an end, Lord 8 Deer seized power by entering into an alliance with outsiders (Toltecs) from the "Place of Reeds," probably Cholula in Central Mexico. Their leader, Lord 4 Jaguar, who in many ways reminds us of the "historical Quetzalcoatl," bestowed royal status on him by means of a nose-piercing ritual. At age fifty-two, Lord 8 Deer was killed by men of Lord 4 Wind, the oldest son of Lady 6 Monkey and Lord 11 Wind of the Town of the Xipe Bundle. This Lord 4 Wind then became the strongest power in the Mixtec region. He founded a new capital in Flint Town (Ñuu Yuchi, the archaeological site known as Mogote del Cacique), and he played an important part in founding the dynasties of Achiutla and Tlaxiaco.

Codex Bodley offers a relatively complete review of the complex family relationships among the dynasties of the main *cacicazgos* (community kingdoms) in the Mixteca Alta region and therefore is of unique importance for studying Mixtec kinship, marital alliance policies, and peer polity interaction. Because the genealogies are connected with dates (in the Mixtec calendar system of successive cycles of fifty-two years), *Codex Bodley* is also a crucial document for establishing a chronological framework for Mixtec Postclassic history. The links of the Mixtec ruling families with other historical personages give this chronology important implications as a point of reference for the broader Mesoamerican Postclassic. The first dates in the Mixtec codices are often sacred dates associated with the foundation of *cacicazgos* and dynasties in the mythic past. Alfonso Caso, in his pioneering work, counted them as real chronological indicators and therefore situated the beginning of Mixtec history at the end of the seventh century CE. The careful studies by Emily Rabin have corrected Caso's calculations, and the earliest dates are now held to coincide with the beginning of the Postclassic period (locally designated as the Natividad phase) in the tenth century CE.

[*See also* Pictorial Manuscripts.]

BIBLIOGRAPHY

Anders, Ferdinand, Maarten Jansen, and G. Aurora Pérez Jiménez. *Crónica mixteca: El Rey 8 Venado " Garra de Jaguar" y la dinastia de Teozacualco-Zaachila, Libro explicativo del llamado Códice Zouche-Nuttall*. Mexico City, 1992.

Caso, Alfonso. *Interpretación del Códice Bodley 2528*. Mexico City, 1960.

Jansen, Maarten. "Dates, Deities and Dynasties: Non-durational Time in Mixtec Historiography." In *Continuity and Identity in Native America, Essays in Honor of Benedikt Hartmann*, edited by Maarten Jansen et al., pp. 156–192. Leiden, 1988.

Jansen, Maarten. "Nombres históricos e identidad étnica en los códices mixtecos." *Revista europea de estudios latinoamericanos y del Caribe* 47 (1989), 65–87.

Jansen, Maarten. "La Princesa 6 Mono y el Héroe 8 Venado: Una epopeya mixteca." In *Historia del arte de Oaxaca*, edited by Margarita Dalton Palomo and Verónica Loera y Chávez, vol. 1, pp. 211–237. Oaxaca, 1998.

Spores, Ronald. "Marital Alliance in the Political Integration of Mixtec Kingdoms." *American Anthropologist* 76 (1974), 297–311.

Spores, Ronald. *The Mixtecs in Ancient and Colonial Times*. Norman, Okla., 1984.

Troike, Nancy. "Preliminary Notes on Stylistic Patterns in the Codex Bodley." *Actas del XLII Congreso Internacional de Americanistas* 6 (1979), 183–192.

MAARTEN E.R.G.N. JANSEN

BONAMPAK. *See* Murals.

BORBONICUS, CODEX. The screenfold known today as the *Codex Borbonicus* is arguably the most brilliantly painted of a handful of surviving native-style pictorial manuscripts attributed to the Aztec of Mexico. Beyond its vivid images, this document is notable for the insight it provides into Aztec rituals centered on two ancient Mesoamerican calendric constructs, the 260-day ritual calendar (*tonalpohualli*, "count of days") and the solar-based 360 + 5-day calendar (*xihuitl*, "year"). The *Codex Borbonicus* also exemplifies the manner in which indigenous manuscripts continued to be produced in the first years after the Spanish conquest of Mexico in 1521.

Drawn by indigenous *tlacuiloque* ("artist-scribes") and constructed in the pre-Hispanic format of a *tira*, or extended rectangular strip, it consists primarily of images, here painted on only one side. Brief, explanatory Spanish glosses in sixteenth-century script were also added, some in areas set aside for this purpose and others more randomly placed in unpainted areas. Folded accordion style to form a compact book consisting of individual panels, this flexible format allowed the screenfold to be read in various ways: spread out in its entirety, viewed in sections, or open to individual panels. The off-white, lime-based coating applied to the amate paper smoothed its surface and provided a contrasting pale background for the variety of intense colors utilized. Contrast was also provided by the black framing line that outlines images, most of which represent deities, deity impersonators, and other participants engaged in various ritual activities.

The screenfold retains thirty-six folded panels, approximately 39 by 40 centimeters (15 by 16 inches) each. Examination of its incomplete contents indicates that two panels are now missing from the front and back. The first notice about the screenfold, published in 1778, confirms this loss, for it was described as having forty panels when it was in the library of the Escorial in Spain. The largest of any surviving pre- or post-Conquest screenfold, the *Codex Borbonicus* is physically imposing. This feature raises questions, however, for it would have been unwieldy for practical use in the pre-Hispanic period and too conspicuous for use in the post-Conquest period, when it would have drawn unwelcome attention from Spanish authorities.

Purchased in 1826 for the library of the Chambre des Députés in Paris (now the Assemblée Nationale Française), housed in the former Bourbon Palace, the screenfold became known as the *Codex Borbonicus* (Y120). How it first arrived in France, or earlier in Spain, is unknown. The Mexican scholar Francisco del Paso y Troncoso, who

Tlazolteotl, one of the goddesses who was expelled from Tamoanchan for cutting the flowers that grew from the mouth of the mother goddess, Xochiquetzal, thereby causing the Earth to part from the Sky. *Drawing by Eric Roule from the* Codex Borbonicus *(f. 13).*

published the first intensive study of it in 1898, proposed that French invaders may have taken the screenfold during the Napoleonic wars of the early nineteenth century or during a later intervention in 1823. The loss of the four end panels may be connected with a hasty seizure. The 1898 study was soon followed by the first chromolithographic edition, accompanied by a shorter commentary by the French Americanist E. T. Hamy (1899). Since then, the screenfold has been published in several other editions (1974, 1979, 1997), attesting to its significance for Aztec studies.

A controversial aspect of the screenfold is its original date of execution in the sixteenth century. Because of its native-style images, format, and paper, early studies described it as a pre-Conquest document. The art historian Donald Robertson (1959) proposed that the manuscript was actually post-Conquest, a position vigorously contested by the Mexican scholar Alfonso Caso (1967), often citing Paso y Troncoso's earlier observations. A date in the 1520s, about the time of the Conquest, seems likely.

The *Codex Borbonicus* is prized for its outstanding draftsmanship. The description of its images as "native style" conveys their closeness to late pre-Hispanic painting, with scant signs of European stylistic influence. This assessment is necessarily limited, because all surviving Aztec manuscripts appear to be post-Conquest copies, earlier examples having been destroyed by the upheavals set in motion by the Spanish invasion of 1519. As the finest Aztec ritual manuscript extant, the *Codex Borbonicus* provides the best example of what a pre-Conquest Aztec manuscript must have looked like. It has thus become a touchstone for Aztec pictorial style in general, along with what remains of Aztec painting on surviving murals, ceramic painting, and a few other native-style manuscripts from the Basin of Mexico.

The *Codex Borbonicus* consists of two major and two minor sections. The first major part (3–18) represents a *tonalamatl*, the ritual handbook used by diviners to calculate the fate of a given day. This type of manuscript divided the 260 days of the *tonalpohualli* (calendar) into twenty thirteen-day periods called *trecenas* by the Spaniards. In this highly structured and uniformly presented section, each of the eighteen extant panels features one *trecena*. The *Codex Borbonicus* is the most densely painted and informative of any Aztec *tonalamatl*, although the content of the *Aubin Tonalamatl* from the Otomí-speaking region of Tlaxcala is closely related, indicating the widespread standardization of the *tonalamatl* format, patrons, and rituals throughout Central Mexico. Large-scale figures of the major deity (or deities) that exerted influence on the entire *trecena* appear in a boxed area in the upper left. These lavishly costumed figures are surrounded by standard ritual items (e.g., offerings of foods and liquids, incense burners), as well as other images specific to ceremonies connected to individual days or to rituals performed to ensure favorable prognostications. Two smaller sets of boxes flank this area. One contains images of thirteen of the twenty days ("day signs") and the numerals 1 through 13 (represented as dots), which share space with a rotating series of nine supernaturals, the so-called night lords. The other encloses another rotating series of thirteen supernaturals, the so-called day lords, and thirteen associated flying creatures (birds and a butterfly). The diviner weighed the multifarious mantic powers pictorially represented by these supernatural forces to determine the prospects for carrying out a successful course of action.

The second major section of the screenfold depicts ritual scenes associated with the eighteen annual ceremonies of the solar year, which consisted of eighteen twenty-day periods that the Spaniards called *veintenas* (23–37). Each one was dedicated to a particular deity or deities and featured an attendant set of ritual activities centering on agricultural and social concerns. Engaged in the pertinent rituals are costumed deity impersonators, priests, musicians, and ordinary, simply garbed commoners. Figures are well and colorfully drawn but smaller in scale than the dominant deity figures of the *tonalamatl*. Scale is sometimes arbitrary, for example, a subsidiary image (e.g., a clay pot with offerings) drawn larger than a nearby human participant. In contrast to the rigid grid of the *tonalamatl*, with its hieratic supernaturals, the *veintena* section lacks a consistent organizational plan for representing the varied activities carried out at major temple sites and other locales. The eighteen scenes are distributed among fourteen panels, with some panels divided by drawn black lines to accommodate more than one scene and some scenes extending across panel folds. Some scenes read vertically, whereas others are painted sideways, requiring the viewer to turn the panel (and entire screenfold) to view them. Scenes also vary in detail; some are sparsely depicted, with few participants, whereas others are more complex, with crowded fields and sequential activities. These inconsistencies also suggest a post-Conquest date, because pre-Conquest manuscripts from other areas are more uniformly organized and drawn. Although a few other *veintena* cycles survive, none displays the richness of the *Codex Borbonicus* episodes. These vivid scenes convey the remarkable panoply that characterized these lively and colorful public ceremonies, which were carried out with music, dancing, feasting, processions, costumed performers, and sacrificial offerings.

Whether Aztec artists before the Conquest depicted *veintena* ceremonies or devised this type of representation in the Early Colonial period has also been disputed.

Although no pre-Conquest *veintena* series exists, this does not preclude their having existed at one time, for sixteenth-century texts describe several types of now lost manuscripts. Just as the *tonalamatl* served as a handbook for the diviner, so a similar type of ceremonial manual may have existed to guide priests of the temple in performing the myriad activities of the annual ritual cycle or to instruct novice priests. The fact that the two major parts of the *Codex Borbonicus* would have been used by different kinds of religious specialists and that they represent two distinct types of manuscripts again signals that the screenfold is a post-Conquest compilation, with the possibility that each part originated in a different location. Compilations are characteristic of post-Conquest manuscript copies, whereas pre-Conquest documents generally feature one type of manuscript.

The *Codex Borbonicus* also includes two minor but important sections. Between the *trecenas* and *veintenas* are two facing panels (21–22). Framing them is another rotating series of nine night lords, here associated with fifty-two year signs and numerals related to yet a different calendric construct. Fifty-two years constituted a grand cycle of the two interlocking counts represented by the screenfold's two major sections, the 260-day *tonalpohualli* and 360 + 5-day solar year count. The Aztecs regarded the transition from one fifty-two-year cycle to another as a momentous and potentially disastrous occasion, for on it hinged the continuation of the universe for another fifty-two years. The *Codex Borbonicus* features a unique depiction of the New Fire Ceremony of 1507, which marked this event, and its inclusion indicates the importance of this ritual to the community for which the screenfold was made.

In the center of each panel are two scenes. On the left (21) is the aged primordial couple, Oxomoco engaged in divining with maize kernels and her partner, Cipactonal, holding an incense container and burner. A passage in Book 4 (The Soothsayers) of the *Florentine Codex* links this ancient pair to the invention of the *tonalamatl*, adding that their painted images adorned this book. A mural with a similar scene was recently unearthed in the Templo Mayor of Tlatelolco, painted on one side of a rectangular structure known as the Templo Calendárico, which features reliefs of the days signs of the first three *trecenas* of the *tonalpohualli* carved around the remaining sides. The similarity in style and iconography between these rare divining scenes supports a possible Tenochtitlan–Tlatelolco origin for the screenfold. On the right (22), another actively posed pair represents the two Aztec deities most closely associated with various aspects of the calendar. On the left, in priestly garb, is Quetzalcoatl (Feathered Serpent), who is credited with the creation of the calendar. Facing him on the right is his adversary, Tezcatlipoca (Smoking Mirror), the arch diviner whose "smoking mirror" ornament served as a divining instrument. These two scenes recall surviving fragmentary accounts regarding the origins of time, the calendar, and the relation between the actions of humans and the will of the gods, tales that very likely were once preserved in the oral lore associated with the rituals of the screenfold's two major sections.

The final section (37–38) contains another set of year signs for a fifty-two-year cycle, incomplete because of the loss of the last two panels; a fire drill above the year sign 2 Acatl (Reed) indicates a New Fire year.

Given the elaborate costumes and staging of the *veintena* ceremonies, the unique depiction of the New Fire Ceremony, and the screenfold's outstanding quality, commentators assumed that it must have derived from a major Aztec city, in particular the Tenochca capital of Tenochtitlan. Although this city remains a possibility, another hypothesis proposes another Basin of Mexico area. Although Paso y Troncoso surmised that depictions of Huitzilopochtli, the special deity patron of the Mexica, pointed to a Tenochtitlan origin, H. B. Nicholson (1988) noted that emphasis on the fertility goddess Cihuacoatl, rather than Huitzilopochtli and Tezcatlipoca, argued otherwise. He proposed that prominent appearances of her impersonator during the detailed harvest ceremony of Ochpaniztli (29–32) and other *veintenas* pointed to an origin in the agriculturally rich southern Basin. Because Cihuacoatl was the patroness of Colhuacan and the Aztec New Fire Ceremony was carried out at the hill of Huixachtlan near Itztapalapan, he posited a possible origin in the Colhuacan–Itztapalapan area.

Despite still unresolved questions, the *Codex Borbonicus* remains a stellar example of Aztec manuscript painting, indispensable for an understanding of the visual representation of Aztec calendric constructions and the deities and ritual performances associated with them.

[*See also* Pictorial Manuscripts.]

BIBLIOGRAPHY

Caso, Alfonso. *Los calendarios prehispánicos.* Mexico City, 1967. Detailed study of the Central Mexican calendar, with extended treatment of the *Codex Borbonicus.*

Codex Borbonicus. Manuscrit mexicain de la Bibliothèque du Palais Bourbon. Commentary by E. T. Hamy. Paris, 1899; reprint, Mexico City, 1979. First chromolithographic edition of the *Codex Borbonicus* with a descriptive commentary.

Codex Borbonicus. Bibliothèque de l'Assemblée Nationale—Paris (Y120). Commentaries by Karl Anton Nowotny and Jacqueline de Durand-Forest. Graz, 1974. Photographic facsimile of the screenfold, accompanied by a discussion of its origin and contents by Nowotny and a description by Durand-Forest.

Couch, N. C. Christopher. *The Festival Cycle of the Aztec Codex Borbonicus.* BAR International Series 270. Oxford, 1985. Investigation of the *veintena* section of the screenfold.

El libro del Ciuacoatl: Homenaje para el año del Fuego Nuevo. Libro explicativo del llamado Códice Borbónico. Commentary by Ferdinand Anders, Maarten Jansen, and Luis Reyes García. Madrid, Graz, and Mexico City, 1991. Photographic reproduction of the 1974 facsimile, retitled in honor of the fertility goddess prominently honored in the *veintena* section, featuring a new commentary.

Nicholson, H. B. "The Provenience of the Codex Borbonicus: An Hypothesis." In *Smoke and Mist: Mesoamerican Studies in Memory of Thelma D. Sullivan*, edited by J. Kathryn Josserand and Karen Dakin, pt. 1, pp. 77–97. BAR International Series 402(I). Oxford, 1988. Reconsideration of the origin of the screenfold, proposing a location in the Colhuacan-Itztapallapan area of the southern Basin of Mexico.

Paso y Troncoso, Francisco del. *Descripción, Historia y Exposición del Códice Pictórico de los Antiguos Náuas*. Florence, 1898; reprint, Mexico City, 1979. First extensive study of the screenfold that describes its contents and includes a valuable discussion of its history.

Quiñones Keber, Eloise. "Ritual and Representation in the Tonalamatl of the Codex Borbonicus." *Latin American Indian Literatures Journal* 3.2 (1987), 184–195. Examination of allusions to pre-Hispanic ritual performance contained in the images of the *tonalamatl*.

Robertson, Donald. *Mexican Manuscript Painting of the Early Colonial Period: The Metropolitan Period*. Norman, Okla., 1994 [1959]. Lucid description of the style of the *Codex Borbonicus*, including Robertson's argument for a post-Conquest dating.

ELOISE QUIÑONES KEBER

BORGIA, CODEX. The pictorial manuscript now known as the *Codex Borgia* is a pre-Hispanic screenfold book consisting of fourteen strips of deerskin folded to form seventy-eight pages measuring 26.5 by 27 centimeters. The two outside pages were once connected to covers and not painted; the remaining pages show brilliant polychrome painting on stucco. The *Codex Borgia* is a characteristic product of the so-called Mixteca-Puebla style (Nicholson and Quiñones Keber, 1994). Its precise provenance is not known, but its style and content have parallels in the Cholula-Tlaxcala area, the Tehuacán Valley, and the Mixtec region (Sisson, 1983; Anders, Jansen, and Loo, 1994).

Its first known owner was Cardinal Stefano Borgia (1731–1804), an erudite collector of antiquities, who was connected—first as a secretary, later as prefect—with the Congregation of Propaganda Fide in Rome. The cardinal invited an exiled Jesuit, José Lino Fábrega (1746–1797), to write a commentary on this codex, a work not published until 1899. Fábrega suggests that the codex was saved from being burnt in the sixteenth century and after that was in the possession of various persons in New Spain and Europe until it came in the hands of Cardinal Borgia, who gave it an important place in his "museum" at Velletri. After his death (and a legal battle over the estate), it became the property of the Propaganda Fide. In 1902 it was transferred, together with other documents of the *Fondo Borgiano*, to the Vatican Library, where it is conserved as *Codex Borgia Messicano 1*.

Alexander von Humboldt published a first short note on the existence of the *Codex Borgia*. Drawings made of it by Aglio were included in Lord Kingsborough's monumental *Antiquities of Mexico* (1831–1848). Later, a facsimile edition was sponsored by the duke of Loubat (1898). Fábrega's pioneering commentary presented an impressive synthesis of eighteenth-century Americanist scholarship. By comparing the manuscript with the *Codex Vaticanus* 3738 ("A"), Fábrega was able to decipher some sections. He was soon surpassed, however, by Eduard Seler, whose methodical and detailed iconographic and philological studies laid the foundation for modern codex research. Seler's commentary (1904–1909) is a classic in this field, and much of his descriptive analysis is still valid. Astralistic interpretations which proceeded from the dominant paradigm in Seler's day were corrected by the subsequent work of Karl Anton Nowotny (1961), who emphasized the mantic (divinatory) and ritual character of the scenes. Ironically, shortly thereafter in 1963, Seler's commentary was translated into Spanish and promoted the old German *Astraldeutung* that Nowotny had definitively refuted. For the facsimile edition, brought out by Akademische Druck-und Verlagsanstalt in Graz, Nowotny wrote a special commentary (1976). Both Seler's and Nowotny's works were the basis for other studies (e.g., Spranz, Nicholson, Biedermann). In 1993, a redrawn and restored version of the *Codex Borgia* was published by Díaz and Rodgers, with a descriptive introduction by Bruce Byland. Meanwhile, the work of interpretation had been given new impetus by Ferdinand Anders, Maarten Jansen, Peter van der Loo, Gabina Aurora Pérez Jiménez, and Luis Reyes García. Working together as a research team and proceeding from the insights of Nowotny, they drew on ethnographic data and oral traditions from present-day Mexican Indian communities to the religious (divinatory-ritual) codices. This resulted in new commentaries on the *Borgia* and related codices, published by the Fondo de Cultura Económica in Mexico (1993–1994), together with enhanced reprints of the Graz facsimile editions.

The *Codex Borgia*'s importance to the study of the Mesoamerican region cannot be overstated. As an original work of art by a great master, it combines profound content with an enormous aesthetic value. It is a priest's manual which registers multiple associations among days, directions, and deities in order to formulate the significance of time, to prognosticate the character and vicissitudes of a person born on a certain day or the favorable time to initiate certain enterprises, to warn of possible dangers, to establish the causes of problems, and

Detail of a deerskin almanac. *After Graz edition. Courtesy of Akademische Druck- u. Verlagsanstalt, Graz, Austria.*

to prescribe ritual remedies. The many subdivisions of the calendar and their many associations correspond to the many contexts in which the book had to provide counsel. Thus, it offers unique insights into pre-Hispanic ceremonial practices, visionary experiences, and divinatory discourse. [*See* Calendars and Calendrical Systems, *article on* Mesoamerian Calendar.]

In overview its contents may be characterized as follows. Pages 1–8 give the sacred count of 260 days (*tonalpohualli*), organized in four quarters of five 13-day periods. Each "quarter" occupies two pages and—as we know from other sources—is associated with one of the four world directions. The 13-day periods are written out in full: all day signs are given, in five horizontal rows of thirteen, one above the other, so that each quarter contains thirteen "columns" of five day signs each. The day signs in each column combine with the same number (between 1 and 13). Each column is associated with two divinatory symbols, one above and one below. Several of these can be interpreted with the help of the work of Bernardino de Sahagún (especially book 6) and other sources. Weapon bundles and the combination of water and fire represent war; a burning house or temple indicates destruction. Owls, bones, or the death god taking a prisoner foretell

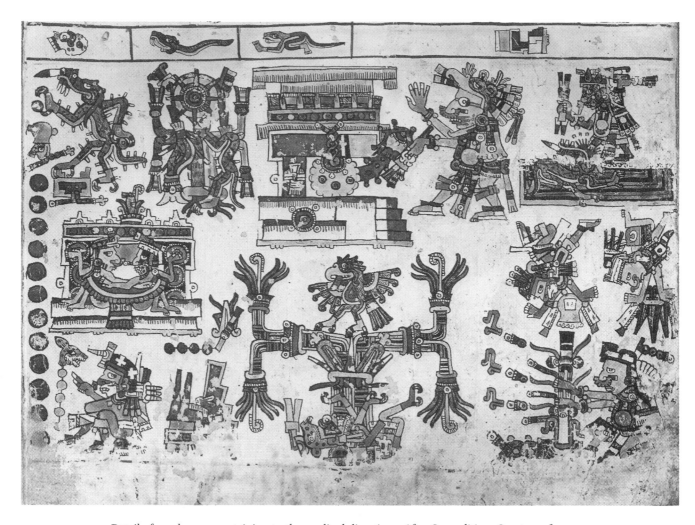

Detail of an almanac pertaining to the cardinal directions. *After Graz edition. Courtesy of Akademische Druck- u. Verlagsanstalt, Graz, Austria.*

death. Intertwined serpents descending from dark skies signal danger and vicious intrigues. Standing vessels symbolize abundance, upturned vessels the opposite. Flowers, jewels, and precious birds are favorable signs that announce happiness and glory.

On pages 9–13, the twenty day signs are listed with their patron deities, whose divinatory aspect is made explicit by symbols. These associations had implications for the character and destiny of those born on a specific day. For example, the patron of the day sign Alligator is the Lord of Our Sustenance (Tonacatecuhtli): an image of a man and woman under a blanket symbolizes procreation and abundance. The patron of the day sign Water is Xiuhtecuhtli, the Fire God: a scorpion announces conflict; water and fire combined may be put to use in a sweatbath but may also represent war. The patron of the day sign Flower is Xochiquetzal, or Flower-Quetzal, goddess of art and pleasure: the breaking of the metate stone announces

death in the family. On page 14, the 260 days are accompanied by the Lords of the Night in cycles of nine; their divinatory aspect is symbolized by a temple (good), crossroads (bad), and a plant or water (indifferent).

Pages 15–17 depict the patrons of childbirth ruling over the twenty day signs, divided in five sequential segments of four days each. First the gods are shown opening the child's eyes with a bone perforator, making it aware of life and at the same time of its ritual obligations. Then they present the child—that is, let it be born. Seizing the umbilical cord, the deities manifest their influence over the child's destiny. Finally, five goddesses determine the aspects of nursing during the days in question.

The twenty day signs are shown on page 17 distributed over the body of Tezcatlipoca. This association has implications for the character of the days: for example, Flower is associated with his tongue, so those who are born on such a day will master the art of oratory.

On pages 18–21, eight images are associated with the fifty-two columns of five days of the *tonalpohualli* (as presented on pp. 1–8). Each shows a patron deity and the negative aspects for certain activities during those days: death and destruction resulting from vicious intrigues threaten successively the house of the noble man, the priest, the woman who goes for water, the ballplayer, the traveler (merchant or ambassador), the farmer, the woodcutter, and the couple.

In the upper register of page 22, the first two "quarters" of five 13-day periods (as on pp. 1–8) are associated with images of deer. Their first period is for decorating and venerating the dead animal; the second is for hunting it. The lower register of page 22 and pages 23–24 give an alternative list of the twenty day signs with patron deities or divinatory signs, or both.

Page 25 is devoted to the twenty-day period following the day 10 Movement, up to the famous day 4 Movement (the calendar name of the present sun, or era). This is divided among four deities, patrons of war: the "Flayed One," Xipe; the rain god, Tlaloc; the ancestral lord Qhyo Sayo (4 Serpent-7 Serpent, known from the Mixtec sources); and the archetypal hunter, Mixcoatl. On page 26, four deities rule over the cult for the dead; each one dominates a segment of four days of the twenty-day period (cf. pp. 15–17).

On pages 27–28, we find prognostications of climatic patterns in the different calendrical periods. The rain god is shown as a central force with a double aspect, bringing water and war, seeds and death. His aspects differ according to the world direction with which he is associated. The thirteen-year period starting with Year 1 Reed and the 65-day period starting with day 1 Alligator are associated with the east: cloudy skies, abundant rain, fertile earth. The periods of the north suffer from heat, plagues of insects, stony and sterile earth. In the west, we encounter cloudy skies, too much rain, inundations. The south brings heat, drought, and plagues of mice. The second page (p. 28) shows the character of the rainwater and of the responding feminine force of seeds and earth during successive years with specific sacred days.

The central chapter on pages 29–47 is to be read top-down, after turning the codex 90° to the left. Important parallels are to be found in the Mixtec *Codex Nuttall* (pp. 15–19), in the frescoes of Ocotelulco in Tlaxcala, and in Maya iconography (e.g., the tomb of Pakal). The ceremonies are shown taking place in a specific cult center which contains, among others, a temple of heaven (like the central sanctuary of Tilantongo) and a temple of Cihuacoatl (like the Tlillan of Xochimilco, represented in the *Codex Borbonicus*). The extraordinary value of this presentation is that it goes far beyond a description of the cult: it conveys an ecstatic religious experience and a symbolic worldview. Objects are represented as animated spirit beings: vessels become "god-pots." Trance is represented by snakes (vision serpents). Priests in shamanic ecstasy share the mysterious existence of the gods and themselves become spirit matter, depicted as serpents with bodies of night and wind.

There are nine rituals, which focus on the magical passages from darkness to light, from death to life, and from sacrifice to the creation of fertility and power. Rite 1 (pp. 29–32) starts with a penis perforation scene in the Temple of Cihuacoatl—its walls are the body of the goddess and that of her vegetal manifestation, *piciete*. In a god-pot, the hallucinogenic black ointment is prepared which makes it possible for priests to enter trance. [*See* Shamanism, *entry on* Pre-Hispanic Shamanism.] The self-sacrifice of the goddess (i.e., of a person consecrated to her) releases a spirit force, which is bathed like a new-born child and made into a holy bundle. The sacrificial knife, the "child of Cihuacoatl," is placed in a god-pot in the patio before the temple and venerated as a deity by priests dancing in the night. The following rituals are introduced (or ordered) by the high priest or priestess, represented as Cihuacoatl, from whose breast the force and words come to set the ceremony in motion. Sacrifices are made for the temple of heaven. The holy bundle is opened. Various sacrificial ceremonies result in the magical creation of maize. A nose-piercing ceremony and the making of the New Fire are also described. The ninth rite (p. 47) is the creation (or invocation) of the Tonaleque and Cihuateteo (the archetypal father as a manifestation of Macuilxóchitl, with the animating force of the sacrificed warrior, and the archetypal mother as a manifestation of the earth goddess, with the magical power of women who have died in childbirth).

On pages 47–48, the thirteen-day periods in the western and southern quarters (cf. pp. 1–8) are shown under the patronage of five different manifestations of the Cihuateteo and Tonaleque, with implications for cult actions to obtain strength and purification. The lower registers of pages 49–53 offer large composite scenes of trees, temples, deities, and divinatory images associated with the four world directions and the center. The upper registers of these pages show the patrons of the four Year Bearers (the four day signs used for naming the years); each patron is accompanied by another god who rules the following three (non-Year Bearer) day signs. In the upper left-hand corner of page 53, the character of each of the twenty day signs is expressed by its position on a deer hide.

Pages 53–54 offer five manifestations of the Venus god, Tlahuizcalpantecuhtli, who attacks certain segments of society and nature as he becomes visible on certain days: successively water, the community, maize, the authorities, and the warriors. There is an important parallel in the Maya *Codex Dresden*, where these images are put in the context of an almanac that registers the appearances and aspects of Venus. In the following pages, six deities influence the traveling of merchants or ambassadors (p. 55); the life-giving force of Quetzalcoatl influences the odd thirteen-day periods, while the death god, Mictlantecuhtli, rules the even ones (p. 56); and the 52 columns of five day signs are divided among six pairs of deities, as patrons of marriages (p. 57).

Prognostications for married couples, according to the sum of the numbers in their calendar names, appear on pages 58–60. Logically there are 25 possibilities, ranging from 2 (= 1 + 1) to 26 (= 13 + 13).

Pages 61–70 are devoted to the twenty 13-day periods with their patrons and divinatory images. There is great similarity with the list of patrons of the individual day signs (pp. 9–13).

The sun god Tonatiuh appears on page 71 as a warlord on his throne, surrounded by the thirteen ominous birds associated with the thirteen numbers. On page 72, the twenty day signs are distributed over the bodies of four deities, surrounded by four great serpents, associated with the four directions. In the center there is a black spider. Possibly the image provides a clue to identifying the divine powers that might cause sickness in certain parts of the body during specific days. Page 73 offers an image of the contrary forces of Mictlantecuhtli and Quetzalcoatl similar to that on page 56. This time, each god influences a segment of the twenty-day period. The character of each sign is further specified by its location on a body part of the combined image. The twenty day signs on page 74 are combined with the Cihuateteo and Tonaleque, probably indicating divinatory aspects for home and family life.

On pages 75–76, the four quarters of 13-day periods are subdivided into units of seven and six columns, each under the supervision of a deity. The patrons of the first and second segments of the eastern 13-day periods are the rain god, Tlaloc, and the sun god, Tonatiuh, respectively. The following divisions are under the patronage of the death god, Mictlantecuhtli, and the mother goddess, Tlazolteotl (north), the maize god and Venus (west), Malinalteotl (the god of the herb *malinalli*), and Macuilxochitl (south).

[*See also* Pictorial Manuscripts.]

BIBLIOGRAPHY

Anders, Ferdinand, and Maarten Jansen. *El Manual del adivino: Libro explicativo del llamado Códice Vaticano B (Códice Vaticano 3773)*. Mexico City, 1993.

Anders, Ferdinand, Maarten Jansen, and Luis Reyes García. *Los templos del cielo y de la oscuridad: Oráculos y liturgia, Libro explicativo del llamado Códice Borgia (Mus. Borg. P.F. Messicano 1)*. Mexico City, 1993.

Anders, Ferdinand, Maarten Jansen, and Peter van der Loo, with Eduardo Contreras Martínez and Beatriz Palavicini Beltrán. *Calendario de pronósticos y ofrendas: Libro explicativo del llamado Códice Cospi (4093)*. Mexico City, 1994.

Biedermann, Hans. *Jade, Gold und Quetzalfedern*. Graz, 1989.

Díaz, Gisele, Alan Rodgers, and Bruce E. Byland. *The Codex Borgia: A Full-Color Restoration of the Ancient Mexican Manuscript*. New York, 1993.

Fábrega, José Lino. *Interpretación del códice Borgiano. Anales del Museo Nacional de México*, vol. 5. Mexico City, 1899.

Loo, Peter L. van der. *Códices, Costumbres y Continuidad*. Dissertation, Leiden University, 1987.

Nicholson, H. B. "Religion in Prehispanic Central Mexico." In *Handbook of Middle American Indians*, edited by Robert Wauchope, vol. 10, pp. 395–446. Austin, Tex., 1971.

Nicholson, H. B., and Eloise Quiñones Keber, eds. *Mixteca-Puebla: Discoveries and Research in Mesoamerican Art and Archaeology*. Culver City, Calif., 1994.

Nowotny, Karl Anton. *Tlacuilolli, die mexikanischen Bilderhandschriften, Stil und Inhalt, mit einem Katalog der Codex Borgia Gruppe*. Monumenta Americana. Berlin, 1961.

Nowotny, Karl Anton. *Codex Borgia*. Graz, 1976.

Seler, Eduard. *Codex Borgia: Eine almexikanische Bilderschrift der Bibliothek der Congregatio de Propaganda Fide*. 3 vols. Berlin, 1904–1909. Spanish translation, *Comentarios al Códice Borgia*. Mexico City, 1963, 1988.

Sisson, Edward B. "Recent Work on the Borgia Group Codices." *Current Anthropology* 24 (1983), 653–656.

Spranz, Bodo. *Göttergestalten in den mexikanischen Bilderhandschriften der Codex Borgia-Gruppe: Eine ikonographische Untersuchung*. Acta Humboldtiana. Wiesbaden, 1964. Spanish translation, *Los dioses en los códices mexicanos del Grupo Borgia: Una investigación iconográfica*. Mexico City, 1973.

MAARTEN E.R.G.N. JANSEN

BORGIA GROUP OF PICTORIAL MANUSCRIPTS.

In pre-Hispanic Mesoamerica, bark paper and vellum screenfolds served as pictographic-hieroglyphic "manuals" to guide specialists in techniques of calendrical divination that were based, above all, on the *tonalpohualli*, a 260-day cycle of 13-day and 20-day periods whose days, arranged in various configurations and influenced by different deities, sacred birds, and other forces, connoted fortunate or unfortunate auguries. These diviners were constantly consulted to ascertain whether a particular day was favorable or unfavorable, particularly days of birth and other significant events in the life of the individual and the community.

Few of these divinatory manuals survived the vigorous efforts of the Spanish missionaries to destroy them. However, repositories in Italy and England today hold five specimens that are closely related stylistically and iconographically and were probably carried early to Europe as curiosities. In 1830–1831, they were first published in their entirety as colored lithographs of copies made by an Italian artist, Agustino Aglio, in volumes 2 and 3 of Lord Kingsborough's monumental *Antiquities of Mexico*. They were baptized the "Codex Borgia Group" by Eduard

Seler, who in 1887 began publishing a series of important elucidations of their contents. They are best known today as the codices *Borgia*, *Vaticanus B* (Biblioteca Apostolica Vaticana, Rome), *Cospi* (Biblioteca Universitaria, Bologna), *Fejérváry-Mayer* (National Museums and Galleries of Merseyside, Liverpool Museum), and *Laud* (Bodleian Library, Oxford). All have been considered pre-Hispanic, although recently one scholar has argued, somewhat unconvincingly, that *Cospi* is post-Conquest.

Two other native tradition pictorials, one pre-Hispanic and the other colonial, are stylistically and iconographically similar to those of the Borgia Group and are sometimes included in it. The first, painted on a single vellum sheet and most commonly designated *Fonds Mexicain 20*, was collected by Lorenzo Boturini in Mexico in the eighteenth century and is now in the Aubin-Goupil collection, Bibliothèque Nationale, Paris. The second, the *Codex Porfirio Díaz*, consists of 10 pages of a vellum screenfold in the Museo Nacional de Antropología, Mexico City. Also known as the *Codice de Tututepetongo*, it appeared in the community of that name in the Cuicatec-speaking region of northern Oaxaca in the late nineteenth century.

With no reliable information concerning when, where, and by whom they were obtained and sent or carried to Europe, ascertaining the proveniences of the five "core members" of the Borgia Group has proved quite difficult. Seler, who achieved considerable success interpreting them utilizing ethnohistorical data largely from the Basin of Mexico and surrounding territory, vacillated between Puebla-Tlaxcala and the Gulf Coast, finally preferring the former area. He was convinced—mainly because of the depiction in three members of the group of versions of the *atl tlachinolli* ("sacred war") symbol (which he had first identified)—that they had been produced by Nahua speakers. However, this is hardly determinative, for, as Nicholson pointed out in 1966, this metaphor also existed in Mixtec, Otomí, and probably other Mesoamerican languages. In 1927, the discovery of the altar paintings of Tizatlan, Tlaxcala, stylistically and iconographically quite close to *Borgia* and *Cospi*, considerably reinforced the opinions of those who favored their Puebla-Tlaxcala provenience.

Then, in a series of studies beginning in 1963, the art historian Donald Robertson argued vigorously for an origin—with the possible exception of the *Codex Vaticanus B*—of the group in the Mixtec-speaking area of western Oaxaca. This view was in conformity with the growing "pan-Mixtec" approach, wherein Mixtec speakers were largely credited with spreading "their" style throughout Late Postclassic Mesoamerica. Responding in part to Robertson's views, Nicholson in 1966 reexamined the provenience problem, questioning the pan-Mixtec approach and favoring a Puebla-Tlaxcala provenience, at least for *Borgia* and *Cospi*. Archaeologists connected with Richard MacNeish's 1960–1965 Tehuacán Project argued, mainly from ceramic evidence, for a Tehuacán Valley origin for *Borgia*; others have agreed, citing additional archaeological data and the evidence of costume. In 1990 and 1991, the discoveries of Postclassic polychrome murals at the sites of Ocotelulco, Tlaxcala, and Tehuacán Viejo (La Mesa), Puebla, stylistically and iconographically close to *Borgia*, provided further support for a Puebla-Tlaxcala origin for it and *Cospi*. Many now favor a Gulf Coast provenience for the stylistically nearly identical codices *Fejérváry-Mayer* and *Laud*, but there is still considerable difference of opinion concerning that of *Vaticanus B*.

In the closing years of the eighteenth century, José Lino Fábrega, a Mexican Jesuit exiled in Rome, undertook a laudable pioneer effort to elucidate the iconography of the *Borgia*. It was not until Eduard Seler entered the field, however, that significant progress was made. Utilizing to the full his "Rosetta Stones," the twin annotated codices *Telleriano-Remensis* and *Vaticanus A*, and relevant pictorial and written data in Sahagún and other colonial ethnohistorical sources, the German scholar, in articles and commentaries published mainly between 1887 and 1909, achieved considerable success, particularly on the identificatory level. He had much less success interpreting the deeper levels of meaning of the Borgia Group's rich, variegated imagery; here he was hampered by his predilection for astral explanations, particularly his earlier "Venusian obsession" and his later, even more pervasive "lunar obsession."

Since Seler's epochal researches, a number of significant studies of the Borgia Group as a whole and of its individual members have appeared, often accompanying new facsimiles. Of special importance have been Karl Nowotny's *Tlacuilolli* (1961), a comprehensive illustrated catalogue and discussion of the Borgia Group and related western Mesoamerican pictorials, and Bodo Spranz's illustrated catalogue of the iconographic elements of the members of the Group (1964, 1973). Nowotny often corrected and improved on Seler's interpretations. Among his more significant advances was his recognition that *Borgia* Section 21, *Vaticanus B* 12, and *Laud* 2 probably involved marriage prognostications based on adding the numerical coefficients of the couple's day signs; that *Borgia* Section 19, *Fejérváry-Mayer* 9–11, and *Laud* 9 appear to concern the merchants and auguries for the days of their departure on mercantile expeditions (a view further elaborated by Eric Thompson in 1966); and that *Fejérváry-Mayer* Sections 3, 4, and 16, *Laud* 6 and 9, and *Cospi* 4 pictorialized ritual prescriptions of the type known to survive among some of the modern Tlapanec, Mixtec, Tequiztlatec, and Mixe of Guerrero and Oaxaca, where they were employed for arranging carefully counted, bundled, and piled offerings before images of various deities. Rejecting Seler's Venusian interpretations, Nowotny also grappled with the remarkable complex and unique central Section 13 of *Borgia*, instead suggesting that these eighteen pages imaged sets of rituals, including some featuring sacred bundles, that were conducted in the temple(s) that owned *Borgia*.

Many lesser studies of aspects of members of the Borgia Group have appeared through the years. Beginning with the excellent (for their time) facsimiles of *Borgia*, *Vaticanus B*, *Cospi*, and *Fejérváry-Mayer* that were financed between 1896 and 1901 by the Duc de Loubat, numerous facsimiles of the five core members of the group have been issued and are now available. In 1964–1968, the Secretaría de Hacienda y Crédito Público, Mexico, published, in four volumes, a partial reedition of Kingsborough's *Antiquities of Mexico* that includes their reproduction in color photographs, with new Spanish commentaries by José Corona Nuñez, largely derived from those of Seler. Of particularly high quality have been the facsimiles issued since 1966 by the Akademische Druck- und Verlagsanstalt, Graz, Austria, latterly collaborating with the Fondo de Cultura Económica in Mexico. Their recent (1993–1994) facsimiles of *Borgia*, *Vaticanus B*, *Cospi*, *Fejérváry-Meyer*, and *Laud* were accompanied by important new commentaries, in Spanish, by Ferdinand Anders and Maarten Jansen, and various collaborators. These studies, building on the earlier work of Seler and Nowotny but taking into more consideration relevant modern ethnographic data, provide the most comprehensive, up-to-date interpretations of the members of this tiny but precious remnant of Mesoamerica's religious and divinatory pictorial literature, which opens a fascinating window into the ideological world of the New World's most advanced indigenous civilization.

[*See also* Borgia, Codex; Cospi, Codex; Fejérváry-Mayer, Codex; Laud, Codex; Vaticanus B, Codex.]

BIBLIOGRAPHY

Aguilera, Carmen. "A New Approach to the Codex Cospi." In *LAIL Speaks! Selected Papers from the VII International Symposium on Latin American Literatures*, edited by Mary H. Preuss, pp. 51–55. Culver City, Calif. 1990. Argues that the *Codex Cospi* is post-Hispanic.

Anders, Ferdinand, and Maarten Jansen. *Manual del Adivino: Libro explicatico del llamado Códice Vaticano B. Codex Vaticanus 3773, Biblioteca Apostólica Vaticana*. Mexico City, 1993. Facsimile of the screenfold and commentary on it, with a general discussion of the ritual and divinatory system with which the members of the Borgia Group are concerned.

Anders, Ferdinand, and Maarten Jansen, with Alejandra Cruz Ortiz. *La Pintura de la Muerte y de los Destínos: Libro explicativo del llamado Códice Laud, Misc. 678, Bodleian Library, Oxford, Inglaterra*. Mexico City, 1994. Facsimile of the screenfold and commentary

on it, with discussion of the Mesoamerican religious-ritual system and a reproduction of and commentary on the ten pages of the Cuicatec *Codice de Tututepetongo (Porfirio Díaz)* that feature ritual-divinatory material similar to that in the Borgia Group.

Anders, Ferdinand, Maarten Jansen, and Gabina Aurora Pérez Jiménez. *El Libro de Tezcatlipoca, Señor del Tiempo: Libro explicativo del llamado Códice Fejérváry-Mayer, M/12014, Free Public Museum, Liverpool, Inglaterra*. Mexico City, 1994. Facsimile of the screenfold and commentary on it; introduction includes a summary index of all the sections of the members of the group, noting those that are parallel and labeling the principal theme of each.

Anders, Ferdinand, Maarten Jansen, and Luis Reyes García. *Los Templos del Cielo y de la Oscuridad, Oráculos y Liturgía: Libro explicativo del llamado Códice Borgia (Museo Borgia P.F. Messicano 1), Biblioteca Apostólica Vaticana*. Mexico City, 1993. Facsimile of the screenfold that gives its name to the group, and commentary on it.

Anders, Ferdinand, Maarten Jansen, and Peter van der Loo, with José Eduardo Contreras Martínez and Beatriz Palavicini Beltrán. *Calendario de Prognósticos y Ofrendas: Libro explicativo del llamado Códice Cospi, Biblioteca Universitaria de Bolonia, 4093*. Mexico City, 1994. Facsimile of the screenfold and commentary on it; introduction includes an extended discussion of the problem of the provenience of the Borgia Group.

Caso, Alfonso, "El culto al sol—Notas a la interpretación de W. Lehmann." In *Traducciones mesoamericanistas*, vol. 1, pp. 177–190. Mexico City, 1966. Updating, with corrections and additions, of Lehmann 1966; includes color photographs of original of *Fonds Mexicain 20*, Bibliothèque Nationale, Paris, and an early copy in the Museo Nacional de Antropología, Mexico City.

Glass, John B., and Donald Robertson. "A Census of Native Middle American Pictorial Manuscripts." In *Handbook of Middle American Indians*, vol. 14, *Guide to Ethnohistorical Sources, Part 3*, edited by Howard F. Cline, Charles Gibson, and H. B. Nicholson, pp. 81–252. Austin, 1975. Useful descriptive and bibliographic entries on all members of the Borgia Group.

Lehmann, Walter. "Los cinco mujeres del oeste muertas en el parto y los cinco dioses del sur en la mitología mexicana." In *Traducciones mesoamericanistas*, vol. 1, pp. 147–177. Spanish translation of article originally published in *Zeitschrift für Ethnologie*, 37 (1905), 848–871. Interprets the iconography of *Fonds Mexicain 20*.

Nicholson, H. B. "The Problem of the Provenience of the Members of the Codex Borgia Group: A Summary." In *Summa anthropologica en homenaje a Roberto J. Weitlaner*, pp. 145–158. Mexico City, 1966. Examination of the problem of the proveniences of the members of the Borgia Group.

Nowotny, Karl A. *Tlacuilolli: Die mexikanischen Bilderhandschriften, Stil und Inhalt. Mit einem Katalog der Codex-Borgia Gruppe*. Monumenta Americana, 3. Berlin, 1961. Comprehensive survey of the Borgia Group and related western Mesoamerican native tradition ritual-divinatory pictorials, with a useful catalogue of their contents.

Robertson, Donald. "The Mixtec Religious Manuscripts." In *Ancient Oaxaca: Discoveries in Mexican Archaeology and History*, edited by John Paddock, Stanford, 1966. Comparing them with the style of the historical/genealogical pictorials from the Mixteca, particularly the *Codex Zouche-Nuttall*, he attributes the members of the Borgia Group—with the possible exception of *Vaticanus B*—to this area.

Seler, Eduard. "Der Codex Borgia und die verwandten aztekischen Bilderschriften." *Zeitschrift für Ethnologie* 19 (1887), 105–114. Landmark article, discussing and comparing the five core members of whom he was the first to define as the Codex Borgia Group.

Seler, Eduard. *Codex Fejérváry-Mayer: Eine altmexikanische Bilder-*

handchrift des Free.-Public-Museums in Liverpool (12014/m) auf Kosten Sr. Exz. des Herzogs von Loubat herausgegeben. Berlin, 1901. English translation by A. H. Keane, Berlin, and London, 1901–1902. First thorough commentary on a member of the Borgia Group, with due attention to the other members of the group.

Seler, Eduard. Codex Vaticanus No. 3773 (Codex Vaticanus B), Eine altmexikanische Bilderschrift der Vatikanischen Bibliothek, herausgegeben auf Kosten Sr. Exz. Des Herzogs von Loubat. Berlin, 1902. English translation by A. H. Keane, Berlin and London, 1902–1903. Thorough commentary on this screenfold, with systematic comparisons between parallel sections in other members of the Borgia Group.

Seler, Eduard. Gesammelte Abhandlungen zur Amerikanischen Sprach- und Altertumskunde. 5 vols. Berlin, 1902–1923. English translations of most of the articles, 6 vols., edited by Frank Comparato, Culver City and Lancaster, Calif., 1990–1998. Well-illustrated volumes of collected articles, published between 1884 and 1923, by one of the greatest Mesoamerican scholars of this period.

Seler, Eduard. Codex Borgia, Eine altmexikanische Bilderschrift der Bibliothek der Bibliothek der Congregatio de Propaganda Fide [Rom], herausgegeben auf Kosten Sr. Exz. des Herzogs von Loubat. 3 vols. Berlin, 1904–1909. Spanish translation, 3 vols., Mexico City, 1963. Constitutes the capstone of Seler's extensive elucidations of the members of the Codex Borgia Group.

Sisson, Edward B. "Recent Work on the Borgia Group Codices." Current Anthropology 24 (1983), 653–656. Report on the deliberations and frequent differences of opinion of the scholars who attended the 1982 Summer Research Seminar of Dumbarton Oaks, Pre-Columbian Studies, and a concomitant conference devoted to the Codex Borgia Group; favors a Puebla-Tlaxcala origin for Borgia and Cospi, and a more southerly provenience for the others.

Spranz, Bodo, Göttergestalten in den Mexikanischen Bilderhandschriften der Codex Borgia-Gruppe: Eine ikonographische Untersuchung. Acta Humboldtiana, Series Geographica et Ethnographica, 4. Wiesbaden, 1964. Spanish translation by María Martínez Peñaloza, Mexico City, 1973. Well-illustrated, broad survey and classification of the iconographic elements of the imagery of the five core members of the Borgia Group.

H. B. NICHOLSON

BOTURINI, CODEX.

A set of central Mexican annals, the *Codex Boturini* chronicles the Mexica migration from Aztlan to the Valley of Mexico. The manuscript takes the form of a screenfold (a long strip of native bark paper (*amatl*) folded like an accordion) and presents its account through pictorial images and date glyphs painted in black and red inks. Crafted by indigenous hands, the *Codex Boturini* probably dates from the mid-sixteenth century and comes from Mexico-Tenochtitlan.

Using an indigenous calendar, the codex covers roughly two hundred years (1 Flint Knife–6 Reed, c.1168–1355 CE). The narrative overlaps with and parallels other accounts from Central Mexico, including the *Codex Aubin*, *Codex Azcatitlan*, and *Mapa de Sigüenza*. Here, however, the founding of Tenochtitlan, later imperial affairs, and colonial events receive no attention; only the Mexica migration, overseen by Huitzilopochtli, is registered. The opening scene of the *Codex Boturini* depicts Mexica de-

parting from the island of Aztlan in boats in 1 Flint, the year of auspicious beginnings. In presenting this event through firmly outlined images and glyphic signs set against an unpainted ground, this scene sets the stage for the manuscript's visual repertoire. All the key events in the *Codex Boturini*—battles, New Fire ceremonies, and portentous sojourns at Tollan, Chapultepec, and Coatepec—rely on the juxtaposition of small figures and large expanses of open space.

When fully extended, the screenfold measures 549 by 19.8 centimeters, and its figures traverse twenty-two panels. Instead of a continuous sequence of years, however, blocks of date glyphs alternate with narrative scenes, effectively punctuating temporal sequences with crucial events. The flow of dates is therefore momentarily but repeatedly suspended so that human action can unfold. In this Nahua account, then, neither time nor event takes priority: temporality and history structure each other.

Although the remnants of a few Nahuatl glosses appear on the *Codex Boturini*, the forms, composition, and *amatl* support align the annals with pre-Conquest paintings. Glyphic elements, body proportions, footprints, and the method of calendrical reckoning further tie the *Codex Boturini* to pre-Hispanic record keeping. The manuscript has thus been seminal in reconstructions of pre-Hispanic history and modes of representation. Scholars have also assessed how it parallels and diverges from other representations of Mexica history. Questions that remain unresolved include who, after the Spanish conquest, would have sought pictorial records like this, and how this kind of document would have answered Early Colonial desires.

The *Codex Boturini* (also known as Tira de la Peregrinación and Tira del Museo) formed part of Lorenzo Boturini Benaduci's collection. Since 1871, it has resided in the Museo Nacional de Antropología e Historia in Mexico City (MNA 35–38). In modern times, the codex has emerged as an emblem of Mexica history. Since the early nineteenth century, both original and copied versions have been displayed in Europe and Mexico. At present, a monumental reproduction appears carved into a stone wall above all who enter and exit the Museo Nacional in Mexico City.

[See also Migrations.]

BIBLIOGRAPHY

Boone, Elizabeth Hill. *Stories in Red and Black: Pictorial Histories of the Aztecs and Mixtecs*. Austin, Tex., 2000. Discussion of structure and content of *Codex Boturini* and other Aztec annals, pp. 197–237.

Códice Boturini (Tira de la Peregrinación). Mexico City, 1975. Facsimile of screenfold.

Corona Nuñez, José. "*Códice Boturini o Tira de la Peregrinación*." In *Antigüedades de México basadas en al recopilación de Lord Kingsborough*, vol. 2, pp. 8–29. Mexico City, 1964. Offers commentary

Through mythical visions, the god Huitzilopochtli told the priests that the Aztecs should leave Aztlán and journey to the south. *Courtesy of Museo Nacional de Antropología, México, D.F.*

on the screenfold along with discussion of other manuscripts in the Kingsborough collection.

Glass, John B. "Códice Boturini." In "A Census of Native Middle American Pictorial Manuscripts," in *Handbook of Middle American Indians*, vol. 14, edited by Howard F. Cline, *Guide to Ethnohistorical Sources*, part 3, pp. 100–101. Austin, Tex., 1975. Summary of the physical attributes, contents, collection history, reproduction, and publication of the codex.

Robertson, Donald. "Tira del Museo." In *Mexican Manuscript Painting of the Early Colonial Period*. Norman, 1994. Analysis of the stylistic and iconographic features of the codex; compares the *Boturini* to other sixteenth-century pictorials from Central Mexico.

DANA LEIBSOHN

BOURBON REFORMS, laws issued by Spain and measures taken from the mid-eighteenth century to 1810, by both metropolitan and colonial Spanish governments, to expand the effective power of the Crown and to increase fiscal revenues; additional measures involved social and educational matters. "Bourbon" refers to the dynasty of Spain at that time, but the thrust of the process belongs to the reign of Charles III (1759–1788) and to cabinet ministers like the Count of Aranda in Spanish affairs and the visitor-general in colonial matters (and later minister of the Indies) José de Gálvez. Some measures were for immediate execution, while others were gradual. Some were intended for the entire empire (like the expulsion of the Jesuits), and some were local in scope. The consequences of all blended thoroughly to establish a comprehensive transformation of the state.

To understand the rationale behind the Crown's reforms, the nature of the traditional Spanish political system must be considered. While local matters were carried on with great autonomy, jurisdictions overlapped, so decision making tended to be consensual. In Spanish-dominated America, these traits became magnified. Blaming such a system for the decadence of Spain since its unification in 1492, the reformers advocated an authoritarian, vertically structured, and highly centralized scheme of government. The effectiveness of their measures, however, varied. Some goals were achieved, and some backfired; many historians argue that their ultimate consequence was the independence of the many nations of Spanish America. In total, the results were extremely complex.

Some of the Bourbon reforms affected the Mesoamerican cultures of New Spain directly; however, to consider these cultures out of context would be misleading. Their interaction with European civilization was two centuries old and more, in some cases, and contacts were increased in the eighteenth century amid a global transformation in social, spatial, and demographic conditions. The reform measures discussed here show only one aspect of the new complex reality.

By 1750, the basic unit of organization for Mesoamerican peoples was the corporate *pueblo de indios*, an essentially political institution that had experienced many changes during the Colonial period. Most *pueblos* were very small, as a process of fragmentation had raised their number to some three thousand in all of New Spain, but they had remained operational. Through their *cajas de comunidad* (corporate treasuries), the *pueblos* managed land, livestock, money, and other goods. *Cofradías* (religious fraternities) performed similar functions. Both enjoyed considerable autonomy, although local Spanish officials and priests constantly intervened. Sources of income for the *pueblos* included fees and proceeds from managing their goods and property (e.g., land leased to Spaniards or to other *pueblos*). Money was spent on royal tribute, public works, social services, and religious festivities. There was generally an annual surplus. The political significance of the *pueblos* was evident in 1767—the visitor-general Gálvez punished a series of riots in the province of Michoacán with the suppression of its *repúblicas* (autonomous governments of the *pueblos*). With the exception of that case, official policy did not point to the destruction of the *pueblos*, still the main source of the royal tribute. Grants of corporate property (especially the 600-*vara fundo legal*) increased in compliance with established legal practices. Unorganized settlements, as on some ranches, were incorporated into new *pueblos* regardless of the mix of ethnic origins. The result, if not planned or desired, was at least most welcome by the government. The *pueblos* became ever smaller corporations (nearly 4,300 by 1810).

Direct intervention in the affairs of the *pueblos* began with the Contaduría General de Propios, an office established in 1766 to audit the *cajas de comunidad*. The initial scheme was designed to raise funds and to spend them wisely (e.g., support of a schoolteacher in every *pueblo*). The turning point, however, was the promulgation of the *Ordenanza de intendentes* (1786), source of a radical transformation in the structure of colonial government. The *Ordenanza* established *intendencias* (provincial governments), empowered to deal with fiscal matters. They aimed at dismantling the 250-year-old system of local administration, to which *pueblos* were closely linked, and to abolish such practices as the *repartimiento de efectos* (forced trade) by which the surpluses of the *pueblos* passed to the local elites. The aim of these measures, however, was not social improvement—or at least not without previously satisfying the needs of the state.

Cajas de comunidad did not escape the *Ordenanza*'s comprehensive aim. First, they were put under strict official control; the amount to be spent in festivities was reduced, special permission was required for any extraordinary expense, and so on. Second, corporate estates were not to be managed directly by the *pueblos* but leased to raise money. Third, any surplus of the *cajas* had to be sent to provincial capitals as savings in the *cajas reales* ("royal chests"), targeted to "useful ends." Money was first loaned to local entrepreneurs, then it was concentrated in Mexico City and used for government expenses, and eventually funneled into Spanish financial adventures, such as the Real Compañía de Filipinas and the Banco de San Carlos. Returns, if any, seldom went back to the *pueblos*. When the government was in need, which happened all too often, money was taken from the *cajas*

as a donation. The process generated a huge amount of accounting and red tape.

Many *pueblos* switched their economic activities to the *cofradías*, which were less exposed to official control—but in the end, the Roman Catholic church managed also to take them over. Most bishops followed the steps of civil authorities and claimed that the *cofradías'* assets were church property (since the *pueblos* had argued that they were the patron saints' property). So, in one way or another, the *pueblos* lost much of their wealth.

Regional differences had always existed in Mesoamerica, but the *intendencias* introduced new ones. New variations derived from specific conditions or policies in any given *intendencia*, or to the attitude of their particular officers. Reforms hit especially hard in Michoacán, where *pueblo* governments were reestablished around 1793, but only to reinforce the extractive process (the support given by *pueblos* in this province to insurgent leaders after 1810 becomes understandable in this light). In Oaxaca, the reforms did not amount to much, the interests of traditional *repartimientos* being an effective deterrent to radical innovations. In Yucatán, there had always been a provincial government, so structural changes were less profound; instead, the central issue involved the church and *cofradías*. Indirect effects of the reforms were particularly evident in Veracruz, where the tobacco monopoly (decreed in 1764), and the organization of militias (some of them with mulattoes and/or blacks) had an enormous impact on the rural population. Provincial differences increased when the *intendencias* became the federal states of Mexico, each with its own legislation after independence in 1821.

BIBLIOGRAPHY

Archer, Christon I. *The Army in Bourbon Mexico (1760–1810)*. Albuquerque, 1977. Analysis of the colonial army that conveys an excellent perspective on the Bourbon era.

Castro Gutiérrez, Felipe. *Nueva ley y nuevo rey: Reformas borbónicas y rebeliones populares en Nueva España*. Mexico City, 1996. Provides extensive discussion on the response of the *pueblos* of Michoacán to reform measures.

Farriss, Nancy M. "Propiedades territoriales en Yucatán en la época colonial: Algunas observaciones acerca de la pobreza española y la autonomía indígena." *Historia Mexicana* 118, 30:2 (1980), 153–208. Excellent discussion of the church's assault on *cofradía* properties.

Farriss, Nancy M. *Maya Society under Spanish Rule: The Collective Enterprise of Survival*. Princeton, 1984. Outstanding book on Colonial-era Yucatán; devotes its final chapters to analyze events of the Bourbon era as a "second conquest."

Hamnett, Brian R. *Politics and Trade in Southern Mexico (1750–1821)*. Cambridge, 1971. Presents a well-documented study of events and conditions in Oaxaca before and after reforms were introduced.

Ouweneel, Arij, and Simon Miller, eds. *The Indian Community of Colonial Mexico*. Amsterdam, 1990. Unique compilation, includes articles by Bernardo García Martínez, Stephanie Wood, Danièle Dehouve, Asunción Lavrin, and William B. Taylor, among others, on some of the major issues in the late eighteenth century.

Ouweneel, Arij. *Shadows over Anáhuac: An Ecological Interpretation of Crisis and Development in Central Mexico (1730–1800)*. Albuquerque, 1996. Illustrates how Bourbon Reforms and other factors eroded New Spain's economic prosperity.

Tanck, Dorothy. *Pueblos de indios y educación en México colonial*. Mexico City, 1999. The ultimate study of *cajas de comunidad*; offers a detailed, splendidly documented analysis of their management.

BERNARDO GARCÍA MARTÍNEZ

BRASSEUR DE BOURBOURG, CHARLES ETIENNE

(1814–1874). French priest, Americanist, historian, and philologist. Brasseur was born into a family of shopkeepers in Bourbourg, a medieval town in northern France. Enthusiastic about Flanders' history, he wrote several essays about local folklore, which enabled him to enter literary circles. In 1837, during the constitutional monarchy, Brasseur came to Paris with French poet Alphonse-Marie-Louis de Prat Lamartine's support to work for political newspapers, among which was *Le Monde*, which sought the democratization of power. In 1840, he entered for two years the seminary of Ghent. He wrote moralistic novels, a success that provided him the money for his travels and his future publications. In 1845, he was ordained in Rome and went to the seminary of Quebec, where he taught church history based on Rohrbacher's works and where he tried without success to establish a Dominican monastery. Brasseur resigned from the seminary in 1846 and traveled to Boston, where he was appointed vicar-general. There he read H. H. Bancroft and William H. Prescott, whose works about the Spanish conquest of Mexico persuaded him to devote his talent to Americanist studies. He then returned to Rome, where he studied Kingsborough's *Antiquities of Mexico*, the *Codex Borgia*, and the *Codex Vaticanus A*. In 1848, Brasseur was appointed chaplain of the French legation in Mexico. There he copied many manuscripts found in the libraries or given to him by Mexican scholars. He was particularly drawn to the manuscript works by Ramón y Ordoñez, who argued that the native Americans had their origins in Chaldea (Mesopotamia). In 1851, Brasseur returned to Paris, where he became involved in French Americanist circles. In 1854, he traveled to Guatemala and was appointed ecclesiastical manager of Rabinal in 1855. There he learned the Quiché language and collected ethnographic data. In 1857, Brasseur concocted a new hypothesis about the origin of native Americans: Scandinavia. In 1859, another journey took him through the Isthmus of Tehuantepec, Chiapas, and Guatemala. On his return to France, he published the Ximénez manuscript of the *Popol Vuh*, and his *Grammaire de la langue quichée*, which contained the *Rabinal Achi* drama, as well as his first theories about the civilization of Atlantis. In 1863, he visited the Quiriguá and Copán archaeological sites. Intrigued by the inscriptions on the stelae, he stopped in Madrid on his way back to Paris to search for relevant documents. The manuscript of the *Relación de las cosas de Yucatán* of Diego de Landa that he found there was considered by Americanists as the primary discovery of the nineteenth century. He then undertook his work on the deciphering of Maya hieroglyphic writing. In 1864, he returned to Mexico as a member of the French Scientific Commission to study the Maya area. When he returned to Europe, he located in Madrid a Maya hieroglyphic screenfold, original and unknown. Brasseur undertook its study, calling it the *Codex Troano* (now part of the *Codex Madrid*). In it, he believed he recognized the history of Atlantis, concluding that this "lost civilization" was of American origin. In 1871, he visited Palenque and decided that he had read the *Codex Troano* backwards. Brasseur died in Nice in 1874 after having sold his Americanist collection of books and manuscripts.

BIBLIOGRAPHY

WORKS BY CHARLES ETIENNE BRASSEUR DE BOURBOURG

Histoire des nations civilisées du Mexique et de l'Amérique centrale, durant les siècles antérieurs à Christophe Colomb, écrite sur des documents originaux et entièrement inédits, puisés aux anciennes archives des indigènes. Paris, 1857–1859. Presents interesting sources and historiographic information about Americanist studies.

Popol Vuh. Le livre sacré et les mythes de l'antiquité américaine, avec les livres héroïques et historiques des Quichés. Ouvrage original des indigènes de Guatemala, texte quiché et traduction française en regard, accompagnée de notes philologiques et d'un commentaire sur la mythologie et la migration des peuples anciens de l'Amérique composée par des documents originaux et inédits. Paris, 1861. Presents Brasseur's theories about migrations of Mesoamerican Indians.

Grammaire de la langue quichée, espagnole-française, mise en parallèle avec ses deux dialectes, cakchiquel et Tzutuhil. Avec un vocabulaire et suivi d'un essai sur la poésie, la musique, la danse et l'art dramatique chez les Mexicains et les Guatémaltèques, avant la conquête, servant d'introduction au Rabinal-Achi, drame indigène. Paris, 1862. First publication known of the *Rabinal Achi*, an important source for native Mesoamerican literature and ethnohistory.

Relation des choses du Yucatán, de Diego de Landa, texte espagnol et traduction française en regard. Avec une grammaire et un vocabulaire abrégés français-maya, précédés d'un essai sur les sources de l'histoire primitive du Mexique et de l'Amérique centrale etc. d'après les monuments égyptiens et de l'histoire primitive de l'Egypte d'après les monuments américains. Paris, 1864. First translation in French. Presents Brasseur's theories about relations between Egyptian and Maya cultures.

Manuscrit Troano. Etudes sur le système graphique et la langue des Mayas. Paris, 1869–1870. Presents Brasseur's decoding method. Important for the facsimile.

GENERAL REFERENCE

Escalante Arce, Pedro Antonio. *Brasseur de Bourbourg. Esbozo biográfico*. San Salvador, El Salvador, 1989. Most important work published concerning Brasseur's biography.

Mace, Carroll Edward. "Charles-Etienne Brasseur de Bourbourg, 1814–1874." In *Handbook of Middle American Indians: Guide to Ethnohistorical Sources*, edited by Robert Wauchope, Vol. 13, pt. 2, pp. 298–325. Austin, Tex., 1973. Very reliable article about Brasseur's theories.

NADIA PRÉVOST URKIDI

BRUJERÍA. *See* Witchcraft, Socery, and Magic.

BUNDLES. Sacred bundles (*tlaquimilolli* in Nahuatl) occupy an important place in the Mesoamerican religious universe. The Franciscan friar Andrés de Olmos, one of the best chroniclers of pre-Hispanic Aztec civilization, asserts that these bundles constituted "the principal devotion of the Indians." However, the documents available on this subject are parsimonious: some representations are in codices, and summaries or brief allusions in the chronicles. The secret and elitist character of the rites dedicated to the *tlaquimilolli* during the pre-Hispanic period, as well as the persistence of clandestine cults dedicated to them during the era of evangelization, undoubtedly explains the discretion of these sources.

The Nahuatl word *tlaquimilolli* means "wrapped thing" and comes from the verb *quimiloa*, "to wrap something in a piece of fabric." The verb also expresses the act of placing a dead body in a shroud. In fact, the *tlaquimilolli* were held to be created from the remains of dead divinities. In Teotihuacan, it was said, the deities Nanahuatl and Tecuciztecatl threw themselves into burning coals and transformed themselves, respectively, into the sun and moon. In order to set itself in motion, the sun demanded the sacrifice of all the gods. These departed ones left pieces of fabric which their followers wrapped around sticks inlaid with jade stones and the skins of jaguar and snake. Each *tlaquimilolli* bore the name of a divinity, and the indigenous people "valued them more than the figures in stone and wood." Other stories associate the origins of sacred bundles with particular divinities: the Mixcoatl bundle was formed with ashes, or from a silex knife, taken from the cremation of the goddess Itzpapalotl; the Aztec adored Huitzilopochtli's loin-cloth, or a *tlaquimilolli* containing his bones; the inhabitants of Texcoco venerated the thighbone of Tezcatlipoca, or a bundle formed from a mirror wrapped in pieces of fabric. Each of the objects making up these bundles could fulfill the function of a relic in itself: Yacatecuhtli and Amimitl were represented by sticks, Curicaueri by an obsidian knife, Quetzalcoatl by a jade stone, Cinteotl by an ear of corn, and so on. We can thus define *tlaquimilolli* as objects or relics associated with a divinity which are wrapped in pieces of fabric; excluded from this category are zoomorphic or anthropomorphic representations.

The sources reveal the multiple functions that the Indians attributed to *tlaquimilolli*. They constituted, first and foremost, an instrument of privileged communication with the divinity. Through the intermediary of the *tlaquimilolli*, the priests knew the divine will: the route of migrations, what offerings or sacrifices to make, or what wars to fight. The sacred bundle also symbolized the political power granted by the divinity: the Quiché of Guatemala received the *pisom c'ac'al* ("glorious bundles") from their mythical ancestors as symbols of their preeminence over other peoples. In Classic Maya writing, the glyph T 684, which represents a bundle, expresses access to power. The *tlaquimilolli* were also associated with war. The Tlaxcaltecans used arrows contained in a sacred bundle to foretell the outcome of a battle. The warrior power generated by certain bundles is illustrated by the conquests of the god Mixcoatl, whose exploits were interrupted as soon as his *tlaquimilolli* was taken from him. Finally, the possession of the sacred bundles of Tlaloc, Chicomecoatl, Cinteotl, and Chalchiuhtlicue was supposed to ensure rain and good crops.

The rituals celebrated in honor of the sacred bundles are not well known, but they involved offerings of incense, flowers, and blood from autosacrifice or, more rarely, from sacrificed victims. For example, sacrifices called "from the gladiators" in relation to the sacred bundles are represented in the *Codex Nuttall* and the *Codex Becker I*. *Tlaquimilolli* were also important in the rites of inauguration of the Mexican kings and their ministers. Secluded in a building, they communed with the sacred bundles of Huitzilopochtli and Tezcatlipoca, the two divinities closely associated with royal power. The future leaders wore the pieces of fabric decorated with bones that covered these bundles, thus identifying themselves with these two gods during their mythical passage to the underworld. These rites reflected the symbolic death of these nobles before their "rebirth" as kings and ministers.

The *tlaquimilolli* were the receptacles of a divine force which was concentrated in one or several objects linked in a metaphorical or metonymic way to the chosen divinity. From the Classic period on, the cult of sacred bundles is attested among numerous indigenous groups dispersed throughout Mesoamerica. The divinities worshiped in the form of *tlaquimilolli* defy all attempts at classification; in fact, they might be embodied as statues as well as in bundles. What, then, was the specific relation of *tlaquimilolli* to anthropomorphic representations? The relation to history allows us better to determine their characteristics. The sacred bundles materialized the divine presence that revealed itself to humans during a particular stage of their history—the moment of the birth of a chosen people, or the time of their establishment in a promised land. The *tlaquimilolli* functioned as identity symbols and frequently were said to be the origin of the name of a group or of a place where they settled. As a result, the origin of sacred bundles often coincided with the beginning of a new era, as in Teotihuacan, where their appearance was linked to the creation of the sun and moon. Another example is the adoration of the dress of Huitzilopochtli following his miraculous birth on the Hill of Coatepec, symbol of the emergence of a new sun and the dawn of the Aztec era. Moreover, the inauguration of the king, already identified with a sacred bundle, was assimilated with the birth of the sun and of the new era.

As a witness to the inauguration of the history of a people, the *tlaquimilolli* served as material evidence of a divinity or of an eponymous hero and preserved the memory of a group, cementing that group by expressing its identity. At the frontier of mythic and human history, the sacred bundle materialized and concentrated acts of divine protection and the founding events of ethnic identity.

BIBLIOGRAPHY

Broda, Johanna. "Relaciones políticas ritualizadas: El ritual como expresión de una ideología." In *Economía política e ideología en el México prehispánico*, edited by Johanna Broda and Pedro Carrasco, pp. 221–255. Mexico City, 1978. Detailed analysis of the functions of the Aztec rulers, crowning ceremonies, and the participation of the king in rituals.

Durán, Diego. *Book of the Gods and Rites and the Ancient Calendar*. Edited and translated by Doris Heyden and Fernando Horcasitas. Norman, Okla., 1971. Chronicles the late sixteenth century, including rare notes on sacred bundles.

Graulich, Michel. *Montezuma ou l'apogée et la chute de l'empire aztèque*. Paris, 1994. Excellent biography of Motecuhzoma II, including a detailed description of the rites of inauguration.

Historia de los mexicanos por sus pinturas. In *Teogonía e historia de los mexicanos. Tres opúsculos des siglo XVI*, edited by Ángel María Garibay K., pp. 23–90. Mexico City, 1965. Chronicle containing fundamental myths related to the sacred bundles.

Olivier, Guilhem. "Les paquets secrets ou la mémoire cachée des Indiens du Mexique central (XVᵉ–XVIᵉ siècles)." *Journal de la Société des Américanistes* 81 (1995), 105–141. Detailed study of the myths of the origin, composition, and functions of the sacred bundles, with a new interpretation of the rites of inauguration of kings.

Sahagún, Bernardino de. *Florentine Codex: General History of the things of New Spain*. 12 vols. Translated and edited by Charles E. Dibble and Arthur J. O. Anderson. Santa Fe, N.M., 1950–1981. Veritable encyclopedia of the sixteenth-century Nahuatl world, including rare observations on sacred bundles and a detailed description of the rites of inauguration.

Stenzel, Werner. "The Sacred Bundles in Mesoamerican Religion." *Proceedings of the XXXVIII International Congress of Americanists* 2 (1970), 347–352. Pioneer study of sacred bundles, including comparisons with the rites of the Indians of North America.

Thévet, André. "Histoyre du Mechique, manuscrit français inédit du XVIᵉ siècle." *Journal de la Société des Américanistes* 2 (1905), 1–41. French translation of a lost manuscript of Fray Andrés de Olmos, including important observations on the sacred bundles.

Townsend, Richard F. "Coronation at Tenochtitlan." In *The Aztec Templo Mayor*, edited by Elizabeth H. Boone, pp. 371–411. Washington, D.C., 1987. Analysis of the rites of inauguration of the Mex-

ican kings as related to the sacred architecture of the Templo Mayor.

GUILHEM OLIVIER
Translated from French by Susan Romanosky

BURGOA, FRANCISCO DE (1604–1681), Dominican friar and principal chronicler of the region of Oaxaca in southern Mexico during the Colonial period. He was born in 1604 in the town of Teozapotlán, or Zaachila, in what is now the state of Oaxaca; his parents were descended from conquistadors. He professed as a Dominican friar in 1620, received sacerdotal orders in 1625, and served as vicar in various indigenous communities, such as Guaxolotitlan in the Valley of Oaxaca and the Mixtec settlements of Tecomaxtlahuaca and Almoloyas (west of the present-day state of Oaxaca), where he learned the native language. He taught theology in the convent of Santo Domingo in the city of Antequera (the present-day city of Oaxaca) and became its prior in 1644. Subsequently, he occupied the post of prior at the Dominican convent of Yanhuitlán in the Mixteca Alta. In 1649, he was named provincial of his order, and in 1656 he represented his province in Rome; in 1662 he again became provincial.

Fray Francisco de Burgoa wrote two books, along with other brief texts. The first, *Palestra historial*, was published in Mexico City in 1670. The second, published in the same city in 1674, was entitled *Geográfica descripción*. Because of these works, unique of their kind in the history of Oaxaca, Burgoa is considered the chronicler of this region. With the purpose of recording and keeping as an example for the future what was almost forgotten about the work of the first brothers of his order, he wrote about the Dominican friars who came to New Spain in the sixteenth century and founded the province of San Hipólito Mártir de Guaxaca. Burgoa considered his two books to be the first and second parts of the same work: the history of his province.

Burgoa employed a baroque style, exceedingly erudite and difficult to read. His work is full of constant praises of the evangelizing labors of the brothers of his order; he described in great detail who they were and the work that they accomplished in teaching doctrine to the Indians while struggling to destroy the native religion. He considered native religion the work of the devil and referred to it with contemptuous, derogatory terms, such as "a group of barbarous vices" and "dishonesties." He included various descriptions of the old religion, the idols revered by the Indians, cave worship, oracles, and sacred sites.

Burgoa's concept of history permeates his work. For him, human history was part of a divine plan that led to the redemption of the human race. In this view, the Dominicans' labors helped to carry out God's will and were a central part of this sacred task. In this vein, Burgoa often discovers parallels between the Dominicans' labors and moments in Jewish history from both Hebrew scripture and the New Testament. He also dedicates long paragraphs to establish analogies between what is recounted in the Indian communities and the actions of the prophets and saints. Forming part of this historical vision, he describes, at times in considerable detail, aspects of seventeenth-century society, with special reference to the Dominicans' labors, their churches and convents, and considerable information about their buildings and sacred objects. He tells of the founding of the city of Antequera in 1523 and speaks of the indigenous communities, the life of workers in the mines, the abuses of the *alcaldes mayores* (Spanish judges), epidemics, and droughts. His description of the countryside, the roads, the vegetation, and the climate is exceedingly rich.

His two works contain information about the pre-Hispanic history of the indigenous population of Oaxaca; they provide details concerning the politics, wars, and rivalries of this period. Because Burgoa held many important posts in the province and learned the Mixtec and Zapotec languages, he took the time to talk with *caciques*, with other Indian leaders, and with the elders, who related their own views of history. His books are particularly rich in historical and ethnohistorical information, despite their cultural biases.

[*See also* Dominicans.]

BIBLIOGRAPHY

Burgoa, Francisco de. *Palestra historial de virtudes y ejemplares apostólicos: Fundada del zelo de insignes héroes de la sagrada orden de predicadores en este Nuevo Mundo de la América en las Indias Occidentales* [1670]. 3d facsimile ed., with introductory studies by Andrés Henestrosa, Guido Múnch Galindo, María Isabel Grañén Porrúa, and Elvira Quintero García. Mexico City, 1997.

Burgoa, Francisco de. *Geográfica descripción de la parte septentrional, del Polo Ártico de la América, y Nueva Iglesia de las Indias Occidentales, y sitio astronómico de esta provincia de predicadores de Antequera Valle de Oaxaca: En diez y siete grados del Trópico de Cáncer: Debaxo de los aspectos, y radiaciones de planetas morales, que la fundaron con virtudes celestes, influyéndola en santidad y doctrina* [1674]. 3d facsimile ed. Mexico City, 1997.

García Mora, Carlos, and Jesús Monjarás Ruiz. "Un acercamiento a la corografía evangélica de Francisco de Burgoa." In *La ciudad y el campo en la historia de México: Memoria de la VII Reunión de Historiadores Mexicanos y Norteamericanos*, vol. 2, pp. 853–856. Mexico City, 1985.

María de los Angeles Romero Frizzi
Translated from Spanish by Scott Sessions

BUTTERFLIES.

With their graceful movements and vibrant colors, butterflies have been an inspiring source of beauty and wonder among many cultures of Mesoamerica. Representations of butterflies abound in the art of Classic and Postclassic highland Mexico. Even the brilliant feather mosaics of the Aztec recall the minuscule, iridescent scales of butterfly wings. As well as being esteemed for its beauty, the butterfly occupied important symbolic domains. As creatures associated with warmth, daylight, and flowers, butterflies were commonly identified with gods of fertility and abundance in Postclassic Central Mexico. Xochipilli, the "flower prince" god of music and dance, is often depicted with a stylized butterfly around his mouth, especially in *xantil* incense-burner figures from the Teotitlan del Camino region in Oaxaca. The fertility goddess Xochiquetzal, or "flower quetzal," often wears a butterfly nosepiece as well as butterflies in her headdress. The early colonial *Codex Kingsborough* illustrates a magnificent feather-mosaic shield that portrays Xochiquetzal as an upward-flying butterfly; Carlos Beutelspacher (1988) notes that the wing form and markings identify this butterfly as the lovely *Papilio multicaudatus*, common in the Valley of Mexico. It is no coincidence that the names of both these deities contain the Nahua word for "flower" (*xochitl*), which is widely identified with sensuality in Mesoamerica. Butterflies, too, were related to joy and sensual pleasure in Central Mexican thought.

Both butterflies and flowers were strongly identified with the sun in Central Mexico and were central components in the solar war cult. Aztec and other highland Mexican warriors wore images of butterflies into battle. The goddess Itzapapalotl ("obsidian butterfly"), a spectral, bellicose deity of war and strife, frequently appears with sharp blades lining her wings. Although it may seem curious that fierce warriors appeared in battle bearing butterflies, these fragile creatures were credited with almost supernatural bravery. An Aztec text, recorded by Fray Andrés de Olmos, portrays the mundane event of a moth or butterfly falling into a flame as a heroic act of self-sacrifice. [*See* Olmos, Andrés de.] The passage also mentions that by this selfless act, the butterfly metamorphoses into a flame. Butterflies commonly represent fire in Central Mexican iconography, as if the flickering flames were compared to fluttering butterflies. The metamorphosis of caterpillar into butterfly probably had powerful symbolism for the solar war cult. At death, warriors were wrapped in cloth bundles and burned, a process recalling the transformation of the apparently lifeless chrysalis into a vibrant butterfly. In fact, it is known that the souls of slain warriors were thought to become butterflies and other flying creatures that dwelt in the celestial paradise of the sun.

Among the earliest portrayals of butterflies in Mesoamerica are Middle Formative Olmec jades of anthropomorphic figures with butterfly wings (Figure 1). An Olmec jadeite pendant discovered in Costa Rica apparently represents a pupa partly transformed into a butterfly, suggesting that the Olmec, too, were fascinated by the

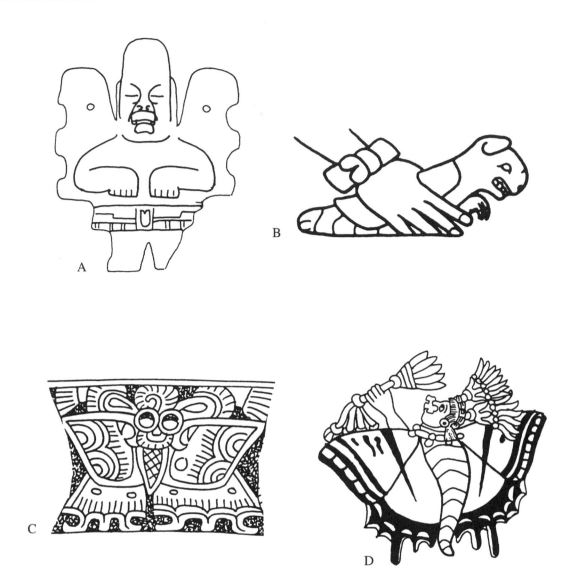

FIGURE 1. Portrayals of butterflies in ancient Mesoamerica: (A) Jade anthropomorphic butterfly, Middle Formative Olmec; (B) Probable representation of butterfly pupa, detail of Olmec jade pendant, Middle Formative period; (C) Teotihuacan representation of *Papilio multicaudatus*, detail of Early Classic ceramic vessel; (D) Xochiquetzal as *Papilio multicaudatus*, detail of representation of feather mosaic shield, *Codex Kingsborough. Drawings by Karl A. Taube.*

process of metamorphosis. Despite their clear interest in floral symbolism, the Classic Maya curiously employed little butterfly imagery; when butterflies are portrayed, they are in the style of Teotihuacan, where there are abundant representations of these creatures. Beutelspacher (1989, 29) notes that the same species found with the Xochiquetzal representation, *Papilio multicaudatus*, also appears in Teotihuacan art. This same butterfly, with its diagnostic wing form and marking, also occurs commonly in Teotihuacan-style art from the Escuintla area of southern coastal Guatemala.

Teotihuacan butterflies are often portrayed with fanged jaguar mouths and the goggled eyes commonly shown by warriors; both probably allude to the militaristic role of butterflies in Central Mexican thought. Gods and warriors at Teotihuacan often wear a stylized butterfly nosepiece, a convention that continued in Late Postclassic Central Mexico. As in Aztec imagery, butterflies represented the souls of dead warriors at Teotihuacan (Berlo 1983; Taube, 2000). The composite incense burners of Teotihuacan and the Escuintla region portray warrior mortuary bundles like those known for the Late Postclassic

Aztec (Taube). Diego Durán notes that the Aztec placed images of mortuary bundles in a shrine known as a *tlacochcalli* ("house of darts"), and many Teotihuacan composite censers are ornamented with dart butts, marking them as "dart house" shrines. A number of Escuintla examples portray the metamorphosis of the butterfly soul out of the mortuary bundle, and the composite censers were likely intended to conjure the souls of warriors through fire offerings.

Following the fall of Teotihuacan, the butterfly warrior cult continued to thrive among the Early Postclassic Toltec. At Tula and Chichén Itzá, Toltec warriors commonly wear large, stylized butterfly pectorals, probably references to the fiery butterfly soul. In addition, a series of bas-reliefs was reportedly discovered on the Cerro de Malinche at Tula, portray flying butterflies. Already present among the Toltec and the even earlier inhabitants of Teotihuacan, the Aztec butterfly warrior cult was an ancient concept that linked the Aztec to earlier great centers of ancient Mexico.

BIBLIOGRAPHY

Berlo, Janet. "The Warrior and the Butterfly: Central Mexican Ideologies of Sacred Warfare and Teotihuacan Iconography." In *Text and Image in Pre-Columbian Art: Essays on the Interrelationship of the Visual and Verbal Arts*, edited by Janet Berlo, pp. 79–117. Oxford, 1983. Discusses the relation of Teotihuacan butterfly symbolism to that of the Aztec; posits that the Aztec concept of warrior butterfly souls was present at Teotihuacan.

Beutelspacher, Carlos C. *Las mariposas entre los antiguos mexicanos.* Mexico City, 1988. Describes butterfly imagery and symbolism of Central Mexico, including the portrayal of particular species; discusses some of the major deities identified with butterflies, including Xochiquetzal, Itzapapalotl, and Xochipilli.

Durán, Fray Diego. *The History of the Indies of New Spain.* Translated and annotated by Doris Heyden. Norman, Okla., 1994.

Taube, Karl A. "The Turquoise Hearth: Fire, Self-Sacrifice, and the Central Mexican Cult of War." In *Mesoamerica's Classic Heritage: From Teotihuacan to the Great Aztec Temple*, edited by Davíd Carrasco et al., pp. 269–340. Niwot, Colo., 2000. Explores the symbolism of warfare in Central Mexico, with focus on fire and butterflies; mentions identification of warriors with butterflies, and explores the concept of metamorphosis and rebirth.

KARL A. TAUBE

C

CABILDO. In creating New Spain, colonial officials recast native communities as *pueblos* and placed them within regional units of civil and ecclesiastical administration. Fundamental to this process was the imposition of the *cabildo*, the Spanish municipal council. Colonial laws repeatedly reinforced the principle that every *pueblo* was to have a *cabildo*, whose election, composition, and function were to be strictly standardized. In practice, like many other aspects of the Colonial-period Mesoamerican *pueblo*, the *cabildo* was a kind of veneer; the principal men of native communities adopted, altered, and interpreted the *cabildo* according to local traditions and requirements.

The two most prominent posts in the *cabildo* were those of *alcalde* (mayor) and *regidor* (councilman). A 1618 royal edict recognized that numbers of officials would vary according to *pueblo* size but ordered that the principal offices conform to the ratio of one to two—for example, two *alcaldes* and four *regidores*. The model of two and four was the one most commonly mandated (e.g., the late sixteenth-century decrees for Yucatán by the *oidor* [visiting judge] Tomás López Médel). In practice, native *cabildos* featured as many *alcades* and *regidores* as they deemed necessary. Tenochtitlan in 1600, for example, had eight *alcaldes* (two for each section of the city) and a dozen *regidores*. Cacalchen (Yucatán) had three *alcaldes* and six *regidores* in 1647, but six years later it had four and five, respectively. Such variations in numbers were ubiquitous in Central Mexico and Yucatán; Mixtec *cabildos* more often conformed to the two-and-four model.

The Spanish model also included one *escribano* (notary) and a number of *alguaciles* (constables); in native *cabildos*, the latter, as well as additional officers such as *mayordomos* (majordomos), could be and were added according to local administrative needs. In 1553, for example, Coyoacán had eight *alguaciles* to complement its eight *regidores*. An edict of Philip IV permitted notaries and *alguaciles* to buy lifetime appointments, but in some native *cabildos*, nobles held other posts in perpetuity too. In fact, *cabildo* offices tended to be held by prominent native men according to local considerations of class, dynastic privilege, factional maneuvering, systems of rotational representation (important in Nahua, Mixtec, and Yucatec Maya *cabildos*), and other dynamics of sociopolitical organization and individual career patterns. The position of notary, for example, was highly prestigious in Colonial Mesoamerica. Unlike his Spanish counterpart, a native notary was likely to be noble, perhaps descended from a long line of notaries, and he could go on to become community governor; he was the only *cabildo* member to receive a salary.

Another set of officers with Spanish titles, such as *fiscal* and *sacristán*, were not technically *cabildo* members but held offices related to local church and *cofradía* (sodality) administration. However, most Mesoamerican communities regarded all officeholders as members of a single body of principal men; in many *pueblos*, the same prominent individuals held multiple posts, producing significant overlap between *cabildo* and *cofradía* officers. Furthermore, below the level of Spanish-titled *cabildo* posts were numerous additional positions that retained pre-Hispanic titles. Thus, unlike those of Spanish *cabildos*, the boundaries around Mesoamerican *cabildos* were ambiguous.

The responsibilities and expenses of the *cabildo* included maintaining the written records of the community (such as wills and land sales); adjudicating local disputes; collecting tribute; funding trips to the city to present petitions; providing carriers for the mail service; maintaining community roads and public buildings, such as the *audiencia*, or *cabildo* building, possibly a jail and a hospital, and a guesthouse for visiting Spaniards; maintaining the community granary and ensuring that the sick, the imprisoned, and the very poor did not starve; and administering community property, such as assigning unused community fields and managing the community cattle ranch.

The relationship between native *cabildos* and native community rulers was also ambiguous. Spanish officials recognized two types of local ruler: the hereditary lord, whom Spaniards usually called *cacique*, Arawak for "chief"; and the appointed or elected ruler, typically called *gobernador* (governor). Both were seen as contributing to local political stability, as long as the ruler's authority was balanced by that of a *cabildo* whose membership did not include the ruler. In practice, the native governor tended to function as *cabildo* head, and the *ca-*

CABRERA, MIGUEL

cique's position either faded in importance or merged with that of the governor.

Toward the end of every year, all the principal men of the community would gather to elect the next *cabildo*, in theory according to merit, but in practice according to local factional politics. Elections often involved elaborate community ritual and festivity. The governor played a major role in the factional and electoral process and in many regions avoided annual election himself. Like all other aspects of the Mesoamerican *cabildo*, the governor's role was subject to much local and regional variation.

The flexible way in which the *cabildo* system was imposed, interpreted, and used by native communities allowed for continuities in local politics and the perpetuation of native self-government. The *cabildo*, thus, was a crucial Colonial Mesoamerican institution.

BIBLIOGRAPHY

Bayle, Constantino. "Cabildos indígenas en la America Española." *Missionalia hispanica* 8 (1951), 5–35. Classic early study of the topic in Spanish.

Gibson, Charles. *The Aztecs under Spanish Rule: A History of the Indians of the Valley of Mexico, 1519–1810.* Stanford, 1964. Chapter 7 is the classic early study of the topic in English.

Haskett, Robert. *Indigenous Rulers: An Ethnohistory of Town Government in Colonial Cuernavaca.* Albuquerque, 1991. Places the *cabildo* in the context of community politics in one corner of Central Mexico.

Lockhart, James. *The Nahuas after the Conquest: A Social and Cultural History of the Indians of Central Mexico, Sixteenth through Eighteenth Centuries.* Stanford, 1992. Good starting point for further reading, especially pp. 30–44.

Restall, Matthew. *The Maya World: Yucatec Culture and Society, 1550–1850.* Stanford, 1997. Chapters 5, 6, and 20 explore how the Maya of Yucatán adopted and adapted the *cabildo*.

Terraciano, Kevin. "Ñudzahui History: Mixtec Writing and Culture in Colonial Oaxaca." Dissertation, University of California, Los Angeles, 1994. Chapter 4 includes detailed discussion of Mixtec *cabildos*.

MATTHEW RESTALL

CABRERA, MIGUEL (1695–1768). Probably the best known of colonial Mexican painters. Cabrera was born in the city of Oaxaca. according to his 1768 will, and has been identified as the Miguel of a 1695 Oaxaca baptismal record, "son of unknown parents," whose godparents were Gregorio Cabrera and Juana Reyna, both mulattos. In an earlier will of 1760 and in his 1739 marriage banns, the painter's full name is given as Miguel Mateo Maldonado y Cabrera.

Cabrera's first known work is a lost 1732 composition reproduced in an Italian print of Juan Diego displaying his *tilma* ("cloak") with the Virgin of Guadalupe, so doubts exist about whether the painter is indeed the Miguel of the 1695 baptismal document, as it would be unusual for a painter to be doing his earliest work at almost age forty, unless he had been a subordinate for many years within another master's shop. Even if the date on the print is mistaken and should be 1752, as some scholars think, Cabrera's first known dated painting, a portrait of Fray Toribio de Nuestra Señora (Mexico City, San Fernando), is from 1740, which only increases the chronological difficulty. Another problem is that of Cabrera's racial origins. In the nonscholarly literature, much has been made of Cabrera's alleged indigenous, or *mestizo*, identity. In fact, in the marriage record of Andrea Maldonado Cabrera, who could well have been the painter's sister, she is identified as Spanish, as is Cabrera's own eldest daughter in another marriage document.

In any case, Cabrera was certainly in Mexico City by the late 1730s. In general, his work shows the assimilation of the style of Juan Rodríguez Juárez (1675–1728) and his circle. In 1722, Juan and his brother Nicolás (1667–1734) had established the Academy of the Art of Painting in Mexico City. In contrast to the dramatic tone and nervous brushwork of the best known painters among their older contemporaries, especially Cristóbal de Villalpando (c.1645–1714), the Rodríguez Juárez brothers integrated movement and drama within the measured tone learned from their father, Antonio Rodríguez (1639–1691). However, Cabrera's direct master may have been José de Ibarra (1685–1756), who claimed Juan Correa (c.1646–1716) as his teacher, but who knew the Rodríguez Juárez academy, because he was working in Juan's atelier at the time of the latter's death. Cabrera refers to Ibarra with great respect in his text on the Virgin of Guadalupe, *Maravilla americana*, published in 1756.

These antecedents point to basic realities of the world of painters in Mexico City in the eighteenth century. Their lives were centered on a guild system, which, to a great extent, was intertwined with family histories. At the same time, they were seeking to expand their education through study, and thus to increase their professional standing. The Rodríguez Juárez academy is the first of several initiatives to establish more formal training for painters. Cabrera himself would participate in an attempt to found another academy in 1753. Indeed, Cabrera's career manifests the importance that painters could attain in New Spain. He became official painter to the archbishop of Mexico City, a title that had not existed previously. Cabrera's account of his examination with several colleagues of the original image of the Virgin of Guadalupe is fundamentally an apology for the art of painting, an expressive vehicle so important that it had served to materialize the Virgin's real presence in the New World.

Cabrera's preserved works number close to four hundred, and he must have had a considerable workshop. The archbishop of Mexico City, the Jesuits, whose novitiate and church at Tepotzotlán he decorated, and other religious orders were his patrons, as well as wealthy individuals, such as the miner José de la Borda, for whom he worked in the church of Santa Prisca in Taxco. Cabrera's paintings range from tiny works on copper to enormous canvases and wall paintings. He also designed altarpieces and funerary monuments. In addition to his many religious compositions, he executed excellent portraits of his contemporaries, as well as of important personages in the history of New Spain, such as the protagonists of the story of the apparition of the Virgin of Guadalupe, and Sor Juana Inés de la Cruz. He is also the author of a *casta* ("racial mixture") series. His paintings display a sense of ample space and brilliant coloring applied in smoothly flowing brushstrokes. Actions are relatively calm. The sweetness of expression, especially of his religious figures, was much appreciated during his lifetime and in the nineteenth century and, despite occasional criticism, continues to appeal.

[*See also* Castas Paintings.]

BIBLIOGRAPHY

Burke, Marcus. *Painting and Sculpture in New Spain: The Baroque.* Mexico City, 1992. General treatment in English of seventeenth- and eighteenth-century painting.

Carrillo y Gariel, Abelardo. *El pintor Miguel Cabrera.* Mexico City, 1966. Monograph that established the basis for subsequent studies of Cabrera.

Tovar de Teresa, Guillermo. *Miguel Cabrera, pintor de cámara de la reina celestial.* Mexico City, 1995. Most recent monograph and catalog with excellent photographs.

CLARA BARGELLINI

CACAO. The plant from which chocolate is derived, *Theobroma cacao*, is a rather spindly understory tree of the tropical forest. On its trunk and branches, each plant bears vast numbers of tiny flowers that are pollinated by midges. The mature fruits are large (0.3 meter; 1 foot), ridged pods, containing flattened seeds, called "beans," surrounded by a sweet, white pulp. Although the raw pulp can be eaten or transformed into a mildly alcoholic drink, several thousand years ago the Mesoamericans discovered how to process the beans into cocoa, chocolate. This process has four steps: (1) removing the seeds and pulp from pod and fermenting the mass until the resulting liquid drains away; (2) drying the cleaned beans; (3) roasting the beans; and (4) grinding the beans on a heated metate. The complex chocolate flavor is not apparent until all four steps are complete. The resultant chocolate paste was dried into cakes and then mixed with hot water and flavorings; the liquid was poured from one vessel into another until the froth, a delicacy appeared. Today this beating and frothing is accomplished with a wooden *molinillo*, a Spanish colonial introduction, consisting of several rings on a rod, which is twirled. Solid chocolate is rarely mentioned in the early sources, although the Aztec used it as military rations while on the march. The flavorings used included honey or maize-stalk syrup for sweetness (the copious use of sugar from cane in chocolate is a Spanish innovation), chiles, and various spices, such as the prized ear flower (*Cymbopetalum penduliflorum*; Nahuatl, *nacaxochitl*).

Linguistic data suggest that it was the Olmec of the Gulf Coast who first discovered this complex process, perhaps by 1000 BCE. *Cacao*—the basic word for chocolate, the bean, and the tree in many Mesoamerican languages—appears to be of Mixe-Zoquean origin. This was probably the language of the Olmec civilization, and both the word and the process may have been spread by them to other Mesoamerican cultures.

There is direct archaeological evidence that the chocolate drink was in use by the fifth century CE in highland Mexico: depictions of the tree and its pods appear on pottery vessels and censers of the Teotihuacan civilization. In northeastern Guatemala, an Early Classic period royal tomb at the Lowland Maya site of Río Azul contained an offering jar painted with the Mayan glyph for "cacao"; this jar proved to have chocolate residue within it. The painted or carved texts on thousands of Late Classic Maya cylindrical vessels from elite burials indicate that they once contained chocolate, and one Codex Style vessel in the Princeton Art Museum depicts their use in the mixing process.

Ethnohistoric sources indicate that chocolate was a semisacred drink, reserved for the Mesoamerican elite (which, among the Aztec, included the warriors). It was taken during banquets and religious rituals; it was never used in cooking. Among the Maya, and perhaps also the Zapotec, chocolate was often used to solemnize and seal marriage pacts. Aztec and probably Maya royal palaces contained vast stores of dried cacao beans, destined to be transformed into the myriad gourd bowls of chocolate that were drunk at royal feasts, such as that described by Bernal Díaz del Castillo for the Aztec emperor Motecuhzoma Xocoyotzin.

BIBLIOGRAPHY

Coe, Sophie D., and Michael D. Coe. *The True History of Chocolate.* London and New York, 1996. The story of chocolate from pre-Columbian times, through its introduction to Europe, until modern times.

Stuart, David. "The Río Azul Cacao Pot: Epigraphic Observations on the Function of a Maya Ceramic Vessel." *Antiquity* 62 (1988), 153–157. Identification of the Maya glyph for "cacao" on a vessel with chocolate residue.

Young, Allen M. *The Chocolate Tree: A Natural History of Cacao.* Washington, D.C., 1994. The botanical history of cacao, with important observations on its cultivation and diseases.

MICHAEL D. COE

CACAXTLA, an archaeological site found in 1975 in the Valley of Tlaxcala. A peasant working his plot found the remains of a mural and reported it. Thus began the excavations to rescue the murals and the building that contained them. Yet Cacaxtla was first described in the sixteenth century: "The Olmeca made of this their main settlement and populated it, [giving] size and strength to their buildings . . . and thus the . . . barbicans, walls, basins, and bastions show that it was the strongest thing in the world" (see Muñoz Camargo 1984). Cacaxtla was mentioned in the Mexican Republic's *Archaeological Atlas* in 1946 and again when Pedro Armillas (1946) surveyed the Cacaxtla and the Xochitecatl areas. He described both sites, within the region he called Southwest of Tlaxcala, as having monumental architecture, which he connected with the Olmeca-Xicalanca presence. Nowadays it is not possible to speak of Cacaxtla without mentioning Xochitécatl, because they are both part of the same site. [*See Armillas, Pedro.*]

The Epiclassic period was characterized by extensive human movements and migrations throughout Central Mexico. In the Basin of Mexico and the border regions, such centers of power emerged as Xochicalco in Morelos, Xochitécatl-Cacaxtla in Tlaxcala, and Tenango in the state of México, among others. Cacaxtla's urban complex was spread over the irregular topography in a rectangular form of 1700 by 800 meters (5,500 by 2,500 feet). The impressive defense system formed by a wall, numerous slopes, and nine basins made it strategically inaccessible. The main gate was to the west and was guarded by a sentry box. The cultivated area was on the lower levels and the domestic habitation terraces on the upper. The Great Platform was Cacaxtla's most important feature. It is an enormous platform of 200 by 110 meters (650 by 350 feet), 25 meters (80 feet) high, supporting both the most important cult and residence areas. The palace has a patio with porticos, various rooms, the Courtyard of the Shrines, and the North Plaza. The palace murals harmoniously join the Maya naturalistic style of human figure with the glyph tradition that emerged from Teotihuacan.

Cacaxtla's chronology is based on radiocarbon dating associated with the buildings that the murals were in, as well as the ceramic sequence provided by Diana Molina (1986). This pottery is ranked as the most characteristic of the Epiclassic period, particularly the red-on-brown and the stick-polishing wares. The theater-type braziers are similar to those of the Teotihuacan tradition and associated with the rain god Tlaloc. Also common are the tripod vessels with carved decoration, painted with symbolic motifs, like the Venus symbol. In the category of domestic ceramics, there were bowls, pots, and a new item—*comales* of several diameters for grilling tortillas and other maize-based batters. There were also tripod plates with solid supports, used for eating; they had the traditional red stripes over a cream background—a local tradition similar to the Coyotlatelco ceramic that was typical in the Epiclassic period.

One of the major finds in Cacaxtla was the mural paintings. From the several influences—Teotihuacan, Maya, Xochicalcas, and others—the art style has been described as eclectic (Foncerrada de Molina 1993). Numerous interpretations have been given about the meaning of these murals. The Mural of the Battle, painted on two slopes in B Building (c.650 CE), presents a narrative scene nearly 26 meters (80 feet) long about the fearful armed fight between two clearly differentiated ethnic groups. The winning group has grayish-brown skin, a big nose, and no cranial deformation; they are armed with round shields, obsidian knives, dart launchers (*atlatls*), and spears. The defeated, by their facial profiles and the deformation of

Cacaxtla, a late Classic site in the Mexican highlands. *Courtesy of Visual Resources Collection, The University of Texas at Austin. Ferguson Collection.*

their heads, have been identified as Maya. They appear naked and wear only plumes, pectoral vests, earplugs, and some jade jewels. In A Building, two scenes are special; both are painted on a red background. The southern wall clearly presents a Maya dressed in a bird outfit and helmet, riding on a plumed serpent. The northern wall shows a man dressed in a jaguar outfit and helmet, standing on a jaguar-skinned serpent. This character has a bundle of darts dripping water from one end. The building's jambs are also of interest. On a blue background, two characters appear: a jaguar-man who pours water into a Tlaloc pot and a Maya with a snail, from which emerges a little red-haired man—probably representing the sun.

Together with paintings newly discovered in the Red Temple and other buildings of the Great Platform, various interpretations have been offered about the Olmeca-Xicalanca origin (López Austin and López Luján 1996). The eclectic style tells of a very intense intercultural relationship, with city-states that included numerous ethnic groups. Many blanks in the archaeological record of Cacaxtla indicate the need for further excavations there.

Cacaxtla obtained dominance over the Valley of Tlaxcala. Since this valley was very fertile, it was probably controlled by a dominant class that stored and later distributed the harvest. Cacaxtla was also able to control the trade routes that took products from the Gulf Coast to the Central Highlands. The trader or dealer portrayed at the Red Temple is a most important representation. Another important iconographic element has to do with war, represented in the Mural of the Battle. Some scholars have interpreted it as a holy war, while others see it as two ethnic groups—Olmeca-Xicalanca versus the Maya.

A peculiar phenomenon occurs in Xochitécatl-Cacaxtla. During the Formative (Preclassic) period, the site has a strong occupation. It is abandoned during the Classic period, then in the Epiclassic period is populated again. At that point, it acquired an important political role. The task remains to explain who these people were, where they came from, why they left, and why they returned.

BIBLIOGRAPHY

Armillas, Pedro. "Los Olmecas-Xicalanca y los sitios arqueológicos del suroeste de Tlaxcala." *Revista Mexicana de Estudios Antropológicos* 3 (1946), 137–146.

Foncerrada de Molina, Martha. *Cacaxtla: La iconografia de los Olmeca-Xicalanca.* Mexico City, 1993.

López Austin, Alfredo, and Leonardo López Luján. *El pasado indígena de México.* Mexico City, 1996.

Molina, Diana. "La cerámica de Cacaxtla." In *Cacaxtla, lugar donde muere la lluvia en la tierra,* edited by Sonia Lombardo. Mexico City, 1986.

Muñoz Camargo, Diego. *Relaciones geográficas del Siglo XVI: Tlaxcala.* Mexico City, 1984.

MARI CARMEN SERRA PUCHE

CACHES. *See* Offerings.

CACIQUES. The Spanish conquistadors adopted *cacique*, the Arawak term for "ruler," during the Conquest and settlement of the Caribbean area, and they then used it throughout Mesoamerica. Initially, the term *cacique* was used to designate the traditional rulers and their successors—*tlatoani* (plural, *tlatoque*) in Nahuatl, *yya* in Mixtec, and *batab* in Maya—who were crucial to early Spanish administration; they thus neglected the proper indigenous terms for "hereditary ruler," and in time, this facilitated the divergence between indigenous concepts of hereditary rule and the Colonial-era *caciques*.

In the sixteenth century, *caciques* enjoyed many of the traditional rights and perquisites of indigenous rulers. They received the tribute and labor of commoners, the produce from substantial properties worked by dependent laborers, and, in regions with a market system, taxes from the local marketplace. They contracted marriage alliances with other ruling families. [*See* Marriage Alliances.] *Caciques* were also among the first to introduce European material culture into indigenous communities: they built Spanish-style houses, acquired Spanish furnishings, and wore Spanish clothes. They engaged in such Spanish-style commercial enterprises as sheep and cattle ranching and the raising of silkworms. Many owned black slaves. *Caciques* also acquired certain new privileges, such as the right to carry swords or firearms and to ride horses or mules. They adopted prestigious Spanish surnames and the honorific title *don*—or, in the case of a *cacica* (the wife of a *cacique* or, less often, a female ruler), the title *doña*. When the Spaniards first introduced municipal councils (*cabildos*) in indigenous communities, the *cacique* in the first post-Conquest generation almost always filled the highest office of governor (*gobernador*) and typically served for life, a reflection of the hereditary nature of indigenous rulership. He was often called by the Spanish title *cacique y gobernador* to signify this dual role.

Caciques actively sought the confirmation and protection of rights associated with rulership from Spanish authorities, and they increasingly claimed their landholdings as private property. Spaniards called the ensemble of rights, privileges, and properties that pertained to the title of *cacique* the *cacicazgo*, by analogy with Spanish *mayorazgo*, or "entail." (An alternate term was *señorío*, derived from *señor* ["lord"], which Spaniards also used to refer to indigenous rulers.) *Caciques* used the new alphabetic writing and Spanish documentary genres to cement their claims in the Spanish domain. *Cacique* families often safeguarded papers related to the *cacicazgo*—genealogies, testaments, baptismal records, land titles, land grants, bills of sale, maps, and plans of houses and properties—many of which have been preserved because they were submitted as evidence in litigation over *cacicazgo* succession and rights.

In the sixteenth century, the title *cacique* technically meant the heir of a pre-Conquest ruler and the single possessor of a *cacicazgo*, but practice was rarely so simple. Spaniards at times ignored the multiple rulers present in many Mesoamerican regional states, effectively elevating one to a dominant position with the designation *cacique*. In constituent parts of a regional state, Spaniards might elevate a leading personage to *cacique* status, thereby creating a ruler where none had existed before. Regional variation also had its effect. Mixtec notions of rulership emphasized the ruling couple, and, after the Conquest, the Mixtec rulers were usually presented as *cacique* and *cacica*. The Mixtec *cacica* ruled in her own right and was much more than the male ruler's consort, though the creation of the office of governor, for which only males were eligible, excluded *cacicas* from the official, political decision-making functions of the community. Over time, a tendency toward male *cacicazgo* succession evolved as Mixtec *cacique* families sought to ensure joint control over the *cacicazgo* and the office of governor. In the isolated and impoverished Sierra Zapoteca (Oaxaca), social stratification was less marked than in the large regional states of the valleys of Mexico and Oaxaca, and Early Colonial *caciques* exercised little power and acquired little wealth. *Caciques* in the Sierra Zapoteca, and in other remote regions such as the Maya Highlands, typically did not even have their status formally recognized by Spanish authorities.

The position of the affluent and influential sixteenth-century *caciques* eroded over time. Epidemics led to the loss of population and tribute income. Spanish authorities restricted the tribute taken by *caciques* and progressively eliminated exempt tribute categories, including the dependents of rulers. In regions where Spaniards were numerous, they steadily appropriated the lands, goods, and retainers of *caciques*. Indigenous commoners, some of them former dependents, also challenged *caciques* over rights to land. The position of *cacique* and the office of governor also became separate over time. The Conquest and sixteenth-century epidemics often brought about crises in *cacique* succession, and Spanish authorities took the opportunity to install nonrulers as governors. Henceforth, *caciques* had to compete for the office with other contenders, typically persons of the same class and potential rivals for the traditional rulership as well as the governorship. In the sixteenth and seventeenth centuries, some *cacique* lines died out. Others faced legal challenges between rival heirs or over the succession of a *mestizo*, a

technical violation of the law. Increasingly, *cabildo* officers openly challenged *caciques* over the rights and privileges of *cacicazgos*, especially landholdings.

Yet the story of *caciques* after the sixteenth century is not one of simple loss and decay. Social stratification persisted in indigenous communities throughout the Colonial period, and *caciques* continued to enjoy considerable status, wealth, and power in some regions. In Yucatán, where the Spanish presence and economy were weak, *caciques* dominated the *cabildos*, though opportunities to amass great wealth were limited by the relative poverty of the region. In Oaxaca, *cacique* prominence did not rest on political power—*caciques* had lost their monopoly of the *cabildos* and shared power with Spanish magistrates—but rather on the independent economic basis of substantial landholdings entailed as *cacicazgos*; a few of these were larger than most Spanish estates in the region. Oaxaca *caciques* had obtained legal confirmation of their landholdings in the sixteenth century, before Spanish demand had developed and used them as the basis for diverse commercial enterprises.

In Central Mexico, the picture was apparently more complex. By the eighteenth century, *cacique* no longer usually meant the holder of a *cacicazgo* who claimed descent from a pre-Conquest ruler. The connotation of *cacique* broadened, and the number of *caciques* proliferated. The children of a *cacique* (or *cacica*) all might successfully adopt the title *cacique*. A branch of a *cacique* family might attempt to secure authorization to establish a new *cacicazgo*, perhaps buttressed by the possession of papers related to an older *cacicazgo* or the presentation of manufactured ones. *Cacique* status also became linked to municipal officeholding, especially the position of governor. Individuals sought *cacique* status for its exemption from tribute and compulsory labor service. Yet *cacique* also might still mean the holder of a hereditary *cacicazgo*, though *cacicazgos* here were rarely on the scale of those in Oaxaca and may have been confined to the eastern Nahua region, where the pre-Conquest noble house (*teccalli*) had been especially prominent. By the Late Colonial period, *cacique* came to mean what *principal* once had: any prominent and reasonably wealthy indigenous person.

The numbers of *caciques* fluctuated dramatically from community to community. In Cuernavaca and Tepoztlan, the term *cacique* was used sparingly, and only two or three dynasties were likely to vie for the office of governor and general prominence; in Puebla, by contrast, the title *cacique* was used extensively. Late Colonial *caciques* pursued diverse occupations: some were artisans, others itinerant merchants, and still others the owners of mule trains. Some *caciques* were landless, whereas others possessed large estates still called *cacicazgos*. In one case in Tecali (Puebla), *cacicazgo* lands were not privately owned

CALAKMUL 117

but were held by sibling-based kin groups descended from the original recipients of sixteenth-century Spanish grants.

In the Late Colonial period, the power of *cacique* families no longer rested on descent from a pre-Conquest ruler. *Caciques* had secured rights to land through proper Spanish titles, and the indigenous origins of the *cacicazgo* hardly mattered. Some *caciques* controlled considerable wealth and power, and many were highly acculturated, marrying non-Indians. Powerful *caciques* were virtually indistinguishable from *hacendados*—both held land by virtue of Spanish title, both might be *mestizos*, and both might take similar positions in conflicts over land with local indigenous communities. As *caciques* became increasingly intertwined with Hispanic society, they were at pains to confirm their identity as Indians in order to maintain such privileges as tribute exemption and *cacicazgo* properties that rested on Indian status.

[*See also* Social Stratification.]

BIBLIOGRAPHY

Chance, John K. *Conquest of the Sierra: Spaniards and Indians in Colonial Oaxaca.* Norman, Okla., 1989. Ethnohistory of the isolated, impoverished, and ethnically diverse Sierra Zapoteca (Oaxaca), which emphasizes the social and political consequences for indigenous communities—including the position of *caciques*—of the forced trade in cotton textiles and cochineal dyestuff.

Chance, John K. "Indian Elites in Late Colonial Mesoamerica." In *Caciques and Their People: A Volume in Honor of Ronald Spores*, edited by Joyce Marcus and Judith Francis Zeitlin. Anthropological Papers, University of Michigan Museum of Anthropology, 89. Ann Arbor, 1994. Typology of eighteenth-century Indian elites, which attributes the key differences in elite structure to regional variations in the degree of elite market integration and of direct coercion by non-Indians.

Chance, John K. "The Caciques of Tecali: Class and Ethnic Identity in Late Colonial Mexico." *Hispanic American Historical Review* 76 (1996), 475–502. Investigation into the meaning of the title *cacique* in the Central Mexican community of Tecali (Puebla); argues that although *cacique* status involved both class and ethnic dimensions, ethnic factors became dominant in the late eighteenth century.

Farriss, Nancy M. *Maya Society under Colonial Rule: The Collective Enterprise of Survival.* Princeton, 1984. Sweeping history of the pre-Conquest Yucatec Maya, which details the social, economic, and political roles of the hereditary rulers called *caciques* by the Spaniards.

Gibson, Charles. *The Aztecs under Spanish Rule: A History of the Indians of the Valley of Mexico, 1519–1810.* Stanford, 1964. Comprehensive history of the Central Mexican Indians, which examines the social, economic, and political roles of *caciques*.

Haskett, Robert. *Indigenous Rulers: An Ethnohistory of Town Government in Colonial Cuernavaca.* Albuquerque, N.M., 1991. Ethnohistory of Indian town government in the central Mexican jurisdiction of Cuernavaca; emphasizes the political basis of *cacique* power in the eighteenth century and the link between the title of *cacique* and the office of governor.

Horn, Rebecca. *Postconquest Coyoacan: Nahua–Spanish Relations in Central Mexico, 1519–1650.* Stanford, 1997. Multifaceted study of Nahuas and Spaniards in the Central Mexican municipality of Coyoacan; includes one of the fullest studies of a single *cacique* group.

Lockhart, James. *The Nahuas after the Conquest: A Social and Cultural History of the Indians of Central Mexico, Sixteenth through Eighteenth Centuries.* Stanford, 1992. Comprehensive social and cultural history of the Nahuas after the Conquest, based entirely on Nahuatl documents, which examines the evolution of concepts and the terminology of nobility and rulership.

Restall, Matthew. *The Maya World: Yucatec Culture and Society, 1550–1850.* Stanford, 1997. Study of Colonial-era Yucatec Maya society based primarily on Maya-language documents; places the study of indigenous rulers within the context of the corporate body, the *cah*.

Taylor, William B. *Landlord and Peasant in Colonial Oaxaca.* Stanford, 1972. Study of landholding in the Valley of Oaxaca, which demonstrates the persistence of the large indigenous estates called *cacicazgos* throughout the end of the Colonial period.

Terraciano, Kevin. *The Mixtecs of Colonial Oaxaca: A History of Ñudzahui Writing and Culture.* Stanford, forthcoming. Fascinating study of Mixtec writing and culture, based on a diverse body of pictorial and alphabetic texts; includes a discussion of Mixtec rulers and *caciques*.

REBECCA HORN

CAKCHIKEL. *See* Kaqchikel.

CALAKMUL, a major site in the Petén, the southern Maya Lowlands, southeastern Yucatán Peninsula, Campeche, Mexico. Today a ruined city, Calakmul was one of the largest and most politically important urban centers in the Maya area from about 600 BCE to 900 CE. Calakmul had numerous tributary centers and dependencies, and it served as the administrative capital of a 13,000-square-kilometer regional state (first outlined as a four-tiered political unit by Joyce Marcus [1973, 1976]). The area occupied by this regional state is conserved within the Calakmul Biosphere Reserve, conceptualized by the Centro de Investigaciones Historicas y Sociales de Universidad Autónomo de Campeche (CIHS/UAC). The 723,000 hectare reserve protects a priceless record of Maya cultural development, as well as a rich and diverse natural environment (Folan et al. 1995).

In 1931, biologist Cyrus L. Lundell conducted the first scientific investigations at Calakmul. He was guided by chewing-gum sap (chicle) collectors from the collection center of Don Francisco Buenfil Palma; these collectors have located hundreds of ancient Maya sites within the Petén. Archaeologists sponsored by the Carnegie Institute of Washington, D.C., mapped the center of Calakmul during the 1930s. From 1982 to 1989 the CIHS/UAC substantially mapped and selectively excavated a portion of this regional capital. The core area is represented by a plaza 200 by 50 meters (660 by 165 feet) on a platform of almost 2 square kilometers. Stucco-covered structures with roof combs and with carved and polychromed façades were built concentrically. The 6,250 stone and wood thatched habitations, sacred structures, and other fea-

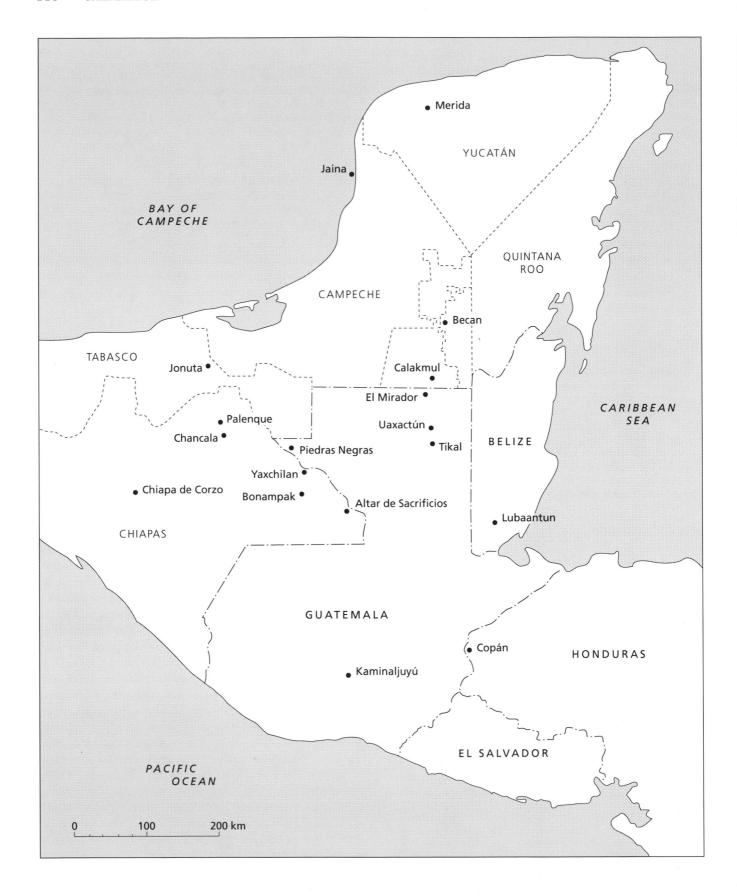

tures were mapped by Jacinto May Hau et al. (1990) during eighty-seven months of work.

Calakmul's significance as a major polity was ascertained by demonstrating its connection to other capitals and other sites in the Maya area. Marcus (1987) conducted in-depth analyses of 118 stelae from Calakmul to determine the political relationships between sites. Calakmul's emblem glyph was mentioned on monuments in more than seventeen cities outside its realm, including Palenque, Piedras Negras, Tikal, Caracol, and Copán. Dynastic monuments from 431 CE to 800 CE revealed twelve rulers or more, including "Jaguar Paw." Political alliances enabled Calakmul to maintain control of its realm.

Calakmul represents one of the most powerful of the Maya capitals. It organized the great numbers of people and the materials that were essential to reflect the ruling power, which had been garnered through the essence of divine status, based on legendary and mythic ancestors. The early 800 BCE to 250 CE center was overlaid by the later 250 CE to 900 CE city. Major structures associated with the central plaza include the 50-meter (165-foot) high Structure I, whose temple is collapsed; its base is larger than Temple 4 at the Maya site of Tikal in Guatemala.

Structure II, 55 meters (185 feet) in height on an imposing 140 by 140 meter (460 by 460 foot) base, has a Late Classic nine-room vaulted palace, with a roof comb built near its summit. It was one of the largest buildings in ancient Mesoamerica. Its façade, built in the first century CE, is covered by wide staircases and more than sixty rooms, in which a variety of activities were conducted. It housed several tombs containing jadeite mosaic masks and polychrome pottery, including a Codex Style vase from Structure IIH, which was excavated by Abel Morales Lopez. Large *huitz* (mountain masks) on the façade have been excavated by Mexico's Instituto Nacional de Antropología e Historia. The analysis of some sixteen thousand lithic artifacts, tons of potsherds, and bone and shell artifacts from Structure II revealed a habitational/culinary unit. This was associated with cottage-type industries related to tool-kit, lapidary, and confectionery production, along with the distribution of finished products, which provided an example of the public building concept, as suggested by Kent Flannery (1998).

Structure III (c.300–400 CE), the Lundell Palace, is a vaulted twelve-room building, with three roof combs. One of Calakmul's earliest known rulers was buried in a royal tomb within it that included three jadeite mosaic masks and three jadeite plaques with incised hieroglyphic writing (Alvarez and Armijo 1989–1990; Pincemin 1994).

Structure VII, at the northern end of the plaza, was a public structure that housed the burial of an eighth-century CE governing member of Calakmul. His tomb was accompanied by a jadeite mosaic mask and more than twenty-two hundred artifacts, including a finely worked pendant, decorative ear plugs, and beads (Domínguez and Gallegos 1989–1990). In contrast to the huge Maya site of Tikal, more jade than obsidian was found at Calakmul. Sources of obsidian (volcanic glass) were determined by Geoffrey Braswell; much of the obsidian from public Structure II came from the Guatemalan Highlands, while a great deal of the obsidian from palace Structure III came from the Mexican Highlands—which suggests different trading partners for the inhabitants of the two structures. (This evidence does not corroborate the empire level of sociocultural integration in the Maya Lowlands, as suggested by Simon Martin and Nikolai Grube on the basis of epigraphic data, with Calakmul as the major capital of a Maya empire.) Imports like basalt, hematite, and some cherts came mainly from Belize and Guatemala, and sea shells came from the Caribbean Sea. Very few ceramic vessels and only a dozen or so figurines were imported into Calakmul, which suggests a very limited exchange of non-perishable manufactured goods—in contrast to the active and major trade routes envisioned by some. Cacao remains possible as a trade item, as do other non-durables, such as salt and cotton.

The detailed settlement pattern and the demographic data that were analyzed by Laraine A. Fletcher et al. (1987), based on a formula developed for the Maya site of Cobá in Quintana Roo (Folan, Kintz, and Fletcher 1983)—where only 55 percent of structures were considered habitations—suggests that 22,000 people (1,000 per square kilometer) lived within the 22-square-kilometer central area of Calakmul, surrounded by a partially modified *arroyo* and a *bajo*. An additional 30,000 residents may have occupied the remaining mapped section and surrounding area. Central Calakmul housed 37 percent more people than the occupied area of central Tikal, previously considered the most populous urban center in the Maya area. Little evidence for the "regal-ritual" model for the Lowland Maya has been found. The area surrounding central Calakmul apparently extends to the opposite side of the *bajo*, linked by a *sacbe* (Maya raised road) that is visible on the remote-sensing imagery provided by the U.S. National Aeronautics and Space Administration (NASA). This *sacbe* may extend 37 kilometers (24 miles) southwest to El Mirador, Guatemala.

Calakmul, like Cobá (Folan, Fletcher, and Kintz 1979),

Facing page: Southern Maya Lowlands. *Map courtesy of William Folan.*

was an arboreal mosaic, with zapote, mamey, and ramón trees planted in the low moist areas called in Mayan *chum uuc'lu'um*. Habitations were built on higher, drained ground. Calakmul slopes downward for 35 meters (110 feet) toward El Laberinto *bajo*, a large seasonal swamp. María del Rosario Domínguez Carrasco tested this *bajo* and discovered that the Maya developed raised platforms within it, from which they exploited an abundant supply of chert to make stone tools. Crops of maize, beans, and squash were planted in distant upland slash-and-burn fields, along the edges of *bajos*, on elevated platforms, and on *cuyitos* (small, naturally raised mounds within *bajos*, similar to those later excavated by Richard Hansen around Nakbe, Guatemala), which protected seeds from excessive moisture and rot. A second crop was planted on and between the *cuyitos* in a four-step process that made possible a minimum of two or more crops per year during periods of regular rainfall, according to Gunn, Folan, and Robichaux (1995). The Maya developed stone, walled enclosures for kitchen gardens, in which they grew chiles, tomatoes, herbs, and medicinal plants. Richard Adams has suggested that some of the smaller apsidal or rectangular structures in the Petén may represent the residences of immigrants who moved into urban centers during periods of major development. This was perhaps part of a push/pull process that occurred in Lower Central America.

Paleoclimatological research on the monthly discharge of the Candelaria River made possible an analysis of the prehistoric climate of the Southern Maya Lowlands. The findings were utilized to create a climatic regression model for this region throughout the past three thousand years (Gunn, Folan, and Robichaux 1995). The rains waned around 850 CE, depriving Calakmul's population of sufficient precipitation for horticultural activities. A lack of groundwater made them dependent on thirteen reservoirs, one covering more than 5 hectares. Then the reservoirs dried up, leaving insufficient water for daily needs. This contributed to Calakmul's downfall, combined with lower fertility rates and migrations that began in the wake of this drought. People moved to regions with more dependable water, such as Lago Petén Itzá in Guatemala, and the coastal areas. The collapse involved several major inland polities in Campeche and Guatemala, which continued until hierarchical political systems disintegrated beyond recovery.

BIBLIOGRAPHY

Alvarez Aguilar, Luis Fernando, and Ricardo Armijo Torres. "Excavación y consolidación de la Estructura 3 de Calakmul, Campeche." *Información*, CIHS/UAC, 14 (1989–1990), 42–55. Account of the excavation of Structure III during the 1984–1985 season at Calakmul.

Domínguez Carrasco, Rosario, and Judith Gallegos G. "Informe de trabajo del Proyecto Calakmul, 1984. Estructura 7." *Información*, CIHS/UAC, 14 (1989–1990), 56–84. Detailed description of the excavation of Structure VII and Tomb 1 at Calakmul.

Flannery, Kent V. "The Ground Plans of Archaic States." In *Archaic States*, edited by Gary Feinman and J. Marcus. Santa Fe, N.M., 1998. Another offering by Flannery toward the better understanding of settlement patterns.

Fletcher, Laraine Anne, Jacinto May Hau, Lynda M. Florey Folan, and William J. Folan. *Un análisis estadístico preliminar del patrón de asentamiento de Calakmul*. Campeche, 1987. Preliminary analysis of Calakmul's settlement pattern.

Folan, William J. "CA Comment: The Late Postclassic Eastern Frontier of Mesoamerica, Cultural Innovations along the Periphery. Authored by John Fox." *Current Anthropology* 22.4 (1981), 321 and 346. Early effort to understand Maya cultural development and its collapse, based on precipitation patterns through time and space in the Maya Lowlands.

Folan, William J. "Calakmul, Campeche: A Centralized Urban Administrative Center in the Northern Petén." *World Archaeology: The Humid Tropics* 24.1 (June 1992), 158–168. Analysis of the six-hundred sites, aguadas, and stelae located ethnoarchaeologically within the 723,000-hectare Calakmul Biosphere Reserve.

Folan, William J., Laraine A. Fletcher, and Ellen R. Kintz. "Fruit, Fiber, Bark, and Resin: Social Organization of a Maya Urban Center." *Science* 240.4394 (1979), 697–701. Pioneering effort to record and interpret the distribution of economically useful trees in the Classic Maya urban center of Coba, Quintana Roo.

Folan, William J., Ellen R. Kintz, and Laraine A. Fletcher. *Coba a Classic Maya Metropolis*. New York and London, 1983. Contains the maps and analysis of the detailed settlement pattern of Coba, Quintana Roo.

Folan, William J., Joyce Marcus, and Frank Miller. "Verification of a Maya Settlement Model through Remote Sensing." *Cambridge Archaeological Journal* 5.2 (1995), 277–282. Reports on an early attempt to locate and explain the *sacbe* (Maya road system) at Calakmul by remote sensing technology.

Folan, William J., Joyce Marcus, Sophia Pincemin, Maria del Rosario Domínguez, Laraine A. Fletcher, and Abel Morales. "Calakmul: New Data from an Ancient Maya Capital in Campeche, Mexico." *Latin American Antiquity*. 6.4 (1995), 310–334. Summary of archaeological efforts at Calakmul to 1988.

Gunn, Joel D., and Richard E. W. Adams. "Climate Change, Culture and Civilization in North America." *World Archaeology* 13 (1981), 87–100. Broad, insightful analysis of the development and collapse of Mesoamerica and other cultures, as affected by climate change.

Gunn, Joel D., William J. Folan, and Hubert R. Robichaux. "A Landscape Analysis of the Candelaria Watershed in Mexico: Insights into Paleoclimates Affecting Upland Horticulture in the Southern Yucatán Peninsula Semi-karst." *Geoarchaeology: An International Journal* 10 (1995), 3–42. Represents a record of the paleoclimatology of the Maya Lowlands, based on the discharge of the Candelaria River in Campeche, Mexico.

Marcus, Joyce. "Territorial Organization of the Lowland Classic Maya." *Science* 180 (1973), 911–916. Early sociopolitical model of the Maya Lowlands.

Marcus, Joyce. *Emblem and State in the Classic Maya Lowlands: An Epigraphic Approach to Territorial Organization*. Dumbarton Oaks, Center for Pre-Columbian Studies. Washington, D.C., 1976. A more profound analysis of the 1973 article.

Marcus, Joyce. *The Inscriptions of Calakmul: Royal Marriage at a Maya City in Campeche, México*. University of Michigan Museum of Anthropology, Technical Report 21. Ann Arbor, 1987. Illustrations and analysis of the dynastic texts of Calakmul known through 1987.

May Hau, Jacinto, Rogerio Cohuoh Muñoz, Raymundo Gonzalez Heredia, and William J. Folan. *El Mapa de las ruinas de Calakmul. Campeche, México.* Campeche, 1990. Represents the map of Calakmul, drawn at 1:6,760 for reading comparison with the earlier map of Tikal, Guatemala.

Pincemin Deliberos, Sophia. *Entierro en el palacio.* Campeche, 1994. Very complete description and analysis of Calakmul's Tomb 1, in Structure III.

Ruppert, Karl, and J. H. Denison Jr. *Archaeological Reconnaissance in Campeche, Quintana Roo, and El Petén.* Carnegie Institute of Washington, D.C., 595. Washington, D.C., 1943. Results of the Carnegie Institute's pioneer efforts at Calakmul and environs, including El Mirador.

WILLIAM J. FOLAN

CALENDAR ROUND. The scholarly term for the permutation of the 260-day cycle and the 365-day year to form a period of 18,980 (= 52 × 365 = 73 × 260) days. The term "calendar round" (CR) refers both to a date that is specified in terms of these two cycles and to the 52-year period that commensurates them. Much Mesoamerican historical chronology was framed in terms of this cycle, or of dates of these kinds, or both; the form of this usage varied somewhat from culture to culture.

As an explicit calendar with fixed beginning and ending years, the CR is known for certain only in Central Mexico; cycles beginning in 1 Flint were emphasized in some traditions, while 1 Rabbit cycles figure prominently in the Mexica tradition. In Aztec sources, the New Fire rite, performed in 2 Reed, signified the transition from one 52-year cycle to the next. Nahua narratives from the sixteenth century concerning the "world ages" specify the number of years that each era lasted, from its creation to its destruction, and these are always exact numbers of CRs.

Pre-Columbian Mesoamerican historical records specify CR dates in two ways. A peculiarly Lowland Mayan practice is to juxtapose the position of the day in the ritual calendar to its position in the 365-day year. A given combination occurred only once within a given 52-year cycle, but it also occurred every multiple of 52 years before and after. This double specification is, strictly, what "calendar round date" means. Not all combinations are possible; because 260 and 365 have a common multiple of 5, only every fifth divinatory calendar date can be synchronous with a given day in the 365-day year, and conversely. There are likely Preclassic examples, but the earliest securely dated instances are from c.300 CE.

The rest of Mesoamerica specified the ritual calendar position of the event and the name of the year in which it fell. The 261st through the 365th days of the year are the same dates in the ritual calendar as the 1st through the 105th, while the 106th through the 260th occur just once. As a result, 155 of the ritual calendar dates have just one position in a given year, and the information is functionally equivalent to that in a Mayan CR date. For the other 105 ritual calendar dates, two different CR dates in the same year, 13 months apart, are consistent with the recorded date. The earliest instances are from Monte Albán and date archaeologically to the Late Preclassic Monte Albán I period.

CR dates of either type secure events in a longer historical framework than do the divinatory calendar or year dates alone. Their contexts often secure their position in spans longer than 52 years: either explicitly, by association with other calendar cycles (among Lowland Mayans, a tie to the long count was the norm); or implicitly, by reference to known historical individuals (CR dates rarely occurred more than once per reign).

[*See also* Calendars and Calendrical Systems; New Fire Ceremony.]

JOHN S. JUSTESON
and TERRENCE KAUFMAN

CALENDARS AND CALENDRICAL SYSTEMS.
[*This entry comprises three articles:*

　Mesoamerican Calendar
　Christian Calendar
　Correlation of Calendars

The first article outlines the basic structure and mechanics of the Mesoamerican calendar; the second article discusses the Christian calendar, including its implementation in Mesoamerica and its various divisions, feast days, and prescriptions; the third article summarizes the theories and debates concerning the correlation of dates among various Mesoamerican calendrical systems and the Christian calendar. For related discussions, see Calendar Round; Day-Signs; Divinatory Cycle; Festivals and Festival Cycles; Long Count; New Fire Ceremony; Saints; *and* Year Cycle.]

Mesoamerican Calendar

Two coordinated calendrical systems were attested almost throughout Mesoamerica, from Michoacán to the Guatemala highlands: a 260-day divinatory calendar important in Mesoamerican cosmology and in individual lives, and a 365-day year that structured community events (their details are described in the other articles of this entry). Several other systems are known from only one or two Mesoamerican cultures. Caso (1967) and Lounsbury (1978) provide important syntheses of Central Mexican and Mayan systems, respectively.

The 260-day and 365-day calendars are attested in uncontroversially dated records from about 300 BCE to 250 CE among Zapotecs, Mayas, and Epi-Olmecs. All putatively earlier dates have been vigorously challenged, but the consensus is that both systems began much earlier. Since the sixteenth century, most communities have lost both of these once universal calendars, but one—or, rarely, both—has survived in diverse linguistic groups through the twentieth century.

These pan-Mesoamerican calendars were based in part on the vigesimal (base 20) numeral systems common to indigenous Mesoamerican languages. There were thirteen groups of 20 successive, named days (called *veintenas* by Mesoamericanists after the Spanish word for "score") in the 260-day divinatory calendar, and eighteen 20-day "months" subdivided the 365-day year (with five extra days at the end). These distinct 20-day components were evidently considered comparable enough that they were called by a single term in many (probably most) Mesoamerican languages. The sharing of *veintenas*, conceptualized in a uniform way, along with the fact that 5 (from the five extra days ending the year, the *nemontemi*) divides 20 exactly, resulted in structural relationships of these two systems with one another and with other temporal cycles.

One prominent relationship is the fact that only four *veintena* days can begin any year or fall at any particular position within a year, so the year bearers—divinatory calendar dates that effectively "name" years—can fall on only four days in the *veintena*, and year names cycle through those days in a fixed order. The *trecena* (13-day) position advances by 1 each year, so the year names advance according to an elegantly simple pattern over a period of 52 years, and then repeat.

Other Important Calendrical Divisions and Cycles. The year cycle was reworked in some areas to accommodate vigesimal numeration in time counts.

The most straightforward adjustment was the Kaqchikel Maya system. The year's length was changed to 400 days, yielding a strict vigesimal count of days in powers of 20; the Kaqchikel form of the pan-Mayan word **ha7b'* ("year"; the asterisk indicated a reconstructed form) referred to this 400-day period, and a higher vigesimal unit (the *may*) of twenty 400-day years also seems to have been used. This year had twenty months of twenty days each, and no extra days; a single day (*A:j*, "Reed") was always the year bearer. The calendar round had no place in this system, and the cycle of year names repeated after just thirteen years. This 400-day year is known only from documents pertaining mainly to the Colonial period, but as an application of Mesoamerican numeration it may be older; it may be reflected in Lowland Maya accession dates, which seem to cluster strongly with respect to a 400-day cycle.

By 36 BCE, lowland Mayans or Epi-Olmecs had made a more elaborate adjustment—the long count. This system used 360 days as a canonical year length; among the Mayans, the word *ha7b'* ("year") was used for both this period and the older 365-day year (*tu:n* referred to anniversaries using either year length—i.e., to years as stations in time—and not, as is often stated, to the 360-day year per se). The structural properties of this year were similar to those of the 400-day year in having a single *veintena* day (*A:ja:w* "Lord") as ruler of the year; in thereby distinguishing just thirteen distinct, named years; and in achieving greater historical depth by including higher vigesimal multiples of the 360-day year in the system. It evidently went further in using a 400-year unit. Because the expression of numeral structure in the long count conforms to that of number words in Mixe-Zoquean languages but violates Mayan canons, it probably originated among Epi-Olmecs.

The only other calendrical cycles well documented in more than one group are the 9-day cycles of Central Mexico, Oaxaca, and the Maya Lowlands. Lowland Mayan texts attest several cycles unattested elsewhere. Prominent among them are several regionally distinct, formalized lunar calendars, in which true lunar months are counted in groups of up to six; most of the other Mayan cycles, like the 819-day count, are imperfectly understood.

Commensuration and Cosmology. A standard practice of Mesoamerican calendar specialists was the commensuration of calendrical cycles with one another and with natural cycles (that is, the construction of larger cycles whose length was a multiple of the lengths of each embedded cycle). Such commensuration seems to have structured Mesoamericans' knowledge about the temporal patterns of celestial events. For example, after a lunar eclipse occurred on a given divinatory calendar date, it could occur on alternate full moons near that same date. Remarkable results of this sort were also achieved in analyzing the cycles of Venus and Mars, which survive in hieroglyphic tables. Such results presumably validated the use of these formal calendar devices, and especially of the divinatory calendar as a model for sacred time (see Justeson, 1989).

Theories of Origin. The best evidence concerning the origin of the divinatory calendar is linguistic. Its roots are very ancient, possibly going back to the earliest phases of a shared Mesoamerican culture. There is scant evidence for calendar notations in Olmec art or writing, although ubiquitous images of a lord with a "breath bead" at the face have been misunderstood as representations of a day 1 Lord/Face. Nonetheless, the vocabulary of Mayan day names shows that the system was ancient, because some of these names—**tinhahx*, **b'e7n*, and **manik'*—underwent very ancient changes in pronunciation, probably well before 600 BCE in the case of **tinhahx*.

The divinatory calendar seems to have begun in a lowland environment, where all ten animals named in the

A stone sculpture containing solar elements and the calendrical sign 6 Rabbit. (Diameter: 18 inches.) *Courtesy of Museo Nacional de Antropología, México, D.F.*

reconstructed list would be found. This has suggested an origin among Mixe-Zoquean speaking Olmecs, and the Mayan names are consistent with such antiquity. Evidence from lexical borrowings confirms that speakers of Mixe-Zoquean languages were involved in the development or spread of the system. Most suggestive is the pre-proto-Zapotec borrowing of three animal names from Mixe-Zoquean, evidently a calendrical complex because all three are Mixe-Zoquean words for animals associated with the divinatory calendar. One, *mma-ni7*, "animal," from Zoquean **mʉ7a* "deer" plus proto-Zapotec **ni7* "classifier for animals," was borrowed early in the Zapotec era, since it was itself borrowed into Lowland Mayan as *manik'* in Preclassic times.

Speculative astronomical correlates, and a connection to fertility and reproduction based on the close approximation of 260 days to the time from missed menses to birth, are widely suggested as bases for the length of the divinatory calendar. The structure of the system, however, militates against explanations in which the length of the cycle is anything but a side effect of the lengths of the two constituent cycles. What needs explaining is why these two cycles became associated. There were other short ritual cycles in Mesoamerica—a 9-day cycle, a 4-day directional cycle, and perhaps a 7-day cycle—and interesting patterns in the commensuration of each of them with the 20-day cycle, basic to Mesoamerican counting, would surely have been observed. But it was the results for the 13-day cycle that happened to be stunningly successful in the astronomical realm; on this basis, its commensuration with the *veintena* may have become recognized for its cosmological significance, its relation to childbirth, or both.

The conceptual richness behind the divinatory system that led to the cycle of named units of the *veintena* is suggested by the case of the 20th day name: "Macaw" in Mixtec, "Blowgunner" in Quichean, and "Lord" in most other Mayan languages. It seems inescapable that the name relates in some way to the story (reflected on a mural in the Mixteca, as well as in the *Popol Vuh* and elsewhere) of young lords shooting a macaw in a tree with a blowgun.

Regional Variations and Developments. Calendars that were closely similar in most respects sometimes differed in the calibration of certain structural features. One of the most pervasive variations is in the differing placement of the *nemontemi* (the five "nameless" days). Changing the placement of these five days would change the year bearer unless there was a parallel shift, by the same number of *veintenas*, in the absolute timing of the days in the divinatory calendar. Some Nahua towns did apparently differ from one another in the timing of their divinatory calendar dates by multiples of 20 days; for example, these dates seem to have fallen 20 days earlier in Tlatelolco than in Tenochtitlan, and 20 days earlier among Epi-Olmecs than among Lowland Mayans.

Calnek identifies a likely historical example of this kind of shift, as well as the mechanism that produced it. In Tenochtitlan, the year 2 Reed lasted 385 days in 1507, with the month Izcalli both beginning and ending that year, but the next year was 3 Flint, as usual; one sequence of 20 days from the ritual cycle must also have been repeated during 2 Reed. The year bearer system and the sequence of year bearers were thereby maintained, and the *nemontemi* fell on the expected days of the divinatory calendar, but divinatory calendar dates fell 20 days later, and what had been the first month became the last. All these features also seem to characterize the relation of the Epi-Olmec divinatory calendar and 365-day year to their Lowland Mayan counterparts.

Mesoamericanists now recognize that there must have been moments when these codified calendar systems were adjusted, because of ethnographic evidence that not all features of all Mesoamerican divinatory calendars, or all features of all vague years, were completely synchronous. Nonetheless, since the integration of the structures of Mesoamerican calendars would have been disrupted by any localized, short-term adjustments, a fixed and inviolable canonical length for calendrical cycles was probably part of the background operating assumptions of Mesoamerican calendar specialists, and any adjustments must have been very carefully designed. In particular, it is unlikely that there could have been a regular adjustment of the 365-day year to the seasons; the scholarly consensus is that such adjustments rarely or never happened, and the difference between the solar year and the vague year need not have been perceived as a problematic discrepancy.

Many groups' calendars show the influence of other Mesoamerican cultures on their structure or vocabulary. The most typical and straightforward cases of influence involve one language borrowing vocabulary from another. Many Mixe day names, for example, are borrowed from Zoquean; they are ordinary Zoquean words for the concepts to which the Mixe day names correspond. Some Mixe *trecena* (thirteen-day period) terms were also borrowed from Zoquean—evidently from Zoque in particular, given the word *kuy* for "seven." Mixe traditions also state that they got their calendar from Zoques. Similarly, certain K'iché and Kaqchikel month names were borrowed from Nahua.

Some evidence for calendrical influence is less direct. Most attested Zapotec day names are identifiable as ordinary Zapotec words whose meanings are directly related to general Mesoamerican day name vocabulary; for example, the second day name, <-ee>, <-ii>, comes from Proto-Zapotec *p+e:7* "wind." A few have uniquely discrepant meanings from a Mesoamerican standpoint, like =*ttella* "knot" for the 10th day (usually "dog"), and =*inna* "maize farming" for the 15th day (usually some kind of bird), but these meanings agree with the forms of the signs for these days in the hieroglyphic texts at Monte Albán. For two day names, we have no etymology. Yet loan words in general vocabulary provide evidence of interaction between Zapotecs and Olmecs, or early Epi-Olmecs, that involved the calendar; and the use of a knotted-cloth day sign at Xochicalco and in Ñuiñe inscriptions reflects the ultimate origin of their day sign notations in Zapotec writing.

Swanton and Doesburg (1996) identify a remarkable example of diffusion of an abstract pattern of calendar names in Oaxaca. In Mixtec, eighteen *veintena* names do not come from Mixtec general vocabulary; only the words for "wind" and "water" occur both as day names and in their everyday meanings, and the linguistic origins of the other day names are unknown. In Chocho-Popoloca, whose names differ from those of Mixtec, somewhat more than half the day name vocabulary has been worked out in detail; all of it differs from the general vocabulary except, again, "wind" and seemingly "water."

[*See also* Calendar Round; Day-Signs; Divinatory Cycle; Festivals and Festival Cycles; Long Count; New Fire Ceremony; Year Cycle.]

BIBLIOGRAPHY

Caso, Alfonso. *Los Calendarios Prehispánicos*. Mexico City, 1967.
Justeson, John S. "Ancient Maya Ethnoastronomy: An Overview of Hieroglyphic Sources." In *World Archaeoastronomy*, edited by Anthony F. Aveni, pp. 76–129. Cambridge, 1989.
Lounsbury, Floyd G. "Maya Numeration, Computation, and Calendrical Astronomy." In *Encyclopedia of Scientific Biography*, edited by C. C. Gillispie, pp. 759–818. New York, 1978.
Swanton, Michael W., and G. Bas van Doesburg. Some Observations on the Lost Lienzo de Santa María Ixcatlan. (Lienzo Seler I). Baessler Archiv 44 (1996), 359–377.

JOHN S. JUSTESON
and TERRENCE KAUFMAN

Christian Calendar

The Julian calendar was inaugurated in Rome in the time of Julius Caesar because of the chaotic condition of the earlier Roman calendar. That calendar apparently had only 10 named months and we do not understand how it worked. The first six months were named after deities, from Janus to Juno. The remaining four months were numbered 7th, 8th, 9th, and 10th (September to December). It was decided by Caesar to institute a system of twelve named months—approximately twelve lunations—and was based on a year of 365¼ days, a reasonable approximation to both the tropical and the sidereal year. It may have been supposed that these were the same. The emperor's own name was applied to the month we call July and his adopted son's name was applied to August. The names were apparently regarded as continuing the deity sequence.

February was assigned only 28 days in three years out of four and 29 days every fourth year. The others were assigned either 30 or 31 days in order to make up a year of 365 days. A week cycle of seven days was in use, and there was an era count based on the traditional date of the foundation of the city of Rome. There were other era bases in use in the Roman Empire, of which the count from the founding of the Seleucid era was the most important. With minor modification, this continued in use among the Jewish people. The Christians had two important era bases, counted from the birth of Jesus and from his execution, but scholars differed on just when these events had happened, and the two bases were sometimes confused. The dating of the Easter cycle, associated with Jesus' execution, was a combination of lunar data, the seven-day cycle, and the spring equinox.

Special services commemorating the deaths of important individuals, especially those who had been killed for their beliefs, developed into a pattern of saints' days now used by the Roman Catholic and Orthodox churches. The association of particular saints with particular professions led to the concept of patron saints. Eventually, every day commemorated several saints, and various annual festivities of pagan groups who had become Christians were incorporated and their gods Christianized or equated with existing saints. Thus, Dionysus, god of wine, became Saint Denis, patron saint of Paris. Occasionally, churches were built so that the sun would shine on the altar on the day of the patron saint of that church, but with the slightly inaccurate Julian calendar, this would gradually cease to be true.

The Julian calendar was introduced to Mexico by the Spaniards. The structural correspondence between the Julian and Mesoamerican calendars immediately caught the attention of both groups. The process by which native beliefs were Christianized was strongly aided by the fact that Mesoamerican deities were associated with specific dates in both the 260-day sequence and the 365-day sequence. Hence, equations could be made either on the basis of similar attributes or on the basis of chronological position in the year. A near coincidence in time of similar festivals would have been particularly striking; however, such a correspondence would rapidly have shifted apart at a rate of 25 days per century. The slower but increasingly obvious slippage of the tropical year relative to the Julian year had led a series of popes, starting with Clement VI in 1344, to consider reforming and correcting the calendar. This was achieved under Pope Gregory XIII, and the new calendar was announced in a papal bull headed *Calendarium gregorianum perpetuum*, "the perpetual Gregorian calendar." The correction came into effect on 4 October 1583 in all Catholic countries. From that time forward, calendrical festivals would fall at seasonally appropriate points.

The hierarchical structure of the church was closely associated with the determination of appropriate festival dates and the associated community events. In many indigenous communities, this evolved into a political hierarchy operating in partial independence from the Spanish government structure. Some groups retained the religious hierarchy but removed it from control by church authorities. In many cases, the only contact communities had with members of the formal church hierarchy was the occasional visit of a priest. In the first century of Spanish domination many large churches and cathedrals were built, and ceremonies inside the churches were usually conducted by priests. Accompanying festivities outside the church usually included parades and dancing under indigenous direction. These festivities often included dramas, drawn in part from native traditions of religious drama and in part from medieval morality plays. Particular dramas were timed to coincide with a particular date either in the Spanish (Gregorian) calendar or in the surviving indigenous calendar. In some cases, they incorporated historical traditions about the Spanish conquest or about some local historical figure revered as a saint. Such plays often served as a relatively safe way of presenting historical and social criticism of the Spaniards.

During festival periods, people came to town from surrounding villages and farms as far as 120 kilometers away. At other times, relatively few people lived in the town, usually elected officials of the indigenous groups. Often markets were held at the same time as church services; earlier markets held at five-day or twenty-day intervals might be replaced by markets at seven-day or twenty-eight-day intervals. During the twentieth century, Protestant evangelists who insist that no work shall be done on the Sabbath (Sunday) have created major rifts within communities between those who accept traditional ways and the Protestant converts.

It has been postulated that the "empty ceremonial center" of this sort is an ancient indigenous pattern and applied to major Mayan archaeological sites. However, more recent studies have shown conclusively that the Maya sites were densely populated by a permanent, urban population and there is no archaeological or historical evidence for an intermediate period when this idea may have arisen. Conversely, the concept was present in Spain, most notably in the Easter ceremonies connected with the Black Virgin of El Rocio. Here a permanent population of a few hundred people became, during holy week, a temporary population estimated as high as a million people who came from all over Spain by traditional forms of transport—principally walking, in oxcarts, or riding horses. Many wealthy people had large homes in El Rocio which were occupied only during holy week and a short time before and after.

Syncretism was typical of ceremonies throughout Latin America. At Cholula, ceremonies associated with Mayauel, a goddess of pulque and of the moon, associated with childbirth and healing, were replaced by festivities of the Virgen de los Remedios, a new aspect of the Virgin Mary whose cult emphasized healing. Among the Yaqui, a deer dance is regularly performed during Easter ceremonies and is associated with the *matachine* dance, a figure dance with two facing rows of male dancers, one set regarded as officially "female." The impressive nature of the Yaqui deer dance led to its adoption and adaptation by the Mexican National Ballet, a fascinating example of reverse acculturation in which it has lost its calendrical associations.

The only surviving dance ceremony that seems to reproduce a pre-Columbian calendrical festival is the so-called *Volador* or flier dance that still survives in a few areas. The most notable example occurs at Papantla among the Totonac people of Vera Cruz. On a small platform atop a tall pole stands a single dancer. Four other dancers, wearing bird costumes, are fastened by long ropes to the pole. The ropes are each wrapped around the pole thirteen times, so that the ends are tight up at the top and the "fliers" swing in ever-widening circuits, reaching the ground on the thirteenth circuit. This ceremony, held around the summer solstice, clearly symbolizes the pre-Columbian cycle of 52 years, with each "flier" symbolizing one of the four days with which the pre-Columbian years could begin.

Among the Maya of Yucatán there persists in many areas a rain ceremony heavily laden with pre-Columbian religious symbolism. Specially made corn tortillas are stacked in thirteen levels and marked with directional symbols. A table is erected with corners carefully oriented to the cardinal directions. Four boys, identified with four different species of "frogs," stand at the corners and make noises regarded as appropriate to the particular species. Prayers in Mayan are directed to God the Father, to the sun, and to the rain gods. There is no feeling that this ceremony is in any way opposed to official Catholic ceremonies. Rain ceremonies are less firmly tied to the calendar than many other ceremonies, but the gods themselves have both Maya and Christian names, with appropriate festival dates.

In only one area of Mexico do true native temples, dedicated to native gods, survive—among the Cora and the neighboring Huichol. Even here, villages also have patron saints with Spanish and Christian names.

There are other components in the cultural mix that may have calendrical features. One of the early leaders of a revolt against the Spaniards was an escaped black slave who used a form of divination that combined Aztec and African elements. It seems safe to say that even the least acculturated native groups were strongly influenced, directly or indirectly, by Spanish religious ideas about the festive calendar and the church hierarchy. Conversely, many widespread and fully Catholicized ceremonies seem to show components derived from native Mesoamerican religious ideas.

[*See also* Saints.]

BIBLIOGRAPHY
Richards, E. G. *Mapping Time: The Calendar and Its History*. Oxford, 1998.
Thompson, D. E. *Maya Paganism and Christianity: A History of the Fusion of Two Religions*. Middle American Research Institute, Publication 19. Salt Lake City, 1954. See pp. 19–35.

DAVID H. KELLEY

Correlation of Calendars

The importance of aboriginal calendars in ritual and other aspects of Mesoamerican life was noted by many missionary priests, travelers, and colonial administrators, and later by ethnographers who described and recorded the cultures of contemporary Mesoamerican ethnic groups. In the second half of the nineteenth century, accurate drawings of hieroglyphic inscriptions at archaeological sites and the publication in facsimile of surviving examples of pre-Columbian books ("codices") written in hieroglyphs were beginning to show the fundamental importance of the calendar to the ancient Maya. By about 1890, owing in large part to the work of Ernst Förstemann, it was understood that the pre-Columbian Maya calendar represented in the archaeological inscriptions and in one of the codices dealt with a very long period of time and numbered consecutively each day that had elapsed since the first day of the calendrical era, thousands of years ago. If this calendar could be correlated with the Christian calendar, then many of the important written records of this ancient American civilization could be placed in historical time, dated accurately to the day.

Attempts to correlate the pre-Columbian Maya calendar with the Christian calendar have used two different kinds of correlations—astronomical and historical. Strictly astronomical correlations have proved to lack enduring scholarly value, for two reasons. First, because of the limitations of pre-Columbian Maya astronomy, precision to the day could not be expected unless the astronomical correlation were based on dated records of visible eclipses. Except for one possible occurrence, no such records exist. Other kinds of astronomical events known to be relevant to the pre-Columbian Maya (planetary heliacal-rise events, moon-age data, and solstices and equinoxes) are subject to observational error that precludes to-the-day precision. Second, it has been generally understood that astronomical correlation would be necessary only if there had not been calendrical continuity from pre-Conquest to post-Conquest times, but it is now clear that such continuity did exist. The role of astronomy in calendrical correlation has, therefore, become one of serving as a broad check on alternative historical correlations.

Historical correlations are based on the now well-documented continuity, at least up to the time of the Spanish conquest, of the 260-day calendrical cycle in much of Mesoamerica, including the Aztec and Maya areas in which the first European historical records were written. The Maya calendar used in Yucatán at the time of the Conquest contained all of the components of the much earlier Classic calendar (the 365-day *haab* with 20-day months and a 5-day intercalary period, 360-day *tuns* grouped into 20-*tun katuns*, and, of course, the 260-day cycle of 20 named days and 13 coefficients); however, it used a different, less redundant recording system that did not provide an explicit statement of the number of days completed since the beginning of the Maya calendrical era. Historical accounts written in Yucatán in the very early Colonial period by both Spanish and Maya authors provide dates for some important sixteenth-century events in both the Christian (Julian) and Maya calendrical systems, but these dates are often incomplete, lacking to-the-day precision. It is from such data that a Maya–Christian correlation has been determined.

The principal steps in the argument leading to the accurate correlation, as developed and refined by J. T. Goodman, J. Martínez Hernández, and J. Eric S. Thompson, are the following.

(1) Several partially conflicting historical references nevertheless agree that a *katun* 13 Ahau (a 20-year *katun* that ended on a day 13 Ahau in the 260-day sequence) ended sometime between the Christian years 1536 and 1541.

(2) Calendrical information in the *Chronicle of Oxkutzcab*, a Mayan-language historical document of the Xiu family of Yucatán, includes the day of the Maya month (the day in the 365-day *haab*) on which a *tun* ends for a sequence of twelve years, from 1533–1534 to 1544–1545. The Maya year covering parts of 1539 and 1540 contained a *tun* ending on a day 13 Ahau 7 Xul. This is taken to be the end of the *katun* 13 Ahau mentioned in other documents (there could be no other *tun*-ending day 13 Ahau between 1536 and 1541).

(3) Because a day 13 Ahau 7 Xul that is also a *katun* ending recurs only every 18,700 years (approximately), it can be calculated from the internal structure of the Maya calendar alone that the end of *katun* 13 Ahau in 1539 corresponded to the Long Count date 11.16.0.0.0 in the pre-Conquest notation. What the *Chronicle of Oxkutzcab* does not tell us is the day in the Christian year on which 11.16.0.0.0 fell.

(4) Information about the year 1553 written by Diego de Landa, bishop of Yucatán, says that a Maya year (*haab*) began on 16 July 1553 (Julian calendar); in the Maya calendar, this New Year day was 12 Kan 1 Pop. The Julian Day Number, or JD# (a day count used by Western astronomers), of 16 July 1553 is 2,288,488. It follows automatically from the structure of the Maya calendar that a day 12 Kan 1 Pop is exactly 5,004 days later than a day 13 Ahau 7 Xul. The addition of 5,004 days to 11.16.0.0.0 produces a Long Count date of 11.16.13.16.4, which indicates a Cumulative Day Count (CDC) of 1,704,204 days since the beginning of the Maya calendrical era. If the Maya CDC of Landa's New Year day (1,704,204) is subtracted from the JD# for that day (2,288,488), the remainder (584,284) is the presumed correlation constant, or the JD# of the first day of the Maya calendrical era. However, 584,284 is not the accurate correlation constant, because Landa's information was not exactly correct.

(5) The Maya–Christian correlation must be corrected by one day to make it agree with the more firmly documented Aztec–Christian correlation. Several historical sources, both Aztec and Spanish, support the dating of Cuauhtémoc's surrender to the forces of Cortés as having occurred on 13 August 1521 in the Julian calendar and 1 Couatl (Serpent) in the Aztec 260-day sequence. Based on the very high probability that the 260-day sequence was absolutely synchronized in Central Mexico and the Maya area, the day of Cuauhtémoc's surrender should have been a day 1 Chicchan (the equivalent of Serpent) in Yucatán. However, use of a correlation constant of 584,284 results in calling 23 August 1521 a day 2 Cimi, the day after 1 Chicchan. The conclusion is that the Maya New Year fell one day earlier in the Christian year 1553 than Landa said it did–on 15 July, not 16 July. (Perhaps Landa collected his information several years earlier but forgot to adjust for the extra day in the Julian leap year of 1552; Maya New Year really did fall on 16 July from 1548 through 1551.) This one-day correction means that although the CDC of 11.16.13.16.14 12 Kan 1 Pop is unchanged (1,704,204), it is now to be subtracted from the JD# of 15 July (2,288,487). The result of the subtraction, 584,283, which is called the "Modified Thompson 2" correlation coefficient, is the accurate statement of the relationship between the Maya and Christian calendars. The correlation of a Maya date is achieved by reducing that date to its CDC, adding 584,283, and translating the resultant JD# into a Julian or Gregorian calendar date, as appropriate.

The "11.16," or Goodman-Martínez-Thompson (G-M-T) correlation family discussed here, is in good agreement with the constraints imposed by the interpretable astronomical content of the pre-Columbian inscriptions and codices. Furthermore, it fits well with radiocarbon dates run on appropriate samples using modern techniques. There is no longer any significant probability that competing correlation families (256 years earlier or later, for example) could be correct.

A variant of the 11.16 correlation based on a correlation constant of 584,285 has been used in recent decades by some North American epigraphers because it has seemed to fit better with their interpretations of astronomical references in the pre-Columbian record. This correlation, for which there is no ethnohistorical warrant, resulted from a calendrical misunderstanding by J. Eric S. Thompson in the 1920s. When additional dated stelae allowed Thompson to recognize his misunderstanding, he repudiated the erroneous correlation constant in 1950 in favor of the correct one, 584,283.

BIBLIOGRAPHY

Aveni, Anthony F. *Skywatchers of Ancient Mexico*. Austin, Tex., 1980. Brief discussion, in Appendix A on pp. 204–210, of the uses and limitations of astronomically based correlations.

Caso, Alfonso. *Los calendarios prehispánicos* (Universidad Nacional Autónoma de México, Instituto de Investigaciones Históricas, Serie de Cultura Nahuatl, Mongrafías, 6). Mexico City, 1967. Comprehensive treatment, on pp. 41–90, of the evidence bearing on the correlation of the Aztec and Julian calendars.

Edmonson, Munro S. *The Book of the Year: Middle American Calen-*

drical Systems. Salt Lake City, 1988. Comprehensive and authoritative review of all calendars used in Mesoamerica before and after the Spanish conquest; systematic consideration of how native calendars are correlated with one another and with the European calendar. This is the most important single source on Mesoamerican calendars.

La Farge, Oliver. "Post-Columbian Dates and the Mayan Correlation Problem." *Maya Research* 1 (1934), 109–124. Presents evidence of uniformity of the 260-day count across Mesoamerica, which led to the recognition of Landa's one-day error.

Morley, Sylvanus G. "Appendix II. The Correlation of Maya and Christian Chronology." In his *The Inscriptions at Copan,* pp. 465–535. Carnegie Institution of Washington Publications, 219. Washington, D.C., 1920. Summarizes and evaluates the basic data of Maya ethnohistory on which the correlation is based. These data are referred to by later authors but usually not repeated.

Thompson, J. Eric S. *Maya Chronology: The Correlation Question.* Carnegie Institution of Washington Publications, 456; Contributions to American Archaeology, 14. Washington, D.C., 1935. Provides the basic justification for the 11.16 correlation, reviewing the earlier work of J. T. Goodman and J. Martínez Hernández.

Thompson, J. Eric S. *Maya Hieroglyphic Writing: An Introduction.* Carnegie Institution of Washington Publications, 589. Washington, D.C., 1950. Summarizes the Aztec data that require a one-day correlation of Landa's 1553 information, leading to the "Modified Thompson 2" correlation constant.

HARVEY M. BRICKER
and VICTORIA R. BRICKER

CALENDAR WHEELS. The term *calendar wheel* generally refers to Colonial-period images that display cycles of time in a circular format. Central Mexican calendar wheels incorporate the eighteen annual festivals or the 52-year cycle. In the Maya area, calendar wheels depict a cycle of 13 Katuns. The only known pre-Hispanic Katun wheel appears on a stone turtle from Mayapán (Miller and Taube 1993).

The earliest known Colonial-period calendar wheel is actually shown in a square format, on pages 21 and 22 of the *Codex Borbonicus,* an Aztec screenfold that divides the 52-year cycle into two parts. The *Codex Aubin,* also known as the *Codex of 1576,* shows the 52-year calendar in a rectangular format on a single page. Most other calendar wheels use a circular format. The Boban calendar wheel, an early sixteenth-century calendar on native paper, depicts the Central Mexican cycle of eighteen festivals in clockwise rotation, with Arabic numerals used to total the number of days; virtually all the text is in Nahuatl. Some paired festivals share the same glyph, but they are represented in different sizes, the first being the "small feast" and the second the "great feast." In the center, a 7 Rabbit date (1538) appears with text and images that refer to Tetzcocan town officers.

Fray Bernardino de Sahagún's *Florentine Codex* calendar wheel displays the Aztec 52-year cycle in counterclockwise rotation, using thirteen concentric circles. The Arabic numbers 1 to 13 appear in four spokes that end

with different year-bearer signs, which mark the four cardinal directions, with east at the top. It seems to be based on one in Sahagún's *Manuscrito de Tlatelolco,* compiled from 1561 to 1565 as part of the *Códice Matritense del Real Palacio.*

About 1581, Fray Diego Durán recorded a calendar wheel linking Central Mexican concepts of time and space with the 52-year cycle. There, four colored spokes radiate from the center and bend around to form a counterclockwise circle of time, beginning with 1 Reed (east and green), moving to 2 Knife (north and red), to 3 House (west and yellow), and 4 Rabbit (south and black). The Tovar calendar of about 1585 follows Durán's calendar, except that the wheel is rotated so that the Reed years are to the right of the page, rather than at the top.

Mariano Fernández de Echeverría y Veytia copied seven Central Mexican calendar wheels for a work yet unfinished at his death in 1780 (see Glass 1975). His calendar wheel no. 1 depicts a 52-year cycle, clockwise, starting with 1 House in 1649 and ending with 13 Knife in 1700. No. 2 displays the 260-day *tonalpohualli* cycle. The twenty day signs, in a central circle, have Arabic numbers 1 to 13 spiraling counterclockwise, from the center, repeating twenty times. An outer circle displays all fifty-two years with year-bearer glyphs and Arabic numbers; the glosses are all in Nahuatl. No. 2 is similar to the Tlaxcalan calendar created by Friar Francisco de las Navas in 1551 (see Reyes Garcia 1993). The spiral form of both may be derived from one in Toribio de Benevente Motolonía's *Memoriales* (1549). No. 3 is the only one of the group that is square. Veytia copied his calendar wheels from several sources, but the originals are uncertain except for no. 4, based on one acquired by Gemelli Careri in Mexico in 1697; the original is now lost, but a version published in 1700 displays symbols for the eighteen festivals and the phases of the moon in two inner concentric circles. No. 5 is derived from a lost Tlaxcalan calendar of unknown date in the Boturini Collection and displays the eighteen festivals clockwise. The last two are closely related; no. 6 has twenty day signs arranged clockwise. This same calendar wheel is repeated in simplified form in the center of no. 7, where Arabic numerals substitute for the dots associated with the twenty day signs. An outer ring records twenty years, rather than fifty-two, and glosses label each year-bearer with *verano* or *v* for "summer."

The *Books of Chilam Balam* display Maya calendar wheels with the 13 Katuns, representing a cycle a few years short of 260 years (see Bowditch 1910). Generally, the Katun wheels use Arabic numerals and display time clockwise. The calendar wheel in the *Chilam Balam of Chumayel* (c.1782) has radiating spokes with Katun numbers, Ahau faces, and the Mayan name for each Katun, with Katun 13 Ahau showing a cross that marks east. The *Chilam Balam*

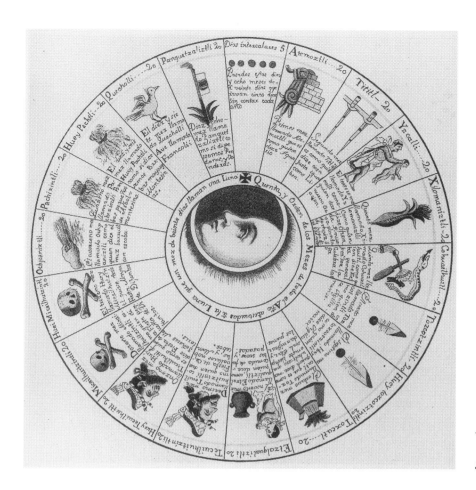

Veytia's Calendar Wheel number 5 (after 1907 edition). *Photograph courtesy of Susan Milbrath.*

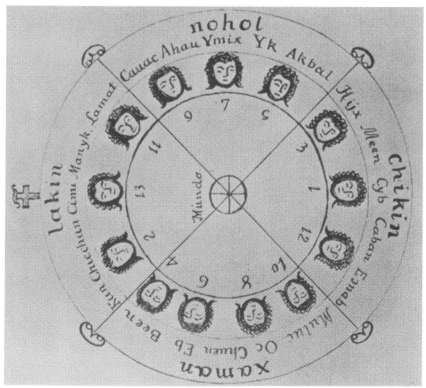

Wheel from Chilam Balam of Kaua (after Bowditch 1910). *Photograph courtesy of Susan Milbrath.*

of Kaua depicts a similar cross, with 13 Ahau labeled *lakin* ("east"), in a calendar wheel of 1789 (see Glass 1975); here, the Ahau faces are linked with the Ahau number and *roy*, the Spanish word for "king." Four spokes mark intercardinal points with small Venus glyphs, which probably show the observed horizon extremes of the planet (Milbrath 1999). *Chilam Balam* calendar wheels continued to be made as late as the nineteenth century.

[*See* Chilam Balam, Book of.]

BIBLIOGRAPHY

Bowditch, Charles. *The Numeration, Calendar Systems, and Astronomical Knowledge of the Mayas*. Cambridge, Mass., 1910. Includes discussion of Maya calendar wheels from the *Chilam Balam* books.

Durán, Diego. *Book of the Gods and Rites of the Ancient Calendar*. Translated and edited by Fernando Horcasitas and Doris Heyden. Norman, Okla., 1971. Major ethnohistorical work that illustrates and describes a 52-year calendar wheel.

Glass, John B. "A Census of Native Middle American Pictorial Manuscripts." *Handbook of Middle American Indians*, edited by Howard F. Cline, Vol. 14, pp. 81–252. Austin, Tex., 1975. Comprehensive annotated list of pictorial manuscripts of the pre-Hispanic and Colonial periods.

Milbrath, Susan. "Decapitated Lunar Goddesses in Aztec Art, Myth, and Ritual." *Ancient Mesoamerica* 8(1997), 185–206. Study showing how lunar months and eclipse cycles were integrated in Aztec art and calendar cycles.

Milbrath, Susan. *Star Gods of the Maya: Astronomy in Art, Folklore, and Calendars*. Austin, Tex., 1999. Extensive study of Maya astronomy, recorded in pre-Hispanic art and calendar cycles; with surviving Maya practices.

Miller, Mary E., and Karl Taube. *The Gods and Symbols of Ancient Mexico and the Maya*. London, 1993. Major work that synthesizes research on pre-Hispanic religion in Central Mexico and the Maya area.

Reyes García, Luis. *La Escritura Pictográfica en Tlaxcala*. Tlaxcala, 1993. Comprehensive study of Tlaxcalan codices; includes two important calendar wheels from Tlaxcala.

Sahagún, Bernardino de. *Florentine Codex: General History of the Things of New Spain*, translated by A. J. O. Anderson and C. E. Dibble. Salt Lake City, 1953. Chronicles native accounts of Aztec astronomy and related calendar cycles.

SUSAN MILBRATH

CALMECAC. In Tenochtitlan, the *calmecac* were the residences of Aztec priests who served in the temples of individual gods. Certain rituals were performed in the *calmecac*, and it was also the place where young men were educated and trained for the priesthood. Some sources describe the *calmecac* as a single unit; others state that each temple had a hall in which the priests resided. The best information on the *calmecac* buildings is in Fray Bernardino de Sahagún's sixteenth-century *Historia general*, in which he listed the various kinds of religious structures in Tenochtitlan. [*See* Sahagún, Bernardino de.] Of seventy-eight buildings, seven are named as the *calmecac* of particular temples; they are the following.

Mexico *calmecac* was connected with the main temple, and its priests performed the daily ritual of burning incense at the shrine of Tlaloc. Their own patron god was Quetzalcoatl, whose image was kept in the *calmecac*. Huitznahuac *calmecac* was the residence of the priests of Huitznahuatl, or Tlacahuepan, younger brother of Huitzilopochtli; these priests burned incense daily in the Huitznahuac temple. Tlillan *calmecac* was the residence of the priests of the goddess Cihuacoatl. According to Fray Diego Durán, Tlillan was the temple where the image of Cihuacoatl was kept. Tlalxicco was another temple connected with Tlillan *calmecac*; in it the priest of Tlillan burned incense when Mictlanteuctli was sacrificed during the feast of Tititl. Yopico *calmecac* was the residence of the priests of Xipe, whose image was kept in the temple called Yopico. Tlamatzinco *calmecac* was associated with the temple Tlamatzinco and with the gods Tlamatzincatl and Mixcoatl. Two *calmecac* were connected with fire deities: Tzonmolco *calmecac* with the fire god Xiuhteuctli, and Tetlanman *calmecac* with the goddess of the hearth, Cuaxolotl Chantico.

Two other structures are described as priestly residences, although the name *calmecac* is not applied to them: Pochtlan for the priests of Yacateuctli, the god of merchants, and Atlauhco for the priests of the goddess Huitzilincuatec, probably another name of Ilamateuctli. The *amanteca*, or feather-workers of Amantlan, had a *calmecac* located next to the *calpulli* and temple of the merchants. There is also a reference to a *calmecac* named Tezcacoac, where a child was given a ritual uncle and aunt during the feast of Izcalli.

A priest called the Mexicatl *teohuatzin*, who had authority over all other priests and supervised all religious observances, was also in charge of the training of the youths who entered the *calmecac*. The Huitznahuac *teohuatzin* assisted in the many duties of the Mexicatl *teohuatzin*, and the Tepan *teohuatzin* was particularly in charge of the youths.

The boys who entered the *calmecac* were sons of the nobility and of the wealthy; they were presented to the *calmecac* as children but took up residence at approximately fifteen years of age. The general name for all the inmates of the *calmecac* was *tlamacazque* ("givers"), a term applied to all priests, especially those of the rain cult. They passed through a series of four ranks: (1) Upon entering, the boys were "little priests" (*tlamacaztoton*), whose work was to clean the temples and gather the objects necessary for religious observances. (2) In the next step, they were called simply *tlamacazque* and were organized in teams that took turns keeping watch and calling the hours with trumpets during the night; they also were the main participants in the ceremonies of the feast of

Etzalcualiztli. (3) At the next rank, a priest was called *tlenamacac* ("fire-giver"), referring to the ritual of censing the idols with copal; priests of this rank were assigned to individual gods and temples. (4) From among them were chosen the two high priests, called *quequetzalcoa* ("plumed serpents"): the *totec tlamacazqui* ("our lord priest"), serving the national god Huitzilopochtli, and the Tlaloc *tlamacazqui* ("Tlaloc priest"), who was dedicated to the rain god.

The young men in the *calmecac* were also trained for warfare and could advance in a series of military grades according to the number of prisoners they took. Those who had captured prisoners of war no longer resided permanently at the *calmecac* but went there for ceremonial occasions. Those who had not captured prisoners were called *cuicanime* ("singers") and remained in the *calmecac*. The *calmecac* was also a place for training in highly skilled crafts.

Another institution similar to the *calmecac* was the *telpochcalli* ("youths' houses"). These were schools and residences for commoners who were trained for public works and for warfare. Their patron was Tezcatlipoca, especially in his manifestation as Yaotl Telpochtli. [*See* Tezcatlipoca.] They passed through a series of four ranks that were similar to the grades of the youths in the *calmecac* (see above).

In Tetzcoco, the building in which the king's children were educated is in one source called *tlacatecco*, whereas the children of commoners were trained in the *calmecac telpochcalli*. In Tenochtitlan, the *tlacatecco* is described as the building where the sacred bundle (*tlaquimilolli*) with the relics of Huitzilopochtli was kept and where newly elected rulers fasted for their initiation. There were also residences for women performing religious service, especially those called the "elder sisters" (*ipihuan*) of Huizilopochtli, who participated in the cult of the god.

The *calmecac* was basic to the education of the children of the nobility, training them to participate in public life, especially in the priesthood but also in warfare, government, and other activities, such as record-keeping. Some positions in the military and administrative organization were held by commoners, but the highest positions went to men of noble birth who had been trained in the *calmecac* in both military and religious activities. Men who had held priestly offices entered the upper level of government. Thus the institution of the *calmecac*, like the *telpochcalli*, reflects the close connections of the religious, military, and political hierarchies. The *calmecac*, then, was an essential part of the promotional ladder that selected the personnel of government and regulated social mobility.

[*See also* Temple Complexes.]

BIBLIOGRAPHY
Calnek, Edward E. "The Calmecac and Telpochcalli in Pre-Conquest Tenochtitlan." In *The Work of Bernardino de Sahagún, Pioneer Ethnographer of Sixteenth-Century Aztec Mexico*, edited by J. Jorge Klor de Alba et al., pp. 160–177. Albany and Austin, 1988.
                                PEDRO CARRASCO

CALPULLI. In pre-Hispanic Mesoamerica, Nahua political units in the Valley of Mexico were subdivided into a number of residential territorial segments, which were corporate groups with collective responsibilities in the economic, political, and ceremonial organizations of the state. The basic political unit—the town or city (in Nahuatl, *altepetl*)—always included such segments, which were defined territorially either as separate settlements or as wards within a single continuous settlement. In some cases, rural dependencies were inhabited by people from the various wards of the city.

All these segments were called *calpulli* (or *calpolli*) in Nahuatl; in Spanish sources, they are termed *parcialidades* or *barrios*. Nahuatl terminology does not distinguish clearly the different levels of social segmentation, so the word *calpulli* can be applied to any such segments at any level. One must be aware of assigning to it too precise a meaning in terms of settlement type and social or political significance. In migration stories, the groups coming from Aztlán are in some sources called *altepetl*, as migrating groups, which would establish separate polities; other sources call them *calpulli*, as wards in a big city. Within a given township, *calpulli* is used for the major territorial divisions and also for their subdivisions. Literally, *calpulli* means "big house," and in some cases it refers to a building or temple. The locative form, *calpulco*, denotes the houses where members met for religious functions; in Tenochtitlan, these were inside the ceremonial center, along the wall.

Other words have meanings that overlapped those of *calpulli*. For example, *tlaxilacalli* denotes a settled area or neighborhood; it was roughly synonymous with *calpulli* and became more common in post-Conquest times. Also *tlayacatl* refers to territorial divisions at the highest level of segmentation, which the Spanish called *cabecera*, meaning a town or ward with its own ruler; it is applied to the chiefdoms of Chalco, to the four *cabeceras* of Tlaxcala, and to the four major subdivisions of Tenochtitlan. The term *chinamitl* ("fence") is used in some documents for a local settlement, and *chinancalli* ("fence house") is also given as synonymous with *calpulli*.

The social solidarity of the *calpulli* members was strengthened by their common ethnic origin, their distinctive culture, and their own patron deities. The traditional histories of some groups provide good examples.

The Tolteca-Chichimeca from Tollan settled a number of *calpulli* in Cholollan and later sent settlers to neighboring areas, where they were described as *calpuleque* ("*calpulli* people"). The city's central settlement around the main pyramid consisted in early post-Conquest times of six *cabeceras*, each including a number of wards; each *cabecera* also had a number of outlying subject settlements. The population of five of the six *cabeceras* were the Tolteca-Chichimeca groups who had settled in the city; another *cabecera*, Colomochco, was made up of people who moved into the city during a later period.

In the Acolhuacan area of the eastern Basin of Mexico, the new settlers after the Toltec breakdown were Chichimeca led by Xolotl, who started the ruling dynasty of Tetzcoco. He admitted three groups who came from the west, of which the Acolhua settled in Coatlichan and gave their name to the region. Two groups, the Chimalpaneca and the Tlailotlaque, came later, during the reign of Quinatzin, the great-grandson of Xolotl. The Tlailotlaque worshiped Tezcatlipoca and painted historical records; probably some of them were merchants. Later on, in the time of Techotlalatzin, son of Quinatzin, four other groups—Mexitin, Tepaneca, Colhua, and Huitznahua—came from Colhuacan, the important center of Toltec culture in the southern Basin, which collapsed at that time. Each of those six groups occupied a ward in Tetzcoco and in other towns of Acolhuacan.

In Chalco, a number of immigrant groups had settled, and their ethnic composition was similar to that of the Acolhuacan. The Teotenanca group had arrived already subdivided into six *calpulli*. The Mexica, as they left Aztlan, were divided into four *calpulli*. Later, their city, Tenochtitlan, was also divided into four parts, with many subdivisions called *calpulli* and *tlaxilacalli*. All those polities whose traditional histories describe a *calpulli* organization were of Toltec origin.

Alonso de Zorita (1891) defined the *calpulli* as lineages, each with a chief similar to Spain's *pariente mayor* ("senior kinsman"); he also compared them with the tribes of Israel. This suggests some kinship basis for *calpulli* membership, and many scholars have held that they were clans; however, in Spain, *parientes mayores* were the heads of noble families, and Zorita's general statement may merely imply separate ethnic origins for many of the territorial subdivisions.

The sources do not give any rules regarding descent or marriage in relation to the *calpulli*. What little is said about these questions indicates an absence of fixed rules, and the study of concrete cases in early post-Conquest census and marriage records confirms this. It is significant that sixteenth-century Spanish writers report patrilineal exogamous groups among the Mayan-speaking peoples of Yucatán and Guatemala, while no such reports exist for the Nahua area, about which much more was written. Concepts of Nahua-area kinship or descent are expressed by terms other than *calpulli*.

There were lineages among the ruling dynasties (*tlatocatlacamecayotl*, "royal line"), but there was no patrilineal exogamy; on the contrary, marriages among agnates were at times preferred. But *calli* ("house") also means "household" or "family," in forms such as *cencaltin* ("people of one house"), so that *calpulli* or *cencalpultin* ("people of one *calpulli*") is a "big household," a residential group whose members can also be related by kinship. Early Colonial-period records show that some neighborhoods were formed by a group of households, most of whose members were somehow related by kinship to the local leader of the community or were his servants.

Several sources describe the *altepetlalli* and *calpullalli* ("city land," "*calpulli* land") as major legal categories, used for the subdivisions of the city and its farming population. The *calpulli* as a body held land from the time of their arrival in the Basin area, when they occupied certain lands for themselves and their successors. The community, as a whole, had collective responsibility for the distribution of land and the rendering of tribute and labor services demanded of the farmers. A farmer had permanent rights of usage over an individual plot, as well as the right to transmit it by inheritance, although this right was conditional on the payment of tribute and services. If a farmer failed to cultivate the land, left to settle in a different ward, or died without heirs, the land reverted to the common fund of the ward and could be assigned to someone else. The chief of the ward had a field assigned for his support which was cultivated for him by the ward members. The *calpulli* elders met with him several times a year to discuss community affairs.

Not all *calpulli* had the same amount of land. As the settlers arrived, some groups arriving first took possession of large tracts; later arrivals might not have found enough available land. A ward could then rent land to members of other wards who were short of land, and the proceeds were used for the common public expenditures of the ward. Within a given *calpulli* there were also important differences in the amount of land held by members, since some farmers with many relatives and servants assumed the obligation to cultivate several plots. Other residents might have no land at all and were servants of wealthy members or worked at odd jobs.

The division into wards also showed a certain relation to the social division of labor. Some wards were inhabited by the ethnically dominant groups, included a higher proportion of noble houses, and had as their leaders the leaders of the city-state as a whole; other wards belonged to ethnic minorities or consisted predominantly of commoners. Professional merchants and skilled artisans had their own wards. When a craft was practiced in several wards, craftsmen were organized for purposes of tribute collection or worship of their patron gods into groups that cut across territorial ward divisions. These were also called *calpulli*, although they were not residential units.

The ward was also a unit of administration within the overall political system. Each ward had labor-draft leaders and tribute collectors (*tlayacanque, tequitlatoque*), and the military organization also took the *calpulli* as a base. Young men were trained for war in the youths' houses (*telpochcalli*), of which there were many in the various neighborhoods. The *calpulli* also had important roles in the ceremonial organization. The major *calpulli* had their own patron deities, and they held lands whose revenue supported their cult.

Ethnic groups other than the Nahua had institutions similar to the *calpulli*; there are reports for Tarascans, the Mixtec, and the Highland Maya. Modern ethnographic accounts also discuss the subject for all major areas.

[*See also* Civil-Religious Hierarchy; Political Organization and Development, *article on* Pre-Hispanic Cultures; Property and Land Tenure.]

BIBLIOGRAPHY

Carrasco, Pedro. "Social Organization of Ancient Mexico." In *Handbook of Middle American Indians*, edited by Robert Wauchope, vol. 10, pp. 349–375. Austin, Tex., 1971. Shifts the emphasis to the *calpulli* as a social segment with various corporate functions, relegating kinship to the process of recruitment and reproduction.

Lockhart, James. *The Nahuas after the Conquest*. Stanford, 1992. Broad study of the Colonial period; includes a discussion of the *calpulli* as part of the cellular organization of Indian towns.

Monzón, Arturo. *El calpulli en la organización social de los tenochca*. Mexico City, 1949. Presents the *calpulli* as ambilateral clans, participating in all aspects of social life.

Zoria, Alonso de. "Breve y sumaria relación de los señores y maneras y diferencias que había de ellos en la Nueva España." In *Colección de documentos para la Historia de México*, edited by Joaquín García Icazbalceta, vol. 3, pp. 71–227. Mexico City, 1891. Major colonial source about the *calpulli*.

PEDRO CARRASCO

CANDELARIA, MARÍA DE LA (also known as María de la Cruz) (c.1698–1716), a Tzeltal Maya woman, leader of the Rebellion in Chiapas, 1712. In June 1712, María López, daughter of the sacristan of Cancuc in the Alcaldía Mayor district of Chiapas, announced to the town's Tzeltal inhabitants that the Virgin Mary had appeared to her in the forest and asked that a chapel be built in her honor. This event was the culmination of two decades of political and social turmoil in Chiapas—a period characterized by poor harvests, a system of tribute that was especially onerous for Indians in mountainous regions, repeated conflicts among the Spaniards, one native rebellion and several mutinies, and a proliferation of miracles and prophets. Cancuc's Dominican friar opposed María's claims and attempted to suppress news of the supposed apparition by ordering the young woman and her father flogged. The people of Cancuc, however, sided with María, expelled the friar, and built the chapel.

During July, word of the miracle spread throughout the Maya region, drawing increasing numbers of Indians from neighboring towns to the chapel. Then on 8 August, in the presence of a multitude assembled before the chapel, María López, who had taken the name María de la Candelaria, proclaimed that there would no longer be any tribute, no king or bishop, no *alcalde mayor*—and that the Virgin had ordered the annihilation of all Spaniards, including the clergy. Some thirty Indian towns of the Chiapas highlands answered this call and rose up against Spanish domination. Over the three and a half months of the rebellion, military captains appointed by María de la Candelaria and Sebastián Gómez de la Gloria (a Tzotzil from Chenalhó who claimed to have risen to Heaven and conversed with the Holy Trinity, the Virgin Mary, and the apostle Peter) commanded the rebel army. Meanwhile, Indian vicars also named by them replaced the Spanish clergy in the churches of the rebel towns, saying Mass, administering the sacraments, and preaching the miracle of the apparition of the Virgin in Cancuc.

With the arrival of Spanish military reinforcements from Guatemala, the Spaniards managed to capture Cancuc on 21 November. Gradually, they recovered control of the large region that had joined the rebellion. After the rebels' defeat, María de la Candelaria escaped in company with her father, husband, brother, and brother's wife. For three months they were hidden in various Tzotzil towns. Pursued by the Spaniards, they eventually took refuge in the forest of Chihuisbalam, in an unpopulated region between the Valley of Huitiupán and Yajalón, where they remained for three years, virtually without contact with the outside world. María de la Candelaria died in childbirth on or about 20 February 1716. Some two weeks later, the rest of the family was discovered by an Indian from Yajalón who informed the Spanish authorities. During the trial that followed their capture, María de la Candelaria's father, Agustín López, admitted that he and his four companions had concocted the Virgin's apparition to put an end to Spanish rule in Chiapas.

Although the memory of the Cancuc Rebellion remains alive in Tzeltal and Tzotzil towns to this day, the modern versions center on the figure of Juan López, a rebel captain who was executed by the Indians. María de la Candelaria appears to have been completely forgotten by the native people of Chiapas.

BIBLIOGRAPHY

Bricker, Victoria Reifler. *The Indian Christ, the Indian King: The Historical Substrate of Maya Myth and Ritual.* Austin, 1981. Anthropologically oriented study of rebellions in the Maya region.

Brinton, Daniel G. *María Candelaria: An Historic Drama from American Aboriginal Life.* Philadelphia, 1897.

Gosner, Kevin. *Soldiers of the Virgin: The Moral Economy of a Colonial Maya Rebellion.* Tucson, 1992. Detailed monograph on the 1712 rebellion and its economic causes. Its characterization of the period preceding the rebellion as one of economic crisis, however, is open to debate.

Viqueira, Juan Pedro. *María de la Candelaria, india natural de Cancuc.* Mexico City, 1993.

Viqueira, Juan Pedro. *Indios rebeldes e idólatras. Dos ensayos históricos sobre la rebelión india de Cancuc, Chiapas, acaecida en el año de 1712.* Mexico City, 1997. Examination of the regional dynamics of the rebellion and the religious beliefs of the Indians who participated in it.

JUAN PEDRO VIQUEIRA ALBÁN
Translated from Spanish by Jan Rus

CANDELARIA, NUESTRA SEÑORA DE LA. One of the most widespread Roman Catholic festivals in Mexico, that of Our Lady of Candlemas, is celebrated on the second day of February. The feast day is associated with the purification of the Virgin and the presentation of the child Jesus in the Temple, forty days after his birth. In Europe, Candlemas was celebrated with a benediction and the distribution of candles; in many places public processions were held. Veneration of the *Virgen de la Candelaria* was carried to New Spain, although it did not become an object of pilgrimage in Mexico City, as did other aspects of the Blessed Mother. Nevertheless, there is a church built in her honor to the east of downtown Mexico City, in the pre-Hispanic section of Ometochtitlan ("The Place of 2 Rabbit," a deity associated with pulque, an alcoholic beverage). The name of the neighborhood today is La Candelaria de los Patos ("Candelmas of the Ducks"). By the eighteenth century, the church was supported by a large group of midwives and the members of a *cofradía* (religious fraternity), whose main purpose was the purchase and sharing of candles, some of which were used *ex voto* (as a votive offering).

Like many others, the feast of Candlemas was adopted into the Mesoamerican agricultural calendar. To this day, on the second of February, Indian communities bless the seeds they will plant. The date falls into the dry season, which ritually lasts until the third of May, when the day of the Holy Cross is celebrated.

The festival of Candlemas is particularly important in Tlacotalpan, Veracruz. Between 1783 and 1786, a shrine was erected there on a parcel of land donated by a Spanish settler. The statue of the Virgin, carrying the child Jesus and resting her feet on a half moon, is dressed in elaborate robes. On her day, the villagers decorate a barge and transport the statue across the Papaloapan River.

Other places also celebrate Candlemas, such as San Juan de los Lagos, Talpa, and Lagos de Moreno in the state of Jalisco. Pilgrims begin arriving in the villages at the end of January. They come to make religious vows or to participate in the festivals, which feature music, dances, markets, cockfights, and bullfights.

The feast of Candlemas has another aspect that is more modern in origin: the custom of designating "godparents" for the child Jesus. Gatherings of family and friends for this custom take place in most parts of Mexico. On the sixth of January, as part of the celebration of Epiphany, everyone at a supper receives a piece of a traditional *rosca de reyes* ("kings' cake"). An unknown number of small figures of Jesus are hidden in the cake, and those who find them are designated "godmothers" and "godfathers." The "godparents" are charged with hosting a big supper party on the day of Candlemas, when tamales and atole are served generously.

BIBLIOGRAPHY

León, Imelda de, ed. *Calendario de fiestas populares.* Mexico City, 1988. Useful state-by-state guide to Mexico's most important religious and civic ceremonies; all Candlemas festivities observed in Mexico are reported.

Ramírez Leyva, Edelmira, Guadalupe Ríos de la Torre, and Marcela Suárez Escobar. *De candelas y candelitas.* Mexico City, 1992. Overview of folklore and traditions concerning candles and Candlemas in the Colonial era and in modern Central Mexico.

XAVIER NOGUEZ

CANEK, JACINTO (?–1761), Hispanicized Maya rebel. José Jacinto Uc de los Santos, who took the royal Itzá surname of Can Ek (the last Maya king of the Petén Itzá, who had been subjugated by the Spanish in 1697), led a short-lived, indigenous uprising in 1761 in Cisteil (or Quisteil), a remote village in southeastern Yucatán. Although Canek and six hundred of his Yucatec Maya followers were killed by colonial authorities, the ill-fated uprising would leave a vivid impression on the mid-nineteenth-century Maya who revolted against Yucatecan rule during the apocalyptic Caste War (1847–1902). The uprising took the Spanish by surprise, because the region had been relatively peaceful since the protracted conquest of the Yucatán Peninsula in the 1540s. Colonial documentation about the revolt—including the minutes of the Mérida city council, correspondence between Yucatán's governor and the viceroy of New Spain, and anonymous diaries—is ambiguous, contradictory, and self-serving. That has led both nineteenth-century historians and modern scholars to debate Canek's motivations and aspirations and to question the brutal overreaction by the Spanish to the revolt.

Canek was an orphan (although historians disagree as to whether he was born in Campeche or Mérida), brought up and educated by Franciscans in the main friary in Mérida. Although orphans were often taken in by Spanish families and treated as domestic servants, the religious education (in Spanish and possibly Latin) that Canek received at the monastery was unusual, akin to what the Maya nobility had received from friars just after the Conquest. Some have surmised that he was a precocious youngster, but he soon fell into a dissolute life, and the Franciscans responded by sending him away. Historians believe that his upbringing, education, and subsequent ouster by the Franciscans contributed to Canek's bitterness toward colonial rule and the Roman Catholic church, as well as his identification with the Maya. For a time, Canek became a baker in Mérida's Santiago barrio before finding his way to the new hamlet of Cisteil, in the parish of Tixcacaltuyú. Why Canek went there is unclear, but he had the profile of the quintessential rebel leader—someone who had his feet in the world of the Spanish and the Maya, who clearly had some experience beyond the confines of Cisteil, and who had been disillusioned with and marginalized from the dominant culture that had educated him.

Cisteil was founded as a new settlement in the Late Colonial period. Almost all of the rebels were recent arrivals, having moved there from other communities. The neighboring *hacienda* of Huntulchac was sold in October 1761 to one of the region's largest landowners. This cattle and maize *hacienda* was an important motor of the local economy, and the sudden change in ownership threatened to undermine existing labor arrangements between Cisteil's villagers and Huntulchac.

On 19 November, villagers in the midst of planning for the festival honoring the town's patron saint became intoxicated; they then killed a merchant who had refused to sell them liquor. Uc de los Santos delivered a stirring speech that night, which expressed strong nativist sentiments and called on the Maya to destroy the Spanish. Seeking to legitimate his movement among the Yucatec Maya, Canek apparently assumed the name Can Ek and added to it Chichán Motecuhzoma, or "Little Montezuma" (whom he may have learned about from his Franciscan upbringing). The *Books of Chilam Balam*, colonial Maya texts that cryptically combined prophecy and narrative, had predicted that the descendant of the king of the Itzá (the royal family that originally ruled the Postclassic-period civilization of Chichén Itzá) would one day return to defeat the Spanish conquerors. Canek also steeped his rhetoric in the Christian vernacular, criticizing church officials for neglecting *visita* towns like Cisteil,

promising to abolish certain church taxes, and castigating priests for licentious behavior. He also denounced the unpopular tribute requirements and labor drafts that continued to exist in peripheral regions like Yucatán until the 1770s. Canek, however, did not abolish the unpopular sale of indulgences, requiring instead that his followers pay them to him in cloth, as tribute. He named himself king in a ceremony in the Cisteil church, where he donned the regalia of the town's Virgin Mary. Purportedly proclaiming a holy war against Spanish rule, Canek sent messengers to nearby villages enlisting their support and boasting that British logwood cutters in present-day Belize would join their rebellion.

After an initial skirmish in which a small detachment of Spanish horsemen was annihilated by Cisteil villagers, the Spanish regrouped and sent five hundred troops to the town on 26 November. Although the Indians outnumbered the Spanish three to one, the better equipped Spaniards triumphed, losing thirty to forty men in the battle to the Indians' six hundred. The town was razed, but Canek and 125 of his followers were able to elude capture. They were subsequently caught in Sibac, near Huntulchac, and taken back to Mérida to stand trial. There were reports of localized, collateral uprisings as far away as Tizimín in the east and Lerma near Campeche to the west. On 30 November, unsubstantiated rumors swept Mérida that the Indians who lived in the poorer barrios were arming themselves for a rebellion. The embattled Spaniards moved quickly to make an example of Canek and the other captives. On 7 December, he was taken to Mérida for trial and execution, suffering the agony of broken limbs and flesh torn off with pincers while still alive; his body was burned and his ashes thrown to the wind. Eight other leaders were hanged and their bodies taken down from the gallows and quartered, with the remains publicly displayed. The rest of the captives got off relatively lightly, with public whippings and the loss of their right ears.

The viceroy of New Spain later rebuked Yucatán's governor for the brutal and excessive manner in which the rebellion was quelched. History's judgment of the Canek uprising has been more ambiguous. Nineteenth-century New World chroniclers, such as Eligio Ancona and Juan Francisco Molina Solís, were more obsessed with the idea of an Indian king than the Maya were. Distraught over the devastation inflicted by the Caste War Maya, these writers readily linked Canek to the Caste War rebel Jacinto Pat. Ancona and Molina Solís emphasized Spanish barbarism, because they wanted to demonstrate that colonial rule was despotic and especially cruel to the Maya. Although disagreement about the Canek uprising remains, the grievances that Canek raised about the Roman Catholic church, autocratic rule, mistreatment, the revolt's millenarian character, and the tensions between communities and *haciendas* were all very much in evidence during the Caste War.

[*See also* Caste Wars.]

BIBLIOGRAPHY

Abreu Gómez, Ermilo. *Canek: History and Legend of a Maya Hero.* Translated, with an introduction, by Mario L. Dávila and Carter Wilson. Berkeley, 1979. Fictional account of the rebellion that accentuates Spanish cruelty and indigenous heroism.

Ancona, Eligio. *Historia de Yucatán desde la época mas remota hasta nuestros días.* 4 vols. Mérida, 1878–1880. Principal nineteenth-century chronicle of the revolt, written by a local liberal politician and historian, that emphasizes the Spanish overreaction and the importance of Canek's appropriation of the title of the Indian king.

Bricker, Victoria Reifler. *The Indian Christ, the Indian King: The Historical Substrate of Maya Myth and Ritual.* Austin, 1981. This work by a historical anthropologist is the most detailed analysis of the primary and secondary accounts of the revolt; Bricker believes that Yucatecan historians twisted the facts of the Cisteil revolt to suit their own needs.

Farriss, Nancy M. *Maya Society under Colonial Rule: The Collective Enterprise of Survival.* Princeton, N.J., 1984. Contains a thoughtful and judicious analysis of the rebellion. By emphasizing the lack of unrest in the region, the author emphasizes the exceptionality of the Canek revolt.

Patch, Robert W. *Maya and Spaniard in Yucatan, 1648–1812.* Stanford, Calif., 1993. Patch provides new data concerning the origins of the rebels, their grievances with the *repartimiento* and indulgences, and the formation of the town of Cisteil.

Ríos, Eduardo Enrique. "La rebelión de Canek, Yucatán, 1761." *Boletín de la Sociedad Mexicana de Geografía y Estadística* 54 (1940), 483–495. The first scholarly analysis to utilize significant primary materials of the revolt, including revealing correspondence between the viceroy of New Spain and the governor.

ALLEN WELLS

CANINES. The dog (*Canis familiaris*), a descendant of the wolf (genus *Canis*), was the only common domesticated animal in pre-Hispanic Mesoamerica. Dogs may have come to the Americas with the first human migrations of hunter-gatherers. Dog remains have been found associated with those of humans dating to c.3000 BCE in the Tehuacán Valley in Mexico. Dogs may have been used for protection. As hunters themselves, dogs surely guided and helped human hunters in some societies. There is also a long tradition of dogs being fattened and consumed as food (as in Asia), usually on special occasions; dog remains were found in food middens at the Olmec site of San Lorenzo in Veracruz (c.1200 BCE).

After the Spanish conquest, in the sixteenth century, Friar Diego Durán reported seeing dogs for sale in a Mexican market, which meant to him that pre-Christian rites were still being celebrated. Diego de Landa, the first bishop of Yucatán, found extensive evidence for the Maya sacrifice of dogs, which continued into post-Conquest times. The Aztec, or Mexica, sacrificed dogs at the time of the winter solstice. Another sixteenth-century friar,

Bernardino de Sahagún, observed that a dog would be buried with its Mexica owner.

Human burials throughout Mesoamerica and in other parts of the Americas contain dog remains or dog effigies—often ceramic vases or figurines—because the old and wide belief is that a dog helps the dead over a body of water to the underworld. Late Classic Maya (600–900 CE) vases and carvings show a lord accompanied to the underworld by a dog. Even in the twentieth century, Lacandón Maya have been buried with palm-frond "dogs." Dogs have other associations with the dead: they bury bones in the earth and dig them up. Maya vases show dogs in underworld scenes with a skeletal rib cage, a "death's-eye" collar, or a scarf worn by human sacrificial victims. The Maya death god had a dog as a companion. "Dog" was a day name; in the Mexica calendar, the death god was patron of that day.

Many modern narratives tell of dogs leading hunter-owners into caves to confront the underworld lords, who are the masters of game animals (usually, the dog-owner has been overhunting). The cave of Naj Tunich in Guatemala, which is filled with Classic Maya paintings, was discovered by a hunter whose dog had chased a deer into it.

The underworld is also the earth, where plants grow. Dogs or dog effigies are still offered in planting rites, sometimes buried in the corners of a field. In Mexica myth, the god Xolotl changes himself into a maize plant. Xolotl, the patron deity of the Mexica ballgame—a sacrificial rite—was a skeletal, dog-faced or dog-bodied god, who was Venus as the Evening Star and the twin or noc-

Long thought to carry the souls of the dead to the underworld, the dog was the only domesticated animal in pre-Hispanic Mesoamerica. Plumed coyote, stone sculpture. (Height: 18 inches.) *Courtesy of Museo Nacional de Antropología, México, D.F.*

turnal equivalent of Quetzalcoatl, the Morning Star. Xolotl and/or Quetzalcoatl, depending on the version of the myth, go to the underworld to shed blood on the bones of the dead, to effect the new creation of humankind. In another account, Xolotl returns to the underworld to retrieve maize seed. Maya dog depictions have a ragged ear (a result of leishmaniasis, or chiclero's ulcer), and Xolotl is sometimes depicted with torn ears.

Early Spanish chroniclers described hairless dogs. These were usually represented in ceramic effigies with wrinkled skin; their rib cages and spines show. Barkless dogs were also mentioned.

In recent times, the Kekchí Maya see the Morning Star as a dog running ahead of the sun. The dog's relation to Venus and its role as guide of the sun probably developed from its role in hunting. In myth, the sun, like ancestral figures, is often a hunter.

Some New World origin myths tell that people were turned into dogs at the time of a great flood. In Mesoamerica and beyond, there are versions of a myth in which the only survivors of the flood that destroyed the earlier creation of humankind are a man and a dog. The dog turns into a woman, and the couple are progenitors of a new group of people.

Dogs are related to fire as well as to water. In the Maya *Dresden Codex* and on Late Classic Maya vases, a dog holds a burning torch or has a torch for a tail. The fire attribute may stem from a panting dog of the tropics or from the volcanic earth in which the Mesoamerican dog digs; dogs generally have a connotation of heat.

The coyote (*Canis latrans*), a wild canine, has a wide natural range in North America, but it is not found in dense forest vegetation. The coyote is also not ubiquitous in Mesoamerican art and myth, but the dog is. Coyotes are most prominent in Mexican Highland art and lore. Mural paintings at Teotihuacan show them with sacrificial knives or human hearts, or in the act of killing deer; coyote warriors are also depicted, as they are in later Central Mexican codices. The Mexica god Huehuecoyotl ("very old coyote") is portrayed playing a drum in the *Codex Borbonicus*; the great deity Tezcatlipoca, who turned people into dogs at the time of the flood, sometimes changed himself into a coyote. In myths from the Oaxacan highlands, dogs turn into coyotes. Like the dog, the coyote has associations with death, the underworld, and maize. There are some confusions between dog and coyote, and between those animals and a Mexica mythical animal, the *ahuitzotl*, a doglike aquatic creature, usually depicted with vegetation. It lured people to death by drowning. Sahagún reported complex beliefs about this creature.

The Mesoamerican fox, the gray fox (*Urocyon cinereoargenteus*), is another wild canine, which prefers rugged, stony regions; it does not appear in densely forested lowlands. Sahagún noted that it was called a "cave-dweller"; it is remarkable, however, as the only canid capable of climbing trees, which it does to escape, to rest, or to seek fruit, birds, or eggs. Gifted and subtle, a fox is seen near human habitations only when it wants to be seen. It leaps on its animal prey as a cat pounces on a mouse.

In the Maya *Popol Vuh* manuscript, the fox is one of the first animals to find maize, and the theme also occurs in more recent lore. Foxes may steal the farmers' maize as well as their chickens. In world folklore, foxes appear as tricksters and shamans. Like the coyote, the fox can be an ill omen, presaging death.

BIBLIOGRAPHY

Baus de Czitrom, Carolyn. *Los perros de la antigua provincia de Colima*. Mexico City, 1988. General archaeological information about dogs, as well as pictures of West Mexican ceramics.

Benson, Elizabeth P. "The Chthonic Canine." *Latin American Indian Languages Journal* 7 (1991), 95–107. Brief summary of dog lore in Mesoamerica and South America.

Berrin, Kathleen. *Feathered Serpents and Flowering Trees*. San Francisco, 1988. Murals of Teotihuacan, with discussion of art and archaeology and illustrations of coyotes and coyote warriors.

Durán, Diego. *Book of the Gods and Rites and the Ancient Calendar*. Translated and edited by Fernando Horcasitas and Doris Heyden. Norman, Okla., 1971. Observations of a sixteenth-century Dominican friar, including his notes on dogs.

Grady, Wayne. *The World of the Coyote*. San Francisco, 1994. Photographs and natural history.

Grambo, Rebecca L. *The World of the Fox*. San Francisco, 1995. Natural history and pictures, with some material on the gray fox.

Landa, Diego de. *Landa's Relación de las cosas de Yucatán*. Edited by Alfred M. Tozzer. Papers of the Peabody Museum of American Archaeology and Ethnology, Harvard University, 18. Cambridge, Mass., 1941. The richest early source on the Maya.

Pohl, Mary. "Maya Ritual Faunas: Vertebrate Remains from Burials, Caches, Caves, and Cenotes in the Maya Lowlands." In *Civilization in the Ancient Americas: Essays in Honor of Gordon R. Willey*, edited by Richard M. Leventhal and Alan L. Kolata, pp. 55–103. Cambridge, Mass., 1983. Report on fauna from archaeological excavations, with information on the extent and context of dog remains.

Sahagún, Bernardino de. *Florentine Codex: General History of the Things of New Spain*. Book 11. Edited by A. J. O. Anderson and C. E. Dibble. Monographs of the School of American Research and the Museum of New Mexico, 14. Santa Fe, N.M., 1963. This important early source includes both descriptions of dogs and beliefs about them.

Schwartz, Marion. *A History of Dogs in the Early Americas*. New Haven and London, 1997. Natural history and pre-Hispanic art, archaeology, and folklore involving the dog; the most extensive examination of this subject.

ELIZABETH P. BENSON

CANNIBALISM. Ceremonial cannibalism, the ritual eating of human flesh, probably had a long existence in Mesoamerica, although evidence for its ancient history is thin. Splintered bones found in refuse deposits in the Pre-classic Olmec site of San Lorenzo, Veracruz (c.1200–900 BCE) suggest cannibalistic practices, and similar bone deposits have appeared at Teotihuacan in the Valley of Mexico (c.600–400 BCE). The wide geographic spread of cannibalism is clearer. Sixteenth-century reports of the practice come from the Tarascan in Michoacán and from the Yucatec, Itzá, and Lacandón Maya in southern Mexico and Guatemala. The most detailed information comes from extensive texts in Spanish and Nahuatl describing ancient Aztec culture. Christopher Columbus was responsible for naming the practice after the Carib or Arawak Indians of the Caribbean: "cannibal" derives from *caribal* ("eaters of human flesh"). In fact, Spanish explorers experienced cannibalism at first hand. After witnessing the ritualistic consumption of four of his shipwrecked companions, Jerónimo de Águilar (who would become one of Fernando Cortés's translators) escaped with his remaining friends from wooden cages in which they were being fattened by their Maya captors.

Theories about cannibalism vary widely. The sixteenth-century Spaniards often saw it as a pagan practice and a result of devil worship. More recent theories tend to fall into four broad groups: (a) cannibalism never existed but rather was fabricated by the Spanish to justify conquest; (b) it served to exert economic and sociopolitical control; (c) consuming human flesh corrected a protein deficiency in a largely vegetarian diet; or (d) cannibalism's roots lay in religious symbolism centering on communion with deities or other powerful forces.

The first theory, that cannibalism was a sixteenth-century Spanish fabrication, flies in the face of a wealth of evidence. Not only are references to cannibalism numerous in earlier histories; many references appear in Nahuatl. A stew made from human flesh and corn was called *tlacatlacualli* ("people-food"). Nahuatl would not have developed such linguistically well-formed words to describe cannibalism if it had been unknown. The Spanish certainly used the suppression of cannibalism to justify their own excesses, but that alone does not mean it never existed.

The second theory, that cannibalism served economic or sociopolitical purposes, has some credibility, although it is insufficient fully to explain cannibalism's presence. Among the Aztec, for example, sacrificial cannibalism was most commonly associated with war rituals; and although war possessed religious symbolism, it was also an effective means of economic expansion and territorial control. Moreover, sacrifice and cannibalism were used to deter criminal acts: those breaking the Aztec penal code could be sacrificed and eaten. Yet other cannibalistic rituals did not serve expansionist goals but rather brought rain and agricultural fertility. And not all offerings were war captives, criminals, or slaves; sometimes elite men or women of admirable character became the central ritual dish. Hence, economic, political, or social control can explain some facets of cannibalism, but not all. Moreover, such explanations do little to aid understanding of how the ancient Mesoamericans themselves viewed the practice.

The third theory, first promoted by Michael Harner (1977), suggests that cannibalism among the Aztec was due largely to a protein deficiency in their predominantly vegetarian diet. According to Harner, as the population in the Valley of Mexico grew to extremely large numbers, protein deficiencies developed because the people had few domesticated animals and hunting no longer provided enough meat. Moreover, religious rituals served as an incentive for young men to participate in expansionist wars. One could climb socially through war victories, and the privileged also enjoyed protein-laden cannibalistic meals.

Bernard Ortíz de Montellano (1978) argues against Harner's theory on several levels. Ortiz contends that the Aztec diet was actually sufficient to serve the population's needs, because hunting game was not the only source of protein. Corn and beans, when prepared in lime and eaten together, provide a complete protein. Moreover, the Aztec kept fish hatcheries and domesticated turkeys, other birds, and dogs for food. They also ate almost anything that "walked, swam, flew or crawled" (Ortíz, 1990, p. 115), including rattlesnakes, mice, iguanas, armadillos, frogs, and insects, some of which provided excellent protein. Furthermore, cannibalism never provided enough protein to make a nutritional difference. The usual ritual focus on limbs (thighs were especially prized) meant cannibals often ate the least nutritional part of the body, and the meal was shared so that no one got very much, and even the elite could not have gained much nutrition in this way. Moreover, to make a difference in one's health, one cannot defer adequate nutrition until adulthood, yet children would not have derived benefits from cannibalism. Besides, a captor often was prohibited from eating his own captive. The Mexica, moreover, employed more efficient responses to nutritional deficiencies: they terraced their hillsides and expanded their highly efficient *chinampa* system of wetland agriculture; and wars of expansion brought in tribute, including large quantities of agricultural products. Finally, cannibalism occurred primarily during harvest festivals, when other resources were most plentiful: Why correct a nutritional deficiency when it is least problematic? Ortiz concludes that cannibalism served no appreciable nutritional need and was practiced primarily for religious reasons.

The fourth theory focuses on cannibalism's religious roots. The practice merely extended the logic of the more widespread practice of sacrifice, human and otherwise. At least for the Aztec, some argue that all sacrifice was based on a feeding exchange among the world's various living beings. All things could maintain life in the Aztec cosmos, so not just people and animals were hungry—gods, trees, streams, and mountains also were living beings in need of nourishment. In every sacrificial ritual, someone fed someone to someone else. The meal usually consisted of something small: quail, a bit of blood from one's earlobe, or a humanlike deity figure made of amaranth dough. In some rituals, however, actual humans served as the meal.

According to the *Florentine Codex*, in a typical Aztec warrior sacrifice, first the heart was extracted from the captive offering, and then the primary sacrificial priest offered it to the sun or to whatever deity required it. Often a priest fed the deity by rubbing a bit of blood on the lips of a statue. Then the priests rolled the corpse down the temple steps, where old men collected it and took it back to the neighborhood house to divide among its captors. Each captor took his portion home, but only his family could eat it. He could not, for the captor was seen as the captive's "son." Afterward, the cleaned bones were hung on a pole outside the family's house; like seeds, bones carried the fertile powers of generative life. Moreover, sacrificial offerings became deities, so that their sacralized flesh might feed both humans and gods. Thus, once the living had been fed, the leftover bones were kept to generate new life.

In a Quiché Maya myth, the *Popol Vuh*, the Hero Twins sacrifice themselves in an underground bonfire; their bones are ground like corn and spread in the river like seeds, which results in another birth for the twins—first as fishermen, then beggars, then powerful warriors, and finally as the sun and moon. In the same myth, gods shape people from ground maize. Similarly, in an Aztec myth, the god Quetzalcoatl travels to the underworld to retrieve human bones from which people are to be made. After the bones have been accidentally dropped, gnawed by quail, bled on by Quetzalcoatl, and ground like corn, the goddess Cihuacoatl finally forms people from them. And so the tale ends: because gods sacrificed themselves to make people, people must sacrifice themselves for the gods. They are the stuff of godly tortillas: the Aztec leader Tlacaellel urged his warriors into battle by telling them they were going to a marketplace to buy fresh tortillas for their god Huitzilopochtli. Aztec and Maya alike are corn, and corn comes from the gods. So, to be fed, one must feed oneself to the gods. Cannibalistic rituals make perfect sense in such a universe.

BIBLIOGRAPHY

Berdan, Frances F. *The Aztecs of Central Mexico: An Imperial Society.* New York, 1982. Excellent summary of major theories on cannibalism and sacrifice, pp. 111–118, includes evidence for an economically based interpretation.

Durán, Diego. *Book of the Gods and Rites and the Ancient Calendar.* Translated by Doris Heyden and Fernando Horcasitas. Norman, Okla., 1971. Major primary source of examples of Mexica cannibalism.

Harner, Michael. "The Ecological Basis for Aztec Sacrifice." *American Ethnologist* 4 (1977), 117–135. Classic article arguing for a nutritional basis for cannibalism.

Landa, Diego de. *Yucatan before and after the Conquest* (Relación De Las Cosas De Yucatán). Translated by William Gates. New York, 1978. Important primary source containing examples of Maya cannibalism and sacrifice, as well as a wealth of information on the Colonial-period Maya.

Ortíz de Montellano, Bernard R. "Aztec Cannibalism: An Ecological Necessity?" *Science* 200 (1978), 116–117. Best rebuttal of Harner's nutritional theory for cannibalism.

Ortíz de Montellano, Bernard R. *Aztec Medicine, Health, and Nutrition.* New Brunswick, N.J., 1990. Describes in detail sources for Mexica nutrition.

Popul Vuh: The Definitive Edition of the Mayan Book of the Dawn of Life and the Glories of Gods and Kings. Translated by Dennis Tedlock. New York, 1985. Primary source containing the story of the Hero Twins in the underworld and the creation of people.

Read, Kay A. *Time and Sacrifice in the Aztec Cosmos.* Bloomington, 1998. Contains a translation from Nahuatl of the tale of Quetzalcoatl retrieving the bones to make people and offers an overall logic for sacrifice, of which cannibalism is one type.

Sahagún, Bernardino de. *The Florentine Codex: A General History of the Things of New Spain.* Translated by Arthur J. O. Anderson and Charles E. Dibble. Monographs of the School of American Research, 14. Santa Fe and Salt Lake City, 1953–1982. Extensive primary source for descriptions of Aztec cannibalistic practices.

KAY A. READ

CANTARES MEXICANOS. What has come to be known as Aztec poetry—actually, song texts—can be traced mainly to a single source, the *Codex Cantares Mexicanos*, preserved as item 1 in a nine-item manuscript miscellany catalogued as 1628-bis at the Biblioteca Nacional, Mexico City. From internal dates, it is clear that the Cantares manuscript was prepared between 1585 and 1597. In Nahuatl, filling 85 folios recto and verso, the work is a compilation of earlier transcriptions, now lost, to which glosses and headings had been added. Many of the songs treat post-Conquest events and personalities or are devoted to Christian themes; several can be linked to dates ranging from 1550 to 1581. Others may have been composed earlier, even before the Conquest of 1521. At least some of the songs were composed or performed "here in Mexico" (i.e., Mexico City), as the texts have it, and a few "here in Azcapotzalco" (8 kilometers northwest of the center of Mexico City).

Two of the known productions of the celebrated missionary–ethnographer Bernardino de Sahagún (*Memoriales con escolios* and *Psalmodia christiana*) show correspondences with the Cantares. This suggests that the songs could have been collected at his behest, and it is possible that at least one of the scribes was Sahagún's Indian assistant, Antonio Valeriano of Azcapotzalco. The Cantares manuscript, however, is unsigned.

Content. The ninety-one songs are made up of short stanzas averaging about thirty words each, presented in the manuscript as hanging paragraphs (of which there are about 1,700). Many of the songs have eight stanzas; most have more, and the longest has 114.

From internal evidence and the contemporary ethnography of Sahagún and other observers, we know that such songs were performed to the accompaniment of the upright skin drum (*huehuetl*) and the horizontal log drum (*teponaztli*), each capable of producing two tones spanning an interval such as a fifth or a major third. Gongs, horns, and other instruments could be added; the full program might include costumed dancing, often with mimicry.

Two-tone drum cadences are preserved in the manuscript as vocable mnemonics utilizing the four syllables *ki, ko, ti,* and *to,* written *qui, co, ti, to.* Because the *i* (as in the English word *elite*) is produced high in the mouth, and the *o* low, and because the *k* sound in the Cantares is never reiterated without an intervening *t,* it has therefore been proposed that the vowels indicate pitch while the consonants represent tempo (as in the tonguing used by modern woodwind players, who project the breath by alternating the tip of the tongue and its base—the *t* and the *k*—in quick passages, using only the *t* in slow movements). Thus, for example, the Cantares' *ti co ti co* represents quick tempo with two tones, whereas *to to to* indicates slow tempo, on the lower tone only. The melodic lines of the songs are not recorded, nor is it possible to detect meter from a study of the texts.

Verbally the texts are rich, though there is much repetition in the vocabulary, with persistent references to flowers, songs, birds, and jewels along with verbs that express coming, arriving, coming to life, greening, blossoming, scattering, and descending. Two principal locales, earth and heaven, are constantly mentioned, together with the names of warrior kings and heroes. War is the pervasive subject; the dance floor, or stage, is envisioned as a battlefield.

Among the kings memorialized, not surprisingly, is the famous Motecuhzoma. In song 70, the singer says, "As a song you're born, O Motecuhzoma," and in song 83, rehearsing the final battle against the Spaniards: "I've been born . . . I've been brought to life, I, the Chichimec Motecuhzoma." (Here "Chichimec" is a prideful designation, implying hardihood and ancient lineage.)

A few of the songs appear to tell a story unrelated to battle and rebirth, yet the twin themes emerge nonetheless. In song 55, devoted to the Nativity story, the singer manages to get the Three Kings slain on the battlefield of "Bethlehem" and then finally envisions "songs" that are "born anew."

In a similar vein, a few of the pieces rehearse fifteenth-century battles between the Mexica and their enemies, notably the Chalcayotl ("Chalcan piece[s]"), recalling the war with Chalco around 1460, and the Matlatzincayotl, reenacting King Axayacatl's victory over Matlatzinco around 1478. These songs, or their prototypes, might well have been composed before the Conquest.

A number of the pieces are satirical, such as the *huehue cuicatl* ("old-man song[s]"), in which decrepit warriors are imagined as "coughing, spitting, spluttering" on the battlefield. In the parodic "female" songs, lesbian themes are developed by male performers in women's dress; yet once again, the setting is the battlefield.

Comparison with Other Sources. A much smaller sixteenth-century manuscript, the *Romances de los señores de la Nueva España,* contains songs that are similar to some of the simpler, shorter pieces in the Cantares Mexicanos. Twenty quite different songs, evidently pre-Conquest, are appended to book 2 of Sahagún's great *Historia.* These twenty presumably belong to the genre called *macehualiztli,* or dance associated with service to the gods. Songs found in the Cantares and the *Romances* are *netotiliztli,* or dance associated with worldly entertainment. This useful distinction was made by Sahagún's contemporary, the historian known as Motolinía, in his *Memoriales* (part 2, chap. 27).

Interpretation. The *netotiliztli* have been controversial, or at least troubling, since they were first noticed by Spaniards in the 1500s. According to Sahagún, "No one understands what they say, because their *cantares* are very obscure," and "there is no one who really understands them, except themselves alone" (*Historia,* book 10; *Psalmodia*). But Fray Diego Durán, another of Sahagún's contemporaries, while conceding that the phrases at first seemed "nonsensical," decided that "afterward, with discussion and conference, they're admirable sentences" (*Libro de los ritos,* chap. 21). Astutely, the Spanish academician Francisco Cervantes de Salazar wrote around 1560, "In these [songs] they speak of conspiracy against ourselves" (*Crónica de la Nueva España,* book 6, chap. 102).

In the early 1600s, the puzzling texts were inherited by a new generation of historians, who combed the manuscripts for fragments to incorporate in their own works. Most industrious among these writers was the *mestizo* chronicler Fernando de Alva Ixtlilxochitl, who assumed that the songs had been composed by the historical figures named in them, especially his own ancestor, King Nezahualcoyotl of Tetzcoco. Since the texts occasionally refer to the kings in the first person (e.g., "I, Nezahualcoyotl"), Alva Ixtlilxochitl's attributions have seemed reasonable to various writers down to the present. The Cantares as a whole yield a more coherent reading, however, if one assumes that the singer is speaking with the voice of the old kings, envisioned as spirits of the dead—ghosts—brought to life through the power of music. This interpretive approach, moreover, fits well with the numerous songs (some of them dated) in which post-Conquest "kings," or *gobernadores*, are summoned to earth from the sky world shortly after their deaths.

Although no pre-Conquest composers or singers are named in the manuscripts, five of the songs in the Cantares are unambiguously attributed by the native glossator to these four composers: Don Francisco Plácido (fl. 1551–1578), Cristóbal de Rosario Xiuhtlamin (fl. 1550), Don Baltasar Toquezcuauhyo (fl. 1563?), and Tececepouhqui (fl. after the Conquest). Plácido has two songs; the others, one each.

Several of the songs in the old manuscripts carry glosses such as *icuic nezahualpilli* ("song of Nezahualpilli," a pre-Conquest king of Tetzcoco) or *de Nezahualcoyotl* ("of Nezahualcoyotl"). But one also finds *tlaloc icuic* ("song of Tlaloc," the rain god) and *de Atlixco* ("of Atlixco," a geographical name). The "of," whether taken from Nahuatl or Spanish, means "pertaining to," not "authored by." As for the *icuic nezahualpilli*, this is explicitly *quitlali cuicani tececepouhqui* ("the singer Tececepouhqui composed it").

Although a few of the songs are satisfactorily attributed to post-Conquest singers, as noted, it would appear that authorship was not jealously guarded. Nearly one-tenth of the Cantares consists of material that is repeated within the manuscript, always with minor variations. In addition, several Cantares passages have close variants in the *Romances*. Evidently the songs passed from singer to singer orally; this is true even of a lengthy, complicated song of obviously recent composition, the Tlaxcaltecayotl ("Tlaxcalan piece"), entered in the Cantares as no. 66 and again, with variations, as no. 91. The purpose of the Tlaxcaltecayotl is to reenact the final battle of the Conquest of 1521 (as in no. 83, mentioned above). Here the singer summons the ghosts of those who participated in the historic events; he humiliates the warriors of Tlaxcala, who sided with the Spaniards; he recalls some of the more satisfying incidents of the battle ("he's come to take a lance from the Spaniards," "they've captured the Conquistadores' guns"); and he predicts a future Mexica dynasty. Material like this in active circulation provides evidence of a mid-sixteenth-century revitalization movement in which singers imagined the return of dead rulers and the restoration of Mexico's glory, contributing a vivid chapter to the history of Colonial Mexico not otherwise documented in surviving sources.

[*See also* Poetry, Songs, and Prose Sources.]

BIBLIOGRAPHY

Arbuthnot, Nancy Prothro. *Mexico Shining: Versions of Aztec Songs.* Colorado Springs, 1995. Concise overview of the Cantares with free versions of 39 songs or parts of songs.

Bierhorst, John. *Cantares Mexicanos: Songs of the Aztecs.* Stanford, 1985. Complete Nahuatl-English edition; extensive commentary treats the sixteenth-century Cantares activity as a revitalization movement.

Bierhorst, John. *A Nahuatl-English Dictionary and Concordance to the Cantares Mexicanos with an Analytic Transcription and Grammatical Notes.* Stanford, 1985. Companion volume to the preceding.

Garibay K., Angel María. *Poesía náhuatl.* Vol. 1. Mexico City, 1964. Complete Nahuatl-Spanish edition of the *Romances de los señores de la Nueva España.*

Karttunen, Frances, and James Lockhart. "La estructura de la poesía náhuatl vista por sus variantes." *Estudios de Cultura Náhuatl* 14 (1980), 15–64. Compares variant song texts preserved in the Cantares and the *Romances.*

León-Portilla, Miguel. *Fifteen Poets of the Aztec World.* Norman, Okla., 1992. Excerpts from the Cantares and the *Romances,* attributed to Nezahualcoyotl, Nezahualpilli, and other pre-Conquest figures.

Peñafiel, Antonio. *Cantares en idioma mexicano: Reproducción facsimilaria del manuscrito original existente en la Biblioteca Nacional.* Mexico City, 1904. Photographic facsimile of the Cantares Mexicanos.

Segala, Amos. *Literatura náhuatl: Fuentes, identidades, representaciones.* Mexico City, 1990. Spanish translation of the French edition of 1989, largely devoted to the Cantares Mexicanos; reviews competing interpretations.

Stevenson, Robert. *Music in Aztec and Inca Territory.* Berkeley, 1968. Summarizes the writings of early Colonial observers; describes native instruments in detail; discussion of two-tone drumming is outdated.

Tompkins, Ptolemy. *This Tree Grows Out of Hell: Mesoamerica and the Search For the Magical Body.* San Francisco, 1990. Includes an interpretive essay on the Cantares Mexicanos.

Treviño, Adrian, and Barbara Gilles. "A History of the Matachines Dance." *New Mexico Historical Review* 69 (1994), 105–125. Describes the *matachines* of New Mexico as a ghost-summoning revitalistic activity comparable to the sixteenth-century Cantares movement in Mexico.

JOHN BIERHORST

CANTONA, a site situated on a lava flow, east of the highlands of Central Mexico, at an elevation of 2500 to 2600 meters (8,000 feet) above sea level, with a surface area of 1267 hectares, was a large fortified city that competed first with Cholula and Teotihuacan and later with the largest and most important of the Central Highland cities. At Cantona, the architectural complexity, settlement pattern, and construction elements and solutions differ from those generally known for Mesoamerica. Its concentrated population was distributed in residential units enclosed by high walls, in which nuclear or extended families lived in houses on platforms. During its apogee from 650 to 950 CE, there were more than eight thousand of these independent residential units, allowing for an estimate of its population at some 90,000 ± 10,000.

An extensive and complex network of roads for internal circulation had been built with streets elevated above the level of the terrain, as well as enclosed within it. Twenty-four ballcourts have been identified, twelve of which possess aligned architectural groups formed by a pyramid at the end, one or two closed plazas, and the court. Important features include the absence of cementation for joining the building stones, which are fitted one above another, as well as plaster or stucco on the wall exteriors. The religio-civic architectural structures have a covering of finished stone (*tezontle* or *cantera*), and in the domestic constructions only the flat part of basalt stones were sought for their exteriors. Another distinguishing and characteristic feature of Cantona is its asymmetry; nothing is symmetrical about its layout, the façades, or the number of superimposed sections of principal structures. It is an intentionally planned asymmetry, not due to a lack of control or care in construction, that seemingly tries to negate what is symmetrical and "well-proportioned" in contemporaneous cities.

Cantona was occupied from 150 CE to about 1000 or 1050 CE, during which time two great periods of development are clearly discernible. The first ranges between the second and seventh centuries; its road system is similar to those found in the majority of known settlements throughout Mesoamerica, and the residential platforms were not enclosed by peripheral walls. The structures have a better finish than those of the subsequent phase. The vertical *talud* face was used often for the foundation walls; engraved panels decorated principal buildings; and a phallic cult existed, among others. The size of the settlement during this period has not yet been established. The second period, from about 650 and 950 CE, was the time when all the roads of internal circulation were built; also built were causeways, paved with stones, which crossed the lava flow and led east, to other minor settlements at the edge of the valley. The residential units were enclosed within peripheral walls, and although platforms were reutilized, the principal civic-religious structures were abandoned and others were constructed. Sixteen to eighteen ballcourts were in use, including ten of the twelve aligned architectural groups. Some of the enclosed plazas with the vertical *talud* face were reutilized but this form was no longer built; the architectural character became sober and, as in the case of the earlier period, mortar was not used to join the building stones and symmetry was not sought. This was the time of Cantona's maximum—the period in which it was the largest settlement in the Central Highlands. It controlled nearly all the basin from the east and a good part to the north. Cantona traded in obsidian, whose mines in Oyameles were greatly exploited. The economy was also based on agricultural production obtained in the valleys to the west and east of the lava flow, as well as the tribute of the cities, towns, and villages under its direct control. Obsidian from the Oyameles deposit has been found by researchers in the Tehuacán Valley, in the Mixtequilla, the Isthmus or Tehuantepec, and places in Tabasco, all of which document Cantona's trading range. In the eleventh century, this great fortified city declined. The causes that led to Cantona's abandonment are still unknown, although the closing of various causeways, the reduction of streets, and the increase of watchtowers inside the settlement all suggest great internal instability.

BIBLIOGRAPHY

Ferriz, Horacio. "Caltonac, a Pre-Hispanic Obsidian-Mining Center in Eastern Mexico? A Preliminary Report." *Journal of Field Archaeology* 12 (1985), 363–370. Study of the obsidian deposits near Cantona; offers information about the obsidian in other deposits in Mexico.

García Cook, Ángel. "Cantona." *Arqueología Mexicana 11* 10 (1994), 60–65. Reports on initial excavations in Cantona; describes the various architectural units (streets, residential units, plazas, ballcourts) available for public examination.

García Cook, Ángel. *Cantona Guía. Mexico City, 1994.* With information uncovered in the initial excavations conducted in Cantona, it offers a general overview of the large city and describes the architectural units available for public examination.

García Cook, Ángel. "Exploraciones arqueológicas en Cantona, Puebla." *IV Coloquio Pedro Bosch Gimpera. Mexico City, 2000.* Describes some of the architectural units and elements present in Cantona; gives dimensions and distinctive features; details the asymmetry of the architectural elements, based on Ballcourt Group 7.

García Cook, Ángel, and Beatriz Leonor Merino Carrión. "Investigación arqueológica en Cantona, Puebla." *Arqueología* 15 (1996), 55–78. Discusses the Cantona Archaeological Project; indicates earlier investigations conducted at the site; describes explorations and restorations and details the principal characteristics of each.

García Cook, Ángel, and Beatriz Leonor Merino Carrión. "Cantona: Urbe prehispánica en el Altiplano Central de México." *Latin American Antiquity* 9.3 (1998), 191–216. Presents an expanded overview of Cantona's geographical location, previous investigations, archaeology, architecture, and material culture (ceramics, lithics, skeletal remains, and sculpture); proposes four successive occupations for the site.

León, Nicolás. "Los monumentos arqueológicos in Cantona." *Seminario Literario Ilustrado* 3.127 (1903), 249–250. Description of Cantona, its topographical location and architecture; offers a chronology and suggests the name must have been Caltonal ("house of the sun"), giving the site a Nahuatl affiliation.

López de Molina, Diana. "Arqueologia de superficie y estudios urbanos, el caso de Cantona." *Revista Mexicana de Estudios Antropológicos* 32 (1986), 177–185. Based on aerial photography as confirmed in the field; reports on the architectural characteristics of Cantona—the number of residential units, the quantity, size, and distribution of the mounds examined, the number of ballcourts registered, as well as a general overview of the "acropolis" where the large ceremonial center of the city was found.

Saussure, Henrie de. "Découverte des ruines d'une ancienne ville mexicaine située sur le plateau de L'Anahuac." *Bulletin de la Société de Géographie* 15 (1858), 275–294. First description of Cantona, introducing its geographical location to the scientific world with detailed explanation of the efforts undertaken to find this enormous city; discusses the settlement, its buildings, and the surrounding countryside.

ÁNGEL GARCÍA COOK
Translated from Spanish by Scott Sessions

CARACOL. Situated approximately 600 meters (1,800 feet) above sea level in the Maya Mountains of Belize, Caracol is the largest Late Classic period (550–900 CE) archaeological site known from the southern Maya Lowlands. At approximately 650 CE, this ancient city supported more than 115,000 people, who utilized extensive agricultural terraces within a widely distributed but highly integrated settlement system. The archaeological site covers 177 square kilometers, is believed to contain over 36,000 structures, and is characterized by a radial causeway system that extends out from the site epicenter as far as eight kilometers (5 miles).

Caracol was discovered in the 1930s by men searching for timber and chicle. Initial visits proved the site to be relatively rich in carved stone hieroglyphic monuments, which are rather rare in Belize. In the early 1950s, an expedition to the site was led by Linton Satterthwaite of the University Museum of the University of Pennsylvania. This early research resulted in the creation of a map of the central part of the site, the excavation of several tombs, the recording of the site's known stone monuments, and the transportation of about a dozen monuments to the University Museum in Philadelphia. Further research on the monumental architecture in the site's epicenter was undertaken during the mid-1950s by A. Hamilton Anderson, then archaeological commissioner of British Honduras. In the late 1970s, one of the site's many outlying agricultural terrace systems was investigated by Paul Healy of Trent University. Since 1983, central Caracol and its outlying residential settlement have been under continuous investigation by the University of Central Florida's Caracol Archaeological Project, directed by Diane Chase and Arlen Chase.

Just as the carved stone monuments of Caracol initially drove interest in the site, Caracol's hieroglyphic history has continued to alter interpretations of the Classic Maya world. Much of the basic data on Caracol's stelae and altars, including a preliminary statement concerning the site's ruling dynasty, were published in 1981 by Carl Beetz and Linton Satterthwaite. Subsequent investigations by the Caracol Archaeological Project have led to the discovery of new stone monuments and inscriptions that significantly amended the dynastic and political history of the site. Especially important have been painted texts found in royal tombs and records of Late Classic conquests; one, included on a circular ballcourt marker discovered in 1986, records a major defeat of the site of Tikal, Guatemala, in 562 CE.

Particularly significant for work at Caracol has been the correlation of archaeological data with hieroglyphic history. This conjunctive research has confirmed some hieroglyphic statements, but it has also pointed to problems in relying on strictly hieroglyphic material for interpreting Maya prehistory. For example, archaeological data have demonstrated that Caracol's population increased dramatically after the victory in 562 CE. At least 115,000 people were present at the site by 650, making it the largest known city in the southern Maya Lowlands at the time. The archaeological record also demonstrates that Caracol's Late Classic population enjoyed more widespread prosperity than is characteristic of other sites in the southern Lowlands. Caracol's immense size and archaeological record seem to support hieroglyphic statements concerning the site's role in political events of the early Late Classic period. However, very little hieroglyphic history at Caracol dates from between 650 and 800. Caracol's "emblem" glyph is not widely found in the southern Lowlands, and the inhabitants did not erect a significant number of stelae during this time. This lack of a monumental record has led some to suggest that Caracol's successes had waned by 650; however, the archaeological record demonstrates that Caracol was most populous and prosperous at and after this time. Thus, a conjoined use of archaeology and epigraphy provides the most reasonable reconstruction of Caracol's ancient past.

Hieroglyphic History. Although the archaeological record indicates that Caracol was settled by 600 BCE, the written history for the site begins much later. A retrospective hieroglyphic text from Caracol notes that the site's dynasty originated in 331 CE (8.14.13.10.4 in the Maya Long Count). The initial "founder" was followed by at least twenty-eight additional rulers. A late 8 Baktun date opens the text on one of the earliest monuments from the site—a badly shattered stela that was cached under a Late Classic altar. Although several hieroglyphic texts may be correlated with individuals who lived before the Late Classic period (before c.550 CE), much of the site's hieroglyphic history comes from stone monuments that date to the early part of the Late Classic. These texts contain historic information that relates predominantly to four key individuals. Lord Water, also known as Yahaw Te K'inich, acceded to Caracol's throne in 553 CE (9.5.19.2.1). The defeat of Tikal is placed within his reign (9.6.8.4.2) on a monument erected by one of his sons. While some epigraphers have suggested that this defeat occurred because of an alliance with Calakmul, Mexico, archaeological data from Caracol cannot be mustered to support this assertion. Yahaw Te K'inich probably died before 599, when the Caracol throne was passed to the first of two of his sons. The elder son, Lord Flaming Ahau or "Ruler IV," was born in 575 (9.7.2.0.3) and acceded to the throne in 599 (9.8.5.16.12). Most of the monument texts relating to him are badly eroded, so that little is actually known about his reign. He was succeeded by his better-known brother, Lord K'an II, who was born in 588 (9.7.14.10.8), acceded to the throne in 618 (9.9.4.16.2), and died in 658 (9.11.5.15.9). Lord K'an II created numerous texts commemorating his military conquest of Naranjo, Guatemala, a site 42 kilometers (25 miles) distant, which appears to have become a second capital for Caracol's ruling dynasty between 631 and 658 (if not later). Approximately one month before his death, Lord K'an II witnessed the accession of his successor, Lord Hok Pol, to the Caracol throne on 9.11.5.14.0. Lord Hok Pol was still ruling in 680, but after this date Caracol's Late Classic dynastic history becomes murky. There are sporadic monuments and texts at the site from the next one hundred years, but the written history of Caracol is largely unknown until the Terminal Classic era (780–900 CE), when carved monuments are again plentiful in the archaeological record. Lord Hok K'auil ushers in a new era of historical records after 798 CE and is followed by textual data relating to at least two other rulers. Caracol's hieroglyphic record falls silent after 859; however, archaeological data indicate that the site epicenter was occupied and rebuilt by a prosperous elite until approximately 895, when burning and on-floor debris suggest that the downtown area was sacked.

Spatial Layout. Caana, an immense elevated palace and temple complex that still rises 43.5 meters above the jungle floor, marks the visual and physical center of Caracol. At least for the Terminal Classic, and probably for earlier periods as well, the archaeological data indicate that the Caracol ruler resided and held court in one of the palace compounds that ring Caana's summit. Architectural form indicates that access to this architectural complex was tightly controlled. Three separate temples command all but the south side of the summit plaza. Within the raised substructures of these temples, important royal relatives and family were buried in elaborate tombs, many of which were painted with red lines and panels; black-line hieroglyphs on the red panels date these burials to the early part of the Late Classic period.

Caana dominates the Caracol epicenter in terms of its sheer size, but other large formally constructed groups occur to its immediate east, west, and south within an area covering approximately one half a square kilometer. These architectural arrangements include formal plazas demarcated by pyramids and stelae, as well as a series of more specialized palace compounds, presumably used for residential and administrative purposes. Dense settlement and agricultural terraces, intersected by numerous ancient roadways, surround the epicenter and extend outward in all directions as far as eight kilometers. The site

of Caracol cannot be understood without reference to its settlement and extensive road system.

Five causeways, many of which bifurcate and split into multiple radiating roads, bind the site epicenter to outlying architectural nodes. Unlike many Maya sites which have all their central architecture concentrated in the site epicenter, Caracol's major plazas and their associated architecture are embedded within the surrounding settlement. A ring of major plazas, or termini, was established at a distance of approximately three kilometers (2 miles) from the site epicenter at the beginning of the Late Classic era (after 550 CE). Following the explosive population growth that then occurred, a second ring of termini was linked by causeways to Caracol's epicenter. This second ring of termini incorporated preexisting architectural nodes (presumably already serving administrative purposes), 4.5 to 7.8 kilometers distant, into the site's settlement system. By the end of the Late Classic, residential settlement and agricultural terraces completely filled in the areas between Caracol's causeways and this second ring of termini, so that all possible areas of the site were inhabited or intensively farmed.

Results of Archaeological Excavations. Besides excavation in outlying residential groups, intensive investigation of Caracol's central architecture has been undertaken by the University of Central Florida Caracol Archaeological Project. These excavations have revealed an initial settlement of the site epicenter around 300 BCE. Deep probes within Caana's substructure platform have shown that this complex was already thirty-five meters high by the end of the Late Preclassic period (before 250 CE). Impressive Late Preclassic deposits have also been recovered in the buildings surrounding the A Plaza, which took the form of an "E Group," or astronomical observatory, by this date. A simple burial with thirty-two vessels and almost five thousand shell and jadeite beads, dating to 150 CE, has also been recovered from the epicenter's Northeast Acropolis. Impressive Early Classic (250–550 CE) tombs have been recovered from the epicenter's A Group, South Acropolis, and Central Acropolis. Late Classic specialized deposits are found throughout the epicenter. Most epicentral buildings have yielded on-floor Terminal Classic remains; the majority date to the decade immediately preceding the onset of the tenth century. Even later remains are associated with the A Plaza.

Excavations within the outlying settlement area have tested more than one hundred residential groups and recovered more than two hundred burials. These investigations indicate an initial settlement of the Caracol region by 600 BCE and a final, but minimal, occupation in the eleventh century CE. Perhaps the most interesting aspect of the settlement research relates to the overall prosperity of the outlying population and their uniform cultural identity. This is seen especially in human interments and ritual caches. Almost half of the burials found at Caracol contained the remains of multiple individuals. Approximately seventy-five of the recovered residential interments were housed within formally constructed tombs; the majority of these were Late Classic in date. About 22 percent of the recovered burials from Caracol also contained individuals with teeth that were inlaid with hematite or jadeite—a numerical percentage far greater than is known from any other Maya site. A formal caching complex, consisting of larger lidded urns, often modeled with human faces, and smaller lip-to-lip dishes that sometimes housed one or more human digits, was also found throughout the residential settlement (as well as in the site epicenter). Many residential groups also contain partial or whole incense burners, either within tombs or associated with the stairways of eastern buildings that functioned as shrines or mausoleums. All these features are found both within the epicenter and in outlying residential groups, and they have been interpreted as part of a distinctive Caracol identity that may have been fostered by the site's elite. The widespread general prosperity observed among the bulk of Caracol's population may well have resulted from and was fostered by successful warfare.

Summary. Caracol's epigraphic history suggests that it was a significant force in the political arena of the Late Classic southern Maya Lowlands. Its size, settlement layout, prosperity, and uniform cultural identity indicate that Caracol followed a somewhat distinctive developmental path. The deemphasis of the site's hieroglyphic record following 650 CE, during an era when great prosperity is evident in the site's archaeological record, highlights a need to reconcile epigraphic interpretation with archaeological reconstruction in the southern Maya Lowlands.

[See also Southern Maya Lowlands.]

BIBLIOGRAPHY

Beetz, Carl, and Linton Satterthwaite. *The Monuments and Inscriptions of Caracol, Belize.* University Museum Monograph 45. Philadelphia, 1981.

Chase, Arlen F. "Elites and the Changing Organization of Classic Maya Society." In *Mesoamerican Elites: An Archaeological Assessment*, edited by Diane Z. Chase and Arlen F. Chase, pp. 30–49. Norman, Okla., 1992. Documents the existence of an extensive middle level of Maya society at Classic period Caracol.

Chase, Arlen F., and Diane Z. Chase. *Investigations at the Classic Maya City of Caracol, Belize.* Pre-Columbian Art Research Institute Monograph 3. San Francisco, 1987. Provides a background to research at Caracol and a summary of important finds of the first three archaeological field seasons.

Chase, Arlen F., and Diane Z. Chase. "More than Kin and King: Centralized Political Organization among the Late Classic Maya." *Current Anthropology* 37 (1996), 803–810. Counters the view that Maya political units comprised "segmentary" states and documents that Caracol was at the heart of a "unitary" state.

Chase, Arlen F., and Diane Z. Chase. "Scale and Intensity in Classic Period Maya Agriculture: Terracing and Settlement at the 'Garden City' of Caracol, Belize." *Culture and Agriculture* 20 (1998), 60–77. Presents detailed terrace maps and documents the existence of intensive agriculture and its integration with residential settlement at Classic period Caracol.

Chase, Arlen F., and Diane Z. Chase. "Late Classic Maya Political Structure, Polity Size, and Warfare Arenas." In *Anatomia de Una Civilizacion: Aproximaciones Interdisciplinarias a la Cultura Maya*, edited by Andres Ciudad Ruiz et al., pp. 11–29. Madrid, 1998. Uses Caracol as an example to define the intellectual underpinnings for three different models relating to Maya political structure and size.

Chase, Arlen F., and Diane Z. Chase. "The Royal Court of Caracol, Belize: Its Palaces and People." In *Royal Courts of the Ancient Maya*, edited by Takeshi Inomata and Stephen D. Houston, in press. Boulder, Colo., 2000. Documents the composition of Caracol's royal court and provides detailed plans of its palaces.

Chase, Diane Z., and Arlen F. Chase. *Studies in the Archaeology of Caracol, Belize.* Pre-Columbian Art Research Institute Monograph 7. San Francisco, 1994. Provides detailed documentation relating to the ecology, soils, architecture, settlement, *chultuns*, caves, shell, lithics, ceramics, hieroglyphs, and human burials at Caracol.

Chase, Diane Z., and Arlen F. Chase. "Maya Multiples: Individuals, Entries, and Tombs in Structure A34 of Caracol, Belize." *Latin American Antiquity* 7 (1996), 61–79. Documents the prevalence of multiple interments at Caracol and places the site within broader cultural practices in the Maya area and elsewhere.

Chase, Diane Z., and Arlen F. Chase. "The Architectural Context of Caches, Burials, and Other Ritual Activities for the Classic Period Maya (as Reflected at Caracol, Belize)." In *Functions and Meaning in Classic Maya Architecture*, edited by Stephen D. Houston, pp. 299–332. Washington, D.C., 1998. Documents widespread ritual patterns that are in evidence at Caracol and demonstrates the existence of a Caracol "identity."

Chase, Diane Z., and Arlen F. Chase. "Classic Maya Warfare and Settlement Archaeology at Caracol, Belize." *Estudios de Cultura Maya* 23 (2000), in press. Conjunctively presents Caracol hieroglyphic and settlement data related to the archaeological interpretation of Maya warfare during the Classic Period.

Martin, Simon, and Nikolai Grube. "Maya Superstates." *Archaeology* (1995), 41–46. Provides an original, but strictly hieroglyphic, interpretation of centralized Maya political organization during the Classic period.

Schele, Linda, and David Freidel. *A Forest of Kings: The Untold Story of the Ancient Maya.* New York, 1990. Chapter 5 provides a hieroglyphic interpretation of Caracol's impact on the southern Maya Lowlands, based on newly discovered texts.

ARLEN F. CHASE
and DIANE Z. CHASE

CÁRDENAS, LÁZARO

CÁRDENAS, LÁZARO (1894–1970), Mexican soldier and politician. In 1938, Lázaro Cárdenas, the president of Mexico from 1934 to 1940, nationalized the foreign oil companies that were seen as exploiters of the nation's oil fields. Soon afterward, he requested donations from Mexican citizens to help compensate the companies. Impoverished women donated the only gold they ever possessed, their wedding bands, suggesting something about Cárdenas's ability to move his compatriots. In fact, in a country where secular mythology has long flourished, Cárdenas remains an object of myth. It is as if Mexican social realities, its gulfs between the wealthy and the poor, promote reverence for a specific type of individual, the openhearted person willing to reach out to the poor. In the case of Cárdenas, he has been characterized as the Mexican Franklin D. Roosevelt, as the Mexican Mahatma Gandhi, and as a successor to Emiliano Zapata's heritage of agrarian democracy.

Yet the Cárdenas myth is at once compelling and false. It is compelling because it points to Cárdenas's complex accomplishments; it suggests something of his response to the 1910–1920 revolutionary clamors for the return of stolen lands, since he redistributed more land than all his post-Revolutionary predecessors combined. In addition, the myth reminds us of the oil appropriation, and it reminds us of his weekly telephone conversations with peasants seeking to break out of worlds of political anonymity. At the same time, there is something disturbing about this portrayal. While Cárdenas's political behavior sustained the representation of a man of deep humanity, the myth is nonetheless partly based on inaccuracies and omissions. The inaccuracies seem to be based on a principle of equivalence, a principle that proceeds something like this. Surely a man so concerned about poverty must have come from poverty; surely a man who lent his ear so many times to Mexican Indians must have himself been an Indian; surely he must have come from an impoverished indigenous past.

This was not the case. Instead, Cárdenas was born 21 May 1894 to a rural middle-class family in the village of Jiquilpan, Michoacán. His father was a merchant and innkeeper, his mother a housewife. At a time when most Michoacanos were poor, some desperately so, and scouring the woods and fields for wild foods to feed their families, Cárdenas's family ate meat regularly.

Insofar as his ethnic origins are concerned, Cárdenas was *mestizo*, like the Mexican majority. Although Tarascan Indians lived in the Michoacán region near Jiquilpan, nonetheless, Cárdenas's response to them was based on his ardent admiration for what he viewed as the Indian world plus a deep ignorance of the nature of that world. His ignorance of that world, in turn, emerged from his own cultural singularity. In a place as devoutly Roman Catholic as northwestern Michoacán, Cárdenas was deeply and sincerely anticlerical. Thus, much about Tarascan culture—characterized by devotion to popular Catholic ritual—remained obscure to him.

Cárdenas's cultural ignorance may have partially accounted for what has not been sufficiently emphasized about the man. In fact, Cárdenas possessed a profound reticence, a quiet ability to put himself aside, allowing others to explain their positions, their needs. By opening unsuspected worlds to him, Cárdenas's reticence functioned as a supplement to the broken formal education of this man who had left school at age twelve to help support his family. It probably sustained him in 1913, when he joined the Mexican Revolution under the eventual tutelage of Plutarco Elias Calles, a military and political man whose inflexibility fueled a desire to create an equally domineering Mexican national government. Cárdenas's poise probably sustained him during his 1928–1932 governorship of Michoacán, during which his political rivals—large landowners and Catholic peasants seeking to create "Jesus's world on Earth"—largely undercut his political programs.

As president, Cárdenas's character was tested and he found himself besieged. The Revolution and the years of government by his post-Revolutionary predecessors had revealed both domestic and foreign elites' continuing determination to dominate the country, along with a complex array of popular demands. Cárdenas's response revealed his willingness to utilize military and political coercion. Thus, he forced Calles to leave the country, convinced the U.S. government to accept the nationalization of the Mexican oil fields, and employed pre-Revolutionary rural bosses (*caciques*) to promote his program in the countryside. Yet it was Mexican peasants who effectively taught him to remove himself from the fray and heed them. When those allied with Cárdenas attempted to teach Indians the "Indian" songs and dances that they themselves had invented, the peasants remained quiescent; when Cárdenas imposed rural bosses who intensified the violent conflict over land, however, the peasants rebelled, forcing Cárdenas to listen. The peasants' abilities surprised him, as they amassed an array of weapons to destabilize his government.

Thus, the tales about Cárdenas's days patiently listening to the life histories of rural Mexicans are both legendary and true. These paired traits enabled Cárdenas to develop a country where, though capitalism still dominated, peasants could plausibly believe that their presence in their country had at last been recognized.

MARJORIE R. BECKER

CASAS GRANDES. During the sixteenth century, at the time of the Spanish conquest, civilized, urban high cultures occupied a territory with a northern boundary across Central Mexico, along the Pánuco, Lerma, Santiago, and Sinaloa rivers. At the same time, and on the other side of this frontier, the Aztec recognized a very large and arid territory that they called "the land of the Chichimecs," or "La Gran Chichimeca," as it was later called by the Spaniards. The Chichimecs, who were then living closer to the Aztec Empire, were hunters and gatherers, without fixed settlements. Farther to the north, "the Chichimeca lords extended their realms more than 2,000 leagues in length and almost 2,000 leagues in width" (Driver and Driver 1963) and "in this northern part between the two seas are the provinces of Florida, Cíbola, Quivira and New Mexico besides many others not yet known," according to the commentary by Antonio de Herrera y Tordesillas. This historical information clearly indicates the great extension of the Gran Chichimeca, where besides nomadic groups, there also were Chichimecs who were excellent farmers, living in large villages, such as the Pueblos. Earlier, there had been the Hohokam ("farmers of the desert"), the Anasazi ("the old people"), and the Paquimé, or Casas Grandes, as their settlement was named by the Spaniards in 1565.

From very early times, the Mesoamerican chiefdoms and states traded with these northern Chichimecs and from about 1 to 1000 CE established colonies in the Gran Chichimeca. The Mesoamerican cultivated plants—maize, beans, and squash—had reached the northern lands long before the colonies were established, but with them came the traditional Mesoamerican symbolism for religious, political, and economical power, especially in the important centers of Snaketown (Arizona), Pueblo Bonito (New Mexico), and Casas Grandes (in the Mexican state of Chihuahua). From these northern Chichimecs, Mesoamericans gained the knowledge of the bow and arrow, which would drastically change war and the hunt, as well as luxury products, such as seashells and minerals. Turquoise, especially, became a desired commodity. [*See* Turquoise.]

Casas Grandes in Chihuahua was a trading center of great importance from 1200 to 1450 CE, and its industries, especially a series of beautiful ceramic wares, were transported as exchange commodities to many settlements in northern Mexico and the southwestern United States. Casas Grandes received shell from coastal Baja California, Sonora, and Sinaloa; feathers and macaws from Mesoamerica; and turquoise from the New Mexico mines, which it redistributed in all directions. Casas Grandes is considered a city, by researchers, in the sense that the huge settlement, which had a very clear extension and limits, included specialized quarters—habitational, ceremonial, and marketplace, with streets, water, and sewer systems. A grand and efficient irrigation system was built, which began in the Sierra Madres to the west to serve rich agricultural lower valleys that were close to the city. Many smaller sites along the nearby rivers were under the control of Casas Grandes, both to the north and east and across the Sierra Madres to the west. These included areas of eastern Sonora, which were part of its economic and political territory. Pathways, signal towers, and hillside fortresses were also built by the people of Casas Grandes, which helped delimit their sovereignty.

The cultural life of Casas Grandes belongs to the northern traditions of the Gran Chichimeca, as is evidenced by its architectonic and artistic styles, as well as its way of solving the local irrigation problem. A few very important elements found by researchers in the city, however, suggest the presence of Mesoamerican elites, who must have played an important role in the economic (and perhaps the political) networks that dealt with some Mesoamerican states to the south. Such elements include the ballcourt, the macaw cult, the stepped greque decorative pattern, copper bells, and representations of the Mesoamerican gods Tlaloc, Xipe, and Xiuhcoatl. There was also use of the "back shield," music rasps, the plumed serpent, and the skull-trophy cult.

The Casas Grandes culture had its roots in earlier northern "pit house" village cultures, dated as early as 7500 BCE, lasting until the Paquimé period (1200 CE). Paquimé then evolved through several stages of development, only to end with a period of decadence. During that stage, foreigners destroyed it by fire and vandalism, about 1450 CE.

A century later, the first Spaniards to visit Paquimé wrote: "This large city . . . contains buildings that seemed to have been constructed by the ancient Romans. . . . There are many houses of great size, strength, and height. They are of six and seven stories, with towers and walls like fortresses. . . . The houses contain large and magnificent patios paved with enormous and beautiful stones" (Obregon 1584).

BIBLIOGRAPHY

Braniff, Beatriz, and Marie Areti Hers. "Herencias Chichimecas." *Arqueologia* 20 (1998).

Cordell, Linda S. *Prehistory of the Southwest*. New York, 1984.

Dean, Jeffrey, and John C. Ravesloot. "The Chronology of Cultural Interaction in the Gran Chichimeca." In *Culture and Contact: Charles C. Di Peso's Gran Chichimeca*, edited by Anne I. Woosley and John C. Ravesloot, pp. 83–103. Albuquerque, 1993. The authors revise the original chronology proposed by Di Peso (1974).

Di Peso, Charles. *Casas Grandes: A Fallen Trading Center of the Gran Chichimeca*. Amerind Foundation, 1974.

Driver, Harold E., and Wilhelmine Driver. "Ethnography and Acculturation of the Chichimeca-Jonaz of Northeast Mexico." *International Journal of American Linguistics* 26.4 (1963), 9. The authors refer to Ixtlilxochit, who wrote a history of the Chichimeca, completed around 1616.

Hammond, George P., and Agapity Rey, trans. and eds. *Obregon's History of the 16th Century Explorations in Western America . . . 1584*. Los Angeles, 1928.

Haury, Emil W. *The Hohokam, Desert Farmers and Craftsmen*. Tucson, 1976.

Herrera y Tordesillas, Antonio de. *The General History of the Vast Continent and Islands of America . . .* Translated by Captain John Stevens, vols. 5–6. London, 1726.

Kirchhoff, Paul. "Mesoamerica: Its Geographic Limits, Ethnic Composition and Cultural Characteristics." In *Heritage of Conquest*, edited by Sol Tax, pp. 17–20. Glencoe, Ill., 1952.

BEATRIZ BRANIFF CORNEJO

CASO, ALFONSO (1896–1970), celebrated for his extraordinary intellectual drive and powerful leadership abilities in helping to found modern archaeological science, as well as Mexico's most significant anthropological institutions. The work of Alfonso Caso y Andrade introduced new methods in the study of pre-Hispanic Mesoamerican history, iconography, and archaeology; it also considered the nature and struggles of contemporary indigenous peoples. During his lifetime, Caso received many awards, honorary degrees, and expressions of appreciation for his innovative methods and ideas.

Caso was born into a family where ideas and critical thinking were encouraged. His father was an engineer and his older brother Antonio was a distinguished philosopher, whose ideas in post-Revolutionary Mexico had a powerful impact on the national debates about the nature and future of Mexican society. Alfonso married María Lombardo Toledano, with whom he had three children, Beatriz, Andres, and Eugenia. By the age of twenty-four, Alfonso had received his law degree from the National School of Jurisprudence of the Universidad Nacional de México with highest honors, and he began to publish essays and teach courses on epistemology, philosophy of law, and the arts. This systematic legal training would mark his aggressive archaeological and administrative work throughout his life.

While a young lawyer, Caso's interests met a turning point during a visit to the then-remote hilltop ceremonial center of Xochicalco in Mexico's state of Morelos. The art and architecture of Xochicalco fascinated him and turned his mind to the archaeological study of pre-Hispanic Mexico. While he continued to work in legal projects associated with Mexican banking and commercial institutions, he began a program of study at Mexico's Museo Nacional. There, he took classes in pre-Hispanic history, ethnology, and archaeology with such influential teachers as Eduard Seler, Hermann Beyer, and Manuel Gamio, with whom he often debated, posing alternative interpretations. At the age of twenty-nine, he obtained a master's degree in philosophy (with a specialty in archaeology) from the Escuela de Altos Estudios, again with highest honors; from that point, he dedicated himself to the knowledge of pre-Hispanic cultures and contemporary indigenous peoples. His rigorous methods of interpretation were evident in his first essay on *patolli* and other pre-Hispanic games, and it was clear to his colleagues and teachers that a powerful new professional voice had arrived.

One of the major debates of the time concerned the nature and causes of evolution in indigenous American, and especially Mexican, cultures. On one side was the conservative view that significant changes in the Americas only took place through cultural diffusion from the older, more advanced civilizations of Egypt, China, India, or other Old World peoples. The other side, backing independent invention, argued that New World peoples were not only separated in space and time from Old World cultural evolution but had also developed their own styles of complex cultures without significant outside stimulus. Caso argued intensely for independent invention and, throughout his career, focused on understanding cultural evolutionary stages, developments, and influences. He often reiterated his position that Mesoamerican peoples developed their own institutions, cultures, and civilizations. With this evolutionary problem and others in mind, he founded in 1927 the journal *Revista mexicana de estudios antropologicos*, which became a creative outlet for many researchers who began to devise studies and report on results about Mesoamerica as a whole, as well as specific sites, problems, and meanings.

Influenced by the work of his teachers Seler and Gamio, and deeply concerned about understanding the symbols of pre-Hispanic Mexico, Caso set out to revise the understanding of indigenous iconography. He wrote on Mexica sculpture ("El Teocalli de la Guerra Sagrada," 1927); on Zapotec stelae (*Las estelas zapotecas*, 1928); and embarked on a thorough interpretation of the codices ("Mapa de Teozacualco," 1949; "Mapa de Xochitepec," 1958; "Vindobonensis," 1953, and others). Concerned, as was Paul Kirchhoff, with developing a more inclusive overview of Mesoamerica, Caso came to appreciate and insist on the importance of the Oaxaca region—as a major cultural area, beside the Maya and the Mexica—in the evolution of pre-Hispanic cultures. His work on Zapotec stelae convinced him that Zapotec culture had undergone powerful transformations, from both internal and external social developments. His vision of Oaxaca as a major cultural area was completely vindicated by subsequent studies.

Caso's reputation as a leading archaeologist expanded in 1931, with his excavation at Monte Albán in Oaxaca, which led to the discovery of Tomb 7; there, an elite burial yielded extremely fine ritual objects. For the next six years, Caso as chief archaeologist and his close colleague Ignacio Bernal explored the monumental structures in the Great Plaza of Monte Albán—the tombs, palaces, and monuments with inscriptions and iconography. The archaeological team explored 180 tombs; careful analysis of tombs 7, 104, and 105, as well as the larger ceremonial center of Monte Albán, led to worldwide fame. There was a new appreciation of both Caso and the royal lineages of the wider Oaxaca cultures, including those of the Zapotec and Mixtec peoples. Caso soon became the director of the Museo Nacional, and he was awarded his first honorary doctorate, *honoris causa*, from the Universidad Nacional Autónoma de México.

In 1936, Caso published his *La religión de los aztecas*, which initiated a series of books and articles in which he attempted a new understanding of the philosophical foundations and patterns of Aztec thought. This book was followed, for the next thirty years, by important essays on numerous topics, including the correlation of the Christian and Aztec calendars, the Toltec site of Tula, the Tarascan calendar, the Olmec cultural complex, various Mesoamerican codices and other calendars, human sacrifice, paradise in the murals of Teotihuacan, Indian identity, and a widely popular book in Spanish and English, *People of the Sun*. One of his most important contributions was his series of articles and debates with others about the history and nature of the Mesoamerican *tonalpohualli*, or "calendar"; he showed that its time depth reached at least as far back as Teotihuacan and, more significantly, that despite the variety of Mesoamerican calendars, they all shared the same basic religious, mathematical, and aesthetic principles.

When Lazaro Cardénas became president of Mexico in 1936, he recruited Caso to lead in the national efforts to stimulate economic growth and pride in the Mexican peasantry, an appreciation for indigenous cultures and arts, and a florescence of Mexican nationalism. Caso became instrumental in the reorganization of institutions dedicated to the invigoration of the anthropological sciences in Mexico and the creation of the Instituto Nacional de Antropología e Historia. Both the Instituto Nacional and the Escuela Nacional de Antropología e Historia were founded under Caso's directorship in 1939–1940. Caso served as director until 1944. This experience stimulated him to study and protect the living Indian arts and communities of Mexico. Demands for his leadership, stimulated by his achievements and fame, resulted in his directorship of Ensenanza Superior e Investiagacion Cientifica de la Secretaría de Educación Pública (SEP) in 1944. Almost immediately, he became the provisional rector of the Universidad Nacional Autónoma de México for six months, stepping down in March of 1945; he then became secretary of Bienes Nacionales e Inspeccion Administrativa that December. During the next four years, he received one award after another, including recognition in France, Great Britain, Ireland, and Mexico. In 1949, he founded the Instituto Nacional Indigenista, which he directed until his death, although he dedicated, in the words of Ignacio Bernal, "at least one day a week," to archaeology. The study and support of indigenous life and cultures absorbed the last two decades of his life.

Caso believed that the Indian peoples of Mexico had undergone intense discrimination in the post-Colonial period and had been painfully marginalized from the benefits of modernizing Mexico. He was a member of the Comision Nacional de Libros de Texto Gratuito, and he worked to bring educational opportunities to indigenous communities, including the printing and free distribution of books and other educational material.

His long-awaited "El tesoro de Monte Alban" was published in 1969, and it described with clarity and emotion each one of the precious ritual objects and funerary architecture that had caused a worldwide sensation thirty years before. In 1970, just two weeks before his death, his *magnum opus* was published, entitled *Reyes y reinos de la Mixteca*. These two volumes represent more than forty years of research into the Mixtec writing found in codices, lienzos, and archives. In sum, Caso was a public intellectual who dominated, sometimes unfairly, the Mexican anthropological community between 1930 and 1960. Today's scholars consider his greatest contributions to have been his study of Zapotec tombs and writing; the interpretation of codices; the reconstruction of Mixtec dynastic history; his understanding of Mexica religion and iconography; and his work on the pre-Hispanic calendar. Caso is periodically eulogized as the founder of Mexico's most significant archaeological institutions and its anthropological sciences. As a symbol of his significance, his remains were reburied, in 1974, in the Rotunda of Illustrious Men in Mexico City.

DAVÍD CARRASCO
and LEÓNARDO LÓPEZ LUJÁN

CASTAS PAINTINGS. The pictorial genre known as *castas* ("castes") is one of the most compelling artistic manifestations from the Colonial period. Most were created in eighteenth-century Mexico, although a few examples also survive from the Viceroyalty of Peru. These works depict the complex process of race mixing (*mestizaje*) among the three major groups in New Spain—Indian, Spanish, and African. Most *castas* paintings comprise sixteen scenes on separate canvases or copper plates, although occasionally the scenes are on a single, compartmentalized surface. Each scene portrays a man and a woman, with one or two of their progeny, accompanied by an inscription that identifies the race or racial mix depicted.

Castas paintings were created for the Spanish and the *criollos* (Spaniards born in the Americas). Early examples were commissioned as gifts to the king of Spain, and other sets were sent by viceroys to the Real Gabinete de Historia Natural (Royal Natural History Collection), founded in Madrid in 1771. The Spanish archbishop in Mexico, Francisco Antonio Lorenzana (1766–1772), brought back with him to Toledo a set of *castas* paintings, and the viceroy Antonio María Bucareli (1771–1779), in addition to owning "six castes of Indians," sent a set to his niece in Spain. *Castas* paintings were also displayed in the homes of both Spaniards and *criollos* in New Spain. In fact, *castas* paintings became extremely popular in the second half of the eighteenth century, and more than one hundred sets are known. While many are unsigned, others are signed by masters, such as José Alfaro, Arellano, Ignacio María Barreda, Luis Berrueco, José Bustos, Miguel Cabrera, Ignacio de Castro, Francisco Clapera, José B. Guiol, Mariano Gutiérrez, Andrés de Islas, José Joaquín Magón, Luis de Mena, José de Páez, Antonio Ruíz, Sebastián Antonio Salcedo, and Ramón Torres. The genre's popularity is related to the overall concern in Europe and the Americas with race, and with the then-growing science of natural history.

Although the production of the paintings spans the entire eighteenth century, the early sets, from before 1750, differ notably from those created after 1760. A number of the early paintings were commissioned by viceroys and ecclesiastical authorities as a way of presenting to the Crown the variety of racial mixing in New Spain. For example, the Duke of Linares (1711–1716) and the auxiliary bishop in Puebla, Juan Francisco de Loaiza, both commissioned sets from prominent painters. On one level, these early examples reveal a special concern with the construction of a particular self-image. In a manner similar to that of royal portraiture, these works provided a vision of reality to be scrutinized by the elite, mainly by imperial authorities. All the different *castas* are clothed luxuriously, which reveals a desire to export an image that underscores the colony's wealth. One of the earliest portrays a mulatto woman (with an inscription in Spanish) "Rendering of a Mulatto, Daughter of a Black and a Spaniard in Mexico City, Capital of America on the 22nd of the Month of August of 1711." The careful attention given to the figure's attire and jewelry, in addition to stressing the colony's wealth, reveals the artist's wish to bring her importance to the foreground, a fact clearly corroborated by the work's inscription. Two other early sets from 1720 (by Juan Rodríguez Juárez and perhaps his brother Nicolás) also stress the luxury of the different *castas*; their canvases are not numbered, suggesting that they were intended to portray the different *castas* equally. These early paintings offer a proud vision, where race mixing is presented as an ineluctable fact of the colony and that, despite the proliferation of *castas* there, society remained orderly and prosperous. On another level, the early paintings may also be interpreted as visual manifestations of racial variety—and, by extension, nature's variety—created by God. The idea was that God demon-

strates divine grandeur by creating all shades of flowers and humans of many colors, a very popular one during the seventeenth and eighteenth centuries.

The *castas* pictorial genre reached its apex during the second half of the eighteenth century, coinciding with the implementation of the Bourbon Reforms in Spain. [*See* Bourbon Reforms.] Those created after 1760 seem to have a very different purpose than early examples. They stress the colony's racial and social hierarchy, by emphasizing a progression. First, there are figures considered to be of "pure" race (that is, Spaniards), lavishly attired or engaged in occupations that indicate their higher status (merchants; bearers of arms; the possessors of culture who are reading or sitting next to their writing implements; those partaking in the leisure activities of eating, playing cards, playing music). As the family groups become more racially Indian and/or African, their social status diminishes, as exemplified by the more modest—and often tattered—clothing and by the trappings of their trades (street vendors, water sellers, shoe-repairers, etc.).

Later paintings may also offer specific social commentaries. Those that portray the mix of Spaniards and Africans or of Indians and Africans often show the African figure as violent. This may be explained by the preoccupation of Spanish authorities with keeping strict racial and social boundaries, to ensure the survival of the Spanish imperial body politic in the colony. Each individual therefore occupied a specific socioeconomic niche, defined largely by race, with Spaniards at the top and Africans at the bottom—the last to enter the New World colonies, and as slaves. The terminology for the mixed people aims at establishing the degree of purity (whiteness) and the presumed degree of debasement (blackness). The post-1760 sets stress the colony's social hierarchy by carefully numbering each scene. They also include a rich classificatory system within which the surrounding objects, food products, flora, and fauna are clearly positioned. These disparate items link the paintings with the burgeoning European interest in natural history in the second half of the eighteenth century, as well as the growing need to classify every aspect of the realm of nature.

[*See also* Cabrera, Miguel; Mestizaje.]

BIBLIOGRAPHY

García Sáiz, María Concepción. *Las castas mexicanas: Un género pictórico americano.* Milan, 1989.

Katzew, Ilona, ed. *New World Orders: Casta Painting and Colonial Latin America.* New York, 1996. (Exhibition Catalog.)

ILONA KATZEW

CASTE WARS. The so-called Caste Wars of Yucatán represent one of the most successful and prolonged Indian revolts in the history of Mesoamerica. For more than fifty years, from 1847 to 1901, Maya rebels in eastern Yucatán maintained their independence and resisted efforts by the provincial government to conquer them. They experienced considerable military success against a politically fragmented Yucatecan (i.e., European colonial) militia, forcing its soldiers to evacuate all of the large towns throughout Yucatán with the exception of the capital, Mérida, and Campeche. Even after the Yucatecan counterattack and the rebels' withdrawal from these towns, the Maya of eastern Yucatán successfully established and maintained a society free from Yucatecan encroachment until the beginning of the twentieth century.

The Caste Wars must be understood within the economic and political context of Late Colonial and post-Independence Yucatán. By the end of the eighteenth century, Yucatán's rural population had expanded considerably as its population grew and non-Indians migrated to rural towns. Economic opportunities, primarily the production of sugar cane, attracted development and land consolidation in the south and east of the peninsula. Shortly after independence from Spain, in 1821, the Yucatecan congress passed a series of laws which both facilitated and encouraged this economic development. By the 1840s, the alienation of peasant lands had increased precipitously, forcing much of this peasantry to abandon their own lands and to work as indebted laborers on large estates. This had a dramatic effect on the Maya peasantry and precipitated the Caste Wars.

The political issues most relevant to the outbreak of the Caste Wars were confrontations between liberals and conservatives at the national and state levels, and the constant factionalism within and between Yucatecan towns and cities. Following independence from Spain, there emerged liberal and conservative political parties, known respectively as the Federalist and the Centralist parties. On three occasions between 1839 and 1847, violent conflicts between the Federalists and the Centralists erupted in Yucatán; in each instance, Maya peasants were enlisted with promises of land and the reduction of church fees and state taxes. The peasants never received the land or the reduction in taxes that they were promised—but they did procure weapons and experience in using them. Moreover, these political revolts and their violent resolutions both heightened the level of political violence in the countryside and taught the disaffected rural peasantry that violence was an acceptable and realistic means of satisfying their desires.

Who were the disaffected peasants who participated in the Caste Wars? The traditional view held by Yucatecans at the time of the revolt, and further promulgated by Yucatecan historians, is that the rebels were Maya Indians and that the Caste Wars were a racial conflict. These writers argue that the Maya hatred of non-Indians unified them into a cohesive rebel force. More recently, however, scholars have contended that, although the majority of the rebels were Indians, many non-Indian peasants also rebelled. These non-Indians shared similar grievances with their Indian counterparts. Some of them, including Bonifacio Novelo and José María Barrera, were important leaders in the Indian army and in the cult of the Talking Cross which followed the initial violence. Hence, this war was a conflict between "castes" (ethnic groups) only to the extent that rebelling non-Indians identified with their Indian collaborators and shared common grievances with them.

Although the rebels' grievances included the alienation of land, their strongest complaints related to a disparity between Indians and non-Indians in civil taxation and church fees. The dominant theme in their leaders' correspondence is that laws should apply equally to all Yucatecans, regardless of their race or ethnicity.

The Caste Wars began in the eastern towns of Yucatán. In July 1847, Colonel Eulogio Rosado, commandant of the eastern, non-Indian town of Valladolid, received reports that Indians were amassing arms in the area of Tihosuco and Chichimila, immediately to the south. One report suggested that Bonifacio Novelo, Jacinto Pat, and Cecilio Chi were plotting against the "white race." Shortly afterward, Manuel Antonio Ay, *cacique* of Chichimila and a friend of Chi, was arrested for taking part in this plot and executed. Rather than quelling a possible rebellion, the execution of Ay incited it: following Ay's execution, on 30 May 1847, Cecilio Chi and his troops attacked the town of Tepich, killing all but one of its non-Indian inhabitants. This massacre is regarded as the beginning of the Caste Wars.

Rebel victories quickly ensued. Much of the rebels' success, however, was due to the Yucatecans' inability to resolve their own political differences. In order to defend his government from an attempted coup in Mérida, Governor Santiago Méndez recalled his troops from the east, leaving its towns inadequately guarded. The Maya rebels acted quickly. By the end of 1847, many rural towns in the east—including Tihosuco, Tixualahtun, Tekuch, Tahmuy, Huumku, Tesacs, Xocen, Kanxoc, Chichimila, Tekom, Ebtun, Dzitnup, Cuncunul, and Kaua—were in rebel hands. By March 1848, the rebel forces had forced the Yucatecans out of their stronghold in the east, Valladolid. By May 1848, the rebels had sacked all the towns to the east and south of Mérida, including the non-Indian towns of Izamal and Bacalar. June 1848 marked the high point of the rebel advance.

For reasons that are still unclear, the rebel advance stopped at this time, and its army began to disband. One interpretation suggests that this coincided with the planting season and that many rebels left the war to tend their fields. Another explanation is that the rebel forces found willing recruits in areas to the east and south of Mérida, but that the Maya closer to Mérida refused to participate in the revolt and even aided in repelling it. In any event, the Yucatecan army, revitalized with help from abroad, succeeded in pushing the rebels eastward; by December 1848, it had recaptured most of the towns it had lost earlier. The rebels retreated into the forests in the east, and the Indian leaders began to consider establishing a new government there.

With military defeat, conflict erupted among the rebel leaders, and both Cecilio Chi and Jacinto Pat were murdered. Hoping to stem the tide of these defeats and to quell internal conflicts among their own ranks, the new leaders—Venancio Pec, Florentino Chan, Bonifacio Novelo, and José María Barrera—shifted the nature of the rebellion from a military crusade to a religious one. In order to revitalize their forces, these leaders sought divine intervention.

During the summer of 1850, near a small *cenote* (sacred well) in eastern Yucatán, José María Barrera established the town of Chan Santa Cruz ("Little Holy Cross"), which became the capital of the rebel Indians for the next fifty years. Barrera erected a cross at this site which became the focal point for a new religion based on direct communication with God. The Talking Cross dictated God's will to the leaders of the Indian rebels. Consequently, this group and its territory became known as the Cruzob. The Cruzob remained independent from Yucatán until 4 May 1901, when General Ignacio Bravo defeated them and occupied Chan Santa Cruz.

When the Caste Wars initially began, they were not a racial conflict between Indians and elite Yucatecans. Instead, they may have been localized conflicts between and within the rural towns to the east. Nevertheless, the heightened sense of rural violence, combined with the Yucatecans' fear of armed Indians, led them to classify the suspicious Indian movements in the east as preparations for a revolt. Whether this was the beginning of a war against the white race or not, the Yucatecans' response to it defined it as such, and the rebels responded accordingly. They conducted a malicious military crusade to expel the creole elite from the rural countryside. The tenuous nature of the rebels' military movement revealed itself in their defeat when conflict erupted among their leaders. Finally, as hope grew dim and conventional weapons no longer led them to victory, the Maya rebels found revitalization in supernatural means, and the cult of the Talking Cross was born.

BIBLIOGRAPHY

Baqueiro, Serapio. *Ensayo histórico sobre las revoluciones de Yucatán dede el año de 1840 hasta 1864.* 3 vols. Mérida, 1878–1887. Detailed military history written from the perspective of a nineteenth-century Yucatecan historian.

Bricker, Victoria R. *The Indian Christ, the Indian King.* Austin, 1981. Discusses the Caste Wars as a revitalization movement.

Dumond, Don. *The Machete and the Cross: Campesino Rebellion in Yucatan.* Lincoln, Neb., 1997. Most recent comprehensive account of the Caste Wars and their aftermath, the cult of the Talking Cross.

González Navarro, Moisés. *Raza y Tierra: La Guerra de Castas y el henequén.* Mexico City, 1970.

Patch, Robert. "Decolonization, the Agrarian Problem, and the Origins of the Caste War, 1812–1847." In *Land, Labor, and Capital in Modern Yucatan,* edited by J. T. Brannon and G. M. Joseph, pp. 51–82. Tuscaloosa, Ala., 1991. Investigates the alienation of Indian lands and its causal role in the Caste Wars.

Reed, Nelson. *The Caste War of Yucatan.* Stanford, 1964. First comprehensive account of the Caste Wars in English.

Rugeley, Terry. *Yucatan's Maya Peasantry and the Origins of the Caste War.* Austin, 1996. Detailed analysis of the first half of the nineteenth century in Yucatan, based on numerous primary documents.

CHRISTOPHER M. NICHOLS

CATHEDRALS. *See* Churches and Cathedrals.

CATHOLICISM. *See* Christianity, *article on* Catholicism; Missionization; Priests, *article on* Catholic Priests; *and* Roman Catholic Church.

CAVES. Charged with sacred meaning, in many cultures caves symbolize the center, a source of fertility. Therefore, settlements have often been situated near caves to tie the community to the cosmovision of its members. In the Maya area, many communities are associated with sacred caves and take their names from them. This association of structures, sacred caves, and toponyms is clear in Teotihuacan, Mexico, where we find Oztoyahualco ("in a circle of caves") and Oztoticpac ("over the cave"). So strong was this tradition that when a cave did not exist in a desirable location, an artificial cave might be carved out in order to lend sacredness to a structure.

Caves are found in many types of soil: in basalt rock, limestone, karst, salt pits, sandstone, dolomite, gypsum, halite, and chalk. They may be formed by the movement of earth, by compression, by tectonic action, or by volcanism. Lava that flowed from the volcanoes, which indigenes thought of as the blood of these fiery mountains, created many caverns which eventually Mesoamericans used for habitation and for rituals.

The tunnel-like cave under the Pyramid of the Sun at Teotihuacan, Mexico, was created by lava flow a million years ago. This pyramid was constructed around 200–100 BCE over a primitive shrine, which in turn had been built over a subterranean cave. The tunnel or lava tube ends

120 meters from the entrance of the pyramid's west side, in a chamber in the form of a four-petaled flower, possibly symbolizing the four world quarters. The Great Pyramid was constructed in such a way that the flower-form chamber lies almost directly beneath its center. This chamber shows work by human hands, though the cave-tunnel is natural. The position of the cave indicates that the pyramid was intentionally built here in order to preserve and honor the ritual space. It may have been the destination of pilgrimages, or an oracle may have used it.

All caves in Mesoamerica were considered sacred: the place of creation, where celestial bodies, gods, humans, and sustenance for people were born. In some cultures, the sun and moon were said to have originated in a cave. The god Cinteotl, "Divine Maize," was created in a cave, and the grain that gave him his name was guarded by *chaneques*, dwarflike men who protect the earth's riches. The cave, the womb of the earth, was also the place of creation for certain ethnic groups. From Chicomóztoc, "Seven Caves," seven groups of people emerged; best known in this mythical birth are the Aztec, founders of Mexico-Tenochtitlan.

Caves, however, were also places of death and entrances to the underworld. Sacrifices of children to water deities took place in caves. In some regions the ancestors' spirits were said to maintain a supernatural government in caves and to protect the living. *Graniceros*—individuals who were struck by lightning and thus "chosen"—control the weather and perform their rites in caves, especially in the Iztaccihuatl volcano.

Stalactites and stalagmites, found in many caves, were frequently considered to be supernaturally created figures of gods or saints. In the cave at Balancanché, Yucatán, close to Chichén Itzá, there is an offering placed eight centuries ago dedicated to the gods of the underworld, consisting mainly of censers, figurines of the rain god Tlaloc, and associated objects. The cave was used as a ceremonial space for honoring the water deities.

Art is also present in numerous caverns in the form of painted and bas-relief wall decorations. In Mexico, two well-known examples of painting are the Olmec figures in Juxtlahuaca, Guerrero, and jaguar-bird-human figures at Oxtotitlan. Art in bas-relief is present in Chalcatzingo, Morelos, where a priestly individual who may represent an oracle is depicted within a cave, and in the majestic cavern at Loltún, Yucatán, where a warrior figure is sculpted at the entrance. A spectacular example of cave art is at Naj Tunich in the limestone hills of Petén, Guatemala; represented here are Maya personages, a ballplayer (now defaced), erotic scenes, and long columns of hieroglyphs.

[*See also* Chicomóztoc.]

BIBLIOGRAPHY

Brady, James E. "Caves and Cosmovision in Utatlan." *California Anthropologist* 18 (1991), 1–10.

Hermitte, M. Esther. *Poder sobrenatural y control social en un pueblo Maya contemporáneo*. Mexico City, 1970.

Heyden, Doris. "An Interpretation of the Cave underneath the Pyramid of the Sun in Teotihuacan, Mexico." *American Antiquity* (1975), 131–174.

Stone, Andrea. *Images from the Underworld: Naj Tunich and the Tradition of Maya Cave Painting*. Austin, Tex., 1995.

DORIS HEYDEN

CEMPOALA. Flourishing from the twelfth to the sixteenth century CE, Cempoala was the first urban settlement the Spaniards saw on the American continent. Its name in Nahuatl means "twenty waters" or "abundant waters." The southernmost Totonac *señorío*, its southern border was the Huitzilapan River, known today as the Río La Antigua, named for the Spanish settlement found a few kilometers upstream from the Gulf of Mexico. Its geographic coordinates are 19° 29′ N by 96° 27′ W, and it is found on the coastal strip of the Gulf of Mexico a few kilometers from the Veracruz-Tuxpán federal highway.

Beginning in 1440, the Mexica exhibited a growing interest in the lands of the Gulf Coast, and in 1458, they began their first military incursion, supposedly punitive, for the death of some Aztec merchants. In 1463, the region was definitively subjugated, and places such as Ahuilazpan, Cuetlachtlan, Cuauhtochco, Oceloapan, Cempoala, and Quiahuitzlan paid tribute to the Triple Alliance, although Cempoala does not appear in the tribute pages of the *Codex Mendoza*.

On 22 April 1519, the conqueror Fernando Cortés disembarked in Challchiucuecan, and on 15 May, he arrived at Cempoala, which he planned to name Villaviciosa or Seville because of its abundance, size, and splendor. On 29 May 1520, the battle began in Fortified System 4 between Cortés and Narvaez, which the former won. The last significant event in the city of Cempoala occurred in December 1521, when important negotiations took place between the officials of the Villa Rica de Veracruz and the *veedor* Cristóbal de Tapia, the former defending the interests of Cortés, the latter the government of New Spain. In 1526, Cortés passed through Cempoala on the way back from his expedition to Hibueras (Honduras). Subsequently, the city gradually was abandoned and lost in history until it was rediscovered by Francisco del Paso y Troncoso in 1891.

Twelve fortified systems are distributed over 1.5 square kilometers (0.58 square mile). These systems represented the centers of each barrio, or *calpulli*, which were characterized by a population united through kinship ties. Ceramic analysis suggests a probable multiethnic coexistence, the Totonacs, on the one hand, and local coastal traditions, on the other. The settlement area, including the sectors of agricultural production, is estimated at 7 square kilometers (2.7 square miles), with a population of between fifteen thousand and twenty thousand inhabitants. The city's water management is outstanding in terms of irrigation, as well as its system for supplying water to the different fortifications and individual homes via closed and hidden hydraulic ducts. The water was taken in at the highest part of the city from the Actopan River, passed through the city, and ended up in the agricultural lands below the city.

Besides the sacred architecture expressed in temples, altars, and shrines, there were elite residences, as well as houses reflecting a more modest form of stylistic elements than the architecture of Cempoala. These houses had thatched roofs and were built on small stone platforms with packed earth in the center covered with a smoothed layer of lime and sand. They have a stairway in front with balustrades on both sides. The elite residences were placed over a stone foundation with various superimposed sections, as in the case of the temple where Xicomecóatl, the Fat Cacique, resided (which is not the main temple of the site). The sacred architecture of Cempoala is characterized above all by its porticos at the foot of the buildings with a rectangular base and continuous, hollow supports at the center of the flat roof, and crenelations along the edges that allude to Tlaloc and occasionally Xolotl. The walls of the fortified systems have continuous step-fret crenelations. The plans of the buildings are usually rectangular, although there are also round ones dedicated to Ehecatl, the wind god. Interior decoration varies. In the case of Las Caritas and El Pimiento, the walls were covered with ceramic skeletons painted white. Other buildings had polychrome murals with ideograms referring to the moon, the sun, and Venus combined with allegorical forms. The architectural style in form and type of construction resembles that of the Central Highlands during the Postclassic period. The sculpture associated with the architecture is ceramic or a plastic material, such as the Chac Mol that Paso y Troncoso found at the foot of the building of the Chimeneas, which no longer exists.

In terms of archaeological research at Cempoala, there have been three main projects: La Comisión Exploradora headed by Paso y Troncoso in 1891, and two conducted by the Instituto Nacional de Antropología e Historia, 1942–1949 and 1979–1982, led by José García Payón and Jürgen Brüggemann, respectively.

[See also Gulf Coast.]

BIBLIOGRAPHY

Brüggemann, Jürgen K., et al. *Zempoala: El estudio de una ciudad prehispánica.* Mexico City, 1991.

Galindo y Villa, Jesús. "Las ruinas de Zempoala y el templo de Tajín." *Anales del Museo Nacional de Antropología* (1912).

García Payón, José. "Zempoala, compendio de su estudio arqueológico." In *Zempoala: El estudio de una ciudad prehispánica.* 1991.

JÜRGEN K. BRÜGGEMANN

CENOTES. Derived from the Yucatecan Maya *tz'onot*, cenotes are deep sinkholes in limestone with a pool at the bottom that are found especially in Yucatán. The Yucatán Maya live on karst topography—cracked and fractured limestone where water quickly drains through the numerous openings in the rock. Even the heaviest rainfall soon disappears underground, leaving a dry surface. As the slightly acidic rainwater flows underground through cracks and crevices, it enlarges these openings by dissolving carbonate minerals. Caverns are soon hollowed out along fracture lines. Further subsurface dissolution and the force of gravity cause the ceilings of caves to fall in, resulting in linear or almost circular cavities. Cenotes develop when the roof of a cave collapses, forming a depression in the landscape that is deep enough to reach water.

This process of fracturing, draining, and internal corrosion turns the environment of northern Yucatán into a vegetation-filled semi-desert where water is a crucial resource. Settlements, both ancient and modern, surround the cenotes.

Rain is essential for maize farming, especially when tassels appear, and Mesoamerican religions reflect this concern. The Maya felt that there was a relationship between rainfall, cenotes, and caves; they revered all three of these phenomena. Shrines and offerings are frequently encountered in Yucatecan caves. Small offerings are pleasing to the rain gods, so the miniature grinding stones and plates found at Balancanche cave, together with actual representations of the deities, indicate the main focus of the cave cults. Redfield and Villa, in their classic study of *Chan Kom*, tell us that contemporary villagers believe the rain gods fill their calabashes at cenotes, then drop the water on their fields.

Sacrifices and offerings were thrown into cenotes at Chichén Itzá, Dzibilchaltún, and other places. The cenote cult at Chichén Itzá, where human sacrifices took place, is described by sixteenth-century chroniclers, especially Landa. These accounts describe the massacre of a group of Xiu pilgrims as they crossed Coccom land in an attempt to end a drought by making offerings at the sacred cenote of Chichén Itzá. The self-sacrifice of Hunac Ceel, who evidently threw himself into the cenote and returned with a prophecy, is a pre-Columbian incident in the history of Chichén Itzá recorded in the Books of Chilam Balam.

Archaeological exploration of the Chichén Itzá cenote

Dzibilchaltún's sacred cenote, *Xlacah*, measures 30 meters (100 feet) across and 43 meters (140 feet) deep. *Courtesy of Visual Resources Collection, The University of Texas at Austin. Ferguson Collection.*

was started by the Mayanist archaeologist Edward Thompson, who dredged the bottom between 1904 and 1911. Later studies in 1967–1968 relied on scuba equipment. These operations recovered quantities of offerings, including quality ceramics, basketry, fine textiles, jade, turquoise, gold objects, copper, carved wood, and obsidian. The collection, including materials that had been brought to Yucatán from distant places, is frequently cited as evidence indicating the high degree of Maya craft specialization and the importance of pre-Columbian commerce.

Skeletal material from the cenote included males and females, both adults and children. The high percentage of young individuals is reminiscent of the sacrifices of children in honor of the central Mexican rain deities.

Other cenotes, especially the one at Dzibilchaltún, have also yielded large collections. These explorations, together with the frequent historical references and contemporary Maya practices, suggest that the cenote cult was a widespread phenomenon.

[*See also* Mesoamerica, *article on* Geography.]

BIBLIOGRAPHY

Coggins, Clemancy Chase, ed. "Artifacts from the Cenote of Sacrifice, Chichén Itzá, Yucatán." In *Memoirs of the Peabody Museum of Archaeology and Ethnology, Harvard University*, vol. 10. Cambridge, 1992.

Coggins, Clemency Chase, and Orrin C. Shane. *Cenote of Sacrifice: Maya Treasures from the Sacred Well at Chichén Itzá.* Austin, 1984.

Tozzer, Alfred M. "*Chichén Itzá and Its Cenote of Sacrifice: A Comparative Study of Contemporaneous Maya and Toltec.*" In *Memoirs of the Peabody Museum of Archaeology and Ethnology, Harvard University*, vols. 11 and 12. Cambridge, 1957.

EDWARD B. KURJACK

CENTRAL MEXICAN PICTORIALS. The Aztec and their neighbors in and around the Valley of Mexico relied on painted books and records to document almost all aspects of their lives. Painted manuscripts recorded their history, science, land tenure, tribute, and sacred rituals; the religious and calendrical manuscripts revealed prognostications for the future and thereby guided the Central Mexicans in their decisions. After the Spanish arrived in the sixteenth century, the European conquerors, friars, and chroniclers remarked on the quantity and range of pictorial codices, praising particularly the veracity of the indigenous maps, histories, and tribute lists. Under Spanish domination, the Aztec continued to think and express themselves visually, and the Spaniards, for their part, came to accept and rely on the painted manuscripts as valid and potentially important records. Thus, the native tradition of pictorial documentation and expression continued strongly in the Valley of Mexico several generations after the Conquest, with the latest examples of this tradition reaching into the early seventeenth century. Manuscript painting is the only native art form to survive this long before it succumbed to European modes of expression. A result of this longevity is that hundreds of pictorial manuscripts have survived from the Basin of Mexico and its environs, more than from any other part of Mesoamerica.

It is ironic, however, that none of these surviving codices is indisputably pre-Conquest in date. All show some level of European influence, whether stylistic or organizational. The pre-Conquest divinatory and religious books in particular were burned by zealous friars or simply fell into disuse, and other painted manuscripts perished in the general destruction that ushered in Spanish control.

Several codices from the Valley of Mexico were long considered pre-Columbian until Donald Robertson, in his pioneering book *Mexican Manuscript Painting of the Early Colonial Period* (1959), successfully argued for their colonial status. These are the *Codex Borbonicus* and the *Tonalamatl Aubin*, both examples of the divinatory codex, or *tonalamatl* (literally "day book"); the *Codex Boturini* or Tira de la Perigrinación, an annals history of the Aztec migration; the Plano en Papel de Maguey, a map of *chinampa* ("drained field") and house plots in the vicinity of Tenochtitlan; and the *Matrícula de Tributos*, an imperial tribute list. All are painted on native paper in the native style. As Robertson pointed out, however, all but the *Matrícula* contain images that show European stylistic influence, and the *Matrícula* is constructed in the European fashion as a bound book of leaves instead of in the native tradition as a screenfold or roll.

The richness and wide range of the native tradition are revealed by these and other colonial pictorials, by transcriptions and translations of pictorial codices rendered into texts, and by the descriptions left by the Spaniards. Some authors, such as the royal Spanish chronicler Peter Martyr, the Franciscan friar Toribio de Benavente Motolinía, the Spanish judge Alonso de Zorita, and the *mestizo* historian of Tetzcoco Fernando de Alva Ixtlilxochitl, speak directly about the manuscript tradition and mention many of the pre-Conquest genres. Other writers mention pictorial manuscripts and painted records in passing; the conqueror Fernando Cortés, for example, refers to indigenous maps and the impressive tribute records of the Aztec ruler Motecuhzoma. Extant colonial codices are even more direct evidence of pre-Conquest prototypes.

Indigenous painted manuscripts from Central Mexico fall roughly into three broad categories, although the categories overlap: religious and divinatory books; histories of various types; and practical documents, such as tribute rolls, maps, and court records. In the sixteenth century, two new genres arose to serve specifically Spanish readers. These were the cultural encyclopedia, a book specifically created under Spanish patronage to document aspects of Aztec religion and culture, and the Testerian catechism.

The sacred and religious books of the Aztec focus on humankind's relationship with the supernatural world.

These include cosmogonies that explained the formation of the previous and present world; they exist in Nahuatl translation and in Alva Ixtlilxochitl's description. Ceremonials or protocols for rituals guided the priests in their performance of rites and festivals; examples include the paintings of the eighteen monthly feasts in the *Codex Borbonicus*, as well as the painted and written descriptions of similar feasts in the cultural encyclopedias (*Magliabechiano Group* codices, *Codex Telleriano-Remensis*, etc.). Divinatory codices, or *tonalamatls*, mentioned by many chronicles, survive in the *Tonalamatl Aubin* and the almanac section of the *Borbonicus*, which preserve the native form virtually intact, and in the almanacs included in such cultural encyclopedias as the *Codex Telleriano-Remensis*, *Codex Tudela*, and Fray Bernardino de Sahagún's *Florentine Codex*. By providing the prognostications for the different days, weeks of thirteen days, and larger units of time, these *tonalamatls* allowed the day keepers or calendar priests and the diviners to know the forces that affected events and personal actions. They were the essential guides for balanced living. Motolinía also mentions specialized divinatory books for marriage prognostications and the naming of infants, as well as books of dreams. Songs and the orations of the elders, called *huehuetlatolli*, were also painted in books, although no examples survive.

Aztec historical books embrace both the mythical and the secular past, for most of the extant histories begin when the Aztec and their neighbors leave their mythical homelands to journey to their destined locations. The histories almost always pertain to a specific polity, recording the people's origin (often emerging from caves), their migration to their present location, the founding and securing of the polity, conquests and alliances, the succession of rulers, and other noteworthy events. Two types of history can be discerned. Migration histories focus on the people's distant origin and on the long and arduous journey they took to arrive at their present homeland; they culminate in the founding of polities. Imperial histories then carry the historical record forward from this founding, some even carrying the story through the Spanish invasion and occupation. Most Aztec histories are organized as annals, where a ribbon of consecutive year signs forms a spine along which historical events are painted. These annals were called *xiuhtonalamatl* ("the book of the counting of the years"). The best known annals are the codices *Aubin*, *Azcatitlán*, *Boturini*, *Mendoza* Part 1, *Mexicanus*, and historical part of the *Telleriano-Remensis*.

Narratives of migrations and foundings of territory were also painted as maps, where events moved over territorial presentations. Such cartographic histories include the *Tetzcocan* codices *Codex Xolotl* and *Mapa Tlotzin*, the *Mexica Mapa Sigüenza*, and the *Cuauhtinchan*

Maps 1 and *2*. The form and nature of pre-Conquest genealogies are suggested by the Circular Genealogy of Nezahualcóyotl and the genalogy in the front of the *Codex Mexicanus*. All these historical codices were created by and for civic leaders and rulers.

Painted manuscripts also documented the practical and even the mundane aspects of Aztec life. Maps, painted on sheets of paper or hide or on large cotton cloths (*lienzos*), recorded territorial lands or organized vast territories. Cortés relied on such maps when he marched to Honduras after subduing Tenochtitlan. Paintings also kept record of the lands worked and owned by individuals, the neighborhood groups (*calpullis*), and distinct communities; they identify boundaries and show how land was distributed. The Plano en Papel de Maguey is such a land record, as are more Europeanized documents such as the Oztoticpac Lands Map from Tetzcoco and the many property plans that were painted on European paper.

Tax and tribute lists include such imperial tribute rolls as the *Matrícula de Tributos* and the tribute section of the *Codex Mendoza* (its cognate), which list goods received in Tenochtitlan from the far reaches of the Aztec realm. Regional tribute documents such as *Codex Azoyu 1* from Tlapa have also been preserved. In the Colonial period, indigenous painters occasionally recorded the goods and services given over to Spanish authorities. Examples are the *Codex Huejotzingo, Codex Osuna,* and *Codex Kingsborough,* which entered into archives as painted testimonies in court cases of official investigations. The *Osuna* and *Kingsborough* were painted as formal complaints. Such court documents, or painted testimonies, were common before the Conquest and continued afterwards. The painted testimony concerning the whereabouts of the idols of the Templo Mayor, for example, was offered up in an Inquisition case in the 1530s.

Economic and practical documents, in addition to the histories, were maintained and held by the community leaders, where they would be available for consultation and amendment. Those of imperial scope were gathered in the metropolitan centers, which featured large libraries of codices. The *mestizo* historian Juan Bautista Pomar remarked particularly on the great royal archive in Tetzcoco, which the Spaniards and Tlaxcalan burned in 1520. Many community archives continued their roles after the Conquest, enabling Spanish authorities to draw on the native pictorials in order to settle disputes over land or inheritance.

As the Spanish friars confronted and tried to adjust to colonial Aztec life, they introduced new genres of manuscript painting that met their own needs. The ethnographic projects of the friars, especially the Franciscans and the Dominicans, as well as official Spanish interest in Aztec history and culture, led to the production of cultural encyclopedias. These compendia of native customs stem not from Aztec roots but from the late medieval encyclopedia tradition of Europe, which classified culture according to broad categories, embracing such topics as religion, the calendar, burial customs, and history. Friars looking to document Aztec culture thus had native painters illustrate on European paper their gods and rites, their calendars, and their histories. The friars then had explanatory texts added to clarify the paintings for Spanish readers. The native painters referred to or copied older originals, drawing images from their own cultural traditions, but the manuscripts they created were fundamentally European in purpose, organization, and audience.

A number of these cultural encyclopedias were painted and annotated in the middle and second half of the sixteenth century. The *Codex Mendoza*—a three-part codex that records Aztec imperial history, the tribute sent to Motecuhzoma, and an ethnography of a typical Aztec person from birth to death—was commissioned by the viceroy Mendoza to send to the European Emperor Charles V. An anonymous mendicant friar had the prototype of the *Magliabechiano Group* of codices created to picture and describe a broad range of Aztec religious beliefs and customs. Although the prototype is lost, the codices *Magliabechiano, Tudela, Ixtlilxochitl,* and others were derived from it. The so-called *Huitzilopochtli Group*—composed of the *Telleriano-Remensis* and its copy, the *Codex Vaticanus A/Ríos*—is also the product of mendicant interest in Aztec culture.

The ethnographic projects of the Franciscan friar Bernardino de Sahagún and the Dominican friar Diego Durán resulted in cultural encyclopedias that were primarily textual but still retained a large pictorial component, forming impressive and thorough records of Aztec culture. These cultural encyclopedias were originally created to be circulated among the evangelical friars in Mexico who wished to understand Aztec culture. Several, such as Sahagún's *Florentine Codex* and Durán's *General History*, were then prepared in clean copies to be sent to Spain.

A second new genre was the pictorial catechism, often called Testerian manuscript, which records the texts of the catechism in a rebus system with images being translated into a set series of words or sounds. Such manuscripts reflect European theories of memory and instruction.

The painted manuscript record from Central Mexico has been a fundamental resource for understanding the arts, ideology, and lifeways of the Aztec and their neighbors. The histories provide a pictorial record of indigenous rulers, their reign dates, their deeds, and important events that happened in their polities, such as conquests, droughts, and famines. Divinatory codices are keys to understanding Aztec iconography and religious ideology. Tribute records and maps enable scholars to understand the organization of the Aztec Empire on local as well as imperial levels. Cultural encyclopedias gather many of these genres together in one document. Because they give specific and detailed information on Aztec culture that is not revealed in the archaeological record, these colonial codices from Central Mexico are especially valuable resources for archaeologists, art historians, and historians of Mesoamerican culture.

[*See also* Aubin, Codex; Aubin Tonalamatl; Borbonicus, Codex; Boturini, Codex; Durán, Diego; Ixtlilxochitl, Codex; Magliabechiano, Codex; Mendoza, Codex; Mexicanus, Codex; Olmos, Andrés de; Osuna, Codex; Ríos, Codex; Sigüenza, Mapa; Telleriano-Remensis, Codex; Tovar, Juan de; Tributos, Matrícula de; Tudela, Codex; Xolotl, Codex.]

BIBLIOGRAPHY

Baudot, Georges. *Utopia and History in Mexico*, translated by Bernard Ortíz de Montellano and Thelma Ortíz de Montellano. Niwot, Colo., 1995. First published as *Utopie et histoire au Mexique*. Toulouse, 1977. Describes the ethnographic projects of the first friars in Mexico and discusses the pictorial and textual manuscripts they sponsored.

Boone, Elizabeth Hill. "Pictorial Documents and Visual Thinking in Postconquest Mexico." In *Native Traditions in the Postconquest World*, edited by Elizabeth Hill Boone and Tom Cummins, pp. 149–199. Washington, D.C., 1998. Explains how and why the tradition of manuscript painting continued in post-Conquest Mexico.

Boone, Elizabeth Hill. *Stories in Red and Black: Pictorial Histories of the Aztec and Mixtec*. Austin, Tex., 2000.

Glass, John B. "A Census of Middle American Testerian Manuscripts." In *Handbook of Middle American Indians*, edited by Robert Wauchope and Howard Cline, vol. 14, pp. 281–296. Austin, Tex., 1975.

Glass, John B. "A Survey of Native Middle American Pictorial Manuscripts." In *Handbook of Middle American Indians*, edited by Robert Wauchope and Howard Cline, vol. 14, pp. 3–80. Austin, Tex., 1975.

Glass, John B., in collaboration with Donald Robertson. "A Census of Native Middle American Pictorial Manuscripts." In *Handbook of Middle American Indians*, edited by Robert Wauchope and Howard Cline, vol. 14, pp. 81–252. Austin, Tex., 1975.

Kubler, George, and Charles Gibson. *The Tovar Calendar: An Illustrated Mexican Manuscript ca. 1585*. New Haven, 1951. Excellent discussion of colonial interest in the Aztec cycle of eighteen monthly feasts; includes a listing of pictorial and textual sources for these feasts.

Mundy, Barbara, E. *The Mapping of New Spain: Indigenous Cartography and the Maps of the Relaciones Geográficas*. Chicago, 1996.

Nicholson, H. B. "Pre-Hispanic Central Mexican Historiography." In *Investigaciones contemporáneos sobre historia de México. Memorias de la tercera reunión de historiadores mexicanos y norteamericanos, Oaxtepec, Morelos, 4–7 de noviembre de 1969*, pp. 38–81. Mexico City, 1971.

Robertson, Donald. *Mexican Manuscript Painting of the Early Colonial Period*. New Haven, 1959.

ELIZABETH H. BOONE

CENTRAL MEXICO. There are ongoing debates concerning when the first human group colonized Central Mexico.

Hunters and Gatherers and the Development of Sedentism. Even though archaeology has not yet disclosed firm evidence, artifacts such as those found in Tlapacoya, México (21,700 ± 500 years BP) and Caulapan, Puebla (21,850 ± 850 years BP) seem to indicate that, as early as 20,000 years ago, hunter-gatherers were exploiting diverse ecological zones in the Central Highlands. The presence of crude lithic artifacts suggests their elementary technological level. At Tlapacoya, an archaeologically well-documented site in the Central Highlands, subsistence of humans based on hunting and gathering in the late Pleistocene period is inferred from the remains of the three hearths filled with ashes and associated with bones of extinct animal species, in conjunction with lithic artifacts made by percussion techniques, principally choppers, end scrapers, and side scrapers, as well as obsidian flakes and crude blades.

Firmer evidence for the presence of early human groups whose life was based essentially on seasonal transhumance (moving to follow the availability of animal and plant resources) was obtained from a series of sites such as San Bartolo Atepehuacan (Mexico City), La Cueva del Tecolote (Hidalgo), San Juan Chaucing (Tlaxcala), and El Riego, as well as the Coxcatlán caves of the Tehuacán Valley, Puebla. The lithic assemblages, composed of projectile points (Clovis and Folsom) and other points, indicate that their subsistence activities depend increasingly on hunting small game and collecting wild plants. Hunting in this region had a different emphasis than in the North American Great Plains; in Mesoamerica big-game hunting occurred to some degree, but it never constituted a primary food-procuring activity and ceased to be practiced by the end of the Pleistocene.

Grinding stones and mortars manufactured by pressure flaking and abrasion, and artifacts made with plant fibers—nets, bags, and ropes—together with botanical and faunal remains and human feces, have been recovered from El Riego, Aveja, and Coxcatlán caves in the Tehuacán Valley, El Tecolote Cave (Hidalgo), and Santa Isabel Iztapan (México); this evidence suggests that incipient plant domestication was occurring around 9,000 years ago. The first domesticated plants identified in the archaeological records were a type of squash, chili peppers, and avocados, corresponding to the El Riego phase in the Tehuacán Valley. These domesticated plants nonetheless had very minor importance in the diet of those early populations. Botanical evidence implies that the subsistence economy still depended strongly on the gathering of wild plants, while the zoological remains indicate that the procurement of medium-sized and small animals for food gradually diminished in importance.

During this early stage of history, the process of social evolution was extremely slow. For thousands of years, people lived in precarious conditions, selecting caves and rock shelters as well as open areas for habitation sites. The basic social organization was probably that of the band. When food resources were scarce and survival problematic, these early hunters and gathers separated into small social units, basically constituted of single families, a type of social organization Richard S. Mac-Neish has termed a "microband." Their presence is represented by campsites with a short, seasonal occupation. During optimum conditions of abundant food resources, these microbands reorganized temporarily into "macrobands," where several families aggregated into a larger social unit. This social flexibility of fissioning and regrouping in response to environmental conditions was probably the essential characteristic of the early human groups who colonized the region.

At this level of social evolutionary development, transhumance was the basic human mobility pattern. There were exceptions, as in the case of lacustrine environments, exemplified by the Zohapilco-Tlapacoya site on the lakeshore of Chalco-Xochimilco, México. The ecological conditions of this site provided people with seasonally diverse subsistence resources which allowed them to remain there for much longer periods.

Plant Domestication, Incipient Agriculture, and Full Sedentism. Nomadic life was gradually transformed into semi-sedentism. One of the primary factors that initiated this process was the domestication of plants such as squash, chili peppers, and amaranth, and especially the appearance of primitive maize, the staple grain which is considered the mother of Mesoamerican civilization. In fact, the close relationship between human groups and their plants constituted the essence of Central Mexican cultures.

Nascent agriculture required people to stay longer in one place. At this stage, the importance of domesticates in the subsistence economy was still inferior to that of wild foods.

The technological base of these early agriculturists does not show radical changes. Lithic artifacts were still widely used, though objects of smaller size and better finish quality predominated. Artifacts made of bone and other perishable materials were undoubtedly also utilized. The material culture of these early semi-sedentary people was frugal and limited, but the presence of abundant body ornaments and the nature of burials suggest that they engaged in ritual practices.

Slowly but steadily, productive economy based on agriculture gained an increasingly more dominant place in subsistence activities. People experimented by trial and error in plant manipulation and gained better knowledge of plant biology, as well as an increasing variety of more productive cultivated plants, and the importance of agriculture as a source of daily foodstuffs increased concomitantly. By 3000 BCE, more than one-fifth of the dietary base was provided by domesticates, while meat consumption decreased. This new form of subsistence economy, in conjunction with other factors, fueled social evolution from the migratory band to the sedentary village.

One technological innovation intimately related to sedentism is the invention of pottery. The earliest evidence of ceramics in the Central Highlands, found in the Tehuacán Valley, was dated at around 2300 BCE. This pottery was made crudely and was similar to the earliest pottery of Mesoamerica, the Pox pottery found at Puerto Marquéz, Acapulco.

During the long movement toward the establishment of sedentary life, people began to use more open areas for habitation, though they were still using caves and rock shelters as well. They constructed small semi-subterranean houses of oval form, such as one in the Tehuacán Valley that has been dated around 3000 BCE.

Villages, Civic-Religious Centers, and Social Complexity. By 2500 BCE, some groups in the Basin of Mexico, such as the people settled at Zohapilco, developed sedentary agricultural communities. Naturally, they complemented their subsistence with other products, especially lacustrine resources, obtained by hunting, gathering, and fishing. The establishment of fully sedentary communities, the gradual preponderance of agriculture over other subsistence activities, better storage systems, technological innovations, population growth, and increasing long-distance exchange are some of the principal factors that stimulated the process of regional integration and political centralization—in other words, social evolution. Each region, however, took its own path toward the emergence of a heterogeneous and non-egalitarian society.

In the context of early hierarchical society, the Olmec phenomenon merits special attention. Although there are still many unresolved questions regarding the evolution of the Olmec and related cultures in Mesoamerica, there is consensus that the Olmec were one of the oldest complex societies with a clear presence of elite and ruling groups, as well as other specialists. Most of the Central Highlands was incorporated in the Olmec cultural sphere, but this does not imply the establishment of Olmec colonies in this region. The wide spread of Olmec cultural traits can be explained by extensive social, political, and economic networks among the nuclear Olmec area and Central Highlands communities which adopted Olmec traits but modified them according to their own needs.

The Olmec phenomenon reached the different parts of Central Highlands at different times; for example, the Puebla-Tlaxcala area manifested Olmec traits earlier than other areas. During this period, corresponding to the Early Formative, the Basin of Mexico and the Toluca Valley were still functioning as marginal areas, though Olmec influence is clearly detectable. In Morelos, some sites show the presence of Olmec elements during the Early Formative, but in places like Chalcatzingo (Morelos), the height of Olmec impact occurred later, after 700 BCE. Other important sites displaying Olmec influence are Las Bocas, Tlatilco, Coapexco, Zohapilco-Tlapacoya, and Calixtlahuaca.

Olmec influences are especially manifest in a distinctive ceramic style consisting of exotic bottle forms, flat-bottomed or slightly concave-bottomed plates of whiteware, black vessels, white-rimmed blackware, and red-on-white ware. These are decorated with white or red painting, resist painting, and incised, excised, or rocker-stamped motifs. In addition, there are hollow ceramic dolls with characteristic baby faces, clay figurines which suggest fertility rituals, masks, stone sculpture with Olmec iconography, jade and obsidian objects, hematite mirrors, and other objects. Many of these articles were obtained by elites and politico-religious leaders through long-distance exchange. This differential access to—and control of—specific nonlocal resources legitimized their social status and political power.

Population increased steadily during the Early and Middle Formative. Settlement patterns start to show hierarchical distinctions. Though the majority of sites are scattered hamlets and small villages, some—like Cuicuilco and Chalcatzingo—became regional centers. The locations of some settlements, such as Terremote-Tlaltenco and Ticomán, suggests that they specialized in particular activities.

In contrast, other regions—such as Tula, the Toluca Valley, and adjacent areas—played a marginal role. The differences among the settlements were based more on size than on internal complexity, such as the presence of public and monumental architecture. Nevertheless, in the Toluca Valley in this early stage of social development, the high-altitude zone (even above 2,800 meters) was colonized by early settlers, implying that their subsistence activity was still strongly complemented by gathering, fishing, and hunting.

Studies of demographic composition, based principally on mortuary practices, show increasing differentiation between groups. Non-egalitarian societies were established; the upper sector was an elite group who engaged in religious as well as secular activities and who controlled and manipulated ideology, as in the Olmec religion. This constituted one of the central forces that stimulated integration among the regions of Mesoamerica, as well as social transformation. Below the elites, there were craftsmen, including some full-time specialists. The base of the society was the low-status population of peasants. Representations of the fire god, Huehueteotl, and of antecedents of Tlaloc and Xipe in Cuicuilco—the deities who would become the central figures of Mesoamerican cosmology—suggest that religion had evolved into an institutional force.

The development of a productive economy based on maize agriculture is worth special mention. By the Middle Formative, there is firm archaeological evidence that indicate the practice of irrigation and the construction of terraces in the regions of Tehuacán and Morelos. These technological innovations permitted better control of cultivated plants and increased agricultural productivity.

These early Mesoamerican societies evolved steadily during the subsequent period. Some centers kept growing and produced monumental civic-religious architectures, as in Tlapacoya and Cuicuilco in the south of the Basin of Mexico, and probably Cholula in Puebla. Other centers, such as Chalcatzingo, declined. The causes of this process were multiple, and distinct in each case. Cuicuilco, for example, was privileged by its strategic location, which allowed it to control exchange routes between the Basin of Mexico and Morelos, and by its favorable environmental conditions, which permitted the inhabitants to exploit not only the fertile soil but also lacustrine and forest resources.

States Society and Urbanism: Teotihuacan and Other Centers. Toward the end of Formative, around the beginning of the Christian era, hierarchical differentiation among settlements became more defined, population increased, and the regional panorama of the Central Highlands became more complex. Urbanism was taking definite form in the Basin of Mexico, a region which became increasingly important in the history of Mesoamerica, while other regions of the Central Highlands (with the probable exception of Puebla-Tlaxcala) moved more slowly toward social complexity. Two representative sites exhibit accelerated urbanization: Cuicuilco in the south of the Basin of Mexico, which was probably the first civic-religious center of the Late Formative period, with a series of monumental buildings; and Teotihuacan, which was growing rapidly in the northeast of the same region. These two centers were functioning as the focal points of the Basin of Mexico, in that not only was the population of the region concentrated in them but also the major manifestations of social complexity.

Cuicuilco was abandoned around the first century CE.

The eruption of the Xitle volcano was probably one of the many causes that truncated this first manifestation of the urban process in the southern Basin of Mexico. With the decline of Cuicuilco, the south lost its dominant position, and the political organization of the Basin suffered a radical change; Teotihuacan survived to evolve into Central Mexico's only supraregional center.

Of the many possible factors that made Teotihuacan the most powerful pan-Mesoamerican political system in the following centuries, we may mention the following: political and social organization able to control a large labor force; efficient control of the circulation and distribution of certain natural resources and manufactured products, such as the obsidian of Otumba and Sierra de las Navajas, and Thin Orange pottery; its strategic location on the natural corridor which connected the Basin of Mexico with eastern and southeastern Mesoamerica; direct access to springs and to the lacustrine environment of Texcoco; and abundant resources for construction, such as pyroclastic material (*tezontle*), basalt, and tufa.

By the Tzacualli (50 BCE–150 CE) and Miccaotli (150–200 CE) phases, Teotihuacan represented the first full-scale urbanism and mature state society in Mesoamerica. The city was laid out with a north–south orientation and was planned with an orthogonal grid in which the Street of the Dead was the central north–south axis. The urban process advanced, parallel to the increasing domination of Teotihuacan during the Classic period. By the Tlamimilolpa phase (200–400 CE), Teotihuacan had reached its maximum surface area of 22.5 square kilometers and completed the construction of its main public structures. Along with the Street of the Dead, there were plazas, palaces, elite residences, major pyramids like those of the Sun and the Moon, Quetzalcoatl, and Ciudadela, markets, and large workshops. Other urban elements included more than two thousand apartment compounds, waterways, a grid system of streets, potable water, and a drainage system.

During the Xolalpan phase (400–600 CE), Teotihuacan reached its apogee. The city absorbed a great proportion of the population of the Basin. This growth accompanied an increasing disparity between the center and the rural settlements in the region.

The supraregional scale of the Teotihuacan system, including its huge urban population, required a well-structured sociopolitical organization, in which religion and ideology as well as the secular bureaucracy played important roles. Teotihuacan was capable of sustaining its direct control over the Basin of Mexico and adjacent regions in order to procure basic natural resources and probably grain. It also developed an efficient system of controlling the long-distance exchange network, through which its people distributed products manufactured in the urban center and obtained luxury materials from other Mesoamerican areas. Teotihuacan thus incorporated the vast region of Mesoamerica.

In the political sphere, the state maintained the status quo through complex interactions. With some regions, such as the Maya area, Teotihuacan established political alliances. With others—the Toluca Valley (Azcapotzaltongo) to the west, the Tula region to the north (Chingú), or Veracruz (Matacapan)—which lay far beyond its symbiotic regions, Teotihuacan secured its domain by imposing colonies. These centers probably controlled by Teotihuacan collected tribute, extracted natural resources, and manufactured products on behalf of the metropolis. With still other regions, interaction was via long-distance exchange.

At the time of its apogee, Teotihuacan had developed a complex state society with hierarchically structured, heterogeneous classes. Some were dedicated to the subsistence economy, while others were craft specialists. The society was ruled by the elite, whose main activities were religion, politics, warfare, and the administration of long-distance trade. There is no consensus regarding the ethnic affiliation of its core population, but the urban center was inhabited by various ethnic groups from different regions of Mesoamerica, as in the Oaxaca "barrio."

The direct or indirect domination and influence of this powerful state are evident in archaeological material, including ceramics, lithics, architecture, settlement patterns, and mortuary practices. Certain ceramics—such as cloisonné polychrome, Thin Orange, and Copa wares—were exported directly from the urban center; others were imitated by distant communities. The pattern of city planning and orientation, as well as the architectural style Teotihuacan had established, were copied by other centers in the Highlands of Mexico. Figurines and representations of deities like Tlaloc and Huehueteotl also suggest the strong influence of Teotihuacan.

Teotihuacan's Relations in the Central Highlands. With a few likely exceptions like Cholula, no center comparable to Teotihuacan in scale and complexity had developed during the Classic in the Central Highlands. The entire region in effect constituted a symbiotic zone for this metropolis. To the south in Morelos, especially in its eastern portion, Teotihuacan influence provoked changes in regional population organization; the San Ignacio site was functioning as the only center in this portion of the valley.

To the west of the Basin was the Toluca Valley, where during the Terminal Formative and the Early Classic period settlement patterns register a clear population decrease. In subsequent periods this tendency was reversed, presenting a definite population movement for recolonization of the region. This trend accelerated steadily until the collapse of Teotihuacan. Many new sites were founded, especially in the lower part of the valley.

This basic settlement tendency continued without radical change from at least the Middle Formative, when the southern half of the valley, including the central area around the present city of Toluca, became the demographic high-density zone, probably because of its favorable environment. From a regional perspective, the settlement pattern had a predominantly rural character in which the majority of sites are small and most of the population was probably dispersed.

During the Middle and Late Classic period, some sites had grown into regional centers which controlled neighboring populations. These centers of minor scale, with little public architecture, were situated in strategic positions and controlled the circulation of certain local and exotic products, but they also established strong relationships with Teotihuacan. A similar situation is evident in other parts of Central Mexico, including the Valley of Puebla-Tlaxcala and the Tula region, where Teotihuacan apparently controlled important limestone sources.

Decline of Teotihuacan and Political Fragmentation. The process which led to Teotihuacan's demise probably started when this supraregional center was still at its height. The factors and causes were many and complex; some were provoked by internal crises, while others originated in external problems, such as invasion of groups from the north, notably the Otomí. An event that is characterized by many archaeologists as the collapse of the Classic world was the ecological devastation caused by both human activities and climatic changes, which led to agricultural crop failures. Long-distance exchange networks were obstructed by newly developed city-states such as Xochicalco.

With the disintegration of the political and economic system led by Teotihuacan, a new historical stage began. During this transitional period, the Epiclassic (650/750–900/950 CE), some of the main characteristics of the Postclassic period germinated. The effects can be observed not only in the Central Mexican Plateau but also in other Mesoamerican regions with which Teotihuacan had established strong relationships.

One of the most conspicuous aspects of the end of Teotihuacan is a change in settlement patterns. The city apparently still functioned as the largest center of the Basin of Mexico even after the destruction of the main sections of the urban center and the loss of four-fifths of the estimated peak population—a decline at its peak from 150,000 people to about 30,000. This dramatic reduction corresponded to a massive centrifugal population movement from Teotihuacan toward more sparsely populated areas in the Basin. This demographic reorganization might explain the sudden resurgence of sites in the eastern portion of the Basin, especially in Tetzcoco and Chalco, while the western portion around the Guadalupe range and Azcapotzalco was still a focal area with a major concentration of settlements.

From the regional point of view, in spite of these changes, the Basin kept its basic settlement pattern, implying a degree of continuity in regional organization from the Classic to the Epiclassic. In adjacent regions such as Toluca, Morelos, Puebla-Tlaxcala, and Tula, a strong increase of settlements occurred in the Epiclassic. This has been attributed principally to a massive population dispersal into these regions from Teotihuacan.

Another aspect of the Epiclassic settlement configuration in the Central Highlands was political fragmentation. There was no major center like Teotihuacan; instead, there were discrete settlement clusters with a certain degree of autonomy, separated by almost uninhabited zones which functioned as frontiers. These groups, roughly similar in population, were clustered around an administrative center of the same level of hierarchy. Naturally, some of these centers grew to the detriment of others: Cacaxtla and Xochitécatl in Tlazcala, Xochicalco in Morelos, Teotenango in the Toluca Valley, Azcapotzalco and Portezuelo, Xico, and some other sites in the Basin of Mexico.

The post-Teotihuacan period was characterized by the appearance of a ceramic complex typified by red-on-brown vessels, referred to as the Coyotlatelco complex. Regarding its origin, opinion is divided: some argue that this ceramic complex originated in the northern or western periphery of Mesoamerica; others, without denying that certain elements of this pottery seem to have arisen in those marginal regions, view Coyotlatelco as a ceramic complex from somewhere in the Basin of Mexico, probably Teotihuacan. Some archaeologists consider that the transition between the Classic and the Epiclassic was a rather sharp break, while others posit a more gradual change. In either case, the Coyotlatelco complex spread quickly in most parts of the Central Plateau, especially in areas which had established a close relationship with Teotihuacan, such as the Tula area and the Toluca Valley, and to a lesser extent in Puebla-Tlaxcala, eastern Morelos, and the Bravo Valley. Western Morelos, especially around Xochicalco and the northwestern state of Mexico, had developed its own Epiclassic cultures.

Tula and a New Political Organization. Some regional centers, such as Xochicalco, declined shortly after the Epiclassic. Others—Azcapotzalco, Cerro Portezuelo, and Tlalpizahua in the Basin of Mexico, Tula in Hidalgo, and Teotenango in the Toluca Valley—continued their trends of expansion during the Early Postclassic period. By this time, historical processes present great complexity. Indeed, our understanding of them can be confused by indiscriminate use of information available from written documents.

Tula (950–1000/1200 CE) and Cholula were two major centers in the Central Plateau. This newly developed historical setting is important to understanding social and political processes in the Central Highlands, and especially to the Postclassic in the Basin of Mexico. At its apogee, urban Tula covered about 16 square kilometers and had about 60,000 inhabitants, of whom the majority were non-food producers and specialized craftsmen. It has been suggested that this urban center controlled the circulation of certain critical resources such as obsidian and of ceramics including Plumbate ware from southern Mesoamerica and Fine Orange pottery from the Gulf Coast. Tula differed from other major centers in the Central Highlands in ways that contributed to its sudden collapse after a considerably short span of explosive growth.

The development of Tula as the dominant center in the northwestern Central Plateau was an important historical event. Tula established the militaristic political system that would characterize Late Postclassic society. The warlike tendencies that were the essence of Toltec society were manifested in the iconography of the *coatepantli*—decorated with jaguars and coyotes eating human hearts as well as skulls—in the architecture of the *tzompantli* (skull rack), and in pilasters of warrior figures and monumental stone sculptures like the impressive Atlantids.

The dominion of this state is clearly evident in the Basin of Mexico, especially in its northern area and also in sites such as Tlalpizahua in the southeast. The southern half of the Basin was more directly influenced by the enigmatic center of Cholula, east of the Sierra Nevada and a major focal site in the Central Highlands, whose history needs to be better known. In general, the settlement pattern of the Basin implies a strong tendency to ruralization, inferred from its predominance of sites of low hierarchical level and its dispersed population distribution. At about the same time as the Toltec expansion in the Tula region, Teotenango and Calixtlahuaca were growing in the Toluca Valley, transforming the Matlatzinca into a hegemonic state whose political domain extended beyond the upper Lerma Basin.

Hegemonic States and Aztec Predominance. Tula ended rather suddenly around 1156 CE. The causes of its fall included internal ethnic conflicts, climatic changes, and the disintegration of its tributary system and long-distance exchange networks.

Around the twelfth century, massive population movements from the northern periphery, often referred to as the "invasion of the Chichimecs," brought changes in the social and political scene of the Central Highlands. Conflict and political fragmentation characterized the period immediately after the demise of the Toltec state. Then a series of small polities established control over its adjacent settlements. Each of these political units maintained rather clear frontiers, consisting probably of contested zones.

Archaeology alone cannot decipher many fundamental aspects of the highly complex Postclassic phenomenon, nor can ethnohistory. Though the latter offers important and useful information about this unsettled period, using it often contributes to biased interpretations.

The post-Tula political fragmentation is evidenced by a series of modest regional centers which established local tributary systems. Xaltocan, an Otomí polity, controlled the north of the basin; Azcapotzalco—ethnically composed of the Otomí, Matlatzinca, and Nahua—and Tenayuca, a Chichimec center, became important focal points on the western side of Lake Texcoco, while Coatlinchan and Tetzcoco represented the Acolhua of the eastern side. Of these, Azcapotzalco was the leading polity and grew into a powerful hegemony at the end of the fourteenth century. Then Tetzcoco slowly expanded its political power to become the principal rival of Azcapotzalco, a conflict which ended in direct confrontation between them. In the south, the densely settled Chalco-Xochimilco region established small tributary systems controlled by a series of minor regional centers. In this politically fragmented situation, the Mexica were apparently obliged to establish alliances with other important groups in the Basin of Mexico.

Political fragmentation in the Middle Postclassic (or Early Aztec) period is also expressed in ceramic regionalism. In the south, the wide distribution of the Aztec I complex suggests a possible relationship with Cholula, a major center on the eastern side of the Sierra Nevada. Contemporary with the Aztec I complex was Aztec II, distributed mainly in the northern Basin of Mexico. The same phenomenon occurs in the Toluca Valley, where three different ceramic complexes have been identified, indicating a possibly multiethnic population of the hegemonic Matlatzinca, the Otomí, and the Mazahua.

In the Basin of Mexico, the Mexica founded their capital on the small island of Tenochtitlan, and in its center they built the temples of Huitzilopochtli and Tlaloc, as well as other religious structures. Later, a segment of the Mexica moved to an adjacent island, establishing their capital, Mexico-Tlatelolco. For some decades, this and Mexico-Tenochtitlan existed as independent political entities. In 1430 CE, the Mexica and their allies, the Acolhua of Texcoco and Tlacopan, defeated the Tepaneca of Azcapotzalco and founded the Triple Alliance, a suprastatal hegemonic organization which functioned essentially for the benefit of Tenochtitlan. The independence of the two adjacent cities ended in 1473, when Tenochtitlan conquered Tlatelolco. After that, these two centers fused to become Tenochtitlan-Tlatelolco, which was connected to the mainland by a series of causeways. At its height, the city was not only the most densely populated center (150,000 to 200,000 inhabitants) of Mesoamerica but also the most complex and perfectly planned urban metropolis, with a sophisticated hydraulic infrastructure.

By this time, the Late Postclassic states were tightly structured by hierarchically differentiated social classes. Even though population in the Basin of Mexico experienced extraordinary increase, rising to an estimated one million, these states were well integrated politically and economically. With the development of a highly complex society, the number of non-producers also increased, especially in urban centers like Tenochtitlan, where the majority of the population was comprised of non-agriculturists.

The economic base for sustaining the huge regional population with its increasing number of elites and other non-food-producing groups was solidly founded on agriculture, the primary economic activity of majority of the inhabitants of the smaller centers. A remarkable Late Postclassic economic innovation was the transformation of lakeshore alluvium and lakebed, which previously had little use, into intensively productive agricultural land by means of *chinampa* (drained field) and other hydraulic technology. The forceful extraction of tribute and the control of long-distance trade networks also helped to guarantee the economic supremacy of the hegemonic state.

To ensure preeminence, the Triple Alliance incorporated neighboring states which were still reluctant to form part of the system, but without destroying their basic political and social structures. The presence of the Aztec III ceramic complex, figurines, stone sculptures, architectural style, and lithic artifacts implies that the Triple Alliance penetrated all dimensions of the society of that time. Tenochtitlan left firm evidence of its abundant material culture, not only in principal sites such as Teotenango, Calixtlahuaca, Malinalco, Tepoztlan, Tula, and many other centers, but also in rural contexts.

The Triple Alliance also undertook expansionist enterprises. The history of the Central Highlands testifies to the profound impact of this aggressive policy. The conquered vast regions of Mesoamerica—Central Mexico, Oaxaca, the Gulf Coast, and Huasteca, to name but a few. Their political and economical domain soon expanded over the territory of ancient Mexico from coast to coast, with few exceptions. One region that resisted the constant hostility of the Mexica was Tlaxcala. Allied with Cholula and Huexotzingo, the Tlaxcalans succeeded in maintaining some autonomy from the Mexica, but otherwise, the Triple Alliance controlled most of the Central Highlands.

The Mexica Empire succumbed to the Spanish conquerors in 1521. With this ended the power and the glory of the state that dominated the vast region of Mesoamerica for centuries.

BIBLIOGRAPHY

Adams, Richard E. W. *Prehistoric Mesoamerica*. Norman, Okla., 1991. Excellent synthesis of the history of Mesoamerica.

Armillas, Pedro. "Gardens on Swamps." *Science* 174 (1971), 635–661. Discussion of *chinampa* agriculture in the Basin of Mexico.

Diehl, Richard A. *Tula: The Toltec Capital of Ancient Mexico*. London, 1983. Synthesis of the evolution of Tula and Toltecs.

Diehl, Richard A., and Janet Catherine Berlo, eds. *Mesoamerica after the Decline of Teotihuacan A.D. 700–900*. Washington, D.C., 1989. Series of articles on the decline of Teotihuacan and post-Teotihuacan phenomenon seen from different regions of the Central Plateau.

Foncerrada de Molina, Marta. *Cacaxtla: La iconografía de los Olmecas-Xicalanca*. Mexico City, 1993. Stylistic and iconographic analysis of the murals of Cacaxtla, Tlaxcala.

García Cook, Angel. *El desarrollo cultural en el norte del Valle Poblano-Tlaxcalteca: Inferencia de una secuencia cultural, espacial y temporalmente establecida*. Mexico City, 1976. Comprehensive overview of settlement patterns and cultural history of the northern valley of Puebla-Tlaxcala.

Grove, David C. *Chalcatzingo: Excavations on the Olmec Frontier*. London, 1984. Synthesis of Chalcatzingo, one of the important Olmec sites in the highlands of Mexico.

Hassig, Ross. *Aztec Warfare: Imperial Expansion and Political Control*. Norman, Okla., 1988. Important work which explains the processes of Aztec expansion.

Hirth, Kenneth. "Xochicalo: Urban Growth and State Formation in Central Mexico." *Science* 225 (1984), 579–586. Synthetic article which presents auther's interpretation of the evolution of Xochicalco, Morelos.

Jiménez Moreno, Wigberto. "Síntesis de la historia pretolteca de Mesoamérica." In *Esplendor del México antiguo*, edited by Carmen Cook de Leonard, vol. 1, pp. 1019–1108. Mexico City, 1959. Introduces the term "Epiclassic" to denote the transitional period between the Classic and Postclassic.

López Austin, Alfredo. "Organización política en el Altiplano Central de México durante el Posclásico." In *Mesoamérica y el Centro de México*, edited by Jesús Monjarrás-Ruiz, et al., pp. 197–234, Mexico City, 1985. Excellent overview of the political processes which characterized the Central Highlands of México during the Postclassic horizon.

Lorenzo, José Luis, and Lorena Mirambell, eds. *Tlapacoya: 35,000 años de historia del lago de Chalco*. Mexico City, 1986. Useful information on the early hunters and gatherers of the Basin of Mexico.

MacNeish, Richard S., ed. *The Prehistory of the Tehuacan Valley*. Vol. 3, *Ceramincs* Austin, Tex., 1970. Excellent ceramic analysis of the Tehuacán Valley, Puebla.

MacNeish, Richard S., ed. *The Prehistory of the Tehuacan Valley*. Vol. 4, *Excavations and Reconnaissance*. Austin, 1972. Basic information on settlement patterns in the Tehuacán Valley.

Manzanilla, Linda Rosa. "La zona del Altiplano Central en el Clásico." In *Historia antigua de México*, edited by L. R. Manzanilla and Leonardo López Luján, vol. 2, pp. 139–173. Mexico City, 1994. Synthesis of the cultural history of the Classic horizon in the Central Highlands.

Millon, René. "Teotihuacan: City, State, and Civilization." In *Supplement to the Handbook of Middle American Indians*, edited by Victoria R. Bricker and Jeremy A. Sabloff, vol. 1, pp. 198–243. Austin, Tex., 1981. Excellent overview and description.

Niederberger, Christine. *Paléopaysages et archéologie pré-urbaine du Bassin de México*. Mexico City, 1987. Synthesis of social and cultural evolution of early human groups settled in the Basin of Mexico.

Piña Chan, Román, ed. *Teotenango: El antiguo lugar de la muralla: Memoria de las excavaciones arqueológicas*. 2 vols. Mexico City, 1975. Basic information on Teotenango, based on excavation reports and analyses of archaeological materials.

Sanders, William T., Jeffery R. Parsons, and Robert S. Santley. *The Basin of Mexico: Ecological Processes in the Evolution of Civilization*. New York, 1979. Basic reference book on archaeology on the Basin of Mexico, which explains the evolutionary processes from band to state.

Serra Puche, Mari Carmen. *Xochitecatl*. Tlaxcala, 1998. Comprehensive overview of Xochitecatl, an important Epiclassic site of Tlaxcala.

Sugiura Yamamoto, Yoko. "Desarrollo histórico en el Valle de Toluca antes de la conquista española: Proceso de conformación pluriétnica." In *Estudio de cultura Otopame*, vol. 1, pp. 99–122. Mexico City, 1998. Comprehensive outline of cultural history and the process of multiethnic formation in the Valley of Toluca.

Weaver Porter, Muriel. *The Aztecs, Maya and Their Predecessors: Archaeology of Mesoamerica*. 3rd ed. New York, 1993. Excellent, comprehensive synthesis of the pre-Hispanic history of Mesoamerica.

YOKO SUGIURA YAMAMOTO

CEREMONIAL CENTERS. Throughout the complex and diverse historical developments of Mesoamerican cultures, ceremonial centers have served to organize and renew social and symbolic life. From the earliest signs of burial practices in "Archaic" traditions in Mesoamerica (8650 BCE), through the rise of urban centers and the formation of imperial strategies, and up to the present search for Aztlan among Mexican Americans, humankind has struggled to discover, construct, and renew places of cosmological orientation and social stability. Whether as group burials, dance courts, home altars, sweatbaths, *altepetl*, pyramid mounds, hieroglyphic stairways, capital cities, cathedrals, or pilgrimage sites, these ceremonial centers demonstrate the human need for *orientatio*, the participation in places that carry the prestige of the creation and the capacity to organize and renew the cosmos.

Ceremonial centers, small and large, represent this dual sense of orientation in their morphology and material substance, dynamics of exchange, and cosmic symbolism expressed in stone, color, and other media. They serve as ritual theaters for the acting out of cherished cosmological, ethical, and political ideas and patterns. In elaborate examples associated with Maya, Aztec, Mixtec, and Zapotec cities, with Christian churches, and with nationalist political buildings, the various ceremonial structures or precincts may be imprinted with symbols, statues, faces, or events that reveal the prestige of a people or place in social and geographical space as well as their religious commitment to the earth (agriculture, mining,

herding) and its spirits, and to the sky (celestial bodies, weather, astronomy) and its gods.

To understand the extraordinary social and symbolic power of many Mesoamerican ceremonial centers, it is important to recall that Mesoamerica was one of the seven areas of primary urban generation—that is, the cultures where human beings managed the great transformation from pre-urban to urban society (the others are China, Mesopotamia, Egypt, the Indus Valley, Nigeria, and Peru). In those parts of Mesoamerica where urban centers came to direct and sometimes dominate society at large, the entire ecological complex of agriculture, population, trade, and social hierarchy was regulated by monumental ceremonial centers which contained a multitude of buildings such as temples, markets, platform mounds, pyramids, palaces, stelae, terraces, and ballcourts. These sites, whether monumental or local, had centripetal and centrifugal powers that functioned together to achieve a social sense of integration and balance. On the one hand, these places functioned as magnets attracting people, gods, goods, and priestly and state authority into their precincts. Once within these cosmological and dramatic environments, people, objects, and ideas underwent processes that changed their values and potentials either subtly or dramatically. Typically, the ceremonial center would disperse its participants and objects back out into the wider society as carriers of the prestige and changes generated from the encounters at the center of the world.

During the past fifteen years, there has been considerable debate about the extent of "ceremonial" control over the complex systems of political and economic developments in Mesoamerican settlements. Concerned with understanding the evolution and interaction of sacred cities and secular systems, scholars have used the alternate terms of "organizational centers," "galactic polities," and "regal-ritual centers" in their attempts to elucidate the different types of urban settlements that dominated parts of Mesoamerica. One advance appears in the work of William Fash, whose attention to the dynamics among market, secular, and ritual systems led him to employ the term "civic-ceremonial centers." The most persuasive model may still be Paul Wheatley's discussion of the nature of the ceremonial center, wherein he shows that monumental ceremonial centers operating with a predominantly religious focus subsumed a growing number of secular functions and social activities under a religious cosmology and ceremonial lifestyle. The evidence from Mesoamerica shows that, especially at Copán, Palenque, Monte Albán, Mitla, Yaxchilán, Teotihuacan, Tula, and scores of others, urban ceremonial precincts became the key instruments for the creation of political, economic, sacred, and social space. The Maya stelae, Zapotec palaces, Toltec ballcourts, Mixtec stonework, and Aztec sac-

The ceremonial center of Bonampak. The covered building (*top right*) contains the famous murals. *Courtesy of Visual Resources Collection, The University of Texas at Austin. Ferguson Collection.*

rificial stones were constructed and used as symbols of cosmic, social, and moral order which both reflected and influenced secular activities. It was the ceremonial style of political leadership and economic exchange that infused the redistributive institutions with sanctified prestige and organizational efficacy. In my terms, these centers were places of world making, world centering, and world renewing. The sacred city itself thus became a monumental ceremonial center par excellence.

How Olmecs "Remade" the World. An early example of monumentalizing a ceremonial center that remade the natural world into a civic-ceremonial precinct is found in the Olmec culture, where the earth was reshaped as a means of religious expression and political authority. The Olmec media for symbolic and political expression were jade, basalt, clay, and earth itself in the forms of caves, hills, and mounds like the one used at the site of La Venta, where jaguar motifs and giant heads sculpted in stone embroider a small, swampy, stoneless island. In the heart of this carefully planned site stands one of Mesoamerica's first monumental ceremonial centers, which contains altars, a courtyard, rectangular structures, and a great pyramid in the form of a fluted, cone-shaped natural structure 140 meters (420 feet) in diameter and 30 meters (100 feet) high. Its outer surface of alternating rises and depressions gives it the appearance of a volcano. Nearby, archaeologists found the buried remains of two youths, heavily covered with thick cinnabar pigment and accompanied by offerings of jade beads and stingray

spines. This ceremonious concern for the dead buried near the heart of a sacred precinct shows a special relation between certain human groups and the *axis mundi*. A number of other caches containing jade, jaguar mosaics, and pierced concave mirrors made of iron ore were excavated at La Venta, evidence of the elaborate artwork, long-distance transportation of materials, and religious commitments embedded in the ceremonial center.

How Palenque "Centered" the World. An impressive example of the centripetal powers of ceremonial centers is found in the Maya site of Palenque, where the rulers, deeply concerned with legitimizing their family trees, constructed a symbolic panorama of cosmic trees within their building program. The rich images and clusters of symbols in Maya art show that they shared an agricultural mentality; that is, they were profoundly committed to the continual regeneration of the plant and animal world as a cosmic analogy to their political world. This mentality sprang from the insight that agriculture and hunting are not just profane skills but deal with sacred powers and life forces that dwell in the seeds, furrows, rain, animals, and sunshine. The tense and dramatic cosmic cycles that enfold civic and ceremonial life became the models for political order and provided the supreme emblems of daily life. One such emblem, an example of world centering, was the elaborately carved cosmic tree found in the famous Tomb of Pacal and in the series of cosmic trees that adorn the Temple of the Foliated Cross and the Temple of the Cross. The prodigious symbols of *orientatio* associated with these trees leave no doubt that the entire Maya cosmos, with its agricultural, trading, and political programs, was anchored in these temple locations. In the case of Pacal's tomb, the tree emerges out of the earth—the underworld, shown as two gaping skeletal jaws—and extends upward where jeweled dragons represent the heavens. The trunk of the tree is marked with mirror symbols, indicating that it has brilliance and power, or in Maya religion, sacred reproductive energy. The top of the tree has bloodletting bowls outlined with beads of blood, representing ritual-sacrificial practices. A double-headed serpent bar (the ruler) is wrapped around the branches of the world tree, from which emerge fleshed dragon heads with open mouths (the earthly level). This complex symbolizes the dynamic relationship by which the human community works and revolves around the sacred ruler. The work of agriculture, with its intense dependence on rain, irrigation, planting, and sowing, is represented in the central image of the Temple of the Foliated Cross, which is a composite of the four sacred trees associated with the four directions of the universe. The tree is transformed into a flowering corn plant, but instead of producing ears of corn, the plant bears the heads of young males, which rest on the leaves. In Maya thought, the beauty of young males may symbolize the ripe maize, which in turn represents the young male ruler ascending or "sprouting" to the throne.

Places of Political, Economic, and Sacred Renewal. The capacity of ceremonial centers to symbolize and participate in the renewal of civic, political, and ritual institutions appears throughout Mesoamerican history, from pre-Hispanic cultures to contemporary societies. For instance, at the monumental Templo Mayor of Tenochtitlan, archaeologists discovered that the Aztec enlarged the temple seven times, with five extra façades, but always kept intact the basic dual symbolism of the rain god Tlaloc and the tribute/war god Huitzilopochtli. As Eduardo Matos Moctezuma has shown, the symbolic and ritual life of this imperial shrine unified the patterns of forced tributary payments from hundreds of communities with the agricultural and hydraulic subsystems of food production. This temple was the site par excellence for the celebration of warfare and the incitement of warriors to leave the capital and endure the vicissitudes of fighting far from home. It was here that the social stratification of warriors, with their complex emblems of rank and valor, was memorialized and legitimated. And it was the site of intense devotions to the vital forces of rain, water, and fertility, and the systems of farming carried out by the masses of Mexica peoples. These rebuildings were part of a decisive imperial program to enlarge the empire, ensure the renewal of agricultural and trading traditions, and revitalize the theological formulations of the priestly elites. In fact, as the studies of the *Codex Mendoza* by Francis Berdan and Patricia Anawalt have shown, there was a parallel growth in the size and ornamentation of the Aztec Templo Mayor and the geographical extensions and magnification of the riches of the empire. The ceremonial center was both a mirror and a generator of political and economic expansion.

Moving into the Colonial period, we find that the entire Christian program of missionization through participation in churches with *atrios*, altars, saints, and vaulted Christian symbolism was based, in part, in the commitment to build a "Nueva España," a new Spain or a renewed Spain in the New World. An effective expression of this program was the efforts of "brick and mortar priests" and others who devoted themselves to building countless parish churches and chapels containing ceremonial altars, confessionals, pulpits, bells, images of saints, and sacristies. These Christian ritual and ceremonial centers became, in the words of William B. Taylor, "mediating points between the congregation of the divine and gathering places for public expression and rites of passage." Baptisms, marriages, masses, confessions, and numerous other rituals took place in and around these sacred pivots, stimulating devotions to cosmic meanings and social ties. These churches and their ritual furniture also had a clear political purpose as "seats of parish priests' authority as magistrates of the sacred in the world" (Taylor, 1996, p. 3). At places like Tepeyac, where the Virgin of Guadalupe appeared to Juan Diego at the site of an Aztec ceremonial center, a new *mestizo* form of Catholic piety, devotion, and ceremonial center was created that contributed to the renewal of both indigenous and imported religious ideas and practices. For almost five centuries, there has been a program of building, rebuilding, and renovating the expanding ceremonial precinct of the Basilica of the Virgin of Guadalupe. The history of this site illustrates the classic patterns of centripetal and centrifugal organization of the wider society. On the one hand, Guadalupe's Christian shrine draws millions of pilgrims every year who deposit their prayers and their money at the many altars, images, and shops. On the other hand, the symbol of Guadalupe has spread throughout Mexico, the United States, and the world as her images appears on banners, medals, murals, motorcycles, and tattoos, and in homes, bars, taxicabs, and churches. And as with all ceremonial centers, the impact of these changes spread to the economic and civic ordering of daily life.

Another Mesoamerican example appears in the more modest Dia de Los Muertos altars and rites. Whether as home altars, cemetery shrines, or public displays in parks, universities, or civic centers, the Day of the Dead sites—a mixture of European and indigenous traditions—depend on a central shrine or installation that attracts people, images, gifts, foods, and eventually the spirits of the dead. These centripetal altars and decorations become the focused sites of ritual activities that include incensing, praying, meditation, and pilgrimage; these ceremonial activities both break the flow of status quo activities and renew social, economic, and spiritual relations between the living and the dead.

The search for the security and renewal of a ceremonial center with primordial prestige is symbolized today in the growing interest among Mexican Americans—especially artists, poets, anthropologists, and college students—in locating the mythical Aztlan and identifying it as one of the "origins" of Chicano culture. Aztlan was the place of seven caves on an island where a patron god spoke to the ancestors in dreams and inspired them to go in search of a new homeland. Many Mexican Americans feel that the loss of ancestral lands, discrimination against Mexican traditions in the United States, and the limitations of classical European intellectual traditions to express their worldview call for the identification of an indigenous Mesoamerican homeland, lineage, and cultural heritage in the southwestern United States. Perhaps these Chicanos, searching for a new orientation, are repeating the ancient quest of the peoples of the *Popol Vuh*, who announced, "Let us go ourselves and search, and we shall see for ourselves, whether there is something to guard our sign." Wandering and feeling that they were without guardians, "they heard news of a city and went there."

BIBLIOGRAPHY
Anawalt, Patricia, and Francis Berdan. *The Codex Mendoza*. Los Angeles, 1995.
Carmack, Robert M., Janine Gasco, and Gary H. Gossen. *The Legacy of Mesoamerica: History and Culture of a Native American Civilization*. Englewood Cliffs, N.J., 1996.
Carrasco, Davíd. *Religions of Mesoamerica: Cosmovision and Ceremonial Centers*. 1998.
Elizondo, Virgilio. *Guadalupe: Mother of the New Creation*. Marynoll, N.Y., 1997.
Fash, William L. *Scribes, Warriors and Kings: The City of Copán and the Ancient Maya*. London, 1993.
Taylor, William B. *Magistrates of the Sacred*. 1996.
Wheatley, Paul. *Pivot of the Four Quarters: A Preliminary Enquiry into the Nature and Origins of the Chinese City*. Chicago, 1968.

DAVÍD CARRASCO

CHAC. *See* Rain Deities.

CHACMOOL, a sculpture of a human figure seated on the ground, with the upper back raised, head turned to a near right angle, legs drawn up to the buttocks, elbows on the ground, and hands holding a vessel, disk, or plate on the stomach where offerings may have been placed or human sacrifices enacted. The term *chacmool* is derived from the name "Chaacmol," which Augustus Le Plongeon in 1875 gave to a sculpture that he and his wife Alice Dixon Le Plongeon excavated within the Temple of the Eagles and Jaguars at Chichén Itzá; he translated *Chaacmol* from Yucatecan Mayan as the "paw swift like thunder." The name, he said, was given by the ancient Maya to a powerful warrior prince who had once ruled the city and was represented in the sculpture. In an article on the archaeological work of Le Plongeon by Stephen Salisbury, Jr., published in 1877 in the *Proceedings of the American Antiquarian Society*, the name Chaacmol was changed to *chacmool* (an archaic Yucatecan Mayan word for the "puma").

The *chacmool* excavated by the Le Plongeons was hidden near the village of Pisté, about 1 kilometer (a half mile) from Chichén Itzá, while they waited for permission from the president of Mexico, Lerdo de Tejada, to ship it to Philadelphia for the Centennial Exposition of 1876. The sculpture was discovered, however, and then paraded with great fanfare into Mérida, the capital of Yucatán. The Yucatecans considered it a great cultural treasure and put it on display, but within a short time Mexico's new president, Porfirio Díaz, recognized its importance and sent an armed military contingent to Mérida to bring it to Mexico City, where it has remained.

*Chacmool*s have been found in Central Mexico and in the Yucatán Peninsula, with the greatest number concentrated at the Toltec archaeological site of Tula in Hidalgo and Chichén Itzá in Yucatán. A *chacmool* excavated from the Aztec Templo Mayor in Mexico City in the early 1980s was found fully painted in several colors. At Tula and Chichén Itzá, a *chacmool* was usually placed in the antechamber of a temple, presumably to receive offerings or for sacrifice. Aztec *chacmool*s exhibit the rain god Tlaloc's iconography, and the one unearthed at the Templo Mayor was found on the side of the Great Temple dedicated to Tlaloc. Maya *chacmool*s also have the Tlaloc characteristics, and Tlaloc iconography is incised on the ear ornaments of the *chacmool* excavated at Chichén Itzá by Augustus and Alice Le Plongeon.

Twelve *chacmool*s have been located at the Toltec city of Tula, fourteen at Maya Chichén Itzá, one without provenience is stylistically Aztec, and two are from the Aztec Templo Mayor in Mexico City. Other *chacmool*s have been found at the archaeological site of Cempoala, in the states of Michoacán and Tlaxcala, and at the Maya site of Quiriguá in Guatemala. A sculpture identified as a Classic period Chalchihuites culture proto-*chacmool* that was excavated at Cerro del Huistle, Huejuquilla el Alto, in the state of Jalisco may indicate that the *chacmool* had its origin in North Central Mexico.

In Central Mexico, no antecedents of the *chacmool*

A polychromed and stuccoed *chacmool* found on the side of the Great Temple of Tenochtitlan. Note the incised ear ornaments typical of Maya *chacmools* dedicated to Tlaloc. (Height: 30 inches; length: 46 inches.) *Courtesy of Museo del Templo Mayor, México, D.F.*

have been located at the important archaeological sites of Teotihuacan, Cacaxla, and Xochicalco, and there are no examples of the sculpture in the surviving manuscripts from Central Mexico. No proto-*chacmool*s have been found in the Maya area; but stylistic similarities to the *chacmool*—the reclining position of a figure in a Classic-period mural at the Maya site Bonampak, the position of "captive" figures in Maya bas reliefs at Classic sites, and the form and function of the Postclassic *chacmool*—have been used to explain the origin for the *chacmool* in the Maya area.

BIBLIOGRAPHY

Desmond, Lawrence Gustave, and Phyllis Mauch Messenger. *A Dream of Maya: Augustus and Alice Le Plongeon in Nineteenth Century Yucatan.* Albuquerque, 1988. Provides an account of the lives, archaeological work, and theories of the Le Plongeons within the context of the developing field of archaeology during the last quarter of the nineteenth century; the excavation of the *chacmool* at Chichén Itzá is described in detail.

Graulich, Michael. "Quelques observations sur les sculptures Mesoamericaines dites 'Chac Mool.'" *Annales Jaarboek* (1984), 51–72. Study of the *chacmool* and its place in Mesoamerican religious practices, including human sacrifice and as an intermediary between man and the gods of rain, water, and fertility.

Hers, Marie-Areti. *Los Toltecas en tierras Chichimecas.* Mexico City, 1989. A chapter is given to a sculpture identified as a proto-*chacmool*, which was uncovered during excavations at Cerro del Huistle, Huejuquilla el Alto, in the state of Jalisco, Mexico; it is placed within the Chalchihuites culture of the Classic period.

Le Plongeon, Augustus. *Queen Móo and the Egyptian Sphinx.* New York, 1896. Considered by the author his most important work, in which he sets forth his evidence that the Maya were the founders of the Egyptian civilization. The *chacmool* is presented as the likeness of Prince Chaacmol, one of the rulers of Chichén Itzá in the Yucatán Peninsula.

Miller, Mary Ellen. "A Re-examination of the Mesoamerican Chacmool." *The Art Bulletin* 67.1 (1985), 7–17. Study of the *chacmool*, based on art historical and archaeological evidence, which gives spatial distribution, stylistic development, religious meaning; it places the origin within the Maya area.

Salisbury, Stephen, Jr. "Dr. Le Plongeon in Yucatan." *Proceedings of the American Antiquarian Society*, 69 (1877), 70–119. This article, based on reports sent to Salisbury by Le Plongeon, was published at the height of Le Plongeon's reputation as an archaeologist, when he had financial support from the American Antiquarian Society; herein, the Le Plongeon name "Chaacmol" was changed to the term *chacmool*.

LAWRENCE G. DESMOND

CHALCATZINGO, a major Formative (Preclassic) period center in the Mexican state of Morelos, and the only site in the Central Highlands with Olmec-like stone monuments. It is the most extensively investigated Formative site in the region, and it provides insights on the emergence of cultural complexity, Formative lifeways, and extraregional interactions there.

Located in the Amatzinac River Valley, the site lies at the base of the two massive granodiorite hills that rise abruptly from the valley's flat landscape. A nearby spring provided its early farming inhabitants with an ample water supply. Initial exploration by Eulalia Guzmán in 1934 described the site and five unusual bas-relief rock carvings. Excavations in 1953 by Román Piña Chan confirmed Chalcatzingo's Formative date and reported additional carvings. Extensive excavations of the ancient village and its domestic and public architecture began in 1972 in a project codirected by David Grove, Jorge Angulo, and Raúl Arana. That research discovered many more stone monuments and defined three major temporal phases in the site's Formative archaeological record: the Amate phase (1500–1100 BCE), the Barranca phase (1100–700 BCE), and the Cantera phase (700–500 BCE).

The initial settlers, at about 1500 BCE, were farmers who grew maize, beans, and squash near their hillslope houses. They had modest buff-colored pottery bowls decorated with red rims. By 1100 BCE, the settlement had become a large village that was the valley's chief center. The pottery used during the late Amate phase is typical of Morelos in general and specifically the Tlatilco site in the western Basin of Mexico: red-on-brown bottles and bowls, and D-2 and K-type clay figurines. Chalcatzingo's regional importance is evidenced by its public architecture, a long earthen platform mound, 2 meters (7 feet) tall, the earliest known example of public architecture in that region. The mound was of such importance that it was maintained, rebuilt, and enlarged several times during the subsequent five hundred years; it is the largest pre-500 BCE platform mound known in highland Central Mexico.

The appearance of new pottery types (white-slipped bowls and jars, and B- and C-type figurines) about 1100 BCE initiated the Barranca phase, during which the local

The ancient Formative site of Chalcatzingo. *Courtesy of Visual Resources Collection, The University of Texas at Austin. Ferguson Collection.*

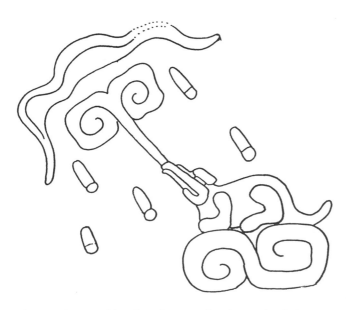

Olmec-style crocodilian breathing wind and rain cloud, from Monument 14, Chalcatzingo. *Drawing courtesy of Karl A. Taube.*

population modified the site's natural hillslopes into a series of broad terraces, perhaps to provide large horizontal agricultural plots and house areas. The Barranca-phase village remained the largest settlement in the valley. Chalcatzingo reached its greatest size and extraregional prominence in the Cantera phase of 700 to 500 BCE, during which its Olmec-like monuments were created. The settlement was dispersed across the hillside terraces. The houses had thatched roofs; front walls of cane that were coated with mud plaster; and back and side walls of adobe bricks. Cooking was done primarily on charcoal braziers made of pottery. Cantera-phase ceramic vessels and figurines reflect an elaboration of Barranca-phase types. Those who died were commonly buried beneath the floors of their houses. Excavations of one Cantera-phase house uncovered thirty-eight burials (almost ten times the average), including some in stone-lined graves, wearing jade jewelry. Such traits distinguish that house from all others and suggest it may have been the residence of the site's leadership.

Thirty-four stone monuments with bas-relief have been recorded at Chalcatzingo. They cluster in two site areas. Those south of the large platform mound were carved on the cliff face and boulders of the Cerro Chalcatzingo, and they express mythico-religious themes. In contrast, the carvings in the northern site area are associated with rectangular stone platforms. They depict individual personages, perhaps village rulers, and they include the earliest carved representation of a woman in Mesoamerican monumental art. Also in the north, situated within a stone-lined patio, is the only Olmec-style throne as yet known outside the Gulf Coast Olmec area.

Chalcatzingo perhaps rose to importance by performing a middleman role in the trade of desired commodities between Central Mexico and centers to the east and south, including Olmec centers. Although the people of Chalcatzingo created Olmec-like monuments, they were not themselves Olmec, since their pottery, figurines, and other objects of daily and ritual use are like those found at other Formative villages in Central Mexico and different from those found in the Olmec realm.

Chalcatzingo declined in prominence and was abandoned about 500 BCE. Minor resettlement occurred during the Late Formative and the Late Classic periods. In the Postclassic period, a small shrine was built on the mountainside near one of the Cantera-phase carvings, perhaps to venerate that ancient monument.

[See also Art and Architecture, article on Pre-Hispanic Period.]

BIBLIOGRAPHY

Grove, David C. *Chalcatzingo: Excavations on the Olmec Frontier.* London and New York, 1984. Highlights the major archaeological discoveries and monuments at Chalcatzingo; discusses the site's possible interactions with Gulf Coast Olmec centers.

Grove, David C., ed. *Ancient Chalcatzingo.* Austin, 1987. Comprehensive archaeological report of twenty-eight chapters, ten appendices, and hundreds of illustrations; provides detailed information and discussions on almost every aspect of the art and archaeology of Chalcatzingo and its external relationships.

Guzmán, Eulalia. "Los relieves de las rocas del Cerro de la Cantera, Jonacatepec, Morelos." *Anales del Museo Nacional de Arqueología, Historia, y Etnografía* 5 (1934), 237–251. Initial report on the discovery of Chalcatzingo and its monuments.

Piña Chan, Román. "Chalcatzingo, Morelos." *Informes* 4, Instituto Nacional de Antropología e Historia. Mexico City, 1955. Report of the first excavations at the site and comments on Chalcatzingo's possible role during the Formative (Preclassic) period.

DAVID C. GROVE

CHALCHIHUITES–ALTA VISTA. The Chalchihuites culture of northwestern Zacatecas and south-central Durango is the best-known Mesoamerican culture of the North Central frontier region. The present knowledge of this culture is essentially the result of forty-five years of research conducted by the late J. Charles Kelley. Kelley distinguished the Chalchihuites area into two contiguous regions centered on the Suchil and Guadiana river basins; differentiation was based on chronology, with the Suchil region's social system developing and peaking during the Classic period. The Suchil regional climax (called the Alta Vista phase) became the base for the Northern Mesoamerican expansion of sedentary villagers into the neighboring central valleys of Durango; from that, the Guadiana regional system developed, subsequently flourishing during the early Postclassic period. Both regional systems played key roles in the cultural dynamics of the northern frontier during their corresponding periods.

The Suchil regional sequence has been defined in two tributaries of the Suchil; the Río Colorado and Río San Antonio valleys, where the earliest Mesoamerican presence is known as the Canutillo phase. The basic Mesoamerican village-and-agriculture complex began there about 2000 BCE and possibly before. The initial wave of Mesoamericanization is viewed as the regional component of the extensive Canutillo-Malpaso horizon that expanded out of Western Mexico into and across much of central (Malpaso Valley) and northwestern Zacatecas.

An important question posed by the Canutillo phase is the process involved in its origin. Was it the result of the rapid colonization of the northern regions by simple *campesino* groups expanding out of the Bajío, western Michoacán, and the Altos de Jalisco regions about 1 CE? Was it the result of the acculturation of local Loma San Gabriel seminomadic groups into simple sedentary Mesoamericans—or a coalescence of both processes? These questions were at the center of Kelley's well-known "soft diffusion" model for the expansion of the northern Mesoamerican frontier.

Radiocarbon dating suggests that by 350 or 400 CE the simple Canutillo village farmers were on their way to developing what later became the most extensive mining industry of Mesoamerica. By 470 CE in the Río Colorado Valley, work was begun on the construction of the ceremonial site of Alta Vista, which was to become the most important and complex site in the Suchil region. Research in the neighboring regions of the Suchil-Chalchihuites culture, pertaining to the interim from 450 to 600 CE, is still in process—which does not permit elaboration on the cultural dynamics of the Late Canutillo phase. Any core-to-periphery interpretations about the northern frontier must await work from the Bajío region through to the Malpaso region.

The Alta Vista phase (600–850 CE) was an intense period of Mesoamerican cultural development in the Suchil region, during which the Suchil-Chalchihuites culture peaked as a social system. During the Alta Vista phase, the mining industry for pigments in the Suchil region reached its most extensive development It was also during this phase that turquoise from Cerrillos, New Mexico, appears in Suchil contexts, which indicates the presence of a Northern Mexican exchange network that reached the American Southwest.

Most of the major structures uncovered to date in the site of Alta Vista belong to this phase. The site is unique among Mesoamerican ceremonial centers—the site was not laid out at random, but was precisely located through a calculated geographic triangulation, determined from the Cerro del Chapín, a mesa some 5 kilometers (4 miles) to the southwest of Alta Vista. On the Chapín mesa, two pecked circle-cross petroglyphs, similar to those of Teotihuacan are found. Major structures in the ceremonial compound of Alta Vista were built on large square court banquette masonry platforms, which contain central altars. The large court banquettes of Alta Vista are oriented diagonally to the cardinal points. The major entrance to the site is outlined by a serpent wall that leads into the three-temple complex, composed of the Sun Pyramid, the Temple of the Skulls, and the Temple of the Hearths. Excavations in the Hall of Columns (originally excavated by Manuel Gamio in 1908) has recently yielded a number of elaborate subfloor burial offerings, in which the iconography of the eagle and serpent calls attention to both Huichol and Mexica (Aztec) mythologies. Alta Vista is known for its astronomical observatory, from which the local elite calculated solar cycles, with major observations on the spring equinox and the summer solstice.

The site has Classic-period Central Mexican iconography, ideological concepts, and construction elements similar to those at Teotihuacan. The dating of such elements will help in defining the cultural dynamics involved, with a time frame of c.550 to 650 CE of greatest importance if Alta Vista may be tied to Teotihuacan through an exchange system—or if the idea of a Teotihuacan diaspora, as proposed by Kelley and Jiménez Moreno, is in order. At present, the latter seems more possible. Between 1956 and 1961, both Jiménez Moreno and Kelley arrived at the conclusion, through separate avenues of research, that the Tolteca-Chichimeca, the ancestors of the Postclassic Toltecs of Tula, probably had originated from the region of the northern Zacatecas—and the Chalchihuites culture in particular. Kelley described traits from the Suchil region (the Hall of Columns, the Tezcatlipoca cult and the warrior cult, and the skull rack) as ideological components of the Tolteca-Chichimeca. Thus the idea of a bidirectional movement, involving the Central Highlands and its northern periphery, became established as a general working hypothesis. The complexity of this process remains key to understanding northern frontier dynamics during the Classic period.

During the Alta Vista phase, people from the Suchil region began colonizing southern and central Durango, in what became the basic Mesoamerican occupation of the Guadiana region. The site of Alta Vista was abandoned about 850 to 950 CE, with the Suchil regional system also coming to an end at that time. The subsequent Guadiana regional system of early Postclassic-period Durango again represents an important aspect of Mesoamerican trade systems. As the valleys of Durango, in sites such as Schroeder and Cañón del Molino, developed into a complex social system, such intrusive artifacts and iconography as ceramic pipes, spindle whorls, ceramics, and copper ornaments attest to direct ties between the Guadiana regional elite and the Aztatlán culture of the Pacific Coast—in what Kelley described as the Aztatlán mercantile system. This extensive exchange system probably extended from the area of Oaxaca and Puebla through Western Mexico to the Pacific coast, where it then met inland, trans-Sierra, at Guadiana. Kelley suggested that from the Guadiana region, the exchange system went northward into the Casas Grandes region of Chihuahua. Research is still needed on the regional segments of this postulated mercantile system, to prove its existence as one of the major trade networks of ancient Mesoamerica.

[*See also* North Central Mexico.]

BIBLIOGRAPHY

Aveni, Anthony F., Horst Hartung, and J. Charles Kelley. "Alta Vista (Chalchihuites), Astronomical Implications of a Mesoamerican Ceremonial Outpost at the Tropic of Cancer." *American Antiquity* 47 (1982), 316–335. Provides the basic functions and interpretations for the observatory at Alta Vista.

Kelley, J. Charles. "Archaeology of the Northern Frontier: Zacatecas and Durango." *Handbook of Middle American Indians*, vol. 11, edited by Gordon Ekholm and Ignacio Bernal, pp. 768–801. Provides the basic outline of the Chalchihuites culture.

Kelley, J. Charles. "The Mobile Merchants of Molino." In *Ripples in the Chichimec Sea*, edited by Frances J. Mathien and Randal H. McGuire, pp. 81–104. Provides the basic outline for the Aztatlan mercantile system.

Weigand, Phil. "Mining and Mineral Trade in Prehispanic Zacatecas." *Mining and Mining Techniques in Ancient Mesoamerica*, edited by P. C. Weigand and G. Gwynne. *Anthropology* 6.1–2 (1982). Excellent description of the mining industry of the Chalchihuites culture.

PETER JIMÉNEZ

CHALCHIUHTLICUE. Around 1535, in the region of Xochimilco, the Franciscan missionary friar Bernardino de Sahagún destroyed a "stone idol" placed in the interior of a fountain where the Indians had been accustomed to offer copal incense. It was undoubtedly a statue of Chalchiuhtlicue ("Her Skirt Is Jade"), the water goddess of the Aztec. She may have been one of the descendants of the "Great Goddess," the major goddess of Teotihuacan in

Detail of the water goddess Chalchiuhtlicue. *After Graz edition. Courtesy of Akademische Druck-u. Verlagsanstalt, Graz, Austria.*

the Classic period, who is widely represented on frescoes and identified on the monumental statues known as the Goddess of Water and the Idol of Coatlinchan. In Aztec statuary of the Postclassic period, Chalchiuhtlicue is sometimes confused with the maize goddesses Xilonen and Chicomecoatl. A deity that the Tlaxcaltecans called Matlalcuye ("Possessor of Blue Skirt") appears in several pictographic manuscripts (e.g., codices of the Borgia Group, *Codex Borbonicus, Codex Telleriano-Remensis*) as patron of the day Snake (Coatl) and of the thirteenth month, which begins with 1 Reed (Ce Acatl)—two calen-

dar signs associated with water and fertility. Included among her ornaments are a helmet made of the head of a serpent, two black rectangles painted on her cheeks, a jade necklace, a mirror or a disk worn as a pectoral, and a triangular cape (*quechquemitl*) or a skirt (*cueitl*) decorated with jade (*chalchihuitl*); the last is the source of her name.

Born on the day 7 Rain (Chicome Quiahuitl), Chalchiuhtlicue was the wife of the rain god Tlaloc and the mother of Tecuciztecatl, the moon god. Under the name Iztac Chalchiuhtlicue, she gave birth to the Mimixcoa, who fought the first holy war in order to nourish the sun and the earth. Chalchiuhtlicue was associated with the Sun (age) of Water (Atonatiuh), or Sun of Jade (Chalchiuhtonatiuh), which was destroyed by a flood. To her wrath was attributed a great flood caused by the rupture of an aqueduct constructed under the historical King Ahuitzotl. Called Apozonallotl ("Foam of Water") and Acuecueyotl ("Wave"), she was also the Atlacamani ("Temptress") who engulfed ships.

During the feast of Etzalcualiztli, the water merchants and the boatmakers offered her a slave, who was sacrificed along with a representation of Tlaloc. In Huey Tozoztli, a young girl attired as Chalchiuhtlicue was slain and thrown into the whirlpool of Pantitlan. Chalchiuhtlicue shared with Huixtocihuatl, goddess of salt water, the title of "Oldest Sister of the Tlaloque" (the rain deities). Because they were divinities of rain and mountains, they were worshipped during the *veintenas* (20-day months) of Tepeilhuitl and of Atemoztli in the form of amaranth seed statues representing mountains.

Midwives would invoke the name of Chalchiuhtlicue when they washed newborns in order to purify them. Likewise, healers would call on the goddess when they practiced hydromancy in order to find the *tonalli* (spirits) of sick children. Under the name of Chalchiuhuehue—also worshipped by the Pipil of Nicaragua—she presided over marriage ceremonies. Depicted in jade, symbol of water and abundance, Chalchiuhtlicue personified the precious element of life, as this invocation of a midwife illustrates: "Here is thy mother, the mother of all of us, Chalchiuhtlicue. Take it [the water], receive it. Here is wherewith thou will endure, wherewith thou wilt continue to live on earth."

BIBLIOGRAPHY

Báez-Jorge, Felix. *Los oficios de las diosas: Dialéctica de la religiosidad popular en los grupos indios de México.* Jalapa, 1988. Presents important ethnographic findings related to the current indigenous myths and rites devoted to water divinities.

Códice Borgia. Edited by Eduard Seler. 3 vols. Mexico City, 1963. Detailed study of the most important pre-Hispanic religious pictographic manuscript, including several depictions of Chalchiuhtlicue.

Durán, Diego. *Book of the Gods and Rites and the Ancient Calendar.* Edited and translated by Doris Heyden and Fernando Horcasitas. Norman, Okla., 1971. Includes rare notes on rites devoted to Chalchiuhtlicue.

Nicholson, Henry B. "The Iconography of the Deity Representations in Fray Bernardino de Sahagún's *Primeros Memoriales*: Huitzilpochtli and Chalchiuhtlicue." In *The Work of Bernardino de Sahagún, Pioneer Ethnographer of Sixteenth-Century Aztec Mexico*, edited by Jorge Klor de Alva et al., pp. 229–253. Austin, 1988. Detailed iconographic study of pictographic representations and statues of Chalchiuhtlicue.

Sahagún, Bernardino de. *Florentine Codex: General History of the Things of New Spain.* Translated and edited by Charles E. Dibble and Arthur J. O. Anderson. 12 vols. Santa Fe, N.M., 1950–1981.

Veritable encyclopedia of the Nahuatl world of the sixteenth century, containing rare iconography, rituals, and terminology related to Chalchiuhtlicue.

GUILHEM OLIVIER
Translated from French by Susan Romanosky

CHALMA, the most important Christian pilgrimage site in Central Mexico, a shrine dedicated to Jesus Christ crucified. Chalma is located southwest of Mexico City and is part of the municipality of Malinalco in the state of México. The climate of the region is warm, with semitropical vegetation. It is a mountainous area crossed by deep ravines. A shallow river, fed by clear, cool spring water, flows by the shrine, creating a lush green zone.

Although there is little information about the pre-Hispanic cults in the area, the ancient Mesoamerican inhabitants of the settlement of Ocuillan (now Ocuilan de Arteaga), worshiped the powerful god Oztotéotl (the god of the cave) at a nearby cave. This deity was related to the Central Mexican gods Tezcatlipoca and Tepeyólotl and also to the rain gods Tláloc and Chalmécatl. Opinions differ as to the meaning of the place name. The meaning of Chalma might derive from the word *challi* ("rupture, fissure, opening"). If this is so, Chalma translates as the "place where the opening occurs or spreads out," probably referring to the unique manner of Tezcatlipoca's birth—the earth opened, and he emerged from it.

According to tradition, in 1539 during the feast of Pentecost, an apparition of Jesus on the cross appeared to villagers in the same ancient cave where Oztotéotl had been worshiped. The Augustinian friars of Ocuillan found in the cave a figure of the Mesoamerican god smashed to pieces. The interior of the cave was strewn with fragrant flowers. According to another version, "heavenly angels" had placed a crucifix in the cave.

After the Spanish conquest of the early 1500s, the first Christian worship in the area of Chalma took place close to the cave. In 1643, a primitive church was constructed in a nearby plain. The Augustinian order administered the cult and chapel for many years, before deciding to construct a monastery and buildings to house the pilgrims who came to worship. By the end of the Colonial period, the complex was known as the Royal Convent and Sanctuary of Our Lord Jesus Christ and Saint Michael of the Caves of Chalma. In time, both the religious and secular buildings were enlarged and changed. Today the church, constructed in traditional ecclesiastical cruciform groundplan, has a Neoclassical façade that faces south. The original wooden sculpture of the Chalma crucifixion was destroyed in a fire at the end of the 1700s. It is said that the present cross was sculpted using pieces of the original. The wooden sculpture represents a dramatic, dark-skinned dead Jesus, bleeding from his wounds. It is located on the main altar, in a Neoclassical gilded canopy called a ciborium. Standing above the crucifix is the figure of the archangel Michael. In some representations of Our Lord of Chalma, Jesus is flanked by the Virgin Mary and Saint John the Evangelist.

At Chalma, the principal festivals are held during the first Friday of Lent, during Holy Week, and during the days between the celebration of Pentecost (the coming of the Holy Spirit) and the following Thursday. Throughout that period in spring, the faithful hold dances and vigils and place huge wooden crosses, some up to 7 meters (25 feet) tall, at the top of hills that overlook the site. Local confraternities (*cofradias*, religious societies), congregations, civic groups, and labor unions participate in the celebrations. At the end of the festivities, the crosses are removed and stored until the next year, when they are refurbished in the atrium of the shrine, then taken into the hills and, again, placed in plain view of the village.

Today, Chalma is widely recognized as a major pilgrimage center. Throughout the year, thousands of the faithful come to pray and offer petitions at the shrine. They are generally the urban and rural poor. Most come from the Federal District and the state of México, though large groups of believers undertake to walk to Chalma from as far away as the states of Morelos, Puebla, Tlaxcala, Hidalgo, and Querétaro. Upon their arrival at the shrine, the pilgrims (*chalmeros*) may crown themselves with flowers. They take part in dances under an ancient *ahuehuete* tree that grows near the shrine, or they dance in the atrium of the church (this is especially true for those who visit Chalma for the first time). Others bathe in the cold waters of the Chalma River, as an act of purification or to obtain a cure. A large number of objects from requested or conceded "miracles" hang from the *ahuehuete* tree: crutches, orthopedic limbs, casts from broken bones, clothes, locks of hair, teeth, and even the umbilical cords of newborn infants. Our Lord of Chalma is renowned as the "patron of difficult causes." One of the ways to invoke him is through dance. Pilgrims with problems gather not only to offer supplications but also to dance for long hours, asking that their prayers be answered.

Chalma has become a village, grown from poverty and without planning, yet its sanctuary has become a place of interest to both Mexicans and foreign tourists. It is close enough to Mexico City, Cuernavaca, and Toluca to provide a weekend getaway for inhabitants of those cities. The Augustinians still administer the monastery, but secular clergy administer the shrine and its services.

[*See also* Crosses and Crucifixes.]

BIBLIOGRAPHY

González Leyva, Alejandra. *Chalma: Una devoción agustina.* Toluca, 1991. The role of the members of the Order of Saint Augustine in the evangelization of the Chalma region in New Spain.

Sardo, Joaquín. *Relación histórica y moral de la portentosa imagen de N. Sr. Jesucristo crucificado aparecido en una de las cuevas de S. Miguel de Chalma.* Mexico City, 1810. The Augustinian friar Joaquín Sardo (1760–1823) wrote this account at the time he was prior in the convent of Chalma. In 1979, the Biblioteca Enciclopédica del Estado de México (Toluca) published a facsimile edition, with a brief introductory note. Sardo's work has become a standard reference, and the first chapters—those dealing with the "miracle"—have been reproduced in popular but inaccurate versions.

Schneider, Luis Mario. *Cristos, santos y vírgenes.* Mexico City, 1995. Short but useful note on Chalma and its cult; includes prayers, festivities, and a basic list of references.

XAVIER NOGUEZ

CHATINO.

CHATINO. In the Sierra Madre del Sur of Oaxaca, about 40,000 Chatino people reside in some fifty-five communities; forty of these are in eight *municipios* within the district of Juquila and the rest are in the district of Sola de Vega. Chatino is a Macro-Mayan language in the Zapotecan family, with three major variants: Highland, Zenzontepec, and Tataltepec. Subvariants of Highland Chatino are the most widely spoken. The Zenzontepec dialect is also spoken in Tlapanalquiahuitl and Tlacotepec; the Tataltepec dialect is used only in that *municipio*.

Economy and Social Organization. The Chatino are part of a classical colonial matrix, in which—unable to support themselves solely on their own lands—they must sell their labor to surrounding coffee plantations. Most Chatino are smallholders, rarely owning more than 5 hectares of land. They grow maize, beans, and squash in swidden (slash-and-burn) fields; where there are suitable lands, they also have small coffee plots. Production, however, usually falls short of subsistence needs, and many of the Chatino work seasonally on coffee plantations. Although pay and living conditions on plantations are poor—workers live in lean-tos and must provide their own food—families work on them an average of three to four months a year, staying three or four weeks at a time. The economic demands of the civil-religious hierarchies that organize village life also encourage families to produce cash crops or sell their labor. These age-graded hierarchical offices organize redistributive exchange systems in Chatino communities; through them, the people share the risks inherent in peasant life by distributing food at ritual meals. Since sponsors of saints' fiestas are obligated to pay expenses involved out of their own pockets, they are in constant need of money.

There are two market towns to which the Chatino take their produce: Santa Catarina Juquila and Nopala. Because the shrine of Virgin of Juquila attracts many pilgrims, Juquila has always been the more important political, economic, and religious center of the two. Since the

1930s, *mestizo* coffee buyers in Juquila have dominated the coffee trade and have become *caciques* (political bosses). [*See* Caciques.] Rivalries between competing *caciques*, which wear the masks of different political parties, has led to increasingly bloody struggles among their followers. This violence was greatly exacerbated when the Chatino began to plant coffee trees on their remaining communal lands in the early 1950s. Before that time, Chatino authorities, fearing coffee would led to privatization, would not allow the coffee to be planted on communal lands. When coffee prices hit an all-time high in 1950, they were unable to stop the planting. Because some barrios had more suitable lands than others, bitter conflicts erupted between them, dividing villages into feuding factions. Ever since, homicide rates have been sixteen to twenty-nine times the national average in Chatino villages that grow coffee.

Religion, Ritual, and Myth. Beneath a surface of Roman Catholic saints, rituals, rosaries, masses, and prayers beat the hearts of older Mesoamerican cosmologies, rituals, and ancient myths. Although Chatino myths include many ancient Mesoamerican stories—that of Sun and Moon and the Lord of the Animals—their oral literature also incorporates European and African influences. The Earth Lord, for example, is represented as a wealthy *hacendado* who enslaves those who fall into his debt.

The Chatino believe the earth is an island surrounded by water, floating in a multilayered cosmos of heavens and underworlds. Connecting these layers are "doors," through which pass various spirits and deities, such as the sun, moon, wind, rain, mountain, and forest gods. Doors are entrances to "houses." Since the Chatino equate "house" with "body," the mountain that is the house of the rain god *is* the rain god. Such equations not only map their cosmos onto the landscape but also provide a common framework for transactions among human beings, animals, spirits, demons, ancestors, and the gods.

Chatino ritual starts from the premise that all good things flow from the supernatural guardians who are identified with mountain peaks and other features of the landscape. To maintain the stability of the universe and meet their needs, people must pay tribute to the gods. In rituals, candles are lit and offerings are made in a series of conceptually larger and more inclusive houses—one's home, the church, the cemetery, cornfields, and mountaintops. Symbolically, these offerings convey the cultural message that just as the gods return one's offerings manyfold, money and other wealth invested in reciprocity and redistributive exchange within the community are similarly multiplied. If these rituals are not done, the gods become angry and show their vexation by causing illness, injuries, poor harvests, financial troubles, and even death.

[*See also* Economic Organization and Development, *article on* Post-Conquest Cultures.]

BIBLIOGRAPHY

Bartolomé, Miguel Alberto. *Narrativa etnicidad entre los chatinos de Oaxaca: Cuadernos de los centros regionales.* Mexico City, 1979. Spanish translations of Chatino folk tales.

Bartolomé, Miguel Alberto, and Alicia Barabas. *Tierra de la palabra: Historia y etnografía de los chatinos de Oaxaca.* Colección científica, Etnología 108. Mexico City, 1982. Regionally focused ethnography; presents a good account of working conditions on plantations.

Cordero Avendaño de Durand, Carmen. *Stina jo'o Kucha = El santo padre Sol: Contribucion al conocimiento socio-religioso del grupo etnico chatino.* Oaxaca de Juarez, 1986. Materials primarily drawn from San Juan Quiahije; contains detailed description of Chatino ritual and provides Chatino texts of the key orations that are part of them.

Greenberg, James B. *Santiago's Sword: Chatino Peasant Religion and Economics.* Berkeley, 1981. Study of Santiago Yaitepec that attempts to explain the economic and policial dimensions of the *cargo* system and Chatino ritual.

Greenberg, James B. *Blood Ties: Life and Violence in Rural Mexico.* Tucson, Ariz., 1989. Study of blood feuds and factional struggles among *caciques* in Santa Catarina Juquila that explores their impact on culture, social organization, and people's lives.

Hernández Díaz, Jorge. *El café amargo: Los procesos de diferenciación y cambio social entre los chatinos.* Oaxaca, 1987. Study of Chatino coffee growers in San Miguel Panixtlahuaca.

Hernández Díaz, Jorge. *Los Chatinos: Etnicidad y organización social.* Colección "Del barro nuestro," 2. Oaxaca, 1992. Ethnography focused on San Miguel Panixtlahuaca.

Pride, Kitty. *Chatino Syntax.* Summer Institute of Linguistics Publications in Linguistics and Related Fields, 12. Norman, Okla., 1965. Grammar based on the Yaitepec variety of Highland Chatino.

Pride, Leslie, and Kitty Pride. *Chatino de la Zona Alta, Oaxaca.* Edited by Yolanda Lastra. Archivo de Lenguas Indígenas de México. Mexico City, 1997. Chatino-Spanish texts in Highland Chatino.

JAMES B. GREENBERG

CHENES. The Chenes cultural tradition flourished in northeastern Campeche and southern Yucatán through the course of the Mesoamerican Late Classic (c.600–900 CE) and Early Postclassic (900–1250 CE) periods. The term "Chenes" derives from the Maya toponym *chen*, a place name for "well," in current use by the modern Maya of the region. Chenes architecture is essentially characterized by range or palacelike structures with vertical façades elaborately sculpted in deep relief, with serpent-mouth or bicephalic monster portals for entranceways. The archaeological zone of Hochob is considered the largest and most diagnostic site yet identified with the Chenes tradition. Although Chenes apparently represents a variation of the Río Bec cultural tradition, and its architectural style is thought to antedate that of the Puuc tradition, both Puuc and Río Bec are thought to represent distinct regional architectural styles and cultural traditions of central Yucatán.

All three styles share the use of palacelike structures with vertical façades elaborately sculpted in deep relief. However, the Río Bec style combines elaborate towers with rounded corners and false or miniature temples and the serpent-mouth or bicephalic earth-monster portal characteristic of the Chenes tradition. Furthermore, whereas the Chenes and Río Bec styles incorporate elaborately sculpted façades that employ deep relief from the base of the façade to the summit of the roofline, Puuc architecture is characterized by range structures with elaborately sculpted and geometrically complex mosaic upper cornice and frieze elements situated atop otherwise plain cut-stone façades.

The Chenes style is identified largely with the elaborate sculptural and architectural embellishments associated with palace and civic-ceremonial patterns unique to the Late Classic. As such, it is best exemplified by the architecture of the sites of Hochob (Structure 2), Dzibilnocac, Santa Rosa Xtampak, El Tabasqueño, Dzehkabtun, and related Río Bec sites such as Chicanná (Structure II) and Hormiguero (Structures II and V), each of which incorporates massive sculpted friezes, serpent motifs identified with the Maya creation deity Itzamná, or the iconography of the bicephalic earth-monster of Xibalba (the Maya underworld). Chenes-style architectural influences are also evident in monuments at the sites of Chichén Itzá (Nunnery, East Wing), Uxmal (Temple IV), and Kabah (Palace of the Masks), among others. In addition, antecedents of the Chenes style have been identified by George Kubler (1984) at Holmul and with Temple 22 at Copán, Honduras.

The widespread use of the bicephalic earth-monster portal and the elaborately carved frieze decorations of Chenes-style temples, palaces, and civic-ceremonial buildings in central Yucatán led David Potter (1977) to infer that the so-called Chenes style is actually just one variant of a "central Yucatán style" that includes both Chenes and Río Bec. Potter's hypothesis contrasts with those who view Chenes and Río Bec as regionally and culturally distinctive traditions centered on central Yucatán. The site of Hormiguero provides one example of the confluence of Río Bec and Chenes styles in the form of Structure II, where the Chenes earth-monster portal is flanked by Río Bec towers. Given the adoption of the serpent-mouth portal in sites such as Kabah and Chichén Itzá, it is likely that the portal is the architectural manifestation of a specific civic-ceremonial function such as that documented by ethnohistorical accounts for the Late Postclassic Central Mexican site of Malinalco, state of México. In

The Río Bec style of Chenes architecture can be seen in the rounded corners and the intricately sculpted façade of Structure I at Xpuhil—the Maya word for "place of the cattails." *Courtesy of Visual Resources Collection, The University of Texas at Austin. Ferguson Collection.*

the latter instance, buildings associated with the earth-monster portal were devoted to rituals and rites of passage specific to bloodletting and the initiation of Eagle and Jaguar Knights of the Aztec era (c.1425–1521 CE). Whereas in central Yucatán the serpent-mouth portals are thought to portray either the Maya creator deity Itzamná or the bicephalic earth-monster, throughout the Central Highlands the serpent-mouth portal was identified with Tlaltecuhtli, the earth-monster deity and the portal to the underworld (Mendoza, 1977).

As to the origins of the style, current perspectives indicate that the Chenes, Río Bec, and Puuc traditions provide more or less direct evidence of a succession of Putún or Chontal Maya incursions into central Yucatán from the delta regions of the Grijalva and Usumacinta rivers of the Mexican Gulf Coast. Similar evidence points to the view that the Putún eventually overran the Classic Maya centers of Seibal, Yaxchilán, and Altar de Sacrificios, as indicated by the presence of Gulf Coast Fine Orange pottery, which is culturally associated with the aforementioned sites and regions of the Tabasco delta. Therefore, the Chenes, Río Bec, and Puuc architectural traditions are seen to represent offshoots of this broader pattern of Mexicanized Maya, Putún, Chontal, and Itzá intrusions into the Maya Lowlands. Much of this pattern has been interpreted to coincide with the growth of Putún and Itzá mercantile interests in riverine and overland trade routes of the northern and southern Lowlands during the Late Classic period. Clearly, the development of spectacular cities with elaborately adorned palaces is just one hallmark of the success of the Putún and Chontal Maya in securing mercantile interests in the Yucatán Peninsula.

[See also Puuc; Río Bec.]

BIBLIOGRAPHY

Heyden, Doris, and Paul Gendrop. *Pre-Columbian Architecture of Mesoamerica*. New York, 1973. Excellent resource for the study of Mesoamerican architecture, with detailed site and architectural feature plans of the major Mesoamerican sites.

Hunter, C. Bruce. *A Guide to Ancient Maya Ruins*. Norman, Okla., 1974. Comprehensive archaeological site guide to the study and exploration of Maya ruins in Mexico and Central America.

Juárez Cossío, Daniel. "El clasico en el area maya." In *Atlas historico de Mesoamerica*, edited by Linda Rosa Manzanilla and Leonardo Lopez Lujan, pp. 98–102. Mexico City, 1989. Detailed region-by-region assessment of the archaeology and chronology of the major cultural traditions and civilizations of Mesoamerica.

Kubler, G. A. *The Art and Architecture of Ancient America: The Mexican, Maya and Andean Peoples*. 3rd ed. New York, 1984. General overview of the art and architecture of ancient America, with special reference to ancient Mesoamerica.

Mendoza, Ruben G. "Worldview and the Monolithic Temples of Malinalco, Mexico: Iconography and Analogy in Precolumbian Architecture." *Journal de la Société des Américanistes* 64 (1977), 63–82. Analysis of the cosmology and iconography of the rock-cut temples of Malinalco, Mexico, with special reference to the symbolism of the serpent-mouth portal.

Potter, David. *Maya Architecture of the Central Yucatan Peninsula, Mexico*. New Orleans, 1977. Excellent comparative overview and architectural survey of central Yucatán, conducted by the Middle American Research Institute of Tulane University.

Weaver, Muriel Porter. *The Aztecs, Maya, and Their Predecessors: Archaeology of Mesoamerica*. 3rd ed. New York, 1993. Detailed overview of the cultures and civilizations of ancient Mesoamerica, with a comprehensive summary of the relevant literature and chronological development of the region.

RUBEN G. MENDOZA

CHERT. In parts of Mesoamerica, especially those that were distant from obsidian outcrops, chert was the primary material used in making stone tools. Chipped-stone tools of chert were of great significance throughout Mesoamerica, owing to the absence of hard metals and the brittle nature of obsidian (a volcanic glass). Chert tools were used in a variety of forms: axes and adzes for woodworking, thick biface celts for stoneworking and forest clearance, oval bifaces for hoes (which bear the distinctive glossy polish acquired in such tasks), and weapon tips for hunting and warfare. Barbara Luedtke (1991) has characterized chert as sedimentary rock composed of microcrystalline quartz; under this general name, she lists flint, jasper, agate, novaculite, and others. For Mesoamerica, the geological distribution of artifact-quality cherts has been documented by research done in Belize, the Yucatán Peninsula, Campeche, Chiapas, Oaxaca, and Tabasco. There are, however, few detailed modern studies for Mesoamerica of chert outcrops, quarrying, tool production and distribution, and tool function.

The cherts of northern Belize are undoubtedly the best known, beginning with the British government-sponsored geological survey by A. C. S. Wright and others (*Land Use in British Honduras*, London, 1959). From 1979 to 1995, the Colhá Project examined chert utilization from Preceramic times (c.2500 BCE) to the Middle Postclassic. Extensive research has demonstrated that the site of Colhá was a rural, craft-specialized community with standardized production of chert tools beginning as early as the Middle Formative (Preclassic). By Late Formative times, and continuing into the Late Classic, more than a hundred chert workshops mass-produced both utilitarian and symbolic lithics for Maya consumers in northern Belize and beyond (Hester and Shafer 1994). Even after Colhá was abandoned in the eighth century CE, its chert outcrops attracted Early and Middle Postclassic peoples who produced weapon points and exported them to other Postclassic groups, whose sites have been surveyed in northern and coastal Belize.

In Guatemala, several research projects involving chert artifact manufacture have been carried out in the Petén. Aldenderfer (1991) describes chert outcrops in the central Petén Lakes region, where the nodules were used for local production of nonstandardized lithics. At Río Azul, Black and Suhler (1986) have excavated several biface-production workshops that utilized local coarse-grained cherts; a similar situation has been documented in studies under the direction of Fred Valdez in adjacent western Belize.

Clark (1988) has studied the chert resources utilized at the site of La Libertad in the Mexican state of Chiapas. He mapped the outcrops, examined manufacturing techniques, and conducted experiments with the raw materials at that site that were used by the ancient peoples. Clark's research on chert in Chiapas has also included studies in the highlands, as well as ethnoarchaeological studies of Lacandón Maya chert point-making. Other important studies in Mexico include the work of Whalen (1986) and Parry (1987) in Oaxaca. Whalen focused on

The Maya city of Cerros, in northern Belize, was a trading center for chert tools, salt, and obsidian during the Formative period. *Courtesy of Visual Resources Collection, The University of Texas at Austin. Ferguson Collection.*

the sources of cherts, ignimbrites, and chalcedonies used at the site of Guila Naquitz, while Parry's work detailed eight chert sources used during the Oaxaca Formative period for making flake tools and projectile points. Hernández Ayala and Jiménez Váldez (1981) have reported on the chert, chalcedony, jasper, and rhyolite sources in the San Mártir River region of Tabasco; these were used in the workshop production of bifaces and eccentrics for local use during the Maya Late Classic period.

Much research is needed in Mexico on chert sources and lithic production. This is especially important for the Central Mexican Late Postclassic period, when there were finely made bipointed bifaces (some up to 46 centimeters/ 18.5 inches long), often involved in Aztec sacrifice and ritual. Similarly, at Copán in Honduras, the source of the fine brown chert, used to make the spectacular Maya anthropomorphic eccentrics, remains unknown.

[*See also* Lithic Technology.]

BIBLIOGRAPHY

Aldenderfer, Mark. "The Structure of Late Classic Lithic Assemblages in the Central Petén Lakes Region, Guatemala." In *Maya Stone Tools*, edited by Thomas R. Hester and Harry J. Shafer, pp. 119–142. Madison, Wis., 1991. Describes chert resources, tool-manufacturing strategies, shapes of common tool forms, and the microwear data suggesting tool functions.

Black, Stephen L., and Charles K. Suhler. "The 1984 Río Azul Settlement Survey." In *Río Azul Reports, No. 2, The 1984 Season*, edited by Richard E. W. Adams, pp. 163–192. San Antonio, Tex., 1986. Reports testing of workshops near Río Azul, where gray to pink-gray coarse cherts were made into bifaces for local use.

Clark, John E. *The Lithic Artifacts of La Libertad, Chiapas, Mexico: An Economic Perspective*. Provo, Utah, 1988. Detailed look at a chert technology based on the use of local stream cobbles to make simple, basic tools; notes the import of exotic forms, such as stemmed macroblades from northern Belize.

Hernández Ayala, Martha I., and Gloria M. Jiménez Váldez. "Presencia litica en las tierras bajas noroccidentales del area Maya." *Revista mexicana de estudios antropológicos* 27.2 (1981), 117–130. Derived largely from Hernández Ayala's 1981 thesis on the archaeology of the Río San Pedro Mártir region of Tabasco, Mexico, this article provides excellent illustrations of chert workshops and the artifacts produced at these localities.

Hester, Thomas R., and Harry J. Shafer. "The Ancient Maya Craft Community at Colhá, Belize and Its External Relationships." In *Archaeological Views from the Countryside: Village Communities in Early Complex Societies*, edited by Glenn M. Schwartz and Steven E. Falconer, pp. 48–63. Washington, D.C., 1994. Summarizes the chert resources, workshops, and volume of production at Colhá and details two kinds of consumers for its exports: "primary," for utilitarian tools (often recycled), and "peripheral," largely elite distribution of stemmed macroblades and symbolic eccentrics.

Luedtke, Barbara E. *An Archaeologist's Guide to Chert and Flint*. Los Angeles, 1991. Definitive study of chert origins, their geology, chemistry, mechanical properties, as well as specific chert types.

Parry, William J. *Chipped Stone Tools in Formative Oaxaca, Mexico: Their Procurement*. Ann Arbor, Mich., 1987. Details the geologic sources, production technology, tool function, and household associations of chert artifacts in Middle and Early Formative sites, including San José Mogote.

Rovner, Irwin, and Suzanne M. Lewenstein. *Maya Stone Tools of Dzibilchaltún, Yucatán, and Becan and Chicanna, Campeche*. New Orleans, 1997. Good overview of lithics research in the Maya area, through an updating by Lewenstein of Rovner's 1975 doctoral dissertation.

Whalen, Michael E. "Sources of the Guila Naquitz Chipped Stone." In *Guila Naquitz: Archaic Foraging and Early Agriculture in Oaxaca*, edited by Kent V. Flannery, pp. 141–146. Orlando, Fla., 1986. Documents the quarry sources of poor-quality siliceous stone, including chert, in the Valley of Oaxaca; tools made from these materials are described in a chapter by Frank Hole in the same volume.

THOMAS R. HESTER

CHICANISMO. In his seminal study of Mexican immigration to the United States, Manuel Gamio first documented the use of the word he spelled *chicamo*. He showed that native "American Mexicans" in Texas around 1900 used *chicamo* as a derogatory term for more recently arrived Mexicans (Gamio, 1930, 1971, pp. 129, 233, 259). The term has since gone through significant conceptual and orthographic changes (see Acuña, 1982; Beltrán-Vocal, Hernández-Gutiérrez, and Fuentes, 1999; Córdova et al., 1986, 1990; de la Torre and Pesquera, 1993; Maciel and Ortíz, 1995; Mangold, 1971, 1972; Rendón, 1971; Velez-I., 1996). During the late 1950s, "Chicano" (also spelled "Xicano") largely transformed from a pejorative term for "Mexican immigrant" into a positive self-identifier of U.S. natives of Mexican descent. By 1959, high school students of Mexican descent identified themselves proudly as "Chicano," defined as "Mexican born on the U.S. side of the border/*un mexicano del otro lado*" or "Mexican American/*mexicoamericano*."

"Chicano" took on a narrower, more leftist, working-class and militantly nationalist Mexicentric connotation, especially among college-educated young adults of Mexican descent, from the mid-1960s through the late 1970s. During this period, a growing number of them also resisted Eurocentric and "Anglo" (English-speaking) dominance by utilizing pre-Colonial native images and symbols, while drawing *indígena* ("indigenous") identity and inspiration from a variety of Mesoamerican traditions, including Apache, Aztec-Mexica, Maya, Chinanteca, Huichol, Hopi, Toltec, Tarascan, Tzotzil, Pima, Purépecha, Pueblo, Yaqui, and Zapotec. By the end of the 1970s, "Chicanismo" denoted the consciousness of the shared struggles for human and civil rights known as the "Chicano movement," which emphasized the *mestizo* (mixed race) and *obrero* (working-class) bases of the U.S. Mexican-descent population (see Muñoz, 1989; Gómez-Quiñones, 1990). This movement transformed the ways both immigrant and native Mexicans in the United States thought about their past, present, and future.

During the 1980s and 1990s, the evolving definition of "Chicano" became even broader, encompassing more nationalities, classes, and ethnic groups while strengthening its *indigenista* covenant. At the start of the twenty-first century, growing numbers of U.S. natives and immigrants claim various national origins and descents—not only in Latin America but also in Western Europe—but also identify as "Chicano" (or "Xicano") on the basis of their ideological commitment to Chicanismo.

One of a series of panels from José Antonio Burciaga's mural "The Last Supper of Chicano Heroes." Detail of mural "The Mythology and History of Maíz." *Photograph courtesy of Carlos G. Vélez-Ibáñez.*

Central among the outstanding artistic representatives of Chicanismo is José Antonio Burciaga, whose book, *Drink Cultura-C/S* (1993), and murals—*Mythology of Maiz* and *Last Supper of Chicano Heroes*—explore its core meanings. Burciaga's work can grant a broader understanding of Chicanismo. He reflects both its political energy and its ephemeral artistry by examining, in his words, "the ironies in the experience of living within, between and sometimes outside, two cultures . . . Mexican by nature, American by nurture, a true 'mexture' . . . the damnation, salvation, the celebration of it all."

Burciaga and many other Mexican American academics, artists, and activists combine complex critiques of U.S. society's racial, gender, and economic biases with communal commemorations of Mesoamerican cultural treasures and social tragedies. Out of this combined critique and celebration has evolved a contemporary Chicanismo with academic and artistic actions energized by creative transculturation processes and a renewed vision of equality and democratic potential. Many of these manifestations demonstrate direct links to both the pre-Hispanic past and present Mesoamerica. For example, Burciaga's murals illustrate four major themes of his Chicanismo: the joint power of the creative earth and Mexican labor forces; political transformation through powerful leadership; family links extending back to pre-Hispanic times in Mesoamerica; and the transculturated vision of complex indigenous identification, imagination, inspiration, spirituality, and wisdom.

Topics in Burciaga's *Drink Cultura* range from the symbolic significance of "c/s" (*con/safos*) as a Chicano graffiti sign-off to a cheeky proposal for a national magazine for *los muertos* (the dead), as well as jalapeño pepper–induced gastronomic ecstasy and the significance of the holiday Cinco de Mayo (Fifth of May). His essay "The Last Supper of Chicano Heroes," on his murals in the Chicano-theme student residence at Stanford University (called Casa Zapata), describes his view of the essence of Chicanismo. Using the mythically significant number 6 as a constant (six humans, six corn stalks, six animals, and six ant tunnels in the shape of a rib cage), Burciaga painted *The Mythology of Maiz* (1985–1987) representing elements of the many Maya myths surrounding maize. Four different colors of maize represent the four cosmic directions. As a satirical comment on the Judeo-Christian concept of creation, Burciaga represents a Chicano transformation of Michelangelo's Adam, complete with head scarf, goatee, sunglasses, cigarette, ornate cross, and teardrop tattoos. In Burciaga's own words: "The central background color is a vibrant combination of white, yellow, orange to red, representing the energy of creation. The green cornstalk forms a wreath above where a mountain range stretches out representing the southwestern desert of Aztlán."

Burciaga originally conceived the central panel of his three-part mural as a depiction of Christ and his apostles at the Last Supper, dining on tortillas, tamales, and tequila instead of bread and wine, but in response to a negative reaction of some students, he replaced the figures with those of thirteen Chicano heroes. This response is exemplary of the Chicanismo practice of incorporating the voices of oppressed people into the creative process. The artist conducted a survey of Stanford Chicano students and Chicano community activists, asking them to list their thirteen heroes, with explanations for their choices. The stratified results of the 140 responses showed that the younger students scattered the votes over a total of 240 candidates, while the older activists concentrated their votes on sixty who played important parts particularly during the 1960s and 1970s. The survey responses collectively reimagined the Chicano hero or heroine as a mythical, historical, symbolic, military, or popular culture figure. Burciaga set the entire collection of heroes in a Mesoamerican *milpa* or cornfield complete with tassel tops. Tall Tolteca monoliths stand on each side framing the Last Supper mural. La Virgen de Guadalupe (called Tonantzin in Nahuatl), the spiritual heroine of Mexico and patroness of the Americas, lofts above the heroes with a beautiful multicolored ribbon stretching overhead from one *Tolteca atlante* to the other. At her feet flies a rarely painted *angelito negro*.

Sitting at the center of the table is Ernesto "Che" Guevara, the Argentine-born Cuban revolutionary hero killed while leading guerillas in Bolivia. Three seats away sits Martin Luther King Jr., the assassinated civil rights leader who inspired efforts for equality all over the world; not all Chicano heroes are of Mexican descent. The other eleven heroes are, though. Ricardo Flores Magón, an exiled Mexican revolutionary intellectual, published community newspapers and organized political parties in San Antonio, Texas, and Los Angeles, California; he died in Leavenworth Federal Prison from beatings received for leading an escape of more than seventy prisoners. Benito Juárez, a Zapotec native of Oaxaca, became Mexico's greatest president during the late 1800s and wrote the often-quoted *"El respeto al derecho ajeno es la paz"* ("respect for another's rights is peace").

Sor Juana Inéz de la Cruz (1648–1695), a Mexican nun and poet, wrote works that are receiving increasing attention among feminists. Tomás Rivera, born into a Crystal City, Texas, migrant farmworker family, became an award-winning writer and higher education leader; he served as the first Chicano president of the University of Texas at El Paso and the University of California at Riverside. Ernesto Galarza, who came as a child to the United States from Jalisco, received a doctorate from Columbia University, and pioneered an exemplary multidisciplinary style of Chicano community-centered activist scholarship which combines organizing farm laborers and writing critical analyses of their political and economic conditions, autobiographical prose, poetry, and children's literature.

Emiliano Zapata, the indigenous Mexican revolutionary leader, remains a heroic icon for *campesinos* (rural people) from Chiapas to California. César E. Chávez, the founder of the United Farm Workers (UFW), dedicated his life to the cause of improving the living and working conditions of laborers in the fields of California. Dolores Huerta, co-founder of the UFW, has continued the struggle since Chávez's death. Luis Valdéz is head of Teatro Campesino (an activist theater company) and a professor at California State University at Monterey Bay, as well as an award-winning writer and director of plays and the films *Zoot Suit* and *La Bamba*. Frida Kahlo, the daring German-Mexican surrealist painter, is a contemporary feminist icon. Directly above her stands her husband Diego Rivera, the revolutionary Mexican artist. Burciaga depicts her between Luis Valdéz and Joaquin Murieta, a native Sonoran who migrated to northern California during the gold rush of the 1850s and became a legendary, Robin Hood–like outlaw, purportedly to avenge his wife's rape-murder by white miners.

Tubrucio Vázquez, an educated poet who turned outlaw following a fight that killed a "Yankee" constable, stands over Che's right shoulder between two dining hall workers. To Diego Rivera's right is Geronimo, the legendary Apache leader, with Willie Velásquez, founder of the Southwest Voter Registration Education Project standing on the other side.

Other figures chosen for the mural include President John F. Kennedy and his brother Robert Kennedy; Gabriela Mistral, the Chilean writer who in 1945 became the first Latin American to win the Nobel Prize for literature; the Nicaraguan freedom fighter Augusto C. Sandino; several workers at the mural site, Stern Hall, such as John Towns, a native Texan of African descent; Carlos Santana, the guitarist who revolutionized Latino rock; Ignacio Zaragoza, the Texas native who commanded the Mexican army that toppled the French troops in Puebla on Cinco de Mayo in 1862; Luisa Moreno, an upper-class Guatemalan artist who became a labor organizer among U.S. Latina workers and students during the 1930s and later was deported to Mexico as an undesirable alien during the McCarthy era; *Los Angeles Times* reporter and editorial writer Rubén Salazar, the award-winning newspaper and television journalist killed by a police tear gas projectile while sitting in an East Los Angeles bar on 29 August 1970, shortly after an unprovoked police attack on the Chicano Moratorium March against the Vietnam War. La Muerte (Death) received enough votes to stand behind the thirteen major heroes—a heroine, the great avenger, and savior from *la vida* (life).

Despite this diversity, Chicano heroes in the late 1980s were perceived as mostly of Mexican descent; as revolutionary, working-class males of color, well-educated, and prematurely dead. Most gave their lives—some violently—to the struggle for social justice. Burciaga summed it up by painting the following words on the tablecloth: "And to all those who died, scrubbed floors, wept and fought for us."

A movement called "Xicanisma" is a contemporary extension of twentieth-century Chicanismo that is ideologically rooted in the Chicana feminist "Mexic Amerindian" consciousness, which rejects *machismo*, exclusionary ethnocentrism, and nationalism while emphasizing indigenous tendencies toward interdependence and cooperation that transcend gender, class, race, and geographic boundaries (Castillo 1994). The form "Xicanisma" appears increasingly as an orthographically distinctive identifier and definer of a U.S.–Mexican consciousness that embraces feminists, cultural guerillas, and our Amerindo lineages.

BIBLIOGRAPHY

Acuña, Rudy. *Occupied America: The Chicano Struggle for Liberation.* New York, 1982.

Beltrán-Vocal, María Antonia, Manuel de Jesús Hernández-Gutiérrez, and Silvia Fuentes, eds. *Mapping Strategies: NACCS and the Challenge of Multiple (Re) Oppressions: Selected Proceedings of the XXIII Annual Conference of the National Association of Chicana and Chicano Studies held in Chicago, Illinois, March 20–23, 1996.* Phoenix, Hermosillo, and Sonora, 1999.

Burciaga, José Antonio. *Drink Cultura-C/S—Chicanismo.* Santa Barbara, Calif., 1993.

Castillo, Ana. *Massacre of the Dreamers: Essays on Xicanisma.* Albuquerque, N.M., 1994.

Códova, Teresa, et al., eds. *Chicana Voices: Intersections of Class, Race, and Gender.* Albuquerque, N.M., 1986, 1990.

De la Torre, Adela, and Beatríz M. Pesquera, eds. *Building with Our Hands: New Directions in Chicana Studies.* Berkeley, 1993.

Gamio, Manuel. *Mexican Immigration to the United States: A Study of Human Migration and Adjustment.* Chicago, 1930; repr. New York, 1971.

García, Ignacio M. *Chicanismo: The Forging of a Militant Ethos among Mexican Americans.* Tucson, Ariz., 1997.

García, Mario T. *Memories of Chicano History: The Life and Narrative of Bert Corona.* Berkeley, 1994.

Gómez-Quiñones, Juan. *Chicano Politics: Reality and Promise, 1940–1990.* Albuquerque, N.M., 1990.

Maciel, David, and Isidro D. Ortíz, eds. *Chicanos and Chicanas in Contemporary Society.* Boston, 1995.

Mangold, Margaret M. *La Causa Chicana: The Movement for Justice.* New York, 1971, 1972.

Muñoz, Carlos. *Youth, Identity, Power.* London, 1989.

Rendón, Armando. *Chicano Manifesto: The History and Aspirations of the Second Largest Minority in America.* New York, 1971.

Rosenbaum, Robert J. *Mexicano Resistance in the Southwest: The Sacred Right of Self-Preservation*. Austin, Tex., 1981.

Vélez-I., Carlos. *Border Visions: Mexican Cultures of the Southwest United States*. Tucson, Ariz., 1996.

JOSÉ B. CUÉLLAR

CHICHÉN ITZÁ. The ancient community of Chichén Itzá is situated in the north central part of the Yucatán Peninsula lowlands. The UTM coordinate that registers Chichén Itzá in the *Archaeological Atlas of Yucatán* is 16Q CT365870 (Garza and Kurjack, 1980, p. 101; Fig. 1). Collapse sinkholes exposing the water table (cenotes), dry sinkholes, and quarries are the dominant physiographic features on the surface of Chichén Itzá. The main architectural groups of the site are near physiographic features that offered access to water, rich soil, and limestone. The two largest cenotes, known as Xtoloc and the Sacred Cenote, are at the site center, and this area has a concentration of massive constructions, vaulted buildings, and elaborate architecture. Several dry sinkholes are situated at the center as well as around the periphery of Chichén Itzá, and the soil within them is fertile and maintains constant moisture, so it was probably used for intensive agriculture year round. Limestone and calcium carbonate, known in northern Yucatán as *sascab*, were obtained from several quarries at the site center and in the surrounding area. *Sascab* and natural limestone blocks of various sizes were used in the construction fill of buildings and causeways. Other, carefully worked stones were used to cover the internal and external walls of buildings or sculpted into zoomorphic, anthropomorphic, or geometric elements to decorate the façades.

Historical Background. The conqueror Francisco de Montejo the Elder, in 1533, was the first European to attempt to establish a Spanish settlement at Chichén Itzá. Montejo succeeded for a brief period and used the main buildings at the site center as his headquarters. However, constant attacks by the Maya forced Montejo and his soldiers to withdraw from Chichén Itzá. The Franciscan bishop Diego de Landa mentioned the existence of pre-Hispanic constructions at Chichén Itzá and drew a sketch map of El Castillo, its main building, and mentioned the Venus Platform, the Sacred Cenote, the small temple at the edge of the Sacred Cenote, and Causeway 1, which links the Sacred Cenote with the Great Terrace, on which El Castillo, the Venus Platform, and other important buildings stand.

Several travelers and explorers visited Chichén Itzá between 1840 and 1900. They produced a large number of descriptions and drawings of the archaeological remains and natural features associated with them, as well as the first photographs of the buildings whose façades were preserved and still standing. Baron Emmanuel von Friederichsthal visited Chichén Itzá in 1840, Benjamin Nor-

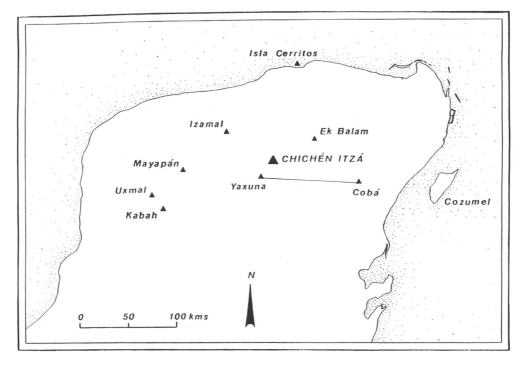

Chichén Itzá and other Northern Maya lowlands sites. *Courtesy of Rafael Cobos.*

El Castillo or Structure 2D5. *Photograph courtesy of Rafael Cobos.*

man in February 1842, and John L. Stephens and Frederick Catherwood a month later. Friederichsthal published his travel impressions in 1841, and the others published their accounts in 1843. These works include general comments on El Castillo, the Great Ballcourt, the Monjas Complex, El Caracol, and the first sketch maps of El Castillo, the Monjas Complex, and La Iglesia.

Visitors to Chichén Itzá during the 1870s and 1880s came with photographic equipment and recorded more accurately the condition of several buildings. They offered their own hypotheses regarding cultural ties between Chichén Itzá and other parts of Mexico and even the rest of the world. For example, Désiré Charnay noticed similarities between the architecture and sculpture of Chichén Itzá and Tula in Central México, which led him to argue that the "Toltec" of Tula influenced the Maya of Chichén Itzá. Augustus Le Plongeon suggested that the Maya founded world civilization and transported their ceremonies and rituals to Greece, Egypt, Mesopota-

mia, and India. To test his hypothesis, Le Plongeon conducted the first archaeological excavations at Chichén Itzá, first at the Eagles and Tigers Platform in 1875, and then at the Venus Platform in 1883. Le Plongeon used photographs, drawings, and notes to record his archaeological findings in 1883.

The 1880s marked the end of half a century of travelers and explorers devoted exclusively to recording and describing buildings, and the beginning of archaeological excavations at the site by amateur archaeologists such as Teobert Maler and Edward H. Thompson. In 1892, Maler partially excavated the Temple of the Little Tables, 250 meters southeast of El Castillo. He found several pieces of sculptures, including Atlantean figures, columns, serpent tails, and a *chacmool*. The *chacmool* is a type of anthropomorphic sculpture characteristic of Chichén Itzá which depicts the trunk of an individual reclining at a 45-degree angle, with elbows resting on a flat surface and supporting the trunk, while the legs are retracted and the face looks to the side. Stephen Salisbury coined the term based on the appellation *chaacmol*, given by Le Plongeon to one of the sculptures found in his 1875 excavation.

Between 1894 and 1903, Thompson excavated several structures at Chichén Itzá: the High Priest's Grave, a small mound to the east of the High Priest's Grave, a ballcourt, the Temple of the Little Tables and a mound associated with this temple, the Monjas Complex, and a cistern, or *chultún*, near the House of the Phalli. Ceramic vessels, jade beads, arrow points, and shell ornaments are some of the items found by Thompson, who is best known for his explorations of the Sacred Cenote.

During the spring and fall of each year between 1904 and 1907, Thompson dredged the Sacred Cenote. He thus recovered a broad sample of archaeological materials, including ceramic vessels, jade ornaments, obsidian blades and beads, shell ornaments, limestone tools, chert tools, objects made of wood, gold and *tumbaga* ornaments, and fragments of textiles. In 1909, instead of dredging, Thompson dived into the Sacred Cenote; however, this proved to be dangerous due to the presence of roots and debris under the calm waters of the *cenote*.

Archaeological investigations resumed at Chichén Itzá in 1924, when a professional team of archaeologists led by Sylvanus G. Morley of the Carnegie Institution of Washington launched a ten-year project at the site. The team excavated and consolidated the Temple of the Warriors, the Temple of the Wall Panels, El Caracol (or the Observatory), La Casa Redonda, El Mercado, and the Temple of the Three Lintels. The Carnegie Institution also produced the first map of a large area, with major architectural groups, platforms with small masonry buildings, platforms with no evidence of construction, ten causeways, cenotes, dry sinkholes, and lime quarries.

Beginning in the late 1920s, the Mexican government's Department of Archaeological Monuments initiated excavations at Chichén Itzá. The buildings investigated between 1927 and 1951 included El Castillo (north and west sides), the Great Ballcourt, the Skull Rack or Tzompantli, the Eagles and Tigers Platform, and the Venus Platform. In the 1930s, the Mexican government created the Instituto Nacional de Antropología e Historia (INAH); its archaeologists have since investigated the Sacred Cenote as well as buildings belonging to major architectural complexes of the site.

In 1961 and 1967–1968, the Sacred Cenote was again explored; the search produced archaeological materials similar to those recovered by Thompson. Archaeological work conducted at Chichén Itzá in the 1980s and 1990s focused on the excavation and restoration of buildings at the site center and periphery. Constructions such as El Castillo (east and south sides), the Western Colonnade Hall, the High Priest's Grave and associated structures, and the Temple of the Big Tables have been investigated and completely restored. Mapping and excavations conducted at the periphery of Chichén Itzá have also yielded important data in the form of ceramics, settlement patterns, and obsidian.

History. The archaeological evidence suggests that Chichén Itzá was occupied for nearly two thousand years, from 300–200 BCE up to the sixteenth century CE. Although the settlement changed during the Preclassic, Classic, and Postclassic periods, at the end of the Classic period, Chichén Itzá transformed into a complex community, reached its apogee, and eventually collapsed.

Preclassic and early classic periods. The earliest occupation at Chichén Itzá dates to these two periods. The evidence consists of ceramic materials, which include the following types of the Tihosuco and Cochuah ceramic complexes: Nolo Red, Xanaba Red, and Tipikal Red-on-striated. These early ceramic types of Chichén Itzá are contemporaneous with Late Nabanché (350 BCE–150 CE) and Xculul (150–250 CE) ceramic complexes of Komchén and Dzibilchaltún, respectively, and with the Tihosuco ceramic complex of Mayapán.

Late classic and terminal classic periods. Chichén Itzá used to be depicted as a settlement that arose in the Early Postclassic period (900–1200 CE) after the collapse of Classic Maya sites. The rise of the city during that period was associated with the "Toltec" of Tula in Central Mexico, who arrived at the site, conquered it, established their rule, and coexisted with a large Maya population (see especially Tozzer, 1957). There were two main reasons for dating Chichén Itzá to the Early Postclassic period: the interpretation by ethnohistorians, historians, and archaeologists of events recorded in Yucatecan historical documents of the sixteenth and seventeen centuries; and the strong influence of the diffusionist model that dominated anthropological and archaeological interpretations between 1930 and 1960.

The traditional view that depicts Chichén Itzá as an isolated site belongs to the past; several archaeologists work-

El Caracol or Structure 3C15.
Photograph courtesy of Rafael Cobos.

ing in the northern Maya Lowlands have seriously questioned it. The ceramic evidence and settlement data make it difficult to explain the rise and existence of Chichén Itzá after the collapse and abandonment of other northern Maya capitals, such as Cobá and Uxmal. It is also hard to believe that Chichén Itzá interacted only with Tula, a site 1,500 kilometers (1,000 miles) away in Central Mexico.

The results of ceramic and settlement analyses conducted over the past twenty years at Chichén Itzá and other pre-Hispanic communities in eastern, central, and western Yucatán show that Chichén Itzá rose at least 150 years earlier than was traditionally claimed. Dating the florescence, apogee, and collapse of Chichén Itzá between 700/750 CE and 1000/1050 places this site within the same chronological framework as other northern Yucatán Classic Maya settlements that were experiencing similar transformations. In fact, ceramic evidence and settlement data from Chichén Itzá suggest a gradual transformation of this site until it reached its hegemonic status at the end of the Terminal Classic period, between 900 and 1050 CE.

Taking into account the vessel forms and ceramic types of the Sotuta ceramic complex, as well as settlement data, we recognize an early and a later phase of occupation. The early phase is defined by the presence of Thin Slate ware, Chichén Unslipped ware (but no hourglass censers), Chichén Slate ware, Chichén Red ware, and Fine Orange. The occupation is further characterized by architectural groups formed by temples, altars, range structures, colonnaded halls, and gallery-patio structures, such as the Initial Series Group and the Southwest Group. Hieroglyphic texts dating to the ninth century are associated with the early Sotuta ceramics. Obsidian blades from Ucareo, Michoacán (western Mexico) and turquoise disks from the Chalchihuites region, Zacatecas (northwestern Mexico), were among the commodities that arrived at Chichén Itzá during the early phase of occupation.

Early Chichén Itzá was contemporaneous with other Maya communities such as Uxmal, Dzibilchaltún, Yaxuná, Ek Balam, Cobá, Caracol, Tikal, Palenque, and Copán. Beyond the Maya area, it was also contemporaneous with Xochicalco in Morelos, Cacaxtla in Tlaxcala, Tula in Hidalgo, and Azcapotzalco in the state of México.

The late phase of occupation at Chichén Itzá is characterized by the presence of Chichén Unslipped ware (including hourglass censers), Chichén Slate ware, Chichén Red ware, Fine Orange, Plumbate ware, and Fine Buff Orange. Thin Slate ware and hieroglyphic texts are absent in this phase.

During the late phase, the Great Terrace and buildings standing on it became the center of the site. This center concentrated massive constructions and a large volume of vaulted buildings. A temple, altar, and gallery-patio structures became the architectural pattern characteristics of the site center and peripheral groups. El Castillo, the Venus Platform, and the gallery-patio in front of the Venus Platform exemplify the late architectural pattern. Obsidian from Ucareo and turquoise from Zacatecas continued arriving, but other commodities were also imported: obsidian blades from Pachuca, Hidalgo (Central Mexico), and Ixtepeque, eastern Guatemala; Plumbate vessels from the western Guatemala highlands; jade from the Motagua Valley in eastern Guatemala; and gold and *tumbaga* from Costa Rica and western Panama.

Chichén Itzá functioned as a hegemonic state after 900 CE, and this state controlled small communities around its periphery and established its own trade port on the northern coast of Yucatán. At Yulá and Halakal, five kilometers from Chichén Itzá, Sotuta ceramics, architecture, and hieroglyphic texts associate the sites with Chichén Itzá. Cumtún, another small settlement, is linked to Chichén Itzá by Causeway 3, six kilometers long.

After 900 CE, Isla Cerritos functioned as the trade port of Chichén Itzá on the northern coast of the Yucatán Peninsula. Archaeological materials uncovered at Isla Cerritos show that obsidian, turquoise, Plumbate vessels, and marine materials such as shells were brought to the city from here.

During the late phase of occupation, Chichén Itzá was contemporaneous with Uxmal, Cobá, Caracol, Palenque, and Copán. Non-Maya settlements such as Tula in Central Mexico and El Tajín in northern Veracruz were also contemporaneous.

Postclassic period. The beginning of this period is represented at Chichén Itzá by the presence of the Xcanchakan Black-on-cream and Kukula Cream types of the Hocaba ceramic complex, which are found either on the surface or in upper levels of the West Colonnade, the Southeast Colonnade, the Temple of the Wall Panels, and the Monjas Complex. During the Early Postclassic period (1050/1100–1200/1300 CE), occupation at Chichén Itzá was reduced and construction activity ceased. It seems that the users of Xcanchakan Black-on-cream and Kukula Cream ceramics were squatters who occupied Terminal Classic period constructions. Contemporaneous settlements include T'ho, Acanceh, Dzibilchaltún, and Mayapán.

The end of the Postclassic period at Chichén Itzá is characterized by the presence of Chen Mul anthropomorphic modeled censers, cast copper, manikin scepters made of wood, and tripod vessels containing copal and incense, which were thrown into the Sacred Cenote as offerings. Between 1200/1300 CE and the sixteenth century, Chichén Itzá functioned as a ceremonial center for pilgrims who came to worship and present these offerings to the Maya deities. During the two or three centuries before the arrival of the Europeans, Chichén Itzá was contemporaneous with Mayapán and Tulúm.

[*See also* Northern Maya Lowlands.]

BIBLIOGRAPHY

Andrews, E. Wyllys, IV. *Balankanche, Throne of the Tiger Priest.* Middle American Research Institute Publication 32. New Orleans, 1970. Analysis of Sotuta ceramics and other archaeological remains found in the Balankanche cave.

Brainerd, George W. *The Archaeological Ceramics of Yucatan.* University of California Archaeological Records, 19. Berkeley and Los Angeles, 1958. First detailed analysis of ceramic materials found at Chichén Itzá.

Braswell, Geoffrey E. "El Intercambio Prehispánico en Yucatán, México." In *X Simposio de investigaciones arqueológicas en Guatemala, 1996*, edited by Juan Pedro Laporte and Héctor L. Escobedo, vol. 2, pp. 545–555. Guatemala City, 1997. Results of Chichén Itzá obsidian artifacts assigned to their geological sources in Guatemala and Mexico.

Cobos, Rafael. "Chichén Itzá y el Clásico Terminal en las Tierras Bajas Mayas." In *XI Simposio de investigaciones arqueológicas en Guatemala*, edited by Juan Pedro Laporte and Héctor L. Escobedo, vol. 2, pp. 791–799. Guatemala City, 1998. Uses archaeological materials to explain contacts between Chichén Itzá and other regions within and beyond the Maya area.

Cobos, Rafael. "Chichén Itzá: Settlement and Hegemony during the Terminal Classic Period." In *The Terminal Classic in the Maya Lowlands: Collapse, Transition, and Transformation*, edited by Don S. Rice, Prudence M. Rice, and Arthur A. Demarest. Boulder, Colo., in press. Analyzes contemporaneity between Chichén Itzá and other northern Maya settlements for the Late and Terminal Classic periods.

Coggins, Clemency C., ed. *Artifacts from the Cenote of Sacrifice, Chichén Itzá, Yucatán.* Memoirs of the Peabody Museum of Archaeology and Ethnology, 10.3. Cambridge, Mass., 1992. Results of analyses conducted on artifacts found in the Sacred Cenote by Edward Thompson.

Coggins, Clemency C., and Orrin C. Shane III, eds. *Cenote of Sacrifice: Maya Treasures from the Sacred Well at Chichén Itzá.* Austin, Tex., 1984. Illustrates and describes artifacts recovered in the Sacred Cenote by Edward Thompson.

Dávalos Hurtado, Eusebio. "Return to the Sacred Cenote." *National Geographic* 120.4 (1961), 540–549. Illustrates archaeological artifacts found in the cenote during the 1961 exploration.

Desmond, Lawrence G., and Phyllis Mauch Messenger. *A Dream of Maya: Augustus and Alice Le Plongeon in Ninteenth-Century Yucatan.* Albuquerque, N.M., 1988. Analysis of Le Plongeon's life as an explorer in Yucatán.

Garza Tarazona de González, Silvia, and Edward B. Kurjack. *Atlas arqueológico del estado de Yucatán.* 2 vols. Mexico City, 1980. Provides data regarding the location and investigations of Chichén Itzá.

Landa, Diego de. *Relación de las cosas de Yucatán* [1864]. 8th ed. With introduction by Angel María Garibay. Mexico City, 1959. Mentions the remains of pre-Hispanic Chichén Itzá in the sixteenth century.

Lincoln, Charles E. *Ethnicity and Social Organization at Chichén Itzá, Yucatán, México.* Ph.D. diss., Harvard University, 1990. Analyzes the Sotuta ceramics and their association with settlement data.

Littlehales, Bates. "Treasure Hunt in the Deep Past." *National Geographic* 120.4 (1961), 550–561. Illustrates and comments on the exploration of the Sacred Cenote in 1961.

Piña Chán, Román. *Informe preliminar de la reciente exploración del cenote sagrado de Chichén Itzá.* Instituto Nacional de Antropología e Historia, Serie Investigaciones, 24. Mexico City, 1970. General comments on the 1967–1968 exploration of the Sacred Cenote.

Ruppert, Karl. *Chichen Itza: Architectural Notes and Plans.* Carnegie Institution of Washington Publication 595. Washington, D.C., 1952. Illustrates and describes buildings mapped between 1924 and 1949 by the Carnegie Institution of Washington.

Smith, Robert E. *The Pottery of Mayapan.* Papers of the Peabody Museum of Archaeology and Ethnology, 66. Cambridge, Mass., 1971. Uses type-variety analysis to classify the Sotuta ceramics uncovered at Chichén Itzá by the Carnegie Institution.

Tozzer, Alfred M. *Chichen Itza and Its Cenote of Sacrifice.* Memoirs of the Peabody Museum of Archaeology and Ethnology, 11–12. Cambridge, Mass., 1957. Uses history and iconography to explain the cultural history of Chichén Itzá and northern Yucatán.

RAFAEL COBOS

CHICHIMEC. The ethnonym Chichimec (in Spanish, Chichimeca) is derived from the Nahuatl word *chichimec-atl* (plural, *chichimeca*), which the Nahua applied to peoples who lived north of Mesoamerica. Karttunen's *Analytical Dictionary of Nahuat* defines *Chichimeca* as "a person from one of the indigenous groups of northern Mexico considered barbarians by Nahuatl speakers. . . . This has both a negative 'barbarous' sense and a positive 'noble savage' sense. The word is possibly derived from *chichi* meaning 'to suckle,' but is not, as is often stated, related to the words for 'dog,' 'rags,' 'patches' or 'bitter'" (Karttunen 1983, p. 48). Nigel Davies (1977, p. 160) suggests that the derivation from *chichi* ("to suckle") lends the notions of newness or youth to the word. Thus, the barbarousness of the Chichimecs relates to their uncivilized culture and their situation as newcomers when some of them moved from their northern homeland into Mesoamerica in late prehistoric times. Rudolph van Zantwijk (1985, p. 308) suggests that *chichimecatl* is a Nahuat corruption of a word from an original Chichimec language, perhaps meaning "eagle."

The uses of the term are complex. The Nahua applied it to all the peoples of northern Mexico (as opposed to the sedentary agriculturalists of Mesoamerica) who shared certain common cultural traits: nomadism; use of the bow and arrow as the principal weapon and hunting instrument; primitive dwellings such as straw huts or caves; no agriculture or pottery; and worship of sky deities representing the sun, moon, and stars. The Chichimecs had no temples or idols, but they practiced animal and human sacrifice in which the victim was hung from a scaffold and shot with arrows. They lived on wild fruits, roots, game, and fish, and they often went naked. They were feared for their expertise and brutality in war.

In fact, the Chichimecs were never one people and did not share a common language. They include the Pames,

Guachichiles, Zacatecs, Guamares, Otomís and other peoples farther north. Those groups (such as the Otomís and some Pames) who lived closer to the civilized peoples of Mesoamerica adopted some of their neighbors' cultural traits and religious beliefs and practices.

The name Chichimec also refers in a general way to northern peoples, probably of varying levels of cultural development, who moved into Mesoamerica at different times. In this sense, the word also denotes the Toltecs, who dominated Mesoamerica after the fall of Teotihuacan from about the ninth to the twelfth centuries, and the Mexicas or Aztecs.

As used by Nahuatl speakers, the term *chichimeca* (singular, *chichimecatl*) referred to the peoples who lived north and west of the Valley of Mexico, and also to those living in the Valley who were descended from these peoples. In Mesoamerican iconography, Chichimecs are often portrayed with bows and arrows, rough clothing, and dogs. In this usage, the word has a more symbolic than ethnological meaning. The Aztecs and the Tlaxcalans considered themselves to be descendants of Chichimecs who moved into the Valley of Mexico during the period before the founding of Tlaxcala and Tenochtitlan. The Aztecs, in particular, claimed that the patrimony of their leaders was based on the union of Chichimec leaders and descendants of the Toltec ruling lineage. As used by Nahuatl speakers, the word *Chichimeca* carries the connotations not only of "barbarian" and "noble savage," but also of "ancestor."

The Nahuatl term also refers more specifically to the people who came into the Valley of Mexico after the fall of the Toltec capital of Tula in the twelfth century, led by a chieftain known as Xolotl. In the *Codex Xolotl*, this individual is depicted as a Chichimec leader of six clans who lived near the legendary Chicomoztoc, some distance north of the valley. Five years after the fall of Tula in 1175 CE (5 Flint), Xolotl and his Chichimec followers invaded the valley and founded an empire comprised of territory previously ruled by the Toltecs. According to this account, Xolotl's Chichimecs eventually became civilized. They abandoned their Chichimec language, learned to speak Nahuatl, and adopted agriculture and the modes of dress of the civilized peoples of the Valley of Mexico. The fourteenth- and fifteenth-century rulers of the Valley of Mexico city-states of Azcapotzalco, Texcoco, and Tenochtitlan traced their lineages back to Xolotl. The veracity of this story is in doubt; the *Codex Xolotl* contains many contradictions concerning important figures and events, and the genealogy is confused. There is little archaeological evidence to support the story's assertion of the sudden fall of the Toltec capital. The ability of simple bands of hunters and gatherers to conquer within a short period of time and subsequently rule a large civilized population has also been questioned.

As used by the early Spanish conquerors of Mexico, the word *Chichimeca* has a number of meanings. It denotes the inhabitants of the province of Nueva Galicia (the modern states of Querétaro and Guanajuato) in northern Mexico against which the Spanish fought the Chichimeca War between 1550 and 1590. These peoples were mostly Guachachiles and Zacatecs. Most, though not all, of them displayed the cultural characteristics that were traditionally considered "Chichimec." The name also denotes all northern natives, regardless of culture, who resisted Spanish colonization and were, therefore, legally eligible to be enslaved or exterminated. In this context, natives who were guilty of apostasy, attacked Spaniards without provocation, rebelled against the Spanish monarch, or prevented Spaniards from traveling freely and peaceably could be considered *Chichimecas*.

There are also several contemporary uses of the term. The word has been used by the archaeologist Charles DiPiso and others to refer to the inhabitants of North and West Mexico and the U.S. Southwest during all historic and prehistoric eras. The anthropologist George Castile applied the term to all North American natives living north of the Valley of Mexico as an alternative to the term "Indian." These two uses of the term are controversial and rarely encountered in the current literature.

Chichimeca is also the name of a small group of people, also called Chichimeca-Jonaz, who live near San Luís Potosí at the Misión Chichimeca. This mission was founded sometime in the sixteenth century by Franciscan missionaries but later came under the direction of the Jesuits. Although it retains its original name, the community is no longer a mission. Some of this group speak a language they call "Chichimec" and consider themselves to be the descendants of the Chichimecas who fought against the Spanish in the sixteenth-century Chichimeca War, led by a chieftain named Chupitantegua. The majority of the inhabitants consider themselves to be *mestizo*, and the way of life in Misión Chichimeca that of a typical *mestizo* rather than Indian community.

[*See also* Mixton War; Toltec; Tolteca-Chichimeca, Historia.]

BIBLIOGRAPHY

Castile, George. *North American Indians: An Introduction to the Chichimecas.* New York, 1949. A controversial extension of the ethnonym.

Davies, Nigel. *The Toltec Heritage from the Fall of Tula to the Rise of Tenochtitlan.* Norman, Okla., 1980. Contains an excellent chapter on the Chichimecs and a comprehensive discussion of the legend of Xolotl.

Davila Aguirre, J. de Jesús. *Chichimecatl: Origen, cultura, lucha y extinción de los Galardos Barbaros del Norte.* Saltillo, 1967. Comprehensive discussion of the culture of the peoples of northern Mexico, with a concise historical overview.

Driver, Harold E., and Wilhelmina Driver. *Ethnography and Acculturation of the Chichimeca–Jonaz of Northeast Mexico.* Bloomington, 1963. Contains comprehensive ethnohistorical background.

Gradie, Charlotte M. "Discovering the Chichimecas." *Americas* 51.1 (1994), 67–88. Discussion of the origin and use of the meanings of the word by the Aztecs and the Spanish.

Karttunen, Frances. *An Analytical Dictionary of Nahuat.* Austin, 1983.

Kirchoff, Paul. "Civilizing the Chichimecs: A Chapter in the Culture History of Ancient Mexico." *Latin American Studies* 5. University of Texas, n.d.

Powell, Philip Wayne. *Soldiers, Indians and Silver: The Northwest Advance of New Spain, 1550–1600.* Berkeley, 1952. The classic work on the Chichimeca War.

Powell, Philip Wayne. "The Chichimecas: Scourge of Silver Frontier in Sixteenth-Century Mexico." *Hispanic American Historical Review* 25 (1945), 315–338. Early article presenting a classic view of the Chichimecs.

Sahagún, Bernardino de. *Florentine Codex: General History of the Things of New Spain.* Edited and translated by Charles E. Dibble and Arthur J. O. Anderson. 12 vols. Santa Fe, N.M., 1950–1981. Monumental work on Aztec civilization, including information on the Chichimecs and the Aztecs' presumed Chichimec origins.

Van Zantwijk, Rudolph. *The Aztec Arrangement: The Social History of Pre-Spanish Mexico.* Norman, Okla., 1985.

CHARLOTTE M. GRADIE

Chicomóztoc from the *Historia Tolteca-Chichimeca. Photograph courtesy of Blas Roman Castellon Huerta.*

CHICOMÓZTOC. Derived from Nahuatl *chicome* ("seven"), *oztotl* ("cave"), and *-c* ("place"), this is the mythic place of origin of the seven tribes and their deities who populated Central Mexico. In symbolic terms these caves within a hill have been compared to the wombs from which the various peoples were born; another possible association is with the seven orifices of the human body. In either case, this term is associated with the origin, birth, or beginning of a group of people, both mythic and historical. The best-known of them are the Mexica (Aztec) who started their migration from Aztlan and a nearby place called Chicomóztoc, along with the Matlatzinca, Chalca, Colhua, Tecpaneca, Acolhua, and Tlahuica peoples. Some chronicles add the Toltec, Michuaca, Huexotzinca, and Tlaxcallan. In all accounts, the Mexica were the last to leave the place of origin. Other incidents in Chicomóztoc involved Ilancueytl, who gave birth to a flint knife, which fell to earth from the sky; from its pieces, sixteen hundred humans were created. Another story says that Chicomóztoc was the birthplace of men who initiated long generations: Xelhua, Tenoch, Ulmecatl, Xicalancatl, Mixtecatl, and Otomitl, all born of the divine couple Iztac Mixcoatl and Ilancueytl.

Attempts have been made to equate Chicomóztoc with geographical places since the eighteenth century. Some historians proposed Florida as its site; others suggested a small Central Mexican town near Tula called Chapa de Mota; and still others asserted that Chicomóztoc was to be identified with the archaeological ruins of La Quemada in the Central Mexican state of Zacatecas. Not one of these ideas has been substantiated by historical or archaeological facts. Most likely, the use of this term in chronicles refers to a legendary account, usually employed to validate political rule.

The caves, as places of origin and entrances to a lost paradise, are frequently depicted in codices, reliefs, and mural paintings of various periods and incorporate geographical and mythic glyphs. In Mesoamerica, caves are usually symbols of creation and life. Chicomóztoc is one name for these places, but there are also Colhuacán ("place of grandparents"), Teocolhuacan ("place of divine ancestors"), Tamoanchan ("house of birth"), and Cincalco ("house of maize"), among others. All these names refer to caves as places of respect and veneration. Formally, the caves are represented as a flower with four petals; this is exemplified in archaeological monuments beginning in the Olmec period, and in pictorial manuscripts, such as the *Historia Tolteca-Chichimeca*, in which Chicomóztoc is figured as seven caves within an arched hill, with people inside. These caves, too, resemble a petaloid flower.

Archaeologically, the caves found in hills were associated with the gods of rain and agriculture. Some caves have also been located below pyramidal structures in several sites. A good example of this pattern is the cave found below the Pyramid of Sun at Teotihuacan, a large tunnel more than 100 meters (330 feet) long, which ends in four natural concavities that were enlarged by human work. These caves may be seen as the shape of a flower, which suggests that the concept of Chicomóztoc as a holy place of origin had a long tradition in Mesoamerica that predated the Mexica.

[*See also* Caves.]

BIBLIOGRAPHY

Heyden, Doris. "Caves, Gods, and Myths: World-view and Planning at Teotihuacan." In *Mesoamerica: Sites and World-views*, edited by Elizabeth P. Benson, pp. 1–39. Washington, D.C., 1981. Comparative overview of the symbolic significance of caves in Mesoamerica, especially Teotihuacan, with a discussion by other specialists.

López Austin, Alfredo. *Tamoanchan y Tlalocan*. Mexico City, 1994. Extensive discussion of mythical places in Mesoamerica, according to sixteenth-century sources and modern ethnographic information.

BLAS ROMAN CASTELLON HUERTA

CHILAM BALAM, BOOKS OF, from the Yucatán Peninsula, are Maya compilations of knowledge on history, prophecy, religion, ritual, literature, the calendar, astronomy, and medicine—written in the Mayan language, using European script and paper. The contents of the books include surviving pre-Hispanic information, as well as descriptions of aspects of the Spanish culture being assimilated by the Maya during the Colonial period. Although many more of these sources are thought to have existed as recently as the nineteenth century, nine works are now available for study.

Typically named for their presumed places of origin,

these are the *Books of Chilam Balam of Chan Cah* (also known as the *Chan Kan*), of *Chumayel*, of *Ixil*, of *Káua*, of *Tekax*, of *Tizimín*, and of *Tusik*. At least one more was preserved through the interest of Juan Pío Pérez, who made copies of numerous old Maya documents from about 1835 until his death in 1859. An 1837 copy of a *Book of Chilam Balam of Maní* is included in his *Codex Pérez*, which is also thought to incorporate parts of the *Chilam Balam of Ixil* (Barrera Vásquez and Morley 1949, 14) and the *Chilam Balam of Káua* (Craine and Raindorp 1979, xvi). The *Chilam Balam of Nah* is named for two men from Teabo, José María Nah and José Secundino Nah, who signed it and are credited with authorship.

The word *Chilam*, or *chilan*, is a title meaning "mouthpiece" or "interpreter of the gods," and *balam* means "jaguar." Hence these works may be thought of as the "Books of the Jaguar Priest." Since *Balam* is a common Yucatec family name, the titles could also be translated as the "Books of the Prophet Balam" (Barrera Vásquez and Morley 1949, 10, 12–13; Roys 1967, 3). They are named for a specific prophet who probably lived in Maní during the late fifteenth through early sixteenth centuries. This *chilan* gained renown because of his apparent prediction of the impending arrival of the Spanish conquerors, as is described in the 1579 *Relación* of the town of Mérida (de la Garza et al. 1983, 1:69) and quoted in the 1633 *Historia de Yucatán* of Bernardo de Lizana (Jiménez Villalba 1988, 123–125). Some texts are repeated in several of the manuscripts (Barrera Vásquez and Rendón 1948), and it is evident that the books were recopied for many years. The extant versions generally date from the early eighteenth through the nineteenth century, but phrasing used in them can be traced to the sixteenth century (Roys 1967, 5–6, 186–187). Miram (1988, 1995) has provided transcriptions of the *Books of Chan Cah* (or *Chan Kan*), of *Chumayel*, of *Ixil*, of *Káua*, of *Nah*, of *Tekax*, of *Tizimín*, of *Tusik*, and the *Pérez Codex* (without the Treaty of Maní, a historical document). A concordance of the other books with the *Chilam Balam of Káua* has been published, as well (Miram and Miram 1988).

The project to transcribe the *Books of Chilam Balam* and assemble the concordance were part of a broader study, with the purpose of identifying the European sources that influenced the development of those Maya manuscripts. Miram (1994) concluded that of the nearly one thousand pages comprising the entire corpus, approximately 62 percent of the content can be traced to the European literature; she regards the remaining portion as being of pre-Conquest origin, although some sections are clearly derived from both cultural traditions. These include information on such topics as how to express dates in the Christian and Maya calendars. The indigenous material consists of predictions for the fates of persons, according to the place of their birth in the *uinal* (a period of 20 days). Also of pre-Conquest origin are the prophecies for *katun*s (calendrical periods of 7,200 days, or about 20 years), *tun*s (periods of 360 days), and *haab*s (periods of 365 days), as well as passages on the "Language of Zuyua," a series of riddles used to authenticate rulers. As the *Chilam Balam of Chumayel* relates (Roys 1967, 89), the examiner might, for example, request that the respondent bring him the sun. Presumably because of training received through his family, the qualified leader would know that he should produce a very large fried egg. Additionally the manuscripts prophesy the return of the pre-Hispanic culture hero Quetzalcoatl.

The presence of European content in the *Books of Chilam Balam* is readily apparent in some passages and more subtle in others. For example, the European zodiac and features of Christian religion are mentioned throughout the manuscripts, and the concentric crystalline spheres of Ptolemaic astronomy are illustrated in the *Chilam Balam of Ixil* (Paxton 1992, Figure 9.1). It is less obvious, however, that the medicinal recipes follow the patterns of Greek and Islamic treatments, rather than the Maya incantation approach, while relying on plants found only in the New World (Miram 1994; also see Roys 1931, xx–xxi). Peter Tschohl (unpublished 1969 and 1972, cited by Brotherston 1992 and Miram 1994; also see Parker 1996) has traced the origin of the interrogation of the maiden Theodora described in the *Chan Cah* (or *Chan Kan*) and *Káua* manuscripts, and in the *Pérez Codex*, to the tales of the *Thousand and One Arabian Nights* (which are written in Arabic, Islamic in tone, and originated in the region of Arabia, Persia, and India. Since Spain had been under the Islamic rule of the Moors from 711 to 1492, the tales were known there). In the Maya version, some questions from the tales were omitted, to limit the discussion to matters of local interest. As Brotherston and Miram have observed, the inclusion of the *Arabian Nights* subjects in the *Books of Chilam Balam* provides cultural information because of such selectivity.

Some *Chilam Balam* passages pertaining to the various intervals of the Maya calendar may well be transcriptions from the hieroglyphic texts of the pre-Hispanic codices (Thompson 1950, 297–302). The post-Conquest statements demonstrate a fundamental premise of the civilization—that history is prophecy. As is stated directly in the narrative on the Katun 10 Ahau (named for the day of the *tzolkin*, or 260-day calendar cycle, on which the *katun* ended) in the *Pérez Codex* (Craine and Raindorp 1979, 169), ". . . the Katun 10 Ahau begins. Here are its history and its predictions." The Maya expected events that had occurred in a particular *katun* to repeat nearly 256 years later, when the following *katun* bearing the same name fell in the calendar cycle.

The historian Ralph Roys (1967, 184) has in fact noted that many major political disturbances took place in *katun*s named 4 Ahau or 8 Ahau. In 1697, Spanish conquerors used their understanding of these prophecies to try to convince the Maya of Tayasai, Guatemala (who had emigrated from Yucatán), to surrender peacefully and become Christians. The argument advanced by the Spaniards was that the change was appropriate because Katun 8 Ahau had returned (Villagutierre Soto-Mayor 1983, 75, 248–250). The Maya at first agreed; then they offered resistance in battle. The fight was brief and dispirited, apparently because the Maya were aware that defeat was inevitable in Katun 8 Ahau (Barrera Vásquez and Morley 1949; see Jones 1989 for similar examples). Following the political subjugation of the Maya by the Spanish, the *Books of Chilam Balam* became crucial tools for preserving the pre-Hispanic civilization, so elements of their tradition are still to be found in the oral literature of Yucatán (Burns 1983).

The *katun* prophecies that report events involving Maya leaders and Spaniards have been used in the correlation of the Maya and European calendars, since the dates of the same encounters are also fixed in Spanish historical records (Thompson 1937). The pre-Hispanic occurrences in the *katun* histories have been cited in reconstructions of the major military dominations of Yucatán (Tozzer 1957, Roys 1954, Roys 1962, Thompson 1970, Ball 1986), as well as in explanations of the original populating of the peninsula, through migrations described as a "great descent" and a "little descent" (Tozzer 1957, 23–24, Barrera Vásquez and Morley 1949). Some of the pre-Hispanic lineage founders and other leaders described in the accounts are treated as celestial deities, indicating the practice of ancestor reverence.

The *Books of Chilam Balam* preserve aspects of the unified preconquest Maya view of time, religion, and spatial planning. This consolidation is clearly expressed in an ideal map of the cosmos painted on pages 76 and 75 of the pre-Hispanic *Madrid Codex*, where calendrical cycles are related to deities and the five sectors of the universe (*Codex Tro-Cortesianus* [*Codex Madrid*] 1967, Paxton forthcoming). The five sectors are the center and four perimeter areas limited by the horizon positions of sunrise and sunset on the solstice dates. In the *Chilam Balam of Chumayel* (Roys 1967, 132), these directions are superimposed on a wheel that shows the recycling sequence of 13 *katun*s. The four divisions of the horizons are the implicit reference for the directional placements of world trees, birds, foods, deities, lineages, events, and intervals of time as mentioned in the books. The texts also describe

Places of origin of the extant *Books of Chilam Balam. Courtesy of Meredith Paxton.*

the directionally oriented activities of "burners," which evidently are postconquest survivals of torch-bearing deities illustrated in the pre-Hispanic codices (Craine and Reindorp 1979, 21). The directions created by the apparent annual motion of the sun are further reflected in the *Books of Chilam Balam* by descriptions of ceremonial pilgrimages (*tzol peten*; Hanks 1988).

The information on the calendar, history, ritual interrogations, and other aspects of Maya life found in the *Books of Chilam Balam* has proved to be invaluable to the study of the pre-Hispanic people. Further, the linguistic constructions of these texts and their general similarities to the hieroglyphic manuscripts from the pre-Conquest era have greatly aided in glyphic decipherment (Álvarez Lomelí 1974; Bricker 1985, 1990a, 1990b; Miram 1994) and other studies of the codices. Barrera Vásquez and Morley (1949) and Gibson and Glass (1975, 379–387) have provided helpful commentaries on the individual *Books of Chilam Balam* (used in compiling the descriptions here), as well as extensive lists of references. The citations of manuscript lengths are from Miram and Miram (1988) or from Gibson and Glass (1975); see also Weeks (1990).

Chan Cah (also the Chan Kan), Book of Chilam Balam of. Two possible places of origin have been identified for a single manuscript. Gibson and Glass (1975, 382) associate a *Book of Chilam Balam* with the village of Chan Kan (near Peto) in the Yucatán Peninsula, and Hires (1981, 3) adds that it was acquired there by Loring Hewen in 1955. Hector M. Calderón (*Manuscrito de Chan Cah* 1982, v) credited Alfredo Barrera Vásquez with correcting the title to *Chan Cah*. Calderón states that the manuscript was discovered in Chan Cah, Quintana Roo, during the 1960s and that Hewen donated it to the Instituto Nacional de Antropología e Historia in 1963.

length: 128 pages
date: mostly 1820s (Hires 1981, 12) or possibly between 1823 and 1845 (Héctor M. Calderón in *Manuscrito de Chan Cah* 1982, vi–vii)
present location: Instituto Nacional de Antropología e Historia, Mexico City
photographic reproduction: Manuscrito de Chan Cah (1982)
commentaries or other editions: Hires (1981)

Chumayel, Book of Chilam Balam of
length: 107 pages
date: 1782 (Roys 1967, 7)
compiler: Juan José Hoil (Roys 1967, 7)
present location: Princeton University Library, Princeton, N.J.
photographic reproduction: Gordon (1913)
commentaries or other editions: Barrera Vásquez and Morley (1949, 19–20), Roys (1967), Edmonson (1986).

Numerous editions of this work have been published; besides English and Mayan, it is available in Spanish (Mediz Bolio 1930), French, and Italian.

Ixil, Book of Chilam Balam of
length: 88 pages
date: Roys (1946, 93) stated that the second page mentions 1701 as the current year. He was of the opinion that the content of the *Ixil* is so similar to portions of the *Káua*, which he dated to the last decade of the eighteenth century, that it must have been contemporary.
present location: Biblioteca Nacional de Antropología of the Instituto Nacional de Antropología, Mexico City
photographic reproduction: Glass (1964, pl. 70); Paxton (1992, figs. 9.1 and 9.3)
commentaries or other editions: Roys (1946)

Káua, Book of Chilam Balam of
length: 141 leaves
date: Roys (1946, 100) dated the manuscript to the last decade of the eighteenth century because "the dates 1789 and 1793 are associated with quotations from Spanish almanacs of apparently recent date."
present location: Princeton University Library, Princeton, N.J. and unknown (Weeks 1990, 77–78).
commentaries or other editions: Barrera Vásquez (1942); Barrera Vázquez and Morley (1949, 19–20); Bricker and Miram (forthcoming). Roys (1931) has compiled remedies for health problems from various sources, including the *Káua*.

Maní, Book of Chilam Balam of (included in *Pérez Codex*)
length: As many as four books may have existed in *Maní*. The copies in the *Pérez Codex* (176 pages) may preserve parts of three. The sources being copied by Pérez were not completely identified; pages 50–64 are from an "almanac from the archive of Maní," and pages 65–137 are from a *Book of Chilam Balam of Maní* (Gibson and Glass 1975, 383).
date: October 25, 1837, at Ticul (with notation on page 170)
copyist: Juan Pío Pérez
present location of Pérez Codex: Museo Nacional de Antropología, Mexico City (Archivo Histórico del Instituto Nacional de Antropología e Historia)
photographic reproduction: Craine and Raindorp (1979, 134–138)
commentaries or other editions: Barrera Vásquez (1942); Barrera Vásquez and Morley (1949, 13–16); Craine and Raindorp (1979)

Nah, Book of Chilam Balam of
length: 64 pages

date: 1857 (Roys 1946, 102), with entries continuing as late as 1896 (Tozzer 1921, 191). Roys suggested that part of the *Nah* was copied from the *Tekax,* and subsequent examination has upheld this view (*Manuscritos de Tekax y Nah* 1981).

compilers: José María Nah and José Secundino Nah (Miram 1994, 211)

present location: Princeton University Library, Princeton, N.J.

photographic reproduction: Gubler and Bolles (2000); *Manuscritos de Tekax y Nah* (1981)

commentaries or other editions: Barrera Vásquez and Morley (1949, 21); studied by Roys (1931)

Tekax, Book of Chilam Balam of

length: 37 pages transcribed from photographs; 28 pages are now known to exist (*Manuscritos de Tekax y Nah* 1981, Introduction, p. 2)

date: 1833 (Roys 1946, 101)

present location: History Archive, Instituto Nacional de Antropología e Historia, Mexico City

photographic reproduction: *Manuscritos de Tekax y Nah* (1981)

commentaries or other editions: Barrera Vásquez and Morley (1949, 21); Gibson and Glass (1975, 386)

Tizimín, Book of Chilam Balam of

length: 54 pages

date: unknown. The parish priest of Tizimín had owned the book for many years before he inscribed the date, March 23, 1870, when he gave it as a gift (Barrera Vásquez and Morley 1949, 18)

present location: Museo Nacional de Antropología, Mexico City

photographic reproduction: *El libro de Chilam Balam de Tizimín: Museo Nacional de Antropología, Mexico City* (*Cod. 35–66*) (1980)

commentaries or other editions: Barrera Vásquez and Rendón (1948); Barrera Vásquez and Morley (1949, 18–19); Edmonson (1982); Makemson (1951); Thompson (1951)

Tusik, Book of Chilam Balam of

length: 58 pages

date: 1875 copy of material includes the date 1628; existence reported by Alfonso Villa Rojas in 1936

present location: Tusik? Slightly different copies are in Germany and Mexico (Héctor M. Calderón in *Chilam Balam de Tuzik* 1996, 7)

photographic reproduction: *Chilam Balam de Tuzik* (1981 and 1996)

commentaries or other editions: Villa Rojas (1945, 73)

Other Books of Chilam Balam. The *Chilam Balam of Oxkutzcab* has been treated as a possible inclusion in the *Codex Pérez,* but according to Barrera Vásquez and Morley (1949, 20–21) this is in error, and no evidence supports the survival of the document. *Books of Chilam Balam of Teabo* (or possibly of *Tabi,* not the same as the *Nah*) and of *Telchac* are mentioned by Genet and Chelbatz (1927, 42). The *Books of Chilam Balam of Hocabá,* of *Nabulá,* of *Peto,* of *Tihosuco,* and of *Tixcocob* are known primarily from references by Tozzer (1921, 191–192; also see Genet 1934, 67–68). Barrera Vásquez and Morley (1949, 21) were of the opinion that the *Teabo* is the same as the *Tekax,* and Weeks (1990, 78) concurs. Tozzer thought the *Hocabá* was the same as the *Káua,* because the owner of the *Káua* had once resided in Hocabá. The *Códice de Calkiní* (Barrera Vásquez 1957), which relates historical and geneological information, is also known as the *Crónica de Calkiní* and the *Book of Chilam Balam of Calkiní* (Gibson and Glass 1975, 379; Weeks 1990, 66).

[*See also* Poetry, Songs, and Prose Sources.]

BIBLIOGRAPHY

Álvarez Lomelí, María Cristina. *Textos coloniales del Libro de Chilam Balam de Chumayel y textos glíficos del Códice de Dresde.* Universidad Nacional Autónoma de México, Centro de Estudios Mayas. Mexico City, 1974.

Ball, Joseph W. "Campeche, the Itza, and the Postclassic: A Study in Ethnohistorical Archaeology." In *Late Lowland Maya Civilization, Classic to Postclassic,* edited by Jeremy A. Sabloff and E. Wyllys Andrews V, pp. 379–408. Albuquerque, 1986.

Barrera Vásquez, Alfredo. "El pronostico de los 20 signos de los días del calendario maya, según los Libros de Chilam Balam de Kaua y de Maní." In *Proceedings of the 27th International Congress of Americanists (1939),* 27A.1:470–481. Mexico City, 1942.

Barrera Vásquez, Alfredo. *Códice de Calkiní.* Biblioteca Campechana, 4. Campeche, Gobierno del Estado, 1957.

Barrera Vásquez, Alfredo, and Sylvanus G. Morley. *The Maya Chronicles.* Carnegie Institution of Washington, 585. Washington, D.C., 1949. Includes English translation of the statements by Barrera Vásquez concerning survival of a *Book of Chilam Balam of Oxkutzcab* (first published as *El Códice Pérez.* See *Revista Mexicana de Estudios Antropológicos* 3.1, 1939).

Barrera Vásquez, Alfredo, and Silvia Rendón. *El libro de los Libros de Chilam Balam.* Fondo de Cultura Económica. Mexico City, 1948. Partially translated in Bárrera Vásquez and Morley (1949).

Bricker, Victoria R. "The Use of Logosyllabic Principles of Writing in the Book of Chilam Balam of Chumayel." *International Journal of American Linguistics* 51.4 (1985), 351–353.

Bricker, Victoria R. *A Morpheme Concordance of the Book of Chilam Balam of Tizimin.* Middle American Research Institute, Tulane University, 58. New Orleans, 1990a.

Bricker, Victoria R. *A Morpheme Concordance of the Book of Chilam Balam of Chumayel.* Middle American Research Institute, Tulane University, 59. New Orleans, 1990b.

Bricker, Victoria R., and Helga-Maria Miram. *An Encounter of Two Worlds: The Book of Chilam Balam of Káua.* Middle American Research Institute, Tulane University, 68. New Orleans, forthcoming.

Brotherston, Gordon. *Book of the Fourth World.* New York and Cambridge, 1992.

Burns, Allan F. *An Epoch of Miracles: Oral Literature of the Yucatec Maya.* Austin, 1983.

Chilam Balam de Tuzik. Mexico City, 1981; 1996.

Codex Tro-Cortesianus (Codex Madrid) Museo de America Madrid. Introduction and Summary by Ferdinand Anders. Codices Selecti, 8. Graz, Austria, 1967.

Craine, Eugene R., and Reginald C. Raindorp, eds. and trans. *The*

Codex Pérez and the Book of Chilam Balam of Maní. Norman, Okla., 1979. English translation based on the 1949 Spanish translation by Ermilio Solís Alcalá (*Códice Pérez. Traducción libre del maya al castellano.* Mérida, Liga de Acción Social); also on comparison with photographs of the original in the Peabody Museum of American Archaeology and Ethnology, Harvard University.

Edmonson, Munro S., trans. and annot. *The Ancient Future of the Itza: The Book of Chilam Balam of Tizimin.* Austin, 1982.

Edmonson, Munro S. *Heaven Born Merida and Its Destiny: The Book of Chilam Balam of Chumayel.* Austin, 1986.

Garza, Mercedes de la (coord.), Ana Luisa Izquierdo, María del Carmen León, and Tolita Figueroa. *Relaciones histórico-geográficas de la gobernación de Yucatán.* 2 vols. Mexico City, 1983.

Genet, Jean. "Mélange maya-quichés." *Revue des Études Mayas-Quichees* 1.2 (1934), 64–80.

Genet, Jean, and Pierre Chelbatz. *Histoire des peuples Mayas-Quichés (Mexique, Guatemala, Honduras).* Paris, 1927.

Gibson, Charles, and John B. Glass. "A Census of Middle American Prose Manuscripts in the Native Historical Tradition." In *Handbook of Middle American Indians,* vol. 15, part 4, pp. 322–400. Austin, 1975.

Glass, John B. *Catálogo de la coleccion de códices.* Museo Nacional de Antropología, Mexico City, 1964.

Gordon, George B. *The Book of Chilam Balam of Chumayel with Introduction by G. B. Gordon.* University of Pennsylvania, The Museum, Anthropological Publications, 5. Philadelphia, 1913. This copy has been reproduced as Mayan Studies 6, Aegean Park Press, Laguna Hills, Calif., 1993.

Gubler, Ruth, and David Bolles, eds. *Book of Chilam Balam of Na.* Culver City, Calif., 2000. Includes a facsimile, with edited Mayan text and translation to English.

Hanks, William F. "Grammar, Style, and Meaning in a Maya Manuscript." *International Journal of American Linguistics* 54.3 (1988), 331–365. Includes a review of *Heaven Born Merida and Its Destiny: The Book of Chilam Balam of Chumayel,* translated and annotated by Munro S. Edmonson.

Hires, Marla Korlin. "The Chilam Balam of Chan Kan." Ph.D. diss., Tulane University, 1981. Includes a transcription and translation to English.

Jiménez Villalba, ed. *Historia de Yucatán,* by Bernardo de Lizana, [1633]. Madrid, 1988.

Jones, Grant D. *Maya Resistance to Spanish Rule: Time and History on a Colonial Frontier.* Albuquerque, 1989.

El libro de Chilam Balam de Tizimin: Museo Nacional de Antropología, Mexico City (Cod. 35–66), introduction by Karl Herbert Mayer. Graz, Austria, 1980.

Makemson, Maud Worcester, transl. *The Book of the Jaguar Priest.* New York, 1951.

Manuscrito de Chan Cah, trans. by Héctor M. Calderón. Mexico City, 1982. Maya and Spanish text in transcription and translation.

Manuscritos de Tekax y Nah. Mexico City, 1981. Includes a transcription of the *Nah* and its translation to Spanish.

Mediz Bolio, Antonio. *Libro de Chilam de Chumayel. Traducción del idioma maya al castellano.* Ediciones del "Repertorio Americano," San Jose, 1930.

Miram, Helga-Maria. *Transkriptionen der (Transcriptions of the; Transcripciones de los) Chilam Balames.* 3 vols. (1:*Ixil, Chumayel, Nah*; 2:*Tekax, Chancah, Tizimin*; 3:*Tusik, Codice Pérez*). Hamburg, 1988; vol. 4 (*Kaua I & Kaua II*). Hamburg, 1995.

Miram, Helga-Maria. "The Role of the Books of Chilam Balam in Deciphering Maya Hieroglyphics: New Material and New Considerations." In *Seventh Palenque Round Table,* edited by Merle Greene Robertson (gen. ed.) and Virginia M. Fields (vol. ed.), pp. 211–216. San Francisco, 1994.

Miram, Helga-Maria, and Wolfgang Miram. *Konkordanz der Chilam Balames.* 6 vols. Hamburg, 1988.

National Geographic. "Archaeological Map of Middle American, Land of the Feathered Serpent." Researched and compiled by George E. Stuart. *National Geographic* 134.4 (1968), supplement.

Parker, Margaret R. *The Story of a Story across Cultures: The Case of the Doncella Teodor.* Colección Támesis, Series A, 161. London, 1996.

Paxton, Merideth. "The Books of Chilam Balam: Astronomical Content and the Paris Codex." In *The Sky in Mayan Literature,* edited by Anthony F. Aveni, pp. 216–246. New York and Oxford, 1992.

Paxton, Merideth. *Cycles and Steps: the Cosmos of the Yucatec Maya.* Albuquerque, forthcoming.

Roys, Ralph L. *The Ethno-botany of the Maya.* Tulane University, Middle American Research Series, 2. New Orleans, 1931.

Roys, Ralph L. "The Book of Chilam Balam of Ixil." *Notes on Middle American Archaeology and Ethnology,* Carnegie Institution of Washington, Division of Historical Research 3.75 (1946), 90–103.

Roys, Ralph L. *The Maya Katun Prophecies of the Books of Chilam Balam, Series I.* Carnegie Institution of Washington, 606. Washington, D.C., 1954.

Roys, Ralph L. *The Political Geography of the Yucatan Maya.* Carnegie Institution of Washington, 606. Washington, D.C., 1957.

Roys, Ralph L. "Literary Sources for the History of Mayapan." In *Mayapan, Yucatan, Mexico,* pp. 25–86. Carnegie Institution of Washington, 619. Washington, D.C., 1962.

Roys, Ralph L., trans. and ed. *The Book of Chilam Balam of Chumayel.* Norman, Okla., 1967. Originally published as Carnegie Institution of Washington, 438. Washington, D.C., 1933.

Thompson, J. Eric S. *Maya Chronology: The Correlation Question.* Carnegie Institution of Washington, 456. Washington, D.C., 1937.

Thompson, J. Eric S. *Maya Hieroglyphic Writing: Introduction.* Carnegie Institution of Washington, 589. Washington, D.C., 1950.

Thompson, J. Eric S. "Review of: *The Book of the Jaguar Priest,* by Maud W. Makemson." *American Anthropologist* 53.4 (1951), 546–547.

Thompson, J. Eric S. *Maya History and Religion.* The Civilization of the American Indian Series, 99. Norman, Okla., 1970.

Tozzer, Alfred M. *A Maya Grammar, with Bibliography and Appraisement of the Works Noted.* Papers of the Peabody Museum of American Archaeology and Ethnology, Harvard University, 9. Cambridge, Mass., 1921.

Tozzer, Alfred M. *Chichen Itza and Its Cenote of Sacrifice: A Comparative Study of Contemporary Maya and Toltec.* Memoirs of the Peabody Museum of Archaeology and Ethnology, Harvard University, 11–12. Cambridge, Mass., 1957.

Villa Rojas, Alfonso. *The Maya of East Central Quintana Roo.* Carnegie Institution of Washington, 559. Washington, D.C., 1945.

Villagutierre Soto-Mayor, Juan de. *History of the Conquest of the Province of the Itza* [1701], translated from the second Spanish edition by Brother Robert D. Wood, S. M., edited and with notes by Frank E. Comparato. Culver City, Calif., 1983. Originally published in Spanish.

Weeks, John M. (compiler). *Mesoamerican Ethnohistory in United States Libraries, Reconstruction of the William E. Gates Collection of Historical and Linguistic Manuscripts.* Culver City, 1990.

MERIDETH PAXTON

CHILIES. Chili as a fresh or dried fruit has been the basic condiment in the Mesoamerican diet. Of the fifty wild species of *Capsicum* native to the American continents, five are cultivated. *Capsicum annuum* is the common chili of Mesoamerica. *Capsicum chinense* is widespread in central and northern South America and is the "habanero" chili of southern Mesoamerica. Archaeological seeds of *Capsicum* from Tehuacán date to about 7000 years ago and probably represent the wild plant; domesticated forms have been recovered from later sites in the Valley of Mexico, Oaxaca, and Tamaulipas. Domestication occurred along with other Mesoamerican crops and resulted in hundreds of forms that are classified today into fifteen major types (such as jalapeño, ancho, cascabel, guajillo, mulato, miahuateco, de chorro, de ramos, pasilla, mirasol, serrano, and others). Each type of chili with its characteristic form, size, and color grows under specific conditions so that different forms can grow from sea level to the high mountains. "Chiltepín," the wild form of the dry tropical forest, is still much appreciated.

The morphological diversity is also paralleled by its flavors and the pungency due to a substance called capsaicin in the placenta (the tissue between the fruit wall and the seed). The *Florentine Codex* describes many of the dishes and sauces that used varied chilies as ingredients; at least six degrees of pungency were noted. Mesoamerican markets offered a great diversity of chilies, a colorful and sensorial delight that one can appreciate even today in Mexico. Tributes of chilies to the Aztec Empire from at least thirty communities have been documented and illustrated in such codices as *Códice Mendocino*, *Códice Yanhuitlán*, and *Códice Sierra*.

Chilies, along with maize, beans, and squash, were part of the diet of those who ascended into the Tlalocan paradise. Tlatlauhqui cihuatl ichilzintli was a sister of Tlalolc and Chicomecóatl. Chili is represented in glyphs such as those found at Monte Albán. Archaeological evidence in the form of *molcajetes* (nahuatl: *molcaxitl*) attest to the antiquity of chili as dietary complement and are still used today for making chili sauces. The famous Mexican sauce, mole, is Postconquest in origin. Nonetheless, it includes ingredients of Mesoamerican origin, along with exotic components.

The fruits of chili were combined with other plants and employed in treating such illnesses as cough, ear infections, infected gums, wounds, diarrhea, and constipation. The irritating smoke of burnt chilies was used as a form of punishment of disobedient children.

Chili is derived from the plant's Nahuatl name *chili*. It is also known as *ic* in Mayan cultures, *guiiña'* by the Zapotec, *yaha* by the Mixteco, and *niiv* by the Mixe.

BIBLIOGRAPHY

Laborde Cancino, J. A., and O. Pozo Campodonico. *Presente y pasado del chile en México*. Mexico City, 1984.
Long-Solis, J. *Capsicum y cultura: La historia del chilli*. Mexico City, 1998.

ROBERT A. BYE

CHIMALPAHIN QUAUHTLEHUANITZIN, DOMINGO FRANCISCO DE SAN ANTÓN MUÑÓN.

It has taken centuries for the seventeenth-century Nahua annalist Chimalpahin to receive the recognition that he is due, though he is now celebrated as Chalco's Mesoamerican historian laureate and is the namesake of a museum there. Born in Tzaqualtitlan Tenanco, a subdivision of Amecameca (Amaquemecan), Chalco, on 26 May 1579, he was the grandson of the late Don Domingo Hernández Ayopochtzin, a seventh-generation descendant of the founding king of the polity. Don Domingo was learned and esteemed, especially for his education and his record-keeping skills in the ancient tradition.

It seems that Chimalpahin was baptized "Domingo Francisco," a sure sign of his commoner status, because neither of his parents held titles of nobility. Nevertheless, Chimalpahin's father, Juan Agustín Ixpintzin, inherited his father-in-law's collection of manuscripts, which suggests the son had some status in the community. By the 1550s, Amecameca was a Dominican province, and Chimalpahin was probably educated by friars at its monastery. It is also likely that he pored over the numerous pictorial histories his grandfather had collected. Almost all of them concerned Tzaqualtitlan Tenanco, an aspect of ethnopatriotism typical of Nahua Mexico; however, in 1547 Viceroy don Antonio de Mendoza had requested an accounting of the histories of all Amecameca in order to determine the rightful rulers. To this end, ancient texts were taken from many noble houses and studied by a native judge sent by the viceroy. New histories were written as well. Don Rodrigo de Rosas Xoecatzin, a nobleman from another part of Amecameca, is reported to have served as amanuensis to the judge.

Otherwise, Chimalpahin furnished little direct evidence about his life experiences, and it is only through fragmentary anecdotes and other emendations in his texts that we know anything about him. He did record that at the age of fourteen he moved to Mexico City, where it was his good fortune to live and work in the ward of Xolloco at a small church called San Antonio Abad. Xolloco was in the old Tenochtitlan quarter of Moyotlan (San Juan), just two kilometers south of the *zócalo*, so it was a locale of much activity. Chimalpahin resided at San Antonio at least until 1624, when the church was closed by city officials.

Just who furnished Chimalpahin with the expensive ink, paper, and leisure to write his histories is not certain, but it is likely that his patron was San Antonio's priest, Fray Agustín del Espíritu Santo, whom Chimalpahin called *notlaçotatzin* ("my precious father"). Fray Agustín knew the famed Jesuit Nahuatl orator Juan de Tovar, and the two men were instrumental in the indoctrination and instruction of young native elites from Amecameca.

In Mexico City, Chimalpahin moved between the Spanish and Nahua worlds. There is evidence in his writings that he returned to Amecameca from time to time. On more than one occasion he interviewed notable elders—both men and women—to obtain information for his history of Tzaqualtitlan Tenanco. There he also made use of their ancient manuscripts, which he described in some detail regarding size, content, and ownership. He used diverse Nahuatl terms to identify the various texts—telling evidence of a strong, centuries-old literary tradition. He recorded that he was gathering all the information, reordering it, and then writing a book (*amoxtli*) so that future generations would know their illustrious past. His industry generated a wealth of extant information about Nahua culture from a unique indigenous perspective, a treasure that would have otherwise been lost. That he wrote in Nahuatl for a Nahua readership speaks to his optimism about his people's future.

Chimalpahin reveals nothing of the circumstances in Mexico City that prompted his vocation as a historian. Certainly his education, family background, and intelligence played a role; and at some point in his early twenties (c.1600–1610), his occupation, at least part time, was that of *copista*. A chronological catalog of his writings is difficult to establish because not all the texts are dated, but it is evident that much of his earliest work entailed the transcription to alphabetic script of a variety of pictorial documents. Most were anonymous and without provenience, although he gave credit when he could.

These earliest accounts were essentially a miscellany about Mexico Tenochtitlan, Tlatelolco, Tetzcoco, and other *altepetl*; they included royal genealogies, migration accounts, and stories of conquest, along with *altepetl* histories. They date as early as 670 CE and cover nearly one thousand years. They are rich and precious accounts, and Chimalpahin copied and transcribed them into his *xiuhtlapohualli*, or annals. Typically, each account begins with a cross mark at the top of the page and the familiar *Nican ompehua* . . . ("Here begins . . ."), although he starts some texts with Spanish headings. Otherwise, Chimalpahin seldom titled his accounts, and they have come to be known by various Spanish labels—the "Relaciones," the "Diario," the *Exercicio quotidiano*, and so forth. There is nothing equivalent in American history written by a known indigenous author in his own language and signed by the author.

Chimalpahin's methodology was to survey dozens of texts and to corroborate the information by comparison with other accounts and by asking Nahua elders about them. He often traveled to other towns to examine additional materials. Whenever possible, he named his sources. One well-known reference is to a portion of a Nahuatl account by Hernando de Alvarado Tezozomoc;

heretofore known as the *Crónica mexicayotl*, it is in fact written in Chimalpahin's characteristic language and style. Moreover, the text contains information from other sources with entire portions authored by Chimalpahin alone. In his annals in general, there is much visual and aural imagery; from the "black and red" (pictorial) manuscripts he incorporates speeches by kings, pronouncements from gods, and conversations between relatives, thereby conserving the vitality of Nahua voice and perspective.

While he was living in Mexico City, Chimalpahin probably did not mix socially with either indigenous or Spanish elites; nevertheless, he knew many of them and recorded their activities in a personal journal which is a Colonial manifestation of his *xiuhtlapohualli*. Pious and devoted to Catholic ritual, he tells of many church-related events. But he also reports on the comings and goings of viceroys, activities in the Philippines, and the ravages of epidemic disease, floods, and earthquakes in the capital. He sometimes adds, *ynin huel* ("truly, this happened"). Characteristically, information about New Spain's indigenous peoples declines as time passes.

At some time during his twenty years of writing, he began to sign himself "don Domingo de San Antón Muñón Chimalpahin Quauhtlehuanitzin." "Don" was a title used by Colonial indigenous nobility; "Domingo" was one of his birth names, probably after his grandfather; "San Antón" referred to the church where he lived and worked; "Muñón" was the family name of San Antón's patrons; and "Chimalpahin Quauhtlehuanitzin" were the names of two famous noblemen from Tzaqualtitlan Tenanco, the latter having ruled as king (1418–1465). Chimalpahin signs himself thus with only slight variations in most of his histories; however, in Mexico City he was probably known only as "Domingo de San Antón."

Chimalpahin also had access to Spanish books. He made a copy of Francisco López de Gómara's *Conquista de México*, though how he managed to come by that forbidden book is not known. The Spanish conquest, however, had little impact on his perception of Nahua history. For Chimalpahin, the golden age of Nahua life ended with the Aztec's subjugation of his Chalca ancestors in the 1460s.

His literary erudition is remarkable but little appreciated. For example, he extracted whole sections on world geography from Enrico Martínez's *Reportorio de los tiempos* (1606) and ecclesiastical treatises from Fray Juan Bautista's *Sermonario en lengua mexicana* (1606) and then interpolated them in his annals. He was also familiar with the works of classical authors like Sophocles and the theologians Saint Augustine and Saint Thomas Aquinas.

Chimalpahin stopped working on his Mexico City journal in mid-sentence in 1615, but he continued to research and write other texts, the most notable being the history of his home town in the 1620s. The last date to be entered was 1631. We do not know of his life after San Antón was closed, and there is no mention of him by any of his contemporaries. His histories, more than one thousand folios, eventually became part of the library of Mexico City bibliophile and savant Don Carlos Sigüenza y Góngora (1645–1700), who added a brief note about Chimalpahin in his journal. Over time Chimalpahin's histories were dispersed; they are now held at the Bibliothèque Nationale of Paris; the Bible Society Library, Cambridge University Library, England; the Newberry Library, Chicago; and the Archivo Histórico at the Instituto Nacional de Antropología e Historia, Mexico City.

Despite his obscurity during the Colonial period, Chimalpahin nearly became a national icon during the Independence era. Carlos María de Bustamante, a champion of liberation from Spain, decided that Chimalpahin should be celebrated as a symbol of Mexico's glorious indigenous heritage. He felt that Chimalpahin's version of the *Conquista de México* (and surely his other works) should be published. Bustamante solicited funds from all the newly formed states of Mexico in support of Chimalpahin and his scholarship. Several states sent as much as several hundred pesos (in exchange for a given number of books), and Bustamante published a seriously flawed Spanish-language edition of the *Conquista* manuscript. That there was no further mention of Chimalpahin was not the fault of Bustamante but rather the result of the upheavals in politically unstable Mexico. It would be another century and a half before Chimalpahin's great history of Indian Mexico found a ready audience.

BIBLIOGRAPHY

Chimalpahin Cuauhtlehuanitzin, Domingo Francisco de San Antón Muñon. *Society and Politics in Mexico Tenochtitlan, Tlatelolco, Texcoco, Culhuacan, and Other Nahua Altepetl in Central Mexico: The Nahuatl and Spanish Annals and Accounts Collected and Recorded by don Domingo de San Antón Muñon Chimalpahin Quauhtlehuanitzin, Codex Chimalpahin.* 2 vols. Edited and translated by Arthur J. O. Anderson and Susan Schroeder. Civilization of the American Indian Series, 225. Norman, Okla., 1997.

Chimalpahin Cuauhtlehuanitzin, Domingo F. de S. A. M. *Die Relationen Chimalpahin's zur Geschichte México's. Teil 1, Die Zeit bis zur Conquista 1521; Teil 2, Das Jahrhundert nach der Conquista (1522–1615).* Edited by Günter Zimmermann. Universität Hamburg, Abhandlungen aus dem Gebiet der Auslandskunde, vol. 68, Reihe B (Völkerkunde, Kulturgeschichte und Sprachen), vols. 38, 39. Hamburg, 1963, 1965.

Chimalpahin Cuauhtlehuanitzin, Domingo F. de S. A. M. *Historia de las conquistas de Hernando Cortés, escrita en español por Francisco López de Gómara, traducida al mexicano y aprobada por verdadera por Juan Bautista de San Antón Muñon Chimalpahin Quauhtlehuanitzin, indio mexicano.* Edited by Carlos María de Bustamante. 2 vols. Mexico City, 1826.

Chimalpahin Cuauhtlehuanitzin, Domingo F. de S. A. M. *Memorial breve acerca de la fundación de la Ciudad de Culhuacan.* Edited and translated by Victor M. Castillo F. Mexico City, 1991.

Chimalpahin Cuauhtlehuanitzin, Domingo F. de S. A. M. *Octava relación: Obra histórica de Domingo Francisco de San Antón Muñon Chimalpahin Cuauhtlehuanitzin.* Edited and translated by José Rubén Romero Galván. Mexico City, 1983.

Chimalpahin Cuauhtlehuanitzin, Domingo F. de S. A. M. *Relaciones originales de Chalco Amaquemecan escritas por Don Francisco de San Antón Muñon Chimalpahin Cuauhtlehuanitzin.* Edited and translated by Silvia Rendón. Mexico City and Buenos Aires, 1965.

Chimalpahin Cuauhtlehuanitzin, Domingo F. de S. A. M. *Troisième relation et autres documents originaux de Chimalpahin Quauhtlehuanitzin.* Vol. 2. Edited and translated by Jacqueline de Durand-Forest. Paris, 1987.

Durand-Forest, Jacqueline. *L'Histoire de la Vallée de Mexico selon Chimalpahin Quauhtlehuanitzin (du XIe au XVIe siècle).* Vol. 1. Paris, 1987.

Schroeder, Susan. *Chimalpahin and the Kingdoms of Chalco.* Tucson, 1991.

Schroeder, Susan. *Chimalpahin y los reinos de Chalco.* Translated by Joaquín Francisco Zaballa Omaña. Mexico City, 1994.

SUSAN SCHROEDER

CHIMALPOPOCA, CODEX. One of the most frequently cited sixteenth-century Nahuatl texts, the *Codex Chimalpopoca* documents the pre-Conquest history of the Valley of Mexico and serves as a primary source for Aztec mythology. It is best known for its stories of the hero-god Quetzalcoatl.

Formerly kept at the Museo Nacional de Antropología, Mexico City, the manuscript had disappeared by 1949 and must now be studied in the 1945 facsimile edition of Primo Feliciano Velázquez. It was penned sometime after 1590 (judging by its Jesuit-inspired orthography) and is a compilation of three earlier alphabetic-script writings—the first and third in Nahuatl, the second in Spanish. Because published editions have omitted the Spanish section, the name "Chimalpopoca" has often been applied only to the parts in Nahuatl. All three are described here.

Annals of Cuauhtitlan. Composed in 1563 with additions as late as 1570, as stated by the anonymous author, the Annals of Cuauhtitlan takes the form of a pre-Cortésian *xiuhpohualli* ("year count"). Thus, events are dated by the year names of the 52-year calendrical cycle (1 Reed, 2 Flint, etc.), starting with a 1 Reed that may be correlated with 635 CE. In that year, it is written, the ancestral Chichimecs—or proto-Aztecs—emerged from Chicomóztoc ("Seven Caves") and began their migration south toward the future city of Cuauhtitlan. [*See* Chicomóztoc.]

Year by year, the author recounts the history of the Cuauhtitlan people, whose capital was destined to be the fourth center in the Valley of Mexico after the Triple Alliance cities of Tenochtitlan, Tetzcoco, and Tlacopan. The history of Tenochtitlan itself is also carefully treated and becomes the main subject of the annals from 3 Rabbit (1430) to the year the Spaniards arrived, 1 Reed (1519). It was in 1430 that Tenochtitlan, seat of the Mexica Aztec and future site of Mexico City, embarked on its epoch of glory. A protracted war had just been won, with the result that the people known as Tepaneca, thereafter seated in Tlacopan, were forced to end their long tyranny over the Mexica. The detailed account of this Tepaneca War and of its origins, going back to a year 6 Reed (1407), makes for one of the most significant passages in the Annals. Along the way, it contributes to the biography of Nezahualcóyotl, future king of Tetzcoco, presented as Tenochtitlan's ally and the war's hero.

Earlier passages dated 1 House (817 CE) through 7 Rabbit (1070) are devoted to a history of Tollan, the ancient Toltec capital at the northern end of the Valley of Mexico and the fabled precursor of Aztec civilization. Here we find an extended account of the late Toltec ruler Topiltzin Quetzalcoatl, who fled Tollan and was taken into the skies as a deity. A child of virgin birth ("placed in his mother's belly when she swallowed a piece of jade"), Quetzalcoatl became a ruler of impeccable saintliness. He refused to make human sacrifices "because he greatly loved his subjects, who were Toltecs; snakes, birds, and butterflies that he killed were what his sacrifices always were." But "sorcerers" tricked him into drunkenness and incest, causing him to flee to the eastern seashore, where he cremated himself; he then passed through the underworld and reappeared as the morning star. The shapely story, with its echoes of the life of Jesus, is gratifying to readers with European sensibilities—who should be careful to note that it is part of a Colonial text not free from missionary influence. Nevertheless, the Annals of Cuauhtitlan offer a wealth of precise, unacculturated detail not only on the pre-Conquest sequence of wars and kings but also on such topics as statecraft, the tribute system, human sacrifice, manufactures, engineering, clothing, land tenure, and the role of women.

Ponce's *Relación*. The *Breve relación de los dioses y ritos de la gentilidad* ("Short account of the gods and rites of the heathens"), by the Indian cleric Pedro Ponce de León (1546?–1628?), takes up three leaves (six sides) of the forty-three-leaf codex. In Spanish, it provides fragmentary notices on Aztec deities, rites of passage, farmer's rituals, medicine, and winemaking.

Legend of the Suns. Occupying the last eleven leaves (twenty-two sides) of the codex, the so-called Legend of the Suns, with its cosmological stories blending into an account of Mexica history, stands as the only creation epic known to have survived in the Nahuatl language. Dated 22 May 1558, the work is apparently a narration,

or reading, of an old-style pictographic book now lost. Using demonstrative phrases ("This sun was . . . ," "These people were . . . "), the anonymous narrator seems to be pointing to pictures.

The first sun to be created, we are told, was simply "destroyed." The second sun was blown away by wind; the third, consumed by fire. During the time of the fourth sun, the earth and its people were destroyed by water. After the flood, the god Quetzalcoatl descends to the underworld and—in one of the most quoted episodes in Aztec mythology—brings back bones from which the present race of humans will be formed. Mictlantecuhtli ("Dead-Land Lord") tries to stop him, but Quetzalcoatl says, "No, I'm taking them forever." In response, Mictlantecuhtli causes the bones to be nibbled; thus the origin of human mortality.

In subsequent passages, Quetzalcoatl discovers maize; the fifth sun (the sun of today) is created; human sacrifice is instituted to nourish the sun; and a pair of mysterious heroes, Xiuhnel and Mimich, engage in a deadly sexual combat with two deer women. Now begins the succession of worldly military conquests, followed by the rise and fall of Tollan and, finally, the history of the Mexica down to the Spanish conquest.

A few of the tales, notably the flood myth and the story of the discovery of maize, are still extant in Mesoamerican oral tradition. The Legend of the Suns has inspired modern Mexican poets, including Octavio Paz, who could write (with reference to the story of Quetzalcoatl and Mictlantecuhtli), "For Mexicans, death sees and touches itself: it is the body emptied of the soul, the pile of bones that somehow . . . must bloom again" ("Mexico and the United States," *New Yorker*, 17 Sept. 1979).

BIBLIOGRAPHY

Bierhorst, John. *The Mythology of Mexico and Central America.* New York, 1990. Texts and geographical distribution for the basic Mesoamerican myths; references to Legend of the Suns.

Bierhorst, John. *Codex Chimalpopoca: The Text in Nahuatl with a Glossary and Grammatical Notes.* Tucson, Ariz., 1992.

Bierhorst, John. *History and Mythology of the Aztecs: The Codex Chimalpopoca.* Tucson, Ariz., 1992. Annals of Cuauhtitlan and Legend of the Suns in English, keyed to the Nahuatl text (see preceding title); includes a subject guide.

Brundage, Burr Cartwright. *A Rain of Darts: The Mexica Aztecs.* Austin, Tex., 1972. Colorful Mexica history with many references to the *Codex Chimalpopoca.*

Brundage, Burr Cartwright. *The Fifth Sun: Aztec Gods, Aztec World.* Austin, Tex., 1979. Detailed overview of Aztec mythology with references to the *Codex Chimalpopoca.*

Garibay, K., Angel María. *Teogonía e historia de los Mexicanos: Tres opúsculos del siglo XVI.* Mexico City, 1979. Three sixteenth-century texts on Aztec religion and mythology: *Historia de los Mexicanos por sus pinturas, Histoyre du Mechique,* and Ponce's *Relación.* In Spanish.

Tschohl, Peter. "Das Ende der Leyenda de los Soles und die Übermittlungsprobleme des Códice Chimalpopoca." *Baessler-Archiv*, n.s. 37.1 (1989), 201–279. Includes a photo-facsimile of the long-missing last two sides of the Legend of the Suns, as preserved in an eighteenth-century copy.

Velázquez, Primo Feliciano. *Códice Chimalpopoca: Anales de Cuauhtitlan y Leyenda de los Soles*. Mexico City, 1945. Spanish translation and photo-facsimile of the codex, except the *Relación* of Ponce and the last two sides of the Legend of the Suns (see the two preceding titles); the reprint of 1975, in a smaller format, is less legible.

JOHN BIERHORST

CHINAMPA AGRICULTURE. *Chinampas* are plots of soil built up on wetlands of a lake or freshwater swamp for agricultural purposes. They are very narrow rectangular islets, with proportions that ensure optimal moisture retention. The term *chinampa* derives from Nahuatl and means "surrounded by rush," referring to the organic material of the shores used to reinforce their structure. The porosity of the soil and the narrowness of the plots allow the water from nearby canals to seep in and provide for a continuous, stable, and intensive agriculture. Since *chinampas* are built in lacustrine and swampy areas of freshwater, as well as in regions subject to periodic flooding, the peasants obtain from that ecosystem the aquatic plants for building and rehabilitating the plots, mud to set up seedbeds, and slush to irrigate and fertilize the beds, as well as the water needed to maintain the moisture and ensure continuous production. The very shape of the plots facilitates the manual operations of agriculture, such as the transportation and the spreading of mud over the seedbeds that are set along their edges, the manual irrigation as needed, and the transportation of crops and young plants. The lavish lacustrine ecosystem not only ensures the stability of the agricultural system but also provides a plethora of other food resources, such as migratory and permanent aquatic birds, fish, insects, frogs, and algae, all of them protein sources. There are also tequesquite, reeds (*Typha* spp.), and other aquatic plants for weaving rush mats, ropes, and other items.

Chinampas flourished during the pre-Hispanic era in the lacustrine system of the Basin of Mexico, where they still exist, although degraded by ecological changes and the unrestrainable urbanization process of Mexico City. Their evolution and the peculiarities of their operations are well known from the ample variety of existing archaeological, historical, and ethnological records. Scholars have found that *chinampas* made up one of the most intensive agricultural systems, from the perspective of soil usage and, moreover, were among the world's most productive irrigation systems of the preindustrial era. The demographic and civilizing development of the Aztec period (fourteenth to sixteenth centuries CE) was linked to the production capacity of this form of agriculture, as well as to the existence of a complex network of interconnected channels and dikes also built during that period for controlling the level, flow, and quality of water for navigation. The Basin of Mexico *chinampas* were first built during the Early Formative period in lacustrine communities in the south of the basin. By the sixteenth century, *chinampas* covered an area of approximately 120 square kilometers (46 square miles) on the southern lakes of Chalco-Xochimilco, plus vast central areas around Mexico-Tenochtitlan, as well as a small extension of wetlands to the north (Xaltocan).

The construction technology of the plots is known through historical sources and present-day oral testimonies. On the basis of such information, scholars have distinguished two types of plots and techniques. The first corresponds to the lacustrine *chinampas* (the "inlake" plots, according to Angel Palerm's terminology): structures made up of the accumulation of aquatic plants, mud, and soil, in which ditches have been dug to open channels and give shape to a rectangular islet. The second type is drained and raised fields ("inland" *chinampas*, according to J. L. Lorenzo's terminology), present in swampy areas with deficient drainage. These were built by opening ditches (making the later channels), to delimit the plot and heap the soil and mud, thereby raising the structure above the water level. The operations concluded with the planting of a willow variety (*Salix* spp.), called ahuexotl or ahuejote.

Horticulture in the *chinampas* includes the following: seedbeds made of muck in which the seeds and cuttings are set in small cubes for later transplantation to the final beds; the actual transplantation; the use of coats of stubble from the harvests to protect the plants from freezes and insulation; fertilization by mud, slush, aquatic plants, and bat guano (for chile pepper plants); and weeding, podding, and other manual tasks for each plant. The tools, all handled manually, require a sizable labor investment but yield plentiful harvests. An average yield of 200 kernels for each kernel of maize planted, or of 80 hectoliters (8 tons) per hectare, was obtained in the *chinampas*, according to the records for 1911. Other important crops were those of tomato (*Lycopersicon esculentum*), green tomatillo (*Physalis ixocarpa*), chile pepper (*Capsicum annuum*), beans (*Phaseolus vulgaris*), squash (*Cucurbita pepo*), chayote (*Cucurbita ficifolia*), and the grain amaranth (*Amaranthus leucocarpus*). The seedbeds of amaranth were later transplanted to nearby drylands): chia (*Salvia hispanica*); flowers, cempoalxóchitl (*Tagetes erecta*) and dahlias (*Dahlia coccinea*); and edible herbs. After the Spanish conquest, the peasants adopted introduced species, which added variety; they also began to use animal manure for fertilizer and metal tools for horticulture.

Chinampas and raised and drained fields also existed outside the Basin of Mexico. Archaeologists have found evidence of their existence in other flooded, swampy, and lacustrine areas of tropical and subtropical Mesoamerica, including the valleys of Teotihuacan, Toluca, Huexotzingo, and Nautla, the plain surrounding the Candelaria River, the Bec region, the Petén, the Motagua River, and Ulúa. After the Conquest, more *chinampas* were built in the valley of Toluca and the Zacapu marsh, among other regions.

[*See also* Agriculture.]

BIBLIOGRAPHY

Armillas, Pedro. "Gardens on Swamps," *Science* 174.4010 (1971), 635–661. Excellent summary of archaeological research on *chinampas* in the Basin of Mexico.

Rojas Rabiela, Teresa. *La agricultura chinampera. Compilación histórica.* Mexico City, 1993. Twelve of the most important articles on *chinampas*, including one by José Antonio de Alzate, written in 1791.

Siemens, Alfred H. *Tierra configurada. Investigaciones de los vestigios de agricultura precolombina en tierras inundables costeras desde el norte de Veracruz hasta Belice.* Mexico City, 1989. Compilation of the author's main works, plus recent writings concerning the usage in pre-Columbian times of the flooded lowlands that extend from Yucatán to the north of Veracruz.

Sluyter, Andrew. "Intensive Wetland Agriculture in Mesoamerica: Space, Time and Form." *Annals of the Association of American Geographers* 84. 4 (1994), 557–584. With the help of maps, the author makes a spatial-temporal analysis of intensive agriculture in the wetlands and raised fields of Mesoamerica.

Wilken, Gene C. "Drained-field Agriculture: An Intensive Farming System in Tlaxcala." *The Geographical Review* 61.2 (1969), 215–241. One of the earliest works on the methods used by the peasants on drained lands in the southeast region of Tlaxcala.

TERESA ROJAS RABIELA

CHINANTEC. Contemporary Chinantec communities in the state of Oaxaca, Mexico, are subdivided by dialect, habitat, and culture into four (or possibly five) main groups. The identifying terms Hu-hmei, Wa-hmi, and Dzah-hmi are used by groups inhabiting the central, eastern, and western subregions, respectively; no comparable terms are reported for the northern and northwestern groups. Chinantecan is a branch of the Otomanguean language family, with the Amuzgan and Popolocan languages its closest relations. Chinantecan is estimated to have separated from those branches about thirty-five hundred years ago.

Throughout recorded history, Chinantec settlements have been confined to the basin of the Papaloapan River. When discovered and subjugated by the Spanish in 1520–1521, indigenous Chinantec settlements were adapted to lowland, humid riverine areas. These settlements suffered the loss of 80 percent or more of their population during the first half-century of European rule, primarily to introduced diseases, such as smallpox and measles, against which the Chinantec had no natural resistance. The survivors of these epidemics then lived in dispersed small hamlets of eleven to fifteen residents.

To protect their new subjects from the unhealthy conditions of the lowlands and to create larger settlements, which would be more easily administered by civil and church authorities, colonial administrators congregated residents of these scattered hamlets into relatively large towns on high ridges of the nearby Sierra Madre Oriental. In the process, the Indians were ordered to destroy all physical vestiges of their former hamlets, effectively eradicating structural reminders of their history and traditional adaptations. Although some of the Chinantec have since reestablished themselves in the lowlands, others remain on the high ridges.

Subsistence gardening, supplemented in the lowlands by cash crops of coffee and tobacco, is the basis of Chinantec economy. Most contemporary communities govern communally owned tracts in addition to smallholdings for subsistence cultivation. A few communities also control extensive communal forest lands. Substantial property in some communities is also held and worked as *ejidos* (commons) on lands the federal government expropriated from foreign-owned banana plantations in the first half of the twentieth century.

Although considerable variation exists among communities, the core of all Chinantec social organization is the nuclear family, with a tendency toward extension through the Roman Catholic sponsorship called *compadrazgo* ("godparent"). Until the 1940s, many Chinantec communities were also organized around corporate groups, some of which held exclusive rights to parcels of communal land. Barrio (neighborhood) structures were elaborate in some communities, marked by distinctive chapels, and they could include socio-ritual organizations and marriage prohibitions. Since the mid-1950s, the barrio has lost importance as the axis of social organization.

Municipal political organization is similar to that in most other parts of rural Mesoamerica and is based on a civil-religious hierarchy (the *cargo* system). In it, all married men are expected to serve a variable number of years in unremunerated public office; men living in outlying hamlets must usually serve in the municipal center (*cabecera*). Passing through these grades, each associated with increasing community responsibility, a man eventually attains the status of respected elder (*anciano* or *principal*). Such individuals, steeped in tradition, were granted enormous respect and viewed as collectively responsible for their community's welfare. Today, however, many young and middle-aged men defer or even refuse *cargo* service. The loss of these candidates, who are attracted by greater income-earning opportunities outside rural areas, has led some *municipios* to diminish radically the number of *cargo* positions to be filled.

Today, the obligatory use of Spanish in Mexico, in negotiating community matters with state and federal authorities, has placed great importance on bilingualism and literacy. Moreover, recognition of the value of experience in both Mexican cities and in the United States, as well as the power that accrues to individuals who send regular remittances in support of family and municipal enterprises, has led to the creation of semiofficial advisory councils of young and middle-aged men who continue to reside outside the community or have done so in the recent past. Such councils, variously known as *la mesa de los jovenes* or *los caracterizados*, reflect a radical shift in power from older men respected for their links with tradition to younger men who are more sophisticated, and presumably more effective, in dealing with the world beyond the *municipio*. Today, as in the past, women in most Chinantec communities tend not to participate in formal political activities, but they enjoy high social status and are not submissive to men.

In the later twentieth century, alliances between various Chinantec *municipios* were formed to protect their respective communal forests from foreign exploitation or to challenge such federal resettlement policies as those related to construction of the Cerro de Oro Dam. Significant numbers of expatriates from highland Chinantec *municipios*, who reside in the United States, collaborate politically and socially with like-minded Mixe, Mixtec, and Zapotec expatriates in organized efforts intended to protect the civil and political rights of their home communities.

BIBLIOGRAPHY

Barabas, Alicia M. "Mesianismo chinanteco: Una respuesta politico-religiosa ante la crisis." *Revista mexicana de ciencias politicas y sociales* 23.88 (1977), 53–85. Unique account of a vision of the Virgin which appeared offering assistance to peasants threatened by immanent relocation from ancestral lands scheduled for flooding by a new dam.

Barabas, Alicia, and Miguel Bartolome. *Hydraulic Development and Ethnocide: The Mazatec and Chinantec People of Oaxaca, Mexico.* Copenhagen, 1973. Analysis of the difficulties encountered by indigenous populations obliged to relocate from areas flooded by the Cerro de Oro dam, and the inadequate support provided them by government agencies.

Bevan, Bernard. *The Chinantec. Report on the Central and South-eastern Chinantec Region*, vol. 1, *The Chinantec and Their Habitat.* Mexico, 1938. Pioneering ethnographic tour of some lowland communities that emphasizes the difficult terrain and the way the Indians have adapted to it.

Chance, John. "Colonial Ethnohistory of Oaxaca." In *Ethnohistory*, supplement to *Handbook of Middle American Indians*, edited by Ronald Spores, pp. 165–189. Austin, Tex., 1986. Compelling presentation of how levels of development of indigenous political organization influenced regional responses to Spain's colonial administration in Oaxaca.

Cline, Howard F. "Civil Congregations of the Indians in New Spain, 1598–1606." *Hispanic American Historical Review* 29 (1949), 349–369. Excellent description of the forced resettlement of Indians and destruction of their former villages.

Cline, Howard F. "Civil Congregation of the Western Chinantla, New Spain, 1599–1603." *Americas* 12 (1955), 115–137.

Gerhard, Peter. *A Guide to the Historical Geography of New Spain.* Cambridge, 1972. Superb guide to how the Spanish administered their Indian subjects and the diverse responses of the latter.

Hopkins, Nicholas. "Otomanguean Linguistic Prehistory." In *Essays in Otomanguean Culture History*, edited by J. K. Josserand et al., pp. 25–64. Nashville, Tenn., 1984. The best contemporary effort to establish the historic relationships between groups speaking Otomanguean-related languages.

Rubel, Arthur J. "Ritual Relationships in Ojitlan, Mexico." *American Anthropologist* 57 (1955), 1038–1040. One of the few descriptions of *barrio* and ritual kinship organization among Chinantecs.

Rubel, Arthur J., Carl W. O'Nell, and Rolando Collado Ardon. *Susto, a Folk Illness.* Berkeley, 1984. Description of some aspects of social and political organization of a Chinantec *municipio* in a comparative framework.

Weitlaner, Roberto J., comp. *Relatos, mitos y leyendas de la Chinantla.* Edited by María Sara Molinari, María Luisa Acevedo, and Marlene Aguayo Alfaro. Mexico City, 1977. Stories, legends, and myths collected over many years from several Chinantec communities.

Weitlaner, Roberto J., and Carlo Antonio Castro G. *Papeles de la Chinantla, I: Mayultianguis y Tlacoatzintepec.* Mexico City, 1954. Broad description of the cultures of two neighboring and otherwise unknown communities.

Weitlaner, Roberto J., and Howard F. Cline. "The Chinantec." In *Handbook of Middle American Indians*, edited by Evon Z. Vogt, vol. 7, pp. 523–552. Austin, Tex., 1969. Authoritative interpretation of Chinantec history and institutions in the absence of an archaeological record.

ARTHUR J. RUBEL and C. H. BROWNER

CHOLULA, one of the key religious centers of ancient Mexico, is located in the Puebla-Tlaxcala Valley, on the outskirts of the modern capital of Puebla. It is near the base of snow-covered volcanoes that include the periodically active Popocatépetl ("smoking mountain"). The city is surrounded by some of the most fertile agricultural land of central Mexico. Dependable rains between May and September are supplemented by runoff from the mountains during the dry season, and perennial streams converged near ancient Cholula to form a marshy lake. The alluvial subsoil has a high clay content that was used to produce high-quality ceramics, including the renowned Cholula polychrome of the Postclassic period.

Cholula played a fundamental role in determining cultural practices throughout the central highlands. As an important market center, merchants from Postclassic Cholula traded exotic goods throughout Mesoamerica in exchange for beautifully crafted pottery and textiles decorated in the Mixteca-Puebla style. Cholula was also the site of one of the architectural wonders of the Americas, the Great Pyramid Tlachihualtépetl ("man-made mountain"), the largest and oldest continuously used structure in the New World.

The high clay content of the subsoil around Cholula was used to produce such high-quality ceramics as this polychrome vessel found in Chamber 3 of the Great Temple of Tenochtitlan. (Height: 13 inches.) *Courtesy of Museo del Templo Mayor, México, D.F.*

Research at Cholula has focused on the ceremonial center, with excavations on the surface, the interior, and around the base of the Great Pyramid. Archaeologists have cut 8 kilometers (5 miles) of tunnels into the pyramid, which exposed four major construction phases that had been built up during some fifteen hundred years. Limited explorations have also been conducted in the urban zone of the ancient city. In addition to the archaeological research, Cholula was the subject of numerous ethnohistorical accounts about the Postclassic and the Early Colonial-period occupations. In combination, the sources relate a twenty-five-hundred-year history of the religious center.

The earliest evidence for occupation at Cholula dates to at least 1000 BCE, when a village flourished near the lakeshore. Scattered artifacts from this initial settlement have been found covering an area of about 2 square kilometers. Decorated kaolin-slipped pottery and baked clay figurines indicate participation in a pan-Mesoamerican ideology that has often been identified with the Olmec of the southern Gulf Coast.

The Late Formative (Preclassic) period remains of 500 to 1 BCE consist primarily of diagnostic ceramics in the construction fill of the pyramid mounds. Several contemporaneous sites in the Cholula region (such as Coronan-go, Coapan, and Acatepec) indicate that Formative-era Cholula was but one of a number of similar centers at approximately the same level of political complexity. This situation changed dramatically by the end of the Late Formative period, however, when Cholula emerged as a regional center, as indicated by the construction of the initial stages of the Great Pyramid and the abandonment of contemporaneous sites within the immediate vicinity.

The earliest stage of the Great Pyramid was probably built toward the end of the Late Formative period. It measured 120 meters (400 feet) on a side and 17 meters (55 feet) high, with *talud-tablero* architecture on its façades. Two elements of the Great Pyramid provide insight into why Cholula developed as a great center while other sites in the vicinity were abandoned. First, the Great Pyramid was built over a spring, which was perceived as a portal linking the mortal world with the supernatural underworld. A cosmological principle incorporated into the layout of the Great Pyramid was its orientation, with the east–west axis aligned at 24 to 26 degrees to the north of west; this orientation corresponds to the position of the setting sun at the summer solstice, and suggests a solar significance for religious practices centered there.

In the Classic period, Cholula grew to approximately 4 square kilometers, with a population of about 10,000 to 15,000. Stage 2 of the Great Pyramid was probably built during this period. It measured 180 meters (600 feet) on a side and reached a height of 35 meters (115 feet). Its architectural style was unique, with each side consisting entirely of steps, thereby allowing access to the top from all directions.

The public architecture of Cholula proclaimed its distinctiveness from Teotihuacan, the great urban center in the Valley of Mexico, through its orientation and style, yet domestic material culture showed closer affiliation. Both pottery forms and surface treatment at the two sites were very similar, and clay figurines suggest that the two cities may have shared aspects of domestic religion. In addition, Cholula had direct access to green obsidian from the Cerro de las Navajas source, which has often been associated with Teotihuacan's economic network. In sum, residents of Classic Cholula may have shared elements of ethnic identity with Teotihuacanos even if state-level ideologies differed.

The Epiclassic period (700–900 CE) is a dynamic one in Central Mexico, with dramatic developments caused by the collapse of imperial Teotihuacan and the movement of various groups, including the Maya, to fill the resultant power vacuum. Polychrome murals at the nearby site of Cacaxtla indicate marriage alliances with ethnic groups from the southern Gulf Coast. [*See* Marriage Alliances.] Cholula may have been the Central Mexican hub for this highland–lowland interaction. In fact, an elite burial of a

The Patio of the Altars at Cholula. *Courtesy of Visual Resources Collection, The University of Texas at Austin. Ferguson Collection.*

Maya lord (with distinctive cranial deformation and pyrite and jade inlaid teeth) suggests that Maya elites may have lived in Cholula at the time.

Ethnohistorical accounts describe the arrival in Cholula of Olmeca-Xicallanca immigrants from the Gulf Coast, and how they defeated—literally "consumed"—the inhabitants who survived after the Classic period. Archaeological evidence from the Patio of the Carved Skulls indicates a less violent transition, however, as the material culture associated with a sequence of elite residential patios suggests a gradual blending of Classic and Postclassic traits.

Several lines of evidence indicate an important change in Cholula's religious orientation beginning in the Epiclassic period. A mural painted on a *tablero* of the Patio of the Altars depicts an elaborate polychrome feathered serpent. Stamp-bottom grater bowls feature numerous iconic referents to Quetzalcóatl, especially as Ehécatl the god of air or wind. Ethnohistorical accounts clearly identify Cholula as the cult center for Quetzalcóatl, and they describe Quetzalcóatl as a priest of the Olmeca-Xicallanca.

The Olmeca-Xicallanca added a third construction stage to the Great Pyramid (Stage 3) that then measured 350 meters (1,165 feet) on a side and 65 meters (215 feet) in height. The architectural facades of Stage 3 again used a Teotihuacan-like *talud-tablero* format, as a symbolic claim that Cholula was the legitimate inheritor of Teotihuacan's socioreligious legacy. Cholula, however, combined numerous other iconographic elements from Oaxaca, the Gulf Coast, and the Maya heartland, creating an artistic program that proclaimed a message of internationalism; the resulting symbolic system evolved into what has been labeled the Mixteca-Puebla stylistic tradition. Cholula polychrome pottery combines bright colors in codex-style designs that create a symbolically charged ware now synonymous with the Mixteca-Puebla horizon of the Postclassic, which began to appear as early as 900 CE.

The southern side of the Great Pyramid featured a large plaza, known as the Patio of the Altars, which received its name from monolithic altars of *tecalli* (onyx) that lie on opposite sides of the courtyard. On the eastern side, Altar 1 combines horizontal and vertical slabs that form a stela/altar group. While the western altar (Altar 2) does not have a corresponding stela, most likely a stela (Altar 3) now located at the base of the stairs leading to the Great Pyramid was originally part of a stela/altar group with Altar 2. All these monoliths are carved with a low-relief volute border, similar to carvings at El Tajín.

An extensive mural from an early phase of the Patio of the Altars depicts ritual practice at the site. Known as the "Drunkards Mural" (*Bebedores*), more than a hundred people are represented in the act of drinking what is generally interpreted as fermented maguey sap (*pulque*). The figures are sprawled on what appear to be platforms of the Great Pyramid; some are shown with animal faces, as if they are in the process of transforming into their animal spirits.

Jutting out from a façade of Stage 3, a massive addition (Stage 3b) was built onto the western side of the Great Pyramid. It features a sculpted stone *tablero*, representing an interlaced mat motif—a pan-Mesoamerican concept that indicated political authority. In front of the staircase is a large, rough-hewn stela with a rectangular hole cut through it; a horizontal slab at its base creates another stela/altar group. Stage 3b faces onto a broad plaza, across which is an unexplored mound known as Cerro Cocoyoc.

The fourth and final construction stage of the Great Pyramid was probably added during the Early Postclassic period, enlarging the mound to 400 meters (1,312 feet) on a side and engulfing some earlier structures, such as the Edificio Rojo. No finished surface to Stage 4 has been exposed by excavators, however, so it is unclear whether the new construction was ever completed or if facing (finishing) stones were stripped off for subsequent building projects. The possibility that construction was suddenly halted and/or that dressed stones were stripped off may be linked to evidence from the Patio of the Altars, where the massive stone stelae were thrown down and systematically smashed. That destruction probably corresponds to the arrival of Tolteca-Chichimeca immigrants from the Valley of Mexico, as described in their own origin myth, the *Historia Tolteca-Chichimeca*. The Polychrome ceramics from the surface of the Great Pyramid date the abandonment to about 1200 CE.

A new ceremonial center to the northwest of the Great Pyramid was built by the Tolteca-Chichimeca, around their Pyramid of Quetzalcóatl. Ethnohistorical accounts describe the political and religious organization of Late Postclassic Cholula. The religious administration was led by two priests, the Aquiach and the Tlalchiach. Civil affairs were administered by a council of representatives from the six wards of the city. At that time, the city of Cholula measured about 8 square kilometers, with a population of 30,000 to 50,000. It remained an autonomous polity, independent from the contemporaneous Aztec Empire, and often in league with Tlaxcala and Huexotzinco against the Triple Alliance in the ritualized Flowery Wars. [*See* Triple Alliance.]

Cholula, as the cult center of Quetzalcóatl, played a key role in the religion, politics, and economy of central Mexico. Pilgrims from many parts of Mesoamerica visited the temple of Quetzalcóatl; the Spanish chroniclers compared Cholula to both Rome and Mecca, as a center of worship and pilgrimage. Nobles came to receive confirmation of their titles, and therefore the authority to rule. The temple complex probably included schools to train priests, as well as libraries to store religious and genealogical manuscripts. The *Codex Borgia* is one of several extant pictorial manuscripts that may have originated in Cholula. Another aspect of the god Quetzalcóatl was as the patron of the *pochteca*, the long-distance merchants who traveled throughout Mesoamerica, acquiring valuable and exotic goods that were then sold in Cholula's marketplace.

When the Spanish arrived in Central Mexico, Cholula was one of the largest and richest cites in Mesoamerica. Cortés and his soldiers were led to Cholula by their Tlaxcalan allies, and in one of the most horrifying events of the Conquest they ambushed and massacred the assembled nobility of the city. The Pyramid of Quetzalcóatl was torn down and replaced by the Cathedral of San Gabriel. Excavations in the courtyard of the cathedral have yielded more than 650 burials from the Cholula massacre, which offer tragic testimony.

Colonial-period Cholula continued many of its pre-Columbian traditions, as the process of adapting to European rule was deflected in part by the construction of the city of Puebla de los Angeles 10 kilometers (6.5 miles) to the east. Even though Puebla usurped much of Cholula's political, religious, and economic importance, Cholula continued as a center of indigenous culture. The Great Pyramid, for example, which had been partly abandoned during the Late Postclassic period, reemerged as the focus of long-distance pilgrimages to the shrine of the Virgin of the Remedies, located at its summit. Thus, Cholula continues to the present day as one of the primary religious centers of Mexico. It is an important site for archaeological as well as ethnographic studies of traditional Mesoamerican culture.

[*See also* Art and Architecture, *article on* Pre-Hispanic Period.]

BIBLIOGRAPHY

Carrasco, Pedro. "Los barrios antiguos de Cholula." *Estudios y documentos de la Región de Puebla-Tlaxcala* 3 (1971), 9–87. Provides a detailed description of the social organization of Late Postclassic Cholula, based on ethnohistorical accounts.

Historia Tolteca-Chichimeca [1560]. Edited and translated by Paul Kirchhoff et al. Mexico City, 1976. Early Colonial-era document in Nahuatl, with illustrations, that recounts the migration of the Tolteca and Chichimeca groups to the Puebla Valley, including their stay in Cholula.

López Alonso, Sergio, Zaíd Lagunas Rodríguez, and Carlos Serrano Sánchez. *Enterramientos humanos de la zona arqueológica de Cholula, Puebla*. Colección Científica, 44. Mexico City, 1976. Description of burials from the ceremonial center of Cholula; although narrow in focus, this is the best report on findings from the Proyecto Cholula.

Marquina, Ignacio, ed. *Proyecto Cholula*. Serie Investigaciones, 19. Mexico City, 1970. Collection of articles on the archaeological, historical, and cultural studies made by investigators from the Proyecto Cholula.

McCafferty, Geoffrey G. "Reinterpreting the Great Pyramid of Cholula, Mexico." *Ancient Mesoamerica* 7 (1996), 1–17. Description and interpretation of the construction history of the Great Pyramid.

McCafferty, Geoffrey G. "Reconsidering Cholula Ceramics and Chronology." *Ancient Mesoamerica* 7 (1996), 299–323. Describes archaeological evidence for the culture history of Cholula, with special attention to the ceramic assemblages of the different periods and the radiocarbon dates used to construct the chronological sequence.

Mountjoy, Joseph, and David A. Peterson. *Man and Land in Prehispanic Cholula*. Vanderbilt University Publications in Anthropology, 4. Nashville, Tenn., 1973. Description of excavations on the campus of the University of the Americas, Cholula, including Formative (Preclassic), Classic, and Postclassic loci.

Nicholson, Henry B., and Eloise Quiñones Keber, eds. *Mixteca-Puebla: Discoveries and Research in Mesoamerican Art and Archaeology*. Culver City, Calif., 1994. Collected articles on the Mixteca-Puebla stylistic tradition, including several papers on Cholula polychrome wares.

Noguera, Eduardo. *La cerámica arqueológica de Cholula*. Mexico City, 1954. Classic study of Cholula ceramics, with color illustrations and description of early investigations.

Suárez Cruz, Sergio. *Un entierro del Clásico superior en Cholula, Puebla*. Cuaderno de Trabajo, 6. Puebla, 1985. Monograph describing results of a rescue excavation at the Great Pyramid that discovered the skeleton of an elite Maya male.

Suárez Cruz, Sergio, and Silvia Martínez A. *Monografía de Cholula, Puebla*. Cholula, 1993. Describes the archaeology of Cholula.

GEOFFREY G. MCCAFFERTY

CHONTAL. *See* Tequistlatec.

CHOROTEGA. *See* Manguean.

CHORTÍ. The Chortí Maya people live in eastern Guatemala and near the Honduras border, on both sides of the tributary that flows past the renowned archaeological site of Copán (in Honduras) to join the Motagua River near the archaeological site in Quirigua, once a satellite city of Copán. The present-day population lives mainly around the market towns of Camotan and Jocotan, on this tributary, and also around La Unión (to the north) and Olopa (to the south). The *ladino* (monolingual Spanish-speaking) population in this area is in the minority, concentrated in the river valley and on the lowest slopes, while the Chortí speakers (adolescents and adults are actually bilingual) live in the traditional Maya dispersed-settlement pattern on the higher and less fertile ground, mostly between 600 and 1200 meters (2,000 and 4,000 feet) elevation. Each family is separated from its neighbors by hundreds of meters. The Chortí practice swidden (slash-and-burn) agriculture, growing maize, beans, and squash in a patchwork of fields; one family's *milpas* (fields) may be widely separated by fallow and cultivated land that is used by others.

Many religious ceremonies, including curing ceremonies, are performed in or around a family's dwellings by the head of that family, sometimes with the assistance of part-time specialists. These religious and medical specialists practice for fees in money or in kind, in much the same way that others make craft items—sisal-fiber wares, rush mats, baskets, or pottery—for sale in markets.

The welfare of the community, and consequently much of its belief system and ritual, centers on the rains associated with the two annual passages of the intertropical front. The belief system has many Maya elements, overlaid and influenced by Roman Catholic and Spanish traditions. For example, the ancient Maya rain god Chac, usually depicted in Classic Maya art as wielding a stone axe, has become for purposes of public worship a syncretized San Miguel, who makes rain nowadays by chopping at clouds with his sword. Within the Chortí belief system, four or more beings—known as *ah patnaar* ("worker") or *tš'ahk*—perform this same function. Other members of the pantheon, such as the Kumiš, or culture-hero child, appear to be even less affected by European contact.

The Chortí language belongs to the Cholan subgroup, along with its extinct near-neighbor and relative Choltí, once spoken to the north of the Motagua Valley, and Chol and Chontal, still spoken in the states of Chiapas and Tabasco, Mexico. "Chortí" is not a name in current use among the people. Among Mayan languages, Chortí (and Choltí) have a distinctive fully ergative predication system, in which transitivity (transitive versus intransitive) and aspect (perfective versus imperfective) are the paramount category distinctions, and in which possessives and subjects of transitive predications are marked by the same prefixes, while subjects of all intransitives are marked differently. Chortí also has a well-developed system of derivational affixes marking the transitivity and modality of each predication.

BIBLIOGRAPHY
Fought, John G. "Chortí (Mayan): Phonology, Morphophonemics, and Morphology." Ph.D. diss., Yale University, 1967.
Fought, John G. *Chortí (Mayan) Texts: I*. Philadelphia, 1972.
Wisdom, Charles. *The Chorti Indians of Guatemala*. Chicago, 1940.

JOHN G. FOUGHT

CHRISTIANITY. [*This entry comprises two articles. The first article presents an overview of the Roman Catholic beliefs and practices introduced to Mesoamerica and their reception and transformation by Mesoamerican cultures; the second article discusses the various denominational Evangelical Protestant beliefs and practices introduced into Mesoamerica. For related discussions, see* Baptism; Calendars and Calendrical Systems, *article on the* Christian Calendar; Churches and Cathedrals; Confession; God; Pilgrimage; Roman Catholic Church; *and* Saints.]

Catholicism

Mesoamerica, at the time of the Spanish conquest, was a region that had a highly developed religious worldview. The Mexica (Aztec), the Maya, and a host of other peoples practiced diverse but essentially similar religious and spiritual traditions. These traditions had been developed through many centuries, perhaps beginning with the Olmec people, whose civilization originated about 1400 BCE. The spirituality of Mesoamerican peoples centered on such concepts as creation, sacrifice, prayer, penance, a fall, and the passage of time. Religion and daily life were inseparable (as they were for many Spaniards).

In Mesoamerica, these sophisticated and devout peoples lived in a landscape dominated by their temples and natural forces. Some of their beliefs appeared, on the surface, to be quite similar to some believed by the new European arrivals. There was the Aztec legend, for example, about their wanderings in the wilderness, which sounded much like the biblical story of the Exodus. They were also familiar with a type of baptism, a form of communion involving the ingestion of pastries, the use of crosses, and the concept of a deity born of a virgin. They practiced a type of confession. The Mesoamerican myth of Quetzalcoatl told of a figure who, in many ways, seemed to resemble Jesus. All this led the early Christian missionaries to posit a previous era of evangelization or even, perhaps, a Hebrew origin for the inhabitants of the Americas. At times, from alarming practices, the missionaries assumed that Satan was "sowing confusion" among their new charges.

Mesoamerica entered the concerns of the Roman Catholic church in the early sixteenth century, when Cortés launched his epic conquest of the Aztec Empire. Shortly thereafter, Spanish influence and Spanish arms entered forcibly into the Maya regions, under the leadership of Francisco de Montejo and Pedro de Alvarado. Though inspired by the usual desires for gold and glory, Cortés was also motivated by a desire to spread the Christian gospel. Jerónimo de Mendieta, an early Franciscan missionary to New Spain, wrote of Cortés as a "new Moses" who had come to free the Mexica from the snares of the devil. Cortés was viewed by sixteenth-century Spaniards as a heaven-sent servant of God, a tool of divine providence; moreover, he was sent to make amends for the protestations of Martin Luther in Europe. It seemed to Mendieta that those souls who had been lost to the Protestant Reformation in Europe would be made up in a rich harvest of American souls. Not only was Cortés a conquistador; he was also a missionary. Cortés gave many signs of his own fervor and devotion and, in his campaign to take the Aztec capital of Tenochtitlan, was accompanied by two priests: Father Juan Díaz, a secular priest (one who lives in the world, not within a religious order), and Father Bartolomé de Olmedo, a friar and priest of the Mercedarian order. Olmedo was particularly eager to convert the newly encountered people; he baptized, erected crosses, and destroyed idols. Even he was no match for the fervor of Cortés, who marched behind a banner bearing the cross and often had to be restrained by Olmedo in his zealous desire to extirpate idolatry and human sacrifice. [*See* Cortés, Fernando.]

Almost immediately after the fall of Tenochtitlan, organized missionary activity began in Mexico. The first organized mission comprised Franciscans, under the leadership of Fray Martín de Valencia; they are commonly referred to as "the twelve," a reference to their apostolic intentions as well as to their actual number. Cortés had requested that the king send members of the mendicant orders, and he met these first barefoot missionaries on their arrival in Mexico City in June 1524. That same year, two Franciscan missionaries, Juan Godinez and Juan Díaz, accompanied the conquistador Pedro de Alvarado into what is now Guatemala. From there, missionaries began to spread throughout Central America. By 1547, with the erection of the Friary of San Francisco in Campeche, the Franciscans had established themselves in the Yucatán Peninsula as well.

These early Franciscan missionaries were products of a reform that had been initiated in Spain by Cardinal Jiménez de Cisneros, who combined Christian beliefs with the humanistic values of such writers as Francis Bacon, Tommaso Campanella, Desiderius Erasmus, and Thomas More. For many of the early missionaries to the New World, it offered the opportunity to begin again, to create a sort of Christian utopia. Inspired by the example of the early Christian church, the friars often found that the indigenous peoples were ideal subjects for their experiment in creating the perfect Christian society. Yet they had also to live with the fact that the church in Mesoamerica was under the nearly total control of the Spanish Crown. The papacy, in the persons of Pope Alexander VI and Pope Julius II, had granted almost total jurisdiction over the church in the Americas to the Spanish monarchs. Thus, the first missionaries fulfilled three codes: their presence and activity helped to legitimize the Conquest; they launched a major cultural and sociological experiment; and they spread the Christian faith.

Although the earliest organized missions were entrusted to the Franciscans, these were followed in 1526 by friars of the Dominican order and in 1533 by the Augustinian friars. Relations among these orders were not always cordial—for example, the Franciscans and the Dominicans battled for jurisdiction in Guatemala—but these three orders were to dominate the history of evangelization in Mesoamerica until the arrival of the Jesuits in 1572. After that date, increased attention was given to the European portions of society, and many of the early missions were turned over to the secular clergy (those who did not belong to an order). Active missionary work then tended to shift to remote areas, such as the southwestern portion of the present-day United States. [*See* Dominicans; Franciscans.*]

The first missionary era had been a time of great enthusiasm. It is estimated that the early friars in New Spain had baptized between four and nine million persons by 1536; but by the 1570s, enthusiasm had waned, and many of the indigenous peoples, baptized or not, had fallen prey to European epidemics. So many died that the missionaries feared that the native American peoples might soon disappear from the face of the earth; and they had found that beneath a veneer of Christianity, there still lurked many of the ancient beliefs and practices. The first missionaries had hoped to create a pure and untainted form of Christianity, but the reality was the beginning of a long process of syncretism. Roman Catholicism was indeed being incorporated into the culture, but in ways that were unexpected, which became disturbing to many of the friars.

The lessons conveyed by the first missionaries and the doctrine they imparted were necessarily simple. In some cases, baptism had obviously been administered without extensive (or any!) preparation. Usually, however, the friars tried to convey the message that there was one creator God, and that He had a son called Jesus, who was the Messiah but also God; Jesus's mother, the Virgin Mary, was not. They also taught about original sin, eternal life, and angels and demons. Among the last were to be counted the gods that the Indians had hitherto worshiped. This knowledge was generally considered sufficient for baptism, though there was often post-baptismal instruction in the catechism. At times, the new Christians were instructed much more thoroughly. In addition to learning basic prayers such as the Our Father and the Creed, the indigenous peoples might also be taught the Hail Mary and the Salve Regina. They learned about the Mass, the various sacraments, and the essentials of leading a moral life according to Christian precepts. The Indians were also to submit freely to the authority of church and Crown.

It is not surprising to find Indians who resisted the new faith, and it is even less surprising that they often blended their ancient faith with Catholicism. Evidence of continued paganism sometimes engaged the attention of ecclesiastical authorities, such as when Christian saints were seen as new deities or, if the missionaries were not cautious, the crucifix was seen as a novel form of human sacrifice.

The methods used by the early missionaries to convey their teachings had to be innovative. They were faced with a variety of languages and a religious worldview that, despite all outward similarities, was quite alien to European sensibilities. At first, the friars used crude forms of sign language. Then they moved to the use of interpreters; children were especially helpful because they quickly learned both Spanish and Latin from the friars. Schools were introduced almost immediately into New Spain. Children would often be gathered after the Mass to learn the catechism; then they were sent out to teach others. Children of the ruling class were often accepted as boarders and were expected to become leaders of their people in both secular and religious matters. In at least one instance, in Tlaxcala, the young Christians were overly enthusiastic about the new faith—they killed a native priest, certain that he was a demon.

It was essential that the missionaries learn the indigenous languages, if only to hear confessions without the embarrassing presence of an interpreter. From the very beginning, all the friars dedicated themselves to language study as a key to communication and familiarity with the cultures of the conquered peoples. They prepared numerous printed works that reduced the native languages to written form and compiled books of grammar and vocabulary. A number of the friars became multilingual; a handful learned as many as ten indigenous languages. In addition, the missionaries tried to promote Nahuatl, the language of the Aztec, as a sort of universal Mesoamerican language. In a somewhat paternalistic manner, the friars often felt called to protect "their" Indians from the Spaniards and their vices; toward that end, they often preferred Nahuatl to Spanish as a common tongue for their charges. Since abilities varied, there were friars who never adequately mastered a native tongue. These men often developed more innovative methods of teaching and preaching. Fray Jacobo de Testera and Fray Luis Caldera made use of large pictures. Other friars used music effectively, in one case having the Ten Commandments sung in Nahuatl. Sometimes teaching methods became rather extreme, as when Testera threw animals into an oven to give children some idea of hell. Other tools of conversion included architecture, theater, dances, and processions. There was a conscious attempt to impress the conquered peoples with magnificent structures and sumptuous ceremony. Numerous plays were written and performed; these were usually in indigenous languages and took as their content Bible stories, Spanish history, or moral messages. Toribio de Benavente Motolinía noted that the Indians enthusiastically decorated their new churches and utilized crosses, banners, gold, and feathers in their religious processions, in which the children marched and danced.

It was not enough for friars to learn the local languages, since they also needed to have some familiarity with the culture and beliefs of the conquered peoples. Ironically, although their goal was to destroy the so-called superstitions and heresies of the indigenous peoples, the early friars preserved in their writings much of what is still known of Conquest-era societies.

Perhaps a great failure of the early evangelizers was the lack of wholesale recruitment of indigenous peoples into the ranks of the clergy—although this was discussed very early in the Colonial era. The ordaining of Indians may even have been the original intent of the Franciscan bishop Juan de Zumárraga, when he established a school for the sons of the Aztec nobility at Tlatelolco. Even more surprising is the fact that, with very few exceptions, the native peoples were not admitted to the Eucharist during the sixteenth century; they were seen, for the most part, as "not ready" to receive Communion. The result was a perennial lack of vocations among the indigenous peoples and the general posting of European clergy. These factors had a crucial effect during later centuries and they still affect the region today.

The early friars were, however, often extremely vocal in the defense of the Indians. A famous example was the Dominican friar and bishop Bartolomé de las Casas. After an experience of conversion in his own life, Las Casas preached against cruelty toward the Indians, and he led the opposition against the *encomienda* system, which exploited native laborers. In Mesoamerica, his most interesting experiment involved an attempt at peaceful conversion in Chiapas, an area of violent resistance; his initial success caused the region to be known thereafter as Verapaz, or "True Peace." Las Casas had to face an even greater challenge, from Spain, because some there questioned whether the inhabitants of the New World were rational human beings. A council was convened at Valladólid in 1550 to decide the issue. The inconclusive results of the debate between Las Casas and Juan Ginés de Sepúlveda meant that the newly conquered people often fell prey to the Spanish need for a local labor supply.

An unusual feature of the early Mesoamerican church was the weak episcopal control over missionary activities. In the bull *Expone nobis nuper fecisti* of 1522, Pope Adrian VI allowed the mendicant clergy to assume the authority they needed to fulfill their missionary task. This authority was given to all friars who were working in an area where there was no bishop or where the bishop was more than two days' journey away. The only exceptions were that the friars could not do those things for which episcopal ordination was absolutely essential, such as ordaining priests. Even where the usual church structures were put into place, the earliest bishops in Mesoamerica were often members of the mendicant orders; the first two bishops in Mexico City, for example were the Franciscan Fray Juan de Zumárraga (1528–1548) and the Dominican Fray Alonso de Montúfar (1553/54–1572).

Although not frequently mentioned, the secular clergy were also active among the Mesoamerican peoples. Near Mexico City, Vasco de Quiroga founded a community called Santa Fe, based on Thomas More's *Utopia* (1516). His model village, which once numbered close to 30,000 inhabitants, was entrusted to the Augustinian friars. Quiroga initiated a second group of communities in Michoacán under the same name. Although called "hospitals" and they indeed were places to tend to the sick and offer hospitality to travelers, they were much more. They comprised educational institutions, places of employment, homes, gardens, and places of worship. The "hospitals" at Michoacán eventually became famous for their handicrafts, and Quiroga attempted to have them function as ideal Christian communities run on quasi-monastic lines. In time, Quiroga became a civil official in Mexico City and was eventually consecrated as bishop of Michoacán, serving in that capacity for close to thirty years (1537/8–1565).

In Central Mexico, and later throughout Mesoamerica, tremendous numbers were added to the church because of the devotion to the Virgin Mary and the saints, especially to the Virgin of Guadalupe. Oddly enough, given their own devotion to Mary, the Guadalupe cult was not favorably received by the mendicants; it seems to have been sponsored primarily by the secular clergy and the bishops, so a certain professional jealousy may have arisen. Such specific devotions to nondivinity alarmed the friars, because they seemed to provide an avenue for little-disguised idolatry. Too many Indians seemed to confuse the Virgin Mary with the goddess Tonantzin, whose shrine had been located on the site where the 1531 apparition at Guadalupe occurred. Nevertheless, the veneration of the Virgin of Guadalupe has persisted and grown, and her image is now present in every corner of Mexico and wherever Mexicans now live. It is perhaps the most powerful example of how Roman Catholicism has been adopted and adapted by the Mesoamericans.

During the seventeenth and eighteenth centuries, the number of priests and religious personnel increased in Mesoamerica, and the earlier fervor of the missionaries was frequently channeled into internecine disputes among churchmen. The church acquired considerable wealth and entered into every facet of colonial life; it played a major role in agriculture, education, moneylending, and expansion of the frontiers. A very potent force in Mesoamerican society was the Society of Jesus. Until 1767, the Jesuits played an extremely important role in the new society. [*See* Jesuits.] The Inquisition came to the New World, and religious houses for women became numerous, especially in Mesoamerica's cities and towns. One nun, Sor Juana Inés de la Cruz (1651–1695), was destined for literary immortality. Soon the region had a disproportionate number of priests, nuns, and brothers—some of questionable morals, and many lacking the zeal and optimism of their predecessors. Increasingly, the church focused its attention on Spaniards (*criollos*) and on the growing number of *mestizos*. Missions among the native peoples continued to be very important, but the evangelizing impulse was generally directed to such frontier regions as Texas, Coahuila, and California.

After a tremendous expenditure of energy, the results of the first evangelization were ambiguous. There was a massive influx of Indians into the Catholic church, but some commentators, such as Pedro Cortés y Larraz, an eighteenth-century bishop of Guatemala, thought that the native peoples had never truly received Christianity. Others noted that European Christianity had originally been the result of certain syncretic compromises, and from that point of view, the lingering contributions of Maya and Mexica serve to enrich the Christian church. Since many of those who survived the great plagues had descendants who were part Spanish, in a real sense, the Conquest has resulted in a new and fascinating odyssey that is still in progress.

[*See also* Baptism; Calendars and Calendrical Systems, *article on the* Christian Calendar; Confession; God; Jesus; Judas; Pilgrimage; Roman Catholic Church; Saints.]

BIBLIOGRAPHY

Chauvet, Fidel de Jesús. *Los franciscanos en México (1523–1980) historia breve*. 2d ed. Mexico City, 1989. Good but brief overview of Franciscan history in Mexico from the earliest days of the Conquest until 1980.

Coe, Michael D. *The Maya*. 4th ed. New York, 1987; repr. 1991. Though this work has only a short section on the post-Conquest period, it is a good introduction to the Maya before the Conquest.

Dussel, Enrique, ed. *The Church in Latin America, 1492–1992*. Maryknoll, N.Y., 1992. Anthology that gives an up-to-date overview of Latin American Catholic church history from the Colonial era to the age of liberation theology; particularly helpful are the chapters on Central America and Mexico by Rodolfo Cardenal and María Alicia Puente, respectively.

Gibson, Charles. *The Aztecs under Spanish Rule: A History of the Indians of the Valley of Mexico, 1519–1810*. Stanford, 1964. Especially good work for the Colonial-era life of indigenous Mexicans.

Gossen, Gary H., ed. *South and Mesoamerican Native Spirituality: From the Cult of the Feathered Serpent to the Theology of Liberation*. Vol. 4 of *World Spirituality: An Encyclopedic History of the Religious Quest*, edited by Ewert Cousins. New York, 1993. Especially helpful chapters are "The Mayan Faith," by Miguel León-Portilla, and "The Cult of the Virgin of Guadalupe in Mexico," by Louise M. Burkhart.

Graulich, Michel, *Myths of Ancient Mexico*. Norman, Okla., 1997. Readable, concise explanation of Mesoamerican cosmology and belief.

Greenleaf, Richard E. "Persistence of Native Values: The Inquisition and the Indians of Colonial Mexico." *Americas* 50 (1994), 351–376. Based on extensive archival research, presents a balanced view of the Indians' less pleasant encounters with religious authority and reveals much about the mindset of the missionary friars, native peoples, and ecclesiastical authorities.

Latourette, Kenneth Scott. *A History of Christianity*. Vol. 2. San Francisco, 1975. General history of the Christian church; helps to place the early history of the Mesoamerican church in a broad context.

Liss, Peggy K. *Mexico under Spain, 1521–1556*. Chicago, 1975. Similar to Gibson (1964) but restricted to the initial phase of colonization.

Lopetegui, Leon, and Felix Zubillaga. *Historia de la Iglesia en la América Española desde el decubrimiento hasta comienzos del siglo XIX*. Madrid, 1965. Attempt, from a Roman Catholic perspective, to give a historical overview of Latin American church history; good work to read in conjunction with Dussel (1992).

Meyer, Michael C., and William L. Sherman. *The Course of Mexican History*. 4th ed. New York, 1991. Excellent overview of Mexican history, particularly useful in providing recommendations for further study.

Motolinía, Toribio. *Motolinía's History of the Indians of New Spain*. Translated and annotated by Francis Borgia Steck. Washington, D.C., 1951. Chronicle written between 1536 and 1541; good one-volume source that gives a contemporary view of New Spain from the vantage of one of the earliest missionaries.

Neill, Stephen. *A History of Christian Missions*. Vol. 6 of *The Pelican History of the Church*. Baltimore, 1964; repr. 1966. Places Mesoamerica in a broad context, but with the advantage of dealing only with the history of missions.

Phelan, John Leddy. *The Millennial Kingdom of the Franciscans in the New World*. 2d ed. Berkeley, 1970. Fascinating study that does much to explain the motivation of the early Franciscan missionaries and gives the reader a good sense of the currents of European spirituality and culture that produced them.

Ricard, Robert. *The Spiritual Conquest of Mexico: An Essay in the Apostolate and the Evangelizing Methods of the Mendicant Orders in New Spain, 1523–1572*. Translated by Lesley Byrd Simpson. Berkeley, 1966; repr. 1982. Originally published in French in 1933, the classic work in this area; Ricard tends to take a positive view of early missionaries without overlooking their faults entirely; still arguably the best introduction to this topic.

Schmidlin, Joseph. *Catholic Mission History*. Edited and translated by Matthias Braun. Techny, Ill., 1933. One of the first attempts to write a comprehensive and scientific mission history from a Roman Catholic point of view; though somewhat dated, still a good companion to the works of Latourette (1975) and Neill (1964).

Woodward, Ralph Lee. *Central America, a Nation Divided*. 2d ed. New York, 1985. Excellent one-volume history of Central America; though not focused on church history, it is helpful since many other works about the Colonial period focus on the Valley of Mexico.

DANIEL P. DWYER, O.F.M.

Evangelical Protestantism

Until recently, the study of the history of Christianity in Latin America understandably focused on the history of the Roman Catholic church and, for the late twentieth century, on liberation theology as the most dynamic new development. The explosive growth of evangelical and Pentecostal churches since the 1960s, however, has prompted a new wave of scholarship on Protestant history in Mexico and Central America. At first, this new scholarship was polarized between left intellectual and liberationist Catholic interpretations, which viewed recent evangelical movements as wittingly or unwittingly serving the interests of Cold War era U.S. imperialist interests, and missionary histories that were frankly partisan on behalf of the new movements. More recent, revisionist academic scholarship attempts a subtler analysis that moves beyond these polarities.

Protestantism (in Latin American discourse, *evangélicos* refers to all Protestant groups, not just to the low church movements called "evangelical" in English) had the popular status of a foreign heresy in much of Latin America through the Colonial period; it was, for instance, the original concern of the Mexican Inquisition. Nonetheless, there had long been significant Protestant enclaves south of the U.S. border, such as the German community in Brazil, or the Moravian Miskito Indians in eastern Nicaragua, or other areas under Dutch or English colonial hegemony, such as Surinam and Belize. The Protestant presence was also felt in the diplomatic and scientific communities, including such figures as Alexander von Humboldt and John Lloyd Stephens in the nineteenth century.

North American Protestant culture exerted influence in consequence of the Mexican-American War of 1846–1848 (when the northern third of Mexico became U.S. territory), and again in the wake of the Spanish-American War in 1898. Meanwhile, the postcolonial governments of Latin America began to provide new openings for Protestantism. Religious freedom was legislated in Mexico in 1857, and a succession of Liberal (laissez-faire positivist) governments devoted to capitalist progress and development sought to weaken what they saw as the retarding influence of the Roman Catholic church and the indigenous *cofradías* (religious confraternities).

North American Protestant churches eagerly sought to exploit these new openings in the spirit of "Spiritual Manifest Destiny." The mainline Protestant denominations, such as Methodists and Presbyterians, made a succession of "comity agreements," culminating in the Congress of Panama (1916), where they divided Latin America into various Protestant spheres of operation. Meanwhile, a second wave of competing "faith missions" was launched, representing various fundamentalist affiliations such as the Assemblies of God. The most influential of the latter was the group known as the Central American Mission (CAM), which established bases in the early 1890s. One issue that fiercely divided the fundamentalist churches was the question of whether to learn and utilize indigenous languages in the missionary effort. Opponents feared that it would weaken their assimilationist ideal for Native American populations, but eventually the commitment to use native languages as a conversion strategy prevailed through the massive campaign begun in the

1930s by a group called (in the United States) Wycliffe Bible Translators and (in Latin America) the Summer Institute of Linguistics (henceforth, WBT-SIL). The two designations obviously served, respectively, to signal the missionary purpose for American supporters and to present an image of disinterested scholarly endeavor to Latin American authorities. This project's growth leveled off in the 1940s and 1950s, but then—for a variety of reasons that is the subject of current scholarly analysis—evangelical Protestantism, and particularly Pentecostal churches, experienced rapid growth in many Latin American countries, which has continued until the present.

The stories and the corresponding analyses of this explosion of "Holy Ghost" spirituality are locally distinct in the various countries and regions. A particularly dramatic instance that has attracted much study is the case of Guatemala. As in much of the rest of Latin America, the modest beginnings of Protestant evangelizing in postcolonial Guatemala rested with individual *colporteurs*, or Bible distributors, in the early nineteenth century. The liberal-progressive president Justo Barrios (1871–1885) specifically invited Protestants into the country to foster economic development and to counter the traditional power of the Catholic church and the *cofradías*. The Presbyterian church, the American Bible Society, and other mainstream Protestant groups date their modern movements in Guatemala to 1892, and by 1902 they were experiencing sufficient success to arrive at a comity agreement dividing up their missionary territory. These mainline Protestant churches were moderately liberal in today's sense of the term—especially the Presbyterians, who represented the new Social Gospel movement, which stressed advocacy of social justice along with evangelization.

In contrast, the fundamentalist "faith missions," such as the Central American Mission, did not favor the Social Gospel movement; they devoted their efforts single-mindedly to saving souls by rescuing them from enslavement to what they called "Christo-paganism," their word for indigenous folk Catholicism. William Cameron Townsend, the founder of WBT-SIL, the son of a poor California tenant farmer, put at the center of his preaching a fervent opposition to Catholic "witchery" and to the extravagances of indigenous Catholic *costumbre*—the customs associated with fiestas, *cofradías*, shamanism, and *cargo* (rotating ceremonial responsibilities), all of which smelled of devilry and waste to these Protestants.

The cultural and political mix in Guatemala was further complicated by the revolutionary reformist governments of Juan Arévalo (1945–1951) and Jacobo Arbenz (1951–1954). As secularizers, both presidents sought to limit the power of the Catholic church, which gave further openings to Protestantism. The Presbyterians supported both these governments; the more fundamentalist groups, however, were wary of their socialist tendencies and were appalled by actions such as the nationalization of the United Fruit Company. The decisive date of 18 June 1954 saw the overthrow of Arbenz by a military coup supported by the U.S. Central Intelligence Agency and the installation of the conservative Castillo Armas. It was followed by a half-century of discord, revolution, counterinsurgency, and civil war, with elements of religious war.

The conservative Catholic hierarchy supported Armas, and there was at first a wave of popular hostility directed at Protestants in many Indian towns. Meanwhile, however, the group known as Catholic Action—originally a conservative movement in Spain aimed at countering secular modernity, and active in Central America in resistance to secularizing progressive regimes—had gradually become radicalized, under the influence of the Maryknolls, in the directions of liberation theology. The left-leaning social activist teachings of the movement's catechists generated conflict on the one hand with indigenous traditionalists (the *cofradías* and the *costumbristas*), and on the other with rejuvenated fundamentalist groups such as Latin American Missions (LAM), which had come increasingly under the patronage of the religious right in the United States. A similar pattern of religious and political polarization was occurring simultaneously in El Salvador, Nicaragua, and Chiapas, Mexico.

A crucial turning point in this recent religious history was the earthquake of 4 February 1976, which marked the advent of "disaster evangelism" on a massive scale. This combination of material aid and proselytizing was nicknamed *lámina por ánima* ("a tin roof for a soul"). These efforts resulted in a spectacular growth in converts to fundamentalism, rising from 5 to 20 percent of the population in a decade. At the other end of the Christian spectrum in the increasingly polarized religious culture of Guatemala were the Catholic radical catechists, who promoted a process of political self-awareness, or *conscientizacíon*, that was perceived by the conservatives as aligned with the armed revolutionary movement in the Maya Highlands. The government-military counterinsurgency came to a head during the presidency of José Efraín Ríos Montt, an evangelical Christian affiliated with the California-based Church of the Word (Verbo) who came to power in a military coup. His presidency (1982–1983) happened to coincide with the centennial of Protestantism in Guatemala, celebrated with a crusade by Luis Palau, the Latin American Billy Graham. It was more significantly marked by violent repression of genocidal proportions, as Ríos Montt's *fusiles y frijoles* ("guns and beans") campaign sought to exterminate the popular base of support for the guerrilla movement.

As David Stoll has argued in detail, this extreme violence in the countryside created yet another opportunity for the expansion of fundamentalist Protestantism as an "apolitical" and therefore safe option for peasants caught between two armies. There is a widespread perception among scholars that this apolitical stance, based on Paul's injunction in Romans 13:1 to abide by the powers that be, amounted in fact to evangelical collusion with military repression. Although some conservative academics (e.g., Sherman 1997) continue to whitewash the presidency of Ríos Montt and to deny the scale of murderous destruction, the Recovery of Historical Memory Project (REMHI), undertaken in the wake of the peace accords of 1996, aims at memorializing the martyrs and victims of those years of repression.

With the Cold War era violence ended, the ongoing story of religious continuity and change in Guatemala resumes. Liberation theology seems to have peaked as a dynamic force, to be supplanted to a degree within the Catholic fold by the charismatic movement (sometimes called Catholic Pentecostalism), and by yet another wave of Protestant fundamentalism—a Neo-Pentecostal movement that has been called the "Prosperity Gospel," which proclaims the entitlement of people of faith to worldly success. Meanwhile, the Pan-Maya and other indigenist movements have introduced yet another factor into the religious mix: self-consciously Maya Christian churches, both Catholic and Protestant, which are fervently anti-assimilationist and dedicated to indigenous cultural survival and revitalization.

Many recent scholars have attempted to analyze the dynamics of religious change in late-twentieth-century Latin America, and to try to account for or explain the explosive growth of fundamentalist and Pentecostal movements. (It is estimated that more than one-fourth of Guatemalans may now be Protestant-affiliated, and the Protestant population of the other countries of Central America ranges from 10 to 20 percent.) Factors held to account for the increasing success of Protestant evangelization include support in coping with alcoholism, promoting education and entrepreneurship, bettering health and hygiene, providing solace or strategies of adaptation, or simply new social space in the face of unsettling and bewildering social change (for an overview of these analyses, see Annis, 1987, pp. 78–79).

Sheldon Annis provides an elegant schema to describe and explicate the respective Catholic and Protestant cosmovisions in a Maya town in Guatemala. The traditionalist Maya Catholic culture he designates as driven by *"milpa* [family corn-plot] logic," which encompasses the retention of a communally based but not cost-efficient horticulture, willingness to cooperate in the "culture tax" to support local *cofradías* and fiestas, and a preference for a "contextualized" (i.e., Maya-grounded) Christian practice. The evangelical cosmovision Annis designates as the "anti-*milpa* nexus," encompassing a rejection of and noncooperation with the traditional "culture tax" and associated activities, a development-driven preference for more cost-efficient ways of farming or otherwise generating individual or family income, and, in religious culture, a rejection of "contextualized" Christianity in favor of assimilation and a theology that focuses solely on the faith commitment to Christ as personal savior, along with the presumption that prosperity is faith's natural outcome.

This evangelical nexus, Annis argues, is a contemporary Central American realization of the thesis propounded by Max Weber in *The Protestant Ethic and the Spirit of Capitalism*, characterized in the Mayan evangelical context by the phrase *del suelo al cielo* ("from the dirt floor to heaven"). Another way of summing up the distinction between the two world views, Annis proposes, resides in the idea that in the Catholic traditionalist value system, land *is* wealth, whereas in the evangelical value system, land is a means to wealth.

A similar comparative analysis of traditionalist and evangelical value systems in rural Chiapas has been undertaken by Eber (1995), with similar results. Once again, the evangelical community staunchly opposes *cooperación* with the *cargo* and *cofradía* systems as manifestations of wastefulness and idolatry. Eber found this rejection of traditional mores especially pronounced with regard to ritual and recreational uses of alcohol, a prominent aspect of every fiesta: traditionalist *costumbristas* embraced its use; Catholic Action catechists recommended moderation; and evangelicals insisted on absolute prohibition. Because the traditionalists saw the evangelical rejection not simply as the other group's option but as a stance destructive of community, the disagreement led to fierce civil conflict in the 1980s. This resulted, for instance, in the Protestants of Chamula being expelled from the town to settle in a Protestant refugee camp that still exists on the outskirts of San Cristóbal de las Casas.

The period of extreme violence seems to be winding down in much of the region, and the various religious sects have resumed their wary coexistence and competition. The evangelical churches continue their steady growth in much of Central America and in the southern and southeastern regions of Mexico, and the Catholic Church apparently finds more rejuvenation in the charismatic Renovacionista (Renewal) movement, sometimes called Catholic Pentecostalism or even Catholic Protestantism—perhaps the ultimate tribute to contemporary Protestant influence in Mesoamerica.

BIBLIOGRAPHY

Annis, Sheldon. *God and Production in a Guatemalan Town*. Austin, Tex., 1987. Readable and extremely insightful comparative analysis of work, wealth, and values according to Maya Catholic traditionalism and the new Protestant ethic.

Eber, Christine. *Women and Alcohol in a Highland Maya Town: Water of Hope, Water of Sorrow*. Austin, Tex., 1995. Feminist analysis of responses to village tradition among Catholic traditionalists and women who converted to evangelical Protestantism as a liberating option from domestic drunkenness and debt, but at the cost of community.

Garrard-Burnett, Virginia. *Protestantism in Guatemala: Living in the New Jerusalem*. Austin, Tex., 1998. Most comprehensive study to date of the evolution of the various Protestant movements in Guatemala in the nineteenth and twentieth centuries.

Garrard-Burnett, Virginia, and David Stoll, eds. *Rethinking Protestantism in Latin America*. Philadelphia, 1993. Seven essays, including a revisionist analysis of Protestantism in El Salvador, and an essay by Linda Green on how evangelicalism offers a valuable social space for Maya widows in Guatemala.

Gossen, Gary. "Life, Death, and Apotheosis of a Chamula Protestant Leader: Biography as Social History." In *Ethnographic Encounters in Southern Mesoamerica: Essays in Honor of Evon Zartman Vogt, Jr.*, edited by Victoria Bricker and Gary Gossen, pp. 217–229. Austin, Tex., 1989. Deliberately neutral presentation of the life of a conflicted and controversial figure who was murdered in the context of religious polarization.

Hullam, Anne Motley. *Beyond Missionaries: Toward an Understanding of the Protestant Movement in Central America*. Lanham, Md., 1996. Useful brief overview, with valuable notes and bibliography.

Martin, David. *Tongues of Fire: The Explosion of Protestantism in Latin America*. Oxford, 1990. Valuable overview of the history of evangelical and Pentecostal Protestantism throughout the whole region south of the U.S. border.

REMHI [Recovery of Historical Memory Project]. *Guatemala: Never Again! The Official Report of the Human Rights Office, Archdiocese of Guatemala*. Maryknoll, N.Y., 1999. One-volume English abridgement of the four-volume report on civil/religious violence during the decade of ethnic cleansing, issued under the guidance of Bishop Juan Gerardi, who was assassinated two days after the report's release.

Samandú, Luis, ed. *Protestantismos y procesos sociales en Centroamerica*. San José, 1990. Valuable collection including case studies in Guatemala, El Salvador, Honduras, Nicaragua, and Costa Rica.

Schäfer, Heinrich. *Protestantismo y crisis social en América Central*. San José, Costa Rica, 1992. History and taxonomy of the millenarian Protestant movements that flourished in the period of social crisis marked by violence and counterinsurgency.

Scotchmer, David. "Convergence of the Gods: Comparing Traditional Maya and Christian Maya Cosmologies." In *Symbol and Meaning beyond the Closed Community: Essays in Mesoamerican Ideas*, edited by Gary Gossen, pp. 197–226. Albany, N.Y., 1986. Valuable comparative cosmology by an anthropologist and Presbyterian missionary.

Scotchmer, David. "Life of the Heart: A Maya Protestant Spirituality." In *South and Meso-American Native Spirituality*, edited by Gary Gossen, pp. 497–525. New York, 1993. Historical analysis, along with a presentation of Maya Protestant spirituality focusing on the themes of the peace in conversion to Christ, and ideals of peace in the created and social orders.

Sherman, Amy. *The Soul of Development: Biblical Christianity and Economic Transformation in Guatemala*. Oxford, 1997. Frankly apologetic presentation of the role of evangelical Protestantism (and of the policies of Ríos Montt) according to the neo-conservative "culture and development" school, in opposition to cultural relativism, liberation theology, and what the author chooses to call "Christo-paganism."

Stoll, David. *Between Two Armies in the Ixil Towns of Guatemala.* New York, 1993. Controversial interpretation of the dynamics of the period of intense civil war and repression in Guatemala, arguing that significant numbers of Maya peasants were supporters neither of the military government nor of leftist guerillas, and were drawn more to the escapism offered by evangelical and Pentecostal Protestantism than to the social activism of liberation theology.

Stoll, David. *Fishers of Men or Founders of Empire? The Wycliffe Bible Translators in Latin America.* London, 1982. Somewhat polemical journalistic study of the controversial evangelical project.

Stoll, David. *Is Latin America Turning Protestant? The Politics of Evangelical Growth.* Berkeley, 1990. Comprehensive, detailed journalistic overview of the explosive growth of evangelical Protestantism across the whole of Latin America, focusing on important case studies in Guatemala, Nicaragua, and Ecuador.

GEORGE L. SCHEPER

CHUJ. *See* Q'anjob'al.

CHURCHES AND CATHEDRALS. The importance of church construction in the New World derives from two basic and related facts: that conversion to Roman Catholic Christianity of the indigenous populations in the newly discovered lands was the ideological justification for the Spanish conquest; and that church buildings were considered essential for Roman Catholic worship. Thus the number, scale, and decoration of churches in New Spain are eloquent indexes of both Spanish determination and the success of their colonization. Many types of churches were built, and cathedrals are generally outstanding because of their central locations and scale. The variations among church buildings resulted from differences in function, patronage, and location.

Church construction for Spaniards and *criollos* (New World–born Spaniards) meant the occupation of territory. Setting up the cross and the celebration of the Mass were among their first actions on taking possession of a new place; these involved the immediate creation of a ritual space, which was preliminary to the erection of a structure—an *enramada*—for repeating the liturgy. Although such initial *enramadas* were temporary, they were part of a continuum, with the climax the designation of a permanent sacred area and the construction of a solid church building that would become the focus of local life.

The fundamental role of church buildings, as well as their symbolic function, was recorded in the 1573 ordinances for the planning and establishment of towns in the Spanish empire. The central city square (plaza) was to be flanked by the cathedral or parish church and by the principal government building. To this day, this combination signals the center of towns throughout Spanish America. Often, the main church had its own atrium, an open space set off from the public square, which in the New World was generally a very large area. Thus the pattern was that of a sacred, enclosed open-air space in permanent relationship with the open-air secular space. The arrangement was repeated on a smaller scale for the churches in the towns. Not only religious events but also commerce, civic celebrations, and casual encounters would always have a church building as a reference point. On countless colonial maps, towns and cities are indicated by the shorthand representation of a church building.

The earliest churches constructed in the New World no longer exist, largely because the materials used were not lasting. Also, many towns changed their urban layout and even their location during the initial years of Spanish rule, as Franciscans, Dominicans, and Augustinians covered central New Spain with networks of their monasteries (*conventos*). Few archaeological efforts in Mexico have been directed toward clarifying the history of post-Conquest settlements; however, at Huejotzinco, one of the first Franciscan settlements, archaeology has revealed two early churches. Both were basilicas in plan, with wooden roofs, and thus different from the present-day massive, single nave, vaulted building, which became the more usual type of church in indigenous towns after the mid-sixteenth century.

Churches are not the only constructions within the monastery complexes, built as we know them after the initial evangelization efforts had been successful. In front of the church is a walled atrium, spacious enough to contain the population of the town and surrounding area for liturgical and paraliturgical activities. Its main entrance is usually on axis with the church nave, but its space is largely defined by elements that characterize its use as an open-air church as well: a central stone cross, an open chapel, and corner *posa* chapels. The open chapels (*capillas de indios*) are fundamentally presbyteries in which the Mass can be celebrated for the crowds in the atrium. Although liturgy outdoors was certainly not unknown in Europe, the variety and architectural invention of the open chapels of New Spain are unrivaled. Next to the church was the monastery, always with a cloister, where the friars lived and where visitors could be accommodated.

These buildings display a variety of styles and decorative elements that were in keeping with the complexity of local situations, as well as of the sixteenth century in Europe. The friars who often directed, and certainly supervised, construction came from different places and backgrounds, as did the European craft and guild masters who worked at the monasteries and who trained native artists and artisans. Gothic, Mudejar, and various Renaissance elements were combined in the roofing, portals, and architectural details, including vast stretches of narrative and iconic wall painting. The work of building was largely the responsibility of the native communities. An important issue relates to native cooperation in the fortress church. The idea derives from references in Colonial-era texts and from the actual appearance of some mission complexes. Their massive, unbroken wall surfaces have details reminiscent of military architecture, such as crenellations and guard towers. Taken at face value, scholars had accepted the view that the complexes were defensive structures, but now the military elements are generally perceived as symbolic of the idea of the "fortified city of God," the heavenly Jerusalem that the friars were constructing in the New World.

In addition to the central monastic complex, smaller churches and chapels were built in native towns. Many were for the various community groups, or sometimes associated with certain activities, or localized in their own *barrios* and with specific confraternities. In time, some of the large central churches became the parish churches of *mestizo* communities; the small churches proliferated as confraternities and local devotions increased. Then, early constructions were remodeled and new ones were built.

The mission efforts of the Jesuits took place in areas very distant from Mexico City, since the mendicant orders (Franciscan, Augustinian, and Dominican) had covered the entire central territory before the Jesuits' arrival in 1571. No early Jesuit buildings survive, but documents speak eloquently of the large basilican Jesuit churches in the Sinaloa missions at the end of the sixteenth century. Still extant are seventeenth- and eighteenth-century Jesuit mission churches in Mexico's states of Sinaloa and Sonora (including Arizona in the United States), Baja California, Durango, Coahuila, and Chihuahua. Many are of considerable architectural interest and were decorated by local craftsmen, as well as by works sent out from metropolitan centers, mostly Mexico City. In some cases, notably in the Lower Tarahumara, the construction and decoration of the mission churches closely resembled those of the secular (nonfraternal order) churches in nearby cities and towns of Spanish and *casta* populations.

Of the three mendicant orders in New Spain during the first half of the sixteenth century, the Franciscans continued to engage extensively in missionary work in the seventeenth and eighteenth centuries. The various provinces, and especially the friars of Propaganda Fide—working out of San Fernando in Mexico City, La Santa Cruz in Querétaro, and Guadalupe just outside of Zacatecas—established missions in Central America, in the Sierra Gorda, and throughout what is now northern Mexico and into Texas. After the 1767 expulsion of the Jesuits by the Crown, many Jesuit missions were put into Franciscan hands and so owe them much of their present-day appearance. In many of such later missions, particularly in

the Sierra Gorda complexes, although the plans of the church buildings are like those of any eighteenth-century parish church, the Franciscans once again utilized the sixteenth-century scheme of a large atrium with a central cross, an open-air chapel, and *posa* chapels. Also, as in the sixteenth century, the seventeenth- and eighteenth-century missions followed and accompanied European colonization.

The establishment of Spanish towns was just as important for colonization as the missionary efforts in the native communities. By definition, a cathedral is the church of a bishop and so implies the existence of a Roman Catholic community. In the New World, bishoprics were therefore established, and the cathedrals were eventually built in important urban areas: in Tlaxcala (1525), Mexico City (1529), Oaxaca (1534, then called Antequera), Tzintzuntzan (1536, moved to Pátzcuaro in 1550), Ciudad Real (1539, today San Cristóbal de Las Casas), Guadalajara (1545), Mérida (1561), and Durango (1620). Much later, in 1777, a bishopric was established at Linares in Nuevo León, and then in Sonora in 1779. Bishoprics not only manifest the existence of a Roman Catholic community; they are necessary for its very formation and consolidation, since only bishops have the authority to administer the sacraments of Confirmation and Holy Orders. The earliest bishoprics of New Spain generated some of the areas of conflict into later centuries. The struggles over cathedrals involved issues of European domination over native peoples and, therefore, the very presence of the church in New Spain.

Charles V ensured the existence of a bishopric in the New World as soon as possible. In 1519, he requested of Pope Leo X its establishment and exercised his right as king of Spain to name bishops. The first was located in Cozumel in 1519; shortly after, this diocese was settled at Tlaxcala, home of some native allies of the Spaniards. Tzintzuntzan-Pátzcuaro, another of the early bishoprics, was also in a predominantly native community, that of the Tarascos. These two bishoprics testify both to the early conversion of their populations and to their importance as agents of subsequent colonization.

The cathedral of Pátzcuaro was the only one in New Spain that explicitly acknowledged a New World situation. Bishop Vasco de Quiroga wanted a new architecture for the new Christian community. His cathedral was planned as a single presbytery with five naves radiating from it, perhaps corresponding to different native groups; however, this extraordinary building was never finished. Furthermore, the diocese of Tlaxcala was moved to Puebla in 1543, while that of Pátzcuaro went to Valladolid (Morelia) in 1580. These facts demonstrate the decline of native populations in the second half of the sixteenth century, and their subordination to the colonizers.

They also demonstrate the shift away from the utopian vision of the friars during the initial phases of evangelization. Many of the early bishops had been members of the regular clergy, but with time the secular clergy came to dominate the church and the cathedrals of New Spain, especially after the Council of Trent.

The grand cathedrals in major cities of New Spain were generally built after the much more modest early churches. From the beginning, both royal patronage and local participation (in the form of native labor and contributions by the colonists) constituted the basis of construction. With the exception of the building at Pátzcuaro, which is today the church that houses the Virgin of La Salud and which had no architectural following, the cathedrals of New Spain are the last in the tradition of the great European cathedrals, whose characteristics had been established by medieval times. They followed the cathedrals in Spain that were still being built or remodeled during the fifteenth and sixteenth centuries, especially in Andalusia after the *reconquista* (from the Moors, 1492 CE). Like them, they are large rectangular buildings with an inscribed transept; and like them, they are usually dedicated to the Virgin (who symbolizes the Christian church), and they also prominently display images of the apostles (who are the foundation of the Christian church as an institution). The interior provides spaces for ceremonies that involve the bishop and the members of the cathedral chapter, in both the nave and the apse; the interior also provides space for the devotions of lay people in the side chapels, patronized by the confraternities often associated with social status and commercial activities, notably through the guilds. Day-to-day parish activities have their own spaces, either in a side chapel or in an adjoining building (the *sagrario*).

Although the cathedral of Guadalajara displays Gothic-vault construction, the others are fundamentally Renaissance buildings with Baroque and Neoclassical elements and furnishings—since, as everywhere, cathedrals took a long time to finish in the New World. The first architects came from Spain, bringing the treatises that were to serve repeatedly as models and references for the architecture of the New World. The usual plan of New Spain's cathedrals includes a nave with side aisles and two rows of side chapels. In the cathedrals of Mexico City and Puebla, which shared architects during the early stages of construction, the inscribed transept and the nave have higher elevations than the side aisles and chapels. Although the dome of the cathedral of Mérida had been erected by 1597, the one on a drum that crowns Puebla cathedral, built by bishop Juan de Palafox by 1649, established the model for many subsequent domes in New Spain. Palafox is the prime example of a bishop who understood the intimate relationship between the construction of his cathedral and the affirmation of the secular church. Through his efforts the cathedral of Puebla was largely completed before that of Mexico City, which was not entirely finished until the early nineteenth century.

Cathedral construction concentrated material and human resources. The principal architects, artists, and artisans contributed to the building and decoration, and their work had great impact on later buildings of all kinds. Echoes of the formal elements of the cathedrals may be seen in other buildings of each cathedral city. Fundamental innovations first occurred at the cathedral of Mexico City, and were emulated throughout the viceroyalty (an example is the construction beginning in 1718 of the Retablo of the Kings by Jerónimo Balbás).

As cathedrals became the architectural centers of the principal cities, parish churches became the symbols of stability for neighborhoods, towns, and settlements. They were administered by the secular clergy under the authority of the bishop; by the eighteenth century, most of the early churches founded by the friars had also become secularized. The typical parish church is a single nave building with a transept crowned by a dome. A good number of the secularized sixteenth-century churches acquired domes as well. A few important parishes, particularly in northern New Spain, have a central nave, two side aisles, and an inscribed transept; documents indicate that these were built with the idea that they might become cathedrals—as happened at San Luis Potosí, Zacatecas, and Chihuahua—although not until the nineteenth century.

In the seventeenth and eighteenth centuries, the decoration of the churches became more elaborate. Just as light from the domes provided drama and focus inside churches, sculpted portals, often movemented in plan and framed by towers, drew attention to the entrances. The interiors, although simple in plan, were expected to be filled with elaborate altarpieces (*retablos*) that concealed and transformed the bare, straight walls. These fundamentally Baroque effects differed by area. Although the types of buildings are the same, their materials, decoration, and colors vary. Glazed tiles, bricks, alabaster (*tecali*), and painted and even gilded plasterwork became typical of the Tlaxcala-Puebla area, from which tiles and alabaster were exported to the rest of the viceroyalty. Limestone of as many hues as there were quarries characterized buildings in different places—greenish in Oaxaca, gray in Mexico City, and white in Durango. Variations were also developed in proportions and in technical matters that related to local soil conditions and to the relative frequency of earthquakes. Before the late eighteenth century, the windows of churches had been increased in number and size, to provide more uniform lighting, as was consonant with Neoclassical tastes.

All these differences and developments testify to the existence of local artisans and workshops, in many specialties, with the experience of generations. The workshops and the guilds that regulated them had their start within the monastery and cathedral projects. Many of these workers were native, but their family origins were not necessarily in the places where their production is found. Since the Conquest, there had been great movements of native groups and of individuals; many people—mulattos and other *castas*, as well as Europeans—worked in construction by the seventeenth century, and they moved to the work sites.

Besides the central presence of cathedrals and parishes, the urban spaces of cities and large towns were marked by other churches. All the mendicant orders that had been a part of the original evangelization had churches there, and other orders did as well. In plan and in decorative elements, these were not significantly different from the parish churches, except for the iconography of their portals and altarpieces. Only for the Franciscans and the Carmelites can a case be made that a certain simplicity was consciously promoted, at least in some instances of construction, though not of interior furnishings. The Jesuits, who had trained architects among them, built some of the most interesting buildings in New Spain; their city churches, many associated with colleges, are notable for their size, the originality of their plans and elevations, and for the richness of their architectural sculpture and interior furnishings. The churches of nuns' convents were of a particular type—with a single nave and two side entrances—since the entire choir area, where one would expect to find the main entrance, was occupied during the liturgy by the nuns and was never accessible to the general public.

In the imported European tradition, civilization implied urban life, be it in a native town or in a large *mestizo* and *criollo* city; therefore, all the churches described have been urban buildings, because their existence is involved with the life of an established Christian community. There were, however, some churches in decidedly nonurban settings. These ranged from the few Carmelite establishments in out-of-the-way places (*desiertos*), to the numerous domestic chapels of the *haciendas* and of native dwellings, to chapels erected for the images that involved miraculous events. For the miraculous shrines, some important sanctuaries were developed, with large and spectacular church buildings, especially that of the Virgin of Guadalupe, outside Mexico City, or that of the Virgin of Ocotlán, outside of Tlaxcala. Although towns grew around them, and the architecture of the more elaborate churches is closely related to urban developments, the focus remained on the image, its sanctuary, and the celebrations centered there. The great numbers of pilgrims would find themselves in a setting where some of the distinctions and hierarchies of race, class, and social position—so present in their ordinary lives and usual places and routines of worship—were temporarily attenuated.

BIBLIOGRAPHY

Angulo Íñiguez, Diego, et al. *Historia del arte hispanoamericano*. Barcelona, 1945–1956. Fundamental source on all of the art of Spanish America; gives very extensive treatment to Mexican architecture.

Baird, James Armstrong. *The Churches of México, 1530–1810*. Berkeley, Calif., 1962. Basic, clearly written book in English.

Bargellini, Clara. *La arquitectura de la plata. Iglesias monumentales del centro norte de México: 1640–1750*. Mexico City and Madrid, 1991. Study of the cathedral of Durango and of the parish churches of the region.

Bargellini, Clara. "Representations of Conversion: Sixteenth Century Architecture in New Spain." In *The Word Made Image. Religion, Art and Architecture in Spain and Spanish America 1500–1600*, pp. 91–102. Boston, 1998. Historiographic treatment of the subject, with particular attention to recent controversies.

Bérchez, Joaquín. *Arquitectura mexicana de los siglos XVII y XVIII*. Mexico City, 1992. Uneven study that, however, places much due attention on the use of treatises by architects in New Spain.

Berlin, Heinrich. "Three Master Architects in New Spain." *Hispanic American Historical Review* 27 (1947), 375–383. One of several articles by this important scholar, on specific architects in the light of archival research.

Catálogo de construcciones religiosas del Estado de Hidalgo. Mexico City, 1929–1932. This monumental work as well as similar volumes about Yucatán were the first efforts at completely cataloguing the colonial architecture of Mexico; for many years nothing more was done, but in the 1970s Mexico's Instituto Nacional de Antropología e Historia began anew to produce catalogs of buildings that are national patrimony—a project still incomplete. Recently, local efforts have been made to publish, notably in Michoacán.

Díaz, Marco. *La arquitectura de los jesuitas en Nueva España*. Mexico City, 1982. Every building is illustrated and its basic history is traced; emphasizes the originality of Jesuit architecture in New Spain.

Fernández, Martha. *Arquitectura y gobierno virreinal*. Mexico City, 1985. Well-documented study of the *Maestros mayores* of Mexico City in the seventeenth century—the principal architects of major buildings and their patrons.

Gustin, Monique. *El barroco en la Sierra Gorda*. Mexico City, 1969. Basic study of the eighteenth-century Franciscan missions of that area.

Kubler, George. *Mexican Architecture of the Sixteenth Century*. New Haven, 1948. Excellent study and still the book most worth reading on the topic.

McAndrew, John. *The Open-Air Churches of Sixteenth-Century Mexico*. Cambridge, Mass., 1965. Fundamental study of these constructions.

Sigaut, Nelly, ed. *La catedral de Morelia*. Morelia, 1991. Only for this Mexican cathedral have all the documents become fully available; this collection explores various aspects of the history of the cathedral and its construction, which answer many questions about the development and governance of these institutions and their buildings.

Toussaint, Manuel. *La catedral de México y el Sagrario Metropolitano.* Mexico City, 1948. 2d ed., 1972. The author was the founder of modern art-historical studies in Mexico; he began his work on the building as a young man and this is the result of his efforts.

Toussaint, Manuel. *La catedral y las iglesias de Puebla.* Mexico City, 1954. Relatively slight volume, but still the most reliable study of these important buildings.

Vargas Lugo, Elisa. *Las portadas religiosas de México.* Mexico City, 1974. Examines the formal characteristics of the portals of Mexican Colonial-period churches, probably the architectural element that has attracted the most attention.

CLARA BARGELLINI

CIPACTLI. Among the most powerful and esteemed creatures of Mesoamerica are the great aquatic caimans and crocodiles of the family Crocodylidae; of the alligator and caiman subfamily, the Alligatorinae, there are no alligators and only one caiman (*Caiman crocodilus*) in this region. The caiman is limited in both numbers and range, extending from the south no farther than northern Guatemala and Belize, so it is absent from the Gulf Coast region. It is found on the Pacific Coast as far north as southeastern Mexico, however. Crocodiles have a far wider range in Mesoamerica; of the two species present, the American crocodile (*Crocodilus acutus*) enjoys the broadest range—on both coasts near the northern borders of Mesoamerica and south to northern Colombia and western Ecuador. A fragmentary vessel from the Postclassic site of Amapa (Nayarit) depicts a probable American crocodile native to the local region. The average size of the American crocodile is far larger than that of the caiman; the crocodile can attain 7 meters (23 feet) in length but is usually about 3.6 meters (12 feet). Although there is undoubtedly overuse of the term "caiman" in Mesoamerican studies, there was probably little differentiation between caimans and crocodiles in native Mesoamerican thought; indeed, iguanas and even swordfish were conceptually linked to crocodilians.

Among the Aztec (Mexica), the American crocodile was known as *acuetzpali* ("water lizard"). Whereas this word denotes an actual creature, the better-known Aztec term "Cipactli" apparently alludes to a mythic supernatural being. As the first Aztec day name of the 260-day calendar, *Cipactli* is equivalent to the Zapotec day name *Pichijlla.* According to Seler (1990–1998), both the Nahuatl and Zapotec terms mean "the spiny." In fact, among the more striking traits of crocodiles and caimans in Mesoamerican art is the series of large spines running down the back and tail, clearly representing the prominent dorsal and caudal scales of these creatures. These sharp scales gave rise to two of the basic symbolic meanings of caimans and crocodiles in ancient Mesoamerica: their identification with the sacred ceiba tree and the surface of

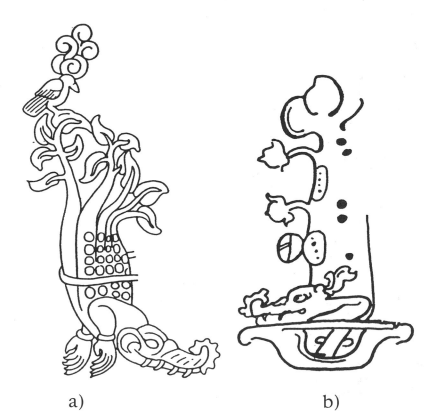

FIGURE 1. Maya portrayals of crocodilian world trees: (a) Crocodilian world tree, Izapa Stela 25, Late Preclassic period; (b) Late Classic portrayal of world tree in ceramic bowl. *Drawings courtesy of Karl A. Taube.*

a)   b)

the earth. Among the ancient Maya, the ceiba (*yax che*) commonly constitutes the pivotal world tree, and it frequently appears as a crocodile or caiman with its tail raised up into the sky (Figure 1a–b). Young ceibas are covered with conical spines, recalling the spiny backs of crocodiles and caimans. One of the earliest representations of the crocodilian world tree appears on Izapa Stela 25, a monument dating to the Late Preclassic period. The curiously segmented tail is commonly found in ancient Mesoamerican portrayals of crocodilians, including Middle Formative Olmec examples. Aside from the ceiba, the ancient Maya also portrayed the central world tree as a maize plant. In one well-known Late Classic scene of the maize god emerging out of the turtle earth, he is epigraphically named the "maize god crocodilian," evidently referring to his role as the world tree.

The crocodile and caiman can also portray the world itself in Mesoamerican thought. In this metaphor, the earth with its sharp peaks is a great crocodilian floating on the primordial sea. The earliest depiction of this concept appears on Kaminaljuyú Stela 9, which portrays a man standing on a caiman or crocodile as the basal earth. The earth crocodilian probably also appears on Kaminaljuyú Monument 2, a massive throne or altar. According to Lee Parsons, both Kaminaljuyú monuments date to approximately the sixth century BCE. In Classic and Postclassic Maya art, the crocodilian appears in basal registers of monumental scenes, again alluding to the earth. In addition, a number of colonial sources pertaining to the Yucatec Maya refer to an earth crocodilian. In the Late Postclassic Borgia Group of codices from Central Mexico, a crocodile or caiman frequently depicts the surface of the earth. According to the Aztec creation account in the *Historia de los mexicanos por sus pinturas*, Cipactli was a great caiman-like fish that swam in the primordial waters; from this creature, the earth was made. Classic Maya as well as Late Postclassic Central Mexican crocodilians are frequently portrayed with fish tails. In addition, both at Early Postclassic Chichén Itzá and among the Aztec, crocodilians can be portrayed with the snout of a swordfish (*acipaquitli*). It appears that the Aztec Cipactli embodied the concept of a monstrous, spiny creature swimming or floating in water.

Unlike those of mammals, the bones of crocodilians and other reptiles continue to grow throughout the lifetime of the animal. A crocodilian the size of the earth would truly be an antediluvian creature, and possibly for this reason they are widely identified with cycles of calendrics and creation in ancient Mesoamerica. As the first of the twenty day names of Late Postclassic Central Mexico, Cipactli was identified with origins and beginnings of both calendrical cycles and events of myth and history; the patron of this day is the wizened old creator god To-

nacatecuhtli, who frequently appears in this context with a primordial human couple. *Imix*, the Maya equivalent of the day name *Cipactli*, refers to the waterlily and, by extension, to standing water. Not only is *Imix* the first of the twenty day names; it is also the first day of the Long Count cycle, which always ends on the twentieth day name, *Ahau*. Two closely related Late Classic vessels portray a palace scene of the mythic beginning of the present Long Count cycle in 3114 BCE. A crocodilian is prominently set atop the palace roof, presumably identifying it as the place of this being.

Among the Formative-period Olmec and the pre-Hispanic Maya peoples, crocodilians were identified with rain-bringing wind, probably because of the widespread belief that wind and rain clouds are "breathed" out of cave openings in the earth. A series of Olmec-style bas-reliefs from Chalcatzingo in the state of Morelos portrays crocodilians breathing rain clouds from their upturned mouths. Portable green stone Olmec sculptures depict crocodilians in similar positions, indicating that they are probably also breathing. In the Late Preclassic period of Izapa, the Maya crocodilians are commonly supplied with a cross-sectional conch shell on the nose (Figure 1b). The form is essentially identical to the cut-conch wind jewel, the *ehecailacacozcatl*, worn by the Aztec wind god Ehecatl-Quetzalcoatl. The placement of this element on Maya crocodilian snouts associates their breath with wind. The Quirigua Zoomorph P, however, constitutes the most ambitious Maya portrayal of the crocodilian earth as the creator of wind and rain. The great face of this being has the typical crossed-band eyes of Classic Maya crocodilians, as well as their conical teeth and rough scutes (external bony plates), here marked with glyphic texts. Both of the cut-conch breath volutes that emerge from the corners of the mouth contain the Maya rain god Chak, carrying a water jar, which indicates that the creature is breathing rain clouds from its cavernous maw. The principal breath element of this cosmic beast is the massive Altar P', placed directly before the face of Zoomorph P. The altar portrays Chak emerging from a stone marked with the Maya wind sign, once again identifying cloud-bearing wind with the breath of the crocodilian earth monster.

BIBLIOGRAPHY

Garibay, Angel. *Teogonía e historia de les Mexicanes: Tres opúsculos del siglo XVI*, 3rd ed. Mexico City, 1979. Contains text of *Historia de los Mexicanes por sus pinturas* (pp. 23–66).

Grenard, Steve. *Handbook of Alligators and Crocodiles.* Malabar, 1991. Detailed descriptions of physical characteristics, behavior, and geographic distribution of living species of crocodilians.

Seler, Eduard. "The Animal Pictures of the Mexican and Maya Manuscripts." In his *Collected Works in Mesoamerican Linguistics and Archaeology*, 2nd ed. Lancaster, Calif., 1990–1998. In a section devoted to the crocodile (pp. 273–277), Seler discusses Mesoamerican conceptions of crocodilians; pre-Hispanic depictions of crocodilians are included, particularly from Central Mexican manuscripts.

Taube, Karl. *Itzam Cab Ain: Caimans, Cosmology and Calendrics in Postclassic Yucatan.* Research Reports on Ancient Maya Writing, 26. Washington, D.C., 1989. Discusses symbolism of crocodilians among the Postclassic Yucatec, particularly the concept of the crocodilian as the earth and its relation to creation and calendrical cycles; Yucatec data are compared with conceptions of crocodilians from Late Postclassic Central Mexico.

KARL A. TAUBE

CITIES. *See* Urbanization.

CITY-STATES. *See* Community Kingdoms *and* Political Organization and Development, *article on* Pre-Hispanic Cultures.

CIVIL RECORDS. The establishment of a town council was an integral part of Spanish efforts to reorganize Mesoamerican regional states along the lines of a Spanish municipality after the Conquest. Each indigenous town council (*cabildo*) had its own scribe (*escribano*), who wrote native-language documents that dealt with mundane legal matters and were intended primarily for a local audience. These civil or notarial-type records represent the continuation of the long-standing Mesoamerican tradition of written recordkeeping. They also reflect the introduction of the technologies of alphabetic writing and Spanish documentary genres—testaments, sales and grants of land, minutes of *cabildo* meetings, petitions, and *cofradía* (religious association) records. Above all, civil records were practical, written to claim and protect rights or material resources that might be legally challenged. Most of those extant today have been preserved because they were submitted as evidence in legal disputes (especially over land) or during *composición* proceedings (the process by which land titles were legally confirmed), when they became incorporated into the titles of Spanish estates. Modeled on Spanish documentary genres that incorporated Spanish legal notions, native-language civil records themselves became instruments of cultural transformation in post-Conquest Mesoamerican communities.

Civil records captured only sporadic scholarly attention before the 1970s. To date, most studies concern Nahuatl—the language best represented in the surviving materials—followed by Maya, Mixtec, and Cakchikel; research on Otomí and Zapotec is in progress. Civil records are also extant for Chocho, Cuicatec, Mixe, Quiché, Tarascan, and Totonac, but these await scholarly attention. Civil records with fully developed conventions appear in Nahuatl from the 1540s and in Yucatec Maya from the 1550s. Most Nahuatl documents originated in the Nahua heartland of central Mexico; some come from Nahua satellite communities as far away as Saltillo to the northeast and Guatemala to the south. Still others come from non-Nahua communities where Nahuatl served as a lingua franca in the early Colonial years. Mixtec scribes first wrote alphabetic texts in Nahuatl, switching to their native language only in the final quarter of the sixteenth century. The time of greatest florescence of documentary production in terms of quantity, quality, and diversity varies: roughly 1580–1610 for Nahuatl, 1670–1720 for Mixtec, and 1770–1820 for Yucatec Maya. This pattern reflects the greater degree of contact with Spaniards and the faster rate at which towns acquired *cabildos* and appointed scribes in central and south-central Mexico than in Yucatán. Throughout the Colonial period, notarial-type records written in Spanish were utilized at times in indigenous communities. Nobles—typically among the first bilingual residents of native communities—might obtain such Spanish-language documents as testaments and land titles to secure their rights and possessions beyond the indigenous domain. In the late eighteenth century, many Nahua and Mixtec scribes switched to recordkeeping in Spanish in response to growing legal discrimination against native-language records and their own increasingly bilingual skills.

Certain conventions characterize the corpus of mundane indigenous-language documents. Civil records typically note the date of composition, identify the community of origin, and list the names of the interested parties and witnesses. Most have elaborate openings and explicit endings, replete with stock formulas. These features derived at least in part from Spanish documentary models, which native-language civil records tend to follow closely. Other features are rooted in pre-Conquest oral tradition: colloquial speech, textual markers that signal separate units (a bequest of a will or the section of a land boundary) or transitions in spoken dialogue, and the broad nature of witnesses. Also reflecting pre-Conquest patterns is an emphasis on the indigenous regional state (and its constituent parts) that pervades the corpus; it constitutes the primary manner by which individuals identified themselves. (The absence of the term *indio*, which Spaniards used to designate indigenous people as a group, is notable here.) Pictorial representation persisted into the sixteenth century in the Nahua and Mixtec regions (Maya writing had had a weak pictorial component before the Conquest), but it appears primarily in genres typical of pre-Conquest recordkeeping, such as tribute lists, cadastrals, and histories. With the exception of certain land-related genres, pictorials are largely absent from civil records—even from testaments, which usually concern landholdings.

Testaments make up perhaps half of all extant mundane indigenous-language records. They are highly standardized and follow Spanish models closely in wording and structure. The typical preamble consists of an invocation of the Holy Trinity, the recitation of some tenets of faith, the identification of the testator by name and community, and the statement that the testator is sick of body but sound of mind. The body of the testament is an enumeration of bequests that proceeds item by item, each signaled by an indentation, dash, or other textual marker, and sometimes by ordinal numbering. The first bequests often specify burial and masses to be performed on behalf of the testator's soul, together with the provision for the sale of property to pay for them. The remaining bequests usually concern houses and land. Pious donations to the church, *cofradías*, and cult of the saints, along with a reckoning of debts to be paid or collected, may follow. Each bequest often ends with an admonition that its provisions are to be carried out or are not to be violated. The final section names the executor (*albacea*) and witnesses and records the date.

The prevalence of the Spanish-style written testament suggests a close indigenous precedent. The written testament apparently drew on a testamentary speech act whereby the dying person made his wishes known during a ceremonious gathering, and traces of that ritual practice appear in the documents. Following Spanish documentary conventions, indigenous-language testaments typically use the third person to refer to executors or potential heirs. But they also contain spontaneous, declamatory statements that may disinherit a potential heir or admonish the listeners to enforce the testator's wishes. These admonitions are often cast in language that suggests a forceful command. Such statements would have no legal purpose in a Spanish testament; they make sense only if directed at an audience. The nature of witnesses in mundane indigenous-language records also suggests an oral ritual. Witnesses to Spanish testaments typically included three adult males whose purpose was to attest to the actual signing of the document. Witnesses to indigenous testaments were greater in number and more diverse—municipal officials, women, potential heirs, and neighbors—and their role was correspondingly broader: they represented the community and attested not only to the distribution of the property but also to the testator's authentic right to it. The written testament also retained much of the function of the pictorial genealogies found in codices and *lienzos*: they served to legitimate the claims of high nobles, but now before Spanish authorities. The connection is quite direct in certain Mixtec genealogies, where the pictorial abruptly ends with an individual whose testament is attached. [*See* Lienzos.]

The preambles of testaments are drawn from Spanish documentary tradition and constitute the most straightforwardly doctrinal statements found in mundane indigenous-language documents, yet preambles typically shed little light on popular piety because they are strongly formulaic. They are often riddled with errors, suggesting that scribes, bored or impatient with the repetitive task, wrote them hastily or carelessly. Variation in detail reflects local style and the preferences of individual scribes more than it does divergence in doctrinal content. The preambles of Mixtec testaments stand apart in that they include direct statements made by testators that reflect an indigenous form of popular Christianity. Whereas the preamble embodies doctrine, the body of the testament concerns the mundane affairs of community and household. The form of expression is less formulaic and employs a more vernacular vocabulary. Above all, the actual behavior of individuals comes to the fore. Whole arenas of indigenous life appear—kinship, gender, inheritance, wealth, material culture, the cult of the saints, and above all, land. Some testaments are essentially land documents.

The centrality of land to indigenous communities accounts for the abundance of land documentation, the second largest body of civil records after testaments. Indigenous communities adopted the full repertoire of documentary genres used to certify individual holdings in the Spanish tradition—bill of sale, grant or donation, and act of possession. Land records based on Spanish models tended to be drawn up—and to approach Spanish models more closely—when the transaction involved a Spaniard, though many record transfers within the indigenous community. The bill of sale (*carta de venta*) was the most common genre, highly conventional and uniform in format. Bills of sale typically mention the date, the names and home communities of buyer and seller, and the location, dimensions, and price of the land. They also commonly include admonitions, as well as other statements—as to the ownership of the land, type of land involved, alleged reasons for the sale, or proposed use of sale money—which address both indigenous and Spanish concerns that the sale is legitimate. Like admonitions in testaments, these statements reflect indigenous oral tradition and would have had no place in a Spanish bill of sale.

Legal ownership in the Spanish tradition was confirmed when the buyer took ritual possession of the land. In the Spanish proceedings, the seller or the local Spanish official led the buyer across the boundaries of the land parcel, after which the buyer threw stones and pulled twigs and tufts of grass in symbolic gestures of ownership. If a house was included in a sale, the buyer might symbolically shove the seller and others out of the house. Officials drew up a document to record the act of possession (*posesión*), which the buyer kept along with the bill of sale. Indigenous communities quickly adopted the Spanish-style act of possession and the related document, which may accompany the bill of sale proper. Documents of possession vary in length and extent of detail; they commonly express ritual elements rooted in the pre-Conquest oral tradition, especially evident in the large number of witnesses (apparently whole neighborhoods) who consented to the proceedings. Other elements of pre-Conquest land ritual—feasting, drinking, and the presentation of payments or gifts—apparently took place too, though because they were attuned to Spanish conventions, scribes rarely recorded them.

Indigenous scribes also wrote documents more directly concerned with the affairs of the *cabildo*, including council minutes, election records, and petitions. With the exception of petitions, much of this material consists largely of lists of Spanish names and offices. The municipal election report is a complete list of newly elected officers sandwiched between mainly formulaic opening and closing sections. The council minutes from sixteenth-century Tlaxcala—the only known set from a Colonial-period indigenous municipality—consist of opening formulas, brief summaries of *cabildo* deliberations, and a list of members in attendance, with occasional speeches and fuller minutes. They provide the fullest evidence on *cabildo* officers, career and recruitment patterns, municipal economic enterprises, and support for religious organizations and activities. The petitions written by *cabildos* to Spanish authorities are generally longer, more varied, and less formulaic than election records and council minutes. Petitions sought to defend community lands, lighten tribute demands, or challenge local priests (for violent behavior, sexual misconduct, or the neglect of their responsibilities), and they often initiated litigation. They could be highly partisan (or even falsified) in order to promote the interests of one political faction in electoral or land disputes. Petitions, election records, and council minutes all exhibit traces of pre-Conquest oratory and declamatory style. Petitions address Spanish authorities in obsequious and reverential language and refer to the petitioners (often members of the nobility) in humble, deferential terms that were characteristic of pre-Conquest speechmaking.

The scribe associated with the municipal *cabildo* (or church) also kept the records of the local *cofradía*, or lay brotherhood. *Cofradías* supported masses, feasts, the maintenance of altars in the local church, and the burial of its members. *Cofradía* records include written constitutions and rules (often translated from Spanish), membership lists, and detailed accounts of cult-related expenses and the monetary contributions made by each member. They shed light on *cofradía* membership, officers, finances, and religious observances, but they rarely concern doctrinal matters or the actual beliefs of the members.

Over all, the civil records written by indigenous scribes provide a perspective internal to the indigenous community. Their pragmatic purpose to communicate among ordinary indigenous people about mundane affairs means that civil records reach the level of individuals and deliver scholars from the generalized accounts written by Spaniards. The language itself provides indigenous categories and modes of organization not found in Spanish-language documents; they shed light on pre-Conquest (and pan-Mesoamerican) patterns and suggest a greater survival of pre-Conquest elements than Spanish documents do. Yet mundane indigenous-language documents above all reflect the dynamics of post-Conquest social and cultural change. Spaniards and Spanish influence appear everywhere, transforming local societies to some degree. Evidence of the influence of Spanish on local languages abounds, providing the basis for historical linguistics, phonology, and dialectology. Yet contact with Spaniards was uneven, and indigenous-language civil records indicate the pronounced regional variation that characterized Mesoamerica, both before and after the Conquest.

BIBLIOGRAPHY

Anderson, Arthur J. O., Frances Berdan, and James Lockhart. *Beyond the Codices*. Berkeley and Los Angeles, 1976. Indispensable introduction to the types and conventions of mundane Nahuatl documents, with a selection of representative texts in transcription and translation.

Cline, S. L. *Colonial Culhuacan, 1580–1600: A Social History of an Aztec Town*. Albuquerque, N.M., 1984. Innovative social history of the central Mexican municipality of Culhuacan, based primarily on a collection of Nahuatl testaments from the late sixteenth century.

Haskett, Robert. *Indigenous Rulers: An Ethnohistory of Town Government in Colonial Cuernavaca*. Albuquerque, N.M., 1991. Wide-ranging study of indigenous town government in colonial Cuernavaca, based heavily on Nahuatl documents, including a large corpus of election records.

Hill, Robert M., II. *Colonial Cakchiquels: Highland Maya Adaptations to Spanish Rule, 1600–1700*. Fort Worth, Tex., 1992. Concise historical ethnography of the Cakchikel of highland Guatemala that rests in part of Cakchikel Maya documents, including testaments, bills of sale, and community titles.

Horn, Rebecca. *Postconquest Coyoacan: Nahua–Spanish Relations in Central Mexico, 1519–1650*. Stanford, 1997. Multifaceted study of Nahuas and Spaniards of the central Mexican municipality of Coyoacán, based heavily on Nahuatl notarial documents; includes a detailed discussion of the bill of sale genre.

Kellogg, Susan. *Law and the Transformation of Aztec Culture, 1500–1700*. Norman, Okla., 1995. Compelling analysis of changing notions of property, gender, and kinship among the Nahua of post-Conquest Mexico City that relies in part on Nahuatl testaments and land records submitted as evidence in property disputes.

Kellogg, Susan, and Matthew Restall, eds. *Dead Giveaways: Indigenous Testaments of Colonial Mesoamerica and the Andes*. Salt Lake

City, 1998. Anthology that analyzes Spanish and native-language testaments of indigenous men and women from Colonial Mesoamerica and the Andes as source, genre, and instrument of cultural transformation.

Lockhart, James. *Nahuas and Spaniards: Postconquest Central Mexican History and Philology*. Stanford, 1991. Excellent articles explore the characteristics and significance of Nahuatl documents in terms of philology, ideology, and social and cultural history; with transcriptions and translations of selected texts.

Lockhart, James. *The Nahuas after the Conquest: A Social and Cultural History of the Indians of Central Mexico, Sixteenth through Eighteenth Centuries*. Stanford, 1992. Comprehensive social and cultural history, based entirely on Nahuatl documents, that includes a succinct discussion of post-Conquest writing and documentary genres.

Lockhart, James, Frances Berdan, and Arthur J. O. Anderson. *The Tlaxcalan Actas: A Compendium of the Records of the Cabildo of Tlaxcala (1545–1627)*. Salt Lake City, 1986. Compendium of the unique *cabildo* records from sixteenth-century Tlaxcala that includes an analytical introduction, a calendar of *cabildo* sessions, and a selection of sessions in transcription and translation, introduced with brief commentary.

Restall, Matthew, "Heirs to the Hieroglyphs: Indigenous Writing in Colonial Mesoamerica." *Americas* 54 (1997), 239–267. Succinct overview of indigenous-language documentation that emphasizes genres, conventions, and patterns of production.

Restall, Matthew. *The Maya World: Yucatec Culture and Society, 1550–1850*. Stanford, 1997. Sweeping study of Colonial Yucatec Maya society, based primarily on Maya-language documents, that considers alphabetic writing and documentary genres, including testaments, land sale records, petitions, and election reports.

Terraciano, Kevin. *The Mixtecs of Colonial Oaxaca: A History of Ñudzahui Writing and Culture*. Stanford, forthcoming. Fascinating study of Mixtec writing and culture, based on a diverse body of pictorial and alphabetic texts, including a significant corpus of Mixtec civil records.

REBECCA HORN

CIVIL-RELIGIOUS HIERARCHY. Variously known as the *cargo*, fiesta, or *mayordomía* system, the civil-religious hierarchy refers to a constellation of political and religious offices (Roman Catholic) found in many Indian peasant communities in highland Spanish America, especially in Mesoamerica. Traditionally, it has been a central part of the culture of such communities, playing an important role in political administration and religious ritual and in defining the parameters of prestige and economic stratification. Though now faded or dismantled in many places, the civil-religious hierarchy has been a basic staple of Mesoamerican ethnography since the 1930s, particularly in the highland regions of Central Mexico, in the Mexican states of Oaxaca and Chiapas, and in western Guatemala.

The system in its classic form consists of two hierarchically arranged sets of offices linked by a custom of individual (or household) sponsorship of religious fiestas for Catholic saints. Positions, or *cargos*, may be elected or appointed by outgoing officials, and the term of office normally is one year. The political offices have to do with local civil administration, whereas the religious offices are concerned with the care and ritual celebration of the saints. Religious *cargos* may be part of *cofradías*, the sodalities devoted to particular saints, or they may consist of *mayordomías*, in which single individuals or couples each take on the responsibility for organizing and financing a fiesta. Adult males, as representatives of households, gradually ascend these twin ladders of *cargos* during their lifetimes, with appropriate "rest periods" along the way, often alternating between civil and religious posts. "Passing one's *cargos*" brings prestige to the office-holder, his spouse (whose participation in fiesta preparations is critical), and his household. The nature and number of offices involved vary considerably from place to place, although the main political offices have been established by colonial and national governments; officeholders who make it to the top and serve in the most prestigious posts become respected and influential elders, or *principales*, who have met their communal obligations. *Cargo* careers involve major commitments of time and money in the service of one's community, and steps along the way are sometimes planned years in advance. Sponsorship of religious fiestas, including the obligatory meals, refreshments, and rituals, can be very expensive, and although the sponsor may receive help from others, he may easily spend more than a year's annual income on a three-day celebration.

Scholars differ over the relationship of the civil-religious hierarchy to pre-Hispanic Mesoamerican culture. Carrasco (1961; 1990) points to pre-Hispanic precedents for individual sponsorship of fiestas, whereas Chance and Taylor (1985) stress the historical discontinuities of this practice. Whatever the antecedents, there is general agreement that *cargo* systems originated in the Early Colonial period, when the Spanish imposed the *cabildo*, the Castilian form of town government, on preexisting indigenous city- or town-states. [*See* Cabildo.] This was a form of indirect rule in many respects, and Indians often had considerable latitude to manage their own affairs and assert their local identities. While outwardly complying with Colonial-era demands for tribute and labor, Indians appropriated these new political offices for their own purposes, merging them with their own local political traditions, and making them into quasi-obligatory vehicles of community service. The first formally established *cargo* systems were civil systems with a single ladder of prestige. The higher offices of *gobernador*, *alcalde*, and *regidor* were articulated in complex ways with Spanish political and commercial interests and served to funnel resources—in the form of tribute and payments for commodities—out of the community. On the inside, the political hierarchy was a primary determinant of community stratification; service in the higher *cargos* became an important avenue to elite or *principal* status, whereas lower cargos were reserved for commoners, or *macehuales*.

Catholicism was also an early European introduction, yet *cofradías* and a full array of religious offices were slower to develop and did not emerge in many regions until the seventeenth and eighteenth centuries. Again, indigenous peoples refashioned these offices and rituals, merging Catholic with native beliefs and carrying out syncretic forms of ritual that priests often disparaged. The sponsorship of these activities during the Colonial period was collective, most often undertaken by *cofradías* with proceeds from their own land or livestock. Individual sponsorship of fiestas was less common, and religious offices generally were not part of the ladder of prestige, which continued to be defined in civil terms for most of the Colonial period.

The development of a ladder of religious offices and its fusion with the civil ladder in a genuine civil-religious hierarchy was mainly a nineteenth-century phenomenon. The chief stimuli were expropriations of *cofradía* property by the church and the prohibition of communal support of religious fiestas by Spanish and later national political officials. These actions stemmed from concerted efforts of both church and state to strengthen their control over rural communities (often for fiscal purposes) and from the growing liberal antipathy of the period toward corporate forms of property. With collective forms of fiesta sponsorship under attack, individual officeholders came under pressure to maintain community rituals by financing fiestas themselves. At the same time, the colonial status differences between elites and commoners were being dismantled, and there was growing concern in the villages that each household should help shoulder the burden of maintaining the cult of the saints. The historical outcome of these factors, Chance and Taylor (1985) have argued, was the classic form of the civil-religious hierarchy first discerned by ethnographers in the mid-twentieth century. Compared to the colonial civil hierarchy that preceded it, this civil-religious structure brought with it a new emphasis on internal activities and obligatory economic redistribution for all members of the community. Civil-religious systems are more inward-looking, more involved with local ritual and local identity, and less concerned than their civil predecessors with representing the community to external political or church authorities.

It also has been argued that the twentieth century ushered in a second major transformation of *cargo* systems, from civil-religious to religious in character. Religious *cargo* systems, organized for the manifest purpose of serving the local saints, are twice as common as those of the civil-religious type in the recent ethnographic literature. Revolution and political reforms in Mexico and Guatemala for the first time opposed the whole concept of the politically autonomous indigenous community, and in many villages civil offices have been divorced from the local ladder of prestige and become appendages of higher-level political systems. This process has destroyed many civil-religious hierarchies, but others have adapted to the challenges by transforming themselves into religious *cargo* systems. Such changes have meant yet another step inward and a renewed emphasis on internal ritual affairs.

A detailed description and analysis of one such religious system in Zinacantán, Chiapas, in the 1960s can be found in Frank Cancian's *Economics and Prestige in a Maya Community* (Stanford, 1965), which shows that a *cargo* system with individual fiesta sponsorship is not incompatible with significant wealth and status differences. Although serving *cargos* could be expensive, the system was not an economic leveler, as some had argued, but instead legitimized existing economic differences—with wealthier men taking the more expensive *cargos*—and accentuated differences in prestige. A related debate flourished over whether *cargo* systems are primarily mechanisms of economic redistribution within their communities, or whether they are vehicles of colonial and neocolonial expropriation, siphoning wealth out of the hands of Indians and into those of priests and *mestizo* merchants. Subsequent research has shown, however, that either alternative might be emphasized in different times and places, depending on the context. Thus, colonial civil cargo systems were geared more toward expropriation, whereas an ethnographic study of a present-day Chatino community in Oaxaca found both expropriation and redistribution to occur in approximately equal proportion (see James B. Greenberg, *Santiago's Sword*, Berkeley, 1981).

Recent ethnography has led to a more nuanced view of the relationships between *cargo* hierarchies and their political and economic settings, just as historical research has shown how these systems have changed during the last four hundred years. Today, however, *cargo* systems of any type increasingly are harder to find, as peasant communities become integrated in new ways into national and transnational contexts. Increasing impoverishment has led to the breakdown of some systems in places where villagers lack the resources to keep their traditions alive. Wealthier communities find it harder to maintain *cargo* systems as extra-communal aspirations become more important to more people, class divisions become more entrenched, and a consensus on ritual activities becomes more difficult to maintain. In Zinacantán, for example, the thriving religious hierarchy of the 1960s had lost much of its significance by the 1990s, weakened by new inequalities stemming from the introduction of new employment opportunities (see Cancian 1992). Maintenance of a *cargo* system is a conservative strategy, an attempt to assert local autonomy and community identity in the face of external pressures. Wherever this autonomy is compromised or becomes undesirable for the community's inhabitants, *cargo* systems can be expected to weaken or disappear. As civil-religious and religious hierarchies fade into the recent past, historical rather than ethnographic treatments of this institution may be expected to predominate.

BIBLIOGRAPHY

Cancian, Frank. "Political and Religious Organization." In *Handbook of Middle American Indians*, edited by Robert Wauchope, vol. 6, pp. 283–298. Austin, 1967. Overview and synthesis of ethnographic research and interpretations.

Cancian, Frank. *The Decline of Community in Zinacantán.* Stanford, Calif., 1992.

Carrasco, Pedro. "The Civil-Religious Hierarchy in Mesoamerican Communities: Pre-Spanish Background and Colonial Development." *American Anthropologist* 63 (1961), 483–497. Discusses pre-Hispanic antecedents and the colonial origin of the system.

Carrasco, Pedro. "Sobre el origen histórico de la jerarquía político-ceremonial de las comunidades indígenas." In *Historia, antropología, y política: Homenaje a Angel Palerm*, edited by Modesto Suárez, vol. 1, pp. 306–326. Mexico City, 1990. Response to questions raised by Chance and Taylor (see below) regarding indigenous antecedents.

Chance, John K., and William B. Taylor. "*Cofradías* and *Cargos*: An Historical Perspective on the Mesoamerican Civil-Religious Hierarchy." *American Ethnologist* 12 (1985), 1–26. Discusses pre-Hispanic antecedents, adds new data on the colonial origins of the system, and presents an argument for the emergence of the civil-religious hierarchy in the nineteenth century in four Mexican regions.

Monaghan, John. "Fiesta Finance in Mesoamerica and the Origins of a Gift Exchange System." *Journal of the Royal Anthropological Institute* 2 (1996), 499–516. Integrates ethnographic with historical analysis of fiesta sponsorship in a Mixtec community in Oaxaca.

Rus, Jan, and Robert Wasserstrom. "Civil-Religious Hierarchies in Central Chiapas: A Critical Perspective." *American Ethnologist* 7 (1980), 466–478. Presents an argument for the emergence of civil-religious hierarchies in the late nineteenth and early twentieth centuries in response to changes in the regional economy.

Slade, Doren L. *Making the World Safe for Existence.* Ann Arbor, 1992. Study of religious ritual in a Nahua community in the Sierra Norte of Puebla, Mexico.

Smith, Waldemar R. *The Fiesta System and Economic Change.* New York, 1977. Comparative study of economic factors that promote and threaten *cargo* systems in the Maya highlands.

Stephen, Lynn, and James Dow, eds. *Class, Politics, and Popular Religion in Mexico and Central America.* Washington, D.C., 1990. Contains ethnographic essays by Lynn Stephen, Frank Cancian, and Duncan M. Earle on *cargo* systems among the Zapotec of Oaxaca and the Maya of Chiapas, as well as a review article by John K. Chance presenting the case for the emergence of religious *cargo* systems in the twentieth century.

JOHN K. CHANCE

CLIMATE. *See* Mesoamerica, *article on* Geography.

COBÁ. The ancient Maya ruins of Cobá are situated in Quintana Roo state, Mexico, in the northeastern quadrant of the Yucatán Peninsula, at 87° 40′ west longitude and 20° 30′ north latitude. The central portion of the ruined city lies about 45 kilometers (30 miles) inland from the Caribbean coast. The small modern town of the same name, part of the municipality of Cozumel, is within the central portion of the archaeological zone.

Cobá lies in the tropics, subject to alternating wet and dry seasons which, on average, differ somewhat from those in the rest of the northern peninsula, where the rainy season generally runs from June through October and the dry season from November through May. At Cobá, rain can occur in almost any time of the year, but there is a short dry period in February and March, and a concentration of rain from September through November.

The natural setting of Cobá is distinguished by a northwest-to-southeast arc of large lakes—Cobá, Macanxoc, Sacalpuc, and Yax Laguna—and a fifth feature, Sinacal, a seasonally swampy depression to the south. Such features are relatively rare in this region of karst limestone and relatively small changes in elevation. The Cobá land surface is one of sharp, pitted limestone exposures and outcrops, and mostly reddish soils, often intermixed with and underlain by extensive deposits of *sascab*, or calcareous sand. This soil is shallow, except in some depressions in the limestone.

The forest canopy in the archaeological zone of Cobá is relatively high, particularly in areas of ruins marked by high structures. Folan et al. (1983) summarize the Cobá vegetation as a two-story semi-evergreen seasonal forest, with only the ramon trees on the archaeological mounds forming a climax forest community. Aside from the ramon trees, the Cobá canopy includes mahogany, mastic trees, and wild figs. The lower tree story includes hackberry, laurel, and many palms. Lianas are abundant, as well as orchids and Spanish moss—the last is particularly evident in the Cobá Group at the site. On a map of greater scope, the rain forest at Cobá appears as a northeastern extension of the rain forest that covers much of Guatemala's northern panhandle, in contrast to the drier, lower thorn forest that characterizes the rest of the north.

The first clearly recorded visit of outsiders to Cobá took place in 1886, when two men from Mérida, Yucatán, José Peon Contreras and D. Elizade, visited the place and produced several drawings of mounds. The site was uninhabited at the time, although sporadic settlement evidently took place in the latter part of the nineteenth century. In 1891, Teobert Maler visited Cobá and photographed the intact building atop the Nohoch Mul, the largest mound at the site. Thomas Gann reached Cobá in 1926, mistakenly thought he had discovered it, and produced the first detailed description of the site center.

The first concentrated archaeological exploration of Cobá took place between 1926 and 1930, when various members of the Carnegie Institution of Washington project at nearby Chichén Itzá visited the ruins. The report by Thompson, Pollock, and Charlot (1932) was the first to show the astonishing system of *sacbeob*, the ancient roads that distinguish the enormous site. Later investigators, notably Alfonso Villa Rojas and, shortly afterward, Victor Segovia Pinto, followed the *sacbe* between Cobá and the site of Yaxuna, 100 kilometers (60 miles) to the west. In 1974, William J. Folan and a team traced another *sacbe* to the ruins of Ikil, 24 kilometers (18 miles) distant.

Other contributors to the knowledge of Cobá include Carlos Navarette, Alejandro Martínez Muriel, and Linda Manzanilla. In 1976, Antonio Benavides Castillo and Fernando Robles, working under the direction of Norberto González Crespo of Mexico's Instituto Nacional de Antropología e Historia (INAH), produced an extensive map of the Cobá *sacbe* system and accompany mound groups. A detailed map showing 30 percent of the central area was added to the record by Folan and colleagues in 1983. The urban center of ancient Cobá lies in the general area of the lakes and includes the largest concentrations of monumental architecture, all interconnected by various *sacbeob*.

The Cobá Group, on the northern edge of Lake Macanxoc, is dominated by a single tall pyramid, the so-called Iglesia, which overlooks several large palace-type quadrangles of possible elite residential structures arranged around small, deep plazas, as well as a ballcourt, one of two known at the site. The Nohoch Mul Group contains the largest structures at the site: the great pyramid itself and, just to the west, an enormous multistory complex featuring a grand stairway. The latter faces the unique Xaibe structure, a conical structure that may have served to mark a "crossroads" in the *sacbe* system. The Macanxoc Group of mounds is distinguished by its well-preserved stelae, which include rare examples of the calendrical Long Count expressed in its fully expanded form, in order to express the date of the beginning of the last creation cycle, equal to our 12 August 3114 BCE. There are thirty-one known carved stelae at Cobá mainly in the central area, and mostly with texts and dates too eroded to read. Stela 20 bears a date translatable to 780 CE, corresponding to the Late Classic period of the Maya archaeological record.

Other clusters of elite residential architecture occur near the city center, including the Chumuk Mul Group, and at the terminus of ancient roads that radiate outward from the site center. The Xkukican Group, for example, lies about 14 kilometers (9 miles) out, at the end of Sacbe 8; others are situated similarly, and at various distances.

From all the available evidence, Cobá appears to have functioned as a major urban center and regional capital throughout the Late Classic period, although it was occupied much earlier, during the Late Preclassic. The occurrence of broken and reused monuments, including badly eroded monument fragments restuccoed and employed in Postclassic times, indicates that following a long period of abandonment, at least the central portion of Cobá was reoccupied. This is reinforced by the presence of numerous Late Postclassic buildings, all in the distinctive style of Tulum and other late coastal sites nearby, superimposed on the old Classic period platforms and pyramids. Examples of this juxtaposition appear in the Nohoch Mul pyramid and the structures and altars in the Pinturas Group.

[*See also* Northern Maya Lowlands.]

BIBLIOGRAPHY

Benavides Castillo, Antonio. *Los caminos de Cobá y sus implicaciones sociales (proyecto Cobá)*. Mexico City, 1981.

Folan, William J., Ellen R. Kintz, and Laraine A. Fletcher. *Coba: A Classic Maya Metropolis*. New York and London, 1983.

Manzanilla, Linda, ed. *Cobá, Quintana Roo: analisis de los unidades habitacionales Mayas*. Mexico City, 1987.

Thompson, J. Eric, Harry E. D. Pollock, and Jean Charlot. *A Preliminary Study of the Ruins of Cobá, Quitana Roo, Mexico*. Washington, D.C., 1932.

GEORGE E. STUART

COCEI. This Zapotec political movement emerged in Juchitán, Oaxaca, Mexico, in 1973. The founders of the movement were radical students, especially Héctor Sánchez, Daniel López Nelio, and Leopoldo de Gyves (Polín). As the movement's name COCEI (Coalición Obrera Campesina Estudiantil del Istmo, or Worker-Peasant-Student Coalition of the Isthmus of Tehuantepec) indicates, the organization is a regionally based, leftist political coalition. It developed as an alternative to the corrupt, *cacique* (boss)-dominated Juchitán branch of the PRI (Partido Revolucionario Institucional) Mexico's longtime ruling party.

After a series of successful strikes and protests in the 1970s, right-wing gunmen killed about a dozen Coceístas, including Víctor Pineda Henestrosa, an activist who became a martyr for the movement. Sympathy for COCEI grew in Juchitán, and in 1981 the coalition, in alliance with the Mexican Communist Party, won the municipal elections. Juchitán became the first city in Mexico since the Revolution to be controlled by the left. It was also a rare community in contemporary Mesoamerica, because Indian people dominated the local political system.

From 1981 to 1983, COCEI's self-proclaimed People's

Government promoted Isthmus Zapotec culture and language and the struggles of Zapotec peasants and workers. Although the movement has many followers in other Isthmus Zapotec towns—such as San Blas Atempa, Unión Hidalgo, and Comitancillo in Oaxaca—its primary focus has been control of land and political power in Juchitán. COCEI's localism and ethnic ideology, rooted in a politicized vision of Zapotec rebellions since Spanish colonial times, has limited alliances with other Mexican Indians and national political parties. Yet COCEI's emphasis on Zapotec ethnic pride, combined with the brilliant artistic and literary production of Juchiteco intellectuals, who are linked to the Casa de la Cultura in Juchitán, stimulated a Zapotec cultural renaissance in the Isthmus of Tehuantepec. Francisco Toledo, a world-renowned Zapotec painter, epitomizes the fusion of political commitment and cultural production in Juchitán.

COCEI's ouster from office in 1983 by the Mexican military brought widespread attention to Juchitán, especially among the leftist intelligentsia and the artistic community of Mexico. As during recent events in Chiapas, journalists and anthropologists came from around the world to observe the conflict between a local Indian political movement and the Mexican army and PRI-run government. Unlike the EZLN (Ejercito Zapatista de Liberación Nacional) in Chiapas, however, COCEI engaged in nonviolent political actions. After several years of repression, COCEI returned to Juchitán City Hall as part of a bipartisan municipal government in 1986. Since 1989, COCEI has governed Juchitán and Coceístas have won numerous positions as representatives and deputies in local, state, and federal government. COCEI's founder, Héctor Sánchez, was also a strong candidate for Oaxaca governor in the 1998 elections. The history of COCEI provides an important example of indigenous empowerment in contemporary Mexico.

[*See also* Zapatista National Liberation Army.]

BIBLIOGRAPHY

Campbell, Howard. *Zapotec Renaissance: Ethnic Politics and Cultural Revivalism in Southern Mexico.* Albuquerque, N.M., 1994.

Campbell, Howard, ed. *The Politics of Ethnicity in Southern Mexico.* Nashville, Tenn., 1996.

Campbell, Howard, Leigh Binford, Miguel Bartolomé, and Alicia Barabas, eds. *Zapotec Struggles: Histories, Politics and Representations from Juchitán, Oaxaca.* Washington, D.C., 1993.

HOWARD CAMPBELL

CODEX _____. *See under latter part of name.*

COFRADÍA. In the Colonial period, a *cofradía* (sodality) was an organization of laymen dedicated to the financing of religious ceremonies and charitable works, as well as to the promotion of the personal piety of its members. According to church law, the election of the *cofradía* leaders and the administration of its finances were to be supervised by the parish priest. Most *cofradías* were supported by the donations of members and at times by an endowment of land or funds. All such organizations were under the royal patronage of the king of Spain, and according to law (*Recopilación de Indias*), they were to have written constitutions approved by the bishop and also by the monarch.

In the four thousand legally recognized Indian towns of Colonial Mexico (officially called *pueblos de indios*), there existed another type of organization also called a *cofradía* or *hermandad* ("brotherhood"), which differed substantially from the ecclesiastical *cofradías* as described. It was an endowment of livestock, money, beeswax, and land managed by a *mayordomo*, who reported to the elected Indian officials of the municipal council, which in the Colonial period was called the *república*. Generally all or part of the goods had originally belonged to the communal property of the town. Often the only member of this type of trust-fund *cofradía*, or *cofradía de república*, as it could be called, was the *mayordomo*. A 1704 survey showed that in some regions of San Luis Potosí, the Indian municipal officials, when asked to describe the town's communal possessions, gave data on the goats and cattle of the *cofradías*, as well as on rented municipal land; in Ameca, Nueva Galicia, the *república* was in the process of transferring to newly founded *cofradías* what previously had been municipal belongings. In Yucatán and Oaxaca at the end of the seventeenth century, the towns were also establishing cattle *haciendas* under the title *cofradías*, as a means of avoiding the interference of local Spanish authorities who stole from town coffers or absconded with communal cattle. As a *cofradía*, the goods were nominally under the supervision of the priest rather than of governmental officials.

Both types of *cofradías*—the ecclesiastical and the *cofradía de república*—helped to support religious festivities held at various times during the year, but the largest part of the funding and the leadership of the celebrations was the responsibility of the Indian municipal council. Each town had communal lands set aside to form a municipal treasury, consisting of the product of the harvest or of the rent received for agricultural properties. Another source of funds was an obligatory contribution (the "*real y medio*"), collected from each head of household. Much of the annual municipal income was used to support the principal religious celebrations: the feast day of the patron saint of the town, Corpus Christi, Holy Thursday, and the three "Pascuas"—Christmas, Easter, and Pentecost.

The leading role of the local civil government in sponsoring the sacred ceremonies was characteristic not only of the Indian towns but also of the municipal governments of Spanish cities and villas in Colonial-era Mexico. All spent large amounts on religious fiestas because one of the most important obligations of government was to offer public worship to God and thereby gain divine protection for the locality. Such activities also demonstrated the organizational ability of the local leaders and unified the people under their rule. The plentiful food, drink, and fireworks that followed the Mass and procession made these celebrations high points of the year for the townspeople.

When the Spanish inspector general José de Gálvez came from Spain to Mexico in 1765, he wanted to curb extensive religious expenditures in the Spanish and Indian municipalities, just as the king had been doing in Madrid and the rest of Spain since 1760. Budget cuts were ordered in the "regulations" drawn up for the main cities and, starting around 1773, for the Indian towns throughout the viceroyalty. Gálvez also established a separate government accounting office, Propios, Arbitrios y Bienes de Comunidad, to issue the newly written rules for each locality and to scrutinize their annual financial reports. These regulations ordered that instead of spending almost all of its annual income, each Indian town was to send at least half to the viceregal treasury, where it was to be safeguarded for use in times of emergency. (In fact, a good part of these savings were sent to Spain in the form of loans and donations to the king, rather than being returned to the towns when famine and epidemics occurred.) The rules prohibited using municipal funds for most religious celebrations, authorizing only one or two: the patron saint's day and Corpus Christi. Expenditures of town money for fireworks, dance attire, communal meals, flowers, incense, and music were not allowed. The payment of the schoolteacher with town income was authorized, at times taking priority over fiesta expenditures.

As a result of the government's supervision of the town treasuries, a practice existing for many years, the use of municipal properties by the cofradías, was called into question by the viceregal authorities. The director of the accounting office complained to the viceroy in 1775 that many Indian repúblicas were transferring, or "unnaming," communal land and cattle and applying them to entities that they "denominated" cofradías. He requested that, since such cofradías were illegally founded, they should be abolished and their properties returned to the municipal treasuries, where their use could be limited by the new regulations. If they remained in the cofradías, the Indians could continue spending all the income on religious festivities, where, according to the accountant, noisy gatherings and drinking—unproductive and harmful—were the main attraction and the cause of the Indians' ruin.

As a result of the new government policies, neither the Indian officials nor the parish priests were inclined to admit that many cofradías were operating with municipal endowments. The nature of these cofradías and hermandades was revealed, however, during the pastoral visits of various bishops at the end of the eighteenth century. Three factors indicated the existence of a cofradía de república rather than an ecclesiastical, membership-type cofradía: the intervention of the república in its foundation; the naming of the mayordomo by the town authorities; and the supervision of cofradía accounts by the república. In the dioceses of Guadalajara and Oaxaca, the bishops found that many priests had little knowledge of the operations of the cofradías and, at most, signed the annual financial report in exchange for a cash payment.

In the archdiocese of Mexico, the prelate took into account three royal decrees: one (1776) declared that to continue in existence, the cofradías and brotherhoods had to obtain the approval of the king; a second (1783), that those without such license were to be abolished; and a third (1791), that at cofradía meetings and any other gathering having the intention of forming a new brotherhood, a government official had to preside. In keeping with these mandates, the archbishop at times suppressed small or debt-ridden cofradías, either of Spaniards or of Indians; in some cases, however—probably to enable the avoidance of the new laws—he immediately renamed the Indian associations "pious works" and let them continue in operation under the town council, although he ordered closer scrutiny of their finances by the priest.

Bishop Antonio Alcalde of Guadalajara obtained a royal decree in 1789 that prevented the intervention of the government in the cofradías of his diocese until the matter was further investigated. The bishop of Michoacan insisted to the viceroy that a 1682 law gave the prelates permission to authorize new cofradías, with the understanding that royal approval was implicit in the episcopal license; he also complained that the accountant's negative report on the cofradías was inspired by his desire to gain advancement and was based on isolated cases or unproven assertions. He noted that under government restrictions the repúblicas could rarely recover their savings from the viceregal treasury in times of trouble. In fact, the cofradías were providing meat and money for the townspeople in such emergencies.

Cofradías in the dioceses of Guadalajara, Oaxaca, Puebla, and México engaged in commercial and productive operations: cattle, sheep, and goat raising; money-lending, with 5 percent interest for Indians and 20 percent for non-Indians; regional trading in cloth, candles, rice, fish, and cotton; production of cochineal and pulque; and the sale of salt. These activities were carried out at a profit, at times between 25 and 100 percent. Some *mayordomos* established commercial circuits, regularly traveling long distances between the coast and the highlands. In this way, municipal authorities served as intermediaries between the town's economy and that of the rest of the region, conserving the communal structure while participating in the wider *mestizo*-Spanish economy. In Oaxaca, the bishop, recognizing the way the *cofradías* operated, ordered that each year the pious associations should turn over 5 percent of their capital to the priest for religious ceremonies and church expenditures; this enabled the Indians to use the rest of the profits for other outlays, such as salaries to shepherds, communal meals, profits for the *mayordomos*, and the accumulation of funds in the *cofradía*.

At the end of the eighteenth century in some areas of Michoacán, individual *mayordomos* without *cofradía* backing were appointed, probably by the *república*, to sponsor a specific religious celebration; to do so, they had to employ their own resources or collect funds from the inhabitants. This probably occurred because the municipal treasuries could no longer finance the accustomed number of festivals, and the existing *cofradías* did not have enough income either. In most other areas, however, there are signs that the *cofradías de república* were able to increase their contributions to the main celebrations and to finance other customary ones once the towns were prohibited from sponsoring them. The greater participation of the *cofradías* in town activities at the end of the Colonial period was due, therefore, not to the decline of municipal government and the strength of the brotherhoods, but rather to the strategy developed by the *repúblicas* in response to the change in governmental fiscal policy: the towns just transferred communal possessions to the *cofradías* to evade the new regulations on municipal property.

The great majority of Indian *cofradías* were named for and dedicated to Christ, the Virgin Mary, and the souls in Purgatory, in keeping with the ecclesiastical mandates to encourage these advocations. Such names were born by 82 percent of those in Michoacán in 1776 and by 73 percent of those in Oaxaca in 1804. The rest had saints' names, generally that of the town's patron.

Of the Indian *cofradías* in Colonial Mexico at the end of the eighteenth century, it can be estimated that 20 percent were ecclesiastical, with various classes of members, and supported mainly by donations; another 10 percent were controlled by the parish priest for his own benefit; 5 percent had been taken over by *mayordomos*, who operated them independently of the Indian town officials and of the parish; and the remaining 65 percent were *cofradías de república*, trust funds, often based on municipal properties, and administered by a *mayordomo* under the supervision of the Indian municipal authorities.

The central point of ethnic identity and communal participation in Colonial Mexico was the town and not the *cofradía*, which was supplemental and subordinate to the *república*. The main positions in the Indian town were civil ones: *gobernador*, *alcalde*, *regidor*, and *escribano*. Not only was the *república* responsible for financing and leading the most important religious celebrations; it also collected the tribute, administered justice at the local level, supervised communal agricultural land, managed the municipal finances, maintained public order, and served as the legal representative of the town and its inhabitants in judicial disputes. The manner of financing religious festivals was generally not individual but rather collective, either by the *república* and its municipal treasury or by the *mayordomo* and the *cofradía* trust fund.

Further research should clarify regional differences in the structure and operation of the *cofradías*, as well as changes that occurred when the *república* was abolished by the Constitution of Cadiz in 1812 and by the 1824 Constitution of independent Mexico. It is possible that after independence, in places where the Indian civil leaders of the towns were replaced by non-Indian authorities of the new municipal councils, the former transferred to posts in the *cofradías* so as to continue directing Indian activities and protecting communal properties.

[*See also* Civil-Religious Hierarchy.]

BIBLIOGRAPHY

Bergoza y Jordán, Antonio. *Cuestionario de Don Antonio Bergoza y Jordán, obispo de Antequera a los señores curas de la diócesis.* Edited by Irene Huesca, Manuel Esparza, and Luis Castañeda Gúzman. Oaxaca, 1984. One of the few published primary sources of ecclesiastical reports on the operation of *cofradías*.

Chance, John K., and William B. Taylor. "Cofradías and Cargos: An Historical Perspective on the Mesoamerican Civil-Religious Hierarchy." *American Ethnologist* 1 (1985), 1–26. Groundbreaking article reviews previous anthropological and ethnohistorical studies, concluding that historical evidence demonstrates that the individual *mayordomía* and alternative *cargo* system between civil and religious hierarchies were not frequent in the Colonial period but rather developed after independence.

Dehouve, Danièle. "El pueblo de indios y el mercado: Tlapa en el siglo XVIII." In *Empresarios, indios y estado: Perfil de la economía mexicana (siglo XVIII)*, edited by Arij Ouweneel and Cristina Torales Pacheco, pp. 86–102. Amsterdam, 1988. Insightful and detailed description of the role of communal organizations in regional production and commerce.

Farriss, Nancy. *Mayan Society under Colonial Rule: The Collective Enterprise of Survival.* Princeton, 1984. Indicates that *cofradía* and municipal community possessions were interchangeable in colonial Yucatán and explains the role of *cofradía* cattle haciendas.

Lavrin, Asunción. "Rural Confraternities in the Local Economies of New Spain: The Bishopric of Oaxaca in the Context of Colonial

Mexico." In *The Indian Community of Colonial Mexico: Fifteen Essays on Land Tenure, Corporate Organizations, Ideology and Village Politics*, edited by Arij Ouweneel and Simon Miller, pp. 220–249. Amsterdam, 1990. Comprehensive analysis of income sources and economic activities of *cofradías* in Oaxaca in 1804, according to reports by fifty-nine parish priests. (For complete transcription of the original reports, see Bergoza y Jordán.)

Pietschmann, Horst. "Agricultura e industria rural indígena en el México de la segunda mitad del siglo XVIII." In *Empresarios, indios y estado: Perfil de la economía mexican (siglo XVIII)*, edited by Arij Ouweneel and Cristina Torales Pacheco, pp. 71–85. Amsterdam, 1988. Presents data on Indian municipal treasuries and *cofradías* as mechanisms of production and commerce, operating with relative autonomy in regional markets.

Tanck de Estrada, Dorothy. *Pueblos de indios y educación en el México colonial, 1750–1821*. Mexico City, 1999. Chapter on municipal treasuries and *cofradías*, based on Colonial-period episcopal and governmental documents; describes strategies of Indian towns facing restrictive government fiscal policies.

Taylor, William B. *Magistrates of the Sacred: Priests and Parishioners in Eighteenth-Century Mexico*. Stanford, 1996. Detailed chapter on *cofradías* provides legal information and analysis of conflict between church and state over *cofradías* in the dioceses of Guadalajara and México.

DOROTHY TANCK DE ESTRADA

COLEGIO IMPERIAL DE SANTA CRUZ DE TLATELOLCO.

During the sixteenth century, the Colegio de Santa Cruz was an important initiative in the evangelization and education of Indian neophytes in central Mexico by Franciscan missionaries. Created to improve local government and colonial administration in the Indian towns, this college for a time provided advanced instruction to descendants of the pre-Hispanic nobility at Santiago Tlatelolco (Mexica Tenochtitlan's twin city, which survived as an Indian settlement on the outskirts of colonial Mexico City). The foundation of the college represented a triumph for those Spaniards who regarded Indians as equal to the conquerors in intellectual potential—those who were convinced that a rigorous education would lead to an indigenous priesthood and, therefore, wider and deeper conversion to Christianity.

On 6 January 1536, with great ostentation, Viceroy Antonio de Mendoza, Bishop Juan de Zumárraga, and the president of the *audiencia* (high court) Sebastián Ramírez de Funleal opened the college. The students, between eight and ten years old, were the sons of baptized Indian leaders from towns throughout central Mexico. Once their studies were completed, they were to return to their home communities to assist in religious and civil administration.

Arnaldo Basacio, García de Cisneros, Andrés de Olmos, Juan de Gaona, Juan Focher, and Bernardino de Sahagún were among the early Franciscan friars who taught in the college. They were missionaries with outstanding academic preparation, conversant with native languages, and remarkably dedicated to their work in the New World and to support for the Indians.

For boarding students, life at the college followed Franciscan rules. Their weekly routine depended on the subjects they were taking and the religious and daily activities required. Entering students were instructed in personal hygiene, European customs, and their own family genealogies traced back at least to their four grandfathers. The literate students studied the arts, Latin grammar, Scholastic theology, rhetoric, logic, philosophy, liturgy, music, and Native American medicine. An Indian physician from Xochimilco was responsible for instruction in the last subject. The first class consisted of about seventy students, but the Franciscans planned to increase enrollment to at least three hundred.

When the first cycle of study was completed four years later, the results were mixed, from the Franciscans' perspective. None of the more accomplished students was disposed to the celibate life and other requirements of a religious vocation. This result discouraged Bishop Zumárraga, one of the leading benefactors of the college and advocate to the Spanish Crown. Thereafter, the college narrowed its educational aims, abandoning plans to train an indigenous clergy. This change gratified the opponents of higher education for Indians—who asserted that the natives were incapable of more than a rudimentary understanding of complex and abstract ideas.

In 1545, the Franciscans considered their labors at the college finished and decided to put it in the care of the most capable of the first generation of graduating students. These graduates elected a rector, council members, and teachers and drew up bylaws for governing the college; however, various circumstances complicated this task. First, many of the students died in the great epidemic of 1545. Then, in 1546, the financial support of the Spanish Crown was reduced from 1,000 to 800 *pesos de minas*; after 1558, royal support for the college seems to have ceased altogether. Some Indian leaders helped with rents and donations, but they covered only a small part of the costs of operating the school. The financial problems resulted in a drastically reduced curriculum and a student body drawn mainly from Indian communities in and near Mexico City. The dwindling number of scholarships, in particular, led the college to accept more day students, who studied only reading, writing, and Latin. Finally, the meager resources of the college became evident in the deterioration of its buildings.

In 1570, the Franciscans took over the college again, but without encouraging results because of the devastating epidemics of 1564 and 1576, as well as lack of support from royal authorities and colonists. The Colegio Imperial de Santa Cruz continued operation as a primary school for the Indian children of Tlatelolco to the end of the Colonial period, but its best years were long past. Yet its first fruits, though meager in quantity, were impressive in quality. At least fifteen students graduated as excellent Latinists, with a wide knowledge of the European and Nahua high cultures of that time. They became untiring collaborators in the Franciscan evangelizing enterprise as translators, coauthors, compilers of ancient and new learning, and especially as teachers of the younger friars. Among these indigenous scholars and teachers were Antonio Valeriano (teacher of the famous Juan de Torquemada), Alonso Vejarano, and Martín Jacovita.

[*See also* Olmos, Andrés de; Zumárraga, Juan de.]

BIBLIOGRAPHY

Kobayashi, José María. *La educación como conquista.* 2d ed. Mexico City, 1985. A first approach to educational work in New Spain, considering its Hispanic and pre-Columbian roots.

Ocaranza, Fernando. *El imperial Colegio de Indios de la Santa Cruz de Santiago Tlaltelolco.* Mexico City, 1934. Selection of Franciscan documents concerning the administration of the college through the Colonial period.

Steck, Francisco Borgia. *El primer colegio de América: Santa Cruz de Tlaltelolco.* Mexico City, 1944. First history of the college, based on Franciscan documents; indispensable reading for the topic.

M ARIA I SABEL E STRADA T ORRES

COLOMBINO-BECKER, CODEX. The *Codex Colombino-Becker* is a pre-Hispanic Mixtec pictorial manuscript that depicts the political history of the great Mixtec ruler Lord 8 Deer "Jaguar Claw." Seven fragments of the original codex have survived, totaling forty pages. These fragments are now grouped into two separate parts: four fragments, containing twenty-four pages, form the *Codex Colombino,* which is in the Museo Nacional de Antropología, Mexico City (inventory no. 35-30); the other three fragments, of sixteen pages, make up the *Codex Becker* I at the Museum für Völkerkunde, Vienna (inventory no. 60306). Additional parts of the manuscript are still missing. Besides this fragmentation, pictorial elements in most of the painted scenes have been deliberately destroyed, and some pages bear texts in the Mixtec language that are not related to the contents of the codex.

Several editions of both the *Colombino* and the *Becker* have been published. The most commonly used facsimile of the *Colombino* is accompanied by the commentary of Alfonso Caso (1966), and that of the *Becker* by the notes of Karl A. Nowotny (1961). For some of the history depicted in the *Colombino-Becker,* there are cognate accounts in other Mixtec codices, particularly the *Zouche-Nuttall.*

Before the pictorial text of the *Colombino-Becker* can be interpreted, its fragments must be reassembled in their original sequence. Some of the placements suggested by Caso are physically impossible. In essays published between 1969 and 1974, Nancy P. Troike analyzed the measurements, design, and functioning of the seven fragments and was able to combine them into three large sections. The original sequence of pages in the *Colombino-Becker,* including those now lost, is then as follows: missing pages; Section I (*Colombino* pages 1–15, 17–19); missing pages; Section II (*Colombino* pages 20–24, *Becker* pages 1–4a); missing pages; Section III (*Becker* pages 5–14, *Colombino* pages 16–16a, *Becker* pages 15–16); missing pages.

The text of the *Colombino-Becker* is primarily an account of the major political events in Lord 8 Deer's rise to prominence in the Mixteca and shows only the activities that directly relate to his gaining power; his personal life, such as marriages and children, is excluded. At this time it is not possible to give absolute dates for these events because the chronology proposed by Caso (1949) contains flaws, and the corrected chronology by Emily Rabin has not been completed.

The original opening pages of the *Colombino-Becker* are missing. The extant pages of Section I begin when Lord 8 Deer is seventeen years of age. From other Mixtec codices, it is known that he was born from his father's second marriage. Over the next three years, he carries out a series of rituals and meetings to become the ruler of Tutuepec, then spends two years solidifying his position through a long series of conquests. After these battles, which are completed when he is twenty-two years old, the text of the *Colombino-Becker* skips forward twelve years. No pages are missing; the events of these years were simply not pertinent to the story of his political rise. When the next series of events begins, he is thirty-four years old. He opens negotiations with Lord 4 Jaguar, who has recently conquered the Coixthauhuaca area, but his ambassadors are rejected, and he requests supernatural support. He wins a ballgame against Lord 4 Jaguar, who is forced to grant him the nose-perforation ritual that makes him a great lord. The remainder of Section I shows Lord 8 Deer consolidating his situation.

Following some missing pages, Section II is devoted to an arduous journey by Lord 8 Deer and Lord 4 Jaguar into an underworld realm in order to secure a prediction of their futures from a solar supernatural, Lord 1 Death. They enter this region through a ballcourt, cross a violent river, and press forward against bizarre opponents. The last surviving page of this short section shows the two men, along with Lord 8 Deer's older half-brother, Lord 12 Movement, receiving their predictions.

Again there are missing pages. Then Section III begins with the murder, under mysterious circumstances, of Lord 12 Movement, and shows in detail the elaborate funeral ceremonies Lord 8 Deer holds for him. Lord 8 Deer blames the murder on the two sons of Lord 12 Movement's sister and sacrifices them in spectacular rites. However, rather than this being a just punishment, Troike (1974) suggests that Lord 8 Deer had Lord 12 Movement killed so that he could blame the two brothers and in this way eliminate the last remaining male descendants of his father's first marriage.

Lord 8 Deer is forty years old when he triumphantly takes power. The *Colombino-Becker* then shifts its focus from him to his younger murderer, Lord 4 Wind, a half-brother of the two sacrificed men. The text skips ten years and shows Lord 4 Wind beginning his plot when Lord 8 Deer is fifty years old. The actual murder occurs two years later, and Lord 4 Wind is shown watching as Lord 8 Deer is stabbed. For a while Lord 4 Wind is able to conceal his role in the murder, but three years later Lord 4 Jaguar discovers the truth and tries to capture him. To prevent war, the solar supernatural Lord 1 Death intervenes and forces Lord 4 Jaguar to grant Lord 4 Wind the nose-perforation that makes him a great lord. The extant pages of the *Colombino-Becker* end with rituals hailing Lord 4 Wind.

Even in its present fragmented and damaged form, the pictorial text of the *Codex Colombino-Becker* presents an outstanding narrative of political activities in the Mixteca in the Early Postclassic period. No other manuscript shows so clearly the maneuvering that is essential when an ambitious man aspires to a position of power that would not ordinarily be his. If the missing pages of this codex are ever found, they will surely enlarge and deepen our understanding of the political struggles reflected in the life of Lord 8 Deer.

[*See also* Pictorial Manuscripts.]

BIBLIOGRAPHY

Caso, Alfonso. "El mapa de Teozacoalco." *Cuadernos Americanos* 47.5 (1949), 145–181. Sets forth the fundamentals of reading Mixtec codices.

Codex Becker I. Issued with Karl A. Nowotny, *Codices Becker I/II.* Codices Selecti, vol. 4. Graz, 1961. Photographic facsimile of codex accompanied by interpretative notes.

Codex Colombino. Issued with Alfonso Caso, *Interpretación del Códice Colombino.* Mexico, 1966. Facsimile of codex accompanied by interpretative notes.

Troike, Nancy P. "Observations on the Physical Form of the Codex Becker I." *Archiv für Völkerkunde* 23 (1969), 177–182. Measurements and physical description of the Becker fragments.

Troike, Nancy P. "Observations on Some Material Aspects of the Codex Colombino." *Tlalocan* 6.3 (1970), 240–252. Measurements and physical description of the *Colombino* fragments.

Troike, Nancy P. "The Structure of the Codex Colombino-Becker." *Anales del Instituto Nacional de Antropología e Historia* 2.7 (1971), 181–205. Analyzes how the design and form of the surviving fragments control the sequence in which they can be arranged.

Troike, Nancy P. *The Codex Colombino-Becker.* Dissertation, University of London, 1974. Reassembles the codex fragments in their correct order and gives the first narrative interpretation of the pictorial text.

NANCY P. TROIKE

COLONIAL ADMINISTRATION. Historians have traditionally emphasized the Spanish origins and character of colonial administration in Mesoamerica. This system, however, resulted not from the simple displacement of indigenous governing traditions and institutions by Spanish ones, but rather from the complex interplay between the two. The indigenous imprint on colonial administration was first established several decades ago with the pioneering work of Charles Gibson. Indigenous-language research, in particular, has deepened our understanding of indigenous polities and their significance to colonial administration since Gibson wrote. At the time of the Spanish conquest, Mesoamerican peoples lived in complex states that had well-established mechanisms to channel the tribute and labor of commoners to dynastic rulers and a body of high-ranking nobles. The Spaniards initially had no incentive (or capability) to reorganize these Mesoamerican states, so they used them to appropriate indigenous resources. After the Spaniards dismantled the so-called Aztec Empire, they superimposed colonial administrative jurisdictions directly on the extant indigenous states throughout Mesoamerica. The most thoroughly studied of these state types are the Nahua *altepetl*, the Mixtec *ñuu*, and the Maya *cah*.

Spaniards initially administered Mesoamerican peoples through the *encomienda* system, which they established immediately following the military conquest of the 1520s. The *encomienda* was a grant to an individual, in almost all cases a prominent Spaniard, of the tribute and labor of the people subject to an indigenous ruler. Thus, the *encomienda* was based on the Spanish recognition of indigenous rulership, and it took its particular shape and size from the indigenous state. To administer the *encomienda*, the Spaniards drew on their own tradition of hierarchically ranked settlements. They designated what they perceived to be the most prominent settlement as a *cabecera*, or head town, and designated the outlying settlements subject to the ruler as *sujetos*, or subject towns. This ranking of the constituent parts of the indigenous state violated the indigenous principle that no one part stood above the others, but it did not radically alter the polity's internal organization. Indigenous officials initially collected tribute and organized labor crews in the customary manner and then directed them to the recipient of the *encomienda* grant, or *encomendero*.

After the assignment of *encomiendas*, the Spaniards established ecclesiastical jurisdictions. In Spain, an individual attended religious services and received the sacraments through membership in a parish. The Spaniards established Indian parishes throughout the Mesoamerican countryside, with the indigenous state again serving as the basis for the colonial jurisdiction. Spanish authorities also attempted to reshape the indigenous state along the lines of a Spanish municipality with the introduction of a Spanish-style municipal council, or *cabildo*, beginning in the 1530s. In the prevailing pattern, one indigenous state ruled by one dynastic ruler was designated both an *encomienda* and a parish and was governed locally by a Spanish-style *cabildo*. Ideally, the borders and constituent parts of these jurisdictions coincided, a reflection of the indigenous state that had given them shape.

Indigenous population decline, Crown restrictions, and the growing number of Spanish immigrants who sought access to indigenous labor but had not received *encomiendas* together contributed to the decline of the *encomienda* system. As the *encomienda* weakened, the Crown extended royal government into the countryside with the designation of administrative jurisdictions called *corregimientos* or *alcaldías mayores* (with no meaningful distinction between the two titles; *alcaldía mayor* is used here). Crown officials initially designated *alcaldías mayores* to administer *encomiendas* that had escheated (reverted) to the Crown, but over time the entire Mesoamerican countryside was divided into them, whether still held in *encomienda* or not. The extension of royal authority into the Mesoamerican countryside was thus gradual and uneven. *Alcaldías mayores* were established in some areas in the 1530s, but they were not extended even to most parts of Central Mexico until around the mid-sixteenth century. In Yucatán, where the *encomienda* persisted until the late eighteenth century, such royal administrative jurisdictions were not established until the reforms of that time. Like the *encomienda*/parish, the *alcaldía mayor* was based on the indigenous state. In Central Mexico, the *alcaldía mayor* was a larger jurisdiction than the others, typically made up of several indigenous states, each with its own *cabecera-sujeto* arrangement. The *cabecera* of the largest indigenous state in the *alcaldía mayor* served as the headquarters of the jurisdiction's highest Spanish official, and, over time, the other *cabeceras* became secondary administrative centers where deputies, or *tenientes*, were headquartered.

The Spanish reliance on indigenous structures and organization initially reinforced the integrity of the indigenous state and enhanced its importance, yet tensions quickly emerged that led to its decentralization over time. The normative pattern of a one-to-one relationship between an indigenous state with one dynastic ruler and the *encomienda*/parish with its *cabecera/sujeto* arrangement did not always work out so neatly in practice. The size and complexity of Mesoamerican states varied greatly. At times, Spaniards divided up a large state or grouped together smaller ones. States often had double or even multiple rulerships or were themselves made up of constituent states, each to some extent separate and autonomous and with its own ruler(s). The Spaniards often ignored or did not recognize double or multiple rulerships or the constituent entities within a large, complex indigenous state. Designation as a *cabecera* effectively enhanced the standing of one entity and its rulers to the exclusion of others. The leaders of *sujetos* resented tribute and labor obligations to the *cabecera* as well as the requirement to attend Mass and receive the sacraments there; they sought to control their own tribute and labor resources and to elect their own officials. Resentment heightened as the building campaigns of the major churches located in the *cabecera* came to a close and *sujetos* sought similar marks of municipal distinction. The interests of a priest stationed outside the *cabecera* who harbored hopes of his own parish coincided with those of the *sujeto* leaders anxious to rid themselves of *cabecera* obligations.

The uneven fit between indigenous structures and the colonial jurisdictions contributed to the pursuit of independent status by *sujeto* leaders. The various campaigns in the late sixteenth and early seventeenth centuries to congregate indigenous populations (especially in the wake of population decline), known as *congregación*, might further complicate the situation. Still later, population growth and the desire for autonomous representation or the legal recognition of a land base (on the basis of late-seventeenth-century legislation) also contributed to the pursuit of independent status. Although *cabecera* status initially rested on Spanish recognition of an indigenous rulership, other attributes came to be associated with it over time—a town council with its own governor, designation as a parish, even a jail or marketplace. These attributes eventually replaced the original criterion, and more and more *sujetos* gained independence based on them, resulting in the decentralization of the indigenous state.

In central Mexico, the pursuit of independent status by *sujetos* was under way by the late sixteenth and early seventeenth centuries, whereas in the Mixteca it took shape in the second half of the seventeenth and the eighteenth centuries. The pursuit of independent status at times occurred in stages, with the construction of a jail or designation as a parish first. Such developments might attract less immediate protest from the *cabecera* than the outright election of a full *cabildo*, and, once in place, they could be used to bolster the *sujeto*'s case. The election of a *cabildo* might also proceed in fits and starts—first an *alcalde*, then other officers, and finally a governor. Ethnic difference, strategic location, or geographic distance from the *cabecera* could hasten a bid for independence. Other factors could forestall it. In contrast to the Nahua *altepetl* and the Mixtec *ñuu*, the Maya *cah* did not fragment over time, a reflection of both the relatively weak Spanish presence and indigenous organization. (In contrast to its parallel units among the Nahua and Mixtec, the *cah* apparently had no internal subdivisions.) Spaniards, not least the civil and ecclesiastical officials responsible for a jurisdiction, also influenced the political fortunes of *cabeceras* and *sujetos*.

The highest Spanish official in the royal administrative jurisdiction (*corregimiento* or *alcaldía mayor*) held the title *corregidor de indios* or *alcalde mayor*, with no distinction in function. These district magistrates were prominent Spaniards and initially included the relatives of *encomenderos* or disappointed candidates for *encomiendas*. Others were new arrivals from Spain, typically drawn from the viceroy's retinue. District magistrates held short-term appointments, commonly for five years or less. Most were one-time appointees, but at least some were professional administrators who served in various districts over the course of their careers. Although they were often present in their districts, most magistrates remained based in Mexico City. As in other levels of Spanish government, the district magistrate held administrative, judicial, and legislative powers. He carried out the directives of the viceroy, to whom he reported. (The line of authority ran from district magistrate to viceroy to the Crown.) He received Indian tribute payments on behalf of the Crown. He presided at meetings of the indigenous *cabildo* if he was present, typically only for annual elections. The magistrate also presided over the district's Spanish court, where he settled disputes concerning both Indians and Spaniards. The magistrate's court represented a new avenue of appeal for Indian commoners, who might use it to challenge indigenous rulers. In rendering decisions, the magistrate might impose Spanish notions of justice and political authority.

The magistrate had to contend with other groups—both Spanish and Indian—in the administration of his district. Priests in pastoral service constituted the other main official Spanish figure in an *alcaldía mayor*, and their education and profession placed them among the local Spanish elite. (By the mid-eighteenth century, a small but significant number of parish priests presented themselves as Indians of noble ancestry.) As a district authority, the priest might ally himself with the magistrate, at times even serving as his deputy. Nevertheless, the authority of magistrates and priests overlapped—each served as a check on the other—and they frequently found themselves as adversaries. Indian officials understood this situation and, in moments of internal dispute, perhaps over an election, one faction typically sought the support of the magistrate while the other turned to the priest. Interaction among the magistrate, priest, and Indian officials typically took place in the *cabecera*, the site of the main church, the magistrate's headquarters, and the core of the district's non-Indian population. The magistrate's staff, which typically included a deputy, constable, notary, and interpreter, was drawn largely from the district's Spanish population. The *teniente* was typically a member of a prominent landowning or commercial family who might also have close ties to indigenous leaders in the district. In the magistrate's absence, the *teniente* carried out all duties associated with the position—presiding over court, granting possession in land sales, and witnessing legal documents. Thus, he was advantageously positioned to further his own economic interests as well as those of his close associates. He frequently served successive magistrates, providing the administration with some continuity. The *teniente* quickly introduced incoming magistrates to local procedures, and responsible for day-to-day affairs, he was central to the magistrate's own economic enterprises in the jurisdiction.

The assumption of office entailed certain expenses for a district magistrate. An appointee from Spain incurred heavy travel expenses for his family and entourage. On arrival, he had to post the bond (*fianza*) required by the Crown to ensure payment of revenues collected on its behalf. In 1677, Charles II introduced the sale of appointments (to generate revenue for wartime expenditures), a practice which continued at least through the mid-eighteenth century. The price of an appointment varied greatly, a reflection of the commercial opportunities in a particular district. Some positions sold for small amounts, others for small fortunes. Additional taxes or fees often increased the cost of the appointment. Once the magistrate assumed office, the district's indigenous population provided him with such necessities as food, firewood, and fodder, as well as domestic servants. He also received a salary drawn from tribute collected in the district. Salaries thus reflected the wealth of the particular district and varied considerably throughout Mesoamerica. Yet salaries in general were notoriously low—the Crown sought to minimize administrative expenses—and often did not even cover administrative costs. To profit from their short-term appointment, magistrates invested in commercial endeavors.

An appointment provided instant credit, which could be used to invest in goods to be sold for profit, primarily in the Mexico City market. In districts with a significant indigenous population, control of tribute monies and maize also provided access to capital. (The Crown tolerated the use of tribute revenue as long as it reached the annual fleet in time to sail for Spain.) Above all, district magistrates hoped to generate quick profits from whatever economic enterprise was profitable in the local economy: financing of silver mining in Zacualpan, livestock ranching in Tehuantepec, cochineal production in Oaxaca, or indigo production in Guatemala. (A magistrate did not generally invest in large-scale agricultural enterprises in the district to which he had been appointed.) At times, the incoming magistrate would conduct an official review (*residencia*) of his predecessor's tenure in office, learning in the process all he needed to know about local commercial opportunities. He also relied on the district's Spanish population to instruct him in customary procedures.

Initially, magistrates extracted products from their districts to sell to the cities and mining centers. By the Late Colonial period, the trading pattern had reversed itself: magistrates coerced Indians to purchase animals or merchandise, often at inflated prices or of inferior quality. This forced trade was called *reparto de mercancías*. In eighteenth-century Puebla, magistrates advanced mules and horses to Indians to be repaid in eggs, which were then sold in Mexico City. In Yucatán, agents advanced cash and raw cotton to be repaid in beeswax and cotton mantles, both traditional products based on indigenous structures of production. One of the most lucrative *repartos*, in Late Colonial Oaxaca, demonstrates the crucial role of merchants, as least in the richer districts with export products. A merchant, often from Mexico City, financed the incoming magistrate—he posted the *fianza*, paid tribute revenues to the royal treasury, and advanced the costs of cochineal production. The magistrate in turn advanced credit to the district's Indians to produce cotton, cotton mantles, and cochineal dyestuff. He used his political authority to ensure Indian production and to guarantee the merchant financier (*aviador*) a monopoly on trade in the district. The magistrate's deputy—an agent of the merchant-*aviador* who could not be removed without his consent—oversaw the actual operation of the *reparto*. When cochineal production peaked in the 1770s, the Oaxaca district was one of the most highly valued in all of New Spain and commanded one of the highest prices.

The commercial activities of district magistrates were largely illegal, though royal officials tolerated them as long as they did not lead to rebellion; Indians actively resisted the demands and at times protested with violence. The Crown sporadically attempted reform, including legalization and closer regulation, but nothing like the sweeping administrative measures of the late eighteenth century. In 1786, the Crown created a new administrative position between the viceroy and the district magistrate called an *intendente*, or intendant. The intendant received a substantial salary and held broad authority over an *intendencia*, or intendancy, a provincial jurisdiction larger than the *alcaldía mayor*. District magistrates were replaced with subdelegates, named by and responsible to the intendant; twelve intendancies oversaw roughly 150 subdelegates. These reforms, which aimed to break the link between district magistrates and their merchant partners and to end the district trade monopolies enjoyed by the Mexico City and Cádiz merchant houses, also pro-

hibited the *reparto*. Yet they ultimately failed to achieve their goals. With the prohibition of the *reparto*, merchants withdrew their capital and *subdelegados* were unable to find *fiadores* (backers). Trade declined considerably. *Subdelegados*, who received no formal salary, protested bitterly and soon returned to the commercial practices of their predecessors.

Although certain eighteenth-century ordinances challenged the monopoly trading privileges of district magistrates, others effectively enhanced their political position and contributed to a discernible shift in Late Colonial district-level politics. The balance of power in the traditional "triangle of authority" between magistrates, clergy, and Indian officials tipped heavily toward magistrates. Late Colonial reforms effectively eroded the parish priest's role in local affairs, restricting his customary right to supervise Indian elections, oversee community treasure chests and *cofradía* funds, police public morality and incarcerate parishioners, and promote schools. These policies sharpened the traditional jurisdictional disputes between magistrates and clergy. Tension escalated. In contrast to priests, who were typically *criollos*, district magistrates tended to be Peninsular-born and increasingly had a military (rather than legal) background; they were less reluctant to use force than their predecessors had been. At the same time, the number of priests grew with the foundation of new parishes, many in the process of secularization. Sensitive to changing royal policy, Indians turned to Spanish courts. Litigation proliferated, concerning such issues as elections, clerical fees (especially in the wake of the 1767 *arencel*, or schedule of clerical fees), and secularization. Conflicts between *cabeceras* and *sujetos* flourished, fueled by such Late Colonial trends as population growth, the increase in the number of non-Indians resident in the countryside, and the growing number of parish priests, each of whom desired his own parish. New bases of political power emerged, including the "legal entrepreneurs," whose power rested on litigation skills that became increasingly important in Late Colonial Mexican districts.

BIBLIOGRAPHY

Chance, John K. *Conquest of the Sierra: Spaniards and Indians in Colonial Oaxaca.* Norman, Okla., 1989. Ethnohistory of the isolated, impoverished, and ethnically diverse Sierra Zapoteca (Oaxaca); emphasizes the social, political, and economic consequences for indigenous communities of the forced trade in cotton textiles and cochineal dyestuff carried out by the *alcaldes mayores*.

Gibson, Charles. *Tlaxcala in the Sixteenth Century.* New Haven, 1952. Pioneering study of Indians and Spaniards in sixteenth-century Tlaxcala; reconstructs the offices of Spanish provincial government and portrays its relationship with the Tlaxcalan *cabildo* as generally cooperative and its efforts to halt Spanish intrusion into the province as largely ineffective.

Gibson, Charles. *The Aztecs under Spanish Rule: A History of the Indians of the Valley of Mexico, 1519–1810.* Stanford, 1964. Comprehensive study of the Indians of the Valley of Mexico; established the direct relationship between the Nahua regional state, or *altepetl*, and Spanish civil and ecclesiastical jurisdictions.

Hamnett, Brian R. *Politics and Trade in Southern Mexico, 1750–1821.* Cambridge, 1971. Excellent study of the *repartimiento* in Late Colonial Oaxaca.

Horn, Rebecca. *Postconquest Coyoacan: Nahua–Spanish Relations in Central Mexico, 1519–1650.* Stanford, 1997. Multifaceted study of Nahuas and Spaniards in the Central Mexican province of Coyoacan; examines the evolving relationship between Spanish administrative jurisdictions and the Nahua *altepetl*, as well as the local activities and associations of the *corregidor* and his staff.

Lockhart, James. "The Magistrate of Zacualpan." In his *Nahuas and Spaniards: Postconquest Central Mexican History and Philology*, pp. 243–261. Stanford and Los Angeles, 1991. Intimate, engagingly written portrayal of the commercial and familial affairs of the late sixteenth century *alcalde mayor* of Zacualpan, a silver-mining district southwest of Mexico City.

Lockhart James. *The Nahuas after the Conquest: A Social and Cultural History of the Indians of Central Mexico, Sixteenth through Eighteenth Centuries.* Stanford, 1992. Comprehensive social and cultural history based entirely on Nahuatl documents that includes an excellent discussion of the post-Conquest *altepetl*.

Patch, Robert W. "Imperial Politics and Local Economy in Colonial Central America, 1670–1770." *Past and Present* 143 (1994), 77–107. Examination of the commercial activities of Spanish magistrates in Late Colonial Central America, which rested on indigenous structures of production and integrated the region into a network of trade with such products as cacao, cochineal, and cotton textiles.

Patch, Robert W. *Maya and Spaniard in Yucatan, 1648–1812.* Stanford, 1993. Study of the economy and society of Yucatán, with attention to the region's relatively long-lived *encomienda* and the *repartimiento* in wax and cotton textiles.

Restall, Matthew. *The Maya World: Yucatec Culture and Society, 1550–1850.* Stanford, 1997. History of the Yucatec Maya, based on Mayan-language documentation, which argues for the centrality of the Maya provincial state, or *cah*, to administrative structures throughout the Colonial period.

Taylor, William B. "Conflict and Balance in District Politics: Tecali and the *Sierra Norte de Puebla* in the Eighteenth Century." In *The Indian Community of Colonial Mexico: Fifteen Essays on Land Tenure, Corporate Organization, Ideology, and Village Politics*, edited by Arij Ouweneel and Simon Miller, pp. 270–294. Amsterdam, 1990. Close reading of district politics in the eighteenth-century Intendancy of Puebla, with particular attention to the rivalry between the district magistrate (and his lieutenants) and the parish priest, its impact on local Indian communities, and the shift in the balance of power away from parish priests with the implementation of the Bourbon Reforms.

Taylor, William B. *Magistrates of the Sacred: Priests and Parishioners in Eighteenth-Century Mexico.* Stanford, 1996. Monumental study of priests and parishioners in eighteenth-century Mexico with a thorough discussion of district-level politics and attention to the "triangle of authority" among magistrates, parish priests, and Indian officials.

Terraciano, Kevin. *The Mixtecs of Colonial Oaxaca: A History of Ñudzahui Writing and Culture.* Stanford, forthcoming. Fascinating study of Mixtec writing and culture based on a diverse body of pictorial and alphabetic texts that examines the evolving relationship between Spanish administrative jurisdictions and the Mixtec regional state, or *ñuu*.

REBECCA HORN

COLORS. Unlike the gray and lifeless stone monuments seen today, Mesoamerican buildings of the past were plastered in white and awash in vibrant colors. The architectural remnants of today are dim reminders of the vitality of these ceremonial centers. Pigments of black, blue, red, and yellow decorated ancient Mesoamerican temples and palaces. Murals of deities, animals, kingly exploits, and many other subjects were painted with an assortment of colors. Ancient cities such as Tikal, Bonampak, Tula, Teotihuacan, Cholulu, Chichén Itzá, and Tenochtitlan were all brightly painted.

Pictorial books, the pre-Hispanic texts, were composed of a series of images. Often these images depicted the activities of gods and heroes, divinatory calendars, and conquests and tribute. Invariably, the artisans who crafted these books used brilliant colors to communicate their messages. Ceramics, stone carvings, and other art objects were also adorned with various colors.

Pre-Hispanic texts also depict body painting. Specific colors and arrangements of colors represented the attributes of gods and humans. For example, a red-striped body represented human sacrifice. Black stripes on the face and yellow hair were associated with the fire god Xiuhtecuhtli, or Ixcozauhqui ("Yellow Face"). White was often associated with the bleached bones of the god Mictlanteuchtli, the lord of the dead, who resided in the underworld. Painted images in these books indicate that body painting was an important feature of Mesoamerican ritual life. Just as colors adorned the temples that were the focus of ceremonial activity, practitioners of the ceremonies used colors to adorn their bodies.

Color was therefore an important feature of Mesoamerican symbolism. At the level of practice, colors could symbolize specific material phenomena: yellow for the sun, red for blood, and blue for water. Often, certain colors were associated with specific cardinal directions. There was, however, no one-to-one correlation between a color and a particular aspect of material life. Colors were often associated with several things at once, so that the meaning of specific colors was multivalent. At the level of ideology, colors could be intimately associated, for example, with a deity, a geographical location, a specific ritual activity, or all of these.

On temples where human sacrifices took place and on pictorial books that represent the activities of the gods, blue and red consistently refer to water and blood. Ceremonies dedicated to fertility deities, such as Chac among the Maya and Tlaloc among the Aztec, underscored the relationship between water and blood; thus, stylized depictions of these deities and adornments on their temples prominently utilized blue and red.

The use of colors was part of the total sensual experience of being in the city. Participation in ceremonial events, as well as everyday activities, meant being surrounded by rich sensory stimuli, including music and sound, light and dark, smells and tastes, and colors. The affective use of color, therefore, gave people the sense of being intimately integrated into Mesoamerican social and cosmological realities.

[*See also* Dyes and Pigments; Painting.]

BIBLIOGRAPHY

Boone, Elizabeth Hill. *Codex Magliabechiano and the Lost Prototype of the Magliabechiano Group*. Berkeley, 1983. Complete analysis of the Mixtec tradition.
Pasztory, Esther. *The Murals of Tepantitla, Teotihuacan*. New York, 1976. Analyzes murals at ancient city of Teotihuacan in order to understand their world view.
Quiñones Keber, Eloise. *Codex Telleriano-Remensis: Ritual, Divination, and History in a Pictorial Aztec Manuscript*. Austin, 1995. Explores the Mexica iconographic and ceremonial traditions.

PHILIP P. ARNOLD

COMETS. Like the Moon and the planets, comets are seen to move with respect to the background stars. They are usually visible for several weeks or months. To the naked eye, the diffuse head and extended tail of a comet distinguish it from the pointlike plants and stars. Comets, therefore, are noticed, and although they are relatively infrequent, they were represented in ethnohistoric Mesoamerican documents and in ethnographic references to traditional sky lore.

In Nahuatl, the language of the Aztec, a comet was known as a "smoking star" (*citlalin popoca*); an equivalent term, *budz ek*, is preserved in Maya dictionaries compiled in Colonial-period Yucatán. In general, comets were regarded worldwide as disturbing omens. Fray Bernardino de Sahagún, the Franciscan who documented sixteenth-century Aztec tradition (in his *General History of the Things of New Spain*), noted that the Aztec interpreted comets as celestial messages of impending catastrophe. They linked the comet to the fate of the king, who might die or be imprisoned. War and famine might also be signaled by a comet. The sixteenth-century Dominican Fray Diego Durán described the reaction of Motecuhzoma II, the Aztec ruler, to a "marvelous and terrifying comet" that appeared in the midnight sky ten years before the arrival of Cortés. In his *History of the Indies of New Spain*, Durán explained that Motecuhzoma's growing anxiety prompted him to consult with Nezahualpilli, the king of Tetzcoco, who explained that the comet signaled destruction of the established order in Mexico. Although some comets documented in Central Mexican codices can be dated and confirmed by references in historical astronomical records from China, the comet of 1519 mentioned by the chronicler Fray Juan de Torquemada is a fabrication; its association with the Conquest, however, reflects the prevailing attitude about comets. According to Ulrich Köhler (1989), comets continue to be regarded as war heralds among the Nahua of the Sierra Puebla.

Although some comets—like Halley's Comet—return periodically, their cyclic behavior goes unrecognized without the establishment, preservation, and systematic review of a written archive of dated celestial events. There is no evidence that Mesoamericans knew of cometary periodicity. The first Mexican record of Halley's Comet is a comet symbol associated with the year 1531 ("13 Reed"), which appears in the *Códice en Cruz*, a year-by-year pictorial compilation of significant events. Other early post-Conquest references to comets are collected in the *Codex Vaticanus A* and *Codex Telleriano Remensis*.

Traditional ideas about comets have been preserved among some indigenous present-day peoples in Mesoamerica. The Quiché Maya of highland Guatemala refer to comets as *uje ch'umil* ("tail of the star"). To them, comets foreshadow epidemics. Early in the twentieth century, the Maya of northern Yucatán expected trouble when a comet appeared. Köhler (1989) encountered comet anxiety among the Tzotzil Maya of Chiapas.

Although traditional Mesoamerican comet lore is sparse, enough survives to confirm that comets functioned thematically in that part of the New World much as they did in the Old World. Defying the regular deportment of the Sun, Moon, planets, and stars, comets arrived unannounced and intruded temporarily with warnings of calamity.

[*See also* Stars and Constellations.]

BIBLIOGRAPHY

Aveni, Anthony F. *Skywatchers of Ancient Mexico*. Austin, Tex., 1980. Pioneering, comprehensive survey of indigenous astronomy in Mesoamerica.
Köhler, Ulrich. "Comets and Falling Stars in the Perception of Mesoamerican Indians." In *World Archaeoastronomy*, edited by Anthony F. Aveni, pp. 289–299. Cambridge, 1989. The most detailed source on the subject.
Krupp, E. C. *Beyond the Blue Horizon: Myths and Legends of the Sun, Moon, Stars, and Planets*. New York, 1991. The only modern, worldwide, cross-cultural survey of celestial mythology, with analysis of its function.

E. C. KRUPP

COMMUNITY KINGDOMS. [*This entry comprises four articles:*

Central Mexico (Nahua)
Oaxaca (Mixtec and Zapotec)
Maya Highlands
Maya Lowlands

The first article discusses the organization and development of Nahua community kingdoms in Central Mexico; the second article discusses the organization and development of

Mixtec and Zapotec community kingdoms in Oaxaca; the third article surveys the organization and development of community kingdoms in the Maya Highlands; the final article focuses on the organization and development of community kingdoms in the Maya Lowlands. For related discussions, see Political Organization and Development, *article on* Pre-Hispanic Cultures; Rulers and Dynasties; *and* States and Empires.]

Central Mexico (Nahua)

Pre-Hispanic sovereign states or polities, most of which were tributary to the Aztec Empire by the time of European contact, are often called "community kingdoms." Some scholars refer to them as "city-states" or *señoríos*, which stress their rather small territorial extension and the limited scope of their political power; however, these names also suggest the social and political complexity most of them achieved. In Nahuatl, they were called *altepetl* (plural, *altepetl* or *altepeme*). Historians gradually have come to prefer this original designation, *altepetl*. A reasonable translation of *altepetl* could be "principality," and most *altepetl* were comparable in size and political standing to a modern small state, such as Liechtenstein. Some, however, became substantial and powerful kingdoms, such as Xaltocan (not Nahua but Otomí), as well as Tlacopan, Tetzcoco, and Tenochtitlan, to mention only those in the Valley of Mexico. The Nahuas distinguished a major *altepetl*, like Tenochtitlan, as a "great altepetl" (*hueyaltepetl*).

The origin of *altepetl* in Central Mexico goes back at least to the Epiclassic period. Archaeological evidence points to the central organization and relative importance of certain settlements that flourished after the downfall of Teotihuacan (from c.650–700 CE), such as Cantona and Xochicalco, and later Tajín and Tula. There were probably many more, less outstanding but essentially similar centers. Written sources confirm the existence of dozens of Central Mexican kingdoms by the fourteenth and fifteenth centuries. They were in an almost constant state of war and eventually dominated or were dominated by their neighbors. The emergence of the Triple Alliance, formed by three *altepetl* (Tenochtitlan, Tetzcoco, and Tlacopan), was the initial stage in a major process of centralization, based mainly on tribute imposition over individual *altepetl*, sometimes reinforced with matrimonial alliances. Occupation or disintegration of conquered *altepetl* was not the rule. The Tarascan kingdom of Michoacán in western Central Mexico, outside the Nahua sphere, achieved what seems to have been a higher degree of political integration.

Each *altepetl* or kingdom produced its own particular history, in most cases heavy with mythical interpretation.

Known to us through native and Spanish paintings, writings, and documents, such histories associate the origin of most *altepetl* with particular tribes or groups that acquired distinctiveness through a sequence of migrations and settlements. Any history of a particular kingdom mentions a tutelary god, a founding king (or hero) and his lineage, and a territory having natural features associated with it, such as mountains or rivers. The word *altepetl* literally means "water-mountain," a reference to the surroundings and sources of life, so it bears a symbolic representation of the material basis of the kingdom. The king (*tlatoani*) served as an intermediary between his people and the god. Political legitimacy or sovereignty (*tlatocayotl*; sometimes taken as equivalent to *altepetl*) depended on continuity of the ruling lineage and the fulfillment of ritual duties.

A key element in the distinctiveness of a kingdom was its proper name, generally a toponym such as Ocotelolco, Zacatlan, Cuauhtinchan, Chollolan, Chalco, or Tenochtitlan (their people, respectively, were called Ocotelolca, Zacateca, Cuauhtlinchantlaca, Chollolteca, Chalca, and Tenochca). Most migrant groups tended to associate the name with their origin as well as with their final settlement. Consequently, the toponym of each kingdom had historical significance and sometimes was reminiscent of tribal beginnings. Toponyms appear overwhelmingly in all sorts of archaeological and documentary evidence, either pictographic or written, recording successions of kings, wars, and conquests. Most of these toponyms are *altepetl* names.

By 1520, about one hundred kingdoms, or *altepetl*, existed in the predominantly Nahua highlands of Central Mexico, and two hundred more in the adjacent, culturally diverse, and then highly populated sierra regions. Michoacán comprised a much smaller but comparable array. These figures are approximate, since no comprehensive lists or maps are available. Just before the Spanish arrived, Tenochtitlan and its allies had absorbed a few dozen *altepetl* and imposed tribute on most of those remaining. Only a few managed to remain independent; the eight or so Tlaxcalan kingdoms were the most conspicuous in this group. In all of Mesoamerica there were about fifteen hundred kingdoms, and the Triple Alliance at its peak controlled nearly half of them. [*See* Aztec.]

Before and after the conquest of Tenochtitlan, the Spaniards took control of individual kingdoms, or *altepetl*, one by one. These were then administered through the *encomienda* (a device designed by the conquerors to maintain the operation of existing tribute systems) and subsequently reorganized corporatively as *pueblos de indios*, which were still called *altepetl* in Nahuatl. Each had some degree of autonomy and local government. Consequently, there were important continuities between pre-

Hispanic polities and colonial *pueblos*, with population, ruling lineages, and territories basically unchanged. For this reason, the history of the *altepetl* in Early Colonial times greatly enhances our otherwise poor knowledge of their late pre-Hispanic past.

By 1520, a typical Nahua *altepetl* of Central Mexico, whether independent or tributary, was ruled by a hereditary king (*tlatoani*), and internally divided into a number of wards or sections, each organized as a *calpulli* and/or headed by a particular lord or *teuctli*. One or more of these sections could comprise a diverse, even non-Nahua population, the result of former conquests or alliances. Common people included a more or less diversified elite, free tributaries, workers attached to the land (or to a particular *teuctli*), and sometimes slaves. Some polities were more complex, as a result of the interaction of several (usually three or four) distinctive and sometimes contrasting constituents. There were also leagues or commonwealths formed by a number of kingdoms, as in the Tlaxcala region.

Bonds of allegiance within a kingdom were related to tribute, ritual obligations, and performance in war, which were reciprocated with administration, land grants, justice, and religious leadership. Boundaries appear to have depended on the presence of people who recognized such bonds of allegiance and identified themselves as subjects of a given *tlatoani*, rather than on definite territorial demarcation. Kingdoms were frequently bordered by fringes of uninhabited or sparsely populated land, such as mountains, ravines, or swamps, whose resources could be collectively exploited.

Far from being the closed, homogeneous, or exclusive conglomerates that ethnic communities tend to be, the kingdoms, or *altepetl*, of Central Mexico reached the complexity that is to be expected of developed political bodies; their supposed tribal origins lay in the remote past. This fact, true even of the smaller ones, proved to be crucial to their persistence as autonomous corporations throughout the Spanish period.

[*See also* Altepetl.]

BIBLIOGRAPHY

Carrasco, Pedro. *Estructura político-territorial del imperio tenochca: La Triple Alianza de Tenochtitlan, Tetzcoco y Tlacopan*. Mexico City, 1996. The most recent overview of the topic; clear explanation of concepts and institutions.

García Martínez, Bernardo. *Los pueblos de la Sierra: El poder y el espacio entre los indios del norte de Puebla hasta 1700*. Mexico City, 1987. History and cartography of the Nahua and Totonac kingdoms of the eastern sierras of Central Mexico.

Gibson, Charles. *The Aztecs under Spanish Rule*. Stanford, Calif., 1964. A pioneering and now classic book; provides a detailed survey of the kingdoms within the Valley of Mexico.

Lockhart, James. *The Nahuas after the Conquest*. Stanford, 1992. A sophisticated discussion of the nature and structure of the *altepetl* and other political organizations.

Pollard, Helen P. *Tariacuri's Legacy: The Prehispanic Tarascan State*. Norman, Okla., 1993. The most recent comprehensive work on Michoacán.

Schroeder, Susan. *Chimalpahin and the Kingdoms of Chalco*. Tucson, Ariz., 1991. Examines the evolution of several closely related *altepetl* in the Valley of Mexico, with particular attention to sociopolitical units of different levels.

BERNARDO GARCÍA MARTÍNEZ

Oaxaca (Mixtec and Zapotec)

Two major states—one centered at Teotihuacan in the Basin of Mexico and one at Monte Albán in the Valley of Oaxaca—dominated the Classic-period pattern of cultural integration in highland Mesoamerica. During the Classic period, the political status of some smaller Zapotec and Mixtec community kingdoms varied considerably. Most Zapotec towns were probably dependent subsidiaries of Monte Albán. The Mixtec towns were independent, parts of small alliance groups, or, in a few cases, dependent on Monte Albán.

The decline of the two major states, at about 750 CE and 800 CE, respectively, did not mean the end of political integration in the region. In fact, these centers remained locally powerful well into the Postclassic period. The decline of their pan-regional power meant that their broad political reach was replaced by numerous smaller centers, including Mixtec and Zapotec community kingdoms, such as Teposcolula, Chalcatongo, Tejupan, Achiutla, Jaltepec, Tilantongo, Jalieza, Zaachila, Tlacolula, Mitla, and Etla, among many others. During the Postclassic period, the preexisting political structures changed as Classic-period alliances between Mixtec and Zapotec communities were dissolved. In the absence of Monte Albán's unifying power in the region, those groups that had been connected to it were transformed, so new alliances were built between Zapotec and Mixtec community kingdoms. Some former Zapotec and Mixtec dependencies of Monte Albán then emerged as new foci of power.

The many Mixtec and Zapotec community kingdoms became the paramount force for regional integration within each area, and intermarriage between elites of these two groups cemented relationships between them. Despite these changes in the political structure of the region during the Classic period, the underlying benefits of inter- and intraregional interaction persisted. Astute politicians in each ethnic group forged a new system that would maintain those benefits in the new Postclassic world. Although the ethnicities and histories of the two areas were distinct, the pattern of intermarriage of elite members of these two groups remained. This is well illustrated in the links between the ruling families of Zaachila, Teozacoalco, and Tilantongo, as documented in the *Codex Zouche-Nuttall* and on the *Mapa de Teozacoalco*.

Most Mixtec and Zapotec community kingdoms were likely ruled by a royal couple and not by a king alone. Kevin Terraciano (1994) has found that an important Mixtec term for their own polity was the *yuhuitayu* (the reed mat that is the seat of the ruling pair); he has argued persuasively that this word embodies the conception of the polity as an entity formed by a marriage that binds together the hereditary lands owned by each member of the couple. The political unit lasted as long as both spouses lived, but it did not necessarily survive them. Because separate tracts of land could be inherited by different heirs, the composition of the *yuhuitayu* could readily change in each generation. Mixtec historical codices contain examples of intergenerational change in allegiance. Stability was not vested in the land that belonged to a kingdom at any one time because that could change. Rather, it lay in the alliance contracted between the families of a man and a woman. This may be why documents like the codices and colonial records emphasize alliance through marriage rather than territory or place. Further, it may explain why place and alliance were recorded on portable, perishable, and alterable documents like codices, rather than on stone monuments. Similar considerations might also help to explain the existence of more than one *cacique* in a single town, a situation noted in some Colonial-era accounts of Zapotec community kingdoms of the Valley of Oaxaca. This observation suggests a complex and changeable system of inheritance and alliance. John Pohl (1994) has recognized extensive alliance corridors that were maintained by Mixtec and Zapotec communities and their allies, which stretched from the Basin of Mexico to the Valley of Oaxaca and beyond.

The organization of government within those kingdoms may be divided into four groups of offices. The first was the ruling family, and the others were composed of hereditary nobles. Pohl (1994) identified the second and third groups as intricate ministerial or cabinet-level departments within the community kingdom. The second group was the long-recognized council of four priests, the *dzutu sandidzo ñuhu*, which maintained and venerated the sacred bundles of the ruler's ancestors and, in so doing, validated the divine aspects of the ruling lineage. Among their tasks was ensuring the stability of succession in the *yuhuitayu*, by maintaining the cult of its leaders as supernaturals. The third group was a set of four sacrificial *yaha yahui* priests, who regulated tribute payment and market exchange; precisely how these priests functioned is not fully understood, but the intricacy and importance of their role, and the iconic similarity of sacrifice, exchange, and tribute, are now evident from John Monaghan's *The Covenants with Earth and Rain* (Norman, Okla., 1995). A fourth group of nobles lived in subsidiary communities and served as rural administrators, though it is possible that the second and third groups also had this function.

Taken together, these four groups—the rulers, the bundle priests, the sacrifice and exchange priests, and the rural administrators—constitute a preliminary conception of the structure of leadership in Mixtec community kingdoms. The rulers of the polity had paramount power and were seen as divine. A group of priests maintained the cult of their divinity, ensured smooth succession, and administered many day-to-day functions of government for the rulers. A second group of priests controlled sacrifice—through its performance and through their regulation of tribute, trade, and the economic functions of the state. There were also noble administrators who resided in subsidiary communities.

A similar organization has been detected among Colonial-period Zapotec polities by Kent Flannery and Joyce Marcus (*American Scientist* 64, pp. 374–383), with the obvious implication that they also existed in Postclassic community kingdoms. Flannery and Marcus identified four varieties of administrators: a ruler, the *coquitao*; a group of noblemen that oversaw smaller dependent communities, the *coqui*; a staff of priests who lived and worked in the community capital, the *bigaña*; and a group of tax or tribute collectors, the *golaba*. These four groups are analogous to the system of governance described for the Mixtec. Michael Lind and Javier Urcid (*Notas Mesoamericanas* 9, pp. 78–111) noted intriguing archaeological evidence, which suggested that the roots of this community-kingdom structure may have existed as early as the Classic period in Zapotec communities.

The similarities and differences in the organization of Oaxacan community kingdoms suggest wider patterns of kingdom organization. The extent to which these patterns are relevant to other peoples and other parts of highland Mesoamerica remains to be determined.

BIBLIOGRAPHY

Appel, Jill. "A Summary of the Ethnohistoric Information Relevant to the Interpretation of Late Postclassic Settlement Pattern Data, the Central and Valle Grande Survey Zones." In *Monte Albán's Hinterland*, Part I: *The Prehispanic Settlement Patterns of the Central and Southern Parts of the Valley of Oaxaca, Mexico*, edited by Richard Blanton, Stephen Kowalewski, Gary Feinman, and Jill Appel, pp. 139–148. Ann Arbor, 1982. Ethnohistoric study of Zapotec community kingdoms at the time of Spanish conquest.

Balkansky, Andrew. "Urbanism and Early State Formation in the Huamelulpan Valley of Southern Mexico." *Latin American Antiquity* 9.1 (1998), 37–67. Discussion of the origins of Mixtec community kingdoms and the roles of local and interregional factors in their development.

Byland, Bruce, and John M. D. Pohl. *In the Realm of 8 Deer: The Archaeology of the Mixtec Codices*. Norman, Okla., 1994. Ethnohistorical and regional archaeological evidence for the development of Mixtec community kingdoms, from the Classic to the Postclassic, and of relationships between Mixtec and Zapotec kingdoms.

Flannery, Kent, and Joyce Marcus, eds. *The Cloud People: Divergent*

Evolution of the Zapotec and Mixtec Civilizations. New York, 1983. Information on the development and organization of Zapotec and Mixtec community kingdoms.

Jansen, Maarten E.R.G.N., Peter Kröfges, and Michel R. Oudijk. *The Shadow of Monte Albán: Politics and Historiography in Postclassic Oaxaca, Mexico.* Leiden, Netherlands, 1998. Presents an interpretation of the interrelationships between Mixtec and Zapotec community kingdoms that contrasts with Byland and Pohl (1994).

Kowalewski, Stephen. "Internal Subdivisions of Communities in the Prehispanic Valley of Oaxaca." In *Factional Competition and Political Development in the New World,* edited by Elizabeth Brumfiel and John Fox, pp. 127–137. Cambridge, 1994. Concise presentation of the development of internal structure in Zapotec kingdoms, presented from the perspective of a broad settlement survey.

Pohl, John. *The Politics of Symbolism in the Mixtec Codices.* Nashville, Tenn., 1994. Pohl's definitive presentation of codical information about the political organization of Mixtec community kingdoms.

Smith, Mary Elizabeth. *Picture Writing from Ancient Southern Mexico: Mixtec Place Signs and Maps.* Norman, Okla., 1973. Still the best discussion of how to read the Mixtec codices.

Spores, Ronald. *The Mixtecs in Ancient and Colonial Times.* Norman, Okla., 1984. Spores's most recent and his best discussion of ethnohistoric evidence for the operation of Mixtec kingdoms in the Colonial period.

Terraciano, Kevin. "Ñudzavui History: Mixtec Writing and Culture in Colonial Oaxaca." Ph.D. diss., University of California, Los Angeles, 1994. Insightful new investigation of Colonial-period writings in the Mixtec language, which reveals much about the way the Mixtec understood their own community organizations.

BRUCE E. BYLAND

Maya Highlands

Most of the Postclassic period (900–1520 CE) communities mentioned in the approximately thirty ethnohistories across highland Guatemala have been identified archaeologically, and so we have a fairly complete view of how lineage complexes of specific kinship groups changed. Disaffected lineage segments realigned or fissioned to form new towns based on degrees of genealogical proximity. The Highland Maya were organized like segmentary lineages and galactic polities. The Postclassic sequence spans about twenty-five generations; this was foreshortened into thirteen historical episodes, each represented by a particular Quiché ruler. The Quiché dominated the "community kingdoms" and provide most of our information.

Early Postclassic Katun Confederacy. Maya ethnohistory commences in about the ninth century CE, when the various legendary leaders gathered during a dark night at deserted Tulan (Tollan) in the western Maya Lowlands. Premised on the cosmology of the solar calendar, the "fire" of the sun (government) was extinguished, and a new calendrical period of night ensued. The ancestors journeyed east to the "sunrise," guided by the light of the planet Venus, and founded new settlements in the Guatemala highlands. The thirteen migratory groups chronicled in the *Popol Vuh* are the Quiché, Rabinal, Cak-

chiquel, Tzutuhil, Lamakib-Kumatz-Tuhal-Uchaba (Sacapultec), Ch'umila, Quiba, Batena, Akul, Qan Chahel, and Balam Kolob. Upon entering the highlands, they congregated at ChiPixab, which has a small temple today, and then fanned out to establish their own towns. ChiPixab lies at the foot of a twin-peaked mountain, Cerro Mamah, at the headwaters of the Río Usumacinta leading from Tulan. The twin peaks of Cerro Mamah represented the mythic Hero Twins, Hunahpu and Ixbalanque, who journeyed through the dark underworld to combat the Xibalban lords in the ballgame, a metaphor of battle. The historical journey into the highlands paralleled the mythic adventures of the Twins in the underworld. The Venus calendar scheduled events of war for this era of constant conflict against the local Highland Maya.

The genealogy-based political relationships among the allied lineage groups (*amak*) is borne out geographically and in settlement patterns. Each group built a fortified residential site (*tinamit*) and an adjacent mountaintop shrine (*sakiribal*, "place of the dawning") to observe the heavens and keep the statue of its patron deity (*cabawil*). Each small shrine temple was aligned to a slightly different aspect of Venus, as the planetary harbinger of the sunrise. Sharing a tutelary god helped the intruders when they had to call on their dispersed kindred for assistance in the protracted wars against the indigenous Vukamak Maya. Each of the thirteen groups was literally within sight of Cerro Mamah, a beacon for signaling collective endeavors. Immediately south of Mamah, the three Quiché segments were spaced three kilometers (two miles) apart at Hacawitz (Nima Quiché), Amak Tam (Tamub), and Uquin Cat (Ilocab). The deity of Hacawitz at its namesake site symbolized Venus as well as the father of the Hero Twins in myth, Hun-Hunahpu, and God-I (the maize god of the Classic period). The seven primary sites of the Quiché enclave, which include the towering shrines PaTohil and P'Awilix, also aligned to the key stations of Venus. For example, when viewed from P'Awilix, a Venusian conjunction commenced over PaTohil. Both the Cakchiquel at Paraxone and the Rabinal at Tzamaneb were spaced about twenty kilometers (twelve miles) from Mamah. North of Mamah, the three Sacapultec sites centered on the *sakiribal* shrine, Cerro ChuPacbalam, with its sacred jade outcrop near the summit. The Toltec and Feathered Serpent lineages at the Sacapultec's Tuha maintained a talking oracle and the calendar stone, which were recognized by the less highly ranked allies across the western highlands. Tuha was thus the font of prophetic icons.

Quiché Segmentary State. The onset of the Late Postclassic period (c.1100 CE) saw profound reordering among and between the Quichean communities; ceramics, lithics, and architectural styles changed. One generation after fleeing the conflagration of Hacawitz (c.eleventh century CE), the Quiché came to speak for and then control the thirteen dispersed peoples of the former confederacy. With this control of the corporate symbols, the Quiché relocated a short distance south to build Utatlan, a capital with the grandeur of Tulan and the seat of the solar calendar. In a calendrical metaphor, the sun rose to create a new state and a new temporal cycle (called a "sun" in the *Popol Vuh*). The office of Feathered Serpent and its namesake first ruler (*ahpop*) were transferred to Utatlan from Tuha. Under Quiché dominion, all the original thirteen groups, except for the Sacapultec, relocated to small cliff-ringed cities. Buildings in the new architectural style of finely cut masonry, *talud-tablero* balustrades, I-shaped ballcourts, and small round temples, were coated in lime plaster to symbolize the sacred buildings of the solar light. The new Quiché patron deity, Tohil, either fused with the local patron god or was seated alongside him in a twin temple.

The chronicles narrate that the thirteen groups were militarily forced into submission, commencing with the higher-ranked Sacapultec in the north and the Tzutuhil in the south—reflecting the *axis mundi* of the ancestors—followed by peoples to east and west, reflecting the solar trajectory. Tribute was paid to the Quiché under the auspices of Tohil. The geopolitical distribution of sites within the Quiché state modeled the circular carapace of both the World Turtle and the solar calendar with its three concentric rings, which were quadripartitioned into thirteen sections. Each of the thirteen provincial groups was ascribed a specific celestial identity, so that, in concert, they represented the full solar calendar. Cadet Quiché lineages from Utatlan built plazas that were reduced versions of their home city with the provincial centers.

Fissioning of Rival States. Under the seventh Quiché ruler, the Cakchiquel rebelled and relocated to Iximché to found a rival state, as recounted in the *Annals of the Cakchiquels*. Soon the Sacapultec, Tzutuhil, Balamiha, and Rabinal also broke loose and initiated small polities (e.g., Rabinal Achi). Four states were engaged in a series of wars when the Spaniards arrived in 1524: the Quiché allied with the Tzutuhil against the Cakchiquel and Pipil of the Pacific piedmont. However, while the Aztec intermarried and thus allied with the Quiché around 1510, the Spaniards sided with the rival Cakchiquel and established the first Guatemala City at Iximché.

BIBLIOGRAPHY
Brown, Kenneth L. "Postclassic Relationships between the Highland and Lowland Maya." In *The Lowland Maya Postclassic*, edited by Arlen F. Chase and Diane Z. Chase, pp. 270–281. Austin, Tex., 1985. Argues that the Quiché did not emigrate from the lowlands but evolved in the highlands from trading contact with Teotihuacan.
Carmack, Robert M. *Quichean Civilization*. Berkeley, 1973. Encyclo-pedic analysis of the major and minor ethnohistoric chronicles written by or about the Quichean peoples from the Postclassic through the Colonial periods.
Fox, John W. *Maya Postclassic State Formation*. Cambridge, 1987. Archaeological evidence for the migration of the Quichean ancestors from Chontalpa of the Mexican Gulf lowlands into the Guatemalan highlands, and for the step-by-step unfolding of the Quiché state according to segmentary lineage principles.
Fox, John W. "On the Rise and Fall of *Tulans* and Maya Segmentary States." *American Anthropologist* 91 (1989), 656–681. How prophecy and decentralized leadership functioned in the migration to the east, the spacing of sites within the Early Postclassic Quichean confederacy, and the economics of segmentary state expansion during the Late Postclassic.
Fox, John W. "Political Cosmology among the Quiché Maya." In *Factional Competition and Political Development in the New World*, edited by Elizabeth M. Brumfiel and John W. Fox, pp. 158–170. Cambridge, 1993. How the sequence of thirteen rulers structured Quiché history and political development, and how conquered peoples were added to the Quiché state according to the principles of the solar calendar.
Fox, John W., Garrett W. Cook, Arlen F. Chase, and Diane Z. Chase. "Questions of Political and Economic Integration: Segmentary versus Centralized States among the Ancient Maya." *Current Anthropology* 37 (1996), 795–801. Examines whether the Classic and Postclassic Maya were organized into centralized or segmentary states.
Recinos, Adrian, and Delia Goetz, trans. *Annals of the Cakchiquels*. Norman, Okla., 1953. Written between 1493 and 1600, this work provides a detailed history of the political events of the Cakchiquels from the time of the migration from Tulan through their split with the Quiché, to the arrival of the Spaniards.
Sahlins, Marshall D. "The Segmentary Lineage: An Organization of Predatory Expansion." *American Anthropologist* 63 (1961), 322–345. Concise view of how African lineages among pastoralists expand and incorporate conquered peoples.
Tedlock, Dennis, ed. and trans. *Popol Vuh: The Mayan Book of the Dawn of Life*. New York, 1985. Provides the genesis myth for the Quiché in the first three parts (creations or "suns"); part four is political historiography of the alliances and military campaigns and the accomplishments of particular rulers from the legendary chiefs who entered the highlands and who dwelt at Hacawitz, to the more historically specific rulers and military leaders at Utatlán.

JOHN W. FOX

Maya Lowlands

The earliest Lowland Maya kingdoms arose ultimately from Formative-period agrarian communities, drawing on religious and lineage-based sources of leadership authority. Although institutionalized kingship (*ahaw*) followed by several centuries the rise of the earliest cities—at El Mirador, Nakbe, and Calakmul—in the late first millennium BCE, formalization of kingship solidified a religious, military, and social authority whose scope already differed markedly from leadership of households, lineages, or farming villages. Through strategic conquest and alliance, kings of one of the earliest Maya polities, Calakmul, achieved dominion over much of the lowlands from the early centuries of the common era until at least the late seventh century. Other alliances were smaller or shorter-lived. Throughout the pre-Hispanic period individual kingdoms coalesced and dissolved repeatedly, at disparate times and rates.

Judging from the texts and iconography of the Classic period (250–900 CE) and from ethnohistoric accounts, the heart of a Maya kingdom was its capital and its king; its body was the populace—the community. This was true of the largest and most powerful Classic kingdoms, such as Tikal, Copán, Caracol, or Calakmul, as well as for the more abundant smaller polities. What varied markedly among specific kingdoms was the precise articulation between heart and body, between ruler and ruled, across space, and through time.

Kings. By Late Classic times, the officials we call "kings" bore the theocratic title *k'ul ahaw*, which we understand as "holy lord." Rule most commonly passed from father to son, although sometimes one brother succeeded another. Women occasionally governed, at least as regents, and interdynastic marriages were often crucial to political strategy. Dynastic sequences are known for several kingdoms; the longest documented is Tikal's, with more than thirty sovereigns spanning seven centuries. Despite the sumptuous royal tombs, impressive building programs, and texts extolling military exploits, marriage alliances, and visits by honored foreign leaders, royal authority was clearly subject to challenge. Titles for subsidiary lords proliferated in the Late Classic, suggesting growing recognition of sub-royal entitlements. A "council house" (*popol na*) is material evidence that Copán's ruler shared formal governance with high-ranking nobles by the late eighth century CE. *Multepal*, joint governance with no clear paramount, was institutionalized at Chichén Itzá in the ninth century, although kings continued to govern elsewhere at that time, as in Cobá and Uxmal.

Capitals. The seat of authority was the royal capital; its civic core was marked by imposing stone temples, palaces, and administrative buildings, with adjoining plazas often spacious enough for thousands to gather at public events. Individual buildings were arranged intentionally to enhance the ruler's authority, drawing on the symbolism of the cardinal directions, centrality, or relative elevation. In ballcourts, kings reenacted primordial supernatural contests, often ritually vanquishing living rivals who had been defeated earlier in battles. In many capitals, public displays of portrait sculptures, dynastic genealogies, and records of military victories reinforced royal authority.

Truncated pyramidal platforms were identified as sacred, ceremonial mountains; the buildings at their summits were places of power, metaphorical cave entries to the otherworld. Rulers reinforced their claims to super-

natural authority with each emergence from such buildings. The importance of location was frequently attested by the rebuilding in place of successive versions of temples—as in Tikal's North Acropolis or Copán's Acropolis. The Tikal royal palace (Structure 5D-46) was accorded respect differently, by being maintained over four centuries, while adjoining spaces were modified and filled with new construction.

Communities. The communities governed as kingdoms varied widely in size and organizational complexity, as well as in the degree of control that kings and nobles exerted over their support population. Although these three characteristics were not yoked inseparably, larger kingdoms tended, not surprisingly, to more internal complexity and tighter integration.

Eighth-century Tikal, for example, had more than sixty thousand residents in its capital city, spread over about 120 square kilometers. Many argue that the Tikal king's dominion extended far beyond the capital environs, over a domain of nearly two thousand square kilometers and a population exceeding four hundred thousand, including smaller-scale subsidiary polities. Calakmul, Caracol, and Cobá were similarly impressive in areal expanse and demographic scale. In contrast, smaller kingdoms like Quiriguá had capitals at most a few square kilometers in extent, and populations of probably only several thousand.

Within and beyond the capitals, variable elaborations of residential architecture and domestic possessions map the social standing of occupants in extended-family compounds. Some of the grandest mark long-established lineages with high local standing, like Group 9N-8 in Copán's Sepulturas sector. Dispersed compounds of high-status families were often the focus of wardlike social integration, as at Copán, Quiriguá, or Caracol. At times, formal causeways joined spatially discrete sectors within capitals, as in Copán, Caracol, or Xunantunich, or they linked separate cities within a polity, as with Cobá-Yaxuna.

Most of the populace held far less social, economic, and political power. They included craft specialists, bureaucrats, retainers living with or near patrons, and especially the many farming families who provided the kingdoms' economic underpinnings. Farmers likewise lived in extended family compounds, both within cities and in more rural settings. Leaders of agrarian settlements were intermediaries with officials in the capitals; a hierarchy of Classic-era political titles (e.g., *ahaw*, *sahal*) suggests parallels with leadership hierarchies recorded in post-Conquest times. As authority in the cities waned, these local leaders often became more active and prominent in social, ritual, and economic integration. Life histories of individual kingdoms are distinguished by ebbs and flows in centralization.

In the largest, most densely populous kingdoms, however, authority became concentrated ever more firmly in the hands of king and nobles. Formality, uniformity, and sheer scale suggest that the extensive agricultural terracing of Caracol was centrally commissioned and controlled. Sophisticated hydraulic engineering for large-scale water capture at Tikal and elsewhere likewise bespeaks centralized management for economic and ritual purposes. Thus did kings both exert and extract authority through control of resources vital not only to physical sustenance but also to ritual practice and belief, mirroring the fundamental kinship and religious origins of their office.

BIBLIOGRAPHY

Culbert, T. Patrick, ed. *Classic Maya Political History: Hieroglyphic and Archaeological Evidence.* Cambridge, 1991. Papers from the 1986 School of American Research Advanced Seminar, comprising critical early synthesis of textual and material evidence for Maya political history, structure, and change.

de Montmollin, Olivier. *The Archaeology of Political Structure.* Cambridge, 1989. Detailed consideration of ancient Maya political organization, analyzing diverse forms of relevant archaeological evidence.

Fash, William L. *Scribes, Warriors and Kings: The City of Copán and the Ancient Maya.* London, 1991. A readable, detailed analysis of one of the best-known Maya kingdoms.

Fox, John W., Garrett W. Cook, Arlen F. Chase, Diane Z. Chase, and Arthur A. Demarest. "The Maya State: Centralized or Segmentary." *Current Anthropology* 37 (1996), 795–830. Combining commissioned articles and commentary, critiques current models for organization of ancient Maya states.

Houston, Stephen D. *Maya Glyphs.* Berkeley, 1989. Short, readable overview of Maya writing and its subject matter.

Marcus, Joyce. *Mesoamerican Writing Systems: Propaganda, Myth and History in Four Ancient Civilizations.* Princeton, 1992. Reviews critically the structure, content, and ancient uses of texts in Maya, Zapotec, Mixtec, and Aztec societies.

McAnany, Patricia A. *Living with the Ancestors: Kinship and Kingship in Ancient Maya Society.* Austin, Tex., 1995. Analyzes the emergence of Maya ancestor veneration, arguing its direct linkage to exclusionary land-tenure practices and the development of social inequalities.

Sabloff, Jeremy A., and John S. Henderson, eds. *Lowland Maya Civilization in the Eighth Century A.D.* Washington, D.C., 1993. Proceedings of the 1989 Dumbarton Oaks conference offer thematic perspectives on Lowland Maya civilization at its Late Classic peak.

Schele, Linda, and David A. Freidel. *A Forest of Kings.* New York, 1990. A pathbreaking and provocative perspective on Maya history and civilization.

Sharer, Robert J. *The Ancient Maya.* 5th ed. Stanford, 1994. Comprehensive review of development and organization of ancient Maya civilization.

WENDY ASHMORE

COMPADRAZGO. The institution of *compadrazgo*—known to anthropologists as ritual kinship, ritual sponsorship, or fictive kinship—is widespread in Latin America at all levels of the sociocultural spectrum. Its geographical distribution extends from the United States throughout Mesoamerica, the Caribbean, and South America. The institution in its various forms is functionally significant in a variety of contexts ranging from egalitarian peasant societies to highly stratified urban settings. *Compadrazgo* is an important mechanism of social interaction that affects groups ranging in size from the hamlet to the nation, and it not infrequently constitutes a system with clearly defined regulatory principles.

Compadrazgo is a familiar concept in the anthropological vocabulary, but it does not have a unitary terminological meaning, and several definitions have been proposed by anthropologists working in Latin America and Europe. In Mesoamerica, where *compadrazgo* exhibits its most complex and diversified form, it may be characterized as follows. *Compadrazgo* is a relationship established between two individuals, two married couples, or a fixed number of related people (kinsmen and nonkinsmen) through the link of a person, religious image, or material object or occasion—the mediating entity. The mediating entity is the necessary condition for the relationship, but in time it becomes passive, and the structural and functional importance of *compadrazgo* is permanently vested in the relationship obtaining between parents, kinsmen, or owners of the mediating entity and the sponsors for the occasion. This is the aspect of *compadrazgo* that approaches the characteristics of real kinship and acquires the configuration of a system which transcends the structure and form the institution had in Europe, its place of origin. Each occasion corresponds to a *compadrazgo* type, which entails specific social, economic, religious, and ceremonial aspects. The types vary in their intrinsic and symbolic importance and in the degree to which their concomitant events and activities are institutionalized. They are categorized along several dimensions, but most distinctly as sacramental (based on sacraments of the church) and nonsacramental types.

The basic *compadrazgo* terminology is standard throughout Mesoamerica. Sponsors are universally addressed and referred to as *padrino* ("godfather") and *madrina* ("godmother") of the mediating entity, who (or which) is designated by the term *ahijado* ("godson") or *ahijada* ("goddaughter"). Even if the mediating entity is an image or object, it is referred to as the *ahijado*, and the sponsors are referred to as the *padrinos* of the object. The godparents and the parents, kinsmen, or owners of the mediating entity refer and address each other as *compadre* ("cofather") and *comadre* ("comother"). This terminological triad obtains for all *compadrazgo* types, although some significant terms of address and reference vary with type, as does the extension of the ritual kinship terminology.

The origins of *compadrazgo* can be traced to the fourth century CE, when ritual sponsorship became a requirement accompanying the main Christian rites of passage. Sidney Mintz and Eric Wolf (1950) traced the evolution and changing functions of the institution through the Dark Ages, the Middle Ages, and the Renaissance into modern times. Sponsors were chosen to stand *in loco parentis* for baptism, marriage, and other occasions in the life cycle. Thus, the basic relationship established by *compadrazgo* was between *padrinos* and *ahijados*, and in most of Europe this has remained basically unchanged until the present. This is the form of *compadrazgo* that was introduced in Mesoamerica by the mendicant friars in the sixteenth century.

Baptism was the first *compadrazgo* type that was introduced, followed by marriage, confirmation, and death and burial. These four sacramental types were the model of *compadrazgo*, which within three generations began to expand and to acquire a much more complex form and a different emphasis. By the middle of the seventeenth century, *compadrazgo* was well on its way to becoming what the institution is today: a complex system of relationships which transcends its strictly religious functions and acquires important social features resembling those of real kinship. This transformation was entailed by two main processes. First, there was a shift from the *padrinos–ahijados* relationship to the *compadres–compadres* relationship as the main feature of the institution. The former did not disappear, but the latter acquired much more structural significance, endowing *compadrazgo* with a component like real kinship. The second process was the continuous expansion of *compadrazgo* beyond the original sacramental types; this continued until the twentieth century and ultimately acquired the constitution of a system.

First, *compadrazgo* was extended to include individual religious-ceremonial events, such as giving a child a scapulary, presenting a child in church at the age of three, or cleansing a sick person. Until about 1630, the mediating entities were persons; from then on, *compadrazgo* was extended to images, objects, and occasions. This was a radical change and became fully institutionalized by the beginning of the nineteenth century. The most salient types were blessing of a saint or image, coronation of the Virgin, blessing of the child Jesus at home and in church, and erection of a cross as an intensification act. Throughout the nineteenth century, *compadrazgo* was extended to more social and material occasions: setting the foundations of a house, blessing a new house, sacralizing the finding of a twinned fruit or vegetable, and other events. The last step in the evolution of *compadrazgo* took place in the twentieth century, when several types were added to the system: graduation, sacralizing the celebrations of silver and gold wedding anniversaries, celebrating the handsel (first use) of new utensils, and other occasions.

By about 1970, *compadrazgo* had become a complex system including more than thirty-five types. There is a good deal of variation in the form and incidence of *compadrazgo* in Mesoamerica, and what follows is a summary of its most common parameters of variation.

All sacramental types are present in most Indian and rural *mestizo* communities and in urban environments. The highest incidence of *compadrazgo* involves social or religious occasions; probably the types of lowest incidence are those in which the mediating entities are material objects or secular occasions. Thus, in addition to sacramental types, most communities have from five to ten nonsacramental types. The average Indian or rural *mestizo* community has ten to fifteen *compadrazgo* types, with *mestizos* tending to have more than Indians. In urban environments, the average is probably ten types. With small variations, the main structural features of *compadrazgo* in all communities are essentially the same: the basic relationships, ritual kinship terminology and behavior, and the nature of the mediating entities. The functions of *compadrazgo*, however, may vary significantly according to the degree of modernization and secularization and the rural-urban cleavage. To understand and explain the institution, it is useful to detail its main structural and functional features for comparative purposes.

Recognizing the overlap of *compadrazgo* and kinship is essential for understanding the functions and structure of *compadrazgo*. Of special significance is whether individuals choose *compadres* mainly from among their kinsmen or from nonrelated people. This and related practices have implications for assessing the dimensions of egalitarian versus stratified, sacred versus secular, and other features. Given the similarities, overlaps, and spheres of action of *compadrazgo* and kinship, it is important to describe and analyze ritual kinship terminology and behavior in order to position *compadrazgo* properly and refine its analysis.

There is a significant dichotomy between egalitarian-horizontal and stratified-vertical *compadrazgo* which characterizes a wide spectrum of *compadrazgo* systems, both communally and regionally. It determines the basic nature of *compadrazgo*: as a sacred context, it emphasizes reciprocity, exchange, and the absence of outright maximization; and as a secular context, it stresses the maximization of social, economic, and even political goals. There are, of course, intermediate systems.

The symmetrical or asymmetrical structure of a *compadrazgo* system interacts with the previous dichotomy.

Symmetrical *compadrazgo* is almost always egalitarian-horizontal and sacred, and mostly realized in rural environments; asymmetrical *compadrazgo*, in contrast, is mostly associated with stratified-vertical and secular situations, usually in urban environments.

Prescriptive, preferential, and optional *compadrazgo* types are distinguished. The complexity and elaboration of *compadrazgo* systems in Mesoamerica vary significantly, particularly with reference to the rural-urban cleavage. This variation is most apparent in the contexts and constraints underlying the processes of recruitment, selection, and establishment of *compadrazgo* relationships.

The distinction of private-individual versus public-communal *compadrazgo* types, more than any other salient structural feature, exemplifies the complexity, pervasiveness, and communal and regional importance of the institution. The realization of public-communal types is one of the main mechanisms that connect the community to the wider world. For example, an important public figure outside the community may become the *padrino* of an entire primary school graduating class.

Compadrazgo choice and its situational contexts are intimately related to the wider context of community culture and society. The structure of *compadrazgo* choice and the situational contexts in which it is embedded illustrate how *compadrazgo* is articulated with other systems and domains at both communal and regional levels. It is perhaps the most significant determiner of the main function of an instance of *compadrazgo*: Does it serve to expand social relationships, to consolidate relationships already established, to complement kinship relationships, or some other end?

Compadrazgo in Mesoamerica is still a vigorous and widespread institution in innumerable rural and urban contexts, and future ethnographic or comparative studies should recognize the domains suggested here. In rural contexts, *compadrazgo* complements kinship and sometimes rivals it; it occasionally has become more important than kinship in the social, religious, and even economic organization of a community. In urban, national environments, *compadrazgo* may have similar functions, but it is more significant as a means of organizing patronage and political action.

[*See also* Institutions, Projects, and Meetings.]

BIBLIOGRAPHY

Anderson, Gallatin. "Il Comparaggio: The Italian Godparenthood Complex." *Southwestern Journal of Anthropology* 13 (1971), 635–661. Compares Mediterranean ritual kinship sponsorship with *compadrazgo* in Mesoamerica.

Deshon, Shirley K. "Compadrazgo on a Henequen Hacienda in Yucatan: A Structural Re-evaluation." *American Anthropologist* 65 (1963), 574–583. The first study of *compadrazgo* that used quantitative data to illustrate the mechanisms of choice and the generation of *compadrazgo* links.

Foster, George M. "Cofradía and Compadrazgo in Spain and Spanish America." *Southwestern Journal of Anthropology* 9 (1953), 1–28. Good comparison of the institution in Spain and Latin America, emphasizing the differences between ritual kinship sponsorship and *compadrazgo*.

Gillin, John P. *Moche: A Peruvian Coastal Community*. Institute of Social Anthropology, 3. Washington, D.C., 1945. One of the earliest publications containing a rather complete description of *compadrazgo* types; a useful source for comparative purposes.

Gudeman, Stephen. "The *Compadrazgo* as a Reflection of the Natural and Spiritual Self." *Proceedings of the Royal Anthropological Institute* (1971), 45–71. Contains some insightful interpretations on the ideological and ideational configuration of *compadrazgo*.

Ingham, John M. "The Asymmetrical Implications of Godparenthood in Tlayacapan, Morelos." *Man* n.s. 5 (1970), 281–289. Makes some important points about the structure and implications of *compadrazgo*.

Mintz, Sidney W., and Eric R. Wolf. "An Analysis of Ritual Co-parenthood (Compadrazgo)." *Southwestern Journal of Anthropology* 6 (1950), 341–368. Deservedly the best-known source on *compadrazgo*; contains both ethnographic and ethnohistorical analyses, the latter an elegant account of the origin and evolution of the institution from classical times to the present, including some of its pre-Hispanic antecedents in Mesoamerica.

Nutini, Hugo G. *Ritual Kinship: Ideological and Structural Integration of the Compadrazgo System in Rural Tlaxcala*. Princeton, 1984. Exhaustive structural and functional analysis of *compadrazgo*, including ideology, comparative dimensions, and regional and wider socioreligious and economic implications.

Nutini, Hugo G., and Betty Bell. *Ritual Kinship: The Structure and Historical Development of the Compadrazgo System in Rural Tlaxcala*. Princeton, 1980. Describes thirty-one regional *compadrazgo* types, places the institution in the context of community culture and society, and provides a historical account of the institution from the Spanish conquest to the present.

Paul, Benjamin D. "Ritual Kinship: With Special Reference to Godparenthood in Middle America." University of Chicago Microfilm Series, 1686. Chicago, 1942. The first general description of *compadrazgo* in Mesoamerica; fairly extensive account of types, functions, and activities.

Ravicz, Robert S. "Compadrinazgo." In *The Handbook of Middle American Indians*, edited by Robert Wauchope, vol. 6, pp. 238–252. Austin, Tex., 1967. One of the best comprehensive assessments of *compadrazgo* in Mesoamerica; illustrates the differences between ritual kinship sponsorship and *compadrazgo*.

Sayres, William C. "Ritual Kinship and Negative Affect." *American Sociological Review* 21 (1956), 348–352. Demonstrates that *compadrazgo*'s extreme social control of aggressive behavior may also produce disruptive and disharmonious results.

Thompson, Richard A. "Structural Statistics and Structural Mechanics: An Analysis of Compadrazgo." *Southwestern Journal of Anthropology* 27 (1971), 381–403. Perhaps the most original and profitable attempt to explain *compadrazgo* selection by the use of formal and statistical techniques.

Van den Berghe, Pierre L., and Gwendoline Van den Berghe. "Compadrazgo and Class in Southern Mexico." *American Anthropologist* 68 (1966), 236–244. Able analysis of the interrelationship of regional class stratification and *compadrazgo*.

HUGO G. NUTINI

CONFESSION. The Roman Catholic sacrament of confession, or penitence, was introduced to Mesoamerica by evangelizing friars in the sixteenth century. According to doctrine, any Christian who commits a mortal sin is condemned to Hell unless he or she confesses and receives absolution from a priest. The priest assigns penances; if these are not completed before death, the soul will spend additional time in Purgatory before entering Heaven but will not be condemned. Like European Roman Catholics, indigenous Mesoamerican people were expected to confess annually during Lent, before marriage, and when near death. The number of confession manuals written in indigenous languages attests to the importance of this ritual and the challenges it presented to priests who, across a considerable linguistic and cultural divide, were expected to interrogate people about intimate details of their lives. The manuals guide priests and penitents through the mortal sins and the Ten Commandments but also often attend to such local conditions as the methods by which merchants cheated customers in the marketplaces and curing practices deemed idolatrous by the church.

Pre-Conquest Mesoamericans had some rituals of confession. In some areas, women confessed any misdeeds to their midwives in order to facilitate childbirth. A Mexica rite described in the work of the Franciscan ethnographer Bernardino de Sahagún (*Florentine Codex*; see translation by Arthur J. O. Anderson and Charles E. Dibble, Santa Fe, 1950–1982) was associated with the female divinity Tlazolteotl ("Filth Deity"), the patron of adultery, promiscuity, and immorality in general. Part of the rite entailed an oral confession directed to the trickster-like deity Tezcatlipoca. Clad only in a paper skirt, the participant performed penance at the crossroads shrine of the Cihuateteo, deified women who had died in childbirth, then left the skirt at the shrine and slipped home naked. The Franciscan Diego de Landa wrote that the Yucatec Maya confessed their sins—particularly theft, homicide, sexual misconduct, and false testimony—when they were sick or otherwise in danger, telling them to the priests or to their parents or spouses. Some contemporary Maya shamans use confession when diagnosing the cause of an illness or, in the case of the Lacandón, appeasing an offended deity.

In principle, the Roman Catholic rite of confession gave priests considerable control over indigenous people's behavior, or at least knowledge about it. The Mexican Inquisition, founded in 1571, exempted indigenous people from prosecution for religious crimes, so confession was one of the few tools priests had to seek out practices that the church deemed idolatrous or otherwise immoral. In practice, the sacrament never worked very well as a tool of doctrinal or social oversight. Many did not participate, and those who did gave notoriously "bad" confessions, from the priests' perspective: they concealed or miscounted some of their sins; they did not display adequate contrition; they did not take responsibility for acts performed when inebriated; and they would not spontaneously confess certain acts, such as premarital sex and usury, that they did not consider sinful.

Eliciting a "good" confession required considerable effort and linguistic skill, both of which priests often lacked—especially during the Lenten season, when one priest might have to confess many hundreds of individuals from several language groups. Many priests had adequate training in at least one language, typically Nahuatl in Central Mexico, but speakers of other tongues often had to confess in Nahuatl or through an interpreter, which was understandably inhibiting. Priests had little success over all in inculcating a fear of Hell among people who did not traditionally view the afterlife in terms of reward and punishment and who attributed some of their acts to superhuman forces. Moreover, native people did not view the human self as a battleground between immortal soul and corrupt flesh. Many felt fear and mistrust toward the priests, who were outsiders to their communities and sometimes corrupt and abusive—even to the point of soliciting sexual favors while confessing women. Priests attributed the indigenous people's perceived failings to their general "coarseness" and lack of theological sophistication, but the situation may more accurately be interpreted in terms of cultural differences and the unequal power relations between nonnative priests and native parishioners.

Among contemporary Mesoamerican peoples, participation in confession varies, depending on the extent of contact with priests, which is limited and sometimes hostile in rural areas, and on local attitudes, which are often negative. People influenced by the Catholic Action movement are more likely to partake of the sacraments than are practitioners of local folk Catholicism; converts to Protestantism have abandoned the rite.

[*See also* Roman Catholic Church.]

BIBLIOGRAPHY

Borremanse, Didier. "The Faith of the Real People: The Lacandón of the Chiapas Rain Forest." In *World Spirituality: An Encyclopedic History of the Religious Quest*, vol. 4, *South and Meso-American Native Spirituality*, edited by Gary H. Gossen and Miguel León-Portilla, pp. 324–351. New York, 1993. Describes contemporary Lacandón rituals of appeasing the gods, including confessions of sins.

Burkhart, Louise M. *The Slippery Earth: Nahua-Christian Moral Dialogue in Sixteenth-Century Mexico*. Tucson, Ariz., 1989. Analysis of Nahua moral concepts and the friars' attempt to adapt Christian morality into the Nahuatl language.

Klor de Alva, Jorge. "Contar vidas: La autobiografía confesional y la reconstrucción del ser nahua." *Arbor* 131 (1988), 49–78. Examines the implications of sacramental confession for Nahua views of the self and relates the introduction of the rite to colonial domination.

Lewis, Oscar. *Life in a Mexican Village: Tepoztlán Restudied.* Urbana, 1963. Gives some information about participation in confession and other sacraments for a Nahuatl- and Spanish-speaking village in Central Mexico.

Maurer Avalos, Eugenio. "The Tzeltal Maya–Christian Synthesis." In *World Spirituality: An Encyclopedic History of the Religious Quest*, vol. 4, *South and Meso-American Native Spirituality*, edited by Gary H. Gossen and Miguel León-Portilla, pp. 228–250. New York, 1993. Discusses Tzeltal rejection of Catholic confession and use of traditional confession during curing rites.

Ricard, Robert. *The Spiritual Conquest of Mexico.* Translated by Lesley Byrd Simpson. Berkeley, 1966. Although its "spiritual conquest" model is outdated, it is a useful source of information on the friars' evangelizing practices and discusses their introduction of confession.

Taylor, William B. *Magistrates of the Sacred: Priests and Parishioners in Eighteenth-Century Mexico.* Stanford, 1996. Detailed study of relations between indigenous villagers and parish priests, including information on participation in and attitudes toward confession.

LOUISE M. BURKHART

CONQUEST NARRATIVES. Historical writing about the Spanish conquest of Mesoamerica began during the Conquest era itself, and ever since, this event has held the interest of scholars and general readers alike. Interpretations of the Conquest are shaped by the individual biases of the writers and by the politics and culture of their eras. The conquest of Central Mexico is recounted in a large number of sixteenth-century narratives. Firsthand accounts by Spaniards and Indians, victors and vanquished, allies and antagonists form the basis of the primary documentation. These accounts include participant accounts by both Spaniards and indigenous people, histories by Spanish friars based on indigenous sources, and histories from both sides of indigenous city-states actively engaged in the military conflict. Indigenous sources are both alphabetic and pictorial, with alphabetic texts in Spanish as well as in Nahuatl and Maya. Spanish and Indian interpretations of the Conquest were written in the Colonial era, and the Conquest became an important issue in Mexico after political independence in the nineteenth century.

The documentation from Spaniards consists of pleas from conquerors to the Crown for rewards for their services (*benemérito* petitions), a standard Spanish genre. The Crown did not directly fund expeditions; instead, it issued licenses to prominent men to explore, conquer, and settle territory in Spain's name. Participants provided their own arms and supplies and were not paid wages, but instead received a share of the wealth seized in the conquered territory. The leader of an expedition usually became the governor of the territory. In order to secure material rewards, conquerors drafted petitions describing their contributions to the conquest. Thus, the construction of conquest narratives was usually special pleading.

The best-known accounts are from Central Mexico, especially those of Fernando Cortés and of Bernal Díaz del Castillo, author of *The True History of the Conquest of New Spain.* Cortés's accounts were widely circulated in Europe contemporaneously with the Conquest. They are not only part of the historical record but also shaped it. His failure to give credit to other participants contributed to the factionalism characterizing post-Conquest New Spain. Díaz del Castillo's *True History* is a gripping, detailed chronicle, begun initially as a *benemérito* petition and finished in the mid-sixteenth century. He consciously wrote a history of the Conquest. In his own view, he was countering the inaccuracies of Francisco López de Gómara's 1552 panegyric to Cortés. Díaz's classic circulated in New Spain during his own lifetime but was not published until 1632. He had a phenomenal memory for detail—or could create convincing fiction where memory faltered.

Most Spanish participant accounts stress the chronicler's personal valor and deeds, but virtually all give a providential interpretation of the Conquest. For these men, history was not a realization of human will and desires, but rather the will of God, Divine Providence, in accord with the Christian worldview. They considered themselves instruments of God's will; though the outcome was difficult to achieve, it was in accordance with divine plans.

The historical record of the Conquest includes a number of Indian accounts, including *benemérito* petitions by the Spaniards' allies and narratives by defeated Indians. There are alphabetic accounts by Nahua, Maya, and Purépecha (Tarascans) of Michoacán. Several chronicles in Spanish from the Nahua or Maya perspective are from secondary city-states or particular families allied to the Spaniards. There also exist several chronicles of the Conquest by the vanquished, written in Spanish, Nahuatl, or Maya.

Spaniards' indigenous allies in the Central Mexican towns of Tlaxcala, Tetzcoco, and Huexotzinco wrote *benemérito* accounts for individual families and entire indigenous communities. Authors of such histories in the mid to late sixteenth century were not military participants but sought special recognition for their towns' services to the Crown. These men had cultural and biological links to the Spanish world in that they were technically *mestizos* (of mixed Indian-European descent), but they were part of the indigenous culture and acted as advocates for their towns. The most prominent was Diego Muñoz Camargo, author of the *Historia de Tlaxcala* and the *Relación geográfica*. Similar in type is Juan Bautista de Pomar's account for Tetzcoco.

A descendant of Tetzcoco's last king, Don Fernando de Alva Ixtlilxochitl, wrote a lengthy chronicle based on indigenous sources. It is noteworthy for its strident condemnation of Spanish cruelties, reminiscent of the anti-conqueror rhetoric of Bartolomé de las Casas. From Alva Ixtlilxochitl's viewpoint, all his kinsmen's and city's aid to the Spaniards not only resulted in no material reward but also brought dishonor in their own eyes. This account did not circulate widely in the Colonial era, but it was published in the early nineteenth century, as Mexicans began reinterpreting the Spanish conquest.

In the mid-sixteenth century, Spanish mendicants recorded indigenous accounts of the Conquest, particularly by the losers, as part of their program to study indigenous culture and facilitate the Indians' conversion to Christianity. The Conquest was the major political event for Indians who actively fought the Spaniards; the conflict also had religious significance for both victors and vanquished. The Franciscan Bernardino de Sahagún recorded an entire chronicle of the Conquest from the Tenochtitlan-Tlatelolco perspective in the *Florentine Codex* (1576) in Nahuatl and Spanish. He revised it in 1585 to give a more pro-Spanish perspective. Another mendicant friar, the Dominican Diego Durán, wrote the *History of the Indies of New Spain* (1581). Both men dealt with the Conquest in Central Mexico, basing their accounts on indigenous informants and written sources. When they began collecting information in the mid-1550s, the intellectual climate favored such investigations, but by the time they finished in the late sixteenth century, it was hostile to implicit or explicit criticisms of the conquerors' actions. Durán's *History* lauds Cortés, as does Sahagún's 1585 revision. Neither friar's work saw publication during his lifetime. For the Maya region, the Franciscan Diego de Landa's *Relación de las cosas de Yucatán* has some material from the indigenous viewpoint. For the Purépecha, the Franciscan Martín Jesús de la Coruña's account, *The Chronicles of Michoacán*, presents the indigenous view of the Conquest without editorial comment.

Some indigenous accounts mention omens of the Conquest—earthquakes, comets, the birth of monsters, and other events interpreted as foretelling change. Omens appear mainly in accounts from defeated groups. Modern scholars conjecture that Indians were attempting to explain their defeat to themselves. The Spaniards had a religious interpretation of the Conquest, and so did the Indians. Their notions of fate and their initial belief that the Spaniards were gods may have helped the Mexica and other indigenous peoples to come to terms with their catastrophic defeat.

Alphabetic texts in Nahuatl and Maya, written by and for indigenous readers, have recently gained prominence. Early mendicants taught a few indigenous men how to write their own languages alphabetically. From the mid-sixteenth century to the end of the Colonial period, alphabetic texts in Nahuatl and Maya were written for indigenous consumption, including accounts of the Conquest. Accounts appeared as early as the mid-sixteenth century; the *Annals of Tlatelolco* date from as early as 1528. This work, written only in Nahuatl, extols Tlatelolco's valor in resisting the Spaniards and asserts that its warriors (and even its women) were more active in resisting the Spaniards than the men of Tenochtitlan. The Tlatelolcans attribute their failure to fate or to turncoat or cowardly allies (or both), and assign themselves a valorous role in the face of all odds.

The larger pre-Hispanic genre of annals—year-by-year lists of important events, including natural phenomena, such as earthquakes, comets, and droughts—provides additional material on the Conquest. Several annals exist that include the years of the Conquest, but these do not give a high profile to the invasion. This absence may indicate the low importance those events held for the writers' towns. Even the account directed to the Nahua by a grandson of Motecuhzoma II, Don Hernando de Alvarado Tezozomoc, only briefly mentions the Conquest. However, the annals written or copied by the seventeenth-century, Jesuit-educated Chimalpahin have much information on it. Annals also exist for the Maya region, written alphabetically in Maya.

Primordial titles, an indigenous written genre of the mid-Colonial period, often include information about a town's role in the Conquest. These documents were histories and descriptions of a town's territory, often written to assert as true claims not previously recorded by local historians or entered into the official colonial record. These accounts often gloss over the town's resistance to the Spaniards or make claims of having allied with them, whether or not the town actually did.

The Nahua and Maya had written historical traditions in pictorials before the arrival of Europeans, so maintaining it in the Colonial period was an extension of previous practice. Alphabetic texts applied a new technology that was enthusiastically adopted by indigenous scribes. Pictorials dealing with the conquest of Central Mexico usually depict key events—the march to Tenochtitlan, the meeting of Cortés and Motecuhzoma, the Alvarado massacre, and the final siege. Doña Marina, Cortés's cultural translator and consort, is prominently shown in several pictorial sources. The most famous set of pictorials is the *Lienzo de Tlaxcala*, known only from later copies, but pictorials with the same subject matter and in the same style were published in Diego Muñoz Camargo's *Historia de Tlaxcala* and his 1581 *Relación geográfica*. Both Sahagún's and Durán's accounts also contain pictorials. Other Central Mexican pictorials include the *Codex Telleriano-Remensis* and *Codex Vaticanus A* (two versions of the same sixteenth-century pictorial text), the *Codex Aubin*, and the *Codex Azcatitlan*. For the Purépecha peoples of west-central Mexico, the *Chronicles of Michoacán*, the Conquest is shown pictorially, including omens and a request for help from Motecuhzoma. There are no known pictorials from the Maya area.

The conquest of Central Mexico continued to fascinate not only Spaniards in Mexico and elsewhere but also other Europeans. For English-language readers, the literature on the conquest of Mexico was enriched by translations of Spanish accounts; Bartolomé de las Casas's *A Short History of the Destruction of the Indies* was published in translation as early as 1585. It fueled anti-Spanish sentiments strongly rooted in political and religious rivalries. The eighteenth century saw renewed English interest in the Conquest, particularly as they expanded their own territories into the Spanish-controlled Caribbean. In 1753, Don Antonio de Solís (1610–1686), historiographer of the Spanish Crown, published his history. In 1767, when the Crown expelled the Jesuits from its territories, Francisco Clavigero was exiled to Italy along with fellow Jesuits; there, he wrote (in Italian) a history of Mexico, *Storia antigua de Mexico*, including the Conquest. It was published in England in 1787.

In early post-Independence Mexico, creole nationalists, seeking to reinterpret the Spanish period, began publishing studies of the Conquest with a decided anti-European bias. Nationalists from Independence onward glorified the indigenous resistance to the Spaniards and denigrated their Indian allies as traitors. Nationalists and *indigenistas* recognized the value of Book 12 of Sahagún's *Florentine Codex*, but his 1585 revision containing pro-Spanish material was pushed into the shadows. Particularly affected by nationalist revisionism was the role of Doña Marina, who was depicted as turning against her "own" people (she was not Tenochca). One exception to the nationalist embargo on lauding indigenous allies was Alva Ixtlilxochitl's anti-Spanish account, extensively published in Mexico under various titles, including *Horribles crueldades de los conquistadores de México* (1829). William Hickling Prescott's *History of the Conquest of Mexico* (1843) had great impact on English speakers' perceptions of the Conquest in the nineteenth and twentieth centuries. The most recent trend in studies of the Conquest is the inclusion of Indian perspectives, whether Spanish allies or their opponents. As pictorials and alphabetic texts in Indian languages are made available, multifaceted interpretations of the Conquest become possible.

[*See also* Conquests, *article on* Spanish Conquest; Cortés, Fernando; Díaz del Castillo, Bernal; Durán, Diego; Muñoz Camargo, Diego.]

BIBLIOGRAPHY

Alva Ixtlilxochitl, Fernando. *Ally of Cortés*: *Account 13 of the Coming of the Spaniards and the Beginning of Evangelical Law*. Translated by Douglas K. Ballentine. El Paso, 1969.

Bricker, Victoria. *The Indian Christ, the Indian King*: *The Historical Substrate of Maya Myth and Ritual*. Austin, Tex., 1981.

Burrus, Ernest J. "Religious Chroniclers and Historians: A Summary with Annotated Bibliography." In *Guide to Ethnohistorical Sources, Part II*, edited by Howard F. Cline, *Handbook of Middle American Indians*, vol. 13, pp. 138–185. Austin, 1973.

Chimalpahin, Antonio Muñon. *Codex Chimalpahin*. Translated and edited by Arthur J. O. Anderson and Susan Schroeder. Norman, Okla., 1997.

Clavigero, Francisco. *The History of Mexico*. New York, 1979.

Cline, Howard F. "Selected Nineteenth-Century Mexican Writers on Ethnohistory." In *Guide to Ethnohistorical Studies, Part II*, edited by Howard F. Cline, *Handbook of Middle American Indians*, vol. 13, pp. 370–422. Austin, 1973.

Codex Azcatitlan. Introduction by Michel Graulich, commentary by Robert H. Barlow. Paris, 1995.

Codex Telleriano-Remensis: *Ritual Divination, and History in a Pictorial Aztec Manuscript*. Edited by Eloise Quiñones Keber. Austin, 1995.

Cortés, Hernando. *Five Letters to the Emperor*. Translated with introduction by J. Bayard Morris. New York, 1969.

Coruña, Martín de Jesús de la. *The Chronicles of Michoacán*. Translated and edited by Eugene R. Craine and Reginald C. Reindorp. Norman, Okla., 1970.

Díaz del Castillo, Bernal. *True History of the Conquest of New Spain*.

Durán, Diego. *The History of the Indies of New Spain*. Translated and annotated, with an introduction by Doris Heyden. Norman, Okla., 1994.

Fuentes, Patricia de. *The Conquistadors*: *First-Person Accounts of the Conquest of Mexico*. Edited and translated by Patricia de Fuentes. Norman, Okla., 1999.

Glass, John B. "A Survey of Native Middle American Pictorial Manuscripts." In *Guide to Ethnohistorical Sources, Part 3*, edited by Howard F. Cline, *Handbook of Middle American Indians*, vol. 14, pp. 3–80. Austin, 1975.

Glass, John B., with Donald Robertson. "A Census of Native Middle American Pictorial Manuscripts." In *Guide to Ethnohistorical Sources, Part 3*, edited by Howard F. Cline, *Handbook of Middle American Indians*, vol. 14, pp. 81–252. Austin, Tex., 1975.

Himmerich y Valencia, Robert. *The Encomenderos of New Spain, 1521–1555*. Austin, 1991.

Klor de Alva, J. Jorge, H. B. Nicholson, and Eloise Quiñones Kleber. *The Work of Bernardino de Sahagún, Pioneer Ethnographer of Sixteenth-Century Mexico*. Albany, 1988.

Landa, Diego de. *Landa's Relación de las cosas de Yucatán*. Papers of the Peabody Museum of American Archaeology and Ethnology, Harvard University. Cambridge, Mass., 1941.

Landa, Diego de. *Yucatán before and after the Conquest*. Translated with notes by William Gates. New York, 1978.

Lockhart, James, ed. and trans. *We People Here*: *Nahuatl Accounts of the Conquest of Mexico*, Repertorium Columbianum, 1. Berkeley, 1993.

López de Gómara, Francisco. *Cortés*: *The Life of the Conqueror by His Secretary*. Translated and edited by Lesley Byrd Simpson. Berkeley, 1964.

Muñoz Camargo, Diego. *Relaciones geográficas del siglo xvi: Tlaxcala.* Edited by René Acuña. Mexico City, 1984.

Prescott, William Hickling. *The Conquest of Mexico.* New York, 1843.

Restall, Matthew, ed. and trans. *Maya Conquistador.* Boston, 1998.

Sahagún, Bernardino de. *Florentine Codex: Book 12—The Conquest of Mexico.* Translated by Arthur J. O. Anderson and Charles E. Dibble. Salt Lake City, 1975.

Sahagún, Bernardino de. *The Conquest of New Spain, 1585 Revision.* Translated by Howard F. Cline, introduction and notes by Sarah Cline. Salt Lake City, 1989.

Solís, Antonio de. *The History of the Conquest of Mexico by the Spaniards.* Translated by Thomas Townsend. 3rd ed. 2 vols. New York, 1973.

Vázquez de Tapia, Bernardino. *Relación de méritos y servicios del conquistador.* Mexico City, 1972.

Warren, J. Benedict. "An Introductory Survey of Secular Writings in the European Tradition on Colonial Middle America, 1503–1818." In *Guide to Ethnohistorical Sources, Part II,* edited by Howard F. Cline, *Handbook of Middle American Indians,* vol. 13. Austin, 1973.

SARAH CLINE

CONQUESTS. [*This entry comprises two articles. The first article provides a historical overview of Mesoamerican conquests in pre-Hispanic times; the second article assesses the stages and processes of the Spanish conquest of Meso-american communities. For related discussions, see* Conquest Narratives; Cortés, Fernando; *and* Warfare.]

Pre-Hispanic Period

The term *conquest* can be defined as "the process of taking possession by violent means," more simply, "to acquire by force." The conquest of people and their territory can be temporary or permanent. Archaeologists have become increasingly interested in conquest, because as more sites are excavated, evidence for violence and subjugation is being found throughout the ancient world. Mesoamericanists are also assessing the extent to which warfare shaped the rise, maintenance, and fall of the various ancient societies; they see conquest as only one of several factors that shaped them, including competition for resources, demography, labor and social organization, political structure, economic interaction, and religious practices.

When Mesoamerican societies became chiefdoms, intervillage conflict seems to have become widespread. Some of the earliest evidence for conflict—the burning of villages and the sacrifice of prisoners—was dated to the first millennium BCE. As early as 600 BCE, sacrificed prisoners were carved in stone in the Valley of Oaxaca. By 300 BCE, men were buried in mass graves in Belize. Such archaeological evidence of conflict comes as no surprise, since anthropologists have long noted that raiding was endemic to contemporary chiefly societies. Yet raiding—which includes the burning of enemy villages and the kill-

ing of their defenders, but usually not the annexation of their land—was more characteristic of chiefdoms than was conquest. With the rise of Mesoamerican states between 150 BCE and 300 CE, raiding on a large scale was accompanied by conquest. With increased populations and tribute collection to support a bureaucracy, states usually have armies that can occupy and retain the lands of the defeated. Nevertheless, small-scale conquests at irregular intervals were more typical of Mesoamerican states than was widespread conquest. True imperial conquest on the scale of the Aztec Empire was rare. Only occasionally did the archaic states embark on major campaigns of territorial expansion that incorporated dozens of linguistic groups into a large empire. The archaeological evidence for territorial conquest and large-scale warfare increased as states were formed, and as populations and armies grew. By the first millennium CE, expansionist states succeeded in annexing new territories, but such direct control rarely endured for more than a few centuries.

Researchers are increasingly interested in the motives for warfare, but it is rare to discern them without written texts. Only after hieroglyphic writing and pictographs were deciphered was there any idea about the motives for warfare in Mesoamerica; these included the elimination of rivals for the throne, revenge for alleged insults, and retribution for a previous defeat. Other causes may have been border disagreements; acquisition of land, goods, resources, and labor; and the rebellion of subordinate peoples to free themselves from onerous tribute demands.

One Mixtec pictorial convention for "conquest" was to show a spear thrust into the upper right side of a hill. This Mixtec place, "Hill of the Mask," was conquered by 8 Deer Tiger Claw in 1044 CE. *Drawing courtesy of Joyce Marcus.*

Cycles of Conquest. Since warfare is not continuous, but tends to fluctuate over time, it has recurring and alternating cycles of expansion and contraction, reconquest and retreat. Many Mesoamericanists believe that such first-generation states as Teotihuacan and Monte Albán arose after one member of a group of chiefdoms subjugated its neighbors, establishing the latter as subject provinces of the larger polity. Archaeological evidence includes the sacrifice of hundreds of males in military paraphernalia (at Teotihuacan), as well as the building of defensive walls and the listing of incorporated regions (at Monte Albán).

The transition from chiefdom to state was more rapid in some regions than others—as was the later decline of states. New states might endure for a few hundred years or for less than a century. When they collapsed, they lost many of the subject polities they had incorporated. Following their collapse, such large states did not become chiefdoms but tended to retain their organizations as small states. They might then regroup and expand into the lands of other polities, forging second-generation states.

Maya conquests. The Maya portrayed "prisoner galleries" in carvings and depicted their rulers treading on the bodies of captives. There are so many Maya texts and scenes documenting warfare that it is amazing that earlier scholars perpetuated the idea that the Maya were a peaceful people. Battles were recorded in texts carved from 300 to 900 CE at many Classic Maya sites, including Tikal, Palenque, Yaxchilán, Piedras Negras, Quiriguá, Caracol, Naranjo, and Seibal. Even for the era before Maya writing, there is archaeological evidence in the form of fortifications, mass graves, and militaristic iconography, suggesting that warfare had become important.

Mixtec conquests. Although the Mixtec region of the Mexican states of Oaxaca and Puebla has a very long archaeological sequence, little is known about Mixtec conquests before the Postclassic period (900–1500 CE). By then, they were being recorded in the deerhide books now called codices. Such conquests usually involved the hereditary lords, who subjugated one or more towns. In the codices, "conquest" was conveyed by depicting an arrow thrust into a hill or place-sign; that pictorial convention had a counterpart in the Mixtec language, because one Mixtec expression for conquest was "to put an arrow into the lands of another." A second expression for conquest was "to burn the town"; its pictorial counterpart showed red flames attached to a hill sign. A third Mixtec depiction of conquest involved a victorious ruler grasping the hair of a defeated lord. (Grasping the hair of a defeated rival was a convention also used by the Maya, Aztec, and ancient Andeans, as well as other New World peoples.)

The most impressive conquests of any Mixtec lord were

Carved stone monument (c.50 BCE) from the archaeological site of Izapa, Mexico. The victor (*at right*) holds the decapitated head of a high-status victim, whose spurting blood is stylized as precious beads and long feathers. Witnessing this event is another high-status individual who is being carried in an elaborate litter. *Drawing courtesy of Joyce Marcus.*

those of the eleventh-century ruler 8 Deer Tiger Claw, who succeeded in conquering about a hundred towns, temporarily unifying the Mixtec Highlands and Mixtec Coast into a single large state. According to the codices, 8 Deer began life as the son of the second wife of the lord of Tilantongo; as such, he was outranked by his older half-brother who was the son of his father's first wife. In 1030 CE, when 8 Deer was nineteen and his half-brother was thirty-three, their father died and the half-brother assumed the throne of Tilantongo; 8 Deer assumed the rulership of a lesser town, Tututepec on the Pacific coast of Oaxaca, to which his mother had ties. From his coastal base, 8 Deer established an expansionist militaristic state, attacking such neighboring peoples as the Chatino and Zapotec. In 1048, learning of the death of his half-brother, 8 Deer was able to succeed him and, for a time, ruled from both Tututepec and Tilantongo, linking Lowlands and Highlands. He also continued to conquer other towns until, in 1063, he lost a battle to two rivals who had allied against him. At that time, 8 Deer was taken prisoner and sacrificed, and his large state fragmented into many smaller polities (*cacicazgos*).

Tarascan conquests. The Tarascan kingdom had an army so powerful that it usually won its battles against the Aztec Empire. Each time the Aztec tried to expanded westward, into the buffer zone that separated them from the Tarascan realm, they were beaten back. Documents record that in 1480 CE, the Tarascans were aided by their neighbors, the Matlatzinca, to produce a fighting unit of fifty thousand that defeated thirty-two thousand Aztec warriors; thirty thousand Aztec were killed. In 1489, to protect their eastern border, the Tarascans established a series of forts stretching from the Lerma River to the Balsas River basin. They placed loyal men at these forts and controlled them from their capital, Tzintzuntzan. In 1515, during a major incursion, they again defeated the Aztec.

Zapotec conquests. One of the longest historical sequences to show the importance of conquest is that of the Zapotec. During the formation of the Zapotec state (whose capital was Monte Albán in the Valley of Oaxaca), three hundred stones were carved, each depicting a sacrificed prisoner. From 150 BCE to 100 CE, the Zapotec expanded their territory, incorporating areas beyond the Valley of Oaxaca, by conquest, colonization, and political alliance. During the centuries following Zapotec state formation, many outlying provinces regained their autonomy. Still later, episodes of warfare and conquest occurred, but no later Zapotec kingdom was as territorially extensive as the early one centered at Monte Albán.

A renowned battle in Zapotec history was fought at Guiengola in the Isthmus of Tehuantepec. There, the Zapotec, under their ruler Cocijoeza, battled the Aztec to a stalemate. To formalize a truce between them, a marriage was arranged between the Zapotec ruler and an Aztec princess. Arranging such marriages was intended to reduce the likelihood of future warfare; this marriage made Cocijoeza the son-in-law of the Aztec ruler Ahuitzotl.

Spanish Conquest of the Aztec. The sixteenth-century Colonial-era accounts make the Aztec Empire into Mesoamerica's most "warlike" society. Archaeological evidence shows, however, that the Tarascan, Zapotec, Maya, Mixtec, and others were also interested in militaristic expansion; the territorial extent of the Aztec Empire was just far more extensive than any other when the Spaniards arrived. In the preceding century, the Aztec had expanded against their weaker neighbors but were unable to conquer their most powerful rivals, the Tlaxcalans and Tarascans. The Aztec had then isolated and worked around these unconquered rivals.

The Spanish conquest was led by Fernando Cortés, who in 1519 brought with him about four hundred men and sixteen horses. After landing on the Veracruz coast, Cortés acquired help from three sources: (1) Gerónimo de Aguilar, a Spaniard who had been shipwrecked near the Yucatán Peninsula, married a Maya woman, and learned the indigenous strategies of Mesoamerican warfare; (2) Malinche, an indigenous woman who spoke Nahuatl and Mayan and who later learned Spanish; and (3) thousands of Tlaxcalan warriors, bitter enemies of the Aztec, who were willing to fight beside Cortés. Aiding the Spaniards in their conquest of the Aztec was smallpox, an Old World disease that led to epidemics and the death of hundreds of thousands of Mesoamericans. The Spaniards had such European weapons as cannons, crossbows, steel swords, and metal lances, as well as insider knowledge, from informants, who told Cortés the "situational ethics" or conventions of Aztec warfare. The Spaniards learned from the Tlaxcalans that the Aztec would surrender if their ruler Motecuhzoma (often written Montezuma) was taken prisoner or killed. Capturing the Aztec ruler thus became their goal.

At first, the Spaniards were not regarded as an enemy by the Aztec, since they failed to follow the Mesoamerican custom of sending ambassadors to declare war. From the Aztec perspective, true enemies would declare war, then engage the Aztec in battle in an open place away from their capital city. Since the Spaniards had done neither of these things, they were not considered a threat, and they were allowed to enter the capital city. Furthermore, it was harvest time (November), and most Aztec men were busy in their fields; the traditional enemies would not have engaged in war during that season because they, too, had a rule of "no war during harvest time."

Within a week of entering the Aztec capital of Tenochtitlan, the Spaniards were able to take Motecuhzoma prisoner. To resolve the situation, the Aztec ruler offered Cortés one of his daughters in marriage. This was a typical conflict-resolution strategy, but it did not work because Cortés claimed that he was already married—and, in fact, Cortés was interested in conquest and gold, not a marriage alliance with an Aztec ruler. After (allegedly) killing Motecuhzoma, the Spaniards fled to Tlaxcala, where they were embraced as friends. Later the Spaniards attacked many Aztec tributaries, thereby gaining allies who fought with them in 1521, when they returned to Tenochtitlan. The combined Spanish and Mesoamerican armies succeeded in conquering the capital on 13 August 1521.

Conclusions. Until the 1980s, researchers considered conquest to be a late phenomenon in Mesoamerica, perhaps restricted to the period 900 to 1500 CE. As a result, many working on earlier periods thought that they could ignore this topic. Increasing evidence shows that competition, conflict, and violence existed even before the formation of the first Mesoamerican states. Thus archaeologists are not only looking for evidence of burned villages, mass graves, and fortifications, but are finding such evidence. Like other sociopolitical and economic events, conquest played a role in both the creation and the destruction of Mesoamerican states.

[*See also* Warfare.]

BIBLIOGRAPHY

Berdan, Frances F., et al. *Aztec Imperial Strategies*. Washington, D.C., 1996. Comprehensive view of Aztec conquests.

Feinman, Gary M., and Joyce Marcus, eds. *Archaic States*. Santa Fe, N.M., 1998. Chapters compare New World and Old World states; some emphasize evidence for warfare (see below, Webster 1998).

Hassig, Ross. *Aztec Warfare*. Norman, Okla., 1988. Detailed synthesis.

Keeley, Lawrence H. *War before Civilization*. New York, 1996. Broad informative overview.

Marcus, Joyce. "Dynamic Cycles of Mesoamerican States." *National Geographic Research & Exploration* 8 (1992), 392–411. Evidence shows that conquest and territorial expansion were crucial in the formation of the Maya, Zapotec, and other Mesoamerican states.

Marcus, Joyce, and Kent V. Flannery. *Zapotec Civilization*. New York, 1996. Case study that shows the role of conquest in the rise of a highland Mexican state.

Smith, Mary Elizabeth. *Picture Writing from Ancient Southern Mexico*. Norman, Okla., 1973. Discusses Mixtec warfare and captive-taking.

Webster, David. "The Study of Maya Warfare: What It Tells Us about the Maya and about Maya Archaeology." In *Lowland Maya Civilization in the Eighth Century AD*, edited by Jeremy A. Sabloff and John S. Henderson, pp. 415–444. Washington, D.C., 1993. Good discussion of current views on Maya warfare.

Webster, David. "Warfare and Status Rivalry: Lowland Maya and Polynesian Comparisons." In *Archaic States*, edited by Gary M. Feinman and Joyce Marcus, pp. 311–351. Santa Fe, N.M., 1998.

JOYCE MARCUS

Spanish Conquest

The Spanish conquests of the major regions of Mesoamerica—the Aztec Empire of Central Mexico, the Tarascan Empire of Western Mexico, and the Maya peoples of the Yucatán Peninsula and Guatemala—were all organized and financed in the colonies. The last three were assembled in Central Mexico after the Spanish victory there.

Cuba's governor, Diego Velázquez, sponsored two voyages to the little-known Yucatán Peninsula and Central Mexico in 1517 and 1518. The second voyage learned of a powerful empire in the interior, and Velázquez decided to send a major expedition (*entrada*) to investigate, giving its command to his associate, Fernando Cortés. Cortés, from an established family in Medellín, Spain, journeyed to the Indies in the early 1500s. He participated in several campaigns against native societies and rose in rank and wealth. In 1511, Cortés assisted Velázquez in the conquest of Cuba. He gained an *encomienda*, became a government official, and married. Thus, by 1519 he was experienced in warfare and enjoyed some authority and

wealth, qualities needed by an expedition leader (*adelantado*).

Cortés had nearly 450 men and sixteen horses when he landed on the Yucatán coast. There he gained the services of Jerónimo de Aguilar, a longtime captive of the Maya who had learned their language. Farther along the Mexican coast, a community the Spanish defeated gave Cortés some young women as tribute. One of them, later called Doña Marina or La Malinche, spoke Nahuatl and Mayan and soon learned Spanish. Through her, the Spaniards could readily communicate with the peoples of Central Mexico. Soon she became Cortés's close companion and advisor, informing him about the beliefs, practices, and expectations of the various Mexican ethnic groups.

Initial Advance and a Spanish Defeat. On 21 April 1520, the expedition disembarked on the shore of the Aztec Empire. Its governor soon arrived to welcome them. Cortés explained that he was an envoy from a powerful foreign monarch assigned to meet the Aztec emperor, Motecuhzoma II. The Aztec treated the Spanish well, and the latter founded a town, which they named Veracruz. This action, following Spanish tradition, gave the expedition its own political identity. It enabled the participants to claim independence from Governor Velázquez and status as an autonomous body, which promptly selected Cortés as its leader. The expedition soon dispatched a ship with representatives and treasure to Spain to win the monarch's sanction.

Delegates from the province of Cempoala invited Cortés to visit, and its ruler expressed his people's dismay at the Aztecs' exorbitant tribute demands. Cortés thus began to learn of widespread dissatisfaction among the empire's subordinated provinces. He entered into an alliance with Cempoala and returned to Veracruz. There he heard of planned treason by Velázquez supporters among his men. He responded by executing the two ringleaders and ordering his ships stripped of supplies and then sunk. These actions left the expeditionaries no recourse but to join Cortés's march toward the Aztec capital of Tenochtitlan, an island city far in the interior.

The expedition soon entered the still independent but economically isolated province of Tlaxcala, whose army regularly resisted Aztec assaults. The Tlaxcalan troops attacked the Spaniards, suspecting them to be Aztec allies. They fought in the manner typical of sedentary Mesoamerican societies, assembling their army of many thousands into closed ranks in an open area away from settlements and never attempting surprise attacks. They advanced methodically, launching arrows and javelins to disrupt their opponent's formation before engaging in close combat with their primary weapon, the *macana*, a wooden club commonly edged with sharp obsidian chips. They wore little protective gear; even their shields were decorative.

The Central Mexican style of warfare stressed man-to-man fighting, with the primary goal of capturing one's opponent for later sacrifice. Although some thousands of warriors might be in battle formation, only the small fraction in the front lines engaged the enemy at any one time. The remainder served as support personnel until they moved up to fight. Finally, being hierarchically structured, these armies retreated if their commander was killed or their battle standard captured. Only rarely were actual towns assaulted, noncombatants killed, or food and crops destroyed.

The Spanish, however, came from a European tradition of more comprehensive warfare which stressed killing one's opponent and disabling his army; cities, crops, and noncombatants too were often subject to attack. Cortés's force never included more than a few harquebusiers (soldiers armed with portable guns), for they were of little use in the open field against a numerous foe. It contained a somewhat greater number of crossbowmen, but three-quarters of the force throughout the campaign was composed of infantrymen bearing swords (or pikes) and shields. These men fought in groups for greater impact and mutual assistance.

They received strong support from the small number of cavalry. The horsemen attacked in groups that could break up any opposing formation, except on broken ground or steep mountainsides. The cavalry could also outflank an opposing army and provide superior reconnaisance. Finally, it could assist beleaguered infantry units, rescuing them or providing cover while they rested. Because of these multiple advantages, in open territory even small Spanish forces were nearly invincible against native armies.

After some days of unsuccessful combat, the Tlaxcalan troops decided to support the Spanish against the Aztecs. Cortés's expedition resumed its advance, now accompanied by a few thousand Tlaxcalans. At Cholula, the next city, Cortés ordered a massacre of its leaders, claiming he needed to strike first to cripple a plan to seize the Spaniards.

On 8 November 1519, Cortés's expedition reached Tenochtitlan, where the Spaniards were welcomed on a causeway by Motecuhzoma, and housed in an imperial palace. Within a week, Cortés seized Motecuhzoma, having determined to rule the empire through him—a long-standing Spanish tactic. But the Aztec royal family soon began to disobey the emperor and to seek a replacement.

Meanwhile, Governor Velázquez had launched an expedition under Pánfilo de Narváez to take Cortés prisoner and place the undertaking once again under his authority. Cortés learned of this soon after Narváez landed and set out to intercept the expedition with about two-thirds of his force. His contingent was outnumbered at least two to one, but Cortés never planned to fight an even battle.

Some of his men entered Narváez's camp to tell his followers of the riches and people that Cortés already controlled and of his willingness to share with them. When Cortés's force rushed Narváez's camp at night, the latter's men quickly surrendered and joined the opposition.

In Tenochtitlan, meanwhile, Pedro de Alvarado, Cortés's replacement, fearing an uprising during an Aztec celebration, had struck preemptively and slaughtered many unarmed people. This sparked a massive uprising that besieged the Spanish in their palace. Even when reinforced by Cortés's returning force, the Spanish could not fight their way out of the city. Moreover, the Aztec royal family had replaced Motecuhzoma with a new emperor, Cuitlahuac. It is recorded that when the repudiated ruler appeared on the palace's roof to beg for peace, his former subjects stoned him, and he died later that night.

The Spaniards decided to sneak out of the capital around midnight of 30 June 1520. But as they bridged one of the many gaps in the causeway, they were discovered and attacked from all sides, especially from canoes on the lake. Only about one-third of the Spaniards arrived safely on the mainland. They then fought off a pursuing Aztec army and reached the safety of Tlaxcala.

Spanish Siege of Tenochtitlan. Cortés now understood that he could defeat the Aztecs only by brute military force. Three factors greatly assisted his renewed campaign. First, his expedition regularly received new men and supplies from the Caribbean colonies. By the time he began his siege, his newly equipped force had doubled in size. Second, smallpox afflicted Central Mexico; previously unknown in the Americas, it caused tremendous mortality, killing perhaps one-third of the region's population. This epidemic ravaged the Aztec and Cortés's allies alike, but the Aztec suffered greater harm, since Cuitlahuac died of it. He was succeeded by his young nephew, Cuauhtémoc. Moreover, the command structures in both civil society and the military were badly disrupted. The Spanish, however, remained an intact fighting force. Finally, Cortés now understood the fragility of the Aztec Empire and offered protection to the many provinces that abandoned it. Even Tetzcoco, a member of the Triple Alliance, sided with the invaders. These peoples provided laborers and supplies to the Spanish, though few native allies may actually have fought alongside the Spanish against the Aztec.

To control the vast lake surrounding Tenochtitlan, Cortés had his men construct thirteen brigantines, each of which could transport twenty-five men, twelve of whom rowed. When launched, these boats protected the Spanish detachments advancing up the causeways and reduced the amount of goods entering the besieged city by canoe.

Cortés divided his men, horses, and allies into three units, each of which proceeded up a causeway. He still aspired to seize Tenochtitlan intact and several times led charges directly into the city. But these all failed, and the Aztec captured and sacrificed dozens of Spaniards. More than once, Cortés himself was almost captured.

Although decimated by disease and shortages of food and water, the defenders of Tenochtitlan held out resolutely. To his dismay, Cortés realized that the capital had to be razed to be defeated. Hence, he ordered his armies to advance only a short distance each day, and to have their allies tear down all the buildings taken and use the rubble to bridge the network of waterways. The Spanish pursued this strategy for some weeks, destroying the heart of the city and driving the survivors to its outskirts. On 13 August 1521, Cuauhtémoc tried to flee by boat to the mainland, but he was captured by a brigantine. With his surrender, the Spanish victory over Central Mexico was secure. The defeated natives never again organized a major uprising against colonial rule.

Spanish Campaigns of Conquest outside Central Mexico. Several isolated mountain societies in the southern province of Oaxaca held out resolutely against repeated Spanish incursions until the 1550s, but they could not enlarge their resistance. The Spanish used terror tactics and enslavement in these campaigns, but they gained territory slowly against these determined defenders.

The powerful Tarascan kingdom, to the northwest of the Aztec Empire, suffered from the smallpox epidemic and witnessed the Spanish destruction of Tenochtitlan. The Tarascans therefore admitted a small Spanish expedition into their capital Tzintzuntzan in late 1521. They accepted the division of their society into *encomiendas* in 1523. In 1530, a rapacious Spanish governor, Nuño de Guzmán, sentenced the Tarascan ruler to death for allegedly undercutting colonial policies. With his demise, the kingdom ceased to be an intact indigenous polity.

Francisco de Montejo, one of Cortés's lieutenants, undertook the conquest of the Maya of Yucatán in 1527, assisted by his son and nephew of the same name. The peoples of the peninsula, however, lacked a centralized political structure and instead were divided into at least sixteen provinces, which were usually subdivided as well. Each had to be defeated separately, and Spanish withdrawal from a region usually resulted in a reassertion of independence. Furthermore, because they practiced slash-and-burn agriculture, Maya communities could sometimes withdraw entirely into the back country.

The Maya style of warfare also created great difficulties for the Spanish. They used the densely overgrown countryside to set ambushes for the invaders, who could not take full advantage of their horses in this terrain. The defenders also constructed barricades along narrow paths and rapidly fired arrows from cover. Maya forces often fled when a battle turned against them.

At one point, the Montejos were forced to abandon the Yucatán Peninsula, but they returned and founded the capital of Mérida in 1542. Few Spaniards ventured to the region, though, because of its lack of precious metals and the inhabitants' military capacity. Over the ensuing decades, bitter rivalries between Maya ethnic groups and decimation of the native population by epidemic diseases aided the Spanish advance. Still, at the end of the Colonial period, independent Maya communities occupied at least the eastern third of the peninsula.

Pedro de Alvarado, another of Cortés's associates, led the conquest of Guatemala beginning in 1524. The characteristics of its peoples were broadly similar to those of the Yucatán, though Guatemala was more mountainous, and the Spanish enjoyed only moderate success. Disease and native rivalries, however, again aided the invaders' cause. Guatemala City was founded in 1524, but it was relocated twice before being firmly situated in 1541 at present-day Antigua.

[*See also* Conquest Narratives; *and* Cortés, Fernando.]

REFERENCES

Chamberlain, Robert S. *The Conquest and Colonization of Yucatan, 1517–1550.* Carnegie Institution Publication 582. Washington, D.C., 1948. Narrative of the early Spanish campaign in Yucatán that reflects the perspectives of the Spanish sources.

Chance, John K. *Conquest of the Sierra: Spaniards and Indians in Colonial Oaxaca.* Norman, Okla., 1989. Considers the conquest of mountain-dwelling peoples in the South and subsequent patterns of cultural change and retention.

Clendinnen, Inga. *Ambivalent Conquests: Maya and Spaniard in Yucatan, 1517–1570.* Cambridge Latin American Studies, 61. Cambridge, 1987. Fresh, compelling perspective on the Spanish military and religious presence in early colonial Yucatán and the responses of the native peoples.

Clendinnen, Inga. "'Fierce and Unnatural Cruelty': Cortés and the Conquest of Mexico." *Representations* 33 (Winter 1991), 65–100. Explains the course and outcome of the Spanish campaign against the Aztec, based on recent findings in ethnohistory and textual analysis.

Cortés, Fernando. *Letters from Mexico.* Edited and translated by Anthony Pagden. New York, 1971. Provides the best translation and commentaries of Cortés's letters to the Spanish monarchy about his actions in Mexico.

Farriss, Nancy M. *Maya Society under Colonial Rule: The Collective Enterprise of Survival.* Princeton, 1984. Systematic, comprehensive history of the dynamic Mayan response to Spanish impositions.

Hassig, Ross. *Aztec Warfare: Imperial Expansion and Political Control.* Norman, Okla., 1988. Comprehensive, well-documented examination of Aztec military practices and imperial arrangements.

Hassig, Ross. *Mexico and the Spanish Conquest.* New York, 1994. Incorporates indigenous perspectives on the Spanish conquest and argues that Cortés's native allies were the decisive factor in defeating the Aztec.

Jones, Grant D. *Maya Resistance to Spanish Rule: Time and History on a Colonial Frontier.* Albuquerque, 1989. Innovative examination of the independent Maya communities of eastern Yucatán, their cultural perspectives and expectations, and their acceptance of certain Spanish cultural patterns.

Lockhart, James, ed. and trans. *We People Here: Nahuatl Accounts of the Conquest of Mexico*. Repertorium Columbianum, 1. Berkeley, 1993. Modern translation of early native accounts of the conquest of Mexico, with extensive introduction and notes.

Lovell, W. George. *Conquest and Survival in Colonial Guatemala: A Historical Geography of the Cuchumatán Highlands, 1500–1821*. Kingston, Ont., 1985. Careful and sensitive rendering of the reasons and dimensions of change among the peoples of this region of Guatemala.

Thomas, Hugh. *Conquest: Montezuma, Cortés, and the Fall of Old Mexico*. New York, 1993. Thorough consideration of all significant aspects of the conquest of Mexico, including various interpretations.

Warren, J. Benedict. *The Conquest of Michoacán: The Spanish Domination of the Tarascan Kingdom in Western Mexico, 1521–1530*. Norman, Okla., 1985. Largely narrative treatment of the first decade of Spanish–Tarascan interaction in western Mexico.

JOHN E. KICZA

CONSERVATION AND RESTORATION.

The Spanish *Conquistadores* and the chroniclers of the early sixteenth century admired and wondered at the architecture and city planning of Mesoamerican peoples. Fernando Cortés and Bernal Díaz del Castillo, a soldier in Cortés's army, have left us glowing descriptions of Tenochtitlan, the capital city of the Aztec.

However, the appreciation of pre-Hispanic architecture did not signify the desire to conserve it. After the fall of Tenochtitlan, for military and political reasons Cortés ordered the razing of the city. Over its remains was built Mexico City, the capital of New Spain. In other parts of Mesoamerica, many pre-Hispanic buildings served as quarries for the construction of Christian churches and *haciendas* of the Spanish settlers. In the following centuries, the interest in indigenous cultures continued but was mainly focused on historical research in the archives and the collecting of codices and manuscripts, as well as a few antiquities.

The first official archaeological expeditions in Mesoamerica took place in 1784–1786, when the government of Guatemala ordered the exploration of Palenque. Antonio del Rio, who commanded one of the expeditions, boasted of the destructive tactics he used in the exploration of the city. Documentation, which is the first step in the conservation of cultural heritage, received further impetus when King Charles IV ordered a survey of New Spain to find and record ruins and other pre-Hispanic remains. Although these expeditions denote a certain preoccupation of the Spanish Court and of the colonial governments in archaeological remains, there was not yet any concern for the safekeeping of this heritage. Times, however, were changing; in the late eighteenth century, developing cultural nationalism and an awareness of the historical and social values of the ancient Mesoamerican heritage led to demands for its conservation.

The nineteenth century saw numerous travelers and artists who traversed the region describing and illustrating the ruined cities. Eventually, toward the end of the century, these romantic and adventurous travelers gave way to no less adventurous but more scientific explorers. Men like Alfred Percival Maudslay and Desiré Charnay pioneered scientific archaeological research in Mesoamerica. Again, despite the growing interest in Mesoamerican archaeology, there were no attempts to restore pre-Hispanic sites, beyond small-scale clearing and consolidation, as well as the collecting of antiquities for museums and private collections.

Formal conservation of archaeological sites began in 1891, when the Peabody Museum of Archaeology and Ethnology, Harvard University, reached an agreement with the Honduran government to explore and restore the ruins of Copán. In Mexico, official restoration of monuments did not begin until 1901, when Leopoldo Batres was commissioned to "repair and consolidate" the Building of the Columns in Mitla. In the following years, Batres would carry out restoration work at Teotihuacán, Xochicalco, and other sites throughout Mexico. His work has been severely criticized, but he was a pioneer in the field, and he did try to protect and preserve the authenticity of the archaeological monuments.

It is useful to define some related terms as they are understood by the majority of archaeologists and conservators in Mesoamerica.

Conservation: all activities directed toward the safeguard of cultural heritage and its values in order to transmit them to the future. It includes actions such as identification, documentation, protection, and restoration.

Restoration: activities or processes physically conducted on the cultural object with the purpose of safeguarding and maintaining it and prolonging its existence. Restoration has several aspects, the following among others:

Reintegration: restitution of original but dismembered parts to their original position and function.

Integration: addition of clearly recognizable elements to ensure the conservation of the object or to make its form understandable.

Reconstruction: reproduction of parts or the whole of a cultural object with new materials similar or identical to the original.

By the early decades of the twentieth century, restoration at several sites was undertaken, associated with archaeological explorations directly sponsored by the governments of the region or by authorized private institutions. Between 1917 and 1920, extensive restoration was carried out by the Dirección of Arqueología of Mexico at Teotihuacan and other sites. The Carnegie Institution of Washington, D.C., began work almost simultaneously at Uaxactún, Guatemala, and at Chichén Itzá in Yucatán, Mexico.

With few exceptions, the quality of most of these restorations was satisfactory, especially considering that they were among the first attempts at restoration of Mesoamerican architecture.

By this time, the governments of Mexico and of the Central American countries had become aware of the worth of their archaeological heritage and expended more efforts in its conservation. Conservationist legislation was passed in Mexico, which considerably improved the decrees that had been in effect—though largely disregarded—since Colonial times. Archaeological sites and objects became state property, and no excavation or restoration work could proceed unless authorized by the government. Guardianships were established at the sites, and some maintenance was undertaken; objects recovered during excavations were cared for in museums. All this eventually led to the founding in 1939 of the Instituto Nacional de Antropología e Historia (INAH), which authorizes and coordinates all archaeological excavation and conservation in Mexico. Shortly thereafter, similar legislation was passed and corresponding institutes were established in several Central American republics and Belize.

However, as the archaeological projects increased in number and extent, the quality of the restoration work decreased considerably. From the 1940s to the early 1970s, undue and exaggerated importance was given to the massive reconstruction of pre-Hispanic architecture. Some of these reconstructions were based on hypotheses or on analogies with other buildings or even other sites, thus reducing the factual and historical value of the restored buildings. Cases of undue, exaggerated reconstruction occurred during this period on numerous buildings at Monte Albán, Tula, Uxmal, and Cholula in Mexico and at Tikal and Mixco Viejo in Guatemala, among others.

It is difficult to pinpoint the exact reasons for this phenomenon; however, some of the motivations can be generalized.

1. Governments, realizing the economic potential of tourism to archaeological sites, wanted spectacularly reconstructed buildings, which, they assumed, would have greater appeal to mass tourism. What they got were massive interventions, which physically preserved the monuments but diminished their authenticity and historical value.
2. It was erroneously believed that the restoration of pre-Hispanic buildings was the sole responsibility of the field archaeologist in charge of the excavation.
3. Archaeologists mostly ignored or rejected international experiences and recommendations, such as the Venice Charter of 1964, as not being applicable to pre-Hispanic structures in Mesoamerica.

4. Archaeological remains were seen as a powerful medium to increase national pride and unity, more so, it was thought, if the ruins were "returned to their original splendor."

By the early 1970s, a reaction was felt against the massive reconstructions and other misguided treatments of ancient Mesoamerican architecture. The First Latin American Regional Seminary on Conservation and Restoration, which met in 1973 in Mexico City, agreed to "condemn the proliferation of works that, far removed from the spirit of the Charter of Venice, falsify and annul values of the monument. . . . [W]e reject reconstructions such as those practiced at Cholula. . . ." Other meetings with multidisciplinary participation, as well as several publications, affirmed these views and recommended changes in the objectives and practice in the conservation of Mesoamerican sites. It was pointed out that reconstructions were detrimental not only to the values of the monuments but also to archaeological research, as they led to comparisons and inferences based, not on facts, but on hypotheses and analogies.

In more recent years, most archaeologists concur on the need for a more interdisciplinary approach that requires the active participation of architects and other specialists in the many aspects of restoration and conservation. A better balance has been attempted between archaeological research and conservation, and it has been shown that they can be complementary and beneficial to both. It is hoped that the increased use of nondestructive geophysical techniques will reduce the damages inherent in traditional archaeological excavation.

The validity of the Venice Charter has been upheld, and there is agreement on its main principles: respect for authenticity and for the original materials, avoidance of restoration based on hypothesis, emphasis on historical as well as aesthetic values, the prohibition of reconstruction in archaeological buildings, and the acceptance of limited integration as the only valid intervention. The need is felt, however, for national or regional guidelines that conserve the spirit of the Venice Charter and adapt it to the region's specific problems and experiences.

The desirability of tourism is recognized, but there is deep concern for the danger it poses to archaeological sites. The need is felt to improve many aspects of the infrastructure, such as services, presentation, and maintenance, and to elaborate better and more comprehensive management plans for all the Mesoamerican sites in order to preserve and enhance the many values—aesthetic, historic, scientific, educational, and economic—of the ancient Mesoamerican cultural heritage.

BIBLIOGRAPHY

Bernal, Ignacio. *A History of Mexican Archaeology*. London and New York, 1980. Highly readable and informed history.

Molina-Montes, Augusto. *La restauración arquitectonica de edificios arqueológicos*. Mexico City, 1975. Review of international theories on restoration and their application in Mexican archaeological practice. Currently out of print.

Molina-Montes, Augusto. "Archaeological Buildings. Restoration or Misrepresentation." In *Falsifications and Misreconstructions of Pre-Columbian Art*, edited by Elizabeth H. Boone, pp. 125–141. Washington, D.C., 1982. Overview of theory and practice of restoration, with detailed examples of some restorations of Mesoamerican buildings.

Schavelzon, Daniel. *La conservación del patrimonio cultural en América Latina*. Buenos Aires, 1990. Not easily accessible, but the most complete critical history on the conservation of Mesoamerican archaeological sites.

AUGUSTO MOLINA-MONTES

CONSTELLATIONS. *See* Stars and Constellations.

CONVENTS. *See* Monasteries and Convents.

COPAL. *See* Incense.

COPÁN, ancient Maya city that mirrors the beauty of the physical landscape in which it flourished—a fertile, well-watered mountain valley in western Honduras at an elevation of 600 meters (2,400 feet) above mean sea level. Best known for the abundance and great artistry of its stone sculpture, Copán reached its apogee during the Classic period under a dynasty of sixteen rulers that reigned from 426 to 820 CE. At its peak, the supporting population comprised some 25,000 people, divided along class lines and, for the most part, concentrated in the urban wards next to the civic-ceremonial center. Owing in part to its location on the less densely populated southeastern margins of the Southern Maya Lowlands, Copán was able to expand over a wider terrain than many of its contemporaries in the Peten and is thought to have controlled a domain greater than 250 square kilometers. While the vast majority of the population consisted of commoners engaged in agricultural pursuits, many also engaged in part-time craft production. Members of the nobility were scribes, sculptors, warriors, ballplayers, craftspersons, and councillors.

Copán was among the first of the ancient cities to attract the attention of Western travelers, scholars, and the public at large, especially after the publication of John L. Stephens's *Incidents of Travel in Central America, Chiapas, and Yucatán* (1841). Half a century later, Alfred Maudslay made an expedition to Copán and other sites; he produced the first plaster casts of some monuments and the useful photographs and drawings of all the free-standing sculptures at Copán, assigning the letters and numbers to the stelae, altars, and structures that are still used today (Maudslay 1896–1902). Subsequent investigations by several institutions in the twentieth century have yielded tremendous insights into Maya culture and history; Copán's artistic and literary creations fire the imagination of visitors, including many Maya pilgrims from Guatemala and Mexico.

The study of the Copán Valley settlements has provided a number of insights into the lifeways and diverse social landscape of the people who supported this Classic Maya kingdom. The ecological survey and mapping of ancient settlements, begun under the direction of archaeologist Gordon R. Willey in the mid-1970s, marked the beginning of a long-term, multidisciplinary analysis of the physical environment and its use over time. Specialized studies have been conducted on the local flora, fauna, rainfall patterns, geology, river geomorphology, soils, pollen, agricultural technology, human demography, diseases (diagnosed from human skeletal remains), and the way these changed through time. The agricultural fertility of the alluvial bottomlands next to the river was the primary incentive for human settlement in the valley during the mid-second millennium BCE. By 1000 BCE, sedentary village horticulturalists began constructing large, elevated stone platforms for their houses. Burials placed beneath house floors were accompanied by incised ceramic vessels and jadeite offerings, which demonstrate active participation in the larger Mesoamerican material and idea exchange systems of the so-called Olmec horizon. From 250 to 400 CE, Copán was home to a chiefdom that erected stone sculptures in the "pot-belly" tradition and participated in the Usulutan ceramic sphere. The chiefdom was likely based in Copán's Northwest Platform—a large building complex to the north and west of the larger, later, and much better known center that Sylvanus Morley (1920) dubbed "the Acropolis."

A new chiefly lineage established the first substantial buildings in the Acropolis, which was situated along the western bank of the Copán River. The "founder" of this new order and his successors proved highly successful at unifying the various political factions in the surrounding region, and people were drawn to their center's economic and other attractions. Economic opportunities, public ceremonies, and feasts drew people toward it; local population growth was soon augmented by immigration from areas farther afield. The fertile alluvial bottomlands that were the impetus for the initial colonization of the Copán Valley filled with human settlements. In the following three centuries, subsequent population expansion onto the adjacent alluvial flatlands and foothills created tremendous stress on the few lands left for agriculture and firewood procurement, which led to deforestation, soil erosion, and, eventually, the inability of the city to feed itself.

Founding of the Acropolis. Both archaeological remains and textual accounts indicate that the Acropolis was founded by an interloper from outside the Copán Valley, named in the hieroglyphic texts as K'inich Yax K'uk' Mo'. Later inscriptions state that K'inich Yax K'uk' Mo' "arrived" in December of 426 CE, some three days after he first grasped the insignia of rulership (*k'awil*). The origins and development of the Acropolis from that point onward were the focus of an eight-year multi-institutional research and conservation endeavor that was designed and directed by William L. Fash (1998), called the Copán Acropolis Archaeological Project. Its tunneling beneath Copán's final-phase temple-pyramids revealed that Yax K'uk' Mo' set the agenda for the new center by building the first versions of Temple 26 (devoted to dynastic lore), the ballcourt, and Temple 11, in an arrangement that was to be respected and embellished upon by all future rulers there. He did this for the important Period Ending of 9.0.0.0.0 in the Long Count, as recorded on Copán's first monument with glyphs, the Motmot floor marker.

Other Acropolis Project investigations beneath the final version of Temple 16 have shown that Yax K'uk' Mo' was buried in a *talud-tablero* building (known as the Hunal Structure) discovered at the core of the Acropolis by Robert Sharer and his colleagues (1999). Constructed in pure Teotihuacan *talud-tablero* style, this building was decorated with painted murals that also recall the great city of Teotihuacan in the Basin of Mexico. The form and decoration of this funerary temple, and the subsequent Late Classic portraits (in Teotihuacano garb), as well as the texts, show that both Yax K'uk' Mo' and his successors wanted him to be remembered as having strong affiliations with the great city in the Basin of Mexico. Several glyphic texts refer to him as a "Lord of the West," and the analysis of his bone chemistry reveals that he was not a native of the Copán Valley. The Motmot floor marker, Maya-style ballcourt, and bone chemistry all suggest that Yax K'uk' Mo' had very strong ties with the rulers of Tikal, a Maya city whose royal line was at one point usurped by Teotihuacan (Stuart 2000). Sharer and his colleagues (1999) have shown that the original nucleus of the Acropolis included three buildings, including Hunal, grouped around a courtyard. Succeeding his father in the office of K'ul Ahaw ("Holy Lord") of Copán in 437 CE, Ruler 2 immediately embarked upon an ambitious building program, creating a series of buildings, with associated art and inscriptions in Early Classic Maya style.

Over the ensuing four centuries, the successors of K'inich Yax K'uk' Mo' rebuilt the Acropolis and its constituent buildings and courtyards several times. Particularly grandiose construction projects were undertaken by Ruler 7 ("Waterlily Jaguar"), 10 ("Moon Jaguar"), and 12 ("Smoke Imix God K"). Hunal Structure was the centerpoint for all subsequent versions of this civic-ceremonial center,

which from its inception included temples, administrative buildings, a ballcourt, and the royal residence, but grew more elaborate and grandiose with the reign of each new sovereign. Ruler 10 commissioned two of the most ornately embellished structures investigated to date, the Ante Structure and the lovely Rosalila, built above the successors to Hunal and the tomb of the founder (Agurcia 1997). Rosalila, its predecessors, and its successors all bear the name and religious symbolism of the first ruler in their façade sculptures, modeled in stucco in the case of Rosalila and its predecessors, and in stone beginning with the reign of Ruler 12.

Late Classic Kings. Reigning supreme during the glory days of the Copán kingdom, Ruler 12 was in power longer the any other king in the city's history, from 628 to 695 CE. At that time, the Acropolis was the center of a vast and complex domain, with more craftspersons, architects, and sculptors than ever before in its employ. A new high-relief sculpture style was lavished on the building façades, also decorated with tenoned mosaic-stone pieces, rather than the modeled stucco that had been used in the Early Classic Acropolis. Ruler 12 commissioned more stelae and altars than any other Copán king; this included a set of six stelae, erected at selected spots throughout the valley in 652 CE, to sacralize the geography and the role of the K'ul Ahau and his ancestors (especially K'inich Yax K'uk' Mo', named on two of the stelae). Shortly before this date, Ruler 12 oversaw the installment of a ruler at Quirigua, some 70 kilometers (45 miles) to the northwest, as recorded on that ruler's accession monument, Altar L— which indicates that Copán's twelfth ruler held political sway over matters far from his regal-ritual center. The death of this long-lived king was marked by the construction of one of the largest tomb chambers in the Maya area, stocked with hundreds of offerings in ceramics, shell, jade, and such perishable materials as wood and gourds (Fash et al. 2000). Atop his grave was built the Esmeralda Structure, soon to be covered over by the final version, Structure 26, with its famed Hieroglyphic Stairway. Commenced by Ruler 13, but not completed until the reign of Ruler 15, the stairway and the temple at its summit constitute a dynastic encyclical and the longest surviving pre-Hispanic Maya text. The inscription states that its purpose was to honor the memory of Smoke Imix God K, whose death, burial ceremonies, and tomb are cited in three passages of the text (Stuart 1997).

Ruler 13 has been variously known as "XVIII Jog," "18 Rabbit," and most recently by his aboriginal name, "Uaxaclahun Ubah K'awil" ("18 are the images of K'awil," a patron god of Maya royal lineages). He took the high-relief sculptural tradition, begun in the reign of Ruler 12, to new heights in his own architectural masterpieces: Temple 22 and the final version of the Copán ballcourt.

The Great Plaza and ballcourt at Copán. *Courtesy of Visual Resources Collection, The University of Texas at Austin. Ferguson Collection.*

He is best known, however, for his nearly full-round stelae, erected in the Great Plaza, each commemorating important rituals that he performed to mark the passage of the Period Endings in the Long Count calendric system that occurred during his reign, from 695 to 738 CE (Baudez 1994). On Stela A, he cites Copán as one of the four Maya kingdoms "on high," along with Palenque, and the two great rival metropoli of Tikal and Calakmul. The hegemony that Copán had previously held over Quirigua came to an abrupt and violent end in 738 CE, when Uaxaclahun Uban K'awil was captured in battle and beheaded by his counterpart from Quirigua, K'ak' Tiliw (known also as "Two-legged Sky" or "Cauac Sky"). His death was viewed as martyrdom in Copán, where the Hieroglyphic Stairway text records that he was killed on that fateful day "with his flint [weapon], with his shield." All his architectural and sculpture monuments in the Great Plaza were maintained, rather than displaced or built over, by the city's final rulers.

The humiliating loss of this great patron of the arts was responded to in an innovative manner by his successor, Ruler 14 (known as "Smoke Monkey"). Rather than continuing in the tradition of erecting stelae and altars in his own honor, this ruler instead built a new and highly decorated version of Structure 22A on the Acropolis, identified by Barbara Fash (1996) as the Council House. On its façades, he publicly portrayed each of the nine members of the council, seated above toponymic glyphs that name the wards or places that each of them represented in the deliberations that took place there. The building is labeled by ten large mats that gave it its name as "Popol Nah" (in Yucatec) or "Popol Otot" (in Cholan), either Council House or "Community House," as cited in numerous dictionaries and other documents of the Colonial period. The K'ul Ahau is portrayed above the councilors in the roof crest, and the building was also provided with a dance platform and a food-preparation area. Dance is frequently mentioned in conjunction with the Council House in the Colonial-era documents, which also refer to feasts held immediately following council meetings. Ruler 14 reigned for eleven years (738–749 CE) and did not erect any other monuments as far as is now known.

Ruler 15 completed the Hieroglyphic Stairway and temple of Structure 26, in 757 CE, extolling the achievements of all his predecessors in office and placing his own portrait (Stela M) squarely before the stairs, at its base. This is the longest pre-Hispanic hieroglyphic text to survive the Spanish conquest; it details the life histories of the first fifteen kings and portrays them in grand style, as powerful warriors, bearing lance and shield. The text in the temple atop the pyramid is recorded in two scripts, in parallel columns: the first, in the elaborate Classic Maya "full figure" style; and the parallel inscription (presented as the first in each pair of columns), which relays the same information in a glyphic style that incorporates elements from Central Mexican (i.e., Teotihuacan) iconography and picture writing (Stuart 2000). This temple and earlier monuments here refer to the place of the bull-rushes (ancient "Tollan"). Its text and the Teotihuacan-derived iconography worn by most of the rulers on the stairway and temple serve to highlight the affiliations that the founder of this Maya dynasty established with the great metropolis of the north. Ruler 15 also commissioned Stela N, placed at the base of the nearby Temple 11, which bears his portrait on the south side, and that of Ruler 14 on the north side.

After the death of Ruler 15, the last great king of Copán, Yax Pasah ("Great Dawn") ushered in a new era. As ruler, this son of a royal woman from Palenque is perhaps best know for his portrait on Alter Q, where he had himself and all fifteen of his predecessors portrayed and cited by name. During his early years in power, he created some of the largest and most imposing architectural monuments in the Maya world—the final versions of Temples 11, 16, and 21A. Temple 11 was the most imposing and also bore the most texts, including eight temple panels, the Reviewing Stand text on the West Court side, and an outset inscribed sculpture panel on the side of the Hieroglyphic Stairway plaza. The massive two-storied Temple 11 was embellished with the tallest and most elaborate sculpture façades ever undertaken at Copán, or perhaps any other Maya city. Temple 16 and its companion monument Alter Q are an ode to the dynasty's founder; they carry both texts and imagery that evoke his ties to Teotihuacan.

During the middle and later years of Yax Pasah's long reign (763–c.822 CE), he dedicated a series of small sculptures—altars, stone censers, and circular bases for censers with inscribed dates—both at his royal residence (Andrews 1996) and elsewhere, to mark the passing of the Period Endings and the ceremonies that he and others performed on those occasions. His name also appears on a series of inscribed benches or "thrones," in the domiciles of the patriarchs of noble families who lived in the valley's elite residential compounds (Sanders 1989). The abundance of these and other sculpture monuments in so many palatial noble quarters has led Fash (1988) to suggest that the end of the dynasty may have come about because of the limited number of political posts available (the nine places represented in the council house) vis-à-vis the much larger number of men who sought to occupy them. Many of the building façades and architectural sculptures that made Copán the most expressive of Maya cities are now on display at the Sculpture Museum in Copán, with a full-size replica of the lovely Rosalila temple as the centerpiece.

Divine Kingship Ends—and the Aftermath. The political problems caused by the burgeoning of the elite class during four centuries of dynastic rule, as well as the breakaway of Quirigua and other formerly subsidiary centers, resulted in the loss of vital tribute to Copán pre-cisely when most needed. In building the city center in the middle of the most fertile land, the dynasty's founders inadvertently created an enormous problem for future generations. By the eighth century CE, the city had engulfed all the best soils in the alluvial bottomlands; this forced agriculture up into the adjacent piedmont, which was eventually also covered by residences of the rapidly expanding population. Consequently, the maize, beans, and squash that had always formed the mainstay of the diet had to be cultivated on thin, upland slopes, which washed away in the massive erosion of the early ninth century CE (Webster 1999). Deforestation of the valley was primarily due to the need for cooking fuel for the thousands of hearths in the bustling city; with each passing year, Copán became less able to provide for its own needs in terms of food and potable water.

Archaeological evidence indicates that the years following the death of Yax Pasah saw a number of destructive actions in the temples, palaces, and monuments of the royal line (Andrews 1996). The private ancestral shrine of Yax Pasah (Structure 29) was burned and toppled, as was his funerary temple (Structure 18), and the Council House (Structure 22A). Fragments of human bone, jade beads, and an inscribed marble vessel from the tomb of Temple 18 suggest that the tomb of Yax Pasah was looted and then ransacked as part of this destructive process. The offering caches found inside the sculpture panels on the stairways of Temple 11 and 16 were also looted and, in some cases, their sculptures rolled down the stairs. Many of the families residing in the urban core of the city continued to live there for another generation or two, but by the mid-tenth century CE, most of the valley was abandoned. A group of immigrants from the region of central Honduras or western El Salvador built a modest village 150 meters (500 feet) south of the Acropolis in about 975 CE (Manahan 1996). They scavenged sculptures from the funerary temple of the last king and other nearby buildings for their house foundations, as well as the occasional household shrine—reminders of the glory that once had been. There was no other occupation of any size in the valley thereafter, until well after the first Spanish description of Copán (and first mention of it by that name), penned by Diego García de Palacios in 1576. When he asked who built the ruins, the few local inhabitants of the region replied that they did not know, but they did manage to provide Palacios with a hieroglyphic book—the final whereabouts of which remains one of the enduring mysteries of ancient Copán.

[*See also* Southern Maya Lowlands.]

BIBLIOGRAPHY

Agurcia Fasquelle, Ricardo. "Le Temple du Roi Soleil et son evolution au coeur de l'Acropole de Copán." In *Les Mayas au pais de Copán*, pp. 91–100. Milan, 1997.

Andrews, E. Wyllys V. "A Late Classic Royal Domestic Compound at Copán." Paper presented at the 61st Annual Meeting of the Society for American Archaeology, New Orleans, 1996.

Baudez, Claude F. *Maya Sculpture of Copán: The Iconography*. Norman, Okla., 1994.

Fash, Barbara W. "Copan's House of Lords." *Natural History* 105.4 (1996), 30–31.

Fash, William L. "A New Look at Maya Statecraft from Copán, Honduras." *Antiquity* 62.234 (1988), 157–169.

Fash, William L. "Classic Maya Dynastic Architectural Programs at Copan and Other Sites." In *Function and Meaning in Classic Maya Architecture*, edited by Stephen D. Houston, pp. 223–270. Washington, D.C., 1998.

Fash, William L., Harriet F. Beaubien, Catherine E. Magee, Barbara W. Fash, and Richard V. Williamson. "The Trappings of Kingship among the Classic Maya: Ritual and Identity in a Royal Maya Tomb." In *Fleeting Identities: Perishable Material Culture in Archaeological Research*, edited by Penelope Drucker. Carbondale, Ill., 2000.

Fash, William L., and Barbara W. Fash. "Building a World-View: Visual Communication in Classic Maya Architecture." *RES* 29/30 (1996), 127–147.

Manahan, Thomas Kam. "An Early Postclassic Settlement in Copan." Paper presented at the 61st Annual Meeting of the Society for American Archaeology, New Orleans, 1996.

Maudslay, Alfred P. *Archaeology. Biologia Centrali-Americana*. 5 vols. London, 1889–1902.

Morley, Sylvanus G. *The Inscriptions at Copan*. Carnegie Institution of Washington, 219. Washington, D.C., 1920.

Sanders, William T. "Household, Lineage, and State at Eighth Century Copán." In *The House of the Bacabs, Copán, Honduras*, edited by David L. Webster. Washington, D.C., 1989.

Schele, Linda, and David A. Freidel. *A Forest of Kings*. New York, 1990.

Sharer, Robert J., Loa P. Traxler, David W. Sedat, Ellen E. Bell, Marcello A. Canuto, and Christopher Powell. "Early Classic Architecture beneath the Copan Acropolis." *Ancient Mesoamerica* 10 (1999), 3–23.

Stephens, John L. *Incidents of Travel in Central America, Chiapas, and Yucatán*. New York, 1841.

Stuart, David S. "Hieroglyphes et histoire de Copán." In *Les Mayas aux pais de Copán*, pp. 101–110. Milan, 1997.

Stuart, David S. "'The Arrival of Strangers': Teotihuacan and Tollan in Classic Maya History." In *Mesoamerica's Classic Heritage: From Teotihuacán to the Aztecs*, edited by Davíd Carrasco, Lindsay Jones, and Scott Sessions, pp. 465–514. Boulder, 2000.

Webster, David L. "The Archaeology of Copan, Honduras." *Journal of Anthropological Research* 7 (1999), 1–53.

WILLIAM L. FASH

COPPER. *See* Mining and Metalwork.

CORA. The Cora, or Nayalita, people reside within a series of *comunidades indígenas* (colonial land grants) and *ejidos* (contemporary agricultural communes) in the eastern highlands and river valleys of the state of Nayarit, Mexico. There is no agreement on the size of their population, though some twenty-five thousand seems reasonable.

Their pre-Hispanic (before the 1530s) and pre-Conquest history (1530s to 1722) is poorly understood. During the 1600s, the Tonati region was the most important, drawing ceremonial tribute from three nearby provinces. A series of chieftains, or "kings," provided the leadership for a fierce and prolonged resistance to the Spanish order, but the burning of Tonati and the ruling family's mummies by the Spanish in 1722 ended Cora independence. Since the resistance had been so strong, the region was assigned to the Jesuits and was organized into a special province, Nuevo Toledo. [*See* Jesuits.] The area became a refuge region and also provided migrant labor for the coastal salt works, the agricultural plantations, and the gold and silver mines of surrounding zones.

The Cora language is very closely related to Huichol and Tequal; all are members of the Totorame subfamily of Southern Uto-Aztecan. Nahuatl, introduced to the region after 1722, had a mild impact represented by lexical borrowings. There exists a modest degree of dialect variation among the Cora, but all the varieties are mutually intelligible; Huichol and Cora are as well, if the speakers agree to simplify their speech.

Traditional society today is strongly organized around a series of Colonial-era and Roman Catholic offices. The civil-religious system, involving a hierarchy of governors, judges, and *mayordomos*, was until recently central to the region's social organization. Government programs such as those of HUICOT and the National Indian Institute (INI), the penetration of political parties (especially the PRI [Partido Revolucionario Institucional]), and the growing presence of Protestant missionaries have fundamentally altered the older order, though it continues to show resilience. Each *comunidad* has its own variant of the aforementioned traditional organizations. The pueblo of Jesús María may have a *mexicanero* (Tlaxcaltecan or Caxcan) barrio, thus incorporating ceremonial ideas from non-Spanish sources after 1722. Certainly, Colonial-period and contemporary sociocultural systems were (and still are) composite and highly syncretized, though the degree varies considerably from place to place. The differing subregional emphases given to the Cora "Trinity" of Father, Son, and the Virgin Mary—and their indigenous counterparts, including six cardinal directions and the nature gods—makes generalization difficult.

The masked dances celebrating the Catholic festival cycle are accompanied by a strong regional musical tradition. Lineages, though agnatic in focus, have strong female participation in determining overall membership, inheritance, and ritualism. Traditional curers play important roles in folk medicine. Some of the most valued singer-curers are Huichols. Intermarriage occurs with other Native Americans, especially Huichols and Tepecanos. Less frequent are unions with *mestizos*, though they are more common today, as acculturation accelerates. Day-wage labor in the region's cities and farms, as well as migration to the United States, is increasing. A prize-winning novel about the Cora, very popular though with ethnographic flaws, is Miguel Angel Menédez's *Nayar* (1940, reprinted 1978).

BIBLIOGRAPHY

Grimes, Joseph, and Thomas Hinton. "The Huichol and Cora." In *Handbook of American Indians*, vol. 8, pp. 792–813. Austin, Tex., 1967.

Hinton, Thomas. "The Cora Village: A Civil Religious Hierarchy in Northern Mexico." In *Culture, Change and Stability: Essays in Memory of Olive Ruth Barker and George C. Baker, Jr.*, pp. 44–62. Berkeley, 1964.

Hinton, Thomas. "Indian Acculturation in Nayarit." In *The Social Anthropology of Latin America: Essays in Honor of Ralph Leon Beals*, pp. 11–35. Los Angeles, 1970.

Jáuregui, Jesús, ed. *Música y danzas del Gran Nayar*. Mexico City, 1993.

Weigand, Phil C. *Ensayos sobre el Gran Nayar: Entre Coras, Huicholes y Tepehuanos*. Mexico City, 1992.

Weigand, Phil C. "Las Sociedades Huicholas antes de la llegada de los Españoles." In *Memoria de la Benemérita Sociedad de Geografía y Estadística del Estado de Jalisco*, edited by María Pilar Sánchez, pp. 407–432. Guadalajara, 1997.

PHIL C. WEIGAND

CORREGIDORES AND ALCALDES MAYORES.

As Spain formulated the best way to govern the Indians of New Spain, it began in 1530 to name *corregidores*—local magistrates and judges, the governors of *corregimientos*—in the *pueblos* (towns) that were no longer included in *encomiendas*. *Corregidores* were salaried royal officials appointed directly in Spain, or in New Spain by the viceroy. Besides their salary, at the beginning of the system they received food, forage, fuel, and other commodities and services from the Indians of their jurisdictions. In addition to the *corregidor*, each *corregimiento* had one or more lieutenants, a city constable, a scribe, and an interpreter of Indian languages. One of the main functions of the *corregidores* was to collect the royal tribute. As of 1550, they were given civil and criminal jurisdiction in cases involving conflicts between Indians and Spaniards. In 1558, they were entrusted with overseeing the accounts of the community coffers, into which went both the tribute collected and the additional surplus produced by the Indian *pueblos*.

In an attempt to centralize the government of the Indies, the Crown between 1530 and 1550 named *corregidores* in places where *encomiendas* became vacant and reverted to royal jurisdiction. During this transitional period it was not uncommon for *encomenderos* to be granted the additional title of *corregidor* in settlements that were outside the jurisdiction of their *encomiendas*. Thus, during the sixteenth century the monarchy recovered jurisdiction over Indian communities that it had formerly granted to private parties through the *encomienda* system. The *corregimiento* then became the government entity closest to the Indian *pueblos*, a position it retained without significant alteration until 1786, when the system of *intendencias* was established.

From the outset, the wages of these royal officials came from the Indian tribute tax, which enabled the *corregidores* to make improper use of those funds. For that reason, in 1611 the Crown prohibited them from intervening directly in the management of community accounts. These officials' greed, however, prompted them to become involved in trade and other economic dealings with the natives, though these were prohibited to them. From the last third of the sixteenth century to the end of the Colonial period, they traded with the Indians, often forcing them to take part in these dealings. Many *corregidores* thus obtained huge profits.

The forced distribution of goods functioned in three ways. The most common form during the sixteenth century was the distribution of money for the purchase of some Indian product—for example, maize for supplying the cities, or cochineal, a natural dye exported for the textile industry. Throughout the Colonial period, money and cotton were also distributed to ensure the production of cloth. *Corregidores* distributed small livestock (sheep, goats, and swine) and meat in the sixteenth century, and larger livestock (horses, mules, and oxen) for agricultural tasks in later times.

The system guaranteed extraordinary profits, since the *corregidores* bought cheaply from the Indians and sold to them at high prices. It constituted a sure market because of its coercive nature. The trade conducted by these royal officials was consolidated to such a degree in the colonial economy that the traders of the Consulado (merchant guild) of New Spain financed the voyages to America of *corregidores* named in Spain in exchange for the services they would provide as liaisons with Indian communities for the purchase and sale of different kinds of goods. As time went by, a great many products came to be distributed under this system. Most were produced within New Spain itself and intended for Indian consumption, but some were products imported from Spain, the Philippines, Ecuador, or Peru. Because they were involved in trading and dealing on such a large scale, the *corregidores* often fulfilled their roles as local justices poorly. By the eighteenth century, the value of the trade that was subject to forced distribution was far greater than the tribute taxes the Indians paid to the Crown.

The Spanish system of exploitation and oppression was embodied in the figure of the *corregidor*. Colonial archives record rebellions against these officials by Indian *pueblos* who denounced the abuses, which, as justices, they had committed against the natives through the arbitrary exercise of power and as distributors of goods.

BIBLIOGRAPHY

Gibson, Charles. *The Aztecs under Spanish Rule (1519–1810).* Stanford, 1964. Presents how, when, and where the *corregidores* were established in the Valley of Mexico, with their jurisdictions and salaries.

Megenus Bornemann, Margarita. "Economía y comunidades indígenas: El efecto de la supresión del repartimiento forzoso de mercancías en la Intendencia de México, 1786–1810." *Mexican Studies* 5.2 (1989). Examines the impact that the suppression of the *repartimiento de mercancías* had on the indigenous economy, and compares the agrarian structure of the intendancy of Mexico with those of the Puebla-Tlaxcala and Oaxaca regions, which have been studied by other historians.

Pastor, Rodolfo. "El repartimiento de mercancías y los alcaldes mayores novohispanos: Un sistema de explotación de sus orígenes a la crisis de 1810." In *El gobierno provincial en la Nueva España, 1570–1787,* edited by Woodrow Borah. Mexico City, 1985. The only theoretical analysis of the *repartimiento* system and its impact on the colonial economy; interesting interpretation of the evolution of the institution during the Colonial period.

Patch, Robert. *Maya and Spaniard in Yucatan, 1648–1812.* Stanford, 1993. Presents the *repartimiento* system in Yucatán, which differs substantially from other regions in New Spain.

Pietschmann, Horst. "El comercio de repartimientos de los alcaldes mayores y corregidores en la región Puebla-Tlaxcala en el siglo XVIII". In *Estudios sobre política indigenista española en América.* Valladolid, 1977. Quantitative regional analysis of the merchandise the *corregidores* distributed among the Indians in the eighteenth century.

MARGARITA MEGENUS BORNEMANN

CORTÉS, FERNANDO

CORTÉS, FERNANDO (1485–1547), Spanish explorer. Cortés—whose given name also appears as Hernando and Hernán—was born in Medellín, a small town in Extremadura in southwestern Spain. Although he was to achieve fame as the leading *conquistador*, little in his early life foretold that outcome. The only son of *hidalgo* (secondary nobility) parents with little income, Cortés received formal education at Salamanca but did not compete his law degree. At the age of twenty, he embarked for Hispaniola, where he settled as a colonist and notary. In 1511, he participated in the conquest of Cuba under Diego Velázquez, who as its first governor appointed Cortés his personal secretary. The appointment enabled Cortés to settle into a quiet life with a prosperous *encomienda* and an administrative career.

For eight years, Cortés showed no interest in expeditions launched from Cuba, but in 1518 he secured from Velázquez appointment as captain of a large fleet of twelve ships. He set sail in February 1519 with about five hundred Spaniards, a few Caribbean Indians, and sixteen horses. Cortés's military experience was almost nonexistent, but he proved to be an effective leader of his small army and won early victories over the coastal Indians.

Moreover, he quickly grasped the political complexities of the vast territories under the control of the Aztec ruler, Motecuhzoma II, and he accordingly devised a daring and ultimately successful strategy of alliances with both Motecuhzoma's disgruntled subjects and his enemies.

The two-year campaign culminated with the fall of Tenochtitlan, the Aztec capital, on 13 August 1521. In 1528, Cortés sailed back to Spain for the first time. Emperor Charles V knighted him with the title of marquis of the Valley of Oaxaca and gave him extensive territories and a huge *encomienda* of Indian laborers, but he never recovered the post of governor general of New Spain, which he had held for a few years after the conquest. Instead, he made use of a grant to explore the northern Pacific coast in the 1530s, with mixed results. Back in Spain in 1542, he spent his last years there in a rather quiet retirement with Juana de Zuñiga, his second wife, first in Valladolid and then in Seville, where he died on 2 December 1547.

Cortés sent five long *relaciones* (dispatches) to his king, detailing his progress in the conquest of Mexico and later his administration of New Spain. The five reports, commonly known as the *Cartas de relación* ("Letters of relation"), were written between 1519 and 1526 in various places and circumstances.

The first dispatch, known as the *Carta de Veracruz*, was signed in Veracruz, on 20 July 1519, by the council members of the recently founded city, but its style and content clearly reveal Cortés's authorship. It begins by describing two expeditions launched from Cuba by Governor Velázquez, which brought vague news of a rich and populated area north of Yucatán, ruled by a great lord. It narrates in detail the events of the third expedition, that led by Cortés in 1519. After reconnoitering the coast of the Yucatán Peninsula, Cortés founded the city of Veracruz and broke away from Velázquez. Sinking his ships to prevent retreat, he led his men in a long march to Tenochtitlan, the capital of the vast Aztec Empire. The *Carta* ends with a detailed list of rich presents he is sending to the emperor.

The second letter was signed in Segura de la Frontera, and recently founded city in Tlaxcala, on 30 October 1520. Cortés narrates the wars and alliances that he conducted on the way to Tenochtitlan, and at the same time provides vivid descriptions of the land and the peoples he encountered. Cortés's ethnographic account culminates in his splendid description of the great city, its buildings and institutions, and the court of Motecuhzoma, whom he had arrested in a daring move to secure the conquest. Even though he shows disdain for the Aztec religion, and particularly the widespread practice of human sacrifice, Cortés expresses deep admiration for the high degree of civilization he has seen—to the point of frequently comparing Aztec achievements with those of Arab and Christian civilizations. The latter part of the letter recounts his victorious skirmish with a rival expedition sent by Velázquez, by then Cortés's declared enemy, and the Spanish retreat to Tlaxcala after they were expelled from Tenochtitlan by the Aztec. Throughout the letter, Cortés justifies his shaky legal position by skillfully laying out the political and religious benefits that might derive from his enterprise. Cortés no doubt understood the political implications of his enterprise. Fully aware that the territories he intended to subdue were a radically new geographic entity, he created a distinct administrative province for them, called New Spain. This was the first time the name of a European nation was used with the adjective "new" to name an American territory.

In his third letter, signed in Coyoacan, Mexico, on 15 May 1522, Cortés narrates his successful siege of Tenochtitlan, which concluded the conquest of Mexico in June 1519, as well as his reorganization of the country under Spanish rule. This included the founding of cities and the development of agriculture and mining, as well as further land and sea expeditions to the outer limits of New Spain, which one year after the conquest had almost doubled the territories formerly controlled by Motecuhzoma. Cortés's view of the political and economic importance of New Spain is revealed in his suggestion that Charles should replace his title of Holy Roman emperor with "emperor of the world." New Spain, he states, can be a double platform for the expansion of the Spanish Empire: not only into the American continent but also into East Asia, based on the newly created harbor of Acapulco on the Pacific coast.

The fourth letter, signed in Tenochtitlan (later called Mexico City) on 15 October 1524, dwells on the same themes. Cortés, who by then had been appointed governor of New Spain, portrays himself as an indefatigable administrator and faithful subject of his king. Although he had won his legal feud with Velázquez, Cortés's enormous power and prestige continued to make him the object of envious rivals in both Mexico and Spain, and he devotes the latter part to defending himself against accusations of embezzling state funds.

The fifth letter, signed in Tenochtitlan on 3 September 1526, can be divided into two parts. In the first, Cortés narrates his painful and ultimately useless expedition to Honduras through impenetrable jungle and mountainous territories unknown to Europeans, and his equally challenging return by land and sea. His two-year absence from Mexico City had been the cause of constant turmoil. To his dismay, on his return he was stripped of his authority and subjected to a judicial inquiry. The second part of the letter is an impassioned self-defense and a summary of his loyal services to God, king, and country.

One can hardly overstate the tremendous impact that the *Cartas de relación* had in Cortés's time. Although the first and fifth letters remained unpublished until the nineteenth century, the other three quickly became known in Europe. Fourteen editions in Spanish, Latin, Italian, and German were published between 1522 and 1532. Their success doubtless stemmed not only from the immediacy and the importance of the content, but also from Cortés's remarkable ability to narrate and analyze those facts, to describe their geographical and social contexts, and ultimately to extract political and economic implications from them. Although the extent of Cortés's formal education has been the subject of debate, even his declared enemy, Bartolomé de las Casas, who knew him well, admitted that he spoke Latin. He clearly possessed a keen intelligence and an extraordinary ability to grasp the complex realities of imperial politics, and his administrative experience gave him an intimate knowledge of law.

Because the conquest of Mexico was widely perceived by contemporary Europeans as a heroic deed that contributed decisively to the expansion of the Spanish Empire, the *Cartas de relación* have traditionally been compared with the Julius Caesar's *Gallic Wars*, an analytical narrative of the Roman conquest of France. Although similarities exist, Cortés—unlike Caesar—did not write a detached historical account of the facts well after the completion of the conquest and therefore addressed to a universal readership; his personal dispatches to the king related several events as they were unfolding. Yet the comparison is not without merit: Cortés's *Cartas* have long been perceived, read, and published as a single historical text unified by the author's beliefs and a solid determination to carry out his enterprise. Throughout his text, Cortés perceives his actions framed by a clear project of conquest, which he deems a necessary and almost inevitable God-mandated and Church-approved service to Christianity.

Cortés's view of the Spanish conquest, the native inhabitants, and the colonial society that he helped to create had an enormous influence in shaping the predominant outlook of contemporary Europe on those matters. Columbus had defined the New World as an exotic group of islands populated by naive and rather primitive "Indians." Cortés turned this view upside down, first by describing Mexico, especially the hinterland, as a physical environment radically different from the Caribbean—in many ways, closer to the European climate and landscape. In addition, his encounter with the sophisticated societies of Mesoamerica led him to establish a hierarchy of the inhabitants of Mexico—curiously, he never called them "Indians"—from the savage Otomí to the refined

Aztec. His detailed description of Tenochtitlan and the royal court abounds in praise and favorable comparisons with contemporary Europe and even classical antiquity.

This admiration, however genuine, has obvious limitations. Like most of his contemporaries, Cortés had no doubts about the superiority of Christian nations and their right to impose a new political and religious order after the conquest. He also favored the *encomienda* system as the only practical way for a small European minority to rule and acculturate the natives. Yet he was also convinced that the highly structured social hierarchy of the Mexica, Tlaxcalans, and other natives should be recognized and assimilated into the new colonial order. Many local *caciques* and other dignitaries were kept in their offices, and he claimed and obtained Spanish recognition for their nobility status. Perhaps most important, he favored integration through both social and cultural assimilation. Cortés, who himself had several offspring by Mexican women (including his interpreter and confidante, Malinche), promoted the education of the Mexican upper class in Christian principles and its eventual integration into the Spanish way of life through marriage with the *conquistadores*. The result was the quick development of a *mestizo* group, who were destined to be the predominant ethnic group in New Spain. Finally, the process of assimilation was enhanced by a massive program of agricultural innovation. By the time Cortés's death, New Spain was self-sufficient in all formerly European products, from wheat to silk and wine, as well as in farm animals.

The ultimate legacy of Cortés's writings was thus to alter radically the European view of the New World, from a region of exotic Caribbean islands inhabited by primitive people to a friendly, Europe-like land populated by civilized societies who could easily absorb the new order imposed on them. It would not be far-fetched, therefore, to say that Cortés's writings laid the foundation of America as the land of opportunity for Europeans.

[*See also* Conquests, *article on* Spanish Conquest; *and* Malintzin.]

BIBLIOGRAPHY

Cortés, Fernando. *Letters from Mexico.* Translated and edited by Anthony R. Pagden, introduction by J. H. Elliott. New York, 1971; repr., New Haven, 1986.

Cortés, Fernando. *Cartas de relación.* Edited by Angel Delgado-Gomez. Madrid, 1993.

Gibson, Charles. *The Aztecs under Spanish Rule.* Stanford and Oxford, 1964.

Gomara, Francisco Lopez de. *Historia de la conquista de México.* Edited by Joaquín Ramírez Cabanas. 2 vols. Mexico City, 1943.

Guzmán, Eulalia. *Relaciones de Hernán Cortés a Carlos V sobre la invasión de Anahuac.* Mexico City, 1958.

Madariaga, Salvador de. *Hernán Cortés, Conqueror of Mexico.* London, 1942.

Martínez, José Luis. *Hernán Cortés.* Mexico City, 1990.

Orozco y Berra, Manuel. *Historia antigua y de la conquista de México.* Vol. 4. Mexico City, 1880; repr., Mexico City, 1960.

Thomas, Hugh. *The Conquest of Mexico.* London, 1993.

Wagner, Henry R. *The Rise of Fernando Cortés.* Berkeley, 1944.

ANGEL DELGADO GÓMEZ

COSMIC TREES. Pre-Hispanic texts, also referred to as pictorials or storybooks, often depict the cosmological structure of the universe. Although the subject matter of these texts varies widely, trees are often represented in various contexts as an important element in the proper functioning of the cosmos.

The structure of the Mesoamerican world was based on the opposition of male and female tendencies, which was also expressed as hot and cold. This view presented a dual structure of opposing elements that divided the universe into four cardinal directions. Thus, the cosmos had four quarters. At each corner of this universe were cosmic trees, as well as four rain deities who held up the sky. In addition, along the central axis of the cosmos ran paths that were traversed by various other gods and spiritual forces. From the four great cosmic trees, the influences of the gods of the upper and lower worlds radiated toward the central point, the earth. Thus, all things in the world, including human beings, were created and sustained by the activity of the gods at the four directions. Their movements (*olin* in Nahuatl) were directed toward earth by means of the cosmic trees, which functioned like antennas and thereby directed and ordered all material existence.

In the Yucatán Peninsula, Belize, and Guatemala, trees played a dominant role in Maya ceremonial life. The Maya built their great cities in the lowland jungle, which could not support large human populations. Maya survival depended, therefore, on their knowledge of trees. Stone monuments (stelae) erected at their ceremonial centers depicted the succession of kings as well as their exploits in war and sacrifice, and these often featured trees. Kings, like cosmic trees, were understood to be intermediaries between human beings and gods. Through the king, human beings could interact with deities of the sky and the underworld, or the hidden beings responsible for material life. The king's association with the tree, therefore, represented his position as someone who could migrate between worlds. His primary responsibility was to ascend and descend along the trunk of the cosmic tree to communicate and interact with divine beings.

Trees were often the focal points of ceremonies. During a festival dedicated to the god of rain and fertility, for example, the Aztec would cut the tallest, fullest, most beautiful tree they could find. They carefully tied the branches to the trunk and cut it down so as to prevent it from touching the ground. They brought the tree back to the temple of the rain god and set it up in the god's courtyard. This tree was then attached to four other trees by means of twisting straw ropes on which hung tassels of grass. This was a ceremonial representation of the Mesoamerican conception of the cosmos described above.

Cosmic trees were seen as a critical link between human beings and the gods, and earthly trees were reflections of their cosmic counterparts. Human interactions with trees therefore entailed a host of hidden realities.

BIBLIOGRAPHY

Arnold, Philip P. *Eating Landscape: Aztec and European Occupation of Tlalocan*. Niwot, Colo., 1999. Discusses the importance of fertility rites for the way the Aztec meaningfully inhabited their material world.

Carrasco, Davíd. *Religions of Mesoamerica: Cosmovision and Ceremonial Centers*. San Francisco, 1990. Excellent overview of the religious dimensions of Mesoamerican traditions.

Heyden, Doris. "Trees and Wood in Life and Death." In *Chipping Away on Earth*, edited by Eloise Quiñones Keber, pp. 143–152. Lancaster, Calif., 1994. Exhaustive investigation of representations of trees in ancient Mesoamerican texts and the ways those concepts translated into their religious understandings.

López Austin, Alfredo. *The Human Body and Ideology: Concepts of the Ancient Nahuas*. Translated by Thelma Ortíz de Montellano and Bernard Ortíz de Montellano. 2 vols. Salt Lake City, 1988. Impressive interpretation of Mesoamerican conception of the human body and how it was intimately connected to the cosmos.

PHILIP P. ARNOLD

COSMOVISION. A large part of the cosmovision of sedentary agricultural peoples is based on concepts inherited from their nomadic ancestors, especially those who, for millennia, complemented their hunting, fishing, and resource gathering with the cultivation of domesticated plants. Mesoamerican peoples thus inherited, among other concepts, an initial idea of dualism and practices that sought communication with the supernatural, especially through psychotropic means. It is also certain, however, that around 2500 BCE sedentarism began to transform the economy, social organization, population distribution, and relations among different indigenous groups; and with this, culture in its totality had to respond to new ways of life. From the earliest times in Mesoamerica, the preeminence of maize gave this plant and its growth cycle the character of an archetype, and it reinforced the perception of the earth as a fecund mother from whom everything is received and to whom everything must return. The mortuary remains of agricultural villagers, buried beneath the floors of their homes, reveal belief in a benevolent, intimate relationship between the dead and their living family members. It is possible that relations between the cultivators of distant villages

strengthened with the cohesive idea of common descent from a first divine ancestor and protector. Moreover, the marked division of the year into two seasons, wet and dry, acquired agricultural resonance and primordial importance for the early Mesoamericans.

From earliest times, Mesoamerica was characterized by permanent contacts and exchanges among agricultural villages which permitted the existence of a common history and from it, a cultural unity. The concepts of cultivators were integrated with a congruence generated in the rationality of daily life and social communication. In this manner, over centuries, a complex of fundamental ideas was integrated to form the core of a common body of thought shared by many different ethnic groups. This complex of ideas, quite resistant to historical change, can be called the "hard nucleus" of Mesoamerican cosmovision. The constituent elements of this hard nucleus were systematically interrelated so that they were self-adjusting and could incorporate new elements of culture, accommodate existing ones, and substitute for those lost in order to give meaning to the remaining components of social thought. Thus, despite great historical changes and considerable regional, linguistic, and ethnic diversity, a basic tradition developed as a result of intense communication among Mesoamerican peoples, and the tradition simultaneously permitted this communication to continue.

Above this initial hard nucleus of Mesoamerican tradition, social and political changes were developing over the course of centuries. Around 1200 BCE, with the emergence of social hierarchies, nascent groups of authority were able to justify their preeminence on the basis of the cosmovision generalized during the long period of egalitarian societies. Thus, rulers portrayed themselves as liminal beings who communicated with the sky, the underworld, and the earth, as though they were the mouthpieces of the mountains and cosmic trees. They presented themselves as intermediaries and spokespersons of the supernatural. The idea of lineage was supported in the common origin of the society's members, but within lines of privileged descent. The rulers were "elder siblings," representing the first divine ancestors.

The abundant iconography of this period illustrates the power of these central cosmological ideas. The concept of the fecund mother earth is depicted in clay figurines of women with wide hips and other maternal traits. It has been suggested that the small two-faced or two-headed figurines related to the dual division of the cosmos. More explicit are the representations of human faces, one half with flesh, the other half skeletal; we know from earlier times the symbolic connections between the rainy season and death, and the dry season and life. Images of gods—already identifiable, such as the Old Fire God—as well as recognizable symbols of the Mesoamerican calendar appear. This period gave rise to a formidable pan-Mesoamerican iconographic movement. Its promoters, the Olmec, stylistically essentialized these generalized cosmic principles and propagated them depicted on objects of high artistic and economic value. Rulers throughout Mesoamerica found symbolic and aesthetic support for their positions in these items of prestige.

Around 400 BCE, Mesoamerica began to be the setting of great rivalries among villages struggling for regional dominance. Already in this period, the link between cosmovision and politics clearly was being expressed, above all, the magnificent temple constructions that seem to reflect a need to affirm and display authority. Architectural monumentality would gradually increase until it arrived at the extraordinary proportions of the Pyramid of the Sun at Teotihuacan or of El Tigre at El Mirador, Guatemala. Notable during this period is the great division created between systems of knowledge and systems of recording thought. Generally speaking, we can say that in the eastern part of Mesoamerica the calendar, numeration, and writing became exceedingly complex, while simpler forms were maintained in the western part.

From the second century CE on, great human concentrations and technological, economic, social, and political development produced the emergence of cities, the concentration of power in hegemonic centers, expanded commercial relations, and a heightened degree of cultural splendor. Capitals were constituted on principles and models of knowledge and religion. Mesoamerican splendor was manifested in the complexity of cosmological thought, especially the increase of deities, opulent rituals, and artistic development. Knowledge was concentrated among groups of specialists, presumably priests, who worked intensely in the service of the courts. The activities of these savants seem to have revolved around three central preoccupations: rain, destiny, and political authority. Differences were accentuated between knowledge and the recording of thought, which paradoxically developed in the Maya area and not at Teotihuacan, the most powerful capital in Mesoamerica. This apparent contradiction may be explained by the fact that the Maya, who elevated the royal figure to enormous heights as an almost-deified "elder sibling," needed to link dynastic history with divine events, knowable by way of the calendar and the movement of the stars, and with events mentioned in the monumental inscriptions. Teotihuacan, on the other hand, was a capital in which ethnic diversity led to other political forms that did not require such complex, onerous systems.

From the seventh to ninth century CE, many of the great capitals gradually collapsed. Teotihuacan was the first to fall, and its misfortune seems to have provoked a chain reaction. Mesoamerican cosmovision was radically transformed and influenced by political instability, the readjustment of interregional relationships, demographic mobilization and the associated emergence of new multiethnic capitals, the penetration of northern peoples, and an increase in militarization and wars. The new cosmovision emphasized warfare and human sacrifice, which increased considerably, especially among peoples struggling for hegemonic expansion. In this period, two figures rose to preeminence: the god Feathered Serpent and his mythical city—the place of reeds, the place of the dawn—from which various human groups left to settle the world and establish themselves before the first sunrise. Feathered Serpent and the city of the dawn became the banner of a political current seeking to impose multiethnic regimes and to subject the old dynasties to a new and more complex order. The "elder siblings" were incorporated with new functions into the multiethnic political complex, validated by and under the presidency of Feathered Serpent's representatives in the world.

Late in the second decade of the sixteenth century, European invaders began imposing themselves on Mesoamerica. From this time on, indigenous thought was profoundly affected by Christianity. The colonial regime produced a fragmentation that led to the birth of new cosmovisions in which Mesoamerican and Christian elements were united in diverse formulations and proportions.

Cosmovision and Praxis. The history of Mesoamerican cosmovision and the current persistence of indigenous concepts reveal how the hard nucleus has maintained coherence of thought. Mesoamerican cosmovision was a product of daily life in agricultural societies. In a process spanning millennia, it was gradually shaped in a rational, though unconscious, manner through the action of humans facing nature and themselves. Humans assimilated their experiences, confronting and abstracting them to form bodies of congruent concepts; this allowed them, conversely, to construct a reality in which their perception of the world and action facing that world acquired a particular meaning. The order and logic of daily practice underlying the abstraction returned to the abstraction refined through the coherence of constant human communication. Cosmovision served as a guide for action. An ebb and flow, therefore, existed between the abstraction of the cosmovision and everyday practice. Cosmovision, though never explicitly formalized, was reflected in all concrete realms of human activity, and particularly in mythology and rituals.

The hard nucleus created during the time of the first cultivators supported the historical changes of subsequent hierarchical social differentiation, the formation of complex societies, and the birth of the state. Great historical transformations were shaping the peripheral layers of the cosmovision, but the nucleus guaranteed the great overriding, permanent existence of a millennial tradition. Today, despite the shock of the Conquest and the difficult conditions of colonial life, many elements of the hard nucleus have survived among Mesoamerican descendants.

Basic Composition of the Cosmos. Mesoamerican thought was profoundly binary. Mesoamericans imagined a cosmos shaped by complementary opposites. Everything—including the gods—consisted of two types of substance. One was masculine, hot, superior, dry, luminous, strong, and vital; the other was feminine, cold, inferior, humid, dark, weak, and mortal. All beings manifested a predominance of one of the substances, but no pure formulation of a single substance existed. For example, the solar deity, of a hot and dry nature, displayed contrary elements in his disk in the form of green stones symbolizing water. Likewise, the rain god, cold and wet, held a "hot" lightning bolt in one of his hands. Any division of an entity immediately produced a new binary composition in each of the resulting parts.

The concept of duality had one of its clearest expressions in divinities, who were often represented as conjugal pairs indicating the specific attributes each of the pair's members had in a sector of the cosmos. The most unitary expression of divinity, the Sole God, could divide itself into the Great Father and the Great Mother, and each exercised power in his or her corresponding part of the cosmos.

In spite of the fact that all beings consisted of the same two substances, a separation existed between creatures and uncreated beings. In simple terms, it can be said that uncreated beings were composed solely of a subtle, light matter, imperceptible to humans under normal conditions. Creatures, on the other hand, had both this type of matter and a perceptible, hard, heavy covering that linked them to decay, destruction, and death. Obviously, the concept of creatures composed in part of divine substance corresponds to a perspective that gives "spirit" to all beings in the world. All creatures—even inanimate ones such as minerals—had this spirit, with which specialists could communicate by using appropriate language.

Myth explains how things are composed of spiritual essence and heavy matter. Before the world existed, the Great Father and Great Mother expelled a large group of their children from the divine realm because of a transgression they had committed. They sent them to settle what would become the world of humans and the kingdom of the dead. The Great Father and Mother also commissioned one of their children, the Sun, to rule the world they would form. The expelled children went through mythic adventures that prepared them to be converted into creatures. The Sun underwent the rite of sacrifice and was reborn as the astral body that illuminates the world. At sunrise he killed all the other gods, transforming them into creatures subject to the cycle of life and death. The process of dying formed a hard, heavy covering. In this account, each member of a particular class of mortal being derived from a certain deity, who remained within that being as an essence covered by the perishable, destructible, heavy matter of mortality. This explains why all individuals of the same sort—dogs, for example—have common characteristics, and why, in spite of the fact that individual dogs die, their species continues in the world. The "dog-spirit," which is a part of the "dog-deity," imprisoned at the moment of the sunrise, descends into the world of the dead when an individual dog dies, but it is recycled when another dog is conceived, entering the maternal womb to return to the world. It is not exactly a reincarnation, but rather a reutilization of "dog essence."

Characteristics of the Divine. In order to understand why the gods occupy the interior of all creatures, it is necessary to describe in detail their characteristics, according to Mesoamerican thought. Gods are personal beings; that is, they possess reason, will, passions, and faculties of communication among themselves and with humans. They are immortal; the "death" of the gods, which condemned them to live in the world of humans and the world of the dead, does not signify their annihilation, but rather their subjection to a life-and-death cycle. When an individual containing a portion of a deity as essence dies, this portion must go to a great subterranean repository of death, where it waits to be reutilized. Gods differ among themselves, and so humans attribute to them the diversity of beings in the world. Each deity transmits his or her particularity to the type of being believed to have come from that deity.

Gods are agents of action, for they have the ability to modify the areas of the world within reach of their specific power. They occupy the world of humans as well as the divine realms of the cosmos. Their powers, however, are limited. They may act only in specific areas, on specific beings, in specific moments. They rule by cosmic law and have very particular needs and desires. When they travel in the world of humans, they are vulnerable to the passing of time and must be nourished. They are both divisible and able to be reconstituted; that is, their substance can be fragmented so that they can exist in various parts of the cosmos at the same time. For example, portions of the same god could simultaneously be in the sky, in the kingdom of the dead, inside mountains, in his or her temple, and within stone or wooden images. Their parts also can also be reincorporated. Finally, the gods are both fusible and divisible. This implies that a god can unite with another to form a more complex deity, or can divide its substance to form two distinct gods, distributing its qualities between them. This explains why all the gods together form the Sole God, the sum of all divinity, and why they can fragment themselves to occupy the interior of all creatures, no matter how small. It is not surprising that a Mesoamerican could believe in a single rain god and, at the same time, four rain gods, with four different colors, occupying the four directions of the world; or in a fire god with three separate personae to inhabit, respectively, the sky, the kingdom of the dead, and the land in between; or in a deity called God 13, the sum of the thirteen celestial deities; or God 9, the sum of the nine deities of the underworld.

Geometry and Dynamics of the Cosmos. The cosmos is made up of three great levels: the sky, the underworld, and the intermediate level corresponding to the realm inhabited by humans. Myth explains the division by the existence of a ravenous, feminine, chaotic monster that inhabited the water of a great celestial ocean. Her figure corresponds to a cold, aquatic animal—a fish, a toad, or more often a crocodile—with teeth and fangs. The feminine monster was divided into two halves, constituting the sky and the earth. Its nature changed from feminine to masculine/feminine, separated into two portions. The monster's desire to recover its ancient form occasioned a universal flood. The gods raised the sky anew and placed it on five columns to avoid another cataclysm.

The definitive separation and creation of the intermediate space had numerical symbolism. The lower part, or the kingdom of the dead, was divided into nine levels. The same number of layers above formed the upper celestial levels. The intermediate space, where the sun, the moon, Venus, the stars, comets, clouds, and the wind circulated, had four levels. Thus, from the earth's surface to the highest celestial level the strata added up to thirteen, a masculine number linked to good fortune; the underworld levels, totaling nine, gave that number a feminine and less fortunate value, because it was related to death.

Horizontally, there were four great quadrants, each assigned a specific color. The distribution of the colors, however, varied a great deal within the different Mesoamerican traditions. The central part of the terrestrial plane formed the sacred space inhabited by the fire god. In each of the four quadrants of the world was located one of the cosmic columns, characterized by the color corresponding to its position. The fifth and principal column occupied the center and served as the *axis mundi*. The columns were considered gods and took arboreal form—either different-colored ceiba trees or separate species of trees. Their trunks were hollow and filled with the hot forces of the sky and cold forces of the underworld, in perpetual opposition. Thus, there would be four

rain gods and four fire gods, distinguished by their four corresponding colors.

These trees were considered the highways of the gods. This idea corresponds with the Mesoamerican concept of time as a substance constantly coming to earth, invading everything, and transforming creatures with the specificity of its force. Time actually consisted of gods who, according to their particularities, affected the world in the form of destinies. Their realms of origin were the sky and the underworld. Inside the trees, divine struggle produced combinations of time, and the sun transported the resulting forces from the sky and radiated them to the entire surface of the earth. On earth, the time-gods worked in their specific ways on every creature, for a game of affinities and oppositions existed between gods and mortal beings. Thus, for example, a day that had the dog god in its composition would be favorable to dogs and to humans named after the dog day sign, and it would facilitate the latter's livelihood.

The gods, subject to the laws of the calendar, had to follow a strict, immutable order. Each temporal unit followed the previous one, being formed and leaving the tree in its turn. The tree in the east went first, then north, then west, then south, then back to the east, and so on. Therefore, times were spatially marked, and there were days corresponding to each direction: the "ceiba" days corresponded to the east, the "wind" days to the north, the "house" days to the west, and so on.

The time-gods were distributed in cycles of distinct dimensions. There were groups of seven, nine, thirteen, twenty, etc., and they combined to form more complex deities made up of day cycles of 260, 360, 365, 18,980, etc. The 260-day cycle was divinatory, the 360-day cycle served for historical records, and the 365-day cycle pertained to labor and religion, because it established the order of the principal festivals dedicated to the gods. Humans could anticipate the march of time by mathematically calculating the successions, knowing the character of each one of the time-gods, and anticipating the result of the combinations of the distinct cycles. Prediction was a complex task to which many of the priests in the service of the courts were dedicated.

Cycle of Life and Death. The year, divided into two seasons—wet and dry—was thought to be dominated by the two opposing, complementary forces of the cosmos. The wet season corresponded to the powers of the underworld, while the Sun ruled during the dry season.

The mother goddesses and the rain gods pertained to the powers of the underworld. Inside the great sacred mountain, there was a large pot that served as the dwelling of the rain god. Inside the pot was all the water that would come to the world, leaving as clouds of rain or hail through the mouths of caves, rising through springs, or running through subterranean rivers to the sea. Inside there were also "hearts" or "seeds" of mortal beings. These "hearts" were gods who calmly waited to return to the surface inside the body of an individual to whom their type of essence would be provided. In addition to the water and "hearts," there were the terrifying feminine forces of germination and growth. At the beginning of the rainy season, these forces were liberated from their enclosure and covered the surface of the earth with verdure. Cultivators deposited the seeds inside the earth and prayed for the arrival of the complements that would make the plants sprout. The sown seeds were united with the invisible ones, or "hearts," the forces of growth, and the water of the rains. The seed germinated, the plant sprouted, and, finally, fruit arrived. With the feminine work concluded, the rains stopped; then celestial authority took over governing the world so that the fruit matured in the sun's rays. The cultivators bid farewell to the rains—to the powers of death—thanking them for their benevolent action. They liberated the powers of growth with ceremonies of the first fruit and burned the stubble so that the water the earth had absorbed, converted by the action of fire into clouds of smoke, would return to its subterranean depository to complete the great cycle.

The process had as its archetype the worldly agricultural cycle of maize, and it served to explain the cyclical processes of all mortal beings. If a tree fell, if a bird died, if a stone was pulverized or calcinated, its "souls" abandoned its corporeal remains and went to occupy their provisional place in the container of the great mountain, one of the places that made up the kingdom of the dead.

The mountain of the rain god had its replicas in all the mountains of the world, which were ordered hierarchically. Each settlement had its own mountain filled with particular riches: the rains and the reproductive potential of humans, plants, and animals. The administration of the mountains' contents fell to human specialists who requested the departure of the resources and averted excesses of their liberation, principally the devastating effects of hail or the "cold" diseases which rose into the world in the form of malignant winds.

The idea of cycle was one of the most important in Mesoamerican cosmovision. Complementary opposites were not polar but, rather, dynamic values whose existence in the world was indispensable and obligatory. Death, for example, engendered life; it was incarnated in the pregnant woman whose dark womb, filled with water, generated life; or life, incarnated in the warrior figure of the sun, caused death to ensure the continuity of the world. The absolute triumph of one of the opposing forces would extinguish existence. Perpetual struggle alternating between triumphs and defeats was necessary.

Humans as Part of the Cosmos. The human body is one of the most important sources for the formulation of ideas about the cosmos, and its daily maintenance generates a large part of the explanations of the processes that humans believe are replicated in the universe. Mesoamericans thought that, like all other mortal beings, humans were composed of a perceptible, hard, heavy substance and a divine, light substance that constituted their animistic entities. Each of these entities had specific functions and explained a complex of human particularities.

The principal animistic entity was the "heart" (not strictly the visceral organ that served as a receptacle, but its invisible interior that generated life force and human specificity). Its origin, as in all creatures, was the deity from whom the species had been created. In the case of their own existence, however, Mesoamericans had to explain problems stemming from a non-evolutionary vision of the world—the mythic perspective that all kinds of creatures began their existence with immutable characteristics. If all human beings were essentially equal, how could differences among human groups be accounted for, when these differences had supposedly existed since primordial time? The mystery of language, for example, had to be explained. Humans were characterized by language, which differentiated them categorically from animals. Language thus formed a part of human essence obtained at the beginning of the world. Humans, however, spoke different languages. The answer to this dilemma was carved out in myths responding to two moments of creation, one specific and the other generic. Human beings—men and women—were formed in the Place of Creation by their patron deity, but this does not signify, directly, their emergence into the world. For this, there were complementary myths that spoke of the life of human beings in a kind of antechamber of the world, where they existed as undifferentiated groups until exiting their enclosure through seven caves and in waves of seven by seven. In this departure, each group received its language, its professions, its ethnic characteristics, and its sacred bundle, and, of course, it remained under the protection of its patron deity, who was a portion of the generic patron deity. The groups spread throughout the land, each occupying the site its particular patron deity indicated, and awaited the first sunrise with which mortal time was initiated. In each settlement, the patron deity occupied the mountain that enclosed the riches and was in charge of distributing water, food, health, protection, and reproductive power from it in exchange for adoration and moral rectitude from the protected.

Other animistic entities accompanied the human "heart." Just as the "heart" explained the individual's similarities to his or her group originating from the common patron, other entities justified individual particularities. Among them, the force of destiny stands out; it was radiated by the sun and introduced to the child by way of ritual. One day soon after birth, the child underwent a ceremony in which a portion of the time then dominant would definitively occupy the body of the newborn. Obviously, a favorable date was chosen so that the time-god would be integrated into the animistic complex of the child in the form of his or her name, destiny, and character. This radiation was a treasure that humans had to be attentive to throughout their lives in order to take maximum advantage of the benefits and avoid the harmful effects of their "day."

These and other entities, permanent or transitory, constituted the identity of the individual. The human, therefore, was conceived as an exceedingly complex being, composed of heterogeneous, sometimes contradictory units that had to be integrated to live a healthy and moral life. Harmony had to be sought internally as well as in the social, natural, and supernatural environments. Health depended in good part on the appropriate ingestion of food; some kinds were considered cold and others hot, and these were combined so as to maintain the organism in equilibrium. Likewise, the restoration of lost health had to be achieved with medicines contrary in nature to the diseases invading from the celestial realm, which caused, among other things, the deterioration of the organism, or to those from the underworld, which occasioned swelling and other symptoms characteristic of bad "colds."

The death of a human being meant the disintegration of the individual's component parts. Existence in another world after life was the destiny of only one of the animistic entities, the "heart." The other elements dissolved in the world, were dispersed, or were left to wander. The "heart" followed the path of all invisible seeds: it went to the world of the dead and suffered the torments of being cleansed of its mortal experience. It arrived, after a long journey, at a point where, cleansed of the particularities of its existence, it lost its individuality and could be used again in another human being.

The documentary sources, however, also speak of privileged deaths that gave a glorious existence to the deceased. Those dying an aquatic death passed a time in the paradise of the rain god, enjoying the exuberance of the vegetal seeds of the subterranean repository and contributing their work to administer the riches of the world. Men who died in combat went to work in the house of the sun, accompanying it in its daily journey from the east; women who died giving birth to their first child accompanied the sun on its nightly journey from the west.

[See also Colors; Cosmic Trees; Creation Myths; Dual-ity; Fertility; Human Body; Sacrifice and Ritual Violence; Soul; Underworld.]

BIBLIOGRAPHY

Aveni, Anthony F. *Skywatchers of Ancient Mexico*. Austin, 1980. General study of Mesoamerican astronomical knowledge, based primarily on archaeological remains.

Boone, Elizabeth Hill, ed. *Ritual Human Sacrifice in Mesoamerica*. Washington, D.C., 1984 Collection of studies on one of the most disturbing ritual practices of ancient Mesoamericans, written by specialists.

Broda, Johanna. *The Mexican Calendar as Compared to Other Mesoamerican Systems*. Vienna, 1969. Study of the some of the calendrical problems of the ancient settlers of Central Mexico.

Carrasco, Davíd. *Religions of Mesoamerica: Cosmovision and Ceremonial Centers*. San Francisco, 1990. Synthesis of the beliefs and practices of Mesoamerican peoples, with emphasis on Mexica and Maya thought.

Caso, Alfonso. *The Aztecs: People of the Sun*. Translated by Lowell Dunham. Norman, Okla., 1958. Work of diffusion; classic general study of Mexica deities.

Edmonson, Munro S. *The Book of the Year: Middle American Calendrical Systems*. Salt Lake City, 1988. General comparative study of calendars and the development of time measurement in Mesoamerican tradition.

Freidel, David, Linda Schele, and Joy Parker. *Maya Cosmos: Three Thousand Years on the Shaman's Path*. New York, 1993. General study of the development of Maya religious and cosmological thought through iconographic and epigraphic analysis.

Graulich, Michel. *Mythes et rituels du Mexique ancien préhispanique*. Brussels, 1987. Examines the religion and mythology of peoples of the Basin of Mexico during the Postclassic period.

León-Portilla, Miguel. *Aztec Thought and Culture: A Study of the Ancient Nahuatl Mind*. Translated by Jack Emory Davis. Norman, Okla., 1963. Studies ancient Nahua thought through textual and philological analysis.

León-Portilla, Miguel. *Time and Reality in the Thought of the Maya*. Translated by Charles L. Boilés and Fernando Horcasitas. Norman, Okla., 1973. Examines the concept of time among the ancient Maya through documentary sources and philology.

López Austin, Alfredo. *Tamoanchan, Tlalocan: Places of Mist*. Translated by Bernard R. Ortiz de Montellano and Thelma Ortiz de Montellano. Niwot, Colo., 1997. Studies cosmic topology and its significance, the foundations of Mesoamerican mythology, concepts concerning vegetation, and the life and death cycle.

López Austin, Alfredo. *The Myths of the Opossum: Pathways of Mesoamerican Mythology*. Translated by Bernard R. Ortiz de Montellano and Thelma Ortiz de Montellano. Albuquerque, 1993. Examines the foundations of mythology in Mesoamerican tradition from the pre-Hispanic past to the present.

Miller, Mary Ellen, and Karl Taube. *The Gods and Symbols of Ancient Mexico and the Maya: An Illustrated Dictionary of Mesoamerican Religion*. New York and London, 1993. Accessible reference work written by specialists of Mesoamerican religion and iconography.

Nicholson, H. B. "Religion in Pre-Hispanic Central Mexico." In *Handbook of Middle American Indians*, edited by Robert Wauchope, vol. 10, pp. 395–447. Austin, 1971. One of the classic studies of pre-Hispanic religion, particularly preoccupied with the taxonomy of deities.

Ortiz de Montellano, Bernard R. *Aztec Medicine, Health, and Nutrition*. New Brunswick, N.J., and London, 1990. General study of the beliefs and practices of the Mexica and their contemporaries concerning health, disease, nutrition, life, and death, with an evaluation of their efficacy from the point of view of current science.

Schele, Linda, and Mary Ellen Miller. *The Blood of Kings: Ritual and Dynasty in Maya Art*. New York and Fort Worth, 1986. Iconographic and epigraphic analysis examining the relationships between politics and religion in the Maya world, emphasizing conceptions of contact with the otherworld.

Taube, Karl. *The Major Gods of Ancient Yucatan*. Washington D.C., 1992. Revision of the traditional denomination of Maya deities and study of their functions and iconography.

Thompson, J. Eric S. *Maya History and Religion*. Norman, Okla., 1970. A classic study of Maya thought.

ALFREDO LÓPEZ AUSTIN
Translated from Spanish by Scott Sessions

COSPI, CODEX. Also known as the *Codex Bologna*, the *Codex Cospi* is a Late Postclassic (1200–1521 CE) manuscript painted in the Mixteca-Puebla style and be-

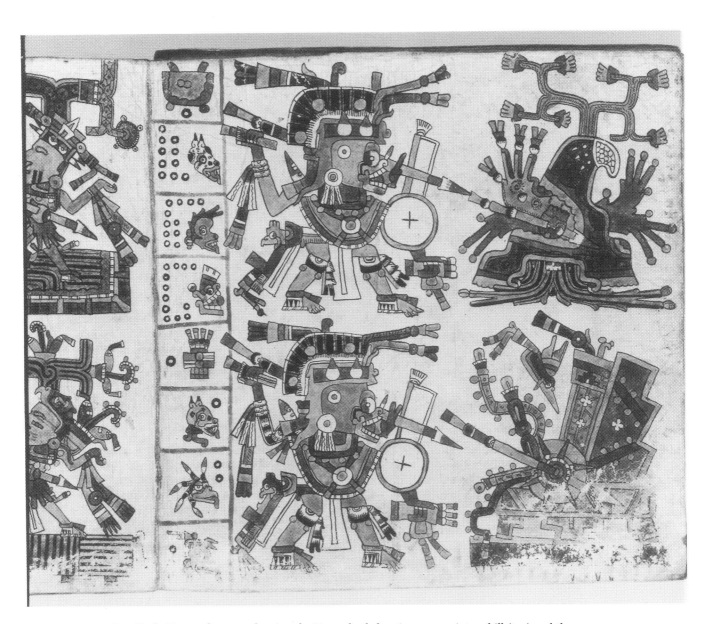

Detail of a Venus almanac, showing the Venus lord shooting arrows into a hill (*top*) and throne (*bottom*). From the *Codex Cospi*. *Courtesy of Biblioteca Universitaria, Bologna.*

longs to the so-called Borgia Group. The contents of the manuscript are of a religious and divinatory character. Its exact place of origin is unknown.

The first known owner of the codex was Count Valerio Cospi, a citizen of Bologna, who gave it to Marquis Ferdinando Cospi for his collection of curiosities. The cover of the manuscript bears an inscription in Italian which, translated, reads: "Book from Mexico [rubbed out: 'from China'] given by Count Valerio Zani to Marquis Cospi on the 26th day of December 1665." The reference to China, later corrected, indicates that at the time of presentation to Cospi, knowledge of the actual origin of the manuscript had been lost. Presently the manuscript is in the library of the University of Bologna (manuscript no. 4093).

The physical manuscript consists of four segments of deerskin that have been glued together and folded into twenty approximately square pages in so-called screenfold fashion. Its total length is 364 centimeters, and the average width of the pages is 18.2 centimeters. The deerskin is covered with a thin layer of stucco on which the polychrome scenes are painted. The protective cover of Italian parchment that bears the aforementioned inscription was added, presumably in Italy. The front side of the screenfold has twenty pages, and the back side has eighteen (because of the added covers). Thirteen pages of the front side (1–13) and eleven pages of the back side (21–31) have been painted; the remaining pages are left blank. The two sides are clearly the work of two different artists, judging by the different execution of details and the far greater skill displayed by the painter of the front side.

The first scene on the front side (pp. 1–8) presents an *in extenso* almanac of the *tonalpohualli* (260-day calendar) that is characteristic of all the Borgia Group codices. Between two tiers of divinatory and ritual prescriptions, the 260 days of the *tonalpohualli* are shown, but without their numerical coefficients. They are arranged in five tiers of 52 (the days read from the lower left of p. 1 to the upper right of p. 8). Cognates of this almanac appear in the codices *Borgia* and *Vaticanus B*. The same type of division, in abbreviated form, can be found throughout the Borgia Group. The Cospi almanac also shows the Nine Lords of the Night, each associated with a particular day.

The second scene of the front side (pp. 9–11) shows the Venus god, Tlahuizcalpanteuhtli, spearing five different entities, arranged over a division of the *tonalpohualli* of 65 × 4 days. The particular four-day periods were considered dangerous times for the speared entities. Cognate scenes occur in the codices *Borgia*, *Vaticanus B*, and *Dresden*.

The third scene of the front side (pp. 12–13) shows a division of the *tonalpohualli* in 5 × 52, arranged over four quarters dedicated to the cardinal points. Gods, or priests dressed as gods, present offerings in front of temples showing positive or negative auguries. Cognate scenes appear in the codices *Borgia*, *Fejérváry-Mayer*, and *Laud*.

The back side pictorially describes rituals that involve counted bundles in front of deities. The rituals are intended for obtaining good luck and protection in several activities. Similar scenes are found in the codices *Fejérváry-Mayer* and *Laud*.

[*See also* Borgia Group of Pictorial Manuscripts; Mixteca-Puebla Style.]

BIBLIOGRAPHY

Anders, Ferdinand, Maarten Jansen, and Peter L. van der Loo. *Calendario de pronósticos y ofrendas: Libro explicativo del llamado Códice Cospi.* Mexico City and Graz, 1994. Provides a full commentary, discussions of provenance, and history of manuscript and its interpretations.

Loo, Peter L. van der. "Voicing the Painted Image: A Suggestion for Reading the Reverse of the Codex Cospi." In *Writing without Words*, edited by Elizabeth Hill Boone and Walter D. Mignolo, pp. 77–86. Durham and London, 1994. Attempt to read the text out of the picture writing, using present-day indigenous traditions.

Nowotny, Karl A. *Tlacuilolli: Die Mexikanischen Bilderhandschriften, Stil und Inhalt.* Berlin, 1961. Fundamental study for modern interpretations of the Borgia Group.

PETER LODEWIJK VAN DER LOO

COSTUME. *See* Dress, Costume, and Adornment.

COTZUMALHUAPA, one of the most important polities of the Late to Terminal Classic periods (c.600–1000 CE) in southern Mesoamerica. (A variant spelling is "Cotzumalguapa.") At that time, a major ceremonial complex (known today as the Cotzumalhuapa Nuclear Zone) developed on the Pacific coastal piedmont of central Guatemala. This complex included a settlement area extending at least six square kilometers between and around three major centers with monumental architecture and sculpture, now known as Bilbao, El Baúl, and El Castillo. The area was linked by a system of causeways and bridges. The major sites boast large stone-faced platforms and pyramids, many adorned with monumental sculptures that display a unique art style and writing system.

More than 150 monuments are known from the Cotzumalhuapa Nuclear Zone, including carved boulders, stelae, staircases, pillars, and other architectural elements. Sculptures were carved in a variety of ways, ranging from bas-relief to full round. The Cotzumalhuapa style is characterized by its treatment of human figures, which dis-

Monument 2 from La Gloria, Santa Lucia Cotzumalhuapa, Guatemala, which provides a typical example of the Cotzumalhuapa sculptural style. This sculpture depicts the face of a supernatural known as the Manikin Death God. Dimensions of carved surface: 1.34 × 0.8m (4 feet × 2 feet). *Photograph courtesy of the Oswaldo Chinchilla Mazariegos.*

play strong and highly individualized facial features combined with flat but well-proportioned bodies, often depicted in dynamic poses. Monuments display complex scenes in which two or more individuals interact with one another or with supernatural beings. Individuals are often shown with "speech scrolls," which take the form of complex vines that grow to enormous lengths, bearing a variety of flowers and fruits.

Much of Cotzumalhuapa iconography remains obscure, but the importance accorded to individualized human figures suggests that the subject matter relates largely to the power of rulers and nobles as political leaders and mediators with the gods. Major themes include the presentation of offerings, exchange of symbols, human sacrifice, and the ballgame. [*See* Ballgame.] Among the variety of supernatural beings that appear as sculptures, the most ubiquitous is the Manikin Death God, a small skeletal being with distinctive attributes. Deities of Central Mexican origin, such as the rain god Tlaloc, are also found. Scenes are often accompanied by texts in the little-known Cotzumalhuapa writing system, which shares features with systems of Oaxaca and Central Mexico.

Most signs are probably calendric, indicating dates or names of individuals.

Outside the Nuclear Zone, Cotzumalhuapa-style sculpture is found throughout a wide region extending more than 150 kilometers (95 miles) along the Pacific coastal piedmont, as far as the present-day frontier between Guatemala and El Salvador. The style is also found in the Antigua Guatemala valley of the central highlands. A discontinuous distribution, with sculptures clustered around major peripheral sites, such as Palo Gordo and Los Cerritos Norte, suggests that political relations between those sites and the Nuclear Zone mediated the adoption of this regal style in peripheral areas. The precise relationship among sites over the entire region is unknown, but there are strong indications that the Cotzumalhuapa Nuclear Zone was the dominant political and cultural power center of the Late Classic in southern Guatemala. The style's range of distribution probably included areas of diverse ethnic and linguistic composition, making identification with a specific group uncertain.

The Cotzumalhuapa area had a long history of occupation, going back to the Middle Formative (Preclassic), with important cultural developments during the Late Formative. El Baúl Monument 1 has one of the earliest known hieroglyphic inscriptions in Mesoamerica, with a Long Count date of 37 CE. This early development remains poorly known archaeologically.

BIBLIOGRAPHY

Chinchilla Mazariegos, Oswaldo. "'Peor es Nada': El origen de las esculturas de Cotzumalguapa en el Museum für Völkerkunde, Berlin." *Baessler-Archiv* n.s. 49 (1996), 295–357.

Chinchilla Mazariegos, Oswaldo. "Settlement Patterns and Monumental Art at a Major Pre-Columbian Polity: Cotzumalguapa, Guatemala." Ph.D. diss. University of Michigan, 1996.

Parsons, Lee A. *Bilbao, Guatemala: An Archeological Study of the Pacific Coast Cotzumalhuapa Region.* 2 vols. Milwaukee, 1967–1969.

Thompson, J. Eric S. *An Archaeological Reconnaissance in the Cotzumalhuapa Region, Escuintla, Guatemala.* Washington, D.C., 1948.

OSWALDO CHINCHILLA MAZARIEGOS

COVARRUBIAS, MIGUEL (1904–1957), Mexican artist and archaeologist. He was born in Mexico City, into a wealthy and politically prominent family, and he died in the same city. At various stages in his life, Covarrubias was a caricaturist, book illustrator, muralist, writer, ethnographer, archaeologist, collector of pre-Columbian antiquities, teacher, and ballet director. Along with his American colleague Matthew W. Stirling, he was the codiscoverer of the Olmec civilization. [*See* Stirling, Matthew W.]

His early art career in New York, drawing caricatures for such magazines as *Vanity Fair* and *The New Yorker*, also gave him the ability to seize the salient characteristics of the ancient objects that interested him and to reach deeply felt understandings about major styles and their evolutionary succession. This talent enabled him to perceive the precocity of the Olmec styles over all others in Mesoamerica.

In 1930 and 1933, Covarrubias and his American-born wife, Rosa Yolanda, traveled to Bali. The book that resulted from Miguel's ethnographic studies and drawings and Rosa's photographs, *The Island of Bali* (1937), is still considered by specialists the best single work on the subject and a classic of anthropological research. His fascination with indigenous dance that began in Bali was later to be rekindled with his work for the National Ballet of Mexico. In addition, it was his work in Bali that initiated his conviction—developed in later books—that the cultures of Asia had been connected with those of pre-Columbian America through trans-Pacific diffusion.

Following the completion of six mural maps for the Pacific House of the San Francisco World's Fair of 1939, Covarrubias returned to Mexico. Subsequently, he received a Guggenheim Foundation grant to travel throughout southern Mexico during the 1940s, collecting and drawing ethnographic, archaeological, and historical data on the peoples of Veracruz and Oaxaca. At the same time, he had begun collecting ancient Mexican art, particularly jade and other pieces in the style identified as "Olmec" by Marshall Saville and George C. Vaillant; many of these consisted of pottery and figurines from the site of Tlatilco in the Valley of Mexico, then being demolished by brickyard operations. After visiting Matthew Stirling and his wife, Marion, at their excavations at the site of La Venta, Tabasco, he attended the conference Mayas y Olmecas in Mexico City, convened by the Sociedad Mexicana de Antropología. There, he presented a comprehensive paper on the origin and development of the Olmec style—the first and still one of the finest treatments of Olmec art and culture in print. The conclusions reached by him, Stirling, and Mexican colleagues such as Alfonso Caso in the 1942 conference volume were that this newly defined civilization was the oldest in Mesoamerica and that it was the *cultura madre* ("mother culture") from which all other native civilizations had evolved.

By this time, Covarrubias had become an archaeologist, and he was a regular participant in the La Venta excavations, making drawings of the major finds as they appeared. He had also been a witness to Alfonso Caso's spectacular tomb discoveries at Monte Albán in Oaxaca. Based on this and on his extensive travels, he produced *Mexico South* (1946), profusely illustrated with his own drawings, maps, and watercolor paintings, and with Rosa's photographs. Besides the well-researched, and in some respects unique, ethnographic data on the contemporary peoples of the Isthmus of Tehuantepec—the Huave, Zapotec, and Mixe-Zoqueans—the book contained Covarrubias's overview of the primacy of the Olmec culture of the Gulf Coast plain. This view had been vehemently opposed by Mayanists such as J. Eric S. Thompson and Sylvanus G. Morley, but before the use of radiocarbon dating, Covarrubias and his colleagues found themselves in a minority regarding the early temporal position of Olmec civilization. [*See* Morley, Sylvanus Griswold; Thompson, J. Eric S.]

For some time, Tlatilco had been a special interest of Covarrubias and, in 1942, he began archaeological explorations at the site with Hugo Moedano. Among the burials that they excavated were some containing Olmec-style ceramic figurines, along with figurines in styles known at the time to be Formative (Preclassic) in date, thus confirming his belief in the great age of the culture. Unfortunately, other than one detailed drawing of a rich interment, these investigations were never properly published. About Tlatilco, his socialist political beliefs led him to the hypothesis, expressed in several articles and in a later book, that this large village represented the arrival of an aristocratic Olmec class from the Gulf Coast low-

A double caricature of Miguel Covarrubias and his photographer wife, Rosa Covarrubias, who took most of the photographs in his two best-known books, *The Island of Bali* and *Mexico South*. *Original Covarrubias drawings courtesy of Michael D. Coe.*

lands, to hold sway over an underclass of local, peasant natives with a far simpler way of life.

Covarrubias had planned a three-volume work on the indigenous art and cultures of the Western Hemisphere, to be published by Alfred A. Knopf in New York. The first volume, *The Eagle, the Jaguar and the Serpent* (1954), covered North America north of Mexico and contained his ideas about trans-Pacific contacts, a subject in which he had never lost interest. The second, *The Indian Art of Mexico and Central America* (1957), while it had very little on the Maya or on Central America (he had little regard for the "baroque" art of the Maya), nevertheless was the best treatment of Mesoamerican culture history that had yet appeared. Particularly influential on later thinking about the Olmec was a chart in which he traced the various Mesoamerican rain gods down to an Olmec "were-jaguar" representation. Because of Covarrubias's unexpected death in 1957, the final volume on South America was never completed. In his last years, he had been director of the National Ballet of Mexico, producing and designing the scenery and costumes for several ballets based on pre-Spanish Mexican themes, such as *Los Cuatro Soles* ("The Four Suns") to music by Carlos Chávez. He had also taught the art of Mesoamerica at the Escuela Nacional de Antropología e Historia in Mexico City.

In retrospect, Covarrubias was one of Mexico's most influential artists and scholars. His great painterly abilities and his skill as a writer brought the beauty of Balinese and pre-Columbian culture to a wide and appreciative audience. His profound understanding of Olmec art—partly intuitive and partly based on archaeological research—foreshadowed all subsequent research on that ancient civilization.

BIBLIOGRAPHY

García-Noriega y Nieto, Lucía, ed. *Miguel Covarrubias: Homenaje.* Mexico City, 1987. Catalog of an exhibition in honor of Covarrubias, with essays on all aspects of his career and an extensive bibliography.

MICHAEL D. COE

COYOTES. *See* Canines.

CRAFT PRODUCTION. Mesoamerican peoples produce a great variety of craft items for domestic needs, subsistence production, ritual life, and for barter or sale in marketplaces. Craft objects are made and used in rural and urban settings and coexist along with mass-produced industrial goods. This persistence attests to the importance of handmade objects and their manufacture for economic survival, social organization, and the creation and reproduction of cultural identity. Recent research documents changing materials, technologies, and designs for many crafts, with its primary emphasis on the effects of the growing tourist and export markets.

A Mesoamerican Model. Specialization among most or all residents of a village or certain *barrios* within villages, towns, and cities is a historical characteristic of Mesoamerica that continues today. Neighboring households practice the same *oficio*, the hereditary manual trade, and they use nearly identical processes and technologies to generate objects with unique characteristics in locally specific styles. For the larger region, members of different communities or barrios often specialize in complementary trades, such as pottery, basketry, weaving, embroidery, metalworking, stone carving, woodworking, baking, and candy confection. The household model for organizing production still dominates in most places and settings from peasant communities to urban contexts despite the fact that nonhousehold labor is common to meet seasonal demands and in workshops geared to commercial production. Diversification occurs across geographical regions and ecological zones. This organizational model originated in pre-Hispanic societies, and many forms of manufacture introduced in the Colonial and modern periods conform to it.

Because of local specialization, marketplaces and periodic religious fairs where artisans and merchants gather to exchange or sell their goods have central importance in Mesoamerica. Varied and overlapping relationships exist for circulating craft objects, among them gift exchange, barter, and sales for cash in rural or urban markets. Newer outlets include sales to stores and boutiques in tourist centers and to individuals or organizations exporting crafts abroad.

The highly characteristic, localized styles that emerge from this pattern allow researchers to identify the precise origin of most objects. Community specialization among artisans also facilitates the transmission of skills and embeds craft objects and their production in particular forms of social organization. For these reasons, certain handmade objects are essential to the creation of local identities, and the continual practice of an *oficio* is a crucial feature of Mesoamerican social and economic life.

Types of Craft Production. Artisanry for local uses tied to subsistence activities and religious practice continues as an important form of production that is often overlooked by researchers. This includes the manufacture of tools and implements for various aspects of work in farming, construction, fishing, wild plant gathering, animal husbandry, and cottage industries, and of utensils for preparing traditional foods. Another category includes specialized objects for fiestas, offerings to the dead, curing ceremonies, and agricultural rituals. These crafts often are produced seasonally, and the objects usually are sold or exchanged in rural marketplaces or urban "popular" neighborhoods.

The most startling development in the second half of the twentieth century has been the extraordinary demand for crafts by tourists and residents of industrialized countries. This worldwide phenomenon has greatly affected artisans in Mexico and Guatemala, and it has received considerable attention from researchers who attempt to evaluate its economic, social, and cultural implications. The differing situations must be considered—among them traditional crafts sold to new buyers, changed forms within a traditional trade for new markets, and the creation of entirely new handcrafted objects that are exclusively for sale. These factors, along with significant regional variation, make generalization difficult; not surprisingly, opinions differ regarding the long-term impact of this international market on local artisans, their communities, and the craft objects.

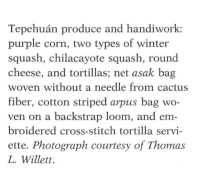

Tepehuán produce and handiwork: purple corn, two types of winter squash, chilacayote squash, round cheese, and tortillas; net *asak* bag woven without a needle from cactus fiber, cotton striped *arpus* bag woven on a backstrap loom, and embroidered cross-stitch tortilla serviette. *Photograph courtesy of Thomas L. Willett.*

Research Problems. Debate surrounds the characterization of craft production when it is intensified and becomes integrated into global markets. Based on changing relationships within workshops, some researchers conclude that artisans have become rural proletarians, petty commodity producers, or home-based "workers" who are dependent on wages. Others find that craftspeople can maintain cultural differences and exercise considerable economic autonomy while relying on cash from selling their goods. An important variable is whether artisans practice subsistence agriculture or have become completely dependent on monetary income from their craft. An additional economic consideration is whether producers or family members achieve direct access to the market. When most artisans in a community or region obtain substantial monetary returns by partially controlling commercial networks, selling crafts can strengthen social and cultural cohesion. Intensified production also alters the division of labor and the management of cash in households, with significant consequences for relations among persons of different genders and different generations.

The research that focuses on craft objects shows greater concern for their symbolic properties. Substantial data demonstrate that crafts are essential to cultural identity and the transmission of cosmology in Mesoamerica. Certainly, this is true for textiles, which have been studied most extensively, but the way that other crafts fulfill similar functions requires some research. A few researchers suggest that commodification breaks down the traditional meanings associated with these objects. Yet the emphasis on the cultural meanings attached to crafts by consumers may actually exaggerate the impact of external valuation on an artisan's perception of his or her work. A crucial analytical distinction must be made between the significance of the object and its production for the artisan and the consumer's relationship to an object purchased or viewed on display in galleries or museums. These very different processes of elaborating meaning require ethnological study sensitive to contemporary circumstances: Mesoamerican artisans and first-world consumers operate in vastly different cultural and economic contexts despite their connection through the market.

Debate also surrounds the impact of commodification on design, materials, and workmanship. Many observers report deteriorating quality among commercial crafts, but market forces in themselves do not fully explain this. In large part, producer standards depend on the level of remuneration and on the ability of adequately compensated artisans to maintain or even improve quality. Contrary to popular stereotypes, experimentation with materials and new designs are historical constants among artisans. In some instances, commercialization appears to stimulate innovations not necessarily inimical to Mesoamerican cultural and aesthetic sensibilities. Once again, careful attention to many interrelated economic, social, and historical variables is required to assess specific cases.

[*See also* Tourism.]

BIBLIOGRAPHY

Buechler, Hans, and Judith-Maria Buechler. *Manufacturing against the Odds: Small-Scale Producers in an Andean City.* Boulder, 1992. Excellent discussion of cottage industries and commercial craft production in Bolivia; provides invaluable comparative material for similar cases in Mesoamerica.

Good, Catharine L. "Painting Local Meanings, Domesticating Money and Markets: Nahuatl Bark Cloth Artists of Mexico." *Museum Anthropology* 20.3 (1996), 11–25. Case study that analyzes the benefits of craft commercialization for one indigenous society by focusing on how artistic imagery and cash income facilitate cultural reproduction.

Nash, June, ed. *Crafts in the World Market: The Impact of Global Exchange on Middle American Artisans.* Albany, N.Y., 1993. Collection of case studies, based on long-term research; also contains essential bibliographical references for key issues.

Sandstrom, Allen, and Pamela Effrein Sandstrom. *Traditional Papermaking and Paper Cult Figures of Mexico.* Norman, Okla., 1986. Provides a detailed study of one ancient Mesoamerican craft used in rituals today.

Schaefer, Stacey. "The Loom and Time in the Huichol World." *Journal of Latin American Lore* 15.2 (1989), 179–194. Demonstrates how weaving reproduces cosmology in a native Mesoamerican culture.

Schevill, Margo Blum, Janet Catherine Berlo, and Edward B. Dwyer, eds. *Textile Traditions of Mesoamerica and the Andes: An Anthology.* New York, 1991. Anthology that documents important cases in which the authors consider women's roles, along with the production, marketing, and symbolism of textiles.

Stephen, Lynn. *Zapotec Women.* Austin, Tex., 1991. This case study of a successful weaving community emphasizes the impact of intensive commercialization on women and Zapotec culture as a whole.

Turok, Marta. *¿Cómo acercarse a la Artesanía?* Mexico City, 1988. Excellent introduction to the major ethnological issues that surround both traditional and commercial forms of craft production in Mexico.

CATHARINE GOOD

CREATION MYTHS. Pre-Hispanic sources on Mesoamerican creation myths are scarce; there are some Classic Maya inscriptions (at Palenque, Quiriguá), Mixtec codices, and some iconography, especially on Maya vases. The imperfectly deciphered inscriptions are short and allusive. The non-Maya, pre-Hispanic or Colonial pictorial codices, which allude to complex stories in concise drawings, were essentially memoranda for oral poets or historians, but they are almost incomprehensible without commentary. The same is generally true of the iconography; it is useful only inasmuch as it depicts myths known from other sources. The bulk of our information, therefore, comes from texts written in the European alphabet.

Only three offer a continuous cosmogony: the Quiché-Maya *Popol Vuh* (PV) and the Mexica *Historia de los Mexicanos por sus pinturas* (HMP) and *Leyenda de los Soles* (LS). Fragmentary documentation for the Maya is found mainly in the *Books of Chilam Balam* and in the works of Landa and Las Casas; for the Aztecs, we have the *Histoyre du Méchique* (HM), the work of Sahagún, Mendieta's and Torquemada's fragments copied from Olmos, and the codices *Telleriano-Remensis* and *Vaticanus A* (CTR, CVA); and for the Mixtecs, the work of Fray Gregorio García. Several other sources offer interesting details. Ethnography provides modern variants of ancient myth cycles that may be helpful for a better understanding of ancient myths and may substantiate the continuity and the fundamental unity of Mesoamerican thought.

With the exception of the *Popol Vuh*, most of these texts (e.g., HMP) are fragmentary, out of context, or splintered, because the events are arranged in an annalistic order. The HMP and the LS were commissioned by Motecuhzoma II to support his religious reforms and his revision of the myths. Although they are essentially oral traditions, manipulations by the authorities are detectable. Myths were also incompletely written down because of lack of interest on the part of the Spanish scribes or to conceal key events from the inquisitive monks.

Usually creation is initiated by a supreme divine couple—Ometecuhtli and Omecihuatl ("Lord" and "Lady of Twoness") among the Nahuas. The very names stress the importance of duality. Other supreme couples are "1 Deer Lion Serpent" and "1 Deer Jaguar Serpent" among the Mixtecs, and Itzamná and Ixchel among the Guatemalan Maya. By their breath or word, or by other means, the supreme creators make children and sumptuous palaces, a celestial city, or the paradise of Tamoanchan. The last is a place of harmony, of the union of opposites, where death is unknown. According to the atypical HMP, the supreme creators beget four children: the red and the black Tezcatlipocas, Quetzalcoatl, and Huitzilopochtli. After six hundred years, the first two order their younger brothers to create fire, a half sun, the first humans, the calendar, the lords of the underworld, twelve other heavens (the thirteen heavens are figured in the *Codex Vienna*, p. 1), and the gods of water and the earth. The first humans beget a son, Piltzintecuhtli; the gods make a woman for him, called Xochiquetzal.

The birth of Piltzintecuhtli involves a transgression that the created beings usually commit in their celestial or paradisiacal abode. A goddess (called, depending on the source, Xochiquetzal, Tlazolteotl, Itzpapalotl, Cihuacoatl, Xquic, or another name), seduced by a god (Piltzintecuhtli, Ppizlimtec in the *Chilam Balam* of Chumayel, Hun Hunahpú, or Tezcatlipoca), picks a blossom or eats a fruit of a forbidden tree, which breaks. According to

some versions, the creator goddess gives birth to a flint knife, and her frightened children expel it from the celestial city. Other primordial transgressions are the tearing into pieces of a monstrous crocodile named Tlalteotl (an earth deity) or playing the ballgame. The Maya of Guatemala claim that certain sons of the supreme couple attempted an art of creation without the permission of their parents. In many of these examples, the transgression symbolizes the first sexual relations: "to pick a blossom" is a metaphor for sexual intercourse. The HM explains that Piltzintecuhtli seduces Xochiquetzal (the scene is depicted in Sahagún's *Primeros memoriales*). In the Olmos version, the earth, fecundated by the flint knife thrown from heaven, gives birth to sixteen hundred gods, the very culprits expelled from heaven. The to-and-fro movement of the ballgame (and of fire sticks—or, in modern version, of the violin bow) is also regarded as procreative. But the fundamental sin of the creatures is pride: they place themselves equal with their creators by usurping their privilege of procreating or by taking life without asking permission to do so.

As a result of the transgression, the tree of paradise (symbolizing the link between creators and creatures) is ruptured; the lesser gods are "rejected and exiled" (according to Olmos) on earth or in the underworld, in darkness, and they are condemned to die. There are also positive effects. Xochiquetzal gives birth to Cinteotl ("maize god"), who is also associated with useful plants, fire, and Venus—the first light of the world. Other texts explain that these plants were born from Tlalteotl's body, cut in two parts. By appearing in the east, Maize God-Venus (or, among the Classic Maya, First Father Hun-Nal-Ye, perhaps "1 Maize Revealed"; Centeotl among the Totonac; Ehecatl among the Mixtec) rises in the sky and makes the surface of the earth appear by driving the waters that covered it away into the sky. Henceforth, the eternal life in paradise is replaced by earth, sex, mortality, the succession of generations, the feeble light of Venus, and the instruments of culture: the useful plants, maize, and the domestic fire.

During the first years in darkness on earth, the created beings die and descend to the underworld. Contact is lost with heaven, light, and the supreme duality. The lost paradise and contact with the supreme creators have to be regained. This is the task of famous heroes, such as the Hero Twins, Xbalamque and Hunahpu, sons of Xquic, who was fecundated by the fruit of the forbidden tree. They descend into Xibalba, the underworld, to defeat the Lords of Death who killed their father. After several trials, they sacrifice themselves by jumping voluntarily into a fire and destroying their heavy, material, terrestrial bodies, which prevent them from ascending to heaven. They die and are reborn; they conquer the lords of Xibalba,

Death and Darkness; they disinter their father and finally appear as Sun and Moon. It is noteworthy that the Twins are associated with maize; in contemporary myths, the hero is often the maize deity.

The well-known and still widespread myth of the creation of the Sun and Moon at Teotihuacan is a variant of the foregoing episode. When told in its proper context, it follows the exile on earth of the gods who expelled their flint-knife brother. The heroes are Quetzalcoatl-Nanahuatl and Tecciztecatl, whose sacrifices are the prototypes of Aztec human sacrifice: they represent the two main categories of victims, the warriors and the bathed slaves. Before offering their lives, they do penance. Tecciztecatl, rich and self-confident, offers coral instead of his blood, precious feathers, gold, and copal. Quetzalcoatl, a poor warrior, draws blood from his own body and burns the scabs of his wounds as incense. Then, at midnight, they are to jump into a huge bonfire. Tecciztecatl tries first, but the heat frightens him. But Quetzalcoatl-Nanahuatl does not hesitate: he throws himself into the fire, dies, descends to the land of the dead where he conquers death, emerges with booty, and rises as the sun. Tecciztecatl follows, but since he had been afraid and jumped into a cooler fire (or into ashes), he becomes only the moon.

The myth clearly concerns the creation of the sun and the earth, as the Aztec informants stated, but it has much more to do with death and resurrection. Through their voluntary sacrifice, the Hero Twins manage to reestablish contact with the supreme creators. Quetzalcoatl-Nanahuatl is solemnly enthroned by them in heaven. He brings light into the world and dries out the earth, thus introducing the day and the dry season, which keeps the earth from rotting. With him begins a state of equilibrium based on the alternation of light and darkness, day and night, dry and rainy seasons. He even becomes the very residence in the afterlife for fallen heroes, the Morning House of the Sun. The moon, appearing next, becomes or establishes the other happy afterworld of the Aztec dead, the paradise of Tlaloc, called On the Moon.

In the *Popol Vuh*, after their sacrifice the Hero Twins vanquish the lords of Xibalba. In some versions of the Aztec myth, too, the sun conquers the forces of darkness. He kills the lord of the night, the Morning Star, and refuses to move forward unless all the gods exiled on earth are immolated to feed him with their blood and hearts. The necessity of feeding the sun, as proclaimed in this probably late Aztec version, is negated in Sahagún's variant, where, in spite of the sacrifices of the gods, the sun does not move.

The Mexica HMP and LS add another myth, which recounts the first war waged to nourish the deities Sun and Earth. Again there is a transgression, but this time by humans. Sun gives rich weapons to four hundred Mimixcoa so that they can kill animals and offer them to their "father and mother," Sun and Earth. But the four hundred neglect their duty. Then five younger Mimixcoa are commissioned to kill the four hundred, which they do. From that time, man-hunting in sacred warfare replaces animal-hunting. In Aztec ritual, the sacrificed warriors usually represented the four hundred Mimixcoa.

The myth of Teotihuacan reportedly tells the story of the beginning of the present era, but the ancient Mesoamericans conceived of several ages of the world, or "Suns," as they called them, because an era as well as a year was assimilated to a day, with a rising and setting of the sun. It is possible to distinguish two different traditions: one, older and more widespread, with four Suns, and a more recent Aztec one with five Suns. The version with four ages is documented among the Maya and from the Valley of Puebla and the Mixteca. In these two regions, the Suns were named from the cataclysm by which they were to end, and each one was also the name of an element. The sequence was 4 Water, 4 Wind, 4 Fire, and 4 Earth. There was a clear idea of evolution and progress from one era to another—noticeable, for example, in the

Xochiquetzal weaving at the tree of Tamoanchan; in front of her, her seducer, Tezcatlipoca (reactualization of the myth during the festival of *atamalcualiztli*). *After Sahagún,* Códice Matritense *f. 254r. Drawing courtesy of Michel Graulich.*

foods of each age. When the Aztecs arrived after the end of the Toltec Empire, they introduced a fifth, "quintessential" Sun, which encompassed the four others: the Sun of Movement. They also changed the first and the fourth Sun so as to break any idea of the evolution of civilization before their own age, and to end the fourth Sun by a total disaster, a great flood. The Aztec sequence was Earth, Wind, Fire, Water, Movement. The idea that the Suns were the stage of a struggle between the two hostile brothers Tezcatlipoca and Quetzalcoatl may also be a recent development. Tezcatlipoca was the first Sun; Quetzalcoatl knocked him down and succeeded him; Tezcatlipoca came back as the third Sun, and Quetzalcoatl as the fourth. The fifth pertains to Tezcatlipoca-Huitzilopochtli. The last change made by the Aztecs had their Sun begin in the eleventh century, although the common date (LS, HMP) for the beginning of the present Sun was around 700 CE.

The adventures of tutelary deities are also those of their people. The wanderings of the Toltec, the Aztec-Mexica, or the Quiché from their lands of origin to their promised lands are the equivalents of the heroes' journey in the underworld. The Quichés' arrival in their promised land coincides with the first rising of the sun and the beginning of the sacred war against the natives of their new territory.

According to the CVA and the CTR, the fourth Sun was the age of the Toltec and of their ruler Quetzalcoatl. Their history is structured by the typical mythic events noted above. They are turned out of their paradisaical land of origin for having tried to overthrow the legitimate ruler, and they migrated to the east. Near Colhuacan in the Basin of Mexico, their leader Mixcoatl is killed by his brothers, the four hundred Mimixcoa, guided by Apanecatl (associated with the moon), Zolton, and Cuilton. His posthumous son, Quetzalcoatl, disinters his remains and buries them in a hill called Mixcoatepec. The Mimixcoa want to inaugurate Mixcoatepec by lighting a fire on its summit, but Quetzalcoatl emerges from the top of the hill and lights it. His angry uncles attack him, but Quetzalcoatl kills and sacrifices Apanecatl and the other Mimixcoas.

This myth is actually a ritualized transformation of the birth of the sun at Teotihuacan and a variation on themes of the *Popol Vuh*. Like the Hero Twins, Quetzalcoatl avenges the death of his father, overtakes the moon and other representatives of darkness, and emerges to make fire. The parallelism with the birth of the sun is more evident in the myth of Huitzilopochtli's birth at Coatepec. Later, Quetzalcoatl arrives at Tollan, which becomes his capital, and founds his empire: the sun rises, and the Toltec era begins. The peculiarity of Toltec history is that there is information only about its beginning and its end.

At the end of Tollan, Quetzalcoatl is seen again, but now diametrically opposed to the triumphant rising sun. Instead of being young and poor like Quetzalcoatl-Nanahuatl, he now is old, ugly, rich, and rather lunar, like a setting sun. In his penance he offers precious feathers, gold, and coral—exactly as Tecciztecatl did. Young, he was a warrior, always on the move; now he is a king-priest and never leaves his palace. Tollan has become a land of unending abundance, with enormous ears of maize and plenty of everything. There is no death or illness. The Toltec are righteous and happy, and they live in perfect harmony, praying only to the supreme creators. It is paradise again.

The fall of Tollan, as told by the Aztec, is the end of a Sun and a repetition of the end of Tamoanchan. Quetzalcoatl's hostile brother, Tezcatlipoca, manages to make him drink pulque; Quetzalcoatl (called Nacxit Xuchit in the *Chilam Balam* of Chumayel), now drunk, has sex with his sister Quetzalxoch, or Xochiquetzal. As a consequence of this transgression, the tree shatters and Quetzalcoatl realizes that the Toltecs must leave Tollan. It is again the expulsion from paradise, the setting of the sun, the intrusion of darkness, death, illness, and war into the world—the end of an era. Exiled, Quetzalcoatl descends to the underworld before burning himself and becoming Venus, the first light of a new era, the Aztec fifth Sun.

When the Mexica tell of their origins, they model the story on the existing mythic structure. They too live in a land of origin where death is unknown, called Aztlan. They too challenge the preeminence of the legitimate king, and their ruler tries to equal his superior. Therefore, the tree breaks, as depicted in the *Codex Boturini*. They wander, guided by the image of their tutelary deity, who promises them a land from which they will conquer the world. The central event of their migration is in Coatepec, near Tollan, where Coyolxauhqui and his four hundred brothers want to settle without asking their god's advice. Furious, the god decides to materialize. As a ball of feather down, he enters the body of their mother, Coatlicue ("Snake Skirt") on the Coatepec hill. When her children see that she is pregnant, they want to kill her and prepare themselves as for war. They climb the hill, but as soon as Coyolxauhqui reaches the top, Huitzilopochtli-Sun is born; he kills first his elder sister, then the four hundred Huitznahuas—that is, the moon and the stars. This myth is a variation of Quetzalcoatl's triumph at Mixcoatepec, of the creation of the sun at Teotihuacan, and of the triumph of the Hero Twins over the underworld in the *Popol Vuh*. The sources explicitly state that the events of Coatepec were reenacted every year in Mexico-Tenochtitlan, on its main pyramid called Coatepec, during the major festival of Panquetzaliztli.

Among the main themes of these myths are the transgression, the expiation through sacrifice, and the attainment of a glorious new life—the mythic justification for human sacrifice is the victory over the forces of darkness. In most cases, the transgression amounts to a negation of the superiority of the creators or the rulers; this pride is the principal fault in Mesoamerican thought, as illustrated by many Aztec discourses and Maya texts. But at the same time, another main theme seems to contradict the basic rule of respect for the creators, the parents, the first ones, the elders, the rulers. The theme of the poor but valiant younger ones—the newcomers, the migrants or nomads who conquer their rich and powerful autochthonous elders—is a constant in all these ancient myths, and in modern ones as well. The Hero Twins, presented as hunters, triumph first over their elder brothers, agriculturists and refined artists, and then over their mighty great-uncles, the lords of Xibalba. Quetzalcoatl-Nanahuatl outdistances his elder kinsman (brother, in some versions) Moon; the five Mimixcoa defeat their four hundred elders; Quetzalcoatl defeats his uncles; and Huitzilopochtli defeats his sister and elder brothers. The insurgent Quiché, Toltec, or Mexica conquer the indigenes of their promised lands. Yet this revolutionary theme applies only against abusive elders who neglect their duty.

Another important recurrent theme concerns false appearances. Those who are to lose, to be conquered, are systematically characterized as figures who try to deceive but are deceived by false appearances: the lords of Xibalba manage to deceive the parents of the Hero Twins but are deceived by the youths. Young Quetzalcoatl-Nanahuatl makes true offerings at Teotihuacan, but when old in Tollan, he makes delusive ones, like Moon. At Mixcoatepec, his uncles are deceived by Quetzalcoatl, who manages to make fire first; the four hundred Huitznahuas are deceived by the appearance of Coatepec, an island in a lake, and imagine it to be the promised land. One more recurrent theme is the solar coding of an era, an empire, a people; but the hero can also be Maize, who descends into the underworld and conquers death (or bad weather, in modern myths) and returns to life on earth.

The Five Suns legend and the transformation of the Mixcoatepec myth into the myth of Coatepec are examples of how myths were constantly manipulated to serve political ends. After the Conquest, the same thing occurred. The Aztec, for example, interpreted their defeat as the end of a Sun and distorted Motecuhzoma's image to present him as profoundly culpable because of his pride and cowardice: he was an abusive autochthon confronted by young and valiant newcomers. Quetzalcoatl was also transformed: since in paradisaical Tollan there was no death and no human sacrifice, and since he solely addressed the supreme creators, he was transformed into a kind of religious reformer who could well have been a Christian. Both the Indians and the Spanish clergy cooperated in this transformation, which served to show that the Indians were not vicious human sacrificers—that possibly, they had even been Christians centuries before.

[*See also* Chimalpopoca, Codex; Creator Deities; Popol Vuh.]

BIBLIOGRAPHY

Bierhorst, John. *The Mythology of Mexico and Central America*. New York, 1990. Reprint of a major early compilation.

Graulich, Michel. *Myths of Ancient Mexico*. Translated by Bernardo R. and Thelma Ortiz de Montellano. Norman, Okla., 1997.

Krickeberg, Walter. *Mitos y leyendas de los aztecas, incas, mayas y muiscas*. Mexico City, 1980.

López Austin, Alfredo. *The Myths of the Opossum: Pathways of Mesoamerican Mythology*. Translated by Bernard R. and Thelma Ortiz de Montellano. Albuquerque, N. M., 1993.

Markman, R., and P. Markman. *The Flayed God*. San Francisco, 1992. Popular work with translations of myths but outdated commentary.

MICHEL GRAULICH

CREATOR DEITIES. Mesoamerican thought conceived of the universe and everything in it as having two aspects, at the same time opposite and complementary: masculine/feminine, celestial/terrestrial, solar/lunar, luminous/dark, igneous/aqueous, hot/cold, heavy/light, and so on. The duality—supposed to have existed from the very start—is epitomized in the concept of the supreme creator couple, known among the Nahuas as Ometeotl ("Two God" or "God of Duality"); a single androgynous deity (e.g., in the pre-Columbian Aztec *Codex Borgia*, pl. 61, in the Cholula-Tlaxcala region, Puebla); or two gods forming a single entity. More often, however, the Nahuas spoke of Ometecuhtli and Omecihuatl ("Lord and Lady of Duality"), of Tonacatecuhtli and Tonacacihuatl ("Lord and Lady of our Flesh [or of Corn]"), and of Citlallatonac and Citlalinicue ("He Who Makes Stars Shine" and "Stars' Skirt"). They were also called "Father and Mother of the Gods," "Night, Wind"—that is, invisible and impalpable—or "Lord of the Near and the Adjacent." Ometecuhtli's calendar name was "7 Flower." They all dwelt in Omeyocan ("the Place of Duality"), the uppermost, twelfth or thirteenth layer of the heavens.

The supreme couple is sometimes identified with the Milky Way; one may be identified with the sun (the supreme deity and symbol of godhead) and fire, the other with the moon or with the goddesses of corn or of love (Xochiquetzal). The universe they create is like an extension of their own dual essence. Possibly the Totonac Great Goddess of the Heavens and her husband, the Sun, are a Gulf coast version of Ometeotl. Ometecuhtli and Omecihuatl were also known among the Nicaraos, a branch of the Nahuas who settled in Nicaragua before the rise of the Aztec Empire, but they appear to have been superseded as supreme creators by Tlamacazqui ("The Priest"; Tlaloc, god of the earth and rain) and Cipactonal. In Central Mexican myth, Oxomoco (male) and Cipactonal (female) are presented as divine or, more often, as human creatures, inventors of the calendar and soothsayers, but an evolution toward supreme creatorship like that found among the Nicaraos exists in the Quiché Maya *Popol Vuh*, where the diviners Xpiyacoc (Cipactonal, male) and Xmucané (Oxomoco, female) are very close to the supreme creators. Among the Mixtec, the original couple was "1 Deer Lion Serpent" and "1 Deer Jaguar Serpent," and among the Maya, Itzamná and Ixchel.

The supreme deities are reputed to have created by their word, their breath, or with their "wisdom and omnipotence." In Central Mexico, according to one version, the supreme couple begot four sons, the red and the black Tezcatlipoca, Quetzalcoatl, and Huitzilopochtli, who then created the universe and the other gods. According to the Mixtec myth, the supreme couple created two sons who made a marvelous garden. The acts of these sons are of particular interest because they sketch the motives and first stages of Mesoamerican sacrifice and lay the foundations of the proper behavior toward creators, parents, and elders: they acknowledge their creators' superiority by offering them first incense, then things from a beautiful field (flowers and animals?), and finally, in order to induce them to allow the creation of heaven and earth, the sons' own blood.

Mesoamerican myths usually recount the way these first creatures committed a transgression by holding themselves equal to their parents. Of the Mixtec story, it is known that a great flood drowned many gods. The Quiché Maya myth tells of the flood that punished humans—who had been fashioned of wood—because they did not remember their creators. The Central Mexican myth of the paradise of Tamoanchan explains how a goddess plucked the flower of a forbidden tree (figured in both pre- and post-Columbian codices)—that is, she engaged in sexual intercourse and gave birth to the maize deity. She procreated without permission, thus usurping the privilege of the supreme creators. The same idea prevailed among the Maya of southern Guatemala, who believed that Itzamná and Ixchel had begotten thirteen children. The older ones tried to create men against the will of their parents, but they produced only common household utensils and were thrown into hell. The younger Hunchouen and Hunahau humbled themselves and were allowed to create the universe and the humans.

Other transgressions include tearing a crocodile into pieces in order to make heaven and earth; the expulsion from the sky of a flint knife to which Omecihuatl had given birth; the ignition of fire with fire sticks assimilated

Ometeotl-Tonacatecuhtli figured androgynous (with skirt and *maxtlatl*, and seated as a woman). *After* Codex Borgia *f. 61. Drawing courtesy of Michel Graulich.*

with sexual intercourse; playing the ballgame (considered an act of creation); and drunkenness followed by incest. The result is always the same: the sinners are expelled from their heaven to the earth, in darkness, and are henceforth condemned to be mortal. Their loss of communication with their creators is often signaled by the breaking of a tree, a cosmic axis that symbolizes the union between heaven and earth. Survival after death in a sort of paradise regained can be achieved only by sacrifice—the voluntary destruction of one's heavy, material body in imitation of the heroes of the *Popol Vuh* or those of the Central Mexican myth of the creation of the sun and moon of Teotihuacan.

After the transgression, Ometecuhtli and Omecihuatl retire to the uppermost heaven and become inactive, except that they remain the masters of life and (pro-)creation: they spend their time drilling with their firesticks to produce the sparks of life, the "souls" (*tonalli*), which descend into women's bodies when they conceive. Humans are not expected to worship them with a cult—logically, because the cultic recognition of one's debt to one's creator is in this case the task of the gods; humans must address their own creators, the gods. The situation was different among the Maya, where Itzamná still intervened in the world, had temples, and received a cult; although Itzamná shared many traits with Ometecuhtli, he seems to have evolved differently, remaining more present in his different "extensions," assuming characteristics of the fire god and of secondary creators, and being linked with divination and writing (like Oxomoco and Cipactonal). Some cities did not even consider him as a primary god.

The supreme creators are usually depicted as aged; sometimes they are shown frontally to indicate their relationship with beginnings. In the divinatory sections of the Central Mexican codices, Ometeotl is figured governing the first day, "Crocodile," and the first "week" of thirteen days, "1 Crocodile." His field of action, giving the sparks of life, is indicated by a human couple covered by a blanket—that is, having intercourse. The *Vienna Codex* contains several representations of the Mixtec supreme creators. The Maya god Itzamná is often represented under his multiple aspects.

[*See also* Creation Myths.]

BIBLIOGRAPHY
Anders, Ferdinand. *Das Pantheon der Maya.* Graz, 1963. A complete manual of Maya gods and rituals, to be complemented and updated by Taube (1992).
Freidel, David, Linda Schele, and Joy Parker. *Maya Cosmos: Three Thousand Years on the Shaman's Path.* New York, 1993. Contains stimulating speculations on a Maya "first father" who shares some traits with creator deities.
Graulich, Michel. *Myths of Ancient Mexico.* Norman, Okla., 1997. Detailed analysis of Central Mexican and Quiché Maya mythology.
León-Portilla, Miguel. *Aztec Thought and Culture: A Study of the Ancient Nahuatl Mind.* Norman, Okla., 1963. A pathbreaking book with remarkable passages on the Aztec supreme deities.
Seler, Eduard. *Comentarios al Códice Borgia.* 3 vols. Mexico City, 1963. Classic analysis of a major Central Mexican pre-Columbian pictorial source.
Taube, Karl Andreas. *The Major Gods of Ancient Yucatan.* Dumbarton Oaks Studies in Pre-Columbian Art and Archaeology, 32. Washington, D.C., 1992.

MICHEL GRAULICH

CRIME AND PUNISHMENT. *See* Law.

CRISTOS DE CAÑA. Life-size figures of Jesus in agony on the cross, made in the sixteenth and early seventeenth centuries, are among the great monuments of Colonial-era sculpture in Mesoamerica. Many creators of these figures employed pre-Colonial construction techniques and materials to produce large but very light images that were well suited to processional use. Many of these have a refined European appearance, but the texture and weight are different, and should the surface be broken, they would have looked strange to Spanish eyes.

Early religious chroniclers, including Jerónimo de Mendieta, Juan de Torquemada, and Alonso de la Rea, were intrigued by these portable images; they referred to them as *crucifijos de caña* ("maize-stalk crucifixes") or *los Cristos huecos de caña* ("hollow maize-stalk Christs") and noted that examples had been sent to Spain as curiosities. These references shed little light on the presumed Indian makers and their methods of construction, or their pre-Colonial antecedents. It is only from physical examination of a few broken *cristos de caña* that we can learn something about their manufacture. Over a rough pine and *tzompantle* (a light native wood) frame, peeled maize stalks were applied in short sections to form the head, torso, arms, and legs. The pieces of maizestalk were held together with a thick paste consisting of ground maize pith, orchid-bulb glue, and carpenter's paste, which could be pressed and smoothed into the desired shape. The finished surface consisted of a fine clay stucco, painted and either varnished or burnished. The head and torso were hollow, and the shape of the torso was sometimes supported on the inside with cloth or sheaves of Colonial-era paper.

This combination of materials and techniques was used for the creation of religious images in the Valley of Mexico, Tlaxcala, and especially near Lake Pátzcuaro in the Mexican state of Michoacán. The most famous of these *caña* images were crucifixes, but other figures of Jesus and the saints are known, including the Virgin Mary (such as Our Lady of Zapopan, near Guadalajara, and Our Lady of La Salud in the town of Pátzcuaro). Most of the dozens of surviving examples are still near their probable places of origin in Michoacán and Central Mexico, but there are also renowned *cristos de caña* in the present-day Mexican states of Guanajuato, San Luis Potosí, Jalisco, Zacatecas, and Nuevo León.

These large crucifixes and their materials were rich in possible meanings for those who commissioned, made, and used them in the Colonial period. One modern interpretation centers on the figures themselves, without reference to their materials: oppressed Indians identified with the suffering of Jesus crucified. Another interpretation gives more attention to the materials: these light crucifixes connected Jesus' passage through birth, death, and miraculous resurrection to the regeneration of the sacred food plant, maize (the seemingly dead plant reborn from its planted seed).

The papers that form the torso of the best known maize-stalk crucifix, "El Cristo de Mexicaltzingo," suggest that the materials themselves had symbolic meaning, in sympathy with the literal representation of Jesus sacrificed, partaking of its essence and substance and completing it. Upon investigating, Abelardo Carrillo y Gariel (1949) discovered that the chest cavity and upper arms were formed around pages of sixteenth-century community tax records in native style and substantial fragments of Nahuatl texts in roman script that recount the Passion of Christ. Included also was a stencil (perhaps an embroidery pattern) of Raphael's painting, "Il Pasmo de Sicilia," depicting the fall of Jesus on the road to Calvary. These papers seem to associate the image of Jesus—sacrificed, resurrected, and present in the consecrated host—with the present-day Indian village of Mexicalcingo (through the tax records, especially if they reported collections that paid for this image), thus binding the community to a powerful new means of association with the sacred—through Jesus and the written words that recount his suffering and triumph.

[*See also* Crosses and Crucifixes.]

BIBLIOGRAPHY

Carrillo y Gariel, Abelardo. *El Cristo de Mexicaltzingo: Técnica de las esculturas en caña.* Mexico City, 1949.

Estrada Jasso, Andrés. *Imágenes en caña de maíz.* San Luis Potosí, 1996.

Kubler, George, and Martin Soria. *Art and Architecture in Spain and Portugal and Their American Dominions, 1500 to 1800.* Baltimore, 1959. See p. 164.

Moyssén, Xavier. "Escultura de pasta de caña y piedra." In *Imaginería virreinal: Memorias de un seminario*, pp. 21–24. Mexico City, 1990.

Weismann, Elizabeth Wilder. *Mexico in Sculpture, 1521–1821.* Cambridge, Mass., 1950. See pp. 166–167.

WILLIAM B. TAYLOR

CROCODILES. *See* Cipactli.

CROSSES AND CRUCIFIXES. The cross and the crucifix (the latter term denotes an image of Jesus on the cross) are Christianity's central icons, symbols of the martyrdom of Jesus Christ, whose sacrifice, according to Christian doctrine, brought about human redemption. Crosses and crucifixes played important roles in the Spanish conquest of Mesoamerica. *Conquistadores* raised the cross to claim land, found new towns, and declare the triumph of Christianity. Friars placed crucifixes in churches, chapels, and missions. Typical Colonial-period examples include stone atrial crosses and crucifixes made of maize-stalk paste, or *Cristos de caña*; these objects were produced by indigenous artists under European direction.

Atrial crosses, exemplified by one at the Basílica de la Virgen de Guadalupe which dates from before 1556, originally stood in mission atriums. Carved in a low relief suggestive of pre-Columbian sculpture, the cross is covered with the "Arms of Christ," a standardized group of emblems referring to Jesus' Passion. Although the sculptural technique is clearly indigenous, the emblems and their arrangement closely resemble a fifteenth-century Spanish cross in Daroca, Zaragoza. Other atrial crosses originally displayed embedded obsidian stones, a Mesoamerican sculptural convention which signified the image's life force. These crosses rarely depicted the actual crucifixion, possibly to avoid highlighting the similarities between Jesus' sacrifice and indigenous sacrificial rites. Examples can be found throughout Mexico.

Mexican *Cristos de caña*, polychromed maize-stalk paste sculptures, closely resemble Spanish wood crucifixes. The technique, however, is indigenous in origin, traceable to pre-Hispanic Michoacán, where it was used to model deity figures. When the Franciscans arrived in this area, they taught the Indian artists to make Christian images. The Tlaxcala crucified Jesus of 1550–1600 is a representative example. The sculpture was modeled from a paste of maize-stalks, orchid tubers, and natural glue on an armature, then painted. The resulting figure is extremely light in weight, perfect for carrying in processions.

A number of Colonial sources report Mesoamericans' enthusiastic reception of the cross. Their acceptance may have been conditioned by the existence of crosslike forms such as the world tree throughout the pre-Hispanic Americas. The world tree, an embodiment of the four cardinal directions, was thought to stand at the center of the world. Scholars have identified examples of it at the Maya sites of Palenque, Chichén Itzá, and Izapa, at Olmec La Venta, and at Zapotec Monte Albán. World trees also appear in both Central Mexican and Maya manuscripts.

Another possible reason that Mesoamericans embraced the cross and crucifix was the centrality of penitential bloodletting, human sacrifice, and ritual cannibalism in both their own religion and Christianity. Roman Catholicism's emphasis on Jesus' torture, suffering, and death during the Passion, the importance of transubstantiation (the doctrine that the communion wafer is literally transformed into the body of Jesus before being consumed), and the eternal life that results from Jesus' sacrifice bore an uncanny resemblance to Mesoamerican beliefs. In fact, pre-Columbian Mesoamericans practiced a type of crucifixion, leading one scholar to suggest that the Colonial Mixtec Cross of Topiltepec analogizes Jesus' sacrifice and Mesoamerican human arrow sacrifice (Callaway, 1990, p. 211). Significant evidence also indicates that native Mesoamericans conflated Christian and indigenous cross forms. According to at least two chroniclers, the Tlaxcala Indians called the cross Tonacaquahuitl, or "the tree that sustains our life," a name for the Mesoamerican tree of life as well as a rain god. They also worshiped the cross as a deity, burning incense in its honor.

Native Mesoamericans continued pre-Contact religious practices in association with the Christian cross. They erected crosses at town entrances and crossroads, in houses, and on hills, reportedly as protection against evil. Some natives practiced self-flagellation in front of the cross. In at least two cases, at Cholula and Jilotepec, friars discovered that the Indians' zealous adoration of the cross, which included adorning it with flowers, was intended to honor not the cross but indigenous images secretly buried around it. In the post-Conquest Maya area, natives transformed the cross into a deity called Ca Yum Santa Cruz (Our Lord the Holy Cross) or Yax Cheel Cab, names for the world tree and a water deity (Callaway, 1990, p. 208). The cross and crucifix were also employed in imported Spanish rituals, most notably during Holy Week. At this time, Mexicans carried in procession *pasos* and *imágenes de vestir*, portable sculptures and costumed sculptures, usually of polychromed maize-stalk paste or wood, in reenactments of Jesus' arrest, torture, and death. These realistically painted statues, their verisimilitude heightened by the addition of human-hair wigs, glass eyes, and real clothing, were carried through cities and villages, transforming the landscape into the Way of the Cross.

[*See also* Chalma.]

BIBLIOGRAPHY

Callaway, Carol H. "Pre-Columbian and Colonial Mexican Images of the Cross: Christ's Sacrifice and the Fertile Earth." *Journal of Latin American Lore* 16 (1990), 199–231. Thorough scholarly study of Colonial Mexican crosses, with emphasis on the survival and transformation of indigenous culture; includes a useful summary of previous scholarship and a catalogue of pre-Hispanic Mesoamerican cross forms in sculpture and manuscripts.

Díaz del Castillo, Bernal. *The Discovery and Conquest of Mexico, 1517–1521*. Translated by A. P. Maudslay, edited by Irving A. Leonard. New York, 1956. Important account of the conquest of Mesoamerica from the Spanish point of view, with information on the use of the cross by the *conquistadores*.

Kubler, George. "On the Colonial Extinction of the Motifs of Pre-Columbian Art." In *Essays in Pre-Columbian Art and Archaeology*. Edited by S. K. Lothrop et al., pp. 14–34. Cambridge, Mass., 1961. Influential essay that has significantly shaped the study of indigenous American Christian art by asserting that most of pre-Columbian culture was destroyed during the Spanish conquest; important for the study of atrial crosses.

McAndrew, John. *The Open-Air Churches of Sixteenth-Century Mexico: Atrios, Posas, Open Chapels, and Other Studies*. Cambridge, Mass., 1965. Still an important source on atrial crosses, though the language used to discuss indigenous culture may seem inappropriate today.

Mexico: Splendors of Thirty Centuries. New York, 1990. Comprehensive catalogue from a magisterial exhibition at the Metropolitan Museum of Art, with important essays which summarize Colonial cultural production, including substantive catalogue entries on atrial crosses and *Cristos de caña*.

Monteverde, Mildred. "Sixteenth-Century 'Atrio' Crosses." Ph.D. diss., University of California, Los Angeles, 1972. The most comprehensive study to date of the iconography of Mexican atrial crosses; emphasizes European iconographic and formal precedents.

Moreno Villa, José. *La escultura colonial mexicana*. Mexico City, 1942. The author coined the term *tequitqui* (Nahuatl, "one who pays tribute") as a label for indigenous American Christian art; the first work to identify and discuss pre-Columbian obsidian insets in atrial crosses.

Motolinía, Toribio. *History of the Indians of New Spain*. Translated and edited by Elizabeth A. Foster. Berkeley, 1950. The author was one of the first twelve Franciscan friars to arrive in Mexico in 1524; his account provides important information on Native Mesoamericans' enthusiastic reception of the Christian cross.

Neumeyer, Alfred. "The Indian Contribution to Architectural Decoration in Spanish Colonial America." *Art Bulletin* 30 (1948), 104–121. Influential essay written in dialogue with and in opposition to George Kubler; one of the earliest scholars to endeavor to demonstrate the continued importance of pre-Columbian culture after the Conquest.

Schele, Linda, and Mary Ellen Miller. *The Blood of Kings: Dynasty and Ritual in Maya Art*. Fort Worth, Tex., 1986. Fascinating and groundbreaking study of Mesoamerican blood sacrifice.

Toussaint, Manuel. *Colonial Art in Mexico*. Translated and edited by Elizabeth Wilder Weismann. Austin, 1967. Still the major survey of Colonial art, a good starting point for nonspecialists.

Webster, Susan Verdi. *Art and Ritual in Golden-Age Spain: Sevillian Confraternities and the Processional Sculpture of Holy Week*. Princeton, 1998. Best source on Spanish Holy Week sculpture.

Weismann, Elizabeth Wilder. *Mexico in Sculpture, 1521–1821*. Cambridge, Mass., 1950. The only treatment of Mexican Colonial sculpture in English, thought-provoking and imaginative.

CHARLENE VILLASEÑOR BLACK

CRUCIFIXES. *See* Crosses and Crucifixes.

CRUZ, MARÍ DE LA. *See* Candelaria, María de la.

CUAUHTÉMOC (c.1497–1525), last ruler of independent Mexico-Tenochtitlan. Cuauhtémoc was born the son of Ahuitzotl, eighth ruler of Mexico, and according to several sources, of Tiyacapantzin, a Tlatelolcan princess. His father died in 1502. In his youth, Cuauhtémoc probably attended the ceremonies celebrating the end of a *xiuhmolpilli* (a fifty-two-year cycle) and the kindling of the New Fire.

Cuauhtémoc studied at the main *calmecac* (the priestly school of Tenochtitlan) and took part in several military actions ordered by his uncle Motecuhzoma Xocoyotl. Around 1515 he was appointed *cuauhtlahtoani*, eagle-ruler, to govern Tlatelolco, the town where his mother was born.

When Motecuhzoma Xocoyotl was murdered in 1520 on the eve of Fernando Cortés's abrupt departure from the Aztec metropolis, Cuitlahuac, the brother of Motecuhzoma, was elected as the new ruler. In his brief reign he struggled to drive out the Spaniards from Mexico. Infected in the epidemic of smallpox brought by Cortés's army, he died eighty days later. The Aztec electors and other members of the nobility, conscious of their nation's great danger, looked for the most capable man who could organize the defense against the invaders, who were ready to besiege the Aztec metropolis. In a unanimous vote they chose Cuauhtémoc as their new ruler.

Cuauhtémoc sought the support of the allies of the Aztec, especially the Acolhuaque of Tetzcoco. Unfortunately, Tetzcoco was in the midst of a civil war between Cacamatzin and Ixtlilxochitl, who were fighting for the throne. Moreover, the Totonac, Tlaxcalan, and Cholulan were allies of the Spaniards. In a desperate move, Cuauhtémoc sought the aid of the Tarascan, who refused to help him.

Cuauhtémoc and his people thus were left alone in fending off the attack of the Spaniards. On 30 May 1521, Cortés began the siege of Tenochtitlan; a month earlier he had launched on the shores of Iztapalapa thirteen brigantines that would play a decisive role in the blockade of the island. Cuauhtémoc and his army, indeed all the inhabitants of the city, resisted the attack of Cortés's forces, composed of about two thousand Spaniards and more than eighty thousand Indian allies.

On 13 August 1521, after nearly eighty days of siege, the city surrendered. The Spaniards took Cuauhtémoc and other nobles prisoners. Some time later, in the presence of Cortés, they were tortured by having hot oil poured over their feet.

Although a new rule was imposed in what became known as New Spain, Cuauhtémoc kept his rank of *tlahtoani* or ruler of Tenochtitlan, while remaining a prisoner. When Cortés left Tenochtitlan, in October 1524 to subdue the rebellion of Cristóbal de Olid in Honduras, he brought Cuauhtémoc and the other prisoners along with him.

On their way, while in Izankanak in Chontal territory (present-day Campeche), Cortés accused Cuauhtémoc and Tetlepanquetzal of plotting a rebellion. They were convicted and hanged sometime in February 1525.

Cuauhtémoc is remembered as a great hero and is an emblematic figure of Mexican nationalism. There are many monuments honoring him, and several streets, schools, and even towns bear his name. In February 1949 the archaeologist Eulalia Guzmán claimed to have discovered the remains of Cuauhtémoc, sparking an intense debate.

BIBLIOGRAPHY

León-Portilla, Miguel ed. *The Broken Spears: Aztec Account of the Conquest of Mexico*. Boston, 1992. Presents Nahuatl texts about Cuauhtémoc's deeds during the siege of Tenochtitlan.

Rendón, Silvia. *Quauhtemoc: Tres semblanzas históricas*. Mexico City, 1979. Collection of Indian, Spanish, and modern Mexican testimonies on Cuauhtémoc.

Scholes, France V., and Ralph Roys. *The Maya Chontal Indians of Acalan-Tixchel*. Washington, D. C., 1948. Includes a unique text in Chontal that tells about the death of Cuauhtémoc.

Toscano, Salvador. *Cuauhtemoc*. Mexico City, 1953. Well-written biography of the young ruler.

MIGUEL LEÓN-PORTILLA

CUAUHTITLÁN, ANALES DE. *See* Chimalpopoca, Codex.

CUICATEC. Cuicatec, Trique, and Mixtecan form one branch of the Otomanguean language family. Cuicatec speakers occupy a portion of the northern area of the state of Oaxaca. This area is bounded on three sides by the canyons of the major rivers that form the Cuicatec Cañada: on the south by the Río de las Vueltas, a tributary of the Río Grande, which in turn bounds the area to the west; and on the north by the canyon of the Río Santo Domingo, formed from the combined Río Grande and Río Salado. The eastern boundary extends just over the crest of the Sierra Madre Oriental to the beginning of the lowlands. The Cuicatec were bordered by Mazatec to the north, Mixtec to the west, Chinantec to the east, and Zapotec and Mixe to the south. At the time of the Spanish conquest, the Cuicatec lived in small towns of at most 5,000 people. There appears never to have been a single

Cuicatec "kingdom," but rather a few loosely related villages, connected by affinal ties between the rulers.

The Cuicatec settlements occupied two important ecological zones: a hot, dry zone in the Cuicatec Cañada, where irrigation was required, and a high, cool temperate zone where rainfall agriculture was possible. The contrasting environments have been a defining characteristic of the Cuicatec system from pre-Hispanic times to the present. The lowland villages along the Cuicatec Cañada required irrigation, but this location allowed them to produce products such as coyol palm, as well as lowland fruits such as zapote, chicozapote, and cacao. The Cuicatec Cañada was also a natural north–south travel route through Mesoamerica, and so it was always connected to larger communities in Mesoamerica.

The highland communities were able to grow several important products that were not available in the lowlands. These included maguey, which was used for production of pulque and fiber, and wood, which grew in the higher mountains. In historic times, cochineal and coffee also became important highland products. The highland towns also traded and wove cotton from the lowlands on the eastern side of the Sierra Madre Oriental. The highlands depended on the Cañada villages for food and for most exchange with the rest of Mesoamerica. They obtained lowland and exotic goods by trade for highland products, by renting lowland irrigated lands, or by working in cold seasons for lowland landholders.

After the Conquest, the Cañada towns, lying on a major north–south transportation route, were drawn increasingly into the Spanish world. The lowland villages were taken over by Spaniards raising cattle and crops such as sugar cane and mango. The transportation route was gradually improved. A railroad was introduced in the nineteenth century. Today, a modern all-weather road follows the old route of the Camino Real.

The highland villages were touched by the Spanish conquest, though always through a filter of the Cañada villages. They continued to trade wood and cotton and also grew cochineal (a beetle that produced a red dye) and coffee. The highland villages remained Cuicatec in speech and culture, while the Cañada villages became part of the national Mexican culture. Based on the Mexican census of 1990, today there are 10,000 speakers of Teutila Cuicatec (269 of them monolingual), and 8,500 speakers of Tepeuxila Cuicatec (850 monolingual).

BIBLIOGRAPHY

Hopkins, Joseph W., III. *Irrigation and the Cuicatec Ecosystem: A Study of Agriculture and Civilization in North Central Oaxaca.* Studies in Latin American Ethnohistory and Archaeology, Memoirs of the Museum of Anthropology, University of Michigan. Ann Arbor, 1984. Combines ethnohistorical, archaeological, and ethnological research to follow the Cuicatec from pre-Hispanic times to the present.

Hunt, Eva. "Irrigation and the Socio-political Organization of the Cuicatec Cacicazgos." In *The Prehistory of the Tehuacán Valle*, vol. 4, *Chronology and Irrigation*, edited by Frederic Johnson, pp. 162–248. Austin, 1972. Eva Hunt and her husband, Robert Hunt, published several invaluable studies of the ethnohistory of the Cuicatec.

Spencer, Charles S., and Elsa M. Redmond, with contributions by Oscar Polaco, Richard G. Wilkinson, Dennis Dirkmaat, Robert D. Drennan, Philip T. Fitzgibbons, and Heinz Dehn. *Archeology of the Cañada de Cuicatlán, Oaxaca.* Anthropological Papers of the American Museum of Natural History, 80, 1997. This work combines Spencer's and Redmond's earlier work, with further analysis and addition of other studies. It provides the most comprehensive statement on research on pre-Hispanic Cañada.

Weitlaner, Roberto J. "The Cuicatec." In *Handbook of Middle American Indians*, vol. 7, *Ethnology, Part 1*, edited by Evon Z. Vogt, pp. 516–522, Austin, 1969. Weitlaner was one of the few ethnologists to visit and publish on the Cuicatec.

JOSEPH W. HOPKINS III

CUICUILCO. Cuicuilco, a settlement situated on a small lake in the southwestern part of the Basin of Mexico, dates back to about 1400 BCE. Its development was interrupted in 60 CE by the eruption of the Xitle volcano, which partially buried much of the civic, ceremonial, and domestic architecture under a basaltic lava flow (five meters thick, on average) that extended over an area of approximately eighty square kilometers. Apparently, the settlement occupied about four hundred hectares. Its major structures include the great circular pyramid (Cuicuilco A), which has a diameter of approximately 160 meters and a height of about 21 meters; mounds, platforms, plazas, house structures, bottle-shaped subterranean chambers, and four pyramids to the west (Cuicuilco B); and a small circular pyramid to the southwest, known as Peña Pobre. Recent research shows that the spatial distribution of architectural features, both ceremonial and residential, was related to a lake located to the south and east of the central area, and that alignments were astronomical in nature. Possibly Cuicuilco was an urban center with twenty thousand inhabitants, complex ritual systems, and social stratification, comparable to Teotihuacan during the Late Formative period.

Cuicuilco's location gave the inhabitants access to the abundant flora and fauna of Lake Xochimilco, approximately four kilometers from the site, and to the forests of the nearby Sierra de las Cruces and Ajusco mountain ranges. Springs and flowing water for irrigation were abundant in the vicinity. In this setting, the pre-Hispanic inhabitants of the settlement could both procure and process their food. Hunting, fishing, and gathering complemented the agricultural activities in and around the site. Probably *chinampas* drained fields were important.

Investigations at the site began in 1922, when Manuel Gamio invited Byron Cummings to direct them, assisted by Emil Haury. Although Cummings did not completely uncover the great pyramid, he defined three architectural stages for it and for the altars on the top of the structure. He also found the main ramps to the west and east, and a circular ceremonial monument made with large tabular basalt stones and painted with red geometrical designs. By 1939, Eduardo Noguera completed explorations of burials close to the southwestern foundation of pyramid and the altars at the top of the structure, and refined the ceramic sequence. In 1956, Angel Palerm and Erik Wolf located six mounds and several irrigation systems northwest of the pyramid. In 1957 and 1962, Robert A. Heizer and James A. Bennyhoff, exploring twelve structures mainly at Cuicuilco B, refined the ceramic sequence for the site, based on stratigraphic excavations and radiocarbon dates. The Instituto Nacional de Antropología e Historia conducted rescue operations in 1967 in an area of several thousand square meters, also in Cuicuilco B. Below five meters of lava, ceremonial platforms, round and rectangular residential buildings, burials, and offerings were found. Florencia Müller studied the ceramic collections and developed a typological scheme and a new phasing covering the time from the Middle Formative to the Late Postclassic. Later, minor studies were carried out to uncover the east ramp of the great pyramid; Peña Pobre and the Tenantongo pyramid (probably built after the Xitle eruption) were partially excavated; a residential area (Corregidora-La Ladrillera), approximately two kilometers south of the great pyramid, and residences south of Cuicuilco B were excavated; and regional surveys and paleo-environmental and geological studies were carried out. In 1996, a complex sequence of superimposed altars painted with hematite red on top of the great pyramid was defined, and a monolithic sculpture four meters in height, made from a columnar andesitic block and situated less than three meters southeast of the great pyramid, was excavated. This "stela," partially painted red, has carved geometric designs consisting of rhomboidal and circular patterns—evidence of complex symbolic systems during the Middle Formative.

Undamaged hard-mud floors and a low bench partly covered with corn plants burnt by the heat of the lava were discovered south of the pyramid at a stratum that covered completely the "stela." Cummings interpreted the architectural fill of the bench as a debris stratum resulting from abandonment processes prior to the Xitle eruption, but new evidence proves that the pyramid was still in use at the time of the eruption.

Research carried out on grounds approximately three hundred meters south of the great pyramid has added important new archaeological information. This area was never completely covered by the lava flow, and the eruption did not destroy the lake environment.

At an average depth of two meters below the remains and debris of a paper factory founded in the nineteenth century, the lateral edge of the lava flow was located. It was at least five meters thick and more than 150 meters in length and displayed a typical pillow-lava structure, formed by the rapid cooling of lava when it enters a body of water. The lava flow sealed off the northern shore of the lake and appears to have created a marshy peat deposit in the eastern section. Multiple layers of volcanic ash from Xitle and possibly from Popocatepetl have been detected in the peat. In the western edge of the stratigraphic section, there is also a creek bed with sand, rounded cobbles, and gravel. Two architectural features situated near the southern limit of the lava flow and covered by the lake during the Late Formative evidence hydraulic systems in the vicinity of the main pyramid: a 150-meter-long Formative irrigation canal showing three construction stages, and a 0.80-meter-wide pathway partially covered with pebbles on the western edge.

Ceramics dating between 200 and 950 CE were found on top of the layer of pillow lava. Tlaloc vessels and miniatures and a Huehueteotl sculpture show that, during the Classic and Epiclassic periods, ritual activities were carried out at the lake. The inhabitants of Cuicuilco may have worshiped both water and fire gods. At the end of the first millennium, life at Cuicuilco was again doomed—this time, covered by ash from a volcanic eruption. The site was abandoned and then resettled during the Late Postclassic period. The settlement is an excellent example of how parts of the Mesoamerican world were destroyed repeatedly by nature's forces.

BIBLIOGRAPHY

Cordova, Carlos F. de A., Ana Lillian Martín del Pozzo, and Javier López Camacho. "Palaeolandforms and Volcanic Impact on the Environment of Prehistoric Cuicuilco, Southern Mexico City." *Journal of Archaeological Science* 21 (1994), 585–596.

Cummings, Byron. *Cuicuilco and the Archaic Culture of México.* University of Arizona Social Science Bulletin 4. Tucson, Ariz., 1933.

Delgado, Hugo, Ricardo Molinero, Pablo Cervantes, Jorge Nieto-Obregón, Rufino Lozano-Santa Cruz, Hector L. Macías-González, Claudia Mendoza-Rosales, and Gilberto Silva-Romo. "Geology of Xitle Volcano in Southern México City—A 2000-year-old Monogenetic Volcano in an Urban Area." *Revista mexicana de ciencias geológicas* 15.2 (1998), 115–131.

Haury, Emil. "Cuicuilco in Retrospect." *Kiva* 41.2 (1975), 195–200.

Heizer, Robert A., and James A. Bennyhoff. "Archaeological Investigations of Cuicuilco, Valley of Mexico, 1956." *Science* 127 (1957), 232–233.

Heizer, Robert A., and James A. Bennyhoff. "Archaeological Excavations at Cuicuilco, Mexico, 1957." *National Geographic Reports, 1955–1960* (1972), 93–104.

Müller, Florencia. *La cerámica de Cuicuilco B: Un rescate arqueológico.* Instituto Nacional de Antropología e Historia, Colección Científica, 186, Mexico City, 1990.

Pastrana, Alejandro. "Nuevos datos acerca de la estratigrafía de Cuicuilco." *Arqueología* 18 (1997), 3–16.

Pastrana, Alejandro, and Patricia Fournier. "Cuicuilco desde Cuicuilco." *Actualidades arqueológicas* 13 (1997), 7–9.

Pérez Campa, Mario. "El gran basamento circular de Cuicuilco." *Arqueología mexicana* 30 (1998), 34–37.

Rodríguez Sánchez, Ernesto. "Cuicuilco 'C': Aportes sobre Aspectos urbano-Arquitectónicos en el Formativo de al Cuenca de México." In *A Propósito del Formativo*, edited by María Teresa Castillo Mangas, pp. 45–58. Mexico City, 1993.

Schávelzon, Daniel. *La Pirámide de Cuicuilco: Album Fotográfico, 1922–1980.* Mexico City, 1993.

ALEJANDRO PASTRANA
and PATRICIA FOURNIER

CUISINE. Food and eating were of great importance to the ancient Mexicans. Not only was food important as a source of energy and as a means to placate the sensation of hunger, it had religious, symbolic, and artistic uses as well. It was the most common ritual offering and played an important role in the fiesta system, which specified foods to be eaten, offered to the gods, and abstained from. The artistic depiction of food can be admired in pre-Hispanic sculpture, murals, ceramic vessels, and codices or painted books.

Before the Spanish Conquest, the basic Mesoamerican diet had a common substratum but varied between areas due to climate, plant resources, latitudes, and cultural and ethnic differences. There were certain features, such as a reliance on maize, beans, and squash, complemented by tomatoes and chile peppers, that were common to most cultural groups. Because more information is available about the Aztec or Mexica diet than that of other cultural groups, due to the early and sustained contact between the Spanish and the Aztec, their diet will be used as a model for describing Mesoamerican food traditions in general.

The Aztec had access to abundant food resources and made use of intensive agricultural techniques, such as the *chinampa*, or drained field, system, which could produce up to three crops a year. They also made good use of resources from the lakes of the Valley of Mexico, such as frogs, waterfowl, fish (both dried and fresh), salamanders, and a large variety of insects and insect eggs. Another high-protein food available from Lake Texcoco was algae (*Spirulina geitlerii*), called tecuitlatl and widely used by the local inhabitants. These products provided rich sources of protein, often believed to have been lacking in the pre-Hispanic diet. The turkey and the dog, fattened especially for eating, were the only domestic animals available as good protein sources. Additional protein was obtained through small game hunting.

Many food systems are dominated by a particular food item that is closely identified with the culture and is considered vital to the group's well-being. In pre-Hispanic Mexico, this role was played by maize. It constituted the most respected food item in the Mesoamerican diet and was often considered sacred. Agricultural fiestas, rituals, and ceremonies were carried out, based on the origin of maize and the role it played in the lives of the people. The Aztec believed that humans and maize shared the same essence and that their destinies were closely connected. It formed the basis of the Mesoamerican diet and is believed to have provided 80 percent of the calories. It was also a good source of complex carbohydrates. The domestication and cultivation of maize supported the growth of ancient Mexican civilizations. The Aztec developed many ways of preparing maize, as in tamales, many shapes and sizes of tortillas, and pozole (hominy stew), or simply boiled or roasted. It was often eaten in combination with other vegetables, especially beans, which contributed both protein and lysine to the diet. Amaranth was grown as an alternative to maize and was also produced in large quantities.

The Aztec diet is believed to have been low in niacin, calcium, and riboflavin, but the innovative preparation techniques of maize helped overcome this deficiency. The process, called *nixtamalización*, consisted of soaking the kernels in a solution of mineral lime and water to facilitate the separation of the hull from the kernel of corn, at the same time softening the grain and making it easier to grind. This procedure changed the chemical makeup of maize by increasing calcium and correcting the proportion of certain amino acids. The process improved the quality of protein in maize and made both niacin and tryptophan more available to absorption by the human body. The alkaline processing of maize prevented a niacin deficiency and the occurrence of pellagra, common in other maize-consuming areas.

An abundant supply of fruits and vegetables provided essential vitamins and minerals to the Aztec diet. Important vegetables included beans, squash, chile peppers, tomatoes, green tomatoes, a variety of wild greens, jícamas, nopales (cactus paddles), sweet potatoes, wild onions, chayotes (vegetable pears), and mesquite. Principal fruits, available on a seasonal and regional basis, were the avocado, plum, cherimoya, chokecherry, blackberry, crab apple, guava, zapotes (*Diospyros ebenaster*) of various colors, and mamey (*Calocarmum sapota*).

Pulque (the fermented juice of the agave plant), chocolate, and atole (a semi-liquid form of gruel made with maize dough and water) were the most common beverages, although many others were available. These beverages provided additional sources of protein, calories, vitamins, and minerals.

The Aztec diet is considered to have been adequate to maintain good health and protect against infectious disease. The diet was sufficient in proteins, vitamins, and calories through the consumption of fruits, vegetables, grains, insects, and small game.

Mexican food, as it is known and appreciated today, had its origins in the sixteenth century. European plants and food products that followed the arrival of the Spanish conquerors were combined with local foods and gave birth to a new cuisine. This entailed not only an interchange of food products but also the introduction of new cooking utensils and new techniques of food preparation. European products that had a strong impact on the Mexican diet were wheat, meat and its derivatives, sugar, citrus fruits, vegetables such as onions and garlic, and the herbs parsley and coriander. All of these contributed to the formation of the new food tradition.

During the Colonial period, when the country was known as New Spain, the diet underwent few changes after the sixteenth century. The Spanish attempted to control immigration into the country by giving permits only to subjects of the Crown. Thus, during three centuries, culinary novelties were introduced in New Spain from Spain itself or by way of Spanish officials or immigrants. It was not until the nineteenth century, when Mexico gained its independence, that Mexico was free to establish contacts with other countries without the intervention of Spain.

The influence of Asian food was felt in Mexico as early as the sixteenth century, after the Philippines were conquered by the Spanish in 1562. The Spanish established a trade route between Mexico and the Philippines that was to last 250 years. During this time, at least one and sometimes two ships, known as the Manila galleon, sailed between Manila and Acapulco every year. The galleon brought several new food products to Mexico that have influenced the evolution of Mexican cuisine, among these a variety of spices. Cinnamon, nutmeg, cloves, and black pepper now arrived directly from Asia instead of going through Europe. Mangoes from Ceylon and Malaysia and tamarind pods from India also became important ingredients in Mexican cooking.

The influence of French cuisine arrived in Mexico during the mid-eighteenth century, introduced by the viceroy Francisco de Croix. The Marquis de Croix was born in Flanders and was a well-known connoisseur of French food in general. He brought an entire team of chefs and kitchen help, well trained in French cooking, decoration, and table service. Dishes were given French names, and the marquis became well known for the fine and delicate food served at his table.

Given the different social and cultural levels that made up the population of New Spain, it is not easy to describe the diet as pertaining to only one eating tradition. The

Indian population, despite the variety of new foods on the market, continued eating the traditional diet of maize, beans, squash, tomatoes, and chile peppers. Those residing in urban areas slowly began to incorporate some European foods, such as wheat bread and meat, into their diets, without losing their own food habits.

The *mestizos* or *criollos*, born in New Spain of Spanish parents, accustomed from childhood to the flavors of both countries, were the promoters of the new eating tradition. It may have been the cooks in open-air markets who began blending the two cuisines by selling food that combined products from both cultures, such as chicken-filled tacos and quesadillas served with an Aztec-style sauce made of chile peppers and tomatoes. Indian cooks on the great *haciendas* and church convents and monasteries began adding maize and beans to Spanish-style dishes and stews. Fruits and vegetables of European origin shared space in market stands with local products. The combination of foods from both worlds provided a more varied and nutritious diet for the Mexicans.

In general, products of European origin were considered of greater prestige and more nutritious than local products. Meat, wheat bread, olive oil, wine, sugar, distilled liquor, spices, nuts, olives, and capers were imported or produced locally to meet the demands of the Spanish and *criollo* population. Some foods, such as meat, bread, wine, and olive oil, were taken to New Spain as cultural necessities of the Spanish. Meat and meat-based dishes were the preferred foods of the ruling class. Wheat, in the form of the consecrated host, played a central role in the liturgy of the Roman Catholic Mass. The Spanish preferred wheat bread to tortillas, which they considered inferior food. Wine arrived in New Spain, along with various alcoholic beverages introduced by the Spanish, during the first years after the Conquest. It was principally destined for the tables of the local Spanish, for use in banquets and in rites of the Catholic church. Olive oil was brought to the New World with a well-established prestige as a symbol of peace, hope, and abundance. In New Spain, it was essentially used as a substitute for animal fat during periods of fasting and as fuel to light church lamps. Initially, these products were expensive, scarce, and difficult to acquire, which helped increase their prestige and status.

The social lives of the *criollos* in New Spain constituted a fiesta without end. Historians describe them as spending their time organizing games, charades, parties, bullfights, dances, and theatrical performances. Everything was carried out in an atmosphere of luxury, where etiquette, style, and manners were of the utmost importance. Food and drink played an important role in the fiestas and ceremonies as tools of ostentation and pretension. Elaborate banquets were offered by civic and religious authorities to commemorate the arrival of a new viceroy, the enthronement of Spanish kings, or the births and baptisms of royal princes or princesses. Menus of official receptions, recorded by participating guests or in state documents, indicate that the number of dishes served was more important than the quality of the food. On many occasions, at least ten dishes were prepared for each of the three courses, reminiscent of the medieval banquets in Europe.

Many social changes took place after Mexico achieved its independence from Spain early in the nineteenth century. The period of independence has been described as one of a new discovery of Mexico, this time not by *conquistadores* and missionaries, but by merchants, entrepreneurs, diplomats, and adventurers. After the new government took power, the Spanish were expelled from the country, and many food products that had carried prestige merely by being the preferred foods of the ruling class undoubtedly lost their favored status. Sonia Corcuera de Mancera (1981) describes a culinary revolution at this time when a spirit of nationalism and pride prevailed in the enjoyment of preparing and consuming typically Mexican food. This was part of a conscious effort, formented by intellectuals and government officials, to establish a new national identity. Although they exalted native foods, the cookbooks published in the nineteenth century contained mostly French and Spanish recipes.

Mexico's borders were now open to new contacts and immigrants. It has been said that the food habits of a country are a reflection of the influence of its conquerors, invaders, and commercial contacts. French, German, English, and American merchants arrived to explore the economic perspectives of the new nation. Luis González y González (1973) describes Mexico during the years after independence as a river in commotion, in which French tailors, merchants, shoemakers, and pharmacists, German merchants, and English entrepreneurs came to fish. All of these new contacts left their influence on the evolution of the Mexican diet. The most influential foreign cuisine of nineteenth-century Mexico was French haute cuisine, introduced by the Austrian archduke Maximilian and his wife, Carlotta, who arrived in 1864 to establish the Second Empire. This was a short-lived venture, lasting only three years; however, French influence at state dinners continued throughout the Porfirio Díaz presidency, until his government was overthrown by rebel forces in 1910. French cuisine replaced the heavy Spanish colonial food that had been served at official functions for over 350 years.

The first half of the twentieth century was marked by revolution and upheaval, when people were more concerned about getting enough food to eat, rather than the nutritional or gastronomic state of their diets.

There probably has been a more substantial change in the Mexican diet in the past fifty years than at any time since the arrival of new food products in the early sixteenth century. Many factors have contributed to this change. Migrating farm and factory workers, who cross the border with the United States in search of a better life, return to Mexico, bringing new eating habits with them. Technological improvements and the modernization of kitchen utensils have made cooking a less arduous and time-consuming procedure. These improvements are especially important with regard to preparing Mexico's basic diet of maize, beans, and chiles.

Maize-grinding machines have practically replaced the *metate*, or grinding stone, which previously occupied many hours of a woman's day. Dehydrated tortilla flour, combined with water, produces masa harina and is now used in industrial tortilla-making machines that manufacture tortillas by mass production. Hand-operated tortilla presses, invented for producing tortillas at home, have nearly replaced tortillas patted out by hand. The pressure cooker produces well-cooked beans in one hour, instead of the four to five hours of simmering on a back burner, which provides a substantial saving of cooking gas. Electric blenders have taken the place of the *molcajete* for grinding chiles and tomatoes for hot sauces in everyday cooking.

Today, American food is the most important foreign influence on the Mexican diet. Advertising by transnational companies, effective marketing techniques, and a more open market due to the North American Free Trade Agreement have all played a role in introducing American food products to the Mexican market. Mexicans enjoy American-style convenience foods, snacks, and soft drinks, but at the same time are fearful of losing their basic food tradition that has served them so well for the past two thousand years.

[*See also* Amaranth; Cacao; Maize, *article on* Origin, Domestication, and Development; Nutrition.]

BIBLIOGRAPHY

Corcuera de Mancera, Sonia. *Entre gula y templanza: un aspecto de la historia mexicana.* Mexico City, 1981. An overview of Mexican cuisine from a historical point of view.

González y González, Luis. "El período formativo." In *Historia mínima de México.* Mexico City, 1973. General history of nineteenth-century Mexico.

González de la Vara, Fernán. *La cocina mexicana a través de los siglos: Vol. 2, Época Prehispánica.* Mexico City, 1996. Second of ten volumes on the history of Mexican food.

Katz, S., L. Hediger, and L. Valleroy. "Traditional Maize Processing Techniques in the New World." *Science* 184 (1974), 765–773. Analysis of the changes in the chemical makeup of maize as a result of the *nixtamalización* process.

Long-Solís, Janet. *Capsicum y cultura: la historia del chilli.* Mexico City, 1986. Anthropological approach to the history of the chile pepper from pre-Hispanic times to the present.

Super, John C. *Food, Conquest and Civilization in Sixteenth-Century Spanish America.* Albuquerque, N.M., 1988. Analyzes the influence of food on the colonization of the New World.

JANET LONG-SOLÍS

CULCULCAN. *See* Feathered Serpent.

CULTURAL INTERACTION. Mesoamerica's cultural unity is the product of contacts maintained among its constituent societies for more than ten millennia. A review of this length cannot do justice to the complex cultural interchanges that took place during this span; instead, it will highlight general changes in the nature and local impacts of intersocietal transactions that helped to shape Mesoamerica.

Confronting a domain with as many diverse manifestations as "intersocietal interaction" requires a guide which specifies basic principles useful in discerning patterns within a complex field. No one manual unerringly reveals the truth about intersocietal transactions; diverse approaches, employing varying tenets, are rewarded with different insights. One useful perspective stresses that power relations among interactors strongly influence the outcomes of cross-border transactions. Situations in which one party can direct the actions of others differ greatly from those where no one is in this position. But power is not equivalent to coercion: it is made up of economic, political, and ideological strains, any one of which may be expressed subtly or explicitly in a particular situation.

Economic power is the capacity of one partner to dictate terms of exchange to others. Such inequity derives from the dominant member's monopoly over the production of something needed by all other parties, and/or control of transportation technologies or routes. Able to specify trade relations to disadvantaged societies, monopolists can siphon off resources for their own benefit, transforming local production and distribution systems in the process. Political power exists when agents from one society control social relations and decisions occurring in another. Such authority is usually achieved through military force. Ideological power concerns the efficacy attributed to a belief system developed within one society by members of another. Such estimations of an ideology's potency may lead to its widespread adoption throughout an interaction network and to the attribution of prestige to the value system's propagators.

All three power dimensions converged during Euro-American expansion from the fifteenth century onward.

This experience does not mean that these power variables are inextricably wedded in all intersocietal contacts. The limited transportation and organizational capacities of most ancient societies generated a pattern wherein political power was exercised across a smaller area than its economic counterpart, and both were dwarfed by the territorial extent over which ideological power could extend. Establishing and maintaining military control taxes the administrative and provisioning abilities of a realm more than does participation in long-distance trade, and the spread of ideas can occur without much logistical support from the homeland. It is important to bear in mind, therefore, just what is meant by "inequality" in any interaction scenario, and what the implications of different kinds of power relations might be for contact processes.

Who engages in cross-border transactions and whether migration accompanies contact are other factors that affect the structure and consequences of intersocietal ties. These issues define continua between extreme possibilities. On the one hand, the opposition is between cases where all members of a society have equal access to external contacts and those in which participation is limited to a single person. On the other, contacts involving permanent relocation of entire populations contrast with situations wherein goods and ideas travel without a concomitant movement of people. Focusing on the intersection of these three variables—power, migration, and interaction participation—provides one way to describe and understand contact processes.

Interaction among Equals. The foundation of Mesoamerica's cultural unity was laid with the widespread diffusion of artifact styles, especially stone tool forms, during the Paleoindian period (11,000–7000 BCE) and the transfer of domesticates across much of Mesoamerica in the Archaic (7000–2500 BCE). Cross-border contacts in early Mesoamerica were probably negotiated by individuals acting largely on their own and not as representatives of clearly defined societies. Through such transfers, conducted among equals, people, goods, and ideas traveled great distances in many small steps. Because power differentials within and between populations were not marked, selection of items and concepts to adopt was largely a matter of personal choice. Consequently, there would have been considerable freedom to modify whatever was selected to fit new circumstances. Migration's role in dispersing artifact styles and cultigens is not clear, though it undoubtedly accounts for the area's initial peopling.

Contacts among the Rich and Powerful. The advent of large, hierarchically structured societies within Mesoamerica, beginning in the Gulf and Pacific lowlands by 1500 BCE, changed intersocietal contact conditions.

Transaction volumes rose as burgeoning populations generated increased demand for such prosaic items as stone used in tool production. Much trade among social units, however, was in exotic items that expressed and legitimized novel inequalities *within* societies. Those inequities were enhanced by the efforts of intersocietal entrepreneurs to control the local distribution of imports. Such monopolies converted equals into dependents reliant on a privileged few for prized items.

Intersocietal interactions were, therefore, increasingly restricted to a small portion of a society's total population. Barring the majority from participation in cross-border transactions ensured that exclusive control over valued imports remained in the hands of emergent elites. One means to this end involved drawing conceptual boundaries around intersocietal contacts and permitting only those who possessed the correct array of symbols to take part. International styles—widely distributed, distinctive motifs emblazoned on a variety of media—functioned in this way. They expressed shared understandings and values which united elites living in distinct societies, and they simultaneously distinguished them from subordinates who lacked the knowledge to replicate these forms. Narrowing access to extralocal ties also contributed to strengthening social boundaries. Exotic ideas and goods were no longer directly accessible for most people. Though some cross-border contacts among nonelites probably continued, their intensity declined and they no longer yielded widely dispersed styles.

Emerging disparities in the sizes and organizational capacities of societies did not translate into interaction networks dominated by a single core polity. Mesoamerica's rugged topography, coupled with the absence of draft animals, limited the political and economic impacts of even the largest realms to relatively small territories throughout most of the area's prehistory. Ideological power differences among polities, however, did affect intersocietal contacts.

The Olmec. Recent work suggests that the Gulf Coast Olmec (1200–500 BCE), traditionally viewed as Mesoamerica's "Cultura Madre," encompassed several culturally linked, politically autonomous, hierarchically organized realms that emerged from poorly understood antecedents. These entities are the best-known examples of a set of contemporary, complexly organized realms distributed across the Isthmus of Tehuantepec, down Mesoamerica's Pacific littoral to El Salvador, and in portions of the Mexican and Guatemalan highlands.

The "Olmec phenomenon" consists, in part, of distinctive decorative motifs, including the "fire-serpent," "paw-wing," "were-jaguar," and double-line break, rendered on ceramic vessels and small, portable stone artifacts. More substantial expressions of Olmec symbols are monumental sculptures that appeared relatively early on the Gulf Coast but seem to postdate 900 BCE elsewhere. These carvings include realistically portrayed human heads, tabletop altars whose basal niches contain three-dimensional human figures, and bas-relief carvings that convey natural and supernatural themes. Olmec sculptures are almost invariably found at sites whose large-scale public architecture marks them as centers of elite residence and administration. The same can be said for Olmec designs on greenstone artifacts after c.900 BCE, suggesting their use as status markers. Motifs on ceramics are more widely distributed.

The origin of these designs and their significance within local developmental trajectories are much debated. It may be safest, for the moment, to view the styles comprising the Olmec phenomenon as expressions of widely held beliefs and values that undergirded increasingly intense intersocietal contacts. In some cases, these transactions were controlled by local elites who distinguished themselves from supporters through display of exotic greenstone items and legitimized their preeminence with reference to conceptions of rulership embodied in monumental stone sculpture. Access to Olmec motifs on ceramics was more egalitarian; the symbols sometimes express cleavages among socially equivalent units unrelated to rank, especially where vessels bearing different "Olmec" designs are localized within portions of sites. Variable associations among Olmec symbols hint at complex interaction processes in which concepts were reinterpreted throughout a network spanning most of Mesoamerica.

Tangible goods that moved along with styles include obsidian, mica, ilmenite, hematite, serpentine, jade, and magnetite mirrors from the highlands, and shell, possibly cacao, and elements of ritual paraphernalia—such as turtle shell drums and crocodile mandibles—from the lowlands. Most surviving exchanged goods served as status markers and within cult observances, hinting at linkages among trade, concepts of hierarchy, and religion.

No participant in the Olmec network exercised political or economic power over the whole network. If the Olmec phenomenon was in fact the creation of a single polity, then that realm exercised ideological hegemony across the web, and its symbols defined the nature of intersocietal discourse. Such an argument conforms to the traditional assertion of Gulf Coast preeminence within the network. It is just as likely, however, that the "Olmec" phenomenon is a syncretic mix of innovations derived from numerous sources, and that different centers were involved in creating the overall pattern.

Despite ongoing disagreements, there is general consensus that the Olmec network contributed significantly to Mesoamerica's cultural unification. Symbols expressing concepts of leadership and the supernatural that crystallized and spread within the web are foundations for later Mesoamerican religions and political structures. Similarly, highland–lowland exchange patterns that took shape in the Olmec network persisted throughout Mesoamerican prehistory.

Teotihuacan. This massive urban center dominated the Central Mexican highlands from 100 BCE to 600 CE and continues to exert a shadowy hegemony over archaeological interpretations of Mesoamerican prehistory. Though many agree that Teotihuacan's rulers played some role in developments occurring over large portions of Mesoamerica, the nature of their impact and the mechanisms by which it was achieved are much debated.

Teotihuacan's "influences" are evidenced by the variable dispersal of designs and material items that are somehow linked to the center, but not necessarily to one another. These markers include artifact styles such as slab-footed cylindrical tripods, complexly decorated hourglass *incensarios*, and distinctive figurines; substantial architectural forms, most notably talud-tablero façades; and iconographic elements, including representations of Teotihuacan deities. Teotihuacan exports include green obsidian from the Cerro Navajas mines about fifty kilometers from the city, and Fine Orange pottery; though the latter was manufactured east of the Valley of Mexico, its prevalence at the city has been used to argue for Teotihuacan's control over Fine Orange distribution throughout Mesoamerica. Elaboration of characteristic motifs at Teotihuacan implies their spread from the city. The numerous large Teotihuacan workshops, in which a wide variety of implements were fashioned from Navajas obsidian, point to paramount control over the intersocietal distribution of this stone.

This mixed bag of elements does not reflect a coherent behavioral entity that inevitably diffused in a monolithic way. Such variation undoubtedly echoes diverse interaction processes with equally divergent local effects. Those few settlements where Teotihuacan styles are well represented in prosaic and esoteric realms and exports from the city are numerous—for example, Matacapan in Veracruz and, possibly, Kaminaljuyú in the Valley of Guatemala—may have housed Teotihuacan merchant enclaves. Where evidence for contact is more diffuse, interaction with Teotihuacan was probably indirect and of a different order.

Whatever the dispersal mechanisms, Teotihuacan motifs and goods are usually found in elite contexts outside the Central Highlands. Teotihuacan imagery adorns depictions of rulers carved on stelae in such Lowland Maya centers as Tikal, whereas talud-tablero architecture graces polity capitals as far afield as Dzibilchaltún, Yucatán, and Tingambato, Michoacán. Offerings of goods derived from or inspired by Teotihuacan are also found in ritual settings, including caches and elite burials. The transactions by means of which objects and ideas labeled "Teotihuacan" spread seem, therefore, to have been controlled by local rulers and to have served their political agendas.

Teotihuacan's political power did not extend beyond the Valley of Mexico and the nearby Valley of Morelos, the Plains of Apan, and around the later Toltec capital of Tula. Teotihuacan did, however, enjoy an ideological advantage within an extensive interaction network linking magnates scattered from the Maya Lowlands on the southeast to northern and western Mexico. Symbols associated with the city and expressed through styles rendered in ceramics and stone were the foundations of interelite discourse. This does not mean that all Teotihuacan motifs originated there; growing evidence suggests that they were contributed by a variety of participating societies. As with the Olmec network, the symbol system facilitating intersocietal transactions may well have been an international effort. In this case, however, Teotihuacan's rulers played the dominant role in fashioning and propagating the syncretic product.

The extent to which Teotihuacan's agents exercised economic power is not clear. Some argue that monopolies over the intersocietal distribution of Navajas obsidian and Fine Orange ceramics gave Teotihuacanos a decided economic edge in their dealings with other polities. This advantage may have been augmented by Teotihuacan's control over other minerals (such as El Chayal obsidian from highland Guatemala and cinnabar from northern Querétaro) through establishment of colonies near their sources. Such moves would have enriched Teotihuacan's nobility at the expense of those whose assets were exploited by the foreign interlopers. Others contend that the prevalence of Teotihuacanos outside the heartland is exaggerated, and that most so-called enclaves reflect intense participation by local elites in the Teotihuacan network. Proponents of this viewpoint see exchanges among economic equals rather than the impoverishment of peripheries by a dominant core. The truth may lie somewhere between these extremes; each case of putative interaction requires evaluation in its own context.

The Teotihuacan phenomenon, therefore, seems like a clearer manifestation of the Olmec network. In contrast to its predecessor, intersocietal interaction was more firmly in elite hands, and boundaries separating component societies were starker. Power differentials among polities remained ideological in nature, though variations in economic wherewithal may have been present in muted form.

Tula. Teotihuacan's decline as a political and economic nexus was followed by intense competition among independent polities (750–950 CE). This interval, in turn, was succeeded by a new period (950–1150 CE) of heightened intersocietal contacts reflected, once again, by widespread distributions of styles and goods.

Motifs emblematic of the new web include geometric (e.g., step-frets) and zoomorphic designs (such as feathered serpents) painted on pottery; distinctive forms of incense burners; wheeled ceramic figurines; and sculptural motifs expressing militaristic (e.g., armed warriors shown in profile) along with supernatural themes (including chac mools and feathered serpent columns). Novel architectural forms, best represented by open colonnaded halls and round structures, made their appearance and became dispersed over large portions of Mesoamerica. Goods moving along with these motifs derived from widely separated locales: green obsidian from the Basin of Mexico; Tohil Plumbate ceramics manufactured on the Pacific coast near the Mexico–Guatemala border; and Silho Fine Orange ware, fashioned on the Gulf Coast.

As with the Olmec and Teotihuacan networks, these designs and items do not comprise a functionally coherent package whose components invariably appear together. Such independence implies that these elements had diverse origins, and that decisions to adopt or reject specific ideas and goods were made freely by different interactors. Association of these intersocietal styles and items primarily with elite contexts further suggests that social leaders still controlled cross-border transactions. It was their calculations that determined observed material distribution.

But what variables went into those computations? Traditionally, Tula, situated immediately north of the Valley of Mexico and the capital of the large Toltec state is seen as the center of the network. Tula's considerable size and its overt artistic expressions of militarism lead many to conclude that its rulers used coercion to ensconce themselves at the hub of a trade web stretching as far southeast as the Yucatán Peninsula. Controlling this far-flung net was facilitated by establishment of a large colony at Chichén Itzá in northern Yucatán, about 1760 kilometers (1,100 miles) distant. Numerous detailed sculptural and architectural styles shared between Tula and Chichén Itzá hint at close ties between their rulers. Perceptions of Tula as an expansionistic, militaristic state logically implied that these connections were forged by conquest. Ethnohistoric accounts of migrations eastward from Tula were seen as metaphoric expressions of this invasion.

Better understanding of the Tula and Chichén Itzá chronologies, along with increasing knowledge of their Mesoamerican contemporaries, raises questions concerning this admirably straightforward interpretation. A complex array of factors, arranged in different combinations depending on location and period, was probably responsible for creating the observed archaeological distributions. The extensive spread of pottery designs may express a shared symbol system linking rulers throughout Mesoamerica. Especially intense participation in these transactions may be signaled by adoption of sculptural and architectural styles that required more knowledge of esoteric beliefs and labor to replicate than was the case for ceramic motifs. Goods exchange accompanied the dissemination of ideas, resulting in the dispersal of distinctive pottery and obsidian throughout the elite network. That many of these widely distributed motifs are most elaborately manifest at Tula may signal the importance of its rulers in propagating the international symbol system. Tula's scions were not necessarily the system's creators, however: the pottery motifs in question arose in southern Puebla and northern Oaxaca; Silho Fine Orange and Tohil Plumbate derive from the Gulf and Pacific coasts, respectively; and some have even argued that many "Toltec" sculptural and architectural styles arose first in Chichén Itzá. It may well be that this international style is yet another syncretic conceptual system combining ideas drawn from diverse sources and used to enable cross-border contacts among rulers.

This symbolic vocabulary probably spread through established interelite networks, though ethnohistoric, linguistic, and archaeological evidence indicates that migrations of varying scales contributed to the dispersal. Many of these peregrinations originated in the Gulf Coast. Populations in this frontier between the Mexican Highlands and Maya Lowlands forged cultures composed of features derived from both zones. From 700 CE onward, groups of differing sizes and compositions left this cultural crucible for varied destinations. Most of the incursions were carried out by small, well-organized cadres of warrior-merchants who employed superior military technologies and organizations to dominate much larger autochthonous populations. The Olmeca-Xicalanca, for example, established themselves at such highland Mexican centers as Cacaxtla, where their presence is revealed in architectural and painting styles that synthesize elements derived from Central Mexico and the Maya Lowlands. Beginning around 800 CE, successive waves of "Chontal-Putun" warrior-traders may have been responsible for introducing stylistic and behavioral innovations into a variety of Lowland Maya centers, including Chichén Itzá. The Quiché, Cakchikel, and Tzutujil, who came to dominate highland Guatemala after 1250 CE, also originated on the Gulf Coast. These movements were driven by competition over land and control of high-volume commodity trading throughout Mesoamerica. Migration, therefore, was one mechanism by which the mercantilistic and militaristic spirit of late prehistoric Mesoamerica was disseminated.

The interaction network linking most Mesoamerican rulers from 950 to 1150 is marked by continued elite control over intersocietal contacts. Tula may have exercised some ideological power within the network, even if its residents were not the ultimate creators of the symbol system so well represented at their capital. That advantage did not translate into, or result from, economic and political power exercised over the entire web. Nevertheless, expansionistic realms throughout the network were converting political and economic advantages on the local level into spatially restricted hegemonies. Migration, conquest, and contests over trade were significant factors in expanding and determining the structure of the network in some portions of Mesoamerica.

Imperial Variations. Intersocietal interaction processes change dramatically when one or more participants gain significant economic or political advantages over their partners. As noted earlier, such leverage enables impoverishment of some societies for the enrichment of others. The impacts of these disparities on interaction structures and local developments vary depending on the magnitude of power differences among societies, the extent to which the three dimensions of power coincide, and the spatial and temporal scales over which power is exercised. At one extreme are those cases in which a society enjoys only, say, a limited amount of political power for a short period within part of a web. At the other are situations in which a society exerts overwhelming, long-term ideological, economic, and political mastery throughout the network. Late Mesoamerican prehistory and early history provide examples from both ends of the spectrum.

The Aztec. The Aztec, or Mexica, Empire converted extant Mesoamerican interaction networks into a tribute system that functioned for the benefit of those ruling the Triple Alliance from the Basin of Mexico. The means to this end was military force. Expansion of the empire was calculated to enhance the flow of valuable resources, such as textiles and cacao, into the capital, Tenochtitlan. Conquests were carefully chosen to advance this objective, resulting in an empire that was a patchwork of controlled areas separated by tracts of unattractive territory outside the realm. Beyond the empire's Central Mexican core, conquered polities were not reorganized following imperial designs. As long as subjugated realms paid tribute punctually, they were largely left alone. It is not clear that the Aztecs even exercised ideological hegemony within their empire. No symbol system undergirding interelite contacts and centered on Tenochtitlan has been identified. Though distinctive Mixteca-Puebla polychrome

ceramics may express a conceptual framework for elite interactions, these symbols extend well outside the empire. In short, the interaction web focused on Tenochtitlan was one in which military coercion was used to extract resources from tribute-paying provinces that were not bound to Tenochtitlan by economic dependency or commitment to a common ideology.

The local significance of these transactions is difficult to gauge, though they seem not to have precipitated major changes in the political, economic, or ideological structures of vanquished societies. Both the simplicity of imperial structure and the ephemeral impact of these relations may be due partly to the empire's brief duration: the Aztec realm had been expanding for less than a century when the Spaniards ended further development.

It is important to bear in mind that late prehistoric interaction networks in which the Aztecs participated stretched beyond the empire's boundaries. Tenochtitlan's masters, therefore, did not control the entire web and were forced to deal as equals with representatives of distant polities. The *pochteca*, professional traders and *agents provocateurs* who established enclaves in entrepôts throughout eastern Mesoamerica, mediated these distant transactions.

The Spanish Empire. Arrival of the Spanish in Mesoamerica during the early sixteenth century instituted new interaction processes with dire consequences for the area's native inhabitants. Overwhelming political power, coupled with the crippling affects of contagious diseases, contributed to the rapid subjugation of most Mesoamerican polities. Mercantilist policies instituted in the wake of military victory incorporated Mesoamerica within an international economic network that siphoned off resources, using indigenous and, later, imported slave labor, for the benefit of Spanish royal and commercial institutions. Simultaneously, imposition of a foreign ideological system and oppression of its native predecessors were launched. The upshot was economic impoverishment, social dislocation, and cultural persecution.

The Conquest's effects were not uniform, however. In areas unattractive to the invaders, indigenous populations often controlled economic and ideological resources needed to resist the worst depredations. Zones that contained assets useful to Spanish enterprises, in contrast, became foci of colonial supervision and settlement. Native peoples here were stripped of the means to ward off imposed beliefs and practices and suffered the greatest cultural and economic dislocations. The empire's long history, stretching over three centuries, guaranteed that its effects were as pervasive as they were profound. Even the remotest corners of the realm were eventually entangled in the tentacles of imperial institutions.

The Spanish Empire represented a concentration of

power that operated along all three dimensions and extended over temporal and spatial scales that were regionally unprecedented. Events following independence maintained established interregional inequalities. Spain was now replaced by a sequence of competing First World cores, of which the United States is now the most powerful. Backed by the threat of military intervention, First World control over economic forces of production and transportation ensures Mesoamerica's continued role as a provider of cheap raw materials and a consumer of expensive manufactured items. These transactions, conducted within a Western capitalist ideology, reproduce on a daily basis Mesoamerica's enduring underdevelopment.

[*See also* Acculturation; Mestizaje; Syncretism; Transculturation; Warfare.]

BIBLIOGRAPHY

Blanton, Richard E., and Gary M. Feinman. "The Mesoamerican World-System." *American Anthropologist* 86 (1984), 673–682. Reinterpretation of the Aztec Empire using concepts borrowed from Wallerstein's world systems theory, as presented in *The Modern World System*, vols. 1–2.

Chase-Dunn, Christopher, and Thomas Hall. "Conceptualizing Core/Periphery Hierarchies for Comparative Study." In *Core/Periphery Relations in Precapitalist Worlds*, edited by Christopher Chase-Dunn and Thomas Hall, pp. 5–44. Boulder, Colo., 1991. This effort to redefine Wallerstein's world systems theory for use in prehistoric contexts provides the basis for the distinctions made in this entry between different components of power and their variable spatial distributions.

Clark, John. "From Mountains to Molehills: A Critical Review of Teotihuacan's Obsidian Industry." In *Economic Aspects of Prehispanic Highland Mexico*, edited by Barry L. Isaac, pp. 23–74. Greenwich, Conn., 1986. Reconsideration of the scale and structure of Teotihuacán's obsidian industry, with significant implications for arguments concerning the city's economic hegemony within Mesoamerica.

Farriss, Nancy M. *Maya Society under Colonial Rule*. Princeton, 1984. Chronicles the ways in which Yucatecan Maya contrived to retain some control over economic and ideological resources needed to resist Spanish incursions in this remote portion of the empire.

Flannery, Kent V. "The Olmec and the Valley of Oaxaca: A Model for Interregional Interaction in Formative Times." In *Dumbarton Oaks Conference on the Olmec*, edited by Elizabeth P. Benson, pp. 79–110. Washington, D.C., 1968. Classic article, the opening shot in reconsiderations of what "Olmec" actually means.

Hassig, Ross. *Trade, Tribute, and Transportation: The Sixteenth Century Political Economy of the Valley of Mexico*. Norman, Okla., 1985. Comprehensive account of the Aztec Empire's economic structure and relations with conquered realms.

Miller, Arthur G., ed. *Highland–Lowland Interaction in Mesoamerica: Interdisciplinary Approaches*. Washington, D.C., 1983. Analyses of iconography, ceramics, obsidian, and agricultural technologies contribute to debates concerning the nature of intersocietal contacts; the principal focus is on relations among Teotihuacan and contemporary Lowland Maya realms.

Rice, Don S. *Latin American Horizons*. Washington, D.C., 1993. Collection of essays presenting varied perspectives on periods of intense intersocietal contact in pre-Hispanic Mesoamerica and South America; the Olmec, Teotihuacán, Toltec, and Aztec phenomena are covered in separate essays; extensive bibliographies.

Sabloff, Jeremy A., and E. Wyllys Andrews V, eds. *Late Lowland Maya Civilization*. Albuquerque, N.M., 1986. Essays review a wide range of topics, though special attention is directed to the founding and growth of Chichén Itzá.

Sanders, William J., and Joseph W. Michels, eds. *Teotihuacan and Kaminaljuyú: A Study in Prehistoric Culture Contact*. University Park, 1977. Strong presentation of the argument for a Teotihuacan enclave at the Highland Maya center of Kaminaljuyú and discussion of its implications for regional developments.

Santley, Robert S., Clare Yarborough, and Barbara A. Hall. "Enclaves, Ethnicity, and the Archaeological Record." In *Ethnicity and Culture*, edited by R. Auger et al., pp. 85–100. Calgary, 1987. Clear statement for the existence of Teotihuacan enclaves outside Central Mexico.

Schortman, Edward M., and Patricia A. Urban. "Living on the Edge: Core/Periphery Relations in Ancient Southeastern Mesoamerica." *Current Anthropology* 35 (1994), 401–430. Detailed consideration of the impacts of intersocietal contacts conducted among Maya and non-Maya within a portion of Mesoamerica; provides a more extensive discussion of general concepts used in this review and a larger bibliography.

Sharer, Robert J., and David C. Grove, eds. *Regional Perspectives on the Olmec*. Cambridge, 1989. Essays in this volume present divergent perspectives on the nature and significance of the Olmec interaction network as viewed from different portions of Mesoamerica.

Smith, Michael E. "The Role of Social Stratification in the Aztec Empire: A View from the Provinces." *American Anthropologist* 88 (1986), 70–91. Interpretation of the means by which the Aztec Empire was held together through interelite alliances.

Smith, Michael E., and Cynthia M. Heath-Smith. "Waves of Influence in Postclassic Mesoamerica? A Critique of the Mixteca-Puebla Concept." *Anthropology* 4 (1980), 15–49. Breaks down traditional understandings of Mixteca-Puebla polychrome ceramics into their constituent elements to clarify the significance of this pottery in understanding intersocietal interactions.

Wallerstein, Immanuel. *The Modern World System*. 3 vols. New York, 1974, 1980, 1989. These volumes revolutionized the ways in which intersocietal interaction is perceived archaeologically; Wallerstein's remarks are especially appropriate to understanding Spain's impact on Mesoamerica.

Wolf, Eric R. *Europe and the People without History*. Berkeley, 1982. This eloquent critique of anthropological approaches to understanding culture form and change broadens the scope of inquiry to include the structure of interaction networks; deals mostly with the period of European expansion from the fifteenth century to the present.

EDWARD M. SCHORTMAN
and PATRICIA A. URBAN

CURANDERISMO. *See* Curing and Healing.

CURING AND HEALING. From the beginning of the written record and probably even before then, Mesoamericans have been accustomed to choosing from among many means of preventing, diagnosing, and healing diseases. Settlement of the region was characterized by frequent and extensive contact among distinct ethnic groups driven by commerce, diplomacy, warfare, the formation of states, and the building of empires, all of which contributed to the continuous exchange of health-related information and practices. Nonetheless, many of the present-day region's most important health concepts and practices can be traced either to the precolonial period or the Spanish conquest. Although the details of these overarching concepts and practices vary, variability is distributed not by ethnic group but by municipality.

Illness Causation. Three distinct spirit essences are implicated in illness causation: the *alma* or *sombra*, the *tonal*, and the *nagual*. Beliefs in these spirit essences are widespread throughout the region, but not universal. Each kind of spirit essence is associated with illness, but the mechanisms are diverse, and the locus of the illness-causing agent varies.

It is universally believed that each individual is born with an innate "soul" (*alma/sombra*) which is so intimately bound as to be interchangeable with a person's breath (*respiro*) or voice (*voz*). The *alma* resides within the body but is only loosely attached. As a result, it, or its segments, can be jarred loose by sneezing; it may wander during dreaming; it may be captured by supernatural beings or abducted by a witch. As long as the *alma* or any of its segments cannot return to its corporal host, the latter suffers the illness called *susto* (soul loss).

The *tonal* is an animal counterpart with which an individual is publicly identified at birth. Throughout their lives, the two remain vitally associated even though they may be in separate locations. Therefore, any event such as illness, accident, or injury that harms one also harms the counterpart. In contrast, where *naguals* are recognized, they are associated only with adults who have powerful or contentious personalities. While the *tonal* take any animal form, the *nagual* is customarily a carnivorous predator such as a jaguar, coyote, vulture, or owl. The *tonal* is incapable of agency in illness causation, but the *nagual*'s owner is presumed to manage his or her spirit to inflict illness or other harm on others.

Failure to preserve harmonious relationships both inside and outside the family leaves one susceptible to sickness as supernatural punishment or harmful witchcraft exercised by those presumed to feel offended. The spirits of dead ancestors, considered the guardians of tradition, may also send currents of noxious air (*aires*) into the bodies of individuals who fail to follow codes of proper conduct, or they may place the offender's *tonal* in the path of danger. Illness may also be a punishment for disrespectful behavior toward the many prescient sprites and spirits who inhabit the natural environment. Whereas God (*Dios*) is ubiquitous, these volitional sprites and spirits inhabit caves, lagoons, pools and rivers, uncultivated woodlands, and mountain peaks. These abodes are best shunned to avoid illness, but when this is impossible, permission to

A shaman praying for the soul of a patient at a mountain shrine beautifully captures the orientation of the dynamic relationship between health and features of the natural surroundings. *Photograph courtesy of Professor Emeritus Frank Cancian.*

traverse their spirits' zones of influence, or to hunt or fish the species they protect, must be respectfully requested.

While these external health threats require prudence, the body's internal homeostatic mechanisms also call for constant attention. The essence of good health lies in the body's homeostatic balance. All extremes are avoided because they can unbalance the body, which in its healthy state is characterized by evenly distributed warmth. Extreme emotional states such as anger, envy, and lasting sexual passion, which "heat" the blood, cause "hot" illnesses. Equilibrium is jeopardized when the body is confronted with many kinds of insults: shocks of cold, heat, or moisture that are too strong or sudden to allow selfreequilibration; systemic strain from overwork, excessive exertion, or exhaustion; displaced or "wandering" organs, especially the fontanel, womb, nerves, and *alma*; and the failure of healthy or diseased body fluids to drain owing to a malfunctioning organ or clogged orifice. Illness symptoms signal disequilibrium and suggest the therapeutic sequences that are required to restore homeostasis. The steps taken depend on the kind of imbalance diagnosed, but they generally involve herbs, foods, or other substances that restore balance, or purgatives to unclog the blocked body part.

Diagnosis and Healing. The importance of maintaining balance helps explain the prominence of two of the region's most widely disseminated health practices: diagnosis by "listening" to the blood, and sweat baths. Listening to a patient's blood by feeling the pulse at the thumb, wrist, or elbow determines whether the blood is excessively thick or thin, pumping vigorously or too slowly, weakly, or rapidly. This form of diagnosis is in the repertoire of only the most experienced healers.

Medicinal sweat baths are used throughout the region to maintain or restore homeostasis in males and females of all ages, but they are especially important in post-partum care, when women must replenish the "heat" lost during pregnancy and parturition. Attendance at medicinal sweat baths is limited to family members and midwives or shamanic healers. They are held in structures especially built for the purpose. The heat of the bath, together with "sweeping" the body with a broom of medicinal herbs and prayers to spirit "lords" and environmental "owners," helps the body regain "warmth" and rids it of noxious substances.

Healers and Curing. Illness symptoms are typically treated by a family member until the sick person recovers or the condition is considered too complicated or unresponsive. Diverse groups of healers are available when more specialized care is required. All healers rely on prayer and use medicinal herbs to some extent, although plant use varies by specialty and individual proclivity. Healers can be divided into two large groups based on how they enter practice and the extent to which their practice requires collaboration with the supernatural: empirical and shamanic healers. Midwives, a third group, have characteristics that cut across the two main categories.

Empirical specialists learn their craft through experience, generally beginning by ad hoc experimentation or by apprenticing themselves to experienced healers. Their entry into practice is not dependent on divine election, nor does their success depend on the intercession of powerful spirit forces. Empirical healers include bonesetters (*huesera/os*), who massage and manipulate muscles and reset bones; herbalists (*yerbera/os*), whose expertise lies primarily in the identification and preparation of medici-

nal plants; *limpiadores*, who cleanse intrusive illness from the body using brooms made of medicinal herbs or live chickens or turkeys, hens' eggs, or copal to absorb the sickness for subsequent disposal; and *chupadores*, who suck out intrusive noxious substances through their patients' skin.

Comparatively little is known about the knowledge and practices of the empirical healers who treat commonplace health problems, but the philosophy and practice of shamanic healers (*curandera/os*), who treat illnesses seen as punishment for inappropriate behavior, have been well studied. Shamanic curers are typically called to practice while dreaming or during a "near-death" experience in the course of a serious illness. Although many are initially reluctant to accept their calling, those who resist risk supernatural punishment, usually death. Shamanic curers diagnose and cure illness by means of clairvoyance, prayers, and the proffering of gifts such as sacrificed animals to powerful spirits. Some also use hallucinogenic plants; others employ alcohol, tobacco, or trance to gain audience with the supernatural powers who have the ability to restore health.

Both empirical and shamanic healers are respected in their communities for their specialized knowledge, but the more powerful and successful shamanic curers are usually viewed with ambivalence. They arouse suspicion primarily because they can access supernatural powers others cannot and because the uses to which they put that collaboration are not socially controlled. As a result, they are often singled out for blame when their communities are threatened by epidemics or other catastrophes. Punishment can include banishment from the community or public execution.

Shamanic healers specialize in treating illnesses caused by social infractions, imbalance of the "humors," witchcraft, and "folk" illnesses, particularly fallen fontanel (*caida de la mollera*), surfeit (*empacho*), "anger" sickness (*coraje, muina*), fright illness (*susto*), and evil eye (*mal de ojo*). The healer treats the symptoms of the diagnosed condition until the patient recovers, or until the fruitlessness of the treatment makes it clear that another diagnosis is required and a new treatment is begun. The healer's repertoire includes restoration of the physical or spirit components of the person (e.g., the fontanel or *alma*) as well as restoration of harmonious relationships between the patient and others, including spirits, who form his or her community. Little is known about shamanic treatments for epidemic illnesses like whooping cough, measles, or malaria, despite their prevalence throughout Mesoamerica.

A person may become a midwife through supernatural calling, inheritance, or voluntarily, although apprenticeship training is probably the most common means of recruitment. The extent of prenatal care is variable; where it exists, massage is an essential part. It is used to relax muscles, relieve discomfort, estimate the progress of pregnancy, position the fetus, loosen the placenta in preparation for delivery, and aid post-partum recovery. In some areas, midwives also possess extensive knowledge of herbs to facilitate labor, ease pain, stop heavy post-partum bleeding, stimulate milk production, and facilitate recovery. In some groups, midwives may administer sweat baths along with massage. They may also help to care for the mother and newborn after delivery.

Change. Healing practices have changed dramatically over the past half century. For the most part, these changes have accompanied efforts to incorporate indigenous communities into the region's nation-states. Community health education campaigns, retraining healers, and posting physicians to areas with no previous access to Western medicine are some of the means used to displace traditional indigenous medicine. Roads linking small villages to market towns and cities now provide rural residents greater access to public clinics and hospitals and private pharmacies. At the same time, greater accessibility has encouraged spiritistic, spiritualistic, and homeopathic practitioners to make inroads in previously isolated villages.

In part because of those efforts, the role of traditional healers has been diminishing. The effects have been more apparent among shamans than among empirical healers and midwives, for two main reasons. First, shamans interpret sickness as a sanction for failing to honor traditional codes of conduct; this leaves them vulnerable because, with the growing impact of public education, proselytism, migration, and mass media, these very codes of conduct are in disarray and subject to conflicting interpretations. Second, shamanic healers practice in consultation with powerful supernatural beings. These are the very powers that resident schoolteachers, Roman Catholic priests, catechists, evangelical missionaries, and "progressive" village authorities seek to obliterate. Change in status and influence is far less evident among empirical healers like bonesetters and midwives, whose practices are not devoted to supporting traditional norms of ritual and social behavior. Perhaps most interesting, in the past half century, forces of change have contributed to the emergence of systems which incorporate pre-Hispanic constructs of causality, components of post-Conquest germ theory, and twentieth-century pharmaceuticals. It is in experiencing these ever more complex systems that we see Mesoamericans responding selectively when faced with illness: picking and choosing, retaining and discarding according to individual experience and the constantly changing paradigms of their local communities.

[*See also* Divination; Human Body; Mal de Ojo; Shamanism; Susto; Witchcraft, Sorcery, and Magic.]

BIBLIOGRAPHY

Adams, Richard N., and Arthur J. Rubel. "Sickness and Social Relations." In *Handbook of Middle American Indians*, vol. 6, *Social Anthropology*, pp. 333–355. Austin, Tex. 1967. Analysis of illness as a manifestation of disharmony caused by failure to observe ritual or social expectations in Middle American indigenous communities.

Aguirre Beltran, Gonzalo. *Cuijla: Esbozo Etnográfico de un Pueblo Negro*. Mexico City, 1958. Chapter 13 of this community study offers an unusually detailed and generalizable analysis of the linkage between a person's health status and the well-being of her or his *tonal*, or animal companion.

Berlin, E. A., and B. Berlin. *Medical Ethnobiology of the Highland Maya of Chiapas, Mexico*. Princeton, 1996. Presents the results of an exemplary interdisciplinary investigation of the diagnosis and treatment of illness in neighboring contemporary Maya communities, with emphasis on gastrointestinal conditions; describes significant medicinal plants and variation in plant knowledge and practice based on gender, specialization, and other social characteristics; includes valuable guidelines for studying similar phenomena elsewhere in Mesoamerica.

Browner, C. H. "Criteria for Selecting Herbal Remedies." *Ethnology* 24 (1985), 13–32. Description of the relationship between concepts of reproductive ethnophysiology and medicinal plant use in an indigenous Oaxacan community; reveals the relationship between humoral concepts and broader ethnophysiological principles.

Cosminsky, Sheila. "The Role of the Midwife in Middle America." In *Actas del XLI Congreso Internacional de Americanistas*, pp. 279–291. Mexico City, 1976. Thorough review and analysis of the midwifery literature, including detailed descriptions of variation in recruitment, training, and practices.

Foster, George M. *Hippocrates' Latin American Legacy: Humoral Medicine in the New World*. Langhorne, Penn., 1994. Perspectives on the importance of humoral medicine in the Americas, with emphasis on a Tarascan community.

Groark, Kevin P. "To Warm the Blood, to Warm the Flesh: The Role of the Steambath in Highland Maya (Tzeltal-Tzotzil) Ethnomedicine." *Journal of Latin American Lore* 20 (1997), 3–96. Careful, insightful synopsis of the importance of the steam bath in Mesoamerica from pre-Hispanic to present times, based in part on participant observation; includes an illuminating discussion of the symbolism associated with the steam bath in the Chiapas highlands and the ritual healing involved.

Heim, R., and R. G. Wasson. *Les champignons hallucinogens du Méxique*. Paris, 1958. Description of the chemical bases, preparation, and use of hallucinogenic plants in some Mexican shamanic healing rituals.

López Austin, Alfredo. *The Human Body and Ideology: Concepts of the Ancient Nahuas*. Translated by Thelma Ortiz de Montellano and Bernard Ortiz de Montellano. 2 vols. Salt Lake City, 1988. Seminal compilation of descriptions of how the Nahuatl-speaking peoples of Mexico's central plateau conceived of health and the human body around the time of the Spanish conquest; relies heavily on sources written in Latin and thus reflects Christian European concepts during the post-Conquest period.

Rubel, Arthur J., Carl W. O'Nell, and Rolando Collado Ardon. *Susto, a Folk Illness*. Berkeley, 1984. Innovative analysis of the distribution, causes, and treatment of *susto* (soul loss illness) in three communities of southeastern Mexico; special attention is paid to the relationship between victims' susceptibility to the illness and their social, psychiatric, and biological characteristics.

Sahagún, Bernadino de. *Florentine Codex: General History of the Things of New Spain*. Translated by Charles E. Dibble and Arthur J. O. Anderson. Santa Fe, N.M., and Salt Lake City, 1981. Introduction to the social context in which ideas about the human body and its care were formed by the pre-Hispanic imperial Nahua of Central Mexico; includes vocabularies of external and internal body parts and consideration of how healers went about diagnosing and healing sickness. However, the extent to which generalizations can be made from the Nahuas to other groups is not clear.

Schultes, Richard E. "An Overview of Hallucinogens in the Western Hemisphere." In *Flesh of the Gods,* edited by Peter Furst, pp. 3–54. Westport, Conn., 1972. A noted ethnobotanist reviews the major hallucinogens of the region and provides both the active chemical ingredients of the plants and descriptions of their use by shamanic healers to communicate with the supernatural world.

Vogt, Evon Z. *Tortillas for the Gods.* Cambridge, 1976. Thoughtful, clear analysis of the moral system of a contemporary Highland Maya society, with emphasis on the relationship between moral transgressions and the visitation of illness; contains a useful discussion of how the status of an individual's innate soul (*alma* or *sombra*) and animal counterpart (*tonal*) reflects health.

Watanabe, John. *Maya Saints and Souls in a Changing World.* Austin, Tex., 1992. Thoughtful account of a Guatemalan community documents changes from the 1940s to the 1990s in the attribution of illness causation and analyzes changes in the relative importance of categories of healers.

ARTHUR J. RUBEL and C. H. BROWNER

D

DANCE. In ancient Mesoamerica, dance was more than a means of pleasure and entertainment; it served a wide range of social and religious functions. Many dances were important forms of social interaction, including publicly condoned contact between the sexes. The sixteenth-century Dominican Fray Diego Durán notes that among the Aztec, the diurnal dance of the warriors at the *cuicacalli*, or "house of song," attracted temporary lovers, while future spouses were frequently met during closely chaperoned night dances of maidens and youths. Particular dances marked differences in social roles, including occupation, gender, and age as well as commoner or noble status. Such dances clearly also reinforced identity and cohesion within social groups. In addition, dances dramatized historical events such as victories and the deeds of kings and ancestors. Commissioned by the elite, many such performances enhanced the authority of the noble class. However, dance was also an important medium of social commentary and parody, as clown dancers lampooned the misdeeds of individuals, including those in high office. Fray Diego López de Cogolludo describes the ritual clowns, or *baltz'am*, of the Early Colonial Yucatec Maya: "They are clever in the mottoes and jokes, that they say to their mayors and judges: if they are too rigorous, ambitious, or greedy, they portray the events that occurred and even what concerns the official's own duties, these are said in front of him, and at times with a single word."

Dance was also inextricably tied to ritual and religious belief. Dances commonly marked calendrically timed events, such as the *veintena* festivals of the eighteen 20-day months or the rites heralding the New Year. Many dances were believed to have magical power to conjure gods and ancestors or natural forces, such as wind, rain, or lightning. In the ecstasy of dance, the division between the mortal and supernatural realms could be blurred, a condition augmented by music and a heady atmosphere of sweet-smelling flowers and incense. The collection of Aztec songs known as the *Cantares Mexicanos* has many references to communicating with a supernatural, flowery paradise through song and dance.

A flower incense, flaming all around, spreads sky aroma, filled with sunshot mist, as I, the singer, in this gentle rain of flowers sing before the Ever Present, the Every Near.

A similar paradisal complex appears to have been present among the Classic Maya, where scenes of conjuring through music, incense, and dance are often filled with falling rain or flowers and jewels. The frequent Classic Maya use of dance to express the rebirth and apotheosis of dead kings probably relates to the importance of conjuring ancestors and gods through dance. In the Quiché Maya *Popol Vuh*, the Hero Twins finally best the gods of death by tricking them through dance. Similarly, the use of dance to evoke and conjure revered ancestors was a negation—at least temporarily—of the forces of death and destruction.

As a means of contact between the sexes and a sensual, corporeal art form, dance was closely related to fertility and sexuality. These themes were commonly associated with flowers, which were identified with the soul and afterlife as well as with sensuality, fertility, and reproduction. According to Durán, the "most enjoyed" Aztec dance was the Dance of the Flowers, dedicated to Xochiquetzal, a goddess of physical love and beauty. An important Aztec god of music and dance was Xochipilli, or Flower Prince, an embodiment of youthful vigor and beauty. However, dance and sensuality had a negative aspect related to bestial excess and lust. Another Aztec being, Huehuecoyotl or Old Coyote, was a god of wanton sexuality as well as a deity of song and dance. In the *Codex Borbonicus* illustration of the 13-day *trecena* of 1 Flower, Huehuecoyotl dances before Xochipilli, who beats a drum. Interestingly, both gods are supplied with the twisted red and white headband worn by male inhabitants of Tlaxcala, blood enemies of the Aztec. Along with the coyote, the spider monkey was identified with sexuality and dance among the Aztec and other peoples. The common running position of spider monkeys, with the hands lifted above the shoulders, evokes a widespread Mesoamerican dance pose.

Dance positions are one important means of identifying depictions of performances in pre-Hispanic art. In one of the most widespread poses in ancient Mesoamerican dance, the elbows are lifted near shoulder level away from the central body axis, with the hands near or above head height. During the Classic period, this dance pose was depicted among the Classic Maya and in the famous smiling ceramic figures from the Nopiloa and Remojadas areas of southern Veracruz. Depictions of dancers in this position are also widespread from Late Postclassic highland Mexico, both Mixtec and Aztec. Classic Maya dancers are also identified by their holding one foot, or one heel, slightly above the other, a convention found as well in the murals of Cacaxtla, Tlaxcala. Although the Cacaxtla murals do demonstrate strong cultural ties to the Late Classic Maya, this dance pose is also known for the Aztec and appears in the early colonial *Manuscrit Tovar*.

Items held or worn by performers also signify dance: rattles, flowers, and feather fans. By the Early Formative period (c.1200–900 BCE) such dancers appear in the figurines of Tlatilco and Xochipala. Flowers, whether freshly picked or as artificial feather bouquets, are commonly held by dancers. Among the ancient Maya and Aztec, dancers often flourish fans, quite probably to accentuate particular moves. In one form of dance still known in Mesoamerica, performers carry live snakes which symbolize lightning and rain, a tradition also present among the contemporary Hopi of the American Southwest. Dance costume includes such elements as masks, headdresses, quetzal plumes, metal bells, and shell or jade tinklers.

Some of the earliest complex scenes of dance appear in the ceramic tomb sculpture of West Mexico, dated to the Protoclassic period (100 BCE–250 CE), which feature groups of people engaged in various forms of dance. The most elaborate feature individuals atop tall poles, possibly a form of the *volador* dance. Other sculptures portray complex village scenes in which dancers surround musicians and others performing on a central, circular platform. One common type of dance features the participants encircling a central group of musicians, a form which also appears among the Late Postclassic Mixtec and Aztec.

Many types of dance are documented for the Contact period Maya. In his discussion of Yucatec New Year ceremonies, Fray Diego de Landa describes dances to "avert calamities" during the end of the old year, including the *xibalba ok'ot*, or "underworld" dance, a dance of old women with ceramic dogs, and a stilt dance. His account corroborated by the New Year pages in the pre-Hispanic *Codex Madrid*, which contain scenes of specific dances. Landa also mentions a dance of warriors, *holkan ok'ot*, danced "with a long martial step." The *Popol Vuh* lists a series of performances by the Hero Twins for the underworld lords of Xibalba, including dances of the weasel, centipede, and armadillo, and another with stilts. Episodes of the *Popol Vuh* were celebrated in public performances: a sixteenth-century Kekchí dance portrayed the resurrection of the Hero Twins and the defeat of the gods of death. An important dance drama recorded for the Highland Maya was the Rabinal Achi, or Dance of the

Tun, which featured the capture and sacrifice of an enemy military leader by the inhabitants of Rabinal.

In addition to Colonial documents, pre-Hispanic writing and art depict a detailed and complex array of dances for the Late Classic Maya. The dances often are epigraphically named by the type of object carried, as in the case of a snake dance scene appearing on a lintel from the Yaxchilán region. Rulers depicted on Classic Maya stelae frequently appear in dance costume with elaborate feather headdresses and back racks, and pendant belt tinklers in the form of oliva shell or thin jade celts. The placement of these monuments in plazas suggests that public dances were performed there. Classic Maya writing and art evidences great variety in types of dance, including forms of the snake dance, dances with deity images, deity impersonation, and dances of war, sacrifice, and bloodletting. The maize god was one of the most commonly impersonated beings in Classic Maya dance, with the sumptuous costumes of quetzal plumage and jade alluding to the verdant growth of the corn plant. Animals and demonic supernaturals were also impersonated in dance, and quite often as ritual clowns calling attention to particular social misdeeds. Many such performances featured a comely female character dancing with an old and often grotesque male. The frequently erotic overtones of such dances probably relate to sexual misconduct, one of the more commonly addressed themes in ritual clowning of both contemporary Mesoamerica and the Southwest United States. In many Classic Maya portrayals of ritual clowns, the characters often display highly animated movements, probably to suggest their agitated nature. Nowhere is this uncontrolled cavorting better reflected than in scenes of the death god gleefully dancing for his sacrificial victim, in striking contrast to the dignity and composure seen in typical portrayals of royal Maya dance.

War is a common theme of Classic Maya dance. Many Late Classic Maya vessels feature processions of richly dressed warriors brandishing weapons and war trophies, including dried heads. Their long stride recalls the *holkan ok'ot* warrior dance described by Landa. Like the dancing warrior figures flanking Structure B at Cacaxtla, the Maya figures commonly wear paper streamers hanging from their waists or phalli, another trait shared with the war dance of Postclassic Yucatán.

The murals in Room 3 of Bonampak portray a sacrificial war dance; many of the participants appear with war trophies or axes below celestial images of the sun god. The principal figures perform a bloodletting dance with large, richly ornamented fans of cloth or paper. [*See Autosacrifice.*] Also known in other Late Classic Maya scenes, this dance is widely interpreted as an especially developed form of penis perforation, with the wounded member supporting the projecting fans. However, it is quite possible that such performances are dramatizations of the bloodletting act. Yaxchilán Stela 9 portrays king Yaxun Balam (Bird Jaguar), wearing bloodletting regalia on his limbs and headdress along with the fans emanating from the loins. However, the fans penetrate the loincloth rather than the genitalia of the king. For the aforementioned snake dance scene, the live serpents carried by Yaxun Balam and his companion are being pulled through their loincloths. Although alluding to the cords used in bloodletting, these snakes were obviously not passed through human phalli. In bloodletting dances, the penitential act often may have been celebrated by passing articles through the loincloth rather than the phallus, with the falling blood readily conveyed through bladders or other liquid-filled vessels hidden in the costumes. In the context of warrior dances, the theme of penis perforation seems to be as much a celebration of male virility as a statement of penitence.

Constructed by the last Copán king, Yax Pasah, Structure 10L-18 at Copán contains a series of reliefs portraying the king performing war dances. Nikolai Grube notes that one of the accompanying texts describes a war dance as *kach*, meaning "to tie," quite probably related to the binding of captives and the ropes worn by the dancing ruler. Yax Pasah also commissioned the final program of Structure 10L-16, which features one of the most ambitious three-dimensional portrayals of dance in Classic Maya art. One of the structure's massive stairway blocks contained a portrayal of the founder of the Copán dynasty, K'inich Yax K'uk' Mo', as the sun god performing a victory dance. The outward-turned knee position reveals that the heel-to-heel convention commonly seen in frontal portrayals of dancers does not derive from problems of perspective but is instead an accurate depiction of Classic Maya dance: the toes were turned sharply out from the central axis of the body. The ancestral king engages in the same bloodletting fan dance found at Bonampak and Yaxchilán, with the fragmentary fans projecting from the inverted head of the Perforator God atop the loincloth. In the case of the Copán sculpture, the dynastic founder is portrayed reborn as the sun god in a victory war dance.

In contrast to the ancient Maya, much of our understanding of Aztec dance comes not from pre-Hispanic texts and art, but from early colonial writings in Spanish and Nahuatl. From these accounts, it is clear that dance was a central component of court life. Book 8 of the *Florentine Codex* provides a detailed list of the ornaments worn by rulers during dances, including feather headdress and back devices, gold armbands, lip plugs and other jewelry, jaguar-skin sandals, and quetzal-feather fans. Mention also is made of a headdress in the form of a quetzal bird, and it is likely that the magnificent quetzal feather headdress in the Museum für Volkerkunde in Vienna was such an item. Early descriptions mention a gold bird head, much as if the entire headdress was a living quetzal with outstretched wings and a central, vertical tail. The *Codex Ixtlilxochitl* provides an excellent portrayal of the Tetzcocan king, Nezahualpilli, richly equipped with dance regalia, including a fan and an artificial bouquet, both fashioned of precious feathers. Diego Durán notes that palace dances were frequently performed to honor historical deeds of rulers and ancestors. According to Juan de Torquemada, the Tetzcocan king Nezahualcóyotl established poetry schools which celebrated the deeds of nobles and historic events through refined song and dance. Durán contrasts the slow, solemn dances of the nobility with the "dances of youths," which tended to be merry and even ribald.

As in the case of the Late Postclassic Maya, dances formed an important part of the Aztec celebrations for each of the 20-day months, or *veintenas*, of the 365-day year. The Early Colonial *Codex Borbonicus* contains detailed scenes of these dances. In one passage, dance movements are conveyed carefully with footprints. For the month Toxcatl, a line of dancers hold hands as they encircle the tall Xocotl pole dedicated to the souls of dead warriors. In the month of Ochpaniztli, an elaborate dance features animal characters and figures in the dress of Huastec Maya and Mixcoatl, a war and hunting god. Holding their exaggerated phalli in one hand and a bundle of sticks in the other, the Huastec and Mixcoatl performers file toward an impersonator of the goddess Tlazolteotl, a Huastec-derived goddess of penitential bloodletting as well as purification. It is likely that as in the case of the Classic Maya, this performance is a dramatization of the bloodletting act, with the hand-held sticks referring to the sticks or straws passed through penitential wounds in homage to Tlazolteotl. A pair of Aztec life-size ceramic statues probably refer to the same performance. Wearing the unspun cotton headband and ear pennants of Tlazolteotl, the figures denote Huastec, who commonly display Tlazolteotl attributes in Aztec art. In the area of the loins there is an article of folded paper surrounding a now missing cylindrical element, quite probably the projecting phallus.

In Mesoamerica, many forms of native dance have continued to the present day. During the Early Colonial period, indigenous dances and accompanying music were commonly adapted to Christian celebrations, including passion plays and festivities devoted to saints. Although he approved of dances supporting the authority of native noble families, Durán also warned against dances in honor of native gods: "If he sees a couple of men in front of the others wearing different adornments and dancing different steps, going and coming in the direction of those that lead the dance, creating a merry din occasionally, ending with a whistle or pronouncing unintelligible words—let him be aware that these men represent gods, that the feast is for them, with both secret and public dancing."

One of the most impressive pre-Hispanic dances was the *volador* ceremony, in which figures descended like circling birds from ropes twisted around a tall pole. It is still performed by the Totonac in the Papantla region of Veracruz and the Quiché Maya of highland Guatemala. Many forms of ritual clowning that appear in contemporary dances can be readily related to performances of ancient Mesoamerica. Although certainly of pre-Hispanic origin, the Quichéan Rabinal Achi was first transcribed in the mid-nineteenth century and is still performed in Rabinal. The Dance of the Conquest, chronicling the defeat of the Quiché by Alvarado, is popular among Maya peoples of highland Guatemala. In the version performed in the Quiché community of Momostenango, the native shaman divines the Conquest and thereby eludes capture and conversion. Thus, an event of political domination and acculturation has been transformed into a performance of native ingenuity and resistance.

BIBLIOGRAPHY

Acuña, René. *Farsas y representaciones escénicas de los Mayas antiguos*. Mexico City, 1978. Describes dances and performances of Late Postclassic and Colonial Yucatán.

Bierhorst, John. *Cantares Mexicanos: Songs of the Aztecs*. Stanford, 1985. English translations of an important body of Nahuatl songs, many of which concern the evocation of heroic historical figures and ancestors through song and dance.

Bricker, Victoria. *Ritual Humor in Highland Chiapas*. Austin, Tex., 1973. Although focusing on contemporary Tzotzil performances of Zinacantan and Chamula, this study analyzes ritual clowning in the broader context of Mesoamerica and the American Southwest.

Freidel, David, Linda Schele, and Joye Parker. "Dancing across the Abyss: Maya Festival and Pageant." In *Maya Cosmos: Three Thousand Years on the Shaman's Path*, pp. 257–292. New York, 1993. Detailed discussion of Classic Maya texts and imagery concerning dance.

Grube, Nikolai. "Classic Maya Dance." *Ancient Mesoamerica* 3 (1992), 201–208. Grube identifies the Classic Maya glyph for dance and discusses Classic Maya texts and attendant imagery pertaining to forms of dance.

Martí, Samuel, and Gertrude Prokosch Kurath. *Dances of Anáhuac: The Choreography and Music of Precortesian Dances*. New York, 1964. Far-ranging work describes dance of both ancient and contemporary Mesoamerica, as well as the Southwest United States.

Taube, Karl. "Ritual Humor in Classic Maya Religion." In *Word and Image in Maya Culture*, edited by William Hanks and Don S. Rice, pp. 351–382. Salt Lake City, 1989. Identifies and discusses ritual clown performances portrayed in Classic Maya art, including figurines, scenes on vessels, and monumental sculpture.

KARL A. TAUBE

DANZAS. As rich and varied as Mesoamerican dance must have been before the arrival of the Europeans, it has left too little tangible evidence to yield any certain reconstruction. The same may be said, however, of medieval European folk dance and drama. Consequently, it is not always easy to know which elements of surviving Mesoamerican *danzas* have their origin in indigenous traditions and which have European roots. (In Mesoamerica, the word *danza* generally refers to ritual dance dramas, and *baile* refers to folk dances with no dramatic narrative in which men and women dance together. The latter tend to be more obviously European in origin.)

More is known about the pre-Conquest dance of the Mexica (Aztec) of Tenochtitlan-Tlatelolco (later Mexico City) than of any other group in the region. There the participation of many people in a single communal dance was an important feature of several of the calendar festivals that dominated their twenty-day months. For example, Ochpaniztli, the Sweeping of the Roads festival, began in late August or early September with the Hand-waving Dance. For eight successive days, from late afternoon until sunset, four rows of dancers bearing marigolds in each hand walked and circled in unified and disciplined silence, accompanied only by upright drums (*huehuetl*). An expanded version of the dance took place at the close of the festival, when crowds of warriors joined in, wearing the gold insignia and quetzal feathers with which they had been honored. The decorated dancers, it is said, filled the whole square with refracted sunlight.

A Serpent Dance took place during Panquetzaliztli, the Raising of the Banners festival, beginning in November. Slaves designated for sacrifice, their merchant sponsors, and other men and women who were to play a role in the festival's sacrificial ritual joined hands to form a line of dancers that snaked around the temple precincts to the accompaniment of rhythmic drumming and song. The dancers recalled both the serpent wall, which enclosed Tenochtitlan's ritual district, and the staff, carved in the form of a snake, which the image of the war god Huitzilopochtli held in his right hand.

The calendar festivals also featured mimetic dances in which individual performers played specific roles. During one dance in honor of the goddess Xochiquetzal, boys in costumes made of fine green, blue, red, and yellow feathers climbed artificial trees that were decorated with fragrant flowers. Imitating birds and butterflies, they passed from limb to limb, pretending to feed on the nectar of the blossoms. As they descended, the "birds" were met by men and women dressed as gods, who fired blowguns at them. Another mimetic dance that drew large crowds was the dance of the fire serpent during the feast of Panquetzaliztli. A priest, concealed within a costume of brightly colored paper and flaming red parrot feathers, with a paper tail some 4.5 meters (15 feet) long and a mobile tongue, danced down the temple steps; according to the eyewitnesses who later spoke to the missionary ethnographer Bernardino de Sahagún, he looked "just like a blazing firebrand" and "like a real serpent."

Warfare was a common theme of narrative dance in pre-Conquest Tenochtitlan. A dance known as *netotelixtli* involved a thousand or more men in feathered headdresses and animal masks, similar to those worn in battle, which identified their wearers as either "eagle" or "jaguar" warriors. They danced in rings, their hands joined, one ring within the other, raising and lowering their arms and heads in unison, while singers recalled the victories of past kings. At times, some of the dancers imitated enemy soldiers, making a considerable effort to catch the nuances of ethnic costume and movement. Then the enemies would be defeated, with all the noise of battle, in a combat dance that celebrated past wars

Dancers representing Aztec warriors in the *danza de la pluma*, Teotitlan del Valle, Oaxaca, July 1994. *Photograph © 1994 Max Harris.*

of conquest. Other dancers played comic roles, imitating drunks or old women for the amusement of the spectators. Rhythmic accompaniment was provided by voices, whistling, upright drums, and horizontal (*teponaztli*) drums, cane flutes, striated bones, and gourd rattles.

Because of their clear association with non-Christian religion, many of these dances were suppressed by the Spaniards. Others, construed as displays of acrobatic skill, survived the Conquest intact. The best known of these is the Danza de los Voladores ("dance of the fliers"). As it is performed today, four *voladores*—accompanied by a fifth playing a flute and a small drum—climb a stripped tree trunk about 24 meters (70 feet) high by means of knotted rope footholds. The four fliers then tie themselves by the waist to a large wooden spool mounted on top of the pole and fling themselves backward from the summit. As the ropes that link the dancers to the spool slowly unwind, the fliers descend head downward in a widening gyre; the spool revolves, forming a tiny rotating dance floor for the musician. Just before they reach the ground, the fliers right themselves and hit the ground running. The musician slides down one of the ropes. Colonial accounts and illustrations of the dance, known from Central Mexico to Guatemala, suggest that the dancers originally wore wings of elaborate featherwork. Interpretations of the dance vary. The sixteenth-century Franciscan writer Juan de Torquemada explained it as a calendrical ritual in which the unwinding of the ropes produces exactly fifty-two revolutions, representing the fifty-two years of the Mexica century. Today's performers say simply that it is "an ancient dance," that it is performed in honor of the sun, or that the dancers represent the gods of the four cardinal points bringing messages from heaven to earth.

Another acrobatic dance that survived the Conquest is the Juego de Palo ("game of the pole"). In 1587, the Franciscan friar Antonio de Ciudad Real saw an elaborate version of this in Mazatlan (now in the Mexican state of Jalisco). One dancer lay on his back with his feet in the air, juggling a carved and painted pole about 1.7 meters (5.5 feet) in length and "a hand's breath around" in time to the beat of a *teponaztli* drum, while others danced around him, singing and shaking gourd rattles. The juggler repeatedly hurled the pole in the air with the soles of his feet, his thighs, or the backs of his calves, catching it in time to the music; he spun it around on one foot while controlling it with the other; finally, he allowed two of the younger dancers to sit astride the pole, one at either end, while he created a seesaw effect for them in time to the music. Although not as widespread as the *danza de los voladores*, the *juego de palo* can still be seen in parts of Guerrero.

Other dances may have survived by adapting to changed circumstances. Incorporation into the conquerors' calendar, whether for the occasional civic pomp of a viceregal entry or the annual liturgical calendar of the church, officially placed the dances in the service of the colonial power, but this could not fully erase the dances' former religious significance. Moreover, the new contexts often suggested new meanings for the dances. The various Danzas del Tigre ("dances of the jaguar") performed throughout Mesoamerica on Roman Catholic holidays are a case in point. The version banned in 1631 by the Inquisition in Tamulte, Tabasco, featured dancers disguised as jaguars who fought, captured, and simulated the sacrifice of a dancer dressed as a warrior. Probably it had its origin in pre-Conquest rites, in which jaguar-warriors fought captive warriors destined for sacrifice. Nowadays the jaguar is more often the object of the hunt, and its killers are wealthy landowners and trackers whose bushy beards, mustaches, and rosy cheeks suggest European heritage. The transformation of the jaguar from hunter to hunted reflects the trauma of the Conquest.

In 1645, Andrés Pérez de Ribas, one of the leading Jesuit missionaries in Mexico, published an account of a dance "formerly dedicated to pagan custom and now dedicated to the honor of him who is king of kings, our Lord Jesus Christ." It was called, he wrote, "the dance of the emperor Motecuhzoma." Fourteen dancers divided into two files were led by another representing the Mexica (Aztec) emperor, Motecuhzoma. All were dressed in costumes that recalled those of Mexica nobles, with "pyramid-shaped diadems covered with gold and precious stones" on their heads and finely embroidered cloaks hanging from their shoulders. Each dancer carried in his left hand a wand of bright green feathers or a cluster of aromatic flowers, and with his right hand he shook a rattle made from brightly painted gourds filled with pebbles. Musical accompaniment included a group of native elders chanting traditional Mexica songs, a *teponaztli* drum, and an imported harp, cornet, and bassoon. Some scholars believe that such dances, adapted from indigenous rather than European models, are the source of New Mexico's Danza de los Matachines ("dance of the Matachines"), Oaxaca's Danza de la Pluma ("dance of the feather"), and other extant *danzas* that feature Motecuhzoma and a court of richly costumed nobles.

Others argue that these *danzas*, along with other combat dances such as the Danza de los Santiagos ("dance of the Santiagos") and the various Danzas de la Conquista ("dances of the Conquest") which are found throughout Mexico and Guatemala, are grounded in an introduced tradition of mock battles between the Moors and the reconquering Christians in Spain. Yet this is not as straightforward as it might seem. Much confusion has been wrought by scholars who have grouped all mock battles between light-skinned European Catholics and dark-skinned non-Christians under the single generic designation Danzas de Moros y Cristianos. In fact, most of the early European mock battles between Moors (or Turks) and Christians were not dances at all, but rather large-scale military exercises that developed from the courtly tournament and eventually passed into the folk repertory in the seventeenth century. Even today, most such performances in Spain take the form of large-scale street theater, which culminates in a deafening, smoke-shrouded battle for a castle. In Mesoamerica, although large-scale battles like this exist, they are far outnumbered by smaller combat dances that dramatize varied themes, such as the Twelve Peers of France, the miraculous victories of Santiago, Aztecs and Spaniards, and—in Guatemala—the confrontation of Pedro de Alvarado and Tecún Umán. The Mesoamerican tradition is also distinguished from its European counterpart by its widespread use of masks. Although the theme of armed conflict between Moors and Christians traveled to Mesoamerica from Spain, the same is not necessarily true of the dance form in which it is now most often represented. The introduced theme may have been appropriated by native peoples as a way of preserving indigenous combat dances in a colonial and Catholic context. Like so much else in Mesoamerica, the present tradition is probably *mestizo*.

One of the more intriguing and widespread characters in Mesoamerican *danzas* is La Malinche. Mistakenly assumed by many scholars to represent Cortés's indigenous mistress and translator of the same name, in the conquest dances she is actually the partner of Motecuhzoma. In such dances, a single dancer openly represents the emperor Motecuhzoma who was defeated by Cortés and discreetly recalls indigenous legends of a messianic Motecuhzoma who will return to drive out foreign invaders. In the imaginative world of the dance, Malinche is both the daughter of the historical Motecuhzoma and the wife of the victorious future Motecuhzoma, thereby sharing and legitimating the latter's power. In the manner of Mexica rulers generally, both Motecuhzoma and Malinche are also mortal representatives of corresponding gods. When, in other dances, Malinche appears without Motecuhzoma, it is probably this divine power that she recalls.

Other components of Mesoamerican *danzas* were clearly brought from Europe. The skirted hobbyhorse that appears in several Mesoamerican *danzas*, including the annual Pecos Bull Dance in New Mexico's Jemez Pueblo, is probably of Catalan origin. Horses were unknown in Mesoamerica before the arrival of the Spanish, and, although other animals were represented in pre-

Conquest rituals, the Mesoamerican skirted hobbyhorse too closely resembles its medieval European counterpart to have developed independently. Other elements of almost certain European origin include the intertwining of ribbons around a pole—a feature of European Maypole dances that has found a home in such varied Mesoamerican *danzas* as Taos Pueblo's Danza de los Matachines and Oaxaca's Danza de los Malinches—and the linked hexagon of raised swords, a common feature of European sword dances that concludes some versions of the Danza de los Santiagos in Mexico's Sierra de Puebla.

Mesoamerican dancers were brought to Europe soon after the Conquest. Two Mexican Indians performed before a private audience in Seville, Spain, in 1522. According to Pietro Martire d'Anghiera (*De orbe novo*, Dec. 5, book 2), a young man armed with the traditional Mesoamerican sword-club or *macuauhitl*, stripped of its obsidian blades, and a reed shield lined with tiger skin "gave an exhibition of battle, first hurling himself upon his enemies, then retreating." He mimed the capture and sacrifice of a prisoner of war (played by his companion), pretending to extract the victim's heart and cut his body into pieces. After changing into a more ornate costume, the young man performed a second dance in which he represented the giving of honor and ceremonial gifts to Mexica rulers. He accompanied himself with a native song and the rhythmic shaking of a circle of bells. After a final costume change, he amused his audience by playing the traditional comic role of a drunkard. Six years later, nearly thirty native entertainers, including jugglers, ballplayers, and dancers, traveled to Spain with Cortés. Two Indians who lay on their backs and juggled a log with their feet, in a version of the Juego de Palo, were the most popular, performing before both pope and emperor.

Indian costumes and dance steps soon became a fashionable part of European royal entries and festive processions. In 1585, eight "Indians," shaking hand-held rattles and wearing costumes characteristically studded with mirrors and crowned with tall feathers, danced in Toledo, Spain, for the Feast of the Assumption of the Virgin. In this instance, as in many others, it is impossible to tell whether the performers were American natives or costumed Europeans. In any case, Spanish interest in exotic Mesoamerica did not wane quickly. As late as 1693, a "dance of Motecuhzoma," noted for the "newness and variety of movements in the Indian style," attracted attention in Seville's Corpus Christi procession. From such contexts, elements of Mesoamerican dance almost certainly passed unnoticed into the European folk repertory, but a thorough study of the influence of indigenous American dance on European folk traditions has yet to be made.

[*See also* Drama.]

BIBLIOGRAPHY

Cline, Howard. "Hernando Cortes and the Aztec Indians in Spain." *Quarterly Journal of the Library of Congress* 26 (1969), 70–90. Illustrated account of the first Mexican performers to visit Spain.

Durán, Diego. *Book of the Gods and Rites, and the Ancient Calendar*. Translated by Fernando Horcasitas and Doris Heyden. Norman, Okla., 1971. Although not as thorough as Sahagún (see below), Durán collected information on Mexica religious festivals from those who remembered them before the arrival of the Europeans.

Esser, Janet Brody, ed. *Behind the Mask in Mexico*. Santa Fe, N.M., 1988. Lavishly illustrated collection of essays on Mexican *danzas*.

Harris, Max. *Festivals of Aztecs, Moors, and Christians: Traditional Dramatizations of Reconquest in Mexico and Spain*. Austin, Tex., 2000. Full account of the tradition of mock battles in Spain and Mexico before and after contact, reading the Mexican performances in particular as sites of resistance to domination by outsiders.

Heth, Charlotte, ed. *Native American Dance: Ceremonies and Social Traditions*. Washington, D.C., 1992. Although this book's primary focus is on the United States, it is full of colorful photographs and includes a couple of good essays on *danzas* farther south.

Markham, Peter T., and Roberta H. Markman. *Masks of the Spirit: Image and Metaphor in Mesoamerica*. Berkeley, 1989. Chapter 12 discusses several versions of the Danza del Tigre.

Martí, Samuel, and Gertrude Prokosch Kurath. *Dances of Anahuac*. Chicago, 1964. The best attempt to reconstruct the choreography of pre-Conquest Mesoamerican dance.

Pérez de Ribas, Andrés. *My Life among the Savage Nations of New Spain*. Translated by Tomás Antonio Robertson. Los Angeles, 1968.

Sahagún, Bernardino de. *Florentine Codex: General History of the Things of New Spain*. Edited and translated by A.J.O. Anderson and C.E. Dibble. 12 books in 13 vols. Salt Lake City, 1950–1982. Chronicles the memories of Mexica elders who survived the Conquest; book 2, in particular, provides invaluable information on Mexica calendar festivals.

Stone, Martha. *At the Sign of Midnight: The Concheros Dance Cult of Mexico*. Tucson, Ariz., 1975. Entertaining account of an American woman's induction into the Concheros.

Toor, Frances. *A Treasury of Mexican Folkways*. New York, 1947. Part 3 offers an easy overview of traditional Mexican dance.

Treviño, Adrian, and Barbara Gilles. "A History of the Matachines Dance." *New Mexico Historical Review* 69 (1994), 105–125. Important article challenging the assumption that the American Danza de los Matachines is of European origin.

Wachtel, Nathan. *The Vision of the Vanquished*. Translated by Ben and Sian Reynolds. New York, 1977. Offers the Danzas de la Conquista as evidence that the trauma of the Conquest remains deeply imprinted on present mental structures in native America.

MAX HARRIS

DAY OF THE DEAD AND TODOS SANTOS.

Todos Santos (All Saints' Day or All Souls' Day), *Día de Muertos* or *Día de los Muertos* (Day of the Dead), *Día de los Difuntos* (Day of the Departed), and *Día de las Ánimas Benditas* (Day of the Blessed Souls) are the most common names by which the combined liturgical feasts of All Saints' Day and All Souls' Day are known in Mexico and most of Latin America. Except for Christmas and Holy

Week (Easter), All Saints' and All Souls' Day is the most important celebration in the yearly cycle of folk Roman Catholicism in Mesoamerica. It is probably in this culture area where the ritual and ceremonial elaboration of Todos Santos acquires its maximal expression worldwide.

The folk manifestation of Todos Santos in Mesoamerica extends well beyond the traditional observation of the feast as practiced in orthodox Catholicism. In Indian and rural *mestizo* communities it acquires significant social, economic, recreational, and even demographic dimensions, many of which extend to urban environments. Todos Santos is a time for homecoming, remembering and propitiating the dead, cementing and intensifying kinship and *compadrazgo* relationships, and sacralizing—albeit temporarily—interpersonal relationships on a community-wide basis. The period extends from five days to a week before 1 and 2 November and seven days to two weeks after these days, which are the heart of the celebration. During this time, country and city come together; the little community becomes the cosmological center of existence, and individuals and families are renewed by remembering their roots and paying homage to those who are no longer present. For a moment, living and dead exist in the same world.

Since the Spanish conquest, the cult of the dead in Mesoamerica has been centered on Todos Santos. In varying degrees, it has evolved into a syncretic complex out of the sixteenth-century interaction of pre-Hispanic polytheistic elements and Spanish Catholic ones. The celebration is not uniform throughout Mesoamerican societies today; rather, it exhibits different manifestations which are largely the result of the nature of local polytheistic manifestations at the time of the Conquest, the degree to which particular regions were subjected to the processes of syncretism and acculturation during the Colonial era, and demographic and cultural variables of more recent origin. Although the belief system that supports the cult of the dead has remained fairly constant, the celebration of Todos Santos varies significantly from region to region. In the physical-ritual manifestation of Todos Santos (its most prominent feature), for example, some regions (e.g., Michoacán and coastal Veracruz) emphasize vigils and the erection of elaborate altars bearing food and flowers in the cemetery; others (Chiapas and highland Guatemala) are noted for the ritual exuberance of processions, dances, and other public displays; still others (the valleys of Mexico and Puebla-Tlaxcala) concentrate on the decoration of home altars and tombs. Some Todos Santos celebrations have become well-known tourist attractions, such as Janitzio in Michoacán and Mixquic within Mexico City.

The feast of All Saints' Day and the liturgical celebration of All Souls' Day go back to the beginning of Western Christendom. Their origins are uncertain, but by the fourteenth century they ranked immediately after Christmas and Holy Week in importance, and their celebration had been fixed on 1 November for All Saints' Day and 2 November for All Souls' Day. Since then, these two feasts have been inextricably related in the liturgy of the Western church. With the Reformation and the rise of modern science during the Renaissance, there was a decline in the ritual and ceremonial underpinnings of Christendom, but in the Catholic New World, the rites, ceremonies, and symbolic meaning of All Saints' Day and All Souls' Day were reinvigorated and in many ways achieved their highest elaboration.

All Saints' Day commemorates individuals who in the service of the church have attained the status of sainthood. Although the transcendentally different natures of the almighty God of Christian monotheism and his underlings, the saints, may be clearly understood by theologians, this has never been the case for significant segments of practicing Christians. Indeed, for sizable segments of Christendom, the proliferation of saints has come to look suspiciously like polytheism and has led to practices incompatible with monotheism. Some anthropologists maintain that most Christians throughout the centuries have been practicing monolatry; that is, in behavior (psychologically) and practice (ritually and ceremonially), no transcendental distinction is perceived between God and the saints, including the manifestations of the Virgin Mary. This is certainly true among traditional Mesoamerican Indians today. Most contemporary Mexican Indians have not internalized the theological distinction between God and saints, and in their actual religious behavior and practice, God is little more than *primus inter pares*, a more powerful deity than the saints. Mexican Indians and rural and urban *mestizos* often rank the village's patron saint higher than the Trinity, or they center their Catholicism on the cult of the Virgin of Guadalupe, in effect abandoning the central tenet of monotheism. The syncretic nature of Catholicism in Mesoamerica is not unique, however: in southern Italy and southern Spain, the saints are conceived as deities of sorts, with powers in their own right, and they are not infrequently arranged in arrays similar to the Classical polytheistic pantheon.

All Souls' Day, 2 November, is a liturgical celebration commemorating the "faithful departed"—that is, those who have died within the fold of the church. In the popular conscience, it developed into a veritable cult of the dead, and by the sixteenth century it had accumulated many beliefs and practices of pagan origin or corruptions of orthodox Christianity. The following are the most noteworthy. During the vigil of 2 November, the souls in Heaven were thought to come back in spirit to bless the households where they died, and souls in Purgatory to come back in the form of phantoms, witches, toads, and other repellent animals in order to scare or harm people who wronged or injured them during their lives. Food offerings were made to the dead in the cemetery, and special offerings were made to prominent departed members of the household; the latter would be ritually eaten by the family after the souls had symbolically tasted the food. Garments that had been worn by particularly good or pious members of the household were displayed on the family altar so that the souls would rejoice on contemplating this display of affection and become effective protectors of their living kinsmen. The way to the house was marked by signposts consisting of flowers and other decorations to help the returning souls find their earthly homes.

It was probably in southern Italy and Spain that the combined celebration of All Saints' Day and All Souls' Day acquired its most elaborate form. By the fifteenth century, the cult of the dead had acquired the trappings of the cult of the saints, and the same position in popular religiosity: both served as intercessors. Those who had led exemplary lives and those who are near God or in Purgatory in the afterlife were both a vehicle for the worship of God and advocates who would entreat God to grant individual or public requests. From the Spanish conquest onward, all these aspects of European folk Catholicism were directly or indirectly introduced to Mesoamerica, where a new, more pagan cult of saints and dead souls arose from interaction with similar aspects of native polytheism.

The pre-Hispanic components of the Mesoamerican cult of the dead were so similar to those of folk Catholicism that a thoroughly syncretic entity was formed. The most significant aspects of polytheism in the syncretic equation were the following: a highly diversified pantheon of hundreds of patron gods and goddesses for practically every human activity, natural phenomenon, and social grouping; a religious ideology that emphasized pragmatism in the relationship between man and the supernatural at the expense of values and morality, which resided in the social structure; a conception of the afterlife as a variegated realm where the dead went to reside in the abode of the god under whose auspices they had died; a pronounced concern with bloodshed and death; and a cult of the dead approaching ancestor worship.

Moreover, the Mesoamerican dead occupied an intercessory position between the living and the gods almost identical to that of Catholic saints. As servants of the gods in the afterlife, the dead were regarded as the best conduit through which the living might entreat the gods. The dead returned to the living at certain times of the year, and they were the subject of much ritual and ceremonial activity, including the consumption of food and the display of items associated with dead kinsmen. The main celebration of the dead took place during the month of Quecholli, from 20 October to 8 November. Even the details of the dead's return were similar, such as the living standing on the roofs of their houses, entreating the dead to return and showing them the way home.

By the end of the seventeenth century, the celebration of Todos Santos had basically crystallized into its present form. The syncretic synthesis is so thorough that it is occasionally difficult to determine whether a trait or practice is of folk Catholic or pre-Hispanic origin. Most of the practices described here are still present in most rural and urban environments; what remains most invariant is the belief system of Todos Santos throughout Mesoamerica.

The foregoing does not do justice to the multiple events, rites, ceremonies, and ancillary aspects of the celebration, which constitute well-known aspects of Mexican and Guatemalan folklore, but a few examples will illustrate them. The cult of the dead is not exclusively vested in the celebration on 1 and 2 November; there are several other occasions when various kinds of dead souls are worshipped and propitiated. In many regions of Mesoamerica, there are several categories of the dead; the most common are those who died as infants, by drowning, in accidents, or as victims of violence. Each of these categories is remembered and honored during the week before 1 and 2 November. The decoration of graves in the cemetery, the elaborate offering of food in the household, and the many kinds of decoration and culinary effort that these activities entail have innumerable regional variations and constitute some of the most significant expressive domains of the yearly cycle. An extensive complex of rites and ceremonies is an integral part of the Todos Santos cycle and usually lasts until the octave of All Saints' and All Souls' Day; it includes dancing, processions, and manifold activities at home, in church, and in the cemetery.

[See also Death.]

BIBLIOGRAPHY

Anguiano, Marina, et al. *Las tradiciones de Día de Muertos en México.* Mexico City, 1987. Good regional description of beliefs and practices.

Carmichael, Elizabeth, and Chloë Sayer. *The Skeleton at the Feast: The Day of the Dead in Mexico.* Austin, Tex. 1992. Very good description and analysis of the various physical manifestations of Todos Santos.

Foster, George M. *Culture and Conquest: America's Pre-Hispanic Heritage.* New York, 1960. Contains useful information on the Spanish background of the cult of the dead in Mesoamerica.

Henning, John. "The Meaning of All the Saints." *Medieval Studies* 10 (1948), 132–167. Excellent account of the evolution of the cult of the dead in Western Christendom.

Lane, Sarah, and Marilyn Turkovich. *Días de los Muertos/Days of the Dead.* Chicago, 1987. Includes some interesting ideas on the belief system and physical realization of Todos Santos.

Lok, Rossana. *Gifts to the Dead and the Living*. Centre of Non-Western Studies, Publication 4. Leiden, 1991. Very good study on the meaning of death and the celebration of Todos Santos in the Sierra de Puebla, Mexico.

López Austin, Alfredo. *Hombre-Dios: Religión y Política en el mundo nahuatl*. Mexico City, 1973. Excellent background for understanding the pre-Hispanic component in the syncretic development of the cult of the dead.

Matos Moctezuma, Eduardo, et al. "Miccahiuitl: El Culto a la Muerte." Special issue of *Artes de México* 145 (1971). Very good compendium of Mexican beliefs and practices.

Navarrete, Carlos. *San Pascualito Rey y el culto a la muerte en Chiapas*. Instituto de Investigaciones Antropológicas, publication 46. Mexico City. Good account of beliefs and propitiation of the dead in Chiapas and Guatemala.

Nutini, Hugo G. *Todos Santos in Rural Tlaxcala: A Syncretic, Expressive, and Symbolic Analysis of the Cult of the Dead*. Princeton, 1988. Exhaustive account of Todos Santos in Tlaxcala today, including the syncretic origins of the cult of the dead in the interaction of sixteenth-century Spanish Catholicism and Mesoamerican polytheism.

Ochoa Zazueta, Jesús Angel. *La muerte y los muertos*. Mexico City, 1974. Contains some interesting notions on the meaning of death and the cult of the dead in Mexico.

Oliver Vega, Beatriz, et al. *The Days of the Dead, a Mexican Tradition*. Mexico City, 1988. Useful compilation of essays on the celebration of Todos Santos in central and southern Mexico.

Sahagún, Bernardino de. *General History of the Things of New Spain*. Santa Fe, N.M. 1982. Best source on the pre-Hispanic components of the syncretic cult of the dead in Mesoamerica.

Sandoval Forero, Eduardo A. *Cuando los muertos regresan*. Cuadernos de Cultura Universitaria, Universidad Autónoma del Estado de México, 8. Mexico City, 1994. Account of the celebration of the cult of the dead in central Mexico under changing conditions.

Sayer, Chloë, ed. *The Day of the Dead*. London, 1990. Interesting compilation of interpretations of the cult of the dead and its pictorial representation by various scholars.

HUGO G. NUTINI

DAY-SIGNS. The set of twenty day names, together with a count of thirteen days (the *trecena*), constitutes the sacred calendar of 260 days known to the Aztecs as the *tonalpohualli*. Words for the twenty days were known by virtually every linguistic group in Mesoamerica (Edmonson, 1988, p. 1). It is possible to correlate across languages not only the day names but also the ordering of days and the system of numbering them: when it was the day 3 Lizard among the Otomí, it was also the day 3 Lizard among the Zapotec.

Among certain ethnic, linguistic, or archaeologically identified peoples, there existed graphic representations for the twenty day names. Although many of the days can be associated between the Central Mexican and Classic traditions, the Maya day-signs tend to be more abstract. Archaeological sites where day-signs have been found include Mone Albán, El Tajín, Cacaxtla, Xochicalco, Maltrata, Piedra Labrada, and Cerro de las Mesas (Berlo, 1989). Stela 1 from La Mojarra, Veracruz, dated at 156 CE, contains two day-signs, Snake and Deer, nearly identical to the Central Mexican day-signs of 1,500 years later; one notable difference is that they are set inside rectangular cartouches and are abstract in design, in the manner of the Maya day-signs.

In Maya dates, a day-sign is placed within another sign, giving the day an added outline, and often three scrolls appear beneath. Houston (1989, p. 35) suggests that the origin of this cartouche is a glyph for 20. A phonetic sign *la* is sometimes infixed into the center scroll, presumably as a phonetic complement for *k'al* ("twenty"). When Maya day-signs occur outside this cartouche, they do not function as day-signs but have logographic or phonetic values, which are often apparently unrelated.

Publications generally list Alligator as the first day name. Tedlock (1992, pp. 93–97) argues that day-keepers in contemporary Guatemala do not conceive of the set of days as having a beginning and an end but rather view them as a repeating cycle. Several investigators, noting the use of similar signs for 20 and "moon," have proposed a lunar origin for the count of twenty days. Thompson (1971, pp. 98–99) believed that the key to the origin of the twenty day names would be found in the semantic correspondences between the Maya head variants for the

TABLE 1. *Head Variants Phonetically Associated with Maya Numbers*

#	GLYPH	YUCATEC MAYA	ENGLISH	YUCATEC MAYA
1	woman's head	*na'* 'woman'	first	[*nah*][1]
2	fist above head	*k'ab'* 'hand'	two	*ka'*
5	man, year-sign headdress	*haab'* 'year'	five	*ho-*
6	axe in eye	*wak'* 'chop'	six	*wak*
8	face with sprout scrolls	*wah* 'tortilla; corn'	eight	*waxak*
9	face with jaguar pelt	*b'aam* 'jaguar'	nine	*b'olon*
10	skull	*laj* 'finish; die'	ten	*lajun*
12	sky	*ka'an* 'sky'	twelve	*lajka'*

[1] *Nah* ("first") is not attested in modern Lowland languages; it is found in Quichean languages.

 # English NAHUATL/MAYA MAYA VALUE

#	English	Nahuatl/Maya	Maya value			
1	Movement earth	*Ollin Kab'an*	kab'/ka			
2	Flint flint	*Tecpatl Etz'nab'*	tok'			
3	Rain year	*Quiahuitl Kawak*	tun/haab'/ku'			
4	Flower flower	*Xochitl Ajaw*	nik/xo			
5	Alligator-waterlily; fist	*Cipactli Imix*	ha'/b'a			
6	Wind wind	*Ehecatl Ik'*	nal			
7	House night	*Calli Ak'b'al*	ak'			
8	Lizard corn	*Cuetzpallin K'an*	wah/wa			
9	Serpent snake?	*Coatl Chikchan*	xa			
10	Death death	*Miquiztli Kimi*				

(continued)

The twenty Mesoamerican day signs. *Mexican signs after Caso 1967: 6–7; Maya signs by Matthew Looper, courtesy of the Maya Hieroglyphic Database Project.*

 # English NAHUATL/MAYAMAYA VALUE

#	English	Nahuatl / Maya	Maya value			
11	Deer hand	*Mazatl* *Manik'*	chi			
12	Rabbit star	*Tochtli* *Lamat*	ek'			
13	Water moon	*Atl* *Muluk*	uh/u			
14	Dog enter?	*Itzcuintli* *Ok*	ok			
15	Monkey monkey	*Ozomatli* *Chuwen*	(se)			
16	Grass jaw/skull	*Malinalli* *Eb'*				
17	Reed	*Acatl* *B'en*	aj			
18	Jaguar jaguar	*Ocelotl* *Ix*				
19	Eagle eagle?	*Cuauhtli* *Men*				
20	Vulture	*Cozacuauhtli* *Kib'*				

The twenty Mesoamerican day signs (*continued*).

TABLE 2. *Head Variants Not Phonetically Associated with Maya Numbers*

#	GLYPH	YUCATEC MAYA	ENGLISH	YUCATEC MAYA
3	circle/plaited headdress		three	*ox*
4	sun 'god'	*k'in* 'sun; day'	four	*kan*
11	Kab'an day sign		eleven	*b'uluk*
13	waterlily monster	13 Muwan (full moon)	thirteen	*oxlajun*

numbers 1 through 13 and the thirteen day names beginning with the day Movement. Recent advances in epigraphy demonstrate a rebus (inexact phonetic) relationship between the number glyphs and the words for the numbers in Mayan languages (Tables 1–2). Furthermore, it can be demonstrated that the relationship between the number glyphs and the day-signs is more than semantic—in some cases it is clearly phonetic. This relationship implies a Mayan language origin for the day-signs, for the *trecena*, and thus for the 260-day calendar (Macri, 1985).

Macri has suggested that the *trecena* and thirteen day-signs beginning with Movement originally signified the waxing moon, from the day of the first visible crescent to the day of the full moon. The head variant for 13 is the waterlily monster, which appears in some examples with the glyph for *winal* ("moon") in its headdress. The thirteenth day after Movement is Water. In the Maya system, this glyph represents the sound /u/. In Yucatec and Ch'olan languages "moon" is *uh*, perhaps originally the day of the full moon.

To expand on this hypothesis, the *Books of Chilam Balam* record in the story of the creation of the *winal* that 7 was added to the 13 to make 20 (Roys, 1967, pp. 39–40). In fact, seven days after the full moon is the third quarter moon. This count of seven days may be the source of the next seven day-signs, Dog through Vulture. Finally, beginning with the third quarter, the moon rises after midnight, initiating a period of approximately nine days when the moon is not visible during the evening. These nine days may have been the original source for the nine-day cycle recorded in Classic Maya dates, related to the nine Lords of the Night in Central Mexican sources. Thus, the lunar cycle was probably the source of the calendrical counts of 7, 9, 13, and 20.

TABLE 3. *Day Names as Personal Names in Classic Maya Texts*

SITE	MONUMENT	NAME
Ikil	Lintel 3	Lady 16 Flower
Palenque	Death's Head	5 Lizard

The earliest example of the use of days of the 260-day calendar in personal names occurs on Monument 3 at San José Mogote, Oaxaca, dated to 600–500 BCE (Flannery and Marcus, 1983). The few examples of personal names in Maya inscriptions occur toward the end of the Classic period (800–900 CE), suggesting that this naming practice was introduced by neighbors from the west, probably Central Mexicans, Mixe-Zoqueans, or Zapotecs (Table 3). Maya glyphic texts also contain examples of structures named with a number and day-sign.

Each day name was associated with auguries that were favorable, unfavorable, or neutral. The augury for any day depended on the combination of the number, the day name, and sometimes the associated Lord of the Night. Thompson (1971, p. 90) found that, according to ethnohistoric and ethnographic sources, the labels "good," "bad," or "indifferent" were not applied consistently. Tedlock (1992, p. 98) suggests that such inconsistencies arise from the complexity of symbolism associated with each of the days. Schele and Grube (1997) list augural glyphs from the almanacs of the Maya codices, including *yutzil* ("its goodness"), *yal* ("has or brings children"), *nichil* ("patches? of flowers"), *chamal* ("death"), *umuk* ("its burial"), *ma utzil* ("no goodness"), and *lob'al* ("evil").

Marcus (1992, pp. 202–206) discusses the frequencies of days found as names of men and women among the Mixtec. Day names alone or numbers alone show no pattern of preference or avoidance; however, a few day-number combinations do appear to have been favored and a few others avoided (that is, they occur more or less often than predicted by chance). This again shows that the favorability of a day rests not just on the day name but on the day-number combination.

The Mesoamerican day-signs have a history longer than 2,500 years. From the beginning, they were firmly linked to the count of thirteen. They may have had a lunar origin, but from their earliest appearance, they were a repeating cycle of twenty days. The twenty day names eventually spread throughout Mesoamerica and are one of the defining traits of the region. They remain in use today among the day-keepers of highland Guatemala.

[*See also* Calendars and Calendrical Systems, *article on* Mesoamerican Calendar.]

BIBLIOGRAPHY

Berlo, Janet Catherine. "Early Writing in Central Mexico: In Tlilli, In Tlapalli." In *Mesoamerica after the Decline of Teotihuacan: A.D. 700–900*, edited by Richard A. Diehl and Janet C. Berlo, pp. 19–47. Washington, D.C., 1989. Excellent summary of scripts in Central Mexico.

Caso, Alfonso. *Los calendarios prehispánicos*. Mexico City, 1967.

Edmonson, Munro S. *The Book of the Year: Middle American Calendrical Systems*. Salt Lake City, 1988. Comprehensive account of the calendar round and the systems of year-bearers.

Flannery, Kent V., and Joyce Marcus. "The Growth of Site Hierarchies in the Valley of Oaxaca: Part I." In *The Cloud People: Divergent Evolution of the Zapotec and Mixtec Civilizations*, edited by Kent V. Flannery and Joyce Marcus, pp. 53–64. New York, 1983.

Houston, Stephen D. *Maya Glyphs*. Berkeley, 1989. Brief introduction to Maya epigraphy.

Macri, Martha J. "The Numerical Head Variants and the Mayan Numbers." *Anthropological Linguistics* 27 (1985), 46–85.

Macri, Martha J. "A Lunar Origin for the Mesoamerican Calendars of 20, 13, 9, and 7 Days." Proceedings of the Oxford V Conference on Archaeoastronomy. In preparation.

Marcus, Joyce. *Mesoamerican Writing Systems: Propaganda, Myth, and History in Four Ancient Civilizations*. Princeton, 1992. Discussion of Mixtec, Zapotec, Aztec, and Maya scripts.

Roys, Ralph. *The Book of Chilam Balam of Chumayel*. Norman, Okla., 1967. Translation of one of the books written in Maya using the Spanish script.

Schele, Linda, and Nikolai Grube. *The Proceedings of the Maya Hieroglyphic Workshop: The Dresden Codex*. Austin, 1997. Summary of recent advances in understanding the Dresden Codex.

Tedlock, Barbara. *Time and the Highland Maya*. Rev. ed. Albuquerque, 1992. Invaluable ethnography of highland day-keepers.

Thompson, J. Eric S. 1971. *Maya Hieroglyphic Writing: An Introduction*. 3rd ed. Norman, Okla., 1971.

Winfield Capitaine, Fernando. *La Estela 1 de La Mojarra, Veracruz, México*. Research Reports on Ancient Maya Writing, 16. Washington, D.C., 1988.

MARTHA J. MACRI

DEATH. The duality of life and death is one of the most important concepts in Mesoamerican thought. By observing what occurred over the course of the year, Mesoamericans recognized a season of rains when everything flourished, and a dry season when everything died. The life/death duality thus took form. We can see its presence in buildings such as the Templo Mayor of Tenochtitlan, the Aztec capital, where part of the temple was dedicated to Tlaloc, the god of water and fertility, and the other part to the war god, Huitzilopochtli.

According to the beliefs of some Mesoamerican peoples, including the Nahua of Central Mexico, individuals could go to one of three places after death. Accompanying the sun in its daily journey was the destiny of warriors who died in combat or sacrifice, or of women who died during childbirth, since it was considered that the birth process was also a battle, and these women were thought to be warriors who accompanied the sun from midday westward to sunset. After four years, the de-

ceased warriors would become birds with beautiful plumage that drank the nectar of flowers. Those who died in relation to water—from drowning, thirst, or being struck by lightning—would go to Tlalocan, the water god's paradise, where summer was eternal and plants were always green. Those who died in any other manner had to journey through a series of dangerous places until reaching Mictlan, the ninth level of the underworld, where they would find the deity couple Mictlantecuhtli and Mictecacihuatl, who were represented as skeletons. There was also a fourth place called Chichicuauhco, where young children who died would be nursed by a tree from whose leaves milk flowed. The destiny of pre-Hispanic people after death was determined by the manner in which they died. In contrast, Christian belief, introduced into Mesoamerica in the sixteenth century, was governed by a moral concept: if one behaves well, one will go to Heaven and enjoy eternal bliss; if one sins, one will suffer the flames of Hell.

[*See also* Day of the Dead and Todos Santos; Death Deities.]

BIBLIOGRAPHY

Matos Moctezuma, Eduardo. *Muerte a filo de obsidiana: Los nahuas frente a la muerte*. Mexico City, 1975.

Matos Moctezuma, Eduardo. *Life and Death in the Templo Mayor*. Translated by Bernard R. Ortiz de Montellano and Thelma Ortiz de Montellano. Niwot, Colo., 1995.

EDUARDO MATOS MOCTEZUMA
Translated from Spanish by Scott Sessions

DEATH DEITIES. Few divinities hold as prominent a place in the intricate Mesoamerican pantheon as do the gods of death. Ubiquitous in pre-Hispanic codices and sculpture, skeletal or partially defleshed images of these deities were already present in the art of the Formative period (1000 BCE–150 CE). The most outstanding examples include a small ceramic head from Tlatilco (state of México), a piece that magisterially synthesizes the life/death duality; a representation of God VIII of the Olmec, a being which Peter Joralemon has identified as the distant ancestor of Mictlantecuhtli in Nahua communities; and a famous relief from Izapa (Chiapas), depicting the entire body of this divinity.

With the exception of Teotihuacan, where representations of them are scarce, it was during the Classic period (150–900 CE) that underworld deities and their symbols acquired orthodox form and were profusely reproduced. Outstanding for their aesthetic quality are the sculptures of La Mixtequilla (Veracruz) and Soyaltepec (Oaxaca). In Maya art, skulls, mandibles, and cross bones are depicted everywhere. In the Postclassic period (1400–1521 CE), the image of God A (the denomination of this Maya god in the Schellhas classification), together with Gods B, D, and E, would become one of the most frequent. No art, however, reveals such an obsession with the symbolism of death as that of the Mexica (Aztec). In an extraordinary manner, Mexica art insists on representing terrifying deities which speak of the fear of the believer and the importance of this cult.

Mictlantecuhtli ("Lord of the World of the Dead"), also known as Ixpuztec ("Broken Face"), Nextepehua ("Scatterer of Ashes"), and Tzontemoc ("He Who Lowers His Head"), was not the only death deity worshiped by the Mexica and their contemporaries. Although of lesser importance, beings such as Mictecacihuatl, Acolnahuacatl, Acolmiztli, Chalmecatl, Yoaltecuhtli, Chalmecacihuatl, and Yoalcihuatl also belong to this complex.

The importance of Mictlantecuhtli in the daily life of Postclassic Nahua is confirmed in their calendar. In the 365-day cycle, he is present in the dual festival consisting of the Miccailhuitontli and Huey Miccailhuitl *veintenas*. In the 260-day cycle, Mictlantecuhtli appears as the sixth Lord of the Day, the fifth Lord of the Night, the patron of the day Dog, and the patron of the *trecena* beginning with the day 1 Flint Knife; his skull is the sign of the day Death.

The Death God also is the key component of the eternal life/death succession. In the *Codex Borgia*, Quetzalcoatl and Mictlantecuhtli are represented as opposing, comple-

Mictecacihuatl, the goddess of the dead. Stone sculpture. (Height: 48 inches.) *Courtesy of Museo Nacional de Antropología, México, D.F.*

mentary principles summarizing the basic cycle of the universe. This same role is revealed in the *Leyenda de los Soles* and the *Popol Vuh*, in mythic accounts where the death gods are confronted and outsmarted by Quetzalcoatl, in the first case, and by the Hero Twins, in the second.

Mictlantecuhtli exercised other functions that seem paradoxical, such as granting and fomenting life. For example, this deity appears as a protagonist in scenes referring to penetration, pregnancy, the cutting of the umbilical cord, and lactation. An explanation can be found in the regenerative power of bones as seeds, which is evident in the journey of Quetzalcoatl into the world of the dead to steal the bones from which human beings would be created, and also in the *Codex Vienna*, where the deities generating lineal descent—the goddesses of pulque and the personified *milpa*—possess skeletal traits.

But surpassing Mictlantecuhtli's generative abilities is his frightening character, which prevails in Mesoamerican cosmovision. His partially defleshed image, with menacing claws, is often associated with animals such as the spider, centipede, scorpion, owl, and bat. The death god, first and foremost, is an insatiable devourer of the flesh and blood of humans. In pictographs, he appears as an active sacrificer armed with an ax or a flint knife, ready to extract the hearts of his victims. Moreover, his nose and tongue take the form of sharp knives. In Maya polychrome vases and codices, God A is depicted participating in executions, and God A' in sinister scenes of autodecapitation, violent death, and sacrifice. It is not strange that the lord of the world of the dead would inspire terror in the indigenous imagination. Perhaps for this reason, in plate 22 of the *Codex Dresden*, God A in two places has the skull sign (T1048), followed by the glyph *bi* (T585a), which together could be read as *xib(i)*. This word is close to the Yucatec term *xibil*, related to the idea of fear.

The images of Mictlantecuhtli and of God A have stereotyped features, with a few variables. Although skeletal representations of this deity are quite common, figures with partially defleshed bodies predominate; these are actually studies of cadavers in the process of decomposition. As a general norm, in place of the head they have a skull, often covered with curly black hair and flanked with large red ears. The ribs are visible, but the extremities usually retain their soft tissue. As in the case of other nocturnal, terrestrial, and underworld deities (such as Mictecacihuatl, Coatlicue, the Cihuateteo, Itzpapalotl, and the rest of the Tzitzimime), ferocious claws take the place of hands and sometimes of feet. Bones are depicted with yellow spots with red dots, signs of osseous and bloody material. The accouterments of this deity are the turquoise crown, small flags, and "stellar eyes" on his head, adornments in the form of rosettes on his front and neck, circular earrings, stoles of white paper, a truss, and sandals.

A fundamental feature of images of the death god and other divinities associated with the lower half of the cosmos is the presence of a liver and gallbladder of exaggerated dimensions. According to Mesoamerican religious tradition, the *ihiyotl*, one of the three animistic entities of the human being, is lodged in both these organs. The liver, like all organs of the abdomen, is symbolically related to the underworld, constituting a semantic complex that integrates within the same logical structure the ideas of femininity, passion and carnal transgression, growth, excrement, trash, and death. From the liver, *ihiyotl* controls life, vigor, sexuality, and the digestive process.

This explains why some names of the god of death refer to putrefaction. For example, the Tarahumara give the Devil the name Huitaru ("He Who Is Excrement"), while the Lacandón and other contemporary Maya call him Cizin ("The Flatulent"). The pre-Hispanic origin of the latter appellative is clear in the glyphic complex T146.102:116, whose phonetic translation is *cizin(i)*. In consonance, Mesoamericans conceived of the underworld as a frightening place of torments, death, putrefaction, and terrible stench.

[*See also* Day of the Dead and Todos Santos; Death; Underworld.]

BIBLIOGRAPHY

Benson, Elizabeth P., ed. *Death and the Afterlife in Pre-Columbian America*. Washington, D.C., 1975.

Brotherston, Gordon. "Huesos de muerte, huesos de vida: La compleja figura de Mictlantecuhtli." *Cuicuilco*, n.s. 1.1 (1994), 85–98.

Graulich, Michel. "Afterlife in Ancient Mexican Thought." In *Circumpacifica: Festschrift für Thomas S. Barthel*, pp. 165–187. Frankfurt am Main, 1990.

Joralemon, Peter David. 1971. *A Study of Olmec Iconography*. Washington, D.C., 1991.

Klein, Cecelia F. "Snares and Entrails: Mesoamerican Symbols of Sin and Punishment," *RES: Anthropology and Aesthetics* 19–20 (1990–1991), 81–103.

López Luján, Leonardo, and Vida Mercado. "Dos esculturas de Mictlantecuhtli encontradas en el Recinto Sagrado de Mexico-Tenochtitlan." *Estudios de cultura Náhuatl* 26 (1996), 41–68.

Mateos Higuera, Salvador. *Los dioses creados: Enciclopedia gráfica del México antiguo*. Vol. 3. Mexico City, 1993.

Matos Moctezuma, Eduardo. "La muerte en el México prehispánico." *Artes de México* 145 (1971), 6–36.

Nicholson, Henry B. "Religion in Pre-Hispanic Central Mexico." In *Handbook of Middle American Indians*, edited by Robert Wauchope, vol. 10, pp. 396–446. Austin, Tex., 1971.

Taube, Karl A. *The Major Gods of Ancient Yucatan*. Washington, D.C., 1992.

LEONARDO LÓPEZ LUJÁN
Translated from Spanish by Scott Sessions

DEER. The white-tailed deer (*Odocoileus virginianus*), one of the larger food animals and the bigger of two deer species present in Mesoamerica, was hunted from very

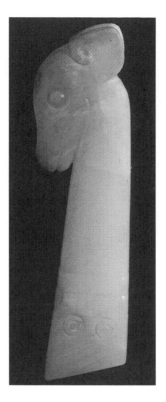

Mexica gods may take the form of a deer; in several codices, gods are sometimes depicted carrying a deer head scepter such as this one found at the Great Temple of Tenochtitlan. *Courtesy of Museo del Templo Mayor, México, D.F.*

early times. Deer might be driven into a large net and speared, caught with nooses or tree snares, or shot with arrows. Speared deer are depicted in Maya and Central Mexican codices; the Maya *Codex Madrid* shows deer in tree snares. Rites celebrated successful hunts, and deer-hunting is still accompanied by ritual in Mesoamerica. Modern hunters ask the underworld earth lords for permission to hunt. Some deer rites take place in caves.

Deer have long been offered in agricultural rites conducted by leaders responsible for the feeding and well-being of the people. In many places, the stag's antlers grow in the same annual cycle as do crops. Deer eat the farmer's crops, and the stag entangles foliage in its branch-like antlers. In modern Yucatán, a rain ritual at a time of severe drought begins with a deer hunt. Deer-hunting scenes on Late Classic Maya vases (600–900 CE) are clearly sacrificial rituals, and vegetation is shown in them. On these vases and in the *Dresden* and *Madrid Codices*, supernatural beings enact a ritual hunt. Some vases show deer being killed when their antlers are shed. Antlers are not easily removable until they are ready to detach from the pedicel base, from which blood then flows. The deer is thought to become young again when it has dropped its antlers; shortly afterward, the new antlers begin to grow.

Deer figure in Mesoamerican origin myths. In some Maya myths, the old man of the original couple was a deer or became a deer when he died; he may have been the grandfather of the sun. All over Mesoamerica, the deer is involved with the sun. In Maya myth, the young man who was to become the sun turns into a deer or hides under a deerskin. As one of the Hero Twins of the *Popol Vuh*, he wears a deer headdress when depicted in Classic Maya art playing ball with the lords of the underworld. Deer-hunting is associated with war and the sacrifice of captives, and human sacrificial victims are sometimes depicted wearing a deer headdress. At least one Maya human sacrifice has been related to deer-hunt sacrifice. [*See* Hero Twins.]

In Mixtec myth from Oaxaca, the original couple shared the calendrical name, 1 Deer. In some versions, they had many offspring, of whom at least one was a deer. A version of an Aztec (Mexica) myth tells how Mixcoatl, a sky and fire god—probably a stellar god—and a legendary hunter, shot with an arrow a two-headed deer who became a woman, was impregnated by Mixcoatl, and gave birth to the culture hero and god Quetzalcoatl. Mexica gods sometimes take deer form—Mixcoatl, for example—and in codices, gods may carry a deer-head scepter; in the *Tonalmatl Aubin*, a codex, such a scepter is shown being used to decapitate a sacrificial victim. Such an object was found as an offering in the Templo Mayor of the Mexica. Many Central Mexican codices were made of deerhide, and sacred bundles were wrapped in the same hide.

BIBLIOGRAPHY

Graulich, Michel. *Myths of Ancient Mexico*. Translated by Bernard R. Ortiz de Montellano and Thelma Ortiz de Montellano. Norman, Okla., 1997.

López Luján, Leonardo. *The Offerings of the Templo Mayor of Tenochtitlan*. Translated by Bernard R. Ortiz de Montellano and Thelma Ortiz de Montellano, Niwot, Colo., 1994. Descriptions of offerings found in the major Aztec temple, with background material and references.

Miller, Mary, and Karl Taube. *The Gods and Symbols of Ancient Mexico and the Maya*. New York and London, 1993. Dictionary of religion and symbolism in Mesoamerica.

Pohl, Mary. "Maya Ritual Faunas." In *Civilization in the Ancient Americas: Essays in Honor of Gordon R. Willey*, edited by Richard M. Leventhal and Alan L. Kolata, pp. 55–103. Albuquerque, N.M., and Cambridge, Mass., 1983.

Taube, Karl. "A Study of Classic Maya Scaffold Sacrifice." In *Maya Iconography*, edited by Elizabeth P. Benson and Gillett G. Griffin, pp. 331–351. Princeton, 1988. On human sacrifice that is related to deer sacrifice.

ELIZABETH P. BENSON

DEITIES. *See* Creator Deities; Death Dieties; Earth Dieties; Fire Dieties; *and* Rain Dieties.

DESERTS. *See* Mesoamerica, *article on* Geography.

DEVIL. Sixteenth-century Spanish theologians in the humanist tradition of Thomas Aquinas, such as Bartolomé de las Casas and Francisco de Vitoria, advocated the view that Mesoamerican religious traditions were a bona fide, if in certain matters misguided, form of "natural religion," lacking in biblical revelation but not idolatrous. First-generation Franciscan missionaries in Mexico, notably Toribio de Benavente Motolinía, at first looked benignly, even admiringly, at some aspects of indigenous religiosity. When it came to bloody sacrifices, in contrast to Las Casas and Vitoria, Motolinía labeled it idolatrous demon-worship (as had Fernando Cortés and Bernal Díaz del Castillo).

The focus of Motolinía's preaching was to persuade Mesoamericans that their deities were in fact devils and their religion a deception created by the devil himself. The sermon purportedly preached by the first Franciscan missionaries to a group of Aztec elders (recorded in Fray Bernardino de Sahagún's 1524 *Coloquios*) tells the whole story of "Paradise Lost"—how the devil followed up the Fall by further deceiving the gentile races into thinking that the devils of hell were their gods. Later missionaries deployed the full range of European taxonomy for diabolism, describing the object of native worship as the "Prince of darkness," "lying demon," and "infernal dragon and bloody crocodile." The devil could, however, be overcome by Christian baptism—as he was by Christ at his own baptism and temptation, and again at the harrowing of hell—these being motifs represented in early Mexican missionary drama.

By the middle of the sixteenth century the missionaries realized that the first wave of conversions had been superficial or even deceptive and that pre-Christian traditions were continuing under the guise of parallel rituals—whose similarities to Christian sacraments were one of the devil's craftiest devices. A major issue for missionaries working in native languages was the translation of Christian terms and concepts. One solution was simply to insert the Spanish word (*diablos* for "devil"). This was soon replaced by suitable Nahuatl, Mayan, or other indigenous terms. Adding negative adjectives to Nahuatl *teotl* ("gods"), to signify "devils," was inadequate and confusing, so they adopted what to their ears were the most negative-sounding names and epithets of local deities (e.g., Tezcatlipoca, Huizilopochtli, Mictlantecuhtli, *tzitzimime* (the star lords of darkness), or *tlacatecolotl* ("horned owl," but connoting "owl-man," a shamanistic sorcerer *nagual*). In Maya areas, they adopted Xibalba (the underworld of the gods) or *kaxtok* ("liar") to signify Hell and the devil, respectively. Early post-Conquest manuscripts show the influence of late medieval depictions of Lucifer.

The problem was that monotheistic Christianity was in moral theology quite dualistic, with moral life understood as ceaseless warfare between spirit and flesh. Conversely, polytheistic Mesoamerican traditions, for all their seemingly dualistic "pairings" of deities, were quite monistic in their cosmovision of necessary balance. Thus, in insisting that Mesoamerican converts refer to the powers of the night or the earth or the underworld (which had traditionally been accepted as necessary components of sacred cosmic balance) as "devils," the persistence of diabolism was unwittingly mandated into folk religious practice as another face of the divine. This ecclesiastical double-bind set the stage for the "extirpation of idolatry" campaigns pursued with especial vigor in such "peripheral" regions of New Spain as Yucatán, Oaxaca, and Michoacán, as well as in the Andes. The brutality and negative impact on Indian communities caused authorities in Spain to repudiate these suppressions as inappropriate and counterproductive; when the Mexican Inquisition was established in 1571, it was confined to *criollos* and *mestizos*. By the eighteenth century, the Inquisition had lost interest in the folk practices of remote villages or adjudicating accusations of sorcery and "pacts with the devil" that obviously derived from community jealousies.

In popular folk Catholicism in Mexico, even today, the devil has largely retained his character from medieval demonology—ultimately powerless to defy the will of God or to bring about the damnation of a human being without the active cooperation of that person's will. Such a folk-devil, as seen in masks and masking impersonators during Holy Week, may be fearsome and repellent but can also be a figure of farcical fun. The devil of Holy Week fiestas is even used for satirical purposes. These fiestas routinely conflate historical epochs and figures—from biblical narrative and pre-Hispanic oral tradition to recollections of the Spanish conquest, Christianization, the Central American and Napoleonic wars, and even current policies of the World Bank. In such conflations it was not difficult for a dissident nativist who was a devout Catholic to argue that the Indians' Jesús was the true Christian God while the Spanish God was really the devil. In Mayan-speaking Guatemala, the self-aggrandizing "way of the Devil" has been used to explain the social and economic ascendency of Ladino over Indian—Indians being the ones who follow the "way of Christ."

The devil thus remains a deeply ambiguous figure in local Mesoamerican Catholicism, ranging from a feared or despised symbol of evil, to a figure of satire and burlesque, to one still resonant of pre-Hispanic veneration. In Maya communities where the venerated ancestral earth lords were consigned by Christian teaching to the designation "devils," Maya Catholics were positioned to honor Jesucristo as the solar deity, *Dios cielo*, while venerating the "demonic" earth lord as *Dios mundo*. Despite the 1950s Catholic Action movement for catechetical orthodoxy, the Roman Catholic church has accommodated nativistic *costumbre* (customs) in strongly traditional towns.

BIBLIOGRAPHY

Bricker, Victoria Reifler. *The Indian Christ, the Indian King: The Historical Substrate of Maya Myth and Ritual.* Austin, Tex., 1981. Encompasses religio-political developments in Chiapas and Yucatán, including passion-play traditions and the talking-cross phenomenon.

Burkhart, Louise. "Doctrinal Aspects of Sahagun's *Colloquios.*" In *The Work of Bernardino de Sahagun: Pioneer Ethnographer of Sixteenth-Century Aztec Mexico*, edited by J. Jorge Klor de Alva, H. B. Nicholson, and Eloise Quiñones Keber, pp. 65–82. Albany, 1988. Astute analysis of a key text, in terms both of linguistic issues and comparative religion.

Burkhart, Louise. *The Slippery Earth/Nahua-Christian Moral Dialogue in Sixteenth-Century Mexico.* Tucson, Ariz., 1989. Groundbreaking comparative study of European Christian and Nahua moral concepts.

Cervantes, Fernando. *The Devil in the New World: The Impact of Diabolism in New Spain.* New Haven, 1994. Indispensable monograph on the subject, relating the representations of the Devil in New Spain both to pre-Hispanic traditions and to the intellectual cross-currents of medieval and early modern Europe.

Clendinnen, Inga. "Ways to the Sacred: Reconstructing 'Religion' in Sixteenth Century Mexico." *History and Anthropology* 5 (1990), 105–141. Reassessment of indigenous Christianity from a phenomenological perspective; and a strong critique of the syncretism school.

Correa, Gustavo. *El Espíritu del Mal en Guatemala.* New Orleans, 1955. Extremely useful introduction to the dynamics of the importation of European Christian ideas about evil, the devil and the demonic into Colonial-era Latin America, as well as literary subgenres that grew out of these motifs.

Gossen, Gary. *Telling Maya Tales, Tzotzil Identities in Modern Mexico.* New York, 1999. Includes an updated essay on the Chamula Festival of Games.

Sahagún Bernardino de. "The Aztec-Spanish Dialogues of 1524" [*Colloquios y doctrina christiana*], translated by J. Jorge Klor de Alva. *Alcheringa/Ethnopoetics*, 4.2 (1980), 52–193. Reconstruction by Sahagún and his indigenous collaborators, some forty years after the fact, of the religious dialogue between the first-generation Franciscans and Aztec elders.

GEORGE L. SCHEPER

DÍAZ DEL CASTILLO, BERNAL (c.1495–1584), author of one of the most comprehensive eyewitness accounts of the Spanish conquest of Mexico. Despite some of his extravagant retrospective claims—written some thirty years after the events—and occasional inaccuracies regarding poorly remembered or secondhand data, his *Historia verdadera de la conquista de la Nueva España* (*True Account of the Conquest of New Spain*) chronicles not only the Conquest but also public affairs in New Spain through the mid-1500s.

Born in Medina del Campo in Old Castile (Spain), Bernal Díaz declared that he arrived in the New World in

1514 on Pedrarias Dávila's voyage to Tierra Firme (now Nombre de Dios in Panama) and that he participated in the first three Spanish expeditions to Mexico—those of Francisco Hernández de Córdoba (1517), Juan de Grijalva (1518), and Fernando Cortés (1519). Although he may not have been on the Grijalva expedition, he was a footsoldier in Cortés's first overland march to the Aztec capital of Mexico-Tenochtitlan in 1519, in the second major offensive that resulted in its fall in August 1521, and a participant in the subsequent events in Mexico until 1524. He accompanied Cortés on the disastrous expedition to Hibueras (Honduras) in 1524–1526 and spent the remainder of his life in New Spain as an *encomendero* (trustee), sustained by the labor and goods produced by his Indians—those inhabiting the areas he held in trust on his *encomienda*. After gaining such grants in the 1520s near Coatzacoalcos in Tabasco and in Chiapas and losing them in the 1530s, Bernal Díaz settled permanently in Guatemala in the 1540s after the first (1539–1541) of his two trips back to Spain to secure further reward for his military efforts. On his second trip (1550–1551), he appeared as a witness in a hearing convened by the Council of the Indies to determine whether *encomiendas* should be granted to current holders' heirs in perpetuity. Successfully opposing such *encomienda* advocates as Bernal Díaz was Fray Bartolomé de las Casas. Bernal Díaz would later vehemently rebut Las Casas's position on the injustice and cruelty of the Conquest in *Historia verdadera*. Bernal Díaz died an octogenarian in Santiago de Guatemala.

Bernal Díaz began to write the *Historia* shortly after his return from Spain to Guatemala in 1551; in 1568, he completed a version that he sent to Spain in 1575 for publication. He continued to work on the manuscript in his possession until his death. During his lifetime and prior to his work's publication, other historians of Mexico, such as the Spanish lawyer and royal official Alonso de Zorita, who in the 1560s wrote *Breve y sumaria relación de los señores de la Nueva España* (*A Brief and Summary Account of the Lords of New Spain*), and Diego Muñoz Camargo, the Tlaxcalan *mestizo* author of *Historia de Tlaxcala* (1576), mentioned Bernal Díaz's writings in their own; at least one local resident in Santiago de Guatemala, the municipal official Juan Rodríguez de Cabrillo, stated in 1579 that he had read Bernal Díaz's manuscript chronicle.

The manuscript that Bernal Díaz sent to Spain was published in 1632, after being emended by Fray Alonso de Remón and Fray Gabriel Adarzo y Santander, whose editorial efforts were aimed at highlighting the work of the Mercedarian order in the Spanish conquest of Mexico. This published version includes a possibly apocryphal chapter (chapter 212), which interprets natural signs and portents reportedly seen by the natives before the Conquest. Bernal Díaz's own manuscript copy, to which his son Francisco later introduced modifications, remained in Guatemala. Transcribed and published in Mexico by Genaro García in 1904–1905 and reproduced by Joaquín Ramírez Cabañas (Mexico City, 1977), it continues to be well regarded. Carmelo Sáenz de Santa María's edition (Madrid, 1982), reproduced by Miguel León-Portilla (Madrid, 1984), is now viewed as the standard edition. Sáenz's attempt to reconstruct a version faithful to the one Bernal Díaz originally intended deletes the Adarzo y Santander additions to the Remón manuscript and supplements its lacunae with sentences from the Guatemala manuscript.

Although Bernal Díaz's *Historia* concentrates on the events of the Spanish conquest in Mexico from 1519 to 1521 (chapters 19–156), the work covers events in Mexico from 1517 to 1568 (chapters 1–18, 157–212) and discusses relevant affairs at the Spanish court, as well as in the seats of governance for Hispaniola and Cuba. Broader in scope than the 1519–1521 campaign in Mexico, which is the heart of the work, Bernal Díaz's objective was to place New Spain in the context of Spain's far-flung kingdoms at the time and to ensure that Mexico would not be eclipsed in importance by the spectacular mineral wealth being generated in Peru.

Regarding his use of historical sources, Bernal Díaz's work should be placed in an intermediate position between Mesoamerican and Castilian sources of the Conquest (León-Portilla, 1984). Bernal Díaz used the published letters of Cortés (1522–1526), Francisco López de Gómara's history of the Conquest (1552), and the just-war theory of Juan Ginés de Sepúlveda, which allowed him to cast the Conquest as just—in response to the perceived Indians' violation of "natural law," with their human sacrifice, cannibalism, and sodomy.

Bernal Díaz also relied occasionally on the Mexican pictorial record. He observed that native paintings provided warfare intelligence to allies or enemies (in chapters 38, 78, and 110); gave historical accounts of significant battles (in chapters 89 and 128); mapped the coast of the Gulf of Mexico (in chapter 102); and preserved native history and culture in ancient books and paintings (in chapter 92). As Keen (1985) pointed out, Bernal Díaz and Cortés are unsurpassed among members of the Conquest generation in their acknowledgment and recording of Mesoamerican cultural achievements and ingenuity. Bernal Díaz's work provides a still partially untapped resource for insight into Mesoamerican culture at the time of the Conquest.

BIBLIOGRAPHY

Adorno, Rolena. "History, Law, and the Eyewitness: Protocols of Authority in Bernal Díaz del Castillo's *Historia verdadera de la con-*

quista de la Nueva España." In *The Project of Prose in Early Modern Europe and the New World*, edited by Elizabeth Fowler and Roland Greene, pp. 154–175. Cambridge, 1997. Examines Bernal Díaz's role as self-styled historian in relation to the Castilian legal tradition.

Díaz del Castillo, Bernal. *The True Story of the Conquest of New Spain*. 5 vols. Translated by Alfred P. Maudslay. London, 1908. The only English translation of Bernal Díaz's entire work (contains some errors); published by the Hakluyt Society.

Díaz del Castillo, Bernal. *The Discovery and Conquest of Mexico*. Translated by Alfred P. Maudslay with introduction by Irving A. Leonard. New York, 1956 and 1981. One-volume digest of the Maudslay translation, consisting of the Hernández de Córdoba and Grijalva expeditions and the Spanish conquest of Mexico through the fall of the Aztec capital.

Díaz del Castillo, Bernal. *The Conquest of New Spain*. Translated by J. M. Cohen. London, 1963. Covers the expeditions of Hernández de Córdoba and Grijalva, as well as that of Cortés, giving a full account of the Spanish conquest through the fall of the Aztec capital.

Keen, Benjamin. *The Aztec Image in Western Thought*. New Brunswick, N.J., 1985. Encyclopedic resource for the period of European contact and the Colonial era in Mesoamerica.

León-Portilla, Miguel. "Introducción." In Bernal Díaz del Castillo, *Historia verdadera de la conquista de la Nueva España*, vol. 1, pp. 7–58. Madrid, 1984. Excellent overview, in Spanish, of Bernal Díaz's life and writing in this three-volume set.

ROLENA ADORNO

DICTIONARIES AND GRAMMARS. The discovery of the Americas coincided with the publication of Antonio de Nebrija's grammar of vernacular Spanish and his Spanish–Latin dictionary. Nebrija's work provided models for the descriptive linguistic efforts carried out by evangelists in Mesoamerica immediately after the Spanish conquest. The importance of Nebrija's models is obvious when the achievement in Mesoamerica is compared with the paucity of material about the languages of the Guanches, indigenes of the Canary Islands, and of the Tainos of the Caribbean islands. The Spanish contacted the Guanches and Tainos before Nebrija's works became available, and these peoples did not survive long enough to have their languages documented with the detailed approach devoted to the mainland languages contacted a quarter-century later.

Mesoamerica is an area of great linguistic diversity. The Mayan language family consists of more than twenty languages, one of which (Huastec) is not geographically contiguous with the others. Nahuatl belongs to a different language family, Uto-Aztecan, whose geographical distribution extends from Central America nearly to the present border of the United States and Canada. A third language family in Mesoamerica is Otomanguean, to which Zapotec, Mixtec, Matlatzinca, Otomí, and many other languages of the region belong. Tarascan is a language isolate with no known linguistic relatives. Totonac and Tepehua are related only to each other. The typological differences across Mesoamerican languages are more on the order of the differences among Chinese, Bantu, Turkish, and German than of those differences between Latin and Spanish that were perceived by Nebrija.

In the half-century following the Spanish conquest of Mexico and Guatemala, more than one hundred books in or about languages of Mesoamerica were published. By 1539, when the first book printed in the Americas (a bilingual catechism in Nahuatl and Spanish) issued from the press in Mexico City, evangelists were working on grammars and dictionaries. Extant early grammars of Mesoamerican languages include Nahuatl (Andrés de Olmos, 1547), Cakchikel (Domingo de Vico, 1550), Quiché (Vico, 1550), Tarascan (Maturino Gilberti, 1558), Tzeltal (Domingo de Ara, 1571), Zapotec (Juan de Córdova, 1578), Otomí (Pedro de Cárceres, 1580), Mixtec (Antonio de Reyes, 1593), Yucatec Maya (Juan Coronel, 1620), Matlatzinca (Diego Basalenque, 1640), Mam (Diego de Reynoso, 1644), Pocomchí (Thomas Gage, 1648), Zoque (L. de González, 1672), Choltí (Francisco Morán, 1685), Chiapanec (Juan de Albornoz, 1691), Mixe (Agustín de Quintana, 1729), Huastec (Carlos de Tapia Zenteno, 1729), and Tzotzil (Josef de la Barrera, 1788). (Language names are given in their Colonial period spellings.)

The grammars listed here are those that have survived, but there is documentary evidence of others that have been lost. The Franciscan Luis de Villalpando is said to have produced a grammar of Yucatec Maya in the mid-1500s, and the Maya Gaspar Antonio Xiu, trained and employed by the Franciscans as an assistant, claimed to have written one too. Before Ara, Francisco de Zepeda produced a grammar of Tzeltal with three other languages, but no copies remain. Andrés de Olmos is said to have composed grammars of Huastec and Totonac, now lost, as well as his surviving Nahuatl grammar. Prior to Olmos's grammar, two other Nahuatl grammars, since lost, were composed by his fellow Franciscans Francisco Jiménez and Alonso Rengel. The Olmos grammar owes its survival to the significant number of copies made; there are six extant manuscripts, no two quite alike.

Printed grammars had better prospects of survival. A Nahuatl grammar by Alonso de Molina was published in 1571 (the same year as Molina's bidirectional Spanish/Nahuatl and Nahuatl/Spanish dictionary). In 1595, Antonio del Rincón's Nahuatl grammar marked an advance in presentation of the morphology and phonology of Nahuatl. This approach was fully explicated and exemplified in the 1645 Nahuatl grammar of his fellow Jesuit Horacio Carochi. Meanwhile, the Augustinian Diego de Galdo Guzmán contributed yet another Nahuatl grammar (1642). Carochi's Nahuatl grammar remained unsurpassed: subsequent Nahuatl grammars, including a "compendium" of Carochi's work by Ignacio de Paredes (1759) for Jesuit instruction, were less insightful and accurate.

Gilberti's 1558 Tarascan grammar was joined in 1574 by another, complete with a dictionary, by Juan Baptista de Lagunas. In 1605, a quarter-century after the publication of the Cáceres Otomí grammar, Alonso Urbano produced a short grammar to accompany a trilingual Spanish–Nahuatl–Otomí dictionary. There are multiple Colonial period grammars of other Mesoamerican languages as well.

The number of different languages described by the evangelists is impressive. At the same time, it is hardly surprising that much attention focused on Nahuatl, the language of the Aztec Empire, which was functioning as the Mesoamerican lingua franca at the time of the Conquest. Spanish civil and religious authorities continued to promote its use and spread it as an administrative language during the Early Colonial era.

The grammars based on Nebrija's grammar of Spanish have been characterized as Eurocentric, constrained by a Latin grammatical straitjacket inappropriate to describing the languages of the Americas. The writers obviously assumed that all languages have prepositions, free-standing pronouns, grammatical gender, and other features of Romance languages. The verb morphology of many Mesoamerican languages, which expresses such features as transitivity, ergativity, specificity, and aspect, posed conceptual and terminological problems for the evangelist-grammarians. Preconceived notions of a certain number and type of "parts of speech" led to empty categories on one hand and underdifferentiation on the other.

Although it was difficult to adapt Nebrija's grammatical framework to Mesoamerican languages, using his Spanish–Latin dictionary as a tool for compiling new dictionaries was less problematical. Most of the early dictionaries are based on it. A manuscript trilingual Spanish–Latin–Nahuatl dictionary in the Ayer Collection of the Newberry Library, for example, is a literal hand copy of the 1516 printed edition of Nebrija. Nebrija's Spanish and Latin are written out in black ink, with Nahuatl glosses entered in red. A Spanish–Nahuatl dictionary based on Nebrija compiled by Alonso de Molina was published in 1555, followed by a bidirectional dictionary in 1571. The Nahuatl–Spanish side of Molina's 1571 dictionary is not a reversal of the 1555 material, but an independent compilation which contains more entries than the Spanish–Nahuatl section and is focused specifically on Mesoamerica. Many items—especially referring to Mesoamerican plants, animals, and foodstuffs—are found only in the Nahuatl–Spanish section of Molina 1571, but a number of Nahuatl items in the Spanish–Nahuatl section are not repeated in the Nahuatl–Spanish one.

Gilberti's bidirectional dictionary of Tarascan was pub-

lished in 1559, a year after his Tarascan grammar. Juan de Córdova's dictionary, published in 1578, is unidirectional Spanish–Zapotec and keeps close to the 1516 edition of Nebrija, but with greatly augmented entries. Francisco de Alvarado's 1593 Spanish–Mixtec dictionary is also unidirectional, based on Nebrija, and expansive. For example, Córdova has 130 entries under the Spanish verb *echar*, and Alvarado has 106, roughly double those under *echar* in Molina's 1555 unidirectional dictionary of Nahuatl.

Alonso Urbano used Molina's 1555 dictionary as a base to compile a 1605 trilingual Spanish–Nahuatl–Otomí dictionary. A manuscript Spanish–Nahuatl dictionary of 1778 by Francisco Xavier Araoz, now in the Tulane University Latin American Library, differs in its inventory from Molina and Nebrija.

There are two Spanish–Maya dictionaries from Yucatán loosely based on Nebrija: the anonymous and undated *San Francisco Dictionary*, and another known as the *Mayathán Dictionary*, thought to be a 1625 work of Diego Rejón Arias. The bidirectional *Motul Dictionary*, compiled after 1577, consists of a Spanish–Maya section and an even more substantial Maya–Spanish section with different content. In this, the *Motul Dictionary* resembles Molina's 1571 Nahuatl dictionary. If the Spanish–Maya section of the *Motul Dictionary* was originally compiled on the basis of Nebrija, however, it underwent such modification that the connection is less obvious than in Molina 1555. A sixteenth-century Cakchikel dictionary, thought to be the work of Juan de Alonso, has entries closely following Nebrija, while Joseph Tirado's 1787 Quiché dictionary departs from Nebrija but shares some of Molina's modifications of Nebrija.

In the mid-sixteenth century, Domingo de Ara used Nebrija as a base for a Spanish–Tzeltal dictionary, later revised and expanded by Alonso de Guzmán (1620). A Tzotzil manuscript dictionary somehow related to Aras/Guzmán was compiled sometime in the latter half of the sixteenth century or at the beginning of the seventeenth. It resembled the *Motul Dictionary* in the size and elaboration of its Spanish–Tzotzil entries, but with different content. A copy was made in 1907, and the original has since been lost. A reconstruction from the copy was published by Robert Laughlin (1988) as *The Great Tzotzil Dictionary of Santo Domingo Zinacantán*.

The initial compilations elicited on the basis of Nebrija's list were edited to fit the context, often (although not always) by omitting items not to be found in Mesoamerica (e.g., "zebra"). Neologisms and borrowings from Spanish for introduced artifacts are recorded (loanwords often have the notations *lo mismo* or *idem*). Some lexicographers devoted their efforts to expanding the depth of coverage of entries in unidirectional dictionaries (as in the cases of Zapotec and Mixtec), while others used their Nebrija-based compilations as the platform from which to launch bidirectional dictionaries (e.g., the *Motul Dictionary*, Gilberti's Tarascan dictionary, and Molina's 1571 Nahuatl dictionary).

In devising writing systems for Mesoamerican languages, grammarians and lexicographers had to deal with the unfamiliar sound systems of the various languages— some with vowel-length distinctions, some with tones, and some with glottalized consonants. They adapted and augmented the Roman alphabet, beginning with the Spanish values associated with each character or digraph: *x* represented [š]; *ch*, [č]; *u* or *hu*, [w]; *cu*, [kʷ]. Generally, [k] was represented by *qu* before the vowels [i] and [e], and by *c* elsewhere; but in writing Maya, the letter *c* was used for [k] in all contexts, hence *ceh* 'deer' rather than *queh*. The character *h*, having become a "silent" letter in Spanish by this time, was available for other uses, so it was sporadically used to represent the glottal stop [ʔ], among other things. Where the grammarian-lexicographers used a character or digraph with a value different from its use in Spanish, they noted that difference. For instance, in Nahuatl *ll* represents a true geminate consonant—one *l* followed by another, as in *calli* 'house'—not its [lʸ] or [y] value in Spanish. Digraphs were used for consonants not occurring in Spanish, such as *tl* for laterally released [tˡ] and *tz* for the affricate [tˢ]. Digraphs were sometimes reversed at ends of syllables: hu/uh [w], cu/uc [kʷ]. Grave, acute, and circumflex accents, the tilde, and the cedilla were also employed, and entirely new characters were invented, such as ɔ (a reversed *c*) of Colonial-period written Maya (since replaced with the digraph *dz*). To provide representation for four consonant sounds of Cakchikel and Quiché, two numbers were adopted as letters: the *tresillo* ɛ (a reversed 3), and the *cuatrillo* 4, which was further augmented with *h* (*4h*) and with a reversed comma (*4ˌ*). Despite these innovations, some phonological contrasts were chronically ignored in Spanish-based orthographies. The glottal stop (often referred to as *saltillo*) often went unrepresented, as did contrastive vowel length and contrastive tone.

The Colonial-period grammars and dictionaries of Mesoamerican languages were tools for evangelization. They had to be accurate and useful to Spanish-speaking priests and friars intent on catechizing, hearing confession, administering sacraments, and preaching sermons in indigenous languages. Awkward, arbitrary, and narrow though some of the grammars may seem from the viewpoint of present-day descriptive linguistics, they represent a monumental response to the linguistic challenge of the Americas. Together with the Colonial-period dictionaries, many continue to be invaluable sources of information about languages still spoken today by indigenous peoples of Mexico and Guatemala.

[*See also* Linguistics.]

BIBLIOGRAPHY

Campbell, Lyle. "Quichean Linguistics and Philology." In *Approaches to Language: Anthropological Issues*, edited by William C. McCormack and Steven Wurm, pp. 223–233. The Hague and Paris, 1978. Section on "Scribal Practice" describes the history of the *tresillo* and *cuatrillo* and the range of phonetic values they have represented in written Quiché, Cakchikel, and other closely related Mayan languages.

Campbell, Lyle. *American Indian Languages: The Historical Linguistics of Native America*. New York and Oxford, 1997. Contains a history of descriptive linguistic work in the Americas, and the most current information about Mesoamerican language family membership and language isolates.

Clayton, Mary. "A Trilingual Spanish–Latin–Nahuatl Manuscript Dictionary Sometimes Attributed to Fray Bernardino de Sahagún." *International Journal of American Linguistics* 55 (1989), 391–416. Detailed study of the early manuscript Nahuatl dictionary in the Ayer Collection of the Newberry Library.

Fisiak, Jacek, ed. *Historical Linguistics and Philology*. Berlin and New York, 1990. Contains articles on the description of Mesoamerican languages in Colonial grammars and dictionaries, by Lyle Campbell and by Una Canger, both with good bibliographies.

Karttunen, Frances. "The Roots of Sixteenth-Century Mesoamerican Lexicography." In *Cultures, Ideologies, and the Dictionary: Studies in Honor of Ladislav Zgusta*, edited by Braj B. Kachru and Henry Kahane, pp. 75–88. Tübingen, 1995. Study of Mesoamerican dictionaries modeled on Nebrija.

Laughlin, Robert M., with John B. Haviland. *The Great Tzotzil Dictionary of Santo Domingo Zinacantán, with Grammatical Analysis and Historical Commentary*. 3 vols. Washington, D.C., 1988. Vol. 1 contains a history of dictionary compilation in Mesoamerica, with emphasis on Mayan languages and a comparative analysis of the content of several sixteenth-century dictionaries.

McQuown, Norman A. "History of Studies in Middle American Linguistics." In *Handbook of Middle American Indians*, vol. 5, *Linguistics*, edited by Norman A. McQuown, pp. 3–7. Austin, Tex., 1972. Concise list of Colonial and modern grammars, dictionaries, and texts in Mesoamerican languages.

Nebrija, Antonio de. *Vocabulario de Romance en Latín: Transcripción crítica de la edición revisada por el autor (Sevilla, 1516) con una introducción*. Edited by Gerald J. MacDonald. Philadelphia, 1973. Edition of Nebrija's dictionary that served as model for a large number of Mesoamerican dictionaries.

Rowe, John Howland. "Sixteenth and Seventeenth Century Grammars." In *Studies in the History of Linguistics: Traditions and Paradigms*, edited by Dell Hymes, pp. 361–379. Bloomington, 1974. Situates the grammars of Mesoamerican languages in the context of grammars of European and non-European languages produced between 1492 and 1699.

Suárez, Jorge A. *The Mesoamerican Indian Languages*. Cambridge, 1983. Detailed study of the languages of Mesoamerica, including a brief history of Colonial-period descriptive work.

Zimmerman, Klaus, ed. *La descripción de las lenguas amerindias en la época colonial*. Frankfurt am Main. 1997. Section I, "Estudios sobre gramáticas y vocabularios de Mesoamerica," contains eight articles about grammars and dictionaries of Nahuatl, Otomí, Tarascan, Zapotec, and Cakchiquel.

FRANCES KARTTUNEN

DIEGO, JUAN (1474?–1548?), according to various traditions, a humble Indian chosen by the Virgin Mary as the carrier of a message to Fray Juan de Zumárraga, the first bishop of Mexico. The Virgin wanted a shrine to be built in the Tepeyac region, where she could show and offer all her love, compassion, and protection. Juan Diego's historical existence has become one of the most controversial topics. Since the eighteenth century, many religious and secular scholars have written in favor of or against his historicity. The information about his life comes primarily from the *Nican mopohua* and *Nican motecpana*. The *Nican motecpana* recounts, in some detail, the lives of Juan Diego, his wife María Lucía, and his uncle Juan Bernardino. Its text clarifies parts that had only been sketched in the *Nican mopohua*. The references in the *Nican motecpana* are extensive and direct. Other native and Spanish sources, written in the sixteenth and seventeenth centuries, add more data that complement or, occasionally, contradict the "official" biography accepted by a good number of members of the Roman Catholic church in Mexico.

Following the most accepted reconstruction of his life, Juan Diego was born in Cuauhtitlán (to the north of Mexico City) in 1474. His original Nahuatl name was Cuauhtlatoa, meaning "he who speaks as an eagle." He was a *macehualli* (commoner) and was married to María Lucía, with whom he shared chastity vows. Juan Diego, his wife, and his uncle were the first group to be baptized into the new faith by Franciscan missionaries in 1524. In 1529, María Lucía took sick and died. Juan Diego turned to his uncle, his only close relative. Juan Bernardino was at that time living in the village of Tolpetlac. Juan Diego left Cuauhtitlán to take up residence in that town. All sources agree Juan Diego saw the Virgin Mary in Tepeyac the first time. She instructed him to tell the bishop of Mexico, Juan de Zumárraga, to build a chapel in her honor. She then left an image of herself on Juan Diego's cloak. On 26 December 1531, two weeks after the miracle of the apparition of the Virgin Mary, a small chapel was erected at the foot of Tepeyac hill to house the sacred image. Bishop Zumárraga put Juan Diego in charge of the chapel. There Juan Diego, living in poverty and abstinence, spent the rest of his life. When he died, he was buried in the chapel. Juan Bernardino died in 1544 at the age of eighty-four.

Other early sources give us information that does not correspond to what is described in this "official" version, although they refer to the same matters. For example, in the *Papeles de notoriedad* (1694), the town of San Juanico (present-day San Juan Bautista Ixhuatepec), a dependency of Tlatelolco, is given as Juan Diego's place of birth. In the *Inin hueitlamahuilzoltzin*, another Nahuatl report on the Mariophany, Juan Diego is described as a very poor commoner who was walking aimlessly, looking for something to eat, when the Virgin made her miraculous appearance. An Indian from Cuauhtitlán declared in 1666 that Juan Diego died in Cuauhtitlán but was buried in Tepeyac (*Informaciones de 1666*).

In May 1990, during a visit to Mexico, Pope John Paul II gave Juan Diego a *beatificación equipolente* ("equivalent beatification"), public recognition of the existence of his cult.

BIBLIOGRAPHY

Noguez, Xavier. *Documentos guadalupanos: Un estudio sobre las fuentes de información tempranas en torno a las mariofanías en el Tepeyac*. Mexico City, 1993. All the sources used above are studied there in detail.

Torre Villar, Ernesto de la, and Ramiro Navarro de Anda, eds. *Testimonios históricos guadalupanos*. Mexico City, 1982. Most complete and updated collection of early Guadalupan texts, with helpful introductory notes; the majority of the works have been transcribed in their entirety. A must for anyone interested in the Mariophany in Tepeyac.

XAVIER NOGUEZ

DIVINATION. The practice of divination is a defining feature of the magico-religious systems of the indigenous peoples of Mesoamerica. The search for hidden knowledge through divinatory techniques has been a primary activity of ritual specialists from the pre-Hispanic period through the Colonial upheaval to the present day. The ancients associated divination with the creation of humankind: in the Maya *Popol Vuh*, the old gods Xpiyacoc and Xmucane engaged in divinatory hand casting while human beings were being created. The Aztec *Codex Borbonicus* shows the original human couple, Oxomoco and Cipactonal, engaged in divining with kernels of maize. This primordial pair is associated with the ritual calendar, and the Aztecs considered them to be the first diviners.

In the 260-day ritual calendar (*tonalpouhque* in Nahuatl), each day was associated with a number, name, direction, animal, sacred tree, or other natural feature, along with a deity; the combined forces of these attributes determined the fate of individuals born on that day. These 260-day signs, or *tonaleque*, were interpreted by a specialist called *tonalpouhqui* ("day counter") who foretold the fate of a newborn to anxious Aztec parents. If the day sign was inauspicious, parents would name the child on a more favorable day. The Aztec consulted these calendrical diviners before any important undertaking. As an indication of how important calendrical divination was for the people of Central Mexico, the great sixteenth-century chronicler of Aztec culture, Bernardino de Sahagún, devotes much of book 4, *The Soothsayers*, in his monumental *General History of the Things of New Spain*, to explicating the meaning of day signs.

Many additional divinatory techniques were employed by the ancient Mesoamericans. People were alert to signs or omens that might foretell future events. In *The Omens*, book 5 of the *General History*, Sahagún documents some of these important signs. He writes about the misfortune of being awakened by the Night Axe or the Bundle of Ashes, two frightening apparitions associated with Tezcatlipoca, or observing a rabbit, red spider, or weasel enter one's house or a weasel cross one's path, or hearing a wild animal cry out. The ancients also made observations of stars and celestial events, and specialists interpreted their meaning. In the period preceding the Conquest, according to Spanish accounts, the Aztec emperor Motecuhzoma Xocoyotl lost authority after the appearance of celestial and other omens foretelling defeat; this gave Fernando Cortés and his allies crucial time to organize against Aztec defenders.

Divination often involved an ambiguous stimulus which was interpreted by an expert trained in a particular technique. A common practice was sortilege, or the casting of lots. A diviner called *tlaolchayauhqui* or *tlaolliqui-tepehuaya* ("he who scatters maize kernels") cast the kernels, sometimes mixed with beans, onto a white cloth. The specialist then interpreted the resulting pattern. This technique is practiced widely by contemporary diviners and is often used to determine the origin of disease. Additional divinatory techniques employed by the ancients included dropping maize kernels in a container of water; observing the surface of water for signs; placing an ill child over a bowl of water to produce a reflection of the sorcerer responsible for the disease; placing a container of water near a patient to determine color changes in the liquid; decapitating a quail and observing movements of its body; determining the direction taken by an insect placed in a quadrant; peering into obsidian mirrors; crystal gazing; feeling the pulse of a patient; interpretation of muscle twitches in the diviner's body; tying knots in cords and prognosticating the fate of a patient by how easily the knots could be loosened; hand casting, or the measuring of a person's forearm with handspans; interpretations of dreams and visions induced by hallucinogenic plants; and releasing a snake to find a thief.

Documents reveal that divination was especially important during the Early Colonial period. Numerous techniques were carried over from the pre-Hispanic era, including observations of reflections, sortilege, belief in lucky and unlucky days, interpretation of signs and omens, interpretation of dreams, and seeking visions. The use of ventriloquism in divination and the casting of bones are techniques that native diviners later borrowed from African slaves. The Spaniards introduced many divinatory techniques familiar to Euro-Americans, such as astrology, palmistry, and card reading. Other European divination techniques that became widespread in Mesoamerica include sortilege using lima beans; breaking eggs under a patient's bed or into a container of water to determine the cause of disease; use of scissors to locate a thief; locating treasure with special sticks; and use of ordeals to identify a guilty party. Divination by alternatives, in which yes-or-no questions are directed at hidden forces controlling the future, derives from both African and European traditions. Examples include rubbing the patient with a chicken or passing a candle over someone suffering from disease. If the chicken lives, the patient will survive; if the candle stays lighted, it is taken as a sign that the patient's disease will be cured.

Divination continues to be a key feature of contemporary Mesoamerican indigenous and nonindigenous magico-religious practice. Maize kernel sortilege is widespread, found throughout the region from northern Veracruz to the highlands of Guatemala. Among Nahua of northern Veracruz, maize kernels are used to divine the origin of disease, the identity of a sorcerer, the location of a patient's lost soul segment, the source of dangerous envy, the identity of a salutary spirit who requires ritual attention, the circumstances of a distant loved one, or the outcome of an important decision. Dream and vision interpretation continue to occupy an important place in indigenous Mesoamerica. Ethnographers report that ritual specialists perform divination by crystal gazing, observing reflections in obsidian, breaking eggs, pulsing, and interpreting patterns in water vapor and copal incense smoke to determine the cause of disease, the identity of a patient's godparents or that of helpful saints, and many other important pieces of information. Ethnographers have shown that the 260-day ritual calendar of pre-Hispanic times continues to organize the work of diviners in parts of Mexico and in highland Guatemala.

Indigenous and nonindigenous peoples in contemporary Mesoamerica often rely on diviners to reveal crucial but hidden information about the future and the past. Diviners' findings guide their clients' responses to problems and help them deal with the uncertainties of life. Reliance on divination is evidence that people in these groups have a worldview in which events and conditions are the result of definite but unseen causes.

[*See also* Curing and Healing; Divinatory Cycle; Shamanism; Witchcraft, Sorcery, and Magic.]

BIBLIOGRAPHY

Aguirre Beltran, Gonzalo. *Medicina y magia: El proceso de aculturación en la estructura colonial.* Mexico City, 1980. Key work by a renowned Mexican anthropologist on magico-religious acculturation in Colonial Mexico, including a detailed discussion of divination.

Colby, Benjamin, and Lore M. Colby. *The Daykeeper: The Life and*

Discourse of an Ixil Diviner. Cambridge, 1981. Contains much information about divination among the contemporary Ixil Maya of highland Guatemala, including discussion of the ritual calendar.

Durand-Forest, Jacqueline de. "La divination dans le Méxique moderne." In *La Divination*, edited by André Caquot and Marcel Leibovici, pp. 151–246. Paris, 1968. Thorough summary of divination among contemporary groups in Mexico.

Nicholson, Henry B. "Religion in Pre-Hispanic Central Mexico." In *Handbook of Middle American Indians*, part 1, vol. 10, pp. 395–446. Austin, Tex., 1971. This key summary of Aztec religion by a foremost authority includes some information on divination.

Quiñones Keber, Eloise. *Codex Telleriano-Remensis: Ritual, Divination, and History in a Pictorial Aztec Manuscript.* Austin, Tex., 1995. Reproduction of the well-known Aztec codex contains a commentary with information on divination and the ritual calendar.

Sahagún, Bernardino de. *General History of the Things of New Spain, Book 4, The Soothsayers and Book 5, The Omens.* Number 14, parts 5 and 6. Translated by Charles E. Dibble and Arthur J. O. Anderson. Santa Fe, N.M., 1979. This single volume of the *Florentine Codex* contains books 4 and 5, listing attributes of Aztec days signs and omens.

Tedlock, Barbara. *Time and the Highland Maya.* Albuquerque, N.M., 1982. Detailed study of divination techniques using the ritual calendar among Quiché Maya in the Guatemalan Highlands.

ALAN R. SANDSTROM

DIVINATORY CYCLE. The divinatory calendar of 260 days is widely known among Mesoamericanists by its Nahua name, *tonalpohualli,* literally "count of days." Structurally, it was a convolution of two component cycles: a series of thirteen days, the *trecena,* whose names typically consisted of the numerals from 1 to 13 in numerical order; and a series of twenty days, the *veintena,* whose names were mostly words for animals, plants, forces of nature, and features of Mesoamerican mythology or cosmology. Each cycle had a standardized beginning and a regular order. Names for divinatory calendar dates were binomial, composed of a name for the position in the *trecena* juxtaposed to the name for the position in the *veintena*—directly reflecting the structure of the overall cycle.

The *Trecena.* In most Mesoamerican societies, the days of the *trecena* were designated by native words for the numbers 1 through 13, in sequential order. (The *Codex Azoyu* provides a unique and mysterious case in which they are the numerals 2 through 14.) Among some groups, like the Mixe, words for some positions in the *trecena* were not native words for numbers. Often, such words are recognizably borrowed from number words in another language—in the Mixe case, from Zoque; sometimes, as in Colonial period Zapotec, words for *trecena* positions are not known to be numerals from any language, and the etymological source of the terms is unknown. In hieroglyphic representations of day names,

even in Zapotec writing, the *trecena* position is always conveyed by a numeral.

Because the words associated with *trecena* positions are typically numerals, Mesoamericanists often refer to these terms as "coefficients" of the day names. However, they do not count or modify the *veintena* names they accompany; the two are simply in apposition. In some languages, this is made clear by the grammatical forms of the words involved. In Nahuatl, for example, *trecena* numerals occur fully inflected, typically with a form of the absolutive suffix *-tli,* while numeral modifiers do not.

Although *trecena* words are not numeral modifiers, they behave like them in terms of word order. In all Mesoamerican languages, in cases documented ethnohistorically or ethnographically, the *trecena* position precedes the *veintena* name, and numeral modifiers precede the nouns they modify. This is true even of Oto-Manguean languages like Zapotec, where numeral modifiers precede but adjective modifiers follow the nouns they modify. In the hieroglyphic inscriptions of several areas, however— notably in the Oaxacan and Xochicalco scripts—numerals normally or often follow the day names. In late records from Central Mexico, numerals show a variety of spatial associations with day signs, and they have no fixed ordering relation with respect to them.

The *Veintena.* Where a native word for the *veintena* is known, it is the same as the word for the 20-day subdivisions ("months") of the 365-day calendar—usually, the word for "moon" in the same language. The *veintena* was analogized to the European week in some sixteenth-century sources.

In most Mesoamerican languages, the names of most *veintena* days are also ordinary vocabulary items. There is substantial agreement across languages and cultural traditions in the meanings of most of these names, and names corresponding in meaning almost always agree in their numerical positions in the *veintena* sequence. This makes it straightforward to reconstruct a very likely original semantic association for most of the days of the *veintena,* and most of the remainder can also be worked out with a fair degree of assurance; Kaufman's results are summarized in Table 1, along with the names and their meanings in colonial Nahuatl, Zapotec, and Ch'olan.

Some languages have some *veintena* names that are not recognizable from the general vocabulary of the same language but that are recognizably borrowed from another language; for example, the Mixes borrowed some *veintena* names from Zoquean. Some *veintena* vocabulary, however, has no known source.

Subdivisions of the Divinatory Calendar. Because 260 is a multiple of many small numbers, this cycle was amenable to subdivision in various ways to serve differ-

TABLE 1. *Reconstructed original meanings for names of days in the divinatory calendar and their names in three colonially attested Mesoamerican systems. Meztitlan Nahuatl forms are added when they disagree with those of the Valley of Mexico; they appear to be more archaic. Zapotec forms are as extracted by Kaufman from Córdova, and from calendars reported by Alcina Franch for the Villa Alta and Choapan regions of Northern Zapotec. Ch'olan forms are from unpublished work by James Fox and John Justeson. Meanings and reconstructed linguistic forms are by Kaufman.*

Reconstructed Original Meanings	Colonial Nahuatl Names	Colonial Nahuatl Meanings	Colonial Zapotec: Córdova	Colonial Northern Zapotec	Colonial Zapotec Meanings	Proto-Ch'olan Forms of Colonial Ch'olan Names	Colonial Ch'olan Meanings
cayman	sipa:ktli		=chilla	=chila	cayman	#nal=chan	first snake/creature (not 'corn snake')
wind	ehekatl	wind	=ii ~ =laa	=ee ~ =laa	wind	7ik'	wind
night	kalli	house	=EEla	=Ela	night	#wotan	god name
lizard (esp. iguana)	kwetzpalin	lizard	=Echl	=Echi	big lizard	k'anan	—
snake	kowa:tl	snake	=zll	=çee	(unknown)	chäk=chan	red snake
death	mikistli / Mez. tzon=tekomatl	death skull	=laana	=lana	smelling like fresh fish, meat	tox	—
deer (not brocket)	masa:tl	deer	=china	=china	deer	manik'	—
rabbit (not hare)	to:chtli	rabbit	=laba	=laba	(unknown)	lam(b)at	—
water	a:tl	water	=niça	=niza	water	mulu..	*water jar?
dog (maybe coyote)	itzkwintli	dog	=tella	=tela ~ =dela	knot	ok	*wild canine (fox, coyote)
monkey (esp. howler)	osomahtli	monkey	=loo	=lao	monkey	b'atz'	howler monkey
tooth or twist	mali:nalli / Mez. i:-tlan	something twisted / one's tooth	=piia	=biaa	soaproot	eb'	instrument for attaching teeth to
reed	a:katl	reed	=ii ~ laa	=ee ~ =laa	reed	b'in	—
jaguar	o:se:lo:tl	jaguar	=Eche	=Echi	jaguar	hix	—
eagle	kwa:wtli / Mez. kwi:xtli	eagle hawk	=nnaa	=ina	cornfield	men or tz'ikin	
sun or buzzard	ko:skakwa:wtli / Mez. teo:tl i:to:nal	buzzard / god's day	=loo	=lao	crow	chab' (maybe chab'an)	
earthquake	oli:n	movement	=xoo	=xoo	earthquake	chab'an (maybe chab')	earthquake (unclear)
flint	tekpatl	flint	=opa	=opa	root of 'cold' and 'dew'	7itz'anab'	
storm	kiyawitl	rain	=aappe	=Epag	face	*chahuk	Thunder
macaw	xo:chitl	flower	=lao	=lao		7ajwal	lord

330

ent purposes. The most common is a division into five groups of fifty-two days each; the only other common division is into four groups of sixty-five days each. These groups are reflected in the structures of tables in manuscripts from several traditions, and they had differing associations with the four world directions. A striking case is the subdivision in the *Borgia* and *Cospi* codices into 81 + 49 (= 130) + 81 + 49 days; Selverstone identifies this as part of a ritual complex, still practiced by contemporary K'iche's, that relates parturition and menstruation to the return of the moon to the same region of the sky (sidereal commensuration). This system probably diffused between Central Mexico and highland Guatemala during the Postclassic period.

Cultural Associations. The day count was a fundamental feature of the lives of ancient Mesoamericans. Several rituals are known to have been scheduled in terms of the day count, including the Yucatec Maya burner ceremonies and the Aztec festival of 1 Flower. Mayan codices contain several astronomical and other tables, all fundamentally anchored in the day count.

People's fates were influenced by the dates of events in the day count. Divination using this calendar is still employed to help determine such influences and to affect the impact of events on individuals; ethnographic accounts are provided by Colby and Colby (1981) for Ixil, by Tedlock (1992) for K'iche, and by Lipp (1991) for Mixes. In one of the most decisive of these influences, people's fates were shaped by their birthdates—an effect so intimate that Mesoamericans were typically named for that date. As a result, the word for "day" also means "name" in some Mesoamerican languages. Recorded day names are amply attested as calendar names of persons in much of ancient Mesoamerica. This practice is notably absent from Mayan hieroglyphic sources, but the favoring of certain *veintena* dates (like Lord) and the disfavoring of others (like Death) among birthdates of rulers reflects the positive and negative portents of divinatory calendar days, and the practice is documented in Colonial Ch'olan records.

Documentation. For some Mesoamericans, like the Huastecs and Zoques, we have no ethnohistoric or ethnographic documentation of the divinatory calendar per se, but calendar names in Colonial baptismal, marriage, and census documents yield nearly complete lists of day names for some groups. The Ch'olan (Maya) and Chocho-Popolocan cases are especially dramatic: few day names are found in temporal records for either group but calendar names of individuals are attested fully enough that Proto-Ch'olan and Proto-Popolocan lists can be reconstructed. In contrast, although a dozen legible Epi-Olmec day signs document the existence of the system for Zoquean from 36 BCE to 533 CE, neither the calendar system

nor Zoquean individuals' calendar names are documented thereafter; its only traces are the name *Tumɥ Chawi7* (Lady One Monkey) of a supernatural being in a modern Zoque story from Chiapas, and Zoque names borrowed into the Mixe divinatory calendar.

[*See also* Calendars and Calendrical Systems, *article on* Mesoamerican Calendar; Divination.]

BIBLIOGRAPHY

Colby, Benjamin N., and Lore M. Colby. *The DayKeeper.* Cambridge, 1981.

Lipp, Frank. *The Mixe of Oaxaca: Religion, Ritual, and Healing.* Austin, Tex., 1991.

Tedlock, Barbara. *Time and the Highland Maya.* Albuquerque, N.M., 1992.

JOHN S. JUSTESON
and TERRENCE KAUFMAN

DOGS. *See* Canines.

DOMINICANS. The first Dominican friars arrived in New Spain in 1526. This mendicant order had been founded three centuries earlier in Castile with the goal of creating an educated brotherhood dedicated to preaching. With the discovery of the New World, the pope had charged the Dominicans (and the other mendicant orders) to convert the natives to Christianity, granting them temporary permission to administer sacraments to the laity and to undertake pastoral work. By the mid-sixteenth century, their numbers in New Spain had grown from the original twelve to more than two hundred friars in approximately fifty convents, or houses.

The original intention was to build a new Indian society free of paganism and based on Christianity—a separate society, similar though inferior to Spanish society. The Dominicans destroyed native temples and altars whenever they could, often building their churches on the ruins. To increase contact with the Indians, they tried to enforce a royal order (1540) which required bringing scattered natives into settlement. The friars often surveyed and laid out these new communities following a standard grid with the church, buildings for the civil authorities, and a plaza (often with a water fountain and whipping post) at the center. The churches could be simple, temporary structures or monuments to Christianity designed to impress the Indians with their size, facilities, and beauty; yet the Dominicans, perhaps because of their emphasis on intellectual pursuits, were not noted as great builders.

The majority of Dominican foundations were near Mexico City and south in present day Puebla, Oaxaca, Chiapas, and Guatemala. These concentrations can be understood in light of territories staked out by other orders, particularly the Franciscans, who had arrived in

New Spain two years before the Dominicans and had already established themselves around Mexico City and to the west and north. The Dominicans quickly anchored themselves in the south, where they faced only minimal competition from other orders throughout the Colonial period. In regions where one order was not clearly dominant, however, orders might vie for control of towns, especially during the first decades of missionary efforts. In Amecameca, strategically situated between Mexico City and Puebla, the community leader welcomed the Franciscans, while in the neighboring town his brother favored the Dominicans. With the help of the latter leader, the Dominicans were able to convince the leaders of Amecameca that they were the more respectable order, and they gained control of that town, too.

These evangelical and territorial interests meant that orders established more convents and churches than there were friars available to staff them. This manpower shortage was never resolved during the Colonial era, and so friars would travel from their assigned convent to surrounding villages at regular intervals and for local feast days. Their contact with these outlying villages was usually infrequent, however, and in their absence they appointed lay assistants, usually chosen from among the village elites.

The Dominicans quickly realized that they needed the support of the Indians, especially their leaders. They generally attempted to work within the existing social system, distributing gifts to *caciques* to win their support and then staging events to display these leaders' Christian worship as an example to others. Dominicans also recognized the importance of learning native languages, and the newly ordained or arrived studied grammars and vocabularies composed by their predecessors, practiced speaking with natives, were tested by examiners "well qualified" in at least three languages, and practiced translating until they were able to compose and deliver sermons on their own. Friars also wrote native-language catechisms and books of sermons that could be memorized.

Dominicans were active participants in some of the sixteenth-century debates about the nature of Indians and their ability to participate in Colonial society and religious life. Dominicans expressed a range of positions on the nature of the Indian: the first provincial, Fray Domingo de Betanzos, argued Indians were childlike and therefore had limited capacities to understand the faith; in contrast, Fray Bartolomé de las Casas was perhaps the most famous defender of Indians and their rational abilities. In general, Dominicans considered themselves the protectors of Indians, particularly against the labor demands of Spanish *encomenderos*, but, with few exceptions, this was a paternal stance toward people whom they regarded as a simple race unable to defend them-

selves. The order's position was that because the Indians were incapable of fully understanding doctrine, they were not qualified to become priests; in 1576, it prohibited Indians and *mestizos* from becoming friars. Although the Crown would later rescind such prohibitions, few Indians joined the order as anything other than servants.

The order did, however, regard Indians as capable of becoming good Christians, even if Dominicans were not as inclined as the early Franciscans to undertake mass baptisms of thousands of potential neophytes as a first stage of conversion. In fact, the Dominicans objected to these mass initiations into the church because they omitted crucial parts of the conversion process. Becoming a Christian first required acquiring an understanding of key elements of the faith, such as the commandments, sins, sacraments, and prayers.

To teach these elements, Dominicans used didactic art, music, processions, and plays, methods they claimed were particularly effective with Indians. They established schools for Indian children with a curriculum generally limited to teaching the catechism. They promoted a typically Dominican conception of the faith, including devotion to Mary through the Rosary. They also taught natives how to dress and eat and trained them in trades, from agriculture to ceramics and raising silkworms. Once educated and baptized, the Indians were to confess and receive communion once a year, usually before Easter, and the early friars used stocks and the whip to encourage them to maintain these practices and lead good Christian lives.

Beyond the round of daily prayers, weekly masses and instruction, annual communion, and observance of high holy days, Dominicans encouraged native *cofradías* ("sodalities") as a way of promoting spirituality as well as generating revenue for the local church and the order. *Cofradías* were established under the direction of friars, and the Dominican influence can be seen in their common dedications to St. Dominic, Our Lady of the Rosary, and Saint Rose. The primary role of these associations was to organize processions and feasts on saints' days, and they collected dues from their members to pay the expenses of these events, including the fees charged by the friars for celebrating mass.

The friars' own lives were supposed to serve as examples to the Indians. This ideally meant long hours in prayer, practicing acts of self-denial such as fasting and forgoing material comforts, protecting their chastity against improper thoughts, and flagellating themselves as a means of imitating Jesus' sufferings. Mystified by the friars' behavior, some Indian spiritual leaders claimed the friars were not normal humans but madmen, or the dead who returned to the earth every night.

Indian reactions to the Dominicans were hardly uniform. They might flee into the country, harass a particularly despised friar, or even—as in the rare case of a 1712 revolt in Chiapas—kill missionaries. On the other hand, they might travel far out of their way to make their yearly confession to a Dominican who knew their language rather than to a closer diocesan priest who did not. Indians did not uniformly accept the new religion, and traditional beliefs were not completely replaced by an official Christianity. Neither did the Dominicans ardently seek out every non-official belief but rather took gains where they could and practiced a limited tolerance out of necessity. John Chance (1994) relates a particularly revealing incident that occurred in 1700, when two Indian assistants to the two Dominicans assigned to the community of Cajonos, Oaxaca, informed the friars of a pagan ceremony soon to take place in a private home. The friars, along with the two Indians and some Spaniards, broke up the ceremony, but the next night an outraged crowd of Indians forced the Dominicans to relinquish the Indian informers who had sought refuge in their monastery. The informers were whipped and killed.

The mendicants were originally sent to New Spain with the power to act as pastors, but without being subject to episcopal authority. Instead of administering "parishes," they administered what were supposed to be temporary *doctrinas de indios* which would be turned over to diocesan clergy once the Indians had been Christianized. From early on, the diocesan clergy sought to reduce the orders' control within the *doctrinas*, complaining that the Dominicans administered sacraments only out of greed for the fees, that they condoned idolatry through their support of *cofradías*, and that they had too infrequent and limited contact with the Indians, or ruled them like despots. The bishops earned from the Spanish crown the rights—however little they could exercise them—to approve new mendicant foundations (1557) and to control their numbers and movements (1574). Dominicans, like the other orders, had no intention of giving up their territories and held onto most of their privileges until 1749 and 1753, when the Bourbons ordered the orders to turn over all but two of their remaining *doctrinas*. The Dominicans did, however, retain some additional *doctrinas* until the end of the Colonial period, particularly in Chiapas and Guatemala, where there were still insufficient numbers of diocesan priests who could speak native languages.

[*See also* Burgoa, Francisco de; Durán, Diego; Las Casas, Bartolomé de.]

BIBLIOGRAPHY

Casas, Bartolomé de las. *In Defense of the Indians.* Translated by Stafford Poole. Illinois, 1974. Presents the learned arguments of the most prominent Dominican defender of Indians' abilities.
Chance, John. *Conquest of the Sierra.* Norman, Okla., 1994.
Dávila Padilla, Agustín. *Historia de la fundacion y discurso de la Provincia de Santiago de México, de la orden de Precicadores.* Mexico City, 1955. Recounts the order's major events and figures in sixteenth-century New Spain.
Gage, Thomas. *A New Survey of the West Indies, 1648.* Edited by J. Eric Thompson. Norman, Okla., 1958. Account of a seventeenth-century English Dominican's travels through Mexico and Guatemala.
Gosner, Kevin. *Soldiers of the Virgin: The Moral Economy of a Colonial Maya Rebellion.* Tucson, Ariz., 1992. Dominicans figure prominently in eighteenth-century Chiapan society and a 1712 Indian revolt.
Kubler, George. *Mexican Architecture of the Sixteenth Century.* New Haven, 1948. Covers Dominican patterns of urbanization as well as their churches and convents.
Mullen, Robert J. *Dominican Architecture in Sixteenth-Century Oaxaca.* Phoenix, 1975. Identifies establishments of Dominican foundations, their styles, and building practices.
Ricard, Robert. *The Spiritual Conquest of Mexico.* Translated by Lesley Byrd Simpson. Berkeley, 1966. Dated, but still the most comprehensive work on the first half-century of mendicant activity in New Spain.
van Oss, Adrian C. *Catholic Colonialism: A Parish History of Guatemala, 1524–1821.* Cambridge, 1986. Includes Dominican roles in organizing a Colonial society.

KAREN MELVIN

DRAMA. Pre-Hispanic Mesoamerica yields little or no evidence of a literary theater in which a prescribed dramatic text was performed by a cast of actors before a single, stationary audience intended to hear every word, see every action, and limit its participation to attention and applause. Some dramatic texts, such as the Quechua *Rabinal Achí* ("Warrior of Rabinal") of Guatemala or the Nahuatl *Güegüence* ("Old Gentleman") of Nicaragua, appear to have survived the Conquest more or less intact. In the former, which is generally believed to be the best example of a drama untainted by European vocabulary, ideas, or historical referents, a prisoner boasts of his martial exploits to his captor and his captor's ruler before being stretched over the sacrificial stone. The drama, which incorporates dance and music as well as carefully composed speeches, was discovered in 1859 in the small town of Rabinal, where it is still occasionally performed. There is also some evidence, in the form of fragmentary dramatic texts, of pre-Hispanic marketplace reenactments of popular mythology and domestic interludes emancipated from strictly religious themes. For the most part, however, even these text-based performances were embedded in a festive and religious context that rendered the relationships among text, performers, and audience far more like those of a communal fiesta than those of the professional theater.

The absence of a substantial body of dramatic texts does not, however, mean that indigenous Mesoamerican cultures lacked a strong theatrical instinct. The calendar festivals that dominated each of the eighteen months of the Mexica year combined historical and mythological narratives, elaborate spectacles, ornate costumes, dance, music, comic relief, and various kinds of mimetic action into grand theatrical displays which straddled the borders between street theater, civic pageantry, and religious ritual. For Ochpaniztli (the Festival of the Sweeping of the Roads), which began in late August or early September, a female slave was chosen to play the role of Toci, the goddess of war. This unfortunate *ixiptla* (impersonator or proxy) was costumed in the same manner as the wooden image of Toci: the upper half of her face was painted white, the lower half black; her dark hair was crowned with white cotton; and she was dressed in a fringed white blouse and short white skirt. Thereafter, she was taken daily through the city to receive homage "as if she had been the goddess herself."

After several days, she was sacrificed and flayed. A naked male priest struggled into her wet skin and was dressed in a blouse and skirt that had been publicly woven by the victim. The sacrifice recalled an early episode in Mexica history (or myth), said to have taken place in 1343, when the daughter of a Culhua ruler had been given to the Mexica as a bride for their god Huitzilopochtli. The girl had been sacrificed and flayed, and a youth dressed in her skin and garments. When, during Ochpaniztli, the new priestly impersonator of Toci chased a number of "terrified" Mexica warriors away from the temple, the mock rout recalled the initial defeat of the Mexica at the hands of the infuriated Culhua. A later mock battle, ranging through the streets of Tenochtitlan (now Mexico City) and perhaps over the surrounding mountains, commemorated the subsequent victory of the Mexica in 1347. Other theatrical elements of Ochpaniztli included communal dances, military parades, erotic caricatures of Gulf Coast Huasteca men (whom the Mexica believed to be negligible warriors but energetic lovers), and a final flight of Mexica warriors, covered in chalk and white feathers as a sign of imminent death, before the bloody, cross-dressed Toci. Thus was inaugurated the Mexica season of war.

The drama of the calendar festivals was not all serious. Early in the festival of Ochpaniztli, "women physicians" staged a mock battle in which they pelted each other with balls made of matted tree moss, reeds, cactus leaves, and yellow marigolds, the goal being to distract the condemned impersonator of Toci and make her laugh. The Jesuit historian José de Acosta wrote in the late sixteenth century of a "humorous interlude" that had been performed as part of a festival in honor of Quetzalcoatl in Cholula. Actors "pretending to be deaf, ill with colds, blind, and one-armed" approached the idol in hope of healing. "Those with colds came coughing and sneezing," the lame limped and complained loudly, and the deaf an-

Moors surround the burning castle. Zacatecas, 1996. *Photograph courtesy of Max Harris.*

swered the god "nonsensically," all of which "made the people laugh uproariously" (*Historia natural y moral de las Indias*, book 5, chap. 30).

After the fall of Tenochtitlan in 1521, newly arrived Franciscan friars adapted both indigenous and European dramatic traditions to the missionary enterprise. Some form of catechetical drama was probably included in the *invenciones* and *danzas* that accompanied the consecration of the first church in Mexico City in 1525. A *Conversion of Saint Paul* was performed by Indians outside the same church in 1530. In 1531 a *Last Judgment* was staged in Tlatelolco, and it may have been revived in Mexico City in 1535. There is evidence of a Passion play in Cuernavaca in the same year.

A flurry of dramatic activity took place in Tlaxcala in 1538. Shortly after Easter, a *Fall of Our First Parents*, notable for the luxuriance of its Garden of Eden, was staged there. Four "rivers" flowed from paradise, nurturing a profusion of flowers and trees, some natural and others made of feathers and gold, all crowded with birds and animals. So many parrots perched in the branches that their screeching disturbed the play, and two wildcats had to be securely tethered because of their ferocity. A quartet of plays telling the story of John the Baptist was performed following the feast of Corpus Christi. These included a comic episode in which the saint's father, who had been struck dumb because of his lack of faith, was addressed in sign language as if he were also deaf, causing much confusion and laughter. In a characteristic integration of theater and real life, the play ended not with the circumcision of the infant saint but with the real baptism of an Indian child, whom the parents named John. In August, the Dominican friar Bartolomé de Las Casas saw a play about the Assumption of the Virgin staged before an audience of "more than eighty thousand people." The play ended with Mary rising "in a cloud," no doubt painted on wood or canvas and manipulated by ropes and pulleys (in the manner of European medieval theater), from one stage to another representing Heaven.

Las Casas remarks of this play: "The apostles, or those who represented them, were Indians, as was the case in all the *autos* [religious plays] that they had previously performed (and it must be taken for granted that no Spaniard takes charge of nor meddles in the *autos* that they put on with them), and the one who represented Our Lady was an Indian man, as were all those who took charge of the play" (*Apologética historia sumaria*, chap. 64). It is generally recognized that the actors, singers, dancers, and musicians in the missionary drama were Indian, and that speeches and songs were in the native language, usually Nahuatl. Las Casas goes one step further, affirming that, at least in Tlaxcala, even those who "took

charge" of the play were Indian. The freedom enjoyed by the Indians in this respect, together with the inherent flexibility of a medium in which scenario or script can only suggest but never fully control performance, rendered the missionary theater an intriguing site for dialogue between European and indigenous points of view.

This is especially true of the theatrical mock battles that quickly became a part of the Colonial Measoamerican scene. Europeans and Mesoamericans both had lively pre-Contact traditions of dramatized conflict, but Colonial mock battles came to be known generically, because of their most common historical referent, as *fiestas de Moros y Cristianos* (festivals of Moors and Christians). By introducing the European theme of conflict between Moors and Christians to Mesoamerica, Spanish colonists may have thought that they were teaching their new subjects to join them in celebrating the divinely ordained victory of light-skinned Christians over dark-skinned "heathens," linking the Peninsular defeat of the Moors in 1492 to the New World defeat of Mesoamericans from 1519 onward. But the theme cut two ways in Mesoamerica: the history being dramatized was not one of conquest but of reconquest, for the Spanish Christians had finally driven out their Moorish invaders. It was this image of liberation rather than that of Spanish victory that attracted indigenous Mexicans to the imported theme. In Colonial festivals of Moors and Christians, a public transcript of Roman Catholic triumph masked a hidden transcript of native reconquest.

The first American *moros y cristianos* was staged in Coatzacoalcos, on the Gulf of Mexico, in 1524, but the most detailed early accounts come from Mexico City and Tlaxcala in 1539. A spectacular trilogy of plays, ending with a *Conquest of Rhodes* that cast Fernando Cortés himself as a Christian hero prophetically liberating the Mediterranean island of Rhodes from the Turks, was staged in the main square of Mexico City early in 1539. Scenic properties were lavish: several distinct stages supporting "more than a thousand Indian musicians and singers"; a number of artificial "castles"; a "city of wood" representing Rhodes; four three-masted sailing ships on wheels that circled the plaza "as if they were on water" and noisily fired their cannon; a number of artificial mountains, rocks, meadows, woods, and springs; and a herd of sheep. *The Conquest of Rhodes* itself seems to have been dominated by a public transcript of Catholic triumphalism, but the two plays that immediately preceded it—known collectively as *The Battle of the Wild Men and the Blacks*— appear to have dramatized, first, a pre-Hispanic battle between Indian tribes, and, second, the Spanish conquest of Mexico. In the latter case, the role of the Conquistadores was played by masked black slaves who were sumptuously dressed, bejeweled, and mounted on horses, discreetly mocking Spanish assumptions of natural superiority and pretensions to grandeur.

The Tlaxcalan decided to go one better and, in June, mounted a *Conquest of Jerusalem*. This represented prophetically the Franciscan dream that a combined army of Christianized Indians would cross the Atlantic, join the European forces of Emperor Charles V, liberate Jerusalem from the Turks, and so usher in the millennium. Again, the staging was spectacular: five three-dimensional scenic cities; several thousand Indians dressed as Turks, European soldiers, and Indian warriors, the latter wearing "their richest plumage, emblems, and shields"; Indian actors playing the Archangel Michael, Santiago, the emperor, the pope, the viceroy of Mexico, and other saints, kings, and dignitaries; red prickly pears and clay balls filled with moistened red earth that exploded on contact to simulate bloodshed; arrowheads that created the same effect; and a barrage of gunpowder, arquebuses, and fireworks. [*See* Santiago.] Intriguingly, the villainous Sultan of Babylon was played by an Indian representing Cortés, and the captain-general of the Moors by another representing Pedro de Alvarado. In all likelihood, the public transcript of the performance conceded the claims of Christianity to Jerusalem, while the hidden transcript argued for the equal justice of Indian claims to Mexico and gave the Indian actors an opportunity to enact the defeat of their own conqueror. When the Sultan Cortés surrendered at the close to an emperor played by an Indian noble and declared himself to be the latter's "natural vassal," it entailed a remarkably sophisticated reversal of the Aristotelian language used by Spaniards to justify the conquest of America. In Tlaxcala, instead, the Spanish "Turks" acknowledged the natural superiority and rightful rule of the indigenous "emperor."

Such mock battles have continued to thrive throughout the Americas. In many cases, they have adapted to New World themes. The Festival of the Volcano in seventeenth-century Antigua (Guatemala) combined an artificial fortress and an artificial mountain—the latter covered with greenery and populated by birds, boars, monkeys, squirrels, and other wild animals—in a day-long mock battle which recalled the capture of rebellious Indian chieftains by Spanish forces in 1526. In nineteenth-century New Mexico, the theme was adapted to reflect more recent battles between Spanish settlers and Comanche raiders. As late as 1929, near Taos, New Mexico, hundreds of local Indians played the part of Comanche warriors in a performance that was so realistic that tourists fled for cover, thinking that real warfare had broken out. In modern Huejotzingo (Mexico), the annual carnival play still enacts a mock battle whose official referent is the defeat of French imperial troops by Mexican national forces at nearby Puebla on 5 May 1862. The largest surviving festival of Moors and Christians is probably that staged at the end of August each year outside the city of Zacatecas (Mexico), where thousands of Christians launch their final attack on the castle from the crest of a hill a mile away, charging down through the scrub and across the intervening valley while cannon fire from the hillsides, the Moorish defenders of the castle fill the air with the smoke of arquebuses, and drum and bugle corps play martial music.

Seasonal religious plays have also continued to thrive. The Franciscan friar Antonio de Ciudad Real saw an Epiphany play staged outside the church of Tlajomulco, Jalisco, in 1587. While the three kings made their arduous way down a steep hill nearby, the crowd was entertained by a brief Dance of Angels and a much longer, comic Dance of Shepherds. When the kings finally arrived at the church, they sought directions from of a ranting, tyrannical Herod before presenting their gifts to the tableau of images that represented the Holy Family. Today's Christmas *pastorelas* focus almost exclusively on the comic antics of the shepherds and the obstacles that Lucifer places in their way as they travel to Bethlehem. Some scholars interpret the comparative neglect of the Holy Family in these plays as a form of resistance to the dominant ecclesiastical narrative. Certainly one wonders at the naïveté of the U.S. cavalry captain, stationed in southern Texas between 1891 and 1893, who innocently lent his uniform to the local *pastorela* troupe so that the character of Lucifer might dress as a cavalry officer!

Easter is also an occasion for a wide variety of indigenous theatrical activities. In Huehuetenango and Totonicapán (Guatemala), a series of dramatic tableaux represent the trial, crucifixion, and resurrection of Jesus. In the Sierra Tarahumara (Mexico), those who play the numerous dancing Pharisees paint their bodies white and dress in white loincloths, red headbands, and turkey feathers. In many cases, the Indians identify with the suffering Jesus and associate the Roman centurions with Spanish Conquistadores and other oppressive outsiders.

[*See also* Danzas.]

BIBLIOGRAPHY

Argudín, Yolanda. *Historia del teatro en México*. Mexico City, 1986. Compact history of the theater in Mexico from pre-Hispanic rituals to today's professional drama.

Burkhart, Louise M. *Holy Wednesday: A Nahua Drama from Early Colonial Mexico*. Philadelphia, 1996. This English translation of and commentary on a Nahuatl Easter play contains an excellent summary of the theatrical, social, and religious conditions in which colonial Nahuatl theater flourished.

Durán, Diego. *Book of the Gods and Rites, and the Ancient Calendar*. Translated by Fernando Horcasitas and Doris Heyden. Norman, Okla., 1971. Although not as thorough as Sahagún, Durán collected information on Mexica religious festivals from those who remembered them before the arrival of the Europeans.

Flores, Richard. *Los Pastores: History and Performance in the Mexican Shepherd's Play of South Texas*. Washington, D.C., 1995. Careful study of the development of the *pastorela* from its roots in Spain to its present interaction with local politics in southern Texas.

Harris, Max. *The Dialogical Theatre*. London, 1993. Argues for the inherently dialogical nature of the theater and focuses, in part 2, on early missionary theater and subsequent folk dramatizations of conquest in Mexico.

Harris, Max. *Aztecs, Moors, and Christians: Festivals of Reconquest in Mexico and Spain*. Austin, Tex., 2000. Full account of the tradition of mock battles in Spain and Mexico before and after the Conquest, reading the Mexican performances in particular as sites of resistance to domination by outsiders.

Horcasitas, Fernando. *El teatro nahuatl*. Mexico City, 1974. Invaluable resource for students of Mesoamerican drama, this is the most complete account of Nahuatl theater in Early Colonial Mexico.

Leinwater, Richard E., ed. and trans. "Rabinal Achí." *Latin American Theatre Review* 1/2 (1968), 3–53. English translation of and commentary on the purest surviving example of a pre-Contact indigenous dramatic text.

León-Portilla, Miguel. *Pre-Columbian Literatures of Mexico*. Translated by Grace Lobanov and Miguel León-Portilla. Norman, Okla., 1969. Survey of pre-Hispanic literature in Mexico, including, in chapter 4, the surviving traces of an indigenous dramatic tradition.

Motolinía, Toribio de. *History of the Indians of New Spain*. Edited and translated by Francis Borgia Steck. Washington, D.C., 1951. Motolinía was the Franciscan guardian of Tlaxcala from 1536 to 1542. His book includes (tr. 1, chap. 15) a detailed account of theatrical activity in Tlaxcala in 1538–1539.

Ravicz, Marilyn Ekhdal. *Early Colonial Religious Drama in Mexico*. Washington, D.C., 1970. Useful introduction to and translation of several religious plays from sixteenth-century Mexico.

Sahagún, Bernardino de. *Florentine Codex: General History of the Things of New Spain*. Edited and translated by Arthur J. O. Anderson and Charles E. Dibble. 13 vols. Salt Lake City, 1950–1982. Chronicles the memories of Mexica elders who survived the Conquest; book 2, in particular, provides invaluable information on Mexica calendar festivals.

MAX HARRIS

DRESDEN, CODEX. Of the four surviving Maya hieroglyphic codices, the *Dresden Codex* is not only the best preserved but also the most beautiful and sophisticated. Its contents are, like those of the other manuscripts, largely of a calendric and ritual nature, with a strong emphasis on divinatory mechanisms based on the 260-day calendar. Although the *Dresden Codex* was among the first Maya hieroglyphic documents to be examined by Western scholars and has been the subject of numerous studies, a considerable portion of it is still poorly understood; yet it remains the most important source for interpreting many aspects of Maya thought and religious belief.

Like all other pre-Hispanic books from Mesoamerica, the *Dresden Codex* takes the form of a screenfold. The pages consist of a paper made from the pounded inner bark of a wild species of *Ficus* (*hu'un* in Maya—a word that became semantically equivalent to "book"). The fiber has been stabilized with the addition of a starchlike glue and its surface whitened with a fine layer of stucco. The 39 pages of the codex were joined together with thin hinges of animal skin, making a single strip of paper 340 centimeters in length. Each page is 20.5 centimeters long and 8.5 centimeters wide. The pages, of which four remain blank, are painted on both sides. In all likelihood, the codex once had wooden covers. The pages are numbered from 1 to 74 in all editions; however, at some point in its history the codex was broken into two parts and the first fragment was replaced back to front, so that reproductions differ in their pagination.

History. Before 1739, when the *Dresden Codex* was acquired by the librarian Johann Christian Götze for the Royal Saxonian Library at Dresden from an antiquarian in Vienna, its history is a matter of assumption and speculation. Neither the location nor date of manufacture is known. A comparison of material objects painted in the book with archaeological finds points to a place of origin on the Yucatán Peninsula. The codex seems to be of Middle or Late Postclassic date (c.1200–1500 CE), but it is quite possible that it represents a copy of a Classic period manuscript. It has been speculated that the book came into Spanish hands when Fernando Cortés landed on the island of Cozumel in 1517. The book may have been sent as part of the "royal fifth" to the Spanish emperor Charles V that same year. From Madrid, it may have made its way to Vienna, the other seat of the Hapsburg kings.

After its acquisition by the Dresden library, five pages of the codex were published by Alexander von Humboldt in his *Vue de cordillères et monuments des peuples indigènes de l'Amérique* (1813), a publication which stimulated early interest in Maya hieroglyphic writing. The first complete reproduction, in the form of hand-colored drawings, was published by Lord Kingsborough in the third volume of his *Antiquities of Mexico* (London, 1831–1848). The first edition to satisfy scientific standards was issued in 1880 by Ernst Förstemann, who also wrote a groundbreaking scientific commentary on the codex which outlined its calendrical and astrological content. Since then, the manuscript has been reproduced in various editions of uneven quality (see Bibliography).

In March 1945, the codex suffered severe water damage after the bombing of Dresden. No restoration has yet been undertaken. The original manuscript is presently on display in the rare book section of the book museum of the Sächsische Landesbibliothek.

Content. Serious research on the decipherment of the *Dresden Codex* began with the pioneering work of Ernst Förstemann. His decipherments of the chronological sections still form the basis of our understanding of the codex. The syntactic structure of the non-calendrical pas-

Two pages from the *Dresden Codex* Venus Table.
Photograph courtesy of Ivan Šprajc.

sages of the hieroglyphic texts and the nominal hiero-glyphs for the gods portrayed were first studied by Paul Schellhas. More recently, several commentaries on the entire manuscript have been published; some focus on the calendrical portions (Thompson, 1972); others supply complete decipherments, transcriptions, and translations of the entire hieroglyphic text as well as its accompanying iconography (Knorozov, 1982; Schele and Grube, 1997; Davoust, 1997).

Most pages of the codex are divided by horizontal black lines into two, three, or four sections, into which scenes and accompanying texts are placed. Each horizontal band, in turn, is divided into several compartments, each containing a scene showing a certain god performing a particular action and an accompanying text of four or six hieroglyphs. Usually, between two and five of these compartments form an almanac of omens based on divisions or multiples of the 260-day cycle.

The codex is further divided into thematic sections, each of which encompasses a series of different almanacs. The content of the larger sections is as follows (pagination follows Förstemann 1880):

Pages 1–15: Miscellaneous almanacs, all based on the 260-day cycle. They record good and bad omens for the days. In addition, these pages seem to represent a general introduction describing different techniques involved in divination.

Pages 16–23: The Moon Goddess; omens for childbirth and different illnesses.

Pages 24, 46–50: Tables for the planet Venus, based on multiples of the 584-day Venus cycle (13 *octaeteris* cycles, each of $5 \times 584 = 8 \times 365 = 2,920$ days).

Pages 51–58: Eclipse tables for the calculation of solar and lunar eclipses, based on cycles of five or six lunations. The total number of days in the table is 11.958, or 405 synodic months.

Pages 58–59: Tables of multiples of 78.

Page 60: A prophecy for the *k'atun* period ending on the day 11 Ahaw.

Pages 61–73: Tables which connect a mythological Long Count date of 16.3.16.14.11.4 9 K'an 12 K'ayab through multiples of 91 with historic dates.

Pages 71c–72c: The sacred day 4 Eb and its bearing on the weather.

Page 74: A prognostication of the end of the universe by a grand deluge on a day 4 Eb.

Pages 25–28: Rituals for the end of the old year and the first day of the new year.

Pages 29a–45: Almanacs dedicated to the different

manifestations of the rain god Chac and suggestions for appropriate food offerings.

Pages 42c–45c: Almanac based on 4 × 65 days, probably related to travels of Chac.

Pages 43b–45b: The planet Mars, based on the 780-day period (= 3 × 260 days).

Page 45a: The arithmetical year of 364 days.

Although the calendrical sections of the individual chapters are widely understood, our comprehension of their syntactic relationships, their precise function, and their meaning within their communicative context is still minimal. The way the codex was read and performed, the audience which attended such readings, and its actual language and style are important aspects of the study of Maya books and literacy in general which still need investigation.

[*See also* Maya Screenfolds.]

BIBLIOGRAPHY

Davoust, Michel. *Un nouveau commentaire du Codex de Dresde, Codex hiéroglyphique maya du XIVe siècle.* Paris, 1997. Translation of the hieroglyphic texts; the analysis of the context rests on Thompson 1972.

Förstemann, Ernst Wilhelm. *Die Mayahandschrift der Königlich öffentlichen Bibliothek zu Dresden*, Leipzig, 1880. Still the best reproduction of the *Dresden Codex*, although printed only in a limited edition and no longer available. A reprint of this edition was published by the Guatemalan press Cholsamaj in 1998.

Förstemann, Ernst Wilhelm. *Commentar zur Mayahandschrift der Königlich öffentlichen Bibliothek zu Dresden*, Dresden, 1901. Groundbreaking publication that lays the foundation of all later work on the calendrical tables of the codex.

Knorozov, Yurii Valentinovich. *Maya Hieroglyphic Codices*. Translated by Sophie D. Coe. Institute for Mesoamerican Studies, State University of New York at Albany, Publication 8. Albany, 1982.

Schele, Linda, and Nikolai Grube. *Notebook for the XXIst Maya Hieroglyphic Workshop, March 8–9, 1997: The Dresden Codex*. Austin, Tex., 1997.

Schellhas, Paul. *Die Göttergestalten der Maya-Handschriften: Ein mythologisches Kulturbild aus dem Alten Amerika*. Dresden, 1897.

Thompson, J. Eric S. *A Commentary on the Dresden Codex: A Maya Hieroglyphic Book*. Memoirs of the American Philosophical Society, 93. Philadelphia, 1972. The most complete commentary on the *Dresden Codex* available, with color reproduction of the codex.

Villacorta C., Juan Antonio, and Carlos A. Villacorta. *Códices Mayas. Reproducidos y desarrollados por J. Antonio Villacorta C. y Carlos A. Villacorta*. Guatemala City, 1930. Reproduction of the three then-known codices in black-and-white line drawings.

Zimmermann, Günter. *Die Hieroglyphen der Maya-Handschriften*. Universität Hamburg, Abhandlungen aus dem Gebiet der Auslandskunde, Band 62, Reihe B (Völkerkunde, Kulturgeschichte, Sprachen), Band 34. Hamburg, 1956.

NIKOLAI K. GRUBE

DRESS, COSTUME, AND ADORNMENT. Unlike the situation in Egypt, far western China, or coastal Peru and Chile, Mesoamerica's humid climate and various burial practices were such that almost no pre-Hispanic garments have survived. Fortunately, the range of clothing worn throughout the area can be reconstructed from depictions found on murals, sculptures, ceramic vessels, figurines and—during the Late Postclassic (1250–1251 CE)—in indigenous pictorial codices, as well as from early Spanish chroniclers' eyewitness accounts. Only a limited number of garment types appear in this archaeological and ethnohistorical record. Each of the regional Mesoamerican cultures displayed its own unique versions, but all reflect the same underlying principle: because clothing requires broad, flat, flexible substances for construction, the size and shape of the fabrics available to a people dictate the nature of the garments they wear.

In Mesoamerica, pre-Hispanic textiles—and even some today—were woven by women on the back-strap loom, a device that produces cloth no wider than the weaver's working armspan of about 1 meter (3–4 feet). Because such woven webs have four completely finished edges—called selvages—a single piece of cloth could be draped on the body directly from the loom to serve as a loincloth or skirt. Wider garments could be constructed by seaming together the selvages of two or more webs. Pre-Hispanic attire was unfitted, with clothing that draped on the body. The basic Mesoamerican apparel was woven of bast (plant stem) fiber. Elite attire was distinguished by the use of the status fiber cotton, as well as by special surface designs and manner of wearing.

Male Clothing. The basic, indispensable male garment, the loincloth, is first portrayed on Middle Formative (Preclassic; 1000–300 BCE) clay figurines from Mexico's central plateau and continued to be worn into the Colonial period. It is a continuous strip of fabric, passed between the legs to cover the genitals and tied about the waist so that its ends hang down in front and back of the body. One variant of this garment consisted of a shorter cloth placed between the legs and then draped over a belt to create short, apronlike coverings in front and back. Both types of loincloth were worn by the Olmec of Mexico's Gulf Coast around 1200 BCE.

During the Classic period (250–750 CE), at the Central Highland site of Teotihuacan, simply dressed clay figurines had short, apronlike loin coverings. Contemporaneous Lowland Maya favored the longer style, with ends hanging down in front and back (see illustration M1). The Aztec of the Late Postclassic wore their loincloths in a distinctive manner, wrapped about the waist so that both of the garment's ends passed between the legs to the front of the body, looped over the waist-encircling "belt," and tied in a large, distinctive knot—the "Aztec knot"—whose short ends fell only to the knees (see M7). This "Aztec knot" is sometimes depicted in the Aztec tribute tallies, to indicate the intended use of those cloths. The distinctive knot apparently was synonymous with virility, be-

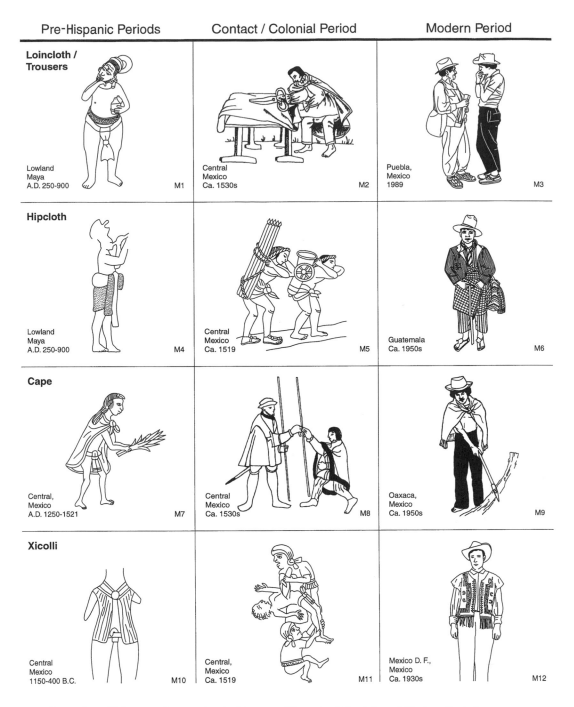

| Pre-Hispanic Periods | Contact / Colonial Period | Modern Period |

Loincloth / Trousers
Lowland Maya
A.D. 250-900 — M1

Central Mexico
Ca. 1530s — M2

Puebla, Mexico
1989 — M3

Hipcloth
Lowland Maya
A.D. 250-900 — M4

Central Mexico
Ca. 1519 — M5

Guatemala
Ca. 1950s — M6

Cape
Central, Mexico
A.D. 1250-1521 — M7

Central Mexico
Ca. 1530s — M8

Oaxaca, Mexico
Ca. 1950s — M9

Xicolli
Central Mexico
1150-400 B.C. — M10

Central, Mexico
Ca. 1519 — M11

Mexico D. F., Mexico
Ca. 1930s — M12

Examples of Mesoamerican male clothing: pre-Hispanic, Colonial, and Modern Periods.
M1: Schele and Miller, plate 58, 1986; M2: Sahagún, Book 10, plate 55, 1950–1982; M3: Photo by Cristina Taccone; M4: Miller, fig. A:2, 1986; M5: Lienzo de Tlaxcala, p. 30, 1892; M6: Wood and Osborne, plate 20, 1966; M7: Codex Mendoza, vol. 3, f. 63r, 1992; M8: Codex Osuna, 1947; M9: Lechuga, p. 69, 1982; M10: Guzman, fig. IV:3, 1959; M11: Codex Magliabechiano, p. 70, 1970; M12: Anawalt, p. 212, 1981.

cause the Nahuatl term for "loincloth," *maxtlatl*, was also used as a male given name.

The hipcloth—a square or rectangular textile that was folded and tied at the waist—was often worn in conjunction with the loincloth by the early Olmec and Lowland Maya (M4), as well as by the Aztec and their Tlaxcalan neighbors (M5). Apparently, the pre-Hispanic Highland Maya also wore the hipcloth; a present-day version of this garment is still known in Solola, Guatemala (M6).

The most status-sensitive of Mesoamerica's garments was the cape, a square or rectangle of cloth that tied about the neck and extended to between waist and ankle. The earliest of Central Mexico's clothed male figures, the Formative figurines of Tlatilco, are sometimes depicted in short cloaks. Some form of cape continued to be worn in Mesoamerica into the Colonial period. Among the Aztec, the cape (*tilmatli*) was a prestigious garment whose fiber, surface pattern, manner of wearing, and length were all reported to have been tightly controlled by the state (M7). According to Fray Diego Durán, only the Aztec ruling class was allowed full-length, richly decorated cotton cloaks; however, research suggests that Colonial-era reports of stringent sumptuary regulations reflect a nostalgic creed more than a pre-Hispanic reality.

Although the loincloth and cape were standard attire throughout Mesoamerica at the time of European contact, the Tarascan people of Western Mexico wore anomalous clothing: males wore fitted briefs, instead of loincloths, and enveloping tunic-like shirts instead of capes. The only Mesoamerican prototypes for this aberrant dress are depicted on mortuary figurines buried more than a thousand years before in the non-Mesoamerican-style deep-shaft tombs of Ixtlan del Rio in Nayarit. Analogs of these garment styles also appear on archaeological figurines from Ecuador, which date from 1500 BCE through the time of Spanish contact.

Elsewhere in Mesoamerica, the cape continued to be worn for some decades after the Conquest (M8), despite the introduction of a completely different manner of male dress that reflected a new concept of clothing construction: tailoring. The Spanish introduced the European practice of cutting and sewing together separate pieces of cloth to create garments that followed the lines of the body (M2). The conquerors also introduced the Old World treadle loom, which could produce broad widths of material, from which the mandated Colonial-period clothing could be constructed.

Sixteenth-century missionary priests insisted that Mesoamerican men wear modest, limb-encasing European shirts and pantaloons (see M2). In reference to these muslin *camisas* ("shirts") and *calzones* ("trousers"), aging Aztec warriors later wryly recalled, "They dressed us in white." Nonetheless, Early Colonial-period men still wore the cape over their European attire (M8). The status and power symbolized by the cape were slow to dissipate, and in certain conservative Mexican villages, it continued to be worn into the twentieth century (M9), though it now has largely disappeared. The white muslin *camisa* and *calzones* continue to be worn in rural areas, but men in Western jeans, T-shirts, and sneakers are increasingly common in Indian marketplaces and festive gatherings (M3). The brimmed Western hat abides, but jeans wearers also don baseball-style caps.

An indigenous form of attire that has moved from lofty pre-Hispanic status to mundane daily wear is the *xicolli*, the Aztec short sleeveless jacket. This garment appears early in the archaeological record, depicted on a few Formative Tlatilco figures (M10), and it was worn by priests at Teotihuacan. Among the Lowland Maya, the jacket served as martial rather than religious attire. For the Aztec, the *xicolli* was special-purpose clothing, ritual dress worn only by gods, priests, rulers, and constables. Since Aztec priests sometimes wore it while performing human sacrifice (M11), it is surprising that it survived the scrutiny of the proselytizing Roman Catholic missionaries. The modern jacket has a new name—*cotorina*—and construction material, wool, as well as a change of status to daily wear, most commonly for winter warmth in Central Mexico's chilly highlands (M12).

Two categories of important pre-Hispanic attire have not persisted into the present. The first is padded armor, protective martial garments stuffed with raw cotton and encased by reeds, animal hide or, most commonly, quilted cloth. The Aztec cotton armor (*ichcahuipilli*) was so effective against indigenous weapons that the invading Spaniards quickly adopted it. Yet these padded garments proved no match for steel swords and lances. The protective attire worn by Mesoamerican ballplayers also did not survive the Conquest. The Spanish missionaries quickly and correctly recognized the ceremonial implications of the often deadly ballgame: ballcourts were places of implacable ritual confrontation, and the players were often dressed accordingly. For example, from the Formative period comes evidence that Tlatilco ballplayers were sometimes attired as though for combat, complete with a mask. Olmec players of that era wore far fewer clothes—often just a protective, hip-encasing garment held in place by a broad belt. The same type of hip padding was still worn at the time of Spanish contact; an animated Tlaxcalan ballplayer was sketched vigorously performing at the court of Charles V of Spain.

Female Clothing. The Spanish missionaries approved of the long, wrap-around skirts and enveloping blouses worn by the women of Central Mexico (F1, F2). As a result, these garments have continued into the present day (F3). A notable exception to the modest dress of Central

Examples of Mesoamerican female clothing: pre-Hispanic, Colonial, and Modern Periods.
F1: Taylor, fig. 6, 1991; F2: Codex Borbonicus, p. 29, 1974; F3: Lechuga, p. 149, 1982; F4: Sayer, p. 38, 1985; F5: Sahagún, Book 8: plate 74, 1950–1982; F6: Cordry, p. 318, 1968; F7: Codex Borgia, p. 59, 1963; F8: Codex Magliabechiano, f. 58r, 1970; F9: Photo by Cristina Taccone; F10: Cordry, fig. 65, 1968; F11: Codices de Tepetlaoetoc, f. 12, lamina B, 1994; F12: Photo by Patricia Anawalt.

Mexico was the clothing worn by Tarascan women, who went about topless, wearing only short, tight skirts despite a chilly climate. Such non-Mesoamerican-style attire reflects the Ecuadorian influence in ancient Western Mexico in women's, as well as men's, attire (see above).

The Mesoamerican blouse (*huipil*), a wide, sleeveless tunic (F6), first occurs in the archaeological record among the Classic Maya (F4). By the Late Postclassic, the *huipil* was the prevalent upper-body garment in Central Mexico, worn by both Aztec (F5) and Mixtec women. Following the Conquest, the *huipil* ceased to be worn in the area to the north of (an imaginary line from) Veracruz to Puebla to the Pacific. Another upper-body garment, the *quechquemitl*, has survived in this northern region; the Aztec term probably derives from Nahuatl *quechtli* ("neck") and *quemi* ("to put on a *manta* or cape"). This garment, unique to Mesoamerica, is composed of two rectangles of cloth joined so that when the "points" are positioned at front and back, a distinctive triangle is formed (F7), but when they are placed over each shoulder, a capelike appearance is created (F9). The *quechquemitl* was the attire of ancient fertility goddesses (F8), and it may have originated in the lush, fertile Gulf Coast region, where it was—and still is—the quintessential female garment.

Another aspect of female attire that has survived into modern times is a distinctive manner of arranging the hair. Aztec females wore their hair long, streaming down to the shoulders until they married; the hair was then arranged in two distinctive "horns," tied up to protrude at either side of the head (F11). In other regions, vines or cords were sometimes braided into the hair to achieve a crownlike effect (F10). The use of wool cords to create a towering headdress continues in the town of Cuetzalan, Puebla, and the *quechquemitl* is worn atop these headdresses (F12).

Costumes with Special Functions. Mesoamerican warrior attire comprised garments that completely encased the trunk and limbs. Although these bodysuits are best known from contact-period Aztec sources, they had ancient antecedents. For example, a Middle Formative Tlatilco dancer-shaman is depicted wearing a body-encasing costume made of overlapping plant material or feathers. At Teotihuacan, men dressed in jaguar suits appear on wall murals, and body-encasing jaguar costumes were worn by the Lowland Maya in rituals depicted on Classic-period polychrome vessels. In Late Formative southern Mexico, similar body-encasing jaguar costumes are shown as ritual attire in certain pre-Hispanic Mixtec pictorials, such as the *Codex Zouche-Nuttall*, as they are in the Central Mexican Borgia Group of codices.

Aztec warriors wore their body-encasing suits into battle, with matching decorative helmets and lofty, ornate back devices of resplendent tropical feathers, to which gold and jade were sometimes added. The shimmering jaguar costumes, all made of feather-covered cloth, were only one of thirteen known warrior-suit styles. Padded armor was always worn beneath this flamboyant feathered attire. Jaguar masks and matching cloth suits are still worn during certain festivals in some rural areas of Mesoamerica.

Costuming was also a part of the dramatic ceremonies that made up Mesoamerica's ceaseless ritual round. During feasts, deity impersonators donned the signature symbolic headdresses, face paint, masks, intricate back devices, and emblematic staffs, shields, and rattle sticks of the gods. From the Spanish chroniclers it is known that most Aztec theatrical ritual attire was created of painted *amate* paper, made from the inner bark of native fig (*Ficus* spp.) or mulberry (*Morus niger*) trees.

Adornment. From the Formative period to the Spanish conquest, the elite of Mesoamerica wore distinctive head adornments. These ranged from the turbans and hair ribbons of the nude Tlatilco figures of the Early Formative to the distinctive Olmec helmetlike headgear depicted on the Colossal Heads; these helmets were probably of cloth and bear evidence of having been tied on.

Classic-period Teotihuacan portrayed wide-frame headdresses bordered by exotic, expensive quetzal feathers, often worn with wide nose ornaments. Teotihuacan is also associated with the tasseled headdress, a diagnostic element of this Central Mexican center that sometimes appears in Classic Lowland Maya art. The Maya—who often represented their names in the imagery of their headdresses—are also distinguished by their towering headdresses. The Early Postclassic Toltec and Maya continued this custom of wearing long, sweeping, quetzal-feather headgear, as did the Late Postclassic Aztec. An icon of the Conquest period is the so-called Crown of Motecuhzoma, now in the Museum für Völkerkunde, Vienna.

Emblematic jewelry served as further elite adornment, some made of mollusk shell. Fray Bernardino de Sahagún, the most encyclopedic chronicler of Aztec life, describes white freshwater gastropod shells, as well as dark-red sections of marine shells set into fish patterns to decorate chief warriors' net capes. Impressive pendants and necklaces made from shells of *Spondylus princeps* have been recovered from the deep-shaft tombs of Western Mexico.

Blue-green stones, including turquoise from the American Southwest, were the most highly prized of gemstones. Gold, too, was valued, but not as much as jade and other green stones. Clear, rose, and smoky quartz crystal also served as elite adornment, notably as lip plugs. The *Codex Ixtlilxochitl* depicts four elite males wearing these labrets, with gold ear plugs and quetzal-feather pompoms in their hair. Another important adornment of the elite was fresh flowers, arranged as long-handled bouquets, and carried on ceremonial occasions but also enjoyed on private ones.

[*See also* Feathers and Featherwork; Weaving.]

BIBLIOGRAPHY

Anawalt, Patricia. "Costume and Control: Aztec Sumptuary Laws." *Archaeology* 33 (1980), 33–43.

Anawalt, Patricia. *Indian Clothing before Cortés: Mesoamerican Costumes from the Codices.* Norman, Okla., 1981.

Anawalt, Patricia. "Analysis of the Aztec *Quechquemitl*: An Exercise in Inference." In *The Art and Iconography of Late Post-Classic Central Mexico*, edited by Elizabeth Hill Boone, pp. 37–72. Washington, D.C., 1982.

Anawalt, Patricia. "Memory Clothing: Costumes Associated with Aztec Human Sacrifice." In *Ritual Human Sacrifice in Mesoamerica*, edited by Elizabeth Hill Boone, pp. 165–193. Washington, D.C., 1984.

Anawalt, Patricia. "Ancient Cultural Exchanges between Ecuador, West Mexico, and the American Southwest: Clothing Similarities." *Latin American Antiquity* 3.2 (1992), 114–129.

Anawalt, Patricia. "A Comparative Analysis of the Costumes and Accouterments of the *Codex Mendoza*." In *Codex Mendoza*, edited by Frances F. Berdan and Patricia Rieff Anawalt, vol. 1, pp. 103–150. Berkeley, 1992.

Anawalt, Patricia. "They Came to Trade Exquisite Things: Ancient West Mexican–Ecuadorian Contacts." In *Ancient West Mexico: Art and Archaeology of the Unknown Past*, edited by Richard Townsend, pp. 233–249. Chicago, 1998.

Cordry, Donald, and Dorothy Cordry. *Mexican Indian Costumes.* Austin, 1968.

Guzmán, Eulalia. "*Huipil y maxtlatl.*" In *Esplendor del Mexico antiguo*, edited by Carmen Cook de Leonard. Mexico City, 1959.

Lechuga, Ruth D. *El traje indigena de México.* Mexico City, 1982.

Sayer, Chloe. *Costumes of Mexico.* Austin, 1985.

Taylor, Dicey. "Painted Ladies: Costumes for Women on Tepeu Ceramics." In *The Maya Vase Book: A Corpus of Rollout Photographs of Maya Vases*, vol. 3, New York, 1991.

Wood, Josephine, and Lilly de Jongh Osborne. *Indian Costumes of Guatemala.* Graz, 1966.

PATRICIA RIEFF ANAWALT

DUALITY. The situation or state in which two forces, elements, or beings act, instead of one, is a fundamental organizing principle in Mesoamerican cultures. It is based in part on observations of nature: light alternates with dark, a rainy season with a dry one, heat with frost, and prosperity with privation. In indigenous views, the world is not static but cyclical, mutable, and motile. Duality does not establish rigid categories; instead, it balances opposing and complementary beings, forces, or states in nature, relationships between people and the gods, family members, and neighbors, and elements of an individual's mind and body. Some modern theoretical approaches (e.g., structuralism) have reduced Mesoamerican classifications to static opposites and have thus ignored their original dynamic fluidity.

In nature, Mesoamerican people saw (and still see) duality not as a duel of opposites but rather as a balance between forces or states that are not intrinsically positive or negative. If any natural element predominates at the expense of others, a catastrophe follows. In the pre-Columbian period, many indigenous groups told stories of a time before the creation of the sun and moon when the world was cold and dark, so it was impossible to plant crops. Yet when the sun appeared, it was stationary and began to incinerate the earth. Only when it moved, and light and heat alternated with cold and dark, could the world sustain life. Hence, in previous world ages, or Suns, when fire, wind, or water were not balanced by different and equally strong forces, they became destructive agents that obliterated all life and ended a world cycle.

Pre-Columbian belief was biased in favor of male deities in number, importance, and activities; frequently, however old otiose creators consisted of male/female pairs, as in the *Popol Vuh*. Some male deities had female counterparts, who were often shadowy figures with less clearly defined functions. Because many Mesoamerican deities were personified principles, natural elements, and places, while others were mythologized human beings, they did not have a corresponding or equal partner.

Most deities had dual aspects, and native people rarely divided them into purely good and evil figures. Gods that cured also killed. The patroness of childbirth also took the lives of women and children during childbirth, and the weather deities sent both needed moisture and drought, deluge, and hail.

Characterizing a spirit as wholly or mostly good or evil often postdated the Conquest. Spanish clergy selected Quetzalcoatl ("Plumed Serpent") of Central Mexico, for example, as analogous to Jesus, and they made Tezcatlipoca ("Smoking Mirror") a demonic figure rather than the mutable trickster of native tradition. [*See* Tezcatlipoca.] European priests sought parallels in indigenous ideology to the Christian God, angels, saints, and demons, and they established an exaggerated dichotomy between native gods.

Pre-Columbian people distinguished between supernaturals and human beings, and this relationship represented a dynamic and unequal balance maintained by the reciprocal exchange of gifts. The deities provided good weather, abundant crops, and a vital and growing family, and they traded these for crops, incense, tobacco, and the hearts and blood that carried human life force. The gods created and sustained the world, and although people were the consumers of natural products, they offered the substances that sustained the gods.

Duality reached its most complete expression in the relationship between men and women. Male and female activities were highly complementary. Men worked in the fields and traveled to other communities to trade, while their wives worked inside the home. Hearth and home stood as the complement to the external area of male activity. In marriage, the male was supposed to be the more active and dominant figure—a distinction often drawn between older and younger siblings as well.

The male/female duality continues to be of great importance to the organization of personal and village life. Correct demeanor and behavior are essential for the wives of important male officeholders. These women become people of authority in the feminine sphere and direct the domestic aspects of civil and religious activities.

Most people saw a distinction between their own communities and the wider world, which included animals, spirits, and unpredictable outsiders with strange habits. Spirits and wild beasts (often the same entities) in the hinterland, on the road, or in other villages made travel away from home and fields dangerous.

Most individuals were neither all good nor all bad; they had a dual nature. Pre-Columbian peoples believed that each day had a character that it conferred on all people born on that date. Some days, and their associated human characters and activities, were positive, but failure to cultivate a positive nature resulted in a negative character. Most good fates contained a counterbalance of negative qualities and possibilities, but negative birthdates did not embody corresponding seeds of good. People with primarily good characters still had bad thoughts and committed bad actions, but a bad character that contained a few good elements did not make a good person.

Physical health required a balance of the dual states of hot and cold, and indigenous peoples had (and continue to have) complex prescriptions for food, activities, and medicines necessary to maintain the correct internal temperature. If the body is too hot or cold, the person becomes ill and perhaps even dies. The health of the mind is intimately tied to the health of the body, and too much or too little heat also affects mental states and attitudes. Cures entail applying hot substances to cold ailments and cold substances to hot diseases.

In life, people established unequal patterns of reciprocal sharing with other human beings and with the deities, but at death, they assumed the status of supernaturals and passed beyond the constraints of human life. Then their relatives asked them for favors. They were expected to provide substantial benefits in the form of crops, children, and successful endeavors. In exchange, their living family members offered food, tobacco, and incense during rituals. Many Mesoamerican people continue to observe this reciprocal relationship in Day of the Dead celebrations.

BIBLIOGRAPHY

Bierhorst, John, ed. *Codex Chimalpopoca*. 2 vols. Tucson, Ariz., 1992. Translation of Nahua texts about the beginning of the world and deities with dual roles and characters.

Sandstrom, Alan R., and Pamela Effrein Sandstrom. *Traditional Papermaking and Cult Figures of Mexico*. Norman, Okla., 1986. Account of modern Nahua reciprocal relations with the gods through ceremonies.

Tedlock, Barbara. *Time and the Highland Maya*. Albuquerque, 1982. Account of modern Maya reciprocal relations with the gods through divination and ritual.

Tedlock, Dennis, ed. *Popol Vuh: The Mayan Book of the Dawn of Life*. New York, 1985. Translation of Maya texts about the beginning of the world and creator couples.

JILL LESLIE McKEEVER FURST

DURÁN, DIEGO (1537–1588), Dominican missionary, historian, and ethnographer. Diego Durán was born in Seville, Spain, and came to New Spain with his family when he was about seven. He grew up in Tetzcoco, in the present state of México, an important learning center where there had been an extensive pre-Hispanic library of books in pictorial form, now called "codices." The inhabitants of Tetzcoco spoke Nahuatl, the language of the Aztec, and the boy soon spoke it as well as his native Spanish. This served him well in his later work among the natives as a friar and as an ethnographer, interviewing Nahuatl-speaking people in rural areas.

Although little is known about Durán's childhood and later personal life, his references to experiences as he interviewed people or observed their activities have allowed us to piece together some details in his biography. When he was still young, his family moved to Mexico City. The boy entered school there. Several institutions educated Spanish and *mestizo* children, as well as Indians of elite families. We do not know where Durán studied, but the polished prose of Tetzcoco did not follow him; his writing style, though colorful and always interesting, does not have the precision and refinement of Bernardino de Sahagún, who came to New Spain as a university-trained adult. Durán was interested in the activities and beliefs of everyone he met: the market people, the Indians who cut wood in the forest, or the women who served his family as domestics and who had once been branded as slaves. Durán commented, too, on the difficult life some of the Spaniards had in the New World. Instead of gold and jewels, many found hardship, poverty, and illness. His acute observations covered innumerable aspects of life in Mexico. Dávila Padilla, in 1625, called Durán's *History of the Indies and New Spain* "the finest account ever written in this field," and Angel María Garibay claimed that Durán was a true ethnographer. Durán's writings thus constitute one of the most valuable sources for students of ancient Mexico.

Durán entered the Dominican Order as a novice in 1556; he later became a deacon in the order's monastery in Mexico City. A number of Dominican monasteries were established around the Valley of Mexico, in what is now the state of Morelos (then the Marquesado), and in

Antequera, now Oaxaca. Durán is said to have been sent to Oaxaca in 1561, but there are no records of his having been there. Rather, he resided in the monastery at Huaxtepec and was vicar at Hueyapan. He wrote that the Marquesado, where these two monasteries were situated, was "one of the most beautiful lands in the world."

Durán did not elicit information from indigenous people with a formal questionnaire, but he consulted elders in the villages and people he met in his daily rounds. He was interested in native pictorial manuscripts or those written in Nahuatl because he believed they could be a key to identifying one of the lost tribes of Israel, from whom he thought the Mexicans might have descended. He also believed that the Mexican culture hero Quetzalcoatl-Topiltzin might actually have been Saint Thomas. He never found proof for these diffusionist ideas, but he did track down a number of documents, evidently pictorial codices, in his search. Unfortunately, he did not preserve them.

Durán, like other religious men in Mexico in the sixteenth century, was dedicated to the evangelization of the natives. The Dominican Order therefore commissioned him to write about indigenous beliefs and ceremonies in Mexico. He wrote that if the work of the ministers "is to be effective and fruitful in their doctrine, to administer the Sacraments one needs more knowledge of the language, customs, and weaknesses of these people." The result of this commission was a three-part work: one volume comprising *The Book of the Gods and Rites* (1574–1576) and *The Ancient Calendar* (1579), and a second volume titled *The History of the Indies of New Spain* (1581). The *History* is based mainly on a document written in Nahuatl, called the *Crónica X* by modern scholars. This document was dedicated principally to the history of the Aztecs, their rulers, and their conquests.

With this wealth of information that followed from Durán's pen, why were his manuscripts lost to the world for centuries? The answer probably lies in waning interest in the religion and beliefs of the Indians during the latter part of the sixteenth century as a result of political and economic consolidation in the country. Furthermore, during the time of Philip II of Spain, the writings of friars in New Spain were expropriated. Durán's manuscripts ended up in the Biblioteca Nacional (National Library) in Madrid, where they are preserved today in the Manuscript Section, catalogued as Vit.24-II.

These documents, now viewed as invaluable segments of Mexican history, lay forgotten until the mid-1800s, when they were discovered by the Mexican scholar José Fernando Ramírez, who had them copied by a scribe. This copy is preserved in the Historical Archive of the National Museum of Anthropology in Mexico (cat. 556 [15585]). Ramírez's copy was published in two parts, in 1867 and 1880. A faulty edition of 1951 was taken from this. Garibay's edition of 1967 is the most reliable in Spanish, although it also relies on Ramírez. The most accurate edition of the *History*, a translation into English from the original Madrid manuscript, appeared in 1994.

We are grateful to Durán for having penned his experiences and memories, which have helped those interested in the history and everyday life of Mexico to understand, in some measure, the culture of a vanished period, with all its fortunes and misfortunes. Durán had promised to produce a "new treatise on things past," but this has never surfaced, if it was in fact written. Durán was ill and old when he finished the *History*, so when he died in 1588, this treatise probably existed only in his mind. If it were to turn up in some dusty archive, the world of Mexican history would indeed be richer.

BIBLIOGRAPHY

Durán, Diego. *Book of the Gods and Rites and the Ancient Calendar.* Translated and edited by Fernando Horcasitas and Doris Heyden. Foreword by Miguel León-Portilla. 2nd ed. Norman, Okla., 1977.

Durán, Diego. *The History of the Indies of New Spain.* Translated and annotated with introduction by Doris Heyden. Norman and London, 1994.

Durán, Diego. *La Historia de las Indias de Nueva España e Islas de Tierra Firme.* Edited by Angel María Garibay. Mexico City, 1967.

DORIS HEYDEN

DYES AND PIGMENTS. The coloring agents in ancient Mesoamerica were dyes, soluble in water and used for textiles, and pigments, insoluble in water and used for painting. Sixteenth-century Spanish writers such as Bernardino de Sahagún recorded some comments on these materials for their economic importance. Related materials are mordants, which fix dyes in textiles, and mediums, which are mixed with pigments to produce paints. Modern chemical analysis of textiles, codices, mural paintings, and other materials have added to the knowledge of the subject. Both ancient and modern writers use color names that may be misleading, since writers are not always specialists and misuse words (e.g., indigo for dark blue, cinnabar for reds). Then, too, in different times and places, the same word may indicate a different material.

White Pigments. In some paintings, whites were the background, but whites were also applied over other colors. The main pigment used was lime (calcite, or calcium carbonate, $CaCO_3$), called *tízatl* by the Aztec. To make it, limestone was burned to produce quicklime, slaked with water, then mixed with sand or inert materials, and applied as the base layer of wall paintings. Stones were also ground with a medium to produce white paint.

Gypsum (naturally occurring hydrated sulphate of calcium, $CaSO_4 \cdot 2H_2O$), called *chimaltízatl*, which was burned and mixed with water, to set as gesso. White clays (kaolin, or China clay, and other unidentified white clays), called *tizatlalli* or *palli*, were also use as white pigments or inert materials, as was the diatomaceous earth, called *tizate*. Whites were also used as mordants for dying or to produce such organic pigments as *sak lu'um, sacalum*, or *castún* ("white powder" in Mayan), the clay mineral palligorkite (also known as attapulgite), or its mixture with sepiolite (meerschaum, a hydrous magnesium silicate, $H_4Mg_2Si_3O_{10}$), the mordant for Maya Blue pigment. The last was also a temper for ceramic clays and was eaten as a remedy for stomach aches; this white earth may have been the *xicaltétl* of Sahagún's informants.

Black Pigments. *Tlilli* is the Aztec name for lampblack (carbon, soot), attained by the smoking of resinous sticks of pine over ceramic pots filled with cold water. The resulting charcoal sticks were used for drawing, but charcoal was also ground to use as carbon black. Graphite (a soft, glossy black carbon found in nature) was kept in decorated ceramic pots. Two mineral blacks were used: magnetite (a black iron oxide, Fe_3O_4), called *tezcatlalli* or *tezcatlilli*, and manganese black (MnO_2), called *wad*. A black ink, called *eek* or *hec*, was obtained using hematoxylin, an extract of logwood (*Haematoxylon campechianun*, or *H. brasiletto*) with a solution of green copperas (ferrous sulfate, $FeSO_4 \cdot 7H_2O$). *Huisache* was an ink from black clay boiled with *huisache* (*Acacia* sp.?) leaves and the bark of *quauhtepoztli*, similar to an ink made by mixing tannins with copperas. In ceramic figures from Veracruz, black was made from bitumen (a natural asphalt), called *chapópotl*.

Red Pigments and Dyes. Three red pigments have been identified; red ocher, clays colored with hematite (Fe_2O_3), called *tláhuitl*, which may refer to the yellow ocher that when fired in a kiln produces the red; cinnabar (HgS), called *tlapalli*; and minium (Pb_3O_4), also known as red lead.

The red dyes included *xochipal* or *xochipalli*, the dyeing flower (*Cosmos solphureus*); the color was obtained from its petals with niter (KNO_3, *tequezquite*) or other mordants, although yellows or browns might be produced. The most important red dye was cochineal, obtained from the bodies of the cactus-eating female insect *Dactilopius coccus*; it proliferates on several species of cactus (mainly *Opuntia ficus-indica*), so the Aztec called it *nocheztli* ("prickly pears' blood"). The dyestuff is carminic acid; when boiled with the crushed leaves of *tézhoatl* (*Conostegia xalapensis*), alum, and copperas, it produces an essence that was formed into small disks called *nochetlaxcalli* (cochineal *tortillas*). Achiote (*Bixa orellana*) is also a source for reds; the dye bixina is extracted from its seeds by boiling water until the color precipitates. To dye cotton yarns, it is mixed with urine. Another red dye is logwood (hematoxylin), called *huizquáhuitl*; it is extracted from the logs of *Haematoxylon campechianun* or *H. brasiletto*, and when exposed to air oxidizes to hematein. With different mordants, it can produce different colors. Hematoxylin is sometimes confused with brazilwood (*Caesalpinia* sp.), which yields the dye brazilin; this oxidizes to brazileina, different substances. A textile dyed with madder has been reported from northern Mexico; madder plants (genus *Rubia*) produce a compound in the root that makes a bright red dye known as alizarin.

Yellow Pigments and Dyes. *Tecozáhuitl* is an earth identified as yellow ocher; after burning, it produces *tláhuitl* as the limonite (clay with hydrated iron oxide) dries, to yield red iron oxide (hematite). Several brown pigments were also obtained from colored earths having iron oxides. Many dyes, when used with different mordants, produced yellow and brown shades. *Zacatlaxcalli* is a yellow dye extracted from a lichen (*Cuscuta tinctoria*); with niter, alum, or gypsum as a mordant, it forms light to dark yellow colors. Similar to the lichen called *cuapastle, quappachtli*, or *cuauhtepoztli*, it produces a better color when mixed with *nacascólotl* (*Caesalpinia coriacea*) and the clay called *palli*.

Green Pigments. There are several green pigments made from minerals: malachite (copper carbonate); green earth; crysocolla; and a copper phosphate that was used for the Teotihuacán murals. *Quíltic* was produced mixing *texotli*, a blue pigment, with *zacatlaxcalli*. *Yapalli* is a green color produced by mixing any yellow with blue pigments.

Blue Pigments and Dyes. Azurite is a copper carbonate similar to malachite and is the only natural blue mineral pigment identified in Mesoamerica. *Matlali* or *matlalin* is a blue obtained from the petals of *Commelina coelestis*, known as chicken herb. *Matlali* is also the name of the blue dye obtained from the Guayacán tree. More resistant and more often used is *muicle* or *mohuitli*, extracted from the plant called *sacatinta* or *mohuitli* (*Jacobinia spicigera*). *Tlacehuili* is the name for native indigo (*Indigofera sufucticosa*), which was extracted from *xiuquílitl*, a New World plant. The indigo dye for exportation to Spain was extracted from *Indigofera tinctoria*, a plant brought in from the Old World. *Tejotlali* or *texotli* is a blue color from Michoacán that was used during the sixteenth century for murals in Christian convents; possibly, it is Maya Blue, the most studied of the Mesoamerican pigments, prepared by dying with indigo the white clay *sacalum* and gently heating it. Seri blue was a pigment used as face paint by the Seri maids; it is prepared with white clay (montmorillonite), the resin from Guyacán (*Guaiacum sp.*), and *Franceria dumosa*.

A purple dye was obtained from the secretions of the shellfish *Purpura patula*; it is like the Phoenicians' Tyrian purple (made from Mediterranean snails). The *Purpura* snails are found on the Pacific coast in the Mexican state of Oaxaca.

Paints. Two drying oils, one extracted from the *chía* (*Salvian chian*) and the other from the *chicalote* (*Argemona mexicana*), were used to make paints. *Tzautli* or *Tzacutli* is an adhesive material taken from the pseudo-bulbs of the orchids *Epidendrum pastoris* and *Bletia campanulata*; it was ground and mixed with gypsum to produce the base layers for the pages of the codices. *Aje*, a fatty substance from the insect *Llavenia axin*, was used to manufacture *maque*, Mexican lacquer.

Mordants. These substances were used in dyes, to fix the colors so that they were insoluble in the fabric fibers. The common mordants were *tequezquite* (niter, saltpeter), alum, white clays, urine, and oxalic acid obtained from *tézhoatl* (*Conostegia xalapensis*).

[*See also* Colors; Painting.]

BIBLIOGRAPHY

Anderson, Arther J. O. "Materiales Colorants Prehispánicos." In *Estudios de Cultura Nahuatl, IV*, pp. 73–83. Mexico City, 1963.

Carrillo y Gariel, Abelardo. *Técnica de la Pintura de Nueva España*. Mexico City, 1983.

Castelló Yturbide, Teresa. *Colorantes naturales de México*. Mexico City, 1988.

Gettens, Rutherford J. "Maya Blue: An Unsolved Problem in Ancient Pigments." *American Antiquity* 27 (1962), 557–564.

Gettens, Rutherford J., and George L. Stout. *Painting Materials: A Short Encyclopaedia*. New York, 1966.

Hernández, Francisco. *Historia de las plantas de la Nueva España*. Mexico City, 1942.

Hoefenk-de Graaff, Judith. *Natural Dyestuffs for Textile Materials: Origin, Chemical Constitution, Identification*. Amsterdam and Brussels, 1967.

Sahagún, Bernardino de. *Historia general de las cosas de la Nueva España. Codice Florentino*. Mexico City, 1956.

Torres Montes, Luis. "Materales y técnicas de la pintura mural de Teotihuacan." *Teotihuacan XI Mesa Redonda*, pp. 17–42. Sociedad Mexicana de Antropología. Mexico City, 1972.

LUIS ALEJANDRINO TORRES MONTES

DYNASTIES. See Rulers and Dynasties.

E

EAGLES. The golden eagle (*Aquila chrysaetos*) is a bird of prey, a raptor that inhabits mountainous and rugged landscapes throughout the Northern Hemisphere, with ranges into Central Mexico, where it is viewed as the most important symbol of mountains and skies and a powerful avatar of the sun. It is a model for warriors, an awesome predator, and a fierce defender of territory. It has a strong beak and large, sharp talons. A splendid flier, it soars effortlessly for hours, rides gale winds, or spirals upward. It can spot a rabbit a kilometer (more than a half mile) away and plummet in a high-speed vertical dive to take the prey.

Platform of the Eagles, Maya-Toltec, Chichén Itzá. *Photograph courtesy of Elizabeth P. Benson.*

Naturalistic eagles, anthropomorphic eagles, and men in eagle costume are common in the pre-Hispanic art of Central Mexico. Eagle-like birds and warriors appear on Teotihuacan murals and vases. Mural paintings at Cacaxtla in Puebla (c.700 CE) depict a battle between eagle warriors and jaguar warriors. On later architectural sculpture at Tula in Hidalgo, as at Chichén Itzá in Yucatán, eagles are portrayed, along with felines, eating human hearts. Eagles and jaguars are paired in scenes of sacrifice in Mixtec codices from Oaxaca, where eagles are also a prominent motif in goldwork.

The eagle was a major Mexica (Aztec) symbol: the tribal and sun god, Huitzilopochtli, had told his people that when they saw the sun (i.e., Huitzilopochtli) in the form of an eagle perched on a cactus whose fruit was red and shaped like a human heart, there they should build their city, Tenochtitlan. The scene—shown on a well-known sculpture, in early manuscripts, and on the present-day Mexican flag—surely had astronomical and geomantic, as well as mythic, meaning.

The Mexica military elite consisted of Eagle Warriors and Jaguar Warriors; their main duty was to provide human hearts to nourish the sun. The Temple of the Sun was called the "House of Eagles" or the "Place of the Great Eagle Vessel" (for sacrificed hearts). Eagle and jaguar thrones were seats of rulership. Eagle feathers were used in the costumes of Mexica gods, priests, warriors, and sacrificial victims; live eagles, eagle skins, and feathered costumes were included on their tribute lists.

Maya depictions of eagles are often identified as the harpy eagle (*Harpia harpyja*), perhaps the world's most powerful eagle; it hunts in the canopy of primary forests and nests in the sacred ceiba tree. It may have inhabited Maya territory in the past, but it has not been reported north of Panama for many decades. Crested eagles seen today in the Maya region are the black-and-white hawk-eagle (*Spizastur melanoleucus*) and the ornate hawk-eagle (*Spizaetus ornatus*), whose traits may have contributed to some mythical Maya birds. Maya bird imagery was a mix of various aspects of eagles, vultures, and hummingbirds, mingled or interchangeable in some contexts.

In Central Mexican and Mixtec calendars, the fifteenth day is "Eagle." The personified form for the *katun* and *baktun* Maya time periods seems to be based on a crested eagle.

Other birds of prey are used symbolically in Mesoamerica. The osprey (*Pandion haliaetus*), a hawk as large as an eagle, sometimes appears in Mesoamerican art, identifiable by the distinctive thick line curving back from the eye. The osprey is usually seen near water, and fish is its primary food; it thus has the symbolism of a water bird, as well as that of an eagle. Other hawks and falcons also share some of the significance of eagles.

BIBLIOGRAPHY
Benson, Elizabeth P. *Birds and Beasts of Ancient Latin America.* Gainesville, Fla., 1997. Pre-Columbian art and lore, with some material on eagles.
Brown, Leslie, and Dean Amadon. *Eagles, Hawks, and Falcons of the World.* Secaucus, N.J., 1989. A thorough, well-illustrated natural history.
Foncerrada de Molina, Marta. *Cacaxtla.* Mexico City, 1993. Pictures, details, and descriptions of the Cacaxtla murals (in Spanish).
López Luján, Leonardo. *The Offerings of the Templo Mayor of Tenochtitlan.* Translated by Bernard R. Ortiz de Montellano and Thelma Ortiz de Montellano. Niwot, Colo., 1994. In addition to descriptions of eagles as offerings, there is discussion of the founding of the city of Tenochtitlan and its major temple.
Sahagún, Bernardino de. *Florentine Codex: General History of the Things of New Spain.* Edited by A.J.O. Anderson and C.E. Dibble. Monographs of the School of American Research and the Museum of New Mexico, 14. Santa Fe, N.M., 1950–1982. This major work by an early observer for the Spanish Crown includes descriptions of Mexica (Aztec) eagle symbolism.

ELIZABETH P. BENSON

EARTH DEITIES. Mesoamerican earth deities embodied the idea of fertility, and more specifically of agricultural fertility. Earth was perceived as the genetrix of all living things, and she was linked to natural phenomena, such as rain: water allowed the staple food crops to grow, and the personified Earth, the Great Mother, then made them germinate and sprout.

Sixteenth-century Mexica (Aztec) ethnohistorical records mention specific domains and functions for each earth deity. Tlazolteotl was associated with weaving or spinning. Others seem to have been related more to political activity; Cihuacoatl, for example, symbolized victory for the Mexica state and the ruling class. Some political rituals were masked under the guise of agricultural ones—for example, the maize rituals, like those associated with Ilamatecuhtli. Most earth deities (e.g., Itzpapalotl) also seem to have been connected with war. Some, moreover, expressed aspects of cosmology, and others were related to sorcery.

There are differences among the earth deities, but there are also many similarities. Allowing for regional variants and functions, most earth deities seem to have performed the same role: promotion of the earth's fertility. The Mesoamerican regions where the Earth Mother cult appears to have been most highly developed were the Gulf Coast (Huasteca) and the *chinampa* (drained marsh field) zone of the Basin of Mexico (modern Mexico City). Tlazolteotl belongs to the Gulf Coast region. In the latter, several goddesses were clearly identified with Gulf counterparts, although they may have had distinct origins. A closely related goddess, *Itzpapalotl-Itzcueye*, seems to have been particularly identified with the earlier, nomadic Chichimec era. Another important goddess, with whom many of these appear eventually to have merged, was Xochiquetzal, who represented the youthful aspect of the mother goddess. The Earth Mother goddesses seem to have been associated with the moon.

Also noteworthy was the martial aspect of the Earth Mother goddesses, especially Cihuacoatl and Tlazolteotl-Ixcuina. Itzpapalotl was considered to have been the first person to die in war. This was directly connected with the role of war in nourishing both the earth and the sun through sacrifice. Itzpapalotl ate deer hearts. Cihuacoatl (Snake Woman) was an important deity to the Mexica, and although she was the goddess of Xochimilco, she was exalted in Tenochtitlan and Tetzcoco, and throughout the Valley of Mexico. Cecelia Klein proposes that Cihuacoatl and her cult were not simply adopted at the time of the Aztec conquest of the southern cities of the Basin of Mexico but rather were forcibly appropriated as a sign of victory. This is suggested by the tradition that the individual who became the first high priest and bore the title of Cihuacoatl was the Aztec war captain Tlacaelel I, half-brother of the ruler Itzcoatl. Some sixteenth-century

Circular stone sculpture depicting Tlaltecuhtli, the Aztec lord of the earth. (Diameter: 37 inches.) *Courtesy of Museo Nacional de Antropología, México, D.F.*

sources associate Cihuacoatl with lasciviousness and forbidden sex, similar to beliefs about Tlazolteotl. In her aspect of Chimalma, Cihuacoatl died in childbirth. Both pregnant women and young children were endangered by her vengeful followers, the Cihuateteo, the souls of women who had also died in childbirth.

Several earth deities had both male and female aspects. An example is Tlazolteotl and Tlaltecuhtli. Tlazolteotl's domain was evil, perversion, lust, and debauchery. She presided over carnal love. She could cause disease, but she could cure as well. She was a goddess of forgiveness through confession. By contrast, Tlazolteotl-Tlaelquani was the Great Parturient, the creative Earth Mother. She was the mother of the fertile earth and also symbolized the earth that receives organic wastes—human and animal excrement, vegetable and fruit remains, fish, fowl, and animal bones—which decompose into humus. She thus symbolized the revitalization of the soil.

Itzpapalotl (Obsidian Butterfly) was also known as Tlazolteotl, Toci, Tonan, Coatlicue, Teteo Innan, and Cihuacoatl-Quilaztli. She was a manifestation of the mother goddess. Itzpapalotl was of Chichimec origin, but the Mexica often incorporated subjugated peoples' deities into their own pantheon. She was connected with war but also with stellar deities. Itzpapalotl embodied the figure of the great Mother Earth Moon. This twofold aspect, in which life becomes death and death life, and one depends on the other, recurs often in Aztec myth and ritual. The colossal sculpture of the earth goddess Coatlicue (Serpent Skirt) at the Museum of Anthropology in Mexico City expresses this notion well: her skirt is decorated with serpents, the great symbols of fertility, and is secured with skull buckles.

The main concept represented by all these deities is agricultural fertility, but war, human sacrifice, and politics were important elements too. The Aztec earth deity Tlaltecuhtli encapsulates this clearly: he was both male and female; he was related to the earth and to agricultural deities such as Mayahuel (goddess of the agave plant) and Tlaloc (god of rain); his cult, however, revolved around warfare and human sacrifice. Thus, Tlaltecuhtli affected both life and death, but the emphasis of his symbolism was on regeneration and life. Tlaltecuhtli is an aspect of the mother goddess, but his dual character is typical of most Mesoamerican deities. The constant overlapping of functions and features among the earth deities indicates that they are all variations on a single theme, associated with the rebirth of the forces of nature and of growth after their apparent death in the dry season. Tlaltecuhtli was considered to be the lord of the earth. According to creation myths, the gods decided that Tlaltecuhtli would bring forth all the food needed to sustain human life. Equally, however, Tlaltecuhtli was linked to

Stone sculpture of Tlaltecuhtli, the earth monster. (Height: 26 inches.) *Courtesy of Museo Nacional de Antropología, México, D. F.*

human sacrifice, because he refused to bring forth fruit if he were not fed with human hearts.

In Aztec sculpture, Tlaltecuhtli figures are frequently carved on the undersides of monuments so that the image of the earth rests directly against the surface of the earth that it symbolized. There are many aspects and variants of Earth Monster representations; a fairly common representation depicts a a "Tlalocoid" conception, in Tlalecuhtli's conventional crouching position with arms upraised, but with a face displaying the rain god Tlaloc's traits.

BIBLIOGRAPHY

Baquedano, Elizabeth. "Aztec Earth Deities." In *Polytheistic Systems*, edited by Glenys Davies, vol. 5, pp. 184–198. 1989.

Baquedano, Elizabeth. "Aspects of Death Symbolism in Aztec Tlaltecuhtli." In *The Symbolism in the Plastic and Pictorial Representations of Ancient Mexico: A Symposium of the 46th International Congress of Americanists, Amsterdam 1988*, edited by Jacqueline de Durand-Forest and Marc Eisinger. Bonn, 1993.

Heyden, Doris. "La diosa madre: Itzpapalotl." *INAH Boletín* 11 (1974), 3–14.

"*Histoyre du Mechique*, Manuscrit français inédit du XVI siècle." *Journal de la Société des Américanistes* (1905).

Klein, Cecelia. *Rethinking Cihuacoatl: Political Imagery of the Conquered Woman*. Oxford, 1988.

Nicholson, Henry B. "Religion in Pre-Hispanic Central Mexico." In *Handbook of Middle American Indians*, edited by Gordon Ekholm and Ignacio Bernal, vol. 10, pp. 395–445. Austin, Tex., 1971.

Sullivan, Thelma D. "Tlazolteotl-Ixcuina: The Great Spinner and Weaver." In *The Art and Iconography of Late Post-Classic Central Mexico*, edited by Elizabet H. Boone, pp. 7–35. Washington, D.C., 1982.

ELIZABETH BAQUEDANO

ECCLESIASTICAL RECORDS. Records of the Roman Catholic church in Mesoamerica go back to the early decades of the sixteenth century, when the first dioceses and religious orders were established and began their missionary, pastoral, and administrative activities. The Archdiocese of Mexico keeps records dating from 1527, and the Franciscan Province of the Holy Gospel (Mexico City) had documents dated 1523 now in the Biblioteca del Museo de Antropología e Historia in Mexico City. Progress in the church's pastoral and administrative activities gave a definitive form to the organization of ecclesiastical records. By the second half of the sixteenth century, there were at least three types of archives: diocesan, parochial, and those of the mendicant orders.

The diocesan archives kept the records originating in episcopal and cathedral offices. Among them are the *libros de gobierno*, records of the bishop's decisions about religious problems in his diocese. Documents on political and religious struggles between the Indian towns and their pastors, or the bishop, appear here and there. Just as important are the records of the ecclesiastical tribunals, such as the Juzgado de Capellanías, which contain a large number of testaments or "pious wills," with information on lineages, family ties, and religious practices and beliefs. The most valuable of all for the study of Mesoamerican cultures are the records of the *provisorato* of the bishoprics. The *provisor*, or vicar general, would take the place of the bishop in judicial matters of the diocese, so he had control over Indian Christian beliefs and practices. This jurisdiction was similar to that of the Inquisition's tribunal over the Spanish and *mestizo* population. During the first half of the sixteenth century, both offices were held at times by a bishop. One was Fray Juan de Zumárraga, the first bishop of Mexico, who—in addition to his ordinary jurisdiction—from 1536 to 1543 held the office of Apostolic Inquisitor, conferred by the Spanish Inquisition. In this capacity, Zumárraga brought to trial about seventy-five Indians accused of pagan practices. These trials' records, however, were kept in the Inquisition office because they were carried out under that jurisdiction. After Zumárraga's harsh death sentence on Cacique Carlos of Tetzcoco, the Spanish Crown withdrew his title as Apostolic Inquisitor. When the Inquisition's tribunal was formally established in Mexico in 1571, the Indian population was excluded from its jurisdiction. From then on, Indian trials for unorthodox practices and beliefs were carried out by the bishops under their ordinary jurisdiction or, if no bishop was available, by missionaries using the prerogatives the pope had granted them.

This ambiguity of ecclesiastical jurisdiction over the Indian population creates problems for the researcher using diocesan records. Geography and chronology provide significant help in this matter. During the sixteenth century, eight dioceses were established in the Mesoamerican region: Tlaxcala, later Puebla, in 1525; Mexico in 1530; Guatemala in 1534; Oaxaca in 1535; Michoacán in 1536; Chiapas in 1539; Guadalajara in 1548; and Yucatán in 1561. Information on the Indian religious practices and beliefs is found in the *provisorato* archives of these dioceses, except for the period 1536–1543 in the diocese of Mexico, when Zumárraga acted as Apostolic Inquisitor. Before the dates of the dioceses' foundation, some missionaries exercised ecclesiastical jurisdiction to bring Indians to trial. The best-known case is that of the Franciscan Fray Diego de Landa, who in 1560 carried out idolatry investigations and trials in Yucatán. The related records are kept not in ecclesiastical archives but in the Justicia and Escribania section of the Archivo General de Indias in Seville. This illustrates the fact that ecclesiastical records are not necessarily to be found in church archives.

Another important section of a diocesan archive consists of cathedral chapter records. The cathedral chapter was the ecclesiastical body that assisted the bishop in the government of the diocese. Its duties included the internal government of the cathedral and its liturgy. It also administered the tithes and other financial affairs of the diocese. Researchers have made excellent use of cathedral chapter records for the study of economic topics. It should be noted, however, that Indian populations were excluded from the payment of tithes, so information on them may be scarce in these records.

The parish archive is one of the richest sources of information on Mesoamerican cultures. Its development was very similar to that in the diocese. The first Mexican church council (1555) prescribed two record books for each parish: baptisms and marriages. The third Mexican council (1585) added a record of confirmations. The 1585 council was explicit as to the contents of each book. The book of baptisms should include the names of the baptized, the parents, and the godparents. The book of marriages should register in one section the names of the groom and bride, their parents, their places of birth, and the names of the witnesses at the wedding. In the same book, but in a different section, the priest should register the dead, including the date of death and the church where the burial took place. The book of confirmations should include the names of the person who received the sacrament, the parents, and the godparents.

The earliest parish records are the books of baptism. Some parishes, such as Tlatelolco in Mexico City, have baptismal records beginning in 1585. Already in these earliest books, some changes begin to appear. Those of Tlatelolco, for example, include the birthplaces as well as the names of the godparents. The books of marriages, dating from the same year, also begin to follow a format different from the one prescribed by the council: instead of registering marriages and deaths in a single book, priests opened a new book exclusively for deaths. Books of confirmations are scarce for the sixteenth century. The importance of these earliest books lies not only in the population data they provide but also in other aspects of Mesoamerican cultures they contain. A good number of them, at least until the second half of the seventeenth century, were written in native languages and probably by native scribes.

Records in parish archives increased quickly. In the sixteenth century, some of them include testaments and wills, as well as confraternities' (*cofradías*) ordinances and administration records, some written in native languages. New parish books were added during the seventeenth century: the *informaciones matrimoniales* with detailed information on family lineages of groom and bride; church inventories, with accounts of church ornaments and images; and, if the town was under the care of a religious order, *directorios*, or guides for the priests on religious celebrations, and the organization and contributions of the parishioners to these feasts.

The archives of the first religious orders to enter New Spain (Franciscans, Dominicans, and Augustinians) are also important for the study of Mesoamerican cultures. The missionaries' writings, letters, memorials, chronicles, and even administrative papers are often the only source left concerning pre-Hispanic cultures. Many of these documents have been published, but a significant number await the attention of researchers. [*See* Augustinians; Dominicans; Franciscans.]

Each religious order had its own archive during Colonial times. As each order was divided into provinces, those formed their own archives. Thus, the Franciscans had six archives corresponding to their six provinces—Santo Evangelio in Mexico City, San Pedro y San Pablo in Michoacán, San José in Yucatán, San Diego in Mexico City, Santiago in Jalisco, and San Francisco in Zacatecas. The Dominicans had four: Santiago in Mexico City, San Miguel in Puebla, San Hipólito in Oaxaca, and San Vicente in Chiapas. The Augustinians had only two: one for the province of Santo Nombre de Jesus in Mexico City, and one for San Nicolás Tolentino province in Michoacán. In addition, the archive of the Franciscan Commissary General of New Spain kept the records of all administrative and judicial matters sent to the Franciscan commissary general in Spain or to the minister general in Rome. Of lesser importance for Mesoamerica are the archives of Franciscan Propaganda Fide colleges, whose missionaries worked mainly north of this region.

In addition to the provincial archives, which might be the equivalent of diocesan archives, the religious orders had local archives in their monasteries, equivalent to the parish archives. In the mid-eighteenth century, the Spanish crown expropriated monasteries in Indian towns to convert them into secular parishes, and most of the monastery records ended up in the parish archives. This was the first misfortune for the religious orders' archives. The second and worse one came in 1859, when the male religious orders of Mexico were suppressed by the government. Most of their provincial archives then went to public libraries. For example, the archives of Santo Evangelio and Jalisco went to the Biblioteca Nacional and Biblioteca del Museo de Antropología e Historia in Mexico City, and to the Biblioteca Pública in Guadalajara. Many documents passed through private hands before reaching the public libraries. Where no public library existed—for example, in Michoacán—the Franciscans were able to keep their provincial archives intact. Some provinces, however, had ceased functioning by the time of their legal suppression; the archive of the Franciscans in Yucatán, one of these, is apparently lost. Archives of other religious orders, the Dominicans and Augustinians, have left little trace of their present whereabouts.

BIBLIOGRAPHY

Cline, S. L., and Miguel León-Portilla. *The Testaments of Culhuacan.* Los Angeles, 1984. Transcription and translation into English of sixty-five Indian wills from the parish of Culhuacan in Mexico City.

Connaughton, Brian F., and Lira González, Andrés, eds. *Las fuentes eclesiásticas para la historia social de México.* Mexico City, 1996. Collection of articles on Mexican ecclesiastical archives, especially diocesan and parochial, and their importance for the study of Mesoamerican cultures.

Garibay Alvarez, Jorge. *Guía de fuentes documentales parroquiales de México.* Madrid, 1996. Short but useful guide to the parochial archives.

Greenleaf, Richard E. *Zumárraga and the Mexican Inquisition, 1536–1543.* Washington, D.C., 1962. Includes a list of the documents on Indian trials, with archival citations.

Mazín Gómez, Oscar. *Archivo capitular de administración diocesana Valladolid-Morelia.* Zamora, 1991. Example of the contents of a cathedral chapter's archive.

Morales, Francisco. *Inventario del fondo franciscano del Museo de Antropología e Historia de México.* Vol. 1. Washington, D.C., 1978. Guide to Franciscan documents; illustrates the various types of documents of a religious order's archive.

Morin, Claude. "Los libros parroquiales como fuente para la historia demográfica y social novohispánica." *Historia mexicana* 21 (1971), 389–418. Calls historians' attention to the importance of parish archives for the study of New Spain's society.

Schwaller, John Frederick. *Guías de manuscritos en Náhuatl* [*Guides to Nahuatl Manuscripts*]: *The Newberry Library* (*Chicago*), *The Latin American Library* (*Tulane University*), *the Bancroft Library* (*Berkeley*). Mexico City, 1987. Includes several documents from parish archives.

FRANCISCO MORALES

ECCLESIASTICAL WRITINGS. [*This entry comprises two articles. The first article presents the historical and hagiographic works written by missionaries, mendicant chroniclers, and church historians during the Colonial* *period; the second article discusses the sermons, prayers, catechisms, theological treatises, and extirpation manuals written by missionaries and church officials during the Colonial period. For related discussions, see Acosta, Joseph de; Burgoa, Francisco de; Durán, Diego; Florencia, Francisco de; Mendieta, Gerónimo de; Missionization; Olmos, Andrés de; and Tovar, Juan de.]*

Historical and Hagiographical Texts

Historical writings were one of the literary genres most widely cultivated by ecclesiastics in New Spain. Though written with historical criteria quite different from those of present-day historians, they contain information on Mesoamerican peoples and their process of Christianization that is not available elsewhere. These texts take various forms. The best known is the so-called religious chronicle, which is characterized by its narrative style. Its principal topic is the historical development of a religious order and its efforts to Christianize Indian communities. By the end of the sixteenth century, these chronicles had a well-defined structure: a section on the origins of the order, one on the conversion of the Indians, a third on the government of the minister provincials, and a final one on its more illustrious members. The last constitutes a real hagiographical text; in fact, parts were occasionally published separately as short biographies.

These religious chronicles do not exhaust the range of ecclesiastical historical writings. In the early decades of the sixteenth century, missionaries began to write historical works with forms and topics quite different from those of the chronicles. Examples are the *Historia de los Indios de la Nueva España*, by the Franciscan Toribio de Motolinía (1490–1569), and the *Historia de las Indias de la Nueva España*, by the Dominican Diego Durán (1537?–1588). Both authors are concerned more with information on Indian communities than with the development of their orders. A different type is exemplified by the *Historia general de las cosas de la Nueva España*, by the Franciscan Bernardino de Sahagún (1499–1590). This work, in spite of its title, is not a proper historical text but an ethnographic one. The *Relación de las Cosas de Yucatán*, by the Franciscan Diego de Landa (1524–1579), and the *Relación de Michoacán*, attributed to the Franciscan Martín de la Coruña (1480–1568) or to Jerónimo de Alcalá (1508–1547?) are similar in purpose. This article discusses writings of a strictly historical character, regardless of their format or title. Ethnographic texts are not included, though they sometimes contain important historical data. Because of their approaches to the evangelization process, we may divide the historical writings by the principal religious orders that produced them. Hagiographical texts are treated in the final section.

Historical Texts by Franciscans. The Franciscans were the missionaries who wrote the earliest historical texts, most of them related to the conversion of the Indians to Christianity. Between 1536 and 1541, Toribio de Motolinía wrote the *Historia de los Indios de la Nueva España*. The title that appears in one of its manuscripts—"Relation on the ancient rites, idolatries and sacrifices of the Indians of New Spain and their marvelous conversion [to Christianity] which God has worked on them"—presages the basic topics that would characterize Franciscan historical writings during the sixteenth century: the culture and religion of the indigenous people, and their conversion to Christianity. Motolinía included some biographical sketches in this work, a practice that would become common in chronicles. Another historical text by the same author, the *Memoriales*, contains very similar material. Scholars have not come to a satisfactory understanding of the relationship of these two works, but both are indispensable for the study of the Nahua peoples of Central Mexico and their conversion.

Jerónimo de Mendieta (1528–1604) opened a second period of historical writing with his *Historia eclesiástica indiana*, written between 1571 and 1604. Though its topics are quite close to those of Motolinía's texts, Mendieta's historical perspective is different. It has a markedly apocalyptic character which envisions Indian Christianity moving from an idealistic origin to a disastrous end. With this work, the Franciscan chronicle reached its standard form, with an ample section on the origin and development of Indian Christianity, another on the activities of the friars, and a final one with biographies of notable friars.

The culminating work among this group of texts is the *Monarquía indiana*, by Juan de Torquemada (1562?–1624). Its subtitle expresses its ambitious objective: "Twenty-one ritual books and Indian Monarchy, with the origin and wars of the Indians in the Western world, their towns, discovery, conquest and conversion [to Christianity] and other marvelous things of their land." Torquemada combines the early historical data of the first Franciscan writers with the accumulated knowledge gathered by later writers. Despite its late date of publication (1615), this text can be considered part of the historiographic trend of the sixteenth century. Many of the sections dealing with the Indians' conversion to Christianity and the history of the Franciscan Order are copied almost verbatim from Mendieta's *Historia eclesiástica indiana*.

As their titles indicate, a general characteristic of these sixteenth-century historical texts is the prominent place accorded to indigenous peoples and the secondary position of the order's development. The Franciscan writers of the seventeenth century redirected their historical approach. Indian communities continued to be an important subject, but the order's historical development became the focus. The great missionary expansion in that century seems to have narrowed the Franciscan sense of history. The production of historical texts is abundant, but the writings are not as fascinating to us as those of the sixteenth century. Two works come from Yucatán, where the Franciscans established the Province of St. Joseph: *Devocionario de Nuestra Señora de Izamal y conquista espiritual de Yucatán*, by Bernardo de Lizana (1580–1631); and the *Historia de la provincia de Yucatán*, by Diego López Cogolludo (1613–1665). Lizana's text, printed in 1633 in Valladolid, Spain, uses the founding of the Izamal Franciscan monastery as a pretext to present the history of the major ceremonial centers near that town. It includes biographical sketches of the first missionaries in Yucatán. Cogolludo's chronicle, printed in Madrid in 1668, follows a structure common in the seventeenth-century chronicles by combining information on civil affairs with ecclesiastical matters. The text also contains an ample biographical section and significant data on missionary activities among the Maya people. For Central Mexico, two chronicles are noteworthy: *Crónica de la santa provincia de San Diego de México*, by Baltasar de Medina (1634–1677?), printed in Mexico in 1682; and *Crónica de la provincia del Santo Evangelio de México*, by Agustín de Vetancurt (1623–1708), printed in 1697. Both chronicles disclose the impact of the Indian missions on the style of historical texts. Medina's work is formed basically around biographies; Vetancurt's, though including an extensive biographical section, centers on Franciscan activities in Indian communities. For the seventeenth century, it provides probably the best information on the religious organization of those communities. Two more seventeenth-century chronicles are worth noting: the *Crónica de la ... provincia de San Pedro y San Pablo de Michoacán*, by Alonso de la Rea (1608?–1661), printed in Mexico in 1643; and the *Crónica miscelánea de la santa provincia de Jalisco*, by Antonio Tello (d. 1653). The first contains information on the evangelization of the Tarascan people; the second, though incomplete, is illuminating on the scantily documented missions of the northern frontier zone of Mesoamerica.

The eighteenth century was also rich in Franciscan chronicles, but these offer few surprises to scholars interested in Mesoamerica. The missionary advance toward the nomadic groups of northern New Spain produced an abundance of writings on the Chichimeca, but few for Mesoamerica. For Central Mexico, we can mention only two significant chronicles, both from Michoacán: the *Crónica de la provincia de Michoacán*, by Isidro Félix de Espinosa (1679–1755), and the *Crónica de Michoacán*, by Pablo Beaumont. Beaumont set out to write the history of the Franciscans in Michoacán from their first contacts

with Tarascan communities to the middle of the eighteenth century, but he reached only the second half of the sixteenth century. The data, generally taken from already published works, add little information on Franciscan activities in Michoacán. Espinosa's chronicle is a more accomplished work, but it does not go beyond the period already covered by Rea in the seventeenth century.

Historical Texts by Dominicans. The earliest and most important texts written by Dominicans came immediately after those of the Franciscans. The prominence of the Dominicans in the Christianization of Mesoamerican peoples is attested by the four religious provinces founded in that region: Santiago de México, San Miguel de Puebla, San Hipólito de Oaxaca, and San Vicente de Chiapas y Guatemala. Equally important was their contribution to the historical literature. Between the end of the sixteenth century and the middle of the seventeenth, Dominicans produced three major chronicles: the *Historia de la fundación y discurso de la provincia de Santiago de México*, by Agustín Dávila Padilla (1562–1604), printed in Mexico in 1596; the *Libro tercero de la historia religiosa de la provincia de México de la orden de Santo Domingo*, by Hernando Ojeda (d. 1615), a continuation of the previous work; and the *Segunda parte de la historia de la provincia de Santiago de México*, by Alonso Franco Ortega (life dates unknown). A characteristic of these three works is the prominent place accorded to biographies. In these, one can perceive nostalgia for a monastic life based on contemplation and study, which seems to have been precluded by missionary activities in Mexico. These chronicles contain unique information on civil and ecclesiastical matters related to the Zapotec and Mixtec communities.

The most valuable seventeenth-century Dominican chroniclers of Mesoamerica are Antonio Remesal (1570–1627?) and Francisco de Burgoa (1600?–1681). Remesal wrote the *Historia de la provincia de San Vicente de Chiapas y Guatemala*, printed in Madrid in 1619. It covers missionary activities not only in Chiapas and Guatemala but also in Oaxaca and Mexico City. Indian communities are its focus. Burgoa wrote two works, the *Palestra historial de virtudes y ejemplares apostólicos*, printed in Mexico City in 1670, and the *Geográfica descripción de la parte septentrional del Polo ártico de la América y Nueva Iglesia de las Indias occidentales*, printed in Mexico City in 1674. Written during the flowering of Baroque literature, these works offer much material on the history of the evangelization of Indian communities in Oaxaca. The *Palestra*, with a biographical emphasis, and the *Geográfica*, with a narrative style, together constitute the best sources on Dominican missionary activities in the Mixtec and Zapotec regions.

A contemporary of these two chroniclers, but without

their literary prestige, is Juan Bautista Méndez (1645?–1703). His *Crónica de la provincia de Santiago de México de la Orden de Predicadores*, only recently edited (Mexico City, 1993), proposes to narrate the early Dominican expansion in Oaxaca, Chiapas, and Guatemala. Méndez used information provided by Remesal and Dávila Padilla. This chronicle offers little about the Indians' conversion to Christianity. Its biographical section is ample, but most of the entries are on missionaries well documented in previous chronicles. Francisco Ximénez (1662–1723) closes this circle of Dominican writers. His *Historia de la provincia de San Vicente de Chiapas* was written around 1720 but not printed until 1929, in Guatemala. Ximénez, like Remesal, provides information on the Indian communities of Guatemala and Chiapas, going back to before the Spanish conquest. He also covers the difficult advance of the Dominicans into the Chol and Lacandón areas and some missionary work in the Verapaz region.

The Dominicans lack the spontaneity and ingenuity of the Franciscan chroniclers, but they offer much historical material on the Mesoamerican Southwest, a region very poorly covered by other printed sources.

Historical Texts by Augustinians. Augustinian friars were present in the Nahua, Otomí, and Tarascan regions of Mesoamerica, and their chronicles complement the information offered by Franciscans for the same area. The first Augustinian chronicler was Fray Juan de Grijalva (1580–1638). His *Crónica de la Orden de Nuestro Padre San Agustín en las provincias de la Nueva España* is a good source of the history of the evangelization of Chilapa, Atotonilco, and Meztitlán, regions not included in the Franciscan chronicles of Jalisco. Like many other chroniclers of his time, Grijalva organized his text around the most notable events during the government of successive minister provincials. The arrival of the Augustinians in the Tarascan communities and their methods of Christianization form part of this chronicle's narrative. If not the center of the text, the Indian communities at least hold a visible place on it.

Esteban García, born in Puebla toward the end of the sixteenth century, is the second chronicler of the Augustinian Order. His *Libro Quinto: Crónica de la provincia agustiniana del Santísimo Nombre de Jesús de México* was meant to be a continuation of Grijalva's four-book work. But more than a complement, García's chronicle is an example of creole pride in the Mexican religious orders. His text is filled with references to the great accomplishments in the province by illustrious Augustinians born in Mexico: Pedro de Agurto, the first creole provincial; Juan de Zapata, bishop of Chiapas and Guatemala; and above all, Bartolomé Gutiérrez, the first Mexican native Augustinian granted the status of "blessed" by the Vatican. His commentaries on ecclesiastical society are noteworthy.

He also offers valuable information on the Christianization of Mesoamerican frontier communities such as Jiliapan and Jalpan.

José Sicardo (1643–1715) closes this series of Augustinian chroniclers with his *Suplemento crónico a la historia de la orden de Nuestro padre San Agustín de México*. This text too was meant to complement previous chronicles, but its narrative reaches only the early years of the seventeenth century. This deficiency is compensated for by an appendix of important sixteenth-century documents. Sicardo's work, unpublished for almost three centuries, is now available in print (Mexico City, 1996).

A second group of Augustinian chroniclers, who came with the establishment of the province of San Nicolás de Tolentino in Michoacán (1602), are represented by Juan González de la Puente (life dates unknown), Diego Basalenque (1577–1651), and Matías de Escobar (1690–1748). Basalenque is the outstanding writer of the group. His *Historia de la provincia de San Nicolás de Tolentino de Michoacán*, printed in 1673, offers the most comprehensive picture of Augustinian evangelization in Michoacán. Though he uses materials from previous chronicles, much of his text is based on original documents. González de la Puente's *Primera parte de la crónica augustiniana de Michoacán*, printed in 1624, is less a historical text than a series of biographies of nine distinguished missionaries in Michoacán. Escobar's *America Thebaida: Vitas patrum [sic] de los religiosos hermitaños de P. San Agustin provincia de San Nicolás Tolentino de Michoacán* is also based on a collection of biographies through which he presents the history of the province as a reflection of the eremitic life of the Desert Fathers of the early church. Escobar's biographies are filled with ascetic exercises and admirable illustrations of Christian virtues. The text also includes bits of information on missionary and pastoral activities in Michoacán.

Other Historical Writings. Of the many texts that remain to be mentioned, those of the Jesuits deserve first place. The Jesuits centered their missionary activity in northern New Spain, outside Mesoamerica, but some of their writings touch significantly on Mesoamerican cultures. The *Historia antigua de México*, by Francisco Javier Clavigero (1731–1787), printed in Italy in 1780, is more ethnographic than historical. The *Historia de la provincia de la Compañía de Jesús*, by Francisco Florencia (1620–1695), is nearer to the chronicles. A complete overview of the missionary activities of the Jesuits is Francisco Javier Alegre's (1729–1788) *Historia de la Compañía de Jesús en Nueva España*, printed in Mexico in 1814.

Other important religious orders were the Mercedarians and the Carmelites. The first was established in New Spain in the last decade of the sixteenth century. Its chronicler, Francisco Pareja (life dates unknown), in

1688 wrote the *Crónica de la provincia de la Visitación de Nuestra Señora de la Merced*. Mercedarians carried out very little pastoral work in Indian communities, but this chronicle is important for the study of the daily life in Mexican monasteries. The Carmelite order was established in 1585 as a contemplative order. Its chronicle, *Tesoro escondido en el santo Carmelo mexicano . . . historia de los Carmelitas Descalzos de la provincia de Nueva España*, written by Agustín de la Madre de Dios in the seventeenth century, is a significant literary piece but is recognized more as a hagiographical text than a historical one.

Hagiographical Texts. Hagiographical texts, the biographies of holy persons, ordinarily formed a section of chronicles. Their main objective was to depict the virtuous life of members of the religious orders. When these texts appeared outside chronicles, nuns, bishops, and other ecclesiastics were also included, and rarely, lay people.

Ecclesiastical writers were quite familiar with the medieval hagiographical literature. The texts of the famous thirteenth-century Dominican hagiographer, Giacomo de Voragine, were present in various libraries of New Spain's monasteries. The medieval Franciscan hagiographical literature also arrived early in the libraries of monasteries and in Indian communities. In fact, the first hagiographical text printed in Mexico was the *Life of Saint Francis* by Saint Bonaventure, translated into Nahuatl by Fray Alonso de Molina in 1577.

The earliest hagiographies were written as independent works and only years later were incorporated into religious chronicles. For example, the life of Fray Martín de Valencia, head of the Twelve First Franciscans, written by his companion, Fray Francisco Jiménez (1480–1560), was later incorporated by Motolinía into his *Historia de los Indios de la Nueva España*. Jerónimo de Mendieta and Pedro Oroz (d. 1597) also wrote a hagiographical collection on Franciscans who died in New Spain before 1585. This text was integrated by Francisco de Gonzaga into his work on the origins of the Franciscan Order, printed in Rome in 1587, and later by Mendieta into his *Historia eclesiástica indiana*.

As a point of departure for the flowering of this hagiographical literature, we can take the life of the blessed Sebastián de Aparicio, written by Juan de Torquemada and printed in 1602. The title of this work, *Vida y milagros del santo confesor de Cristo, fray Sebastián de Aparicio*, announces what would be the favorite topic of this literature in the seventeenth and eighteenth centuries: the life of friars or nuns already beatified or in the process of beatification. Other works of this kind are the *Vida y martirio y beatificación del invicto proto-martir de el Japón, San Felipe de Jesús*, by Baltasar de Medina, printed

in Mexico in 1683, and the *Vida y virtudes heroicas de la madre María de Jesús religiosa profesa en el convento de la Limpia Concepción de la Ciudad de los Angeles* (Puebla), by Francisco García Pardo (d. 1688).

The independent hagiographical texts differed in style and other characteristics from texts written for the chronicles. They were intended to promote a new devotion or to emphasize the practice of Christian virtues in the monasteries as a way of demonstrating that New Spain's church exalted the Christian life as well as its counterpart in Spain. These writings consequently had a local character and contributed to the growing creole nationalism. Their readers as well as their authors came from creole society. From the beginning of the eighteenth century, San Felipe de Jésus was regarded in Mexico City as the saint who "had ennobled our Mexican city." Hagiographies of nuns tended to present the ideals of a feminine religious life in which chastity, self-abnegation, and love of God were extolled.

The hagiographical texts of the religious chronicles were aimed at a different type of reader and thus had a different object. Their readers were principally members of the religious orders, and their objective was to preserve the memory of their founding fathers and other prominent friars in order to provide continuity for their projects, whether evangelization or the sphere of internal life. The styles of these hagiographical texts varied according to the diverse spiritualities of the religious orders and the epochs in which they were written. The early Franciscans, for example, wrote their hagiographies with the evangelical radicalism of the founders of their provinces in mind. Thus, when Mendieta wrote the biographies in the fifth book of his *Historia eclesiástica*, he used the struggle against the enemies of the religious life—"world, demon, and flesh"—as a criterion for choosing the events to be narrated. As a result, his texts are filled with anecdotes related to that struggle: the abandonment of motherland and family to come to the missions, lives of prayer, and ascetic exercises. The Dominicans—for instance, in Dávila Padilla's *Historia de la provincia de Santiago*—underlined the heroic practice of religious vows and engaged in long, erudite discourses on the virtues of their friars. The Augustinian chronicle *America Tebaida* held up for emulation the lives of the early Egyptian hermits.

Various changes are evident in these writings during the Colonial period. After the mid-seventeenth century, the hagiographical section of the chronicles emphasizes not only the virtuous life of the friar but also his position. Often, minister provincials appear in the hagiographical section. The chronicles of provinces with missions on the northern frontier give a special place to friars who died in rebellions at the Indian missions.

The modern reader faces undeniable difficulties in approaching these texts, saturated as they are with marvels or vague formulas for the religious life; yet they offer access to the religious ideas and images that shaped much of social behavior in the Colonial period. Independent hagiographical texts provide material related to creole society's values and behavior; the chronicles illustrate the ideal conduct of the friars working in Indian communities. In both cases, the texts provide unique information for the study of what is today called the history of thought and social responses to the sacred.

[*See also* Acosta, Joseph de; Burgoa, Francisco de; Durán, Diego; Florencia, Francisco de; Guadalupe, Nuestra Señora de; Landa, Diego de; López de Cogolludo, Diego; Mendieta, Gerónimo de; Motolinía, Toribio de Benavente; Olmos, Andrés de; Saints; Torquemada, Juan de; Tovar, Juan de.]

BIBLIOGRAPHY

Baudot, Georges. *Utopia and History in Mexico: The First Chroniclers of Mexican Civilization, 1520–1569.* Translated by Bernard R. Ortiz de Montellana and Thelma Ortiz de Montellana. Niwot, Colo., 1995. Detailed, well-documented study on the first Franciscan writers and their works.

Chávez, Angélico, ed. and trans. *The Oroz Codex.* Washington, D.C., 1972. Hagiographical collection from the sixteenth century; classic example of hagiographical texts.

Lavrin, Asunción. "La vida femenina como experiencia religiosa: Biografía y hagiografía en Hispanoamérica colonial." *Colonial Latin American Review* 2 (1993), 27–52. Following the hagiographies of some Mexican nuns, the author discusses the ideals of female religious life.

León-Portilla, Miguel. "New Light on the Sources of Torquemada's *Monarquía Indiana.*" *Americas* 35 (1978), 287–316. Studies the indigenous sources of Torquemada's chronicle.

Merdader Martínez, Yolanda. *Crónicas y cronistas de la Nueva España: Orden de Predicadores de Santo Domingo.* Tlaxcala, 1984. Illustrative survey on the Dominican writers, with short biographies.

Phelan, John Leddy. *The Millenial Kingdom of the Franciscans in the New World: A Study of the Writings of Gerónimo de Mendieta (1525–1604).* Berkeley and Los Angeles, 1956. Studies the ideas, the cultural and religious background of the famous Franciscan writer.

Rubial García, Antonio. *La santidad controvertida: Hagiografía y conciencia criolla alrededor de los venerables no canonizados de Nueva España.* Mexico City, 1999. Thoughtful study of hagiography and Mexican society.

Steck, Francis Borgia, ed. and trans. *Motolinía's History of the Indians of New Spain.* Washington, D.C., 1951. English translation of one of the classic religious chronicles.

FRANCISCO MORALES

Devotional Texts and Manuals

Works on religious practice played an important role in the cultural development of post-Conquest Mesoamerican societies. Through them the early missionaries, and later the pastors, modeled the religious and moral practices of their parishioners. Devotional texts can be defined as those dealing with pious practices such as prayers, devotions to the saints, novenas, processions, and other expressions of popular religion. Manuals are related to the instruction either of the faithful—for example, catechisms—or of the clergy themselves, such as *confesionarios* (guides for priests hearing pastors confessions). This article also discusses texts intended to regulate the performance of the Roman Catholic church's rites and sacraments.

Devotional Texts. The early establishment of the printing press in Mexico (1539) gave the missionaries, almost from the beginning of their evangelization, a valuable instrument to mold the religious life and practices of the recently converted peoples. The first books printed in Mexico, however, almost ignored the devotional life of Mesoamerican Christianity. Of 178 books printed during the sixteenth century, only three can be considered devotional texts: *Libro de horas* (1567), the *Modo de rezar el rosario* (1576), and the *Psalmodia christiana* (1583). The first, written in Latin, is a collection of psalms to be repeated during the day, following the order of the divine office recited by the clergy, a common practice among the faithful during that century. The second is a brief treatise on how to recite the Rosary, a devotion spread throughout the Catholic Church during the pontificate of Pius V (1566–1572). The last is one of the most notable sixteenth-century devotional tests. Written in Nahuatl by Fray Bernardino de Sahagún, the *Psalmodia* combines the traditional indigenous manner of praying with the Judeo-Christian tradition. This collection of songs (Sahagún calls them psalms) was to be used on principal feast days—a Christian adaptation of pre-Hispanic song and dance performances. Scholars of Nahua literature seem to have a low opinion of the poetic value of these songs, but this text is a notable effort to integrate the rhetorical style of the old religion with Christian devotional forms. An oft-mentioned devotional text, the *Cancionero espiritual*, one attributed to Fray Bartolomé de las Casas, is now considered to be derived from a nineteenth-century history of Spanish literature.

In addition to these printed devotional texts, there are several manuscript ones in Mexican and U.S. public and private libraries. The "Exercicio Quotidiano" (Ayer Ms. 1484, Newberry Library, Chicago) is a Nahuatl text written by Sahagún, containing daily meditations on biblical themes. But even taking into account these manuscripts, it seems certain that the composition of devotional texts was very rare in sixteenth-century New Spain—an unsurprising fact, considering the early missionaries' well-documented concern for an austere and sober piety. In the first decades of the seventeenth century, a few more were published. A work by Alonso de Molina in Nahuatl, instruction in reciting the Rosary, appeared in 1605, as *Ro-*

sario o psalterio de nuestra Señora. In 1611, two devotional texts appeared: the *Breves meditaciones para todo el año*, by the Jesuit Nicolás de Anaya, and the *Camino del cielo*, by the Dominican Fray Martín de León. All three texts continue the austere line of Christian devotions. The *Camino del cielo* includes some devotional practices that characterized the religious life of its period: Holy Communion, Christian death (*arte de bien morir*), and the Mass.

Around the 1650s, the flowering of devotional texts began. To the devotions just noted, new ones were added: prayers for souls in Purgatory, spiritual exercises, and Holy Week devotions. In the 1680s the favorite topic of the Colonial period appeared: devotions to the saints, which with the novenas, *octavas* (the eighth day after the feast day), and *decenas* (ten days of celebrations) dominated religious practice for the rest of the Colonial period. By the end of the eighteenth century, there was hardly a day without a special devotion to a saint. The first day of every month was dedicated to Divine Providence, the third to Saint Francis Xavier, the fourth to Saint Francis of Assisi, the seventh to Our Lady of Sorrows, the eighth to Saint John of God, and so on.

Manual Texts. The production of these texts followed an opposite trajectory from that of devotional texts: abundant in the sixteenth century, but scarce in the seventeenth. An explanation of this trend can be found in the early missionaries' concern for evangelization based on the fundamental teachings of the church rather than on devotions. Thus, one of the most frequently written and published texts during the sixteenth century was the catechism, which was printed in many Indian languages: ten titles in Nahuatl, five in Tarascan, two in Mixtec, two in Huastec, and one each in Zapotec, Quiché, Otomí, and Chuchona (an almost extinct language). This concern for religious instruction also emerges from the analysis of some Spanish catechisms printed in that period in Mexico. For instance, the *Regla cristiana breve*, printed in 1544 by the first bishop of Mexico, Fray Juan de Zumárraga, is an interesting example of Erasmus's influence on the ideas and practices of the first missionaries.

The contexts of these early catechisms allow us to consider further the reasons for the paucity of devotional texts. The *Doctrina breve*, printed in 1546 by Zumárraga, covers not only the Ten Commandments and an explanation of the Articles of Faith but also the most frequent devotional practices: confession, Holy Communion, Mass, and sermons. The *Regla cristiana*, published in 1547 by Zumárraga, contains one chapter on "How to pray in the morning" and another on "How the Christian has to reconsider himself [*recogerse*] every night and examine his acts." These and other texts indicate that the early catechisms were more than mere collections of religious formulas to be learned by heart: many were small treatises on the Catholic faith. For instance, the *Doctrina cristiana en lengua española y mexicana*, published by the Dominicans in 1548, is a lengthy explanation of Christian doctrine in forty sermons.

In addition to this type of manual produced and printed in Mexico, some older works on Christian life originally published in Spain were reprinted in Mexico. Juan Gerson's *Tripartito*, intended to introduce the faithful to the mystical tradition of the church, appeared printed in Spain in 1526 and was reprinted in Mexico in 1544. Saint Bonaventure's *Teología mística* was reprinted three times in Mexico (1549, 1575, and 1594). There were similar works written specifically for Indian communities, such as the *Coloquios de paz y tranquilidad* (1582), written in Nahuatl by the Franciscan Juan de Gaona.

Another topic frequently dealt in manuals was the administration of the sacraments, mainly matrimony and confession. Eight Nahuatl works on matrimony were published during the sixteenth century. Grammars and vocabularies of Indian languages were also well represented in this period, with eleven printed texts: four in Nahuatl, three in Tarascan, two in Zapotec, and one each in Chiapanec and Mixtec.

In the first half of the seventeenth century, manuals dealt with topics similar to those of the sixteenth century. Between 1601 and 1653, ten catechetical works were published in Indian languages: six in Timicuana (a language of northern Florida), two in Nahuatl, and one each in Mazahua and Mayan. Grammars and vocabularies maintained their presence with four works on Nahuatl, two on Mame (Chiapas), one on Zapotec, and one on Timicuana. The administration of the sacraments is also well represented, with fifteen titles, most of them now in Spanish. Mystic and ascetic life is the subject of two noteworthy Nahuatl works: *El libro de la miseria y brevedad de la vida del hombre* (1604), by the Franciscan Juan Bautista, and *Espejo divino* (1607), by the Dominican Juan de Miganjos.

As the seventeenth century advanced, a shift in topics occurred in manual texts; now published sermons predominated. In the 1680s, of eighty ecclesiastical works printed, seventy-four contained sermons while only ten had manual texts.

[*See also* Ruiz de Alarcón, Hernando; Serna, Jacinto de la; Valadés, Diego.]

BIBLIOGRAPHY

Anderson, Arthur J. O., ed. and trans. *Bernardino de Sahagún's Psalmodia Christiana (Christian Psalmody)*. Salt Lake City, 1993. English translation, with well-documented introduction, of Sahagún's devotional text.

Durán, Juan Guillermo. "La transmisión de la fe: Misión apostólica, catequesis y catecismos en el Nuevo Mundo (Siglo XVI)." In *Historia de la evangelización de América*. Vatican City, 1992. General analysis of sixteenth-century catechisms, with a documentary appendix of the catechism of the Third Mexican Council.

García Icazbalceta, Joaquín. *Bibliografía mexicana del siglo XVI*. Mexico City, 1972. Reprint of a bibliographic compilation originally published in 1886.

Garibay, Ángel María. *Historia de la literatura Náhuatl*. 2 vols. Mexico City, 1953. Includes ample discussion of the most important catechetical and manual texts written in Nahuatl during the sixteenth and seventeenth centuries.

Hérnández de León-Portilla, Ascensión. *Tepuztlahcuilolli: Impresos en náhuatl, historia y bibliografía*. 2 vols. Mexico City, 1988. Most complete reference on texts written in Nahuatl.

Medina, José Toribio. *La imprenta en México, 1539–1821*. 8 vols. Santiago de Chile. Best current reference work for printed texts of the Mexican Colonial period.

Vázquez Janeiro, Isaac. *Caeli novi et terra nova: La evangelización del Nuevo Mundo a través de libros y documentos*. Vatican City, 1992. Brief catalog of sixteenth-century books and documents related to the evangelization of Mexico.

FRANCISCO MORALES

ECLIPSES. To the naked eye, eclipses dramatically transform the Sun and Moon, compromising their normal behavior with an interruption of their usual light. Although the timing of eclipses is fundamentally periodic, these events are infrequent and varied enough to be regarded by most peoples as departures from the customary rhythms of the sky.

In a total solar eclipse, the entire disk of the Sun is covered by the Moon's dark silhouette. This dramatic reduction of sunlight allows the much fainter corona, the Sun's outer atmosphere, to be seen. An extended garment of veils, ribbons, and plumes of pearly light, the corona is accompanied by an eerie twilight that envelops the sky and usually by the appearance of planets that would go unseen in a normally bright day. The landscape is stunningly altered, and despite the brevity of totality, the event profoundly affects human behavior. Even a deep partial solar eclipse significantly modifies the lighting, and the incomplete coverage of the Sun's disk is clearly evident.

Lunar eclipses always occur at full moon, and so they convert the full, white disk into an untimely crescent. In a total lunar eclipse, sunlight that leaks through the Earth's atmosphere tints the moon's dark disk with an odd copper-red light. Stars that were lost in the bright moonlight assert themselves until the Moon regains its former brilliance.

Shortly after the Spanish conquest, Fray Bernardino de Sahagún described the Aztec response to eclipses in his *General History of the Things of New Spain*. People were disturbed. They made noise, killed captives, and sacrificed their own blood on behalf of the faltering, troubled Sun. Darkness and the emergence of the *tzitsimime* ("demons of darkness"—most likely Venus and other planets that appear as totality nears) inspired fear of the world's end. Lunar eclipses were also alarming, and pregnant women were judged to be especially vulnerable during those events.

In Yucatán, the Mayan word for "eclipse" incorporated the root for "bitten," and by implication the Sun and Moon are devoured during an eclipse. Various creatures were identified as the hungry predator. Eclipse glyphs in the *Dresden Codex* (the Maya hieroglyphic divinatory almanac from Postclassic Yucatán) are suspended above the gaping jaws of snakes. Detailed analysis by the mathematician Michael Closs (1989) identifies the voracious agent of eclipses as the planet Venus. In the Central Mexican highlands, the eclipse beast was sometimes represented as a jaguar.

Throughout Mesoamerica, people reacted to eclipses and engaged in ritual behavior on behalf of the threatened Sun and Moon, but effective eclipse prediction is demonstrated only by the Postclassic Maya of Yucatán. In the *Dresden Codex*, pages 51 through 58 operate as an eclipse almanac. By matching 405 lunations with 46 cycles of the 260-day ritual calendar, the compiler of this document created an almanac that correctly identifies dates when eclipses are possible. Although detailed interpretations of this table differ, it is a product of systematic observation and record-keeping. Links between this table and the 584-day visual cycle of the planet Venus imply that the Maya's blaming of eclipses on that planet was reinforced—and perhaps inspired—by astronomical numerology.

[*See also* Moon; Planets; Sun.]

BIBLIOGRAPHY

Aveni, Anthony F. *Skywatchers of Ancient Mexico*. Austin, Tex., 1980. Pioneering, comprehensive survey of indigenous astronomy in Mesoamerica.

Aveni, Anthony F., and Edward E. Calnek. "Astronomical Considerations in the Aztec Expression of History: Eclipse Data." In *Ancient Mesoamerica*, in press. Demonstrates that Aztec presentations of history linked significant events with solar eclipses, fulfilling symbolically significant calendric criteria.

Bricker, Victoria, and Harvey Bricker. "A Method for Cross-dating Almanacs with Tables in the Dresden Codex." In *The Sky in Mayan Literature*, edited by Anthony F. Aveni, pp. 43–86. New York, 1992. See pp. 73–81 for more possible eclipse references in Maya codices.

Closs, Michael P. "Cognitive Aspects of Ancient Maya Eclipse Theory." In *World Archaeoastronomy*, edited by Anthony F. Aveni, pp. 389–415. Cambridge, 1989. Comprehensively collects indigenous Mesoamerican eclipse lore from ethnographic sources and innovatively synthesizes Maya eclipse imagery to identify Venus as a primary agent of eclipses.

Justeson, John S. "Ancient Maya Ethnoastronomy: An Overview of Hieroglyphic Sources." In *World Archaeoastronomy*, edited by Anthony F. Aveni, pp. 76–129. Cambridge, 1989. Modern milestone in the literature of Maya astronomy, with detailed commentary on the calendar, planetary and lunar tables, eclipses, constellations and asterisms, and directions.

Krupp, E. C. *Beyond the Blue Horizon: Myths and Legends of the Sun, Moon, Stars, and Planets.* New York, 1991. The only modern, worldwide, cross-cultural survey of celestial mythology, with analysis of its function.

E. C. KRUPP

ECOLOGY. *See* Mesoamerica, *article on* Geography.

ECONOMIC AND TRIBUTE MANUSCRIPTS.

Pre-Hispanic Mesoamerican civilizations required formal systems of recording and accounting to manage the complex affairs of state. It was especially important for political administrations to record assessments and income in taxes and tributes, to keep track of financial accounts of labor duties and personal service, and to maintain censuses of individual tax-paying households. These accounting needs continued under the region's Spanish colonial rule. In general, the documents that resulted from these needs recorded the production and distribution of material goods, and the allocation of land and labor. This article focuses on material goods and labor; the distribution and allocation of land is discussed elsewhere. [*See* Property and Land Tenure.]

Almost all existing pictorial manuscripts with economic content were produced after the Conquest, and only a precious few refer explicitly to pre-Hispanic times. Nonetheless, documents from the Early Colonial period to some extent reflect pre-Hispanic conditions that continued into the Colonial era. The most significant pictorial manuscripts that overtly document pre-Hispanic economies are the *Matrícula de Tributos* and the *Codex Mendoza*, followed by the *Codex Azoyu 2*, *Humboldt Fragment 1*, the initial pages of the *Codex Kingsborough*, and portions of the *Mapa de Quinatzin*. Among the numerous documents that pertain to the Colonial period, a few are especially important for understanding indigenous economies: *Codex Mariano Jiménez*, *Matrícula de Huexotzinco*, *Codex Chavero*, *Codex Sierra*, and the remainder of the *Codex Kingsborough*.

Among the extant pictorial documents that broadly record pre-Hispanic tribute demands, the most thorough and accessible are the *Matrícula de Tributos* and the second section of the *Codex Mendoza*. These documents are nearly identical; it is possible that the *Mendoza* was copied from the earlier *Matrícula*, or that both were copied from a common antecedent. They group geographically neighboring communities into tribute-paying provinces; the more complete document, the *Codex Mendoza*, groups 371 communities into thirty-eight distinct provinces distributed throughout central and southern Mexico. The *Matrícula*, though it is probably the older of the two tallies (and perhaps dates from pre-Hispanic times), lacks

five pages included in the *Mendoza* (for the provinces of Axocopan, Atotonilco de Pedraza, Tlachquiauhco, Tochtepec, and Oxitipan) and has lost glyphs for some communities through wear and tear, especially along the margins. However, this older document is enriched by the inclusion of Nahuatl as well as Spanish glosses. With the exception of community names and personal names and titles, the *Mendoza* glosses and commentaries are almost exclusively in Spanish. These tribute tallies are especially significant for the information they impart on resource availability throughout the empire, the arrangement of political jurisdictions, manufacturing and specializations in the provinces, regional cultural variation as seen in provincial styles of specific material goods, and the needs of the imperial powers as reflected in the demands they made on their conquered subjects.

Additional information on pre-Hispanic tribute obligations is revealed in portions of other pictorial documents. For instance, leaf 2 of the *Mapa Quinatzin* portrays the Tetzcocan palace as a political center administering eight major tribute districts. On a political level, this leaf symbolizes administrative and military domination. On an economic level, it records tribute obligations in goods and services by specific towns, along with their delivery schedules. This document amplifies and expands our knowledge of imperial tribute: while the *Matrícula de Tributos* and *Codex Mendoza* focus on economic control by the Mexica rulers at Tenochtitlan, the *Mapa Quinatzin* illustrates the extent of economic control exercised by Tetzcoco as a second member of the imperial Triple Alliance. Also from this eastern region of the Basin of Mexico, the first part of the *Codex Kingsborough* addresses tributes from the inhabitants of the town of Tepetlaoztoc. Farther south, from Tlapan in Guerrero, come the *Codex Azoyu 2* and its continuation, *Humboldt Fragment 1*. The *Codex Azoyu 2* spans the years 1429–1564 and records tribute owed to local rulers. These tributes, in gold and clothing, were delivered quarterly according to indigenously depicted months (Tlacaxipehualiztli, Etzalcualiztli, Ochpaniztli, and Panquetzaliztli). These documents offer a picture of local-level tribute demands during the time of Aztec hegemony.

Numerous other pictorial documents depict economic flows in Spanish colonial times. The information presented in these codices necessarily reflects colonial conditions, but some details relevant to pre-Hispanic economic life can be extracted from them. The *Codex Mariano Jiménez*, for instance, documents tributes paid by the town of Otlazpan, northwest of the Basin of Mexico, during 1549 and 1550. This codex, supplemented with Spanish and Nahuatl texts, provides native-style pictorial details on periods of tribute collection and types of tribute (including cacao, turkeys, firewood, clothing, agricultural pro-

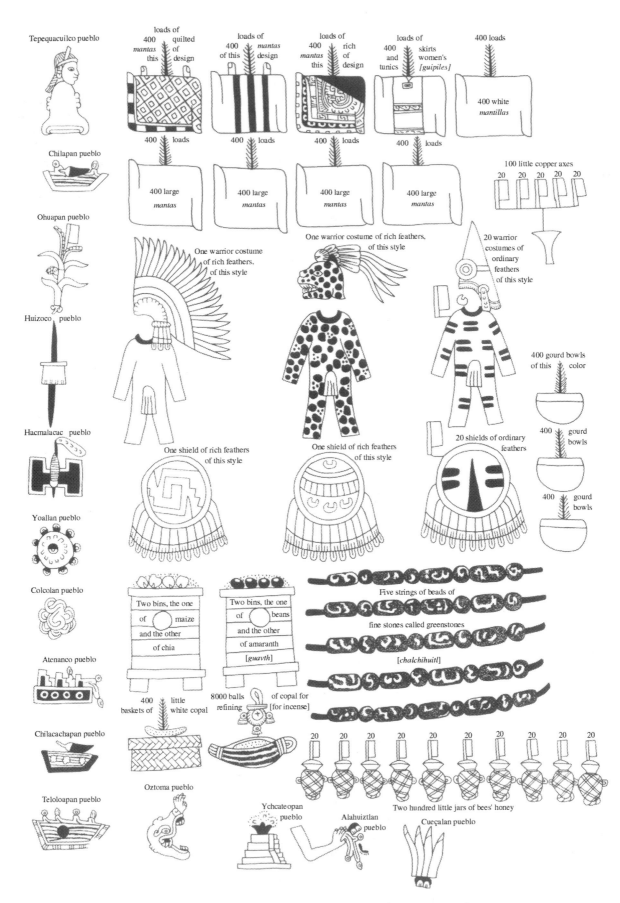

Tepequacuilco pueblo

loads of 400 *mantas* this quilted of design

loads of 400 of this *mantas* design

loads of 400 *mantas* this rich of design

loads of 400 and tunics skirts women's [guipiles]

400 loads

400 white *mantillas*

Chilapan pueblo

400 loads

400 large *mantas*

400 loads

400 large *mantas*

400 loads

400 large *mantas*

400 loads

400 large *mantas*

100 little copper axes

20 20 20 20 20

Ohuapan pueblo

One warrior costume of rich feathers, of this style

One warrior costume of rich feathers, of this style

20 warrior costumes of ordinary feathers of this style

Huizoco pueblo

400 gourd bowls of this color

400 gourd bowls

Hacmalacac pueblo

One shield of rich feathers of this style

One shield of rich feathers of this style

20 shields of ordinary feathers

400 gourd bowls

Yoallan pueblo

Colcolan pueblo

Two bins, the one of maize and the other of chia

Two bins, the one of beans and the other of amaranth [guavth]

Five strings of beads of

fine stones called greenstones

[chalchihuitl]

Atenanco pueblo

Chilacachapan pueblo

400 little baskets of white copal

8000 balls of copal for refining [for incense]

20 20 20 20 20 20 20 20 20

Oztoma pueblo

Two hundred little jars of bees' honey

Teloloapan pueblo

Ychcateopan pueblo

Alahuiztlan pueblo

Cueçalan pueblo

Tribute page from *Codex Mendoza. Courtesy of Frances F. Berdan.*

duce, and personal service). Similarly, parts 2–4 of the *Codex Kingsborough* contain an annual record of tribute demands spanning the years 1522 through 1554. These tributes were paid in goods and services to the local Spanish *encomendero* and offer an interesting comparison with the pre-Hispanic tribute of the town of Tepetlaoztoc, as recorded in the first part of the *Codex Kingsborough*. Farther to the east in the Puebla-Tlaxcala region, the *Codex Chavero* depicts tribute payments during 1571–1579 for seventeen communities in the region, including Huexotzinco. This document is complemented by the *Matrícula de Huexotzinco*, a massive census for that town compiled in 1560. In terms of economics, the *Matrícula de Huexotzinco* identifies many individuals by occupation; many of these specializations were common in pre-Hispanic times, such as stoneworkers, matmakers, painters, featherworkers, and honey-gatherers. This is an invaluable source of information on economic specialization.

Beyond the central valleys of Mexico, the *Codex Sierra* depicts the expenses of the town of Texupan in the Mixteca Baja from 1550 to 1564 in the support and maintenance of its colonial church. Its thirty-one pictorial and glossed pages illustrate not only such Spanish introductions as coinage, candles, and silk, but also native material goods such as turkeys, cacao, carrying frames, and woven maps. Such a pictorial document, amply glossed in Nahuatl, offers a wealth of information on the juxtaposition of indigenous and introduced material culture in the Early Colonial period.

Together, these economic codices provide pictorial documentation on production, specialization, exchange, and tribute from various areas of Mesoamerica. In addition, the information they contain is amplified by numerous textual accounts such as histories, chronicles, and the *Relaciones geográficas*.

[*See also* Mendoza, Codex; Tributos, Matrícula de.]

BIBLIOGRAPHY

Berdan, Frances F., and Patricia Rieff Anawalt. *The Codex Mendoza*. 4 vols. Berkeley, 1992. Comprehensive analysis, description, translation, and color facsimile of the *Codex Mendoza*, which includes a tribute tally of Aztec imperial provinces; condensed paperback version published as *The Essential Codex Mendoza* (Berkeley, 1996).

Boone, Elizabeth. "Manuscript Painting in Service of Imperial Ideology." In *Aztec Imperial Strategies* by Frances F. Berdan et al., pp. 181–206. Washington, D.C., 1996. Analysis of codices as they pertained to Aztec empire-building; places the *Codex Azoyu 2* in this context.

Leander, Birgitta. *Codice de Otlazpan*. 2 vols. Mexico City, 1967. Thorough analysis of the *Codex Otlazpan* in one volume, and a facsimile reproduction of the codex in the other.

León, Nicolás. *Códice Sierra*. Mexico City, 1982. Facsimile reproduction of the *Codex Sierra*, with translations of the glosses and interpretations of the pictorial glyphs.

Matrícula de Tributos. Commentary by Frances F. Berdan and Jacqueline de Durand-Forest. Graz, 1980. Facsimile of the *Matrícula de Tributos*, with descriptions of the codex and its place in the Aztec economic system, and translations of the Nahuatl glosses.

Offner, Jerome A. *Law and Politics in Aztec Texcoco*. Cambridge, 1983. Discussion of the legal life of Tetzcoco, including detailed analysis of the *Mapa Quinatzin*.

Prem, Hanns J. *Matrícula de Huexotzinco*. Graz, 1974. Facsimile of the *Matrícula de Huexotzinco*, with commentary in German and an introduction by Spanish by Pedro Carrasco.

Robertson, Donald. *Mexican Manuscript Painting in the Early Colonial Period: The Metropolitan Schools*. New Haven, 1959. Classic discussion and interpretation of Mexican codices dating from the sixteenth century.

FRANCES F. BERDAN

ECONOMIC ORGANIZATION AND DEVELOPMENT.

[*This entry comprises two articles. The first article discusses economic organization and development among pre-Hispanic Mesoamerican cultures; the second article presents an overview of economic organization and development among post-Conquest Mesoamerican cultures. For related discussions, see* Craft Production; Haciendas and Plantations; Markets; Merchants; Textile Industry; Tourism; Trade and Exchange; *and* Workshops.]

Pre-Hispanic Cultures

The economic system of highland central Mexico is outlined here, with an emphasis on the organization of production and the distribution of wealth.

Ancient Mexico had a politically integrated economy. The government controlled the basic means of production, land, and labor, and accumulated the surplus in the form of tribute. The social division of labor was defined by a stratification system in which members of each estate were assigned different positions in the economic process. Rights to land were assigned to individuals and institutions on the basis of status. Rulers and officials had the right to demand services and tribute and to dispose of the wealth accumulated as tribute. The commoners were the ruled and were obliged to give tribute and labor services.

Rights to land were politically regulated; different types of land were defined according to the institution or social rank of the person to whom the land was assigned. There was the land of the ruler (*tlatocamilli*), as well as other lands assigned to the palace (*tecpantlalli*), a lord (*teuctlalli*), or a nobleman (*pillalli*). These lands were held for life and transmitted by inheritance; others were assigned to support office holders, such as judges. The ruler himself had both office lands, by virtue of his position, and patrimonial lands, inherited from his ancestors. All these types of land were cultivated by various types of peasants.

The lands of towns and barrios (*altepetlalli* and *calpollalli*) were another important category. From these, peasant households received plots for family use, for which they gave labor services and tribute.

There was also "purchased land" (*tlalcohualli* or *milcohualli*) that could be sold, yet with some restrictions. Nobles could sell some types of land to each other, but the commoners could not alienate land without permission.

As a condition for the usufruct of land, the commoner paid tribute both in kind and in labor. In all units of agricultural production larger than the individual commoner household, production was organized on the basis of the land controlled by an official or institution, as well as the labor of the commoners subject to them. Production, therefore, was based on the political control of labor as well as of land.

The lands of the king and the nobility were usually cultivated by commoners from the barrios. In other cases, parcels of land were given to tenants, required to supply the labor necessary for the *tlatoani*'s demesne; peasants under noble landlords are described in some sources as a separate social category of farmhands (*mayeque*).

Another type of labor was that of the so-called slaves (*tlacotin*), individuals who had pledged their labor but otherwise kept their full rights; some prisoners of war became slaves of the rulers. Neither group was a basic source of labor.

Individuals without land paid no tribute. Some men hired themselves out to work as field hands or porters; women hired themselves as weavers. There is no record, however, of any large productive unit relying on wage labor.

The household of farmers was a basic unit of production. It might comprise several married couples, usually related, and occasionally servants and slaves. All members cooperated in the production of goods for household consumption, for exchange in the marketplace, and for payment of tribute in kind; they also gave labor services. Men worked at cultivation, and all knew how to do stonework, build a simple house, make twine or rope, and other simple tasks. Women took care of the children, ground maize, cooked, and made textiles.

The barrio was a corporate unit, with communal administration of the land and collective responsibility for the payment of tribute. The land apportioned to a farming household was transmitted by inheritance, and within a given community there often were great differences in the amount of land held by each household. The lord would not take it away as long as the tribute was paid, but the farmers could not alienate the land without his permission and without having the local ward official record in the register of lands and residents the name of the new landholder, who would assume the tribute obligation. When lands were left vacant, because the holder died without heirs or left the barrio, the official reported this to his superior so that the land could be allotted to a new person; in the meantime, all the villages of that barrio cultivated the land in order to pay the tribute.

Households were also units for craft production. Artisans paid tribute in kind or labor according to their craft and made goods for the market. The principal specialties, found in most villages, were those of carpenters, stoneworkers, masons, potters, basketmakers, mat makers, and sandal makers. Others made paper or salt. The most skilled artisans, many working in the palaces, were the goldsmiths, featherworkers, woodcarvers, sculptors, precious stone workers, and painters. The rulers' wives and servants were skilled weavers.

Artisans passed on their craft to their sons. For their contribution of goods and labor, artisans were organized separately from the farmers. Within a single craft group there were different types of production units; some worked at home, others at the tribute collection house or in the palace.

Because many craftspeople also held land, they must have worked at their craft only part time. They had been granted land from the ruler for their maintenance, but they also received compensation for their work or products. Some specialists—such as hunters, flower makers, and jugglers—lived in various wards supported by their farmer neighbors and had to contribute their services to the rulers, especially for public works and festivals.

Some plots were worked in common for the needs of the barrio, and the land of the barrio chief was also worked in common. For tribute payments and labor drafts, the commoners were organized in teams of twenty or multiples of twenty, under the direction of headmen charged with collecting tribute and taking their teams to provide labor for public works.

The palace of a ruler, and on a smaller scale of a nobleman, was a unit of production and consumption. The lords depended on the labor of their commoners for the construction and repair of their palaces. Their subjects also contributed domestic labor—cleaning and cooking—and brought water, firewood, and food for daily use.

The palace was also the administrative center for the organization of large-scale public works, such as the construction of public buildings, causeways, and hydraulic works. Tribute provided the construction materials and food for the drafted workers.

Goods moved as tribute from the producer to the political superior, whether king or nobleman. Farmers, as well as artisans and merchants, paid a third of what they produced; labor for public works, like military service, was given according to need. The amount of tribute was assessed through procedures that varied from one region to another. In central Mexico, payment in proportion to the amount of land was predominant, but in some places payment was set on a per capita basis.

Each of the kings of the Triple Alliance received provisions as tribute from the peasant communities within his own domain, as well as within the domains of the other two kings. Distant conquered polities also gave as tribute goods of different kinds. A great quantity and variety of products came to the royal storehouses of Tenochtitlan as tribute from the various areas. Foodstuffs were particularly abundant: maize, beans, *huauhtli*, *chia*, chile, cacao, salt, and honey. Raw materials for construction and craft work were wood, lime, cotton, cochineal, and feathers. Manufactured goods included paper, seats made of rushes, mats, gourds, and reed tubes for smoking tobacco. Firewood and copal were also brought in, along with enormous quantities of clothing, warriors' suits, and shields. Gold came as dust, small ingots, or made into jewelry; copper came as small axes or bells. Other products of great value were turquoise beads and jaguar skins. In addition, the local commoners giving their term of domestic service also brought along firewood, turkeys, and fresh produce.

The great variety of goods produced as tribute and the wide range of social groups to which it was distributed indicate that the political organization of the economy entered into all its basic aspects. Nevertheless, this does not give us a complete picture of the economy; the market was another important mechanism of exchange.

Market exchanges were closely regulated. Marketplaces (*tianquizco*) were well-defined areas within specific towns, and markets were held every five or twenty days. Trading outside the marketplace was strictly forbidden, and all transactions were watched over by the market authorities. Exchanges in the marketplace were carried out either by barter or by using as a medium of exchange goods such as cacao beans and certain types of cloaks. Prices are said to have been set by the authorities, but no details are available about this.

The market was attended by the mass of the regional population, who brought in goods they themselves had produced and acquired other kinds of goods for their own consumption. There were also retailers (*tlanecuilo*) who acquired products for resale. The professional merchants (*pochteca*) had their own organization as members of specific barrios; their chiefs (*pochteca tlatoque*) formed a tribunal with jurisdiction over the marketplace and decided in situ all cases that came before them. The merchants called *oztomeca* engaged in long-distance trade and also acted as their kings' ambassadors, for the exchange of gifts with the kings of the towns they visited. In addition, the king himself commissioned merchants to take certain goods to distant provinces for exchange.

The market was important in the circulation of consumer goods, both necessities and luxury items, but it played no significant role in the organization of production, since land and labor were not commodities but were regulated by the government.

The tribute accumulated by the rulers was used in various ways, including productive activities. It provided raw materials for public works and for the palace artisans. Weapons, warriors' suits, and provisions supported the armies. Foodstuffs fed the palace personnel and were distributed at certain ceremonies and as famine relief.

Tribute goods maintained the standard of living of the ruling class and made possible the lavish ostentation during ceremonial distributions of presents at great public events, such as the religious festivals throughout the calendar year, the military victory celebrations, the inauguration of temples, and the installations and funerals of kings, when enormous amounts of wealth were displayed and consumed. The palaces of local kings and of the heads of noble houses (*teccalli*), although on a lesser scale, were similar centers for the accumulation and redistribution of goods.

The process of accumulation and redistribution of goods also met the needs of the general population. Commoners paying tribute benefited from public works and from the redistribution of goods; they received land to support themselves, protection in case of conflict, food in case of famine, and the benefits of the public cult organized by the rulers. Nevertheless, the surplus appropriated by the sovereign supported the kings, lords, nobles, priests, and high-ranking military officers, all of whom lived thus at the expense of the commoners. The ruling class received its income either in the form of grants of land and workers or directly from the goods accumulated as tribute. The redistribution of the surplus shows the economic function of the state as providing for society in general, but also as an organ for government and for the appropriation of surpluses for the ruling class. The economy of ancient Central Mexico was integrated by a political system that controlled the organization of production by its regulation of land and labor. The surplus, in the form of tribute, went to the governing class. The market mechanism was more important than in other controlled economies, such as that of the Inca, but was restricted to the circulation and distribution of consumer goods.

[*See also* Markets; Merchants; Trade and Exchange; Tribute; Workshops.]

BIBLIOGRAPHY

Berdan, Frances F. "Trade, Tribute and Market in the Aztec Empire." Ph.D. diss. University of Texas, 1975. Three important aspects of the economy under the Triple Alliance.

Carrasco, Pedro, and Johanna Broda, eds. *Economía política e ideo-*

logía en el México prehispánico. Mexico City, 1978. Articles by Pedro Carrasco, Frances Berdan, and Edward Calnek, with different approaches to the study of the pre-Spanish economy.

Castillo, F., and Víctor, M. *Estructura económica de la sociedad mexica: Según las fuentes documentales.* Mexico City, 1972. Collected texts from the original sources, with extensive discussion.

PEDRO CARRASCO

Post-Conquest Cultures

Post-Conquest Spanish rule brought drastic economic changes for the peoples of Mesoamerica. Colonial success was predicated on exploiting indigenous labor. Sixteenth-century institutions like the corvée labor drafts of the *repartimiento* sought to integrate and exploit Indian laborers for the benefit of early colonial projects (church building, urban construction, agriculture, and other tasks). Private, commercial enterprises like *obrajes* (textile workshops) forcibly impressed and imprisoned large numbers of Indian laborers. The precipitous decline of the indigenous population from disease during the sixteenth and seventeenth centuries initiated the development of private Spanish agricultural production, such as *estancias de ganado* (livestock ranches), *haciendas* (landed estates), and *ranchos* (smaller units of agricultural production). Other enterprises, such as sugar and henequen plantations and mining operations, also developed. All these enterprises drew on indigenous labor through some combination of coerced labor, free wage labor, or debt peonage, resulting in the temporary or permanent estrangement of large numbers of Indians from their communities of residence.

Simultaneously, other forms of economic extraction exploited Indians in their home communities. Initially, Fernando Cortés rewarded his Spanish *conquistadores* with grants of *encomienda*. Each grantee (*encomendero*) was assigned rights to the tribute and labor of the inhabitants of particular indigenous city-states (*altepetl*). With the termination of the *encomienda* in many areas during the sixteenth and early seventeenth centuries, royal officials sought to articulate indigenous communities into a more fully unified economic and political system. Charles Gibson, in his groundbreaking study (1964), demonstrates the importance of the pre-Hispanic city-state in assigning *encomiendas* and in creating colonial municipalities. Concerning the latter, officials instituted a settlement hierarchy dividing a city-state between an urban head town (*cabecera*), the seat of the pre-Hispanic ruler, and its outlying subject villages (*sujetos*). With the creation of a municipal government (*cabildo*) in each head town, colonial officials delegated indigenous officeholders to collect royal tribute at stipulated intervals. They established community treasures (*cajas de comunidad*) where proceeds from community property and local ex-

actions could be aggregated for tribute, church expenses, and municipal officials' salaries. Meanwhile, the development of the illicit but profitable *repartimientos de efectos* (trade and craft monopolies) of local Spanish magistrates forced Indians to purchase overpriced products, or coerced them into producing goods for remuneration at less than market value. Like royal tribute, these widespread extortions depended on the structure of the municipality and its Indian officials for implementation. The municipal hierarchy declined somewhat during the eighteenth and nineteenth centuries owing to the proliferation of newly designated *pueblos* (towns) that were no longer economically and politically subordinated to the central municipality. Even so, Spanish policy remained explicitly oriented to upholding the economic viability of the *pueblo* through the establishment of governments, grants of community-controlled property (*fundo legal, ejido*), and other corporate institutions to ensure that tribute flowed from these newly independent communities to colonial coffers.

Although indigenous peoples came to be integrated in the developing colonial economy in a multitude of ways, recent studies by historians and anthropologists underscore the resiliency of native society in structuring the economic organization and land tenure within indigenous municipalities and *pueblos*. Some of these findings come from the innovative use of native-language documentation (e.g., Nahuatl, Mixtec, Yucatec Maya), or from previously underutilized documents like indigenous wills (found in either Spanish or native idioms), which provide better insight into indigenous customs. Other researchers more carefully investigate indigenous society in the often neglected eighteenth and early nineteenth centuries, primarily through careful study of Spanish documents. In most studies, rather than assuming a simple dichotomy between cultural persistence or acculturation to Spanish ways, scholars recognize the possibility that colonized peoples constructed new cultural syntheses by incorporating both indigenous and Spanish elements. The challenge is to investigate these developments on a region-by-region basis, to recognize pre-Hispanic antecedents and their economic significance, and then to trace the nature of their duration or decline within the regional colonial economies of post-Conquest Mesoamerica.

Indigenous organizations sometimes acquired a basis in Spanish colonial law that helped to perpetuate their economic significance in the local arena. The Nahua (Aztec) *teccalli*, or noble houses, of Central Mexico's Valley of Puebla represent one example. As stratified social units, pre-Hispanic noble houses organized the division of labor, land tenure, and tribute obligations through a hierarchy of patronage between the head of the noble house (*teuctli*) and his dependent nobles (*pipiltin*), and more generally between the nobles and the noble house commoners (*macehualtin*). Multiple, confederated *teccalli* composed each pre-Hispanic city-state of the Valley of Puebla and continued to structure the post-Conquest municipality. During the mid to late sixteenth century, the Spanish colonial government introduced European notions of private property by endowing noble house leaders with land confirmations and titles of *cacicazgo*, which established a colonial legal basis for this landholding class. The Spanish envisioned *cacicazgo* as the New World equivalent of Spain's *mayorazgo*, a privately owned, legally entailed estate bequeathed by one owner to the next under a jural mandate of primogeniture. These grants, made to a leading noble rather than to all the nobles of a house, ostensibly destroyed the corporate organization of the noble house; however, investigations of the eighteenth century suggest that many nobles remained organized in landholding groups. The heavy development of Spanish *hacienda* agriculture in the Valley of Puebla led to the transfer of tremendous amounts of land from Indian to Spanish control, and to the demise of the noble houses in certain municipalities. In other municipalities, however, noble houses persisted as *cacicazgos* throughout the Colonial period. Where they did, it appears that the imposed Spanish municipality remained economically and politically organized through this institution. Even lands officially designated as municipal corporate properties might be unofficially controlled by nobles at the expense of commoners. By the eighteenth century, in Valley locations like Santa Cruz Tlacotepec or Santiago Tecali, groups of nobles profited by renting their properties to Indian commoners or, just as often, to Spanish ranchers and farmers. Such findings revise those of earlier scholars, like Charles Gibson, who assumed that over time, colonial rule uniformly destroyed the basis for indigenous social stratification.

Across the volcanic divide in the adjacent Valley of Mexico, the term *teccalli* does not appear, and the land tenure regime there came to be organized quite differently than in the Valley of Puebla. The principal subunit of a pre-Hispanic city-state was the *tlaxilacalli*, or *calpulli*, a district or ward (in nearby Morelos, the term *chinamitl* designated much the same entity). These terms could also denote outlying rural hamlets. As with Puebla's *teccalli*, commoners of pre-Hispanic *tlaxilacalli* were integrated into the economy through tributary and labor obligations to the nobility. In the Valley of Mexico, however, the land and commoner retainers of the nobility appear not to be synonymous with the land and commoners associated with particular *tlaxilacalli*. Under colonial rule, Spaniards designated outlying *tlaxilacalli* as municipal subject towns (later, *pueblos*), while *cacicazgo* properties remained separate and distinct from those of the municipality. More-

over, commoners in the colonial *tlaxilacalli*-cum-*pueblo* appear to have retained greater effective control of their individual landholdings than did their commoner counterparts in the Valley of Puebla. Commoners controlled, bequeathed, bought, sold, and rented property with a good deal of autonomy. The *pueblo* asserted its residual, corporate right to lands only in rare cases where particular plots remained unclaimed or unused. Scholars of the region regularly note sixteenth- and seventeenth-century wills dictated by commoners bequeathing land to the next generation. Such patterns contrast sharply with evidence in the Valley of Puebla, where commoner wills are few and nobles thoroughly monopolized post-Conquest indigenous land tenure. More studies of indigenous land tenure patterns in the Valley of Mexico in the eighteenth and nineteenth centuries are needed, however, to understand these trends over time.

To the south, the Quiché and Cakchiquel Maya of highland Guatemala had an organization termed *chinamit* (a Central Mexican Nahuatl loan word). Spanish observers assumed them to be a kin-based lineal descent group (i.e., lineage). But with the exception of a core family of noble leaders that may have constituted a lineage, *chinamit* members shared the same indigenous surname but were not necessarily all related to one another. Much like the Valley of Mexico's *tlaxilacalli*, the *chinamit* constituted a residential and territorial unit with residual jurisdiction over lands, while individual families held and cultivated specific plots. Each *chinamit* might also specialize in craft production. Under colonial rule, they remained significant units in the land tenure of highland Guatemalan municipalities. The Spanish recognized them as *parcialidades* (town sections, or divisions). Although they never established a consistent policy regarding the role of *parcialidades* in a community, Spanish legal decrees resulting from local disputes often reinforced the importance of these units in matters of land management and community government. Hill and Monaghan (1987) demonstrate that the five present-day *cantones* of Sacapulas—landholding entities consisting of properties privately owned by *cantón*—are the direct descendants of the pre-Hispanic *chinamit* and colonial *parcialidades* of that municipality.

Beyond examining the role of indigenous organizations intermediate between household and *pueblo*, Mesoamerican scholars have recently employed colonial wills and litigation documents as a window on the individual household decisions concerning inheritance and land tenure. Again, a good deal of indigenous cultural persistence in the context of Spanish institutions is apparent, together with some interesting regional parallels. For example, household land ownership and inheritance among the Yucatec Maya of Yucatán and the Nahua of Central

Mexico appear to have been structured through strikingly similar principles. Two basic indigenous principles, sibling equivalence and joint ownership, were fundamental to household organization in both regions. With sibling equivalence, all children could expect to inherit equally from both parents. This principle, in turn, contributed to joint ownership, in which groups of siblings—and often cousins—collectively managed their land and property. Kellogg (1995) refers to these collectivities in the context of colonial Mexico City (pre-Hispanic Tenochtitlan) as "corporate sibling-based kin groups." Her study indicates that the early impoverishment of Mexico City's Indians, associated with the massive intrusion of Spaniards, negated the importance of these groups and led to simplified nuclear families by the first years of the seventeenth century. But in other zones, like the Valley of Puebla, data from eighteenth and nineteenth centuries suggest that sibling-based kin groups among the nobility continued to function and, in fact, served to structure the late colonial *cacicazgos* of this region. In Santiago Tecali (modern Tecali de Herrera), preliminary documentary research further suggests that in certain cases, such groups remained intact until at least the first years of the twentieth century of perhaps later. Finally, in the modern context, Sandstrom's ethnographic investigations among the Nahua-speaking inhabitants of Amatlán, in northern Veracruz, finds sibling groups—again, often with cousins, other distant relatives, or non-kin members—clustered together in house compounds of two to eight dwellings. Scattered about in the vicinity of the village, these compounds form a basic economic unit—not only in terms of the exchange of goods and labor that goes on among the households of each compound, but also in structuring the larger land tenure regime of the community. Although Sandstrom does not address the antiquity of this arrangement, his investigations provide ethnographic details possibly applicable to the organization of similar entities investigated historically.

Historians and ethnographers commonly assume not only that the post-Conquest Spanish-imposed *pueblo* articulated local peoples with the colonial and later national government but also that the *pueblo* and its associated institutions largely organized their lives. Recent investigations by no means negate this view, but they demonstrate that indigenous social structures and customs could endure the Conquest and remain central to the internal economic organization of the *pueblo* throughout the Colonial period and perhaps beyond. Future investigations of such phenomena promise a more nuanced understanding of cultural persistence and change in the economic organization of Mesoamerican peoples.

[*See also* Craft Production; Haciendas and Plantations; Markets; Mining and Metalwork; Textile Industry; Tourism; Trade and Exchange.]

BIBLIOGRAPHY

Chance, John K. *Conquest of the Sierra*: *Spaniards and Indians in Colonial Oaxaca*. Norman, Okla., 1989. Explores the impact on indigenous society of Spanish magistrates' illegal *repartimientos de efectos*, organized primarily to extract cotton textiles and cochineal dyestuff from *pueblos* in the remote Sierra Zapoteca.

Chance, John K. "The Caciques of Tecali: Class and Ethnic Identity in Late Colonial Mexico." *Hispanic American Historical Review* 76 (1996), 475–502. Discusses the colonial underpinnings and economic ramifications of the indigenous *teccalli* in the Valley of Puebla.

Farriss, Nancy M. *Maya Society under Colonial Rule*: *The Collective Enterprise of Survival*. Princeton, 1984. Treats comprehensively the economic integration of Maya communities into the colonial order and chronicles changes over time, including an important discussion of the consequences of the eighteenth-century Bourbon reforms for the corporate economy of Maya communities.

Gibson, Charles. *The Aztecs under Spanish Rule*. Stanford, 1964.

Greenberg, James B. *Santiago's Sword*: *Chatino Peasant Religion and Economics*. Berkeley, 1981. Employs the important model of the closed, corporate community to explain the dependent articulation of Yaitepec, a modern indigenous community, into the external economy.

Hassig, Ross. *Trade, Tribute, and Transportation*: *The Sixteenth-Century Political Economy of the Valley of Mexico*. Norman, Okla., 1985. Examines in equal measure the regional economic infrastructure of the Aztec empire and the changes initiated as Central Mexico became part of the Spanish empire.

Hill, Robert M. II. "Social Organization by Decree in Colonial Highland Guatemala." *Ethnohistory* 36 (1989), 170–198. Demonstrates the importance of Spanish administrative decisions in modifying and preserving indigenous *chinamit* as significant political and economic units, leading to variations in modern community organization.

Hill, Robert M. II, and John Monaghan. *Continuities in Highland Maya Social Organization*: *Ethnohistory in Sacapulas, Guatemala*. Philadelphia, 1987.

Kellogg, Susan. *Law and the Transformation of Aztec Culture, 1500–1700*. Norman, Okla., 1995.

Kellogg, Susan and Matthew Restall, eds. *Dead Giveaways*: *Indigenous Testaments of Colonial Mesoamerica and the Andes*. Salt Lake City, 1998. Collected papers from different Mesoamerican regions illustrate the importance of wills as a source for understanding household structure and economic organization, bequest patterns, and clues to the structure of landholdings.

Lockhart, James. *The Nahuas after the Conquest*: *A Social and Cultural History of the Indians of Central Mexico, Sixteenth through Eighteenth Centuries*. Stanford, 1992. Using primarily Nahuatl documentation, comprehensively explores the post-conquest Nahua *altepetl*, including (among many topics) the pattern of landholding within the *calpulli* (*tlaxilacalli*), and the organization of households, and hypothesizes organizational differences between the Valley of Mexico's *calpulli* and the Valley of Puebla's *teccalli*; contains an extended bibliography.

Restall, Matthew. *The Maya World*: *Yucatec Culture and Society, 1550–1850*. Stanford, 1997. With colonial documents written in Yucatec Maya, investigates land tenure and material aspects of life within the colonial Maya *cah* (municipal community), and outlines the indigenous landholding principles of sibling equivalence (*cetil*) and joint ownership (*multial*).

Sandstrom, Alan. "Toponymic Groups and House Organization among the Nahuas of Northern Veracruz, Mexico." In *Beyond Kinship: Social and Material Reproduction in House Societies*, edited by Rosemary A. Joyce and Susan Gillespie, pp. 53–72. Philadelphia, 2000. Ethnographic account of the economic organization of sibling groups associated with house compounds in Amatlán, Veracruz.

Taylor, William. *Landlord and Peasant in Colonial Oaxaca*. Stanford, 1972. Presents an important corrective to models of land tenure based solely on central Mexican data, by detailing over the length of the colonial period the persistence of large *cacicazgos*, the corporate integrity of indigenous communities, and the attenuated development of Spanish haciendas.

Wasserstrom, Robert. *Class and Society in Central Chiapas*. Berkeley, 1983. Ambitiously explores the changing economic conditions and class structure of the highland Maya, focusing especially on the municipalities of Zinacantan and Chamula over the course of the colonial era, the nineteenth-century Liberal reforms, and up to the ethnographic present.

STEPHEN PERKINS

EIGHT DEER (mid-eleventh century–early twelfth century), Mixtec warrior and ruler. Lord 8 Deer "Jaguar Claw" is probably the best-known Mixtec ruler of the pre-Hispanic period. He lived during the time when the traditions of the Classic period were being swept aside by those of the Postclassic. His life was turbulent and adventuresome; he succeeded in seizing power and attempted to create an empire, but he was murdered and his achievements nullified. His political life is recorded in extensive detail in the *Codex Colombino-Becker* and on side 1 of the *Codex Zouche-Nuttall*. His personal life, including his various wives and children, is shown best in the *Codex Bodley*, and also on side 2 of the *Zouche-Nuttall*.

Lord 8 Deer was born in the year 12 Reed, probably sometime after the middle of the eleventh century CE. A more precise dating is not possible at present because the Mixtec year dates in the codices cannot yet be correlated accurately with the modern calendar; the correlation proposed by Alfonso Caso in 1949 is seriously flawed, but the corrected correlation by Emily Rabin has not been completed. Lord 8 Deer was the first son born of his father's second marriage. Since the Mixtec practiced primogeniture, more importance would be given to the first son of the first marriage, Lord 12 Movement, who was eighteen years older than Lord 8 Deer.

At the age of seventeen, Lord 8 Deer began his political activities. Over a period of several years he held meetings, carried out rituals, and played the Mixtec ballgame (reportedly, against a supernatural). When he was twenty years old, he became the ruler of the coastal domain of Tututepec. He spent the next two years conquering a number of nearby sites to consolidate his position.

No surviving Mixtec codex contains any information about Lord 8 Deer's life between the ages of twenty-two and thirty-four. At thirty-four, however, he initiated the events that finally carried him to power. He opened negotiations with Lord 4 Jaguar, who had conquered the Coixtlahuaca area the previous year. Lord 4 Jaguar rebuffed these approaches, but Lord 8 Deer secured supernatural support, and the two men played the ballgame to decide the issue. Lord 8 Deer won and received from Lord 4 Jaguar the coveted ritual nose-perforation that raised his status to that of a great lord. The next year, the two men are said to have made a dangerous trip into the underworld realm of the solar supernatural to win predictions of their futures. Entering the underworld through a ballcourt, they crossed a raging river and battled against unnatural opponents. The solar deity granted predictions to them and to Lord 12 Movement.

The following year, Lord 12 Movement was murdered at age fifty-five, and Lord 8 Deer held lavish funeral rites for him. Lord 8 Deer blamed this murder on the two sons of Lord 12 Movement's sister (who was also Lord 8 Deer's half-sister). The next year, he captured them, but he waited another year before sacrificing them in bloody ceremonies. It is more probable, in fact, that Lord 8 Deer was behind the death of Lord 12 Movement and used it as the excuse to sacrifice the last surviving male descendants of his father's first marriage. With these three deaths, he eliminated all potential family rivals. The next year, at age forty, he celebrated reaching the peak of his power. He then took as his official dynastic wife the sister of the two brothers he had sacrificed; since she was his half-sister's daughter, by marrying her 8 Deer united the families of his father's two marriages. Two years later, the daughter of his own sister became his second wife; there were also three other marriages. Problems arose when his second wife was the first to bear him a son. To merge his father's two families, it was essential that his heir be a son by his first wife, but this child was not born until 8 Deer was forty-seven.

While Lord 8 Deer was concerned with these problems of dynastic succession, a young enemy was plotting against him. Lord 4 Wind was the half-brother of the two men sacrificed by Lord 8 Deer. He formed an alliance with Lord 8 Deer's second wife, whose son had been set aside for the younger heir. Lord 8 Deer was led into an ambush, and Lord 4 Wind looked on as he was killed.

Lord 8 Deer was fifty-two when he died. His nascent empire was divided between the eldest sons of his first and second wives. Several years later, Lord 4 Jaguar uncovered Lord 4 Wind's plot and pursued him. Because the political situation had already been severely unbalanced by Lord 8 Deer's death, we are told, the solar supernatural intervened and forced Lord 4 Jaguar to give Lord 4 Wind the nose-perforation that made him a great lord. Lord 4 Wind married several of Lord 8 Deer's daughters and lived to the age of seventy-two before dying peacefully.

[*See also* Mixtec Group of Pictorial Manuscripts.]

BIBLIOGRAPHY

Caso, Alfonso. "El mapa de Teozacoalco." *Cuadernos Americanos* 47. 5 (1949), 145–181. Sets forth the fundamentals of reading Mixtec codices.

Troike, Nancy P. "The Codex Colombino-Becker." Dissertation, University of London, 1974. Reassembles the codex fragments in their correct order and gives the first narrative interpretation of the pictorial text.

NANCY P. TROIKE

EJIDOS. The Mexican *ejido* system of landholding is rooted in the survival and adaptation of pre-Hispanic communal land use practices and the cultural life they helped to sustain through three centuries of European colonialism and the Industrial Revolution. In Aztec times, much Indian land was held by corporate groups such as the *calpulli*, which was both a land unit and the community of families making their living from that land. The land was dedicated to the homes and agricultural plots of group members and included common access to nearby forest resources. This system, though transformed over time, is one basis of the modern *ejido* (Spanish, "common"). At the same time, the *ejido* derives from a Castilian tradition in which communal lands provided the basis from which the peasantry met their economic obligations to the state. The combination of these two traditions in Mexico meant that communal life had deep indigenous roots and was initially legitimated by the Spanish crown.

After the Conquest, however, land tenure patterns in many part of Mesoamerica shifted away from subsistence-oriented community ownership toward commercial production. That process created deep social divisions in the Mexican countryside as great estates (*haciendas*) encroached on village lands, transformed many peasants into rural wage workers, and threatened their previous way of life. The tensions associated with this social dislocation characterized Mexican history from the mature Colonial period to the agrarian revolution that swept Mexico from 1910 to 1919.

The Ley Lerdo of 1856 legalized the privatization of agriculture that was already under way and revealed the clash of cultures underlying the endemic conflict in Mexican rural society. The law opened up corporate property of both the Roman Catholic Church and villages for sale, as Mexico's Liberal government sought to modernize the country and transform rural Mexicans into freeholding, independent yeoman farmers. The government hoped these small farmers would provide for themselves and be more driven by market incentives; instead, the legislation facilitated the spread of the great estates at the expense of the villagers.

These contradictions were laid bare in the Mexican Revolution of 1910, and that violent upheaval temporarily halted the Liberal project. Spontaneous land distribution began during the armed phase of the revolution when agrarian insurgents began to parcel out *hacienda* land to villagers. Born out of this pressure from below, Article 27 of the Mexican Consitution of 1917 sanctioned the redistribution of land from large private estates back to communities that had been despoiled in the past. The creation of *ejidos* was one of the primary methods employed to this end. An *ejido* is a grant from the Mexican government to a rural community of land that can be worked either individually or collectively but is held in common. Land redistribution was energetically carried out in those regions where agrarian insurrection had been most widespread, but it then slowed until the presidency of Lázaro Cardenas (1934–1940), when more than 49 million acres of land were redistributed—about double the amount distributed by all previous revolutionary regimes combined.

Eligible *ejidatarios* and their descendants enjoy usufruct rights to the land, but before 1992, measures existed to protect common landholdings from being lost through debt or sale; therefore, they could not be bought, sold, or used as collateral. *Ejido* lands can be used for house lots, subsistence crops such as maize, pasture, woodlots, or cash crops such as cotton or sugar. Cash-crop *ejidos* are run as cooperatives and operate much like business enterprises. Today, there are about 3.1 million *ejidatarios* and millions more of their dependents living on 27,410 *ejidos*, which cover one-half of the arable land in Mexico.

Agrarian reform stalled after 1940, however, except for a brief revival during the administration of Luis Echeverría (1970–1976), and it came to an almost complete halt in the 1980s. Since then, the existence of the *ejido* has come under assault by a new generation of modernizers in the Mexican government who, like their nineteenth-century predecessors, hope to attract foreign investment, erode communal land ownership, stimulate private property, and develop a more capital-intensive agricultural sector. The 1992 agrarian law promulgated by President Carlos Salinas (1988–1994) dismantled the hard-won Article 27 and is reminiscent of the Ley Lerdo. It decreed an end to land distribution and established procedures that encouraged the privatization of *ejido* land. The assault on the *ejido* has been justified by the low productivity of Mexico's agricultural sector, but given the history and cultural significance of collective land use in the country, the value of the *ejido* cannot be measured in economic terms alone. The future privatization of collective land will probably benefit a minority of people in the Mexican countryside, while the majority will be driven from the land and into the cities—or, given the incapacity of Mexican industry to absorb them, into the United States.

BIBLIOGRAPHY

Cornelius, Wayne, and David Myhere, eds. *The Transformation of Rural Mexico*. La Jolla, Calif., 1998. Collected essays provide an overview of the social, economic and environmental consequences of *ejido* reform in regional perspective.

Gibson, Charles. *The Aztecs under Spanish Rule*. Stanford, 1964. Seminal study, meticulously researched and providing an in-depth study of pre-Columbian and early Conquest society in the Valley of Mexico, illuminating patterns of continuity and change.

McBride, George McCutcheon. *The Land Systems of Mexico*. New York, 1971. Important geological overview of Mexico's natural resources and an introduction to land tenure patterns and systems of productivity.

Simpson, Eyler Newton. *The Ejido: Mexico's Way Out*. Chapel Hill, 1937. Analysis of Mexico's rural social questions, with attention to indigenous traditions and solutions.

Snyder, Richard, and Gabriel Torres, eds. *The Future Role of the Ejido in Rural Mexico*. La Jolla, Calif., 1998. Collection of essays treating the changing role of the *ejido* in post-NAFTA Mexico, with a good introductory essay.

PAUL HART

EL CEDRAL, the archaeological and paleontological site in Mexico, at Rancho La Amapola, Cedral, San Luis Potosí (located at 23°49′N, 100°43′W). It is at an elevation of 1700 meters (5,700 feet) above sea level, in a basin, with Pleistocene fossil deposits. In the Pleistocene, the site had artesian springs, that, for part of the year, created a fairly extensive lake, surrounded by thick vegetation, a gallery forest with walnut (*Juglans*) and juniper (*Juniperus*). It was very different from today's vegetation of small-leafed species, such as *Opuntia, Yuca, Berberis, Cassia,* and *Graminea*, with only a little *Juglans* and *Juniperus*. The exposed stratigraphy resulted from the lake depositions and relatively wet phases, alternating with the springs' discharges in drier phases. In addition to excavations at the site, the researchers at Rancho La Amapola did the following studies: on stratigraphy, geomorphology, geology, soil analysis, archaeobotany, and archaeozoology. Samples for radiocarbon dating were also collected in this interdisciplinary research project.

The springs in the area attracted many animals. When they died, their bones became part of the sediments. With a visible abundance of Pleistocene fauna, Rancho La Amapola became a promising site for research. The faunal remains are varied. Mammals include the mammoth and the mastodon as well as horses of three sizes (apparently different species), tapirs, cameloids, deer, antelope, and bison. Other animals found included carnivores, such as bear, canines, felines, and rodentia. There were also reptiles, birds, and mollusks recovered from the sediments—and these small animals are good indicators of climate changes.

Human presence at the site seemed logical, since it would be attractive to obtain water for drinking, for bathing, for collecting plants, and for stalking and killing a thirsty animal, which might be butchered right there. A spring is in a potentially dangerous location, especially during dry seasons, so the possibility of a human settlement was not good—yet some human remains were found. Human finds from the first digging season are conclusive: a circular hearth surrounded by mammoth bones dated to $31,850 \pm 1,600$ before present (BP), an obsidian projectile point of the Gary type dated to between 7,000 and 5,000 BP; and there was a flake and a fragment from another obsidian projectile point. Also found, in a zone tested by radiocarbon dating to $21,960 \pm 540$ BP, was a fragment of a horse tibia, broken and used, probably to cut and perforate. A stratum dated to $33,300 \pm 2,700$–$1,800$ BP yielded a discoidal scraper *in situ*, made of chalcedony. Also a stratum older than 15,000 BP contained a limestone nucleus, with evidence of use as a hammerstone. The importance of the few lithic remains at those very early dates is enhanced by the presence of the animal bones with marks of human modifications. They all testify to the presence of man in the site.

Later excavations located seven hearths, dated by the radiocarbon method to points between $37,694 \pm 1,963$ BP and $21,468 \pm 458$ BP. Two other hearths gave an average age of $28,084 \pm 580$ BP: four samples were dated for one of them, with two of the samples dating to $26,323 \pm 827$ BP and the other samples dated to $28,462 \pm 507$ BP and $33,630 \pm 2,066$ BP.

The site, therefore, gives clear evidence of the human presence in northern Central Mexico from at least 35,000 to 21,000 BP. The later human finds of a well-structured lithic industry—including choppers and chopping tools, polyhedric nuclei, projectile points, flakes, blades, and a small circular grindstone—dated to between 7,000 and 6,000 BP. Evidence for both stages are not many at the site, but they are solid. The earliest one features hearths, one isolated and seven others superimposed, associated with the bone fragments of small and medium-size animals. No lithic artifacts have been found in association, although there have been finds in stratigraphically well-dated locations that correspond to the dates of the hearths.

The finds at Cedral must be understood in relation to the ongoing discussion about the earliest date of human presence in the Americas. For those who think 14,000 to 12,000 is the earliest period, materials at the site will be seen not as evidence of human activity but as remains of natural fires. Yet it should be impossible to dismiss their location, variety, dates, and associations—especially the remains of fires with a diameter between 0.6 meters (2 feet) and 1.7 meters (6 feet), concentrated in a small area, in a spot with good access to the lake and the springs.

BIBLIOGRAPHY

Lorenzo, José Luis, and Lorena Mirambell. "Informes anuales de 1977 a 1984 y 1991." Presented at the Consejo de Arqueología, Instituto Nacional de Antropología e Historia. Mexico City, 1977–1984; and 1991.

Lorenzo, José Luis, and Lorena Mirambell. "El Cedral, S. L. P. Un sitio con presencia humana de más de 30,000 aP." ("El Cedral, S. L. P.: A Site with Human Presence from More Than 30,000 BP.") UISPP. Comisión X11. El Poblamiento de América. Mexico City, 1981.

LORENA MIRAMBELL SILVA

ELECTRONIC RESOURCES. Electronic resources have become increasingly relevant for Mesoamericanists from a variety of disciplinary and professional backgrounds. Because the Internet—in particular, the World Wide Web (WWW)—is rapidly displacing the use of external storage media, such as floppy disks and CD-ROMs, this overview is weighted toward resources available on the Internet. Also, this review is limited to resources that provide information that is not available (or possible) in traditional media and that is associated with established scholars or institutions. Because it is the exception rather than the rule for an organization or journal devoted to Mesoamerican research not to have a Web site, such resources are not listed unless they meet the preceding criteria.

A number of Web sites offer general information about Mesoamerican cultures and pointers to other resources on the Internet. The most useful of these is *A Mesoamerican Archaeology WWW Page*, hosted by Thomas Burglin, a cell biologist at the University of Basel, Switzerland (http://copan.bioz.unibas.ch/meso.html). In addition to a categorized list of pointers to other Web sites, newsgroups, and e-mail lists, the site contains bibliographic information, conference announcements and proceedings, downloadable software and data sets, and various documents of interest to Mesoamericanists. Supplementing the many abstracts and indices to published material already available on CD-ROM or by private network through subscription, a few such resources are available directly on the Web. Volumes 56 through 60 of the Library of Congress's *Handbook of Latin American Studies On-Line* (http://lcweb2.loc.gov/hlas/), an annually published bibliography that describes over 5,000 works selected and annotated by more than 130 scholars from a variety of disciplines and nationalities, will be published on the Web. In a more specialized vein, the *Tarlton Law Library Resources on Aztec and Maya Law* (Mike Widener, University of Texas at Austin) provides an annotated bibliography on an underrepresented subject (http://www.law.utexas.edu/rare/aztec.htm).

Many Web sites describe specific archaeological projects. The most extensive of these is the *Yaxuná Archaeology Project*, which documents research in Yucatán, Mexico, being conducted by David Freidel, Tracy Arden, and Charles Suhler of Southern Methodist University. The site offers scholarly essays, detailed excavation reports, and both two- and three-dimensional movie clips of artifacts and site views. A live satellite link is promised for the next field season. *The Belize River Archaeological Settlement Survey/El Pilar*, conducted by Anabel Ford, University of California, Santa Barbara, also contains three-dimensional tours of the site. *The Ancient Limestone Quarries of Nakbe, Guatemala* describes five years of excavation at five Formative (Preclassic) limestone quarries by James C. Woods and Gene L. Titmus of the College of Southern Idaho (http://archaeology.miningco.com/msubexperimental.htm). An interesting feature of this site is an experimental replication of the quarrying process. Other reports include *The El Cayo Archaeological Project* (http://www.ucalgary.ca/UofC/faculties/SS/ARKY/cayo/elcayo.html) (Peter Mathews and Mario Aliphat, University of Calgary), the *K'axob and Xibun Archaeological Projects* (http://www.bu.edu/tricia/title.html) (Patricia MacAnany, Boston University), *Tlahuica Ruins near Cuernavaca* (http://www.albany.edu/~mesmith/tlaruin.html) (Michael E. Smith, University at Albany, State University of New York), and *The Early Copán Acropolis Program* (http://www.famsi.org/projects/sharer.html) (Robert Sharer, University of Pennsylvania Museum, the Instituto Hondureno de Antropología e Historia, and FAMSI). In contrast to the large number of archaeological Web sites that can be classified as "brochureware," the *Latin American Archaeology Database* at the University of Pittsburgh contains raw data sets to complement texts published by the University of Pittsburgh Latin American Archaeology Publications. As the site explains, such data are best left in digital format because they are not useful in print form, and the Web is an ideal medium for their distribution. Currently, the site contains data sets from two site reports, Rueda (1995) and Jaramillo (1996).

A number of high-quality Mesoamerican language resources have been published on the Web. Terrence Kaufman and John Justeson's *Mesoamerican Languages Documentation Project* provides a sophisticated user interface to a set of dictionaries that range in size from 4,000 to 8,000 lexical items, and in which "every effort has been made to collect all the morphemes of the language." The currently available languages are Oluta and San Miguel Chimalapa Soke. John Dienhart's *The Maya Site at Odense University* (http://maya.hum.sdu.dk) features a fully searchable database composed of the data published in

John Dienhart's three-volume work, *The Mayan Languages: A Comparative Vocabulary* (1989). The site currently contains more than 40,000 entries. The Summer Institute of Linguistics Web site (http://www.sil.org) has, in addition to a set of general resources pertaining to ethnology, geography, and advocacy, the *Ethnologue* (http://www.sil.org/ethnologue/), edited by Barbara F. Grimes, which contains demographic and other information on more than 6,700 languages spoken in 228 countries. A useful tool for the creation of language databases, the *Ethnologue* lists over 39,000 language names, dialect names, and alternate names. In an experimental vein, *The Mayan Epigraphic Database Project* (http://jefferson.village.virginia.edu/med/) (Rafael Alvarado, University of Virginia) offers a relational database that links a variety of data sets necessary to conduct epigraphic research—glyph images, glyph readings, calendrical tables, and digital transcriptions of hieroglyphic texts.

A more comprehensive collection of digitized epigraphic material is available on the CD-ROM that accompanies *A Concordance to the Inscriptions of Palenque, Chiapas, Mexico* (Ringle and Smith-Stark 1996). The disk contains a complete catalog of Mayan hieroglyphs that significantly updates Thompson (1962), bitmap images for each entry, and the digital transcriptions of the entire extant corpus of inscriptions found at Palenque. Curiously, although all of the transcribed texts are glossed, individual glyphs are not. Also, in contrast to the Web resources described above, the disk is readable only with computers running the Microsoft Windows operating system.

Although no collections of research-quality images are currently available on the Web, a number of sites display moderately high-resolution photographs, as well as movies of artifacts, buildings, and places. A good starting point is *Mesoamerican Photo Archives* (http://studentweb.tulane.edu/~dhixson/) (David Hixson, Tulane University), which contains dozens of annotated photographs from various regions within Mesoamerica, as well as a comprehensive collection of pointers to other private and institutional collections. For contemporary representations of Mesoamerican culture, see the exhibits at *The Virtual Museum of Mexican Culture* (http://www.arts-history.mx/). *Maya Archaeology* (http://www.maya-archaeology.org/) (Nicholas Hellmuth, Foundation for Latin American Anthropological Research, Brevard Community College) provides technical information about the field of digital photography, as well as photographs and three-dimensional movies of Maya artifacts from museums in Guatemala, Honduras, Mexico, and Belize. Merle Greene Robertson's CD-ROM collection, *The Rubbings of Maya Sculpture*, has high-resolution scans of rubbings made from carved artifacts from eighty-nine sites. The ten-disk set is available for both Apple and IBM-compatible systems from the University of Oklahoma Press. *Maps of the Americas*, from the Perry-Castañeda Library Map Collection at the University of Texas at Austin, has maps produced by the U.S. Central Intelligence Agency of Central and South American regions in both PDF and bitmap file formats.

There are two primary on-line discussion groups available to Mesoamericanists, *The Pre-Columbian History Discussion List* (AZTLAN-L) (e-mail: aztlan-request@listserve.louisville.edu), a moderated e-mail list, and *sci.archaeology.mesoamerican*, an unmoderated newsgroup. Currently, the former is both more popular and more professional than the latter. Well-known scholars in the field participate with enthusiasts on a number of interesting if sometimes unorthodox topics on the e-mail list, whereas a disproportionate amount of time is spent in the newsgroup discussing such issues as the possible transoceanic diffusion. For more traditional academic discourse, the on-line journal *AZTLAN* publishes essays submitted by participants of AZTLAN-L (http://www.cc.ukans.edu/~hoopes/aztlan/). To find out about issues of advocacy, the EZLN Web site (http://www.ezln.org) provides current information on the political situation in Chiapas and Mexico, and CHIAPAS-L, an unmoderated e-mail list, provides a forum for discussing and announcing news about the same topic. Other discussion groups include *Teotihuacan Notes*, a journal of Teotihuacano archaeology and iconography (http://archaeology.la.asu.edu/VM/mesoam/Teo/notes/); NAHUAT-L, an unmoderated e-mail list devoted to Aztec language and culture; H-MEXICO, a moderated e-mail list devoted to Mexican history and studies; H-LATAM, a moderated e-mail list devoted to Latin American history; and the following newsgroups: *soc.culture.mexican*, *soc.culture.honduras*, *soc.culture.costa-rica*, *soc.culture.nicaragua*, *soc.culture.latin-america*, *rec.travel.latin-america*, and *soc.culture.native*.

[*See also* Institutions, Projects, and Meetings.]

BIBLIOGRAPHY

Dienhart, J. *The Mayan Languages: A Comparative Vocabulary*. 3 vols. Odense, Denmark, 1989.

Jaramillo, E. L. G. *The Socioeconomic Structure of Formative 3 Communities*. 1996.

Ringle, W. M., and T. C. Smith-Stark. *A Concordance to the Inscriptions of Palenque, Chiapas, Mexico*. New Orleans, 1996.

Rueda, C. H. L. *Regional Archaeology in the Muisca Territory: A Study of the Fúquene and Susa Valleys*. Pittsburgh, 1995.

Thompson, J. E. S. *A Catalog of Maya Hieroglyphs*. Norman, Okla., 1962.

RAFAEL ALVARADO

EL MIRADOR, a massive Lowland Maya site in a remote area of dense tropical forest in northern Guatemala. El Mirador is an intriguing but still little understood Late

Formative (Preclassic) city; it is situated within the *municipio* of San Andres, Department of Petén, Guatemala, in what is called the El Mirador Basin, located at the base of the Yucatán Peninsula, about 6 to 7 kilometers (3.5 to 4.5 miles) south of the Mexican border. There is a heavy tropical deciduous forest surrounding El Mirador for approximately 125 kilometers (80 miles) in all directions. Most of the variation in the landscape is provided by small *aguadas* (naturally occurring water holes), a few scattered settlements, and a maze of trails and roads.

Although the site would be interesting for its immense size, it has fired the imagination of scholars because its peak of occupation and monumental construction appear to have occurred during the Late Formative period (350 BCE to 200 CE). This challenges the traditional model, which saw the "rise" of Maya civilization in the subsequent Early Classic period (250–600 CE). A series of investigations at El Mirador and elsewhere has begun to reveal a surprisingly complex Formative Maya civilization, which had developed much that was long assumed to have developed later, during the Classic period. El Mirador was "discovered" by *chicleros* ("chicle workers"), searching the tropical forest for *chico zapote* trees, from which chicle gum is extracted. It was the *chicleros* who bestowed the name of El Mirador ("the look out") on the site because of the lofty ancient structures located there, which allowed those who climbed them a rare view of the surrounding terrain. The *chicleros* named not only the site but also many of its principal public architectural complexes; they gave them the names of forest animals, such as *tigre* ("tiger-jaguar"), *danta* ("tapir"), and *monos* ("howler monkeys"). The first Europeans to visit El Mirador and report it to the outside world were Frank Vans-Agnew and Enrique Schufelt, who visited the site in 1926. Later, in 1930, El Mirador was photographed from the air during exploratory flights by Percy Madeira Jr., who was accompanied by archaeologist J. Alden Mason. The photographs and description of the site stirred interest in El Mirador, and it was visited by the Sixteenth Central American Expedition (Second Campeche Expedition), led by Karl Ruppert and John H. Denison in 1933. The next archaeologist to visit the site was Ian Graham in 1962. Graham made a pace and compass map of the main architectural complexes and accurately surmised that structures at the site were mostly Formative. In 1970, Joyce Marcus excavated six test pits in various platforms and buildings at El Mirador, as part of a larger testing program in the northern Petén, directed by Graham. In 1978, Bruce H. Dahlin, then of Catholic University of America and now of Howard University, was the principal investigator of Project Acalches, which began in 1978 at El Mirador and included excavations in *aguadas* Maculis and Limón, three excavations in the Bullard and

Gifford Causeways, and other soil-sampling operations. The most extensive investigations at the site to date were carried out for five seasons from 1979 to 1983: Ray T. Matheny of Brigham Young University and Bruce H. Dahlin were the principal investigators of Project El Mirador. The major efforts of the Matheny team (including, among others, Glenna Nielsen, Richard D. Hansen, Wayne K. Howell, Deanne G. Matheny, Denise Evans Copeland, and Ellen Stutz Landeen) were directed toward determining the periods of construction, occupation, and abandonment of the major architectural complexes and toward establishing a chronological framework for the site by the ceramic studies of Donald W. Forsyth. Dahlin's group continued working in the bajos and reservoirs. Mary Elizabeth Chambers of the Catholic University team initiated studies of the large earthworks or wall system that surrounds the ceremonial precinct in the western portion of the site. Dahlin and his team explored and excavated at the so-called Crossroads and also carried out two seasons of mapping. In 1982, Arthur Demarest, then of the Peabody Museum, Harvard University, and Robert Sharer, of the University Museum at the University of Pennsylvania, with their teams, joined the El Mirador expedition for part of the season to establish stratigraphic excavations in strategic locations for ceramic studies. The work carried out by those groups, while significant, has just begun to reveal a few of the secrets of El Mirador. The logistical difficulties of reaching the site, as well as supplying and otherwise sustaining a group to accomplish work there, are daunting but possible to overcome.

El Mirador must have been a glorious city at the height of its power. Even today, after it has lain largely in a ruined state for almost two thousand years, its massive public constructions soar above the forest floor. The maximum extent of the city is still unknown, but reconnaissance suggests that it covers more than 16 square kilometers. An examination of the known areas of public buildings at the site center show that the city was carefully planned. For example, at least two of the monumental public constructions, the Tigre Complex, facing east, and the Danta Complex, facing west, track the path of the sun. The city contains two obvious aggregations of public architecture: the western precinct and the vast Danta Complex to the east. The western precinct contains a concentration of massive building complexes, including the Tigre Complex, the Central Acropolis, the Monos Complex, the Tres Micos Complex, and many other very large but yet unnamed architectural complexes. This western portion of El Mirador sits on a fairly flat plateau, and its many buildings are encompassed by a wall or embankment system that encloses them on the southern, eastern, and northern sides. On the west, a fairly steep escarpment drops down to the El Mirador Bajo. The wall system included both freestanding segments of walls or embankments and others that are associated with architectural complexes or other features. The mapping efforts of Dahlin's team included the wall and identified a series of possible entrances. Mary Elizabeth Chambers explored and tested several areas of the wall system.

No discussion of El Mirador would be complete without mentioning the east-facing Tigre Complex found on the western side of the precinct. The Tigre Pyramid dominates the complex which, in addition to the Tigre Pyramid, includes the long narrow Tigre Plaza (found on the eastern side of the pyramid) and the structures surrounding it, including Structure 34. The Tigre Complex represents a distinct unit of architectural construction, including approximately 428,000 cubic meters of construction material, and the Tigre Pyramid, with a total height of about 54 meters (165 feet) and with basal dimensions of about 126 by 135 meters (400 by 435 feet), is one of the largest structures ever built by the ancient Maya during any period. Richard Hansen has demonstrated, by way of comparison with some constructions at Tikal, that if a plan view of the base of the Tigre Pyramid is superimposed over a plan view at the same scale of part of the site center at Tikal, it covers the Grand Plaza, Temples I and II, and half of the North Acropolis. The Tigre Pyramid is a truncated platform that rises about 30 meters (100 feet) to an upper landing. The landing was reached by a wide inset stairway and, on the uppermost landing, a central structure rises almost 25 meters (80 feet) and is flanked by two smaller pyramidal structures on the north and south. This triadic pattern of architecture is seen again and again in the public architecture of El Mirador. Excavations in Building 34, which forms the southern end of the Tigre Plaza (in front of the Tigre Pyramid), revealed sophisticated architecture with large painted modeled stucco masks and other modeled elements. Richard Hansen's excavations in the Tigre Complex indicate that all of the public architecture tested was constructed and used during the Late Formative period, although there was some minor Classic-period activity in some areas.

The Central Acropolis and its associated structures are a large complex of public architecture located just to the east and slightly to the south of the Tigre Complex. The Central Acropolis has a base platform of about 342 meters (1,500 feet) east–west and it varies in width, with the central portion being approximately 90 meters (300 feet) wide. The overall area of the Central Acropolis is a little more than 40,000 square meters. While there is some variation (particularly now in its ruined state), the base platform has a generally uniform height of about 7 meters (25 feet). The Central Acropolis plan form is complex,

appearing rather like an inverted T, with the north-facing central portion of the platform projecting forward. Flanking areas of the platform on the east and west contain significant structures that have not been explored, with the exception of a possible palace on the southwestern corner, which is described below. Ray T. Matheny and Deanne G. Matheny, along with others in Matheny's team, explored several structures and areas of the platform on the Central Acropolis. While these investigations were very brief and limited, they strongly suggest that the principal period of construction and use for the Central Acropolis was during Late Formative times. Some limited reuse and minor refurbishment of some structures near the centerline is evident during the Early Classic period, associated, perhaps, with a Termination ritual. An interesting revelation from the single deep probe of the Central Acropolis platform is that there is a substantial Middle Formative-phase platform/construction that was covered by the later massive Late Formative construction. Investigations on the southwestern portion of the Central Acropolis by Ellen Stutz Landeen produced evidence that suggests certain structures to be the residence of elite persons, perhaps even of a ruler of El Mirador.

Glenna Nielsen's investigations in the Central Plaza just in front of the Central Acropolis included extensive excavations in two small "altar-like" structures and other areas. These altar-platforms included large vertical slabs reminiscent of stelae, and two early sculptured stela fragments were found between the platforms and may have been looted out of them. Nielsen's excavations demonstrate that the Central Plaza was a complex area, containing numerous features, and that both the plaza and its structures underwent complex renovations over time. Her investigations clearly show that there was a strong Late Formative-period presence in the southern end of the Central Plaza, probably related to the building program that produced the Central Acropolis and its associated structures. In addition to the Tigre Complex and the Central Acropolis, there are a number of as yet unexplored monumental architectural complexes bordering the large Central Plaza.

The Monos Pyramid is one of the most imposing structures at El Mirador, standing about 42 meters (135 feet) above the surrounding terrain. The Monos Complex, which includes the Monos Pyramid, is located south of the Tigre Complex and, although not as massive as the Tigre and Danta complexes, is a very large and complicated group of constructions located or grouped around immense platforms. Denise Evans Copeland of the Brigham Young University team carried out investigations in the Monos Complex. The Monos Complex appears to cover at least 32,600 square meters excluding the huge plaza adjoining it to the west. The Monos Complex appears to follow the same pattern of the other architectural complexes thus far investigated at El Mirador, with its major construction occurring in a single construction phase during Late Formative times. Dating the huge Monos Pyramid and its three structures is somewhat problematic, because few datable materials were recovered from the limited excavations there; however, the best evidence available indicates it was a Late Formative construction, although its orientation differs slightly from that of the second level of the Monos Complex.

The Danta Complex was explored by Wayne K. Howell. The Danta Pyramid is located almost 800 meters (a half mile) east of the eastern wall system that encloses the large concentration of public architecture on the western side of El Mirador. The Danta Pyramid sits considerably higher than the Tigre Pyramid because it is located on a natural rise. The pyramid faces west and sits, along with approximately fifty other structures, upon a series of great platforms that took advantage of the natural rise in the terrain. The platforms, pyramid, and other associated structures are collectively known as the Danta Complex. As Howell (1989, p. 6) has explained, "the complex rises in a series of four unequal tiers from west to east and is extremely steep on the back or eastern side." Howell estimated that the complex covered some 165,000 square meters. Howell's investigations suggest that all the major architectural features of the Danta Complex were built, utilized, and abandoned during the Late Formative period, with construction of the large platforms beginning after 400 BCE, although further testing of the Danta Acropolis and its buildings will be needed.

Investigations were carried out in various other areas of the site, including explorations in a few residential complexes. Also Bruce Dahlin's team investigated the intriguing area known as the "Crossroads," located approximately 1 kilometer (a half mile) west of the Tigre Complex, which is apparently the terminus of several causeways that converge on the site from outlying areas. The Crossroads may have functioned as an entry and departure point from the western part of El Mirador. Although Dahlin's investigations revealed both Late Formative and Late Classic occupations, the Late Formative occupation appears to be the most intense.

These brief descriptions of some of the architectural complexes of the site give a basic idea of the monumentality and complexity of El Mirador. While many unknown areas of the site remain to be explored and many known areas and architectural complexes have not been tested, it is possible to say that El Mirador's monumental size, architectural complexity, and sophisticated masonry and stucco work indicate that in this area of the Petén, the earliest known ancient Maya city, with all the expected social complexities necessary to manage the in-

tense exchanges between the population and the ecological complex of the wider world, had been created. The labor investment necessary to build and maintain this city, to say nothing of the artistic vision, ceremonial schedules, and political glory of the site, indicates that for several centuries at least El Mirador and perhaps a few of its neighbors achieved the basic ingredients of urban civilization that we associate with later developments at Teotihuacan and among the Classic Maya.

Richard Hansen's investigations at the nearby site of Nakbé have demonstrated that it developed a surprising degree of complexity even earlier, during the Middle Formative period. Not much is known about El Mirador's achievements during that time, since constructions of that period are likely covered by the massive Late Formative architecture (as demonstrated by the probe into the Central Acropolis). Apparently, the El Mirador Basin was an early setting for the growth of complex sociopolitical organizations for hundreds of years, but why this was the case remains a mystery. Much investigation at El Mirador and other nearby sites is needed to help determine the revision of our current models of the "florescence" of civilization among the ancient Maya. At least for now, El Mirador stands as one of the most intriguing and challenging sites in all Mesoamerica, and it beckons our best efforts to understand its history, structure, and significance.

BIBLIOGRAPHY

Bishop, Ronald L. "Analysis por activacion de neutrones de la ceramica de El Mirador." *Mesoamerica* 5.7 (1984), 103–111.

Chambers, Mary Elizabeth. *Reservoir Excavations.* El Mirador Series, Papers of the New World Archaeological Foundation, 62 (forthcoming).

Copeland, Denise E. *Excavations on the Monos Complex, El Mirador, Peten, Guatemala.* El Mirador Series, part 2, Papers of the New World Archaeological Foundation, 60 (1990).

Dahlin, Bruce H. "Climate and Prehistory on the Yucatan Peninsula." *Climatic Change* 5 (1983), 245–263.

Dahlin, Bruce H. "A Colossus in Guatemala: The Preclassic City of El Mirador." *Archaeology* 37 (1984), 18–25.

Dahlin, Bruce H., John E. Foss, and Elizabeth Chambers. *Project Acalches: Reconstructing the Natural and Cultural History of a Seasonal Swamp at El Mirador, Guatemala. Preliminary Results.* Papers of the New World Archaeological Foundation, 45 (1980), 37–58.

Demarest, Arthur A. "Proyecto El Mirador de la Harvard University, 1982–1983." *Mesoamerica* 5.7 (1984), 1–13.

Demarest, Arthur A., Robert J. Sharer, William Fowler, Elenore King, and Judy Fowler. "Las excavaciones." *Mesoamerica* 5.7 (1984), 14–52.

Dixon, Boyd, Dennis Jones, and Bruce Dahlin. "Excavaciones en el complejo Los Cruces, El Mirador, Guatemala," *Mayab* 9 (1994), 18–30.

Forsyth, Donald W. *The Ceramics of El Mirador, Petén, Guatemala.* El Mirador Series, part 4, Papers of the New World Archaeological Foundation, 63 (1989).

Fowler, William R., Jr. *Analysis of the Chipped Stone Artifacts of El*

Mirador, Guatemala. Notes of the New World Archaeological Foundation, 5 (1987).

Hansen, Richard D. *Excavations in the Tigre Complex, El Mirador, Peten, Guatemala.* El Mirador Series, part 3, Papers of the New World Archaeological Foundation, 62 (1990).

Hansen, Richard D., and Mary Elizabeth Chambers. "Monumento 18 de El Mirador: el contexto arqueológico y la iconografía." *Simposio de Investigaciones Arqueológicas en Guatemala,* pp. 313–329. Museo Nacional de Arqueología y Etnologia, Mexico City, 1995.

Hansen, Richard D., and Donald W. Forsyth. "Late Preclassic Development of Unslipped Pottery in the Maya Lowlands: The Evidence from El Mirador." In *Maya Ceramics: Papers from the 1985 Maya Ceramic Conference,* pp. 439–468. London, 1987.

Hoopes, John W. "Analysis de la ceramica del periodo clasico de El Mirador." *Mesoamerica* 5.7 (1984), 93–102.

Howell, Wayne K. *Excavations in the Danta Complex, El Mirador, Peten, Guatemala.* El Mirador Series, Papers of the New World Archaeological Foundation, 60 (1989).

Matheny, Ray T. "Early States in the Maya Lowlands during the Late Preclassic Period: Edzna and El Mirador." In *City States of the Maya: Art and Architecture,* edited by Elizabeth Benson, pp. 1–44. Rocky Mountain Institute for Precolumbian Studies, Boulder, Colo., 1986.

Matheny, Ray T. "An Early Metropolis Uncovered: El Mirador." *National Geographic,* 172.3 (1987), 316–339.

Matheny, Ray T. "Varhainen Mayojen Suurkaupunki Kaivettu esin: El Mirador." *Toivelehti* 3.93 (1994), 43–50.

Matheny, Ray T., and Deanne L. Gurr. "El Mirador, Peten, Guatemala." In *Past and Present in the Americas: A Compendium of Recent Studies,* edited by John Lynch, pp. 130–136. Manchester, 1984.

Matheny, Ray T., and Deanne L. Gurr. *El Mirador, Peten, Guatemala: A Preclassic City.* Authors of film script both in English and Spanish, 28 minutes. Brigham Young University Film, Salt Lake City, 1984.

Nelson, Fred W., Jr. *Trace Element Analysis of Obsidian Artifacts from El Mirador, Guatemala.* Notes of the New World Archaeological Foundation, 3 (1986).

Nielsen, Glenna. "Central Plaza Excavations at El Mirador, Peten, Guatemala: Operations 18 and 27." Ph.D. diss. Department of Anthropology, University of Utah, Provo, 1990.

RAYMOND T. MATHENY
and DEANNE G. MATHENY

EL TAJÍN. The city of El Tajín 20° 28' 35" N, 97° 22' 39" W) is located on one side of the Sierra Papanteca, between two small valleys, with a tropical climate, in the northern part of the Mexican state of Veracruz. It began as a ceremonial center in the Epiclassic period, then became a city with the construction of Tajín Chico. It started to decline in the twelfth century CE, until it was abandoned in the thirteenth century. Subsequently, it was used sporadically as a necropolis. In the areas surrounding the ancient city, we find settlements that correspond to the three great periods in the history of ancient Mesoamerica but not in the city itself, as has been suggested in a few chronological tables (Brüggemann 1991; García Payón 1958; Wilkerson 1990).

Apart from El Tajín, we have not found anything simi-

lar in terms of urban complexity anywhere on the Gulf Coast until the arrival of Cempoala, which corresponds to the Late Postclassic period. El Tajín is, without a doubt, the most important center of its time, and Cempoala emerged as the important center on the Gulf Coast after its decline.

With respect to the layout of the urban settlement, El Tajín should be considered in its first phase as a ceremonial center with a symmetrical axis deviating 20° NE. Four buildings enclosing a central space form the Great Plaza of the Arroyo Group in the central part of the city. Other structures, such as the two associated ball courts, have the same orientation. The function of all of these buildings is ceremonial. In the following developmental period, which we call the urban phase, El Tajín spreads north and changes its orientation to 45° NE. The buildings of Tajín Chico are the major event of this period, providing a residential area for a permanent population dedicated to governmental and religious exercises. Two architectural barriers separate this area from the center of the old city and subdivide the residential area of the ruler and the high functionaries of the government.

The third and final period is characterized by anarchy in the urban layout and social disintegration. Because of the lack of space in the central area and the imposition of partisan forces, the buildings are arbitrarily arranged with respect to the original urban plan. The famous Pyramid of the Niches is the most illustrative example of this.

The decline of the architecture of El Tajín, in quality and beauty, is without a doubt evidenced in the Pyramid of the Niches, adjacent to which an artificial plaza was created with buildings that do not belong to the plaza and do not bear any urban context with the pyramid. The lower section of the building itself is nearly joined to the retention wall and Ballcourt 11.

We have not found any clear system of roads. It seems that there was a system of internal circulation based on interconnected open spaces of different sizes rather than streets, which shows us the little importance in the urban layout of El Tajín of straight lines connecting one point or urban area with another. Some archaeological evidence shows that another urban element existed to drain and protect the structures from the torrential rains of the tropical climate.

Mesoamerican cities are differentiated more by their formal aspects rather than by their religious, political, social, or economic content. After the Formative (Preclassical) period, the Mesoamerican city appears in nearly all cultural subareas, earlier in some places than others. There is no significant difference in the social, economic, or political aspects between the cities of the Classic period and those of the Postclassic. The city produces no qualitative changes, in either time or space. The urban

El Tajín. *Courtesy of Visual Resources Collection, The University of Texas at Austin. Ferguson Collection.*

layout of Teotihuacan or Tenochtitlan is essentially consistent; the differences are formal and stylistic, but the social structure is the same.

In contrast to our understanding of the Aztec, the only sources informing us of social composition and religious activities in the case of El Tajín are the reliefs on the North and South Ballcourts and on the columns of the Temple of the Columns.

The final phase of the process of Mesoamerican urbanization began with the growing contradiction between the established state power and the economic necessities of the community, such as occurred between the Eagle Knights and the *pochteca* ("traveling merchants") in Mexica society. Something similar also seems to have occurred at El Tajín because of the destruction of the urban plan, the scenes of warfare on the column reliefs, and the city's subsequent abandonment.

Art, Architecture, and Thought. In pre-Hispanic Mesoamerican society, as in all traditional societies, religion and civil society were intimately linked, forming a sole reality in which humans blended with deities and vice versa. The concrete, tangible, and sentient mingled with the visionary and cosmogonic. Real life combined the worldly with the transcendental. Any other existence was impossible to contemplate.

Keeping these basic concepts of Mesoamerican existence in mind, where the esoteric and rational is in some manner joined together into a sole unit, it is not strange that themes in artistic production are intimately tied to this vision of the world of deities and humans. Thus, the high priests simultaneously would have been the supreme political leaders. We remember that the Aztec king was the one who personified Huitzilopochtli and had to dance in his festival, just as 13 Rabbit did at El Tajín.

The notion of time as an abstract figure is translated into movement in the concrete realm. Herein lies the importance of the ball game, dedicated to time, in which the ball simulates the universal cosmic game. This form of interpreting the existential reality of Mesoamerican peoples symbolizes the precarious nature of the cosmos and life in general, always at the point of falling into chaos. This traumatic existence was alleviated only by blood from decapitation. Therefore, if the deities and the entire cosmos were at peace, humans also would be, and everyone could expect prosperity, which translated into a bountiful maize harvest that guaranteed group survival.

The articulation of the plastic in space is perceived in different ways by Mesoamerican cultures. What they have in common is the integration of the plastic arts—the genres of sculpture, relief, and painting—within architecture and urban planning when they are related to religion and the state. They can be found in the base of a temple, as in Tula; in the sanctuary itself, such as the paintings in the temple associated with the Great Ballcourt in

Chichén Itzá; in funerary chambers, as in Palenque; and in residences and palaces, as in Teotihuacan, Bonampak, and El Tajín. Mural painting and reliefs can be found outside and inside buildings. Freestanding sculpture, at times, plays a structural role in architecture, as in the case of the *atlantes* of Tula and the columns on the portico of the Governor's Palace in El Tajín. The possibility also exists that it performs a specific function in the ritual within the building where the sacrifice occurs. Architecture itself is articulated not only in isolated buildings but also in groups of various structures that make up an urban space among open and closed spaces. The development of exterior space is a specifically Mesoamerican characteristic in contrast to Western architecture. In terms of design, not only the buildings but also the open spaces, such as plazas, are of integral importance and have to be kept in adequate proportion to invoke the desired effect in the user of the city.

In such a manner is explained the great development of the foundations to the detriment of the building itself. The interior space achieved does not have any rational relation with the effort exerted, which confirms that attaining the interior space was not the principal motivation in the construction of buildings and in the layout of cities. It seems that one of the principal functions of architecture was the persuasion of the masses and the consolidation of the state.

From the perspective of form, El Tajín is distinguished from other Mesoamerican cities by the multiple, varied use of the niche in building façades. Niches could be square or rectangular, large or small, and used abundantly or sparingly in architectural design. At times, they bear a step-fret motif in their interior. The repetition of the niche produces an optical sensation in the spectator that lightens the weight and severity of the mass of the buildings. Generally, we find niches in *tablero* panels or on the ends of balustrades. The *taludes* and superimposed sections of the foundations may vary in number and form. There are buildings with several sections, such as the Pyramid of the Niches and Structure 16 in the Plaza del Arroyo, or with elongated *taludes*, such as Structure 5.

In the construction systems employed, the retention walls of the amorphous nucleus stand out in which natural slabs of local sandstone are cemented with earth and plastered with a sand and lime mortar. In the case of the Pyramid of the Niches, there is a structured nucleus in which the walls of the different sections spring out from the base, and, as a particularity, a flight of stairs runs from the temple on top of the base to the second section, without terminating in a funerary chamber. In some cases, the foundations were painted in a monochrome blue or red color.

Concerning the art associated with the buildings, there are bas-reliefs in stone. The most famous are the ones in the North and South Ballcourts, but also important are those of the Temple of the Columns and the Plaza del Arroyo. The subject matter depicted in the sculptural corpus is predominantly sacred, but it can also be historical, as in the case of the column reliefs.

The first sculptural works belong to the pre-urban phase and come from the buildings of the Plaza del Arroyo. In contrast with the works of the period of florescence, they depict isolated personages, statically presented without any major complications. Subsequently, everything becomes movement and a greater complexity in the way of ideograms and allegorical motifs. The sculptures relate episodes in ritual ceremony or political life, such as the accomplishments of 13 Rabbit. The static phase changes to a dynamism with complex curvilinear forms, as in the Baroque period of Western art.

In mural painting, the subject matter may be abstract-symbolic or figurative-concrete, but also sacred, such as the divine beings and mythological animals in Building 1 of Tajín Chico.

In the time of the apogee of El Tajín, the plastic arts and the architectural design of the building façades have in common the repetition and connecting of plastic elements, such as niches in the architecture and ideograms in sculpture and painting, in such a way that they evoke an aesthetic pleasure that is beyond words and makes the culture of El Tajín unmistakable.

[*See also* Gulf Coast.]

BIBLIOGRAPHY

Bertels, Ursula. *Die Göetterwelt von El Tajín Mexiko.* Münster in Westfalen, Germany, 1991.

Brüggemann, Jürgen K. "Informes técnicos del Proyecto Tajín." *Archivo de Arqueología* (1984–1992).

Brüggemann, Jürgen K. "Apuntes sobre la restauración de edificios prehispánicos." *Boletín del Insituto Nacional de Antropología e Historia (México)* 29 (1990), 24–32.

Brüggemann, Jürgen K. "El problema cronológico de Tajín." *Archivo de Arqueología* (1990).

Brüggemann, Jürgen K. "Analisís urbano del sitio arqueológico de Tajín." In *Proyecto Tajín*, vol. I. Mexico City, 1991.

Brüggemann, Jürgen K. "Seriación del material cerámico procedente de pozos estratigráficos." In *Proyecto Tajín*. Mexico City, 1991.

Brüggemann, Jürgen K. "Otra vez la cuestión totonaca." *Boletín del Insituto Nacional de Antropología e Historia (México)* 34 (1991), 84–85.

Brüggemann, Jürgen K. "La ciudad y la sociedad." In *Tajín*. Xalapa, Mexico, 1992.

Brüggemann, Jürgen K., ed. *Tajín*. Madrid and Mexico City, 1992.

Carrasco, Pedro, Johanna Broda, et al. *Estratificación social en al Mesoamérica prehispánica.* Mexico City, 1976.

Castells, Manuel. *The Urban Question: A Marxist Approach.* London, 1977; Cambridge, Mass., 1979.

Castillo Peña, Patricia. *El catálogo de la escultura de Tajín.* Field report for the 1989–1990 season of Proyecto Tajín. Mexico City, 1990.

DuSolier, Wilfrido. "Principales conclusions obtenidas del estudio de la cerámica del Tajín." In *Congreso Internacional de Americanistas, XXVII sesión, del 5 al 15 de agosto de 1939, Mexico, D.F.*, no. 2, pp. 25–38. Mexico City, 1939.

Elias, Norbert. *The Civilizing Process: The History of Manners*. Oxford, 1994.

Erdheim, Mario. *Prestige und Kulturwandel: Eine Studie zum Verhältnis subjektiver und objektiver Faktoren des kulturellen Wandels zur Klassengesellschaft bei den Azteken*. Wiesbaden, Germany, 1972.

García Payón, José. "Informes sobre las temporados de canto en Tajín." *Archivo de Arqueología*. Insituto Nacional de Antropología e Historia, México, 1939–1970.

García Payón, José. "Evolución histórica del Totonacapan." In *Miscellanea Paul Rivet octogenario dicata*, vol. 1, pp. 443–453. Mexico City, 1958.

Kampen, Michael Edwin. *The Sculptures of El Tajín, Veracruz, Mexico*. Gainesville, Fla., 1972.

Kroster, Paula, and Roman Kroster. "Topografía y cerámica de Tajín." *Anales del Insituto Nacional de Antropología e Historia (México)* 3 (1972).

Ladrón de Guevara, Sara. "Pintura y escultura." In *Tajín*. Madrid and Mexico City, 1992.

López, Austin. *Alfredo Hombre-dios. Religión y política en el mundo náhuatl*. Mexico City, 1989.

Raesfeld, Lydia. *Die Ballspielplätze von El Tajín*. Münster in Westfalen, Germany, 1992.

Rinke, Dorothee. *Wohnbauten in El Tajín, Mexiko*. Münster in Westfalen, Germany, 1992.

Wilkerson, Jeffrey. "Man's Eighty Centuries in Veracruz." *National Geographic* 153 (August 1990).

JÜRGEN K. BRÜGGEMANN
Translated from Spanish by Scott Sessions

EMPIRES. *See* States and Empires *and* Triple Alliance.

ENCOMIENDAS AND REPARTIMIENTOS.

Once the conquest of Mexico-Tenochtitlan had been completed, Fernando Cortés proceeded to distribute the native lords and their people to his officers in a system of subjugation known as *encomienda*. From the moment *encomiendas* were established in New Spain, they were a source of discussion and conflict. At first, King Charles V of Spain was opposed to the creation of *encomiendas*, fearing that the same disaster that had befallen the Caribbean would come to pass in Mexico—a high mortality rate and depopulation. Nevertheless, Cortés argued that this was the only way to compensate the soldiers and gradually populate the land with Christians. In his fourth letter to the King in 1524 (*Cuarta carta de relación*), Cortés stated that he had distributed Indians in *encomiendas* in Coatzacoalcos, Oaxaca, and Colima. In the same year, he formulated the Ordinances of Good Government, in which he ordered that the *encomenderos* (holders of *encomiendas*) be entrusted with destroying native idols and paying a clergyman or monk to teach Christian beliefs to the Indians. He also limited the personal services required of the Indians included in an *encomienda* and prohibited their being forced to pay part of their tribute in gold. From 1526 to 1528, the negative attitude of the Crown subsided, and as a result of the reports it received from the regular clergy came to favor perpetual *repartimientos* ("distributions"), or *encomiendas*. In 1529, however, the Crown reversed its policy again and prohibited the *encomienda*, arguing that it deprived the Indians of their freedom.

The abuses resulting from this institution were described by Fray Bartolomé de Las Casas, who became the staunchest advocate of the Indians and the chief opponent of the *encomienda* until it was partially abolished in 1542. In effect, the New Laws of 1542 ordered that on the death of the owner of an *encomienda*, it would revert to the Crown. This policy produced great discontent among the Spanish *encomenderos*, who saw their source of livelihood threatened. After numerous petitions, in 1545 they managed to have the *encomienda* extended to two lifetimes. That same year, a major epidemic broke out that reduced the native population considerably. In 1549, by royal decree, personal service was eliminated as an integral part of the tributes to be paid within the *encomienda* system. Then, in 1550, with a tour of inspection of Diego Ramírez, there was a reassessment that reduced the tribute to be paid by the Indians. The restrictions successively imposed on the *encomienda* aroused the indignation of the Spanish colonists and led to the 1537 conspiracy of Martín Cortés (see below). Nevertheless, by the 1560s, the Crown had succeeded in subduing the *encomenderos* and their seigneurial aspirations and in consolidating government in the hands of royal officials. By the latter third of the sixteenth century, the importance of the *encomienda* had diminished. Tribute was set on the basis of the number of Indians who should pay a regular rate of one peso and half a *fanega* (approximately 1.5 bushels) of maize. By 1580, the Indian population had declined by 80 percent. All these changes greatly reduced the income of the *encomiendas*.

From the Indians' point of view, the *encomienda* helped to initiate a process whereby their provinces—known in Spanish as *señoríos*—were gradually disintegrated. Although at first the Crown claimed to favor respecting the political and social organization of the natives and taking only the tribute that Motecuhzoma had received as their king, the distribution of Indians in *encomiendas* did not respect the territorial and jurisdictional extension of the former *señoríos*. The president of the Second Audiencia (high court), Ramírez de Fuenleal, pointed out that the provinces or *señoríos* were so large that if they were allotted on the basis of one per *encomendero*, there would not be enough to go around. By 1526, the Crown—fearing the power that could be concentrated in the hands of the *encomenderos*—ordered that the number of Indians granted in an *encomienda* be limited to three hundred. Some of the first *encomiendas* granted by Cortés had contained two thousand or more.

The disbanding of the Indian *señoríos* elicited protests on the part of the native lords. In 1537, the Indian Martín Cortés, who was governor and *cacique* (chief) of the pueblo of Tistla, filed suit against Diego Xaramillo, *encomendero* of Zumpango, claiming that the pueblo of Xilapancingo belonged to that of Tistla. A similar case was the lawsuit brought to court in 1536 by Tlatelolco for control of the *estancias* (estates) of Tepanquilla and others, against Benavides, *encomendero* of Xaltocan. In the 1550s and 1560s, such requests became more numerous. The native lords of Tacuba, Xochimilco, and Tetzcoco, among others, asked for various privileges related to their posts to be restored—for example, the right to receive tributes from the pueblos given to the Spaniards as *encomiendas* or, even, access to Indian lands and labor.

Since the *encomiendas* were not distributed according to the Indian form of organization based on *tlatoani* communities (those dependent on a single native overlord), imperial and local tributary systems were affected. In addition, the new colonial units created confusion about the rights of persons involved in the old and new systems and led, on more than one occasion, to lengthy lawsuits. In principle, the Spanish monarch had succeeded Motecuhzoma as sovereign and, as such, was entitled to receive the tribute that Indian *señoríos* had paid that ruler. The disruption of Indian *señoríos* owing to the allotment of Indians to *encomiendas*, however, undermined the rights that the native lords had over their vassals. The manner in which the tributary system evolved until it was consolidated in the 1580s—when it was determined that each Indian subject to tribute should pay a peso and half a *fanega* of maize—also had considerable impact on the rule of native lords. In the 1550s, the Crown proceeded to regulate the tribute that could be received by the lords from their vassals. Even more significant were the reassessments made by Inspector General Valderrama in 1563. The measures imposed by Valderrama caused the final disruption of relations within the *señorío*. Valderrama incorporated the *mayeques* (people conquered in pre-Hispanic times who had become tenant farmers or sharecroppers on lands they previously owned) of the native lords in tributary registers, while also including the *principales* (Indian leaders, the nonruling nobility), who until that time had been exempt from paying taxes. The tax adjustments made by the inspector general led to a wave of protests on the part of native lords and *principales*.

By the end of the sixteenth century, the Crown had managed to suppress both the *encomenderos* and the native lords by directly administering the tribute paid by Indians. The few *encomenderos* who survived the New Laws or who had perpetual *encomiendas*—for example, the sons of Emperor Motecuhzoma, or the Marqués de Salinas—were made royal pensioners who received a fixed income from the Crown. Thus, by the end of the sixteenth century, the *encomienda* relinquished its status as a major axis for organizing the colonial government and economy.

[*See also* Labor.]

BIBLIOGRAPHY

García Bernal, Manuela Cristina. *Población y encomienda en Yucatán bajo los Austrias*. Seville, 1978. View of the way the *encomienda* was established in Yucatán and the effect it had on the native population.

Gibson, Charles. *The Aztecs under Spanish Rule 1519–1810*. Stanford, 1964. Chapter 4 has a complete description of the *encomienda* and its evolution in the Valley of Mexico.

Megenus Bornemann, Margarita. *Del señorío indígena a la República de indios: El caso del Valle de Toluca 1500–1600*. Mexico City, 1992. Chapter 3 contains an interpretation of the *encomienda* from the Indian perspective and the effect this institution had with respect to their traditional forms of organization.

Miranda, José. *El tributo indígena en la Nueva España durante el siglo XVI*. Mexico City, 1952. Comprehensive outline of the evolution of the tribute system in the sixteenth century, an institution closely related to the *encomienda*.

Miranda, José. *La función económica del encomendero en los orígenes del régimen colonial: Nueva España, 1555–1531*. Mexico City, 1965. The first study that analyzed the economic importance of the *encomienda* in the formation of the early colonial economy.

Simpson, Lesley Byrd. *The Encomienda in New Spain: The Beginning of Spanish Mexico*. Berkeley and Los Angeles, 1950. One of the first attempts to analyze the *encomienda*.

Zavala, Silvio. *De encomienda y propiedad territorial en algunas regiones de la América española*. Mexico City, 1940. An exceptional interpretation of the *encomienda* which ended the debate regarding it and property rights.

Zavala, Silvio. *La encomienda indiana*. Mexico City, 1973. The most complete analysis of the *encomienda* and its evolution during the entire Colonial period, with a comparative overview of the *encomienda* in Spanish America and the Philippines.

MARGARITA MEGENUS BORNEMANN

EPIGRAPHY. [*This entry comprises three articles:*

Maya
Mixtec and Central Mexican
Zapotec

The first article discusses the history and development of the study and interpretation of Maya hieroglyphs and pictography, including major contributions and breakthroughs; the second article presents the study and interpretation of Mixtec and Nahua glyphs and pictography; the third article treats the study and interpretation of Zapotec glyphs and pictography. For related discussions, see Mesoamerican Studies *and* Writing Systems, *article on* Overview and Early Development.]

Maya

The decipherment of Maya hieroglyphic writing has been a very slow process in comparison with the decipherment of similar scripts in other cultures, such as Egyptian and Hittite. The major obstacle to epigraphic success in more than 150 years of intensive research has been a general failure to understand both the nature of the writing system in use among the ancient Maya scribes and the purpose behind the carving of their stone monuments. Real progress along these lines began only in the 1950s.

European knowledge about Maya writing, however imperfect, began with the Spanish conquest. Suppression of the Maya religion by Spanish missionary priests and persecution of native religious practitioners resulted in a decline in practical knowledge of their ancient script among the Maya themselves, and eventually in the total replacement of hieroglyphs with roman letters. Some Franciscan friars—particularly Diego de Landa—learned to read the glyphs, but it is unlikely that by the close of the eighteenth century any Maya could read or write in the ancient system.

Age of Exploration. With the independence of Mexico and the Central American countries, knowledge of the ancient Maya entered a new phase. In 1816, the polymath scientist Alexander von Humboldt published a facsimile of four pages of the *Dresden Codex*, and several decades later Lord Kingsborough reproduced the entire codex in an accurate rendering by an Italian artist. The earliest publication of a Classic Maya inscription—considerably distorted—appeared in 1822, in the Spaniard Antonio del Río's description of Palenque. But it was not until 1841, with the appearance of John Lloyd Stephens's *Incidents of Travel in Central America, Chiapas, and Yucatán*, illustrated by the English topographical artist Frederick Catherwood, that the world learned of the "lost" civilization of the Classic Maya and its wealth of inscribed (but then unreadable) stone monuments.

Stephens recognized that the Maya themselves had built these ancient cities, and also that the writing system of the Dresden manuscript and of the monuments was the same. He also made the prophetic suggestion that, when deciphered, the monuments would prove to record the history of those cities and their rulers. Through perusal of the illustrations in the books by del Río, Stephens, and Humboldt, the biologist Constantine S. Rafinesque realized that in the Maya numeration system, a dot stood for "one" and a bar for "five"—the very first step in the long history of Maya decipherment.

What was lacking through much of the nineteenth century was a real corpus of Maya inscriptions, highly accurate renderings of the texts as good as those produced by French artists and scholars during the Napoleonic campaign in Egypt. These were not to appear until the end of the century, in the form of the magnificent drawings and photographs published by Alfred P. Maudslay in *Biologia Centrali-Americana* (1889–1902), and the equally fine photographic record of the Austrian Teobert Maler. Before this, all efforts toward decipherment were necessarily centered on the codices.

Pioneers of Decipherment. Following Rafinesque's discovery of bar-and-dot numeration, little work was done on Maya writing until the mid-nineteenth century and the appearance on the scene of a French abbé, Charles Étienne Brasseur de Bourbourg. He brought to light one part of the *Madrid Codex* and in 1862 discovered the manuscript of Landa's *Relacíon*. The sixteenth-century Franciscan priest (and later bishop of Yucatán) Diego de Landa is still a figure of controversy. In 1562, he began inquisitorial proceedings against Maya converts whom he accused of idolatry, eventually conducting a great auto-da-fé in Maní at which he burned an unknown number of native hieroglyphic books. Recalled to Spain to answer charges of exceeding his authority, he wrote his famous *Relación de las cosas de Yucatán*, in which he devoted several pages to the Maya writing system, relying on high-ranking native informants for his information. According to Landa, the basis of the system was an alphabet, for which he gives a total of 30 different "letters," along with three examples of how words and brief sentences were written. Unfortunately, Landa's original has been lost: all we have is an early-seventeenth-century copy that was rediscovered in the mid-nineteenth century. It was not until the 1950s that the true nature and importance of Landa's contribution were fully realized: this is the Rosetta Stone of Maya decipherment, the bilingual document that provides the key to the script.

In his enthusiasm over Landa's explanation of the script, Brasseur attempted to apply it as an alphabetic key to the *Madrid Codex*, with ludicrous results. A far better idea of the nature of the Landa "alphabet" was held by the French Orientalist Léon de Rosny, who saw that the entire system was a mixture of phonetic signs and what we would now call "logograms" (symbols representing entire words). Moreover, de Rosny identified the glyphs for the world-directions and recognized the New Year ceremonies in the *Madrid Codex*.

The most consistent nineteenth-century champion of phoneticism in the script, however, was the American anthropologist Cyrus Thomas. In several pioneering essays of the 1880s, Thomas argued that much of the script was phonetic, and, on the basis of Landa's signs, he proposed several readings of glyphs in the *Dresden Codex* which in retrospect have proved to be valid. His greatest opponent was the German Mesoamericanist Eduard Seler, a formidable defender of the idea that the glyphs were largely ideographic—that is, they conveyed concepts rather than phonetic information. It was Seler's view that held sway in Mayanist circles until the mid-twentieth century.

Concurrent with these debates about the nature of the script, major progress was being made toward understanding the calendrics and astronomy in the codices and inscriptions. Here the pivotal figure was Ernst Förstemann, director of the Royal Library in Dresden (where the famous codex was housed). Beginning in 1886 and continuing until his death in 1906, Förstemann published a series of brilliant studies of the codex in which he brought to notice for the first time the Maya Long Count and its starting date at 4 Ahaw 8 Kumk'u, the vigesimal basis of Maya arithmetic, the workings of the 260-day calendar (*tzolk'in*), and the Venus and lunar tables in the *Dresden Codex*. His contemporary, the American newspaper editor Joseph T. Goodman, may have independently discovered the Long Count, but Goodman's chief claim to fame in epigraphic research was his proposed correlation between the Maya and Christian calendars—a correlation that has stood the test of time, with an emendation of only a few days.

Thompson and His Contemporaries. The major figure in Maya research during the first half of the twentieth century was the British archaeologist J. Eric S. Thompson. After establishing the correctness of the Goodman correlation, Thompson turned his attention to the Lunar Series on the monuments. The American engineer John S. Teeple had already shown that this recorded the age of the current moon and its position in a cycle of six lunations; Thompson went on to identify its first glyph ("Glyph G") as a recurring cycle of nine Lords of the Night. In the same vein, he later demonstrated the existence of an 819-day cycle in the inscriptions. More important, he identified "date indicators" which tell the reader to count forward or backward to other dates on the same monument, in effect foreshadowing the epigraphic revolution that was soon to take place.

Thompson was a lifelong opponent of any proposal to read the non-calendrical glyphs phonetically: to him, apart from a few rebus signs, they were entirely ideographic and symbolic, with a host of esoteric associations. Thus, when the American linguist Benjamin Whorf revived the Thomas approach in a 1933 study, Thompson was quick to discredit both him and any other who essayed to use the Landa "alphabet."

The Knorosov Revolution. In 1952, a Soviet journal published an article by the young Russian philologist Yuri V. Knorosov. Contending that the Landa "alphabet" was really a syllabary, Knorosov proposed that the Maya script was logosyllabic in nature: that is, while whole words could be written with logograms, syllabic signs for various combinations of consonant plus vowel were often

attached to these as phonetic indicators. Furthermore, a Maya word with the structure consonant-vowel-consonant could be expressed with two syllabic signs, in which case the second vowel, although suppressed in reading, usually duplicated the preceding vowel (Knorosov called this the "Principle of Synharmony"). Faced with the fierce opposition of Thompson, Knorosov's view of the script initially had few adherents among Mayanists (David H. Kelley was a notable exception), but by the time of the 1979 Albany Conference on Phoneticism in the Maya Script, it had clearly won the day; it is now accepted by all modern epigraphers.

History in the Inscriptions. The second revolution that changed the course of Maya decipherment was the discovery of the historical nature of the Maya inscriptions. This began in 1958 with the identification by Heinrich Berlin of what he called "emblem glyphs"—glyphs with main signs that varied according to the city, but with unvarying affixes. Berlin hypothesized that real history might be written on the monuments, not just calendrics and astronomy.

The Berlin hypothesis was validated in 1960, when Tatiana Proskouriakoff published her groundbreaking article, "Historical Implications of a Pattern of Dates at Piedras Negras, Guatemala." Through examination of a series of stelae, she demonstrated that each series recorded the birth and accession to power of successive rulers of Piedras Negras. Next, she was able to outline the histories of two warlike rulers of Yaxchilan, Shield Jaguar and Bird Jaguar, and to identify personal names as well as verbal phrases of prisoner capture, ritual bloodletting, and other royal activities of both men and women. Almost all of the subsequent development of Maya decipherment has rested on the twin foundations of historical analysis (notably the unraveling of Palenque's dynastic history, beginning with the Mesa Redonda of 1973) and of epigraphic linguistics.

Recent Developments. The pace of decipherment has accelerated greatly over the past three decades. The glyphs for many verbs ("action glyphs") and parentage terms were decoded in the 1970s and 1980s. In 1987, the young epigrapher David Stuart brought out his *Ten Phonetic Syllables*, in which he added to the corpus of syllabic signs and also established the methodology of decipherment through identification of scribal substitutions (phonetic signs substituted for logographic ones). First brought to light by Peter Mathews, the Maya propensity for "name-tagging" personal possessions and other objects has led to the recognition of names for ceramic types, personal adornment, carved monuments, buildings, and places (even supernatural ones).

Classic period painted and carved ceramics have played a prominent role in Maya epigraphy. David Stuart, Nikolai Grube, Stephen Houston, and Barbara McLeod, among others, have shown that the formulaic Primary Standard Sequence that is prominent on many ceramics dedicates the vessel, frequently names the artist/scribe, describes the contents, and identifies the owner or patron. In the same vein, Stuart has shown that Maya artists often signed their works; these include the sculptors who produced the carved monuments. The analysis of secondary texts and scenes on Maya vases has led epigraphers into the supernatural world, with the simultaneous decipherment by Grube, Houston, and Stuart of the glyph for *way*, the occult "alter ego" or co-essence of Maya rulers, personified as an otherworldly, chimeric being.

What of the future? With the identification of the Classic period language behind the texts (including even those in Yucatán) as a proto-Cholan tongue ancestral to modern Chortí, epigraphers are now turning to a precise analysis of the parts of words and sentences, and to the nuances of Maya syntax and discourse. For example, written verbs are no longer merely labeled as "event glyphs" but are now recognized as comprising transitives, intransitives, and passive voice. Simultaneously, earlier readings continue to be tested by the principle of phonetic substitution and through linguistic analysis. The result will be a decipherment as complete as that of Old World hieroglyphic scripts.

[*See also* Writing Systems, *article on* Overview and Early Development; Writing Systems, *article on* Maya.]

BIBLIOGRAPHY

Coe, Michael D. *Breaking the Maya Code.* London and New York, 1992. Popular account of the history of Maya decipherment.

Stuart, George E. "Quest for Decipherment: A Historical and Biographical Survey of Maya Hieroglyphic Investigation." In *New Theories on the Ancient Maya*, edited by Elin C. Danien and Robert J. Sharer, pp. 1–63. Philadelphia, 1992. Presents important details not given by Coe, especially concerning the earliest pioneers of decipherment.

MICHAEL D. COE

Mixtec and Central Mexican

The most prominent products of ancient Mixtec and Central Mexican iconography and writing are the pictographic codices, *lienzos*, rolls, and maps used by the Nahua, Mixtec, and other peoples. Most pre-Hispanic manuscripts were lost during the process of colonization in the sixteenth century; fewer than twenty survived, generally because they ended up as curiosities in the hands of collectors and later became the treasures of libraries and archives, mostly in Europe. This core is enriched by several hundred specimens from the Early Colonial period. The documents that remained in family or community archives were locally seen as related to land titles. Consequently, with the land reforms of the nineteenth century, many of these were sold, either to be concentrated in Mexican institutions such as Archivo General de la Nación and the Museo Nacional de Antropología, or to wander by tortuous and sometimes illegal ways to collections in Europe and the United States.

Early Colonial comments—based on information provided by indigenous experts—provide the key for interpreting these manuscripts. The corpus of signs representing the names of places or individuals, identified by their Nahuatl names in alphabetic script, can be used as a pictographic dictionary. In a similar way, we can learn about the iconography of the deities and the conventions that represent actions, genealogical relationships, and religious symbols. One such "Rosetta Stone" is the *Codex Mendoza*, engravings of which were published as early as 1625 (*Purchas' His Pilgrimes*, London). Systematic studies of ancient Mexican pictorial manuscripts did not start until the eighteenth century: Lorenzo Boturini presented the first catalogue, and the exiled Jesuit Fábrega tried to interpret the most important pre-Hispanic religious manuscript, the *Codex Borgia*, with the help of the colonial *Codex Vaticanus A*. Scholars like Alexander von Humboldt, Joseph Aubin, José Fernando Ramírez, and Ernest Hamy continued this tradition throughout the nineteenth century, clarifying the basic principles of ancient Mexican pictography. At the same time, projects like those of Lord Kingsborough, the Duke of Loubat, and the Mexican Junta Colombina resulted in the publication of the most important codices.

At the turn of the twentieth century, Eduard Seler, Zelia Nuttall, Francisco del Paso y Troncoso, and other scholars brought interpretation to a higher level through meticulous iconological description and philological research. Seler was strongly influenced by the astralistic paradigm of his days, which led him to look for occult astronomical references in the religious codices of the Borgia Group; it also made him and his alumnus Walter Lehmann blind to suggestions as to the possible historical character of a group of codices related to the *Codex Vienna*. By contrast, Nuttall, James Cooper Clark, Richard Long, and Herbert Spinden favoured a historical reading of the latter group of manuscripts, but they were unable to identify their provenience and time depth. Aztec culture and terminology were the main frame of reference.

In his commentary on the *Codex of Yanhuitlan* (1940), Wigberto Jiménez Moreno, author of many significant contributions to the understanding of Central Mexican antiquity, laid the foundation for the study of Mixtec ethnohistory. At his suggestion, Alfonso Caso analyzed the pictographic *Map of Teozacualco*, which accompanied the 1580 *Relación geográfica* of that town in the Mixteca Alta. Caso discovered that the protagonists of a specific group of codices in pre-Hispanic style—the codices *Vienna, Nuttall, Bodley, Colombino, Becker I,* and *Selden*—were also present on the Teozacualco map and were identified there by a gloss as rulers of the Mixtec city states of Tilantongo and Teozacualco. Caso deciphered their genealogical relationships and calculated their time depth by tracing the sequence of associated dates (given in 52-year cycles) back to the end of the seventh century CE. As a consequence, Caso was able to describe in much more detail the lives of two important historical personages already identified by Cooper Clark and Spinden: Lord 8 Deer and Lady 6 Monkey. Caso's results were published in a number of articles, three commentaries with facsimile editions of the codices *Bodley* (1960), *Selden* (1964), and *Colombino* (1966), and a posthumously published synthesis with an inventory of the individuals mentioned in these codices (*Reyes y reinos de la Mixteca,* 1977–1979).

In the meantime, the knowledge of Central Mexican pictography was advanced through a commentary on the *Codex Xolotl* by Charles Dibble (1951) and numerous publications by Robert Barlow. Building on the edition of the *Codex Mendoza* by Cooper Clark (1938), Karl Anton Nowotny analyzed the toponymic hieroglyphs and produced an elementary pictographic dictionary (1959), which was expanded through Hanns Prem's index of onomastic glyphs in the *Matricula de Huexotzingo* (1974) and complemented by studies on phoneticism in Aztec writing by Henry B. Nicholson and Joaquín Galarza. With his profound understanding of the calendar and divinatory (mantic) symbolism, Nowotny showed new ways to interpret the Borgia Group and corrected the astralistic interpretations proposed by Seler. His *Tlacuilolli, die mexikanischen Bilderhandschriften, Stil und Inhalt, mit einem Katalog der Codex Borgia Gruppe* (1961) remains a standard work.

Looking at the codices from an art historian's perspective, Donald Robertson laid the foundation for a stylistic analysis in his fundamental study, *Mexican Manuscript Painting of the Early Colonial Period: The Metropolitan Schools* (1959). Nicholson contributed in a number of publications to the definition of the Mixteca-Puebla horizon style. A debate arose about the provenience of the members of the Borgia Group. Comparing their style and iconography with decorated ceramics, frescoes, and reliefs, some scholars (Nowotny, Nicholson) pointed to Cholula as the great religious center of the Postclassic period, while others (e.g., Robertson) stressed the similarities between the Borgia Group and the Mixtec codices.

During the 1960s and 1970s, a number of magnificent facsimile editions were produced by the Akademische Druck- und Verlagsanstalt (Graz, Austria). Stimulated and supervised by Ferdinand Anders, this project set new standards for quality of reproduction and codicological analysis. A census and synthesis were offered by John Glass and Donald Robertson in the *Handbook of Middle American Indians*, with a comprehensive bibliography (1975, vols. 14, 15). This led to an expansion of editions and commentaries in the last quarter of the twentieth century. Several projects were realized in Mexico (Fondo de Cultura Económica, Instituto Nacional de Antropología, Colegio Mexiquense), and more fine facsimiles were brought out in the United States and Europe.

A landmark in Central Mexican ethnohistory was the new edition of the *Codex Mendoza* (Berdan and Anawalt, 1992). Many other sources have become available, including the *Codez Azcatitlan* (Graulich, 1995), *Codex García Granados* (Noguez, 1988), *Codex Kingsborough* (Valle, 1993) and *Codex of Tlatelolco* (Valle, 1994). Work at the Centro de Investigaciones Superiores en Antropología Social (CIESAS), Mexico City, has focused on the documents of the Cuauhtinchan area: the *Historia Tolteca Chichimeca* was edited with a full commentary by Kirchhoff, Odena Güemes, and Reyes García (1976), complemented by the publication of the *Cuauhtinchan Maps* (Yoneda, 1981), and studies by Reyes García on the whole corpus of pictographic texts related to Tlaxcala (1993). These have become crucial works of reference for the ethnohistory of the Postclassic. Microhistory is combined successfully with contextualization in the wider circle of problems related to social-economic organization (tribute structure), political events, and the interaction of cultural-ethnic groups in the period after the fall of Tula and before the imperial expansion of Tenochtitlan. In this respect, local land documents and tribute lists receive more attention, as do the codices of adjacent areas, which provide examples of local but related historiography: the recently "discovered" *Codex Xicotepec* (Stresser-Péan, 1995), the Otomí codices from Huamantla (Aguilera, 1984) and Huichapan (Reyes Retana, 1992), the Tlapanec *Codex of Azoyú* (Vega Sosa, 1991) and the corpus of pictorial documents from Michoacán (Roskamp, 1999). The connection with other archival documents, *titulos,* and Late Colonial pictographies (the Techialoyan codices) sheds light on indigenous historiography and the resignification of the past in the context of changing social circumstances after the Conquest.

In the course of extirpating native religion, the Spanish missionary friars had several codices painted or copied. The groups of Colonial religious codices that are the result of their projects show complex relationships. One group comprises codices *Tudela* (Tudela de la Orden, 1980), *Ixtlilxochitl* (Van Doesburg and Carrera González, 1996), and Magliabechi (Boone, 1983; Anders, Jansen et al., 1996). Another consists of the *Codex Telleriano-Remensis* (Quiñones Keber, 1995) and its later copy, the *Vaticanus A* (Anders and Jansen, 1996). Modern commentaries focus on syncretism with its changes in form (style) and content (cosmovision).

The pre-Hispanic Borgia Group was published by the Fondo de Cultura Económica: the accompanying commentaries (main author, Maarten Jansen) follow the ideas of Nowotny but go further to propose "readings" of the pictorial scenes, based on comparison of the historical data with present-day indigenous oral tradition and on a study of Mesoamerican symbolic and divinatory language, with its many metaphors. Mantic language often displays a combination of ambiguity and triviality; where the symbols apply to common, daily situations, the actual reading may have a demystifying effect.

Caso's work on the Mixtec codices was continued by a number of scholars. Given the still fragmentary understanding of this corpus, emphasis was on further decipherment. Fundamental is Mary Elizabeth Smith's *Picture Writing from Ancient Southern Mexico, Mixtec Place Signs and Maps* (1973). The ethnohistorical and archaeological work of Ronald Spores clarified the structure of ancient Mixtec society. With a profound commentary on the *Codex Colombino-Becker* (1974), Nancy Troike contributed to the understanding of the life of Lord 8 Deer as a royal drama; she also published articles on various pictorial conventions (e.g., the gestures of the protagonists). The religious dimension of Mixtec worldview was emphasized by Jill Furst in her dissertation on the *Codex Vienna* (1978). Emily Rabin revised the chronology proposed by Caso: according to her calculations, the beginning of Mixtec history coincides with the beginning of the Postclassic era (tenth century CE), and Lord 8 Deer lived from 1063 to 1115 CE.

Gabina Aurora Pérez Jiménez and Maarten Jansen have tried to read portions of the codices in Mixtec, combining ethnohistorical data with the concepts of the living culture. Their commentaries on codices *Vienna, Nuttall, Selden,* and a number of smaller documents have provided new identifications of toponyms and a better idea of the metaphors and dramatic structures underlying the pictographic texts. The need to combine anthropological insights with linguistics and ethnohistory as a base for investigating such religious and literary aspects is further demonstrated by the excellent work of John Monaghan and Kevin Terraciano on aspects of Mixtec cultural semantics. Comparisons with other Mesoamerican texts are necessary and fruitful: the ancient Mixtec discourse of power included themes like the bundle cult and nahualismo, which are also found in the Borgia Group and in Maya iconography. Geographical reality and aspects of material culture may be investigated through archaeological fieldwork. For example, *In the Realm of Eight Deer* (1994), by Bruce Byland and John Pohl, is based on a survey of the Tilantongo area and contains new hypotheses about the sites where the codex events occurred and, in general, about the dynamics of pre-Hispanic Mixtec politics and ideology.

Pictorial documents were not made only in the Mixteca Alta but also in other areas of Oaxaca. Mary Elizabeth Smith and Viola König studied the documents of the Mixteca Baja, while Ross Parmenter defined the *lienzos* of the Coixtlahuaca Valley as a coherent group. The Zapotec corpus has become much better known thanks to contributions by Joseph Whitecotton, Viola König, and Michel Oudijk. The history and contents of the *Cuicatec* codices were elucidated by Bas van Doesburg.

Jansen showed that references to an expedition from the Mixteca to the Cuauhtinchan area (fourteenth century) connect the Mixtec codices with the Coixtlahuaca *lienzos* and these with sources from southern Puebla and Central Mexico. He then linked the Mixtec and Zapotec historiographies by demonstrating that the dynasty of Zaachila in the *Lienzo of Guevea* is also mentioned in the *Codex Nuttall*. Recently, Jansen has proposed even more extensive supraregional connections, by identifying the place Mountain that Opens–Insect (which plays an important role in early Mixtec history) as Monte Albán and by proposing that Lord 4 Jaguar, the important Toltec captain who interacts with Lord 8 Deer, is nobody less than Nacxitl Topiltzin Quetzalcoatl of Cholula. These connections counterbalance the microhistorical approach.

Better understanding of the complex nature of writing and semiotics in general, and of the rich contents of Mexican pictography in particular, has led to a fundamental reevaluation of the codices and *lienzos*. They are no longer seen as primitive rebuses but rather as sophisticated works which utilize a highly developed conventional sign system to communicate all kinds of messages. They transcend linguistic boundaries and express powerful literary contents in an impressive artistic form.

[*See also* Writing Systems, *article on* Central Mexican; Writing Systems, *article on* Mixtec.]

BIBLIOGRAPHY

Anders, Ferdinand, and Maarten Jansen. *Schrift und Buch im alten Mexiko.* Graz, 1988.

Arellano Hoffmann, Carmen, and Peer Schmidt, eds. *Die Bücher der Maya, Mixteken und Azteken: Die Schrift und ihre Funktion in vorspanischen und kolonialen Codices.* Frankfurt am Main, 1988.

Boone, Elizabeth Hill. *Stories in Red and Black: Pictorial Histories of the Aztec and Mixtec.* Austin, Tex., 2000.

Boone, Elizabeth Hill, and Walter D. Mignolo, eds. *Writing without Words: Alternative Literacies in Mesoamerica and the Andes.* Durham, N.C., 1994.

Bricker, Victoria Reifler. *Handbook of Middle American Indians, Supplement 5: Epigraphy.* Austin, Tex., 1992.

Galarza, Joaquín. *Amatl amoxtli: El papel, el libro.* Mexico City, 1990.

Jansen, Maarten, and Luis Reyes García, eds. *Códices, caciques y comunidades.* Cuadernos de Historia Latinoamericana, 5. , 1997.

Jansen, Maarten, Peter Kröfges, and Michel Oudijk. *The Shadow of*

Monte Albán: Politics and Historiography in Postclassic Oaxaca, Mexico. Leiden, 1998.

Quiñones Keber, Eloise. *Codex Telleriano-Remensis: Ritual, Divination, and History in a Pictorial Aztec Manuscript.* Austin, Tex., 1995.

Reyes Garcí, Luís. *La escritura pictográfica en Tlaxcala: Dos mil años de experiencia mesoamericana.* Tlaxcala, 1993.

Rueda Smithers, Salvador, Constanza Vega Sosa, and Rodrigo Martínez Baracs, eds. *Códices y documentos sobre México: Segundo simposio.* Mexico City, 1997.

MAARTEN E.R.G.N. JANSEN

Zapotec

The study of Zapotec writing began in earnest at the turn of the twentieth century with the work of Eduard Seler, Marshall Saville, and Leopoldo Batres. The first systematic effort to classify Zapotec hieroglyphs, however, was that of Alfonso Caso, who, in *Las Estelas Zapotecas* (1928), assigned a letter (A to Z) to each of the principal hieroglyphs.

In 1931, Caso undertook the first of eighteen field season at Monte Albán, a hilltop city at the center of the Valley of Oaxaca, Mexico. Those excavations established a solid chronological framework for the architecture, ceramics, and stone monuments that bore hieroglyphic texts. Caso determined that the earliest Monte Albán monuments with writing dated to Monte Albán Period I (500 BCE), and the latest to Monte Albán Period IIIb–IV (700–1000 CE). In 1975, with the discovery of Monument 3 at San José Mogote, the date for the appearance of Zapotec hieroglyphs was pushed back to 600 BCE, just a century before the founding of Monte Albán. At present, Monument 3 provides our oldest evidence for the Zapotec 260-day calendar. The dot and day sign on Monument 3 can be read "1 Earthquake," the name of the slain captive depicted on the stone. (The Zapotec had the custom of naming children after the day they were born.) With the movement of population from San José Mogote to Monte Albán around 500 BCE, Zapotec writing became increasingly important and abundant, but it was still restricted at this time to Monte Albán.

Caso began his study of Zapotec writing by dividing the hieroglyphs into two groups: those that occurred with numbers, and those that did not. He determined that many signs with numbers had calendric functions (day names, year-bearers), and that some signs without numbers were place-names. To interpret the calendric portions of hieroglyphic texts, Caso relied on Fray Juan de Córdova's 1578 account of the Zapotec calendar. The Zapotec began their day at midday and ended it the following midday. They named the days in the 260-day calendar after animals (deer, monkey) or natural forces (lightning, wind). They called the day *copiycha*, the month *peo*, the 260-day calendar *piye*, and the 365-day year *yza*. The *piye* was divided into four units of 65 days each, called *cociyo*.

Oldest writing shown here at Monte Albán, Oaxaca. *Drawing by Joyce Marcus.*

Each *cociyo* was divided into five units of 13 days each, called *cociy*. The *piye* generated 260 differently named days by combining thirteen numbers (from 1 to 13) with twenty day names.

Because Zapotec children were named after their birthdays, we cannot assume that every sign with a number functioned *only* as a day in the 260-day calendar. We know now that some texts formerly regarded as purely calendric are in fact primarily historical and dynastic, supplying the names of people. To write these personal names, the Zapotec used cardinal numbers: for example, in the written name 6 Deer, a bar stands for 5, and a dot for 1; the resulting number 6 serves as an affix (usually below or to the left) of a deer head.

The Zapotec used ordinal numbers (first, second, third) to specify the birth order of males. The terms were the same ones they used for fingers; thus, the right thumb, *yobi*, was used to designate "first-born son"; the second finger on the right hand, *tini*, referred to "second-born son," and so on. (A different set of terms was used for the birth order of females.)

The leaders of Monte Albán during Period I commissioned some pure hieroglyphic texts—Stelae 12–15 and 17—indicating that a significant threshold had been reached. Writing could now supply the entire message, not just caption scenes or label individuals. Associated with Stelae 12 and 13, Caso discovered a gallery depicting slain captives arranged in four rows. Some captives with earspools, elaborate hairdos, and necklaces were associated with additional hieroglyphs. This early use of writing at San José Mogote and Monte Albán to specify the names of important captives established a pattern seen in later Mesoamerican states, whose leaders used military success to enhance their claims to office.

On the basis of the early texts at Monte Albán, we can define Zapotec writing as a system of signs that show some correspondence to spoken language, follow rules for their combination, and are arranged in columns or rows which indicate reading order. Although Zapotec hieroglyphs were arranged in columns from Period I onward, scholars still disagree on the reading order. Most Period I–IIIa texts were read top to bottom, but some Period IIIb–IV dynastic texts were read from bottom to top. Although some texts may have been read from right to left, most were read from left to right. Variation in writing order and reading order may suggest that scribes had options in constructing their messages. Even though the most common word order in Zapotec today is verb–subject–object, other orders—such as subject–verb–object—are also grammatical.

For a century, scholars have suggested that Zapotec writing was a mixed system of pictograms (depictions of objects signified), ideograms (signs standing for concepts), logograms (signs standing for words), and phonograms (signs representing sounds), with particular use of "rebus writing" based on homonyms. Only recently has the writing been linked convincingly to the Zapotec language, which is tonal and does not feature many affixes. Two factors that contributed to this delay in linking the ancient script to the spoken language were the dearth of lengthy hieroglyphic texts and the limited occurrences of each sign during each time period.

The subject matter of ancient Zapotec writing was historical and political. We can identify the names of individuals, as well as nouns, verbs, and dates. A major addition to that repertoire occurred between 200 BCE and 100 CE, when place-names first appeared. At that time, the Zapotec state was expanding outside the Valley of Oaxaca, so place signs were needed to specify newly incorporated towns or provinces along the frontier. From 100 to 600 CE, the Zapotec continued to write the names of prominent captives, their home towns, and dates of conquest on monuments commissioned as groups, such as the group in the South Platform at Monte Albán.

A major change in the subject matter and format of texts occurred after 600 CE, when Monte Albán's political power was declining. Nobles recorded their ties by descent or marriage to other nobles to legitimize claims to offices at many sites, including Monte Albán, Zaachila, Cuilapan, Lambityeco, Macuilxochitl, Matatlán, Mitla, and Xoxocotlán. Many of these sites were then using writing for the first time. Such dynastic information was presented on a new type of monument which scholars call a "genealogical register." In format and content, these genealogical registers foreshadow the "books" painted by the Mixtec from 1200 to 1600 CE—polychrome screenfolds which contained the dynastic histories of their nobles.

One likely impetus for the emergence of Zapotec writing was the inability of earlier iconography to specify calendric dates and proper nouns (names of people and places). Endemic competition among polities constitutes a probable context for the earliest Zapotec monuments featuring captives. The Zapotec (as well as the Zoque and Maya) show us that writing could predate the emergence of the state, although it reached its greatest development after the state had formed. Zapotec writing and its calendar were influential in the development of later writing systems seen at Xochicalco, Cacaxtla, and Teotenango, and among the Zoque, Nuiñe, and Mixtec peoples.

[*See also* Writing Systems, *article on* Zapotec.]

BIBLIOGRAPHY

Caso, Alfonso. "Zapotec Writing and Calendar." In *Handbook of Middle American Indians*, edited by Robert Wauchope and Gordon R. Willey, vol. 3, part 2, pp. 931–947. Austin, Tex., 1965. Overview of Zapotec writing as well as ancient and modern Zapotec calendars.

Caso, Alfonso. *Los calendarios prehispánicos*. Mexico City, 1967. Compares the Zapotec calendar to the Maya, Mixtec, Aztec, and other calendars.

Marcus, Joyce. "The Origins of Mesoamerican Writing." *Annual Review of Anthropology* 5 (1976), 35–67. Focuses on the origins of the Mesoamerican calendar and writing systems of the Zapotec, Zoque, and Maya.

Marcus, Joyce. "Zapotec Writing." *Scientific American* 242 (1980), 50–64. Illustrates Zapotec writing from different periods and links it to archaeological data.

Marcus, Joyce. *Mesoamerican Writing Systems: Propaganda, Myth, and History in Four Ancient Civilizations*. Princeton, 1992. Develops a theoretical framework to show that Zapotec, Maya, Mixtec, and Aztec writing were both tools and by-products of the competition for leadership positions.

Marcus, Joyce, and Kent V. Flannery. *Zapotec Civilization: How Urban Society Evolved in Mexico's Oaxaca Valley*. New York, 1996. Situates Zapotec writing within its social, political, and evolutionary context, with abundant illustrations.

JOYCE MARCUS

ETHNICITY. The basic Mesoamerican culture pattern was shared by people speaking at least thirty languages, living in a number of ecological zones, and frequently in contact with each other through trade, military activity, migrations, elite intermarriage, and colonization. Such diversity might easily result in communities within which there were several groups that could be called "ethnic"; however, it was only in the highlands of Central Mexico that "ethnicity" was a significant factor—that is, where polities or communities were distingushable. According to Anthony D. Smith (1986), ethnic groups can be distinguished by six features: a collective name, a common myth of descent, a shared history, a distinctive shared culture, an association with a specific or historical territory, and a sense of community solidarity. There were many entities in Central Mexico that displayed those features; they also justified their claim to territory on ethnic grounds.

In Central Mexico, ethnicity can be viewed in several ways. There were large groups called Mexica, Acolhua, Tepanec, Chalca, Tlaxcalan, and so on; although these are ethnonyms, they were derived from the name of the state with which a group was associated, so they are best viewed as nationalities. The name of the state, however, was often derived from that of the ethnic group that furnished its ruling dynasty. Ethnicity as a basis for segmentation or factionalization is best seen in the smaller groups that had a presence in many of the states of the region. These smaller groups bear such names as Acolhua, Chimalpaneca, Huiztnahuaque, Nonoalca, Tenanca, and Tlacochcalca; some others will be listed alphabetically here. Most Central Mexican groups spoke Nahuatl, the prevailing language of the region. Some may have spoken Otomí or Mixtec, but language was not an ethnic marker.

What distinguished them as ethnic groups was, above all, their historical traditions. All the peoples of Central Mexico (and of many other parts of Mesoamerica as well) kept histories of having migrated from someplace else—of having arrived at their present locations after long peregrinations. These migration legends have a number of common features, which Rudolf van Zantwijk (1985) has summarized: the land of origin is far away; departure from it takes place by order of a deity on a date that begins a new cycle; and the people whose history is described always leave their homeland accompanied by other groups, but during the migrations, some people split off. They are divinely guided on the migration, and the place of final settlement is ordained by omens. As these histories approach within three or four centuries of the time when they were recorded, myth tends to give way to history, with realistic dates; the events they describe and their dates tend to be confirmed by the histories of other groups. There are certain recurrent themes. Aztlán was the origin point not only of the seven groups associated with the Mexica but of several other groups that migrated to Chalco. Chicomóztoc (the "Seven Caves") was either a place of origin or a stopping place in the migrations of the Acolhuaque, Chichimec of Xolotl, Itztlacozauhque, Mexica, Tecuanipantlaca, Tepaneca,

and Tlaxcalteca. It was also the place to which the Tolteca-Chichimeca rulers of Cholula went to recruit Chichimec warriors to help them defeat the Olmeca-Xicalanca. Tollan was said to be the place of origin of the Acxoteca, Colhua, Nonoalca, and Tolteca-Chichimeca of Cholula. Several others sojourned there at least briefly: the Acolhuaque, Chichimeca of Xolotl, Mexica, Teochichimeca, Tepaneca, and Tlaxcalteca. The Huitznahuaque, along with the Colhua, Mexica, and Tepaneca, are said to have come to Tetzcoco bearing a Toltec culture. Each of these groups also had its patron deity, which was carried on its migrations and, at least in some cases, spoke as an oracle, guiding the people to their destinations. At their final destination, and sometimes at earlier stops, a temple to this deity was the first structure built. This deity, its temple, and the rituals associated with it were another major feature that defined the ethnic group.

Their histories served as charters—legitimizing the peoples and the possession of their territories—justifying their right to be there. In Chalco, as Susan Schroeder (1991) notes, to have arrived from elsewhere as a group already distinct, with its own dynastic leadership, was the hallmark of a legitimate sociopolitical segment, an *altepetl*. The role of the patron deity in guiding the people on their migrations, or at least the fact that his image was carried on them and was venerated in a temple, lent an air of sanctity to the enterprise. In the Early Colonial period, the histories (minus the non-Christian gods) were sometimes presented in Spanish court cases over land rights or the political status of a community. In 1547, the legitimacy of one of the component segments of Amecameca was called into question because the group lacked an "arrival." Histories were used for similar purposes throughout Mesoamerica and, at least in the Maya area, often involved migrations in relatively recent times. What is exceptional about Central Mexico is simply that the entity involved is an ethnic group.

Two ethnic entities that deserve special attention are the Chichimec and the Toltec. People called "Chichimec" figure prominently in the histories of many states in the valleys of Mexico and Puebla, and they come in many varieties—clearly not always the same people. In pictorial documents, they are often depicted dressed in skins, carrying bows and arrows, and they are described as huntergatherers, sometimes without knowledge of agriculture, and stateless. Yet from archaeological evidence, there had been no hunter-gatherers in Central Mexico for at least three millennia before the Spanish conquest; moreover, these so-called hunter-gatherers were sociopolitically stratified and had the ability to interact with the nobility of established states. Their depiction as "huntergatherers" is understood to be a metaphor, possibly to indicate that they were passing through a period of disorderly wandering, or that they were a people without recognized kings, at least when they first enter history. Many continued to call themselves Chichimec and bore the name proudly, even after they had become the kings of respected states. The rulers of Tetzcoco, who traced their dynastic origins to the Chichimeca of Xolotl, bore the title of *Chichimeca teuctli* ("Chichimec lord"), and their symbol was the bow and arrow. When the Spanish moved north later in the sixteenth century and encountered real hunter-gatherers, they made an association with the Chichimec of the historical legends—but there was probably no direct relationship between the two.

Etymologically, a *Toltec* is "a person of Tollan (Tula)," a city renowned for its achievements in the arts and crafts and for its great and divine kings. To be "Toltec" implies a bearer of high civilization. Most important, a Toltec king was a king of unquestioned royalty. The royalty of an ethnic leader could be legitimized by a marital tie with a royal Toltec lineage and, better yet, could travel "to Tollan" for his installation as king. Some of the smaller ethnic groups of the valleys of Mexico and Puebla are said to have originated "in Tollan" or to have introduced Toltec culture to their place of residence. Since the 1950s, scholars have consistently identified "Tollan" with the single site of Tula, Hidalgo, but recent scholarship has tended toward the view that "Tollan" could also refer to any city whose rulers were accepted as qualified to bestow royalty on others. Tula was probably one such city in the Early Postclassic period. Cholula had a similar role in the Valley of Puebla, and by the early sixteenth century, Tenochtitlan may have been a contender. Even in faraway Oaxaca and the Maya area, princes traveled to "Tulan" to legitimize their royalty, and even some Maya lineages claimed a Toltec origin.

The following were the major ethnic groups of Central Mexico. The list is not complete, and it is not a systematic comparison because the same kind of data is not available for each group. There are some inconsistencies, since a given group might play a different part in the histories of various peoples.

Acolchichimeca: one of the seven groups brought from Chicomoztoc to Cholula by the Tolteca-Chichimeca to fight the Olmeca-Xicalanca.

Acolhuaque: originated in Chicomoztoc, sojourned in Tula, arrived in the eastern Valley of Mexico and were received by the Chichimeca of Xolotl, settled in Coatlichan, and became the ruling dynasty of Tetzcoco. Patron deity was Cocopitl, later Tezcatlipoca. Present in all cities of Acolhuacan.

Acxoteca: early arrivals in Chalco from "Tollan," the first to call themselves Chalca. Patron deity was Acollacatl Nahualteuctli. Present in Tlalmanalco.

Chalca: collective name for peoples of the southeastern Valley of Mexico; departed from Artlán in the Mexica origin myth.

Chichimeca of Xolotl: entered the eastern Valley of Mexico from the Huaxtec area via Chicomoztoc and "Tollan," under the leadership of the chieftain Xolotl. They settled first in Tenayuca and gave rise to the Acolhua ruling dynasty.

Chimalpaneca: people of Toltec culture who came via the Mixtec area to Chalco, then to Acolhuacan during the reign of Quinatzin of Tetzcoco; a Chichimec subgroup that arrived in Cuauhtinchan, in the Valley of Puebla. Present in Tetzcoco and other Acolhua towns.

Colhua: came originally from Teocolhuacan, but moved to "Tollan" and participated in Toltec culture. Moved to the Valley of Mexico and established their capital at Colhuacan, but maintained dynastic continuity from Toltec times and, through marital alliances, bestowed royal legitimacy on newcomers. One group settled in Acolhuacan during the reign of Techotlalatzin of Tetzcoco. After the late fourteenth/early fifteenth-century conquest by Azcapotzalco, groups of Colhua settled in Azcapotzalco, Cuauhtitlan, several cities of Acolhuacan, and Tepeaca in the Valley of Puebla. Patron deities were Cinteotl and Cihuacoatl.

Colomochca: moved to Cholula from the Mixteca, also present in Cuauhtinchan.

Cuauhtinchantlaca: one of the groups brought from Chicomoztoc by the Tolteca-Chichimeca to help them defeat the Olmeca-Xicalanca; settled in Cuauhtinchan.

Huitznahuaque: one of four groups of Toltec culture that came to Acolhuacan during the reign of Techotlalatzin. Patron deity was Tezcatlipoca. Present in Tetzcoco and each main town of Acolhuacan.

Itztlacozauhque: left Aztlán and Chicomoztoc in the twelfth century, came to Chalco, settled in various places, and finally arrived in Amecameca in 1261. Patron deity was Totollin.

Mexica: originated in Aztlán; went to Chicomoztoc, then to "Tollan," then to the Valley of Mexico via Coatepec. Were one of four groups of Toltec culture that entered Acolhuacan during the reign of Techotlalatzin. In the Valley of Mexico, settled for a time in Chapultepec, then in Colhuacan (origin of the first Mexica king); arrived in Tenochtitlan and Tlatelolco in the early fourteenth century, first as allies of Azcapotzalco, then as independent empire builders. Patron deity was Huitzilopochtli. Present in Mexico, Azcapotzalco, and all major towns of Acolhuacan.

Mixteca-Popoloca: came to Cuauhtinchan from Coixtlahuaca, possibly at the behest of Chimalpaneca and Cuauhtinchantlaca. Present in Cuauhtinchan and Tecamachalco.

Moquihuixca: brought by Tolteca-Chichimeca from Chicomoztoc to Cholula, but became a major subgroup in Cuauhtinchan.

Nonoalca: after the fall of "Tollan," moved south from there to settle in Izucar, Zongolica, Teohuacán, Teotitlan del Camino, and Cozcatlan. Also present in Tlatelolco, Tacubaya, Chiautla, Coatlichan, and Xaltocan. One group settled in Chalco-Tlalmanalco, another in Amecameca. Patron deity was Tlatlauhquii Tezcatlipoca.

Olmeca: known variously as Olmeca-Huixtotin and Olmeca-Xicalanca; were old residents of the Valley of Puebla and Chalco. Displaced by Tolteca-Chichimeca, Tlaxcalteca, and others (*not* related to the archaeologically known Olmec of the southern Gulf Coast region).

Otomí: received by Xolotl when they came, along with the Acolhua and Tepanec, to the eastern Valley of Mexico, and settled in Xaltocan. After it was conquered by Azcapotzalco, most fled and settled in Metztitlan, Otumba, and Tlaxcala. Patron deity was Otonteuctli. Center of Otomí-speaking population was in the Jilotepec–Chapa de Mota area and northward and in the Valley of Toluca.

Pinome: emerged as a segment in Cuauhtinchan through elite intermarriage of Mixteca-Popoloca and Chimalpaneca. Present in Cuauhtinchan and Tepeyacac.

Tecuanipantlaca: originated in Chicomoztoc near Aztlán; arrived in Chalco-Tlalmanalco, then moved to Amecameca. Patron deity was Citecatl, also known as Mixcoatl.

Tenanca: came from Aztán via Teotenango; traveled to Tizatepec near Cuitlahuac, then to Chalco, arriving in twelfth century. Sometimes called Teotenanca. They split into two groups—the Tenanco Texocpalco Tepopolla, which became a major part of Chalco, and the Tzacualtitlan Tenanco, of Amecameca. Patron deity was Nauhyoteuctli Xipil.

Tepaneca: from Chicomoztoc via "Tollan" entered the Valley of Mexico, then Xolotl settled them in Azcapotzalco. They were one of the four groups of Toltec culture that came to Acolhuacan during the reign of Techotlalatzin. They were established in a ward of each major Acolhua town. Under Tezozómoc, they came to dominate the entire Valley of Mexico in the late fourteenth century. Patron deity was Otonteuctli.

Tlacochcalca: left with the Mexica from Aztlán. Came from Chicomoztoc; sojourned in "Tollan," then entered Chalco. Present in Chalco Tlalmanalco and Chalco Chimalhuacan. Patron deity was Tlatlauhqui Tezcatlipoca.

Tlailotlaque: came with the Chimalpaneca to Acolhuacan during the reign of Quinatzin; said to be from the Mixtec area. Present in Tetzcoco and other major towns of Acolhuacan. Patron deity was Tezcatlipoca. In Chalco, they came with the Acxoteca, but in the fourteenth century a new segment called Tlailotlacan emerged in Amecameca, probably not connected with the others.

Tlaxcalteca: from Chicomoztoc via "Tollan," or in some accounts left Aztlán with the Mexica. They were brought by the Tolteca-Chichimeca from Chicomoztoc to Cholula to help defeat the Olmeca-Xicalanca. Present for a time in southern Acolhuacan but were driven out; most went to Tlaxcala. Patron deity was Camaxtli.

Tolteca-Chichimeca: arrived in Cholula from "Tollan," then took the city from the Olmeca-Xicalanca. Their leaders went to Colhuatepec Chicomoztoc to bring Chichimec to help them defeat Olmeca-Xicalanca. Patron deities were Tezcatlipoca and Quetzalcoatl.

Totolimpaneca: came from Aztlán Chicomoztoc; arrived in Chalco after the Nonoalca, as hunter-gatherers. They wrested Amecameca from the Olmeca. Patron deities were Mixcoatl, Itzpapalotl; and Ehecatl-Quetzalcoatl.

Totomihuaque: brought by the Tolteca-Chichimeca to Cholula from Chicomoztoc to help defeat the Olmeca-Xicalanca, and settled in Totomihuacan.

These groups all seem to have had social classes; they had or could have their own ruling nobility, as well as a large commoner stratum, but there is no presumption that members of the same ethnic group were linked by kinship. Although some ethnic groups were present in many cities or states, including states that fought each other, there is no evidence that they united to form transnational factions or pressure groups. They were, therefore, important units in state building; often, the different groups were assigned to different governmental functions. As Elizabeth Brumfiel (1994) has noted, ethnicity, with its claim to common history but not necessarily common blood, allowed for enduring relationships between nobles and corporate groups of commoners. Power was in the hands of the nobles, who denied any kinship tie with commoners, but ethnicities bound nobles and commoners together, thus minimizing the potentially disruptive effects of class struggle.

To the west, in the Tarascan state, ethnicity took a different form. The Tarascan language is unrelated to any other in Mesoamerica, and although the Tarascan cultural system conformed to the general Mesoamerican pattern, it had a number of distinctive features. Helen Perlstein Pollard (1994) distinguishes between the Tarascan heartland, a zone of active assimilation, and a zone of ethnic segregation. The heartland was the region around Lake Pátzcuaro and the surrounding highlands, where the Tarascan empire began. The zone of active assimilation was the area absorbed into the Tarascan state after 1440, in which the local population was encouraged to adopt the Tarascan language and culture. The zone of ethnic segregation was the frontier region, inhabited in part by non-Tarascans. Some were refugee groups from Aztec rule, and many of those were organized into ethnic military units, under Tarascan command, to serve as buffers and as cultural brokers on the frontiers between Tarascans and non-Tarascans.

In the Maya area, Yucatán and Guatemala, ethnicity does not appear as a salient feature in the historical or descriptive accounts. The linguistic diversity of the Guatemala Highlands is recognized, but the Yucatán Peninsula is notable for its linguistic uniformity: everyone spoke the Mayan language. It may be significant that although the accounts make no mention of groups that might be called "ethnic," they make frequent reference to large population segments identified as "lineages." In general, lineages held land in common and migrated together. To some extent, these appear to function in the Maya area much as did the ethnic groups of Central Mexico, except that they were composed only of the dominant class.

In Oaxaca, neither ethnicity nor kinship generated significant factions. That is, when Mixtec groups from Oaxaca entered the Valley of Puebla, they became ethnic factions there, yet in Oaxaca itself, the major segmentary divisions were *between* communities rather than *within* communities. The two major linguistic groups of Oaxaca, Mixtec and Zapotec, interacted. In their historical accounts, they took note of linguistic affiliation; however, factions and segments were not formed along ethnic lines, either in practice or in ideological expression—nor were they formed along kinship lines. Kowalewski (1994) has contrasted this situation with those in Central Mexico and the Maya area. He suggests that the Valley of Mexico's marginal position in the Early Postclassic period after the fall of Tula, as well as the competition between groups with ties to various outside powers, was an ideal environment for the development of ethnically based factions. Among the Maya after the Classic-period collapse, there was opportunity for expansion, and John W. Fox (1987) has argued that the Maya segmentary lineage became a mechanism for predatory expansion. In the Valley of Oaxaca, however, a considerable continuity of settlement was ongoing throughout the Classic and Postclassic periods, with little opportunity for expansion into underused land. The ambitious Oaxaca lord, Fox suggests, did better by marrying into an established royal line than by forming a predatory faction.

[*See also* Migrations; Social Stratification.]

BIBLIOGRAPHY

Brumfiel, Elizabeth M. "Ethnic Groups and Political Development in Ancient Mexico." In *Factional Competition and Political Development in the New World*, edited by Elizabeth M. Brumfiel and John W. Fox, pp. 89–102. Cambridge, 1994. Explains how ethnic groups were used in state-building.

Carmack, Robert M. *The Quiché Mayas of Utatlán*. Norman, Okla., 1981. Describes the political function of lineages in highland Guatemala.

Carrasco, Pedro. "The Peoples of Central Mexico and Their Historical Traditions." In *Handbook of Middle American Indians*, edited by Robert Wauchope, vol. 11, *Archaeology of Northern Mesoamerica*, edited by Gordon F. Ekholm and Ignacio Bernal, pp. 459–473. Austin, Tex., 1971. Useful summary of the major ethnic groups of Central Mexico.

Fox, John W. *Maya Postclassic State Formation*. Cambridge, 1987. Describes Maya noble lineages as agents of predatory expansion.

Kowalewski, Stephen A. "Internal Subdivisions of Communities in the Prehispanic Valley of Oaxaca." In *Factional Competition and Political Development in the New World*, edited by Elizabeth M. Brumfiel and John W. Fox, pp. 127–137. Cambridge, 1994. Shows that ethnicity was not a factor in segmentation in the Mixtec–Zapotec area and offers an explanation for this.

McAnany, Patricia A. *Living with the Ancestors: Kinship and Kingship in Ancient Maya Society*, Austin, Tex., 1995. Discusses the political function of lineages in the Maya Lowlands.

Pollard, Helen Perlstein. "Ethnicity and Political Control in a Complex Society: The Tarascan State of Prehispanic Mexico." In *Factional Competition and Political Development in the New World*, edited by Elizabeth M. Brumfiel and John W. Fox, pp. 79–88. Cambridge, 1994. Discusses the role of ethnicity in the Tarascan area.

Reyes García, Luis. *Cuauhtinchan del siglo XII al XVI. Formación y desarrollo histórico de un señorío prehispánico*. Wiesbaden, 1977. Describes ethnic groups of the Valley of Puebla and their history.

Schroeder, Susan. *Chimalpahin and the Kingdoms of Chalco*, Tucson, 1991. Describes ethnic groups in the development of Chalco.

Smith, Anthony D. *The Ethnic Origin of Nations*. Oxford, 1986.

Zantwijk, Rudolf van. *The Aztec Arrangement: The Social History of Pre-Spanish Mexico*. Norman, Okla., 1985. Chapters 2 and 3 contain a good discussion of the origin myths of different peoples of Mexico and the role of ethnic groups in the political structure.

FREDERIC HICKS

ETHNOGRAPHY. *See* Anthropology, *article on* Sociocultural Anthropology.

ETHNOHISTORY. *See* Historiography.

EVIL EYE. *See* Mal de Ojo.

EXCHANGE. *See* Trade and Exchange.

EXHIBITIONS. *See* Museums and Exhibitions.

EZLN. *See* Zapatista National Liberation Army.

F

FAMILY AND KINSHIP. Despite some cultural and temporal variations, widely shared kinship practices and organizing principles can be delineated and traced over time in Mesoamerica. Some of this homogeneity can be traced to Spanish colonialism. The adoption of Spanish bilateral kinship terminology, administrative policies affecting household size and organization, marriage, inheritance, and gender status, and changes to demographic patterns and economic structures all contributed to decreasing the size and importance of extrafamilial kinship units after the Spanish conquest. Nevertheless, many pre-Hispanic kinship principles and practices have continued into the present in traditional communities.

Kinship is a fundamental mechanism for organizing persons into groups, each with its own identity and property, and for creating personal networks among many individuals beyond these groups. Although families are the most visible kinship groups in contemporary Mesoamerica, kinship principles are integrated with the organization and operation of larger-order territorial and economic units. Kin relationships are integral to economic exchanges, social control, recruitment to religious organizations, and urban–rural migration patterns; in the past, kin-based structures played a more fundamental role in organizing all of society. Thus, kinship is not independent of the other factors that integrate persons within society. In Mesoamerica, kinship is intimately interconnected with locality (residence). In practice, a commitment among persons to work together for their mutual benefit within a household or other territorial unit may be as important as biological relationships in the formation of what are usually identified as "kinship" groups. As a strategy for social reproduction, kinship groups and kinlike relationships need not be restricted to persons linked by actual consanguineal (biological) or affinal (marriage) ties, nor are strict rules of descent, marriage, or inheritance imposed that may constrain people's opportunities to optimize their chances for survival. Although patrifilial (father–child) tendencies in descent and locality preference are typical, there is always an element of choice in relationships based on kin ties.

The family is the basic unit for the organization of labor and for the transmission of practical knowledge in traditional communities. More fundamentally, it is the primary focus of loyalty and mutual support and is the major source of social identity and personhood. Names are important symbols of social identity based on kin group membership. Personal names are sometimes passed down through family lines and are bestowed at baptisms or similar familial rites, some of which existed in the pre-Hispanic era. Patronyms (surnames inherited from the father) are commonly employed to indicate membership within a larger network of kin, forming name groups that are often exogamous (out-marrying) as an expression of the closeness of their members' relationships to one another. Name groups also existed prior to Spanish contact, especially among the Maya, and have sometimes been confused with lineages.

Names may also be bestowed based on residence, so that toponyms (place names) which function like surnames are adopted by everyone residing within a locality, whether or not they are kin; this may obscure the distinction between kin ties and co-residence as a mechanism for group membership. Non-kin may be accepted as members based on their cooperation in economic and ritual activities, in effect becoming "fictive" kin through their participation and joint investment in the success of the unit. By their contribution to the agricultural labor needed to sustain the group, and to the ritual activities that maintain the group's spiritual well-being, they effectively express the relationships to others that are expected of kin (and by the same token, actual relatives who refuse to contribute to the group's well-being may be obliged to relinquish membership).

Another ancient and widespread means of expressing group membership and identity is to consider kin group members as descendants of the same ancestors, although it is usually not necessary to trace actual genealogical ties to founding ancestors. The demonstration of a group's common origins is accomplished instead through the curation and ritual veneration of property believed to have been acquired by the ancestors, including land and water rights, heirloom objects, the actual remains of the dead (which in the past were often interred in or near the residence), and such nontangible property as the names and even souls of predecessors. Most domestic groups erect a shrine in the form of an altar or cross for family devotions to ancestors or other spirit guardians. There is a common belief that the house itself contains a soul or spirit, which must be ritually sustained and which is metaphysically linked to the well-being of family members. Evidence for the antiquity of these beliefs includes the archaeological recovery in residential contexts of burials, heirloom items, and objects of ritual use such as bloodletters and figurines, as well as epigraphic and ethnohistoric information on the transfer of names through family lines.

The principal indicators of kinship organization are terminological systems, kin group types, and customs pertaining to marriage, residence, and inheritance. In Mesoamerica, bilateral terminologies are most common, and this was apparently the case even before Spanish contact. Bilaterality reveals a structural equivalence of

Young Tepehuán couple with child in Durango, Mexico. *Photograph courtesy of Michael Hale.*

males and females in the construing of descent ties to their progeny, and it results in a greater emphasis on the coalescence of cognatic rather than unilineal descent groups. Typically, lineal distinctions are made in kin terms for the parents' and children's generations, while cousins and siblings may be called by the same term (a system ethnographers call the Hawaiian type of kin terminology). Indigenous kin terms are frequently differentiated by the sex of the speaker as well as that of the referent, and by the relative age of speaker and referent, indicating the importance of gender and age differences in the operation of relationships among close kin. These differences are also exhibited in the authority and gender structure within families. Elder males typically command the obedience of younger members, which is a frequent source of conflict where the former control family-owned agricultural land. Although male and female children may have equivalent inheritance rights to some property, a patrilineal bias in the transmission of surnames and the control of agricultural land by males are typical. Men and women contribute differently to the household through their complementary labors, so that both genders are necessary for social production; women are responsible for domestic tasks, including weaving, and men for the bulk of agricultural work and some specialized crafts. The Highland Maya area today exhibits far greater variation in kinship terminology than the rest of Mesoamerica, including the Omaha type reported in some Tzeltal and Tzotzil communities. In this kin terminology system, most of the mother's male relatives are referred to by the same term, obscuring generational differences and treating them as a collectivity. The Maya area also has the most instances of the few reported unilineal descent groups.

The basic kin group type is the nuclear family, which may form an independent household. Still today, and much more so in the past, nuclear families are constituents of extended (joint, multiple) families that function as corporate groups. They tend to own or manage agricultural land in common, efficiently pooling the labor of several adult males. The extended family members who form a single consumption unit or domestic group may co-reside as one household with walls erected to separate the nuclear families; or the individual nuclear families may have separate dwellings, often spatially contiguous within a cluster or compound. Such dwelling clusters have been found archaeologically, indicating the longevity of this family type. Even where the nuclear families maintain their own households and budgets, they may cooperate in agricultural labors as a non-residential extended family. The extended family ideally is composed of three generations: a spousal couple with their married sons, who bring their wives into the family (virilocality), and their grandchildren; the adult daughters marry out. However, other compositions are not uncommon, including the inclusion of sons-in-law, widows, and collateral kin into the extended family.

The composition of the extended family is best understood as the outcome of a developmental cycle. The "Mesoamerican developmental cycle of domestic groups," as described by David Robichaux (1997), typically begins with virilocal postmarital residence, as men bring their wives to their father's domestic group until they can establish their own residences, usually near the husband's parents (viri-neolocality). It culminates with the death of the parents and the inheritance of their dwelling by the youngest son. Although this pattern is widespread, variations exist to allow for the exigencies of individual situations, such as a lack of sons, insufficient agricultural land, or the varying market value of men's and women's labor. Another major source of temporary variation in this cycle is the practice of bride service, especially in the Maya area; in the past, this practice required a new husband to live with his wife's family for one or more years before he could bring her to his parent's home (uxori-virilocality).

In the past, young men in many parts of Mesoamerica would live in segregated men's houses prior to marriage, which was typically arranged with the aid of matchmakers, usually in the service of the groom's family. Today, elopement as an alternative to arranged marriage is more common. In addition to bride service, specialized objects were once commonly exchanged between the bride's and groom's households to confirm the marriage. Polygyny, most likely more widespread in the past, is still known, but it represents a tiny fraction of all marriages. Divorce or separation is not uncommon. With the exception of incest prohibitions, other formal marriage rules are generally lacking; however, some customary subdivisions (barrios) are endogamous (in-marrying) or exogamous (out-marrying). Local communities tend to be endogamous in practice.

Although unilineal descent groups were never a dominant organization in Mesoamerica, in the pre-Hispanic period long-lived cognatic corporate groups controlled land and resources, including labor, primarily among the nobility. Members of the noble estate were organized into groups often referred to in the native languages as "houses," which were structurally equivalent to the noble houses of feudal Europe. The heads of noble houses were the lords and rulers, and the houses were apparently considered related to one another in terms of real of fictive kinlike ties. Houses maintained tangible and intangible property over many generations through the recruitment of new members via both marriage and descent, so that some property rights were obtained and held through women as well as men. In some cases, commoners were attached as hereditary clients to the various noble houses.

The best evidence for noble houses (e.g., *teccalli* in Nahuatl) is in Nahua Central Mexico and the Maya area.

Larger territorial units—the customary subdivisions or wards of communities and *municipios*—were also organized by means that parallel or overlap with kinship ties. Variously called *barrio, paraje, calpulli, cantón, chinamitl,* or other local terms, the subdivision typically combines elements of kinship and locality, although there are some non-localized groupings. These subdivisions provide for social and economic interactions among their members, including the same benefits that family members would provide for one another, such as sharing food and labor. These units are also a source of status and identity, and membership may be by birth or marriage within a particular subdivision, or by other demonstrated kin ties to subdivision members. Like families, some subdivisions have their own symbolic identifiers in the form of group shrines, shared surnames, or the expressed belief in a common origin. Although some subdivisions have overt societal roles—such as the sponsorship of religious cults or the regulation of marriage—their function as a means of establishing bonds of relatedness among multiple domestic groups may lie dormant for long periods, to be triggered only by certain events over which intracommunity factions emerge. Many communities, especially in the Maya area, are described as being organized into dual *barrios*, which tend to be endogamous.

Fictive kinship as ritual co-parenthood (*compadrazgo*) is yet another means of creating a kinlike relationship between two or more families for various purposes. Although the *compadrazgo* system is a Spanish introduction, there is evidence for the pre-Hispanic practice of choosing "godparents" as sponsors for children during baptismal or puberty rites in both Central Mexico and Yucatán. It fits within the general practice of extending kinlike ties to others in the community as a means of enlarging personal networks for strategic purposes.

BIBLIOGRAPHY

Carrasco, Pedro. "Social Organization of Ancient Mexico." In *Handbook of Middle American Indians*, vol. 10, *Archaeology of Northern Mesoamerica, Part One*, edited by Gordon F. Ekholm and Ignacio Bernal, pp. 349–375. Austin, Tex., 1971. This detailed description of Aztec society is still influential, although some terms and concepts are now dated.

Chance, John K. "The Noble House in Colonial Puebla, Mexico: Descent, Inheritance, and the Nahua Tradition." *American Anthropologist* 2000, in press. Applies the "house" model to Early Colonial and, by extension, pre-Hispanic Nahua society.

Farriss, Nancy M. *Maya Society under Colonial Rule: The Collective Enterprise of Survival*. Princeton, 1984. Overview of Yucatec Maya kinship and community and the changes it underwent during the Colonial period.

Kellogg, Susan M. "Kinship and Social Organization in Early Colonial Tenochtitlan." In *Supplement to the Handbook of Middle American Indians*, vol. 4, *Ethnohistory*, edited by Ronald Spores, pp. 103–121. Austin, Tex., 1986. Covers the mid- to late-sixteenth-century situation in the Basin of Mexico, updating Carrasco's 1971 article.

Kendall, Carl, John Hawkins, and Laurel Bossen, eds. *Heritage of Conquest: Thirty Years Later*. Albuquerque, N.M., 1983. Chapters by Michael Salovesh and by Joseph Gross and Carl Kendall provide an update of earlier studies of kinship in Mesoamerica.

Lazos Chavero, Elena. "Parentesco y tierra en el sur de Yucatán." In *Memorias del Primer Congreso Internacional de Mayistas*, pp. 295–315. Mexico City, 1992. Provides a clear explanation of the relationship of kinship to locality.

Mulhare, Eileen M., ed. *Mesoamerican Community Organization: Barrios and Other Customary Units*. Special Issues of *Ethnology* 2/3 (1996). Articles by Eileen M. Mulhare, Hugo G. Nutini, John K. Chance, Robert S. Carlsen, Alan R. Sandstrom, John Monaghan, James Dow, Gregory F. Truex, Frank Cancian, and Manning Nash examine various aspects of customary subdivisions, with implications for kinship.

Mulhare, Eileen M. "Mesoamerican Social Organization and Community after 1960." In *Supplement to the Handbook of Middle American Indians*, edited by Victoria Reifler Bricker, forthcoming volume on Ethnology. Austin, Tex., in press. Provides an extensive bibliography on Mesoamerican social organization.

Nash, Manning, ed. *Handbook of Middle American Indians*. Vol. 6, *Social Anthropology*. Austin, Tex., 1967. Has key articles on kinship terminological systems by A. Kimball Romney, local and territorial units by Eva M. Hunt and June Nash, and *compadrazgo* by Robert Ravicz.

Nutini, Hugo G. "Clan Organization in a Nahuatl-Speaking Village of the State of Tlaxcala, Mexico." *American Anthropologist* 63 (1961), 62–78. Describes an unusual "unilineal" organization outside of the Maya area.

Nutini, Hugo G. "A Synoptic Comparison of Mesoamerican Marriage and Family Structure." *Southwestern Journal of Anthropology* 23 (1967), 383–404.

Nutini, Hugo G., Pedro Carrasco, and James M. Taggart, eds. *Essays on Mexican Kinship*. Pittsburgh, 1976. Seminal discussion that generated a greater interest in the role of kinship in contemporary Mesoamerica.

Robichaux, David. "Residence Rules and Ultimogeniture in Tlaxcala and Mesoamerica." *Ethnology* 36 (1997), 149–171.

Sandstrom, Alan. "Toponymic Groups and House Organization: The Nahuas of Northern Veracruz, Mexico." In *Beyond Kinship: Social and Material Reproduction in House Societies*, edited by Rosemary A. Joyce and Susan D. Gillespie, pp. 53–72. Philadelphia, 2000. Describes the operation of kin-based toponymic groupings or residential clusters as "embryonic houses" among contemporary Nahua.

Spores, Ronald, and Kent V. Flannery. "Sixteenth-Century Kinship and Social Organization." In *The Cloud People: Divergent Evolution of the Zapotec and Mixtec Civilizations*, edited by Kent V. Flannery and Joyce Marcus, pp. 339–342. New York, 1983. Brief but informative description of late pre-Hispanic social organization in Oaxaca.

Taggart, James M. "'Ideal' and 'Real' Behavior in the Mesoamerican Nonresidential Extended Family." *American Ethnologist* 2 (1975), 347–357.

Wilk, Richard R., and Wendy Ashmore, eds. *Household and Community in the Mesoamerican Past*. Albuquerque, N.M., 1988. Discusses archaeological indicators of households, the developmental cycle, and possible *barrio*-like subdivisions with emphasis on the Maya.

SUSAN D. GILLESPIE

FARMING. *See* Agriculture *and* Chinampa Agriculture.

FASTING. Refraining from food and water is practiced by many indigenous groups throughout Mesoamerica as part of ceremonial life, but the topic has not been studied extensively. Fasting falls under the broader ethnological category of sacrifice, about which there is an abundant literature. This brief essay describes several forms of fasting observed by ethnographers and considers possible explanations for the practice.

Fasting is not simply the refusal to eat; it includes restrictions such as drinking water only at night, consuming food only at a specific time, and omitting salt or chile from all food. Sexual abstinence frequently accompanies fasting, and both may be observed for periods as short as three days or as long as a year. Fasting is conditioned by age, gender, kinship ties, social position, and specific ceremonial contexts. For example, sometimes these restrictions are required of persons before they assume ritual posts or perform specific ceremonial obligations. Fasting and sexual abstinence are often observed by all participants in certain rituals—such as those performed to bring rain for planting maize or to end a drought—by those departing on pilgrimages to sacred places, and among extended kinship networks during curing ceremonies. These practices may be necessary before people ingest ritual foods or other substances and before they handle ritual objects or religious images.

It is instructive to consider why various forms of fasting and sexual abstinence are so widespread. In Mesoamerican cultures, human action is regarded as a necessary complement to divine and natural forces in order to achieve specific objectives, such as the beginning or cessation of annual rains, the productivity of cultivated plants, harmonious relations between the living and the dead, and fertility among humans and domestic animals. All the components of a ceremony—special foods and flowers, weavings and clothing, candles and incense, fireworks, particular forms of music and dance, and so on—constitute ceremonial offerings in themselves. The overall efficacy of each ceremonial event depends on the proper execution of its complex, interrelated parts.

Some ethnographic data suggest that fasting and sexual abstinence protect humans against natural and supernatural forces that reside in sacred places or that may be released in certain ceremonies. It is significant that these prohibitions most often accompany rituals concerned with diverse aspects of production and reproduction in agriculture, those for preserving or restoring health, and those associated with diurnal or seasonal changes in nature. My research suggests that many Mesoamerican rituals are based on the concept of *fuerza*, or vital energy, which circulates among humans, the souls of the dead, elements of the natural world, sacred places, and ritual objects, including Roman Catholic saints. Ingesting or eschewing certain foods and plants and abstaining from sexual relations enables humans to capture, control, and channel the flow of this energy to desired ends. Through collective ritual action, human communities can ensure the continued functioning of the natural world and the larger cosmological order.

CATHARINE GOOD

FEATHERED SERPENT. The religious art of pre-Hispanic Mesoamerica featured a remarkably rich and varied iconographic bestiary. Most of the more prominent types of regional fauna were represented, but one animal was featured, the serpent, most frequently the rattlesnake. Composite icons, fusing two or more different animals, were also common. The most renowned of these is known as the Feathered Serpent; it combined bird feathers with the body of the snake and, sometimes, crocodilian and/or feline features. At the time of the Spanish conquest, in predominantly Nahuatl-speaking Central Mexico, this icon was named Quetzalcoatl (from *quetzalli*, "quetzal feather" and *coatl*, "snake"). In the Mayan-speaking areas of the Yucatán Peninsula and Guatemala, names of equivalent meaning were Kukulcan (in Yucatec Mayan) and Gucumatz (in Quiché Mayan). The name (and/or title) Quetzalcoatl was used for both a traditional priest/ruler of Tollan (the Early Postclassic Central Mexican imperial capital), and a major god at the time of the Conquest.

The deity displayed multiple aspects. As Ehecatl ("wind"), he functioned as a leading fertility god who was propitiated in round temples. He also played a key role in the cosmogonic myths, was connected with the planet Venus, and possessed important mercantile associations. The Toltec ruler/priest who bore his name was the protagonist of an extensive series of narratives (e.g., "The Topiltzin Quetzalcoatl of Tollan Tale"), which recounted his rise and fall and eventual flight down to the Gulf Coast, where he disappeared, promising eventually to return to reclaim his royal dignity. Quetzalcoatl, Kukulcan, Gucumatz, and related appellatives were also employed as sacerdotal titles, as well as those of political and military offices.

Representations of the Feathered Serpent were featured in various Mesoamerican aesthetic traditions in a variety of forms and diverse iconographic contexts. As early as the Middle Formative (Preclassic) in the Olmec tradition, images of serpents with avian characteristics were represented often on several types of artifacts and monuments. This composite creature, who has been denominated the "Avian Serpent" and "Olmec God VII," appears to constitute an incipient form of the later full-fledged Feathered Serpent, the rattlesnake covered with feathers, probably with at least some of the same celestial and fertility connotations.

Not until the Early Classic period, at the great urban metropolis of Teotihuacan, did the indubitable Feathered Serpent appear as the preeminent iconographic motif, embellishing one of the most elaborate structures ever built in pre-Hispanic Mesoamerica, the Pyramid of the Feathered Serpent. Rising in seven stages, in the center of a vast compound called the Ciudadela (which was the

The pedestal of the Feathered Serpents. *Photograph courtesy of Norberto González Crespo.*

axis mundi of the city), all of its *tableros* (vertical framed quadrangular panels) and *taludes* (sloping surfaces beneath the *tableros*) featured massive stone carvings of feathered rattlesnakes. On the *tableros*, a series of their heads, edged with feather ruffs, project from what may be circular pyrite mirrors. They alternate with platelet-textured reptilian visages lacking lower mandibles, but with feathered eyes, and wearing knotted headdresses garnished with pairs of rimmed circles or "goggles." Carved in relief on both the *tableros* and *taludes* are the undulating bodies of Feathered Serpents, plus conch and scallop shells. The flanking ramps of the stairway on the western face of the structure are also decorated with the projecting Feathered Serpent heads.

There have been many differences of opinion concerning the identification of the other *tablero* head. They have been identified as headdresses on the basis of comparisons with similar images in other iconographic contexts at Teotihuacan. One view regards the creature represented on this headdress as an early version of the crocodilian earth monster, the Cipactli, which served as the first of the twenty day-signs of the 260-day divinatory cycle, the *tonalpohualli*, and which also played a significant role in the Conquest-period cosmogonic myths. Another opinion interprets the headdress creature as the "War Serpent," an essentially ophidian creature that, in many variants, was widely distributed throughout Classic Mesoamerica and (as first proposed in 1952 by Alfonso Caso and Ignacio Bernal) that evolved during the Postclassic into the Xiuhcoatl ("Turquoise Serpent"), a celestial serpentine creature with strong igneous associations.

Archaeological investigations adjacent to and under the pyramid have revealed more than two hundred burials, mostly of young males accoutered as warriors, who appear to have been sacrificed in dedicatory rituals at the time the edifice was constructed, probably about 200 CE, during the Late Miccaotli or Early Tlamimilolpa phase. It has been suggested that the structure might have been built by a powerful ruler in an ostentatious proclamation of his power and piety. In any case, the prominence accorded there to the Feathered Serpent makes it likely that this icon did constitute a symbol of royal command, as it unquestionably did in Toltec and other later Mesoamerican cultural traditions—a view supported by Teotihuacan images of the Feathered Serpent in juxtaposition with a mat, a Mesoamerican symbol of political authority.

Feathered Serpents, in a variety of images, continued to be represented throughout the period of Teotihuacan's dominance. Typical examples, commonly with sectioned bodies, are featured on ceramic vessels and on the numerous murals at the site, usually in border locations, where their fertility connotations are often emphasized by liquid streams that issue from their maws (possibly including blood, which may add an additional sacrificial dimension). An association with the planet Venus, based mainly on the occasional presence of the quincunx device on the creature's body, is also possible but not certain.

In other regions of Classic Mesoamerica, images of ostensible Feathered Serpents are scattered and rare, although in the Lowland Maya region more generalized celestial and terrestrial reptilian monsters, often bicephalic (two-headed), are ubiquitous—particularly the creature known, among other designations, as the "Bearded Dragon." Although some of these zoomorphs are edged with feathers, they appear to represent creatures essentially distinct from the rattlesnake enveloped in feathers that constituted the Teotihuacan Feathered Serpent. They appear to have had both celestial and terrestrial connotations, especially celestial, and they are often associated with royal power, particularly when functioning as the "ceremonial bar" held by rulers. Another important Classic Maya icon, the "Serpent Bird" or "Principal Bird Deity," apparently conceptually related to the Feathered Serpent, was configured quite differently. Subsequent to the fall of Teotihuacan, during the Epiclassic, about 700 to 900 CE, images of the Feathered Serpent proliferated and diffused throughout Mesoamerica. Two important Central Mexican Epiclassic centers, Cacaxtla in Puebla and Xochicalco in Morelos, featured particularly striking manifestations of the icon. At Cacaxtla, a mural displays an elaborately attired, very Mayoid male figure wearing an eagle headdress, holding a version of the bicephalic Ceremonial Bar, and standing on a "bearded" Feathered Serpent.

Eight somewhat similar Feathered Serpents are carved in relief on the *talud* that constitutes the lower stage of the Pyramid of the Feathered Serpent, the most elaborately ornamented structure at Xochicalco. Their undulating bodies are decorated with what have been interpreted as cloud or shell motifs. Positioned within the undulations of those on the northern, eastern, and southern sides are six identical images of Mayoid male figures, sitting cross legged and wearing elaborate "monster maw" feather headdresses. They alternate with six 9 Reptile's Eye (9 Ehecatl?) dates, in elaborately adorned square cartouches. The other relief carvings of this structure, including those on the walls of the temple chamber, consist of numerous repeated images of what appear to be priests and/or rulers, place signs, and calendric dates. It has been suggested that they commemorate some kind of sacerdotal congress or, perhaps more likely, a dynastic/political event. In any case, the emphasis on the Feathered Serpent, Quetzalcoatl, functioning as both patron of calendric wisdom and symbol of political power, would seem to have been a fitting icon to be featured on this elaborately adorned structure.

At another major Western Mesoamerican Epiclassic center, El Tajín, in northern Veracruz, some reptilian images, depicted in the characteristic double-outlined interlocking scroll technique, have been identified as Feathered Serpents—but, if so, they are imaged in a stylized manner quite different from those described above. Yet a relief carving on a large boulder at the site of Maltrata in central Veracruz does portray a Feathered Serpent not too dissimilar in configuration from those of Cacaxtla and Xochicalco. At Cholula, the center of the Quetzalcoatl cult at the time of the Conquest, monumental images of the Feathered Serpent are virtually absent, but symbols associated with the anthropomorphic aspect of the deity are occasionally featured on portable artifacts, including ceramics. In two great centers that emerged late in the Epiclassic and continued to flourish during the Early Postclassic (c.900–1250 CE), the Feathered Serpent truly came into its own: at Tula in Central Mexico and at Chichén Itzá in northern Yucatán. Whatever the explanation for the striking architectural and iconographic similarities between these two distant sites and their exact chronological relationship (which is still controversial), the Feathered Serpent is depicted in quite similar fashion at both, including the icon's most innovative manifestation, the Feathered Serpent column. Another apparent new format was the "patron" position of the undulating Feathered Serpent behind the figure of a warrior/leader, implying a significant relationship between the creature and rulership. Also ubiquitous at both sites is the undulating Feathered Serpent on the cornices of stone benches, or banquettes, edging some rooms. This frequency of Feathered Serpent images, particularly at Chichén Itzá, appears to provide archaeological support for the ethnohistorical traditions that associate both Quetzalcoatl and his Yucatecan counterpart, Kukulcan, with these two leading centers of political and military power.

In the Late Postclassic, the Feathered Serpent continued to play an important role in Mesoamerican art and iconography. Wherever the widespread Mixteca-Puebla stylistic/iconographic tradition prevailed, centered in the Puebla–Western Oaxaca–Gulf Coast region but also dominant in a somewhat more "naturalistic" version in the Basin of Mexico and adjacent territory, it appears as a common image, especially on polychromed ceramics and in the ritual/divinatory screenfold books. It was also frequently depicted in stone sculpture in Central Mexico, where the range of its manifestations was significantly greater than in those of the earlier traditions, principally Toltec, out of which it had evolved. It was most strikingly imaged in sculptures of coiled Feathered Serpents, sometimes with a human face peering out of its open jaws. They also often bear dates and some of the symbols asso-

ciated with Quetzalcoatl. In relief carvings, the "patron" configuration persisted, as well as the undulating Feathered Serpent on banquette cornices and other edging locations. The Templo Mayor of the gods Huitzilopochtli and Tlaloc in the Mexica capital of Tenochtitlan also displayed colossal Feathered Serpent heads at the bases of its stairway ramps, à la Chichén Itzá.

The reason for the spread of Feathered Serpent imagery throughout Mesoamerica during the Epiclassic and Early Postclassic, it was recently suggested, was the military expansion, pursued with messianic vigor, of a millenarian cult or "world religion" that revolved around the deity Quetzalcoatl—which continued into the Postclassic and was at least partly responsible for the spread of the Mixteca-Puebla stylistic/iconographic tradition. There is, however, scant evidence for the existence of organized, proselytizing religious movements in pre-Hispanic Mesoamerica, so it seems hardly necessary to invoke this type of mechanism to explain the widespread distribution of the Feathered Serpent. Rather, the inherent fascination and appeal of this ancient icon that fused a celestial with a terrestrial creature, symbolizing creativity and fertility, the fundamental theme of all Mesoamerican religious systems, probably best accounts for its enduring popularity among so many of the peoples that participated in the New World's most advanced indigenous civilization.

[*See also* Topiltzin Quetzalcoatl; Venus.]

BIBLIOGRAPHY

Bardawil, Lawrence W. "The Principal Bird Deity in Maya Art—An Iconographic Study of Form and Meaning." In *The Art, Iconography and Dynastic History of Palenque*, part 3: *Proceedings of the Segunda Mesa Redonda de Palenque, December 14–21, 1974—Palenque*, edited by Merle Green Robertson, pp. 195–209. Pebble Beach, Calif., 1976. Well-illustrated survey and discussion of the Classic Maya icon that appears to have been conceptually related to the Feathered Serpent.

Berrin, Kathleen, ed. *Feathered Serpent and Flowering Trees: Reconstructing the Murals of Teotihuacan.* San Francisco, 1988. Articles describing and interpreting a large corpus of murals donated in 1976 to the M. H. de Young Memorial Museum, San Francisco, which include some striking images of the Feathered Serpent.

Joralemon, Peter David. *A Study of Olmec Iconography.* Dumbarton Oaks, Trustees for Harvard University, Studies in Pre-Columbian Art and Archaeology, 7. Washington, D.C., 1971. Survey and analysis of Olmec iconography, in which the author identifies what he calls "God VII" as the Feathered Serpent.

López Austin, Alfredo, Leonardo López Luján, and Saburo Sugiyama. "The Temple of Quetzalcoatl at Teotihuacan: Its Possible Significance." *Ancient Mesoamerica* 2.1 (1991), 93–106. Following an analysis of the iconography of the structure, the conclusion is that it was dedicated to "the myth of the origin of time and calendric succession," with the sculptures on its façade representing "the Feathered Serpent at the moment of creation."

Miller, Arthur. *The Moral Painting of Teotihuacan.* Washington, D.C., 1973. Comprehensive survey and discussion of Teotihuacan murals at time of publication, including some that feature the Feathered Serpent.

Nicholson, H. B. "The 'Feathered Serpents' of Copan." In *The Periph-*

ery of the Southeastern Classic Maya Realm, edited by Gary W. Pahl, pp. 171–188. UCLA Latin American Center Publications, 61. Los Angeles, 1987. Discussion of four Classic Copán monuments with images that had been identified by various students as Feathered Serpents; the conclusion, after a review of Mesoamerican ophidian iconography, was that as versions of the "Bearded Dragon," they represent an essentially distinct entity.

Nicholson, H. B. "The Iconography of the Feathered Serpent in Late Postclassic Central Mexico." In *Mesoamerica's Classic Heritage: From Teotihuacan to the Aztecs*, edited by Davíd Carrasco, Lindsay Jones, and Scott Sessions, pp. 145–164. Boulder, Colo., 2000. Illustrated survey and discussion of Feathered Serpent iconography in this period and area, emphasizing its richness and diversity.

Ringle, William M., Tomás Gallareta Negrón, and George J. Bey. "The Return of Quetzalcoatl: Evidence for the Spread of a World Religion during the Epiclassic Period." *Ancient Mesoamerica* 9.2 (1998), 183–232. After a broad survey of the archaeological evidence, the authors advance the hypothesis that the militaristic spread of an organized Quetzalcoatl millenarian religion best explains the wide distribution of Feathered Serpent symbolism during the Mesoamerican Epiclassic.

Sugiyama, Saburo. "Teotihuacan as an Origin for Postclassic Feathered Serpent Symbolism." In *Mesoamerica's Classic Heritage: From Teotihuacan to the Aztecs*, edited by Davíd Carrasco, Lindsay Jones, and Scott Sessions, pp. 117–143. Boulder, Colo., 2000. Surveys the Feather Serpent imagery at Teotihuacan and develops the identification of the head alternating with the Feathered Serpent head on the *tableros* of the Pyramid of the Feathered Serpent as the headdress of the "Primordial Crocodile."

Taube, Karl A. "The Temple of Quetzalcoatl and the Cult of Sacred War at Teotihuacan." *Res* 21 (1992), 54–87. Identifies the head that alternates with the Feathered Serpent on the *tableros* of the Pyramid of the Feathered Serpent as a headdress imaging the "War Serpent," a solar fire serpent ancestral to the Postclassic Xiuhcoatl, that was also widely adopted by Classic Maya rulers, with the structure itself, featuring Feathered Serpent heads emerging from mirrors, apparently an ancestral form of the Tezcacoac, "Place of the Mirror Snake," an Aztec temple connected with war.

Taube, Karl A. "The Rainmakers: The Olmec and Their Contribution to Mesoamerican Belief and Ritual." In *The Olmec World: Ritual and Rulership*, pp. 83–103. Princeton, N.J., 1998. Discussion with numerous illustrations of the "Avian Serpent" in Olmec iconography—the apparent prototype of the rattlesnake covered with feathers that constituted the later Mesoamerican Feathered Serpent.

H. B. NICHOLSON

FEATHERS AND FEATHERWORK.

Featherworking was among the finest of the luxury industries in pre-Columbian Mesoamerica. A wide array of ordinary and exotic feathers was used, and the objects created included warrior costumes, shields, headdresses, banners, fans, capes, and decorative hangings.

At least among the Late Postclassic peoples, featherworking was considered to be a "civilized" craft, and it ranked along with fine stonework and metalwork as a luxury enterprise. Close links were maintained between featherworkers and the nobility, since ornate and elaborate feathered objects were the prerogative of the nobility and served as important visible symbols of their exalted status. The highland Valley of Mexico featherworkers also maintained close ties with long-distance merchants, since the most prized plumes were obtained from distant tropical lowlands through the efforts of those professional traders, the *pochteca*.

The manufacture of feathered objects was well established by the Classic period in Mesoamerica. Feathered accouterments are vividly depicted in Classic Maya sculptures and paintings, and feathered headdresses, fans, and banners are prominent features of Maya iconography (especially in the murals of Bonampak). Feathered adornments are also featured in depictions of nobility and deities throughout other regions of Classic Mesoamerica, including Teotihuacan, El Tajín, and Monte Albán. After the collapse of the Classic period centers, feathered adornments continued to be meaningful symbols of nobility. The enigmatic Toltec were considered by later peoples to have been innovators of featherwork who brought shimmering tropical feathers to the drier highland centers and raised the craft of featherworking to unexcelled heights. However, it is clear that brilliant exotic feathers had adorned highland nobles and deities in earlier times (as at Teotihuacan), and that the transport of feathers constituted a considerable commercial investment by professional merchants. A mural depiction of a merchant's pack frame containing green flowing feathers at the Late Classic/Early Postclassic site of Cacaxtla testifies to the importance of these tropical luxuries in the highlands.

The abundant written documentation on the Last Postclassic peoples (especially the Aztec) offers rich details about the technology and use of feathered artifacts, as well as on the role of featherworkers in the larger society. These esteemed artisans applied both "ordinary" and "exotic" types of feathers to their craft. Ordinary feathers included those plucked from ducks and turkeys, which were dyed and used as the undermost layers in a mosaic object; over them the more precious exotic feathers were laid. Exotic feathers included those from macaws, parrots, hummingbirds, and especially the prized quetzal. The small feathers from these birds formed the top layers of elaborate mosaics or were tied together to form shirts, while the long wing and tail feathers (especially the shimmering tail feathers of the quetzal) were tied into flowing headdresses, fans, banners, bracelets, or back devices.

The feather artisans employed two basic techniques in creating feathered objects. That which produced mosaics required several stages of meticulous preparation. First, a thin, stiff backing of cotton cloth (hardened with glue) was prepared; a design was drawn on a cotton and paper stencil, and this design was applied to the prepared backing. The bottom layer of feathers was then carefully applied to this design; this consisted of ordinary feathers, dyed and then dipped in glue. Shimmering tropical feathers, in their natural colors, were then glued on top of this base, resulting in exquisite objects. The glue was obtained from a type of orchid and was manufactured by Amanteca children. Often, pieces of goldwork were also included in the design, suggesting that goldworkers may have worked closely with featherworkers. A second technique involved attaching long, graceful feathers to a frame and tying them with maguey twine; this yielded eye-catching objects such as flowing headdresses, ornate fans, banners, and tufted armbands.

In Late Postclassic Central Mexico, featherworkers were organized into their own urban districts, where they carried out their craft and instructed their neophytes. The most fully documented featherworking district, or *calpulli*, was Amantlan in Tlatelolco, Tenochtitlan's sister city. These featherworkers therefore became known as Amanteca. Geographically and functionally, they were closely associated with the professional merchants, or *pochteca*. This was a convenient and lucrative association, since the finest feathers employed by the Amanteca in their craft were available only in tropical zones, regions frequented by the far-ranging *pochteca*.

The Franciscan friar Bernardino de Sahagún, in book 9 of his *General History*, mentions two general types of featherworkers: those who worked exclusively for the Mexica ruler, and those who were private artisans. The former were housed in the royal palace and supplied with feathers from the imperial coffers, many of which were undoubtedly obtained through tribute. The royal featherworkers specialized in producing the regalia of the god Huitzilopochtli, the adornments of the ruler, and the gifts the ruler chose to distribute to other high-ranking individuals. It may be assumed that rulers of other powerful cities, such as Tetzcoco and Tlacopan, employed their own cadres of featherworkers. The private featherworkers produced and sold their creations independently of the palace, but probably under some supervision. Although these appear to have been family-based household operations (*Codex Mendoza* 1992, vol. 3, f. 70r), urban guildlike organizations oversaw education and training, quality control, ritual and social activities, and rewards for outstanding achievement.

The creation and use of feathered adornments continued throughout the Colonial period, and some objects (such as feather-adorned greeting cards) were still being produced in the twentieth century. The art of tying feathers to flowing headdresses and fans seems to have disappeared shortly after the Spanish conquest, although the art of feather mosaics continued with some energy for another two or three centuries. These mosaics became

transformed in conformity with the changes wrought by the Conquest: indigenous objects and iconography were replaced by Christian ones. Thus, mosaic shields and warrior costumes disappeared, replaced by the bishop's miter and other ecclesiastical vestments, and depictions of indigenous deities yielded to Christian saints. Nonetheless, some indigenous objects continued to be treasured by their owners after the Conquest, as documented by Anderson, Berdan, and Lockhart (1976).

Only a handful of feathered objects from Late Postclassic Mesoamerica are known today. Among these rare objects are four mosaic shields, a fan, a quetzal headdress, a feathered cape, and perhaps a small disk with a Tlaloc face design. The last, however, may belong to the much larger body of extant feathered objects dating from after the Spanish conquest.

[*See also* Craft Production.]

BIBLIOGRAPHY

Anders, Ferdinand, Francisco de la Maza, Teresa Castelló Yturbide, and Marita Martínez del Río de Redo. *Tesoros de Mexico—Arte Plumario de Mosaico*. Artes de México, 137. Mexico City, 1970. Detailed discussion of Central Mexican featherworking in pre-Columbian and Colonial times.

Anderson, Arthur, Frances Berdan, and James Lockhart. *Beyond the Codices*. 1976.

García Granados, Rafael. "Mexican Feather Mosaics." *Mexican Art and Life* 5 (1939), 1–4. Discussion of Colonial as well as pre-Columbian featherwork mosaic pieces, with abundant illustrations.

Noguera, Eduardo. "Minor Arts in the Central Valleys." In *Handbook of Middle American Indians*, vol. 10, *Archaeology of Northern Mesoamerica*, edited by Gordon F. Ekholm and Ignacio Bernal, pp. 258–269. Austin, Tex., 1971. Description of featherworking of the Late Postclassic peoples of highland Central Mexico.

Pasztory, Esther. *Aztec Art*. New York, 1983. Brief discussion (pp. 278–280) of featherworking from an art historian's perspective, with excellent illustrations in color of several of the extant featherwork pieces.

Sahagún, Bernardino de. *Florentine Codex: General History of the Things of New Spain*. Edited and translated by Arthur J. O. Anderson and Charles E. Dibble. Salt Lake City, 1950–1982. Book 9 contains detailed description of Aztec featherworking, including techniques, rituals, and other activities.

Saville, Marshall H. *The Goldsmith's Art in Ancient Mexico*. Indian Notes and Monographs, Museum of the American Indian, Heye Foundation. New York, 1920. Despite its title, this book contains a wealth of information on feathered artifacts; especially useful is the detailed list of objects known at the time of the Spanish conquest.

Seler, Eduard. "The Jewelry Craft of the Ancient Mexicans and Their Art of Working in Stone and Making Feather Ornaments." In his *Collected Works in Mesoamerican Linguistics and Archaeology*, vol. 2, pp. 270–295. Culver City, Calif., 1991. Translations of the relevant Sahagún materials on featherworking, with abundant notes.

Toscano, Salvador. *Arte precolombino de México y de la América Central*. Mexico City, 1970. Though brief, the discussion of featherworking (pp. 181–186) offers good descriptions of the extant objects in museums.

FRANCES F. BERDAN

FEJÉRVÁRY-MAYER, CODEX. A pre-Conquest ritual and divinatory codex from central Mexico, the *Codex Fejérváry-Mayer* is one of the principal manuscripts of the so-called Borgia Group, a group of seven pictorial manuscripts that are associated by the similarity of their content, arrangement, and general style to the Codex Borgia. Included in the Borgia Group are the *Codex Borgia, Codex Fejérváry-Mayer, Codex Laud, Codex Cospi, Codex Vaticanus B, Aubin Ms. No. 20*, and the reverse of *Codex Porfirio Díaz*. These Borgia Group codices all date from the Late Postclassic or Early Colonial period and contain almanacs that relate the twenty day signs, the thirteen day coefficients, and the 260 days of the ritual calendar to the supernaturals and other elements that carry the mantic associations for different periods of time. Read and interpreted by day-keepers or calendar priests, such divinatory codices revealed the fates of individuals according to the day and period of their birth. The divinatory books were also consulted to determine the best times to plant and harvest, to go forth and return from journeys, to go to war, and to engage in other activities. They also gave the fates of couples considering marriage. There was little in the lives of the Aztec and their neighbors that was not controlled by the fates of the days as revealed in the divinatory codices.

Like most of the other Borgia Group manuscripts, the *Codex Fejérváry-Mayer* is a screenfold book of animal hide (probably deer). Its long hide strip, which reaches 400 centimeters (13 feet) when fully extended, is folded accordion-style into twenty-three leaves measuring 17.5 by 17.5 centimeters (6.9 by 6.9 inches). The first and last leaves are painted on one side only (they were originally glued to the hard covers that once protected the book), but the other leaves are painted on both sides. This yields twenty-two painted pages on each side of the codex. Except for the original covers, the manuscript appears to be complete. The end leaves are now backed with European cloth.

The codex reads right to left, opening and closing with elaborate one-page presentations of the 260-day calendar.

Page 1 of the *Fejérváry-Mayer*, which is the most often reproduced page of all the Mesoamerican codices, is a diagram both of time and of space. It is often interpreted as a cosmogram of the Late Postclassic world. Around a central figure of Xiuhtecuhtli, the lord of the year and of time, the painter arranged the 260 days of the ritual calendar in a multicolored ribbon that defines a Formée cross (often called a Maltese cross). The cross's broad arms are oriented toward the four cardinal directions, with east at the top. Narrower loops between the arms are oriented toward the intercardinal points. The 260 days of the ritual calendar flow along this ribbon in twenty groups of thirteen days, called *trecenas*. Each *trecena* is represented by the first day sign of the period fol-

Tezcatlipoca's body, uniting time and the divine form, as depicted in the reverse of the *Codex Fejérváry-Mayer. Drawing by Rodolfo Avila.*

lowed by twelve dots that serve as spacers standing in for the other twelve days. Beginning with the first day (Crocodile), the count reads counterclockwise around the cross: the first five *trecenas* are associated with east and northeast, the second five with north and northwest, the third five with west and southwest, and the fourth five with south and southeast.

Each arm of the cross, and thus each direction, has its own color: red in the east, yellow in the north, blue in the west, and green in the south. Within the frame of each arm appear the two lords, the directional tree, and the bird that are associated with that direction. These nine lords—two in each direction and Xiuhtecuhtli in the center—are the nine Lords of the Night, who in other contexts influence the fates of the days in sequence. The intercardinal loops have their own plants and animals, and they are topped with birds flying toward the center. Within the birds' bodies, circles around the day signs Rabbit, Reed, Flint, and House distinguish these day signs also as yearbearers. Beside the birds, dismembered body parts of the deity Tezcatlipoca (god of rulership and divination) release blood that flows toward Xiuhtecuhtli in the center, as if the body of the god of divination were nourishing the lord of time at the center. A second set of *trecena* day signs along the intercardinal loops associates the *trecenas* with the directions in yet another pattern.

In this one complex and masterful presentation, the painter has used the regular passage of the 260-day ritual count and the continuity of the *trecenas* to re-create the physical space of the cosmos with its cardinal directions, cosmic trees, birds, and the lords who rule those directions. As it passes, time moves from one part of the cosmos to another, absorbing the mantic meaning associated with each direction. Thus, the ribbon of time describes the cosmos as a physical and geographic entity; at the same time, the physicality of the cosmos inscribes time with mantic meaning. This single diagram, interpreted as a temporal and spatial map of the cosmos, shows how inextricably time is linked to space in the Aztec mind.

Following this cosmogram, the next almanac relates the nine Lords of the Night to days, rituals, and prognostications (pp. 2–4). What then follows on this side of the codex is not another almanac, but a series of nineteen descriptions of rituals that involve quantities of counted items. Each painted description usually features a deity or supernatural, the items used to conduct the ritual (such as balls of rubber, bound sticks, and bloodletters), one or more days signs that signal specific dates, and amounts of items. These amounts are presented as bars and dots—the bar signaling the quantity of five and a dot signaling one—arranged in decided patterns, just as a contemporary diviner might arrange groups of counted items on an altar. Rituals involving bundles of carefully counted and arranged grass and pine needles are still conducted in Nahuatl-speaking areas of Guerrero.

The reverse of the codex contains fifteen almanacs arranged in two distinct and separate registers. An eighty-day almanac (pp. 23a–29a) presents supernaturals manipulating small humans, who have generally been interpreted as infants. Other almanacs present pairs of interacting deities, single deities seated in temples, and deities making offerings before temples. Several almanacs features travelers, characterized by the burdens on their backs and the walking sticks they hold. For this reason, it has been suggested that the *Codex Fejérváry-Mayer* was created to be used by the *pochteca*, or long-distance merchants.

The reverse ends with a full-page presentation of Tez-

Page 1 and view of the entire *Codex Fejérváry-Mayer*. After *Codex Fejérváry-Mayer*, intro. C. A. Burland. *Graz: Akademische Druck- u. Verlagsanstalt, 1971 facsimile edition.*

catlipoca (god of divination and rulership) surrounded by the twenty *trecenas*, each *trecena* signaled by its beginning day sign and the twelve spacers. Just as the first almanac in the manuscript arranged the *trecenas* according to the cardinal directions, uniting time and space, this almanac arranges the *trecenas* according to Tezcatlipoca's body, uniting time and the divine form. Although the *Codex Fejérváry-Mayer* is not the longest or most complex of the divinatory almanacs, it remains a principal resource for understanding the Aztec religion, divination, and calendrics.

Stylistically, the codex belongs generally to the Mixtec-Puebla horizon style, as do the other Borgia Group codices. It lacks the naturalism of manuscripts from the Valley of Mexico and has instead been attributed to the area embraced by Puebla, Tlaxcala, and Veracruz. In draftsmanship, figural proportions, and size, it is nearly identical to the *Codex Laud*, which has been called its stylistic twin; indeed, the two manuscripts are so similar that they may have come from the same workshop. Both manuscripts are in nearly pristine condition. With brilliant colors outlined and directed by the sure hand of a master painter, the *Codex Fejérváry-Mayer* is one of the best preserved of the pre-Conquest codices.

The codex takes its name from two of its previous owners, Gabriel Fejérváry and Joseph Mayer. Its history is unknown before the first quarter of the nineteenth century, when the codex was in the possession of the Hungarian savant Gabriel Fejérváry, who had a notable library and collection of antiquities. It was during this time that Lord Kingsborough included the codex in his monumental *Antiquities of Mexico* (London, 1831). After Fejérváry's death, his nephew sold the codex to the English collector Joseph Mayer of Liverpool, whose large collection of antiquities was given in 1897 to the Free Public Museums of Liverpool, where the codex is now kept. In 1901, the Duc de Loubat published the manuscript in chromolithographic facsimile with a still valuable commentary by Eduard Seler. José Corona Núñez included it in his *Antiquedades de México* (Mexico, 1964), and Miguel León-Portilla edited an excellent but scarce photographic facsimile (Mexico, 1985), interpreting the codex as a merchant's almanac. More recently, outstanding photographic facsimiles have been issued in Graz, Austria (1971) and Mexico City (1994), the latter with a descriptive commentary.

[*See also* Borgia Group of Pictorial Manuscripts.]

BIBLIOGRAPHY

Anders, Ferdinand, Maarten Jansen, and Gabina Aurora Pérez Jiménez, eds. *El libro de Tezcatlipoca, señor del tiempo, libro explicativo del llamado Códice Fejérváry-Mayer*. Mexico City, 1994. Excellent photographic facsimile in color with descriptive commentary.

Boone, Elizabeth Hill. "Guides for Living: The Divinatory Codices of Mexico." In *Precious Greenstone, Precious Feather/In Chalchihuitl*

In Quetzalli: Essays in Honor of Doris Heyden, edited by Eloise Quiñones Keber. Culver City, Calif., 2000. Overview of the Mexican divinatory codices.

Seler, Eduard, ed. *Codex Fejérváry-Mayer: An Old Mexican Picture Manuscript in the Liverpool Free Public Museums*. Berlin and London, 1901–1902. Long the fundamental commentary on the codex; published in both English and German versions.

ELIZABETH H. BOONE

FERTILITY. Agricultural fertility was and continues to be of primary concern for Mesoamerican cultures. Many ritual activities of pre-Columbian people were directed to deities of land and rain. Their understanding of fertility was intimately involved with specific geographical attributes—in particular, bodies of water, mountains, and caves. The Mesoamerican concern with agricultural success was directly related to survival and prosperity. Ceremonies to rain and earth deities were an integral part of most aspects of their socioreligious organization. Therefore, fertility is best discussed as the Mesoamericans' varied attempts to orient themselves to a hidden, cosmological structure on which their material survival was based.

An important step in the development of Mesoamerican urban civilization was the control of agricultural plants. *Chinampas*, or raised fields in shallow freshwater regions, allowed Mesoamerican civilizations to grow enormous amounts of food to sustain their burgeoning populations. Intensive agricultural practices required detailed knowledge of the surrounding landscape. Of particular importance was the control of water, which was accomplished with massive hydrological projects that mixed water and earth in the correct proportions to maximize agricultural fertility. The productivity of the *chinampa* system was not surpassed until the introduction of chemical fertilizers in the twentieth century. [*See* Chinampa Agriculture.]

The Olmec (3000–300 BCE) civilization was the first urban culture to demonstrate a documented ritual concern for agricultural fertility. In their development, the Olmec placed special emphasis on ancestral kings. Giant stone heads of dead rulers were the focal points for ritual events that connected the world of the living with the dead, who were associated with the earth, in order to propitiate spiritual beings directly involved with agricultural fertility. Ancestral leaders acted as intermediaries between human beings and deities of water and earth. The reciprocity between humans and deities of earth was related to the development of architectural innovations like the pyramid, which reproduced the local mountainous topography, an abode for earth deities, and also connected the Olmec with deities of the sky and underworld. In this sense, the pyramid may be interpreted as a vertical axis for human communication with a sacred reality. In

Possible representation of a priest performing crop fertility rites. Mural painting at Tepantitla.
Courtesy of Visual Resources Collection, The University of Texas at Austin. Ferguson Collection.

later Mesoamerican cultures, pyramids were referred to as "mountains of sustenance."

At Teotihuacan (200–700 CE) in Central Mexico, there was a dramatic magnification of Olmec urban planning. Like the Olmec, the Teotihuacan builders sited their Pyramids of the Sun and Moon to correspond to the mountainous topography of the surrounding valley. The massive Pyramid of the Sun was built over a cave that had four chambers extending into the four cardinal directions; it was undoubtedly used for ceremonial purposes. Recent excavations have revealed that a canal encircled this pyramid. It was filled with water from a river that was rerouted through Teotihuacan so that it would flow through the central ceremonial region. These findings emphasize the Pyramid of the Sun's importance as a mountain of sustenance. Teotihuacanos constructed their ceremonial center to promote the ideal of fertility. Therefore, objects from the sea, as well as local objects that symbolized fertility, constituted a major portion of temple offerings.

Teotihuacan was oriented to the appearance of the Pleiades in the western sky by means of a series of "pecked circles" carved into rock or stucco, with points numerically associated with the Mesoamerican divinatory calendar. Pecked circles have been found in the ceremonial center and on surrounding hilltops. The first appearance, or heliacal rising, of the Pleiades in the west corresponded with the beginning of the rainy season and the beginning of the agricultural year. Thus, the entire city of Teotihuacan was organized with reference to the agricultural fertility cycle.

The Maya (200–1300 CE) emphasized the intimate relationship among kingship, sacrifice, divine authority, and fertility. It was the duty of Maya kings and queens to let their own blood, or to perform autosacrifice, from their tongues and/or genitals at particular times of the year. The blood of kings was understood to have a fertilizing effect on the land. In addition, the experience of Maya kings and queens while letting their own blood could induce visions of deities. Ritually burned blood-spattered papers were seen as an appropriate gift to the gods and as having a fertilizing effect on the land.

The Maya, who also practiced *chinampa* agriculture, were intensely involved with intercity warfare. Although political and economic issues played a primary role in these conflicts, the ceremonial reason for war was the taking of captives. Analogous to the autosacrifice of kings, the sacrifice of captured warriors from other polities often took the form of torture in which the victim's blood, associated with his life energy, was understood to promote fertility and prosperity.

The importance of human sacrifice for fertility ceremonies was amplified with the Aztec, or Mexica (1350–1521 CE). As in other Mesoamerican cultures, the Aztec city of Tenochtitlan was sustained by *chinampa* agriculture. Most of the offerings found since 1978 in excavations at the Templo Mayor, the central ceremonial temple of Tenochtitlan, were dedicated to Tlaloc, the Aztec god of rain and fertility.

Wars between rival empires would be fought in order that sacrificial captives could be taken and offered to the gods. Most captives would not be killed on the battlefield but instead would be sacrificed at the temple in the center of the city of their captors. The Aztec arranged these wars, called "flowery wars," with enemy states in order to increase the number of sacrificial victims. Arranged battles and the sacrifice of warriors at ceremonial temples reflected war's fertilizing effect on the earth.

Ceremonies to Tlaloc and other fertility deities often included human sacrifice at specific moments in the agricultural cycle. These sacrifices were understood to release water in proper amounts for growing crops. Blood, which is internal to human beings, directly corresponded with water, which was understood to exist under the ground. Water was Tlaloc's blood, and it was humans' responsibility to give up some of their life (blood) so that Tlaloc could be fed and water released for the entire Aztec community.

BIBLIOGRAPHY

Arnold, Philip P. *Eating Landscape: Aztec and European Occupation of Tlalocan.* Niwot, Colo., 1999. Importance of fertility rites for how the Aztec meaningfully inhabited their material world

Aveni, Anthony F., Horst Hartung, and B. Buckingham. "The Pecked Cross Symbol in Ancient Mesoamerica." *Science* 202 (1978), 267–279. Important analysis of the organization of Teotihuacan based on alignments of architectural features with celestial phenomena.

Broda, Johanna. "Las fiestas Aztecas de los dioses de la lluvia: Una reconstrucción según las fuentes del siglo XVI." *Revista española de antropología americana* 6 (1971), 245–327. Comprehensive outline of rain and fertility gods as described in early colonial sources.

Heyden, Doris. "An Interpretation of the Cave underneath the Pyramid of the Sun in Teotihuacan, Mexico." *American Antiquity* 40.2 (1975), 131–147. Significance of cave symbolism in Mesoamerican traditions.

Matos Moctezuma, Eduardo. *Life and Death in the Templo Mayor.* Translated by Bernard R. Ortiz de Montellano and Thelma Ortiz de Montellano. Niwot, Colo., 1995. Interpretation of Aztec ceremonial life informed by the recent excavations of their central temple.

Schele, Linda, and Mary Ellen Miller. *The Blood of Kings: Dynasty and Ritual in Maya Art.* New York, 1986. Insightful interpretation of the ritual dimensions of Maya kingship through their art and architecture.

PHILIP P. ARNOLD

FESTIVALS AND FESTIVAL CYCLES. Annual festivals are still a prominent feature of Mesoamerican cultures, and they undoubtedly have been through much of the region's human history. This article describes in detail the best documented pre-Hispanic festival cycle, that of the Aztec of Central Mexico.

During the fifteenth and sixteenth centuries, the Aztec created a cultural synthesis of new elements, which they combined with ancient traditions of Mesoamerican cosmovision and perception of nature. An important corpus of evidence for the study of pre-Hispanic calendrics, religion, and society is the information about Aztec calendar festivals compiled by sixteenth-century Spanish chroniclers such as Bernardino de Sahagún and Diego Durán. These materials refer to the celebration of elaborate rituals forming part of the Aztec state cult. There also exist pictographic documents referring to the same topic, principally the *Codex Borbonicus* and the *Primeros memoriales* of Sahagún.

Ceremonies. These festivals depended on the *xiuhpohualli* ("counting of the years"). The second Mesoamerican calendrical cycle (*tonalpohualli*) of 260 days provided the names of the days and the years. Certain rites were fixed by the *tonalpohualli* and repeated every 260 days, but here we are dealing with the solar year of 365 days (*xíhuitl*), which consisted of eighteen months of twenty days and five extra days (*nemontemi*). During each month, a main festival (*ilhuitl*) was celebrated; its name coincided with the name of the month (see Table 1). These festivals generally took place on the last day of the

TABLE 1. *The Aztec Calendar correlation according to Sahagún, General History of the Things of New Spain (Santa Fe, 1951–1982), Book II*

PRE-HISPANIC MONTHS		CHRISTIAN CORRELATION (GREGORIAN DATES)
I	Atlcahualo	12.2–3.3
II	Tlacaxipehualiztli	4.3–23.3
III	Tozoztontli	24.3–12.4
IV	Huey tozoztli	13.4–2.5
V	Toxcatl	3.5–22.5
VI	Etzalcualiztli	23.5–11.6
VII	Tecuilhuitontli	12.6–1.7
VIII	Huey tecuilhuitl	2.7–21.7
IX	Tlaxochimaco-Miccailhuitontli	22.7–10.8
X	Xocotlhuetzi-Huey miccailhuitl	11.8–30.8
XI	Ochpaniztli	31.8–19.9
XII	Teotleco	20.9–9.10
XIII	Tepeilhuitl	10.10–29.10
XIV	Quecholli	30.10–18.11
XV	Panquetzaliztli	19.11–8.12
XVI	Atemoztli	9.12–28.12
XVII	Tititl	29.12–17.1
XVIII	Izcalli	18.1–6.2
Nemontemi		7.2–11.2

month, but there were also minor celebrations or preparatory rites that began twenty, forty, or eighty days before the main festival. In other cases, the rites continued for several days, sometimes twenty or forty days, after the feast. In this way, in the manner of a fugue, a web of ceremonies was created which spanned the whole year and led from one celebration to the next. During the five extra days, the *nemontemi*, the Aztec refrained from all activities, and no religious ceremonies were performed.

The calendar festivals were celebrated with a tremendous display of people and decorative as well as symbolic elements. They were dramatic representations set against the background of the impressive temple architecture of the Templo Mayor of Tenochtitlan. Many ceremonies took place at night, in the glaring light of torches and great fires, or at dawn before the sun rose. The richness of the participants' costumes, with the lavish use of gold, splendid feathers, and beautifully woven materials, combined with the dramatic power of the ceremonies, must have had an overwhelming effect on the spectators. In this tense atmosphere, the rites culminated in the sacrificial slaying of human victims. Myth was enacted and became reality in theatrical setting.

Aztec state cult implied the active participation of the populace and mirrored social stratification. It was the most important ideological expression of political life in an ancient civilization characterized by the institutional integration of socioeconomic, political, and religious functions. These dramatic representations were organized by priests, although rulers and dignitaries also played an active part. Throughout the year, a numerous priesthood with specialized functions dealt with the preparation and organization of these ceremonies.

There were the feasts of the warrior cult, in which the supreme ruler and the warrior nobles participated. The hierarchy of social ranks as a consequence of military achievement was reflected in the right to perform certain ceremonies. Among them was the offering of war prisoners as victims to be sacrificed in the ceremonies. In this warrior cult, which had both ideological and political significance, the Aztec gods Huitzilopochtli, Xipe, Toci, Mixcoatl, and others were venerated. In some of these feasts, the historical mission of the Aztec people as lords of Mexico was reaffirmed (the feast XV Panquetzaliztli), or their past as Chichimec hunters and warriors was ritually evoked (XIV Quecholli). These rites were also related to the cult of the sun and of Venus.

By contrast, the festivals in which the common people participated centered on the processes of production and the fertility cult (the feasts of the deities of rain and maize); they were related to agricultural production and the activities of artisans and other occupational groups. These rites were devoid of the political ostentation of the feasts of the solar cult. Whereas the warrior cult took place at the Templo Mayor, the agricultural rites made symbolic use of the surrounding landscape. During the fifteenth century, the Aztec created a ritual landscape which comprised numerous shrines or sacred places within the Basin of Mexico. The interaction with nature, with sacred mountains and caves and the lake, was of fundamental importance.

Ritual Calendar and Astronomy. There existed a correspondence between the tropical year, the cycles of nature, and Aztec ceremonies. The chronicles supply abundant testimony on this point. Given that such a relation existed, and that ritual functioned to reinforce it, a still unknown method must have been used to maintain the calendar in harmony with the solar year. The correlation with the Christian year given by Sahagún for the Aztec months (allowing for the Gregorian correction of ten days) permits us to establish a correspondence between the natural cycles and the festivals. The interpretation presented here is based on Sahagún. Nevertheless, among investigators there remains active debate over whether periodic corrections were applied to this ritual calendar, and over how the correspondence of the festivals with the tropical year was maintained.

Observation of the annual course of the sun formed the basis of pre-Hispanic calendrics and astronomy. It is possible to establish a symbolic relationship between solar phenomena and Aztec festivals that were celebrated at the equinoxes (II Tlacaxipehualiztli, IX Ochpaniztli), the solstices (XVI Atemoztli, VII Tecuilhuitontli), or the zenith passages of the sun (V Toxcatl, VIII Huey Tecuilhuitl). Nevertheless, we must beware of looking for a direct correspondence between astronomical events and the ceremonies. The relationship was more complex; it was dialectical, and its symbolism was exuberant. Besides the solar reference, the structure of the festival calendar derived from seasonal and agricultural cycles. The division of the year into the dry season (*tonalco*) and the rainy season (*xopan*) was fundamental. Ceremonies dedicated to the deities of rain, maize, and the earth provided the basic calendrical cycle.

Mesoamerica is situated within the tropical latitudes, where the sun passes the zenith twice a year, on its apparent journey toward the Tropic of Cancer (23°27'N), and on its way back. The ancient Nahua said that the sun entered Mictlan, the abode of the dead situated "to the north." Only during the period between the two zenith passages does the sun pass north of the geographical latitude at noon, rather than to the south, as during the rest of the year. The passages of the sun through the zenith also determine the climatological phenomenon of the rainy season. The first zenith passage announces in Mesoamerica that the rains will start soon—the necessary condition for initiating the planting of maize. This causal nexus was expressed in myth and ritual, in ceremonies related to water and maize.

Seasonal, Agricultural, and Ritual Cycles. There were four crucial dates within this ritual agricultural calendar: (1) the beginning of the Aztec year, 12 February; (2) the planting of maize, April 30; (3) the climax of the rainy season and of the growth of the maize plant, August 13; and (4) harvest, October 30. On these dates, the Aztec festival calendar programmed significant rites that can be analyzed in great detail: the feasts I Atlcahualo, IV Huey Tozoztli, IX Tlaxochimaco, and XIII Tepeilhuitl.

These dates were apparently already important in Mesoamerica during the Classic period at Teotihuacan, since they correspond to the alignment of 15.5° by which the Pyramid of the Sun and the Street of the Dead deviate from the cardinal points. This "sacred Teotihuacan orientation" (Aveni, 1980) was later adopted by many other cultures that succeeded Teotihuacan.

In Aztec ritual we can distinguish three groups of festivals that were dedicated to the deities of rain and maize: (1) the cycle of the dry season, which consisted mainly of child sacrifices that took place in the mountains of the Basin; (2) the planting festival in IV Huey Tozoztli, followed forty days later by the feast of young maize and the celebration of the onset of the rainy season in VI Etzalcualiztli, along with the feast of Huixtocihuatl, goddess of salt and the water of the sea, in VII Tecuilhuitontli; and (3) the harvest and beginning of the dry season, celebrated by the cult of mountains and the pulque gods, during the feast of XIII Tepeilhuitl. Sixty days later, in XVI Atemoztli, the worship of the mountain images was repeated in commemoration of the dead.

Thanks to the chroniclers, it is possible to reconstruct these festivals in great ethnographic detail. Here we will only mention some basic traits. In Aztec ritual, child sacrifices occupied a central place. Children were sacrificed in the driest months of the year, from XVI Atemoztli to IV Huey Tozoztli, in order to cause the coming of the rains and strengthen the growth of maize. Children were small beings, like the *tlaloque*, or servants of the rain god. They personified the mountains; they were carried in procession to be sacrificed at the mountain shrines. These sacrifices were conceived as a contract between the rain gods and men: for the sacrifices, the Aztec obtained the rain necessary for growing maize.

In IV Huey Tozoztli, corresponding to April, the rulers of Tenochtitlan, Tetzcoco, and Tlacopan ascended Mt. Tlaloc (4120 meters). At the summit of the sacred mountain, they sacrificed young children. By means of these ceremonies, the kings of the Triple Alliance ritually initi-

ated the agricultural year. Simultaneously, the Aztec performed agricultural fertility rites in temples, fields, and the lake of Mexico.

In VI Etzalcualiztli, during June, the Aztec celebrated the onset of the rainy season by means of the cult of the rain god Tlaloc and the goddess of the lake, Chalchiuhtlicue. During the subsequent months, VII Tecuilhuitontli and VIII Huey Tecuilhuitl, the solar cult (represented by the sacred ballgame) was combined with offerings that symbolized the proper progress of the agricultural cycle: green maize stalks and ears of maize from the irrigation cycle of cultivation—an exuberant symbolism of plant and human fertility.

During XI Ochpaniztli, corresponding to September, they celebrated the birth of the maize god, son of the mother and earth goddess and the solar god Huitzilopochtli. It was not yet the moment of harvest but of first fruit offerings, the first young ears of maize. The *Codex Borbonicus* dedicates several splendid pages to this feast, representing the sacrifice of yet another personification of maize, the goddess Chicomecoatl.

During XIII Tepeilhuitl, at the end of October, they celebrated the harvest with lavish agricultural offerings and the impersonation of the pulque gods. People worshipped the mountains and modeled miniature figurines representing the principal mountains of the Basin; certain other images were also modeled in honor of the dead and the ancestors. The worship of mountains as generators of life was identified with the cult of the dead, who returned to the womb of the earth where maize was kept. Rain was solicited from the mountains; the Aztec believed that during the dry season the mountains stored the water inside, in order to release it again during the wet season. The Aztec state cult permits us to envision the complex cosmovision of pre-Hispanic Mesoamerican society, in which humans tried to control ritually the balance of the forces of nature and to propitiate them for the own benefit.

[*See also* Calendars and Calendrical Systems; Cofradía; Dance; Danzas; Day of the Dead and Todos Santos; Impersonation of Deities; New Fire Ceremony; Pilgrimage; Processions; Rites of Passage; Sacrifice and Ritual Violence; Syncretism; Year Cycle.]

BIBLIOGRAPHY

Aveni, Anthony F. *Skywatchers of Ancient Mexico*. Austin, 1980.

Broda, Johanna. "Las fiestas aztecas de los dioses de la lluvia." *Revista española de antropología de América* 6 (1971), 245–327, Madrid. Comprehensive reconstruction, from data of the chroniclers, of the cycle of Aztec festivals dedicated to the rain gods.

Broda, Johanna. "Ciclos agrícolas en el culto: Un problema de la correlación del calendario mexica." In *Calendars in Mesoamerica and Peru: Native American Computations of Time*, edited by Anthony F. Aveni and Gordon Brotherston, pp. 145–165. BAR International Series, 174. Oxford, 1983. Synthetic interpretation of the correspondence of Aztec calendar festivals to seasonal cycles and agricultural activities, based on the correlation given by Sahagún.

Broda, Johanna. "Templo Mayor as Ritual Space." In *The Great Temple of Tenochtitlan: Center and Periphery in the Aztec World*, edited by Johanna Broda et al., pp. 61–123. Berkeley, 1987. Interpretation relating the findings of the excavation of the Templo Mayor of Tenochtitlan to more general notions of Aztec cosmovision and ritual; it particularly stresses the importance of the mountain cult and the symbolic importance of the sea.

Broda, Johanna. "The Sacred Landscape of Aztec Calendar Festivals: Myth, Nature and Society." In *To Change Place: Aztec Ceremonial Landscapes*, edited by Davíd Carrasco, pp. 74–120. Niwot, Colo., 1991. Detailed analysis of several groups of Aztec calendar festivals, their symbolism, and the creation of a ritual landscape in the Basin of Mexico.

Broda, Johanna. "Astronomical Knowledge, Calendrics, and Sacred Geography in Ancient Mesoamerica." In *Astronomies and Cultures*, edited by Clive Ruggles and Nicholas Saunders, pp. 253–295. Niwot, Colo., 1993. Taking as a point of departure Aztec calendrics and cosmovision, applies an interdisciplinary approach to the study of Mesoamerican archaeoastronomy and ritual landscapes.

Carrasco, Pedro. "La sociedad mexicana antes de la conquista." In *Historia general de México*, edited by Daniel Cosío Villegas, vol. 1, pp. 165–288. Mexico City, 1976. Most authoritative synthesis of Aztec religion and society.

Carrasco, Pedro. "Las fiestas de los meses mexicanos." In *Mesoamérica: Homenaje al doctor Paul Kirchhoff*, edited by Barbro Dahlgren, pp. 51–60. Mexico City, 1979. Suggestive synthesis interpreting the structured whole of Aztec calendar festivals, their ceremonies, and the symbolism of their principal deities.

Carrasco, Pedro, and Johanna Broda, eds. *Economía política e ideología en el México prehispánico*. Mexico City, 1978. Collective volume presenting several important essays of synthesis on Aztec society, ideology, and ritual.

Codex Borbonicus. Commentary by Karl Anton Nowotny. Graz, 1974. Excellent facsimile edition and authoritative critical commentary by the foremost expert on codices, with a pictographic record of the eighteen Aztec calendar festivals.

Durán, Diego. *Historia de las Indias de Nueva España*, 2 vols. Edited by Angel María Garibay. Mexico City, 1967. Besides Sahagún, volume 2 of Durán constitutes the most important sixteenth-century source on Aztec gods and ceremonies.

Graulich, Michel. "La structure du calendrier agricole des anciens Mexicains." *Lateinamerika Studien* 6 (1980), 99–113. This author has developed and presented in numerous publications an interpretation differing from the one presented here of the correlation of Aztec calendar festivals with the Christian year.

Graulich, Michel. "Mythes et rites des vingtaines du Mexque Central préhispanique." 3 vols. Dissertation, Université Libre de Bruxelles, Brussels, 1979–1980. Most comprehensive reconstruction that exists of Aztec calendar festivals, stressing the nexus between ritual and myth.

Graulich, Michel. *Mitos y rituales del México antiguo*. Madrid, 1990. Publication of parts of Graulich's dissertation, an evocative and creative interpretation.

Nowotny, Karl Anton. "Die aztekischen Festkreise." *Zeitschrift für Ethnologie* 93 (1968), 84–106. Erudite interpretation of the structured whole of Aztec calendar festivals; a different perspective from the one presented here.

Sahagún, Bernardino de. *Florentine Codex: General History of the Things of New Spain*. Edited and translated by Arthur J. O. Anderson and Charles E. Dibble. 12 vols. Santa Fe, N.M., 1951–1982. Book II is the basic source on Aztec calendar festivals.

Seler, Eduard. "Die achtzehn Jahresfeste der Mexikaner (Erste Hälfte)." *Altmexikanische Studien*, 2. *Veröffentlichungen aus dem Königlichen Museum für Völkerkunde* 6 (1899), 67–209. First erudite study on Aztec calendar festivals.

JOHANNA BRODA

52-YEAR CYCLE. *See* Calendar Round.

FINCAS. *See* Haciendas and Plantations.

FIRE DEITIES. The Aztec god of fire was the oldest of all the deities. In historical sources he is called by many names, which reflect his varied aspects and dwellings in the three parts of the cosmos. The most common names are Huehueteotl ("Old God"), Xiuhtecuhtli ("Turquoise God"), Ixcozauhqui ("Yellow Face"), and Cuezaltzin ("Red Feather"). He is associated with the original dual god, Ometeotl, by the appellation Teteo Innan Teteo Inta ("Mother and Father of the Gods"). As the god of *axis mundi*, he could inhabit all three parts of the cosmos: sky (Ilhuicatl), earth (Tlalticpac), and underworld (Mictlan). From each of these cosmic locales, the fire god sent his sacred force cyclically to stimulate the regeneration of nature. In the sky, Ixcozauhqui was identified with the sun because both provided *tona*, the vital energy necessary to all life, especially to ripen plants. On earth, the fire god dwelt primarily in the central part (*tlaxicco*, "navel") and at the four "corners." In the domestic sphere Chantico, the goddess of fire, was located at the hearth. The fire god Chicnauhyotecuhtli dwelt in Mictlan, the place of the dead, from which he sent the fire of regeneration to stimulate the growth of plants.

The fire god's main functions were purification, sacralization, and transformation. He was related to creation and renewal. In myth time, he transformed Nanahuatzin into the sun and Tecuciztecatl into the moon when these deities hurled themselves into a primordial fire. He was also the god of time's renewal; his main ceremony was called the New Fire. This ceremony was celebrated every fifty-two years and inaugurated a new cosmic cycle. Another fire celebration took place every four years. Fire's annual ceremonies were Xocotl Huetzi and Izcalli, which divided the year into two parts.

Xiuhtecuhtli was a liminal god because of his presence at moments of transition from one condition to another. At rites of passage, he facilitated changes in nature, in society, and in individuals. He also enabled communication between living and dead persons and between humans and gods.

Huehueteotl was related to the male principle. He was associated with fecundation and reproduction, in conjunction with his opposite, water. He was worshipped in several agricultural rites in which his action renewed the

The fire serpent, Xiuhcoatl. (Height: 38 inches.) *Courtesy of Museo Nacional de Antropología, México, D.F.*

fields, a concept derived from the practice of burning fields before sowing.

One of the fire god's symbolic elements, depicted in the ceremony Xocotl Huetzi, was an upright tree trunk. This represented the *axis mundi*, which both connected and separated earth and sky. The god, in this sense, was the mediator between the hot sky and the cold, wet earth. Thus, Xiuhtecuhtli was the god who preserved the equilibrium between heat and humidity in order to prevent destruction by drought or flood. The Mexica fire cult was an important part of the religious system; the deity's main responsibility was to ensure the world's continuity by renewing it through ritual practices.

[*See also* Old Gods.]

BIBLIOGRAPHY

Broda, Johanna. "La fiesta azteca del Fuego Nuevo y el culto de las Pléyades." *Lateinamerika-Studien* 10 (1982), 129–158. Interesting outline of ceremony of the New Fire in Early Colonial sources.

Durán, Diego. *Historia de las Indias de la Nueva España e islas de tierra firme*. Edited by Angel M. Garibay K. 2 vols. Mexico City, 1967. Sixteenth-century covering native Mesoamerican beliefs and practices.

López Austin, Alfredo. "El dios enmascarado del fuego." *Anales de Antropología*, 22 (1985), 251–285. Interesting interpretation of the fire god in the underworld.

Ruiz de Alarcón, Hernando. "Tratado de las supersticiones y costumbres genticias que oy viuen entre los indios naturales de esta Nueva España" [1629]. In *Tratado de la idolatría supersticiones, dioses, ritos, hechicerías y otras costumbres gentilicias de las razas aborígenes de México*, edited by Francisco del Paso y Troncoso, pp. 17–180. 3d ed. Mexico City, 1953. Seventeenth-century historical source compiles Indian religious practices and conjurations to the pre-Hispanic gods.

Sahagún, Bernardino de. *Florentine Codex: General History of the Things of New Spain*. Translated and edited by Charles E. Dibble and Arthur J. O. Anderson. 11 vols. Albuquerque and Salt Lake City, 1950–1963. Sixteenth-century source for native Mesoamerican beliefs and practices.

SILVIA LIMÓN OLVERA

FISHING. Since the early twentieth century, mainstream research on the development of Mesoamerican culture has focused on small-plot farmers, or *milperos*, living mostly in upland valleys and plateaus, describing them as the springboards of civilizational development. Comparatively recently, however, new research has revised this view by illuminating the important contributions of coastal peoples in this development. It is widely recognized that the foundations of Mesoamerica's great civilizations are not only interior-dwelling agricultural societies but also societies that thrived along the coastal plains, as well as the mutually enriching and synergistic relationships between them.

Mesoamerica's coastal plains offered unique opportunities for the development of prosperous human societies during the Archaic or Formative period. These regions, which are interspersed with fertile river flood plains in close proximity to sheltered bays, briny lagoons, and tidal estuaries, offer fertile lands and an abundant variety of mollusks, crustaceans, fish, birds, mammals, and reptiles. Not only were they propitious places for humans to settle, thrive, and grow, they were conducive to the development of more diverse subsistence systems than those developing in the interior, while also offering greater possibilities for transport and development of trading relationships.

Mesoamerica's coastal environments also posed some serious obstacles to the development of large, permanently inhabited human settlements, in particular, severe storms and catastrophic flooding, which periodically forced coastal dwellers to abandon their living sites. Yet, even if these natural hazards prevented continuous habitation and the growth of large settlements, they otherwise promoted the development of subsistence and economic systems that were more flexible and adaptable than those being developed simultaneously in the interior.

Mesoamerica's earliest *costeños* took up residence along the region's coastal plains during the early Archaic period, between seven and five thousand years ago. They practiced rudimentary forms of agriculture, hunted wild animals and gathered wild plants, and reaped increasingly bountiful harvests of seafood. They left behind huge shell middens attesting to the abundance of those resources and increasingly engaged in trade—at first with their proximate neighbors, and eventually with peoples living at greater distances in the interior.

Although shrimp and mollusks were central in these people's economies, they also produced large harvests of fish, as well as sea turtles, crabs, seaweed, and, on a more limited scale, seabirds' eggs, crocodiles, other reptiles, and marine animals, such as seals, sea lions, and manatees. With the exception of the mollusks, the remains of the other creatures they harvested, as well as the technologies utilized for producing them—including woven nets and fishhooks and harpoon points made from wood and bone—are underrepresented in the archaeological record, owing mainly to their greater perishability as compared with shells. The same is true regarding their watercraft, which became increasingly varied and sophisticated over time, and which figured importantly not only in local harvesting activities but also in coastal trade.

Many of the foods produced by these Archaic-era coastal peoples were preserved by smoking, sun drying, and salting, and salt figured importantly in the development of their trading networks, as well as in the eventual development of more complex societies in the interior. Among the Formative lowland Maya, for example, there was a thriving long-distance coastal trade between the northern and southern spheres. The southern sphere supplied the northern sphere with salt, whereas the northern sphere used the salt to preserve seafood, which it traded with peoples living in the interior. Decorative items made from shells were also important in these trading relationships. This pattern continued throughout the Classic and Postclassic periods, ending only after the first Europeans arrived.

When the Classic civilizations arose, Mesoamerica's coastal societies underwent various transformations. From one sprang Mesoamerica's first civilization: the Olmec. Arising around thirty-two hundred years ago, this first civilization arose not in an upland valley or plateau, but in a lowland environment not far from the coast, in what is now part of the contemporary Mexican states of Tabasco and Veracruz. Other coastal Mesoamerican societies helped to catalyze the rise of Classic civilizations among the interior-dwelling peoples they traded with, continuing to enjoy a thriving trade with these new complex societies throughout the Classic period. Others, however, were not so fortunate and lost much of their au-

tonomy, as they became the exploited coastal-dwelling components of more powerful societies arising in the interior.

The demise of the Classic-period civilizations, followed by the rise and consolidation of the Postclassic ones, prompted the further development of certain coastal societies. In the Maya region, for example, following the collapse of the southern lowland centers around 900 CE, corresponding with the steady decline in their interior economic systems, many people migrated to the coastal regions. Thus, increasingly complex coastal societies began to arise—the renowned "maritime Maya" thriving around the Yucatán Peninsula from 1000 to 1520 CE, for example, who greatly relied upon marine resources and coastal canoe trade.

For the remainder of the Postclassic period, other maritime Mesoamerican societies similarly thrived, their populations continuing to swell, especially along the coastal plains bordering both the Pacific Ocean and the Gulf of Mexico. In those regions, in addition to producing and trading shellfish as their ancestors had for several millennia, they began to erect semi-permanent weirs across narrow estuary channels, making possible huge seasonal harvests of shrimp and fish, which are the forerunners of the *tapos*—fencelike barriers with evenly spaced openings leading into traps—that are utilized by contemporary peoples living along those same coastal plains today. Throughout the remainder of the Postclassic period, other maritime technologies appeared or were further refined (e.g., more sophisticated nets, various watercraft, and the use of torches and bonfires set along the shores at night to attract shrimp, fish, and other prey).

On the eve of Spain's arrival in the New World, prosperous maritime societies could be found along most of Mesoamerica's coastlines. These were especially populous along the coastal plains, thriving there mainly on the basis of flood-plain agriculture, seafood production, and trade. However populous and prosperous they were when the first Spaniards arrived, their social organization was generally less stratified and complex than that of the interior-dwelling peoples inhabiting the highland valleys and plateaus. This made it more difficult for the Spaniards to find uses for them and left them more vulnerable to slaving raids. Simultaneously, disastrous epidemics spread throughout the coastal lowlands as native peoples contracted exotic diseases brought by the Spaniards—which killed them either directly or indirectly as their localized subsistence economies broke down. This unusually rapid depopulation of coastal peoples, especially along the coastal plains, left vast tracts of lowlands virtually empty, which in turn facilitated the rapid growth of cattle-raising haciendas and plantations in these regions.

Along the Gulf of Mexico, the Huastec, whose populous

culture was thriving prior to Spanish contact, had completely disappeared from the coastal lowlands by the end of the seventeenth century. Similarly, on the Pacific coast, the Uto-Aztecan-speaking Tahue and Totorame, collectively estimated to number 170,000 people at the time of Contact, quickly disappeared, whereas the Cora declined from an estimated 150,000 at the time of Contact to around 3,000 by the 1950s. Farther south, the Cuitlatec of Pacific-coastal Guerrero, among whom fishing had been a cornerstone of subsistence prior to Contact, abandoned the coast in the wake of Spanish contact.

Today, where coastal Mesoamericans can still be found living mainly by harvesting seafoods, it is mainly in regions that are otherwise poorly suited for cattle raising and agriculture. Thus, along various arid coastlines today can be found the Mayo in Sinaloa and bare remnants of the Nahua in Michoacán, the Amuzgo in Guerrero, and the Mixteco and Tequislateco in Oaxaca. Similarly, living amid mangrove swamps, marshes, and briny lagoons along the Pacific coast can be found the Huave and Zapotec in Isthmian Oaxaca, while along the coast of the Gulf of Mexico can be found bare remnants of the Mixteco and Nahua in Veracruz and the Chontal in Tabasco. Many contemporary lowland Maya can still be found living around the shores of the Yucatán Peninsula, but today only a few derive their primary livelihoods from seafood production. Otherwise, the lowland Maya's formerly rich maritime culture has virtually disappeared.

The persistence of some Mesoamerican fishing peoples and their maritime cultures was helped for a while by the advent of the international export trade in seafood beginning in the late nineteenth century, particularly in Mexico. Then, during the Mexican Revolution (1910–1924), there was a near cessation of seafood production in many coastal areas. After the hostilities ended and during the era of postrevolutionary reform, government-sanctioned fishing cooperatives were established, mainly for purposes of producing seafood for export. From the 1930s to the 1960s, these inshore coastal fishing cooperatives thrived and their members prospered.

However, by the 1960s, new developments began to marginalize these organizations. Herbicides and pesticides, for example, which were increasingly being used in developing rural agriculture, decimated many important shellfish stocks. In coastal fishing, the widespread adoption of outboard motors and nylon gill nets quickly decimated many important inshore fish stocks. Also devastating was the ascendancy of offshore shrimp trawling fleets, as well as other, better capitalized and more technologically sophisticated approaches to fishing, which competed for limited marine resources.

By the late 1970s, these developments had brought about the depletion of many of the marine resources that coastal Mesoamericans had traditionally relied upon, with crises and complete collapses becoming widespread by the early 1980s. Since then, most of the formerly important marine stocks have remained depressed.

The survival of Mesoamerica's coastal people, especially the survival of their characteristic maritime cultural adaptations, will depend on the resurgence and sustained productivity of the marine resources on which they have depended. With wiser and more effective approaches to fisheries management, the future survival of these people, societies, and maritime-fishing cultures seems practically assured. Without it, they may soon disappear forever.

BIBLIOGRAPHY

Beals, Ralph L. "The Comparative Ethnology of Northern Mexico before 1750." *Ibero Americana*, monograph 2, 1932. Describes the disappearance of indigenous coastal peoples following Spanish contact.

Chevalier, François. *Land and Society in Colonial Mexico: The Great Hacienda.* Berkeley, 1970. Describes rapid depopulation of Mesoamerica's coastal lowlands by slaving, diseases, and other factors, leaving empty lands available for the rapid development of cattle-raising haciendas and agricultural estates.

Coe, Michael D., and Kent V. Flannery. "Early Cultures and Human Ecology in South Coastal Guatemala." *Smithsonian Contributions to Anthropology*, Vol. 3, 1967. Seminal archaeological study of early, Archaic-period coastal peoples on Guatemala's Pacific coast.

Foster, George M. *Culture and Conquest: America's Spanish Heritage.* Viking Fund Publications in Anthropology no. 27. New York, 1960. Discusses items of Spanish material culture introduced into Mesoamerica following contact, including items of fishing technology.

Freidel, David A. "Maritime Adaptation and the Rise of Maya Civilization: The View from Cerros, Belize." In *Prehistoric Coastal Adaptations: The Economy and Ecology of Maritime Middle America*, edited by Barbara L. Stark and Barbara Voorhies, pp. 239–265. New York, 1978. Describes the lowland Maya fishing and maritime cultures from the Archaic through the Postclassic periods.

McGoodwin, James R. "The Human Costs of Development." *Environment* 22.1 (1980), 25–31, 42. Outlines the development of Pacific Mexican coastal fisheries from aboriginal through contemporary times.

McGoodwin, James R. "Human Responses to Weather-induced Catastrophes in a West Mexican Fishery." In *Climate Variability, Climate Change, and Fisheries*, edited by Michael H. Glantz, pp. 167–184. Cambridge, 1992. Discusses periodic catastrophes which constrained development of pre-Columbian coastal settlements.

Stark, Barbara L., and Barbara Voorhies, eds. *Prehistoric Coastal Adaptations: The Economy and Ecology of Maritime Middle America.* New York, 1978. Rich collection concerning Mesoamerica's early maritime peoples, societies, and cultures, from the first coastal inhabitants through Spanish contact.

Wauchope, Robert, ed. *Handbook of Middle American Indians*, vols. 7 and 8 (Evon Z. Vogt, vols. ed.). Austin, Tex., 1969. Essential references regarding the ethnohistory and ethnology of contemporary Mesoamerican peoples, societies, and cultures, including coastal-dwellers.

JAMES R. MCGOODWIN

FLORENCIA, FRANCISCO DE (1619–1695), priest and theologian. Florencia was born in St. Augustine, Florida, at the edge of the Spanish American colonies. He received his early education at the Franciscan school there and then moved to Mexico City, where he studied at the Jesuit Colegio de San Ildefonso. At the age of twenty-three, he became a member of the Society of Jesus.

In Mexico, Florencia taught philosophy and theology at the Colegio de San Pedro y San Pablo. In 1668 he traveled to Madrid and Rome to represent the Jesuit Order as *procurador* of his province, and later to Seville as *procurador* of all the provinces of the Indies. He finally returned to Mexico City, where he was appointed rector of the Colegio del Espíritu Santo in Puebla, and two years later, rector of the Colegio Máximo in the capital.

Florencia was a respected theologian, author, and preacher, renowned for his eloquence and knowledge. While many of his works were published during his lifetime, some appeared after his death. Most were written to promote Mexico's religious shrines or to celebrate the achievements of the Jesuits and the virtues of the people of Mexico.

Florencia and his work represented a creole movement to recognize the divine presence in New Spain through the Virgin Mary and miracles performed by the celebrated religious images, especially the Virgin of Guadalupe. Profoundly convinced of the truth of the apparition account and the miracles associated with that image, Florencia searched for historical proof and tried to convince Rome to authorize veneration of the Mexican Virgin at her shrine and to obtain official sanction of her apparition at Tepeyac in 1531. He pleaded that God wished to give equal value to miracles in Europe and America, and he asserted Mexico's claim to an independent religious tradition.

In his *La Estrella del Norte de Mexico* (Mexico City, 1688; Madrid, 1785) Florencia provided an encyclopedic work in which he describes the Virgin's apparitions by commenting on various sources: Spanish and Mexican, written, oral, and pictorial. He copied, paraphrased, praised, and also refuted historical documents from earlier and contemporary chroniclers and molded them to authenticate his own text. The result is a synthesis of published works, augmented with poetry, songs, legends, and miracles within a tradition of creole and Baroque historiography. Florencia tried to convince his audience of the miraculous origins of the Guadalupe cult and to authenticate the legends of Guadalupe's apparitions. With his writings, he established the foundations of the Guadalupan textual and historical tradition.

Other important works by Florencia are his *Historia de la Provincia de la Compañia de Jesus de la Nueva España* (Mexico City, 1694) and the *Zodiaco Mariano* (Mexico City, 1755). Both offer interesting accounts of the lives of Mexican Jesuits, although confined to praising their virtues, and of the principal miraculous images of New Spain. The latter was edited and added to by Juan Antonio Oviedo (1670–1757) after Florencia died; Oviedo revised the manuscript on the basis of an incomplete draft he found in the Colegio de San Pedro y Pablo, eliminated what he considered deviation, condensed certain parts, and collected narratives about images Florencia did not know.

Together with Miguel Sanchez (who published the first text about the Virgin of Guadalupe in 1648), Luis Lasso de la Vega, and Luis Becerra Tanco, Florencia is often described as an evangelist of the Virgin of Guadalupe. He served as an intermediary between the Mexican people and the church hierarchy in Rome. His books reflect the process of collective creation of forms of Mexican traditional religion and the search for cultural identity by *mestizos* and creoles in seventeenth-century Mexico, an era of repression and control. In spite of his efforts to achieve official recognition of the Mexican Virgin, however, Florencia failed as an intermediary at the time, and it was not until 1754 that her apparition was officially acknowledged.

BIBLIOGRAPHY
Alcalá, Luisa E., "¿Pues para qué son los papeles . . . ? Imágenes y devociones novohispanas en los siglos XVII y XVIII." *Tiempos de America* 1 (1997), 43–56. Attempt to evaluate to what extent Florencia's analyses of miraculous images in New Spain were influenced by creole movements of the time.
Florencia, Francisco de. *La estrella del Norte de Mexico*. Mexico City, 1688; Madrid, 1785. Encyclopedic work on the Virgin of Guadalupe, composed of earlier published texts and augmented with legends, testimonies, images, and poetry collected by Florencia.
Florencia, Francisco de. *Historia de la Provincia de la Compañia de Jesus de Nueva España*. Edited by Juan José Guillena Carrascoso. Mexico City, 1643. First published work on the achievements of the Company of Jesus in Mexico.
Florencia, Francisco de. *Origen de los dos celebres santuarios de la Nueva Galicia. Obispado de Guadalaxara en la América Septentrional (1757)*. 4th ed. Introduction by Miguel Mathes. Zapopan, 1998. One of the many works by Florencia on sanctuaries of New Spain.
Florencia, Francisco de, and Juan Antonio de Oviedo. *Zodiaco Mariano*. Mexico City, 1755; reprinted, Mexico City, 1995. One of Florencia's main works on Mexican Jesuits and the principal miraculous religious images of New Spain, edited and completed after his death by Oviedo.
Maza, Francisco de la. *El guadalupanismo Mexicano*. Mexico City, 1959, 1981. Work on the four evangelists of the Virgin of Guadalupe, including Florencia.
Poole, Stafford. *Our Lady of Guadalupe: The Origins and Sources of a Mexican National Symbol, 1531–1797*. Tucson, Ariz., 1993. Includes material on Florencia, Carlos de Siguenza y Gongora, and the need for documentation.
Santaballa, Sylvia Rosa. "Representing the Virgin of Guadalupe in

Francisco de Florencia's 'La Estrella del Norte de Mexico'." *Colonial Latin American Review* 7 (1998), 83–103. On the works of Florencia as an integral part of two seventeenth-century movements: the Spanish American Baroque and *guadalupanismo*.

FLORINE ASSELBERGS

FLORENTINE CODEX. *See* Sahagún, Bernardino de.

FOLK ART. Since pre-Hispanic times, folk art (*arte popular*) in Mesoamerica has been the primary vehicle through which people have expressed their dreams and fears, courted their lovers, amused their children, worshiped their gods, and honored their ancestors. Today, as in the past, folk art is produced throughout Mesoamerica. Largely because of long-enduring and numerous cultural traditions, made possible by Mesoamerica's ecological diversity and community isolation, it remains a region of rich and varied folk expression.

The Mexican artist and art critic Adolfo Best-Maugard (1923) has stated that "folk art is above all the synthetic expression of the soul of the people, its tastes, its ideals, its imagination, and its concept of life." As in other parts of the world, in Mesoamerica folk art is local, un-self-conscious, community-based artistic expression. For the most part, it is made to serve its place of origin. Folk art also functions as a buffer between the individual and/or the community and the larger physical, social, and spiritual environments. It is a cultural response to demands that come from these sources, helping individuals and communities to cope. Mesoamerican folk art meets the challenges of the physical environment through, for example, special agricultural implements, clothing, house types, and countless daily-use items. Elegant ceramic water-support ensembles from the tropical Zapotec community of San Blas Atempa, Oaxaca, are cultural responses to the local physical environment. Excellent examples of the way that form follows function, every aspect of their construction responds to the challenges of storing cool water. They function in the following way: fresh water is placed in the jar and covered with a ceramic lid; it is then nestled in a broad, shallow dish, half-filled with sand and balanced atop a hollow ceramic female figure, often sculpted and painted in realistic ways. The porous clay of the jar allows water to cool through evaporation; since warm water "sweats" through the walls of the jar, cool water is left inside. This warm water is absorbed by the sand in the dish. Because the jar and dish are elevated, the dirt floors of the local huts are kept dry.

Throughout Mexico, Guatemala, and other parts of Mesoamerica, folk art also responds to demands that emanate from the social environment. Dress, which signals community affiliation in Indian Oaxaca; communal

houses for village officials among the Tlapanec Indians of Guerrero; dolls used to socialize Guatemalan children into their adult roles—these and numerous other examples are traditional artistic responses to local social environments. Finally, folk art responds to local demands in the spiritual environment by facilitating communication between individuals, their saints, and their ancestors. For example, votive paintings allow the faithful to publicly acknowledge favors received from Roman Catholic saints, thereby satisfying sacred vows. Then, too, many objects created for Days of the Dead and offered in village graveyards or on household altars provide dual functions of strengthening ties between generations and, at the same time, easing communication with the deceased.

Folk Art through Time. As in contemporary Mesoamerica, folk art was ubiquitous in pre-Hispanic societies. Set apart from more formal, trend-setting, and self-conscious expression of such great urban centers as Tikal, Monte Alban, and Teotihuacan, where pan-Mesoamerican styles were often born, pre-Hispanic folk art was rural, local, and slower to change than its avant-garde urban counterpart. In addition, the needs of the community at large were met, rather than the demands and tastes of a small but powerful class of the religious and political elite.

With the arrival of the Spanish in the sixteenth century, and the subsequent depopulation of the indigenous world, all the Mesoamerican art changed dramatically. Art associated with the indigenous religious, military, and social power structures was strictly prohibited by the conquistadors and their Roman Catholic priests and, if found, promptly destroyed. Art obscured by remoteness and isolated from the centers of power of the new lords of the region, tended to survive—in some cases, to the present. Art forms not associated with the Spanish maintenance of potential threatening indigenous hierarchies were also left alone and, in many instances, continued to thrive and evolve. Practically all Aztec religious art was destroyed because it threatened new Catholic hierarchies. The pre-Hispanic ceramics—well-made, serviceable, and a threat to no one—persevered.

In general, a great deculturation took place throughout Mesoamerica, and into the cultural vacuum created by the Conquest moved new cultural forms from Spain and elsewhere in Europe—the household altars of Chiapas and Hidalgo; the giant processional figures of Celaya, Oaxaca, and Antigua in Guatemala; the glazed pottery of Guanajuato, Puebla, and Totonicapan; the masked dance dramas of Chichicastenango, Veracruz, Chilapa, San Juan Teotihuacan, and a thousand other villages and towns. All trace their origins to Spain, with few exceptions. In addition, traditional furniture, ironwork, non-Indian textiles, passion plays, votive art in the forms of

Masked dance dramas throughout Mesoamerica can trace their origins to Spain (masked dancer, Guatemala, c.1990). *Photograph courtesy of Marion Oettinger, Jr.*

body parts, testimonial paintings, and countless other forms of Mesoamerican folk culture trace their origins back to Spain.

Something important occurred when these Spanish-rooted folk forms arrived in the Americas—many were immediately changed to meet the needs of the new places, peoples, and cultural conditions. They were transformed into folk art forms palatable to Mesoamericans. Catholic saints, first associated with the Spanish conquerors, were changed and eventually integrated into the lives of the vanquished. Santiago Matamoros (Saint James, the Slayer of Moors) is a good example of this transformation and appropriation; Santiago came to Mesoamerica as the patron saint of Spain and the Spanish army, since the Moors had been defeated in the Iberian Peninsula and expelled to North Africa and other Arab lands in 1492, after dominating Spain from 711 CE. During the siege of Mexico, "Santiago y a ellos!" ("Santiago, and after them!") had been the battle cry of Cortés's army. According to tradition, the saint miraculously appeared dozens of times in Mexico, Guatemala, and elsewhere in the Americas, to assist the Spanish. Soon, this impressive figure was adopted by indigenous peoples, and he assumed new appearances and attributes. In Guatemala, he became the patron saint of mares, and he is still invoked by men looking for a wife. As Altman (1980) has shown, in Sololá, Guatemala, the image of Santiago is still dressed in traditional indigenous attire and paraded through the streets on feast days. Essentially, Santiago has become a valuable member of the community he serves.

Through time, Mesoamerican governments have either supported or reviled traditional popular art. At the turn of the twentieth century, during the rule of the Mexican dictator Porfirio Díaz (1877–1911), official Mexico had little use for folk art and instead looked to the arts of Europe and the United States for inspiration. The Mexican Revolution of 1910 to 1920 changed that; the new order enthusiastically embraced pre-Hispanic and folk art forms in the effort to build a new national identity, based on what was native to Mexico. Similar situations existed in other parts of Mesoamerica and continue into the present. Contemporary Mesoamerican folk art is at the confluence of the many currents mentioned above. It contains persistent elements of Native American cultures; pervasive Spanish elements introduced during the Colonial period; West African motifs brought in during the years of the slave trade; Asian elements that resulted from several centuries of trade between Spain and China via the Philippines; and strong modern influences, notably those of the United States. All are important ingredients in the rich modern recipes for the Mesoamerican folk arts.

Geographic, demographic, historical, and other dimensions often account for the quality and quantity of the folk forms produced in Mesoamerica today. The geographic setting often provides the same materials that have been used through the ages. Therefore, potting communities are always located near sources of clay and the fuels for kilns. Then, too, the persistence of folk art occurs where there are concentrations of indigenous peoples, such as in Oaxaca, highland Guatemala, Chiapas, and the mountains of Puebla. There the artisans still use traditional materials, such as textiles woven on backstrap looms, indigenous-style pottery, objects associated with non-European curing, and other specialties. Another factor may be the historical background of a particular area. The region surrounding Lake Patzcuaro in Michoacán, reorganized in the sixteenth century by Bishop Vasco de Quiroga, is characterized by a network of craft communities that were based on Thomas More's *Utopia*. Tzintzuntzan made pottery, Santa Clara del Cobré produced copper items, and other villages specialized in other things. Today, each of these communities continues to specialize in a particular craft, and each cooperates symbiotically with other communities in the region.

Many Faces of Regional Folk Art. There are many manifestations of folk art in contemporary Mesoamerica, and classifying this material has been difficult. Some scholars have studied folk art according to the materials used, such as wood, metal, straw, paper, and so on. Some study it by time period. Others study it by geographical region. Here, function is suggested as a useful way to organize and study folk materials. Although categories according to function may be fluid, Mesoamerican folk art can be divided into four basic types: utilitarian, ceremonial, recreational, and decorative. Utilitarian folk art—clothing, household furnishings, cooking utensils, equestrian gear, farming and fishing equipment, objects associated with a trade, and other necessary objects—exists throughout Mesoamerica; it is usually made to satisfy both daily and practical needs. Ceremonial folk art, perhaps the most dramatic and visible form of folk expression, is usually associated with celebration, both religious and secular. In this category are the religious statuary for household altars, the votive objects to give thanks for favors received, the sugar skulls to entice the souls of deceased family members back to the family compound during Days of the Dead, and the dance masks used in performance. Some masks are used to disguise identity, transforming the dancers into powerful animals, historical figures, characters of opposite gender, or figures born out of the dreams of shamans. In the Nahua community of Atzacualoya in Guerrero, more than a dozen masked dance dramas are performed each year on 2 February, to celebrate the community's patron, the Virgin of Candelaria. Masks for jaguars, buffoons, Spaniards, monkeys, and dozens of other characters help present tales that are both entertaining and historically significant. Some dance groups are local but some come to the village festival to perform; all use the occasion to honor the Virgin in whose hands rest the well-being of their families, crops, and animals.

Recreational folk art is often whimsical and may be used by children for entertainment and amusement. Dolls, games, toys, and other items are in this category. Recreational folk art often performs other equally important functions. Throughout Mesoamerica, children are given toys that allow them to act out the scenes of real life. Boys are given miniature farming implements, machetes, and fishing tools that are similar to the objects used by their fathers, so that they can move readily into the adult male world. Girls are often given cooking pots, miniature weaving tools, and toy dolls that help prepare them for the adult roles of housekeeper and mother. Puppets are used to entertain, but puppets often teach religious, political, and moral lessons. During the late nineteenth century, Puebla's great puppeteer, Rosete Aranda, performed exciting reenactments, such as the apparition of the Virgin of Guadalupe or the Mexican defeat of the French at the Battle of Puebla.

Decorative folk arts also exist to brighten the corner of an otherwise drab dwelling or to enhance a dress on market day. Into this category are also placed vast array of folk art produced for tourists and for export to the United States, Europe, and elsewhere. Frequently originating from forms used locally, such things are destined for shops and museum shops in Paris, Santa Fe, London, and New York. The wood-carved animals of Oaxaca, once designed to please the simple traditional tastes of neighborhood children, are now meant for collectors and the eclectic tastes of foreign markets. Here folk art is again a coping mechanism, but this time for artists who have found themselves living in a cash economy.

Makers of Folk Art. Men and women, young and old, rural and urban, Indian and non-Indian may be today's folk artists. Most are still part-time specialists—who work as farmers, masons, and fishermen—but they also make folk art for their contribution to a communal festival or for sale, to augment meager incomes. Others are full-time specialists who make textiles, pottery, tin toys, and countless other things to sell locally or for export.

Most folk artists receive their educations informally, by working as apprentices for already established artists, parents, or older siblings. Some, but not many, are self-taught. Most are economically marginal, although those who have connected with export economies are often among the wealthiest members of the community. In spite of the relatively low economic status of most, folk artists are usually held in high esteem by their neighbors, since they are seen as vital links between the past and the present—caretakers of traditional life.

Folk art is constantly changing to meet new times and circumstances. It is born, dies, and is reborn anew each day to face the challenges of modern Mesoamerica. Today, the societies of Mexico and Guatemala are changing at rates far greater than ever before. Improved communications link previously isolated villages to the cultures of neighboring towns and cities and allow for the importation of new materials and ideas. Once heavily populated rural areas are rapidly emptying, as young people are drawn to the cash and opportunities of the cities, and even other countries, leaving older relatives behind to fend for themselves until they can send cash remittances to help them. Folk art and the traditional folk artist have suffered from these changes. Despite them, or perhaps because of them, folk art continues as a vital coping mechanism for individuals as well as communities throughout the region.

Chichicastenango, a town in the center of the Quiché Maya region of Guatemala, has managed to cope with the changing world by providing flexible cultural responses to several audiences. The town plays host to hundreds of thousands of intrusive tourists each year and has organized its market to meet their considerable and complex needs. Income from this "outside" source allows members of the region to survive in the modern, cash-based world, albeit at times only marginally. Yet the town has not forsaken its strong indigenous roots, and throughout the year stages dozens of traditional religious ceremonials that support ancient belief systems. Today, Chichicastenango is a host to two worlds—one of great antiquity and the other of modern and rapid change. The tourist market makes it possible for the traditional society to survive.

BIBLIOGRAPHY

Altman, Patricia. *Santos: Folk Sculpture from Guatemala*. UCLA Museum of Cultural History, Los Angeles, 1980. Brief but useful study of the cult of saints in Guatemala; good illustrations and much data based on field work.

Best-Maugard, Adolfo. *Tradición, resurgimiento y evolución del arte mexicano*. Mexico City, 1923. Manual for teaching the basic elements of Mexican art to students after the Mexican Revolution of 1910–1920.

Martínez Penaloza, Porfirio. *Arte popular mexicano*. Mexico City, 1975. Good examination of folk art within the context of Mexican history.

Mendez, Leopoldo, et al. *The Ephemeral and the Eternal of Mexican Folk Art*. 2 vols. Mexico City, 1971. Two profusely illustrated volumes; the best work to date on the subject.

Morris, Walter F., Jr. *Living Maya*. Photographs by Jeffrey J. Foxx. New York, 1987. Beautiful study of the Maya of Southern Mexico, with strong emphasis on traditional textiles.

Murillo, Gerardo (Dr. Atl). *Las artes populares en México*. Mexico City, 1921. First important study of Mexican folk art in the twentieth century. Part of Mexico's attempt to establish new identity, based on local folk images and pre-Hispanic cultures.

Oettinger, Marion, Jr. *Dancing Faces: Mexican Masks in a Cultural Context*. Washington, D.C., 1985. Discussion of traditional masks in Mexico; complemented an exhibition.

Oettinger, Marion, Jr. *The Folk Art of Latin America: Visiones del Pueblo*. New York, 1992. Overview of Latin American folk art, with strong emphasis on function. Includes materials from seventeen countries; many plates.

Oettinger, Marion, Jr., ed. *The Folk Art of Spain and the Americas: El Alma del Pueblo*. New York, 1997. Catalog for the first exhibition in the United States of Spanish folk art; contains a section on the transformation of Spanish folk art in Latin America, also sections on popular theater, votive art, popular graphics, folk ceramics, and popular furniture.

Rubin de la Borbolla, Daniel F. *Arte popular mexicano*. Mexico City, 1974. Valuable essay on Mexican folk art from pre-Hispanic times to the present.

Sáenz González, Olga, ed. *Arte popular mexicano: Cinco siglos*. Mexico City, 1996. Catalog for extensive exhibition on Mexican folk art; collection of essays by Mexico's leading authorities.

MARION OETTINGER, JR.

FOOD. *See* Cuisine *and* Nutrition.

FÖRSTEMANN, ERNST (1822–1906), Maya scholar who discovered their number system, their use of the "zero," and their calendar system. Born in Danzig on 18 September 1822, he was the son of a professor of mathematics, Wilhelm August Förstemann, and the nephew of librarians, archivists, and physicists. Förstemann became a teacher and librarian and was married in Danzig to Clara Schirrmacher, who died after a year. In 1856 he married Emilie Dette of Wernigerode, where he was then living, and with her had a daughter and two sons.

In 1857, Förstemann published a book on Old Germanic personal names, which won a prize from the Berlin Academy. He followed this, in 1859, with the first systematic study of German place-names, a major academic achievement. In 1865, he became the chief librarian of the Royal Public Library of Dresden. Among the treasures of this library was a Maya codex, now called the *Dresden Codex*, which fascinated Förstemann. In 1880, Förstemann published a fine edition of the *Dresden Codex* with an important commentary, the first such study that can still be taken seriously today. Later, he was to write similar commentaries on the two other known Maya codices.

Förstemann's most basic contribution was the recognition of the Maya number system, as employed in their calendar—with dots for 1, bars for 5, and shells for placeholders (the "zero") in a base-20 system (save that one unit in the third place was composed of only eighteen units in the second place). From this, he worked out the structure of the Maya calendar system, identified the associated day and month glyphs, and recognized the use of the calendar in astronomical tables. He recognized the Venus table, where he was able to determine the glyphs that identified Venus, and the lunar table (now known to refer to eclipses). Förstemann recognized the 177-day intervals of this table as groups of six lunations (but he missed the crucial connection of that interval with eclipses). In the lunar table, he pointed out a partial repetition of glyphs at intervals that were multiples of seven days. He interpreted this repetition as the combining of references to lunations with sidereal lunar months and with the tropical year. Some of his suggestions about planetary tables in the Maya codices are still not adequately appraised.

In the Maya inscriptions, just then becoming available, Förstemann recognized that the glyphs showing the heads of gods of periods (day, month, year, etc.) substituted for the simpler glyphs of those periods. That masterly piece of work laid the foundation both for reading Maya inscriptional dates and for realizing the interrelationships of the Maya religion and their calendar. In the last two years of his life, Förstemann published seven papers on Maya subjects. He died in Charlottenburg and is remembered for his major contributions in two disparate fields of scholarship.

Charles P. Bowditch, a Mayanist, recognized the tremendous importance of German scholarship in Maya matters and paid for a series of translations, some published by the Peabody Museum of Harvard University. These ensured that many important German works, especially those of Förstemann, Eduard Seler, and Paul Schellhas, were made available to English-speaking scholars.

BIBLIOGRAPHY
Schneider, Ernst. "Förstemann, Ernst Wilhelm." *Neue deustche biographie* 5 (1953), 270–271.
Thompson, J. Eric S. *Maya Hieroglyphic Writing: Introduction.* Carnegie Institution of Washington, D.C., 589. Washington, D.C., 1950.

DAVID H. KELLEY

FRANCISCANS. In the history of the Christian evangelization of Mesoamerican peoples, members of the Franciscan Order, or Friars Minor, played a leading role. Throughout the Colonial period, the Franciscan friars maintained extensive contacts with Indian communities within their six assigned provinces—the Provincia del Santo Evangelio (Province of the Holy Gospel) for Central Mexico, San Pedro y San Pedro de Michoacán, Santiago de Jalisco, San Francisco de Zacatecas, San José de Yucatán, and El Santísimo Nombre de Jesús (The Holy Name of Jesus) de Guatemala. Most of these provinces were organized in a similar fashion; they centered on the provincial city where most Spaniards in the region resided and where they constructed their most important monastery. From this center their influence was extended to Indian communities throughout the province.

The Franciscans' early colonial activities were divided into two periods by the late sixteenth-century chronicler Fray Gerónimo de Mendieta. The first began with the arrival of the friars in 1524 and ended with the first wave of secularizations of their *doctrinas* (proto-parishes) in 1556. Mendieta referred to these early decades of activity as the "golden age" of Franciscan labors in New Spain; he regarded the second period, until 1604, as their "silver age." Elsa Malvido (1941) has described a third period, from 1649 to 1750, when the Franciscans were removed from administering their six assigned provinces, which she calls the Franciscans' "iron age." From the mid-eighteenth century on, little is known of the Franciscan enterprise, but judging by the little that has been written, it was a time of decadence for the order.

Mendieta had based his two periods on changes in the Crown's support for the Franciscan friars and in the friars' dedication to Indian affairs and the evangelization

enterprise. During the "golden age," Emperor Charles V of Spain followed the Franciscans' efforts closely and provided financial and diplomatic support, which enabled them to achieve the many gains described by the chroniclers and other Franciscan records: large numbers of Indians baptized, many monasteries founded, and the extensive territory overseen. By contrast, Mendieta saw the Crown's support melting away during the second period in favor of the diocesan clergy, opening the way to secularization of the friars' *doctrinas*.

The work of the Franciscans in New Spain began in 1523, when three Flemish friars—Juan de Ayora, Pedro de Tecto, and Pedro de Gante—reached the central highlands. Their impact as missionaries was limited at first, since two of them died on Cortés's expedition to Central American in 1524, but Fray Pedro de Gante initiated the evangelization process and studied the Nahuatl language

Franciscan monastery of Huejotzingo, Puebla. Sixteenth-century atrium cross in front of church (west façade). *Photograph courtesy of Jeanette Favrot Peterson.*

through his contacts with children of the Indian elite from the city of Tetzcoco. As a result, just as Ayora and Tecto were setting out with Cortés, when the first official mission of Franciscans (known as "the Twelve," in memory of the first Apostles of Christ) arrived, Gante could claim that the first steps toward evangelization of the Indian neophytes had been taken, based on his start toward mastery of the major language of the area.

The Franciscans later applied to other native languages the methods they had used to learn Nahuatl. Within a few years after the arrival of "the Twelve," they achieved an understanding of the language adequate for basic communication with their parishioners. The friars acquired the language by joining Indian children in their games and pooling their knowledge of new words and correct pronunciation of the end of the day. As they accumulated enough words and phrases, they began to compose the first Nahuatl grammars and dictionaries to be used in the pastoral work of friars who were less advanced in Nahuatl.

From those early encounters, the interaction of friars and Indians continued to grow. The new colonial circumstances led to friars who became deeply involved in the daily lives of their Indian charges. They devoted themselves not only to the evangelization of Indian neophytes but also to the defense of Indian communities against threats by European colonists and from attempts to increase taxation on parishioners. They also protested royal decrees that interfered with the good order of Indian affairs. These were not the only ways in which Franciscan friars expressed their interest in Indian life and thought; there was also their strong curiosity about the psychological, economic, and social realities of their parishioners. Consequently, it is not unusual to find in the writings of the Franciscans—Mendieta, Bernardino de Sahagún, Toribio de Benavente Motolinía, Andrés de Olmos, Diego de Valadés, and others—important inquiries into the daily and ceremonial lives of Indians. These early inquiries continue to serve as the foundation of studies of pre-Hispanic social life.

Among the array of Franciscan writings from the sixteenth century, the chronicle written by Fray Bernardino de Sahagún stands out. It is a veritable dictionary of culture, religion, and life among the Nahuas of the Valley of Mexico in the pre-Hispanic period. Along the same lines, but less probing, are writings about other peoples and indigenous Mesoamerican cultures, such as those for the Franciscan province of Yucatán by Diego de Landa and Diego López de Cogolludo, the *Relación de las ceremonias y ritos y población y gobierno de los indios de la provincia de Michoacán*, and the chronicle written by Fray Alonso de la Rea for Michoacán. All these works, with various methods of research and greater or lesser perspicacity,

sought to give close, detailed accounts of the social organization of the indigenous people before the arrival of the Spaniards. Yet the purpose of these writings was not just scientific curiosity; they were actually meant to provide a baseline of information for conversion and to help identify and eradicate vestiges of pre-Hispanic religious rites. The chroniclers thus sought to establish the connections between seemingly mundane practices and the adoration of gods, so that friars in contact with Indians would have the information they needed to root out "superstitious" practices. Even Franciscan writings composed for other purposes, including those written to chronicle the development of the order's provinces in New Spain, include an introductory study of indigenous life in the region. This can be seen in the writings of Mendieta, Juan de Torquemada, and Agustín de Vetancurt for the Provincia del Santo Evangelio de México, all of which include in opening sections extracts concerning salient aspects of indigenous life.

These developments demonstrate the ways that Franciscans of the first generations tried to find different modes of establishing contact with and understanding of the habits, conceptions, and values of the peoples who were to be their parishioners. This deep interest and involvement in Indian lifeways led many Franciscans to seek material benefits for the Indian pueblos they were catechizing. It is not unusual to find that during the first half of the sixteenth century they relocated Indian communities and sponsored public works for the benefit of the community, like the aqueduct built under the supervision of Fray Francisco Tembleque or the first *congregaciones* (congregated settlements), which were intended to promote a Spanish way of life among Indians. Beyond these efforts, the greatest proof of their regard and respect for the Indian population, according to the Franciscans' view of the world, was the friars' willingness to provide Indians with the sacrament of baptism without requiring extensive knowledge of Christian doctrine and to open the sacrament of priesthood to their new converts. These two policies of the Franciscans put them in serious conflict with the diocesan clergy and the other religious orders, especially the Dominicans, who opposed the provision of either of these sacraments to people who knew so little about Roman Catholicism.

The idea of conferring baptism indicated clearly that the Franciscans thought the Indians had the same capacity as Spaniards to live a Christian life. Some of the early Franciscan chroniclers even mention that within the reforming movement of the order, these recently converted Indians had a special place in the creation of a new society, preceding the second coming of Christ—a new society that would be composed only of the friars and the Indians. With respect to the priesthood, proposing to permit neophytes access to this sacrament implied that the separate Spanish and Indian groups comprising Colonial-era society were completely equal, since both could aspire to this most perfect state of human existence. Still, this proposal was debated even within the Franciscan order. In a chapter meeting in 1555, both positions on the question of ordination were debated; Fray Juan de Gaona argued for delay in opening the priesthood to Indians, and Fray Jacobo Daciano represented those who wished to begin the process of ordaining Indians. In this Scholastic-style debate, Gaona forced Daciano to alter his position. The result was damaging to the Indians' legal standing in Colonial-era society. By adopting Gaona's ideas, the Franciscan order condemned the Indians of Mesoamerica to a very long period—centuries—in which they were virtually defined as infants, since only ordination was the equivalent of achieving full adulthood.

From that time on, the Franciscan friars began to view the Indians as people in need of protection—as perpetual minors—and adopted a paternalistic attitude toward them. At the same time, from the late sixteenth century onward, the relationship between Franciscans and Indians began to deteriorate, above all in the sense that Indian communities saw the Franciscans as interfering in their daily affairs. The problems first centered on the friars' demands for the payment of sacramental fees and the performance of other obligations to the church, as well as their attempts to influence the election of officers in Indian pueblos. These problems between Franciscans and Indians increased as time went by; soon the neophytes began to make use of the Spanish courts to halt what they considered injustices done them by the friars. Royal officials began to take notice of other abuses by the friars, especially with respect to excessive charges for the sacraments and unpaid labor for the construction and reconstruction of the Franciscans' monastery-churches. Not surprisingly, some Franciscan writers began to complain of the Indians' lack of gratitude and love for their friar-pastors. Despite the growing incidence of conflicts between the two groups, the secularization of the remaining *doctrinas* administered by the Franciscans—which took place in the diocese of Puebla in 1640 and in the other dioceses of New Spain after 1749—roused some protests against this royal policy of removing the friars from pastoral service. The protests fell on deaf ears. The removal did not take place all at once (like the expulsion of the Jesuits in 1767), but the Crown did systematically execute the secularization order after 1749. With it, the bond that had united the Franciscans with the Indians of Mesoamerica was severed.

As the secularization was carried out, the Franciscans were obliged to assemble in a few monasteries for each province. Most of these were situated in the largest cities of New Spain. Their former churches and monasteries in the *doctrinas* were occupied by diocesan priests. This and other restrictive policies of the Crown, such as limiting the number of individuals who could enter the novitiate of an order, resulted in a further decline in the influence and numbers of Franciscans in all provinces in the center and south of New Spain. The friars' scope of activity was limited to the places where the church was still not well established, principally in the far north—beyond the area of Mesoamerica—and in some remote north-central regions, such as the Sierra Gorda (northern Hidalgo).

[*See also* Gante, Pedro de; Landa, Diego de; López de Cogolludo, Diego; Mendieta, Gerónimo de; Montolinía, Toribio de Benavente; Olmos, Andrés de; Torquemada, Juan de; Valadés, Diego; Zumárraga, Juan de.]

BIBLIOGRAPHY

Baudot, Georges. *La pugna franciscana por México*. Mexico City, 1980. Compilation of articles with special attention to the sixteenth century.

Baudot, Georges. *Utopía e historia en México: Los primeros cronistas de la civilización mexicana (1520–1569)*. Madrid, 1983. Analysis of some sixteenth-century Franciscan chronicles, including Motolinía, Las Navas, Andrés de Olmos, and *La Relación de Michoacán*.

Brading, David A. *Una iglesia asediada: El obispado de Michoacán, 1749–1810*. Mexico City, 1994. One of the few studies to treat the secularization of *doctrinas* after 1749.

Cartas de religiosos de Nueva España, 1539–1594. Mexico City, 1941. Some of the most important documents produced by the Franciscans in the sixteenth century.

Códice Francisco: Siglo XVI. Mexico City, 1941. Includes lengthy reports submitted by provincials of the Franciscan provinces of Mexico and Jalisco in 1570 to Visitador Ovando, with details on regional and local conditions.

Malvido, Eiso. "Los Nouicios de San Francisco en la Ciunad de México. La edad de Hierro (1649–1749)." *Historia Mexicana* 36, No. 4 (1987), 699–738. Sociodemographic article, with special reference to the familial backgrounds of the Franciscan novices.

Mendieta, Gerónimo de. *Historia eclesiástica indiana*. 3d ed. Mexico City, 1980. One of the most important chronicles for the development of the Franciscan mission in the sixteenth century, especially for the Provincia del Santo Evangelio.

Morales, Francisco. *Ethnic and Social Background of the Franciscan Friars in Seventeenth-Century Mexico*. Washington, D.C., 1973. Mainly a study of admission of novitiates to the Franciscan order, with important inferences about the history of the order in the seventeenth century.

Phelan, John L. *The Millennial Kingdom of the Franciscans in the New World*. Berkeley and Los Angeles, 1956. Analysis of Mendieta's writings for a history of Franciscan ideas in sixteenth-century New Spain.

Ricard, Robert. *The Spiritual Conquest of Mexico*. Berkeley, 1966. The classic work on the history of evangelization of Indians in New Spain during the sixteenth century.

Vetancurt, Agustín de. *Teatro mexicano: Crónica de la Provincia del Santo Evangelio de México, menologio franciscano*. 2d ed. Mexico City, 1982. An important source for the seventeenth century; the least studied chronicle of the Provincia del Santo Evangelio.

GUILLERMO ANTONIO NÁJERA NÁJERA
Translated from Spanish by William B. Taylor

FROGS AND TOADS. Frogs and toads—amphibians of the order Anura and collectively called "anurans"—require water to reproduce. Both are most visible and vocalize most loudly during the rainy season in Mesoamerica, and both, usually seen near water, symbolize moisture, earth, and agricultural fertility to Mesoamericans. Although some have brilliant colors, they are often earth-brown or leaf-green. Frogs that live in trees especially emphasize their association with vegetation. At the Mexica (Aztec) Templo Mayor at Tenochtitlan (c.1500 CE), a pair of stone frogs or toads stood flanking the stairway in front of the rain god's shrine. In modern times, frogs are still widely used or imitated in Mesoamerican agricultural rituals; they are thought to be the rain god's companions, his children, or the guardians of his cave or shrine. Toads can be considered manifestations of the earth, which their skin resembles. A toadlike earth monster is often portrayed on Classic Veracruz stone yokes (600–1000 CE), which are related to the ballgame ritual. The Mexica earth deity, Tlaltecuhtli, was sometimes portrayed as a toad with fangs and claws.

Anurans are also metaphors for regeneration: they shed their old skin and look fresh and new. A Classic Maya glyph meaning "birth" is based on a frog. Transformation is a major theme in indigenous American literature, and the anuran conversion from egg to fishlike tadpole to frog or toad is a vivid example of observable transformation in nature.

Many anuran species are nocturnal, which leads to further symbolism; that they move by jumping adds to their interesting characteristics for symbolism. Frogs, which can jump nine times their body length, are more agile than toads and more water-dependent.

Amphibians probably all secrete some skin toxins. Those bearing the most powerful poisons are generally found south of Mesoamerica. The largest toad, *Bufo marinus* (the "marine toad," commonly known by its scientific name), is distributed in lowlands from the southern United States to northern South America. The toxin in its parotid gland is powerful enough to kill a small dog that bites it. For defense, the toad can release toxin contained in "warts" on its skin. Bufotenine ($C_{12}H_{16}N_2O$), a poisonous hallucinogenic alkaloid, is derived from this toxin. At the Olmec site of San Lorenzo (c.1000 BCE), remains of *B. marinus* have been found in middens on different levels, which suggests periodic ritual use. It is not known if ancient people obtained this drug, but the toxin is used in modern folk curing in Mesoamerica.

Throughout the prehistory of Mesoamerica, frogs and toads were prominent in art and lore. Massive toad altars were carved from 200 BCE to 200 CE at Kaminaljuyú and Abaj Takalik in Guatemala, and at Izapa in far southern Mexico. Many Late Classic Maya vases depict a *Bufo* toad the same size as the monkey, dog, or turkey also shown on the vessel. The toad's toxic gland and a glyph meaning "sacred" are drawn on its back. In the Maya calendar, a toad portrays the glyph for the twenty-day *uinal* period. Today, women weaving textiles in the Maya Highlands of Mexico and Guatemala use a design that they call both "toad" and "saint."

[*See also* Hallucinogens.]

BIBLIOGRAPHY

Benson, Elizabeth P. *Birds and Beasts of Ancient Latin America.* Gainesville, Fla., 1997. Information and lore about amphibians in Mesoamerica and South America.

Miller, Mary, and Karl Taube. *The Gods and Symbols of Ancient Mexico and the Maya.* London and New York, 1993. A general book with some information on the lore and myths of toads.

Stebbins, Robert C., and Nathan W. Cohen. *A Natural History of Amphibians.* Princeton, 1995. A general book on amphibians.

Wing, Elizabeth S., and Michael D. Coe. "Faunal Remains from San Lorenzo." In *In the Land of the Olmec*, edited by Michael D. Coe and Richard A. Diehl, vol. 1, pp. 375–386. Austin, Tex., 1980. Description of remains from food middens at this Olmec site, along with some interpretation.

ELIZABETH P. BENSON

G

GAMIO, MANUEL (1883–1960), pioneer Mexican archaeologist. Gamio studied archaeology, ethnology, and anthropology with Nicolás León and Jesús Galindo y Villa at the International School of American Archaeology and Ethnology (established on 11 January 1911 at the Museo Nacional de Antropología in Mexico City). The institution had great impact on Mexican archaeology, particularly when it was under the directorship of Eduard Seler, Franz Boas, and Alfred Marston Tozzer in the early twentieth century.

In 1908, Gamio began his first archaeological exploration at Chalchihuites, Zacatecas. Afterward, he was subdirector of archaeological explorations in Ecuador, under the direction of M. H. Saville. He then returned to Mexico to pursue a master's degree. He went to Columbia University in New York for his doctorate, granted in 1924.

From 1911 to 1925, Gamio explored various sites in Mexico, as general inspector of archaeological monuments but also as director of the International School of American Archaeology and Ethnology: Azcapotzalco, Chichén Itzá, Teotihuacan, Copilco, Chalco, Templo Mayor, and Naucalpan. During this period, he founded the Direction of Anthropology, a government agency for archaeological research, and the journal *Ethnos*. Of particular interest is his stratigraphic excavation at Azcapotzalco (1912), where he established the chronological succession of the Formative (then called the Preclassic), Teotihuacan, and Aztec cultures in the Valley of Mexico.

Gamio's interest in archaeological method was clearly represented in his 1914 article, "Metodología sobre investigación, exploración y conservación de monumentos arqueológicos." In it, he proposed two types of methods: the extensive method, which consisted in characterizing pre-Hispanic cultures through historical sources, archaeological remains, and the geographic setting; and the intensive method, which consisted in detailing these characteristics through abstract and material data: myths, legends, religious and military institutions, technological and artistic productions, architecture, sculpture, human remains, flora and fauna, migrations, abandonment processes, cultural influences, and successions.

Gamio was subsecretary of public education under Mexico's President Plutarco Calles (1924–1928). In 1925,

he was forced to leave Mexico temporarily, when he publicly revealed financial irregularities in the department. He returned to Mexico in 1929, and from 1942 to 1960 was the director of the Instituto Indigenista Interamericano, concerned with Indian affairs.

One of Gamio's main contributions to the field was as editor of the two-volume publication *La población del Valle de Teotihuacan* (1922), an interdisciplinary study in which the nature of archaeology is emphasized as part of anthropology, that is, as a synthesis of the physical, linguistic, and cultural aspects of humankind. In this work, Gamio not only coordinated articles on archaeological explorations in parts of the ancient city of Teotihuacan, such as the Temple of Quetzalcoatl and the Temple of Agriculture, but also envisioned the study of the geological, geomorphological, faunal, floral, and biophysical substrate of the region, the architecture and crafts of the Teotihuacanos, the economic and religious aspects of the Colonial period, and the living conditions of the inhabitants of the valley in the twentieth century. The result of this last issue was important technological and industrial progress for the modern population: meteorological stations; information about new methods to improve cultivation and cattle breeding; a new road from Mexico City to Teotihuacan; commercialization of the maguey-cord industry; pottery workshops; and more. [*See* Teotihuacan.]

Gamio's research concepts provided models for multidisciplinary collaboration in New World archaeology and intellectual endeavors of regional scope that few scholars ever attempt in their careers. He was praised and won awards for his efforts in fieldwork and publication by both the founders of the discipline and his colleagues in New World archaeology.

BIBLIOGRAPHY

Estudios antropológicos publicados en homenaje al doctor Manuel Gamio. Mexico City, 1956. This is Gamio's *Festschrift*.

Gamio, Manuel. *La población del Valle de Teotihuacan*. 2 vols. Mexico City, 1922. Gamio's major contribution to Mexican interdisciplinary archaeology.

Gamio, Manuel. *Arqueología e indigenismo*. Mexico City, 1972. Covers archaeological concepts and methods, as well as Indian matters in Mexico.

Matos Moctezuma, Eduardo. "Don Manuel Gamio. O la otra cara de la moneda." In *Las Piedras Negadas. De la Coatlicue al Templo Mayor*, pp. 79–103. Mexico City, 1998. Presents an overview of some of Gamio's main contributions.

LINDA MANZANILLA

GANTE, PEDRO DE (1491–1572), Franciscan missionary and educator, known by the Spanish name for his native city, Gante (from Ghent). Still, historians do not agree on his Flemish family name or on his place of birth. They suggest three family names based on a Spanish letter written by him in 1529—Peter of Moor, Van der Moere, or Muer—and two birth places, Ayghen-St-Pierre or Yedeghem. According to testimony provided by him in 1535, he was born in 1491, which disproves the longstanding rumor that he was an illegitimate offspring of the emperor Charles V. In 1552, Gante affirmed that he was a close relative of the emperor and had entered into his service as a young man. He probably served only for a short time, because in 1522 he was already a Franciscan friar living in Ghent, then part of the Spanish domain. In the spring of that year, he left Ghent in the company of two Franciscan priests, Juan de Tecto and Juan de Aora. After a short stop in Spain, they arrived in Mexico in 1523. Despite his noble lineage, Gante never accepted priestly ordination and remained a lay brother.

Gante and his two companions established the first Franciscan community of New Spain in Tetzcoco, where he began the activity that would characterize his missionary life: the education of Indians. Gifted in languages, he was one of the first missionaries to learn Nahuatl. When the elected bishop of Mexico, Fray Juan de Zumárraga, arrived in 1528, Gante was his first translator in Nahuatl. He left testimonies of his knowledge of Nahuatl in writings such as the "Testerian catechism," preserved in the Madrid National Library; the "Doctrina Christiana en Lengua Mexicana" (1553), published in Mexico; and a textbook in three languages (Nahuatl, Spanish, and Latin) attributed to him and published in Mexico in 1569.

In 1523, Pedro de Gante founded a school for the children of Indian nobility in Tetzcoco. Following European teaching methods of that time, he taught not only Christian doctrine but also reading, writing, music, and good manners. In 1526, he was transferred to the recently built Franciscan monastery in Mexico City, where he constructed a chapel for the Indians called San José de los Naturales. Next to it, he established a school, where by 1529 he was teaching more than five hundred children.

San José de los Naturales and the Franciscan College of Santiago Tlatelolco were the most important centers of education for Mesoamerican people during the sixteenth century. As of the mid-1530s, the school curriculum included not only reading, writing, and music but also such Spanish crafts as tailoring, shoemaking, carpentry, smithing, and stone-cutting. Pedro de Gante introduced European techniques and models to enrich the fine arts in which Mesoamerican people were already very skilled; for example, sculpture and painting. He saw that Indians learned the use of chisels for woodworking and copied Flemish models. For their part, the Indians brought their materials and techniques to the production of Christian art, and such is the case of a great number of crucifixes made from maize stalks. The Indian artisans trained in this school participated in the construction and decoration of various churches in Mexico, as well as in the monumental sixteenth-century Franciscan monasteries.

Gante's educational endeavor did not distract him from the Franciscans' other missionary activities. He was a renowned preacher, organized splendid devotional services, and amply participated in baptizing Indians. He was considered one of the most important ecclesiastical figures of his time. The second archbishop of Mexico, the Dominican Alonso de Montúfar, said: "The archbishop is not I, but Pedro de Gante." Gante's interest in Indian causes appears in his letters to Charles V and Philip II. With words as strong as those of the Dominican Bartolomé de las Casas, he wrote to Charles V in 1552 complaining that the Spaniards gave better treatment to their dogs than to the Indians.

Gante's death was registered in Mesoamerican codices, among them the *Aubin Codex*. One of the best testimonies of the Indians' appreciation for this Franciscan lay brother is the Nahuatl poem that his students wrote and sang in a religious celebration. It was performed in the Franciscan monastery in 1567, before his death. Its text has been rescued from oblivion and translated into Spanish by Miguel León-Portilla in "An Aztec Laud in Praise of Some Famous Franciscans" (*Franciscan Presence in the Americas*, Washington, D.C., 1985).

[*See also* Franciscans.]

BIBLIOGRAPHY

Barth, Pius. *Franciscan Education and Social Order in Spanish North America*. Chicago, 1950. General survey of the Franciscan educational activities in Mexico.

Chávez, Angélico, ed. and trans. *The Oroz Codex: The Oroz "Relacíon" or Relation of the Description of Holy Gospel Province in New Spain, and the Lives and Founders and Other Noteworthy Men of Said Province, Composed by Fray Pedro Oroz, 1584–1586*. Washington, D.C., 1972. Includes a translation into English of the first biography of Pedro de Gante.

Cortés Castellanos. *El Catecismo en pictogramas de fr. Pedro de Gante*. Madrid, 1987. Presents a detailed study and interpretation of each catechism's pictogram.

Kieckens, F. *Les anciens missionaires belges en Amérique. Fray Pedro de Gante récollet flamand. Premier Missionaire de l'Anahuac (Mexique), 1523–1572*. Brussels, 1880. Best and most complete biography of Gante. Difficult to find even in the best libraries. (The Spanish translation by Enrique Cordero y Torres is entitled *Biografia de Fray Pedro de Gante*. Puebla, 1966.)

Torre Villar, Ernesto de la. *Fray Pedro de Gante. Maestro and civilizador de América*. Mexico City, 1973. Short but well-documented biography; includes five of Gante's letters written from Mexico between 1529 and 1558.

FRANCISCO MORALES

GARIBAY KINTANA, ANGEL MARÍA (1892–1967), rediscoverer of Nahuatl literature. He was born in Toluca, state of México, into a family of limited economic resources, and his father died when he was young. After finishing his elementary studies, he entered the seminary of the archdiocese of México. There, in addition to the ecclesiastical curriculum, he became well versed in classical languages and literature (of the Romans, Greeks, and Hebrews). He also read in Spanish, English, French, German, and Italian. His interest in Nahuatl and Otomí dates to this time. As the seminary's librarian, he spent many hours reading the treasures stored there.

The difficult times of the Mexican Revolution obliged him to interrupt his stay at the seminary, which was temporarily closed. Returning to his family's home, he visited several Indian communities in the state of México, where he practiced the Nahuatl and Otomí languages. Upon his return to the seminary, he was ordained a priest in 1917.

Garibay served for five years as a professor at the seminary. In 1922, he began his work, first as coadjutor and later as rector, in several rural parishes within the state of México. Separated from academia, he did not abandon his intellectual concerns. While in Xilotepec, he prepared a study on the morphology of the Otomí, as spoken in that region. While in Huixquilucan, he published a translation of Aeschylus' *Trilogy of Orestes*; and in San Martín, Tenancingo, and Otumba, he proceeded with his studies of the Nahuatl language and literature. In his regular visits to Mexico City, he acquired whatever publications he found related to the subjects of his interest; this he did mainly by visiting the Porrúa Bookshop, with whose owners he established a close and fruitful friendship.

While in Otumba, he prepared and published his *Llave del Nahuatl* (A Key to the Nahuatl Language, 1940), which proved to be a valuable tool for the study of the language (among the many who used it were Arthur J. O. Anderson and Charles E. Dibble, renowned translators). In the 1940s, he changed his residence to Mexico City upon his promotion as canon of the Basilica of Guadalupe. Around the same time, Garibay began to collaborate with the Universidad Nacional de México. His first collaboration resulted in the publication of *Poesía indígena de la Altiplanicie* (*Indian Poetry from the Highlands*) and *Épica Nahuatl* (*Nahuatl Epics*), both included in the "Library of the University Student" series. From the 1940s, in addition to ecclesiastical duties, he devoted most of his time to studying and translating Nahuatl compositions,

mainly from the *Cantares mexicanos*, and the texts collected by Fray Bernardino de Sahagún.

In 1951, on the fourth centennial of the royal decree and papal bull that established the Universidad Nacional de México, Garibay was awarded an honorary doctorate. In 1953–1954, he published his magnum opus, *Historia de la literatura Náhuatl*, which revealed from a humanistic perspective the richness of the literary productions in that language. The influence of this work on many contemporary Mexicanists, in Mexico and elsewhere, has been decisive. In 1956, he published an annotated edition, with an ample introduction, of *Historia general de las cosas de Nueva España* by Bernardino de Sahagún.

Garibay's relationship with the university became closer when, in 1957, he and a former student, Miguel León-Portilla, joined it as research professors at the Instituto de Investigaciones Históricas. There, they founded the Seminar on Nahuatl Culture and began to publish the review *Estudios de Cultura Náhuatl*. Garibay organized a group of students who devoted themselves to the study of Mexico's Indian past and to research in the fields of Nahuatl language and literature. Besides León-Portilla, the group included Alfredo López Austin, Thelma D. Sullivan, Jacqueline de Durand Forest, and Georges Baudot.

In his last years, Garibay published several valuable works, among them *Veinte himnos sacros de los Nahuas* (1958), *Poesía Náhuatl* (3 vols., 1964–1967), and his edition of Fray Diego Durán's *Historia de las indias de Nueva España e islas de Tierra Firme*. In great part, his modern Nahuatl research in Mexico gave impetus to the field and inspired today's new research.

BIBLIOGRAPHY

León-Portilla, Miguel, and Patrick Johansson. *Angel María Garibay, La rueda en el río*. Mexico City, 1993. Garibay's most comprehensive biography, illustrated with many photographs of him.

Roldán, Dolores. *Biografía de Angel Ma. Garibay K*. Mexico City, 1985. A biography based on Garibay's unpublished journals.

Rublúo, Luis. *Angel María Garibay K. Estudio biblio-hemerográfico*. Mexico City, 1965. Provides a comprehensive bibliography of Garibay's works.

Solé, Alberto Herr. *Angel María Garibay o la confrontación de los orígenes*. Mexico City, 1992. Desciption of the contents of Garibay's archives preserved in Mexico's national archives.

MIGUEL LEÓN-PORTILLA

GARÍFUNA. The Garífuna people, also known as Karaphuna or Black Caribs, are the descendants of Africans of unknown origin and indigenous peoples of the Lesser Antilles, who were termed "Caribs" by early Europeans there. In 1797, after a long period of intermittent and then intensive warfare, they suffered a final defeat by the British on the Lesser Antillean island of Saint Vincent. They were then transported to Roatan, an island off the Caribbean coast of Honduras.

Garífuna mothers and children waiting for the return of the fishermen, Livingston, Guatemala. *Photograph courtesy of Nancie L. González.*

Today the Garífuna inhabit the Central American mainland between Belize and Nicaragua; many also live in New York and other U.S. and Central American cities. Their language, still spoken by a large majority today, is basically South American Arawakan, but it has been strongly modified by extensive contact, at various times, with speakers of Cariban, French, English, and Spanish. Their culture at the time of their removal to Honduras was based on fishing, gathering, the cultivation of manioc and other root crops, the sale of baskets and hand-hewn canoes, and sporadic wage labor for Europeans, especially tasks related to maritime transportation. Their religion, then and now, celebrates the continuation of life after death through ritual communication with their ancestors. This has been successfully syncretized with Christianity, which was first introduced to them in Saint Vincent.

The two thousand or so survivors of the Saint Vincent wars and exodus have prospered in Central America, where they continued their traditional way of life for about 150 years after their arrival. Their settlement preferences in isolated parts of the Caribbean coastline facilitated the preservation of their indigenous culture, while at the same time allowing maximal mobility for the men to travel abroad seeking wage labor. They were welcomed by the Spanish authorities and colonists for their military prowess and for their maritime skills, as well as for their food crops, which are produced largely by the women. Their African heritage was enhanced by the intermar-riage of their women with exiles from the Haitian wars of independence, men forced to flee during the early years of that conflict, who had found refuge near Trujillo, Honduras. During and after World War II, Garífuna men began to work on U.S. ships sailing out of New York, New Orleans, and Mobile. This led to increasing permanent migration to the United States. By the 1960s, women also found the attraction of wage labor in the United States irresistible.

Both in Central America and beyond, many Garífuna have achieved high levels of formal education, but others work in semiskilled or unskilled jobs. Their exotic music and dance, a modern synthesis based on African and South American antecedents, has become popular wherever they live, despite the fact that much of their performance is seen by the elders as a profanation of the ancient religion. The dark color of their skin has led to social problems in Guatemala but has not been a hindrance in Belize or Honduras, where several have achieved positions of considerable authority, influence, and power in education, government, and the Roman Catholic religious hierarchy.

BIBLIOGRAPHY

González, Nancie L. *Sojourners of the Caribbean: Ethnogenesis and Ethnohistory of the Garífuna.* Urbana, Ill., 1988.

Kerns, Virginia. *Women and the Ancestors: Black Carib Kinship and Ritual.* Urbana, Ill., 1983.

Taylor, Douglas M. *The Black Caribs of British Honduras.* Viking Fund Publications in Anthropology, 17. New York, 1951.

NANCIE L. GONZÁLEZ

GENDER ROLES. [*This entry comprises three articles:*

Pre-Hispanic Period
Colonial Period
Contemporary Cultures

The first article provides an overview of gender roles within various Mesoamerican cultures during the pre-Hispanic period; the second article discusses Mesoamerican gender roles during the Colonial period; the third article treats the changing nature of gender roles within contemporary Mesoamerican cultures. For a related discussion, see Gender Studies.]

Pre-Hispanic Period

In general, it is fair to say that most Mesoamerican women worked primarily in or near the home, while most men worked outside and some distance from it. Sixteenth-century authors have left us enough information, albeit riddled with European and male biases, to make it clear that, at the time of the Spanish conquest, women ideally and typically bore principal responsibility for childbearing, food preparation, housecleaning, and laundry. Although it is likely that many women of noble birth had servants to help them with the last three, this prescription probably applied to women of all social classes. Among the Aztec of Central Mexico, the umbilical cord of a newborn girl was buried in the home, beneath her mother's metate, or grinding stone, whereas that of an infant boy was taken away to be buried in the battlefield.

This was so because masculinity was defined largely in military terms in Aztec culture, as it no doubt was among other peoples who frequently engaged in warfare. Throughout Mesoamerica, male gender identity was also closely tied to hunting (including fishing, where relevant) and agriculture, occupations that again tend to draw men away from their homes. There is little doubt that, over all, it was the men who cleared, burned, and tilled the fields in most parts of Mesoamerica. Women, however, often helped with the planting and harvesting and, under certain circumstances, worked at least some fields by themselves. Women, moreover, usually maintained the gardens close to the house, which could include fruit-bearing trees. Most of the herbs that were used for medicinal and magical purposes were apparently grown in household gardens by women, who also bred and cared for domestic animals such as dogs, as well as fowl and sometimes other birds.

The *Codex Mendoza*, a sixteenth-century pictorial manuscript painted by an Aztec artist, makes it clear that childrearing was shared jointly by husband and wife, with the father taking primary responsibility for training

the couple's sons, and the mother for socializing the daughters. Children were taught early to help with the tasks appropriate to their sex. Thus, little boys accompanied their fathers into the fields, carried firewood to the marketplace, and eventually learned to hunt and fish. Girls stayed closer to their mothers and, by the end of their sixth year, had been taught to spin. Weaving and housework were so closely identified with femininity in Aztec culture that infant girls were provided at birth with a broom and a distaff with spindle, as well as a little basket in which to keep their future weavings.

Cloth production was of such importance in pre-Hispanic Mesoamerica that family members of both sexes and all ages probably participated in one or more of its phases, but carding, spinning, dying, weaving, and embroidering were theoretically women's tasks. Within those communities that paid tribute in finished cloth to a more powerful polity, this placed women in an economically strategic position. Women, moreover, seem to have been the principal sellers of woven cloth at the local markets. This shows not only that women did leave home, at least occasionally, for economic reasons, but also that they were free to dispose of their own domestic products. Whether they were further free to keep the items they received in exchange for those products is not known. Women, sometimes together with their husbands, also sold produce and prepared foods and beverages for market, as well as a variety of craft items. They were probably responsible for acquiring such goods, as well; in today's culture, they probably would be identified as the major domestic consumers.

Many goods bought and sold in the markets had been brought from distant lands by professional merchants, called *pochteca* by the Aztecs. Since the *pochteca* were also undercover spies for the government who occasionally got drawn into military skirmishes, it is not surprising that they were almost always male. Supported by a male ethic stressing the virtues of bravery and fortitude, men dominated the military throughout Mesoamerica. There is no convincing evidence that women ever actively participated in organized military offensives, although, in Mixtec painted histories, certain female rulers are depicted doing so. Women's participation in battle was typically limited to their usual roles of food preparers and providers of physical comforts in general.

Although Aztec noblewomen occasionally trained to be scribes, and some helped their menfolk in highly specialized crafts such as featherworking, most Aztec crafts other than textile production were the province of men. Throughout Mesoamerica, women probably molded clay into household vessels, and perhaps figurines, but it was typically men who carved the large stone statues, painted the colorful murals and sacred manuscripts, cast and hammered gold and silver, and polished and inlaid precious stones. Among the Aztec and the Classic Maya, painting and lapidary work were prestigious occupations deemed worthy of a ruler's offspring, and Maya sculptors may also have been of royal blood. In all cases where the identity of a Maya artist is known to us, the artist's name is that of a man. Even the prestigious Aztec craft of featherworking, although it involved the help of women as breeders of birds and feather-dyers, was performed by men.

The priesthoods that arose in the more complex Mesoamerican societies were likewise dominated by men, and there appears to have been a "glass ceiling" that kept women out of their upper echelons. Among the Aztec and the Maya, to judge from Colonial period sources, all high-level positions in the priestly hierarchy were occupied by males. Some Aztec girls were educated along with their brothers at the *calmecac*, a school that trained children of the nobility for service in the temples. Unlike the boys, however, the girls were forbidden to view the statues of the deities they served and apparently did not honor the gods by performing autosacrifice. This parallels Colonial period reports that Yucatec Maya women were not allowed to shed blood to the idols. Nor could Maya women perform—indeed, even attend—human sacrifices. Most Aztec girls did not remain in temple service for more than a few years, instead returning home to marry. Aztec and Maya boys, in contrast, could—if judged worthy—remain in the priesthood for the rest of their lives. Richard Trexler (1995) has proposed that some of these boys were assigned to socially and sexually subservient female roles, serving the higher-ranking male priests within the temples as what anthropologists refer to as *berdaches*.

Although women may not normally have occupied the most powerful positions within the priesthood, their participation was surely greater than Spanish authors would lead us to believe. Betty Ann Brown (1983) has pointed out that although the Franciscan author Bernardino de Sahagún typically mentions only male priests in his earliest text on Aztec ceremonies, his native illustrators show numerous women clearly serving priestly functions. Priestesses also flank the famous icon at the center of the so-called Tepantitla Patio murals at Classic period Teotihuacan in Central Mexico, and they appear in the form of large ceramic figurines from Classic central Veracruz. Among the Yucatec Maya at the time of the Conquest, moreover, one group of old women was permitted inside the temples on certain occasions. These women may have been the Maya counterparts of Aztec graduates of the *calmecac* who stayed on there to teach subsequent generations of young women. There is scattered evidence that a woman occasionally attained the rank of major priestly

oracle. Sharisse and Geoffrey McCafferty (1994) have proposed that the obviously high-ranking individual buried in Tomb 7 at Monte Albán, Oaxaca, was a priestess, possibly identifiable with the female oracle named 9 Grass who figures prominently in the Mixtec historical manuscripts.

If women normally did not dominate the official religious hierarchy in the larger, state-level systems, they nonetheless played active religious roles at the more local, popular level. Elderly women, for example, seem to have excelled at arranging marriages, tending to premarital, marital, and reproductive problems such as adultery and impotence, and delivering babies. Although these tasks may not strike us today as "religious," in pre-Hispanic times successful conception and childbirth were seen as being in the hands of certain female supernaturals. Mesoamerican midwives were often members of the broader professions of herbalist, curer, or doctor, which could entail contact with the gods. A measure of the religious dimension of medical practice in ancient times is the fact that Aztec midwives were permitted to hold their own ceremony in the main temple precinct in the capital.

Although they were primarily charged with domestic duties, including reproduction, Mesoamerican women therefore could participate in numerous occupations that took them, at least temporarily, outside the home. Their value to the political order, however, rested largely on their ability to serve as wives and mothers. In the highly centralized, expansionist society of the Aztec, it was men who occupied the highest official government positions. The only possible exception was a woman named Atotoztli, who was the daughter of the ruler Motecuhzoma I. Atotoztli may have briefly served as regent for her young son Axayacatl until he could eventually succeed his grandfather, who had no brothers who could claim the throne. Royal women are well known to have served as regents for their underage sons at the Classic Maya sites of Palenque, Naranjo, and perhaps Tikal. Palenque and other Classic Maya sites, such as Piedras Negras, also have monuments depicting a newly seated ruler attended by his mother, whose high-ranking lineage was apparently the basis of his right to rule. The rulers of these polities, as in the Mixteca, also often married the younger women in their families to male rulers of other cities with which they wished to form alliances. Mixtec women, however, apparently co-ruled the family's territories, sharing a level of power and prestige not available to royal women in Maya and Aztec dynasties. At times, when a Mixtec king died, his wife thenceforth ruled alone. We also have isolated reports of female rulers, or *cacicas*, governing smaller polities in the more distant provinces outside Central Mexico.

Whereas Mesoamerican women are never reported to

have taken more than one husband, many, if not most, Aztec men of high rank were polygynous. It was usually the principal wife of a ruler who enjoyed the status of "queen," and only the offspring of her union with the king were considered his legitimate heirs. A noble's secondary wives and concubines did not enjoy the same status and privileges as his principal wife. Moreover, within the population at large, it appears that women who never married at all—like married women who did not remain faithful to their husbands—were regarded as social failures and even dangers to society. Aztec adulteresses, like their sexual partners, were publicly executed, while "public women," or women who apparently sold sexual favors in the marketplace, were threatened with being sacrificed.

These "public women," however, should probably be differentiated from another class of Aztec women who were selected by state officials during certain state-sponsored ceremonies to dance and sleep with any distinguished warriors and nobles who requested them. The "pleasure girls," as Sahagún referred to them, were carefully guarded by the matrons at the *telpochcalli*, a school used primarily to train commoner boys to become warriors. In addition to providing temporary social and physical companionship to the elite, these women were trained to sing and dance in state-sponsored ceremonies. Their status, as Margaret Arvey (1988) has shown, was probably fairly high, and there is no evidence that they were not free eventually to leave the *telpochcalli* and marry. As far as we know, however, their male counterparts, who were likewise trained to sing and dance for the benefit of the elite, were never asked or expected to provide sexual favors.

BIBLIOGRAPHY

Arvey, Margaret Campbell. "Women of Ill-repute in the *Florentine Codex*." In *The Role of Gender in Pre-Columbian Art and Architecture*, edited by Virginia E. Miller, pp. 179–204. Lanham, Md., 1988. Argues that, owing to bias and misunderstanding, Spanish sources misrepresent Aztec attitudes toward female sexuality and sexual morality.

Brown, Betty Ann. "Seen but not Heard: Women in Aztec Ritual—The Sahagún Texts." In *Text and Image in Pre-Columbian Art: Essays on the Interrelationship of the Verbal and Visual Arts*, edited by Janet Catherine Berlo, pp. 119–153. Oxford, 1983. Shows how Spanish authors failed to mention the numerous Aztec priestesses depicted by their native illustrators as active participants in major religious ceremonies.

Brumfiel, Elizabeth. "Weaving and Cooking: Women's Production in Aztec Mexico." In *Engendering Archaeology: Women and Prehistory*, edited by Joan M. Gero and Margaret W. Conkey, pp. 224–251. Cambridge, Mass., 1991. Demonstrates that women's roles as weavers and preparers of food and beverages were affected by changing social and economic factors and often deviated from the ideal of the stay-at-home housewife described in Colonial sources.

Burkhart, Louise. "Mexica Women on the Home Front: Housework and Religion in Aztec Mexico." In *Indian Women of Early Mexico*, edited by Susan Schroeder, Stephanie Wood, and Robert Haskett, pp. 25–54. Norman, Okla., 1997. English translation of "Mujeres mexicas en 'el frente' del hogar: trabajo doméstico y religión en el México azteca." *Mesoamérica* 23 (1997), 23–54. Shows that among the Aztec, household work was permeated with religious meaning and regarded as highly important.

Carrasco, Pedro. "Royal Marriages in Ancient Mexico." In *Explorations in Ethnohistory*, edited by H. R. Harvey and Hanns J. Prem, pp. 41–81. Albuquerque, N.M., 1984. Discusses the ways in which a ruler's daughter's rank and lineage were often exploited through interdynastic marriage to lords and rulers of other cities with which a peaceful alliance was desired.

Freidel, David, and Linda Schele. "Maya Royal Women: A Lesson in Precolumbian History." In *Gender in Cross-cultural Perspective*, edited by Caroline B. Brettell and Carolyn F. Sargent, pp. 59–63. Englewood Cliffs, N.J., 1993. Presents evidence of Maya royal women having at times acquired positions of substantial political power.

Joyce, Rosemary A. "Women's Work: Images of Production and Reproduction in Pre-Hispanic Southern Central America." *Current Anthropology* 34 (1993), 255–266. This article is followed on pp. 266–274 by comments solicited from other scholars, as well as a "Reply" by the author; argues that women's labor is represented in a more positive light in small-scale, local artworks, such as ceramics, than it is in monumental imagery commissioned by rulers.

McCafferty, Sharisse D., and Geoffrey G. McCafferty. "Spinning and Weaving as Female Gender Identity in Post-Classic Mexico." In *Textile Traditions of Mesoamerica and the Andes: An Anthology*, edited by Margot Blum Schevill, Janet Catherine Berlo, and Edward B. Dwyer, pp. 19–44. New York, 1991. Establishes the place of spinning and weaving in the construction of Aztec women's gender identity and a female counterdiscourse to the dominant male ideology.

McCafferty, Sharisse D., and Geoffrey G. McCafferty. "Engendering Tomb 7 at Monte Albán." *Current Anthropology* 35 (1994), 143–152. This essay is followed on pp. 153–166 by comment solicited from other scholars, as well as a "Reply" by the authors; accuses previous scholars of male bias, suggesting that the bones found in an elite tomb in Oaxaca are those not of a high-ranking male priest, as was formerly assumed, but rather of an important priestess.

Molloy, John P., and William L. Rathje. "Sexploitation among the Late Classic Maya." In *Mesoamerican Archaeology: New Approaches*, edited by Norman Hammond, pp. 431–444. Austin, Tex., 1974. Surveys the evidence that, through interdynastic marriage, Maya royal women were used to cement political alliances.

Pohl, Mary DeLand. "Women, Animal Rearing, and Social Status: The Case of the Formative Period Maya of Central America." In *The Archaeology of Gender*, edited by Dale Walde and Noreen D. Willows, pp. 392–399. Calgary, 1991. Examines Maya women's role in animal husbandry during the Late Preclassic and Early Classic periods.

Sahagún, Bernardino de. *Florentine Codex: General History of the Things of New Spain*. Translated by Arthur J. O. Anderson and Charles E. Dibble. 13 vols. Santa Fe, 1952–1983. Encyclopedic sixteenth-century report on indigenous Aztec culture, including our best Colonial period information on gender roles.

Sousa, Lisa. "Women in Native Societies and Cultures of Colonial Mexico." Ph.D. diss., University of California, Los Angeles, 1998. Thorough study of archival and textual data, shedding light on the roles of and attitudes toward women in Conquest period Mexico.

Trexler, Richard C. *Sex and Conquest: Gendered Violence, Political Order, and the European Conquest of the Americas*. Ithaca, 1995. Presents a range of Spanish reports of institutionalized male same-sex relations throughout the Americas at the time of the conquest.

CECELIA F. KLEIN

Colonial Period

Colonial Mesoamerica, or New Spain, was a hierarchically organized and ethnically and racially diverse world. Gender roles—the culturally defined and socially enacted roles of women and men—cut across these forms of difference in shaping individuals' lives and experiences. This essay discusses gender and women's roles in three of the main ethno-racial groups in colonial society: indigenous, Spanish, and *casta* (mixed-race) peoples. These roles were in flux throughout the Colonial period, as the gender, class, and ethno-racial systems influenced one another.

Although differences existed in the patterns of gender roles among pre-Hispanic Mesoamerican peoples, scholars agree that complementarity marked many aspects of Mesoamerican gender organization. Some complementary features of gender organization can still be found among contemporary Nahua, Zapotec, and Maya groups. This complementarity would be severely strained during the Colonial period. The arrival of Europeans reinforced aspects of hierarchy that existed during the pre-Hispanic era and also introduced new forms. Gendered aspects of labor, political organization, and religious worship all became transformed, and forms of family life and sexuality were influenced in ways that tended to reinforce male dominance.

In most regions, urban or rural, indigenous women probably still rose each morning to perform an array of household-based tasks similar to those they would have worked at before the arrival of Europeans: grinding maize, preparing drinks such as atole, caring for small animals for household consumption or sale, picking up or sweeping up after their fellow household inhabitants. Across these domains of daily life, a certain continuity can be seen in women's labor patterns. Yet throughout Mesoamerica, indigenous women began to work harder while they lost power and authority.

There was an increase in women's extra-household labor of weaving, marketing, and personal service, work that could be performed within or outside the household, but whose primary purpose was to earn income, to fulfill state-sponsored labor demands, or both. Although forced labor, extracted through the institutions of *encomienda* (forced payments of tribute and/or labor) and *repartimiento* (rotational labor drafts), is usually portrayed as a requirement imposed on indigenous males, women also provided labor that helped fulfill such obligations. In areas like Oaxaca, where cloth flowed directly into the trib-

ute system and women remained the primary textile producers, assessments fell directly and heavily on them, and this remained so throughout the Colonial period. The Nahua, Mixtec, or Maya daughters and granddaughters of rulers and high nobles might avoid such obligations, but by the seventeenth century, enough compression in the native class structure had occurred that most indigenous women felt pressured by state demands and family needs for cloth or cash.

While noblewomen avoided the common and sometimes extreme forms of labor exploitation, the roles of economic, political, and religious authority that noble and some commoner women held during the pre-Hispanic era suffered significant decline during and after the sixteenth century. Women of the colonial indigenous nobility, often referred to as *cacicas* in Spanish, were not permitted to hold office in the Spanish governing system. They retained political influence, however, and expressed it through their roles as community elders or in lawsuits and rebellions. In the Cuernavaca region, for example, noblewomen in the sixteenth, seventeenth, and eighteenth centuries participated in legal actions to protect community resources. In the early eighteenth century, elite and common women joined rioters there protesting a hated indigenous governor and his Spanish allies.

Religion constituted an important arena of transformation for both native women and men, but some aspects of belief and symbols that were female-centered continued to exist, as did some institutionalized religious roles for women, though the latter were much reduced in authority. Transformation in the gendered aspects of religious practice was fundamentally tied to the more male-centered belief system and authority structure of the Roman Catholic Church. For example, Mexica goddesses (such as Cihuacoatl, a powerful warrior goddess, or Tlazolteotl, strongly associated with sexuality) took on increasingly negative associations, and many were forgotten over time. Marian devotion certainly spread to the Americas, but Mary is fundamentally identified as the mother of Jesus and an intercessor between individuals and a male-conceptualized God, not as powerful in her own right. Furthermore, as Mexica priestesses disappeared, native women took on subservient, church-based roles such as sweepers or guards who helped ensure that women and girls attended services. Hardly any Indian women of New Spain became nuns until the eighteenth century, when a convent for indigenous noblewomen was founded in Mexico City. Outside the realm of the church, indigenous women continued to serve as midwives, curers, and matchmakers.

The Iberian presence also had an impact on native family life and gender relations at the household level. It would be a mistake to paint an idealized picture of native family life before the arrival of Europeans: poverty, disruption of family life for reasons of war or diplomacy (through the giving of women to create or solidify kin group and/or political alliances), and violence against women certainly existed. But it would also be a mistake to discount the ways that the Conquest led to change as a result of the introduction of new diseases, demands for labor, forced resettlement of native communities, and introduction of new gender ideologies. In many areas, family size and structure, patterns of authority, and inheritance practices changed in ways that reinforced the rights of men and weakened those of women. The Catholic church actively promoted its family values, including monogamy, chastity, and marriage as a relationship between two individuals rather than between families and kin groups. If native people sometimes resisted these changes by persisting in allowing marriage brokers (often female), families, and communities to play an important role in marriage arrangements, the rhetoric tying female chastity to purity and honor did have some effect, as when indigenous men (like men of other ethno-racial groups) justified violence against their wives through the language of honor.

Although indigenous gender relations were becoming more rigidly hierarchical—perhaps because of the increasing economic burdens placed on women, as well as male absence due to labor demands—women participated in and even led acts of rebellion and resistance against colonial authorities across central and southern Mesoamerica. The impact of Spanish colonial rule generally worked to strengthen the power of husbands and fathers both within and outside households: nevertheless, indigenous women not only provided labor that enabled their families and communities to survive but also continued to exert authority and influence, even though the institutionalized means to do so had been weakened.

Spanish women, too, played a variety of roles in New Spain, even though the Spanish population brought with them a gender ideology that was more restrictive for women than those in place before their arrival. The ideal Spanish woman, according to legal codes and proscriptive writings, was devoted to her religious and familial responsibilities and was submissive and chaste in character, but in everyday life, these women were also active, vital contributors to the developing colony. Although the number of women who migrated from Spain was small in comparison to men, a few fought in the Conquests; many women of the middle and lower classes worked, and some women owned businesses and even administered estates. Prohibited by law from holding office, serving as judges or lawyers, and even from adopting children without permission, Spanish women nevertheless could inherit property and undertake lawsuits. If they chose not to marry, they could enter convents where they could receive an education and rise in the female administrative hierarchy.

One of the most famous colonial intellectuals of the seventeenth century was the creole genius Sor (Sister) Juana Inés de la Cruz, well known for the originality of her insights and the emotional depth of her writings, which address such subjects as science and reason versus emotion, and the double standard that allowed men a privileged position in colonial society. Sor Juana was exceptional even among Spanish women for her literacy and strength of character.

Casta women, whose ethno-racial background could be indigenous, Spanish, and/or African, found it as difficult as native women did to live under the patriarchal, restrictive Spanish gender ideology. They worked in a variety of settings, typically as domestic servants, street and market vendors, laundresses, or midwives. A few were artisans. Toward the end of the Colonial period, women worked in the growing number of tobacco factories, where they were paid lower wages than male workers. Because *casta* women's employment was frequently informal and temporary, their earning power generally was less than men's, but it was still vital because many were single heads of households, widowed, separated, or never married.

Casta and native women also played a major role in the development of the colonial social hierarchy, with its complex class and ethno-racial structure, through their formal and informal—often coerced—liaisons with Spanish men. Such couplings began as early as the relationship between Fernando Cortés and his Nahua translator, Malintzin. Spanish women, too, played a role in the development of cultural diversity. In the Late Colonial period, in Mexico City and other large cities of New Spain, Spanish women began to marry or form relationships with men of other ethno-racial and class groups. Thus, women of all identities and strata contested the boundaries of gender, class, and ethnicity; and along with men, they participated in the productive and reproductive activities that created a vital, turbulent, diverse colonial world.

BIBLIOGRAPHY

Arrom, Silvia Marina. *The Women of Mexico City, 1790–1857.* Stanford, 1985. Comprehensive women's history treating the late Colonial and early national periods.

Gallagher, Ann Miriam. "The Indian Nuns of Mexico City's *Monasterio* of Corpus Christi, 1724–1821." In *Latin American Women: Historical Perspectives*, edited by Asunción Lavrin, pp. 150–172. Westport, Conn., 1978. Provides a history of indigenous women's relationship with the Catholic church, focusing especially on their institutional roles.

Gonzalbo Aizpuro, Pilar. *Familia y orden colonial.* Mexico City, 1998. Illustrates how family and gender interacted with colonial ethno-racial and class hierarchies in the neighborhoods of colonial Mexico City.

Haskett, Robert. "Activist or Adulteress? The Life and Struggle of Doña Josefa María of Tepoztlan." In *Indian Women of Early Mexico*, edited by Susan Schroeder, Stephanie Wood, and Robert Haskett, pp. 145–163, Norman, Okla., 1997. Important study of indigenous women's political roles in and around Colonial Cuernavaca.

Maura, Juan Francisco. *Women in the Conquest of the Americas*. Translated by John F. Deredita. New York, 1997. Overview of Spanish women's experiences and lives during the Conquest and early Colonial periods.

Muriel, Josefina. *Cultura femenina novohispana*. Mexico City, 1982. Important study of women writers, artists, and intellectuals of the colonial period.

Schroeder, Susan, Stephanie Wood, and Robert Haskett, eds. *Indian Women of Early Mexico*. Norman, Okla., 1997. Path-breaking collection detailing the activities, achievements, and social positions of indigenous women across a range of colonial Mesoamerican cultures.

Stern, Steve J. *The Secret History of Gender: Women, Men, and Power in Late Colonial Mexico*. Chapel Hill, N.C., 1995. Insightful study of indigenous women's lives, gender relations, and political culture in colonial Morelos, Oaxaca, and Mexico City.

Tuñón Pablos, Julia. *Women in Mexico: A Past Unveiled*. Translated by Alan Hynds. Austin, 1987. Comprehensive overview of Mexican women's history, first published in Mexico in 1987 as *Mujeres en México: Una historia olvidada*.

SUSAN M. KELLOGG

Contemporary Cultures

Contemporary gender roles in Mesoamerica reflect both dramatic changes as well as strong continuities. Perhaps the most far-reaching change has been the overdue recognition of women as pivotal actors in their societies who are creating new spaces for autonomy. This recognition has revealed the particular forms of subordination under which women labor and their reluctance to appeal to universal notions of gender oppression. The words of an indigenous woman supporter of the the Zapatista Army of National Liberation in highland Chiapas, Mexico, suggest this reluctance: "It doesn't matter to me if my husband walks in front of me on the trail wearing shoes. He needs boots to work in the cornfield, while I work at home. What matters to me is that my husband works hard and respects me." Mesoamerican women and men continually reflect upon and change their gender roles from local knowledge bases.

Influences on gender roles in contemporary times range from economic to ideological. This essay addresses a variety of influences, drawing attention to the day-to-day impact of economic change, specifically on women's strategies to obtain resources to raise their children.

Economic changes have heavily influenced gender roles in the institution of marriage. Although marriage has various expressions throughout the region, a strong tendency has persisted since the Colonial period for a woman to assume the role of wife to obtain a man's resources to raise her children, as well as conform to the community ideals for a woman and mother. The dual complex of *marianismo* (devotion to the Virgin Mary) and *machismo* values women who are saintly, passive, and all-suffering, and men who are virile risk-takers, and this provides a sacred rationale for women's dependence on and subordination to men. In many areas, this ideology has promoted the concept of marriage as a form of women's work. This attitude, combined with women's faith in romantic love and the economic necessity of supporting their children, conflicts with the physical abuse, abandonment, and infidelity that many women experience.

Increasingly in the contemporary era, men and women have had to adapt to new and sometimes hostile economic forces—for example, structural adjustment policies, national debt payments, and scarcity of land. Both men and women have had to migrate in search of work, with the result that women have become more important as cash providers, a pattern that exists to varying degrees throughout Mesoamerica. In recent years, women and men have created numerous strategies to cope with economic changes. In some cases, women combine various strategies that allow them to maintain respect and connection to traditions they value, including marriage.

Women throughout Mesoamerica have expanded dramatically into the informal economy, especially as producers of handicrafts. An increasing number of women work as craft producers, either independently or in artisan cooperatives. Many women seek opportunities to work as artisans that allow them to stay at home, speak indigenous languages, and remain available to their children and families (Nash, 1999). Recently, women in areas such as highland Chiapas, Mexico, have sought increased autonomy by forming smaller collective associations, with assistance from nongovernmental organizations, through which they have been able to rework their culturally specific ideas about gender roles within contexts of cooperation and solidarity. Thus, as Tice describes (1995), Kuna women in Panama work in cooperatives to manufacture embroidered *mola* blouses for sale to the tourist market, a strategy that allows them to remain at home yet contribute economically to their families. At the same time, cooperatives may introduce disruption: Oaxaca, Mexico, where some Zapotec women interviewed by Stephen (1991) were able to use outside connections and skills to protect higher status and income.

Rural Mesoamerican men have long migrated to work, and women have increasingly sought work both in nearby cities and in the factories of northern Mexico (Tiano, 1994). These strategies sometimes provide women with a greater cash income than they might otherwise earn in

Young woman making tortillas on clay *comal. Photograph courtesy of Michael Hale.*

their own communities, but they are often caught up in a cycle of dependency on employers that leaves them with few alternatives.

Women's increased economic autonomy as providers of cash for their households has influenced many women not to marry. Throughout Mesoamerica, both young men and young women are resisting communal controls over their reproduction and production, such as arranged marriages and being restricted from furthering their education or working outside of their homes or communities. Young women's experiences with drunken or abusive kinsmen may also influence them not to marry.

Women are also transforming gender roles through the consciousness-raising and leadership training they gain in religious and revolutionary movements. Beginning in the 1960s, many poor men and women began to critique the unfair burden women bear in their households and communities in workshops led by pastoral workers in the "preferential option for the poor," a social justice orientation within the Roman Catholic church. Although this movement has empowered many poor men and women, the movement has not created a very wide opening for redressing gender inequality. Protestant churches have garnered a large following throughout Mesoamerica. Protestant missionaries have ameliorated some aspects of *machismo* by providing women social, spiritual, and material support and by encouraging men to stop drinking

and act more humbly and respectfully. Some Protestant churches maintain traditional degrees of gender inequality, while others promote egalitarian gender norms.

Throughout Mesoamerica, political military conflicts have altered gender roles in complex ways. Thousands of people have become internally displaced as refugees or have had to flee into exile. Many households are now headed by women. In these contexts of turmoil and dislocation, women and men have transformed gender roles in their search for strategies to survive (Green, 1999).

Some women have joined armed groups, or support bases for these groups, in hope of obtaining greater autonomy and rights. From the 1970s through the late 1990s, women participated as combatants in liberation struggles in Guatemala, El Salvador, Nicaragua, and Chiapas, Mexico. Despite their rhetoric, none of these revolutionary groups has addressed gender inequality on a par with other inequalities they would reform. Spurred on by the contradiction between rhetoric and practice in the Zapatista movement in Chiapas, women of diverse ethnic and class backgrounds are developing new frameworks to incorporate gender into the broader society's analyses of oppression.

Women throughout Mesoamerica have been the victims of violent retribution as a result of their involvement in cooperatives and religious, feminist, and revolutionary movements, and because of their efforts to break away

A Tepehuán man hauling roof grass. *Photograph courtesy of Michael Hale.*

from household and community controls. Rosalva Aída Hernández Castillo and others (1999) describe this experience for women in Chiapas. Women have become politicized through this suffering, as well as through the loss of loved ones during wars and through their growing awareness of the injustices of marginalization. These experiences have compelled women to create women's organizations which assist them in a variety of ways as Stephen (1997) describes for women in Mexico and El Salvador. Although organizing has been helpful to women in gaining rights within the larger society, it has been less successful in helping them obtain greater autonomy within their households, where they struggle for the right to pursue education, to choose whether to marry, and to be free of physical or emotional abuse. Nevertheless, individually and in their groups, Mesoamerican women are challenging the status quo in ways that transform not only gender roles but also society as a whole.

BIBLIOGRAPHY

Beneria, Lourdes, and Martha Roldán. *The Crossroads of Class and Gender: Industrial Homework, Subcontracting and Household Dynamics in Mexico City.* Chicago, 1987. Detailed view of how class and gender interact to marginalize women labor migrants to urban centers.

Eber, Christine. *Women and Alcohol in a Highland Maya Town: Water of Hope, Water of Sorrow.* Austin, Tex., 1995. Detailed ethnographic analysis of alcohol use and abuse in San Pedro Chenalhó, Chiapas, from indigenous women's viewpoints.

Ehlers, Tracy Bachrach. *Silent Looms: Women and Production in a Guatemalan Town.* Boulder, Colo., 1990. Ethnographically rich discussion of women's changing work patterns in San Pedro Sacatepequez.

Green, Linda. *Fear as a Way of Life: Mayan Widows in Rural Guatemala.* New York, 1999.

Hernández Castillo, Rosalva Aida, et al. *The Other Word: Violence and Women, before and after Acteal.* Waterford, 1999. Account from Chiapas.

Menchú, Rigoberta. *I, Rigoberta Menchú: An Indian Woman in Guatemala.* Edited by Elisabeth Burgos-Debray. London, 1983. The most famous Mesoamerican woman social activist recounts her life story.

Nash, June, ed. *Crafts in the World Market: The Impact of Global Exchange on Middle American Artisans.* Albany, 1999. Collection of articles by anthropologists of the production and marketing of crafts in Mesoamerica.

Randall, Margaret. *Our Voices, Our Lives: Stories of Women from Central America and the Caribbean.* Monroe, Me., 1995. Essays and conversations exploring women's views of feminism, socialism, patriarchy, and other factors shaping gender systems.

Rosenbaum, Brenda P. *With Our Heads Bowed: The Dynamics of Gender in a Maya Community.* Albany, 1993. Ethnography exploring gender ideologies and roles.

Rosenbaum, Brenda P. "Women and Gender in Mesoamerica." In *The Legacy of Mesoamerica*, edited by Robert Carmack et al., pp. 321–352. Albany, 1996. Survey of Mesoamerican gender systems from pre-Hispanic times to the present, with excellent overview of current issues in studies of women and gender in the region.

Rovira, Guiomar. *Mujeres de maíz: La voz de las indígenas de Chiapas y la rebelión Zapatista.* Barcelona, 1996. Diverse experiences and perspectives of indigenous women in Chiapas, from roles in the Zapatista movement to struggles for control of their own lives in household and community.

Rus, Diane. *Mujeres de Tierra Fría.* Chiapas, 1997. Women of San Cristóbal de las Casas describe their lives, focusing on the need to work hard to provide for themselves and their children.

Stephen, Lynn. *Zapotec Women.* Austin, 1991. Women's lives in Oaxaca, Mexico.

Stephen, Lynn. *Women and Social Movements in Latin America.* Austin, 1997. Analysis of women's activism in Mexico and El Salvador.

Tiano, Susan. *Patriarchy on the Line: Labor, Gender, and Ideology in the Mexican Maquila Industry.* Philadelphia, 1994. Women's issues related to the factories serving U.S. industry in northern Mexico.

Tice, Karin. *Kuna Crafts, Gender and the Global Economy.* Austin, Tex., 1995. Ethnographic analysis of Kuna women's craft production in Panama.

CHRISTINE E. EBER
and ROBIN O'BRIAN

GENDER STUDIES. Scholarly studies of gender in Mesoamerica did not appear in force until the 1970s, shortly after anthropologists had begun to investigate the ways in which gender has been defined and categorized in other cultures. Like others working in this new field, Mesoamericanists tended from the beginning to focus on women. Their preoccupation with the Maya and Aztec, as opposed to other Mesoamericans, was likewise prophetic of the future direction of the field. The seeds of these early concerns, however, had been sown in the preceding decades. In 1939, a pioneering article on Mesoamerican moon goddesses by the British Mayanist J. Eric S. Thompson initiated a long line of scholarly studies of the role of females in Mesoamerican cosmology and myth. Similarly, the Mexican art historian Justino Fernández's formalist analysis (1954) of the famous stone statue of the Aztec goddess Coatlicue preceded a large number of detailed iconographic examinations of female images. Finally, in a series of articles published in the early 1960s, the North American architectural illustrator Tatiana Proskouriakoff (e.g., 1961) showed, through decipherment of several Classic Maya glyphs that accompany figures previously identified as men, that these figures are actually portraits of royal Maya wives and mothers. The decades preceding the 1970s also saw the first serious ethnohistorical studies of Mesoamerican family structure and Anita Hellbom's (1967) lengthy study of the lives and roles of pre-Hispanic and post-revolutionary women in Mexico.

These early efforts, together with new questions posed by rising feminist voices and several major archaeological discoveries, inspired a growing number of Mesoamerican gender studies during the 1970s. Discovery in 1978 of a large carved stone disk depicting a naked, beheaded, and dismembered woman prompted several formalist and iconographic studies that recall Fernández's work on Coatlicue. Found at the foot of the Aztecs' main temple, the relief portrays a woman quickly identified as Coyolxauhqui (Bell-Cheeks), who in an Aztec migration myth is beheaded by her brother Huitzilopochtli, the state's patron god, for attempting to challenge his leadership. The image raised important questions about sexual mores regarding female nudity, the level of political and military participation by women, and the political meanings and functions of state-commissioned depictions of women. These questions have continued to be addressed to the present time.

Most other studies of the social roles and standing of women that were done in the 1970s likewise focused on Aztec women. Several key essays by Eleanor Leacock and June Nash culminated with an article by Nash (1980), who argued that Aztec women had steadily lost power and status during the process of state formation. Interest in the social status and roles of women also continued among Mayanists, who began to build on Proskouriakoff's discovery that some Classic Maya women had played politically powerful roles. Studies published in the 1970s by John Molloy and William Rathje (1974) and by Joyce Marcus (1976) showed that Classic Maya women of royal blood married rulers of secondary centers to form political alliances.

In addition to the works that grew out of earlier explorations, two new areas of interest opened up in Mesoamerican gender studies during the 1970s. The first focused on issues of sexual behavior and mores. In 1974, Noemi Quezada issued her first exploration into Aztec female sexuality and eroticism. Similarly, studies of sexual deviance and the ways that pre-Hispanic peoples viewed it made their first appearance in the 1970s. A major synthesis of aberrant pre-Columbian sexual practices, including the first serious look at reports of what the Spaniards called "sodomy" at the time of the Conquest, appeared in 1971 in a book by the physician Francisco Guerra. Ethnographic studies that extensively chart modern sexual behavior and attitudes toward sexual norms, including deviance, also first appeared in the 1970s. Probably the most influential has been Victoria Bricker's *Ritual Humor in Highland Chiapas* (Austin, 1973), which includes descriptions and analyses of a number of Highland Maya rites that reinforce sexual values through ceremonial transvestism and burlesqued sexual acts.

In the same period, scholars began producing intensive analyses of present-day indigenous women's social and cultural roles. These studies often expand on and highlight issues touched by earlier ethnographic studies that explored the lives and worldviews of particular ethnic or linguistic Maya groups. In 1973, Beverly Chiñas published a book that dealt with the roles of Zapotec women living in the Isthmus, initiating a trend toward ethnographies focused exclusively on the lives and roles of women today. Such studies continued to be produced throughout the 1980s and 1990s. Most have focused on Maya women, but several recent studies have concentrated on the Zapotecs, and Stacy Schaefer's 1990 dissertation analyzes the lengthy and arduous process by which a Huichol woman in Nayarit becomes recognized as a proficient weaver.

Academic art historians did not seriously enter the field of Mesoamerican gender studies until Magali Carrera (1990) deposited a dissertation at Columbia University on sculptural representations of Aztec women. An important 1983 article pointing out the unreliability of Colonial sources in documenting Aztec women's roles and status was written by the art historian Betty Ann Brown. Brown observed that, whereas the post-Conquest illustrations of Aztec ceremonies painted by Indian artists in manuscripts written by the Franciscan Bernardino de Sahagún depict numerous women participants, Sahagún's text usually mentions only men. To date, the only major work to take up gender in pre-Hispanic lower Central America is Mark Miller Graham's 1985 art history dissertation on the stone sculpture of Costa Rica, which examines the gender symbolism of domestic and agricultural implements.

It was not until 1985 that anthropologists and art historians came together to share their work on gender in Mesoamerica. The proceedings of an interdisciplinary symposium on "The Role of Gender in Pre-Columbian America," held that year at the International Congress of Americanists meeting in Bogotá, Colombia, were published three years later by Virginia Miller (1988). Art historians have since made a number of important contributions to the effort to identify women in the visual record where previously none had been seen. In addition, they have maintained the earlier scholarly interest in the sexuality of pre-Hispanic Mesoamericans. Andrea Stone's analysis in the Miller volume of images of the relation of Maya sexuality to sacrifice was followed by analyses of Classic Maya men dressed in women's clothing and of what Stone and others have perceived as male same-sex intercourse depicted on the cave walls at Naj Tunich, Guatemala.

Fascination with mounting evidence that ancient Mesoamericans perceived gender differently from the modern West led to a number of works after 1970 on androgyny in pre-Hispanic Mesoamerican mythology, in addition to studies of male same-sex behavior that expand on Guerra's work. Alfredo López Austin authored a comprehensive ethnohistorical study of Aztec concepts of the human body, including homosexuality, that first appeared in Mexico in 1980. In 1995, Richard Trexler published a book on Spanish reports of indigenous institutionalized male same-sex relations at the time of the Conquest. A year later, Cecelia Klein presented an essay on the ceremonial roles and meanings of persons of ambiguous gender. During the 1990s, studies of homosexuality among Mexican men today also began to appear. The first serious look at the determinants and concepts of masculinity in a Mesoamerican culture was James Taggart's 1983 study of present-day Nahuatl mythology. Taggart exemplifies the growing number of students of Latin American folklore and popular literature who are contributing to our understanding of notions and representations of gender.

During the 1980s, gender studies took a variety of new directions which were pursued into the 1990s. As Taggart's work had shown, "woman" often serves as a rhetorical device, or sign, in Mesoamerican narrative. This point was reinforced by Susan Gillespie (1989) when she showed how royal women predictably appear in Aztec official mythohistories at moments of rupture and transition, which they thus mark. A 1994 article by Cecelia Klein showed specifically that the motif of the "conquered woman" served as an Aztec metaphor for opposition to state authority. Klein went on to further explore pre-Hispanic Aztec gender symbolism, at the same time that ethnographers such as Jacques Galinier (1990) and Nathaniel Tarn (1984) were beginning to do the same for the modern Otomí and Maya.

Studies of Mesoamerican women's roles and status took a new turn in the 1980s as feminists began to question women's acceptance of male definitions of power. The old assumptions that Mesoamerican women were confined to their homes and children, and that domesticity automatically bestows low levels of status and economic power on women, were now challenged. Not only were there a number of studies focused on specific female roles, such as those of "wife" and "priestess," but the previously low estimation of the value of Mesoamerican women's household labor and products was revised. Mary Pohl and Lawrence Feldman (1982) initiated these efforts in relation to the Maya, to be followed in 1992 by Rosemary Joyce's initial study of Maya visual images of women and men at work. For the Aztec, Elizabeth Brumfiel (1991) examined the archaeological evidence regarding the importance of women's weaving and cooking to the economy, while Louise Burkhart (1997) showed how Aztec women's housework had important social and religious connotations. Some of the most telling arguments in favor of a high status for pre-Hispanic women were co-authored by Sharisse and Geoffrey McCafferty (e.g., 1988), who not only see Aztec women as powerful in the home but have also identified what they see as depictions of high-ranking women at the Classic period Mexican sites of Cacaxtla and Monte Albán.

During the 1980s and 1990s, Mesoamerican gender analyses also shifted our attention to the Colonial period. Sometimes these studies take the form of criticism of colonial representations of women. In 1988, Margaret Arvey published an art historical critique of Sahagún's representation of Aztec "women of ill repute," showing that Sahagún's native artists, in using European illustrations of wanton women as pictorial models, misrepresented the physical appearance, reputation, and status of these women. Similarly, Cecelia Klein (1995) revealed the distorting influence of European notions of Wild Woman on Colonial period artistic and mythological representations of Aztec goddesses.

Other Mesoamericanists turned to the law. In 1984, Susan Kellogg began to study colonial wills and testaments in order to determine what legal rights Aztec women had during the Early Colonial period. Susan Schroeder's work has focused on the economic status and political roles of Aztec noblewomen living in Chalco. Mexican scholars such as Asunción Lavrin and Sylvia Marcos, as well as the French scholar Serge Gruzinski, have extended the earlier interest in sexuality, eroticism, and marriage to the Early Colonial era, while other authors have focused on the nexus among native women, "witchcraft," and the Inquisition. Some studies examine women's roles during the Conquest, in particular those of Cortés's native translator, La Malinche, and the effects of the Conquest on women in Yucatán and Central Mexico. Others have reconstructed the history of the cult and image of Colonial Mexico's best-known religious icon, the Virgin of Guadalupe. As our information and understanding have grown, broad syntheses of Mesoamerican gender have begun to appear. Lisa Sousa's 1998 dissertation examines women in native societies throughout Colonial Mexico, with emphasis on the Mixtec as well as the Aztec. Steve Stern's *The Secret History of Gender* (1995) extends Mexican gender studies into the Late Colonial period. Finally, a historiographic overview of the literature on Mesoamerican women living today, with a discussion of recent trends, has been published by Brenda Rosenbaum and Christine Eber (1992).

The 1980s and 1990s have also seen more incorporation of theory into discussions of Mesoamerican gender. As early as the late 1970s, isolated studies revealed the authors' interest in psychoanalytical and structural paradigms. By far the most influential theoretical models, however, have been Marxism and feminism. María Rodríguez-Shadow's 1988 portrayal of pre-Conquest Aztec women as largely oppressed follows the Marxist tenets first laid out by Eleanor Leacock and June Nash. Feminist thinking, on the other hand, is particularly evident in the writings of scholars working on Mesoamerican women today, who hope that their work will ultimately serve to improve these women's lives. It can also be seen in the work of the pre-Hispanicists Sharisse and Geoffrey McCafferty, as well as that of Elizabeth Brumfiel. All three have been influenced by the feminist archaeologist Margaret Conkey, who has written extensively on the importance of gender studies to archaeology. The work of gender theorist Judith Butler is central to Rosemary Joyce's (1998) recent work on Maya performance of the body, initially presented at the 1996 Dumbarton Oaks Pre-Columbian Studies conference titled "Recovering Gender in Pre-Columbian America." That conference, at which Conkey served as commentator, was the first interdisciplinary gathering of specialists working on gender in pre-Columbian America since the 1985 conference in Bogotá; it was also the first time that pre-Columbian gender studies has been formally recognized by a mainstream institution as an important area of study in its own right.

BIBLIOGRAPHY

Arvey, Margaret Campbell. "Women of Ill-repute in the Florentine Codex." In *The Role of Gender in Pre-Columbian Art and Architecture*, edited by Virginia E. Miller, pp. 179–204. Lanham, Md., 1988.

Brown, Betty Ann. "Seen but Not Heard: Women in Aztec Ritual—the Sahagún Texts." In *Text and Image in Pre-Columbian Art: Essays on the Interrelationship of the Verbal and Visual Arts*, edited by Janet Catherine Berlo, pp. 119–153. Oxford, 1983.

Brumfiel, Elizabeth. "Weaving and Cooking: Women's Production in Aztec Mexico." In *Engendering Archaeology: Women and Prehistory*, edited by Joan M. Gero and Margaret W. Conkey, pp. 224–251. Cambridge, Mass., 1991.

Burkhart, Louise. "Mexica Women on the Home Front: Housework and Religion in Aztec Mexico." In *Indian Women of Early Mexico*, edited by Susan Schroeder et al., pp. 25–54. Norman, Okla., 1997. English translation of "Mujeres mexicas en 'el frente' del hogar: Trabajo doméstico y religión en el México azteca." *Mesoamérica* 23 (1997), 23–54.

Carrera, Magali. "The Representation of Women in Aztec-Mexica Sculpture." Ph.D. diss., Columbia University, 1990.

Chiñas, Beverly L. *The Isthmus Zapotec: Women's Roles in Cultural Context*. New York, 1973.

Fernández, Justino. "Coatlicue: Estética del arte antiguo." In *Ediciones del IV Centenario de la Universidad Nacional*, vol. 15. Mexico City, 1954.

Galinier, Jacques. *La mitad del mundo: Cuerpo y cosmos en los rituales otomíes*. Translated by Angela Ochoa and Haydée Silva. Mexico City, 1990.

Gillespie, Susan D. *The Aztec Kings: The Construction of Rulership in Mexica History*. Tucson, Ariz., 1989.

Graham, Mark Miller. "The Stone Sculpture of Costa Rica: The Production of Ideologies of Dominance in Prehistoric Rank Societies." Ph.D. diss., University of California, Los Angeles, 1985.

Guerra, Francisco. *The Pre-Columbian Mind*. New York, 1971.

Hellbom, Anita. *Indias y mestizas en el México precortesiano y postrevolucionario*, Stockholm, 1967.

Joyce, Rosemary. "Images of Gender and Labor Organization in Classic Maya Society." In *Exploring Gender through Archaeology*, edited by Constance Claasen, pp. 63–70. Madison, Wis., 1992.

Joyce, Rosemary A. "Performing the Body in Pre-Hispanic Central America." *Res: Anthropology and Aesthetics* 33 (1998), 147–165.

Kellogg, Susan. "Aztec Women in Early Colonial Courts: Structure and Strategy in a Legal Context." In *Five Centuries of Law and Politics in Central Mexico*, edited by Ronald Spores and Ross Hassig, pp. 25–38. Nashville, Tenn., 1984.

Klein, Cecelia F. "Fighting with Femininity: Gender and War in Aztec Mexico." In *Gender Rhetorics: Postures of Dominance and Submission in Human History*, edited by Richard C. Trexler, pp. 107–146. Binghamton, N.Y., 1994.

Klein, Cecelia F. "Wild Woman in Colonial Mexico: An Encounter of European and Aztec Concepts of the Other." In *Reframing the Renaissance: Visual Culture in Europe and Latin America, 1450–1650*, edited by Claire Farago, pp. 245–263. New Haven, 1995.

Klein, Cecelia F. "None of the Above: Gender Ambiguity in Nahua Ideologies." In *Gender in Pre-Columbian America*, edited by Cecelia F. Klein. Washington, D.C., forthcoming.

López Austin, Alfredo. *The Human Body and Ideology: Concepts of the Ancient Nahuas*. Translated by Thelma Ortiz de Montellano and Bernard Ortiz de Montellano. 2 vols. Salt Lake City, 1988. English translation of *Cuerpo humano e ideología*. Mexico City, 1980.

Marcus, Joyce. *Emblem and State in the Classic Maya Lowlands: An Epigraphic Approach to Territorial Organization.* Washington, D.C., 1976.

McCafferty, Sharisse D., and Geoffrey G. McCafferty. "Powerful Women and the Myth of Male Dominance in Aztec Society." *Archaeological Review from Cambridge* 7 (1988), 45–59.

Miller, Virginia E., ed. *The Role of Gender in Pre-Columbian Art and Architecture.* Lanham, Md., 1988.

Molloy, John P., and William L. Rathje. "Sexploitation among the Late Classic Maya." In *Mesoamerican Archaeology: New Approaches,* edited by Norman Hammond, pp. 431–444. Austin, Tex., 1974.

Nash, June. "Aztec Women: The Transition from Status to Class in Empire and Colony." In *Women and Colonization: Anthropological Perspectives,* edited by Mona Etienne and Eleanor Leacock, pp. 143–148. New York, 1980.

Pohl, Mary, and Lawrence H. Feldman. "The Traditional Role of Women and Animals in Lowland Maya Economy." In *Maya Subsistence: Studies in Memory of Dennie E. Puleston,* edited by Kent V. Flannery, pp. 295–311. New York, 1982.

Proskouriakoff, Tatiana. "Portraits of Women in Maya Art." In *Essays in Pre-Columbian Art and Archaeology,* edited by S. K. Kothrop, pp. 81–99. Cambridge, Mass., 1961.

Quezada, Noemi. "Erotismo en la religión azteca." *Revista de la Universidad de México* 28 (1974), .

Rodríguez Valdés, María J. *La mujer azteca.* Toluca, 1988.

Rosenbaum, Brenda, and Christine Eber. "Trayendo el margen al centro: mujer y género en Mesoamérica." *Mesoamérica* 23 (1992), 15–25.

Schaefer, Stacy B. "Becoming a Weaver: The Woman's Path in Huichol Culture." Ph.D. diss., University of California, Los Angeles, 1990.

Sousa, Lisa M. "Women in Native Societies and Cultures of Colonial Mexico." Ph.D. diss., University of California, Los Angeles, 1998.

Stern, Steve J. *The Secret History of Gender: Women, Men and Power in Late Colonial Mexico.* Chapel Hill, N.C., 1995.

Stone, Andrea. "Sacrifice and Sexuality: Some Structural Relationships in Classic Maya Art." In *The Role of Gender in Precolumbian Art and Architecture,* edited by Virginia E. Miller, pp. 75–103. Lanham, Md., 1988.

Taggart, James M. *Nahuatl Myth and Social Structure.* Austin, Tex., 1983.

Tarn, Nathaniel. "'Eating the Fruit': Sexual Metaphor and Initiation in Santiago Atitlan." In *Investigacions recientes en el área maya: XVII Mesa Redonda, 21–27 junio 1981,* pp. 401–408. San Cristóbal de las Casas, 1984.

Thompson, J. Eric S. "The Moon Goddess in Middle America." In *Contributions to American Archaeology,* pp. 122–173. Carnegie Institution of Washington Publication 5. Washington, D.C., 1939.

Trexler, Richard C. *Sex and Conquest: Gendered Violence, Political Order, and the European Conquest of the Americas.* Ithaca, 1995.

CECELIA F. KLEIN

GENEALOGICAL MANUSCRIPTS. Although ancestry was clearly a preoccupation of pre-Columbian cultures throughout Mesoamerica, the earliest extant pictorial manuscripts containing dynastic and genealogical information come from the Mixtec area located in the present state of Oaxaca. The Mixtec genealogical manuscripts include the codices *Zouche-Nuttall, Colombino-Becker, Bodley, Seldon,* and *Vindobonensis* (*Codex Vi-*enna), screenfolds painted on long panels of prepared animal hide. The earliest, the *Codex Zouche-Nuttall,* dates from perhaps the fourteenth century, while the latest were completed shortly after the Spanish invasion in the sixteenth century.

These manuscripts are stylistically and thematically consistent. Flat figures painted across the surfaces focus on the life and deeds of rulers and the founding of important royal houses. The manuscripts recount the travels of culture heroes and list dozens of historical locations. Important marriages and births are often displayed, and it is within this context that genealogical information is relayed. Married couples face each other, and births are shown in a variety of ways: individuals may be born from the earth or from a tree; in one instance, an actual birth is shown, with an umbilical cord connecting mother and child.

Historical and genealogical information contained in Mixtec codices was shared with the local inhabitants in ritualized public readings. The sequence of pictured events and actors acted as visual prompts for the orator, who recounted the history and lineage of the great ancestors. Public performance and the material existence of the codices functioned together to promote the genealogical legitimacy of Mixtec rulership and past territorial expansion. At the same time, social contracts made through marriage with other ruling houses were celebrated.

After the Conquest, indigenous genealogies were modified to take into consideration a new European audience. While genealogies still served as historic records for the immediate family and the community, they were also directed toward the Spanish colonial government. In that context, they functioned as legal evidence of ownership in disputes over land titles. In addition, the documents supported claims of ancient royal ancestry and could be used, along with other evidence, in indigenous bids for colonial *hidalgo* (noble) status.

European contact also brought changes in the materials and style of the genealogies, as well as new motifs. Pre-Contact artists had painted primarily on *amate* paper or deerskin; in the sixteenth century, however, most genealogies were produced on imported European paper. Indigenous artists also adopted European stylistic conventions, including contoured rendering of figures and draperies and aspects of aerial and linear perspective. Whole motifs derived from European sources were sometimes modified and used by indigenous artists in order to bridge the conceptual abyss between the two cultures. Examples of this can be found in the *Xiu Family Tree,* from the Maya area, and in the Tarascan genealogy included in the *Crónica de Michoacán,* where the indigenous artists used a modified European Tree of Jesse as a template to show familial relationships. The indigenous progenitors in both images replace Jesse at the base of their family trees.

Most post-Conquest genealogies from Central Mexico are fairly standardized in organization and appearance. Presented in single-page format, family members are organized in double or single columns according to status and order of birth or succession to office. In the Tlaxcalan *Genealogía de Zolin*, for example, the progenitor of the line is visually privileged by his position at the top of the page and is seated inside a house. A simple line indicates familial relationships. In other examples, this line may consist of broken segments, or a rope, a pan-Mesoamerican metaphor for an umbilical cord, may be substituted for the solid line. As in earlier Mixtec manuscripts, in the *Genealogía de Zolin* the married couple face each other. Although figures are shown in profile and in full-figure form, in other genealogies they may be indicated by a head alone. Family members are identified by means of name glyphs attached to the figures.

Genealogical lists appear in many kinds of Colonial-period documents. Although most genealogies were produced as proof of individual legitimacy in regard to traditional landholding and status, many also appear in cartographic-historical manuscripts which focus on a town or group of towns and the physical boundaries of a territory or region held by a group. Visual references to the historical acquisition of that land, with accompanying battles, may also be depicted. Though secondary to the main focus of these manuscripts, genealogical lists are frequently incorporated. The simultaneous appearance of people and places in these documents recalls pre-Columbian traditions in which the fusion of genealogical information and land is essential to the formation and reinforcement of corporate identity.

Perhaps the best-known group of cartographic-historical manuscripts are the *lienzos*. These large-format documents functioned as village charters and often recorded intermarriage between corporate groups. They were meant to be shown publicly during special occasions and were often used as proof of familial or communal ownership of land. In them, the founding lineages are generally depicted next to the relevant township, which is shown in the central part of the visual field. Secondary lineages, if included, tend to be farther from the central field.

Indigenous genealogies were produced throughout the Colonial period, but toward the end of the seventeenth century, the tradition essentially ceased. This resulted from a number of factors. By the end of the Colonial period, some members of the prestigious native ruling houses in Central Mexico had married into the Spanish nobility. Lesser indigenous nobility lost their landholdings over time, so the production of genealogies became less necessary on a practical level. Finally, with the spread of Christianity, genealogies and the ancient power structures they represented were felt by many indigenous people to be antithetical to successful conversion.

[*See also* Bodley, Codex; Colombino-Becker, Codex; Lienzos; Mixtec Group of Pictorial Manuscripts; Selden, Codex; Selden Roll; Vienna, Codex; Zouche-Nuttall, Codex.]

BIBLIOGRAPHY

Boone, Elizabeth Hill. "Prominent Scenes and Pivotal Events in the Mexican Pictorial Histories." In *Códices y documentos sobre México, segundo simposio*, edited by Salvador Rueda Smithers et al., vol. 1, pp. 407–424. Mexico City, 1997. Overview of important events appearing in manuscripts from various Mesoamerican cultures.

Galarza, Joaquín. *Códices y pinturas tradicionales indígenas en el Archivo General de la Nación: Estudio y catálogo*. Mexico City, 1996. Overview of pictorial manuscripts of one of the most important collections in the world; includes hundreds of small black-and-white photographs organized by document type.

Glass, John B. *Catálogo de la colección de códices*. Mexico City, 1964. Classic study of Mexican codices, with brief descriptions and citations of early studies of individual manuscripts.

Glass, John B. "A Survey of Native Middle American Pictorial Manuscripts." In *Handbook of Middle American Indians: Guide to Ethnohistorical Sources, Part Three*, edited by H. F. Cline et al., pp. 3–81. Austin, Tex., 1975. Broad introduction to illustrated manuscripts from various sources.

King, Mark B. "Hearing the Echoes of Verbal Art in Mixtec Writing." In *Writing without Words: Alternative Literacies in Mesoamerica and the Andes*, edited by Elizabeth Hill Boone and Walter D. Mignolo, pp. 102–136. Durham, N.C., 1996. Explores the presence of orality and the performative aspect of Mixtec codices.

Leibsohn, Dana. "Primers for Memory: Cartographic Histories and Nahua Identity." In *Writing without Words: Alternative Literacies in Mesoamerica and the Andes*, edited by Elizabeth Hill Boone and Walter D. Mignolo, pp. 161–187. Durham, N.C., 1996. Study of the linkage between geographic spatial constructions and community as they pertain to Central Mexican indigenous identity.

Monaghan, John. "The Text in the Body, the Body in the Text: The Embodied Sign in Mixtec Writing." In *Writing without Words: Alternative Literacies in Mesoamerica and the Andes*, edited by Elizabeth Hill Boone and Walter D. Mignolo, pp. 87–101. Durham, N.C., 1996. Explores the relationship between body, dance, and text in Mixtec codices.

Pohl, John M. D. *The Politics of Symbolism in the Mixtec Codices*. Nashville, Tenn., 1994. Study relating codices to political and ritual practice and Mixtec social organization.

Robertson, Donald. *Mexican Manuscript Painting of the Early Colonial Period: The Metropolitan Schools*. New Haven, 1959; repr., Norman, Okla., 1994. Classic art historical study of styles and evolution of Central Mexican manuscripts.

CONSTANCE CORTEZ

GEOGRAPHY. *See* Mesoamerica, *article on* Geography.

GEOLOGY. *See* Mesoamerica, *article on* Geological and Natural History.

GLYPHS. *See* Epigraphy.

GOD. When the Franciscans began systematic evangelization of New Spain in 1524, they faced two obstacles: the difficulty of introducing monotheistic ideology with its commitments to a monistic world view into cultures habituated to richly complex pantheons ordered, in part, by primordial dualities; and the barrier of wholly new languages. The friars' first recourse was to depend on symbolic gestures, physical signs, and pictorial representation. Fray Jacobo da Testera was particularly noted for his technique of teaching with pictures and lent his name to a genre of elementary teaching texts called "Testerian catechisms," which depict such basic scenes as a bearded figure pointing a wand to an array of stars, intended to convey the idea of God creating the heavens. As Bishop Palafox expressed it, "In the Indies it is customary to say, and truly, that the Faith enters these poor natives through their eyes" (cited in Taylor, p. 167). The limitations of such pictorial or rebus systems were manifest, however, and language was recognized as another key to successful evangelization.

As early missionaries achieved fluency in native languages, they confronted a crucial decision about whether to utilize indigenous vocabulary for basic religious concepts or to insert Spanish or Latin terminology. First-generation Franciscans were optimistic about building on the parallels they perceived between native and Christian religiosity. In Bernardino de Sahagún's *Colloquios y doctrina christiana* (1564), which represents dialogic encounters between the first Franciscans and Aztec elders, Nahuatl *teotl* and Spanish *dios* are used interchangeably to refer to the Christian God; *teotl* is often paired with *tlatoani* ("authoritative speaker") to give the sense of "divine speaker." Other epithets, such as "true God" and "sole God," were used to distinguish the Christian concept of God; one notes such combinations as *çan ce dios çan ce teotl* ("only one deity, only one god"). Yet the friars also freely adapted for the Christian God epithets routinely associated with Aztec deities, such as *tloque nahuaque* ("posessor of the near, possessor of the far"), regularly used of Tezcatlipoca—at the same time as they sought to emphasize how different the loving Christian God was from the demonic pagan gods.

Similar patterns occur in Maya contexts. For example, a modern Zinacantecan community uses the divine name Yahval Balamil, an amalgam of Biblical Hebrew and Tzotzil Maya. More common Maya epithets for the Christian God include "Celestial Lord" and "Earth Lord" (although the implicit pre-Hispanic primordial duality sits uneasily with Christian monotheism, so that often "Earth Lord" seems rather to complement than to represent the Christian deity).

Later generations of missionaries became wary and preferred to avoid rather than embrace any apparent parallels between pre-Hispanic and Christian religiosity. Second-generation friars such as Diego Durán and Sahagún expressed great misgivings about earlier evangelization efforts. By the mid-sixteenth century, Sahagún came to believe that Christian teaching had been so shallowly planted that it was almost as if it never had been. Even more suspicious clerics, such as Hernando Ruiz de Alcarón in his 1629 *Treatise on the Heathen Superstitions*, saw idolatry everywhere, giving rise to the "idols behind altars" thesis. Debate continues among ethnographers: on the one hand, Madsen, Nutini, Vogt, and Zantwijk emphasize syncretism, pre-Hispanic survivals, and "Christo-paganism" (a view of indigenous folk Catholicism shared by Protestant evangelicals); on the other, more phenomenologically inclined scholars such as Clendinnen, Burkhart, and Avalos emphasize the wholeness of indigenous lived traditions. Recent scholarship strongly suggests that a shared religious vision emerged in which the pre-Hispanic indigenous habits of conceiving and celebrating the sacred were joined to European concepts of God and the Trinity. As Taylor (pp. 59–62) has emphasized, however, it is important to recognize that the process of religious change was and is at any given moment inherently transitional and incomplete, so that we need to go "beyond syncretism" in the sense of any fixed formulation. [*See* Syncretism.]

The Catholic doctrine of the Trinity posed special challenges for missionaries trying to impart a monotheistic theology. It stretched linguistc ingenuity, leading to such misunderstandings as a Nahuatl sentence reading, "There is only one God, who is Father, Son, and Holy Spirit, three persons, only one of whom is the true God" (Fray Juan Bautista, cited in Gruzinski). The Holy Spirit, too, is a relatively rare referent. Calderon suggests that the Holy Spirit as a dove may have become conflated with the Aztec eagle, and Gruzinski reports one militantly nativist governor of the *pueblo* of Tlapacoya who in 1661 claimed to have the Holy Spirit under lock and key inside seven nested caskets. In iconography, God is far less frequent than the multitudinous representations of Jesus, Mary, and the saints. The Testerian catechisms sketched God as a bearded, robed patriarch, and God the Father appears regularly in Trinitarian Baroque paintings, along with Christ and the dove of the Holy Spirit. One distinctive tradition of Mexican art, imported from Spain, is a bold depiction of the Trinity as a clone of three bearded males, looking either like three God the Fathers or like three Jesus Christs. Images of God did frequently appear in colonial altarpieces, especially in the sixteenth century, sometimes not only as a father but also as a celestial judge of humankind. Many depictions showed God as a remote figure at the top of the painting who could, however, be approached through the mediation of Christ and the saints. Another Mexican motif, derived from the medieval European image of God guiding Luke in the painting of the Holy Face of Jesus, is the image of God directly painting the image of the Virgin of Guadalupe on the *tilma* (cloak) of Juan Diego.

As in the popular Spanish Catholicism whence it came, the Catholicism of New Spain tended to present God as a remote power, rather like the Hindu Brahma. Indian communities tended to bring God closer by simply conflating God with Jesus as Lord of Heaven. Native-language documents such as letters, wills, and land titles routinely begin with formulaic invocations of God or the Trinity (as well as Jesus, Mary, or a local patron saint). God's remoteness remained, however, as shown by the fact that virtually no religious occasions, festivals, or processions were devoted to God per se, nor were churches named for God, as they were for aspects of Jesus, Mary, or the saints—or, on occasion, the Trinity. This divine remoteness resulted in some important strategies in folk Catholicism, as shown by folktales that depict the active roles of the saints in bringing God's powers closer to humankind. In one story, recorded by Madsen, the Virgin of Guadalupe not only bargains with but successfully tricks God into granting her will on behalf of a devotee. The day-to-day religiosity that had been associated with the pre-Hispanic deities continued in indigenous communities after conversion to Christianity more in the form of devotions to Jesus, Mary, and the saints than as worship of the God of the theologians.

BIBLIOGRAPHY

Avalos, Eugenio Maurer. "The Tzeltal Maya-Christian Synthesis." In *South and Meso-American Native Spirituality*, edited by Gary Gossen, pp. 228–250. New York, 1993. Reasoned critique of Vogt and other proponents of the syncretism thesis.

Burkhart, Louise. "Doctrinal Aspects of Sahagún's *Colloquios*." In *The Work of Bernardino de Sahagún*: *Pioneer Ethnographer of Sixteenth-Century Aztec Mexico*, edited by J. Jorge Klor de Alva, H. B. Nicholson, and Eloise Quiñones Keber, pp. 65–82. Albany, 1988. Astute analysis of a key text, in terms both of linguistic issues and comparative religion.

Carrasco, Pedro. "Tarascan Folk Religion, Christian or Pagan?" In *The Social Anthropology of Latin America*: *Essays in Honor of Ralph Leon Beals*, edited by Walter Goldschmidt and Harry Hoijer, pp. 3–15. Los Angeles, 1970. Closely argued rebuttal of the syncretism analysis of van Zantwijk's *Servants of the Saints*.

Clendinnen, Inga. "Ways to the Sacred: Reconstructing 'Religion' in Sixteenth Century Mexico." *History and Anthropology* 5 (1990), 105–141. Reassessment of indigenous Christianity from a phenomenological perspective, and a strong critique of the syncretism school.

Durán, Diego de. *The History of the Indies of New Spain*. Translated by Doris Heyden. Norman, Okla., 1994. Important primary source for the history of the Aztec and the beginnings of Christian New Spain as told by a second-generation missionary drawing upon indigenous sources.

Gruzinski, Serge. *The Conquest of Mexico*: *The Incorporation of Indian Societies into the Western World, 16th–18th Centuries*. Cambridge, 1993. Important reassessment, significantly updating the work of Ricard.

Lockhart, James. *The Nahuas after the Conquest*. Stanford, 1992. Important review of new scholarship based on analysis of Nahuatl-language documents.

Mackay, John A. *The Other Spanish Christ*: *A Study in the Spiritual History of Spain and South America*. New York, 1933. Idiosyncratic account reflecting a "liberal humanist" bias characteristic of its time.

Madsen, William. *Christo-Paganism*: *A Study of Mexican Religious Syncretism*. New Orleans, 1957. Tries to make a case for the argument that contemporary Mexican Indian religious practice is more reflective of pre-Hispanic than Christian tradition; an important but dated analysis.

Motolinía, Toribio de Benavente. *Motolinía's History of the Indians of New Spain*. Translated and edited by Elizabeth Andros Foster. Berkeley, 1950. Indispensable primary source for the history of evangelization in New Spain.

Nutini, Hugo G. *Todos Santos in Rural Tlaxcala*: *A Syncretic, Expressive, and Symbolic Analysis of the Cult of the Dead*. Princeton, 1988. Influential study that intends to demonstrate the usefulness of syncretism as a paradigm for ethnographic analysis.

Ricard, Robert. *The Spiritual Conquest of Mexico*. Translated by Lesley Byrd Simpson. Berkeley, 1966. Long the standard work, but the triumphalist "conquest" approach has been superseded by more recent scholarship accessing indigenous sources.

Sahagún, Bernardino de. "The Aztec–Spanish Dialogues of 1524" [*Colloquios y doctrina christiana*]. Translated by J. Jorge Klor de Alva. *Alcheringa/ Ethnopoetics* 4.2 (1980), 52–193. Reconstruction by Sahagún and his indigenous collaborators some forty years after the fact of the religious dialogue between the first-generation Franciscans and Aztec elders.

Sahagún, Bernardino de. *Florentine Codex*: *General History of the Things of New Spain*. Translated by Arthur J. O. Anderson and Charles E. Dibble. Vol. 1, *Introductions and Indices*. Contains "Sahagún's Prologues and Interpolations," his important commentary and explanation of his ambitious project of presenting an encyclopedic survey of Aztec culture and cosmovision as conveyed by trilingual Nahua seminarians working with elders as informants.

Vogt, Evon. "Gods and Politics in Zinacantan and Chamula." *Ethnology* 12 (1973), 99–114. This, like many other works by Vogt, strongly emphasizes the syncretism thesis.

Zantwijk, Rudolf van. *Servants of the Saints*: *The Social and Cultural Identity of a Tarascan Community in Mexico*. Assen, 1967. Strongly presents the argument that popular religious practice is more reflective of pre-Hispanic than Christian ideology; for a critique, see Pedro Carrasco.

GEORGE L. SCHEPER

GOLD. *See* Mining and Metalwork.

GREENSTONE. *See* Jade and Greenstone.

GRINDING IMPLEMENTS. Until the expansion of mechanical grain milling in the twentieth century, broad-surfaced metates (grinding surfaces) and hand-held manos (cylindrical rubbers) were the most important household tools in Mesoamerica. Modern ethnographers estimate the amount of time a woman expended daily in the preparation of maize for tortillas at three to eight hours. Milling and grinding improves the nutritional quality of maize in three important ways:

1. *Size reduction*: Small particles of maize absorb heat and are cooked and digested quickly. Grinding also disrupts protein structures and other barriers to nutrient absorption.
2. *Fractionation*: Removing the less desirable fractions of kernels improves the nutritional quality of maize. The separation of the pericarp (bran) and tipcap prevents the fiber in these fractions from reducing the body's absorption of nutrients. This separation often is accomplished through a combination of lime treatment, light milling, and washing.
3. *Mineral supplementation*: The inadvertent addition of minerals from grinding-stone residue enhances the nutrient composition of maize. In one study, the use of igneous grinding tools increased iron levels in prepared maize by a factor of seven.

In addition, grinding tools have numerous culinary functions secondary to the grinding of staple plant foods. Modern households retain separate equipment to grind chiles, coffee, and other hard foods. Specially designed *morteros* and *tejolotes* (mortars and pestles) have similar uses; the bowl-shaped *molcajete* is useful for processing herbs and other loose or liquid substances.

Tertiary functions of grinding tools include the processing of ceramic temper and pigments (e.g., hematite). Finally, because of their regular shapes, grinding tool fragments were reused as tiles and bricks in construction, as hammerstones and anvils in obsidian production, and for other purposes.

The early evolution of grinding technology paralleled the growing dependence of Mesoamerican populations on plant foods, particularly maize. The earliest metates were little modified from the original boulders; they had round, basin-shaped grinding surfaces most suitable for crushing relatively small amounts of plant food with a small mano and a short, rotary grinding stroke. As dependence on maize increased, tool forms changed to improve the output volume and quality. Metate bodies became longer, broader, and thinner to accommodate an elongated, linear grinding stroke which increasingly emphasized shearing rather than crushing force. Likewise, manos became longer to provide more leverage, but thinner to decrease the weight of repeated strokes. The introduction of lime treatment also contributed to a flattening of metate grinding surfaces; the lime-soaked kernels (*nixtamal*) are softer and more compact, and so more easily controlled.

The rise of complex urban economies and socioeconomic stratification spawned further developments which archaeologists are only beginning to study. The problem areas under investigation include the effects of craft specialization and the appearance of markets on equipment production and exchange; the nutritional and subsistence economics of maize preparation; the social and economic reorganization of maize preparation, including the development of cooperative production among households and the appearance of specialists such as Sahagún's tortilla vendor; and the role of grinding equipment style as an indicator of household social or economic status.

BIBLIOGRAPHY

Biskowski, Martin. "The Adaptive Origins of Prehispanic Markets in Central Mexico: The Role of Maize-Grinding Tools and Related Staple Products in Early State Economies." Ph.D. diss. University of California, Los Angeles, 1997. Explores the role of metates and manos in pre-Hispanic economies of the Teotihuacan Valley, Mexico, and the problems of undertaking such study.

Clark, John E. *The Lithic Artifacts of La Libertad, Chiapas, Mexico: An Economic Perspective.* Papers of the New World Archaeological Foundation, 52. Provo, Utah, 1988. Overview of Formative-period grinding technology and a discussion of analytical methodology.

Cook, Scott. *Zapotec Stoneworkers: The Dynamics of Rural Simple Commodity Production in Modern Mexican Capitalism.* Washington, D.C., 1982. Discusses the social and economic contexts of modern grinding tool production in Oaxaca.

Hayden, Brian, ed. *Lithic Studies among the Contemporary Highland Maya.* Tucson, Ariz., 1987. Edited volume provides unique information on traditional grinding tool production methods, use, and the functional significance of grinding tool design.

Krause, V. M., H. V. Kuhnlein, C. Y. Lopez-Palacios, K. L. Tucker, M. Ruz, and N. W. Solomons. "Preparation Effects on Tortilla Mineral Content in Guatemala." *Archivos latinoamericanos de nutricion* 43 (1993), 73–77. Third in a series of articles by these authors (the other two are in *Ecology of Food and Nutrition* 28 (1992), 279–288 and 289–297) detailing preparation effects and rural/urban differences in tortilla preparation.

Serna-Saldivar, S. O., M. H. Gomez, and L. W. Rooney. "Technology, Chemistry, and Nutritional Value of Alkaline-cooked Corn Products." In *Advances in Cereal Science and Technology*, vol. 10, edited by Y. Pomeranz, pp. 243–307. St. Paul, Minn., 1990. General overview of the nutritional sequences of modern commercial tortilla production; although hand-held grinding tools are not addressed, this article identifies several nutritional and economic issues in the preparation of maize foods.

Spink, Mary. "Metates as Socioeconomic Indicators during the Classic Period at Copán, Honduras." Ph.D. diss. Pennsylvania State University, 1983. Combines archaeological studies of the Classic Period grinding technology with modern ethnographic research in the Copán region.

MARTIN BISKOWSKI

GROLIER, CODEX. Of the four pre-Conquest Maya codices, the fragmentary *Codex Grolier* has the narrowest topical focus and is the most Mexican in its iconography and painting style. Its ten extant pages of native bark paper (sheets 10 and 11 are pieces of the same page) present part of a Venus almanac, one that originally spanned 20 pages. This almanac is unique because it illustrates and gives equal weight to each of the planet's four stations, devoting a page to each, and it is the only extant manuscript to present the iconography of all four stations. In contrast, the other Venus almanacs—in the Maya *Codex Dresden* and in the Codices *Borgia*, *Cospi*, and *Vaticanus B* from central or southern Mexico—all concentrate solely on the aspect of Venus as the Morning Star.

Numbers at the top of the pages express the standardized intervals of Venus phenomena: 90 days for its disappearance at superior conjunction, 250 days for its rising as Evening Star, 8 days for its disappearance at inferior conjunction, and 236 days for its rising as Morning Star. The numbering system employed is unique to the *Grolier*, however, and seems more closely related to Mexican patterns than to Maya ones. Red dots arranged horizontally across the top of the page function as coefficients of 20, to which are added the black numbers that are framed in red like "ring numbers" or bundles. Thus it uses numbers according to both the Maya bar and dot system (day numbers and ringed numbers) and the Central Mexican system of presenting all the dots individually, and combines them uniquely. Like the *Dresden Codex*, the *Grolier* almanac originally presented 65 synodical revolutions; five revolutions were originally pictured, and these were to be read through thirteen times. On each page a column of thirteen day glyphs provides the *tzolkin* (260-day calendar) day name for each station: the uppermost glyph naming the day of the first pass through the table, and the next lower glyphs naming the day on subsequent passes. Calendrically, the *Grolier* is cognate with *Dresden* pages 48, 49, and the left half of 50, using the same temporal intervals, day names, and *lub* or base day (1 Ahau).

The *Grolier's* spatial organization and painting style also vary greatly from those of other Maya codices. The *Grolier Codex* devotes a full page to each station, rather than employing registers, and it lacks hieroglyphic texts altogether. The figural style and iconography of the anthropomorphic figures pictured for each station are a mixture of Maya, Toltec, Mixtec, and Borgia Group features.

The aberrant numeration and topical focus of the *Grolier Codex*, along with its eclectic style and organization, led some scholars originally to question the manuscript's authenticity. However, later study has dispelled the strongest of these objections. The *Grolier Codex* likely came from a mixed culture, where Mayan and Mexican languages were spoken and where Maya and Mexican ideological traditions were enmeshed with each other. The awkward use of pseudo "ring numbers" and the dots representing quantities of 20—this being so at odds with both Maya and Mexican practices—suggest that the artist was working in a cultural frontier zone, far from the hearts of the two traditions but where the edges of the traditions mixed. The manuscript came to the attention

A few pages from the *Grolier Codex* Venus Table. *Photograph courtesy of Ivan Šprajc.*

of the scholarly community only in 1971, when it was exhibited at the Grolier Club in New York. Said to have been found in a dry cave in Chiapas in the 1960s, it is now preserved in the Museo Nacional de Antropología in Mexico City.

BIBLIOGRAPHY

Carlson, John. "The Grolier Codex: A Preliminary Report on the Content and Authenticity of a 13th-century Maya Venus Almanac." In *Calendars in Mesoamerica and Peru: Native American Computations of Time*, edited by Anthony Aveni and Gordon Brotherston, pp. 27–57. Oxford, 1983.

Coe, Michael. *The Maya Scribe and His World.* New York, 1973. First and best facsimile publication of the codex with a description of its content and provenience.

ELIZABETH H. BOONE

GUADALUPE, NUESTRA SEÑORA DE. [*This entry comprises two articles. The introductory article provides an overview of the legends, apparitions, miracles, veneration, cult, ritual activities, and representations associated with Nuestra Señora de Guadalupe; the companion article is a discussion and exploration of the devotion and creative responses to the Virgin de Guadalupe among Mexican American peoples (and others) in the borderlands and Mexican diaspora in the United States. For a related discussion, see Marian Devotion.*]

An Overview

The devotion to the Virgin of Guadalupe is one of the most important phenomena in the history of Mexico. It is commonly regarded as the source and binding force of Mexican nationality (*mexicanidad*) and self-identification. Though preeminently a Mexican devotion and symbol, it has spread throughout the Western Hemisphere, including the United States.

According to the traditional account, the Virgin Mary appeared to an indigenous Roman Catholic neophyte named Juan Diego at the hill of Tepeyac, just north of Mexico City, in December 1531. She directed him to go to Juan de Zumárraga, the bishop-elect of Mexico, and to instruct him to have a church built on that site. Juan Diego did so, but he was initially rebuffed by Zumárraga. The native reported the failure of his mission to the Virgin, who told him to return to the bishop-elect on the following day. When he did, Zumárraga asked for a sign that would confirm the request. Returning home, Juan Diego learned that his uncle, Juan Bernardino, was mortally ill. The next day, he went in search of a priest to minister to his uncle and tried to avoid meeting the Virgin at Tepeyac. She found him, however, and after telling him that his uncle was cured, she directed him to go to

the top of the hill and collect the flowers that were blooming at that cold and barren spot. He did so, folding the flowers in his mantle (now called the *tilma*, from Nahuatl *tilmahtli*). On being readmitted to Zumárraga's presence, Juan Diego opened the *tilma*; the flowers cascaded to the floor, and imprinted on the mantle was the image of the Virgin. The bishop-elect, in tears, asked forgiveness for his skepticism, placed the image on public display, and hastened to construct a small church at Tepeyac (now called Guadalupe).

The story belongs to the classic European genre of apparition accounts. It gives a supernatural origin for a shrine. The Virgin appears to a poor and marginalized person. Ecclesiastical authority is initially skeptical but is won over by a miracle. The Guadalupan apparitions differ from the standard genre, however, in that the Virgin's message is not apocalyptic or penitential but comforting and protective.

Between 1556 and 1648, there are numerous references to a chapel at Guadalupe, but none associate it with apparitions. The sermon of the Franciscan provincial Francisco de Bustamante (1556), a report by the vicar of the shrine, Antonio Freire (1570), and a report by the Viceroy Martín Enríquez de Almansa (1575) all agree that the shrine was built about the years 1555–1556, not in 1531. Enríquez attributes the origin of the shrine to a claim by a herdsman that he had been miraculously cured at the site.

The story of the apparitions as an explanation for the origin of the shrine was first made known by a Mexican priest, Miguel Sánchez, in a book published in 1648, *Imagen de la Virgen María, Madre de Dios de Guadalupe*. For Sánchez, the apparitions were a divine confirmation of the special and elect status of the *criollos* and the city of Mexico. The story came as a surprise to the inhabitants of Mexico. The claim was even made that the story had been "forgotten" in the course of almost a century and a half. In the following year, the vicar of the shrine at Guadalupe, Luis Laso de la Vega, published a book in Nahuatl, *Huei tlamahuiçoltica*, intended for the native population. It included an account of the apparitions—known from its opening words as the *Nican mopohua*—a series of miracle stories (*Nican motecpana*), and hortatory and devotional material (*Nican tlantica*). The claim that this work was written by the Nahua scholar Antonio Valeriano in the early sixteenth century does not rest on solid historical evidence. The book had little impact on the natives, and until the eighteenth century, devotion to the Guadalupe of the apparitions was confined almost entirely to the *criollo* population of New Spain. When an epidemic struck Mexico City in 1736, the civil and ecclesiastical authorities swore an oath accepting Guadalupe as patroness of the city and celebrating 12 December as her

Chapel of El Pocito, Villa de Guadalupe. Chapel marks sacred well by the basilica of the Virgin of Guadalupe. *Photograph courtesy of Jeanette Favrot Peterson.*

feast. This patronage quickly extended to the rest of New Spain and the Spanish Empire.

Contrary to the common assertion that the apparitions brought millions of Indians to Christianity—a claim for which there is no evidence whatever—it was only in the last half of the eighteenth century that the devotion began to spread among indigenous peoples, perhaps as a part of a planned campaign by the church. It was the use of the Guadalupe symbol by Miguel de Hidalgo y Costilla in the revolution of 1810 that made it a symbol of Mexican nationality. In this sense, it acted as a force that bound disparate classes and ethnic groups into one nation.

In more recent times, Guadalupe has been given a wide variety of interpretations. One is that of "spiritual orphanhood," the comforting mother who restored dignity and hope to a native population that had lost all in the Spanish conquest. In this interpretation, it was Guada-

lupe that compelled both church and crown to recognize the humanity of the Indians. Others view Guadalupe as an instrument of evangelization which joined the indigenous past to the Spanish present and thus created the modern Mexican. Similarly, it is asserted that through a conscious syncretism, Guadalupe was substituted for the goddess Tonantzin. There is scant evidence for this, and the nature of that deity is obscure. For feminists, Guadalupe has conflicting meanings: a symbol either of submission to normative patriarchy or of empowerment and liberation. At the present time, a widespread interpretation is that of inculturation, whereby Christian teaching is presented in a native form and permits the indigenous peoples to receive Catholicism in terms and categories consistent with their heritages. Most contemporary interpretations of the Guadalupe phenomenon by theologians and anthropologists view the historical truth or falsity of the apparitions as irrelevant.

[*See also* Diego, Juan; Nican Mopohua; Tepeyac.]

BIBLIOGRAPHY

Burkhart, Louise. "The Cult of the Virgin of Guadalupe in Mexico." In *South and Meso-American Native Spirituality: From the Cult of the Feathered Serpent to the Theology of Liberation*, edited by Gary H. Gossen and Miguel León-Portilla, pp. 198–227. New York, 1993. Perceptive survey of the role of Guadalupe in Mexican religious life.

Grajales, Gloria, and Ernest J. Burrus, comps. *Bibliografía guadalupana (1531–1984)—Guadalupan Bibliography (1531–1984)*. Washington, D.C., 1986. Generally good bibliography, though the authors' biases lead them into accepting questionable works and dates.

Lafaye, Jacques. *Quetzalcoatl and Guadalupe: The Formation of Mexican National Consciousness, 1531–1813*. Translated by Benjamin Keen. Chicago, 1976. Original French ed., *Quetzalcóatl et Guadalupe: La formation de la conscience nationale au Mexique (1531–1813)*. Paris, 1974. One of the most influential modern studies of the impact of Guadalupe on Mexican nationality, it uses a multidisciplinary approach in analyzing the role of Guadalupe in the development of Mexican national consciousness as the unifying factor in an otherwise fragmented society; central is the idea of the hispanization of Quetzalcoatl and the indianization of Guadalupe.

Laso de la Vega, Luis. *The Story of Guadalupe: Luis Laso de la Vega's Huei tlamahuiçoltica of 1649*. Edited and translated by Lisa Sousa, Stafford Poole, and James Lockhart. Stanford, 1998. The only English translation of the entire work, and the first scholarly English translation of the *Nican mopohua*, with philological analysis.

Maza, Francisco de la. *El guadalupanismo mexicano*. Mexico City, 1981. Highly regarded survey, but somewhat sketchy.

Nebel, Richard. *Santa María Tonantzin Virgen de Guadalupe: Continuidad y transformación religiosa en México*. Translated by Carlos Warnholtz Bustillos. Mexico City, 1995. Original German ed., *Santa María Tonantzin Virgen de Guadalupé: Religiöse Kontinuität und Transformation in Mexiko*. 1992. Interesting theological and anthropological analysis of the Guadalupe event and its influence on Mexican life and thought, marred by a certain lack of historical consciousness.

Noguez, Xavier. *Documentos guadalupanos: Un estudio sobre las fuentes de información tempranas en torno a las mariofanías en el Tepeyac*. Mexico City, 1993. Essential survey and analysis of the documentary sources of the Guadalupe phenomenon.

Poole, Stafford. *Our Lady of Guadalupe: The Origins and Sources of a Mexican National Symbol, 1531–1797*. Tucson, Ariz., 1997.

Taylor, William B. "The Virgin of Guadalupe: An Inquiry into the Social History of Marian Devotion." *American Ethnologist* 14 (1987), 9–33. Prize-winning analysis of the influence of Guadalupe in the wider context of Marian devotion in the late colonial and early national periods; Taylor sees it as predominantly a *criollo* devotion spread by *criollo* clergy.

Torres Villar, Ernesto de la, and Ramiro Navarro de Anda, eds. *Testimonios históricos guadalupanos*. Mexico City, 1982. Despite some omissions, a valuable compendium of all the pertinent documents dealing with Guadalupe, each preceded by an excellent bibliographical introduction.

STAFFORD POOLE, C.M.

Meaning and Reception

This article focuses not on the origins of the Guadalupe event but on its expanding, deepening, and liberating power in the lives of Mexicans and others throughout the Western Hemisphere and beyond. Today, Our Lady of Guadalupe is found not only at Tepeyac in Mexico, where she first appeared and left her imprint on the *tilma* of Juan Diego, but also throughout the world, especially in areas of Mexican, Chicano, and Mexican American concentration. Her expanding presence in the consciousness of the people is evident in medals, art, neighborhood murals, hubcaps, tattoos, and even motorcycles. She leads religious processions and *campesino* marches for justice. Immigrants, soldiers, police, and prisoners pray to her for protection in time of need. Celebrations in her honor draw crowds in Los Angeles, New York City, Anchorage, Chicago, and Washington, D.C.

The Guadalupe event, like all other events that have given rise to great religious movements, is mysterious. The story of Our Lady of Guadalupe really begins in 1492, when two humanities who had never suspected the existence of each other suddenly found themselves face to face. Both Europe and the Amerindian civilizations had accomplished great wonders, yet both had also devised various types of violence that appeared logical and even necessary to themselves but incomprehensible to the other. They were as fascinated with each other as they were frightened. The ensuing struggle would be unequal, for the Europeans had definite superiority in the instruments and techniques of war. The European conquest of Mexico was brutal, and the native populations were also decimated by diseases and reduced to being servants of the new masters, alienated in their own land. The beginning of the New World for Europeans might have been the end of the native ways of life for many of the people, but it would not be so.

Conquest had brought the Old World into a new geographical space, but the real New World, the humanity of the Americas, would begin in part with the marvelous apparition at Mount Tepeyac in 1531. Just ten years after the conquest of Mexico, when many of the native people were suffering so much that they simply wanted to die, a dark Virgin Mary appeared to Juan Diego, a lower-class Indian; amid the beautiful singing of birds, she asked him to go to the bishop and demand that a temple be built at Tepeyac where she could show her love and compassion to all the inhabitants of the land. After some difficulties, the bishop asked for a sign, which the Virgin gave to Juan Diego: beautiful Spanish flowers emerging out of the sacred mountain of Tepeyac. She also imprinted her image miraculously on the *tilma* (mantle) of Juan Diego and healed Juan's dying uncle, Juan Bernardino. This is a simplified retelling of the basic elements of the story that is elaborated by Laso de la Vega in the *Nican Mopohua*.

The account of Guadalupe's appearances and compassion is a creation narrative as remembered by the victim-survivors of the Conquest, who were equally the firstborn of the new creation. Whereas European historians wrote about the Conquest, Nahua historians provided us with this creation story—not a conquest, but a birth. The Guadalupe event, as recorded in the *Nican Mopohua*, is a characteristic Nahuatl narrative, a beautiful and carefully constructed Nahuatl poem with contrasting imagery, symbolic communication, tender consolation, radical affirmation, and social inversion through divine intervention. It is a highly complex *mestizo* (Nahuatl–European) form of communication in various ways: the image and the narrative are mutually interpretative, with both Nahuatl and Iberian symbols and styles, which together say new things that neither alone could have expressed. The image of Guadalupe on the *tilma* is visible poetry, while the *Nican Mopohua* poem is audible imagery, and together they constitute a coherent communication. At Tepeyac and throughout New Spain, a new Nahuatl-Christian sacred imagery would erupt and open the way for true spiritual intercourse and innovation.

The gospel through Our Lady of Guadalupe has been kept alive, interiorized, assimilated, and transmitted through song, dance, and personal testimonies. The deep joy that the Guadalupe experience brought about was spontaneously communicated—first among the conquered Indians, and then in time by *mestizo* and *criollo* society. Today it flourishes among the poor, downtrodden, and marginalized throughout the Western Hemisphere. Like the gospel stories of Jesus, the Guadalupe narrative is strikingly simple. It is the Nahuatl proclamation of the Resurrection: "They tried to kill us, but God has raised us to life. They tried to destroy the ways of life of our ancestors, but God has protected us and redeemed us."

Our Lady of Guadalupe has long been the focus of individual and local devotions, testimonies of miraculous favors granted by her, and, most of all, celebrations on her feast day, 12 December. Today she inspires songwriters, poets, artists, and dramatists; personal testimonies of favors granted and the religious imagination of the people continue to expand beyond the confines of the church or organized movements. In popular *telenovelas* (Mexican "soap operas"), she is often addressed at moments of crisis. She is depicted on the hubcaps of "lowrider" cars and tattooed on the backs of prisoners. Many immigrants from Mexico thank her for protecting them from border patrols and helping them to cross the border safely.

In the period 1850–1950, when many Mexican people of the U.S. Southwest were treated like foreigners in their own land and the new immigrants were viewed with disdain, Guadalupana societies gathered people together and gave them a sense of dignity and pride as Mexican Catholics living in an anglophone-dominated Protestant nation. These social-religious groups also gave them a sense of divine protection against the abuses they suffered from many of the structures of society, and even from the church. Her dynamic, intimate presence has kept *mexicanidad* alive in the United States in spite of threats to cultural-religious identity and has given people a sense of cohesion and belonging. Today, programs like the Valley Missionary Program, centered on the pyramid-shrine of Our Lady of Guadalupe in Coachella, California, show how the dynamics of Juan Diego and the Virgin continue to be lived out among Mexican immigrant farmworkers and other marginalized people. This program, designed around the dynamic of the Guadalupe event and narrative, has produced miraculous results in rehabilitating Mexican farmworkers. Like the *Virgen de Guadalupe* herself, such programs affirm continuity with ancient religious roots while offering people an opportunity for healing and liberating transformation.

Our Lady of Guadalupe has important theological and anthropological significance for today. In January 1999, the Roman Catholic church officially proclaimed her the first and greatest evangelizer of the Americas. Others see her as the protector and liberator of the poor, the downtrodden, and the disenfranchised. Today she is beginning to be seen as the beginning of a new creation, the mother of a new humanity, and the manifestation of the femininity of God, with unlimited possibilities for creative and liberating reflection. Juan Diego is seen as the prototype of the new human being of the Americas, and the narrative of the social transformation of her encounters with Juan Diego, of Juan Diego's encounters with the bishop, and of the healing of Juan Bernardino are as miraculous as the image itself. She is not simply an event of the past but a powerful living presence. The consciousness of the people continues to re-create and transmit her loving, compassionate, and healing presence and message. There is a chapel to her next to St. Peter's tomb in St. Peter's Basilica in Rome, and a much-visited chapel to her in Notre Dame Cathedral in Paris. Devotion to her is growing in South Africa, where people see her as a symbol of reconciliation among the races.

Our Lady of Guadalupe is not an element of Catholic dogma, but she is among the most tender, beautiful, and influential truths of American Christianity. In her longevity and the creative uses of her image by diverse peoples, we see that the power of tenderness is greater than the power of dogma. Devotion of the heart emerges not from official doctrine but from the saving truth of the *sensus fidelium*, the "faith memory" of the people that animates their hearts. Guadalupe is certainly a popular devotion, but behind this there is a more profound understanding of reality, truth, humanity, and God. The persistence and force of all long-standing religious movements fascinates and perplexes scientists and historians. Guadalupe offers a way of relating religions and peoples not by opposition, but by synthesis.

VIRGILIO P. ELIZONDO

GUERRERO, GONZALO (late fifteenth century–1536), Spanish explorer from Palos de la Frontera, Huelva, Spain, who died in Puerto Caballos, Honduras. On 11 January 1511, Vasco Nuñez de Balboa wrote to Christopher Columbus to tell of an Indian named Panquiaco who knew of an ocean (the Pacific) on the other side of the mountains. Balboa asked for a thousand men to help find that ocean. The letter was given to Pedro de Valdivia, the regent of Darien, Panama, who sailed for Santo Domingo, but he and his men were shipwrecked off the coast of Jamaica. Nineteen men survived in a small boat for two weeks, with ocean currents carrying them to the Yucatán Peninsula, where the Maya captured them and placed them in cages. Some were executed, but three escaped, including Gonzalo Guerrero. The three served with the troops of Aquincuz, Lord of Xamanzana, who had recaptured them. Soon they learned Mayan, told the Maya about Spain and the Spanish fleet—all of which informed the Maya about what might happen to them.

Aquincuz was succeeded by Taxmar, who gave the slave Guerrero to Nachancan, chieftain of Uaymil-Chetumal; there, he was renamed Nacon ("leader of the troops") and a member of the nobility when he married the chieftain's daughter. During this adaptation to the world of the Maya, he took inspiration from Juan Alonso, who had deserted Governor Diego de Nicuesa's troops in Panama. Alonso was made a captain by the chieftain Careta, and he began to dress like an Indian, but soon he was discovered by Balboa; it is likely that Guerrero and Gerónimo de Aguilar also met him. Eventually, Alonso betrayed Careta, revealing that the Panamanians had gold.

In 1517, Hernandez de Cordoba "discovered" Yucatán and was immediately attacked by Maya warriors who had been advised by Guerrero. During the attack, two Maya were captured (Melchor and Gaspar), then taken to Cuba as interpreters. They told of the shipwrecked Spaniards and their involvement in Maya life. In 1518, Juan de Grijalba was also attacked off the coast of Yucatán, although he managed to rescue from the Maya a Jamaican fisherwoman who had been shipwrecked in 1516. She told them about Guerrero.

Fernando Cortés arrived in Cozumel in 1519 and sent a letter to the shipwreck survivors, "hidden in the braided hair of an Indian," according to Lopez de Gomara—together with green gems for the Indians as ransom. Cortés gave his long-lost countrymen eight days to present themselves to him. Bernal Díaz del Castillo wrote that Gerónimo de Aguilar went to Chetumal to persuade Guerrero to join Cortés. Guerrero responded: "I am married and have three children; these people consider me a chieftain and captain during wartime. Go with God. . . . My face is tattooed. . . . What will they say about me! Besides," he added, "look at my beautiful children."

Aguilar insisted on retrieving Guerrero, but Cortés remarked, "I didn't come for such meager things." Eight years later, in 1527, Francisco Montejo and his lieutenant, Alonso Davila, arrived in Yucatán to conquer the peninsula. Montejo founded the town of Salamanca and set forth to look for Guerrero. Montejo set sail for Chetumal, while Davila went by land. Montejo wrote to Guerrero, inviting him to join them, but Guerrero turned him down, saying, according to the historian Robert Chamberlain, "I am a slave; I have no liberty." Guerrero told Montejo that Davila had died, then told Davila that Montejo had died, thus successfully separating the two.

The conquest of Yucatán was attempted on three occasions. Although the Spanish forces advanced from 1531 to 1533, Guerrero apparently made significant contributions to the Maya war effort, through his familiarity with Spanish combat techniques and technology. In 1536, Guerrero arrived with fifty canoes to help a chieftain from Honduras besieged by the Spaniards led by Andres de Cerezeda. He, in turn, asked Pedro de Alvarado for help. A letter signed by Cerezeda and dated 14 August 1536 reveals: "The chieftain Cicimba explained how, from a harquebus shot, the Spaniard called Gonzalo Aroza died during combat. He is the one who has lived amongst the Indians for more than twenty years, and it is said that he destroyed Montejo." Chamberlain concluded that Gonzalo Guerrero and Aroza are one and the same.

CARLOS VILLA ROIZ
Translated from Spanish by Marthe Imber

GULF COAST. The coastal area of the Gulf of Mexico is characterized by tropical forests and presents a wide environmental spectrum extending from the coast and coastal plain to the *sierras* (mountain ranges). Around the central and northern coast, climates vary from tropical wet to semi-arid, with temperatures between 18°C and the 40s°C, and an annual mean slightly above 24°C, though somewhat cooler in the foothills.

The landscape of extensive plains is interrupted in some places by mountainous areas of lower elevation, such as Otontepec, which rises near Lakes Tamiahua and Chiconquiaco, south of the Nautla River. Los Tuxtlas, flanked by the Papaloapan and Coatzacoalcos areas, in some places rise to more than 1,500 meters above sea level. Because of the poor drainage there, numerous wetlands form; this, together with the coastal mangrove swamps and an extensive hydraulic network of rivers, streams, and lakes comprises around 3,000 kilometers of navigable waters.

These interior waterways, and the sea, were used as routes of communication and cultural exchange of raw materials and luxury objects. Routes linking the coast and coastal plain with the *sierras* and high plains are described in historical sources and evidenced in the archaeological record. Throughout the development of civilization, the exploitation of mangrove swamps, lakes, and rivers through fishing, gathering mollusks, and hunting waterfowl, mammals, and lizards is evident in nearly all pre-Hispanic settlements in the area. Farther inland, the cultivation of tubers, maize, cotton, and cacao was important, along with hunting and gathering and the exploitation of other natural resources.

From south to north, the Gulf Coast had four principal foci of cultural development, each with its own moment of splendor. From the late second millennium to the fourth century BCE, the Olmec culture flourished in southern Veracruz and northwestern Tabasco. Between the centuries around the state of the common era until the ninth or tenth century CE, the cultures of central Veracruz stand out. From the ninth to the twelfth or thirteenth century, the culture of El Tajín was prominent. Finally, after the twelfth or thirteenth century until the moment of European contact, the Huastec and Totonac gave rise to splendid cultural expressions, although the Huastec began to flourish a few centuries earlier. The Huastec occupied the coast and plains of present-day northern Veracruz and southern Tamaulipas. In the interior, their remains are found in eastern San Luis Potosí, northern Puebla, and parts of eastern Hidalgo. To the south, the Totonac were established on the coast between the Cazones and La Antigua rivers and extended inland to Hidalgo and Puebla. Between the Huastecs and Totonac lived smaller groups—Tepehua, Nahua, and Otomí.

Although human occupation of the Gulf Coast dates from several millennia BCE, more salient cultural expressions emerged around 1500 BCE, when groups from the interior of the Coatzacoalcos Basin began to make offerings such as finely polished stone axes (*hachas*), wooden objects, rubber balls, and copal spheres in springs and other sacred spaces, as was customary at El Manatí. These traces are local expressions that centuries later were incorporated into Olmec culture.

Olmec Culture. Around 1350–1300 BCE, groups identified as Mixe-Zoquean, whose prominent cultural features were their pottery and figurines, reached southern Veracruz and northwestern Tabasco from the Pacific coast of Guatemala and Chiapas and intermarried with the local inhabitants. About a century later, the Olmec culture began to flourish; the term "Olmec" designates an artistic style rather than a particular ethnic group of the region, which included some 16,000 square kilometers between Papaloapan and southern Blasillo-Tonalá, reaching inland to the initial spurs of the *sierra*. In a short time, bearers of this culture opened commercial routes and arrived in places as far away as Chiapas and Central America in search of raw materials, which they also sought in Oaxaca and Central Mexico, where they established some "colonies." Evidence of these relations has been found in San José Mogote (Oaxaca), Oxtotitlan and Teopantecuanitlan (Guerrero), Chalcatzingo and Atlihuayan (Morelos), Las Bocas (Puebla), Tlatilco and Tlapacoya (state of México), and other sites.

Of the numerous coastal sites they founded, only a few have been systematically explored: San Lorenzo, Tres Zapotes, Laguna de los Cerros, El Manatí, Loma del Zapote, La Merced, El Macayal, San Isidro de los Almagres, Las Limas, and Arroyo Pesquero in the modern state of Veracruz, and La Venta in Tabasco. Of these sites, the most important politico-religious centers were situated in quite different environments—San Lorenzo in the Coatzacoalcos basin, Tres Zapotes and Laguna de los Cerros in the lower elevations of Los Tuxtlas, and La Venta in marshy lowland terrain. Although the architecture of these centers is of earth, mud, and wood, in La Venta, flourishing between 1200 and 400 BCE, limestone, adobe, and columnar basalt were used. Here, the constructions were aligned on a north–south axis to form plazas and architectural groups covering a little more than a square kilometer. In some of these groups, offerings consisting of figurines, axes, and various objects made of greenstone were deposited. The people carved mosaic serpentine masks with the stylized face of the jaguar, dedicated to the earth, and buried them at a considerable depth.

In a political structure typical of young states with a centralized government, the cult dedicated to the jaguar occupied the foreground in the religious sphere. Attributes of this animal appear in both major and minor sculpture, carved in basalt, serpentine, and jade, achieving exceptional sculptural quality. Prominent in these pieces are representations of human beings in different positions, often wearing elaborate outfits and headdresses. Felines, birds, serpents, fishes, monkeys, and fantastic beings—anthropomorphized or combining feline and reptilian attributes—are found carved on altars, stelae, bas-reliefs, and colossal heads. In sculpture and pottery, a wide variety of symbols appears, such as Saint Andrew's cross in the form of an X, flaming eyebrows, V-shaped cleft foreheads sometimes sprouting maize plants, downturned mouths, the hand-claw-wing complex, and crocodilian attributes. Some of these concepts persisted for centuries and shaped future Mesoamerican religious traditions.

Around the fourth century BCE, assimilated and transformed by the ideas of other groups that arrived in the area, Olmec culture came to its end. Some bearers of its ideas and knowledge emigrated to Chiapas and Central America, while others went to the Central Mexican Highlands, the Middle Usumacinta Basin, and Central Veracruz—areas with which, centuries earlier, they had sustained political and economic relations.

Cultures of Central Veracruz. By the late centuries BCE and the early centuries CE, new and distinct cultural expressions began to flourish in different places in the mountainous massif of Los Tuxtlas, Cerro de las Mesas, the Papalopan Basin, and La Mixtequilla. There, alongside dozens of villages and small settlements, politico-religious centers were established whose public architecture—built primarily of clays, sand, and perishable materials—included large foundations reaching 20 meters in height, and long platforms delimiting plazas and ballcourts. The earliest inscriptions in the area come from Los Tuxtlas. Stela C of Tres Zapotes has a date corresponding to 31 BCE, and 162 CE is recorded on the "Tuxtla Statuette." In the 1980s, the La Mojarra Stela, whose long text depicts the dates 143 and 156 CE, was discovered in the riverbed of the Acula, a tributary of the Papaloapan; the Alvarado Stela was found at the beginning of the twentieth century in the Papaloapan. The former originally had an inscription that was illegible because of erosion, although the depiction of a richly adorned personage apparently yielding to an individual with Olmec features is clear.

Other stelae, some with late inscriptions, come from Cerro de Las Mesas. Stelae 6 and 8, for example, reveal the dates 468 and 533 CE, respectively. Here, in the late 1930s, a mortuary offering was discovered that contained objects dating to the early centuries CE, together with some Olmec pieces in greenstone dating around the tenth to eighth centuries BCE, reused in that burial. In the Remojadas area a little farther north, from the first to the ninth or tenth century CE, the carving of minor clay sculpture reached its culmination in smiling figurines related to the cult of death. In El Zapotal, a site in the semiarid zone of La Mixtequilla, evidence is strong for a cult dedicated to Mictlantecuhtli, the god of death, and to the Cihuateteo, women transformed into goddesses after having died during childbirth. Mictlantecuhtli is depicted life-size, reigning in the underworld, accompanied by these goddesses and numerous smiling figurines. Some of them have jointed extremities, reflecting contacts with Teotihuacan. Relations between that great urban center of the Central Highlands and sites such as Matacapan in Los Tuxtlas are also reflected in the exchange of goods and diverse ideological features, including pottery, architecture, and deities.

Until the early 1970s, in addition to the smiling figurines found in Tlalixcoyan, Dicha Tuerta, Nopiloa, and Remojadas, the best-known sculptural expressions of Central Veracruz belonged to the sculptural trilogy consisting of *yugos*, *palmas*, and *hachas*. The interfaced decoration of these objects gave rise to the artistic style of Central Veracruz, whose distribution exceeded its territorial boundaries, reaching southward to Central America and northward to the Huasteca. This sculptural style is found in the decoration of some of the buildings at El Tajín, especially two of its seventeen ballcourts. In this urban center, the architectural complexes of Tajín Chico, the Arroyo Group, and the Central Group, with its Pyramid of the Niches, are prominent, as well as the Building of the Columns and the Xicalcoliuhqui. In the Pyramid of the Niches and other buildings, chiaroscuro is important in the interplay of volumes and recessed planes. In others, the interplay of light and shadow by means of latticework, or decoration with stone mosaics, elegant bas-reliefs, and fine polychrome mural painting, gives the ancient city exceptional architectural quality. In political, economic, and urban matters, the city was the capital of a similarly named territory in northern Central Veracruz, whose development was based on the agricultural exploitation of three alluvial valleys, on commerce, and on a centralized authority that produced an intense though relatively brief period of splendor from the ninth or tenth century to the twelfth.

Totonac Culture. In the *tablero* panels of the South Ballcourt and in the Building of the Columns—both late constructions in El Tajín—uncharacteristic elements appear. Perhaps at this time the Totonac began to arrive in the area, spreading through the coastal plain and the lower elevations of the *sierra*, as in Vega de la Peña, where some Tajín architectural elements were reproduced. Not until the thirteenth century, however, would all the characteristic features of Totonac culture take shape, including its political organization in small independent states headed by rulers who governed from capital cities such as Cempoala, Misantla, and Quiahuiztlan.

In these classist societies, there was a clear division between nobles and commoners, although sources call attention to a third social group of servants and porters for the nobility who controlled government, economy, and religion. The commoners were dedicated to artisanal production, fishing, and extensive and intensive agriculture by means of simple hydraulic works, diverting water from rivers via canals.

In the Totonacapan, urban centers such as Cempoala had areas differentiated according to their purposes and needs: management, production, exchange, consumption, and symbolic functions. In public plazas, exchange and commerce were conducted in regional products as well as those brought from distant places, including pottery and metals from the Mixteca, alabaster from Puebla, cacao and salt from Campeche, and fine cloth from the Huasteca. In addition to monumental buildings of an administrative and ritual character, there were large temple precincts. The nobility's palaces and residences had gardens, running water, and ducts for removing refuse. The homes of commoners were simple, with only one room without interior divisions.

Huastec Culture. Around the tenth and eleventh centuries, close relations existed between El Tajín and the southern portion of the Huasteca. Of Mayan linguistic affiliation, the Huastecs were organized in independent polities whose political structures, land tenure, and relations of production appear to have had a feudal character. The polities (called *señoríos* in Spanish) were headed by a ruler who resided in the principal politico-religious center, which was divided into *barrios*. Also living there were the nobility allied to the ruler, craft, specialists, and a small bureaucracy. Lesser communities subordinate to the principal center were governed by close relatives of the ruler. From the coast to the initial spurs of the *sierra*, we find cities with monumental architecture in which the constructions sometimes assume circular forms. Ruins of temples, palaces, and even altars with mural paintings reveal the development of the Huasteca. In some places, the people dug artesian wells to obtain water; elsewhere, as in Metlaltoyuca in Puebla and Yahualica in Hidalgo, cities were walled to defend against the invasions of Mexica armies, just as Castillo de Teayo had been when the Toltec were extending their dominion in this region.

Fine examples of Huastec cities are Tabuco and Tumilco in Veracruz, Tamtok and Tamuín in San Luis Potosí, and Zacamixtle, Órganos, and Tepetzintla on the Veracruz coastal plain. These urban centers shed light on the organizational forms of the Huastec polities, whose florescence was based on agriculture and commerce controlled and monopolized by the ruler. Not only agriculture but also marine products, furs, feathers, and a wide variety of cotton cloth were commercialized. Another important product was salt, used not only as a condiment but also as a medicine and as a medium of exchange. Fishing was practiced in rivers and lakes by means of baited hooks, harpoons, baskets, and nets, or else by poisoning the waters. The people preserved fish, shrimp, and skate roe by salting and drying them in the sun, although fish also were, and still are, preserved by smoking them over mangrove wood fires.

[*See also* Cempoala; El Tajín; San Lorenzo-Tenochtitlan.]

LORENZO OCHOA
Translated from Spanish by Scott Sessions